The Tibetan History Reader

The Tibetan History Reader

Edited by Gray Tuttle and Kurtis R. Schaeffer

COLUMBIA UNIVERSITY PRESS

NEW YORK

A special thank you to the Shelley & Donald Rubin Foundation for crucial financial support for the publication of this book.

Columbia University Press
Publishers Since 1893
New York Chichester, West Sussex
cup.columbia.edu

Library of Congress Cataloging-in-Publication Data
The Tibetan history reader / Gray Tuttle and Kurtis R. Schaeffer, editors.
    p. cm.
  Includes bibliographical references and index.
  ISBN 978-0-231-14468-1 (cloth : alk. paper) — ISBN 978-0-231-14469-8 (pbk.) — ISBN 978-0-231-51354-8 (electronic)
  1. Tibet Region—History.   2. Tibet Region—Civilization.   3. Tibet Autonomous Region (China)—History.   I. Tuttle, Gray.   II. Schaeffer, Kurtis R.
  DS785.T495 2013
  951'.5—dc23   2011045303

Columbia University Press books are printed on permanent and durable acid-free paper.
This book was printed on paper with recycled content.
Printed in the United States of America
c 10 9 8 7 6 5 4 3 2 1
p 10 9 8 7 6 5 4 3 2 1

To Shelley and Donald Rubin
for their generous support for Tibetan studies.

May it lead even more students and learners
to greater understanding of Tibet and the Himalayas.

CONTENTS

PART FOUR
Lamas and Patrons
(Thirteenth to Fourteenth Centuries)
Tibet and the Mongols

PART FIVE
Centers of Power and Religious Learning
(Fourteenth to Eighteenth Centuries)

Institutional Growth Beyond Central Tibet

Tibet in a Global Context

PREFACE AND ACKNOWLEDGMENTS

The Tibetan History Reader assembles crucial studies of Tibetan history, organized in a comprehensive chronological framework, to make available concise
yet detailed essays drawn principally from the last half-century of Tibetan studies, most of which have been inaccessible to a general audience. Emphasizing
political, social, and cultural history, this book is designed to introduce Tibet to
university courses on Asian studies, religious studies, and world civilizations. It
is our hope that the *Reader* becomes the first place to which students and scholars of Asia turn when seeking accurate, in-depth information about the history
of Tibet.

This volume complements another volume published by Columbia University Press, *Sources of Tibetan Tradition* (edited with Matthew Kapstein). Where
Sources provides translations of important Tibetan works of literature, the *Reader*
adds important essays on specific aspects of Tibetan civilization, so they work in
concert featuring translated texts and authoritative studies.

The *Reader* follows a chronological and regional outline, surveying the political and institutional history of Tibet from its emergence as an imperial
power in the seventh century to the profound transformations of the modern
period. Each section strikes a balance between the general and the specific,
emphasizing broad historical trends through choice essays on specific topics.

There has long been a need for current, detailed, and readable materials for
teaching about Tibet as part of the Asian humanities curriculum in North

American colleges and universities. The *Reader* is designed to make the veritable explosion of research about Tibet in the last three decades readily accessible in the college classroom, as well as to scholars in other fields who need to consult authoritative studies of Tibet. Tibetan history is a very international endeavor, as can be seen by the diverse contributions here of Americans, Chinese, French, Germans, Italians, Japanese, a Norwegian, and Tibetans. To help bring this vast scholarly knowledge to a general audience, Tibetan personal and place names have been rendered in an easy-to-pronounce phonetic system based on the Tibetan and Himalayan Library (THL) standard developed by David Germano and Nicolas Tournadre. Chinese transliterations have been rendered in Pinyin. Some effort has also been made to standardize the Mongol terms and names, according to the system used in Christopher Atwood's *Encyclopedia of Mongolia and the Mongol Empire* (New York: Facts on File, 2004). All notes have been converted to endnotes, and in general, we have left the Tibetan spellings in the notes as in the original, whether in phonetics (now standardized in the THL phonetics) or Wylie transcriptions. Moreover, the complex and sometimes cryptic references to cited works have been standardized here according to Columbia University Press style. This has sometimes altered the appearance or formatting of the original articles; however, the full citation of the original will lead interested readers to the Tibetan Wylie transcription as well as the original footnotes or parenthetical references. All bibliographic references have been collected at the end of the book.

The work of making these changes was much more extensive than we initially realized it would be, so we have many people to thank. First, our editor, Anne Routon, deserves special thanks for her consistent support of Tibetan studies in general and this project in particular. Funding from the Shelley & Donald Rubin Foundation has been absolutely essential to completing this volume, and we are very grateful to the Rubins as well as Bruce Payne and Alex Gardner for their visionary assistance. In preparing the manuscript for this volume, Ulan, in Tibetan Studies at Columbia University, has played the key role, especially in standardizing the bibliographies; translating the Chinese, Japanese, and German bibliographic references; and generally keeping track of changes and resolving outstanding issues. Stacey Van Vleet, also at Columbia University, and Lindsey Sekreve, at the University of Virginia, tackled the massive task of converting all the Tibetan transcriptions into phonetics and standardizing the Chinese as Pinyin. Geoff Barstow, Benjamin Deitle, and William McGrath at the University of Virginia provided critical assistance at the later stages of the editing, taking several of the most challenging articles through many layers of editing. Finally, thanks are due to Leslie Kriesel for copyediting (and much more) and to Cynthia Col for indexing. We are being quite literal when we say that without the expert assistance of everyone involved in this project, it would never have been completed. Thank you to all!

DATES IN TIBETAN HISTORY AND KEY EVENTS
IN NEIGHBORING LANDS

680	death of Princess Wencheng
680–750	Umayyad caliphate
684–705	reign of Chinese Empress Wu Zetian
704–712	Tibet under the rule of Empress Dowager Tri Malö
710	Princess Jincheng sent to Tibet; marries the future Tri Detsuktsen
712–755	reign of Tri Detsuktsen
739	death of Princess Jincheng
742	birth of Tri Songdetsen
750–1258	Abbasid caliphate
751	defeat of Tang armies by the Abbasids at the Battle of Talas
c. 750–1174	Pāla dynasty rules northeastern India
755	assassination of Tri Detsuktsen and enthronement of Tri Songdetsen
755	An Lushan rebellion exiles Tang court to Sichuan
762	conversion of Tri Songdetsen to Buddhism
763	Tibetan occupation of the Chinese capital Chang'an
c. 767	earliest extant Tibetan writing, the Takdra Lukhong inscription, in Lhasa
779	foundation of Samyé monastery
c. 781	Tibetan conquest of Dunhuang
c. 797	abdication of Tri Songdetsen; succession uncertain
c. 804–815	reign of Tri Desongtsen
815–838	reign of Tri Tsukdetsen, a.k.a. Relpachen, assassinated 838
822	"uncle-nephew" treaty with Tang China
838–842	reign of Üdumtsen (Lang Darma); assassinated; succeeded by Ösung
845	persecution of Buddhism in China
842–c. 900	reigns of Ösung and his son Pelkortsen; local rebellions and final collapse of the empire
851	Governor Zhang Yichao overturns Tibetan rule in Gansu, including Dunhuang
c. 900–1250	*age of fragmentation*
906–1099	*Tibetan polities in northeastern Tibet*
906–1016	Lingchu Serkap (Ch. Liangzhou) Silk Road city under Tibetan rule
mid- to late 10th century	restoration of Central Tibetan Vinaya by monks ordained in Amdo by Lachen Gongpa Rapsel or his successors
c. 950–1685	*kingdom of Gugé in far western Tibet*
960–1279	Song dynasty
958–1055	life of the "great translator" Rinchen Zangpo
shortly after 1000	sealing of Dunhuang "Library Cave"

c. 959–c. 1036	life of Yeshé-ö, Buddhist ruler of Gugé
c. 996	foundation by Yeshé-ö of monasteries at Tabo (now in Himachal Pradesh, India) and Toling, west Tibet
1032–1227	Xixia (Minyak or Tangut) dynasty in northwestern China
c. 996–1035	life of Shenchen Luga, revealer of Bönpo canonical scriptures
997–1099	*Tsongkha kingdom rules in northeastern Tibet*
1012–65	reign of Gyelsé (Ch. Gusiluo), imperial scion in Tsongkha kingdom
1017	Tangpoché monastery founded in Yarlung Valley
1027	introduction of Kālacakra tantra and inception of new calendrical system based upon it
1042	Atiśa (982–1054) arrives in Gugé
1045	Atiśa travels to Central Tibet
1054	death of Atiśa at Nyetang
1057	foundation of Radreng (Reting) monastery by Atiśa's disciple Dromtön (1004–64)
1073	foundation of Sakya monastery by Khön Könchok Gyelpo (1034–1102)
1073	foundation of Sangpu monastery by Ngok Lekpé Sherap
1096	death of Marpa (b. c. 1012), founder of Kagyü tantric lineage
1099	Tsongkha kingdom falls to the Song dynasty
1123	death of Milarepa (b. 1040), poet-saint of the Kagyü
1143	death of Machik Lapdrön (b. c. 1055), female saint and founder of the lineage of Severance
1153	death of Gampopa (b. 1079), founder of Kagyü monastic order
1159	foundation of Katok monastery in Kham by Dampa Deshek (1122–92)
1170	death of Pakmodrupa Dorjé Gyelpo (b. 1110), founder of Pakmodrupa Kagyü order
1169–93	reign of Renzong (b. 1139) in Xixia; extends support to Tibetan Buddhism
1175	foundation of Tsel Gungtang monastery outside Lhasa by Lama Zhang (1122–93)
1179	foundation of Drikung-til monastery by Kyopa Jiktensumgön (1143–1217)
1180	foundation of Taklung monastery by Taklung Tangpa Trashipel (1142–1210)
1193	death of Düsum Khyenpa (b. 1110), First Karmapa and founder of the Karma Kagyü

1193	Indian Buddhist university of Nālandā sacked by Bakhtiyar Khalji
1204	arrival in Tibet of the Kashmiri master Śākyaśrībhadra
c. 1200–1769	Malla kings rule the Kathmandu Valley
c. 1207	Jagaddala in Bengal, among the last of the major Buddhist monasteries in India, destroyed
1211	death of Tsangpa Gyaré (b. 1161), founder of Drukpa Kagyü order, later the state religion of Bhutan
1227	death of Chinggis Khan (b. c. 1167)
1240	first Mongol invasion of Tibet ordered by Köden; razes Radreng (Reting) monastery
1246	Sakya Paṇḍita (1182–1251) meets Köden Khan in Liangzhou, Gansu
1252	Mongol armies under Möngke Khan ravage eastern Tibet
1256	Möngke holds religious debates at Sira-ordos, attended by Karma Pakshi (1206–83), the second Karmapa
1264–1350	**Sakyapa rule, under Mongol authority**
1264	Sakyapa Lama Pakpa (1235–80) appointed leader of Tibet by Qubilai Khan (1215–94)
1268	Mongol-sponsored census of Tibetan households
1271	eastern Mongol empire, under Qubilai Khan, adopts the dynastic title Yuan
1278	xylographic publication of Sakya Paṇḍita's *Logic* in Beijing
1280–1368	Yuan dynasty rules all of China
1285	Hülegü Khan, ruler of Mongols in Persia, assists Drigungpa assault on Sakya
1290	Drigung monastery razed by armies of Qubilai Khan
1299–1923	Ottoman Empire
1304	comparative catalogue of Tibetan and Chinese Buddhist canons completed with Yuan support
1339	death of Third Karmapa, Rangjung Dorjé (b. 1284)
1350	fall of the Sakyapa hegemony
1350–1642	**Pakmodrupa, Rinpungpa, and Tsangpa hegemonies**
1354	Mongols recognize Tai Situ Jangchup Gyeltsen (1302–64) as ruler of Tibet
1361	death of Jonangpa master Dölpopa Sherap Gyeltsen (b. 1292)
1363	death of Longchen Rapjampa (b. 1308)
1364	death of Butön Rinchendrup (b. 1290)
1368–1644	Ming dynasty rules China
1369	Fourth Karmapa, Rölpé Dorjé (1340-83), dispatches mission to Nanjing, China, to celebrate the foundation of the Ming dynasty
1385–1432	reign of Pakmodrupa ruler Miwang Drakpa Gyeltsen

1403	Ming emperor Yongle (r. 1402–24) initiated by Fifth Karmapa, Dezhinshekpa (1384–1415)
1405	foundation of Bön monastery Menri in Tsang by Nyammé Sherap Gyeltsen (1356–1415)
1409	Tsongkhapa establishes Great Prayer Festival in Lhasa and founds Ganden monastery
1410	Yongle emperor publishes Tibetan Buddhist canon (Kangyur)
1416	foundation of Drepung monastery by Tsongkhapa's disciple Jamyang Chöjé (1379–1449)
1418	Choné ruler in southeast Amdo recognized by Yongle emperor; family rules until 1949
1419	foundation of Sera monastery by Tsongkhapa's disciple Jamchen Chöjé (1354–1435)
1419	death of Tsongkhapa (b. 1357)
1432	death of Gyeltsap-jé (b. 1364), Tsongkhapa's successor at Ganden
1435	Samdruptsé (later Zhigatsé) seized by the Rinpungpa, vassals and rivals of the Pakmodrupa
1447	foundation of Trashi Lhünpo monastery at Samdruptsé by Gendün-drup (1391–1474), posthumously held to be First Dalai Lama
1453	fall of Constantinople to Ottoman Empire
1498–1518	suppression of the Gelukpa in the Lhasa region by the Rinpungpa administration
1501–1736	Safavid dynasty in Iran
1526–1858	Mughal empire in northern India
1542	death of Gendün Gyatso (b. 1476), posthumously held to be Second Dalai Lama
1542–82	reign of Altan Khan; invades Amdo and converts to Tibetan Buddhism
1565	fall of the Rinpungpa
1578	Sönam Gyatso (1543–88) receives title of Dalai Lama from Mongol leader Altan Khan
1588	foundation of Kumbum monastery in Amdo by Dalai Lama Sönam Gyatso
1600s–1700s	expansion of Russian empire in Siberia
1603–34	reign of Ligdan Khan of the Chahar khanate, last of the Borjigid line; embraces the Sakya order of Tibetan Buddhism in 1617
1604	foundation of Gönlung monastery in Amdo
1605	Wanli emperor (r. 1572–1620) of the Ming dynasty publishes the Tibetan Buddhist canon

1617 ·   death of Fourth Dalai Lama, Yönten Gyatso (b. 1589), a
                       Tümed Mongol; birth of Fifth Dalai Lama, Ngawang
                       Lozang Gyatso
1618   final defeat of the Pakmodrupa by the Tsangpa regime;
                       Tenth Karmapa, Chöying Dorjé (1605–74), crowned
                       by the Tsangpa as spiritual leader of Tibet
1630   arrival of Oirat (later called Kalmyk) Mongols in the
                       region of Astrakhan, Russia
1634   death of Tāranātha (b. 1575), Jonangpa teacher and
                       historian; foundation of ecclesiastical state in Bhutan
1630s–1756   Zunghar Khanate rules much of central Eurasia,
                       embracing Tibetan Buddhism
1636–1724   Khoshud Khanate, under Gushri Khan and his sons,
                       rules most of Amdo
1638–45   Mahākāla Temple complex established in Mukden,
                       capital of the Manchu Jin dynasty
1642–1959   **Ganden Podrang regime**
1642   the Khoshud Gushri Khan (1582–1655) defeats the Tsangpa
                       regime; beginning of the Fifth Dalai Lama's rule;
                       enthronement of Püntsok Namgyel, first Tibetan King
                       of Sikkim
1644–1911   Qing (Manchu) dynasty rules China
1644–61   reign of Emperor Shunzhi (b. 1638)
1645   construction of the Potala Palace begins
c. 1651   death of Zhapdrung Ngawang Namgyel (b. 1594),
                       Tibetan founder of the Drukpa Kagyü ecclesiastical
                       state in Bhutan
1652–53   journey of Fifth Dalai Lama to Beijing; meets Emperor
                       Shunzhi
1658–1707   life of Mughal Emperor Aurangzeb; Mughal empire
                       reaches largest extent
1661–1722   reign of Qing Emperor Kangxi
1662   death of Chökyi Gyeltsen (b. 1570), tutor of Fourth and
                       Fifth Dalai Lamas and first recognized Panchen
                       Lama (numbered Fourth)
1682   death of Fifth Dalai Lama, concealed by Regent Sanggyé
                       Gyatso until 1696
1684–92   Kangxi edition of Tibetan Buddhist canon published
1700   Lhazang Khan becomes chief of Mongol forces in Tibet
1705   assassination of Regent Sanggyé Gyatso (b. 1653) by
                       order of the wife of Lhazang Khan; Lhazang rules
                       Central Tibet until his death in 1717

1706	death of Sixth Dalai Lama (b. 1683) following his dethronement by Lhazang Khan
1709	foundation of Labrang monastery in Gansu by Jamyang Zhepa (1648–1721)
1717	invasion of Tibet by Zunghar Mongols
1718–20	Kangxi edition of Mongolian translation of Tibetan Kangyur published
1720	Tibetan and Manchu forces repel Zunghars; Seventh Dalai Lama, Kelzang Gyatso (1708–57), installed at Potala Palace
1722–35	reign of Qing Emperor Yongzheng
1723–24	Mongols and Tibetans in Amdo rebel against Manchus but are harshly suppressed
1727–47	Polhané (1689–1747), with Manchu support, rules Tibet
1727–35	Seventh Dalai Lama exiled to Kham
1727	Qing court establishes *amban* as resident envoy in Lhasa; position lasts until 1911
1730–32	publication, under Polhané's sponsorship, of Kangyur at Nartang
1733	completion of Dergé printed edition of Kangyur
1744	completion of Dergé printed edition of Tengyur (canonical commentaries)
1744	foundation of Yonghe gong Gelukpa monastic university in Beijing
1737–96	reign of Qing Emperor Qianlong
1747–50	Tibet ruled by Polhané's son Gyurmé Namgyel, who dies in abortive rebellion against Manchus
1750	Seventh Dalai Lama becomes head of state
1757–77	regency of Sixth Demo Khutughtu (1723–77)
1757–1858	British East India Company rule in India
1768	Prithvi Narayan Shah (1742–75) establishes Shah (Gurkha) dynasty in Nepal
1774	death of Situ Paṇchen Chökyi Jungné (b. 1699), founder of Pelpung monastery in Dergé
1774	East India Company Governor Warren Hastings dispatches George Bogle to Tibet
1777–86	regency of Tsemönling, former chaplain of the Qianlong emperor
1778	Ulan Bator, capital of modern Mongolia, founded
1780	death in Beijing of Sixth Paṇchen Lama, Pelden Yeshé (b. 1738), Bogle's host in Tibet

1786	death of Changkya Rölpé Dorjé (b. 1717), Buddhist tutor of the Qianlong emperor
1792	Nepalese invasion of Tibet repulsed by Qing army; Qianlong emperor enacts reforms of Tibetan administration
1794	Qianlong edition of Manchu translation of Tibetan Kangyur published
1796–1820	reign of Qing Emperor Jiaqing
1804	death of Eighth Dalai Lama, Jampel Gyatso (b. 1758)
1815	death of Ninth Dalai Lama, Lungtok Gyatso (b. 1805)
1814–16	Anglo–Nepal War
1819–44	regency of Tsemönling Jampel Tsültrim Gyatso, scion of Choné's ruling family
1837	death of Tenth Dalai Lama, Tsültrim Gyatso (b. 1816)
1837–65	Nyarong wars in Kham, concluded by Manchu and Central Tibetan intervention
1839–42	Opium War weakens China
1845–62	regency of Radreng (Reting) Yeshé Tsültrim Gyeltsen
1846	British annexation of Ladakh
1850–64	Taiping Rebellion
1851	death of Amdo poet-saint Zhapkar Tsokdruk Rangdröl (b. 1781)
1855	death of Eleventh Dalai Lama, Khedrup Gyatso (b. 1838); Nepalese invade Tibetan border regions
1857	Indian Rebellion (formerly known as the Sepoy Mutiny) aims to overthrow the rule of the British East India Company
1858–1947	British Raj rules India following the dissolution of the East India Company
1861	British annexation of Sikkim
1864–73	regency of Dedruk Khyenrap Wangchuk
1875	death of Twelfth Dalai Lama, Trinlé Gyatso (b. 1856)
1874–1908	reign of Qing Emperor Guangxu
1875–86	regency of Tatsak Ngawang Pelden
1876	birth of Thirteenth Dalai Lama, Tupten Gyatso
1883	anti-Nepalese riots in Lhasa
1884–1908	China governed by Empress Dowager Cixi (b. 1835)
1886–95	regency of Demo Khutughtu Lozang Trinlé
1895	Thirteenth Dalai Lama, Tupten Gyatso, becomes head of state
1899	death of Jamgön Kongtrül (b. 1813)
1904	Younghusband Expedition invades Central Tibet; Thirteenth Dalai Lama flees to Mongolia

1905	Chinese general Zhao Erfeng's campaigns crush monasteries in southern Kham
1906–11	reign of infant Emperor Puyi (1906–67)
1907	Bhutanese monarchy founded; coronation of King Ugyen Wangchuk (1862–1926)
1908	Thirteenth Dalai Lama, still in exile, visits Beijing for imperial audience
1909	Thirteenth Dalai Lama returns to Tibet
1910	General Zhao Erfeng invades Tibet; Thirteenth Dalai Lama flees to India
1912	return of Thirteenth Dalai Lama; Chinese garrison driven from Central Tibet; death of Mipam Rinpoché (b. 1846)
1912–49	Chinese Republic founded following the fall of the Manchu Qing dynasty
1924	Ninth Panchen Lama (1883–1937) flees into exile in China
1924	Mongolian People's Republic founded
1929	Qinghai made a province under the Chinese Muslim Ma family, who oppress the Amdo Tibetans
1933	death of Thirteenth Dalai Lama, Tupten Gyatso
1934	Radreng (Reting) Rinpoché (1911–47) made regent
1935	birth of Fourteenth Dalai Lama, Tenzin Gyatso, in Taktsé, Qinghai
1937	Ninth Panchen Lama dies in Jyekundo while seeking to return to Central Tibet
1938	birth of Tenth Panchen Lama (d. 1989) in Bindo, Amdo
1941	Radreng (Reting) Rinpoché steps down as regent in favor of Takdra Rinpoché
1947	Radreng (Reting) Rinpoché seeks to regain power in abortive rebellion
August 15, 1947	India becomes independent, marking the end of the British Indian Empire
October 1, 1949	establishment of the People's Republic of China under Mao Zedong
1950	Fourteenth Dalai Lama made head of state at age 15
October 24, 1951	Tibet is incorporated into the People's Republic of China by the "Seventeen-Point Agreement"

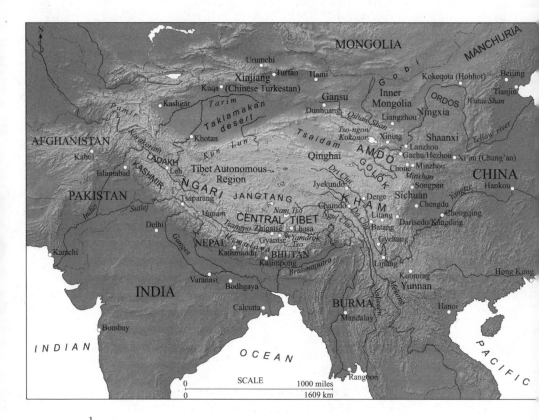

1

The Tibetan Plateau in Modern Asia

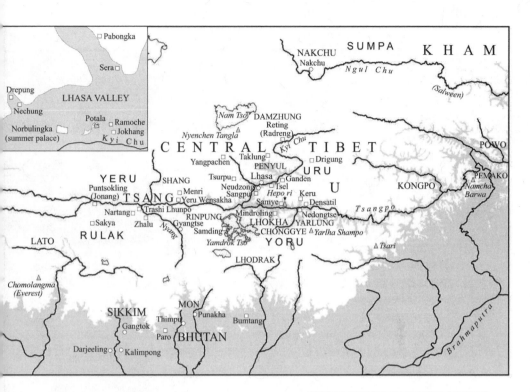

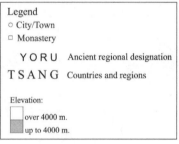

Legend
○ City/Town
□ Monastery

YORU Ancient regional designation

TSANG Countries and regions

Elevation:
over 4000 m.
up to 4000 m.

2

Central Tibet and Ngari

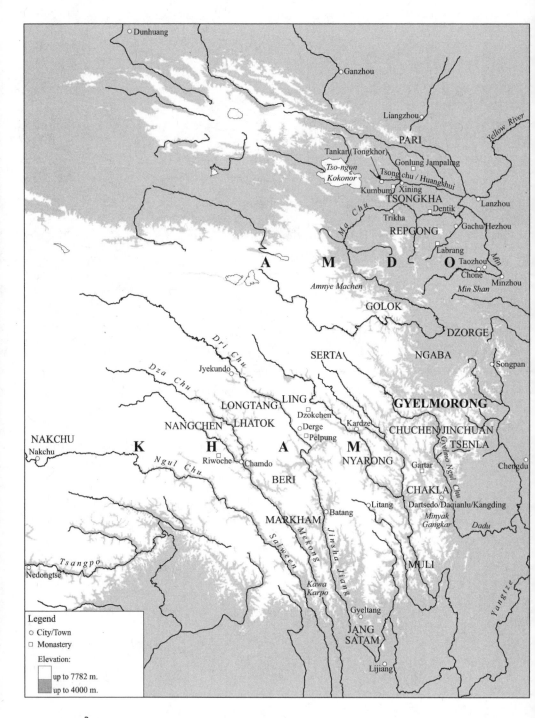

3

Eastern Tibet: Amdo, Kham, and Gyelmorong

The Tibetan History Reader

PART I

From Prehistory to History

Chapter 1

THE PREHISTORY OF THE TIBETAN PLATEAU
TO THE SEVENTH CENTURY A.D.

Mark Aldenderfer and Zhang Yinong

At a conservative guess, the area that we today refer to as the Tibetan cultural region was inhabited by humans around 20,000 years ago; farming settlements were present at least 5,000 years ago. Tibetan history therefore could be said to begin almost 19,000 years before contemporary historians typically pick up the story. But that story is not simple; Aldenderfer and Zhang recognize the politically loaded nature of archaeological and genetic research on the Tibetan Plateau, and they correctly point out that "making explicit correlations between languages, 'races' or ethnic groups, and archaeological cultures is fraught with difficulty." Nevertheless, their work presents the existing evidence on early humans on the Tibetan Plateau as well as the most plausible theories for the origins of these humans. This first article in the *Reader* very appropriately begins with an introduction to the region of Tibet, starting with the entire plateau. The region is massive; if the plateau's quarter of a million square kilometers represented a country's borders rather than just a geographic zone, this country would be the eleventh largest on earth. Moreover, the plateau's average altitude of over 5,000 meters makes Tibet, *on average*, higher than the *highest* peak in the lower 48 United States (California's Mount Whitney at 14,494'). This essay's survey of the plateau's terrain, major river systems, climate, and ecology provides an excellent orientation to the Tibetan cultural region. However, the focus of the essay is the prehistoric evidence for human habitation on the Tibetan Plateau.

THE POLITICAL AND ACADEMIC STRUCTURE OF ARCHAEOLOGY IN CHINA AND TIBET

For the sake of a general understanding of the archaeology of the Tibetan plateau in China and particularly the terms and usage in this article, it is necessary to make clear some possible confusions of the use of the term "Tibet" as well as in the nomenclature and organization of the administrative system for cultural resources in contemporary Tibet, which is currently based on Chinese ideology.

Contemporary Tibet is often vaguely referred to by scholars in different disciplines in terms of its geographical, ethnographic, and political meanings due to the complexity of its historical and current situations. The highest plateau on the earth, the Tibetan plateau, covers more than 2,500,000 square kilometers of plateaus and mountains in central Asia (fig. 1.1). Before 1950, "premodern Tibet," as Samuel calls it,[1] was constituted mainly by three Tibetan regions—central Tibet, Kham (eastern Tibet), and Amdo (northeastern Tibet)—and small population centers in the neighboring countries of Nepal, Bhutan, and India (including much of what is Ladakh and Sikkim today). After its annexation by China in 1950 and following the exile of the Dalai Lama in 1959, the major body of "premodern Tibet" in China was completely separated from that of Tibetan peoples in other Himalayan countries. According to Tibetologist Melvyn Goldstein, the concept of modern Tibet has a twofold meaning: "political

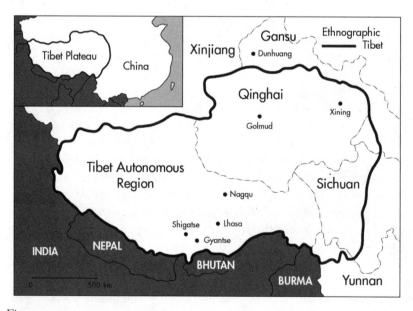

Figure 1.1

The Tibetan plateau, showing political boundaries, major rivers, and the extent of "ethnographic" Tibet. Scale approximate.

Tibet"—a region that used to be ruled by the Dalai Lama and is currently named the Tibet Autonomous Region (TAR) within the Chinese governmental nomenclature, and "ethnographic Tibet"—a much larger area inhabited by all ethnic Tibetan people that covers not only a major part in China but also many regions along the Himalayas in India, Nepal, and Bhutan.[2] While Tibet is still in many areas referred to by some scholars by its former integrity and traditional division, it has been reorganized and fragmented into several parts in China. These parts eventually fell into five contemporary Chinese provinces, including the TAR, Qinghai, Gansu, Sichuan, and Yunnan (fig. 1.1). With the exception of the TAR, Tibetan territory and population only constitute a small part in each of the other four Chinese provinces.[3]

MODERN ECOLOGY AND PALEOENVIRONMENTS

The Tibetan plateau is the highest in the world with an average elevation of over 5000 meters (fig. 1.2). This oft-cited figure, however, obscures its extraordinary topographic and ecological variability. Some of the highest peaks on the planet, barren of life, are juxtaposed to deep valleys that have unique ecologies which have only been explored in the modern era. In this section of the paper, we describe briefly the topographic features of the plateau, its hydrology, climate patterns, and ecological and biome structure. Following this, paleoenvironments are discussed.

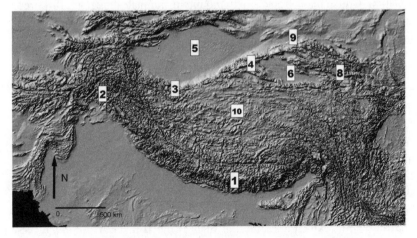

Figure 1.2
Major topographic features of the Tibetan plateau. 1: Himalayas; 2: Karakorams and Pamirs; 3: Kunlun Shan; 4: Arjin Shan; 5: Taklamakan Desert; 6: Qaidam Basin; 7: Qilian Shan; 8: Qinghai Hu (Lake Koko Nor); 9: Hexi (Gansu) corridor; 10: Jangtang. Scale approximate.

Before examining the plateau in detail, it is useful to review the fundamental structuring factors of high mountain and high plateau environments. As I have argued elsewhere, on the basis of the work of many geographers and ecologists, these environments are characterized by environmental heterogeneity, extremeness, low predictability, low primary productivity, and high instability and fragility.[4] Highly dissected topography, combined with altitudinal effects, creates a patchy mosaic of juxtaposed microenvironments with varied spatial and temporal extents. Extremeness (high absolute elevations, very low temperatures, etc.) exacerbates this variability. Low predictability is the degree to which key environmental features have a predictable periodicity. High mountains and plateaus are usually characterized by low predictability. Low primary productivity is typical of high plateaus and mountains since they tend to be quite cold and depending on location, often quite dry. Finally, these environments are highly unstable, with significant risk of hazard such as massive erosion and damaging seismic activity. Resource patches are frequently destroyed though these events.

On the basis of these criteria, the Tibetan plateau is among the most extreme and difficult highland environments on the planet. It is fundamentally a cold, alpine environment where the average temperature in the warmest month is not more than 10°C, and only three portions of the plateau—the Yarlung Tsangpo, Senggé Khebap, and Langchen Khebap river valleys, are *not* alpine by this definition. Since the plateau mostly lies between 30 and 35°N latitude, seasonal climatic variation is strong, with a moderately long winter and relatively short summer, both of which are in great part contingent upon altitudinal zonation. Unlike many tropical high mountain and plateau regions, this strong seasonal variability on the Tibetan plateau improves the predictability of precipitation to an extent.

TOPOGRAPHY

The plateau, created largely by the collision of the northward drift of what was to become the Indian subcontinent and the land mass of what was to become Asia some 40–50 million years ago, apparently reached its modern elevation by at least 8 million years ago, and probably substantially earlier.[5] The Himalayas, the highest mountain range in the world and which stretches in a vast arc along the southern margin of the plateau, were created in this ancient collision. The western and northwestern margins of the plateau are formed by the Karakorams and the Pamirs, which are almost as high as the Himalayas. Although these ranges are cut through by a number of large rivers, and can be traversed over very high mountain passes, the combination of high elevation and extreme topographic ruggedness make access to the southern and western regions of the plateau from these directions quite difficult. The northwestern boundary of the plateau is marked by the somewhat lower Kunlun Shan, which transitions into

the Arjin Shan along the north-central margins of the plateau. The northeastern margin of the plateau is defined by a series of relatively low, parallel mountain ranges, with the Qilian Shan the northernmost of these. In general, these
northern ranges are much lower than those to the south and west, and do not
present as much difficulty for transit. However, as will be shown below, other
topographic factors make this region a harsh environment. Finally, the eastern
boundary of the plateau is marked by a series of northwest-southeast trending
ranges created by major rivers that descend from the interior of the plateau into
north-central China as well as southeast Asia. These valley systems are very
deep and narrow, and rise precipitously toward the plateau. The extreme northeastern corner of the plateau contains the so-called Hexi (or Gansu) Corridor,
where the Machu (Huang He or Yellow) River valley cuts through the mountains,
and which affords relatively easy access to the interior of the plateau from the
steppelands to the north.

The interior of the plateau is divided by other, smaller mountain ranges that
generally run east-west. These ranges define four other major topographic features: the long, relatively narrow Yarlung Tsangpo valley in southern Tibet, the
large, arid Jangtang rangeland that dominates most of the interior of the plateau,
the Qaidam Basin, and the Qinghai Hu Basin, both located in the northeastern
corner of the plateau.

The Yarlung Tsangpo valley and that of its major tributary drainage the
Kyichu, as well as those of numerous smaller rivers, form the modern agricultural heartland of the plateau. Elevations of the relatively flat valley floors range
from 3700 to 3900 meters above sea level. The valley is arid to the west, and
gradually becomes wetter toward the east. The gradient of the river is gentle, and
except in deep gorges, the river and its tributaries tend to form broad, shallow,
braided channels.

Surrounding these valleys are low foothills and sometimes very steep moun-
tainsides. The Yarlung Tsangpo courses through a very narrow gorge between
the two major population centers of Lhasa and Zhigatsé. As the river flows to the
east, it again enters a very deep (over 5200 meters above sea level in depth), almost
impassable, canyon that contains a unique ecology.

In contrast, the Jangtang is an arid, rolling tableland dotted with lakes, some
with areas as large as 1000 square kilometers. The elevation of the southern
Jangtang ranges from 4300 to 4500 meters above sea level, while in the north, it
ranges from 4500 to 5000 meters above sea level. As described by Schaller, "The
terrain varies from valleys hemmed in by rugged ranges, and rolling hills separated by broad, shallow valleys, to enormous flats, the landscape becoming more
spacious and higher from south to north."[6] Vegetation is sparse, and most of the
region is barren rock and soil, but in some places, high groundwater tables create
large expanses of grazing lands.

The Qaidam Basin is a vast depression (when compared to the rest of the
plateau) that ranges in elevation from 2600 to 3000 meters above sea level.

Although a lake once existed in the basin during the Oligocene, during the Pleistocene, it was large and arid.[7] Today it contains a number of small lakes as well as large marshlands that serve as the source of the Machu River. However, the western half of the Qaidam is quite arid, and is covered in varying degrees with shifting, blowing sands, gravel outcrops, and in some places, thick deposits of salts. Small oases fed by glacial meltwaters dot the northern margins of the basin.

The Qinghai Hu basin, at 3200 meters above sea level, is a large grassland surrounding Koko Nor (or Qinghai) Lake. The terrain here is gently rolling, and vegetation more extensive. The lake itself is brackish.

HYDROLOGY

Although best characterized as an arid environment, the plateau is the source to a number of major river systems for the Indian subcontinent, southeast Asia, and China. In the west, the headwaters of the Senggé Khebap (Indus), and one of its major tributaries, the Langchen Khebap (Sutlej), are found on the plateau. We have already seen that the headwaters of the Machu (Huang He) are found in northeastern Tibet. In the east, four major rivers originate on the plateau. From south to north, they are the Yarlung Tsangpo (Bramaputra), Ngülchu (Salween), Dzachu (Mekong), and Drichu (Yangtze). The flow from these rivers is massive; almost 28 percent of the water budget of China comes from the plateau, as does 34 percent of that of the Indian subcontinent.

Over 2,000 lakes of all sizes are found on the plateau, mostly in the Jangtang. The majority of these were formed during the glacial epoch and are now fed primarily by glacial meltwaters or in the southern Jangtang, by convective and some monsoonal rains. As a result of their origins, few have external outlets, and as a consequence, many have brackish or saline waters. Vast salt flats surround some of these lakes, and mining salt for trade primarily to the Indian subcontinent has a long history. These lakes, because of their characteristics and antiquity, are important data sources for tracking paleoenvironmental variability on the plateau, and consequently, they have been the focus of intensive limnological analysis. A number of lakes have sacred significance, probably of great antiquity. Perhaps the most important of these is Lake Mapam (Manasarowar), which is near the famous Mt. Tisé (Kailash). Both of these geographical features are sacred to Tibetan Buddhists as well as Hindus, and are still today the scene of pilgrimage.

CLIMATE

The influence of the Tibetan plateau on global climate patterns is widely recognized.[8] The height and mass of the plateau affect the course of the jet stream, and this has implications for other major wind patterns and weather systems at both regional and global scales. Overall, rainfall intensity and humidity decrease from east to west and south to north. The formation of the plateau 8 million years ago created the conditions for the development of the Southeast Asian summer monsoon and the winter monsoon. The summer monsoon brings moisture to south Asia from across the eastern Indian Ocean as well as the Bay of Bengal, which is the primary source of the southwest Indian Monsoon.[9] It brings significant summer rainfall to the southeastern plateau. However, the Himalayas act as a barrier to this moisture, and they create a rain shadow along their northern margins. Storms traveling up the major valley systems penetrate furthest into the plateau. Summer climate in eastern Tibet is also wet, created in this case by the major low-pressure system that develops seasonally near the source of the Machu and Drichu rivers. Some summer storms cross into western Tibet from the south, but for the most part, these storms do not penetrate deeply into the plateau, leaving most of the Jangtang and the Qaidam Basin semiarid to arid. Winter weather patterns are dominated by the prevailing westerlies, which are split by the mass of the plateau and Karakorams into two streams. Most of the plateau lies within the rain shadow of these winds, and consequently, very little moisture reaches it. Winters tend to be cold and severe, with the most frigid temperatures in the northwest and the warmest in the southeast.

ECOLOGY AND BIOME STRUCTURE

Most authors agree that the plateau consists of 11 biomes which can be placed into three broad altitudinal zones (table 1.1; see fig. 1.3).[10] Ecological structure is strongly determined by latitude and elevation, which in turn affect precipitation. The plateau is a complex mix of biomes, but generally, the northeast and the southeast have the greatest complexity, species diversity, and primary productivity. In contrast, most of the central and western portions of the plateau are quite arid and cold, and therefore have limited species diversity and productivity. The north-central plateau is also home to year-round permafrost, as are some of the high peaks in the west, south, and northeast. The remainder of the plateau, aside from the Yarlung Tsangpo valley and the upper reaches of the Ngülchu, Tsachu, and Machu rivers, is subject to seasonal frozen ground.[11] In short, the bulk of the plateau has very low primary productivity, rendering much of it useful only for pastoral pursuits today, or agriculture that is heavily dependent upon irrigation in less frigid regions. However, it is important to remember that like any high elevation environment, it is also very patchy, and resources are distributed asymmetrically in both time and space.

TABLE 1.1

MODERN BIOME STRUCTURE OF THE TIBETAN PLATEAU

(MASL: METERS ABOVE SEA LEVEL)

Biome	Altitudinal zone
Temperate/subalpine coniferous forest	<4000 masl
Temperate/subalpine deciduous forest	<4000 masl
Temperate/subalpine broadleaf/deciduous forest	<4000 masl
Tropical/subtropical seasonal and rain forest	<4000 masl
Temperate shrublands/steppe	<4000 masl
Temperate steppe	<4000 masl
Temperate desert	<4000 masl
Alpine meadows/shrublands	4000–5200 masl
Alpine steppe	4000–5200 masl
Alpine desert	4000–5200 masl
Ice/polar desert	>5200 masl

Ni, "A Simulation of Biomes on the Tibetan Plateau and Their Responses to Global Climate Change."

PALEOENVIRONMENTS

Some authors have speculated on a deep antiquity for a human presence on the Tibetan plateau (discussed in greater detail below), but there is no convincing evidence of one until late in the Pleistocene. Therefore, our review of paleoclimates of the plateau begins at 50,000 B.P. [before present].

Although data are sparse, at 50,000 B.P. the plateau was dominated by the climatic conditions associated with the end of oxygen isotope stage 4, a period of glacial advance that was cold and arid.[12] Temperatures were colder than in the modern era, and surface water would have been very scarce. Vegetation would have been sparse, and there would have been considerable areas of barren ground, gravel, and rock across much of the plateau. Most of the mountain peaks of the plateau were covered by glacial ice of limited extent.[13] However, large areas around these mountain ranges would have been periglacial in character, and surrounding valley systems would have been subject to severe wind chill. Although being mindful of the complexity of ecological structure on the plateau, much of it is best described as a hyperarid, cold desert at this time.

Between 50,000 and 25,000 B.P. (oxygen isotope stage 3), climatic conditions across the plateau improved. Glacial ice at high elevations retreated substantially, and rising lake levels in most areas of the plateau indicate a significant

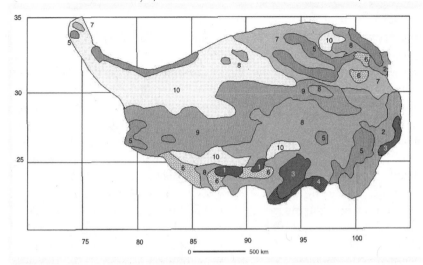

Figure 1.3

Major biomes of the Tibetan plateau (after Ni, 2000). 1: Temperate conifer forest; 2: temperate deciduous forest; 3: temperate broadleaf evergreen forest; 4: tropical seasonal rainforest; 5: temperate shrublands/meadow; 6: temperate steppe; 7: temperate desert; 8: alpine meadow/shrubland; 9: alpine steppe; 10: alpine desert. Scale approximate.

increase in precipitation.[14] It is reasonable to infer that temperatures also increased. As these processes unfolded, desert gave way to steppe formations across the plateau, substantially increasing primary productivity. This in turn would have led to the expansion in range and numbers of the large ungulates native to the plateau. Importantly, these improved conditions may have ameliorated the extreme aridity of the large desert basins just to the north of the plateau (the Taklamakan and Gobi deserts), thus making movement onto the plateau from the north more feasible.

Glaciers resumed their advance after 25,000 B.P., signaling a return to arid and cold conditions across the entire plateau. Some authors, most notably Kuhl, have argued for the presence of a massive ice cap on the entire plateau during Last Glacial Maximum times (22,000–18,000 B.P.).[15] More recent multidisciplinary research has shown, however, that no such ice cap existed at any time in the Last Glacial Maximum or Holocene, and that glacial advances during this period were purely "local" and no more extensive than the glaciers of the oxygen isotope stage 4 advance.[16] Although no ice cap existed, there is no question that plateau climate deteriorated substantially during the Last Glacial Maximum. There is good evidence that the summer monsoon weakened considerably, thereby preventing precipitation from reaching much of the plateau.[17] Glacial lakes that had reached their maximum extents during oxygen isotope stage 3 dropped rapidly in level. Desert once again replaced steppe, and the plateau once again became a cold, arid desert. Some climate models suggest that annual mean temperatures on the plateau ranged from 13 to 2°C lower than in the modern era,[18] conditions harsher than at any time during the Late Pleistocene. This, coupled with increased aridity, would have substantially decreased primary productivity in most plateau biomes.

The Last Glacial Maximum signals the start of a gradual process of desiccation across the plateau that extends throughout the Holocene. However, this general trend is marked by local and regional reversals as well as periods of intensification of the process. For instance, the Qaidam and Qinghai basins experienced a period of hyperaridity from 15,000 to 9,000 B.P. followed by somewhat less arid conditions in the Holocene. The north-central margins of the plateau saw extensive dune formation from 15,000 to 13,000 B.P. However, the eastern portion of the plateau became more humid and warmer from 13,000 to 10,000 B.P. due to the reinforcement of the Pacific summer monsoon,[19] and this supported the growth and expansion of spruce/fir/pine forests, especially in the valley systems that descend to the southeast.[20] Although data are sparse, there is the high probability that broadleaf forest also expanded in the valleys of southeastern Tibet at this time. In contrast, western Tibet remained arid until roughly 10,000 B.P. when a major climatic reversal appeared, creating warm and wet conditions until 9500 B.P. Arid conditions returned and intensified until 4000–3000 B.P., but were interrupted twice by wet pulses at 9500–8700 and 7200–6300 B.P.[21] These pulses apparently stimulated the return of small groves of spruce and fir in sheltered locations and where soil humidity was sufficient. Records of these wet pulses have been recorded for central and northeastern Tibet as well. Temperatures during this period are believed to have been 3–4°C warmer than the present.

At 6000 B.P., forests on the plateau begin to contract, a pattern also seen through much of China. Ren[22] attributes this contraction to human agency, specifically the expansion of agriculture. Although archaeological data from the plateau for this time period are very thin, the timing of forest reduction is consistent with what appears to be the expansion of a Neolithic cultural "package" in the major river valleys of the eastern plateau. Climate change, though, cannot be discounted as a correlative factor, since rainfall diminished and colder temperatures were seen on the plateau after 3000 B.P.[23]

THE ARCHAEOLOGY OF THE PLATEAU

Despite more than fifty years of research on the plateau, it remains the case that we are still ignorant of many of the important historical, evolutionary, and social processes and events that took place upon it through time. In this section of the paper, we will examine the state of knowledge on the following research themes:

the timing of a human presence of the plateau and the changing adaptive strategies of these early foraging peoples, the appearance of Neolithic cultures, and the emergence of cultural complexity. Not surprisingly, these questions will follow a roughly chronological sequence, and include the Paleolithic, Mesolithic (or what passes for it on the plateau), Neolithic, and historic (as defined by Chinese scholars) periods.

PEOPLING THE PLATEAU

Although a number of fossil *Homo* remains, as well as archaic and modern *Homo sapiens* specimens, have been found around the margins of the plateau, specifically in Yunnan and Shaanxi provinces, none have been found on the plateau itself.[24] This has not discouraged speculation, however, that there is a deep antiquity for a human presence upon it. Huang suggests that the initial occupation of the northern fringes of the plateau coincided with oxygen isotope stage 3, and focuses on the date 30,000 B.P. as the most probable time of entry.[25] Tong has argued for an even earlier date of entry before 50,000 B.P.[26]

Radiometric dates and reliable archaeological contexts indicative of a Pleistocene occupation of the plateau are scarce (table 1.2). Huang describes archaeological materials from the Xiao Qaidam site located at 3100 m in the central Qaidam basin (fig. 1.4).[27] Artifacts recovered include simple core and flake tools made of quartzite. Although the deposits from which the tools were recovered were not dated directly, ostracod samples from stratigraphically correlated deposits dated between 35,000 and 33,000 B.P. Brantingham suggest these dates are too early, and argue for a more likely occupation of the site between 22,000 and 18,000 B.P.[28]

Another site of Late Paleolithic age is Chusang, at 4200 meters above sea level and located ca. 85 kilometer northwest of Lhasa along the north branch of the Tolung Chu. First discovered in 1995, the site consists of 19 human hand and footprints impressed into a now-calcified travertine deposit.[29] All the prints were pressed into the same layer of the travertine, and because they had rough, unsmoothed edges, were not likely to have been cut or carved out of the rock. Size differences in the prints suggest that both adults and children were present when they were made. The travertine deposit began as a soft calcitic mud precipitated as dissolved CO_2 degassed and the hot spring water became supersaturated with calcium carbonate. The exact depositional environment of this mud is unclear from the recorded observations. The prints were formed sometime after this deposition, and the mud was subsequently lithified, presumably by the addition of calcium carbonate cement, forming the present hard calcareous travertine deposit. Zhang and Li also discovered what they describe as a hearth near one concentration of prints. Unfortunately, no artifacts of any kind have yet been found near the prints or hearth, but no search was made of the

TABLE 1.2

EARLY CHRONOMETRIC DATES FROM THE TIBETAN PLATEAU

Site	Dates[a]	Comments
Xiao Qaidam[i] 33.0 ± 3.0	Radiocarbon dating of ostracods	
	35.2 ± 1.7	
Chusang[ii]	21.7 ± 2.2	Optically stimulated
	21.1 ±2.1	luminescence
	20.6 ± 2.9	
Koko Nor sites		
Heimahe[iii]	11.1 (13.3–12.9)	Radiocarbon dating of wood
	10.8 (13.0–12.8)	Charcoal
Jiangxigou[iv]	12.4 (15.4–14.1)	Radiocarbon dating of wood
		Charcoal
Layihai[v]	6745 ± 85	Wood charcoal

[a]All dates are reported as uncalibrated radiocarbon years before present unless otherwise noted.

[i]Huang, 1994.

[ii]Zhang and Li, 2002.

[iii]P. J. Brantingham et al., "Speculation on the Timing and Nature of Late Pleistocene Hunter-Gatherer Colonization of the Tibetan Plateau," *Chinese Science Bulletin* 48, no. 14 (2003): 1510–1516.

[iv]Brantingham et al., "Late Pleistocene Hunter-Gatherer Colonization of the Tibetan Plateau."

[v]P. Gai and G. Wang, "Huanghe shangyou Layihai zhongshiqi yizhi fajue baogao" [A Mesolithic Site at Layihai, Upper Yellow River], *Acta Anthropologica Sinica* 2 (1983): 49–59.

site at the time of discovery. Optically stimulated luminescence dating of quartz crystals in the travertine deposits and hearth produced dates ranging between 21,700 and 20,600 B.P. Should this locality be confirmed as an archaeological site of this age, it implies that an occupation of the plateau probably took place somewhat earlier than the Last Glacial Maximum, and that models of extensive ice cover of the central plateau are in error.

Beyond these dated sites, however, there are a number of sites that have been provisionally assigned to the Paleolithic based on typological analysis and cross-dating. Prominent among these are Geting[30] (ca. 4660 meters above sea level), Duogeze[31] (ca. 4830 meters above sea level), Zhuluole[32] (ca. 4800 meters above sea level), Sure[33] (ca. 4500 meters above sea level), Luling[34] (ca. 4700 meters above sea level), Hadongtang and Quedetang[35] (ca. 4100 meters above sea level),

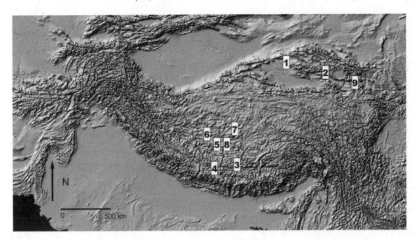

Figure 1.4
Locations of major sites of the Paleolithic and postglacial periods. 1: Xiao Qa-idam; 2: Heimhe and Jiangxigou; 3: Chusang; 4: Sure; 5: Zhuluole; 6: Duogeze; 7: Zhabu; 8: Luling; 9: Layihai.

and Zhabu. These sites are spread across the plateau from the far west (Zhabu) to the south (Sure) to the eastern Jangtang (Geting; fig. 1.4). What they share are assemblages composed of core and simple flake tools as well as tools made on large blades. Assumed tool functions include scrapers, gravers, burins, and unifacial points. Some points and flake tools from Zhuluole and Geting have what some authors describe as a Levallois-like technique.[36] Assignment of these tools to a Paleolithic age are made on comparisons with sometimes very distant sites. For example, the Zhuluole assemblage has been compared to that found at Hutouliang in Hebei Province, some 5000 kilometer to the east.[37] One of the best analogues for Paleolithic comparisons, however, comes from Shuidong-gou, a site just below the eastern margins of the plateau dating between 29,500 to 23,800 B.P. in Ningxia Hui Autonomous Region.[38] The site is composed of two localities—1 and 2. Locality 1 has an assemblage composed of large blades and elongated flakes, some of which have been made with a Levallois-like technique. This assemblage is very similar to those found at sites in the Mongolian Gobi and southern Siberia, but which date much earlier (49,000–33,000 B.P.). Unfortunately, no reliable direct dating of the Locality 1 assemblage has been made, but Brantingham *et al.* argue for a Middle Paleolithic age for the site.[39] However, reliable dates of a similar core-blade technology at Locality 2 range between 29,000 and 23,000 B.P. If this cross-dating is accurate, it suggests a human presence on the far western part of the central plateau at an early date.

A second technological tradition at Locality 2 of Shuidonggou is of interest as well. Madsen et al. describe a bipolar microcore/microblade technology on small pebbles of chalcedony.[40] Not a true microcore/microblade technology, it nevertheless appears to presage the appearance of such technologies later in time, and which are found at numerous sites across the plateau, especially after the Last Glacial Maximum. There is a very real possibility that some of the assemblages found on the plateau and described as microcore/microblade in nature (and thus presumed to be relatively late in time) are in fact more similar to the bipolar technology found at Locality 2. To verify this, however, would require an exhaustive technological reanalysis of these collections.

Brantingham *et al.* report two stratified sites on the shores of Koko Nor at ca. 3100 meters above sea level that were occupied between 12,400 and 10,800 B.P. (table 1.2).[41] Heimahe is a stratified site that contains five stone-lined hearths. No lithics were recovered in the testing, but animal bone was present. The second site, Jiangxigou, has a single unprepared hearth, and with it was found debitage suggestive, but not diagnostic, of a pebble microblade reduction strategy.

Unfortunately, there are no other dated sites of Pleistocene age on the plateau, thus making it difficult to determine routes of entry and the timing of its occupation. Other data types have been pressed into service to examine this problem. Using mitochrondrial DNA evidence, Torroni et al.[42] argue that indigenous Tibetans have a north Asian and Siberian origin of uncertain antiquity. They do not, however, speculate on the process by which these northern populations entered the plateau. One major limitation of the analysis is the very small sample of Tibetans tested. They further suggest that observed mitochrondrial DNA mutations in Tibetan populations were not the result of selective pressures for adaptation to high elevation life. A northern or central Asian genetic contribution to Tibetans has been confirmed more recently by Qian et al., but they do not speculate on a likely date of the appearance of the central Asian genes.[43]

Su et al., using Y–chromosome haplotypes, "postulate that the ancient people, who lived in the upper-middle Yellow River basin about 10,000 years ago and developed one of the earliest Neolithic cultures in East Asia, were the ancestors of modern Sino-Tibetan populations."[44] In this model, a source population moves from the west-central Machu (Huang He, Yellow) river basin onto the plateau into Qinghai sometime around 6000 years ago, and then disperses rapidly across it. This reconstruction places the origins of the Tibetan people very late in time, well into the Holocene. As we will discuss below, while there are some interesting features to this model, it does not accord well with newly obtained data on the Neolithic period on the plateau, nor does it account for the data we have just discussed.

Brantingham et al., taking full advantage of recent archaeological discoveries in northern and central Asia, posit a substantially different model for the peopling of the plateau.[45] Their model takes into account the physiological challenges of life at high elevation, resource configurations, and potential cultural responses. As a species, humans are lowlanders, and are not adapted to high elevation life. To live permanently at altitudes over 2500 meters above sea level requires a suite of behavioral, cultural, and physiological adaptations.[46] Native lowlanders find at high elevations that work capacity is reduced, caloric needs are greater, risks of certain diseases, including respiratory infections and altitude-induced illness are increased, and physiological responses to cold stress are intensified. From a physiological perspective, these challenges can only be overcome by being born at altitude. Their effects can be ameliorated by cultural adaptations that tend to minimize the frequency and distances traveled of residential moves, selective patch choice to reduce the foraging radius, increased logistical mobility for hunting parties, embedded resource procurement strategies, development of a transport capacity, and caching,[47] as well as the controlled use of fire and the adoption of sophisticated clothing.[48]

Using concepts like these, Brantingham and others propose a three-step model for the peopling of the plateau. The first step brings a source population from the low elevation zones north of the plateau (Inner Mongolia, Gansu, etc.) into northwestern China no later than 29,000–25,000 B.P. and possibly earlier. The second step moves these people into the eastern Qinghai lakes region (at elevations between 3000 and 4000 meters above sea level) around 25,000 B.P. but in any case before the extremes of the Last Glacial Maximum. It is during this second step that physiological adaptations to high elevation conditions would commence. The third step, movement to the much higher central plateau, may have occurred at the onset of Last Glacial Maximum conditions, ca. 23,000–22,000 B.P. Although the model remains to be tested, it is in general accord with the mitochrondrial DNA data, sources of technological traditions, and movement across the plateau. Should Chusang on the central plateau date to ca. 21,000 B.P. this would help strengthen the empirical foundations of the model. However, it remains possible that the Qinghai lake sites reported by Brantingham reflect a late (post-Last Glacial Maximum) second-step occupation of the plateau.[49]

CHANGING ADAPTIVE STRATEGIES IN THE LATE PLEISTOCENE AND EARLY HOLOCENE

Between 11,000 and 6000 B.P., the archaeology of the plateau is essentially unknown. With one exception, Layihai in extreme eastern Qinghai,[50] there is no radiometrically dated site known before ca. 5000 B.P. (table 1.2). Consequently, it is difficult to discuss postglacial adaptive strategies with much confidence. It is well known that sites containing a Neolithic cultural package (domesticated plants and animals, ceramics, sedentary life with clear investment in facilities such as houses, ground stone tools) were present on the plateau by 5000 B.P. Although most of these sites are found along the eastern margins of the plateau, some are known from the central portion of the Yarlung Tsangpo valley. Most Chinese sources, as well as western models derived from historical linguistics and DNA analysis, favor a migration or colonization process that brings Neo-lithic settlers to the plateau from the surrounding lowlands. Little consideration is made of possible indigenous cultural transformations, such as a local process of sedentarization, that could have taken place without a diffusion from low-land sources. Neither has there been research to investigate how the pastoral economies, which are the basis of current lifeways across much of the plateau, came into being except within a diffusionist context. Obviously, the movement of people and the diffusion of traits did happen, but a more serious consider-ation of indigenous cultural processes is needed to balance this historical trend.

In the absence of data, we can only speculate on the nature of post-Last Gla-cial Maximum and postglacial cultural adaptations. We begin with the reason-able assumption that population densities across the plateau were very low in post-Last Glacial Maximum times. Environmental amelioration after 18,000 B.P. encouraged the adaptive radiation of humans and plant and animal species. Foragers on the central plateau (should they in fact have been there and sur-vived the extremes of the Last Glacial Maximum) would have been able to exploit new and expanding niches, especially in the major river valleys. In the northeastern and southeastern corners of the plateau, forest expansion implies that lower elevation plant and animal species migrated into higher elevation zones; this in turn may have encouraged foraging groups in these valleys to ex-pand their ranges into the fringes of the plateau. A process like this happened in postglacial times along the western flanks of the Andes.[51] There, foraging groups quickly established permanent residence after the initial "discovery" of the plateau.[52] In the north, however, hyperaridity in the Qinghai and Qaidam basins may have encouraged foraging populations there to jump from the second step (3000–4000 meters above sea level) to the third step (4000–5000 meters above sea level) in Brantingham et al.'s model. This would have taken place between 12,000 and 10,000 B.P. In either scenario, small groups of foraging people likely expanded into the most productive niches across the plateau.

There are a number of preceramic or aceramic sites that probably date to the postglacial and pre-Neolithic period. Most of these sites have microlithic tech-nologies. Microliths and their varied associations continue to vex archaeologi-cal reconstructions of plateau prehistory. Most known sites containing microliths are surface assemblages that have been haphazardly collected, and are thus likely to have unknown sampling biases, making comparisons tenuous. With few ex-ceptions, most assemblages have not been rigorously described, again making it difficult to identify clear technological trends. It also appears that many of these sites are palimpsest occupations created by deflation and erosion. Microliths are also known from excavated sites containing ceramics and bronzes that are clearly of Neolithic or post-Neolithic (i.e. Bronze Age) dates.[53] Finally, it is clear that the term itself—microlith—has been variously defined by Chinese archaeologists.[54] Once applied broadly to assemblages containing small tools, it now has a more restrictive definition based upon the technological definition of microblade

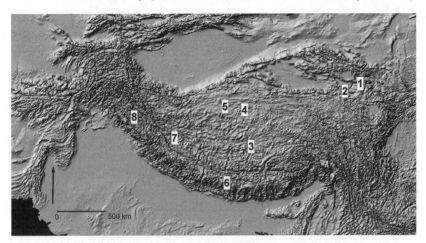

Figure 1.5

Location of major microlithic sites on the plateau. 1: Layihai; 2: Dayutai; 3: central Jangtang sites; 4, 5: northern Jangtang sites; 6: Zhongba, Nyalam; 7: upper Yarlung Tsangpo sites; 8: Rutok.

production (blades with triangular or trapezoidal cross-section and less than 10 mm in width). Within this category, however, authors have described a number of reduction strategies and styles.[55]

In Tibet, Chinese archaeologists often describe two traditions of microlithic technologies—northern and southern (fig. 1.5).[56] The northern tradition includes sites found in Qinghai[57] (Layihai), the central Jangtang, especially near Shenzha, Shuangu, and Banga,[58] and the northern Jangtang (Mani, Sewugang, Suishaole, and Geladandong). The southern tradition is said to include Zhongba and Nyalam,[59] a series of sites along the middle and upper Yarlung Tsangpo valley,[60] and sites near Rutok in far western Tibet.[61] The majority of these sites are aceramic, although they are often found to be mixed with different kinds of stone tools. Also, some technological traditions are thought to extend into later ceramic periods. For instance, Li describes sites with microliths along the middle and upper reaches of the Yarlung Tsangpo and places them into five categories: (1) typical microliths with small flake artifacts, (2) typical microliths with both large and small flake artifacts, (3) small and large flake artifacts, (4) uniform small flake artifacts, and (5) uniform large flake artifacts.[62] In his paper, "typical" microliths are defined as those created by direct percussion on small, funnel-shaped cores. The author speculates that this type of microlith dates from 7500 to 3000 B.P. Microliths are also found with tool forms thought to be of Paleolithic age, such as at Zhuluole.

Technological distinctions define the traditions.[63] In the north, microliths are said to be made on a wide variety of core types, including wedge-shaped, flat, conical and semiconical, and cylindrical and semicylindrical (fig. 1.6). Microblades are produced by pressure flaking, tend to be rectangular in shape, and are generally trapezoidal to triangular in cross-section. These assemblages often have a full range of other small tool types, such as scrapers, points, and burins. In contrast, the southern tradition sites tend to be dominated by flat cores, but also include edge-shaped, boat-shaped, funnel-shaped, and cylindrical cores. Microblades are said to be produced by hard and soft hammering as well as some pressure flaking. Southern tradition microblades, at least from the illustrated examples from the Chinese literature, seem more like blade-like flakes rather than blades made from prepared microcores. Many of these blades exhibit a pronounced curve, and are frequently triangular in cross-section. As in the north, microblades are frequently found with other tool forms, usually flake scrapers and other flake tools.

Brantingham et al. have observed microliths in association with a blade-and-bladelet technology in the northern Jangtang.[64] They speculate that the blade technology could be as old as 25,000 B.P., but more probably dates to 15,000 B.P. They do not, however, believe that microblades are of this antiquity, and instead suggest they are of Neolithic age. Illustrations of the microcores from their sites indicate that these could be comfortably placed within the northern tradition as defined above.

Because of the lack of systematic work on microlithic technology on the plateau, it is difficult to place these traditions into a broader perspective and assess their anthropological significance. Basic chronology is desperately needed to evaluate how and where these tools change across the plateau. Until stratigraphic excavations are conducted, little progress on using microliths as cultural markers or representations of specific cultural adaptations can be made. However, it is possible to speculate briefly on how these tools may have been used by plateau inhabitants. We begin by assuming that microliths are not common until after 15,000 B.P., and quite possibly 10,000 B.P. Elston and Brantingham, using a risk-minimization model, argue that microlithic tools become important in northern Asia (which would include the Tibetan plateau) as part of an adaptation directed at the intensification of large-game hunting in highly variable seasonal environments.[65] They demonstrate that although composite microlithic tools are more expensive to make than bifacial points, they are more lethal killing tools, and were more reliable than bifacial tools, thus minimizing subsistence risk. They further speculate that wedge-shaped cores may have been used in high-risk situations, such as hunting for winter stores in highly variable environments, since tool production was more predictable than with simple boat-shaped cores, which may have been used in less risky contexts. In Tibet, it is interesting to note that wedge-shaped cores form the primary component of the northern tradition, while boat-shaped cores are found in the south. If time is not a factor in this, this suggests that northern foragers faced greater subsistence risk and may have had higher levels of residential mobility than their southern counterparts. This

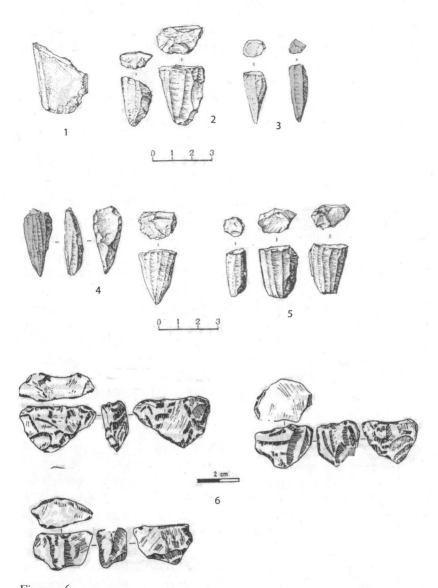

Figure 1.6

Microliths from the Tibetan plateau. 1: wedge-shaped cores, northern and central Jangtang (after An et al., 1982, fig. 3); 2: flat cores, northern and central Jangtang (after An et al., 1982, fig. 3); 3: conical cores, northern and central Jangtang (after An et al., 1982, fig. 3); 4: conical cores, northern and central Jangtang (after An et al., 1982, fig. 3); 5: cylindrical cores, northern and central Jangtang (after An et al., 1982, fig. 3); 6: wedge and funnel-shaped cores, southern Tibet (after Tang and Hare, 1995, fig. 8).

is certainly consistent with modern ecological structure, wherein the Jangtang (the north) is a patchy, arid environment whereas the south (primarily the major river valley systems) is relatively benign by comparison.

THE NEOLITHIC OF THE TIBETAN PLATEAU

As Underhill notes, the Neolithic in China is said to be characterized by "pottery, ground stone tools, sedentism, cultivation, and animal husbandry."[66] This definition has been extended to the Tibetan plateau, but with the clear proviso that the Neolithic there has a number of significant differences when compared to its low-elevation counterpart, and appears also to have a much longer duration. Although there are fewer Neolithic era sites known on the plateau compared to earlier time periods, excavations and data recovery at these sites are far more complete, and consequently, we have a more secure understanding of many aspects of Neolithic lifeways than of the Paleolithic.

How the Neolithic is characterized depends on location. For instance, there are a large number of Neolithic sites known from the extreme northeastern part of Qinghai near its border with Gansu. The western Machu (Huang He or Yellow) River valley has been studied extensively by Chinese archaeologists and consequently, they have extended the Neolithic phase names from this region into this area of the plateau.[67] These are generally applicable to this specific region, but cannot be extended beyond it. Elsewhere on the plateau, archaeological cultures are named after specific sites, such as "Qugong culture" or "Karou culture." As more information is generated, it is likely that these will become phase names for the Neolithic.

There are four areas on the plateau where Neolithic period sites have been extensively examined: the extreme northeastern corner of Qinghai near its border with Gansu, around the modern city of Chamdo at the eastern edge of the plateau near the Dzachu (Mekong) River, at the great bend of the Yarlung Tsangpo river as it turns southward, and on the central plateau in the Yarlung and Kyichu valleys (fig. 1.7). Table 1.3 lists reported radiocarbon dates from these sites. In addition to research at village or habitation sites, there has been considerable work directed at the excavation of burial mounds and tumuli across the plateau, and many of these tombs appear to be Neolithic.[68]

The earliest known Neolithic culture on the Tibetan plateau is found near the modern city of Chamdo at Karou (table 1.3). The site is found at 3100 meters above sea level on a high terrace above the Zachu (Mekong) River. The total site area was estimated to be 1 ha, of which 1800 m^2 was systematically excavated over 2 years (1978–79) by a joint archaeological team of [the] Cultural Relics Administration of the TAR and the history department of Sichuan University led by Chinese archaeologist Tong Enzheng.[69] Although the stratigraphy of the site was

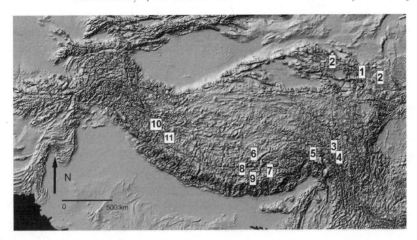

Figure 1.7
Location of major Neolithic and complex period sites. 1: Liuwan; 2: Qinghai Neolithic sites; 3: Xiaoenda; 4: Karou; 5: Neolithic sites at the Great Bend of the Yarlung Tsangpo; 6: Qugong; 7: Qinba; 8: Changguogou; 9: Bangga; 10: Dindun; 11: Kyunglung.

complex, it could be divided into five (not including the modern ground surface) major stratigraphic complexes, which are said to contain evidence of at least two, and most probably three, distinct occupations of the site. Although some archaeologists continue with efforts to make the occupation of Karou as early as possible, the range of occupation fits most comfortably from ca. 4000 to 2000 B.C. No cemetery was located, although one rectangular stone tomb was located near the site and has become the definition of the "Karou tomb type."[70] The earliest occupation level (4) contained the remains of seven structures interpreted as domestic residences. Of these, three were rectangular in form and semi-subterranean in construction, and ranged in size from 13.8 to 24 m² in covered floor area. Two were round or ovoid pit structures, somewhat smaller (10.1–11.4 m² areas) with central hearth features. Two other structures were incomplete. In Level 3, many more structures were present. All but one (a roughly ovoid structure partially destroyed by construction) were rectangular and of semi-subterranean construction. Those with central hearth features ranged in covered floor area from roughly 12 to 34 m²; one structure with what appeared to be multiple rooms or a covered patio had 69 m² of floor area. Smaller structures without hearths (presumably small storage facilities) were adjacent to some of these residences. Reconstructions of both the storage and residences suggest that ladders were used to enter and exit them. In Level 2 (said to be the later occupation), was a single complex of three semi-subterranean structures with interior walls composed of rough, uncut stone. Two of these structures had large central hearths and one

TABLE 1.3

RADIOCARBON DATES FROM THE TIBETAN NEOLITHIC

Site	Date[a]	Calibrated date	Comments
Karou	4955 ± 100	3966–3317[b]	Level 4, early occupation[i]
	4280 ± 100	3104–2616[b]	Level 3, early occupation[ii]
	3930 ± 80	2603–2196[b]	Level 2, later occupation[iii]
Qugong		1742–1519[c]	
		1688–1457[c]	
		1598–1055[c]	
		1523–1323[c]	
		1414–1162[c]	
		1368–102[c]	Ignored by authors as too late[iv]
		1308–930[c]	Ignored by authors as too late[v]
Xiaoenda	3775 ± 80	2459–2012[b]	

[a]Uncalibrated radiocarbon years before present.
[b]Date calibrated by authors using Calib 4.3, and reported as B.C.
[c]Date calibrated by original author using tree-ring intercepts available at the time of publication; reported as B.C.
[i]Bureau of Cultural Relics, Tibet Autonomous Region and Department of History, Sichuan University, Changdu Karou [Karou: A Neolithic Site in Tibet] (Beijing: Wenwu chubanshe, 1985).
[ii]Bureau of Cultural Relics, TAR, Karou: A Neolithic Site in Tibet.
[iii]Bureau of Cultural Relics, TAR, Karou: A Neolithic Site in Tibet.
[iv]Institute of Archaeology, Chinese Academy of Social Science and Bureau of Cultural Relics, Tibet Autonomous Region, "Xizang Guoga xian changguogou xin shi qi shi dai yi zhi" [The Changuogou Neolithic Site in Gongga County, Tibet], Kaogu 4 (1999): 1–10; and Qugong in Lhasa: Excavations of an Ancient Site and Tombs (Beijing: Encyclopedia of China Publishing House, 1999).
[v]Institute of Archaeology et al., "The Changuogou Neolithic Site in Gongga County, Tibet"; and Qugong in Lhasa.

had a bench against one of the interior walls (fig. 1.8).[71] The authors of the report reconstruct this complex with flat roofs, which resemble some modern Tibetan architecture (fig. 1.9).[72] Other features on the Level 2 surface include two stone walkways, a large rectangle of stone of uncertain function, a small stone pen, and circular stone features.

The artifacts recovered from Karou are impressive. Ceramic forms are primarily basins, bowls, and jars, and are for the most part incompletely fired. Decorative motifs are incised and graved geometric patterns with some appliqué, cord-marking, and basket impressions. One vessel shows traces of black

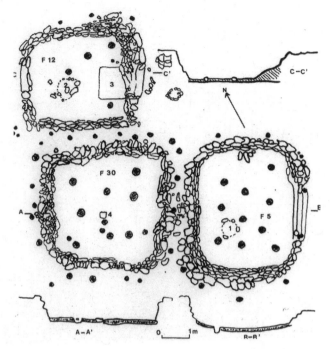

Figure 1.8
Plan view of residential structures found on Level 2, Karou (after Bureau of Cultural Relics, Tibet Autonomous Region and Department of History, Sichuan University, 1985, p. 33).

and red paint. The lithic assemblage includes chipped stone tools, debitage, some microliths, and ground stone and polished tools. Flake tools are much more abundant than microliths. Most of the microlithic cores are conical or polyhedral in form, although some wedge-shaped and boat-shaped cores are present. Bone tools are abundant as well, and include awls, probable weaving tools, needles, and combs. Decorative objects include stone pendants, jade pins, perforated shells, and stone bracelets. The presence of ceramic spindle whorls indicates textile production, but it is not clear what was being spun.

Subsistence at Karou is said to be characterized by a mix of hunting, gathering, and plant cultivation. Animals hunted include red deer (*Cervus elaphus*), roe deer (*Capreolus capreolus*), goral (a small, goat-like antelope; *Naemorhedus goral*), serows (SE Asia wild goat; *Capricornus* sp.), Tibetan gazelle (*Procapra picticaudata*), Chinese water deer (*Hydropotes inermis*), and woolly hare (*Lepus ojostolus*). Unidentified bovids are also present, as are various species of macaques, rodents, and rats. Pigs (*Sus* sp.) are present, and are thought to be domesticated. Plant remains include cultivated millet, chenopods (likely to have been collected), and other plants.

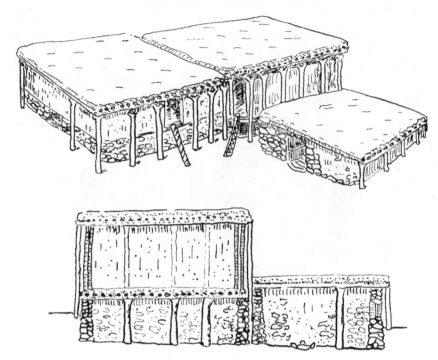

Figure 1.9
Reconstruction of Level 2 structures, Karou (after Bureau of Cultural Relics, Tibet Autonomous Region and Department of History, Sichuan University, 1985, p. 36).

Although the excavators speculate that Karou has similarities to sites in northwestern Sichuan, such as Lizhou,[73] they conclude their evaluation of the site by suggesting that it is a representation of an indigenous Tibetan archaeological culture. Indeed, other sites in the Chamdo area, such as Xiaoenda with its similar cultural content, reinforce this interpretation.[74] Although its occupations are contemporary with the Majiayao, Banshan, and Machang cultures to the north, they are significantly different from these in terms of content, and clearly do not owe their origins to them. As more data are recovered from Sichuan and Yunnan, connections to the plateau from these regions may move from the realm of almost pure speculation to more reasoned analysis.[75]

The second major Neolithic site found on the plateau is Qugong, located 5 km north of Lhasa at an elevation of 3680 meters above sea level.[76] The site is found along the margins of a low hill at the base of higher hills and mountains. The site was heavily eroded, and had also suffered damage from local villagers who used the soil of the terrace for construction projects. Portions of the site were also damaged by intrusive tombs. The original extent of the site was estimated to be ca. 1 ha, and of this, ca. 0.4 ha were excavated. A mortuary component, containing 32 tombs, is found some 300 m to the northwest. According to the excavators, the site could have been occupied as early as 1750 B.C. (table 1.3), and was probably abandoned by ca. 1100 B.C. Note that these occupations are considerably later in time than those at Karou, and they overlap substantially with the Chinese periodization of so-called Chalcolithic and early Bronze Age cultures such as Qijia (ca. 2000 B.C.), Siwa (1300–1000 B.C.), and Xindian (ca. 1000 B.C.) of Gansu and northwestern China.

The deposit is divided into early and late components. The early component had no structural features present aside from a number of ash pits and three tombs. The later component was defined as one of "redeposition," which in this case appears to mean the reworking of the deposit through time. The ceramic assemblage is described by the investigators as "mature," meaning that many of the vessels are finely made and highly fired (especially when compared to the Karou assemblage), and include both hand molded and wheel-thrown examples. Some of the finest ceramics are a highly burnished blackware. However, decoration continues to consist of geometric forms executed by incision, punctuation, and some painting. Forms include bowls, jars, and cups. The lithic assemblage still contains a few microliths made on wedge- or boat-shaped cores, and a wide variety of types, including unifacial points. Grinding stones for both subsistence and pigments (red ochre) are common. Bone tools include awls, needles, points, hairpins, combs, and probable weaving implements. Only one bronze artifact—an arrowhead—was recovered from the site. A detailed analysis suggests it is of local origin. Subsistence practice was not examined in detail for plants (only a pollen analysis was conducted), but faunal remains included examples of yak (*Bos grunnians*), domesticated sheep (*Ovis aries shangi*), musk deer (*Moschus moschiferus*), red deer (*Cervus elaphus*), Thorold's deer (*Cervus albirostris*), domesticated pig (*Sus scrofa*), Tibetan ass (*kiang; Equus hemionus kiang*), dog, and some birds. Not surprisingly, animal husbandry is of great importance, but hunting continues to be a significant part of subsistence effort.

The tombs that are clearly associated with the early deposit are small, square-to-rectangular in form, with walls made of stone. The floors are soil. They contain secondary burials in a flexed position. Only one tomb had grave goods, which consisted of utilitarian ceramics. Unfortunately, it is not clear which tombs from the cemetery component of the site date to the Neolithic, but it seems certain that the majority date to the Bronze Age and later.[77] One of these tombs contained a spectacular bronze mirror, the first found in any archaeological context in Tibet, and of clear Central Asia origin. The dating of the mirror is controversial, but consensus is beginning to emerge that the mirror appeared in this portion of the plateau some time between 800 and 500 B.C. based on the examination of stylistic motifs and its chemical composition.[78]

Other sites associated with Qugong and which have had some systematic work include Changguogou, located south of Lhasa on the north bank of the Yarlung Tsangpo at an elevation of 3570 meters above sea level,[79] Bangga in the Yarlung Valley,[80] and Qinba.[81] Although not radiocarbon dated, the archaeological assemblage, especially the ceramics, at Changguogou, are very similar to those found at Qugong. Excavations at Bangga have uncovered at least one rectangular semi-subterranean house with 24 m² of covered floor area, stone-lined interior storage pits (one of which was used for a secondary burial), and ceramics similar to those at Qugong. Sites thought to be part of the Qugong tradition but which have seen limited work are those in the great bend area (Nyingtri/Nyingchi) of the Yarlung Tsangpo, such as Jumu, Beibeng, and Maniweng, among others.[82]

Most of the authors who have worked with Qugong materials argue that this archaeological culture has its origins in the earlier Karou culture, and as such, it is an indigenous Tibetan development. What is known of it suggests a village-based society with limited social differentiation as indicated by mortuary remains. Qugong likely had trade connections with cultures in Sichuan and possibly central Asia, and certain technologies, like metal working in bronze, had apparently entered the central plateau sometime before this.

If Karou and Qugong are thought to be "Tibetan," the Neolithic cultures in extreme northeastern Qinghai are clearly of lower elevation origin. The dating of Neolithic cultures in this area remains controversial. The Yangshao culture is well known from eastern Gansu and the central Huang He (Yellow) River valley, and is said to date between 5000 and 3400 B.C.[83] Its presence in Qinghai has been debated, and a local culture, Shilingxia, is said to be its extreme western variant.[84] However, it seems more reasonable to regard this culture as an early expression of the following culture, Majiayao (3400–2800 B.C.), which is well defined in Qinghai. Important sites of this culture include Sunjiazhai, Shangsunjia, and Hetaozhuang.[85] They are said to be between 20 and 30 smaller sites in extreme eastern Qinghai that have traces of Majiayao culture, primarily ceramics. This culture is characterized by rectangular semi-subterranean houses, grinding stones, polished stone axes, hoes, large numbers of bone tools, and impressive ceramics painted in red and black with geometric and animal motifs. Sites in Gansu of this culture are known to have broomcorn and foxtail millet as well as hemp fruits. Cemeteries are found near the largest villages, and in the Qinghai sites, burials are secondary and found in wooden coffins. Some burials had significant quantities of painted ceramics accompanying them. The next culture to be found in the region is Banshan (2800–2300 B.C.), which is known in Qinghai primarily from the famous mortuary site of Liuwan.[86] A total of 257 burials of this period were discovered, and burial treatments ranged from secondary to simple, extended burials through multiple burials within the same rectangular wooden coffin. Burials were accompanied by a wide variety of artifacts, including the famous Banshan ceramics, stone tools (both chipped and polished), bone tools, and some decorative objects, including turquoise, bone, and stone beads as well as stone bracelets. The final Neolithic culture in this region is Machang (2300–2100 B.C.). Although best known from Liuwan, there are village sites known from this period in Qinghai, including Machangyan.

Subsistence continues to be focused upon millet, and residential structures are similar to those of the preceding cultures. The majority of burials at Liuwan date to this culture, and while burials are generally similar to those of earlier cultures, the ceramics now have [a] significant number of anthropomorphic motifs as well as geometries that resemble certain characters of early historic writing systems.[87] Some mortuary treatments are impressive—one Machang burial from Liuwan had more than 90 highly decorated ceramic vessels.

One additional source of data on the Neolithic is the very large number of mortuary sites examined by Chinese archaeologists. In comparison to habitation sites, which are usually buried by alluvial or colluvial processes, mortuary sites are distinctive since they often are characterized by above-surface mounds of varying shapes and sizes. Mortuary sites are found along the Nyechu (Longzhi) River in the Lhoka (Shannan) region in southern Tibet, near Nyingtri (Nyingchi) of the Yarlung Tsangpo valley, and near Zhigatsé. Many of these sites have been tested and excavated, but unfortunately, the data recovered from them tend not to be examined systematically, and few of the sites have been dated by radiometric methods. Consequently, typologies of mound types are constructed on the basis of the few sites that have been dated, and by assumptions about site age and affiliation based on cross-dating of artifact types, often from areas far-flung from the plateau. Two archaeologists—Huo[88] and Xiage[89] have attempted to systematize these data for the central and southern parts of the plateau. Despite these efforts, clear patterns are not obvious. Tombs assigned to the Neolithic are described as "stone coffins," are square or rectangular in form, and are made either with large flat slabs for walls and floors, or coursed, uncut stone used to construct walls. An uncommon, more complex form is said to be a stone cyst tomb with an entrance, tunnel passage, and central chamber.[90] Burial goods, if present, tend to be simple decorative objects (stone beads) or small amounts of local ceramics. Burial treatments tend to be flexed, and are often secondary. Some of these tombs, especially those in the vicinity of Karou, are thought to have originated from migrants to the plateau of people from the adjacent, lower elevation valleys on western Sichuan.[91] In short, while tombs are in abundance on the plateau, they currently contribute little to our knowledge of the Neolithic because they have not been systematically dated and associated with habitation sites.

The most controversial question of the Neolithic on the Tibetan plateau is the debate over the origins of what are known today as the Tibetan people. Some authors have argued strongly that the majority of the current ethnic inhabitants of the plateau owe their origins linguistically, culturally, and biologically to migrations of people from east Asian sources during the Neolithic. This issue has already arisen in the discussion of the peopling of the plateau during the Paleolithic. We have already alluded to the shifting meanings of the term "Tibet" and "Tibetan," and thus it should not be surprising that considerable confusion accompanies this debate. Renfrew has summarized current directions

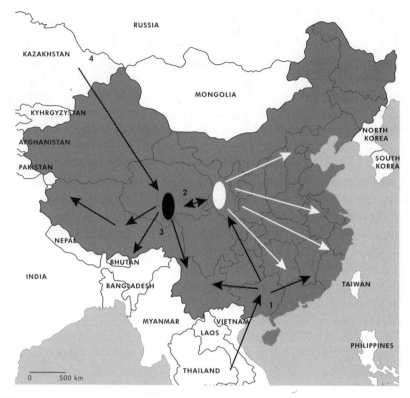

Figure 1.10

Su et al. (2000) model of population and linguistic relationships. 1: proto-Chinese entry into Yellow River drainage between 40,000 and 20,000 years ago; 2: formation of proto-Sino-Tibetan ca. 10,000 years ago; 3: proto-Tibeto-Burman ca. 6000 years ago; 4: central Asian genetic contribution ca. 6000 years ago.

in research that has attempted to correlate in a systematic manner historical linguistics, molecular biology, and archaeological data, and while optimistic about the future of this synthesis, nevertheless observes that making explicit correlations between languages, "races" or ethnic groups, and archaeological cultures is fraught with difficulty.[92] Nevertheless, a number of authors have made the attempt to create such a synthesis for the occupation of the plateau. The most prominent of these are those by Su[93] and van Driem.[94]

Su and others' model asserts that that deep in prehistory, a Southeast Asian population moved into southern China, specifically into Yunnan and Guangxi. Using a specific dominant Y haplotype (M122C), Su *et al.* argue that this south China-based population moved into the central and western Machu (Huanghe, Yellow) river basin sometime between 20,000 and 40,000 B.P. (fig. 1.10).[95] They label this group "Proto-Chinese," which over time genetically and linguistically diverges into what they call "Proto-Sino-Tibetan." Around 10,000 B.P., this population began to grow substantially, and budding daughter populations were forced into new niches, with some of these populations moving further to the west along the Machu. Around 6000 B.P., another linguistic shift occurs, with what are now called "Proto-Tibeto-Burmans," which move from their western Machu and eastern Qinghai focus across the Tibetan plateau. With yet another linguistic split, one group (Baric speakers) moves to the south, crossing the Himalaya, and moving back into northern Yunnan, Bhutan, and northeastern India. Still another group (Bodhic speakers), after having received a significant genetic admixture of an unspecified central Asian or southwestern Siberian population, moves across the entire Tibetan plateau. The authors argue that this model is supported by archaeology[96] and linguistics.[97]

Van Driem's model is similar to that of Su and others but makes a stronger attempt to integrate archaeological data. He begins with a historical classification of Tibeto-Burmese languages, and divides them into two major groups—an eastern and western variant.[98] Of concern here is the eastern group, which can be further subdivided into two groups—northern (Sino-Bodic) and southern languages (which are found in Southeast Asia). Sino-Bodic is split into a northwestern (Bodic) and a northeastern (Sinitic) group of languages. Bodic can then be split into Bodish (the source of languages spoken on the plateau) and Himalayan (various languages spoken along the Himalayan chain as well as Kashmir in the distant west). This language phylogeny is distinctly different than that proposed by Matisoff.[99]

Given the relationships between these language families and their spatial distribution, van Driem proceeds to create a hypothesis of how this patterning can be explained.[100] He postulates the existence by 11,500 B.C. of an ancestral homeland of Tibeto-Burmese speakers in the middle and upper Yangtze (Drichu) river of Sichuan. This population served as the source of the early Neolithic groups in both the eastern (Peiligang) and western (Dadiwan) Huanghe basin. Both areas were occupied as early as 6500 B.C., and van Driem labels them as "Northern Tibeto-Burmese" speakers (fig. 1.11). He suggests that the clearest archaeological correlate of this migration is what he terms the "abrupt" replacement of local microlithic-using cultures by the Dadiwan cultivators.[101] These migrants brought with them cord-marked pottery and polished stone tools, which van Driem takes as cultural and ethnic markers.

The postulated linguistic divergence that created Northwestern Tibeto-Burmese (Bodic) languages is directly correlated by van Driem with the appearance of the Majiayao Neolithic in Gansu and extreme eastern Qinghai, which he dates as early as 3900 B.C. He argues that this group not only migrates onto the plateau proper, ultimately spreading Bodish languages across the plateau, but that it is also responsible for the appearance of what he calls the "Northern Neolithic" cultures of Kashmir by 2700 B.C. This group of Himalayan family language speakers then populates the southern fringes and valley systems of the Himalayan chain after this date. Although he does not mention either Karou or

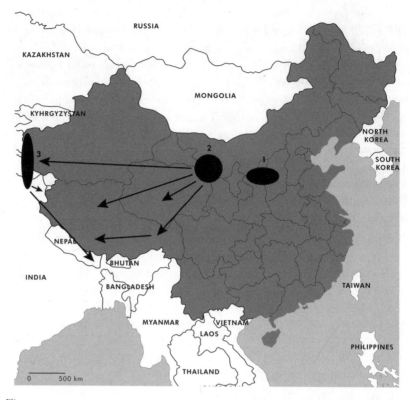

Figure 1.11

Van Driem's (2002) model of population, linguistic, and archaeological relationships. 1: ancestral home of Tibeto-Burman speakers, ca. 11,500 B.C.; 2: "Northern Tibeto-Burmese speakers," ca. 6500 B.C.; 3: Kashmiri "Northern Neolithic," ca. 2700 B.C.

Qugong or any of the other central Tibetan plateau archaeological sites in his model, it is clear that these cultures would be considered derivative from the Majiayao Neolithic, in sharp contrast to the assertions of the Chinese archaeologists who excavated them.

Van Driem discusses the genetic data available at the time and how they integrate with his linguistic model.[102] He argues that the Su *et al.* model is flawed because it is based upon an inadequate sampling of Tibeto-Burman speakers in outlying, but critical, areas of the Himalayas, and further, the linguistic phylogeny is flawed. He asserts that Chu *et al.*'s use of microsatellite markers is a more comprehensive reconstruction of east Asian population relationships, which also included groups from outside the region for comparative purposes, and that it is in general accord with his archaeo-linguistic reconstruction.[103]

What are we to make of these models? While they are broadly plausible, they suffer from a number of problems that limit their utility. Looking first at the genetic data, it is clear that both suffer some methodological defects. Su *et al.'s* model is based upon a very small sample given the complexity of the argument. And while van Driem claims that the Chu and others' model supports his position, a careful reading belies that assertion. As expected, their model shows that Tibetans have a greater genetic similarity with the northern Chinese than they do with other east Asian peoples or groups from different areas. However, when they examine only east Asian populations, their results are surprising, and place Tibetans into a mixed group of southern and northern Chinese. Given this wholly unexpected finding, Cavalli-Sforza, while generally laudatory of the Chu and others' model, suggests these data be viewed with caution.[104] This is especially concerning given that two studies using different genetic markers— Torroni and others and Qian and others—have confirmed the presence of central Asian genes in modern Tibetan populations. We suggest that the Chu *et al.* study has little reliable to say about the peopling of the plateau, and that they offer no support for van Driem's reconstruction.

Both models assume that archaeological cultures are direct material indicators of ethnicity and language. Seldom, if ever, does a single artifact type, burial practice, or stylistic motif unambiguously represent a set of genes or language. Moreover, the models simply assume language dispersal via migration, and as Renfrew and others have pointed out, there are other mechanisms for language dispersal that do not assume the direct, large-scale movement of people.[105] Another problem with the models is that they rely upon selective use of inaccurate and incomplete archaeological data. Both models ignore entirely the central Tibetan Neolithic sites. Their use of the western Machu (Huanghe, Yellow) river data is generally accurately portrayed in terms of cultural content and dating, however, and to be fair to van Driem,[106] he does assert, following Chang,[107] that one important source of plateau population is likely to be the western Drichu (Yangtze) river valleys of western Sichuan.

However, perhaps the greatest flaw of both models is the simplistic way in which migration is conceived. Van Driem offers a number of motivations for Majiayao Neolithic people to move to the west, including ecological calamity, stress, or simply, "tidings of prosperity from the west."[108] Unfortunately, for these models, their authors appear not to have looked carefully at their maps and considered the subsistence technologies of these people in their desire to move them about the landscape. Both models have agricultural peoples from relatively low elevations moving up to the high plateau and across the hyperarid and frigid Jangtang. Only pastoralists thrive in these portions of the plateau, and it is far-fetched indeed to believe that these sedentary agriculturalists somehow moved a Neolithic "package" across the Jangtang and into the far west without significant changes to that package. These models also ignore all of the problems created by hypoxic environments and their effects on human physiology. In short, they assume demic diffusion, rather than some alternative, without thinking seriously of how the subsistence system of the cultures could have likewise been transported, and how these cultures adapted to the known rigors of life at high elevation.

A more plausible model of the appearance of the Neolithic cultural package on the plateau is one that supports a mosaic of both demic and acculturation mechanisms. Demic diffusion is clearly plausible in Qinghai, but the spread of the Majiayao Neolithic package should be limited to Qinghai. Central Tibetan plateau sites have few direct material affinities with these cultures, and we should be looking elsewhere for their sources. We agree with van Driem that Sichuan is a likely source for a Neolithic package, and it is very likely that demic diffusion pushed populations up the major river valleys of the eastern plateau. Instead of moving these Tibeto-Burmese speakers north, then back south again, it is far more parsimonious to move them from Sichuan upward onto the plateau. Karou may have been founded by this demic expansion, and if this is the case, we should find more Neolithic sites expanding up all of the major valley systems sometime after 6000 B.P., a date consistent with Ren's model of agricultural expansion.[109] The mechanism for the expansion of the Neolithic across the plateau could be either demic diffusion or acculturation, but since the data are scanty, it is not possible to test either alternative. However, an acculturation mechanism may be the best explanation for the presence of central Asian or southwestern Siberian genes in Tibetan populations according to Su and others' model if we assume that these genes were those associated with the Mesolithic peoples of the plateau who adopted the Neolithic package or married into it. Qugong, as a descendant of Karou, appears to reflect an indigenous expansion of the Neolithic into new niches further to the west.

Just how complex are the central plateau sites? This question cannot be answered at present simply because few sites have been excavated, and none have yet been placed into a regional scale settlement system. The mortuary data suggest that significant social differentiation had not yet occurred on the central plateau by ca. 1900 B.C. This stands in stark contrast to the Qinghai Neolithic sites, where displays of wealth accompanying burials suggests some social ranking in place in that region by the end of the Neolithic. It is important to remember, however, that both the central plateau and Qinghai are quite simple when compared to cultural developments taking place further to the east in China, such as the Xia Dynasty, which is said to have been founded around 2200 B.C.

TOWARD COMPLEXITY

As we move toward the known complexity and political centralization that accompanies the emergence of the Tibetan empire in the mid-seventh century A.D., it is the case that historical documents, rather than archaeological evidence, serve as the primary record of the period from the end of the Neolithic onward. In China, we now enter the period of the historically known dynasties beginning with the Shang (ca. 1700–1100 B.C.) to the Sui (A.D. 580–618). During this period, China itself saw varying degrees of political centralization, retraction, and territorial expansion. The majority of these dynasties rose in eastern China, and had greater or lesser levels of contact with and interest in the peoples and polities to the west, including what is today known as Tibet. Writing systems first appear in Shang times, and some authorities believe that oracle bone inscriptions dating to ca. 1400 B.C. which describe the Qiang (Ch'iang) people are in fact making reference to inhabitants of the eastern fringes of the Tibetan plateau.[110] Whether this reference is actually specific to Tibetans, or one of many small ethnic groups and tribes that inhabited the western fringe of China, from Gansu southward through Sichuan and into Yunnan, is unknown. Indeed, some authors note that while the Qiang are a recognized nationality within the Chinese state today, the term "Qiang" is a generic Han term for non-Han or is best read as a Han conceptualization of the "other" with a deep antiquity that reflects a distinction between a pastoral and an agricultural lifeway.[111] What seems clear, however, is that the Chinese written record had no clear description of the agricultural peoples of the central Tibetan plateau until much later in time, and most have concluded that the Qiang were ethnically and culturally distinct from Tibetans.[112] In fact, the first written reference by Chinese authors to central Tibet comes during Sui times with the recognition of a pre-empire Tibetan king named Namri Songtsen, who was the father of the first emperor of Tibet, Songtsen Gampo.[113]

Although few other written records of Chinese interest in Tibet can be found, there was considerable contact between Tibetan polities, such as they were, and the Han dynasty (206–209 B.C.). The Han significantly expanded and eventually centralized the Chinese state, and established its capital at Chang'an (Xi'an) in western China. Trade contacts with inner Asia were important, and the Han gained control of the lucrative Silk Road, which runs just along the northern fringes of the plateau eventually entering Gansu and continuing to the east. Small Tibetan polities in Qinghai (often described as "tribes" or "people") such as the Tibetan speaking Sumpa and Azha, undoubtedly benefited from participation in this trade. However, this gives little insight into what these polities might have been like socially and politically.

Tibetan historical records written well after the spread of the empire and found at Dunhuang, a major religious and economic center along the Silk Road found at the very eastern margin of the Taklamakan desert, provide some insight into the immediately pre-empire polities of the plateau. Although these documents are known to be combinations of myth, legend, and history of highly doubtful veracity, as summarized by Haarh[114] and others, the polities on the central Tibetan plateau were probably small-scale chiefly societies that inhabited the major river valleys and tributary streams of the Yarlung Tsangpo drainage (the region of central Tibet known today as Ü-Tsang.) The term "clan" is often used to describe these groups, and these clans (or lineages) persisted as major political factors well after the establishment and fall of the empire. They held territory, and established major strongholds on mountain peaks surrounding the river basins. Warfare was common, as was extensive alliance building. Political leadership is characterized as a form of divine kingship, and religious practice is said to have been based upon shamanic ritual, which included the worship of local mountain deities and animal sacrifice.[115] Haarh notes that these historical sources indicate that one of these probably mythical rulers made contact with Indian Buddhism some five generations before the start of Songtsen Gampo's reign,[116] although the earliest known Buddhist constructions on the plateau are contemporaneous with the establishment of the empire.[117] Economically, these polities were based upon the use of a full suite of animal and plant domesticates that was introduced onto the plateau during the Neolithic, but with the addition of the horse and goat, iron tools, and sophisticated agricultural technologies, including small-scale irrigation systems and terracing.

Unfortunately, there is almost no archaeological evidence of this period in the central Tibetan plateau, and consequently, it is not possible to either examine the veracity of these reconstructions or track the transformations of these polities as they moved toward centralization by the mid-seventh century. A large number of mortuary sites have been located on the central plateau, however, and while many of these have been excavated, few of them have been dated and systematically examined.[118]

Some of the best data on this long period are found, paradoxically, on the Jangtang and in far western Tibet. Although little is known today beyond a handful of specialists, the Zhangzhung (also Shangshung or Zan-Zun) polity once thrived in the high deserts of western Tibet between ca. 500 B.C. to A.D. 625. The origins and evolution of the polity are shrouded in mystery. Legends and fragmentary history speak of migrations of peoples from the west into the homeland of Zhangzhung, but when these occurred is unknown. The nature of the polity is debated: it has been variously described as a small-scale coalition of territorially based lineages, a kingdom,[119] a confederation,[120] a petty state,[121] and an empire. Even the location of Zhangzhung has been disputed, with some authors arguing for a vast, nebulous polity that extended from western Tibet well into northeastern Tibet and beyond.[122] But aside from the myth, legend and apparent mystery, Zhangzhung played a major role in central Asian prehistory and history. It appears to have acted as an important intermediary of trade and the diffusion of knowledge between the Indian subcontinent and the Tibetan plateau, and for a time, was a significant political rival of the emerging Tibetan empire. It also acted as a filter of knowledge and cultural influences from the distant west, including Sogdiana, Persia, and the Hellenistic world.[123] Perhaps of even greater importance was the sponsorship by Zhangzhung of

Bön, a belief system thought by many to be the indigenous religion of much of the Tibetan plateau, and which had a profound influence of the development and evolution of Tibetan Buddhism.

Some of the most interesting data on the pre-Buddhist, possibly Zhang-zhung, occupation of western Tibet are those collected by Bellezza in a series of remarkable exploratory trips across the Jangtang.[124] During his more than a decade of research, he discovered almost 500 archaeological sites which he has placed into four major categories: fortresses (in what appear to be defensible locations), buildings (residential and religious), stela (or standing stones in a variety of configurations), and tombs. Using a combination of local myth and oral tradition, religious texts, and other data, he argues that most of these sites were founded in the period after ca. 1000 B.C. but before the introduction of Buddhism to the northern plateau, which could not have occurred before the establishment of the Tibetan empire in the seventh century A.D., and most probably after its "second diffusion" in the years following A.D. 1000. Unfortunately, Bellezza has no chronological control over these sites since he was unable to collect materials from them or excavate at them. While the majority of these sites are likely to be pre-Buddhist, just when they fall into time and how they articulate within a settlement system is unknowable at this point.

Further to the south, excavations at a number of pre-Buddhist sites have created an empirical basis for chronology in the region. These excavations are a part of a larger collaborative project between western and Chinese archaeologists designed to understand the second diffusion of Buddhism into far western Tibet.[125] During that project, a village site—Dindun—was excavated[126] as were two cemetery complexes, Gebusailu and Sasongtang.[127] The village component consisted of at least 11 structures, of which three were fully excavated. The structures were semi-subterranean built with coursed stone on a rectangular plan (fig. 1.12). Although the number of rooms varied, the placement of features was consistent in them, as was the material culture, which consisted of cord-marked and unslipped plainwares, animal bone (caprids and bovids), ground-stone tools, and metal scrap. The tombs vary in size, shape (circular and rectangular), and construction details (number of chambers, materials used). All, however, are excavated into the ground to varying depths, and one is a shaft tomb, unique in the archaeological record of this region. This tomb contained some scattered human remains, a disarticulated horse, a bronze dagger, small iron artifacts, and ceramics identical to those found at Dindun. Three radiocarbon dates have been run on the village and mortuary complex (2380 ± 80; 2310 ± 60; 2065 ± 60), and using the R–Combine function of Oxcal 3.8,[128] these calibrate into the most probable time frame of 400–100 B.C. These dates place Dindun and the cemeteries within the putative range of Zhangzhung, but the data are clearly insufficient to say that Dindun represents the Zhangzhung archaeological culture. This will require far more systematic excavation at sites across the region.

One of the structures at Dindun had a stela (or standing stone) in a small chamber within it. Two other standing stones were found at the east and west sides of the village.[129] Scattered across Tibet and the trans-Himalaya are literally thousands of standing stones of varied shapes and sizes, and which are found in a diversity of contexts that indicate far more humble, but complex, uses than those devoted to the royal dynasties and their activities. Standing stones first became known to the west at the beginning of the twentieth century when the Tibetologist M. J. Bacot in 1907 described what he called a "megalith" observed in eastern Tibet.[130] Standing stones were subsequently reported by Francke in both western Tibet and Poo in the Langchen Kebap (Sutlej) valley near a village called Dralang.[131] He described them simply as "perpendicular stones," with one further labeled as a "lingam." Perhaps the most important of these early descriptions of standing stones was made by Roerich.[132] During his Central Asiatic Expedition from 1925 to 1928 which explored what was then called Chinese Turkestan, the Altai, western Mongolia, and parts of northern and western Tibet, he discovered a number of archaeological sites with standing stones called by the locals *doring*, but which Roerich labeled menhirs, cromlechs, and alignments.[133] One of these sites, known as Doring, had the remains of an impressive alignment that combined 18 rows of smaller standing stones, a circle of larger ones, and an arrow-shaped alignment pointing due west.[134] Among the speculations he offered as an interpretation of this set of alignments were broad similarities of the Tibetan alignments with the megalithic cultures of western Europe, and the presence of the arrow as a reflection of the indigenous "nature cult," which

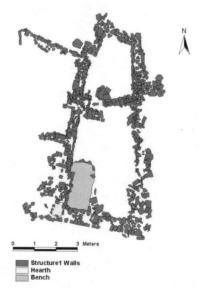

N

0   1   2   3 Meters

■ Structure1 Walls
□ Hearth
▨ Bench

Figure 1.12
Residential structure from Dindun, western Tibet.

he said included sun and fire worship, among other things. Elsewhere, he argued that a thorough examination of Bön manuscripts would help to create a context for understanding the function of these stones.

Chinese archaeologists have examined standing stones as an aspect of mortuary practice and not specifically as an independent cultural manifestation.[135] Most of their research has been devoted to basic descriptions of alignments when encountered, and attempts to classify variation in them within this mortuary perspective. Bellezza has offered a number of potential explanations for their use: stone pillars in various combinations may have had at least four roles, including territorial markers, monuments of clans or chieftains, markers for mortuary sites, and shrines for the worship of indigenous deities.[136] The roles of stelae and monolithic alignments are interpreted through a lens of modern mythological beliefs, ranging from associations with the Gesar epic to persistent features of Bön, including boundary markers and religious symbols.[137]

Many of the stones discussed so far, indeed, the vast majority of those encountered by Roerich, Bellezza, and others on their expeditions, have strong affinities to the standing stones and megalithic monuments found all across north and central Asia and which date from the Bronze Age into historical times.[138] The earliest of these standing stones, which possibly date to the early Bronze Age (ca. 2000 B.C.) are large megalithic constructions which are often elaborately carved; none of these are known from the Tibetan plateau. So-called "deer stones," often found singly as well as in small groups, tend to have images of deer or other animals or weapons carved upon their surfaces, and are frequently found within small rectangular enclosures. Uncarved examples are also known, and these bear a real resemblance to some of the larger standing stones seen on the Jangtang. Those from Mongolia that can be dated by evaluation of the art motifs found upon them tend to fall into the late Bronze Age or early Iron Age (ca. 1000 B.C.–A.D. 500). These general similarities between deer stone complexes and some Tibetan plateau standing stones offer a temptation to date those found on the Tibetan plateau to this antiquity. While this is plausible, it must remain a hypothesis subject to further revision. The cultural affiliation of those who erected these stones are unknown, and as before, it is premature to assign these stones to Zhangzhung people as has been done by some authors.

The only known center of the Zhangzhung polity examined by any scholar is its putative capital, Kyunglung. The Tibetologist Giuseppe Tucci visited it in 1933, and he recorded a number of sacred and secular buildings as well as residential areas.[139] A brief reconnaissance by archaeologists from the Chinese Institute of Tibetology has located a number of mortuary sites in its vicinity. Kyunglung will be studied in detail over the next five years, and fundamental questions about its size, the nature of its settlement hierarchy, and dating, will be addressed. Even these highly limited findings suggest that numerous centers should be found across the plateau, especially in the central valleys.

We have barely begun to understand the basic outlines of the prehistory of the Tibetan plateau, but if this review of what has been accomplished by Chinese and western archeologists over the past 30 years is any indication, we can look forward to continued discoveries that can only be enhanced by the attempt to place these discoveries in a broader Asian context, which will permit not only historical research, but also investigation of major questions of anthropological concern.

NOTES

Due to considerations of space, some portions of the original essay have been omitted.

1. G. Samuel, *Civilized Shamans: Buddhism in Tibetan Societies* (Washington, D.C.: Smithsonian Institution Press, 1993).

2. M. Goldstein and M. Kapstein, eds., *Buddhism in Contemporary Tibet: Religious Revival and Cultural Identity* (Berkeley: University of California Press, 1998).

3. M. Goldstein, *The Snow Lion and the Dragon: China, Tibet, and the Dalai Lama* (Berkeley: University of California Press, 1997); S. Tsering, *The Dragon in the Land of Snows: A History of Modern Tibet Since 1947* (New York: Columbia University Press, 1999). [Editors' note: The Tibetan autonomous administrative units actually make up a majority of Qinghai province, and a large portion of Sichuan province.]

4. M. Aldenderfer, *Montane Foragers: Asana and the South-Central Andean Archaic* (Iowa City: University of Iowa Press, 1998).

5. D. Rowley et al., "A New Approach to Stable Isotope-based Paleoaltimetry: Implications for Paleoaltimetry and Paleohypsometry of the High Himalaya Since the Late Miocene," *Earth and Planetary Science Letters* 188 (2001): 253–268.

6. G. Schaller, *Wildlife of the Tibetan Steppe* (Chicago: University of Chicago Press, 1998), 26.

7. A. Hanson et al., "Upper Oligocene Lacustrine Source Rocks and Petroleum System of the Northern Qaidam Basin, NW China," *American Association of Petroleum Geologists Bulletin* 85 (2001): 601–619.

8. F. Lehmkuhl and F. Haselein, "Quaternary Paleoenvironmental Change on the Tibetan Plateau and Adjacent Areas (Western China and Western Mongolia)," *Quaternary International* 65/66 (2000): 121–145.

9. J. Overpeck et al., "The Southwest Indian Monsoon Over the Past 18,000 Years," *Climate Dynamics* 12 (1996): 213–225.

10. D. H. S. Chang, "The Vegetation Zonation of the Tibetan Plateau," *Mountain Research and Development* 1 (1981): 29–48. J. Ni, "A Simulation of Biomes on the Tibetan Plateau and Their Responses to Global Climate Change," *Mountain Research and Development* 20 (2000): 80–89; Schaller, *Wildlife of the Tibetan Steppe*.

11. Ni, "A Simulation of Biomes on the Tibetan Plateau," 82.

12. Lehmkuhl and Haselein, "Paleoenvironmental Change on the Tibetan Plateau."

13. F. Lehmkuhl, "Late Pleistocene, Late-Glacial, and Holocene Glacial Advances on the Tibetan Plateau." *Quaternary International* 38/39 (1997); and "Extent and Spatial Distribution of Pleistocene Glaciations in Eastern Tibet," *Quaternary International* 45/46 (1998); B. Zheng and N. Rutter, "On the Problem of Quaternary Glaciations and the Extent and Patterns of Pleistocene Ice Cover in the Qinghai-Xizang (Tibet) Plateau," *Quaternary International* 45/46 (1998).

14. Lehmkuhl and Haselein, "Paleoenvironmental Change on the Tibetan Plateau."

15. M. Kuhle, "Reconstruction of the 2.4 km² Late Pleistocene Ice Sheet on the Tibetan Plateau and Its Impact on the Global Climate," *Quaternary International* 45/46 (1998); and "The Pleistocene Glaciation of Tibet and the Onset of the Ice Ages: An Auto-cycle Hypothesis," *GeoJournal* 17 (1988).

16. J. Schäfer et al., "The Limited Influence of Glaciations in Tibet on Global Climate Over the Past 170,000 Years," *Earth and Planetary Science Letters* 194 (2002); Zheng and Rutter, "Pleistocene Ice Cover in the Qinghai-Xizang (Tibet) Plateau."

17. Schäfer et al.,"Influence of Glaciations in Tibet on Global Climate."

18. J. Liu et al., "Palaeoclimate Simulation of 21 ka for the Tibetan Plateau and Eastern Asia," *Climate Dynamics* 19 (2002).

19. Lehmkuhl and Haselein, "Paleoenvironmental Change on the Tibetan Plateau."

20. G. Ren and H. Beug, "Mapping Holocene Pollen Data and Vegetation of China," *Quaternary Science Reviews* 21 (2002): 1395–1422.

21. F. Gasse et al., "Holocene Environmental Changes in Bangong Co. Basin (Western Tibet)," *Paleogeography, Paleaoclimatology, Palaeoecology* 120 (1996): 79–92.

22. G. Ren, "Decline of the Mid-to-late Holocene Forests in China: Climate Change or Human Impact?" *Journal of Quaternary Science* 15 (2000): 273–281.

23. G. Miehe, "On the Connexion of Vegetation Dynamics with Climate Changes in High Asia," *Paleogeography, Paleaoclimatology, Palaeoecology* 120 (1996): 5–24.

24. P. Brown, "The First Modern East Asians?: Another Look at Upper Cave 101, Liujiang, and Minatogawa 1," in *Interdisciplinary Perspectives on the Origins of the Japanese*, ed. K. Omoto (Kyoto, Japan: International Research Center for Japanese Studies, 1999), 105–130; D. Etler, "The Fossil Evidence for Human Evolution in Asia," *Annual Review of Anthropology* 25 (1996): 275–301.

25. W. Huang, "The Prehistoric Human Occupation of the Qinghai-Xizang Plateau," *Götinger Geographische Abhandlungen* 95 (1994): 201–219.

26. E. Tong, "Zhongguo xinan diqu—Ren lei ke neng de fa yuan di" [Southwest China: A Possible Place of Origin for Human Beings]. *Sichuan daxue xuebao* (Chengdu: Sichuan renmin chubanshe) 3 (1983): 3–14; and "Xizang gaoyuan shang de shou fu" [Hand Axe from the Tibetan Plateau], *Kaogu* (Beijing: Kexue chubanshe) 9 (1989): 822–826.

27. Huang, "The Prehistoric Human Occupation of the Qinghai-Xizang Plateau."

28. P. J. Brantingham et al., "Lithic Assemblages from the Chang Tang Region, Northern Tibet," *Antiquity* 75 (2001): 321.

29. D. Zhang and S. Li, "Optical Dating of Tibetan Human Hand- and Footprints: An Implication for the Palaeoenvironment of the Last Glaciation of the Tibetan Plateau," *Geophysical Research Letters* 29 (2002): 1069.

30. Huang, "The Prehistoric Human Occupation of the Qinghai-Xizang Plateau"; F. Qian and X. Wu, "Zang bei gaoyuan Geting shi qi chu bu guan cha" [A Preliminary Observation on the Stone Artifacts Collected from Geting on the Northern Tibetan Plateau], *Renleixue xuebao* (Beijing: Kexue chubanshe) 7 (1988).

31. Z. Liu and F. Wang, "Xizang gaoyuan Dougeze yu Zhabu di dian de jiu shi qi—jian lun gao yuan gu huan jing dui shi qi wen hua fen bu de yingxiang" [Paleoliths from the Duogeze and Zhabu Sites of the Tibetan Plateau—On the Paleo-Environmental Influence on the Distribution of Stone Culture on the Tibetan Plateau], *Kaogu* (Beijing: Kexue chubanshe) 4 (1986): 289–299.

32. Z. An et al. "Paleoliths and Microliths from Shenja and Shuanghu, Northern Tibet." *Current Anthropology* 23, no. 5 (1982): 493–499.

33. S. Hou, *Xizang Kaogu Da Gang* [*Archaeological Survey of Tibet*] (Lhasa: Xizang renmin chubanshe, 1991); E. Tong, "Xizang Kaogu zong shu" [A Summary of the Archaeology of Tibet], *Wenwu* (Beijing: Wenwu chubanshe) 9 (1985): 9–19.

34. An et al., "Paleoliths and Microliths from . . . Northern Tibet."

35. W. Huo, "Jin shi nian Xizang Kaogu de faxian yu yanjiu" [Archaeological Findings and Research in the Last Ten Years], *Wenwu* (Beijing: Wenwu chubanshe) 3 (2000): 85–95; Liu and Wang, "Paleoliths from . . . the Tibetan Plateau," in *Jilong Wenwu zhi* [A Survey of the Cultural Relics in Kyirong County], ed. W. Huo and Y. Li (Lhasa: Xizang renmin chubanshe, 1993). W. Suolang, "Xizang Kaogu xin faxian zong shu" [A Brief Summary of New Archaeological Discoveries in Tibet], in *Nanfang minzu Kaogu* [*Southern Ethnology and Archaeology*], 4 vols., ed. E. Tong (Chengdu: Sichuan daxue chubanshe, 1991), 9–24.

36. A. Chayet, *Art et Archéologie du Tibet* [*Art and Archeology of Tibet*] (Paris: Picard, 1994), 30.

37. Gai Pei and Wei Qi, "Hutouliang Jiushiqishidai wanqi yizhi-de faxian" [Discovery of the Late Paleolithic Site at Hutouliang, Hebei], *Vertebrata Palasiatica* 15, no. 4 (1977): 287–300.

38. D. Madsen et al., "Dating Shuidonggou and the Upper Paleolithic Blade Industry in North China," *Antiquity* 75 (2001): 706–716.

39. P. J. Brantingham et al., "The Initial Upper Paleolithic in Northeast Asia," *Current Anthropology* 42 (2001): 735–747.

40. Madsen, "Dating Shuidonggou and the Upper Paleolithic Blade Industry in North China."

41. P. J. Brantingham et al., "Speculation on the Timing and Nature of Late Pleistocene Hunter-Gatherer Colonization of the Tibetan Plateau," *Chinese Science Bulletin* 48, no. 14 (2003): 1510–1516.

42. A. Torroni et al., "Mitochondrial DNA Analysis in Tibet—Implications for the Origin of the Tibetan Population and Its Adaptation to High Altitude," *American Journal of Physical Anthropology* 92 (1994): 189–199.

43. Y. Qian et al., "Multiple Origins of Tibetan Y Chromosome," *Human Genetics* 106 (2000): 453–454.

44. B. Su et al., "Y-Chromosome Data Evidence for a Northward Migration of Modern Humans Into Eastern Asia During the Last Ice Age," *American Journal of Human Genetics* 65 (1999): 1718.

45. Brantingham et al., "Late Pleistocene Hunter-Gatherer Colonization of the Tibetan Plateau."

46. Aldenderfer, *Montane Foragers*, 19–25.

47. Aldenderfer, *Montane Foragers*, 20–22.

48. M. Aldenderfer, "Moving up in the World: Archaeologists Seek to Understand How and When People Came to Occupy the Andean and Tibetan Plateaus," *American Scientist* 91, no. 6 (2003): 542–550; and "Early Human Occupations of the Tibetan Plateau and Andean Altiplano," paper presented at the American Association for the Advancement of Science, Seattle, WA, 2004.

49. Brantingham et al., "Late Pleistocene Hunter-Gatherer Colonization of the Tibetan Plateau," 1510–1516.

50. P. Gai and G. Wang, "Huanghe shangyou Layihai zhongshiqi yizhi [A Mesolithic Site at Layihai, Upper Yellow River], *Acta Anthropologica Sinica* (Beijing: Kexue chubanshe) 2 (1983).

51. M. Aldenderfer, "The Pleistocene/Holocene Transition in Peru and Its Effects Upon the Human Use of the Landscape," *Quaternary International* 53, no. 4 (1999): 11–19.

52. Aldenderfer, *Montane Foragers*, 142.

53. H. Tang and J. Hare, "Lithic Tool Industries and the Earliest Occupation of the Qinghai-Tibetan Plateau," *Artefact* 18 (1995): 7.

54. P. Gai, "Microlithic Industries in China," in *Paleoanthropology and Paleolithic Archaeology in the People's Republic of China*, ed. Rukang Wu and John W. Olsen (New York: Academic Press, 1985), 225–242.

55. C. Chen, "The Microlithic of China," *Journal of Anthropological Archaeology* 1, no. 3 (1984): 79–115; C. Chen and X. Wang, "Upper Paleolithic Microblade Industries in North China and Their Relationships with Northeast Asia and North America," *Arctic Anthropology* 26, no. 2 (1989): 144–145; Q. Duan, "Xizang xishiqi yicun" [Microlithic Remains in Tibet], *Kaogu yu wenwu* 5 (1989): 87–109; Z. Liu, "Xizang gaoyuan Mafamu hu dongbei an deng san ge di dian de xishiqi" [Microliths from Three Sites on the Northeast Shore of Mapham Lake in Tibet], *Nanjing daxue xuebao* 4 (1981): 87–96; H. Tang, "Lue lun qing zang gao yuan de jiu shi qi he xishiqi" [A Preliminary Research on the Paleoliths and Microliths on the Qinghai and Tibetan Plateau], *Kaogu* 5 (1999): 44–54.

56. Duan, "Microlithic Remains in Tibet"; Y. Li, "Jilong luo long gou de Yalu zangbu jiang zhong shang you de shi qi yi cun—jian lun Xizang gaoyuan xishiqi yi

cun de xiang guan wenti" [Deposits of Stone Implements in the Gyirong Area and the Upper and Middle Reaches of the Yarlung Tsangpo River: A Reference to Some Correlative Questions about the Early Stone Implements in Tibet], *Nanfang minzu Kaogu* 4 (1991): 47–63; Liu and Wang, "Paleoliths from . . . the Tibetan Plateau"; Tang and Hare, "The Earliest Occupation of the Qinghai-Tibetan Plateau."

57. Gai and Wang, "A Mesolithic Site at Layihai, Upper Yellow River."

58. An et al., "Paleoliths and Microliths from . . . Northern Tibet."

59. Tong, "A Summary of the Archaeology of Tibet."

60. Li, "Questions About the Early Stone Implements in Tibet."

61. W. Huo and Y. Li, *Ali diqu wenwu zhi* [*A Survey of the Cultural Relics in Ngari Prefecture*] (Lhasa: Xizang renmin chubanshe, 1993).

62. Li, "Questions About the Early Stone Implements in Tibet," 60.

63. Tang and Hare, "The Earliest Occupation of the Qinghai-Tibetan Plateau."

64. Brantingham et al., "The Initial Upper Paleolithic in Northeast Asia."

65. R.G. Elston and P. J. Brantingham, "Microlithic Technology in Northern Asia: A Risk-Minimizing Strategy of the Late Paleolithic and Early Holocene," in *Thinking Small: Global Perspectives on Microlithization. Archeological Papers of the American Anthropological Association*, ed. R. G. Elston and S. L. Kuhn, 12 (2002): 103–112.

66. Anne P. Underbill, "Current Issues in Chinese Neolithic Archaeology," *Journal of World Prehistory* 11 (1997): 105.

67. K. C. Chang, *The Archaeology of Ancient China* (New Haven: Yale University Press, 1986), 138–150.

68. W. Huo, *Xizang gudai mu Zang zhidu yanjiu* [*Studies on Ancient Tibetan Burial Customs*] (Chengdu: Sichuan ren min chubanshe, 1995); Xiage Wangdui, "Shixi Xizang shiqian shiguanmu de xingshi yu fenqi" [A Tentative Analysis of Types and Dates of Prehistoric Stone Coffin Burials in Tibet], *Xizang yanjiu* (Lhasa: Xizang yanjiu bianjibu) 4 (1998): 40–44.

69. Bureau of Cultural Relics, Tibet Autonomous Region and Department of History, Sichuan University, *Changdu Karou* [*Karou: A Neolithic Site in Tibet*] (Beijing: Wenwu chubanshe, 1985); E. Tong, *Zhongguo xinan minzu Kaogu lunwenji* [*Collected Papers on Ethnoarchaeology in Southwest China*] (Beijing: Wenwu chubanshe, 1990).

70. Xiage, "Prehistoric Stone Coffin Burials in Tibet."

71. Bureau of Cultural Relics, TAR, *Karou: A Neolithic Site in Tibet*, 33.

72. Bureau of Cultural Relics, TAR, *Karou: A Neolithic Site in Tibet*, 36.

73. Bureau of Cultural Relics, TAR, *Karou: A Neolithic Site in Tibet*, 178.

74. Bureau of Cultural Relics, TAR, "Xizang Xiaoenda xinshiqi shidai yizhi shijue jianbao" [Brief Report on the Excavation of Xiaoenda Neolithic Site in Tibet], *Kaogu yu wenwu* (Xi'an: Shanxi sheng kaogu yanjiusuo) 1 (1990); S. Hou, *Xizang kaogu da gang* [*Archaeological Survey of Tibet*] (Lhasa: Xizang renmin chubanshe, 1991).

75. D. Wang, "A Further Typological Study of Neolithic Culture in Yunnan," *Journal of Tibetan Archaeology* 1 (1994): 91–108.

76. W. Huo, "Jin shi nian Xizang Kaogu de faxian yu yanjiu" [Archaeological Findings and Research in the Last Ten Years], *Wenwu* (Beijing: Wenwu chubanshe) 3 (2000); Institute of Archaeology, Chinese Academy of Social Science and Bureau of Cultural Relics, Tibet Autonomous Region, "Xizang Lasa shi Qugong cun xin shi qi shi dai yi zhi di yi ci fa jue jian bao" [Brief Report on the First Excavation of Qugong Neolithic Site in Lhasa, Tibet], *Kaogu* 10 (1991): 873–881; Institute of Archaeology, Chinese Academy of Social Science and Bureau of Cultural Relics, Tibet Autonomous Region, "Xizang Lasa shi Qugong cun shi shi mu fa jue jian bao" [Brief Report on the Excavation of the Qugong Burials in Lhasa, Tibet], *Kaogu* 10 (1991): 927–931; Institute of Archaeology, Chinese Academy of Social Science and Bureau of Cultural Relics, Tibet Autonomous Region, *Qugong in Lhasa: Excavations of an Ancient Site and Tombs* (Beijing: Encyclopedia of China Publishing House, 1999).

77. Xiage, "Prehistoric Stone Coffin Burials in Tibet."

78. W. Huo, "Xizang Qugong cui shi shi mu chu tu de dai bing tong jing ji qi xiang guan wen ti chu tan" [A Preliminary Discussion of the Bronze Mirror with an Iron Handle Unearthed at the Qugong Cyst Tomb, Tibet], *Kaogu* (Beijing: Kexue chubanshe) 7 (1994): 650–661; and "Zai lun Xizang dai bing long jing de you guan wen ti" [A Further Discussion on Questions Related to a Bronze Mirror with Handle from Tibet], *Kaogu* (Beijing: Kexue chubanshe) 11 (1997): 61–69; Institute of Archaeology, *Qugong in Lhasa*; H. Zhao, "Xizang Qugong chutu de tiebing tongjing wenti yanjiu" [Questions Concerning a Bronze Mirror with an Iron Handle Unearthed in Qugong, Tibet], *Kaogu* (Beijing: Kexue chubanshe) 7 (1994): 47–52.

79. Zhongguo shehui kexue yuan, Kaogu yanjiu suo, Xizang Zizhiqu Wenwu ju [Institute of Archaeology, Chinese Academy of Social Science and Bureau of Cultural Relics, Tibet Autonomous Region], "Xizang Gongga xian Changguogou xinshiqi yizhi diaocha baogao" [A Report on the Investigation of the Neolithic Sites in Changgougou, Gongga County, Tibet], *Xizang Kaogu* (Chengdu: Sichuan daxue chubanshe) 1 (1994): 28; Institute of Archaeology, Chinese Academy of Social Science and Bureau of Cultural Relics, Tibet Autonomous Region, "Xizang Guoga xian Changguogou xinshiqi shidai yizhi" [The Changuogou Neolithic Site in Gongga County, Tibet]. *Kaogu* 4 (1999a): 1–10; J. Liu and H. Zhao, "Xizang Gongga xian Changguogou xinshiqi yizhi" [The Changguoguo Neolithic Site in Changguogo, Tibet], *Kaogu* (Beijing: Kexue chubanshe) 4 (1999): 1–10.

80. H. Zhao, "Lun Xizang Bangda yizhi, Qugong wenhua, yu Xizang de shiqian wenming" [On the Bangga Site, Qugong Culture, and Prehistoric Civilization in Tibet], paper presented at the International Academic Conference on Tibetan Archaeology and Art, Beijing, 2002.

81. *Naidong xian wenwu zhi* [A Survey of Cultural Relics in Nedong County] (Lhasa: Xizang renmin chubanshe, 1986).

82. Chayet, *Art and Archeology of Tibet*, 46–47.

83. Underbill, "Chinese Neolithic Archaeology," 118.

84. Chayet, *Art and Archeology of Tibet*, 51.

85. Chang, *The Archaeology of Ancient China*, 142–144.

86. Chayet, *Art and Archeology of Tibet*, 53.

87. Chang, *The Archaeology of Ancient China*, 150.

88. Huo, *Studies on Ancient Tibetan Burial Customs*.

89. Xiage, "Prehistoric Stone Coffin Burials in Tibet."

90. Huo, *Studies on Ancient Tibetan Burial Customs*.

91. E. Tong, "Shilun Chuan xibei shiguanmu de zuqun wenti" [A Tentative Study of the Ethnicity of Stone Coffin Burials in Northwestern Sichuan], *Kaogu* (Beijing: Kexue chubanshe) 2 (1978): 34–45.

92. C. Renfrew, "At the Edge of Knowability: Towards a Prehistory of Languages," *Cambridge Archaeological Journal* 10, no. 1 (2000).

93. B. Su et al., "Y-Chromosome Data Evidence for a Northward Migration," 1718–1724; and "Y-Chromosome Haplotypes Reveal Prehistorical Migrations to the Himalayas," *Human Genetics* 107 (2000): 582–590.

94. G. van Driem, "Neolithic Correlates of Ancient Tibeto-Burman Migrations," in *Archaeology and Language II: Archaeological Data and Linguistic Hypotheses*, ed. Roger Blench and Matthew Spriggs (London: Routledge, 1998); Van Driem, *Languages of the Himalayas: An Ethnolinguistic Handbook of the Greater Himalayan Region*, 2 vols. (Leiden: Brill, 2001); van Driem, "Tibeto-Burman Phylogeny and Prehistory: Languages, Material Culture, and Genes." in *Examining the Farming/Language Dispersal Hypothesis*, ed. Peter Bellwood and Colin Renfrew (Oxford: McDonald Institute for Archaeological Research, University of Cambridge, 2002).

95. Su et al., "Prehistorical Migrations to the Himalayas."

96. L. Cavalli-Sforza, "The Chinese Human Genome Diversity Project," *Proceedings of the National Academy of Sciences of the United States of America* 95 (1998): 206.

97. J. A. Matisoff, "Sino-Tibetan Linguistics: Present State and Future Prospects," *Annual Review of Anthropology* 20 (1991): 469–504; Wang, "A Further Typological Study of Neolithic Culture in Yunnan."

98. Van Driem, *Languages of the Himalayas*, 399.

99. Matisoff, "Sino-Tibetan Linguistics: Present State and Future Prospects."

100. Van Driem, *Languages of the Himalayas*, 408–433.

101. Van Driem, *Languages of the Himalayas*, 417.

102. Van Driem, "Tibeto-Burman Phylogeny and Prehistory," 241–243.

103. J. Chu et al., "Genetic Relationships of Populations in China," *Proceedings of the National Academy of Sciences of the United States of America* 95 (1998): 11763–11768.

104. Cavalli-Sforza, "The Chinese Human Genome Diversity Project," 11502.

105. Renfrew, "Towards a Prehistory of Languages," 24–26.

106. Van Driem, *Languages of the Himalayas*, 419–420.

107. Chang, "The Vegetation Zonation of the Tibetan Plateau."

108. Van Driem, *Languages of the Himalayas*, 423–425.

109. Ren, "Decline of the Mid-to-late Holocene Forests in China," 273–281.

110. R. A. Stein, *Tibetan Civilization* (Stanford: Stanford University Press, 1972), 29.

111. M. Wang, "Searching for Qiang Culture in the First Half of the Twentieth Century," *Inner Asia* 4 (2002).

112. C. I. Beckwith, "Tibetan Science at the Court of the Great Khans," *Journal of the Tibetan Society* 7 (1987): 8.

113. D. Snellgrove and H. Richardson, *A Cultural History of Tibet* (Boston: Shambhala, 1995), 26.

114. E. Haarh, *The Yarlung Dynasty* (Denmark: University of Copenhagen, 1969).

115. Samuel, *Civilized Shamans*, 438–444.

116. Haarh, *The Yarlung Dynasty*, 128.

117. R. Vitali, *Early Temples of Central Tibet* (London: Serindia Publications, 1990).

118. Chayet, *Art and Archeology of Tibet*; Huo, *Studies on Ancient Tibetan Burial Customs*; Xiage, "Prehistoric Stone Coffin Burials in Tibet," 76–89.

119. L. Petech, "Western Tibet: Historical Introduction," in *Tabo: A Lamp for the Kingdom*, ed. D. Klimburgh-Salter (London: Thames and Hudson, 1997), 230.

120. Beckwith, "Tibetan Science at the Court of the Great Khans," 14.

121. G. Tucci, *Preliminary Report on Two Scientific Expeditions in Nepal*, vol. X (Rome: Serie Orientale Roma, Instituto italiano per il Medio ed Estremo Oriente, 1956), 92.

122. K. Chung, "On Zhangzhung," *Bulletin of the Institute of History and Philology Academia Sinica* 4 (1960); Tucci, *Report on Two Scientific Expeditions in Nepal*.

123. Stein, *Tibetan Civilization*.

124. J. Bellezza, *Antiquities of Upper Tibet: Pre-Buddhist Archaeological Sites on the High Plateau. Findings of the Upper Tibet Circumnavigation Expedition, 2000* (Delhi: Adroit Publishers, 2002); *Antiquities of Northern Tibet, Pre-Buddhist Archeological Discoveries on the High Plateau, Findings of the Changthang Circuit Expedition, 1999* (Delhi: Adroit Publishers, 2001), and "Buddhist Archaeological Sites in Northern Tibet: An Introductory Report on the Types of Monuments and Related Literary and Oral Historical Sources," *Kailash* 19, no. 1–2 (2000).

125. M. Aldenderfer, "Piyang: A 10th/11th C A.D. Tibetan Buddhist Temple and Monastic Complex in Far Western Tibet," *Archaeology, Ethnology & Anthropology of Eurasia* 4, no. 8 (2001): 138–146; and "Roots of Tibetan Buddhism," *Archaeology* 54, no. 53 (2001): 610–612. Huo, "Excavation of a Buddhist Temple in Ngari, Tibet, 2002," *Wenwu* 8 (2002): 34–39; and "Two Buddhist Caves Newly Discovered in Tsamda County, Tibet," *Wenwu* 8 (2002): 63–69; W. Huo and Y. Li, "Xizang Zhada Xian Piyang-dong ga yizhi 1997 nian diaocha yu fajue" [Survey and Excavation of the Piang-Dongga Site in Tsamda County, Tibet, in 1997], *Acta Archaeologica Sinica* 3 (2001): 397–426.

126. M. Aldenderfer, "Domestic rdo-ring? A New Class of Standing Stone from the Tibetan Plateau," *Tibet Journal* 28 (2004); and "Archaeology and Ethnicity in Far Western Tibet: The Evidence from Dindun," in *Proceedings of the Tenth Seminar of the International Association for Tibetan Studies*, ed. A. Heller and G. Orofino (Leiden: Brill, 2003); M. Aldenderfer and H. Moyes, "Excavations at Dindun: A Pre-Buddhist Village Site in Far Western Tibet," in *Essays of the International Conference on Tibetan*

Archaeology and Art, ed. W. Huo and Y. Li (Chengdu: Center for Tibetan Studies, Sichuan Union University, 2004), 47–69.

127. China Tibetology Institute, Archaeology Department of Sichuan University and Bureau of Cultural Relics, Tibet Autonomous Region, "Xizang Zhada Xian Piyang dongga yizhi gu mu qun shi jue jian bao" [Brief Report of a Preliminary Excavation of Ancient Tomb Groups in Piyang-Dongga Site of Zhada County in Tibet], *Kaogu* (Beijing: Kexue chubanshe) 6 (2001): 14–31; and "Xizang Zhada xian Gebusailu mudi diaocha" [Survey of the Gebusailu Cemetery in Zhada County, Tibet], *Kaogu* (Beijing: Kexue chubanshe) 6 (2001): 39–44.

128. C. Bronk-Ramsey, "OxCal Program v3.8," in *Radiocarbon Accelerator Unit*, Oxford: University of Oxford, 2002.

129. Aldenderfer, "A New Class of Standing Stone from the Tibetan Plateau."

130. A. W. Macdonald, "Une note sur les mégaliths Tibétains, " *Journal Asiatique* 241 (1953): 64.

131. A. H. Francke, *Antiquities of Indian Tibet*, Archaeological Survey of India 38, Part 1: Personal Narrative (Calcutta: Superintendent Government Printing, India, 1914); and *A History of Western Tibet: One of the Unknown Empires* (London: Patridge, 1907).

132. G. N. Roerich, *The Animal Style Among the Nomad Tribes of Northern Tibet* (Czech Republic: Seminarium Kondakovianum, Prague, 1930).

133. Roerich, *The Animal Style Among the Nomad Tribes of Northern Tibet*, 33.

134. Roerich, *The Animal Style Among the Nomad Tribes of Northern Tibet*, 16.

135. Huo, *Studies on Ancient Tibetan Burial Customs*.

136. Bellezza, *Antiquities of Northern Tibet* and *Antiquities of Upper Tibet*.

137. Bellezza, *Antiquities of Northern Tibet*, 34–38.

138. E. Jacobsen-Tepfer, et al., *Mongolie du Nord-Ouest: Tsagaan Salaa/Baga Oigor. Répertoire des Pétroglyphes d'Asie centrale* [*Mongolia of the Northwest: Tsagaan Salaa/Baga Oigor. Index of Central Asian Petroglyphs*], Fascicule no. 6, 2 vols., ed. Jakov A. Sher and Henri-Paul Francfort (Paris: De Boccard, 2001).

139. G. Tucci, *Sadhus et Brigands du Kailash: Mon Voyage au Tibet Occidental* [*Sadhus and Brigands of Kailash: My Voyage to Western Tibet*] (Paris: Editions R. Chabaud, 1989), 189–199 (1st ed. in Italian, 1937).

Chapter 2

SOME REFLECTIONS ON THE PERIODIZATION
OF TIBETAN HISTORY

Bryan J. Cuevas

Bryan Cuevas investigates the vexed question of how best to periodize Tibetan history—that is, how to usefully divide up the events that Tibetan and other historians have counted as significant into meaningful larger units of time, thereby creating an outline of the *story* of the Tibetan past. Cuevas surveys the range of scholarly assessments of relevant major epochs in Tibetan history, as well as the major political regimes to hold power in Central Tibet (Ü-Tsang). Yet any periodization scheme has its limits, as this exercise in comparative chronology demonstrates. Cuevas makes clear that neither he nor anyone else has tried to apply such periodizations to the wider Tibetan-speaking communities in the eastern Tibetan cultural regions of Kham and Amdo. At present, we simply know too little about the course of history in those areas to attempt such surveys; even when more is known, it is doubtful there will be anything close to the consensus on periodization for Central Tibet. Whether because of environmental or political factors, eastern Tibet rarely supported the kind of strong centralized regime that flourished in Central Tibet. Cuevas relies here mainly on indigenous Tibetan schemes of periodizations of Tibetan history and finds therein two basic lines, one Buddhist, the other political. That is, periodization in Tibetan sources is most often connected to legitimizing claims to either religious authority or local political institutional interests, though often the religious and political are tightly bound together. His dismissal of the typical tripartite Eurocentric model of periodization— "ancient," "medieval," and "modern"—is particularly appropriate, especially because the term "medieval" is often used to lump together so much of Tibetan history (as much as a millennium in some accounts). Although not discussed in this essay, the oft-used division of the "early modern" is rarely applied at present to describe Tibetan history, which is typically categorized as "traditional" until the forcible introduction of the "modern," e.g., Western, concepts and ideologies that entered Tibet with China's communist People's Liberation Army in the 1950s.

History is always expressed as a narrative, a story about the past. To write a story out of the events of the past, historians must give those events a coherent meaning and plot those meaningful events as chapters in a larger narrative. This means that the method of writing history is not simply the recording of a series of past events, or a set of dates. Such a record would not be a history but a mere chronology, and history is never just a chronicle of dates. Historiography, the study of history and the methods employed in how individuals, or a community of people, or a culture come to understand the past and articulate that understanding, presupposes that history by necessity, whether we prefer this or not, is always written in chapters. Periodization—the breaking-up of the past into chapters, or "periods"—is one necessary way historians make sense of the past and also write history.

The question of periodization, however, is one of those topics in historiography that generates fierce debates and can create, and certainly has created, much controversy. The problem of periodization is precisely this problem of how best to characterize and interpret the chapters in a coherent story of the past. As many insightful historians have warned over the years, the articulation of historical periods may indeed be arbitrary and artificial, but rarely is such articulation a neutral, unambiguous, and value-free enterprise.

Having heeded this warning, I choose in this brief essay—perhaps unwisely—to charge headlong into this academic mine-field where success is not only risky, but far from guaranteed. I want to do this because, in my opinion, there has not been much sustained reflection on the critical question of periodization in the historical study of Tibet, despite an ever increasing scholarly interest in Tibetan history and historiographical issues. I see this lack of serious historiographical reflection as one unfortunate consequence of a long-standing and predominant inclination among scholars in Tibetan studies to be concerned only with the development of Buddhism and Buddhist thought in Tibet.

For several generations now, the question of periodization has been dealt with critically, with varying degrees of success, in other related fields of Asian studies, including China, Japan, and India.[1] And, of course, in European studies, the issue is an old one and has been debated for a century or more.[2] But, notwithstanding the major contributions made by scholars of Tibet past and present, it is my contention, unfortunately, that Tibetanists have tended to reflect far too little on what they do as scholars of history, and how historians of Tibet and Tibetans themselves, have divided and articulated Tibet's past into discrete periods. Even though Tibetanists continue to generate and repeat various divisions of time whenever writing about Tibet—whether writing about Buddhist history or the meaning of Buddhism in Tibet or about Tibetan social and political history—Tibetanists rarely, if ever, take up the question of periodization. For whatever reason, few have been willing to openly consider this question or acknowledge that the persistent articulation and interpretation of the periods of Tibetan history, which have generally been accepted uncritically, may still be in need of reassessment.

What follows are just a few remarks intended hopefully to generate some discussion and perhaps even a few constructive debates. I should make clear at the outset that whenever I use the term "Tibet" here, I am referring only to the central and western regions traditionally and collectively called Ü-Tsang and not to the wider Tibetan-speaking communities beyond this regional boundary, such as the eastern provinces of Kham and Amdo (in the present-day west China provinces of Qinghai, Gansu, Sichuan, and Yunnan).

All concepts of periodization, of temporal divisions, are founded on theoretical interpretations of continuity and change. For the purposes of narrative coherence and convenient presentation, historical periods must be distinguished by clearly articulated long-term continuities and the break-up of these continuities by times of transition between periods. The debates over periodization tend always to flare up around where one chooses to locate the transition points rather than how one describes the continuities. The reason this is so is that the transitions and divisions of time always reflect the value judgments and priorities of the classifiers, and those judgments and priorities are often challenged by alternative judgments and priorities. Even when some consensus of agreement is reached on the extent of a period or a point of change, the temporal divisions generated by the interests and priorities of historians working even in the same area are not always articulated uniformly. One group of Tibetan historians, for example, might identify a span of time as the time when so-and-so was in control or doing such-and-such, while another group of scholars might classify a stretch of time when some social, religious, or political movement prevailed, or when an artistic style or literary work was introduced, or when a certain significant event took place. Problems arise when historians require commitment to a particular period scheme as reflecting some sort of metaphysics or ontology, which by definition would invalidate all alternative schemes.[3] The reality, of course, is that organizing the past is necessarily an exercise in interpretation and there is always room for other interpretations. In general, then, rival schemes for dividing up time should not, and indeed cannot, cancel each other out.

We must bear in mind this flexibility of historical interpretation when considering how periods of continuity and change in Tibetan history have been articulated both by Tibetan historians and by scholars of Tibet. I would like to examine briefly below a few of the exemplary periodizations of Tibetan history that have been presented. I will limit my comments to these few indigenous Tibetan schemes, since these by and large continue to serve as a basis for the various periodizations employed by European and American scholars of Tibet.

It is often remarked that Tibetans, like the Chinese, have tended toward a certain preoccupation with history. From the late tenth century onward in Tibet, we see an increased concern for history and historical writing and find ample evidence for the emergence of a truly Tibetan indigenous historiography.[4] Such an interest in history appears for the most part to be based on concerns for legiti-mizing claims to religious authority, but I want to suggest also that this move to lay claim to the authority of history may also have been a response to very real sociopolitical conflicts and local institutional interests. The Tibetan histories that began to appear from this time onward organized the past according to two basic schemes, one in which Buddhist history claimed primacy in determining the divisions of time and another in which political history, or more accurately imperial and later local institutional history, assumed priority.

The periodization of Tibetan history in Buddhist terms was not new. In some of the old Tibetan chronicles unearthed from Dunhuang,[5] for example, we find Tibetan religious history divided into four periods: 1. the period of pre-history when Tibetans were characterized as savage barbarians before imperial authority emerged and before Buddhism was introduced to Tibet; 2. the period of the Buddhist "kings" (tsenpo) from the seventh through mid-ninth century, inaugurated by the emperor Songtsen Gampo, perceived to be an incarnation of the bodhisattva Avalokiteśvara, when Buddhism as a civilizing force was first brought to Tibet; 3. the period of darkness and chaos beginning with the perse-cutions of Buddhism by the evil emperor Langdarma and the collapse of Bud-dhist imperial authority; and finally 4. the period of Buddhist renaissance in Tibet beginning in the late tenth century.[6]

This four-fold model of Tibetan history was widely used in succeeding cen-turies, though occasionally modified and re-cast in either a three-fold or a two-fold scheme. Perhaps the earliest example of a three-fold periodization of Tibetan Buddhist history is the brief thirteenth-century historical work of the Kadampa scholar Chomden Rikpé Reldri, the *Ornamental Flower of the Buddha's Teach-ing* (*Thub pa'i bstan pa rgyan gyi me tog*) composed in 1261.[7] Here we see the fa-miliar religious ordering of historical time emphasizing the spread of Buddhist doctrine in Tibet. Thus, we have: 1. the period of the "early spread of the Bud-dhist teachings" (*tenpa ngadar*),[8] beginning with the miraculous landing of cer-tain Buddhist sutras and other sacred objects on the palace roof at Yumbu Lag-ang during the reign of Lha Totori Nyentsen (b. c. 460) and continuing on through the reigns of the famous Buddhist kings of Tibet, Songtsen Gampo (c. 610–649/50), Tri Songdetsen (r. 755/56–797), and so forth; 2. the period of the "interim spread of the Buddhist teachings" (*tenpa bardar*), beginning with the emperor Yeshé-ö in western Tibet and highlighted by the Buddhist translation activities of Rinchen Zangpo (958–1055); and finally, 3. the period of the "later spread of the Buddhist teachings" (*tenpa chidar*), associated with the new wave of Buddhist translators beginning with Drokmi Lotsawa (992–1074).

The earliest Tibetan Buddhist historians of a two-fold periodization system—essentially identical to the one adopted by Chomden Rikpé Reldri but with the omission of an independent middle period (*tenpa bardar*)—include such Buddhist luminaries as Sakya Drakpa Gyeltsen (1146–1216), Neu (Nelpa) Paṇḍita (thirteenth century), and Bütön (1290–1364).[9] These early Buddhist historians of Tibet clearly demonstrated familiarity with varied concepts of periodization, all based, however, on interpretations of discrete moments in time of religious transformation and transition. Their Buddhist concept of history emphasized the spread of Buddhist doctrine, and more precisely the transmission and diffusion of translations of Buddhist scripture. From a historiographical standpoint, one of the unfortunate consequences of these traditional Buddhist periodizations of Tibetan history is that the rather minimal division of time, marked only by the birth, decline, and rebirth of Buddhist teachings in Tibet, overemphasizes the significance of Buddhist doctrine, oversimplifies the sociopolitical factors causing change, and imposes restrictions on any historian who wishes to articulate a more far-sighted and deeply textured historical narrative of Tibet's past.

As an alternative to this oversimplified religious ordering of history, Tibetan historians have also conceived of continuity and change in political terms and identified periods based on the formation and disintegration of particular regional and institutional hegemonies. Barring evidence in the early Tibetan histories of an explicit interest in the imperial succession of Tibet's royal lineage, we see the primacy of politics in determining historical periods appearing rather late in Tibetan historiographical literature. Though we still find embedded in these later histories the skeletal system of the two-fold *ngadar/chidar* division, usually with an imprecisely dated "dark period" located between the two,[10] the later Tibetan historians' orientations to the past are dominated by the identification of particular regional—albeit religious—hegemonic powers and their shift from one locus to another. One fine example of this type of periodization can be found in the nineteenth-century history of Guru Trashi.[11] At the conclusion of the sixth chapter of this monumental work—a chapter surveying the history of the major Nyingmapa institutions in central, southern, and eastern Tibet and, I might add, a chapter in desperate need of a full critical study in and of itself—Guru Trashi discusses in two separate sections the history of the kings of Degé and the historical rulers of central Tibet.[12] In the latter section, the author employs a scheme for dividing the history of central Tibet into discrete periods defined by the consolidation, fragmentation, and reconstitution of various politico-religious forces and the institutions driving them.

In Guru Trashi's approach to organizing Tibetan history, the past is divided into as many as eleven distinct periods, each characterized by a consolidated axis of power located in a specific time and region. Thus, to mention just a few examples, we have the period of the early kings situated in the Yarlung valley during the early seventh to late eighth century, or the period of Sakya authority, dating from 1268 to 1349, and consolidated at the noble hereditary and monastic estate of Sakya, but extending well beyond its frontiers to the remote Mongol court of Qubilai Khan. Then again, we have the period of the early Ganden Podrang established in 1642 with the rise to power of the fifth Dalai Lama (1617–1682), and ending in 1705 with the assassination of the Dalai Lama's regent, Desi Sanggyé Gyatso (1653–1705), by the orders of the militant Lhazang Khan, ruler of the Khoshud Mongol regime in Lhasa. Guru Trashi's periodization of Tibetan history ends in 1813 when he finished editing the full work. In Guru Trashi's own terms, the completion of the work took place in the period of the regency of the incarnate successors of Demo Rinpoché as de-facto rulers of Tibet.[13]

Following the Chinese Cultural Revolution (1966–1976), Tibetan historical studies in contemporary Tibet and China has become a flourishing academic discipline. In the PRC, conceptions of the periodization of Tibet's past tend to be dominated by conflicting interpretations of the socioeconomic characteristics of each historical period. Although political history still claims primacy in recent Tibetan attempts to divide periods of time, many Tibetan and Chinese historians prioritize a social-scientific approach following a Marxist teleological interpretation, and focus on how Tibetan society can best be understood in a Communist historical framework. For these historians, the issue of periodization is inextricably bound up with Marxist historiography and much effort is expended in articulating the transformation and transitions of pre-Communist Tibet from a slave society to a feudalist one.[14] At this point I do not wish to enter into a discussion of the so-called "feudalism controversy" in Tibetan studies, but I hope it will suffice to mention just one example of this approach to interpreting Tibetan history.[15] I refer to the study of Dungkar Lozang Trinlé, *The Merging of Religious and Secular in Tibet* first published in 1981.[16] Dungkar Lozang Trinlé's work is a fascinating piece of indigenous historical scholarship influenced by non-Tibetan concepts of historiography, namely those grounded in a distinctively Marxist ideology. Despite its overt polemical stance, and the distortions of historical evidence such polemics generally require, the periodization of Tibetan history employed in this work is actually quite conventional by Tibetan standards, and for the most part follows an organizational structure similar to that found in Guru Trashi's study. That is, we still see in Dungkar Lozang Trinlé's division of Tibet's past an emphasis on the formation and eventual disintegration of familiar hegemonic power centers culminating in the rise of the Ganden government and the political office of the Dalai Lamas.

Following this same scheme, but with less emphasis on Marxist polemics, is the contemporary history of Tupten Püntsok, *The Ruby Key: A General History of Tibet* published in 1996.[17] Tupten Püntsok's work is perhaps the most detailed historiographical study to appear in Tibet in recent years. He divides Tibetan history into nine overarching periods marked not only by key political transitions but also fundamental religious, intellectual, socioeconomic, and even scientific breakthroughs. The work is a truly remarkable example of how Tibetan historiography has matured since the establishment of Tibetan academic studies in both China and Tibet. Here, again, we are reminded of the fact that historical classifications reflect the values and priorities of the classifier.

Now that I have a chance to have my own say about Tibetan historical periodization, I would like in conclusion to propose my own approach to organizing Tibetan history. First and foremost, I am not fully convinced that periodization categories contrived in Europe for the study of European history can provide a meaningful structure for the study of Tibetan history. Thus, I would prefer to abandon certain standard western historiographical conceptions of history, and particularly the identification of periods defined by an all-encompassing tripartite sequence divided into "ancient," "medieval," and "modern." The word "medieval" is particularly vague and ill-defined, as we see most recently, for example, in the ambitious three-volume anthology *The History of Tibet* edited by Alex McKay.[18] Here in volume two, Tibet's "medieval period"—subtitled "The Development of Buddhist Paramountcy"—spans an enormous range of over 1,000 years beginning in *c.* 850 and ending in 1895!

It is my opinion that scholars of Tibet who use this word "medieval" have given little thought to the implications of that term. To my knowledge, there has been no open discussion among Tibetanists, and thus little consensus, about the precise dating of the "medieval" period in Tibetan history or even what we should accept as the key defining characteristics of "medieval" Tibetan society. Rather, I hope that scholars of Tibet will be encouraged to conceive of the major periodic divisions of Tibetan history in indigenous terms, or at the very least make attempts to articulate divisions of time that would be consonant with how Tibetans might understand, or have understood, their own history.

So, to conclude. Although I do acknowledge that no periodization scheme achieves complete and satisfactory integration of the history of all Tibetan-speaking regions, including central Tibet (i.e., the current Tibetan Autonomous Region, TAR) and the eastern borderland areas in Kham and Amdo, at present I recommend specifically a periodization of central Tibet into four epochs divided at circa 610 (birth of Songtsen Gampo), 910 (rebellion and fragmentation of the empire), 1249 (Sakya Paṇḍita's appointment as viceroy of Tibet by the Mongol court), and 1705 (the beginning of various foreign occupations in Lhasa; see Appendix 1). My so-called "middle period," which I choose not to call "medieval" but rather "The Age of Monastic Hegemony" (1249–1705), is organized by parallel centers of power—a scheme largely inspired by my reading of Japanese historiography—that is, periods identified by the name of a territorial region and political center and by its affiliated sectarian religious leadership. Thus, for example, I suggest the Sakya Period associated with Sakya Hegemony (1249–1354), the Neudong Period and the Pakmodrupa Hegemony (1354–1478), the Rinpung Period and Zhamarpa Hegemony (1478–1565), the Zhigatsé Period and Karmapa Hegemony (1565–1642), and finally the Lhasa Period and the Gandenpa Hegemony (1642–1705). This third period ends at roughly 1705 with the brief Khoshud Mongol rule over Lhasa under Lhazang Khan and marks the beginning of the fourth epoch, "The Age of Foreign Interests and Occupation" (1705–present) taking us to the present. In the end, having suggested all of this, it may be worthwhile to stress that any system of dating really should reflect the values and priorities of those who may actually be affected by it.

APPENDIX 1: A SUGGESTED PERIODIZATION SCHEME FOR THE HISTORY OF TIBET

IMPERIAL AGE
1. Early Imperial Period (c. pre-610)
2. Late Imperial Period/The Yarlung Dynasty (c. 610–910)
AGE OF FRAGMENTATION
3. Local Hegemonic Period (c. 910–1056)
4. Period of the Emergence of Monastic Principalities (c. 1056–1249)
AGE OF MONASTIC HEGEMONY
5. Sakya Period and Sakyapa Hegemony (c. 1249–1354)
6. Neudong Period and Pakmodrupa Hegemony (c. 1354–1478)
7. Rinpung Period and Zhamarpa Hegemony (c. 1478–1565)
8. Zhigatsé Period and Karmapa Hegemony (c. 1565–1642)
9. Lhasa Period and Gandenpa Hegemony (c. 1642–1705)
AGE OF FOREIGN INTERESTS AND OCCUPATION
10. Period of Khoshud Mongol Rule (c. 1705–1717)
11. Period of Zunghar Mongol Occupation (c. 1717–1720)
12. Period of the Manchu Protectorate and Gelukpa Hegemony (c. 1720–1911)
13. Period of British Interest (c. 1888–1914)
14. Period of Tibetan Independence (c. 1914–1951)
15. Period of Chinese Communist Occupation (1951–present)

APPENDIX 2: SELECTED EXAMPLES OF PERIODIZATION SCHEMES IN TIBETAN SOURCES

(1) **Old Tibetan Chronicles from Dunhuang (c. 8th–10th century)**
1. Pre-Imperial/pre-Buddhist Period (ends c. 630)
2. Period of the Early Spread of the Teachings (*tenpa ngadar*, c. 630–842)

3. Period of Chaos (time-frame uncertain, begins c. 842)
4. Period of the Later Spread of the Teachings (*tenpa chidar*, late 10th century)

(2) **Rikpé Reldri, *Tuppé Tenpa Gyengyi Metok* (1261)**
1. Period of the Early Spread of the Teachings (*tenpa ngadar*, ends early 10th century)
2. Period of the Interim Spread of the Teachings (*tenpa bardar*, mid-10th century)
3. Period of the Later Spread of the Teachings (*tenpa chidar*, late 10th century)

(3) **Sakya Drakpa Gyeltsen, Neu Paṇḍita, Bütön, etc. (c. late 12th–14th century)**
1. Period of the Early Spread of the Teachings (*tenpa ngadar*, c. 600–842)
   *The "Dark Age" (time-frame uncertain, begins c. 842)
2. Period of the Later Spread of the Teachings (*tenpa chidar*) (late 10th century)

(4) **Guru Trashi, *Gutré chöjung* (1813)**
1. Period of the Early Kings (c. 600–798)
   *(nameless interim period, c. 798–1268)
2. Sakya Period (1268–1349)
3. Period of Taisitu Jangchup Gyeltsen and the Pakmodru (1349–1435)
4. Rinpung Period (1435–1565)
5. Period of Karma Püntsok Namgyel and the Karmapa (1605–1642)
6. Period of Desi Sönam Rapten and Gushri Tendzin Chögyel and the Ganden Podrang (1642–1705)
7. Period of King Lhazang and the Khoshud Mongols (1705–1717)
8. Period of Zunghar Suppression (1717–1728)
9. Period of Miwang Sönam Topgyel and Chingwam Talé Batur (1728–1757)
10. Period of the Regency of Demo Rinpoché (1757–1813)

(5) **Dungkar Lozang Trinlé, *Bökyi Chösi Zungdrel Korshepa* (1981/83)**
PRE-ESTABLISHMENT OF THE TIBETAN POLITICO-RELIGIOUS INSTITUTION
1. Period of Bon/pre-Buddhist (ends c. 629)
2. Buddhist Imperial Period (c. 629–869)
3. Period of Chaos in Tibet and Interior China (c. 869–978)
4. Period of the Revival of Buddhism in Tibet (c. 978–1238)
ESTABLISHMENT OF THE TIBETAN POLITICO-RELIGIOUS INSTITUTION
5. Period of Sakya Hegemony and War Between Sakya and Drigung Kagyü (c. 1238–1349)

6. Period of Pakmodru Hegemony and the Rise of the Gelukpa (c. 1349–1432)
7. Period of Civil War Among the Pakmodru Rulers (c. 1432–1448)
8. Period of Civil War Between the Rinpungpa and the Gelukpa (c. 1448–1565)
9. Period of War Between Desi Tsangpa and the Gelukpa (c. 1565–1642)
10. Period of War and Struggles Between the Ruling Class for Political Power (c. 1642–1721)
11. Period of the Decline of the Politico-Religious System and Internal Struggle Among the Ruling Class (c. 1721–1903)
12. Period of the Encroachment of Imperialists and Betrayal of Tibet by the Ruling Class (c. 1903–1949)
13. Period of Rebellion of the Ruling Class Against the Chinese People's Liberation Army (c. 1949–1951)

(6) **Tupten Püntsok, *Bökyi Logyü Chidön Pema Ragé Demik* (1996)**
1. Prehistoric Period (time-frame uncertain)
2. Period of Emerging Order (time-frame uncertain)
3. Period of Pugyel/The Early Kings (time-frame uncertain, ends c. 629)
4. Period of the Buddhist Kings (c. 629–841)
5. Period of Fragmentation (c. 841–1247)
6. Period of Sakya Rule (c. 1247–1349)
7. Period of Pakmodru Rule (c. 1349–1435)
8. Period of the Tsangpa Kings (c. 1435–1642)
9. Period of the Ganden Podrang (c. 1642–1951)

APPENDIX 3: SELECTED EXAMPLES OF PERIODIZATION SCHEMES IN TIBETAN STUDIES

(1) **G. TUCCI, *Tibetan Painted Scrolls* (1949)**
1. Central Tibet from the Fall of the Dynasty to the Mongol Invasion (c. 650–1239)
2. The Sakyapa [= Sakya Period] (c. 1247–1349)
3. Jangchup Gyeltsen's Successors and Struggle Between Pakmodru and Their Ministers (c. 1349–1481)
4. Tsang/"Reds" [Karmapa] Against Dbus/ "Yellows" [Gandenpa] (c. 1481–1642)
5. The Triumph of the "Yellows" and the Loss of Independence (c. 1642–1727)

(2) **P. CARRASCO, *Land and Polity in Tibet* (1959)**
1. The Early Dynasty (c. pre-842)
2. Four Dark Centuries (c. 842–1247)

3. The Sakya and Pakmodru Periods (c. 1247–1641)
4. The Rise of the Gelukpa (c. 1641–1728)
5. The Establishment of Chinese Dominion Over the Dalai Lamas (c. 1728–1911)

(3) **R. STEIN, *Tibetan Civilization* (1962)**
1. The Ancient Monarchy (c. 600–930)
2. The Evolution of Monastic Power (c. 930–1642)
3. The Modern Era (c. 1642–1962)

(4) **D. SNELLGROVE AND H. RICHARDSON, A *Cultural History of Tibet* (1968)**
THE EARLY KINGS
1. Manifestation of Tibetan Power and Introduction of Buddhism (c. 600–866)
THE MIDDLE AGES
2. Foundations of Monastic Life (c. 978–1207)
3. Mongol Overlordship (c. 1207–1368)
4. Resumption of Independence (c. 1391–1578)
THE YELLOW HATS
5. The Yellow Hats Rise to Power (c. 1578–1720)
6. Manchu Overlordship (c. 1720–1888)
7. British Interests (c. 1888–1911)
8. Renewal of Independence (c. 1911–1947)
9. Communist Domination (c. 1950–present)

(5) **V. BOGOSLOVSKIJ, *Essai sur l'histoire du peuple tibetain* (1972)**
1. La société tibetaine avant le VIIe siècle (c. pre-629)
2. Fin du processus d'unification au début du VIIe siècle (c. 629–649)
3. Le Tibet dans la deuxième moitié du VIIe siècle (c. 649–704)
4. Apogée de l'État tibetain au VIIIe siècle (c. 704–804)
5. Déclin de l'État tibetain dans la première moitié du IXe siècle (c. 804–842)

(6) **H. HOFFMAN, "Early and Medieval Tibet" (1990)**
EARLY TIBET
1. Pre- and Early History (c. pre-570)
2. Rise of the Tibetan Empire (c. 570–649)
3. The Period of Regency (c. 649–755)
4. The Zenith of the Tibetan Empire (c. 755–797)
5. The Period of Decline and Disintegration of the Empire (c. 797–842)
6. The "Dark Period" (c. 850–1000)
MEDIEVAL TIBET (not clear in Hoffman when "Medieval Period" begins)
7. The "Second Introduction of Buddhism" (c. 1042–1076)
8. Development of the Theocratic State (c. 1076–1300)

9. Decline of the Sakya Power and the Rule of the Pakmodrupa (c. 1300–1435)

(7) **G. SAMUEL**, *Civilized Shamans: Buddhism in Tibetan Societies* (1993)
1. Tibetan Empire (c. 625–841)
2. The Local Hegemonic Period (c. 841–1276)
3. Mongol Overlordship (13th–14th centuries/c. 1276–1358)
4. Gelukpa Synthesis and Shamanic Reaction (c. 1358–1642)
5. Gelukpa Power and the Rimé Synthesis (c. 1642–1950)

(8) **G. DORJÉ**, *Tibet Handbook with Bhutan* (1996)
1. The Yarlung Dynasty (c. pre-842)
2. Persecution of Buddhism and Disintegration of Empire (c. 842–978)
3. The Later Spread of Buddhism (c. 978–1235)
4. The Sakyapa Administration (c. 1235–1349)
5. The Pakmodrupa Administration (c. 1350–1435)
6. The Rinpung Administration (c. 1478–1565)
7. The Tsangpa Administration (c. 1565–1642)
8. The Depa Zhung [=Lhasa Government] (c. 1642–1951)
9. Chinese Administration (c. 1951–present)

(9) **M. GOLDSTEIN**, *The Snow Lion and the Dragon* (1997)
1. The Imperial Era (c. 630–842)
   *(no mention of a period between 842 and 1207)
2. Tibet and the Mongols (c. 1207–1372)
3. The Rise of the Geluk Sect in Tibet (c. 1372–1888)
4. The British Enter the Picture (c. 1888–1904)
5. The Chinese Reaction (c. 1904–1911)
6. Interlude: De Facto Independence (c. 1911–1933)
7. Chinese Communist Rule: The Mao Era (c. 1949–1976)
8. The Post-Mao Era (c. 1976–1997/present)

(10) **D. MARTIN (based on outline by M. Aris), www.thdl.org** (2002)
1. Early Empire (c. 600–842)
2. Tibet in Pieces (c. 842–1249)
3. Mongol Pressure (c. 1249–1349)
4. Rival Powers (c. 1350–1642)
5. Ganden Podrang Government (1642–1950s)
6. Manchu Pressure (c. 1720–1912)
7. Independence (1912–1950s)
8. PRC Rule (1950s–present)

(11) **A. McKAY**, *The History of Tibet* (2003)
1. The Early Period: Yarlung Dynasty (up to c. 850)
2. The Medieval Period: Development of Buddhist Paramountcy (c. 850–1895)
3. The Modern Period: Encounter with Modernity (1895–1959)

NOTES

I had the honor of delivering earlier drafts of this essay at two seminars organized at the University of Virginia in March 2003 and at Harvard University in April 2004. I wish to thank my colleagues who participated in these events for their generous comments, suggestions for refinement, and for the few lively debates that took place during the sessions and afterward over coffee.

1. Exemplary surveys of the issue of periodization in Chinese studies include Mark Elvin, *The Pattern of the Chinese Past* (Stanford: Stanford University Press 1973); Jacques Gernet, *A History of Chinese Civilization* (Cambridge: Cambridge University Press 1982), esp. 22–25; J. A. G. Roberts, *A Concise History of China* (Cambridge, Mass.: Harvard University Press, 1999); James H.Y. Tai and Marjorie K.M. Chan, "Some Reflections on the Periodization of the Chinese Language," in *Studies in Chinese Historical Syntax and Morphology: Linguistic Essays in Honor of Mei Tsu-lin*, Alain Peyraube and Chaofen Sun, eds. (Paris: École des Hautes Etudes en Sciences Sociales, Centre de Recherches Linguistiques sur l'Asie Orientale, 1999), 223–239; in Japanese studies, see John Whitney Hall, "Terms and Concepts in Japanese Medieval History: An Inquiry into the Problems of Translation," *Journal of Japanese Studies* 9, no. 1 (1983): 1–32; Jeffrey P. Mass, *Antiquity and Anachronism in Japanese History* (Stanford: Stanford University Press, 1992); in Indian studies, see Sabyasachi Bhattacharya and Romila Thapar, eds., *Situating Indian History* (Delhi: Oxford University Press, 1986); Brajadulal Chattopadhyaya, *The Making of Early Medieval India* (Delhi: Oxford University Press, 1994); Romila Thapar, *Ancient Indian Social History: Some Interpretations* (1978; reprint, New Delhi: Orient Longman, 1996) and *Early India: From the Origins to* AD *1300* (Berkeley: University of California Press, 2002), esp. 1–36.

2. Debates about periodization in European studies began in earnest in the nineteenth century. For a helpful overview of the development of these debates, see William A. Green, "Periodization in European and World History," *Journal of World History* 3, no. 1 (1992): 13–53. For recent reflections on several key approaches to dividing up and interpreting the past from the point of view of European and American historiography, see Ludmilla Jordanova, *History in Practice* (London: Arnold, 2000), 114–140.

3. By "metaphysics" or "ontology" here I mean to imply a conception of history in which a specific division of time is held to be objectively established, as "just the way it is." In this sense, a metaphysical or ontological conception of the past is one that views historical constructs such as periodization as unconditionally given and fails to acknowledge the merely conceptual or heuristic nature of such constructs.

4. On the early developments of Tibetan historiography, see the insightful discussions in Matthew Kapstein, *The Tibetan Assimilation of Buddhism: Conversions, Contestations, and Memory* (New York: Oxford University Press, 2000), chaps. 2–4.

5. Much of what scholars know of the ancient Tibetan empire has depended to a great extent on the manuscripts recovered from Dunhuang and preserved at both the Bibliothèque Nationale in Paris (Pelliot Collection) and the British Library in

London (Stein Collection). Materials for the study of these important texts can be found in Marcelle Lalou, *Inventaire des manuscrits tibétains de Touen-houang conservés à la Bibliothèque Nationale, Fonds Pelliot tibétains*, 3 vols. (Paris: Librairie d'Amérique et d'Orient, 1939–61); Jacques Bacot, F. W. Thomas, and Ch. Toussaint, *Documents de Touen-houang relatifs à l'histoire du Tibet* (Paris: Librairie Orientaliste Paul Geuthner, 1940); Spanian Macdonald and Yoshiro Imaeda, *Choix de documents tibétains conservés à la Bibliothèque nationale*, 2 vols. (Paris: Bibliothèque nationale, 1978–79).

6. Rolf A. Stein, *Tibetan Civilization*, trans. J. E. Stapleton Driver (Stanford: Stanford University Press, 1972), 54.

7. Rig pa'i ral gri, *Thub pa'i bstan pa rgyan gyi me tog* (Nepal National Archives; reel no. L493/2). My thanks to Kurtis Schaeffer for introducing me to this little-known work and for sharing with me his notes on the text.

8. For a brief but detailed account of the politics of this period, see Hugh Richardson, "Political Aspects of the *Snga-dar*, the First Diffusion of Buddhism in Tibet," in *High Peaks, Pure Earth: Collected Writings on Tibetan History and Culture* (London: Serindia, 1998), 196–202; see now also Ronald M. Davidson, *Tibetan Renaissance: Tantric Buddhism in the Rebirth of Tibetan Culture* (New York: Columbia University Press, 2005), 61–83.

9. Sa skya Grags pa rgyal mtshan, *Bod kyi rgyal rabs*, in *Sa skya pa'i Bka' 'bum* (Tokyo: The Toyo Bunko, 1968), vol. 4, 295–296, trans. in Giuseppe Tucci, "The Validity of Tibetan Historical Tradition," in *India Antiqua: A Volume of Oriental Studies Presented by His Friends and Pupils to Jean Philippe Vogel, C.I.E., on the Occasion of the Fiftieth Anniversary of His Doctorate* (Leiden: Brill, 1947), 309–322; Ne'u (Nel pa) Paṇḍita Grags pa smon lam blo gros, *Sngon gyi gtam me tog phreng ba*, in *Rare Tibetan Historical and Literary Texts from the Library of Tsepon W.D. Shakabpa* (New Delhi: Taikhang, 1974); and Bu ston, *Bu ston chos 'byung* (Beijing: Krung go bod kyi shes rig dpe skrun khang, 1988), trans. E. Obermiller, *History of Buddhism in India and Tibet* (1932; reprint, Delhi: Sri Satguru, 1986).

10. This mysterious middle period, the so-called "dark age" in Tibetan history, has been described also by Tibetan historians as a "period of fragmentation" (*sil bu'i dus*). See, for example, Nor brang O rgyan, *Bod sil bu'i byung ba brjod pa shel dkar phreng ba* (Lhasa: Bod ljongs bod yig dpe rnying dpe skrun khang, 1991); also Thub bstan phun tshogs, "Bod sil bu'i skabs kyi dus tshigs 'ga' zhig la dpyad pa," in *Krung go'i bod kyi shes rig* 1 (1990): 57–62.

11. *Gu bkra'i chos 'byung* [=*Bstan pa'i snying po gsang chen snga 'gyur nges don zab mo'i chos kyi byung ba gsal bar byed pa'i legs bshad mkhas pa dga' byed ngo mtshar gtam gyi rol mtsho*] (Beijing: Krung go'i bod kyi shes rig dpe skrun khang, 1990).

12. *Gu bkra'i chos 'byung*, 648–938, esp. 922–935 and 935–938. See also Dan Martin, "A Brief Political History of Tibet by Gu ru Bkra-shis," in *Tibetan History and Language: Studies Dedicated to Uray Géza on His Seventieth Birthday*, ed. E. Steinkellner (Vienna: Arbeitskreis für Tibetische und Buddhistische Studien, 1991), 329–351.

13. *Gu bkra'i chos 'byung*, 937 and 1055.

14. For an account of the early development of Chinese Marxist historiography, see Arif Dirlik, *Revolution and History: Origins of Marxist Historiography in China, 1919–1937* (Berkeley: University of California Press, 1978).

15. On the use of the term "feudalism" with reference to Tibetan history, see Stein, *Tibetan Civilization*, 289–292; also, on the controversies surrounding the term "serfdom," the various articles by Melvyn C. Goldstein, "Serfdom and Mobility: An Examination of the Institution of 'Human Lease' in Traditional Tibetan Society," *Journal of Asian Studies* 30, no. 3 (1971): 521–534; "Reexamining Choice, Dependency and Command in the Tibetan Social System: 'Tax Appendages' and Other Landless Serfs," *Tibet Journal* 9, no. 4 (1986): 79–112; "On the Nature of the Tibetan Peasantry: A Rejoinder," *Tibet Journal* 13, no. 1 (1988): 61–65; and critical responses by Beatrice D. Miller, "A Response to Goldstein's 'Reexamining Choice, Dependency and Command in the Tibetan Social System,'" *Tibet Journal* 12, no. 2 (1987): 65–67 and "Last Rejoinder to Goldstein on Tibetan Social System," *Tibet Journal* 13, no. 3 (1988): 64–66.

16. Dung dkar blo bzang 'phrin las, *Bod kyi chos srid zung 'brel skor bshad pa* (Beijing: Mi rigs dpe skrun khang, 1981/1983), trans. Chen Guansheng, *The Merging of Religious and Secular Rule in Tibet* (Beijing: Foreign Languages Press, 1991). Mention should also be made of the recent Chinese publications by Rin chen nor bu, *Bod kyi lo rgyus slob gzi blo gsar jug pa'i bab stegs* [*Teaching Material of Tibetan History*] (Lanzhou: Kan su'u mi rigs dpe skrun khang, 1996) and Xincha Losang Gyatso, *Bod kyi lo rgyus gzhon nu dga' ba'i gtam phreng* [*General Tibetan History*] (Lanzhou: Kan su'u mi rigs dpe krun khang, 1997). In both cases a decidedly Marxist vocabulary is employed for the various periods of Tibetan history, e.g., the "Founding of the Tubo Dynasty and Emergence of Feudal Serfdom," the "Separatist Regimes Period," and the period of "The Peaceful Liberation of Tibet."

17. Thub bstan phun tshogs, *Bod kyi lo rgyus spyi don padma ra'a ga'i lde mig* [*General History of Tibet*] (Beijing: Mi rigs dpe skrun khang, 1996).

18. Alex McKay, ed., *The History of Tibet*, 3 vols. (London: Routledge Curzon, 2003).

Chapter 3

HISTORY AS MYTH

ON THE APPROPRIATION OF THE PAST IN TIBETAN CULTURE
AN ESSAY IN CULTURAL STUDIES

Peter Schweiger

Peter Schweiger, a leading German historian of Tibet, asks: What role has historical writing played in the conservation of Tibetan society? As he explains in this essay, the Tibetan need for a mythic history arose in an era when the culture was coming out of a particularly chaotic time after the fall of the empire. His statements about the stationary nature of Tibetan history writing might be taken as critical by some, but this is not his intention. Instead, Schweiger illuminates the Tibetan tradition's own understanding of the proper place of history: to preserve a link to the past, especially through a direct and unbroken connection. Continuity through time and over historical ruptures is perhaps nowhere better represented than in genealogy. Schweiger illustrates the essentially genealogical structure of Tibetan historiography as well as its connection to Indic patterns. Moreover, as he points out, these patterns are especially useful in legitimating both religious and political institutions (which were usually linked in Tibet).

INTRODUCTION

The range and variety of historiographical literature in Tibet depicts history almost exclusively from the selective perspective of the Buddhist religion. Many Western historians accepted this as a mere shortcoming of the sources, at most explained by a brief reference to the ideological function of Tibetan tradition. However, in Tibetology a similarly selective perception of the sources has frequently emerged, which is based on the usefulness of the sources in relation to the abstraction of historical facts and is a parallel development, so to speak, of the selective perception shown in Tibetan historiography. The former was ultimately, albeit not always explicitly, based on a classification of written sources that distinguishes between "relics," or *Überreste*, and traditional sources. Originally established by Droysen and later further systemized by Bernheim, Kirn, and Brandt, it is today no longer the sole valid classification applied in the science of history because it draws its orientation from purely fact-based historiography.

When, for example, the label "tradition" is used as a basis for the classification of historiographical sources as having low informative value, this is a judgment generated solely by the historian's specific phrasing of the question, not inherent in the source per se. It has become a truism that basically every source, depending on what one seeks to find out, may also qualify as a "relic," since it always communicates additional unintended information. In addition, the trends shown in historiographical sources in particular may be declared the object of historical investigation, given that they betray a great deal about the intentions, ideas, and views of the historiographers and—to use a term coined by Friedrich Nietzsche in his critical examination of scientific history—about the "closed horizon" that encircles the scope of their opportunities as historical beings.[1] By adopting this perspective I am also establishing a connection with the broadly based cross-disciplinary discussion that has emerged in recent years from the field of cultural and social sciences.

The concept of culture on which this essay is based assumes culture to be "a symbolically and textually conveyed process of self-interpretation and construct of meaning."[2] This applies particularly to history—that is, history in the sense of representation. But "textually conveyed" does not on any account mean that culture is completely subsumed in text. In culture, power is always an additional issue.[3]

HYPOTHESIS AND QUESTION

I intend to restrict my analysis to the Tibetan image of history that emerged at the start of the Second Propagation of Buddhist teachings in Tibet, thus from the eleventh century onward, and remained the only valid proposition until well into the twentieth century. In doing this, I will initially undertake a rough outline of the diachronic aspect before focusing on a synchronically based analysis. According to the late Michael Aris, the reason to favor such a methodical focus when writing about Tibet's historiographical literature is that "the literary language used in these texts has not undergone any really significant change during the last millennium."[4] This is primarily due to the unchallenged position occupied by Buddhism in Tibetan society throughout the centuries.

My analysis also examines history as myth. By "myth," I mean that history has been assigned the role of conferring meaning and that normative claims have been derived from it. In this sense, the term "myth" has become established in cultural science[5] and in the science of history in particular.[6]

My starting point is the following thesis:

History, understood as the remembered past, has the function in Tibetan culture of providing a solid basis for, and defining, sociocultural interrelationships in a monocentric culture.

In substantiating this thesis, I will address the following two questions:

1   What happened to bring Tibetan culture largely to a standstill?
2.   How was history reconstructed in Tibetan culture?

DIACHRONIC ANALYSIS

Although the foundations for the development of a culture exclusively oriented to Buddhism were laid as early as the Tibetan Age of Kings (seventh to ninth centuries), some resistance was put up by the influential nobility of the time. In addition, as a closed system of teaching, Buddhism was primarily a court religion and was practiced there side by side with non-Buddhist cults, particularly those associated with the graves of the Tibetan kings. However, a widespread general willingness to accept Buddhist teachings appears to have been established in Tibet at the end of this period: a certain familiarity that could be resumed as a starting point at a later date.[7] This is likely to have had broader causes than the official support of Buddhism by the court, as later Tibetan historiography would have us believe. Other formative influences would certainly have been the many contacts with itinerant Indian yogis traveling to remote regions of the Himalayas as pilgrims and to practice meditation. While such contacts promoted neither the systematic propagation of Buddhist teachings nor a necessarily correct and deeper understanding of them, they allowed a general familiarity to develop with Buddhist and, in particular, Tantric practices as reflected in the formation of religious movements, the followers of which were later known as Nyingmapa and Bönpo. We may also assume that this form of infiltration of Buddhist practice and Buddhist thought did not cease to progress even after the decline of the monarchy in Central Tibet.[8] However, the main focus would probably have been on Tantric and shamanic forms of Buddhism.[9]

In the eleventh century, when the western Tibetan kings initiated the revival of Buddhism in Tibet, they shifted the focus to monastic and academic traditions—a process that reached its peak in the fourteenth century in the academic and to a certain extent also political centers of Sakya and Zhalu.[10] What took place has been described by the Egyptologist Jan Assmann as the act of closure in the process of canonization: the flow of tradition was finally canonized, its content and form defined in universally binding terms as the sole true tradition.[11] The Indian classics of Buddhism were regarded "as the embodiment of the ideas and values to which society had committed itself."[12] In this respect, ancient Tibet wholly corresponded to our image of other premodern societies: "the teachings in question had been accepted as the Truth [*sic*], which remains true however early or late its discovery may be." The idea that the truth was recorded in binding works from the past additionally led to the conclusion that knowledge—albeit broad—was ultimately limited: "everything had been said; everything could be mastered given sufficient time."

Texts require interpretation to ensure that their vitality, recorded once and for all, is retained throughout the passage of time. By institutionalizing interpretation, "a new class of intellectual elites" is created that strives to represent the normative and formative aims of the canon from a position largely independent of social constraints.[13]

Two factors played a decisive role in the final process of fixing the canon in fourteenth-century Tibet:[14] one was the examination of traditions handed down that later survived only as apocryphal accounts; the other was the increasing dearth of living sources of tradition as Islam penetrated into northern India.[15] From this point onward, the tradition fixed in the canon held indubitable validity and was considered to be the veritable ultimate truth—an exalted position transferred to those who invoked the tradition as the ultimate authority and who occupied themselves with its interpretation. By committing themselves to its canon, the members of the Buddhist clergy had finally cemented a monocentric culture in place. "A distinguishing feature of this kind of culture," as Assmann writes, "is its general orientation, the power of a unifying and binding formula which overlays the various codes of cultural communication in practice and which leaves no room for independent thought and autonomous discourse."[16] Although this did not check the creative powers of the bearers of the high culture,[17] evidence of which is furnished by many works of philosophical teaching (*yikcha*) and apologetic texts (*gaklen*),[18] these are exclusively interpretations of canonized writings. Above all, the training of analytical capabilities practiced with the use of this literature moved within the strictly prescribed scope of Indo-Buddhist scholarship. As a result, there was little space for new ideas. We begin to form the image of a culture we would be justified in describing as "stationary." For this assessment is not solely the result of *our* perspective as observers:[19] in fact, as the bearers of the high culture, Tibet's spiritual elite themselves clung to the image of a stationary culture.

The section of the clergy that adhered to apocryphal traditions above and beyond the commonly recognized canon[20] was largely denied any social influence. The Bönpo, who did not recognize the Buddhist canon as binding and produced their own canon in response to the canonization of Buddhist texts, were socially marginalized.[21]

Furthermore, a collective identity was founded and formed by the body of texts and values delimited in the canon, defined as binding, considered to be beyond all doubt and thus sanctified. Sanctification was extended to all who committed themselves to this identity.[22] Thus the image of a "chosen people" was increasingly established in Tibetan society—formulated by the intellectual elite. In Tibet, this awareness of a unique status was based on the idea of being the sole keepers of the one true tradition. Tibet was perceived as the only country in which Buddhism, in its specific Mahāyāna form, had survived in unbroken and undamaged tradition as almost the only doctrine to be accepted by the entire population, while in all other originally Buddhist countries encircling the land of snows it had been ousted completely by other religions or was engaged in permanent competition with them. For this reason, according to Tsewang Norbu, an eighteenth-century intellectual, "this (Tibet) amid the snowy mountains may be insignificant and low in its location, but because of the higher status (of living creatures as human beings) and the true value (of liberation and omniscience or complete enlightenment), this snow-covered Tibet rivals (even) Shambhala in the north."[23]

The goal was to preserve this unique legacy of the one true tradition together with the external conditions required for its maintenance. After the downfall of the monarchy, the clergy in Tibet regarded themselves as the highest guarantors of this heritage. As can also be observed in other places to the present day, this led to clericalization, and ultimately sacralization, of the culture. The authority of the clergy, as the highest guarantor of the sanctified cultural heritage, was not restricted to the route by which salvation could be achieved but also provided guidance in secular matters.[24]

ANALYSIS FROM A SYNCHRONOUS PERSPECTIVE

In the role of historiographers, the clerics now brought history into the service of conserving the culture. In doing so, they did not write history as such, but the history for and about the institution to which they were bound in each case.[25] Tibetan historiography is thus based on a communication situation similar to that of the European Middle Ages. Historiographers were not only dependent on the institution for which they were writing the history but also themselves generally involved in the narrative. As a result, their historical interest was far from dissociated from references to the present and future.

There were but few points of connection with India for this interest, which led to the creation of a wealth of historiographical writings: in addition to the annals known as Vamshāvalî,[26] these points primarily constituted the legend of the life of the Buddha, which supplied Tibetan hagiographers with a range of topoi. It could presumably be linked to early Tibetan family chronicles or similar materials, such as those that had probably been continued throughout the era of the downfall of the Tibetan monarchy and beyond.[27] However, it had arisen above all from people's need to reassure themselves repeatedly of the unbroken connection to their own cultural origins and to legitimize their own sense of mission from these origins. Depending on the proximity of spiritual institutions to individual aristocratic houses, as encountered in Tibetan history, this need could in some cases be intimately connected with the ambition to legitimize a clan's claim to power. This is most obvious in the case of the Sakya and Taklung schools.[28] On the periphery of the Tibetan cultural sphere, there were also regions where the institution of the monarchy survived even in the centuries after the Second Propagation of Buddhist teachings. The Tibetan historiographers who wrote "royal chronicles" (*gyelrap*) under the patronage of a king in this epoch basically derived the royal claim to power from the same cultural roots as, say, those of monastic institutions.[29] Dynastic history was also in the service of religion. Conversely, one of the range of services offered by religion was naturally to place its power of legitimation, and of its associated historiography, at the disposal of secular social relationships if this appeared expedient for the goals prescribed by religion and its institutions.

The form of Tibetan historiography largely follows the pattern of genealogical structure. "As a formal structure, genealogy divides history into a series of biographies linked by the principle of hereditary succession, which regulates both the progression of time and the transfer of property and honor. Viewed from the standpoint of the genre, genealogical chronicles represent a blend of a theoretically different biography with chronography."[30] This pattern formed the basis not only for tracking the lineage and interconnections of clans but also, and primarily, for establishing incarnation series, monastic chronicles or deeds, and spiritual lines of succession (teacher-pupil chains), in which the biographies served as links in the chain of traditions *deliberately* handed down.

The unbroken continuity of such series guaranteed the authenticity of the tradition while passing on to later generations the power of blessing that it drew from its origins. In this sense it possessed a function similar to that accorded to genealogy in myth, understood as a history of the gods: "to transfer the power of the sacred origins to what originated from, was derived from them."[31]

As time progressed and these chains grew longer, concern indeed arose that both their authenticity and the "power of sacred origins" were gradually being eroded. This concern was strongest in the orthodox Buddhist school of Nyingmapa with respect to spiritual lines of succession, since this school, unlike the other Buddhist schools in Tibet, traced its entire tradition, adopted from India, back to the First Propagation of Buddhist teachings in Tibet. The Indian tradition itself was not questioned further. The Nyingma school developed sophisticated concepts enabling the tradition to be "abbreviated" by means of visions and apocryphal literature, to remove any misgivings over its power of blessing and its authenticity from its teachings passed down in this way.[32] This not only resulted in the establishment of new cult traditions but also served to "recharge" existing cults with new powers of blessing.[33] These concepts are based on an understanding of time not as a homogeneous measure of a continuous sequence of events, but rather as a dimension containing "holes" through which

the "power of sacred origins" can repeatedly manifest itself directly and spontaneously in the present. Time is, so to speak, a transparent and porous sheet
through which historic events become visible, always against the founding background of their cultural origins. Events remain bound to these origins not only
through the unbroken nature of their sequence, perceived as a causal relationship, but also through visions, prophecies, promises that continue to take effect
after the death of the salvation figures, wish-granting prayers, and so on. In this
context, history symbolizes the close, continuous connection to cultural origins.

History, in both its orally recounted form and its form that is personally experienced and shaped, provided a means of orientation in the present and future, since it was perceived as a method of organizing the collectively shared
fund of cultural knowledge. Tibetan historiographers moved within a common
and relatively narrow horizon, their stories part of a greater web of meaning,
literally a "context." This context is what we call a culture. The deep semantic
structure of Tibetan culture, which directs the entirety of its surface structure,
determines global structure, creates continuity between disparate phenomena,
and defines what is meant by these phenomena—which, in other words, creates
meaning—had been developed from the core concepts of Indian Mahāyāna
Buddhism.[34] Indian Mahāyāna Buddhism thus shaped the horizons of the way
the consciousness of Tibetan culture as a whole (i.e., the group consciousness
reflected in individual consciousnesses and coupled with collective intention)
perceived the world.[35] At the same time, by doing so it supplied the firmly closed
framework of interpretation that enabled history to be read as meaningful text.[36]
Because of the widespread stasis of Tibetan culture, throughout the centuries,
minor shifts of accentuation were the only changes to this frame of reference for
the reconstruction of the past.

When Buddhism absorbed the Hindu cosmology it also absorbed the concept of cyclical time. These cosmic cycles of the creation and decline of worlds,
however, operate on a different plane from that of historical time. In historical
time, history most certainly has a beginning, in the direction of which it is reconstructed as a linear process. This beginning is the life of the Buddha Shākyamuni,[37] which serves as a fixed point of reference for Tibetan historiography.
In the search for contexts of meaning and development, events in the "shapeless
flow of history"[38] are tested for their ability to be incorporated and are isolated,
selected, reconstructed, and reshaped retrospectively in the direction of this
beginning as part of a more or less unconscious process of perception, thereafter to be presented in a plot, a chain of development that is linked not merely in
a temporal sense but also in a meaningful and causal sense and has a beginning, a middle, and an end.[39]

In his *Poetics*, Aristotle linked the three moments of beginning, middle, and
end with the concept of the "whole."[40] These three nonempirical ideas trans-
form a narrative into a closed, complete form (or dynamic form), and thus into
something in opposition to the open, random nature of life as it is lived. "The

narrative, like the visual perception of form, brings out those elements that form the pattern or plot and that serve as the focus of attention. In addition, by means of the process of smoothing, the narrative works in a similar way to the principle of closure, in which incomplete figures are perceived as whole."[41] History as a narrative thus draws its orientation from perception. But perception also works by assigning significance, a process based on the principles identified in Gestalt psychology under the terms "consistency," "*Prägnanz* (pithiness)," "good *Gestalt*," "Common Fate," and so on.[42]

"Unlike real life, a narrative structure generally revolves around a single 'main plot,' where only those subplots and events are accepted that contribute to the main plot, and all irrelevant occurrences are removed."[43] The plot on which Tibetan historical stories are based is the catalog of actions performed by the buddhas and bodhisattvas for the good of living beings in Tibet by means of emanations and incarnations—actions that manifested less in originality and innovation than in a close-knit sequence of uniform events,[44] simultaneously documenting the unbroken connection to the roots of their own culture. The narrative representation of history thus tended to be schematic literature with a minimal range of variation.[45] As in many other premodern societies, the monocentric nature of Tibetan culture also resulted in the lack of any search for alternative lines of meaning in history. Each presentation of history rewritten throughout the centuries—despite the temporal and spatial narrowness of its focus—was linked in form and content to what is rooted in the collective consciousness as the "right" image of Tibetan history, and reiterated it repeatedly. For this reason, the many depictions of Tibetan history appear to us today to be more or less part of a single "family history."

In Tibetan depictions of history the actions and protagonists take center stage,[46] while social, economic, and political structures take a back seat. In the presentation of interrelationships between the protagonists, complex ideas are reduced to simple binarism. Tibetan tales of history are clearly dominated by the dichotomies of friend-enemy (friend/protector of Buddhist teachings versus enemy of Buddhist teachings), giver-receiver (giver versus receiver of religious instructions and initiations), donor-recipient (donor versus recipient of devotional gifts), protector-protegé, and Buddhist and non-Buddhist (*nangpa-chipa* [literally: insider-outsider]). These basic dichotomies were allocation rules, part of the central code of Tibetan culture, and thus were themselves able to control social behavior. These dichotomies also dispensed the narrow categorical framework of a simple social model of reality, into which more complex social relationships such as those between landowners and dependent peasants and animal herders were sometimes forced in roughly abbreviated form, but generally completely blanked out.[47] This allowed the events of history to be repeatedly relinked into the same familiar patterns, giving a static quality to history as narrative: although the protagonists were replaced by others, the roles depicted (particularly clerics, abbot, teachers, pupils, patron, and so on) and the actions and modes of behavior expected from their players remained the same for centuries, so that the relationships portrayed remained as unchanging as a painted picture. The social persona in its entirety—in other words, the *complete* catalog of roles—is almost invisible, and the individual is completely hidden, although isolated genuinely individual character traits can be made out in exceptional cases. "'The individual' or the individual-in-general is a concept arising rather late in most complex human cultures," writes Victor Turner. Where it appears at an early stage, for example in societies without the written form, it is "often in veiled or restricted form."[48] Yet the individual is "the moral critic who envisages another kind of social or moral order, the creative spark poised and ready to change tradition."[49] Only from the perspective of the individual are the social roles called into question and declared to be a sham.

Tibetan historians were primarily clerics whose scholarship had been honed on the classical literature of Indian Buddhism and its rhetorical tools of style. The literary forms—the "toolbox," so to speak—available to them were thus limited in a different way from those of nineteenth-century European historiographers. The literary models familiar to us, such as romance, tragedy, comedy, and satire, were not in literary use.[50] Historiography, like prayers, religious teachings, instructions concerning rituals and evocations, and so on, was part of a religious system of communication. Given the similarities and overlaps in the intended effect, topics, complexes of ideas and symbols, patterns of events, and arguments from other types of religious text were incorporated into historiography almost of their own accord. Yet unlike these, narrated history did not have a place in rituals and cults, lacking the performative aspect, and instead embodied the fundamental claim to truth of the content laid down in canonical writings.

Historiography, which largely followed the pattern of genealogy, primarily drew its orientation for presenting individual biographies from Indian Buddhist descriptions of an ideal and typical life, with that of the Buddha at the fore, but also including the life of Buddhist ascetics, known as siddhas, and the ideal of the bodhisattva expressed in the Mahāyāna writings. The ideal, and thus exemplary, type of life primarily consists of a gradual progression toward the highest goal of enlightenment and the outward demonstration of the implementation of the bodhisattva's virtues. This resulted in a clear-cut repertoire of unvarying presentations of events that served as a framework for the various biographies. An example of a topos featured in the biographies of outstanding figures who were placed at the head of a line of incarnation would be a life crisis through which the subject of the biography turns to religion or seeks a spiritual teacher. Further commonplaces were primarily the receipt and granting of initiations and religious instructions that produce spiritual progress.[51] Events considered worthy of reporting also included the foundation of monasteries, construction activities in monasteries, the setting up of religious images, pilgrimages, and travel by groups of students. All actions corresponded to the expected pattern of virtuous deeds of body, speech, and mind. The specific virtues of a bodhisattva include compassion and wisdom. Both were documented either by appropriate deeds, which ultimately followed the patterns of their Indian templates, or by descriptions of these qualities as exemplified by the protagonists and their deeds. The Indian templates also specified the topoi attesting to spiritual progress in the lives of the saints: accounts of miracles, visions, and prophecies. Once the life of a protagonist had been classified as holy, miracles were deemed to furnish insight, and visions and prophecies were permitted as meaningful. At the same time, outstanding deeds in the life of the protagonist were regarded as directed by compassion or wisdom. A life not classified as holy was generally[52] deemed not worthy of narration, and was thus mentioned in Tibetan historiography only peripherally or as a disruption that could not be ignored.

One might initially think that unlike, say, the ancient perception of history in the Near East—which attributed striking events in history to the will of the gods or according to which God's will was revealed in history—the Tibetan idea of history had primarily been shaped by the Indian concept of karma and thus saw history as containing an automatic causal connection. This concept was also doubtless reflected in the perception of past time, flanked by the idea of an increasingly degenerate world. As a consequence, a consciousness of imperfection in the present developed and was countered by the depiction of the distant past as an age of glory. In Tibetan historiography, this golden age was not so much the age of the Buddha Shākyamuni as the Tibetan Age of Kings, in which cultural heroes such as the first Tibetan kings and the Buddhist missionary Padmasambhava established the foundations of Tibetan culture. This epoch appeared as the wellspring or beginning of Tibetan culture, and thus was already accorded the achievement of creating identity, linked with the glorification of the events it portrayed. Throughout the centuries, this image of a glorified past exerted a powerful normative and formative influence on Tibetan culture. We need only consider the ideal image of a ruler established by the Indian Buddhist idea of Dharmarāja, yet in a directly "plastic and graphic" form that is perpetually present in the traditional image of the first Tibetan kings; or the codification of law ascribed to the period of rule of Songtsen Gampo (618–649), which was thus legitimized *in principio* and withdrawn from the passage of time; or the "Great Debate of Samyé" at the end of the eighth century, which compresses the decision made in favor of the specific form of Buddhism adopted in Tibet into a single event and a rational power; or the relationship between monks and laypeople that took shape under King Relpachen (815–838 or 842), under which the care of the former was assigned to the latter; or Padmasambhava's conquest of the gods and demons, the pattern of which recurs repeatedly in hagiographies of the Tibetan clergy and is applied continuously in Tibetan Buddhist ritual; and finally, the episode of the murder of King Lang Darma (838 or 842), which presents the justification and location of violence up to and including murder in a Buddhist context. All these and further aspects that make up the traditional image of the Tibetan Age of Kings reveal Tibetan culture and its fundamental achievements (religion, the writing system, laws, the monastery system and monasticism, cultural unity) as created by and for religion, thus simultaneously giving primacy to religion before politics.

Oddly, the guiding function of the concept of karma was now displaced in the Tibetan idea of history by a different guiding principle, or rather collection of principles, that echoed the Christian concept of *Heilsgeschichte* (salvation history)—particularly in its most striking form of the Avalokiteśvara cult. This group of ideas, which took shape as early as the twelfth to early fourteenth centuries,[53] moved into the foreground as a result of changes in power politics from both internal and—primarily—external causes. The particular effectiveness of the Avalokiteśvara concept is based on the idea of the bodhisattva Avalokiteśvara as the embodiment of infinite compassion, thus offering points of association for a devotional cult to the broad mass of the people.[54]

The Avalokiteśvara cult is one of Tibet's most far-ranging bundles of religious concepts, linking the Indian ideal of the bodhisattva with the image of spiritual teachers who undergo reincarnation for the good of living beings, and shaping this connection in a way that affected the fields of politics and salvation history.

In the Maṇi Kabum text, the oldest parts of which date from the twelfth century,[55] King Songtsen Gampo is mentioned for the first time as an incarnation of Avalokiteśvara. Avalokiteśvara is here presented as Tibet's tutelary deity and a direct forefather of the Tibetan people in one of his forms—the monkey bodhisattva who coupled with a mountain demon symbolizing Tārā and begat the six ancestors from whom the six tribes of Tibet descended. Avalokiteśvara is therefore directly responsible for the existence of the Tibetan people.[56]

If Avalokiteśvara had manifested himself in human form in the past, in principle he was able to repeat this act at any time to take exclusive care of *his* people. The Fifth Dalai Lama, Ngawang Lozang Gyatso (1617–82), was the most successful in claiming the Avalokiteśvara concept for himself by embedding it, in word and deed, in a general concept of Tibetan history that presented the dominance of the Gelukpa school under his leadership as the pinnacle and logical conclusion of a continuous process of development. The "chronicle" (*gyelrap*) of the Dalai Lama[57] from the year 1643 was aimed primarily at demonstrating one thing—that Tibet's entire history to date had been directed at a single goal: Gosi Qan (Gushri Khan)'s conquest of Tibet. As stated in the Fifth Dalai Lama's biography, this conquest was crowned with the offering of Tibet as a sacrifice to the Fifth Dalai Lama, the incarnation of Avalokiteśvara, in 1642. And by establishing the Potala at precisely the spot where the ruined palace of King Songtsen Gampo was said to have stood in the past, he claimed the position of the ancient Tibetan kings, making clear to all the claim to preeminence raised by the Gelukpa and their leader. The here and now is thus no longer a mere link in the chain of earthly events, but part of a history planned as if by divine foresight.

Events that have absolutely no direct connection are thus linked to form a meaningful narrative. From the Potala as a base, the physically present Avalokiteśvara, who had accompanied the Tibetans from their mythical beginnings, continued his activities for the good of Tibet.

The plan of salvation on which the narrative was based promised no release from earthly calamity at the end of days. Instead, it offered the assurance of constant ministration by the messianic figures, the assurance of their recurring presence and unfailing efforts to save living beings from the cycle of rebirth, the ocean of suffering. The message was not only that the possibility of salvation is ever-present in Tibet but also that the support and guidance of powerful assistants can always be counted on in realizing salvation.

The bundle of concepts associated with the Avalokiteśvara cult enabled the legitimation not only of secular power but also of its spiritual counterpart. In these terms it was more comprehensive than, for example, the concept of dynastic continuity such as that in place in Ladakh for the legitimation of political power. Other forms of rule were "tried out" after the period of Zunghar rule in Central Tibet (1717–20), but they all failed, and in 1751 the country finally reverted to a form where the Dalai Lama was the head of state and legitimation was derived from the Avalokiteśvara idea.

The Gelukpa, ruled over by the Dalai Lama, successfully utilized the Avalokiteśvara idea and increasingly shaped the communication process as a whole into a pyramidal structure. In this their elite functioned to an ever-greater extent as a controlling factor, aiming to centralize the hierocratic Tibetan "ruling organization"[58] as an institution of salvation to reflect their own ideas.

The complex of central Buddhist concepts bundled in the Avalokiteśvara cult shaped Tibet's remembered history into the ultimate identity-creating myth of the Tibetan people. Its normative and formative power was so extensive that today it has become the focal point of an emerging nationalism. Here the founding myth shifts into its counterpoise, in which the past is represented as a social utopia.[59] The Avalokiteśvara cult is particularly suitable as a symbol of the Tibetan nation-to-be, as the "most satisfactory icons from a proto-national point of view are obviously those specifically associated with a state, i.e. in the pre-national phase, with a divine or divinely imbued king or emperor whose realm happens to coincide with a future nation."[60]

This essay has spanned a wide arc, revealing the central significance of history as a myth for the Tibetan people. In general we tend to associate the concept of "myth" closely with the power of imagination, which establishes images of memories and ideas largely unconnected with reality. In this, reality is assumed to be something that exists independently of ourselves; yet such a definition would exclude many things from our real world that we generally attribute to it without hesitation. In Tibetan culture, history as myth itself was undoubtedly classified among the objective facts of the world and was a part of the real world—just as cars, banknotes, Members of Parliament, football games, and millennium celebrations are part of the real world in our culture of today. How this was possible can be explained with the help of Searle's critique of social ontology: all the entities listed are "things that exist only because we believe them to exist," and are thus not "brute facts" but "social facts" that contain a collective intentionality.[61] In particular, they are "institutional facts," "because they require human institutions for their existence." Institutional facts are only made possible by constitutive rules and exist "only in a set of systematic relations to other facts," frequently involving iterated structures. Institutional facts are created by assigning a function to an entity, something not immanent within that entity. The elements or beings involved need not necessarily be aware of the assignment of the function.

To be more explicit, the institutional fact of "history" was based on the iteration of other institutional facts, primarily the bodhisattvas and the spiritual teachers who underwent reincarnation for the good of living beings. The ability of a human being to be a bodhisattva or reincarnation only exists in relation to the (internal or external) observer and is not immanent within the person involved. We must return to the temporal sequence of the pure events to reach the physical plane of raw facts. This plane is still further back than the perception of events "as something," for "we do not experience things *as* material objects, much less as collections of molecules. Rather, we experience a world of chairs and tables, houses and cars, lecture halls, pictures, streets, gardens, houses, and so forth. . . . Even natural phenomena, such as rivers and trees, can be assigned functions, and thus assessed as good or bad, depending on what functions we choose to assign to them and how well they serve those functions."[62] History was made possible as an institutional fact through constitutive rules, in the forefront of which was that, "In the context of Tibetan culture, history is counted as the implementation of a plan of salvation." Further rules determine, say, what counts as salvation and what as damnation. History was created as an institutional fact by being assigned the function of legitimizing the truth and validity of a canon of values and ideas codified once and for all. History represented, "stood for," the standard connected with this canon. To put it in general terms, the useful function of history was to symbolize, to have meaning— similar to the way a map represents a specific area, or the sounds of our language represent meaning. History was thus accorded a power it does not possess in and of itself.

As a symbol, history was part of the overarching system of symbols that determined Tibetan culture and was the goal of its observers' socialization and acculturation. As a whole, it represented the reality that formed the basis of social behavior, i.e., the reference by which the individual members of society interacted and communicated.[63]

EXCURSUS

One involuntarily wonders why this rigid system remained so astonishingly stable over such a long period, despite all the tension in external relations and in an environment that consisted to a significant extent of different cultures. This stability was due to a number of factors:

First, the inhospitable and remote geographical location of Tibet, which thus appeared an uninteresting target for colonization.

Furthermore, its strategic insignificance over a long period.

Then there is the acknowledgment of the large-scale constellation of powers, scarcely reflected directly by historiographical and even diplomatic Tibetan sources but at best reinterpreted by them, yet always silently implied, which always had profitable aspects for the Tibetan hierocracy. Apart from the brief episode of the Zunghar invasion, this acknowledgment has only been absent in the most recent past; only here, then, can we speak of genuine tyranny.

Finally, there is the fact that many of the emperors on the Chinese throne at the head of a multicentric culture showed great skill in using their familiarity with a variety of cultural formations to further their ambitions in power politics. It must not be forgotten that the "foreign dynasties" in particular were already rooted in cultural diversity, and were thus in a situation that had already been shaped by a range of cultural contacts from the time of their emergence.

Even high-ranking Tibetan clerics attempted to instrumentalize the foreign rulers to benefit their own institutions. However, they generally acted not out of the cynicism of power but in completely unreflective harmony with the categorial framework of their culture, with a powerful sense of mission unique to universalistically oriented religions and with the conviction that they could thus best strengthen their own institution while simultaneously serving the general good. Communication from the Tibetan side was conducted against the backdrop of stereotypical autorepresentations and heterorepresentations,[64] interpreting the interrelationships within Tibet's own hermetically sealed cultural horizon. This interpretation was no longer possible when Tibetan culture underwent direct attack by the *clash of cultures* instigated by Communist China. The Tibetan cultural consciousness responded "with outlines of hetero- and auto-stereotypes which consolidate into 'images' of a national character."[65]

Under the forms of indirect rule developed primarily by the rulers of the Yuan and Qing dynasties for marginal peoples, including a sophisticated religious policy,[66] internal cultural structures were left largely intact. And yet they were far from unaffected. In fact, the indirect rule was assigned a clear-cut control function, also in sociocultural areas, as is shown by the material support and strengthening of the Gelukpa hierarchy[67] and the creation of the religious system headed by the Dalai Lama in Qing-era Tibet. By initiating his radical campaign for a cultural desert, Mao Zedong's Communist China deprived itself of the use of this flexible range of instruments for exercising rule.

CONCLUSION

Finally, here is a summary of the main points:

My starting point was the characterization of the Tibetan idea of history as myth, expressing the view that history was accorded the role of an establishing element that contributed meaning and from which normative claims were derived.

In addition, my thesis proposed that in Tibetan culture, history has the function of codifying the sociocultural conditions of a monocentric culture.

Society became clericalized by the development of a hierarchically structured monastic and academic form of Buddhism combined with the lack of a uniform, centrally organized system of rule. Only the clergy in Tibet had access to any notable widespread infrastructure and organization, and the clergy alone, to echo Max Weber, "held the single, rationalized organized power in their own hands."[68] With few exceptions within the aristocracy, clerical officials were the only ones to have specific abilities such as reading and writing, knowledge of the scriptures, and the art of providing moral interpretations of canonical writings. As the heart of the culture, religion also had a controlling function, which aimed to shape as many activities as possible within society. Debate over traditions not recognized as authentic and the gradual drying up of the Indian sources led to a canonization of handed-down traditions, implying the preservation of the ideas and values fixed in the canon and regarded by the whole of society as binding.

Within this context, history was reconstructed, based on the central cultural code and in the service of a culture codified once and for all. The foreground was occupied not by what was new in history, but by the preservation of what was recognized once and for all as right and valuable. The past was perceived as the unfurling of a cultural programming effected both in the temporal beginning and on the transcendental plane, that is to say, the implementation of a salvation plan that served as the foundation of history.

NOTES

My thanks go to Isrun Engelhardt for her invaluable assistance in identifying the English editions of the secondary literature used.

1. Friedrich Nietzsche, *Untimely Meditations* (Cambridge: Cambridge University Press, 1997), 63.

2. Ansgar Nünning, ed., *Metzler Lexikon Literatur- und Kulturtheorie: Ansätze— Personen—Grundbegriffe* [*Metzler Encyclopedia of Literature and Cultural Theory: Approaches—Exponents—Concepts*] (Stuttgart, Weimar: Metzler, 1998), 301.

3. Here is Lawrence Grossberg's attempt to define the concept of "cultural studies": "While the question of 'what cultural studies really is' may have become impossible to specify for all times and places, we believe that in any given context, cultural studies

cannot be just anything. Even the most open definition of cultural studies here—Tony Bennett's 'a term of convenience for a fairly dispersed array of theoretical and political positions'—is immediately qualified in a way that marks boundaries: 'which, however widely divergent they might be in other aspects, share a commitment to examining cultural practices from the point of view of their intrication with, and within, relations of power.' To work even within that rather broad configuration, of course, requires an analysis of those relations of power and one's place within them" (Lawrence Grossberg, Cary Nelson, and Paula A. Treichler, eds., *Cultural Studies* [London: Routledge, 1992]).

4. Michael Aris in Dan Martin, *Tibetan Histories: A Bibliography of Tibetan-Language Historical Works* (London: Serindia, 1997), 9.

5. Jan Assmann, *Religion and Cultural Memory*, trans. Rodney Livingstone (Stanford: Stanford University Press, 2006), 15, 20, 168, 177, 186; Klaus P. Hansen, *Kultur und Kulturwissenschaft: Eine Einführung [Culture and Cultural Studies: An Introduction]* (Tübingen: Francke Verlag, 1995), 164.

6. Christian Simon, *Historiographie: Eine Einführung [Historiography: An Introduction]* (Stuttgart: Ulmer, 1996), 286.

7. Cf. David Snellgrove, *Indo-Tibetan Buddhism: Indian Buddhists and Their Tibetan Successors* (London: Random House, 1987), 464.

8. Cf. on this Snellgrove, *Indo-Tibetan Buddhism*, 396–407.

9. Geoffrey Samuel, *Civilized Shamans: Buddhism in Tibetan Societies* (Washington, D.C.: Smithsonian Institution Press, 1993), 441.

10. See Snellgrove, *Indo-Tibetan Buddhism*, 396; Samuel, *Civilized Shamans*, 474, 492.

11. Assmann, *Religion and Cultural Memory*, 41. The act of closure "draws the two crucial lines between the canons and the apocrypha, and between the primary and the secondary. . . . Canonical texts are sacrosanct: they call for literal transmission. . . . The canonical text combines the binding force of a legal contract with the sacred authority of a ritual utterance."

12. This and the following two quotations are from British historian Patricia Crone on the culture of premodern societies in general: Patricia Crone, *Pre-industrial Societies: New Perspectives on the Past* (Oxford: Blackwell, 1989), 85–86.

13. See Assmann, *Religion and Cultural Memory*, 43.

14. A brief overview of historical events is given in Paul Harrison, *A Brief History of the Tibetan bKa' 'gyur*, in *Tibetan Literature: Studies in Genre*, ed. José Ignacio Cabezón and Roger R. Jackson (Ithaca, N.Y.: Snow Lion, 1996), 70–94 (chiefly 74–80).

15. Yeshe De Research Project, *Light of Liberation: A History of Buddhism in India*, ed. E. Cook, Crystal Mirror Series, Vol. VIII (Berkeley: Dharma Publishing, 1992), 410, according to which Somanatha was the last Kashmiri pandit to come to Tibet, where he worked with Bu ston on translating Sanskrit texts into Tibetan.

16. Assmann, *Religion and Cultural Memory*, 19: "Canonization means an intervention that subjects the constant flow of traditions that are being handed down to a strict process of selection. This intervention consolidates the selection and sanctifies it, that is to say, it exalts it to the status of an ultimate authority and in this way calls a

halt to the stream of tradition once and for all. From now on, nothing can be added or taken away. The contract turns into the canon."

17. Certain elite groups acted as the bearers of cultural orientation with the function of a supervisory body. In premodern societies, religion was the determining factor of high culture, the core of the culture, so to speak. Crone, *Pre-industrial Societies*, 83.

18. See G. Newland, "Debate Manuals (*Yig cha*) in dGe lugs Monastic Colleges," and D. S. Lopez, Jr., "Polemic Literature (*dGag lan*)," both in Cabezón and Jackson, eds., *Tibetan Literature*, 202–216 and 217–228. (Lopez translates *dgag lan* as "polemics," not "apologetics"; see 222, note 2.)

19. This objection to qualifying a culture as stationary in comparison to our own Western culture and our perception of it as cumulative is raised by Claude Lévi-Strauss in *Structural Anthropology II* (Chicago: University of Chicago Press, 1963), 541, 553. To assess Tibetan culture as "stationary" is by no means to stamp it as "unsuccessful." "A culture defines the range of potential interaction stories of its members. As values are exclusively culture-specific and historic, there is no measure to determine that one culture is more appropriate than another. A culture can only be successful within the prediction interval, which it defines. For this reason, a culture cannot be criticized as unsuccessful from the perspective of another culture." Siegfried J. Schmidt, ed., *Der Diskurs des radikalen Konstruktivismus* [*The Discourse of Radical Constructivism*] (Frankfurt: Suhrkamp, 1996), 47.

20. A fact applying to this specific literature is that it scarcely shows significant deviations or even original new creations, because of the claim established as an analogy to the generally recognized canon that it handed on the truth defined in the "glorious" past unscathed.

21. Bön as it manifested itself in Tibet at the time of the Second Propagation of Buddhism at the latest appears to us to be Buddhist in nature, both in its fundamental philosophy and its practice. However, this does not apply to the tradition as claimed by the Bönpo and as a consequence of their self-perception. The Bönpo were and are also regarded as non-Buddhists by the various Buddhist schools. For Bön literature, see Per Kvaerne, "The Literature of Bon," in Cabezón and Jackson, eds., *Tibetan Literature*, 138–146.

22. See Assmann, *Religion and Cultural Memory*, 127.

23. Peter Schwieger, *Teilung und Reintegration des Königreichs von Ladakh im 18. Jahrhundert: Der Staatsvertrag zwischen Ladakh und Purig aus dem Jahr 1753* [*Partition and Reintegration of the Kingdom of Ladakh in the Eighteenth Century: The 1753 Treaty Between Ladakh and Purik*], MTH, Abt. III, Bd. 7 (Bonn: VGH Wissenschaftsverlag, 1999), 183. For further statements of Tshe dbang nor bu on the outstanding status of Tibet, see 182–183.

24. The way fear of one's own identity and of alienation from one's origins can lead to stasis in cultural forms even today is shown very clearly in the cultural policies of the small Himalayan monarchy of Bhutan. Attempts are made to seal off the country's cultural heritage from outside influences that extend into everyday life (house con-

struction, clothing, art, language, restriction of external contacts from tourism, modern communication methods and media).

25. This means in most cases that their gaze was primarily directed at the history of their own institution. However, like the Sa skya cleric Bla ma dam pa, they could also be inspired and influenced by the ideological guidelines of powerful patrons associated with them—for whatever reasons—who were not direct members of their own institution (see Per K. Sørensen, *Tibetan Buddhist Historiography: The Mirror Illuminating the Royal Genealogies* [Wiesbaden: Harrassowitz, 1994], 35). Tibetan authors created a systematic scheme of classification for historiographical literature. On this, see particularly Andrei Vostrikov, *Tibetan Historical Literature*, trans. R. H. Gupta (Calcutta: Indian Studies: Past & Present, 1970). Cf. also Leonard W. J. van der Kuijp, "Tibetan Historiography," in Cabezón and Jackson, eds., *Tibetan Literature*, 39–56.

26. Cf. August Herrmann Francke, *Antiquities of Indian Tibet, Part II: The Chronicles of Ladakh and Minor Chronicles* (New Delhi, Madras, 1992), 7; van der Kuijp, "Tibetan Historiography," 40.

27. Van der Kuijp, "Tibetan Historiography," 41.

28. For the Sa skya school and the 'Khon clan, see particularly Luciano Petech, *Central Tibet and the Mongols: The Yüan–Sa skya Period of Tibetan History*, Serie Orientale Roma, Vol. LXV (Rome: Instituto italiano per il Medio ed Estremo Oriente, 1990). For the Stag lung school and the closely associated Ga zi clan, see Jeremy Russell, "A Brief History of the Taglung Kagyu," in *Chö-yang (Journal of the Council for Religious and Cultural Affairs of H.H. the Dalai Lama)* (ed. Pedron Yeshi, co-ed. Jeremy Russell) 1, no. 1 (Spring 1986): 120–126; Elena de Rossi Filibeck, "A Manuscript on the Stag lung pa Genealogy," in *Tibetan Studies: Proceedings of the 6th Seminar of the IATS Fagernes 1992*, ed. Per Kværne, vol. 1 (Oslo: The Institute for Comparative Research in Human Culture, 1994), 237–240; Peter Schwieger, "The Lineage of the Noble House of Ga zi in East Tibet," *Kailash* 18, no. 3–4 (1996): 115–132.

29. The most famous examples are *La dwags rgyal rabs*, probably written in the seventeenth century and continued in installments (edited in Francke, *Antiquities of Indian Tibet, Part II*, 19–59), and *Sde dge'i rgyal rabs*, written in the nineteenth century (edited in Josef Kolmaš, *A Genealogy of the Kings of Derge, Sde Dge'i Rgyal Rabs* [Prague: Academi, 1968]). On the legitimation of monarchic rule in the context of Tibetan Buddhism, see Schwieger, *Partition and Reintegration of the Kingdom of Ladakh*, 89.

30. Translated from Gabrielle M. Spiegel, *Geschichte*, "Historizität und die soziale Logik von mittelalterlichen Texten" [History, Historicity, and Social Logic in Medieval Texts], in *Geschichte schreiben in der Postmoderne. Beiträge zur aktuellen Diskussion* [*Historiography in the Postmodern Age: Contributions to Current Discussion*], ed. Cristoph Conrad and Martina Kessel (Stuttgart: Philipp Reclam, 1994), 183f.

31. Translated from Klaus Heinrich, "Funktion der Genealogie im Mythos" [The Function of Genealogy in Myth], in *Parmenides und Jona* (Basel: Stroemfeld, 1982), 11–28, 163–167, reprinted in Klaus Heinrich, *Vernunft und Mythos: Ausgewählte Texte*

[*Reason and Myth: Selected Texts*] (Frankfurt: Fischer Taschenbuch Verlag, 1983), 11–26 (quotation, 12).

32. On the concepts addressed here, see Tulku Thondup Rinpoche, *Hidden Teachings of Tibet: An Explanation of the Terma Tradition of the Nyingma School of Buddhism* (London: Wisdom Publications, 1986).

33. For an example, see Peter Schwieger, "Zur Rezeptionsgeschichte des *Gsol 'debs le'u bdun ma* und des *Gsol 'debs le'u bsam pa khun grub ma*" [The Reception History of the *Gsol 'debs le'u bdun ma* and the *Gsol 'debs le'u bsam pa khun grub ma*], *Zentralasiatische Studien* 21 (1989): 29–47 (esp. 40).

34. The key Mahāyāna concepts include the major concepts of "canonical" Buddhism (*Urbuddhismus*), particularly the idea of karma and the cycle of rebirth, the Four Noble Truths, and the twelve links of dependent origination (Hans Wolfgang Schuhmann, *Buddhismus: Stifter, Schulen und Systeme* [*Buddhism: Sponsors, Schools, and Systems*] [Olten: Walter Verlag, 1976], 80), but primarily comprise the philosophy of the Prajñāpāramitā, Yogācāra, and Mādhyamika schools as they developed in India from the first or second century A.D.

35. Cf. Nünning, *Metzler Encyclopedia of Literature and Cultural Theory*, 534, under "Tiefenstruktur" ("deep structure").

36. The main function of the text is not to faithfully represent a reality outside language, but to produce meaning: "The textual world is composed of concepts and relations between these concepts. Concepts are units of our knowledge, which have formed there as a result of our perception and experience—and which need not necessarily present a faithful picture of the real world." Translated from Heinz Vater, *Einführung in die Textlinguistik: Struktur, Thema und Referenz in Texten* [*Introduction to Textual Linguistics: Structure, Theme, and Reference in Texts*] (Munich: Fink W. Robel, 1994), 43. Hansen expresses it thus, in analogy with Saussure: "Words contain conceivabilities which do not reflect reality, but imbue it with an interpretation." Hansen, *Culture and Cultural Studies*, 61. Cf. also Vater, *Introduction to Textual Linguistics*, 110.

37. This is made clear in, e.g., the section on historiography in *Shes bya rab gsal* (see *Prince Jiṅ-gim's Textbook of Tibetan Buddhism: The Śes-bya rab-gsal [Jñeyaprakāśa] by 'Phags pa Blo gros rgyal mtshan dPal bzang po of the Sa skya pa*, trans. and annotated by Constance Hoog [Leiden: Brill, 1983], 39–43): The fixed point is Buddha's entrance into Nirvāna. The preceding narrative is the history towards this point. The following narrative is the development from this point onward. Thus it outlines that the first Tibetan king appeared one thousand years after Buddha's entrance into Nirvāna. It should be noted that this historical axis does not mark the beginning of the Tibetan calendar. The calendar is based on the Tantric system of teaching, the Kālacakra, ascribed to Buddha Shākyamuni. The Kālacakra came to Tibet after the year 1026. The first year of the Tibetan calendar corresponds to the Western year 1027. See Dieter Schuh, *Untersuchungen zur Geschichte der tibetischen Kalenderrechnung* [*Exploring the History of the Tibetan Calendar*] (Wiesbaden: F. Steiner, 1973).

38. Translated from Hans-Jürgen Goertz, *Umgang mit Geschichte: Eine Einführung in die Geschichtstheorie* [*Handling History: An Introduction to the Theory of History*], (Reinbek bei Hamburg: Rowohlt Taschenbuch Verlag, 1995), 151.

39. This step from the purely temporal connection of events to a causal connection is already taken in many of the works termed "Annals" or "Chronicles," inter alia, e.g., *Deb ther sngon po* (George N. Roerich, *The Blue Annals* [Delhi: Motilal Banarsidass, 1976]), *Deb ther dmar po gsar ma* (Giuseppe Tucci, *Deb t'er dmar po gsar ma: Tibetan Chronicles by bSod nams grags pa*, Vol. I, Serie Orientale Roma XXIV [Rome: Instituto italiano per il Medio ed Estremo Oriente, 1971]).

40. Cf. Paul Ricœur, *Time and Narrative* (Chicago: University of Chicago Press, 1990), 38: "The notion of a 'whole' (holos) is the pivot of the analysis that follows. . . . 'Now a thing is a whole, if it has a beginning, a middle, and an end.'"

41. Donald E. Polkinghorne, *Narrative Psychologie und Geschichtsbewußtsein: Beziehungen und Perspektiven* [*Narrative Psychology and Historical Consciousness: Relations and Perspectives*], in *Erzählung, Identität und historisches Bewußtsein. Die psychologische Konstruktion von Zeit und Geschichte (Erinnerung, Geschichte, Identität 1)* [*Narrative, Identity, and Historical Consciousness: The Psychological Construction of Time and History (Memory, History, Identity 1)*], ed. Jürgen Straub (Frankfurt: Suhrkamp, 1998), 25f.

42. Schmidt, *The Discourse of Radical Constructivism*, 14f. This becomes directly clear in visual perception. Here too, our brain strives to create a meaningful whole and proceeds along exactly these principles of *Gestalt, Prägnanz*, etc.; in other words, it interprets individual phenomena using these principles as a meaningful unit. The principles are subjective by nature. Familiar optical illusions such as Rubin's vase make us aware of these limitations of our perception.

43. Translated from Polkinghorne (*Narrative Psychology and Historical Consciousness*, 25) in analogy with David Carr, *Time, Narrative and History* (Bloomington: Indiana University Press, 1986).

44. Connected with it is a tendency to produce stylized self-images and images of others. As Jürgen Straub writes, "For normative constructions of collective 'pseudo-identities,' however, the self-images and images of others are characteristically highly stereotyped and low in, or completely empty of, experience." Translated from *Personale und kollektive Identität: Zur Analyse eines theoretischen Begriffs* [*Personal and Collective Identity: On the Analysis of a Theoretical Concept*], in *Identitäten: Erinnerung, Geschichte, Identität 3* [*Identities: Memory, History, Identity 3*], ed. Aleida Assmann and Heidrun Friese (Frankfurt: : Suhrkamp, 1998), 100.

45. For the concept of schematic literature, see Matias Martinez and Michael Scheffel, *Einführung in die Erzähltheorie* [*Introduction to Narrative Theory*] (Munich: C. H. Beck, 1999), 136.

46. This is a general feature not only of historic narratives but also of narrative in general. "In the final analysis, narratives have acting and suffering as their themes" (Ricœur, *Time and Narrative*, 56).

47. At most, relationships between clerical landowners and dependents are mentioned, although this relationship is more or less disguised as a spiritual one.

48. Victor W. Turner, *From Ritual to Theatre: The Human Seriousness of Play* (New York: Performing Arts Journal Publications, 1982), 113.

49. Kenelm Burridge, *Someone, No One: An Essay on Individuality* (Princeton: Princeton University Press, 1979), 5.

50. These are the four types of emplotment determined by H. White in European historiography of the nineteenth century. Hayden White, *Metahistory: The Historical Imagination in Nineteenth-Century Europe* (Baltimore: Johns Hopkins University Press, 1973).

51. Robinson once again pointed out that these structural elements are already constituents of the lives of the Indian siddhas. James Burnell Robinson, "The Lives of Indian Buddhist Saints: Biography, Hagiography and Myth," in Cabezón and Jackson, eds., *Tibetan Literature*, 59f.

52. A notable exception is the life of Pho lha nas Bsod nams stobs rgyas (1689–1747). See Luciano Petech, *China and Tibet in the Early XVIIIth Century: History of the Establishment of Chinese Protectorate in Tibet* (Leiden: Brill, 1972), 3f., although it is naturally the life of a ruler regarded as exemplary.

53. See Matthew T. Kapstein, "Remarks on the *Mani bka' 'bum* and the Cult of Avalokiteśvara in Tibet," in *Tibetan Buddhism: Reason and Revelation*, ed. R. Davidson and S. Goodman (Albany: SUNY Press, 1992), 79–93, 163–169 (chapter 4 of this volume); Matthew T. Kapstein, "The Indian Literary Identity in Tibet," in *Literary Cultures in History*, ed. Sheldon Pollock (Berkeley: University of California Press, 2003), 22f; Sørensen, *Tibetan Buddhist Historiography*.

54. Samuel, *Civilized Shamans*, 484, 485.

55. The text of *Mani bka' 'bum* is known as a *gter ma*, its oldest sections allegedly discovered by the *gter ston* or treasure-seeker Nyang ral Nyi ma 'od zer in the twelfth century (1124 or 1136–92?). *Gter ma* texts are apocryphal texts with religious content, which were said to have been hidden by Padmasambhava or one of his pupils at the time of the First Propagation of Buddhist teachings in Tibet and recovered later by a treasure-seeker at the precisely foretold time and under the conditions suitable for the propagation of the text.

56. Samuel, *Civilized Shamans*, 482f.

57. For an English translation, see Ngag dbang blo bzang rgya mtsho, the Fifth Dalai Lama, *A History of Tibet*, trans. Zahiruddin Ahmad, Indiana University Oriental Series No. 7 (Bloomington: Indiana University Research Institute for Inner Asian Studies, 1995); Zahiruddin Ahmad, *Sino-Tibetan Relations in the Seventeenth Century*, Serie Orientale Roma, Vol. XL (Rome: Rome: Instituto italiano per il Medio ed Estremo Oriente, 1970), 131f., 137f.

58. Cf. on the concepts of Max Weber, *Economy and Society: An Outline of Interpretive Sociology*, ed. Guenther Roth, Claus Wittich, and Ephraim Fischoff (Berkeley: University of California Press, 1978), basic sociological terms, 54. On the translation

of the term "Herrschaftsverband" as "ruling organization," cf. also Weber, *Economy and Society*, xciv.

59. On this function of myth cf. Assmann, *Religion and Cultural Memory*, 79f.

60. Eric J. Hobsbawm, *Nations and Nationalism Since 1780: Programme, Myth, Reality* (Cambridge: Cambridge University Press, 1992), 72.

61. See John R. Searle, *The Construction of Social Reality* (New York: Free Press, 1995), 1, 2, 35.

62. Cf. Searle, *The Construction of Social Reality*, 14.

63. Cf. Siegfried J. Schmidt, *Kognitive Autonomie und soziale Orientierung: Konstruktivistische Bemerkungen zum Zusammenhang von Kognition, Kommunikation, Medien und Kultur* [*Cognitive Autonomy and Social Orientation: Constructivist Observations on the Connection Between Cognition, Communication, Media, and Culture*] (Frankfurt: Suhrkamp, 1996), 27, 229.

64. Cf. note 44.

65. Nünning, *Metzler Lexikon of Literary and Cultural Theory*, 10.

66. Cf. Pamela Kyle Crossley, *The Manchus* (Cambridge, Mass.: Blackwell, 1997), 24, 44, 116; Sabine Dabringhaus, *Das Qing-Imperium als Vision und Wirklichkeit: Tibet in Laufbahn und Schriften des Song Yun (1752–1835)* [*The Qing Empire as Vision and Reality: Tibet in the Life and Writings of Song Yun*] (Stuttgart: Franz Steiner Verlag, 1994), 159, 230–233; Rainer Kämpfe, *Die Innere Mongolei von 1691 bis 1911* [*Inner Mongolia from 1691 to 1911*], in *Die Mongolen: Beiträge zu ihrer Geschichte und Kultur* [*The Mongols: Examinations of Their History and Culture*], ed. Michael Weiers (Darmstadt: Wissenschaftliche Buchgesellschaft, 1986), 421f.; Jürgen Osterhammel, *China und die Weltgesellschaft; Vom 18. Jahrhundert bis in unsere Zeit* [*China and Global Society: From the Eighteenth Century to Our Time*] (München: C. H. Beck, 1989), 86f., 90, 105; Petech, *China and Tibet in the Early XVIIIth Century*, 154; Dieter Schuh, *Erlasse und Sendschreiben mongolischer Herrscher für tibetische Geistliche: Ein Beitrag zur Kenntnis der Urkunden des tibetischen Mittelalters und ihrer Diplomatik* [*Decrees and Epistles of Mongolian Rulers for Tibetan Clerics: An Essay on Documents and Diplomacy of Medieval Tibet*], MTH, Dept. III, Vol. 1 (St. Augustin: VGH-Wissenschaftsverlag, 1977), xxvi.

67. Support of the Dge lugs pa resulted in an enormous expansion of monasticism in Tibetan society. According to Goldstein, the number of monks rose from 97,000–98,000 in 1694 to over 319,000 by 1733. Assuming a total population of 2.5 million Tibetans (including Kham), the proportion of clerics was equal to 13 percent of the male population (Melvyn C. Goldstein, *A History of Modern Tibet, 1913–1951: The Demise of the Lamaist State* [1989; reprint, Delhi: Bishen Singh Mahendra Pal Singh, 1993], 21).

68. Max Weber, *The Religion of India: The Sociology of Hinduism and Buddhism* (Glencoe, Ill.: The Free Press, 1962), 284. "Like the bishops of the European Occident in the time of migrations of the nations, the monastic superiors here [Tibet] held the single, rationalized organized power in their own hands." Max Weber, *Gesammelte Aufsätze zur Religionssoziologie II* [*Collected Essays on Religious Sociology*] (1921; reprint, Tübingen: Mohr, 1988), 310.

PART II

Imperial Tibet (Seventh to Tenth Centuries)

NARRATIVES OF TIBETAN ORIGINS

Chapter 4

REMARKS ON THE *MAṆI KABUM* AND THE CULT
OF AVALOKITEŚVARA IN TIBET

Matthew T. Kapstein

The *Maṇi Kabum* is a collection of Buddhist teachings, poetry, myths, and rituals extolling the virtues of worshipping the bodhisattva Avalokiteśvara. Say the six-syllable mantra and you will win the blessing of this totally beneficent being. Recall his past actions for the benefit of Tibetans and you will share in the force that has protected Tibet from time immemorial. Matthew Kapstein surveys three major aspects of the Maṇi tradition. He first outlines the complex development of the literature. Next, he isolates the central themes of the work that he argues constitute a major part of Tibetan Buddhist views on life. Finally, he treats the unique doctrinal and practical teachings of the *Maṇi Kabum*.

The *Maṇi Kabum* is clear that Avalokiteśvara is the preeminent deity of Tibet. What's more, this celestial being has involved himself directly in Tibetan history by incarnating as the famous emperor Songtsen Gampo. As emperor, Avalokiteśvara himself transformed Tibet from a land of barbarian violence and chaos into a civilized Buddhist holy land. Tibet becomes, in the cosmos of the *Maṇi Kabum*, not merely a country among others in Inner Asia, but a blessed realm that was specifically chosen by an omniscient, omnibenevolent being as his special field of activity. In the *Maṇi Kabum*, Tibetan history fuses with Buddhist cosmology to become Buddhist history, the story of the unfolding of the Buddhist teachings in the human realm. Kapstein's essay takes us through the literary and intellectual development of this most Buddhist of Tibetan historical works.

The *Maṇi Kabum*,[1] a heterogeneous collection of texts ascribed to the Tibetan King Songtsen Gampo (d. A.D. 649) and primarily concerned with the cult of the Bodhisattva Mahā-kāruṇika-Avalokiteśvara (Tib. Thukjé Chenpo Chenrezi kyi Wangchuk), has enjoyed a singularly long history of study in the West.[2] As early as 1801 P. S. Pallas had published an account of its first chapters, and in 1838 the intrepid Magyar scholar Csoma de Körös mentioned it by name among Tibetan historical works, thereby creating the false impression that the *Maṇi Kabum* might be regarded as such. A. I. Vostrikov, writing some one hundred years later, sought to provide a more accurate assessment of the *Maṇi Kabum*, saying that it

> . . . contains much interesting material from the point of view of literature and folklore. Its fairly frequent deviations from the dominant views of Tibetan Buddhism are of great interest. As a historical source, however, it is of absolutely no value and cannot be classed under historical works.[3]

More recently, Mme. Ariane Macdonald has reported briefly on her studies concerning the contents and compilation of the *Maṇi Kabum* as a prelude to the study of the legendary biographies of Songtsen Gampo found therein, for, as Mme. Macdonald observes, it is the historico-legendary aspect of the *Maṇi Kabum* that has held the attention of occidental scholars.[4]

In the course of my own reading of the *Maṇi Kabum* and allied literature, I have sought to examine three aspects of this important body of material: the history of the *Maṇi Kabum*'s compilation; its significance for the development of a Tibetan worldview; and its peculiar approach to the problems of Buddhist theory and practice. It is with full awareness that I have been able to give a cursory glance to only a few of the available sources that I present here a tentative statement of my conclusions in each of these three areas.[5]

I

The *Maṇi Kabum* is usually divided into three "cycles" (*kor*):

1. *The Cycle of Sūtras* (*dokor*), which includes various legendary accounts of the exploits of Avalokiteśvara and of King Songtsen Gampo;
2. *The Cycle of Attainment* (*drupkor*), which contains the meditational "means for attainment" (*druptap*, Skt. *sādhana*) of Avalokiteśvara in various aspects; and
3. *The Cycle of Precepts* (*zheldam kyi kor*), containing some 150 short texts, which treat a wide variety of topics, most of which are connected in some way with the systems of meditation focusing upon Mahākāruṇika.[6]

Further, there is a small collection of texts, sometimes referred to as *The Cycle of "The Disclosure of the Hidden"*—after the most renowned of the works found therein—which in some redactions of the *Maṇi Kabum* is appended to *The Cycle of Precepts,* and in others forms by itself a fourth cycle, an appendix to the entire collection.[7]

This entire mass of textual material—usually assembled in two volumes containing about 700 folia in all—was discovered as *terma* by some three discoverers of spiritual treasure (*tertön*) over a period lasting approximately one century, beginning, it appears, in the middle of the twelfth. The Fifth Dalai Lama Ngawang Lozang Gyatso (1617–1682) has summarized its compilation in these words:

> The Dharma protecting King Songtsen Gampo taught the doctrinal cycles [*chökor*] of Mahākāruṇika to disciples endowed with [appropriate propensities owing to their own past] actions and fortunate circumstances, and had the cycles set down in writing. The *Great Chronicle* [*Logyü Chenmo*], which comes from *The Cycle of Sutras,* was concealed together with *The Cycle of Attainment* and *The Cycle of Precepts* beneath the feet of Hayagrīva, in the northern quarter of the central hall [in the Lhasa Jokhang]. Some, including *The Disclosure of the Hidden* and [the remaining portions of] *The Cycle of Sūtras,* were concealed in the right thigh of the *yakṣa* Nāga-Kubera, beneath the hem of his gown. The glorious, Great One of Orgyen [Padmasambhava] well revealed them to Lord Trisong Deutsen, saying, "Your own ancestor Songtsen Gampo has concealed such treasures in Rasa [i.e., Lhasa]." Thereupon, [the King] gained faith and made *The Means for the Attainment of the Thousand-fold Mahākāruṇika, The Disclosure of the Hidden, The Creation and Consummation of the Thousand Buddhas, The Benefits of Beholding [Songtsen Gampo's] Spiritual Bond* [that is, the Jowo Śākyamuni image of Lhasa], and *Songtsen's Last Testament* into [his own] spiritual bonds.
>
> Later, the *siddha* Ngödrup—a yogin who was taken into the following of Mahākāruṇika [by the deity himself], and who lived in the human world for about 300 years—drew forth *The Cycle of Attainment* from beneath the feet of the Hayagrīva in the northern quarter of the central hall and transmitted it to Lord Nyang[-rel Nyima Özer, 1124/36–1204], the incarnation of Tsangpa Lhé Metok [i.e. King Trisong Deutsen]. Lord [Nyang] brought *The Cycle of Precepts* out from beneath the feet of Hayagrīva. Shākya-ö [who is also known as Shākya] Zangpo, a teacher from Lhasa in Üru, [later] brought forth *The Cycle of Sūtras,* as well as *The Disclosure of the Hidden* and so on, from the *yakṣa*-shrine. So it is that this doctrinal cycle had three discoverers. Nonetheless, it is renowned as the treasure of the venerable *siddha* Ngödrup, for he was foremost [among

them]. For that reason, I have not here written [about the *Maṇi Kabum*] in the sections devoted to the doctrinal cycles of the other two treasure discoverers but have placed [all their discoveries belonging to the *Maṇi Kabum*] together at this juncture.[8]

The Great Fifth later reinforces his case for establishing the preeminence of the *siddha* Ngödrup among the revealers of the *Maṇi Kabum*. Speaking of the *Great Chronicle* he tells us that the location in which it was concealed (under the feet of the Hayagrīva image) suggests it to have been among the treasures discovered by Ngödrup. The attribution of *The Cycle of Sūtras* to Shākya-ö, then, must refer to only four of the remaining texts in that section.[9] The Dalai Lama does not mention that the *Great Explanatory*, the colophon of which clearly attributes its discovery to Ngödrup and which belongs to the *Cycle of Attainment*, refers explicitly to the *Great Chronicle*.[10] His hypothesis that the discovery of this latter text preceded Shākya-ö's discoveries thus seems plausible.

In sum, then, the *siddha* Ngödrup would seem to have discovered the original kernel of the *Maṇi Kabum*, consisting of a version of the *Great Chronicle*, *The Great Explanatory Commentary*, and at least three other texts included in *The Cycle of Attainment*, which are explicitly referred to in *The Commentary*.[11] It is by no means improbable that this *tertön* revealed at least some of the remaining works of *The Cycle of Attainment* as well, though the internal evidence on this point is inconclusive.

There appears to be no reason to contradict the traditions that Nyangrel Nyima Özer increased this original body of material with the discovery of *The Cycle of Precepts*.[12] More problematic, however, is the contribution of Shākya-ö, who, as a student of Nyang's disciple Mikyö Dorjé of Latö, probably belongs to the mid-thirteenth century.[13] One text from *The Cycle of "The Disclosure of the Hidden"* is clearly attributed to him, the colophon of which states that it is but one of several works discovered together.[14] The opinion of the Great Fifth concerning his contribution to *The Cycle of Sūtras* has been referred to above. Beyond that, I can only note that I have thus far found no internal evidence that would render it impossible to ascribe the entire *Cycle of "The Disclosure of the Hidden,"* as well as the four works in *The Cycle of Sūtras* mentioned by the Fifth Dalai Lama, to the age of Shākya-ö. Thus, it is certainly possible that the great majority of texts presently included in the *Maṇi Kabum* were in existence by about 1250, though their present arrangement, in the form of a single collection, may still be the product of a later generation.[15]

The tale of the recovery of the texts forming the *Maṇi Kabum* has few variations, reflecting the fact that most of the Tibetan authors who wrote on this topic did so with one and the same *karchak* before them.[16] The most significant variation I have encountered is found in the writings of the learned Jonang Jetsun Tāranātha (b. 1575), who states that:

the means for the attainment of the deity [found in] *The Collected Works of the King [Gyelpo kabum]* and the roots of the precepts appear, certainly, to have been composed by the religious-king Songtsen Gampo. Therefore, they are the actual words of Ārya Avalokita and are really the ancient ancestral religion of Tibet. It is well known that they were concealed as treasures by master Padma [-sambhava]. Moreover, the history and most of the ancillary texts were composed by the treasure discoverer, *siddha* Ngödrup, by Nyangrel, and by others.[17]

While this statement is of great interest for its critical, but not condemnatory, view of the *Maṇi Kabum* as *terma*—as for its assertion that it was Padmasambhava, and not Songtsen Gampo, who concealed the portions Tāranātha regards as being indeed ancient—it does not otherwise alter our conception of the history of the *Maṇi Kabum's* compilation, as outlined above.[18]

Finally, it may be noted that it is not exactly clear when it was that this collection received the name *Maṇi Kabum*, save that it was universally known as such no later than the seventeenth century.[19] Elsewhere, it is entitled *The Collected Works of the Dharma Protecting King Songtsen Gampo*, and even *The Doctrinal Cycle Concerning the Six Syllable (Mantra) of Mahākāruṇika.*[20] The meditational system it embodies is usually referred to as that of *Avalokiteśvara according to the System of the King*, a phrase attested as early as the first half of the fourteenth century, when we find Karmapa III, Rangjung Dorjé (1284–1339) conferring its empowerment on the master from Samyé, Künkhyen Longchen Rapjampa (1308–1363).[21]

II

The mythical portions of the *Maṇi Kabum* develop a distinct view of Tibet, its history, and its place in the world. Three elements which inform this view are outstanding. Two of these were current by the time the *Maṇi Kabum* made its appearance: the belief that Avalokiteśvara was the patron deity of Tibet; and the associated legend of King Songtsen Gampo and his court, in which the King is represented as being the very embodiment of Avalokiteśvara, the founder of *Buddhadharma* in his formerly barbarian realm. The third element may have its origin in the *Maṇi Kabum* itself, though, as we shall see, it was inspired by earlier sources. This is the cosmological vision of the *Maṇi Kabum*, whereby the King's divinity, and the divinity's regard for Tibet, are seen not as matters of historic accident, but as matters grounded in the very nature of the universe.

1. Following the *Maṇi Kabum* and other legendary sources, later Tibetan historians have tended to assign the inception of the Avalokiteśvara cult to the reign of Songtsen Gampo.[22] Thus, for example, Tukwan Chökyi Nyima (1737–1802):

At first, the religious King Songtsen Gampo taught *The Creation and Consummation of Mahākāruṇika* and other precepts *in extenso*, and there were many who practiced them, too. It was at first from this, that [the custom] spread throughout Tibet and Kham of praying to Ārya Avalokita and reciting the six-syllable [*mantra*].[23]

In addition to acting as a teacher in his own right, the King is said to have encouraged and sponsored the establishment of shrines and images, as well as the translation into Tibetan of the fundamental texts of the Indian Avalokiteśvara tradition. The spiritual activity begun by Songtsen Gampo was then continued on a vast scale by his descendant Trisong Deutsen (reigned from 755).[24]

Western authorities have tended to be skeptical about such traditions. They point to the inconclusive evidence of ancient historical chronicles on the subject of Songtsen Gampo's actual commitment to Buddhism and the near absence of archaeological evidence of a widespread cult of Avalokiteśvara in Tibet prior to the eleventh century.[25] At the same time, the known history of the translation of Sanskrit and Chinese Buddhism into Tibetan does establish that canonical texts of fundamental importance for this cult were available in Tibetan by 812, the year of the compilation of the *Denkarma* catalogue of Buddhist texts.[26] One may note, too, that the *Kama* tradition of the Nyingmapa school, which purports to represent an unbroken lineage transmitting teachings that were introduced into Tibet primarily during the reign of Trisong Deutsen and which certainly does include authentically ancient material, accords scant attention to Avalokiteśvara. It is, rather, with the recovery of *terma* texts, above all the *Maṇi Kabum*, that the great Bodhisattva assumes a role of considerable importance for the Nyingmapas.[27] Finally, we should remark that—even among those Tibetan historians who are inclined to accept the validity of the *Maṇi Kabum* and related traditions—there are those who see evidence in it, not of a flourishing Avalokiteśvara cult in ancient Tibet, but rather of a secret transmission from Songtsen Gampo to a small number of worthy adepts, family members, and courtiers, who did not, in turn, transmit the King's teachings to a subsequent generation.[28] In short, the available evidence powerfully suggests that, while ancient Tibet had some familiarity with the Bodhisattva, the cult of Avalokiteśvara, as known to a later age, is a product not of the ancient imperial period but of the "later spread of the doctrine" beginning in the eleventh century.

There can be little doubt that the first great figure to actively promote the practice of meditational techniques focusing on Avalokita was Dīpaṃkara-Śrījñāna, better known as Atiśa (982–1054, and in Tibet from 1042 onwards). Three major systems of instruction on the *Avalokiteśvara-sādhana* may be traced back to the Bengali master.[29] During the latter part of the eleventh century and the beginning of the twelfth several other systems were propounded by Bari Lotsāwa (b. 1040), the *siddhas* Candravajra (Dawa Gyeltsen) and Tsebupa, and by Milarepa's famous disciple Rechung Dorjé Drak (b. 1084).[30] The works relating to these systems which I have thus far been able to consult do not make it clear whether or not these masters regarded Tibet as Avalokiteśvara's special field. But the following passage, attributed to the emanation of the Great Mother, Machik Lapkyi Drönma (1055–1145/53), and thus possibly belonging to the very period we are considering, is of much interest in this connection:

> I have made both Avalokiteśvara and Bhaṭṭārikā-Tārā into special doctrines that are universally renowned. It also appears that the two are our common Tibetan ancestors, and in that they are certainly our "divine portion," infants learn to recite the six-syllable [mantra] at the very same time that they are beginning to speak; this is a sign that the Exalted One has actually blessed their spirits. Thus, it is truly right for us all to make the Exalted One our "divine portion."[31]

The tone of advocacy here is noteworthy. Are we reading too much between the lines if we see here a slight suggestion that Tibetans during the early twelfth century still required arguments that they did, indeed, have a special relationship with the ever compassionate Avalokiteśvara? During the later part of the same century the *Great Chronicle* of the *Maṇi Kabum* is able to state the case with far greater assurance—as in this passage, addressed to Avalokiteśvara by the dying Buddha Śākyamuni:

> There are none left to be trained by me. Because there are none for me to train I will demonstrate the way of nirvāṇa to inspire those who are slothful to the doctrine and to demonstrate that what is compounded is impermanent. The snowy domain to the north [i.e., Tibet] is presently a domain of animals, so even the word "human being" does not exist there—it is a vast darkness. And all who die there turn not upwards but, like snowflakes falling on a lake, drop into the world of evil destinies. At some future time, when that doctrine declines, you, O Bodhisattva, will train them. First, the incarnation of a Bodhisattva will generate human-beings who will require training. Then, they will be brought together [as disciples] by material goods. After that, bring them together through the doctrine! It will be for the welfare of living beings![32]

So there can be no longer any doubt that the Bodhisattva has been assigned to Tibet by the Buddha himself. To the assertion that the Snowy Land is Avalokiteśvara's special field, the *Maṇi Kabum* has lent a semblance of canonical authority.

2. Let us turn now to the legend of King Songtsen Gampo's having been an incarnation of Avalokiteśvara. Mme. Macdonald, in her superb study of the royal religion of this King, has argued that this religion, based in large measure on indigenous Tibetan beliefs, was most certainly not Buddhism. The belief that the

King was, in fact, the Bodhisattva seems then to reflect the opinion of a later age, perhaps one in which the growing community of Tibetan Buddhists sought to reinforce the precedent for its own presence in the Land of Snows.[33] In this, of course, it goes hand in hand with the myth of the Bodhisattva's role as Tibet's spiritual patron. Like this latter myth, the time of the former's origin cannot be established with great precision: when it makes its first datable appearance in 1167—which is probably close to the time of its appearance in the *Great Chronicle* as well—it is presented without reservations as established history.[34]

It is in the portions of the *Mani Kabum* that were discovered latest—viz., during the thirteenth century—that the simple tale of the incarnate King is richly developed, so that his court becomes a veritable Tibetan Camelot. Further, it is in the form of an elaborate romance that the legend of Songtsen Gampo is restated repeatedly, in works like the apocryphal *Kachem Kakhölma* and the semihistorical *Gyelrap Selwé Melong* [*The Clear Mirror*].[35] In this literature—including the *Mani Kabum*—in which the myth of Avalokiteśvara's guiding role throughout the course of Tibetan history is developed, a distinct, unifying theme emerges: the Bodhisattva now functions as a *deus ex machina* of sorts, making benign incursions onto the Tibetan landscape at various critical junctures. As such, he may be projected into present and future situations too, whenever the need for his assistance becomes known. So it is that the *Great Chronicle* of the *Mani Kabum*—looking back on the age of imperial greatness from the vantage point of twelfth-century chaos and uncertainty—closes with this prophetic declaration concerning, one may safely assume, the era of its own discovery, when

> demons will enter the hearts of religious teachers and cause them to blaspheme one another and to quarrel. *Damsi* spirits will enter the hearts of the *mantrins* [*ngakpa*] and cause them to cast great spells against one another. *Gongpo* spirits will enter the hearts of men and cause them to defile themselves and to fight with one another. Demonesses will enter the hearts of women and cause them to argue with their husbands and to take their own lives. *Teurang* [= *theu rang*] spirits will enter the hearts of youths and cause them to act perversely. The *lha, lu,* and *nyenpo* divinities will be disturbed, and the rains will not come during appropriate seasons. Sometimes there will be famine. A time will come when people's merits will decline. So, at that time, if you wish to amass happiness, then pray to Mahākāruṇika-Avalokiteśvara! Recite these six heart-syllables: *Oṃ Maṇi padme Huṃ!* Because all the happiness and requirements of this lifetime come forth from this, it is like praying to the [wish fulfilling] gem. There can be no doubt that in future lives your obscurations will be removed and that you will attain enlightenment. Harbor not divided thoughts about it! Meditatively cultivate Mahākāruṇika! Attain it! Teach it! Expound it! Propagate and spread it! [Thus], the presence of the Buddha is established. The doctrinal foundation is established.[36]

It was during this same period that the custom of propagating the cult of Avalokiteśvara at public assemblies (*tromchö*) seems to have begun, for by the second half of the thirteenth century no less a hierarch than the renowned Karma Pakshi (d. 1283) composed a rite for just that purpose.[37]

What was the result of Avalokiteśvara's ascension to a position of such central importance in the Tibetan world, particularly during a period of grave political unrest?[38] There can be little doubt that the myth of the religious king did much to support the notion that worldly affairs might best be placed in the hands of essentially spiritual leaders. And it is possible, too, that the Tibetan people came to expect their temporal woes to be set aright as before, by the timely intercession of the great Bodhisattva. Can it be any wonder, then, that when Tibet finally achieved a measure of real unity during the seventeenth century—after some seven centuries of strife—it did so under the leadership of a latter day emanation of Mahākāruṇika residing in the ancient capital of Lhasa, and constructing for himself a palace on a hill named after the divine Mount Potalaka? It seems we are in the presence of a Tibetan twist on the Arthurian legend, whereby the once and future king becomes at long last the king, once and present.

3. The *Maṇi Kabum*'s view of Avalokiteśvara's role in Tibetan history and, in particular, his manifestation as Songtsen Gampo develop, as we have seen, themes whose general features had been well defined by the time the first sections of the collection appeared. More eclectic in their formation, and thus more resistant to efforts to understand their evolution, are the cosmology and theogony of the *Maṇi Kabum*. In the short space afforded here, it will be possible to do no more than give cursory treatment to these areas.

The notion that Avalokiteśvara might be regarded as the primordial deity, the point of departure for a unique theogony, was introduced into Tibet no later than the ninth century with the translation into Tibetan of the *Kāraṇḍavyūha-sūtra*, though the theogonic theme is but slightly developed therein.[39] The same *sūtra* presents also a vision of Avalokiteśvara, in which each pore of the Bodhisattva's body is seen to embrace whole world systems, a vision that was later taught by Atīśa in connection with the precepts of *The Four Gods of the Kadampas*.[40]

In the *Great Chronicle*, Avalokiteśvara undergoes a tremendous evolution. Though presented there as the emanation of the Buddha Amitābha, it is the Bodhisattva whose own body gives rise to the thousand *cakravartin* kings and the thousand Buddhas of the Bhadrakalpa, just as the body of the Avalokiteśvara of the *Kāraṇḍavyūha-sūtra* had given birth to the brahmanical pantheon.[41] Moreover, the *Kāraṇḍavyūha*'s vision of the deity is now supplanted by a cosmological vision widely associated in Tibet with the *Avataṃsaka*, but with Avalokiteśvara here occupying a position even prior to that of the great Vairocana.[42] It is, moreover, a novel sense of Tibet's station in the universe that constitutes the most striking innovation: [After Amitābha] had empowered the best of Bodhisattvas, Ārya Avalokiteśvara, to benefit living beings, an inconceivable and immeasurable light radiated forth from his body and magically created [*trül*] many *sambhogakāya*-fields, in which he magically created many *sambhogakāya*-Buddhas. So it was that he benefitted many sentient beings.

> And from the hearts of those *sambhogakāyas* there radiated forth an inconceivable [number of] *nirmāṇakāya*-fields, in which were magically created many *nirmāṇakāya*-Buddhas; and from the hearts of those *nirmāṇakāyas* light radiated forth, which was ineffable and beyond being ineffable. From that Ārya Avalokiteśvara, Bhṛkuṭīs, and Tārās were magically created equal to the number of sentient beings. So, too, did he benefit living creatures.
>
> Again, light emanated from his body and he magically created many world systems, as many as there are atoms in the substance of the world system that is the "middle array" [consisting of one million worlds of four continents each surrounding a Mount Meru]. And in them the innumerable Tathāgatas magically emanated forth to an equal number, whereby he again benefitted sentient beings.
>
> Then from their bodies there radiated forth light rays, which were immeasurable and beyond being immeasurable. At [the tip of] each one there was magically created a Jambudvīpa, in each of which was a Vajrāsana. To the north of each Vajrāsana there was a land beyond the pale, [namely] the Land of Snows; [and in each of these there was] a supreme horse, a destroyer of armies; an eleven-faced Avalokiteśvara; and a Tārā and a Bhṛkuṭī. In each one King Songtsen Gampo and the venerable ladies, white and green, were magically created. Ineffable light rays poured forth from their bodies and they magically created Mahākāruṇikas and six-syllable [mantras] equal to the number of sentient beings. Thus they benefitted living creatures.[43]

The enlightened activity of Avalokiteśvara, his incursion into Tibetan history in the form of King Songtsen Gampo, is no longer an event occurring within the Tibetan historical framework. Rather, Tibet itself is now an aspect of the Bodhisattva's all-pervading creative activity. How could *Buddhadharma* have been artificially implanted in such a realm, the very existence of which is evidence of the Buddha's compassionate engagement in the world? That Tibet is here referred to as being 'beyond the pale' is the fortuitous survival of an outmoded turn of phrase, for it is clear that the *Maṇi Kabum* regards the Land of Snows as no less part of the Buddhist universe than Āryavarta itself.

III

To what end has the *Maṇi Kabum* elaborated its peculiar world view, with its broad ramifications for cosmology, theogony and history? It is my belief that the impulse to explain events in the external world is a consideration of but little importance here. The aim of the *Maṇi Kabum*'s cosmology is, rather, to propagate the cult of Mahākāruṇika and his six-syllable mantra—to demonstrate that this is the most efficacious *sādhana* in this debased age, particularly for the Tibetan people. It is a measure of the emphasis of the *Maṇi Kabum* that merely one third of its total volume is concerned with the themes we have been considering thus far, the remaining two thirds being wholly devoted to the exposition of a unique system of meditation, which is developed throughout the *Cycle of Attainment*, the *Cycle of Precepts*, and the *Cycle of "The Disclosure of the Hidden."* While many aspects of Buddhist metaphysics, psychology, and ritual are referred to and commented upon in these cycles, the *Maṇi Kabum* by and large eschews speculative philosophy and the elaboration of a systematic psychology. Thus, with the exception of the *sādhanas* which are accorded a fairly well established pattern of exposition such as is required by the structure of *sādhana* itself, the doctrinal portions of the *Maṇi Kabum* exhibit much freedom in their development; not confined by a single system, the *Maṇi Kabum* utilizes a variety of systems, calling upon them when they are needed to advance a teaching that, we are told, lies beyond them all.[44] Thus, these instructions that are placed in the mouth of Songtsen Gampo touch upon such diverse topics as: the nine successive vehicles;[45] the two truths;[46] Mahāmudrā;[47] *Dzokpa chenpo*;[48] the sequence of the path;[49] the trio of ground, path, and result;[50] the trio of view, meditation, and action;[51] Trikāya;[52] *et cetera*. But none of these topics is ever allowed to ascend to the position of a central *leitmotif*, one that would unify, to some extent, the *Maṇi Kabum*'s diverse contents. Of this, the *Maṇi Kabum* is itself conscious. The *karchak* tells us that these precepts

> . . . are not all dependent on one another. They are "magical fragments of instruction"—each one benefits a particular individual.[53]

This peculiar term "magical fragment," which so appropriately describes the *Maṇi Kabum*'s many short precepts, is the subject of a detailed definition found in the *Great Explanatory Commentary*:

> "Magical fragments" are so-called because, just as magic appears variously but is without substantial existence, this doctrine of Mahākāruṇika is explained and taught by various means and in various aspects but nonetheless remains the same in that it is an indivisible union of emptiness and compassion. "Fragment" means that each particular division of the doctrine suffices as the occasion for the particular development of [spiritual] experience [by a given] individual.[54]

So the many doctrines referred to by the *Maṇi Kabum* all serve to illustrate the single doctrine of Mahākāruṇika and are thus the bases for an exposition of the central doctrines of the Mahāyāna, those of compassion and emptiness, which, though they are indivisible as aspects of the play of enlightened awareness, must nonetheless be distinguished conventionally. It is from such a perspective that the *karchak* endeavors to summarize the teaching of the *Maṇi Kabum*:

> . . . however many precepts associated with the doctrines of provisional meaning are expounded, they are not the doctrines of Mahākāruṇika unless you have deliberately taken up sentient beings, having seized the ground with loving kindness and compassion. If, because you fear the sufferings of *saṃsāra*, you desire freedom, desire bliss, desire liberation for yourself alone, and thus cannot create an [enlightened] attitude for the sake of sentient beings, then these are not the doctrines of the Bodhisattva Avalokita. If you do not practice for the sake of all living beings, you will not realize Avalokiteśvara. . . .
>
> However many doctrines of definitive meaning are expounded you must recognize the true Mahākāruṇika, Reality itself, mind-as-such, which is empty and is the *dharmakāya*, to be within yourself. Cultivate it! Familiarize yourself with it! Grow firm in it!
>
> If you desire to attain some Mahākāruṇika who "dwells in his proper abode," or desire to behold his visage, or to attain the accomplishments, you will be granted the common accomplishments but will stray far from the supreme accomplishment, Buddhahood.[55]

It appears that, in its emphasis on the union of compassion and emptiness, the teaching of the *Maṇi Kabum* is inspired by the eleventh-century renewal of interest in the path of the Mahāyāna sūtras, particularly as developed in the *upadeśa* of the Kadampa school.[56] But in its discussion of "the true Mahākāruṇika, Reality itself," that is, in its discussion of "doctrines of definitive meaning," the diction of the *Maṇi Kabum* becomes decidedly that of the Nyingma tradition—for example, in its identification of Mahākāruṇika with "the play of intuitive knowing, continuous, fresh pristine cognition."[57]

In sum, then, it may be said that, while the extraordinary variety of the *Maṇi Kabum*'s teaching of doctrine and ritual and the unsystematic way in which these topics are, for the most part, presented, do much to frustrate the attempt to define too strictly a "central doctrine," the teaching of the *Maṇi Kabum* represents, by and large, a syncretic approach to the doctrines of the Nyingmapas and those of the Avalokiteśvara traditions of the *sarma* schools, particularly the Kadampa. Further, through the instructions on the visualization and mantra of Avalokiteśvara transmitted by masters of all the major Tibetan Buddhist schools, as well as by lay *mantrins* and itinerant *maṇi-pas* who preached the bodhisattva's cult far and wide, it was this syncretic teaching that became, for all intents and purposes, Tibet's devotional norm.[58]

In this sketch of the compilation, world view, and doctrine of the *Maṇi Kabum*, some of the many problems raised by this collection have been briefly surveyed, and I have described the approaches by which these problems that have been suggested by my reading in this textual tradition to date might be somewhat resolved. While I hesitate to draw firm conclusions from this first foray into such an enormous body of material, I believe that it is important for the Western student of the *Maṇi Kabum* to recall that the collection's traditional audience did not perceive the mythological portions of the *Maṇi Kabum* to belong to some special category of literature called "myth." For that audience, the *Maṇi Kabum* created an active world view, as does any living myth, and in its *sādhanas* and precepts set forth the means by which one might live in the world thus created—a way which affirms that, in the final analysis, Avalokiteśvara, the embodiment of consummate spirituality and the creative ground of the universe, might be found within each and every individual and is none other than mind itself. I would hope that future exploration in this area would devote more attention than has previous research to the doctrinal aspects of the *Maṇi Kabum* which, representing a particularly rich syncretic development beginning no later than the twelfth century, have much to tell us of the evolution of Tibetan Buddhism during that critical age.

NOTES

Shortly after this article was originally written (Spring 1980), I learned that Michael Aris, *Bhutan: The Early History of a Himalayan Kingdom* (Warminster: Aris & Phillips, 1979, 8–24), included an extended discussion of the *Maṇi Bka' 'bum* that usefully complements the present effort. The obscure *siddha* Dngos grub has been considered in detail in Anne-Marie Blondeau, "Le 'Découvreur' du *Maṇi bka' 'bum* était-il Bon-po?" in *Tibetan and Buddhist Studies*, ed. Louis Ligeti (Budapest: Akadémiai Kiado, 1984), vol. 1, 77–123. A brief hagiography of Nyang ral Nyi ma 'od zer will be found translated in Dudjom Rinpoche, Jikdrel Yeshe Dorje, *The Nyingma School of Tibetan Buddhism*, trans. G. Dorje and M. Kapstein (London: Wisdom Publications, 1991), vol. 1, 755–760. The positive responses of colleagues to this article, during the several years its publication has been delayed, have encouraged me to publish it here without major revision, though I am aware more than ever of its many shortcomings. I am particularly grateful to the late Dezhung Rinpoché for his learned counsel when I first read the *Maṇi Kambum* with him in 1979, and to Mme. A. M. Blondeau for her kind interest in this work.

1. The edition I have utilized for this study is: *Ma ṇi Bka' 'bum: A Collection of Rediscovered Teachings Focusing Upon the Tutelary Deity Avalokiteśvara (Mahākaruṇika); Reproduced from a Print from the No Longer Extant Spungs thang (Punakha) blocks by Trayang and Jamyang Samten*, 2 vols. (New Delhi, 1975). (Hereafter: *Maṇi Bka' 'bum*, followed by volume number in Roman numerals and plate number.)

The blocks for the Punakha edition reproduced here were apparently carved at the request of a certain Mnga' ris sgrub chen Ngag dbang chos 'phel, the disciple of Ngag dbang bstan 'dzin rab rgyas (*Maṇi Bka' 'bum* II. 708). Dr. Michael Aris has kindly informed me that while the former remains unidentified,

> . . . his master . . . was the fourth *'Brug Sde srid* (regn. 1680–1695, lived 1638–1696). He was the first in the line of the *Khri sprul* or *Bla ma khri pa* (of which there have been six). The *Lho'i chos byung* makes him the first Rgyal tshab, the official stand-ins for (sometimes the incarnations of) the 1st *Zhabs drung*. He was one of the greatest and most effective Bhutanese rulers. There is an extremely long biography by Ngag dbang lhun grub, dated 1720, not yet published. (Correspondence: July 18, 1980)

This Punakha edition seems to be based on an earlier edition from Gung thang in Mnga' ris (*Maṇi Bka' 'bum* II. 617).

2. Andrei Vostrikov, *Tibetan Historical Literature*, trans. Harish Chandra Gupta (Calcutta: Indian Studies Past & Present, 1970), 52.

3. Vostrikov, *Tibetan Historical Literature*, 55.

4. Ariane Macdonald, *L'annuaire de l'École Pratique des Hautes Études*, IVe3 section, 1968/69, 528.

5. Recent years have seen the publication of many Tibetan works concerning the Avalokiteśvara cult. Among those that may be of interest to students of the *Maṇi Bka' 'bum* that I have not been able to make use of in connection with the present study are:

    a) *Maṇi Bka' 'bum chen mo* of *Gu ru Chos kyi dbang phyug*, Version A (Thimphu, 1976).

    b) *Maṇi Bka' 'bum chen mo* of *Gu ru Chos kyi dbang phyug*, Version B (Thimphu, 1976).

    c) *Chos 'byung me tog snying po sbrang rtsi'i bcud*, by Mnga' bdag Nyang ral Nyi ma 'od zer (Paro, 1979).

    d) *Chos rgyal Mes dbon rnam gsum gyi rnam thar rin po che'i phreng ba*, by Mnga' bdag Nyang ral Nyi ma 'od zer (Paro, 1979).

    e) *Thugs rje chen po'i rgyud rang byung ye shes*, revealed by Mnga' bdag Nyang ral Nyi ma 'od zer (Paro, 1979).

    f) *Die grosse Geschichte des tibetischen Buddhismus nach alter Tradition Rnying ma'i chos 'byung chen mo*, ed. R. O. Meisezahl. Monumenta Tibetica Historica, vol. 3 (Sankt Augustin: VGH Wissenschaftsverlag, 1985).

6. The basic structure of the *Maṇi Bka' 'bum* is revealed in its *dkar chag* (*Maṇi Bka' 'bum* I. 9–23). It seems that this *dkar chag* is of some antiquity and is identical to the *Yer pa'i dkar chag* referred to by *Maṇi Bka' 'bum*'s editors (I. 19, *mchan*). A similar *dkar chag* served as the basis for the Fifth Dalai Lama's discussion of the contents of the *Maṇi Bka' 'bum*: Ngag dbang blo bzang rgya mtsho, "Record of Teachings Received: The Gsan yig of the Fifth Dalai Lama Ngag dbang blo bzang rgya mtsho," vol. 3 (Delhi: Nechung and Lakhar, 1971), plates 130–153. (Hereafter: Ngag dbang blo bzang rgya mtsho, "Record of Teachings Received," followed by plate number.) The discussion of the "Record of Teachings Received," is, for all intents and purposes, a detailed

commentary on the *dkar chag* and reflects the Dalai Lama's great personal interest in the *Maṇi Bka' 'bum*. It is noteworthy that at least one group of texts listed in the *dkar chag* that was not available to the redactors of the *Maṇi Bka' 'bum* (II. 616–617) could not be located by the Great Fifth either (Ngag dbang blo bzang rgya mtsho, "Record of Teachings Received," 149). The Dalai Lama also mentions one group of texts (Ngag dbang blo bzang rgya mtsho, "Record of Teachings Received," 139–140) that are not to be found in the *dkar chag* but seem to have been in circulation in connection with the *Maṇi Bka' 'bum*. For useful summaries of the *Maṇi Bka' 'bum*'s contents see also: Vostrikov, *Tibetan Historical Literature*, 53–55; and Macdonald, *L'annuaire*, 527–528.

7. In the *Maṇi Bka' 'bum* it forms a separate cycle (II. 619–711), where it is entitled *'Phags pa nam mkha'i rgyal po'i mngon rtogs sogs phran 'ga'*. The title *Gab pa mngon phyung gi skor* is given in the *dkar chag* (I. 22).

8. Ngag dbang blo bzang rgya mtsho, "Record of Teachings Received," 130. This is a restatement of part of the *dkar chag* (*Maṇi Bka' 'bum* I. 21–22). It is of some interest to note that some of the masters mentioned in connection with the compilation of the *Maṇi Bka' 'bum* are also mentioned in connection with the cult of the Lhasa Jokhang. See: *Lha ldan gtsug lag khang gi dkar chag: A Guide to the Great Temple of Lhasa by His Holiness Ngag dbang Blo bzang Rgya mtsho, the Great Fifth Dalai Lama* (Delhi: Ngawang Gelek Demo, n.d.), 78–79.

9. Ngag dbang blo bzang rgya mtsho, "Record of Teachings Received," 131.

10. *Maṇi Bka' 'bum* I. 498 and 584. Mme. Blondeau has suggested to me that the present version of the *Great Chronicle* is of very doubtful attribution. See Blondeau, "Le 'Découvreur' du *Maṇi bka' 'bum* était-il Bön po?" esp. n. 19.

11. *Maṇi Bka' 'bum* I. 504.

12. Ariane Macdonald has advanced the thesis that Nyi ma 'od zer and Mnga' bdag Myang (Nyang) ral were, in fact, two distinct persons, for the latter was used as a familial title among Nyi ma 'od zer's descendents. See her "Une Lecture des Pelliot Tibétan 1286, 1287, 1038, 1047, et 1290: Essai sur la formation et l'emploi des mythes politiques dans la religion royale de Srong bcan sgam po [A Reading of the Pelliot Tibetan (Manuscripts) 1286, 1287, 1038, 1047, and 1290: Essay on the Formation and Use of Political Myths in the Royal Religion of Srong btsan sgam po]," *Études Tibétaines* 203 (1971): 190–391, 203, n. 59. However, the mention of the *siddha* Dngos grub in connection with the lineage of the *bka' brgyad* as well as that of the *Maṇi Bka' 'bum* leads me to believe that such a view may not, in this instance, be tenable, though we cannot rule out the possibility that one of Nyang ral's sons has been conflated with his father. See Blo gros mtha' yas, Kong sprul, *Zab mo'i gter dang gter ston grub thob ji ltar byon pa'i lo rgyus mdor bsdus bkod pa rin chen baiḍūrya'i phreng ba*, in *Treasury of Rediscovered Teachings* (Paro, 1976) vol. I, 371–372; Dudjom Rinpoche, *The Nyingma School of Tibetan Buddhism*, vol. 1, 758.

13. Ngag dbang blo bzang rgya mtsho, "Record of Teachings Received," 151 notes that he was a *bhikṣu*. It appears that the Dalai Lama had access to some specific information about the lesser-known figures in the *Maṇi Bka' 'bum*'s lineage.

14. *Maṇi Bka' 'bum* II. 651.

15. It should be noted that the *dkar chag* seems not to have originally listed any of Shākya 'od's discoveries, but that the account of them forms an appended discussion (*Maṇi Bka' 'bum* I. 22). Perhaps the "original" *Maṇi Bka' 'bum* consisted solely of the discoveries of Dngos grub and Mnga' bdag Nyang, as assembled by the latter or one of his school.

16. E.g., Blo gros mtha' yas, Kong sprul, *Shes bya kun khyab mdzod: The Treasury of Knowledge*, 4 vols. (Paro: Ngodrup and Sherab Drimay, 1976), 1:429.

17. Tāranātha, "Khrid brgya'i brgyud pa'i lo rgyus" [History of the Transmission of the *One Hundred Instructions*], in *Gdams nag mdzod (sic): A Treasury of Instructions and Techniques for Spiritual Realization*, vol. XII, ed. Blo gros mtha' yas, Kong sprul (Delhi: N. Lungtok and N. Gyaltsen, 1971), 356–357.

18. Among *terma*, the *Maṇi Bka' 'bum* is peculiar with respect to its punctuation: it makes use of the ordinary *shad*, instead of the *visarga*-like *gter shad*. It is of interest to compare, too, Tāranātha's mild suggestion that the treasure discoverers composed, rather than found, some parts of the *Maṇi Bka' 'bum* with Sum pa mkhen po Ye shes dpal 'byor's vociferous remarks (Vostrikov, *Tibetan Historical Literature*, 56–57). Cf. M. Kapstein, "The Purificatory Gem and Its Cleansing," *History of Religions* 28, no. 3 (Feb. 1989): 217–244.

19. This is confirmed by the Central Tibetan Ngag dbang blo bzang rgya mtsho, "Record of Teachings Received," the Bhutanese *Maṇi Bka' 'bum*, and the many references found throughout Karma Chags med, *Thugs rje chen po'i dmar khrid phyag rdzogs zung 'jug gi skor* [*Instruction on the Great Compassionate One*], in *Collected Works*, Volume 2 (Bir, H.P., 1974). Chags med, who hailed from Nang chen in Khams, lived during the first half of the XVIIth century. The meaning of the title *Maṇi Bka' 'bum* is somewhat problematic; see Vostrikov, *Tibetan Historical Literature*, 52–53 and Macdonald, *L'annuaire*, 527. The biographies of Guru Chos kyi dbang phyug (see n. 5 above) were perhaps the first works to use this title and may provide the key to its precise interpretation. My own rendering is similar to that of Mme. Macdonald, *L'annuaire*.

20. *Maṇi Bka' 'bum* I. 1 and 10.

21. Bdud 'joms Rin po che, *Gangs ljongs rgyal bstan yongs rdzogs kyi phyi mo snga 'gyur rdo rje theg pa'i bstan pa rin po che ji ltar byung ba'i tshul dag cing gsal bar 'brjod pa lha dbang g.yul las rgyal ba'i rnga bo che'i sgra dbyangs* (i.e. the *Rnying ma'i chos 'byung*) [*The Religious History of the Nyingma*], in *Collected Works*, Volume 1 (Delhi, 1979), 242. Trans. by Dorje and Kapstein in *The Nyingma School of Tibetan Buddhism*.

22. E.g., Bu ston, *History of Buddhism* (*Chos-ḥbyung*), Part II, trans. E. Obermiller (Heidelberg: In commission bei O. Harrassowitz, 1931–32), 183–185. Bu ston's account certainly has some affinity with that of the *Maṇi Bka' 'bum*, though there is no reason to assume that he based himself on that source directly. See, too, 'Gos Lo tsā ba, *The Blue Annals*, trans. G. Roerich (New Delhi: Motilal Banarsidass, 1976 [reprint]), 1006.

23. Chos kyi nyi ma, Thu'u bkwan, *Grub mtha shel gyi me long* [*The Crystal Mirror of Philosophical Systems*] (Delhi: Ngawang Gelek Demo, n.d.), 65–66. Passages such as this

one, found in the work of a leading Dge lugs pa hierarch, suggest that the *Maṇi Bka' 'bum* did not meet with the condemnation in Dge lugs pa circles that the scholar who encounters Sum pa Mkhan po's opinion (n. 19 above) may suppose. See, for example, Macdonald, *L'annuaire*, 531. Discussions with a number of Tibetan scholars, notably the Ven. Dezhung Rinpoché who himself studied the *Mani Bka' 'bum* under a Dge lugs pa *dge bshes*, have convinced me that the Great Fifth's love of the *Maṇi Bka' 'bum* made a lasting impression on the cult of Srong btsan sgam po/Avalokiteśvara within the Dge lugs pa sect.

24. *Maṇi Bka' 'bum* I. 22 and Ngag dbang blo bzang rgya mtsho, "Record of Teachings Received," 131. According to these texts it was Padmasambhava who revealed to Khri srong lde'u btsan the works of his ancestor.

25. These issues are taken up at length in: Macdonald, "The Formation and Use of Political Myths in the Royal Religion of Srong btsan sgam po," and Yoshiro Imaeda, "Note Préliminaire sur la formule *Oṃ Maṇi Padme Hūṃ* dans les Manuscrits Tibétains de Touen Houang" [A Preliminary Note on the Formula *Oṃ Maṇi Padme Hūṃ* in Tibetan Manuscripts of Dunhuang], in *Contributions aux études sur Touen-Houang* (Genève, Paris: Droz, 1979), 71–76. But see also Hugh E. Richardson, "The Dharma that came down from heaven: A Tun-huang Fragment," in *Buddhist Thought and Asian Civilization* (Emeryville, Calif.: Dharma Publishing, 1977), 219–229.

26. Marcelle Lalou, "Les Textes Bouddhiques au temps du Roi Khri srong lde bstan" [Buddhist Scriptures at the Time of King Khri srong lde bstan], *Journal Asiatique* 341 (1953): 313–353. Texts related to the Avalokiteśvara cult that are listed here include numbers 79, 114, 157, 316, 343, 347, 352, 366, 388, 410, 440, 459, and 460.

27. My remarks on the *Rnying ma Bka' ma* are based on conversations with the late Ven. Bdud 'joms Rin po che and the Rev. Mkhan po Thub bstan. Avalokiteśvara is one of the Eight Bodhisattvas in the *maṇḍalas* of the *Sgyu 'phrul zhi khro*, which is associated with the *Guhyagarbhatantra*, and the *Dgongs pa 'dus pa*, the foremost *Anuyoga-tantra*. In the latter he is also found, with Mañjuśri and Vajrapāṇi, as one of the *rigs gsum mgon po*. Avalokiteśvara's wrathful aspect, Hayagrīva, occupies a position of great importance in the *Bka' ma* tradition, particularly in the *Bka' brgyad* cycle. When I state that the *Bka' ma* includes "authentically ancient material," I do so with the understanding that the many threads which are woven together there cannot at present be satisfactorily sorted out.

28. Blo gros mtha' yas, Kong sprul, ed., *The Treasury of Knowledge*, I. 429. Repeated *verbatim* in Bdud 'joms Rin po che, *The Religious History of the Nyingma*, 153–154.

29. These are the *Bka' gdams lha bzhi'i spyan ras gzigs, Skyer sgang lugs kyi spyan ras gzigs,* and *Dpal mo lugs kyi spyan ras gzigs.* Their lineages and precepts have been masterfully summarized by Jo nang Rje btsun Kun dga' grol mchog; see Blo gros mtha' yas, Kong sprul, ed., *A Treasury of Instructions*, vol. XII, 252, 256–257, 394–395, 430–432.

30. See *Thugs rje chen po dang phyag rgya chen po zung 'jug tu nyams su len tshul rjes gnang dang bcas pa* [*The Way to Practice the Union of Avalokiteśvara and Mahamudra, together with the Authorization*], in *Sgrub thabs kun btus* (Sde dge ed.) vol. Ga, ff. 1–8; and Roerich, ed., *The Blue Annals*, 1006–46. The *Thugs rje chen po rgyal ba*

rgya mtsho, introduced by Ras chung pa, became particularly popular among the Rnying ma pas, and among the Karma Bka' brgyud pas, whose hierarchs adopted it as their *yi dam*.

31. Karma Chags med, *Instruction on the Great Compassionate One*, 265.

32. *Maṇi Bka' 'bum* I. 87.

33. Macdonald, "The Formation and Use of Political Myths in the Royal Religion of Srong btsan sgam po," 388.

34. Macdonald, *L'annuaire*, 532.

35. Vostrikov, *Tibetan Historical Literature*, 28–32 and 67–78. The *Bka' chems ka khol ma* is traditionally said to have been revealed by Atīśa. The precise era of its appearance and, hence, its chronological relationship with the *Maṇi Bka' 'bum* have yet to be determined.

36. *Maṇi Bka' 'bum* I. 192–193.

37. Karma Chags med, *Instruction on the Great Compassionate One*, 268–269. See also M. Kapstein, "The Limitless Ocean Cycle," in *Soundings in Tibetan Civilization*, ed. Barbara N. Aziz and Matthew T. Kapstein (Delhi: Manohar, 1985), 358–371.

38. The degree to which even ascetics were affected by this unrest is well indicated in *Maṇi Bka' 'bum* I. 525, where the *yogin* is advised to equip his retreat with weaponry.

39. *Avalokiteśvaraguṇa-Kāraṇḍavyūhah* [*The Magnificent Array of the Qualities of Avalokiteśvara*], in *Mahāyānasūtrasaṁgrahah*, Buddhist Sanskrit Texts No. 17, ed. P. L. Vaidya (Darbhanga, 1961), 265. See, too, the excellent study by Constantin Regamey, "Motifs Vich-nouites et Śivaïtes dans le *Kāraṇḍavyūha* [Vaisnava and Śaivaite Motifs in the *Kāraṇḍavyūha*]," in *Études Tibétaines dediées à la mémoire de Marcelle Lalou* (Paris: Maisonneuve, 1971).

40. *The Magnificent Array of the Qualities of Avalokiteśvara*, 288–292. The *locus classicus* for Atīśa's teaching of this vision is found in the *Lha bzhi bstan pa'i skabs* of the *Bka' gdams glegs bam pha chos*, where I have encountered it. Unfortunately I do not presently have a copy of this text at my disposal and so cannot give the exact page reference. The relevant verses may be found quoted in Karma Chags med, *Instruction on the Great Compassionate One*, 258. See also n. 30 above.

41. *Maṇi Bka' 'bum* I. 34.

42. *Maṇi Bka' 'bum* I. 35–36.

43. *Maṇi Bka' 'bum* I. 29–30.

44. *Maṇi Bka' 'bum* I. 511–512, II. 265–266 and 279. (In notes 45 through 53 it is not my intention to provide a comprehensive catalogue of relevant passages, but rather to signal representative examples.)

45. *Maṇi Bka' 'bum* I. 496–497 and 511–512.

46. *Maṇi Bka' 'bum* II. 584–586.

47. *Maṇi Bka' 'bum* II. 288–289, 531, and 579–582.

48. *Maṇi Bka' 'bum* II. 288, 582–584.

49. *Maṇi Bka' 'bum* II. 182–234.

50. *Maṇi Bka' 'bum* I. 514–519.

51. *Maṇi Bka' 'bum* II. 29–30, 279–280, and 396–397.

52. *Maṇi Bka' 'bum* II. 280. More often, however, the *Maṇi Bka' 'bum* speaks of the *sku drug*, six *kāyas*, e.g. II. 26–27, and *passim*.

53. *Maṇi Bka' 'bum* I. 18.

54. *Maṇi Bka' 'bum* I. 514.

55. *Maṇi Bka' 'bum* I. 20–21.

56. Blo gros mtha' yas, Kong.sprul, ed., *A Treasury of Instructions*, vols. II and III. The intricate teaching of the Bka' gdams pas requires careful study. My statement here is a general one, based on the reading of such sources as those brought together by Kong sprul in the magnificent anthology herein cited.

57. *Maṇi Bka' 'bum* I. 470.

58. Having attended discourses on Avalokiteśvara given by representatives of all the major Tibetan Buddhist traditions, I cannot but observe that the unifying features of this cult are far more apparent than the distinguishing features of the various lineages involved. It would seem that this unity of the cult is what moved 'Gos Lo tsā ba to give it separate treatment in the *Blue Annals*, 1006–46; Blo gros mtha' yas [Karma] Kong sprul to anthologize it separately in the *A Treasury of Instructions*, vol. XI; and Chags med to combine freely precepts derived from its different lineages in his *Instruction on the Great Compassionate One*.

Chapter 5

ON THE TIBETAN HISTORIOGRAPHY AND
DOXOGRAPHY OF THE "GREAT DEBATE OF SAMYÉ"

David Seyfort Ruegg

David Seyfort Ruegg is a prominent scholar of Mahāyāna Buddhism and, though born in America, has taught in France, the Netherlands, and England. The "Great Debate of Samyé" is one of the most famous events in early Tibetan intellectual history. Two Buddhist masters, one from China, one from India, pit their skills against each other in a battle to win the favor of the Tibetan emperor, Tri Songdetsen. The reward is no less than the right to propagate their own Buddhist tradition in this newly emerging Buddhist culture. The moment is characterized as a turning point at which all the major issues treated by subsequent Buddhist philosophers were decided upon. In this moment, Tibet elected to favor a gradual approach to enlightenment over a sudden approach, to turn away from China and toward India in order to develop its Buddhist tradition.

Of course the history of the event and the issues symbolized by it are more complex than this. Since the middle of the twentieth century, European scholars have argued that the debate narrative is a synthetic account of the broad changes that Tibetan culture underwent in the eighth century. Tibetan literati also debated the historical details and cultural significance of the Great Debate. In this essay Ruegg provides an overview of contemporary Euro-American historiography on the event, as well as Tibetan historical writing about it. He shows that the dominant version in Tibetan histories is in great measure a polemic by the new schools of Buddhism against the Nyingma school. He also suggests that, whatever the facts may be, the location of Samyé became through the tale of the debate a "locus of memory" for Tibetan writers attempting to reconstruct the early history of their tradition.

I

Towards the end of the eighth century C.E., during the reign of Tri Songdetsen (r. c. 755–794/7), there took place an event of the greatest significance for Tibetan history and culture which had an enduring influence on later religious and philosophical development in Tibet and was to shape important areas of it. This event was the famous encounter, the so-called "Great Debate of Samyé," between the Chinese *heshang* [Chin., monk] Moheyan (*hashang* Mahāyāna/ Mahāyan) and disciples of Śāntarakṣita including the Indian Kamalaśīla and members of the great Tibetan Ba (Sba, Dba', Dba's) clan such as Yeshé Wangpo and Pelwang.

Since the late 1930s this event, which is now somewhat wrapped in the mists of time, has rightly attracted the attention of European scholars such as Marcelle Lalou, Paul Demiéville, Giuseppe Tucci and Rolf Stein. More recently it has been investigated also by scholars in America and above all in Japan. This work has been of immense importance for our understanding of this eighth century event, although it must be said that much of the more recent research has generally tended to allow the significance of the "Great Debate" for Tibetan civilization and thought to be eclipsed by problems in the history and doctrines of Chinese Chan. (A noteworthy exception to this tendency is the thesis on *Dzokchen* just published by Samten Gyaltsen Karmay: *The Great Perfection* [Leiden, 1988].)

This paper will be concerned with aspects of this encounter as either a historical event or a more or less dehistoricized *topos*, and with its significance in Tibetan historiography and doxography and for the history of Tibetan religion and philosophy.

II

Several thorny questions arise as to what the exact nature of this event was. Indeed, was the encounter between Moheyan and Kamalaśīla a real event having historical authenticity? For the very existence of their reported debate as a historical occurrence has come to be questioned.[1] And one might well ask how a Chinese monk evidently unfamiliar with any Indian language could have actually discussed, much less debated, important questions of Buddhist theory and practice with an Indian pandit who had only recently arrived in Tibet and could scarcely have been fluent in Tibetan, let alone Chinese.[2]

Let us begin with the name given to this encounter by modern scholars. Since Paul Demiéville's path-breaking and masterly *Le concile de Lhasa* (Paris,

1952), it has frequently been called the Council of Lhasa. Now it has to be said that, as depicted in the ancient Tibetan and Chinese documents from Dunhuang as well as in the later Tibetan historical and philosophical literature, this event was no council in the proper ecclesiastical sense of the term, nor was it even a local Buddhist synod. Sometimes the relevant materials take the form of aphorisms or *logia* uttered by Moheyan (and other Heshangs), e.g., in several Tibetan documents from Dunhuang. Alternatively, in Wang Xi's *Dunwu Dacheng zhengli jue* translated by Demiéville, we have a series of more or less polemical questions put by a "Brahman monk" to Moheyan with the latter's replies. And sometimes the materials are set out as a discussion or debate between Moheyan and (mainly) Kamalaśīla's disciples.

In the Tibetan historical literature starting with the various versions of the *Bazhé* and the *Chöjung Metok Nyingpo* of Nyang Nyima Özer, the event is in fact depicted as a debate (*rtsod pa, [g]shags*), with Tri Songdetsen in the middle acting as "witness" and presiding over the assembly. To the monarch's right were the "Simultaneists" led by Moheyan (who seemingly, according to a Tibetan tradition, wished because of his monastic seniority in Tibet to figure as the proponent). And to his left were the "Gradualists" led by Kamalaśīla but represented in the proceedings of the debate mainly by members of the Ba family—Yeshé Wangpo, Pelwang and/or Sangshi(ta)—figuring as the opponents. In other words, the setting is that of a classical debate with proponent (*vādin* = *snga rgol*), opponent (*prativādin* = *phyi rgol*) and witness or arbiter (*sākṣin* = *dpang po*) as described in the Vāda-manuals belonging to the Indo-Tibetan tradition. Although this scenario might perhaps seem out of place at the court of the Tibetan ruler as early as the end of the eighth century, this need not be so. Let us recall that Kamalaśīla's master Śāntarakṣita had commented on Dharmakīrti's *Vādanyāya* where procedures in debate are described. And it should be carefully noted that according to the *Vādanyāya* the procedure of debate is employed not just out of a desire for victory at any price since it is not just *vijigīṣuvāda*, and that it concerns reflexion on what is true (*tattvacintā*) and its proclamation (*khyāpana*), serves the preservation of truth (*tattvarakṣaṇa*) and is engaged in for the purpose of assisting an other (*parānugraha*).[3] It is quite possible that all this was very well known to Śāntarakṣita's and Kamalaśīla's Tibetan disciples towards the end of the eighth century, and that a debate was arranged by the Tibetans and their Indian teacher with just such an end in view.

As for the site of the Great Debate, in the Tibetan sources it is often said to have been the Jangchupling temple at Samyé, the first Tibetan monastic center founded by Śāntarakṣita. Tucci accordingly preferred the name of "Council of Samyé" to Demiéville's "Council of Lhasa."[4] But more recently the appellation "Council of Tibet" has been extensively used by scholars, including Demiéville himself.[5] As has been suggested by Ueyama and Demiéville, it may well be that meetings between participants took place at more than one single place, and in more than a single session.

No cogent reason is however known to me for thinking that Samyé (and perhaps in particular the Jangchupling Temple which Tibetan sources have presented as the site of the encounter) was not, in the technical and legal sense, the venue and in any case the focal point for what was a debate rather than a council in the proper sense. At all events, the appellation "Council of Lhasa" is certainly a misnomer; and the name "Council of Tibet" may be more general and imprecise than need be.

Even though Kamalaśīla's three *Bhāvanākramas* do not report in an historical fashion on any specific debate at an identifiable place with identifiable participants, they do reflect a discussion or debate in a quite dehistoricized form. As for Wang Xi's account in the *Zhengli jue*, it refers only to a Brahman monk (*pho lo men seng*, folio 127a) and not specifically to Kamalaśīla as Moheyan's opponent.

The account found in the Ba Records (*Bazhé*) has not only been questioned as to its historical accuracy and veracity, but it has been ascribed to the fourteenth century; and the classical Tibetan historical tradition on the subject has been described as late.[6] Despite the many problems these Ba Records undoubtedly pose, such a dating would seem to be unduly late. For the account in question is found, in somewhat differing forms it is true, not only in the Supplemented *Bazhé* (that is, the *Zhap takma* version)—which may well have something to do with Atiśa's school since it concludes with his mission in Tibet and which must, moreover, be quite late in its extant version since it refers (p. 54 in Stein's ed.) to the *Sungrap rinpoché [wang] dzö*, i.e., apparently to the *Chöjung* of c. 1323 by Butön (1290–1364), who however himself cites a *Bazhé* (*Rba bzhed*)—but in the presumably earlier "Pure" *Bazhé* (that is, the *Tsangma* version) which itself includes the "Alternative Tradition" on the Great Debate used not only by Pawo Tsuklak Trengwa (1504–1566) but evidently also in the works of Sakya Paṇḍita (1182–1251, who cites a *Pazhé* [*Dpa' bzhed*] apparently in the version of the "Alternative Tradition"), Butön, and much of the Tibetan historical literature. Furthermore, and most importantly, a closely related (if somewhat divergent) account of the "Great Debate" is found in the history of Nyang Nyima Özer (1124/1136–1192/1204). Now, provided of course that it is authentic, this account in the *Chöjung Metok Nyingpo* goes back to a time before Sakya Paṇḍita. Moreover, and very significantly, it is found in the work of a master of the Dzokchen/Nyingma school; and this fact militates against the supposition that the account in question of the Samyé Debate was simply a fabrication of the *sarmapas* intended somehow to discredit the Dzokchenpas (several of whose teachings were compared by Sakya Paṇḍita and other Tibetan authorities with the teachings of the Hashang Mahāyāna).

As for the main participants in the Great Debate, although according to the Tibetan sources Kamalaśīla was the leader of the Gradualists the actual speakers on their side were mainly members of the Ba family (Yeshé Wangpo, Pelwang and/or Ba Sangshi[ta]). Hence the question as to what language Kamalaśīla and Moheyan had in common loses much of its relevance, at least from the point of view of the Tibetan sources. (It is true that in Wang Xi's *Zhengli jue* Moheyan and the unnamed "Brahman monk" are represented as speaking to each other; but this may have to do with the literary presentation adopted by Wang Xi. Kamalaśīla's remarks to Moheyan could in any case have been translated into Tibetan, or even into Chinese.) It seems likely, then, that the language used in the discussions would have been mainly Tibetan, with which Moheyan was presumably familiar after his residence in Tibetan-speaking areas. Chinese may have been employed in addition between some Tibetans and Moheyan and his Chinese associates; and an Indian language might have been in use between certain Tibetans and Kamalaśīla.

By Demiéville and other scholars the "Great Debate" has been characterized as a Sino-Indian or an Indo-Chinese controversy. This description could however lead to a misapprehension as to its nature and purpose, for the discussions were evidently set in train by the Tibetans themselves in order to clarify acute problems of theory and practice that had urgently come to their attention. The Tibetans in fact were then a major power in central Asia; and in view of their intellectual achievements by the beginning of the ninth century (as attested for example in the works of Yeshé Dé), it would seem to be quite unsatisfactory to regard them as nullities only a short time earlier at the time of the "Great Debate," or as nothing but an intellectual *tabula rasa* waiting to be used by others and lacking any philosophical or religious rôle of their own in organizing and carrying through the discussions. As already suggested, it may well have been organized in the way best known to Yeshé Wangpo and his colleagues, namely in the above-mentioned classical Indo-Tibetan form of a debate devoted to reflecting on, proclaiming and preserving what is true (*tattva*).

If this is indeed so, it will also be far from the mark—and quite anachronistic—to regard the "Great Debate" as a more or less politically motivated confrontation between the Indians and Chinese as rival great powers in Central Asia. To the extent that political factors were involved, it would appear that they would have been connected rather less with any possible conflicts between Chinese and Indians than with rivalries between Tibetan clans and the regions with which the clans were linked. Such clannishness may have opposed members of the Ba clan as disciples or supporters of Śāntarakṣita and Kamalaśīla to members of the Nyang (*Myang, Nyang*) and Nya (*Mnya', Snya*) clans as supporters of the *heshangs*; the sources in fact report that Tingngedzin Zangpo of Nyang and Bima (*Bi ma, Bye ma,* etc.) of Nya (*Mnya'*) were in opposition to Yeshé Wangpo of Ba (*Sba*). But because of the nature of our documentation it is hard to pin this down. It has indeed to be borne in mind that a member of this Ba (*Sba*) clan had also earlier been closely connected with *heshangs*, while members of the Nyang as well as of the Ba (*Dba'*) clan are stated in a Dunhuang document to have been disciples of Śāntarakṣita;[7] and in the twelfth century Nyang (*Nyang*) Nima Özer gave an account of the Great Debate, including the defeat of the

Hashang Mahāyāna, that is closely related to (if not completely identical with) what we find in the Ba Records.

III

It would of course be unrealistic to pretend that the Tibetan historical and doxographical sources at our disposal have given us a full and a perfectly accurate and balanced account of exactly what took place at the "Great Debate" of Samyé. The relevant Dunhuang documents in Tibetan, although fairly numerous, are both fragmentary and episodic. (In this respect they differ for example from Wang Xi's *Zhengli jue*, also recovered from Dunhuang.) And the accounts in the classical Tibetan historical literature starting with the *Bazhé* and the other sources more or less closely related to the Ba Records, although reasonably long, are no doubt somewhat formalized and stereotyped to the extent that their authors relate what had become, in part at least, a somewhat dehistoricized *topos*.

It could nevertheless be that these Ba records go back at least in their core to a time soon after the Great Debate, and in any case to the time of the Yarlung dynasty in the early ninth century. (The *Tsangma* version of the *Bazhé* concludes with the accession of Muné Tsenpo.) Nevertheless, if this is indeed so, this would of course apply to their contents only and not to the language of the extant versions of the *Bazhé* (which is scarcely the Old Tibetan of the eighth century even though it contains a number of archaisms).

The later Tibetan historical tradition would appear to have no longer had an entirely clear picture of just what had happened at the encounter between Moheyan and Kamalaśīla's disciples. There was even some uncertainty for Tsewang Norbu (1698/9–1755) as to whether this event took place in the reign of Tri Songdetsen or earlier in that of his father Mé Aktsom (Tri Detsuktsen). After the break caused by the downfall of the Yarlung dynasty and the end of the period of the Early Propagation of Buddhism in the middle of the ninth century, Tibetan historians evidently had as much difficulty in reconstituting their ancient history as the modern Tibetologist does. Accounts found in the Tibetan historical literature in fact seem to reflect the Tibetans' attempts either to rediscover their early history or to constitute tradition, or even to do both of these things at the same time. As a consequence, the "Great Debate" of Samyé often appears in this literature more as a semi-historical *topos* than as an historical event, and the Hashang Mahāyāna as a more or less dehistoricized and emblematic figure standing as it were for a certain typological variety of Buddhism. In connection with the "Great Debate," Samyé itself became so to say a "locus of memory" (*lieu de mémoire*).[8]

IV

Even if we must conclude that our sources on the "Great Debate" of Samyé are neither complete nor perfectly accurate and balanced as *histoire événementielle*, are we then to regard them merely as essentially the fabrications of anti-Nyingma *sarmapas*, as the interpolation of later logic-choppers (*phyis kyi rtog ge pa*),[9] as tendentious tracts, or as polemic directed against the *Chakgya chenpo* (at least in one of its forms) with its teaching described as a *karpo chiktup*, that is, as a unique and perfectly self-sufficient Sovereign Remedy? In other words, if the Great Debate and along with it Samyé both became a "locus of memory," of what nature was this memory?

As reported in our historical and doxographical sources, the religious-philosophical problems that arose in eighth-century Tibet in a form evidently acute and urgent enough to make a discussion/debate and, if possible, a decision about them both timely and necessary appear to be old ones that were in no way simply the product of the particular historical juncture in question, i.e., the simultaneous presence in eighth-century Tibet of both Chinese and Indian Buddhist masters and the resulting encounter and confrontation between their doctrines.

The two traditions of Buddhism facing each other in the accounts of the Great Debate have usually been described as "Gradualism" (*rim gyi jukpa*, etc.) and "Simultaneism" (*chik char gyi jukpa*, etc.) or, as the latter current is often termed by Sinologues, Suddenness or "Subitism." This terminology is parallel to the distinction in Chinese between *jian* and *dun*, reflected in the Tibetan terms *tsé mun/min (pa)* and *tön mun/min (pa)*.

Now, this Gradualism is a method of spiritual training and development that is familiar from a very large number of Buddhist texts available in Sanskrit and Pali or in translations from these languages. The term describes a course of sequential and progressive (*kramena*) cultivation on the Path of the factors conducive to liberation and Awakening through the mediacy of practice and means. As for its opposite, Simultaneism, it too is far from being absent in some form from the classical sources of Buddhism. The corresponding Tibetan term *chik charwa* (etc.)—derived from Tib. *chik char* = Skt. *yugapad* (or *sakṛt*)—describes the immediacy and innate spontaneity of Awakening in and to the pure, original and real nature of Mind. Such simultaneity, or spontaneous and holistic immediacy, is mentioned in a number of classical Sūtras and Śāstras. And typologically (if not genetically) related notions are known from both Sūtras and Śāstras under the names of Buddha-nature (*sangs rgyas kyi rang bzhin*), *tathāgatagarbha*, *prakṛtistha-gotra*, and natural luminosity (*prakṛtiprabhāsvaratā*) of Mind. In the literature of the Vajrayāna related or comparable notions became especially frequent.

Simultaneism and Gradualism as two currents in Buddhism can be described in other words as immediacy in contrast to mediacy, innateness over and against reinforcement, spontaneity over and against effort, and even nature over and against nurture. To use a medical metaphor (a procedure not infrequently used in our sources in this connection), whilst Gradualism can be described as allopathic, employing counteragents (*pratipakṣa*) as remedies against the afflictions/impurities (*kleśa*) that are the impediments (*vipakṣa*) to liberation and Awakening, holistic Simultaneism represents a sort of nature-cure consisting in face-to-face encounter with and recognition of innate and ever-present Mind. As for the Vajrayāna, using as it does the *kleśas* to subdue the *kleśas*, it may be described as homoeopathic. Even though it is sometimes possible to observe a tendency for these last two currents to converge—e.g., in Dzokchen where, however, the Simultaneist tradition of the Hashang Mahāyāna is normally differentiated from Mahāyoga and Atiyoga—it would seem necessary in general to distinguish between the pure naturalness and spontaneous immediacy of Simultaneism and the progressively cultivated effort required in Vajrayāna traditions to achieve liberation and Buddhahood in this very life and body.

Another way of looking at the matter has been in terms of the balance between Tranquility or Quiet (*śamatha* = *zhi gnas*) and Insight (*vipaśyanā* = *lhag mthong*). An extreme version of simultaneist immediacy and innateness may emphasize Quiet by rejecting *vipaśyanā* as analytical, ratiocinative *prajñā*, i.e., *pratyavekṣā* involving mentation (*masas[i]kāra* = *yid la byed pa*). Conversely, an extreme version of gradualist cultivation of analysis may emphasize correct mentation (*yoniśomanasikāra*) and analysis (*vicāra* = *dpyad pa*) at the expense of Quiet.[10] In general, at all events, the out-and-out "Simultaneist" (*chik charwa*) would tend to reject the need for the progressive and alternating cultivation of Quiet and Insight which finally leads to their total integration in a syzygy (*yuganaddha* = *zung du 'brel par 'jug pa*) as taught in so much of classical Buddhism. The Hashang's simultaneist method is described in Tibetan sources on the one side as an extremely etherealized spirituality associated with a quietistic abandonment of all activity (*karman, caryā*), wholesome as well as unwholesome, as being an obstacle to realization, in the same way as white clouds and dark clouds both obscure the sun; and on the other side the Hashang's method is associated with delectation in emptiness (*stong pa nyid la dga' ba*), which is regarded as impurity of theory (*dṛṣṭikaṣaya* = *lta ba'i snyigs ma*)

This is to say that two genuine components of the Buddhist Path such as Quiet and Insight could if carried to excess, and when Ground and Fruit are so to say collapsed by suppressing the stages of the Path, become opposed and be regarded as antithetical extremes rather than as alternating and mutually reinforcing aspects which finally are to be integrated. The "Simultaneist" (*chik charwa*) and the "Gradualist" (*rim gyi pa*) will then appear as irreconcilable. But the co-ordination and final integration of these two currents has been amply set out both in the Śrāvakiyānist and Mahāyānist canonical traditions and in Śāstras. An example of the latter is to be found in the eminently "gradualist" *Abhisamayālaṃkāra*, where the progressive *anupūrvābhisamaya* (Chapter vi) is followed by the single-moment *abhisamaya* of the *ekakṣaṇābhisambodha*

(Chapter vii), which leads on in a second and final moment to the realization of the *dharmakāya* (Chapter viii).

Both these currents are moreover well attested in Chinese Buddhism itself. And there can therefore be no more question of characterizing all of Chinese Buddhism as "subitist" than there is of characterizing Indian Buddhism as exclusively gradualist. Kamalaśīla for one was evidently well aware of both currents. Not only did he comment on the *Avikalpapraveśadhāraṇī* for example, but in the sources he cited in his *Bhāvanākramas* they are mentioned, and their extreme or one-sided versions are rejected. But it is not clear how familiar Moheyan was with the gradualist tradition in Chinese Buddhism–a tradition which was represented for example by his (elder?) contemporary Tankuang who (like Moheyan himself) was in contact with Tri Songdetsen. Thus the encounter in Tibet at the end of the eighth century between the gradualist and simultaneist currents of Buddhism was certainly not between two homogeneous and monolithic national traditions standing in opposition to each other as Indian *vs.* Chinese Buddhism, but rather between two transmission-traditions: that of Moheyan traced back to Bodhidharma (and further to Kāśyapa) and that of Śāntarakṣita and Kamalaśīla (traced back to Nāgārjuna).

It appears that already at that time the Tibetans decided in favor of traditions the authentic transmission of which they considered they could clearly and confidently trace from reliable Indian sources, either written or living. But this did not involve the automatic anathematization of all Chinese traditions, as has been made clear by more than one Tibetan doxographer. Indeed, canonical texts translated from Chinese such as the *Suvarṇabhāsa* and the *Mahāparinirvāṇa* were received into the Kangyur; and an originally Chinese Śāstra such as the great commentary on the *Saṃdhinirmocana* by Wŏnch'uk (Yuanze, 613–696) translated from Chinese by Gö Chödrup/Fa cheng was included in the Tengyur.

Concerning the forms of *Dzokchen* that became known in Tibet, what was especially open to criticism from Tibetan scholars such as Sakya Paṇḍita (Sapaṇ) and some of his successors was perhaps not any and every form of Great Perfection (though the origins of *Dzokchen* were unclear and therefore controversial), but specifically what Sapaṇ termed in his *Domsum ropyé* the "Chinese style" Dzokchen (*rgya nag lugs kyi rdzogs chen*) that he linked with the Hashang Mahāyāna. As for Mahāmudrā, it was certainly not all forms of this teaching, some of which Sapaṇ explicitly accepted, that were the object of his criticism, but what he describes as "latter-day" Neo-Mahāmudrā (*da lta'i phyag chen*) with its doctrine of the "Sovereign Remedy" (*karpo chiktup*) which was also linked with the Hashang. For, as already noted, in the "Alternative Tradition" of the *Bazhé* evidently used by Sapaṇ as well as in the *Chöjung Metok Nyingpo* of Nyang Nyima Özer, the *karpo chiktup* is said to have been taught by the Hashang Mahāyāna. It is perhaps not quite certain whether under this name of Neo-Mahāmudrā Sakya Paṇḍita was criticizing a teaching of Gampopa (1079–1153), or whether it was the more extremely "simultaneist" formulation of the Mahā-mudrā and *karpo chiktup* doctrine found with Zhang Tselpa (1123–1193) that he was attacking.

V

To suppose that Sakya Paṇḍita's use of the term *karpo chiktup and* his juxtapo-sition of what he has termed Chinese-style Dzokchen and Neo-Mahāmudrā with the Hashang's teaching was mainly motivated by tendentious sectarianism and by polemics would seem to be excessive. In this matter, beside the problems of historiography mentioned above which arise in respect to the extant accounts of the "Great Debate" of Samyé, we are confronted by a problem in comparative religion and philosophy, and in particular by a question of typological affinity as distinct from direct genetic dependence.

As already noted, the expression *karpo chiktup*—which properly designates a unique and self-sufficient Sovereign Remedy—has been used metaphorically in several Tibetan sources to describe an "all-at-once" face-to-face encounter with and recognitive identification of innate and pure Mind (*sems ngo phrod pa, sems rtogs pa*) which restores one to one's true natural state by "curing" all afflic-tions and impurities. By Gampopa it was employed to describe an aspect of his Mahāmudrā teaching, and soon afterwards it was used by Zhang Tselpa in a strongly "simultaneist" sense.

It is, as we know, found also in the "Alternative Tradition" of the *Bazhé*, in the *Chöjung* of Nyang Nyima Özer, and in that of Pawo Tsuklak Trengwa (following the "Alternative Tradition") in addition to the works of Sakya Paṇḍita and some of his followers, where the expression is used to characterize simultaneist under-standing and recognitive identification of mind in the Hashang Mahāyāna's teaching.

Now, from a typological point of view, the doctrines in question do appear to be connected in a complex lattice of criss-crossing links. And they are further-more connected with very much older doctrines, problems and even controver-sies that are known from the Indian sources, some of them cited in Kamalaśīla's *Bhāvanākramas*. The opposition between, e.g., the mystical and enstatic on the one side and the intellectual and analytical on the other, and that between Fixation-Bhāvanā (*'jog sgom*) and Inspection-Bhāvanā (*dpyad sgom*), which arise in some Tibetan discussions of the Great Debate, recall a tension between the mystical and the analytical currents in old canonical sources.

Doctrines that are typologically and structurally related are of course very of-ten linked through direct historical derivation and branching. But, clearly, a pair of doctrines may, in addition, be connected with each other typologically without one having to be directly dependent historically on the other. The question then is: Are the links existing between the teachings ascribed to the Hashang

Mahāyāna and certain currents in Dzokchen and Chakchen not only typological and structural but also historical in the sense of direct genetic derivation?
Or are these links typological without any direct historical dependence having
to be postulated?

This is not an easy question to answer. Briefly stated, Sakya Paṇḍita may
have assumed not only typological and structural similarity but also historical
dependence and continuity, and several of his successors appear to have made
the same assumption. Longchenpa (1308–1363), the great Dzokchen master, on the
other hand was evidently prepared to accept a certain typological and structural
similarity between Dzokchen and the teaching of the Hashang without, apparently, positing any sort of genetic dependence; this is natural for him since, as
already noted, his Dzokchen school has differentiated between its Atiyoga tradition and the *chik charwa* tradition of the Hashang (see also the *Samten mik drön*).
But other Dzokchenpas/Nyingmapas have emphasized the differences more
clearly, just as many Kagyüpas have differentiated between Chakchen and the
teachings of the Hashang.

VI

In the present state of our knowledge, the conclusion seems indicated that when
the "theory of the Hashang" was rebutted by masters of the Sakyapa, Kagyüpa
and Gandenpa schools, and when some Dzokchenpa masters also distanced
themselves from it and did not accept it unreservedly, their target was a somewhat dehistoricized position involving ethical and karmic quietism as well as an
"ideoclasm" that tended toward intellectual nihilism and that form of impurity
of theory (*dṛṣṭikaṣāya*) described as delectation in the empty (*stong pa nyid la
dga' ba*). And the theory of the Hashang was identified with the ethical quietism and "ideoclasm" combatted in texts cited by Kamalaśīla. In other words,
the teachings of Moheyan, as known in Tibet chiefly through versions of the *Ba
Records* and related sources, have been taken as an instance of a *type* of theory
and practice already rejected in classical Sūtras and Śāstras.

The existence of typological and structural affinities, and of "family resemblances," between the doctrines in question taught in Tibet and some much
older doctrines found in the Śrāvakayānist and Māhāyanist canons—and in
particular with the *tathāgatagarbha* doctrine (even though the latter doctrine is
only sometimes explicitly evoked in the available sources on the teaching of the
Hashang Mahāyāna and on Simultaneism)—suggests that the acute and urgent
problems that arose at the "Great Debate" of Samyé extend far beyond the specific frame of a particular eighth-century historical juncture when Indian and
Chinese doctrines and masters met in Tibet. Clarification of the problems involved requires both religious and philosophical comparison bearing on the

history of Buddhism in India since early times and the study of the ideas and modes of Tibetan historiography and doxography.

Important though each is, focusing exclusively on the problematic triad formed by the Hashang, (Chinese-style) Dzokchen and (Neo-)Mahāmudrā, on the "Great Debate" of Samyé as an occurrence in eighth-century Tibetan *histoire événementielle*, or on the Sino-Indian and Sino-Tibetan dimensions could have the undesirable effect of obscuring the question of typological affinity and the problem of the relationship between currents that are in fact very old in Buddhism.

To sum up: There exist certain typological affinities and "family resemblances" between the views ascribed to the Hashang Mahāyāna and certain features in both Mahāmudrā and Dzokchen, especially in what has been described as "Neo-Mahāmudrā" and "Chinese-style Dzokchen." But links of direct genetic dependence are more difficult to establish clearly. The full significance of such similarities can only be revealed by historical and doxographical investigation combined with comparative typological and structural analysis. The Tibetologist has then to concern himself not only with trying to reconstruct what actually occurred at the so-called "Great Debate" of Samyé but with what the Tibetan historiographical and doxographical traditions considered to be the importance of this event and *topos*, that is, with its meaning for Tibetan civilization.[11]

NOTES

1. See recently Yoshiro Imaeda, "Documents Tibétains de Touen-Houang concernant le concile du Tibet" [Tibetan Documents from Dunhuang Concerning the Tibetan Council], *Journal Asiatique* (1975):125–146; H. V. Guenther, "'Meditation' in Early Tibet," in *Early Chan in China and Tibet*, ed. W. Lai and L. Lancaster (Berkeley: Asian Humanities Press, 1983), 351 and "Review: Mahāmudrā. Lobsang P. Lhalungpa," *Journal of the American Oriental Society* 109, no. 1 (1989): 151.

2. See for example Daishun Ueyama, "Donkō to Tonkō no bukkyō" [Donkō and Buddhist Teaching in Dunhuang]. *Tōhō Gakuhō* [*Journal of Oriental Studies*] 35 (1985): 169. Paul Demiéville, "Récents travaux sur Touen-houang" [Recent Work on Dunhuang], *T'oung Pao* vol. 56, Livr.1/3 (1970): 42. Imaeda, "Tibetan Documents from Dunhuang Concerning the Tibetan Council," 129.

3. *Vādanyāya*, ed., Svāmī Dvārikādās Śāstri (Varanasi, 1972), 68–71.

4. G. Tucci, *Minor Buddhist Texts, Part II* (Rome: Istituto italiano per il Medio ed Estremo Oriente, 1958), 32, 285–287.

5. Paul Wheatley, "Langkasuka," in *T'oung Pao* 44 (1956): 404–408; Demiéville, "Recent Work on Tunhuang," *T'oung Pao* 56 (1970): 42. See also P. Demiéville, "Deux documents de Touen-houang sur le Dhyana chinois" [Two Dunhuang Documents

on Chinese Dhyana], in *Essays on the History of Buddhism Presented to Professor Zenryu Tsukamoto* (Kyōto: Nagai Shuppansha, 1961), 14, 24.

6. See Imaeda, "Tibetan Documents from Dunhuang Concerning the Tibetan Council," 129.

7. See F. W. Thomas, *Tibetan Literary Texts and Documents Concerning Chinese Turkestan* (London: Royal Asiatic Society, 1951), 2:85.

8. For this concept see Pierre Nora, *Les lieux de mémoire* [*Places of Memory*] (Paris: Gallimard, 1984).

9. See Gtsug lag phreng ba, Dpa' bo, *Chos 'byung Mkhas pa'i dga' ston* [*Feast for Scholars*], ja, f. 122a–b.

10. Incorrect mentation (*ayoniśomanas[i]kārd*) on the contrary is of course recognized as dichotomizing conceptualization (*vikalpa*), and as the source of *karman* and *kleśa*. See for example *Ratnagotravibhāga* i. 56, and *Ratnagotravibhāga*-Commentary, i. 12 and 64.

11. For details see the present writer's 1987 Jordan Lectures published as *Buddha-nature, Mind and the Problem of Gradualism, in a Comparative Perspective* (London: School of Oriental and African Studies, University of London, 1989).

IMPERIAL POLITICS

Chapter 6

THE LINGUISTIC AND HISTORICAL SETTING OF
THE OLD TIBETAN INSCRIPTIONS

Fang Kuei Li and W. South Coblin

This essay introduces the Tibetan language and its earliest extant writings, which are to be found on stone obelisks in Lhasa dating from the eighth century. In contrast to later Tibetan historiography, which emphasized the roles of the emperors as cultural heroes, in early inscriptions the emperors were merely first among equals in the aristocratic clans of Central Tibet. Buddhism did eventually become a tool that could help the emperors take more power, but such incursions on the nobility's prerogatives also led to civil strife. We have some sense of the power of the noble clans to harm or protect the Tibetan emperors from the fact that the very first datable inscription in Tibetan concerns an assassination of one emperor and the protection offered to the next emperor by a loyal minister. And yet the enduring power of the imperial institution to protect the noble families across the generations is precisely the focus of the binding claims made in several of these early inscriptions. The shift of loyal ministers from laity to monks across the decades illustrates the slow but steady growth of the influence of Buddhism on the Tibetan elite. This is in contrast, again, to later Tibetan historians, who see in Songtsen Gampo a dedicated Buddhist. In this respect, it is also important that the early religion of Tibet, including practices called *mi chö*, "the religion of men," cannot be simplistically identified with Bön in this period. Finally, the authors discuss the early diplomatic and military relations between China's Tang Empire and the Tibetan Empire as revealed through these earliest Tibetan inscriptions.

1.1. LINGUISTIC BACKGROUND—THE
TIBETAN LANGUAGE

The Tibetan language comprises a number of rather closely related modern dialects spoken in Tibet and adjacent areas, a classical literary language with a history of more than a millennium, and a modern literary language which has been emerging during the last three or four decades. Tibetan constitutes one of the major branches of the Tibeto-Burman family of languages. It seems to be most closely related to certain ancient and modern Himalayan languages and to tribal languages of the Sino-Tibetan borderlands, but the exact nature of these relationships remains to be systematically determined. Indigenous historical tradition holds that Tibetan was reduced to writing by Tönmi Sambhota during the reign of King Songtsen Gampo (died A.D. 649). Chinese records suggest that writing was in use in Tibet no later than 648,[1] and the Dunhuang Annals for the year 655 make specific reference to its use in the recording of laws.[2] Thus, that the Tibetan script was developed during the first half of the seventh century seems beyond doubt. The earliest datable texts in this script are the Zhöl Inscriptions (dated to shortly after 763). During the reign of King Tri Tsuk-detsen (r. 815–838) the script underwent a reform, which codified the spelling conventions observed from that day to this.[3] Following the suggestion of Miller,[4] the language of texts written between the invention of the script and the spelling reform will be called "Old Tibetan." We shall call the literary language of later times "Written Tibetan." In addition to the inscriptions under study here, Old Tibetan is also represented in the far more extensive text materials discovered in the Dunhuang cave library and at various Central Asian archeological sites. These include historical and folk-literary texts, government and administrative documents, medical works, pre-Buddhist religious materials, the earliest Tibetan translations from the Buddhist canon, etc., etc. The language of the Old Tibetan inscriptions must be studied in concert with that of these non-inscriptional materials, many of which have only begun to be analyzed and understood.

1.2 HISTORICAL BACKGROUND

1.2.1 The Tibetan Monarchy. In the period immediately preceding that with which we are concerned the people of central Tibet lived in clans and tribal units which were gradually combining into larger confederations. These groups were controlled by chiefs or princelings whose power was centered in fortified redoubts. Among the more powerful of these individuals were the princes of Yarlung who, during the late sixth and early seventh centuries, were able to gain supremacy over the chiefs of the Tsangpo River valley and then subjugate the more far-flung groups and confederations of the Tibetan plateau. The conquered leaders united under the new dynasty formed a powerful and restless nobility who often viewed the reigning king as *primus inter pares* and exercised varying degrees of political control over him by serving as *lönchen*, "great ministers," or by obtaining the position of *zhang*, "maternal uncle," through matrimonial alliances with the royal house.[5] Both the Yarlung kings and the noble clans claimed divine origins.[6] Royal assertions of supernatural descent are manifested in a number of titles and epithets in the inscriptions, e.g., *lha* "god," *trülgyi lha* "God Incarnate" or "God of Supernatural Qualities,"[7] *lhasé* "Son of the Gods," and *nam lhap kyi gyelpo*, "King of Broad Heaven"; and direct reference is sometimes made to the origin myth of the royal house. In another text a member of the noble house of Karpo in Kong recounts this dynastic myth in more detail and claims common descent from the legendary royal ancestor, Nyatri Tsenpo.

The nobility bound themselves to the royal house through oaths of fealty, examples of which are preserved in the Dunhuang Chronicle.[8] The kings, for their part, rewarded their vassals' loyalty with grants to them and their posterity, usually including caveats outlining what steps would be taken in the event that one or more of the heirs became disloyal (e.g., the Lhasa Stele of Minister Takdra Lukhong). Later in the royal period such grants were also made to celibate Buddhist monk-officials; and then, it was necessary to specify that the benefits of the grants should devolve upon the heirs of the nearest lay relatives of the grantees.

Datable Tibetan history begins with Songtsen Gampo, one of the greatest Yarlung kings, under whom the power of the dynasty was consolidated and Tibet became a potent force in Central Asia. The reigns of the next three kings, Manglön Mangtsen, Tri Düsong, and Tri Detsuktsen, have been characterized as "the period of the regency" because these rulers were minors when their fathers died, and the great ministers who acted as regents were pre-eminent in affairs of state.[9] The Dunhuang Annals are defective for the year of Tri Detsuktsen's death (754), but they do mention various activities of two important ministers, Bel Dongtsap and Lang Nyezik (744, 746, 747); and they record that Bel and Lang were punished in the aftermath of some sort of disturbance (755, 756).[10] The Zhöl Inscriptions (the Lhasa Stele of Minister Takdra Lukhong) state that Bel and Lang actually murdered the king and then endangered the life of his successor, Tri Songdetsen. Later their disloyalty was discovered and punished as a result of the efforts of Ngenlam Takdra Lukhong, in whose honor the Zhöl pillar was erected. The text goes on to outline Takdra Lukhong's further contributions to the government and particularly the foreign policy of Tri Songdetsen.[11] This king rivaled Songtsen Gampo in greatness, and enthusiastic praise for his internal policies and foreign conquests rings in the Inscription at Chonggyé Bridge. Unfortunately, however, his last years were marred by troubles; and it is possible that his death was not from natural causes.[12] In fact, these circumstances and the identities and chronology of his immediate successors form one of the most vexing tangles in the history of the royal period.[13] The inscriptions at Zha Lhakang (Tri Desongtsen's edicts rewarding the monk Tingngedzin) indicate that there were troubles between Tri Songdetsen and one of his elder sons and that these problems culminated in very difficult circumstances during the minority of the eventual successor, Tri Desongtsen. As described in the text, the new king's guardian and guide during these trying years was a Buddhist monk, Nyang Tingngedzin, who in later times became a valued advisor and minister. This suggests a comparison with the reign of Tri Songdetsen, in which the position of loyal minister and helper was held by Takdra Lukhong (see the Lhasa stele of Minister Takdra Lukhong), a member of the traditional nobility. Now, in the time of Tri Desongtsen, we see a monk in this role. Also of interest here is a passage in the west side of the pillar of Tri Desongtsen's edicts for Tingngedzin where it is pointedly stated that Nyang's contributions are in no way to be considered inferior to those of the powerful Ba family of conservative lay ministers. All this brings to mind the often noted fact that the Yarlung kings saw in Buddhism a force which could be marshaled in their struggles with the entrenched and ever-fractious nobility.[14] One result of this strategy would have been the intrusion of monks into the upper levels of civil administration, where the nobility had been accustomed to exercise paramount influence.[15] The friction generated by the activities of the government bureaucracy becomes apparent in one text, where the noble house of Karpo recounts its own and the royal origin myth, rooted in traditional rather than Buddhist beliefs, and complains of infringement on its prerogatives by royal officials.

Another monk-official who was very influential in the time of Tri Desongtsen was Drenka Pelgyi Yönten. During the reign of the next king, Tri Tsukdetsen who was heavily under the influence of the Buddhist clergy, Pelgyi Yönten became one of the most powerful officials in Tibet. This is revealed by the rank and titles ascribed to him in the Chinese-Tibetan Treaty Inscription of 821–822 and by the prominent position his name occupies in the list of Tibetan signatories to the treaty. Eventually the anger and jealousy engendered among the lay ministers and nobility exploded in a revolt in which Pelgyi Yönten was disgraced and executed and Tri Tsukdetsen was assassinated. These events were followed by the brief reign of Langdarma, during which a vehement reaction against Buddhism set in. The assassination of this king then brought the dynasty to an end.

1.2.2. Religion in the Royal Period. Direct views of the indigenous pre-Buddhist religion of Tibet are afforded by certain Old Tibetan texts and fragments, but these sources are necessarily very difficult to interpret. Some of the old beliefs survive in the modern folk religion (called *mi chö* "the religion of men") and many others have been incorporated into the now highly systematized Bön religion. Recent research has shown that the earlier Tibetological practice of identifying the entire body of pre-Buddhist beliefs as "Bön" is an over-simplification.[16] The Old Tibetan word for the indigenous religion was *tsuklak*, but this was a broad term which also encompassed other concepts, such as the art of government, and later even non-native bodies of thought and tradition.[17]

The ancient religious tradition was animistic and populated the sky, air, and earth with supernatural beings. The vital principle or animist soul was called *la*. Human misfortunes and natural disasters were attributed to the wrath of hostile gods and spirits, and much religious activity centered around identifying and placating the offended entities. Identification could be accomplished by divination techniques such as the casting of lots (*mo*) or interpretation of omens (*té*), usually dream omens (*nyité*), or through trances wherein a shaman's soul was projected into the supernatural realms to search out the source of mischief. Propitiation was accomplished by animal and sometimes human sacrifices; and the conscientious performance of such ceremonies at regular intervals could be expected to forestall future troubles. Sacrifices were also performed to seal oaths, for the frequent oath-swearing of the early Tibetans was an essentially religious act in which the gods were invoked as witnesses.

An important aspect of the indigenous religion was the belief in the divine origin of the kings. As mentioned in section 1.2.1 their titles and epithets identified them as magically changed forms or "sons" of the *lha*, the gods on high; and in the Kongpo inscription the legendary ancestor of the royal house is portrayed as a *cha*, a deity which dwelt in one of the stories of the sky. This belief in the divine nature and origins of the royal house accounts for the need in the ancient mythology to offer rationalizations for the deaths of the kings and the presence of their corpses on earth; and it probably also underlies the great concern of the traditional religion with the elaborate obsequies surrounding royal burials.

Religious history in the royal period is in great part an account of the introduction of Buddhism into Tibet and of its contacts, interplay, and conflicts with indigenous beliefs. It is possible that the Tibetans were aware of Buddhism before the time of Songtsen Gampo,[18] but royal patronage of the new religion did not begin until the reign of this king, who, according to the Karchung Inscription (Tri Desongtsen's vow to support Buddhism), established a chapel at his capital of Rasa (later Lhasa). The same text reports further royal support in the time of Tri Düsong. Traditional Buddhist histories attached undue significance to this early royal interest in Buddhism, leading Tucci to caution:[19] "That the first Tibetan kings were not hostile to Buddhism is probable; but that they all embraced it with zeal is dubious." Tri Desongtsen's vow to support Buddhism indicates continued royal patronage during the long reign of Tri Detsuktsen, but in the later years of this king a reaction set in amongst the aristocracy, and the royal edicts preserved in Pawo Tsuklak Trengwa's *Khepé Gatön* (*Feast for Scholars*, completed 1564) reveal that the practice of Buddhism was actually proscribed by law during the minority of Tri Songdetsen.[20]

The fortunes of the foreign faith changed again with the accession of the new king, for Tri Songdetsen was a firm supporter of Buddhism, who eventually declared it the state religion of Tibet.[21] It was also during this reign that the great temple of Samyé was founded, as celebrated in the Samyé Inscription and reflected in the Samyé Bell Inscription. However, the king was not heavy-handed or militant in his furtherance of the Buddhist cause, and his caution and restraint are reflected in the wording of the Inscription at Chonggyé Bridge. In this text the king's accomplishments are praised in primarily pre-Buddhist terms, but the traditional wording of these encomia is nonetheless carefully and subtly interlarded with Buddhist ideas and terminology.

During the reign of Tri Desongtsen Buddhism became a force to be reckoned with in the political arena. As already mentioned, Tri Desongtsen's edicts for Tingngedzin indicate that the monk Nyang Tingngedzin was very close to the king and had played an active role in the consolidation of his power. The powerful monk, Drenka Pelgyi Yönten, who is mentioned so prominently in the Chinese Tibetan Treaty of 821–822, also attained eminence during this period. Tri Desongtsen's devotion to Buddhism is best illustrated in the inscription celebrating the founding of the chapel at Karchung (Tri Desongtsen's vow to support Buddhism), which portrays the king's reign as a victorious culmination of royal patronage of Buddhism in Tibet. In passing we may also mention the short Trendruk Bell Inscription which is also indicative of royal religious devotion during this period. It is clear, however, that the influence of the old religion was still present, especially among the aristocracy. One inscription, which recounts the royal origin myth and states the complaint of the noble house of Karpo against the state bureaucracy, is couched entirely in traditional language and shows no Buddhist influence at all. Also noteworthy is Tri Desongtsen's funerary inscription. As noted by Tucci[22] the language of this text is predominantly pre-Buddhist and may suggest that royal burials were still primarily the domain of the indigenous religion and its priesthood.[23]

Tri Desongtsen was followed by Tri Tsukdetsen, whose devotion to Buddhism and the Buddhist clergy is reported to have bordered on obsequiousness. His religious attitudes are reflected in the Tsurpü inscription, in which a Buddhist chapel was endowed by the grateful subject, Takzang Nyatsö, who had enjoyed the king's favor. Tri Tsukdetsen's strong reliance on clerical bureaucracy is reflected in the Chinese-Tibetan Treaty of 821–822. It would ultimately lead to the king's murder at the hands of the jealous lay nobility and to the fierce persecutions of Buddhism during the reign of Langdarma.

The rivalry between Buddhism and the indigenous religion during the royal period was in great part an outgrowth of political discord, with the kings wielding the new religion as a weapon in their struggle for dominance over the non-Buddhist nobility. But the royal house was equally adept at using the pre-Buddhist beliefs to its advantage. For example, the kings never abandoned their claims to supernatural origin, and even the pious Tri Tsukdetsen retained his divine titles and epithets (e.g., the Chinese-Tibetan Treaty of 821–822). The old practice of swearing by oath could be used to bind the royal heirs and the nobility itself to the defense of the new religion, with Buddhist deities invoked as witnesses in place of the old gods (the Samyé inscription and Tri Desongtsen's vow to support Buddhism) or even together with them (as in the royal edicts). Because the enemies of Buddhism had used divination and omen interpretation as weapons against the new religion, the kings were at pains to deny the validity of these attacks (Tri Desongtsen's vow to support Buddhism), but they were nonetheless quite capable of citing calamities and ill omens as justification for the abrogation of anti-Buddhist laws.[24] Thus it was that the lines between the indigenous and the new beliefs could be drawn more or less clearly depending on the political exigencies of the time.

1.2.3 Sino-Tibetan Relations in the Royal Period. The political consolidation of the Yarlung dynasty led to the formation of an efficiently organized state with unprecedented military power. Under Songtsen Gampo and his talented minister, Gar Tongtsen Yülzung, the full weight of Tibet's expanding influence pressed upon her neighbors and would continue to be felt by them throughout the royal period.[25] Contacts and conflicts with various contiguous peoples, known from other historical sources,[26] are mentioned briefly in the Chinese-Tibetan Treaty of 821–822 and again in fragmentary passages of another text; but it is relations with China which are by far best reflected in the inscriptional texts. This material begins in the Chinese-Tibetan Treaty of 821–822 (East Face) with the friendly relations between Songtsen Gampo and the Tang emperor, Taizong (r. 627–649), when the famous princess, Wencheng *gongzhu*, was sent to be consort of the Tibetan king. Subsequently, relations between the two states deteriorated into warfare; but the Chinese-Tibetan Treaty of 821–822 indicates that peace was reestablished in the time of Tri Detsuktsen and the Chinese emperor, Xuanzong (r. 713–756), who again sent the Tibetan ruler a consort, Jincheng *gongzhu*. However, the text then adds that amicable relations were disturbed by border incidents.

Moving on to Tri Songdetsen's time we must turn to the Lhasa Stele of Minister Takdra Lukhong. Here we learn that, using the strategy developed by Takdra Lukhong, the Tibetans took advantage of internal disorders in China to attack the Chinese-held areas of Central Asia and successfully isolate their allies, the Azha (i.e., the Tuyuhun) population around Lingzhou (the area of Lingwu in modern Ningxia Province). Subsequently an attack led by Takdra Lukhong was launched against China proper, resulting in the capture and brief occupation of the Tang capital, Chang'an, in 763.[27]

Returning to the Chinese-Tibetan Treaty of 821–822, we find that in the time of Tri Desongtsen efforts of some sort were made to establish peaceful relations with the Chinese, apparently with indifferent success. However, comparing the inscription at the tomb of Tri Desongtsen (lines 22–26, according to Richardson's restored version) it would seem that after considerable fighting some sort of accord was actually achieved before the death of this king.

By the reign of Tri Tsukdetsen both sides were exhausted from years of warfare, and their mutual need for peace led to the signing of the great treaty which forms the body of the Chinese-Tibetan Treaty of 821–822. With the assassination of Langdarma in 842 the centralized Tibetan state disintegrated into warring factions, and the country's role as an important diplomatic and military power came to an end.

NOTES

1. Géza Uray, "On the Tibetan Letters ba and wa: Contribution to the Origin and History of the Tibetan Alphabet," *Acta Orientalia Academiae Scientiarum Hungaricae* 5, no. 1 (1955): 106.

2. Jacques Bacot, F. W. Thomas, and Ch. Toussaint, *Documents de Touen-houang relatifs à l'histoire du Tibet* [*Dunhuang Documents Concerning the History of Tibet*] (Paris: P. Geuthner, 1940–6), 13, 31.

3. The reform is dated to the period 826–827 by Bufan Huang, "'Shangshu' sipian gu Zangwen yiwen de chubu yanjiu" [Preliminary Study of the Translation of Classical Tibetan in Four Articles of the *Shangshu*], *Yuyan yanjiu* 1 (1981): 203–232 n. 3; Y. Wang, *Tufan jinshilu* [*Records of Tibetan Epigraphs*] (Beijing: Wenwu chubanshe, 1982), 9, 13 n. 23. Cf. also Bingfen Luo and Shixing An, "Jiantan lishi shang Zangwen zhengzi fa de xiuding" [Preliminary Study of Revisions of the Tibetan Language Spelling Rules in History], *Minzu yuwen* (Beijing: Zhongguo shehui kexue chubanshe) 2 (1982): 27–35.

4. Roy A. Miller, "Review of: A. Róna-Tas, *Tibeto-Mongolica: The Tibetan Loanwords of Monguor and the Development of the Archaic Tibetan Dialects*," *Language* 44, no. 1 (1968): 147 n. 1.

5. Giuseppe Tucci, "The Sacral Character of the Kings of Ancient Tibet," *East and West* 6 (1955/56): 197; Helmut Hoffmann, *Tibet: A Handbook* (Bloomington, Ill.: Research Institute for Inner Asian Studies, 1976), 197; Hugh E. Richardson, "Ministers of the Tibetan Kingdom," *The Tibet Journal* 2, no. 1 (1977): passim.

6. Tucci, "The Sacral Character of the Kings of Ancient Tibet," 202.

7. Editor's note: The following passage is extracted from a later note referred to here by the authors (p. 82 in the original text): Fang-kuei Li: *Trülgyi lha* "God Incarnate" is a regular epithet of the Tibetan kings and apparently refers to the tradition that the first Tibetan king had been a god in heaven transformed into a ruler of men. The common phrase used with minor variations to denote this tradition is, as in the east face of the pillar I, "he came from among the gods to become the ruler of men." The epithet corresponds in the Chinese version [of the Sino-Tibetan Treaty of 821–822] to the words *sheng* [sage] and *shen* [spirit], which are also common epithets of the Tang emperors. . . . W. South Coblin: For *trülgyi lha* and *lha trül* I prefer the translation "god of supernatural qualities" and shall use this or variations on it when these

terms recur in Tri Desongtsen's edicts for Tingngedzin and Tri Desongtsen's vow to support Buddhism.

8. See, for example, Bacot et al., *Dunhuang Documents Concerning the History of Tibet*, 110, 146–147.

9. Hoffmann; *Tibet*, 42–43.

10. See also Bacot et al., *Dunhuang Documents Concerning the History of Tibet*, 102, 132. For a special study of this period, see Christopher Beckwith, "The Revolt of 755 in Tibet," in *Contributions on Tibetan Language, History and Culture, Wiener Studien zur Tibetologie und Buddhismuskunde* 10, vol. 1, ed. Ernst Steinkellner and Helmut Tauscher (Wien: Arbeitskreis für Tibetische und Buddhistische Studien, Universität Wien, 1983), 1–16.

11. Takdra Lukhong's career has been discussed in Fang-kuei Li, "Notes on Stag sgra Klu khong," in *Contributions on Tibetan Language, History and Culture, Wiener Studien zur Tibetologie und Buddhismuskunde* 10, vol. 1, ed. Ernst Steinkellner and Helmut Tauscher (Wien: Arbeitskreis für Tibetische und Buddhistische Studien, Universität Wien, 1983).

12. Erik Haarh, "The Identity of Tsu-chih-chien, the Tibetan 'King' Who Died in 804 A.D.," *Acta Orientalia* 25 (1960): 122–125; Hoffmann, *Tibet*, 45.

13. The complex events of this time are reviewed in detail in Haarh, "The Identity of Tsu-chih-chien." See also Giuseppe Tucci, *The Tombs of the Tibetan Kings* (Roma: Instituto italiano per il Medio ed Estremo Oriente, 1950), 19–24; Hugh Richardson, *Ancient Historical Edicts at Lhasa and the Mu tsung/Khri gtsug lde brtsan Treaty of* A.D. 821–822 (London: Royal Asiatic Society of Great Britain and Ireland, 1952), I:138–149.

14. Tucci, "The Sacral Character of the Kings of Ancient Tibet," 197.

15. Richardson, *Ancient Historical Edicts at Lhasa*, 136–137; Hugh Richardson and David Snellgrove, *A Cultural History of Tibet* (New York: Praeger, 1968), 94.

16. R. A. Stein, *La civilisation tibétaine* (réédition revue et augmentée) (Paris: l'Asiathèque, 1981), 144; Géza Uray, "The Old Tibetan Sources of the History of Central Asia up to 751 A.D.: A Survey," in *Prolegomena to the Sources on the History of Pre-Islamic Central Asia*, ed. J. Harmatta (Budapest: Akadémiai Kiadó, 1979), 298, especially n. 64 for detailed references to earlier studies.

17. Stein, *La civilisation tibétaine*, 169, especially nn. 206 and 207 for further references.

18. Richardson and Snellgrove, *A Cultural History of Tibet*, 74; Hoffmann, *Tibet*, 126.

19. Tucci, "The Sacral Character of the Kings of Ancient Tibet," 197.

20. Tucci, *The Tombs of the Tibetan Kings*, 47, 52, 98, 101; Hugh Richardson, *Tibet and Her Neighbours: A Presentation of the Historic Facts of Tibet's Relations with Neighbouring States* (London: Tibetan Society of the United Kingdom, 1960).

21. Tucci, *The Tombs of the Tibetan Kings*, 49–50, 100; Hugh Richardson, "The First Tibetan Chos 'byung," *The Tibetan Journal* 5, no. 3 (1980): 68, 71–72.

22. Tucci, *The Tombs of the Tibetan Kings*, 41.

23. It was formerly believed that the inscription at the tomb of Tri Desongtsen contained no references to Buddhism at all; but the recent discovery of a previously unknown portion of the inscription shows this assumption to be false.

24. E.g., in the Second Edict of Tri Songdetsen; see Tucci, *The Tombs of the Tibetan Kings*, 47–48, 98 and Richardson, "The First Tibetan Chos 'byung," 67, 70.

25. For a study of Mgar and his clan, see Li Fang-kuei, "Tufan da xiang Lu Dongzan kao" [On the Tibetan Minister Lù Dongzan], *Papers on the International Conference on Sinology* (Taipei: n.p., 1981), 369–378.

26. For a thorough listing and discussion of these sources, see Uray, "Tibetan Sources of the History of Central Asia up to 751 A.D.," and Christopher Beckwith, "The Introduction of Greek Medicine Into Tibet in the Seventh and Eighth Centuries," *Journal of the American Oriental Society* 99, no. 2 (1979): 297–313.

27. For a discussion of these events, see Fang-kuei Li, "Ma Zhongying kao" [On Ma Zhongying], *Guoli Taiwan daxue wenshizhe xuebao* (Taibei: Guo li Taiwan daxue chuban weiyuanhui) 7 (1956): 1–8; and Li, "Notes on Stag sgra Klu khong."

Chapter 7

THE TIBETANS IN THE ORDOS AND NORTH CHINA

CONSIDERATIONS ON THE ROLE OF
THE TIBETAN EMPIRE IN WORLD HISTORY

Christopher I. Beckwith

When the Tibetan Empire reached deep into Inner Asia at the height of its expansion, what did it encounter? What effects did this encounter have upon the political and cultural history of Asia? Along with the concluding chapter to the seminal work *The Tibetan Empire in Central Asia*, the following article marks a rare attempt to put Tibetan history into a global perspective. Christopher Beckwith is ideally positioned to undertake this, being well-versed in Tibetan, Chinese, Arabic, and Turkic sources. He is concerned especially with a key geographic location in what is now Inner Mongolia: the southern part of the great bend of the Yellow River known as the Ordos. He argues here that the century-long occupation of this region by Tibetans and their allies, as well as their later enduring presence, formed a key bulwark against the spread of Western religions—Manicheanism, Nestorian Christianity, and Islam—into China. This connection helped ensure that the classical Tibetan language and Tibetan Buddhism came to dominate High Asia, stretching eventually from northern Xinjiang to Inner Mongolia, and from the Himalayas to Lake Baikal.

Current opinion among most orientalists with regard to the Tibetan Empire is dominated by the notion that while Tibetan culture was strongly influenced by neighboring civilizations—Indian, Chinese, Iranian, and Central Asian—the Tibetan expansion did not have any lasting effect upon the history of Asia. Thus the idea that Tibetan history is irrelevant for world history—an idea with different origins, to be sure—continues to be reinforced, even by Tibetologists. On the other hand, most historians of Tibet, Mongolia, and the Manchus, as well as a few Sinologists, agree that a thin veneer of later Tibetan Buddhist culture came to be spread across northeastern Eurasia beginning in the Mongol Empire period, and expanded again in the Manchu period. The present paper is an attempt to revise the above conclusions in the light of recent research.

After the outbreak of the An Lushan Rebellion in Tang China in 755 A.D., the Tibetans took advantage of the resulting Chinese military weakness to recapture a vast stretch of Tibetan territory that had been occupied by the Tang during the preceding two or three decades.[1] They did not stop at their old borders, however, but—perhaps seeking revenge—pressed on deeper into China, where they captured the capital, Chang'an, in December of 763.[2] It is not often appreciated that the eastern border of the Tibetan Empire then stayed fixed for a century at a point only a short distance to the west of the Chinese capital. This was the cause of constant worry to the Tang, since the Tibetans could and often did threaten the capital more or less at will. More important than this, however, is the fact that at the same time Tibet also controlled a vast territory further to the north and northwest of Chang'an, the borderlands between the northern steppes and the traditional Chinese realm south of the Great Wall. This Tibetan military domination of the southern Ordos and neighboring regions of northwest China during the late eighth and early ninth centuries seems to have had a long-lasting effect on the history of East Asia.

The Tibetan capture of Liangzhou in 764,[3] and the consequent Tang loss of Hexi *dao* to Tibet meant that the direct routes from China to Central Asia (and, thus, the Western world) were all in Tibetan hands until nearly the end of the Tang dynasty. Japanese historians have long ago noted the significance of this fact. In an article published in 1956, K. Nagasawa argues that this event was a major turning-point for the history of East-West trade because, he says, the Tibetans held onto Liangzhou long after the rest of their Empire had broken up, and furthermore the Tanguts inherited the same area of control from the Tibetans, and kept it even longer.[4] Tibetan control of the area meant—according to Nagasawa—that the bulk of Tang China's silk exports had to go west via the so-called "Uighur route": from North China via the Ordos or Taiyuan (in Hedong, present-day Shanxi) to Zhong Shouxiang cheng (the "Middle City for Receiving Submission"), which was located just north of the great bend of the Yellow River. From there the route passed northward to the Uighur capital on the Orkhon, and thence westward to the Arab caliphate.[5] Although Nagasawa's interpretation is basically correct, the story is somewhat more complicated, and his conclusions should be modified. In addition, while the debilitating effect on Tibet of the protracted warfare with the Uighurs and Chinese has been duly noted by nearly all writers on the subject, the effect of the same warfare on the Uighurs has received little attention. The Tibetan Empire's movement northward from Hexi into territory once under the influence of (or actually controlled by) the Turks—the area from Hami to the Ordos—on the one hand had a great impact on the fate of the Uighur Empire, and on the other helped lay the foundations for the Tangut Empire. The eventual results of these changes were indeed of fundamental importance for later East Asian history.

The Tibetan expansion into the Ordos region seems originally to have been merely an extension of campaigns into the area about Chang'an and into Gansu, along the Silk Road into Central Asia.[6] Through constant use of the Yellow River routes, the Tibetans ended up in an excellent position to raid the prefectures along the Great Wall, both north and south of it. They did so regularly: south from 763 on,[7] and north from 778 onward.[8] Most of the raids included large contingents of Tanguts, Tuyuhun, and others along with the Tibetans.[9] Although the Chinese had settled some Tanguts and Tuyuhun in Guannei [inside the passes] and across the Wall in the southern Ordos—in order to keep them away from their former Tibetan overlords[10]—the Tibetan army apparently brought new contingents of these peoples with them from northeastern Tibet. After the Chinese refused to honor the Tang's part of the bilateral agreement of 783–784 concerning payment to Tibet for military assistance against the rebel Zhuci and his Uighur allies (which Tibetan assistance was decisive in the rebels' defeat),[11] the Tibetan army of Zhang Gyeltsen again entered to attack the prefectures to the near northwest of the capital district.[12] When this move was blunted, he turned northward to begin a campaign of conquest in the southern Ordos. On or about December 10, 786, Yanzhou was taken and garrisoned;[13] by December 26 of the same year, Xiazhou, Linzhou, and Yinzhou were likewise taken.[14] The Tang was duly alarmed; when Zhang Gyeltsen suggested a peace treaty, the Chinese snapped at the chance. By the summer of 787, everything was set for a treaty to be signed at Pingliang. But the Tibetans then turned the tables on the Chinese on July 8, 787, by capturing and carrying off a great number of the Tang generals and other attendants sent to the intended treaty-signing ceremonies.[15] Immediately afterward, his goal largely accomplished, Zhang Gyeltsen ordered the Ordos fortresses destroyed and the garrisons withdrawn.[16] So ended the first period of Tibetan forays into the Ordos proper.

The next stage followed almost without a pause. During the Tibetan-Uighur war over Tang-held Beshbalïq (Beiting, near present-day Urumchi) the Uighurs attacked and defeated the Tibetans at Lingzhou (present-day Ningxia).[17] After the Uighurs captured (not, as often stated, "recaptured") Beshbalïq from Tibet in 792, they pressed the Tibetans southwards, capturing from them Qocho (Gaocheng or Xizhou, in the Turfan Depression) in the same year.[18] The Tibetans, who apparently still held Hami (Yizhou), counterattacked—recapturing Liangzhou and eventually pushing the Uighurs back to Qocho in the West. Tibet also sent armies again into the Ordos region. Although in 808 the Uighurs were able to take Liangzhou and possibly hold it for a short time,[19] the Tibetans responded in the following year by sending 50,000 cavalry to attack an Uighur embassy on its return home from China, somewhere beyond Piti Spring (located north of Xi Shouxiang cheng, the "Western City for Receiving Submission").[20] Tibetan pressure on the Uighurs' most critical lifeline was such that in 816 a Tibetan raid is said to have reached a point only two days' journey from the Uighur capital, Ordubalïq (now known as Karabalgasun).[21] Tibet kept up the pressure, to the point where the Uighurs felt the need to boast to the Chinese in 821 that not only would they be able to protect the Taihe Princess on her way to the Uighur capital in Mongolia, but they would even send out 10,000 cavalry via Beshbalïq and 10,000 via Anxi, to push the Tibetans back.[22] In fact, however, the Uighurs sent at most 3,000 men to the Chinese border near Fengzhou, and there is no record of any actual Uighur move against the Tibetans at this time. Moreover, it was undoubtedly only due to the conclusion of the Sino-Tibetan peace treaty of 821–822, and the Sino-Uighur and Tibetan-Uighur accords of the same year, that the Tibetans did not continue their raids in the Ordos region.[23] It is clear from these events that Tibetan influence then extended across the southern Ordos and the neighboring area south of the Great Wall, southwestward throughout the whole of Gansu and Hexi, and westward as far as Hami and Qocho. With the conclusion of the new treaty, the Tibetan military presence was theoretically restricted to the parts of that territory which were under actual Tibetan administration in 821. Finally, between 849 and 863 most of the Tibetan-ruled areas outside present-day ethnic Tibet were lost.[24]

The most important immediate effect of the nearly century-long Tibetan presence in the Ordos and North China was the movement of a great number of people from areas further west or south into the borderlands of the northern steppe. Some of these people had fled from Tibetan control and had been moved by the Tang in order to keep them away from Tibet. Such were most of the Tuyuhun and Tanguts, moved in the seventh century,[25] and the Shatuo Turks, moved in the early ninth century.[26] The Shatuo and Tuyuhun were soon moved across the Yellow River to the east into what is now Shanxi and Hebei,[27] where they were eventually to become power brokers in Chinese dynastic politics, to help set geopolitical patterns followed by a long succession of northern Chinese dynasties. The Tanguts, however, unlike the Tuyuhun and (ultimately) the Shatuo, seem normally to have retained a close working relationship with the Tibetan Empire during its period of domination over them, and many Tanguts, remnants of the Tibetan armies, were apparently more recent arrivals from their homeland in the northeastern marches of Tibet. Together with some Tibetans who stayed behind, they continued to be active as rebels, bandits, or raiders of one kind or another, long after the conclusion of the international peace of 821–822 and the cessation of imperial Tibetan military activities in the area. The Tanguts' power grew proportionately as that of the Tang declined, so that by the end of the latter dynasty they were for all practical purposes independent. The Tangut Empire established in the eleventh century—with a Chinese-style dynasty later known as Xixia—was territorially more or less a reincarnation of the former Tibetan zone of influence there. The Tangut Empire lasted until its conquest by the Mongols in the early thirteenth century.

The presence of the Tibetan Empire (and later the Tangut Empire) in the lands bordering northwestern China had several far-reaching consequences. One of these was the redirection of international trade: caravans to or from China were forced either to go through Tibetan territory or to go around by a very circuitous route through Uighur Mongolia, and so westward.[28] (Seaborne commerce was not affected at all, except to be encouraged.) Another, perhaps more dramatic, effect of Tibet's movement northward was its impact on the Uighur Empire. Tibet's military presence in Hexi and the neighboring regions helped to separate Mongolia from Zungharia; thus, with simultaneous Tibetan pressure on both the southern Mongolian steppe and the more fertile and prosperous western part of their empire, the Uighurs ended up divided, apparently keeping the bulk of their forces in the West. The Tibetan raids into Mongolia were thus designed to divide, or at any rate had the effect of dividing, the Uighur Empire into two separate halves. The eastern part, with the capital, Ordubalïq, was eventually weakened to the extent that it was easily crushed by the Kirghiz in 840.[29] The destruction of Uighur rule in Mongolia meant the nearly total elimination of Western religious pressure, in the form of Manicheism, on Eastern Eurasia. The remaining followers of Manicheanism, and the numerically weak Nestorian adherents, ultimately disappeared in the face of another world religion, South Asian in origin, namely Tibetan Buddhism.

Of all the effects of the Tibetan expansion, the most long-lasting was not primarily political, but rather cultural in nature. The late Tibetan Empire, its successor states in Liangzhou and Siling (Xining), and finally the Tangut Empire, were all strongly Buddhist states, powerful enough to resist the encroachment of Islam. They allowed Buddhist clerics to pass through and cross-fertilize, for example between Tibet and the Buddhist centers on Wutai shan.[30] Tibetan Buddhist activity in the colonial areas just outside Amdo continued uninterrupted after the breakup of the empire. There was quite a lot of Tibetan Buddhist activity in Shazhou (Dunhuang) even after the Chinese recapture of the city in 848;[31] Tibetan monks were to be found in the armies of the two feuding ministers Lön Gungzher and Zhang Bibi, at the same time.[32] In addition, it is well known that the refugee monks from Central Tibet, including eventually Lhalung Pelgyi Dorjé, the assassin of Langdarma, settled in Amdo after attempting to preach to the Uighurs (presumably those in Ganzhou); this presupposes no open hostility to Buddhism in the area. The Tibetan successor-states in Liangzhou and neighboring areas were pro-Buddhist. When the Tanguts finally occupied this region they simply continued to support an already long-established Buddhist church. Furthermore, Tibetan monks were quite active at the court of the Song dynasty in China, where they assisted in the translation of several important Buddhist texts into Chinese. When the Mongols finally supplanted the Tanguts, they did not disturb the existing Buddhist establishment; on the contrary, they supported it as strongly as their predecessors had. A crucial fact of Tibetan-Mongol relations, one generally overlooked, is that Qubilai, the Mongol Great Khan and founder of the Yuan dynasty in China, was raised by a Tangut nursemaid[33] and grew up in Tangut at the court of his influential cousin Köden. There he met Pakpa Lama, and the Tibetan-Mongol cultural alliance was soon firmly in place. It is clear that the Mongol ruling class (at least) wholeheartedly accepted Tibetan Buddhism by the end of the thirteenth century.[34]

Tibetan culture thus was enabled to expand uninterruptedly northeastwards during the Tangut period and on through the Mongol and Manchu periods, with the eventual result that the dominant high culture of northeastern Eurasia, including (besides Tibet, Mongolia, Manchuria and parts of Siberia, and the southeasternmost corner of Europe) also parts of Northwest China (mainly in Gansu) was Tibetan Buddhist culture, not Chinese culture. It is no accident that foreign accounts of eastern Eurasia written in the nineteenth century liked to refer to Tibetan as the "Latin" of what they called "High Asia"—meaning the vast area dominated by Tibetan Buddhist culture. Chinese and its attendant literary culture was, like Hindustani in India, the province of native scholars, with very few exceptions, whereas Tibetan was the common language of scholars from Tibet, Mongolia, Siberia, Manchuria, and China. One could hardly imagine this happening if the late Tibetan Empire, its successor states, and then the Tangut Empire—the latter a multinational state including Tibetans as one of its most important components—had not maintained a strong Buddhist bulwark against the powerful forces of Islamic expansion that were then eliminating Buddhism from East Turkistan.

In conclusion, the Tibetan Empire's expansion into the Ordos and northwestern Chinese borderlands was merely the beginning of a much greater Tibetan Buddhist cultural empire that continued to spread from Tibet, eventually to dominate nearly the whole of northeastern Asia well into the twentieth century.

NOTES

1. The details of this struggle, and of the topic of the present paper, are properly the subject of a thorough book-length monograph. Here, primary-source reference will be made only to Sima Guang, Zi zhi tong jian [Comprehensive Mirror to Aid in Governance], 10 vols. (Beijing: Zhonghua shuju, 1956; reprinted: Taipei, 1979): the single most important source for Tang-Inner Asian history, though the least utilized. The first Tang armies in Tibet's northeast fell in the twelfth month of 756; see Sima, Comprehensive Mirror to Aid in Governance, 219:7011. For citations of other sources, and a more detailed historical narrative (which omits most of the material on the present subject) see my book, The Tibetan Empire in Central Asia: A History of the Struggle for Great Power Among Tibetans, Turks, Arabs, and Chinese During the Early Middle Ages (Princeton: Princeton University Press, 1993).

2. This followed the Tibetan capture of the whole of Hexi and Longyou in the summer of that year (Sima, Comprehensive Mirror to Aid in Governance, 223:7146–

7147) and the surrender of a Chinese official who helped lead the Tibetan army of over 200,000 soldiers (including Tuyuhun, Tanguts, and others) to the capital (Sima, *Comprehensive Mirror to Aid in Governance*, 223:7150–7157).

3. Li Jifu, *Yuanhe jun xian tu zhi* [*Gazetteers of the Tang Dynasty*] (Taipei, 1973), 40:2v, 557; Liu Xu, *Jiu Tang shu* [*Old Tang Annals*], 16 vols. (Beijing: Zhonghua shuju: Xinhua shudian Shanghai faxing suo faxing, 1975), 196a:5239; Ouyang Xiu and Song Qi, *Xin Tang shu* [*New Tang Annals*], 20 vols. (Beijing: Zhonghua shu ju, 1975), 216a:6088.

4. See Kazutoshi Nagasawa, "Toban no Kasei shinshutsu to Tō-Zai Kōtsū" [Tibet's Domination in Hexi and the Communication Between the West and the East], *Shikan* 46 (1956): 71–81. A number of articles in Japanese would appear (from the titles given in the bibliographies I have consulted) to be directly relevant to this question, as well as to the other problems I treat in this article. However, they have remained inaccessible to me.

5. Nagasawa, "Tibet's Domination in Hexi," 73.

6. In fact, it is likely that the Tanguts—intentionally or otherwise—prepared the way for the Tibetan advance by their raids, mainly in 760 and 761, into the very areas that the Tibetans occupied. See Sima, *Comprehensive Mirror to Aid in Governance*, 220:7060, 7066; 221:7093, 7096, 7097, 7100; 222:7105, 7113, 7114, 7119, 7122, and 7126.

7. Ouyang and Song, *New Tang Annals*, 223:7146–7147.

8. Ouyang and Song, *New Tang Annals*: 225:7251.

9. The Chinese sources unfortunately only rarely mention the other participants explicitly; see Sima, *Comprehensive Mirror to Aid in Governance*, 223:7150; 232:7496, 7501; 241:7774–7775, 7783–7785.

10. This is mentioned in, among other places, the gloss to Sima, *Comprehensive Mirror to Aid in Governance*, 220:7060.

11. Ouyang and Song, *New Tang Annals*, 231–7442; for details, see the discussion in Beckwith, *The Tibetan Empire in Central Asia*. It is notable that the Uighurs were actually at war with China, or there were very hostile relations between the two nations, quite often during the period of the Uighur Empire's existence, specifically, ca. 745–756, 764–765, 775–787; the Uighurs raided or threatened the border in 796, 813, 822, and 840. It was, nevertheless, deliberate Tang policy to cultivate the Uighurs, probably because the Turks, unlike the Tibetan Empire, were no real danger to a united China; they were never able to penetrate very far into the country, nor hold any territory; moreover, they were separated from China by the Gobi.

12. Ouyang and Song, *New Tang Annals*, 232:7470.

13. Ouyang and Song, *New Tang Annals*, 232:7474.

14. Ouyang and Song, *New Tang Annals*, 232:7475.

15. Ouyang and Song, *New Tang Annals*, 232:7486–7487.

16. Ouyang and Song, *New Tang Annals*, 232:7889.

17. Ouyang and Song, *New Tang Annals*, 233:7524.

18. See now the article by Tsuguhito Takeuchi, "The Tibetans and Uighurs in Pei-t'ing, An-hsi (Kucha), and Hsi-zhou (790–860 A.D.)," *Kinki Daigaku kyōyōbu kenkyū kiyō* 17, no. 3 (1986): 51–68.

19. See Beckwith, *The Tibetan Empire in Central Asia*, chapter 6, for further details.

20. Sima, *Comprehensive Mirror to Aid in Governance*, 238:7660, 7666.

21. Liu, *Old Tang Annals*, 195b:5265. Cf. Colin Mackerras, *The Uighur Empire According to the Tang Dynastic Histories: A Study in Sino-Uighur Relations, 744–840* (Columbia: University of South Carolina Press, 1973), 172 n. 250.

22. See the discussion in Beckwith, *The Tibetan Empire in Central Asia*, chapter six.

23. Beckwith, *The Tibetan Empire in Central Asia*.

24. Beckwith, *The Tibetan Empire in Central Asia*.

25. Sima, *Comprehensive Mirror to Aid in Governance*, 220:7060, gloss.

26. Sima, *Comprehensive Mirror to Aid in Governance*, 237:7651–7652.

27. Sima, *Comprehensive Mirror to Aid in Governance*, 237:7661.

28. On international trade during this later period, see the valuable article by Yoshinobu Shiba, "Sung Foreign Trade: Its Scope and Organization," in *China Among Equals: The Middle Kingdom and Its Neighbors, 10th–14th Centuries*, ed. Morris Rossabi (Berkeley: University of California Press, 1983), 89–115. It is important to realize that the fragmented polities of the area encouraged international trade, and made it possible by providing numerous alternative routes. It is notable that one important route for East-West trade passed through the Qingtang kingdom in northeastern Tibet. See Shiba, "Sung Foreign Trade," 100–102.

29. Internecine conflict within the Uighur Empire was primarily responsible for the collapse. Perhaps the Kirghiz, former allies of Tibet, merely succeeded in taking advantage of a situation created by the Tibetan strategists, who were finally unable to do the job themselves. For subsequent events, particularly the fate of the Uighurs who fled to China, see the unpublished dissertation of Michael Drompp, "The Writings of Li Te-yü as Sources for the History of T'ang-Inner Asian Relations," Ph.D. diss., Indiana University, 1986.

30. Already in the early eighth century under Mé Aktsom Tibetan Buddhists are said to have established a connection with the Buddhist centers on Wutai shan (Tib. *Ri wo rtse lnga*), a mountain sacred to Mañjuśrī. According to an account in the Bazhé (*Sba bzhed*) connected to the material on the building of Samyé—and therefore, it would seem, basically reliable—Ba (Sba) Sangshi visited Wutai shan during a trip to China, and when he returned built a small temple, called Nang Lhakhang, "Inner Temple," in the imperial palace precinct at Drakmar. The temple was built "in the shape of Wutai shan." See C. Beckwith, "The Revolt of 755 in Tibet," *Wiener Studien zur Tibetologie und Buddhismuskunde* [*Contributions on Tibetan Language, History, and Culture*] 10, vol. 1, ed. Ernst Steinkellner and Helmut Tauscher (Wien: Arbeitskreis für Tibetische und Buddhistische Studien, Universität Wien, 1983), 13. For further discussion of Sangshi and his journey, see Jeffrey Broughton, "Early Chan Schools in Tibet," in *Studies in Ch'an and Hua-yen*, ed. Robert M. Gimello and Peter N. Gregory (Honolulu: University of Hawai'i Press, 1983), 1–68, especially 5–7 and notes. In 824, during the reign of Relpachen, as is well known, Tibet formally requested the Tang government for a map of the holy mountain; the request was granted. See Paul

Demiéville, *Le concile de Lhasa* [*The Council of Lhasa*] (Paris: Institut Hautes Etudes Chinoises, 1952), 188 n.1.

31. See Géza Uray, "L'emploi du tibétain dans les chancelleries des états du Kansou et de Khotan postérieur a la domination tibétaine" [The Use of Tibetan in the Chancelleries of the States of Gansu and Khotan After Tibetan Domination], *Journal Asiatique* 269 (1981): 81–90; and the paper on Tibetan letters from Dunhuang by Takeuchi, forthcoming in the proceedings of the Csoma de Kôrös Symposium held at Visegrád in 1984.

32. See Beckwith, *The Tibetan Empire in Central Asia*, for details and references.

33. John Andrew Boyle, *The Successors of Genghis Khan* (New York: Columbia University Press, 1971), 241.

34. See C. Beckwith, "Tibetan Science at the Court of the Great Khans," *Journal of the Tibet Society* 7 (1987): 5–11. It should not be overlooked that Tibetan Buddhism had two good chances to be established in the West as well, first through the strong patronage of the Mongol Ilkhans in Persia, and later through the patronage of the Zunghars, whose Kalmyk descendants living on the European shores of the Caspian Sea still follow Tibetan Buddhism. The History of Ilkhanid-Tibetan relations—especially the question of the Tibetan *bakhshis* at the Ilkhanid court, and their influence on non-Buddhist religious beliefs and practices—is a potential goldmine. Besides Tibetan material, there is much in Islamic sources, apparently some in Greek, and probably some in various other languages, waiting to be explored.

PART III

Tibetan Revivals (Tenth to Twelfth Centuries)

Chapter 8

THE TIBETAN TRIBES OF HEXI AND BUDDHISM
DURING THE NORTHERN SONG PERIOD

Tsutomu Iwasaki

Tsutomu Iwasaki makes clear in this essay the thoroughgoing integration of religion and politics after the demise of the Tibetan empire, and shifts the focus from Central to northeastern Tibet. He demonstrates that by the early eleventh century Tibetan Buddhist monks had come to be potent political leaders in a system known as hierocracy: government by the clergy. This part of Tibet, now called Amdo, was known in Chinese as Hexi, meaning "west of the (Yellow) River," and had three main Tibetan centers, one in Xiliangfu (present-day Wuwei, in Gansu province), another in the Tsongkha region (around Xining, Qinghai province), and the third south of Lanzhou, Gansu. He describes the first important postimperial Tibetan polity in eastern Tibet after the fall of the empire: the Tsongkha kingdom, founded in the name of Gusiluo (Tib. *Gyelsé*, or prince), a scion of the Tibetan (Ch. Tufan) imperial rulers. He describes the earliest instances of mass monasticism, of monasteries serving as important centers of economic activity, and of the merging of political and religious power in the hands of monastic figures, all trends that were to become central to the rest of Tibetan history. The Tibetan regimes of this area were eventually caught between the expansion of the Chinese Song dynasty and the rise of the Tangut Minyak (Ch. Xixia) Kingdom. If we speak of a renaissance of Tibetan Buddhist culture in Central Tibet brought about by the reintroduction of Buddhist monasticism, we cannot ignore the role of the Amdo region in keeping Tibetan Buddhist culture alive after the collapse of the empire. Iwasaki's essay emphasizes the continuities and enduring success of Buddhist monastics in the east.

I. INTRODUCTION

The birthplace of Tsongkhapa (1357–1419), the great reformer of Tibetan Buddhism, was the Tsongkha region, and his name means "man of Tsongkha." Ta'ersi [Kumbum], the largest monastery in Qinghai province, is held to have been built on the site of his birthplace.[1] Even in the twentieth century this region continues to flourish as an important center of Tibetan Buddhism, and if we go back in history, we find that Buddhism was thriving already a long time prior to the birth of Tsongkhapa. It was the Tibetan tribes of Hexi, who were active in this region during the Northern Song period, that laid the foundations of the subsequent Buddhist faith here, and in the *Song shi* [*History of the Song Dynasty*] their religion is described succinctly as "revering Buddhism."[2] In the following I would like to discuss the relationship between the Hexi Tibetans and Buddhism.

II. THE XILIANGFU ADMINISTRATION AND BUDDHISM

The main center of the Hexi Tibetans during the Five Dynasties period and the early Song was Xiliangfu (Liangzhou). That the inhabitants of this region were devout Buddhists is evident from the following passage of indeterminate date from the *Song shi* "Tufan zhuan" [*History of the Song Dynasty*, "Account of Tufan (Tibet)]:"

> The prefect (*zhou shuai*) of Xiliangfu lost the support of the people, who held a meeting in protest. The prefect hastily climbed a wooden seven-storied pagoda inside the town and deceitfully shouted to them, "If you attack me, I will set fire to the pagoda!" The people, who set great value on the pagoda, made a promise with the prefect and forgave him.

We know that in the year 998 Xiliangfu had a population of more than 128,000, of whom the greater part were of Tibetan stock,[3] and so the above incident may be said to indicate that Buddhism had become firmly rooted in Tibetan society.

According to the "Tufan zhuan," Zhebu Jiashi, the first person to establish an administration controlled by Tibetans, provided protection for a Chinese monk on his way to India in search of Buddhist scriptures, and his second successor Zhebu Youlongbo asked the Song for gold and five-colored decorations for use in the construction of a pagoda. It is not clear in which monastery this pagoda was to be erected, but in view of the fact that Panluozhi, who took over political power from the Zhebu clan, received gold foil and other materials from the Song in order to repair the two monasteries Hongyuansi and Dayunsi in 1004,[4] it is to be surmised that the pagoda that Youlongbo intended building was connected with the repairs on one of these two monasteries, probably the former. This is because in the same year Panluozhi made a further request of the Song for the dispatch of artisans and gifts of gold, jasper and silk for making repairs on Hongyuansi.[5] These repairs on Hongyuansi were not completed during Panluozhi's lifetime and were continued by his younger brother Siduodu.[6] Thus, judging from the fact that two successive rulers of Xiliangfu devoted considerable efforts to effecting repairs on Hongyuansi, we are no doubt justified in assuming that the pagoda that Youlongbo intended erecting was also connected with this monastery. It was probably a renowned monastery dating from prior to the Tang and the main center of Buddhism in Xiliangfu. Making repairs on this monastery therefore afforded the holders of political power in Xiliangfu a chance of representing themselves to the general populace as patrons of Buddhism and was utilized as an opportunity to ensure the stability of their rule. Dayunsi, the other monastery for the repairs of which Panluozhi also asked the assistance of the Song, is an old monastery still extant today, and it is a well-known fact that the famous Ganyingda stele of Xixia stood in its precincts.[7]

Let us now consider the position of Buddhism under the Xiliangfu administration. During the rule of the Zhebu clan and Panluozhi there were no noteworthy activities on the part of the Buddhist clergy. But with the assumption of power by Siduodu the activities of monks suddenly came to the fore. According to Xu's Song huiyao jigao [Draft Compendium of Institutions During the Song], "Xiliangfu" section, three monks dispatched by Siduodu every three years starting in 1008 were given purple robes by the Song. But this was not so much a manifestation of Siduodu's pro-Buddhist policies as testimony to the fact that these monks were closely involved in the inner workings of the administration, for during the Song period purple robes (ziyi) and the title of master (shihao) were granted upon request to non-Chinese, especially for pacificatory purposes, in accordance with the relationship obtaining between a particular regime and the Song, and it was not necessary for the monk in question to be a monk of any note. It is also known that during the time of Siduodu there were already tribes (fan bu) ruled by monks. Evidence of this may be seen in the name "Lanbuchi" appearing in the following passage from Xu's Draft Compendium of Institutions During the Song, "Xiliangfu" section:

> In the 5th month of the 4th year [of the Jingde era] Siduodu dispatched soldiers, and eighteen leaders (shouling) of the Liugu tribes, including Lanbuchi, brought tributes. They were grateful for the hospitable treatment given them by the Song and expressed their thanks.

As will be discussed in greater detail below, "Lanbuchi" represents a transliteration of rinpoché, the Tibetan term for a reverend lama. The tribe representative of the eighteen Liugu tribes, which constituted the mainstay of the Xiliangfu administration at the time, was, namely, ruled by a monk. But this does not mean that an ordinary monk had risen to a position where he was able to assume political power; it probably indicates rather that a tribal chieftain (*fanqiu*) or his family had taken advantage of the popularity of Buddhism to win over the monasteries and assume their spiritual authority. Thus during the rule of Siduodu there was a marked rise in the influence exerted by Buddhism both in the center of the government and among the tribes, and this formed the prototype of the Tibetan administration of the next generation.

III. THE APPEARANCE OF GUSILUO AND THE RISE OF TIBETAN MONKS

The area inhabited by the Hexi Tibetans outside of Xiliangfu may be divided into two main regions. One is the region extending from the valley of the Huangshui in the upper reaches of the Yellow River to the valley of the Taohe and corresponding to the former home of the Tuyuhun, while the other is the region around the Liupan Mountains on the northern side of the upper and middle reaches of the Weishui, the largest tributary of the Yellow River. During the period of rule by Tufan [the Tibetan empire] the Huangshui Valley was politically the most important area. This region was known as Tsongkha already during the Tang, and its inhabitants appear to have been quite familiar with Buddhism. According to Yamaguchi Zuihō, a monk by the name of Menhashang betook himself to Tsongkha towards the end of the eighth century and there trained disciples, one of whom (named Namkha Nyingpo) traveled from Tibet proper to Qinghai to receive religious instruction.[8] R. A. Stein further notes that the monk who killed the king Langdarma fled to the neighborhood of Xunhua, south of the Yellow River, and he also mentions later examples of monks who fled to this region.[9] These instances probably indicate that Tsongkha had been flourishing as a center of Buddhism from a rather early stage. This region no doubt maintained links with Buddhist circles in Dunhuang and Tibet even in the late Tang and during the Five Dynasties period, and it is to be surmised that it upheld a form of Buddhism tinged even more strongly with Tibetan elements than was the Buddhism of Xiliangfu. Once we enter the Song period, the Buddhist faith of the Hexi Tibetans doubtless flourished even more in response to the movements to revive Buddhism in central Tibet.

The number of monks involved in government further increased with the birth of the Gusiluo regime in Zonggecheng [Tsongkha town, present-day Ping'an, one of the administrative centers for the court of the Tibetan prince, Gusiluo]; the sphere of their influence was not restricted to the Tsongkha region alone, and in the upper reaches of the Weishui, too, the activities of Tibetan monks (*fanseng*) leading various tribes became more noticeable. This coincided with the time when the illustrious general Cao Wei of the Song was in the course of bringing the tribes along the northwestern borders under control,[10] and the movements of the

Tibetan monks were also connected with this. Our attention is first drawn to a passage in the entry for the 2nd month of Dazhong Xiangfu 8 (1015) in Li Tao's *Xu zizhi tongjian changbian* (*The Expanded Sequel to "The Comprehensive Mirror in Aid of Government"*), fasc. 84.

> Cao Wei memorialized the Throne, suggesting that purple robes and the title of master be conferred on four Tibetan monks, one of them Lishi Linbuchi, who held power in the Jingyuan region. The Emperor issued an order in accordance with the request.

At this time Cao Wei was also applying himself to the administration of Yuan-zhou, and Lishi Linbuchi and his colleagues probably stood over and above the tribal leaders and controlled both political and religious power in this region. "Linbuchi" corresponds to the aforementioned *rinpoché* and this title was also used by Li Zun, to be mentioned below, who gave his backing to Gusiluo. Today the title *rinpoché* is generally applied to reverend lamas such as the Dalai Lama and Paṇchen Lama, and the passage quoted above tells us that among the Hexi Tibetans in the eleventh century a *rinpoché* was revered as someone differing from ordinary monks. The conferral by the Song of purple robes and the title of master on these four monks testifies to the fact that they wielded enormous spiritual authority among the tribes of the Jingyuan region. Their special treatment by the Song represented nothing less than the finishing touches to Cao Wei's subjugation of the Jingyuan circuit.

It was also around the second month of 1015 that Li Zun and other chieftains of the Zongge [Tsongkha] tribe installed Gusiluo in the seat of power in Kuozhou [on the banks of the Yellow River, in present-day Hualong County, Qinghai]. Li Zun then began to assume dictatorial powers, leading to the establishment of the Gusiluo regime in Zonggecheng, and already in autumn of the same year an offensive was launched against the tribes of Qinzhou. At about the same time, in the ninth month of 1015, the Song authorities charged Cao Wei with the task of bringing Qinzhou under control and subjugating the tribes living there. Owing to the success of the careful measures taken by Cao Wei in dealing with these tribes, this conflict ended in the total defeat of the Zongge side. But an examination of this confrontation clearly reveals that Tibetan monks were politically active in Qinzhou too. In the *Sequel to "The Comprehensive Mirror in Aid of Government"* fasc. 91, we find the following entry for the fourth month of Tianxi 2 (1018):

> *Jimao*: Cao Wei reported that the Tibetan monk Yumuzhabuqin once gathered together the people in Guweizhou and established a *wenfa*, but that it has now completely collapsed.

Yumuzhabuqin was a Tibetan monk serving under Li Zun, the dictator behind the Zonggecheng administration, and, although only for a short time, he had laid down a *wenfa*[11] in Chuimangcheng in Guweizhou and there established a strongpoint for the Zonggecheng administration. There is no doubting the fact that he took advantage of the Buddhist faith of the Hexi Tibetans living in the upper reaches of the Weishui and, siding with Li Zun's despotic Buddhist regime under Gusiluo, aimed at gaining control over the Tibetan tribes. His rule of Chuimangcheng also ended in total failure following attacks by Zhang Xiaoge, head chieftain (*dushouling*) of the Zhang tribe, and other local inhabitants,[12] but it would appear that influential monks from this region were in fact actively involved in these attacks too. In Li's *The Expanded Sequel to "The Comprehensive Mirror in Aid of Government"* fasc. 93, in the entry for *dingmao*, 1st month, Tianxi 3 (1019), we read that

> the two Tibetan monks Celingbanzhuer and Yilangbowo of Yongning Xing in Qinzhou were granted purple robes in consideration of the fact that they had often both followed the directions of commander-in-chief (*bushu*) Cao Wei.

The fact that these two Tibetan monks Celingbanzhuer and Yilangbowo were granted purple robes on account of their having "often followed . . . directions" is proof that they controlled the tribes of Yongning Xing, and it also points to the existence in Yongning Xing of Buddhist groups that did not submit to Yumuzhabuqin, who was using the authority of Gusiluo for his own ends. Such a state of affairs was by no means restricted to Yongning Xing alone, and a similar situation appears to have been developing in Qinzhou. Qinzhou was at this time already under the control of Cao Wei,[13] and Mangbumalagan, a disciple of the already deceased Tibetan monk Nubunuoer, was granted a purple robe on the grounds that he was "discharging duties." The conferral of a purple robe represented a reward for the services that he had rendered in controlling the Buddhist tribes of Qinzhou and preventing them from yielding to the maneuvers of Yumuzhabuqin, and it means that the Song recognized Mangbumalagan as the successor to Nubunuoer. It is thus evident that in the upper reaches of the Weishui there were Tibetan monks such as Yumuzhabuqin who ranged themselves with the Zonggecheng administration and those who sided with the Song and did not submit to Gusiluo's authority.

It is now time to consider the exact character of the Zonggecheng administration, which aimed at the expansion of its political power even to the extent of taking advantage of the Buddhist faith of the Tibetan tribes in the manner outlined in the above. It should go without saying that the name "Gusiluo" represents a transliteration of the Tibetan *gyelsé* meaning "son of the Buddha."[14] Recently, however, it has come to light that this *gyelsé* was not Gusiluo's personal name but a royal title and that it was frequently used also by his successors, in which cases the Chinese sources translate *gyelsé* in its alternative meaning of "prince."[15] This would suggest that the Hexi Tibetans employed the term *gyelsé* not so much in its Buddhist sense but rather as a title signifying more directly temporal power. It was after his move to Hezhou [present-day Linxia, Gansu] during the Xianping era (998–1003) that Tri Namdéwön Tsenpo (Qinan-lingwenjianbu, "Tsenpo of the descendants of Ösung") changed his name to Gyelsé, and it is clearly mentioned in the *Song shi* "Tufan zhuan," and in the *Luoquan ji* (*The Works of Chang Fangping, Styled Luoquan*), fasc. 22, that its initial meaning was "son of the Buddha" (*foer*). Songchangsijun and other members of the tribes in Hezhou relied not only on Gusiluo's origins but, taking advantage of the Buddhist faith of the Tibetan tribes, purposely adopted as Tri Namdéwön Tsenpo's new name the term *gyelsé*, with the meaning of "son of the Buddha" in addition to that of "prince," in order to facilitate the unification of the tribes. It was probably an ingenious stratagem whereby they sought to superimpose upon his status as a member of the royal family that of a "manifestation of the Buddha" and impress it on the minds of the people. The identification of people in positions of power with buddhas and bodhisattvas was no doubt easy to effect among Tibetans,[16] and it may be assumed that the cult centered on Gusiluo as "son of the Buddha" followed such traditions. But soon after Gusiluo moved to Zonggecheng and installed Li Zun as dictator any elements that might be associated with a "son of the Buddha" seem to have disappeared from the character of Gusiluo. This is clearly demonstrated by the following passage from the account of the Uighurs (Huigu) in Section 4 on "Fanyi" (Barbarians) in Xu's *Draft Compendium of Institutions During the Song*:

> [The king] Guihua and his prime minister Suowenshougui both reported to the Emperor that they were forming a friendship with Prince Zanbu of Xifan.

The original Uighur corresponding to "Prince Zanbu" (Zanbu *wangzi*) would have translated the Tibetan *tsenpo gyelsé*, which, properly speaking, ought to have been translated "son of the Buddha (*foer*) Zanbu." The fact that *gyelsé* is, however, here translated as "prince" (*wangzi*) would suggest that under the Zonggecheng administration, once the situation had settled down, the title *gyelsé*, which had by now gained currency, continued to be used, but only with the political connotation of descendant of the royal house of Tufan. Since the translators on the Chinese side were also familiar with these circumstances, they accordingly adopted a translation more in line with the true state of affairs, and as a result we happen to learn from the above source that Gusiluo's full title under the Zonggecheng administration was *tsenpo gyelsé* (*zanbu gusiluo*). This means that the title of "prince" was in use already from the time of Gusiluo. Initially Li Zun had probably attempted to make maximum use of Gusiluo's spiritual authority. But, as is evident from the failure of the operations against the tribes of Qinzhou, the spiritual authority of Gusiluo had not been established among all the Tibetans in Hexi. The reason for Li Zun's prompt renunciation of monastic orders and return to secular life may also lie in these circumstances.

At this point it will be just as well to consider why Li Zun was able to assume political power in the Zonggecheng administration. Later, when Gusiluo fled Zonggecheng, it was Li Zun's nephew Nasijie who acted as his guide, and even after Li Zun's death Zonggecheng remained under the rule of a member of Li Zun's family by the name of Li Baqin. On the basis of these facts, we are probably justified in assuming that Li Zun was originally a powerful tribal chieftain (*qiuhao*) of the Zongge Tibetan tribes in control of Zonggecheng. When Li Zun installed Gusiluo in Zonggecheng, he initially assumed the position of *lunbu* (Tib. *lönpo*: minister of state), but he also used the title *yingcheng lanbu-chi*. *Yingcheng* probably represents a transliteration of the Tibetan *deng zhang/desi*, meaning "regent," while *lanbuchi* corresponds to the aforementioned *rinpoché*.[17] This means that at first Li Zun held a position in which he was able to exercise both political and religious power on behalf of Gusiluo, but when he realized that Gusiluo's spiritual authority would not take root, he abandoned the title of *rinpoché* and returned to secular life, retaining the title of *yingcheng*[18] and maintaining his position as a political dictator.

IV. THE DEVELOPMENT OF HIEROCRACY

After having parted with Li Zun in 1025, Gusiluo betook himself to Miao-chuancheng [present-day Ledu] with the assistance of Wenbuqi. But he soon fell out with Wenbuqi too and, after having killed him, moved to Qingtangcheng [present-day Xining] around 1032–33. During this time Gusiluo's eldest son Xia-zhan established himself in Hezhou, while his second son Mozhanjiao was based in Zonggecheng; both of them laid down *wenfa* and subsequently fell into violent conflict with their father Gusiluo.[19] Their confrontation was long lasting and continued until the two sons were killed by Gusiluo's third son Dongzhan in the year Jiayou 3 (1058).[20] Political developments among the Hexi Tibetans thereafter evolved around Dongzhan and his adopted son Alige, but with the passing of time political divisions deepened, and the political activities of Tibetan monks became correspondingly more marked. In this section I shall trace the movements of these monks subsequent to the three-cornered confrontation between Gusiluo and his sons.

First, in the case of Xiazhan, when in 1054 he assisted the Song army in re-solving a dispute among the Tibetan tribes of Guweizhou, he received assistance from the tribal chieftain Lijuesa and his elder brother Zunzhuige, the latter a monk, and they were conferred by the Song the rank of army commander-in-chief (*dujun zhu*) and a purple robe respectively.[21] This indicates that these two figures wielded considerable influence in the Xiazhan regime. Then immediately after Xiazhan's death, when there arose the question of his son Mucheng's instatement, the monk Luzun worked actively on his behalf together with the tribal chieftains, and he played a part in winning the allegiance of the tribes throughout Tao, Min, Die, Tang and Wushengjun.[22] It is thus evident that under the rule of Xiazhan and his son monks exerted considerable political influence.

Next, in the case of the Mozhanjiao regime, the leaders in charge of offering tributes (*jinfeng shouling*) and purple-robed monks (*ziyi seng*) Zunlanzhanjiebu, Chenzun and Tangzunchilaqing were each granted a purple robe, silver vessels and other garments by the Song in 1053.[23] Judging from the fact that there were three monks with purple robes, one may assume that the political influence of monks under the Mozhanjiao regime was even greater than under the Xiazhan regime. Of particular interest among these three monks is Chenzun. Following Mozhanjiao's death, the political power of his son Xiasaqiding was, in accordance of the wishes of his grandmother of the Li clan, absorbed by the Gusiluo regime, and Chenzun now appears in Gusiluo's administration as a monk with the title of great master (*dashi*) and was also treated with deference by the Song, being granted the position of a regular army commander of his tribe (*benzi zhengjunzhu*).[24] This treatment may be considered to have been in recognition of his services, and it is quite possible that it was in fact Chenzun who prevailed upon the Li clan to allow the absorption of Xiasaqiding's political power by the Gusiluo regime. Other Tibetan monks involved in the Gusiluo regime included Sengjieba and Caozun, both to be considered in further detail below.[25] It is thus evident that a considerable number of monks were involved in the Gusiluo regime too, but as is equally clear from the above instances and from the examples to be considered below, these monks were not all men of religion alone, and there appear to have been not a few who had been ordained while in fact retaining their positions as tribal chieftains at the head of Tibetan tribes.

In his later years Gusiluo entrusted the affairs of state to his third son Dongzhan, and the death of Gusiluo in 1065 saw the birth of the Dongzhan regime in both name and deed. But at the same time Mucheng, who had inherited Xiazhan's political power, ruled all of Hezhou [now Linxia, Gansu] and stood opposed to Dongzhan, and in addition minor independent regimes were mushrooming throughout the region, making the establishment of a unified administration even more difficult.[26] In dealing with this state of affairs among the Tibetan tribes of Hexi, the Song modified its earlier policies and began to actively develop a policy the aim of which was to prevent the advance of Xixia.[27] From this time onwards the historical sources give even greater prominence to the independent activities of hierocracies led by monks who do not appear to have been associated with the Dongzhan regime.

In 1070 there first occurred an incident in which the two Tibetan monks Jiewuchila and Kangzunxinluojie, lending their support to Mucheng's younger brother Donggu, attempted to establish an independent regime in the important center of Wushengjun (Lintao).[28] They also considered entering into a marriage of convenience with Xixia,[29] and the fact that Tibetan monks directly related to neither Dongzhan nor Mucheng should have backed a grandson of Gusiluo in an attempt to establish a pro-Xixia regime merits our attention. In particular, Jiewuchila had many tribes under his command,[30] and he was evidently a force to be reckoned with. In view of the fact that he had plans for a marriage between Donggu and the rulers of Xixia, it is clear that he was aiming at the establishment of his own regime to replace that of Dongzhan and unify the Hexi Tibetans. His activities call to mind the figure of Li Zun and his backing of Gusiluo. This incident therefore had important implications for the Song too, and although the suppression of those involved was delayed because of a protracted confrontation between the reformist (xinfa) and conservative (jiufa) parties over the question of how to deal with the affair, it was eventually brought to a conclusion with the surrender of the two monks to Wang Shao.[31]

At about the same time Yulongke and Wangqibu, both powerful tribal chieftains in the uppermost reaches of the Weishui, pledged in turn their allegiance to the Song, and 1072 saw the restoration of Wushengjun to Chinese control. In conjunction with these events the Song also established the Xihe circuit, and the influence of its rule began to be felt directly even further afield in Hezhou, Taozhou and Minzhou. This inevitably led to a fierce struggle with Mucheng, who regarded this region as his own sphere of influence, and the Song was to carry out three offensives against him.[32] These offensives, under the direction of Wang Shao, at first proceeded satisfactorily, but then in 1074 Mucheng, joining forces with Dongzhan's general Guizhang, attempted a final major counteroffensive.

On this occasion the Tibetan monk Wenzun, acting in concert with Mucheng, brought the three tribes of Rong, Li and Long to participate in the besiegement of Minzhou. Wenzun was probably a monk native to the vicinity of Minzhou, and he may in fact be regarded as having been a powerful local chieftain who not only had the above three tribes under his command, but also possessed his own tribe. Judging from the fact that, apart from the Long, these tribes do not appear to have taken any real military action and that when Mucheng was put to rout he immediately submitted to the Song,[33] Wenzun was probably not a chieftain originally affiliated with Mucheng, but rather the leader of a regime ruling a particular region who controlled an independent hierocracy in the vicinity of Minzhou and contrived to preserve his political power by skillfully adapting himself to changing political circumstances.

In the fourth month of 1074 Mucheng finally capitulated, and soon afterwards Dongzhan and Guizhang also submitted to Song governance. At the same time there was a sense of growing crisis in Xixia, leading to an intensification of the struggle between the Song and Xixia for the allegiance of the Tibetan tribes, and in the fifth month of 1075 a large tribe living to the north of the Yellow River and ruled by monks tendered its submission to the Song. In reference to this, an entry for the year Xining 8 (1075) in Xu's Draft Compendium of Institutions During the Song "Tufan" section has:

fifteenth of fifth month: The Tibetan monk Libazhan was appointed commissioner of the three ranks (*sanban chaishi*) and frontier military inspector
of his own tribe (*benzi fan xunjian*). Libazhan lives to the north of the
Yellow River; he rules over a large number of tribes and shares borders
with Xixia. It appears that Xixia is bringing pressure to bear on him in an
attempt to win him over. For this reason he was given the above official
titles in order to appease him.

Libazhan is thought to have been in possession of the area along the northern
banks of the Yellow River to the north of Lanzhou.[34] This region was one in
which the Song, Xixia and Dongzhan were contending for domination, and it
was also of considerable political importance, with an independent hierocracy
far more powerful than that of the above-mentioned Wenzun.

In regard to another hierocracy lying within range of direct pressurizing on
the part of Xixia, Li's *The Expanded Sequel to "The Comprehensive Mirror in
Aid of Government"* fasc. 275, records the following events of early 1076 in an
entry for the fifth month of this year:

> *Mouchen*: The military commissioner (*jinglüesi*) of the Xihe circuit says:
> "On *guiyou* of the first month Longjibu and others of the Tibetans tribes
> who have not submitted to the Song encircled [the monastery] Guomangsi
> with troops. The Tibetan monk Baluosidan, the leader Zhebuzun and
> others mobilized troops and held the enemy off, taking thirteen heads.
> Baluosidan and Zhebuzun, who distinguished themselves, and their tribes
> had recently submitted to the Song. . . . Those who distinguished them-
> selves should be appointed commissioners of the three ranks, and in par-
> ticular Baluosidan should be made military inspector of his own tribe
> (*benzi xunjian*), while Zhebuzun and Baluojiyingcheng should be made
> military inspectors (*xunjian*)." The Song administration acted accordingly.

The monastery Guomangsi referred to in this passage corresponds to Guang-
huisi, which still stands today. It lies approximately 60 km to the north-northeast
of Xining, and even in the twentieth century it is an important monastery with
its own *hutuketu* (*qutughtu*) or "living Buddha" and twelve temples under its jurisdiction.[35] The incident described in Li's *The Expanded Sequel to "The Comprehensive Mirror in Aid of Government"* would appear to have been an internal
clash over policy between, on the one hand, the Tibetan monk Baluosidan and
his followers who were prepared to submit to the Song and, on the other, Longjibu
and others who stubbornly resisted all Song overtures. Judging from the fact
that Baluosidan was appointed to the same posts as the aforementioned Libazhan, namely, commissioner of the three ranks and military inspector of his own
tribe, he was doubtless an important chieftain (*daqiu*) exercising control over
tribes in this region, and the fact that he undertook the defense of Guomangsi
would suggest that he was the chief abbot of this monastery. It is also interesting

to note that the struggle for control of Guomangsi confirms the fact that the center of a hierocracy was located, as is only to be expected, in a monastery.

There were, however, not a few monks who aligned themselves with the Dongzhan regime, which had taken over Gusiluo's sovereign power, and who in practice acted as tribal chieftains. In the ninth month of 1076, immediately after the settlement of the Guomangsi incident, a monk by the name of Wang-zun serving under Dongzhan encroached upon territory under the control of the Song and was taken prisoner.[36] He was probably one of the tribal chieftains supporting Dongzhan's regime. Another monk who sided with this regime was Luzun, who together with Dongzhan and Guizhang repeatedly violated the border with the Song during the Xining era (1068–77).[37] He is probably identical to the Luzun who had worked for the instatement of Mucheng twenty years earlier, and in 1080 he was granted by the Song the rank of inspector-chief (*duyuhou*) of the Lusijie tribe. This would suggest that he too was originally a tribal chieftain, ruling over the Lusijie tribe. Later, shortly after the birth of the Alige regime, he is mentioned in a holograph edict issued by the emperor Shen-zong in the tenth month of 1084 to encourage his forces in their offensive against Xixia—"The Tibetan monk Luzun came and gave advice on tactics against Xixia and other matters"[38]—and it is thus evident that he continued to be active as a negotiator for the Song. He represents an interesting example of a Tibetan monk who cleverly conducted himself in accordance with changing circumstances.

It is thus to be seen that during the time of Gusiluo and his successors there was a marked increase in the number of Tibetan tribes that may be considered to have been governed by monks. This does not mean, however, that monks came to assume control of these tribes; rather, as is evident from the examples that we have already considered, it would appear that in actual fact tribal chief-tains took the tonsure and donned the robes of a monk while retaining political authority over their tribes. A case in point is the monk Zunzhuige, who, as already mentioned, was involved in Xiazhan's administration, and his younger brother: they were conferred a purple robe and the rank of army commander-in-chief re-spectively, thus clearly indicating that they had originally been tribal chieftains. We shall now consider the reasons for this increase in the number of tribal chieftains who became monks.

The first point to be made is that Buddhism was flourishing among the Ti-betans throughout Hexi, with the social status of monks rising proportionately, and the position of monks as leaders of the general populace in matters both temporal and spiritual had been established. Li Yuan, who participated in the subjugation of the Hexi Tibetans during the Yuanfu era (1098–1100), makes the following comment in his *Qingtang lu* (*Record of Qingtang*):

> The Tibetans respect monks and invariably turn to them for decisions in important matters. In addition, monks are excused even if they violate the law.

In its entry for *mouzi* in the eighth month of Yuanfu 2 (1099), recording the defeat of Alige's son Xiacheng, Li's *The Expanded Sequel to "The Comprehensive Mirror in Aid of Government"* fasc. 514, indicates that those who had taken monastic orders were given special treatment.

> Then, together with his wife and children, he shaved his head and they became monks and nuns, entering a Buddhist temple to the west of the town. This took place on *gengwu* in the seventh month. It is customary among Tibetans that those who become monks or nuns are not killed. Xiacheng acted in this way simply because he did not want to die.

In its account of Liu Huan's journey to visit Gusiluo in 1041, the *Qingbo zazhi* (*Pure Wave Random Records*), fasc. 10, similarly shows that monks were venerated as people of special status.

> According to Tibetan law, only monks are able to move about freely, and they are also given food and drink. Liu Huan accordingly shaved his head and went wearing a monk's robes.

We may thus assume that one reason for the donning of monks' robes by tribal chieftains was to facilitate control of their tribes through the exercise of both temporal and spiritual authority. It is, however, likely that they did at least possess sufficient religious faith to win the respect of the tribes. When Wang Shao set about winning over the two monks Jiewuchila and Kangzun Xinluojie who had been trying to instate Mucheng's younger brother Donggu, Wang Anshi purposely chose the monk Zhiyuan for this task,[39] and this was probably a tactic that took into full account the Buddhist faith of these two monks. The account of the dispute between Alige and Wenxiqin in the entry for *Xinyou*, sixth month, Yuanyou 5 (1090), in Li's *The Expanded Sequel to "The Comprehensive Mirror in Aid of Government"* fasc. 444, contains the following passage:

> The Tibetan monk Guasidun has more than one thousand people under his rule and is venerated by many people both high and low in this region. He was enraged at the unnecessary slaughter performed by Alige.

Judging from the context, Guasidun was probably a tribal chieftain, and he provides us with a concrete example of a tribal chieftain who was revered among the tribes in his capacity as a monk.

The second reason for the increase in the number of tribal chieftains who became monks is related to various questions concerning monasteries, and there already exists an extremely instructive study on this subject by Satō Hisashi. In a paper entitled "Daruma-ō no shison ni tsuite" (On the descendants of King Darma),[40] he discusses the relationship between monasteries and secular lords, taking as his example the family known as Yarlung-Jowo, which wielded considerable influence in the Yarlung Valley, the birthplace of the ancient Tibetan dynasty. He argues that "it was the secular lords who supported the large monasteries both economically and militarily and who strove to have successive abbots chosen from the same family, thereby monopolizing this position." The reasons for this were that "abbots at the time were entrusted with the social responsibility of arbitrating disputes and wars between secular forces, and it was impossible for an abbot who was a commoner by birth and lacked any real power to perform this important duty. In addition, the monasteries too were no doubt strongly desirous of abbots who had been tribal chieftains in order to enhance their prestige." As regards the reason for a particular family's monopolization of the position of abbot for successive generations, Satō draws the following conclusion: "The abbot's wealth was distinguished from the wealth of the monastic community, but when the abbot died his wealth was inherited by the next abbot or by the monastic community, and it was not returned to the abbot's family. The abbot's family would therefore push strongly for a monk from the same family to succeed him and have his wealth and position transferred to the new abbot. If the family was always contributing to the maintenance of the monastery, its voice would have increasing influence, and in practice this would result in the creation of a branch family taking the form of an abbacy." A situation similar to this would have obtained among the Tibetans of Hexi too. In Xu's *Draft Compendium of Institutions During the Song*, "Gusiluo" section, it is mentioned that when the monk Maqubusiji who had been serving under Gusiluo died, his purple robe was passed on to his nephew, the monk Sengjieba, and this signified abbatial succession within a single family. The earlier instance of the monk Zunzhuige and his younger brother Lijuesa, both serving under Xiazhan, would suggest that the elder brother became an abbot and assumed control of a monastery.

Next we must also consider the question of the economic strength of monasteries. Satō maintains that it was secular forces that supported the monasteries economically, but I consider that the situation was rather such that the secular powers depended on or made use of the economic activities undertaken by monasteries. In an entry for the tenth month in the winter of Tiansheng 3 (1025) in Li's *The Expanded Sequel to "The Comprehensive Mirror in Aid of Government"* fasc. 103, there is the following passage:

> On *gengshen* [an official of] the fiscal commission (*zhuanyunsi*) of Shanxi said: "Cela, the tribal army commander (*fanguan junzhu*) of Qinzhou, and others have made a request to erect a Buddhist temple in Laiyuanxing, and they wish to make it into facilities for travelers and horse traders." The Song agreed to this.

In addition to the fact that monks were the safest travelers, it is to be readily assumed that monasteries played an important role from this time onwards not only in horse trading but also in many other forms of economic activity. The opportunity to secure control of such economic power may also be regarded as a reason for the taking of the tonsure by tribal chieftains.

Finally, we may also add the military use of monasteries. It is a well-known fact that even today Tibetan monasteries are situated in strategically important locations backed by mountains. This was also true in the case of Guangren chanyuan to be discussed in the following section, and even judging from the struggle for the monastery Guomang si mentioned above, it would be safe to say that monasteries served an important function as military strongpoints.

V. THE ACTUAL STATE OF BUDDHISM

This period was a time of revival for Buddhism and, as is symbolized by the entry of Atiśa (982–1054) into Tibet, it was a time of new movements throughout the Buddhist world. In view of the fact that Jangchup Jungné, who was born in 1015 and became the chief abbot of Radreng [Reting] monastery, hailed from the Tsongkha region,[41] it is to be assumed that there was a considerable amount of exchange between the monasteries of central Tibet and the Hexi region. In this section I shall give an indication of the actual state of Buddhism as it was practiced among the Tibetan tribes of Hexi on the basis of references to be found in Chinese historical sources.

There are very few leads for acquainting ourselves with the actual state of Buddhism among the Hexi Tibetans, and the only contemporary inscription is the Guangren chanyuan stele to be found in present-day Guangfusi in Min county.[42] This stele records the early history of this monastery, which was built in Minzhou by the Song as a measure to appease the frontier tribes, and it is of considerable historical value in that it is almost completely undamaged and it is possible to ascertain the date of its erection on the basis of its concluding phrase: "Inscribed on the fourteenth of the eighth month, Yuangfeng 7 (1084)." It describes the religion of the Hexi Tibetans in the following terms:

> The Hexi Tibetans believe in Buddhism. Each tribe, in accordance with its numbers, selects a deity to worship and makes an image of it.

A leading role in the religious affairs of each tribe was performed by the tribal chieftains, who also acted as important patrons of Buddhism. According to our stele, on the occasion of the founding of Guangren chanyuan,

> the tribal chieftains Zhao Chunzhong, Bao Shun and Bao Cheng, who all wielded considerable influence throughout the prefecture, each made donations and erected a Buddhist image. The woods that had stood there were completely cleared, and in their place a magnificent Buddha-hall rises up. The doors to its entrance are kept open, and the gilded Buddhist

image looks even more splendid. They then had a bell cast to announce the time, had the scriptures stored, and devoted themselves to the Buddhist faith.

Zhao Chunzhong corresponds to Mucheng's younger brother Bazhanjiao, while Bao Shun and Bao Cheng correspond to the aforementioned powerful tribal chieftains Yulongke and Wangqibu of Xihe who submitted to Wang Shao. This passage exemplifies the Buddhist faith of the tribal chieftains who went over to the Song, but Gusiluo's successors were also devout followers of Buddhism. Li's *The Expanded Sequel to "The Comprehensive Mirror in Aid of Government"* fasc. 226, mentions that "Dongzhan and Mucheng are cultivating friendship with many monks," and the same work, fasc. 507, in an entry for *gengwu*, third month, Yuanfa 2 (1099), describes the Buddhist faith of Alige in the following manner:

> Xibawen sent word to Alige: "Am I not a distant relative of yours? In addition, I have been reading books about Buddhism for many years, and I am now a monk. Do not be suspicious of me." Alige realized that he was not somebody to be feared and left the matter at that. The Tibetans of Hexi revere the teachings of the Buddha, and Alige in particular took pleasure in devoting himself to the construction of temples and so forth.

Xibawen referred to in this passage was the son of the aforementioned Wen Xiqin, and in a gloss in Li's *The Expanded Sequel to "The Comprehensive Mirror in Aid of Government"* fasc. 511, it is stated that "Xibawen is a person of Buddha lineage (*fozhongren* = *rinpoché?*) and has very many followers." Successive rulers of Qingtangcheng such as Dongzhan and Alige revered Buddhism as the state religion, and their administration also had a Buddhist coloration, as is indicated by Li Yuan in his *Qingtanglu* where, after having noted that the town was divided into an eastern sector and a western sector, he continues as follows:

> The king resides in the western sector. The gate consists of two watchtowers, and behind it there is a middle gate (*zhongmen*) and a ceremonial gate (*yimen*). . . . About two hundred steps to the north of the ceremonial gate there is a large hall. The pillars and beams are colored gold, and the throne is eight to nine feet high and set nine feet apart from where the people sit. [The throne] is surrounded by glazed tiles of blue lapis lazuli, and people refer to it as the imperial court. Even when tribal leaders come for an audience [with the king] they remain outside the tiles, and anyone who steps on them is killed. Next [to the throne] there stands a golden Buddhist image which is several dozen feet high, adorned with pearls, and draped with a cover of birds' feathers.

From these accounts it is to be inferred that the tribal chieftains of the Hexi Tibetans not only ruled their tribes, but also played a central role in religious affairs.

In addition, as is suggested by the instances of Guangren chanyuan and the temple at Laiyouanxing in Qinzhou mentioned in the previous section, the erection of a monastery also provided proof of the strength of secular forces. Let us accordingly next consider the outward appearance of monasteries constructed with such secular assistance. On the subject of Qingtangcheng, where Alige resided, the *Qingtanglu* contains the following passage describing the magnificent spectacle of a large temple complex lying on the western outskirts of the town:

> To the west of the town there flows a river called the Qingtangshui, and it flows into the Zonghe. The land is flat to the east and west, and a monastery has been built here. It is five to six *li* in width and surrounded by a wall, and it has more than one thousand buildings. Large Buddhist images have been carved on the pillars and painted in gold. In addition, thirteen pagodas have been erected and are being preserved. In order to win the hearts of the people, Alige also made Buddhist images.

This monastery corresponds to the "Buddhist temple to the west of the town" mentioned in an earlier quotation from Li's *The Expanded Sequel to "The Comprehensive Mirror in Aid of Government"* as the place where Xiacheng took the tonsure, and it was probably the largest monastery in the whole of Hexi. The *Qingtanglu* further describes how temples stood side by side within the town too:

> Temples account for half of the town. Tiles are used only on the king's great hall and on temples, and the roofs of other buildings, including even the king's palace, are covered in earth.

Qingtangcheng would have had the appearance of a veritable religious city. In 1099, when the town was attacked by the Song general Wang Shan, it was "Buddhist images of gold and silver"[43] and "a triad of golden images adorned with pearl necklaces"[44] that became the targets of pillage, and this reflects the fact that Qingtangcheng had so many temples. In regard to Guangren chanyuan, it was constructed with donations from people such as Zhao Chunzhong, Bao Shun and Bao Cheng, the stele quoted earlier continues with the following description of the monastery itself:

> The monks have fixed quarters, and there are also houses set aside for guests. The storehouses are stocked with provisions, and meals are prepared hygienically. The buildings number in all four hundred and sixty.

One is able to view them in the distance from high mountains and large rivers and beyond thick woods and the town walls. While on their way there or on their return people say in unison to one another, "What a magnificent sight! There has never been such a fine monastery in this region!"

Let us lastly consider the daily life of the Tibetan monks. Again it is the Guang-ren chanyuan stele that serves as the only suitable historical source.

The monks recite from scriptures written from left to right, resembling *pattra* (leaves), and although it is totally incomprehensible because it is in Tibetan, their voices ring out beautifully and flow on endlessly like the waters of a plunging waterfall. From autumn to winter the monks secure a supply of food and do not go outside. Sometimes they simply sit inside their retreats. This is called *zuochan* (seated meditation), and if one performs *zuochan* the mind becomes relaxed and one is able to readily comprehend the teachings of the Buddha. But it is difficult for ordinary people. On the other hand, although Tibetan monks understand the teachings of Buddhism, they do not study the monastic code. They therefore marry and have children, often behave no differently from the laity, and think nothing of eating meat and drinking liquor.

It is as if we were here given a glimpse of life in Tibetan monasteries of the so-called Red Hats (*zha marpa*) prior to Tsongkhapa's reforms.

VI. CONCLUSION

There are many aspects of Tibetan history that remain obscure in the period between the fall of the ancient kingdom of Tufan and the birth of the Dalai Lama's regime. It was during this time in Amdo, an outlying district remote from central Tibet, that the Hexi Tibetans, with Gusiluo, a descendant of the former rulers of Tufan, as their progenitor and wedged in between the Song and Xixia, made their appearance in the eleventh century and shed a light of their own on the stage of history for the span of about one century before vanishing again. Their history had a strongly Buddhist coloring. Both Gusiluo and his successors were devout Buddhists, and the town of Qingtangcheng, their seat of government, looked almost like a religious city. Monks were always in positions of importance within the administration, and they were not simply men of religion but were also involved in the operations of government. Religion was not, however, the prerogative of the ruling class, and each tribal domain had its own deity and monks were accorded special respect. For the tribal chieftains, monasteries represented a focal point for regional rule. As the political power of Gusiluo and his successors gradually waned as a result of the pressure exerted by the Song and

Xixia, tribal chieftains themselves began to don monks' robes. In the state of virtual anarchy that now existed, the concentrated exercise of power was necessary for ruling individual tribes, and this led to the birth of numerous hierocracies, both great and small and endowed with both temporal and spiritual power, throughout the region. It is possible for us to perceive quite clearly in these Tibetan tribes of Hexi the forerunners of the later Buddhist kingdom of Tibet centered on monastic power.

NOTES

1. Furong Kang, *Qinghai ji* [*Account of Qinghai*], in *Zhongguo fangzhi congshu* [*Series of Chinese Local Gazetteers*] (Taipei: Cheng wen chubanshe, 1968).

2. *Song shi* [*History of the Song Dynasty*], fasc. 492, "Liezhuan" [Biographies] 251, "Waiguo" [Foreign Lands] 8, "Tufan" [Tibet]. All names appearing in this paper are given in the form in which they appear in the *History of the Song Dynasty*.

3. Xu Song, *Song huiyao jigao* [*Draft Compendium of Institutions During the Song*] (Beijing: Guoli Beijing tushuguan, 1936), "Fangyou" (Regions) 21, "Xiliangfu."

4. Entry for Jingde 1 (1004) in the *History of the Song*, "Tufan zhuan."

5. Entry for Jingde 1 in Xu, *Draft Compendium of Institutions During the Song*, "Xiliangfu."

6. Xu, *Draft Compendium of Institutions During the Song*, entry for Jingde 2.

7. The section on Xixia in Yan Kejun, *Tieqiao jinshi bo* [*Epigraphical Notes by Tieqiao*], fasc. 4, states: "[this] stele is at Dayunsi in Liangzhou; it was erected during the reign of Chongzong of Xixia in the year Tianyouminan 5 (1095)."

8. Zuihō Yamaguchi, "Toban Shihai Jidai 3: Tonkō no Bukkyōkai [Dunhuang Under Tibetan Rule 3: Buddhist Circles in Dunhuang]," in *Kōza Tonkō 2, Tonkō no Rekishi 2* [*Lectures on Dunhuang 2: History of Dunhuang*], ed. Enoki Kazuo (Tokyo: Daitō Shuppansha, 1980), 227–228.

9. R. A. Stein, *Tibetan Civilization* (Stanford: Stanford University Press, 1972), 69, 71.

10. Tsutomu Iwasaki, "Sokajō Kakushira Seiken no Seikaku to Kito" [The Character and Designs of the Gusiluo Regime of Zonggecheng], *Chūō Daigaku Ajiashi Kenkyū* no. 2 (Tokyo: Chūō Daigaku, 1978).

11. There is much that remains uncertain about the meaning of *wenfa*, but it appears to have been a code of rules laid down by a tribal chieftain when he united a number of tribes and established his sovereignty over them, and its content is thought to have been strongly marked by Buddhist influence. For details see Enoki Kazuo, "Ōshō no Kiga Keiryaku ni Tsuite" [Wang Shao's Administration of Xihe], *Mōko Gakuhō*, no. 1 (Tokyo: Mōko Kenkyūjo, 1940).

12. Iwasaki, "The Gusiluo Regime of Zonggecheng."

13. Iwasaki, "The Gusiluo Regime of Zonggecheng."

14. H. A. Jäschke's *A Tibetan-English Dictionary* (1881; reprint, Delhi: Motilal Banarsidass, 1980), 109b has: "1. prince. 2. son of Buddha, a saint."

15. Ryūichi Suzuki, "Geruse Seitō Toban ōkoku no ōgō" [*Rgyal sras:* The Royal Title of the Kingdom of Tufan in Qingtang], *Yasuda Gakuen Kenkyū Kiyō* 25 (1985).

16. It is, for example, a well-known fact that Srong btsan sgam po, the founder of the kingdom of Tufan, and the later Dalai Lamas were regarded as manifestations of Avalokiteśvara.

17. Xu, *Draft Compendium of Institutions During the Song*, "Fanyi" 6, "Tufan" mentions the name Qinzhan Linbuzhi, thus indicating that *lan* is an error for *lin*.

18. Xu, *Draft Compendium of Institutions During the Song*, "Fanyi" 6, "Gusiluo," mentions a "tribal official (*fanguan*) Li Yingzheng." He is perhaps identical to the Li Baqin who invited Mozhanjiao and his mother to Zonggecheng. The title *yingzheng* was evidently inherited by the Li clan.

19. Tsutomu Iwasaki, "Seika kenkoku to Sōkazoku no dōkō" [The Founding of Xixia and the Movements of the Zongge Tribe], in *Nakamura Jihei sensei kaki kinen tōyōshi ronsō* [*Collection of Papers on Oriental History in Honor of the 70th Birthday of Professor Nakamura Jihei*] (Tōsui Shobō, 1986).

20. Sima Guang, *Sushui jiwen* [*Sushui Notes*], fasc. 12.

21. Li, *The Expanded Sequel to "The Comprehensive Mirror in Aid of Government,"* fasc. 176.

22. Li, *The Expanded Sequel to "The Comprehensive Mirror in Aid of Government,"* fasc. 188.

23. Xu, *Draft Compendium of Institutions During the Song*, "Gusiluo."

24. Xu, *Draft Compendium of Institutions During the Song*. This source erroneously gives *benxian zhengjunzhu* for *benzi zhengjunzhu*.

25. Xu, *Draft Compendium of Institutions During the Song*.

26. Li, *The Expanded Sequel to "The Comprehensive Mirror in Aid of Government,"* fasc. 197.

27. Enoki, *Wang Shao's Administration of Xihe*.

28. Enoki, *Wang Shao's Administration of Xihe*.

29. Li, *The Expanded Sequel to "The Comprehensive Mirror in Aid of Government,"* fasc. 213.

30. Li, *The Expanded Sequel to "The Comprehensive Mirror in Aid of Government,"* fasc. 226.

31. Enoki, *Wang Shao's Administration of Xihe*.

32. Enoki, *Wang Shao's Administration of Xihe*.

33. Li, *The Expanded Sequel to "The Comprehensive Mirror in Aid of Government,"* fasc. 252.

34. Enoki, *Wang Shao's Administration of Xihe*.

35. Liu Yunxin, ed., *Datong Xian zhi* [*Account of Datong County*], Part 2; contained in *Zhongguo fangzhi congshu* (Taibei: Chengwen chubanshe, 1970).

36. Li, *The Expanded Sequel to "The Comprehensive Mirror in Aid of Government"*, fasc. 277.

37. Li, *The Expanded Sequel to "The Comprehensive Mirror in Aid of Government,"* fasc. 291.

38. Li, *The Expanded Sequel to "The Comprehensive Mirror in Aid of Government,"* fasc. 349.

39. Enoki, *Wang Shao's Administration of Xihe.*

40. *Tōyō Gakuhō* 46, no. 4. (1964).

41. Stein, *Tibetan Civilization*, 73.

42. Wei Zhang, *Longyou jinshi lu* [*Epigraphic Records of Longyou*], fasc. 3, "Song," Part 1.

43. Li, *The Expanded Sequel to "The Comprehensive Mirror in Aid of Government,"* fasc. 516.

44. Xu, *Draft Compendium of Institutions During the Song,* "Tufan."

Chapter 9

THE RULERS OF WESTERN TIBET

David Snellgrove

David Snellgrove is one of Britain's great Tibetologists, a veritable giant in twentieth-century European scholarship on Tibet. He is especially well known for his work on the western regions of Tibetan culture, including Nepal's Tibetan communities. This extract from his larger work on Indo-Tibetan Buddhism traces the remnants of the Tibetan empire, in the form of the descendants of the Yarlung kings, as the rulers of western Tibet (Ngari). Although their restoration to power in this region started in the tenth century, the main focus here is on the kings' support for the revival of Buddhism in Tibet in the eleventh century. It is to this period that Snellgrove has traced the beginnings of the Tibetan practice of having a ruler serve jointly as head of state and religious leader. The essay focuses especially on the translator Rinchen Zangpo (958–1055) and the Indian teacher Atiśa (982–1054) as well as their patrons, the religious kings Yeshé-ö and Lhadé, who also supported many other translators, both Indian and Tibetan. It introduces as well the founder of the first indigenous Tibetan religious order, the Kadampa tradition, founded by Dromtön (1005–64). Finally, Snellgrove describes the issues associated with Yeshé-ö and his grandson Zhiwa-ö's famous prohibitions against certain corrupt Buddhist tantric practices as well as the contemporary practice of tantra, which plays such an important part in Tibetan Buddhism.

Western Tibet refers generally to the vast area of upland pastures and mountainous waste lying beyond the province of Tsang, which together with Ü represents Central Tibet. Its limits westward are formed by the massive ranges uniting the

Himalaya and the Karakorum, into which Tibetan-speaking peoples have penetrated deeply, including not only Ladakh, but also Baltistan and Gilgit even
further west. The Tibetans first occupied this far western area in the first part of
the seventh century, but were forced to relax their hold over the more remote
districts as a result of the general breakup of the kingdom in the mid-ninth
century. By this time, however, the land of Zhangzhung lying directly to the
west of Tsang seems to have been fully incorporated into Tibet, now understood as a cultural and linguistic entity, and has never been separated from it
since. As I have argued elsewhere,[1] its language was probably already a form of
Tibetan when this territory was first incorporated, and thus its cultural cohesion
with the rest of the country must have been easily achieved. To begin with the
Tibetans had allowed its administration to continue under its old rulers, but after
several revolts a Tibetan commissioner was appointed, and it is likely that various
Tibetan aristocratic families closely involved in government affairs received estates in the new domain. After the breakup of the kingdom the owners of such
estates would have become self-declared chieftains, as must have happened
elsewhere, and their many contentions and conflicts were the cause of the generally unhappy state of the whole country, resulting in the absence of all historical
records. Later attempts to write the story of this unsettled period are nothing
but more or less intelligent efforts at historical reconstruction. All that appears
to be certain is that some time early in the tenth century a descendant of the last
of the effective Yarlung line of kings was received as titular king of Western Tibet,
now normally known as Ngari (probably simply meaning "royal domain") by the
leaders of one or more Tibetan clans who already ruled there locally. One can
imagine that this was an astute political move on the part of whichever ruling
clan invited him (most likely the Dro clan), for having united one's family in
this way with the representative of the old Tibetan royal house, it would be a far
easier matter to persuade one's neighbors into allegiance or force them into
submission. There is no available account of how the new kingdom was created,
but it probably consisted to begin with of the comparatively small areas to the
south of Mount Kailāsa [Kailash] adjoining what are nowadays the extreme
northwestern limits of the modern state of Nepal, and also the area to the west
of Kailāsa, bordering on the present-day Indian state of Himachal Pradesh. The
first of these is Purang (known to the Nepalese as Taklakot) and the second is
Gugé, where a royal city was built by the new rulers at Tsaparang. From Gugé it
must have been easy to occupy Spiti (now part of Indian territory), while a more
ambitious campaign must have been required for the eventual occupation of
Ladakh. One may note that all these territories adjoin to the south and west
districts of Indian culture, and that Buddhism probably still maintained a hold
in many of the high Himalayan valleys, such as Kulu and Kangra, as it most
certainly did in Kashmir. The vast expanses to the north of Kailāsa were understandably of little interest to the rulers of these Western Tibetan territories, and
thus they only partly correspond to the old kingdom of Zhangzhung. The first

representative of the line of the Yarlung kings to be declared king of Ngari is named Nyima Gön; he was probably the grandson of Ösung, a posthumous son of the assassinated Lang Darma. After the death of Nyima Gön his new kingdom was divided between three sons, although just how the division was made remains uncertain. Ladakh was clearly one unit, while Zangskar and Spiti may have been another, and Gugé and Purang the third unit. Certainly Gugé and Purang seem to be united when they enter our religious history during the life of the Great Translator, Rinchen Zangpo (958–1055), being ruled jointly by King Songngé (grandson of the founder of the western line of kings, Nyima Gön) and his son Lhadé.[2] Songngé adopted the religious life, becoming known by his religious name of Lha Lama (royal Lama) Yeshé-ö (Wisdom's Light). These two royal persons were the Great Translator's main benefactors during the first part of his career. Yeshé-ö died some time toward the end of the tenth century, and Lhadé's son, Ödé, was probably associated with his father as co-ruler. His two brothers, known by their religious names of Jangchup-ö and Zhiwa-ö, devoted themselves to Buddhist works, the younger of the two becoming a renowned translator. At the same time they continued to use royal titles and may also have been involved in the affairs of government together with their elder brother, Ödé. During the reign of his son, Tsedé, a great religious council was held, for which the *Blue Annals* gives the date of 1076. At least one of Tsedé's sons adopted the religious life, and hereafter this remarkable royal family becomes again a bare list of dynastic names.[3] It is remarkable because for the first time in Tibetan history an aristocratic family appears in the dual role of head of state and religious head, sharing these functions between them. This arrangement was adopted, whether in imitation or spontaneously, by some of the new religious orders as they began to shape their destinies, and has thus become a distinctive feature of later Tibetan government.[4] Thus we may note its beginnings in Western Tibet in the tenth and eleventh centuries. The royal family controlled religion in so far as they provided the greater part of the cost of inviting foreign scholars, of financing expeditions to India in quest of ever more books, in building monasteries and temples and in establishing translation "workshops." Despite certain pronouncements against wrong practices, to which we shall refer below, no restraints would seem to have been actually imposed, and thus others remained free to import Buddhist teachings just as they pleased. One may even note that accounts of the so-called second diffusion, while starting with brief stories of the reestablishing of monastic institutions in Central Tibet by monks from the east and then rather more detailed ones concerning the great works done by the religious kings of Western Tibet, go on to tell of the activities of such independent traveling scholars as Drokmi and Marpa, and there is no hesitation in including an approving reference to the activities of the "One Mother" [Machik]. One of the sons of our last named Western Tibetan king, Tsedé, is mentioned as one of the disciples of Dampa Sanggyé. Thus once Buddhism became the accepted religion of Tibet, tolerance of all kinds of religious practices became the norm. Some comment seems to be required concerning the readiness with which Buddhism was generally accepted from the time of its second diffusion, when one recalls the opposition that it faced some two centuries earlier. Moreover it was precisely Western Tibet, then known as the land of Zhangzhung, which was traditionally regarded as the strongest center of Bön. If stories of the triumph of Bön over Buddhism as a result of the assassination of the last Buddhist king, Relpachen, had any truth in them, one would have expected the people of Zhangzhung not only to throw off the political control of Central Tibet, but also to revert to their old religious ways, which in any case were unlikely to have been suppressed in the meantime. There seems to be only one answer to this imaginary situation, and it confirms what I have already written earlier about the need for distinguishing carefully between Bön, as it must surely be understood, and the pre-Buddhist religion of Tibet. They cannot be so easily identified with one another.

As I have stressed just above, the new Western Tibetan kingdoms extended into what is nowadays Indian or Nepalese territory. Purang and Gugé lay immediately to the south and west of Mount Kailāsa, regarded in Indian mythology as the abode of Lord Śiva, and identified with Mount Meru, the center of the universe, according to both Hindu and Buddhist cosmological ideas. This part of the ancient land of Zhangzhung had for many centuries been open to cultural influences from northwestern India, and I have suggested above that the Bön religion that was fostered already in these western limits of the Tibetan plateau was very likely to be a form of partly understood Buddhism, perhaps strongly affected by the vague philosophical ideas and sincere meditational practices of traveling yogins. Spontaneous religious developments of such a kind would have conflicted in no way with the kinds of pre-Buddhist religious customs, which later came into conflict in Central Tibet with Buddhism, once it was introduced officially as the state religion. While at first the followers of these heterodox teachings, known as Bön, understandably objected to the more orthodox forms of Buddhism, when they began to enter the country, in so far as they conflicted with their earlier ideas of what this religion was all about, they would surely have gradually come to realize that their position was a false one, as more and more Indian Buddhist teachings reached Tibet and more and more Tibetans went in search of these teachings in India. Thus Bön in Zhangzhung would have prepared the way for a Buddhist revival, and this had probably largely taken place before the tenth century when the royal Tibetan dynasty became established there. Western Tibet is never again mentioned as a stronghold of Bön, while the Bön tradition has flourished precisely in Eastern Tibet as far away as possible from these genuine Indian sources, which prove so easily the mistaken nature of some of its fundamental assumptions.[5] Thus if I am speculating reasonably, the religious kings of Western Tibet brought order and direction to a process that was already in operation. This alone explains the absence of any suggestion in the early sources concerning this period that any other religious groups were opposed to the fresh initiatives that they supported so generously. They are concerned in their pronouncements only with Buddhism, and while they issue the sternest warnings against the practice of corrupt religion, it is corrupt Buddhism that they have in mind and not another religion known as Bön. The practices that they so strongly disapprove of are precisely those prescribed in some Yoga Tantras and especially in the so-called Supreme Yoga Tantras, namely sexual yoga if performed by those who had taken monastic vows, rites of slaying or otherwise harming living beings, and religious offerings consisting of animal flesh or other impure substances.[6] The Religious King Yeshé-ö seems to have been the first to issue an ordinance on the subject:

All of you tantrists, village specialists,
Must not say, "we are Mahāyānist."
And must reject these erroneous views.
Practice what is taught in the Threefold Scriptures,
What is correct and pure.
Confess the ten sins, which you have previously committed.
If you fail to do so and follow such perverted religion,
You will not deflect the inevitable retribution.
Although it is true as our Teacher has taught
That the Dharma-sphere is essentially void,
You must believe in the law of retribution.
The effects of one's action are not deflected, but follow close behind.
As they do not simply reach a general state of maturation in the four elements
And as the sufferings of the three states of evil rebirths are so terrible,
Reject such evil practice and keep to the Threefold Scriptures.[7]

Toward the end of the eleventh century his grandson, the royal monk-translator Zhiwa-ö proclaimed another warning against wrong tantric practices, adding a whole list of unauthorized Buddhist treatises, said to be indigenous Tibetan productions, the following of which could lead only to evil rebirths. The works listed correspond in many respects to those of the earlier Yoga Tantra tradition, which we have referred to above. It is interesting to note that the Tibetan religious leaders, who were later to be such prolific writers themselves, should be so mistrustful of any Buddhist teaching, which could not be shown to have an Indian original to guarantee it. Thus the reformers were attempting to combat on the one hand malpractices based upon genuine Indian Buddhist tantras and on the other hand any form of Buddhist practice based upon texts that they regarded as spurious. Having listed the many works he willingly would have proscribed, had he been able to, Zhiwa-ö ends thus:

None of these represents the true path, and since they do not result in the achieving of supreme enlightenment, no one should resort to them or accept them as a path. Also those who have taken vows as monks must keep to the monastic rule, and those who have taken up the practice of Secret Mantras must not be in conflict with adherence to the rule, for in the case of (tantras of the) Kriyā, Upa, Yoga class and even the *Guhyasamāja* and others, one should strive to practice without breaking one's vows. Although the Wisdom (= Yoginī) tantras are excellent, there has been much neglect of the teachings proper for a monk owing to ignorance concerning the true meaning of the terminology, and for this reason there is nothing averse, if one does not practice them. In particular the theories of the Great Fulfillment (Dzokchen) are mixed up with those of heretics (viz., Hindu yogins), so if one practices these, one will be led into evil rebirths. Since they thus obstruct perfect enlightenment, in no wise is it suitable to practice them.[8]

It may be interesting to note in passing that the various grades of tantras referred to in this Western Tibetan ordinance correspond still to those of the earlier period[9] and do not yet include a specifically named Supreme Yoga class. However, the *Guhyasamāja* is already recognized as belonging to a rather different category from the Yoga Tantras, and thus it comes to be grouped with the Heruka-type tantras with their circles of yoginīs around the central lord. One suspects that Zhiwa-ö is only paying lip service to them when he says they are excellent, and would rather see them dispensed with altogether. By making the main criterion for orthodoxy the proven existence of an Indian original, the promoters of the new translations seem to have placed themselves in a contradictory situation. They found themselves eventually bound to accept all those tantras described as Supreme Yoga despite the many "heretical" (Hindu) concepts contained within them,[10] while they rejected many far less "heretical" works because of their doubtful provenance. Thus Buddhist teachings were not judged according to their particular merits, but trustfully accepted in accordance with the word of one's teacher, and at this particular stage the teacher was essentially the Indian master. This represents in general the attitude of those responsible for this second diffusion of the doctrine, although we must observe that the freer and more eclectic approach of the earlier period still had many representatives not only in the emerging Nyingma lineages, but also among the leaders of the new sects that were gradually establishing themselves. At the same time all and sundry benefited from the high standards of translation work achieved thanks to the zealous support given by the rulers of Western Tibet. This is best summarized by a quotation from the book the *Blue Annals*:

Furthermore the Royal Lama Yeshé-ö invited from Eastern India the great scholar Dharmapāla, who had many disciples such as the three whose names end in *pāla*, namely Sādhupāla who was the foremost of his disciples in the teaching and demonstration of the monastic rule, as well as Guṇapāla and Prajñāpāla. Their lineage is known as the Monastic Rule of Upper Tibet (Tö Dülwa). Furthermore in the time of Lhadé, Subhūti Śriśānti, known as the Great Scholar of Kashmir, was invited. He translated many of the sūtras and commentarial works of the Perfection of Wisdom class, such as the "Perfection of Wisdom in Eight Thousand Verses," its main commentary (the *Abhisamayālaṃkārāloka*), also the *Abhisamayālamkāratika* and other works. Students of the Great Translator (Rinchen Zangpo) who themselves became skillful translators, made many translations of works from the monastic rule section from the canon, from Perfection of Wisdom literature and from the tantras (*mantra-dharma*). Thus Gewé Lodrö of Ma translated many texts such as the *Pramāṇavārtika* and its matching commentary (*rangdrel*), as well as commentaries by Devendramati and Śākyamati, thus establishing a course for study. Spreading from there, the study of logical philosophy reached the province of Central Tibet. At the same time Khyungpo Draksé, renowned for his great learning, composed many works on logic. All this is referred to as the Old System of Logic. Later the Translator Loden Sherap was responsible for the so-called New System of Logic. The Great Scholar Jñānaśri came to Tibet, although he had not been invited, and many other scholars came, so that numerous good translations could be made. In the time of Ödé the Princely Lord (Jowo Jé, namely Atiśa) was invited and made corrections in the doctrine. During the reign of the son (of Ödé), King Tsedé, in the fire male dragon year (1076), most of the great scholars of canonical works from Central and Eastern Tibet came together for a religious council, known as the Council of the Fire-Dragon Year. They all kept in motion in their various ways the Wheel of the Doctrine. At the same time the Zangskar Translator was working on a translation of the *Nyāyālaṃkāra*. All in all these kings of Ngari in Upper Tibet rendered services to religion such as have no parallel in other countries.[11]

Any detailed account of this period of scholastic activity might seem to make rather difficult reading, as it would consist largely of lists of Indian scholars, their Tibetan collaborators and the works that they translated together. Thus the brief quotation above may serve to give some impression of the work that was done. It may be noted in passing that the term "canon," which I have used to translate *Tripiṭaka* (Tibetan: *Denö Sum*, viz., the three repositories), while referring in the earlier Indian Buddhist period specifically to the three-part canon, consisting of *Vinaya* (Monastic Rule), *Sūtras* (Discourses) and *Abhi-dharma* (Further Doctrine), is applied much more loosely in the later period to include any works regarded by their proponents as authentic Buddhist teaching and thus with no particular regard for the basic meaning of "threefold scriptures." Thus the Tibetans adopted the term in the same rather vague sense. When they later compiled their own canon, the earlier threefold arrangement had no direct relevance. Having separated the texts that were supposedly genuine "Buddha Word" from the works of recognized commentators and exegetes, they arranged the Buddha Word, known as the "Translated Word" (Kangyur) into four general sections, namely Vinaya, Perfection of Wisdom sūtras, other Mahāyāna sūtras, and tantras. Mahāyāna treatises on "Further Dharma," such as those of the Mind Only school, found their way quite properly into the vast set of "Translated Treatises" (Tengyur), so there was never any question of retaining an Abhidharma component as the "Buddha Word." Thus all that their canon retained in common with the early canons of the "eighteen *śrāvaka* sects" was the Vinaya section, which was identical with that of the Indian Mūlasarvāstivādins. Although there are indications that some Mahāyāna sūtras and tantras were already arranged in groups during the later centuries of Indian Buddhism, there was never any Indian Buddhist Mahāyāna Canon for the Tibetans to model theirs on. Thus the process of the conversion of Tibet to Buddhism involved many generations of scholars in the enormous task of seeking out many thousands of texts in India, whether from great monastic centers such as Vikramaśila or Odantapuri, or from the many smaller ones mentioned in Xuanzang's travels, or from individual teachers, especially tantric yogins, in their homes, or in inviting any renowned Indian scholars, who could be persuaded to come to Tibet to assist in the elucidation of the vast literature that had been acquired, and in the preparation of approved translations. It is scarcely conceivable that at any other time in the history of human civilizations such a wholesale importation of so vast a foreign religious culture was achieved in so short a time at such extraordinarily high scholastic standards. The importation of the same Indian Buddhist traditions into China may be considered a comparable undertaking, but this was a rather longer process with its own peculiar difficulties, which made the scholarly standards achieved rather more uneven.

The two great religious figures who stand out on the Tibetan and the Indian side are Rinchen Zangpo, nicknamed the Great Translator (958–1055), and the Great Scholar Dipankaraśrijñāna, usually known as the Princely Lord (Jowo Jé) or Atiśa, who came to Tibet from Vikramaśila in 1042 and remained teaching and guiding there until his death in 1054.[12] Apart from a few significant details, such as his appointment as Head Priest (*Ü Chöné*) and Vajra Master to King Lhadé and his founding of certain important monasteries, very little is known of the Great Translator's life except in rather general terms.[13] While retaining some seemingly quite valid traditions concerning him, presumably collected by his disciple Pel Yeshé (to whom the only known biography is attributed), the eventual compiler of his biography has introduced a certain amount of irrelevant legendary material and stories that seem to belong originally to traditions concerning Atiśa. A large amount of the earlier traditions appear to have been lost or else they were deliberately omitted for some doctrinal reason or other, which now escapes us. Rinchen Zangpo made three expeditions to India, including

Kashmir and the eastern regions (modern Bihar and Bengal), spending a total of seventeen years there, but there are no details of his travels apart from a quite convincing description of how the first expedition began. Thereafter we are left with the impression that having become proficient in the art of "swift-footedness," he traveled everywhere at miraculous speed. Thus in summing up his various achievements, his biographer informs us that "having obtained the mastery of 'swift-footedness' known as 'wish-fulfiller,' he went in six days and returned in six days, while it had previously taken him six months to travel from Tibet to Kashmir."[14] One can scarcely expect a travelogue of the kind produced by Xuanzang from someone who is believed to have traveled at such incredible speed; it would also have been impossible for his companions to keep up with him. Of these there were often quite a number, either fellow scholars or the trained artisans and religious painters whom he brought back with him to work on the many temples that his royal benefactors willingly financed. He is said to have founded one hundred and eight temples, a roundly suspicious number, but a more likely list of twenty-one is also given. He founded several monasteries, Tabo in Spiti, Nyarma in Ladakh, probably Sumda in Zangskar, as well as adding to the royal monastery at Toling in Gugé. Of his many temples, one in particular, which he founded at his birthplace of Reni in Kyuwang, is specially mentioned, but this place remains unidentified.[15] His numerous works of translation and the names of his collaborators, Indian as well as Tibetan, can be reliably abstracted from the colophons of all his productions, which were included later in the Tibetan Canon. His main interests certainly seem to have been tantras and Perfection of Wisdom literature. Tantric works include not only those classed as Yoga (or Mahāyoga) Tantras but also those which were referred to as Supreme Yoga Tantras soon after his time. Thus he translated not only the "Symposium of Truth" and the *Paramāditantra*, which relate directly to Vairocana's fivefold maṇḍala,[16] but also the *Guhyasamāja* and the main *Cakrasaṃvara (Heruka) Tantra*.[17] As we noted from the ordinance of Yeshé-ö, the separation of tantras into the four classes of *kriyā* (action), *caryā* (performance), *yoga* and *anuttarayoga* (supreme yoga), which must certainly have already been known in eastern India at that time and was later to be accepted as more or less a standard arrangement in Tibet, does not seem to have been current in Western Tibet during the period with which we are now concerned. Thus no distinction is made by Rinchen Zangpo and his contemporaries between Yoga Tantras and what are later referred to in Tibet as Supreme Yoga. In any case Rinchen Zangpo remained a celibate monk and there is never any suggestion that he used these tantras for other than meditational exercises.

The arrival of Atiśa (982–1054) in Tibet in 1042 and the twelve or so years that he spent there until his death came to be treated by later Tibetan historical writers as one of the really great events of Indo-Tibetan relations. He was responsible through his devoted disciple Dromtön (1005–64) for the eventual establishing of the first distinctive Tibetan religious order, namely that of the Kadampa, meaning "bound to the (Buddha's) word," which was later transformed under Tsong-khapa's powerful direction in the early fifteenth century into the "New Kadampa" or Gelukpa Order. These two related religious orders, which insisted upon monastic celibacy as the basis for all their religious practice, may be regarded as the representatives of more orthodox forms of Buddhism during the whole millennium that together they almost cover. They have provided a kind of monastic model, which all other Tibetan religious orders (even the Bönpos) have emulated, although these have continued to encourage the freer kinds of religious practice, suitable for noncelibate enthusiasts, to which we have already referred. Neither Atiśa nor Tsongkhapa were radical reformers of the kind that one meets with in the history of Western Christianity, admitting no validity in religious practices except those that are the result of their own prescribed reforms. They are reformers only in the sense that they established reformed orders of monks at times when monastic discipline had become lax in many other religious houses; they might protest against such laxity in general terms, but only rarely did they presume to declare the invalidity of the teachings followed by others, so long as an Indian origin could be shown for them.

The general lines of Atiśa's life are much better known than those of Rinchen Zangpo.[18] He is said to have been the second son of a royal line in eastern India and to have taken up the religious life after a vision of the Goddess Tārā. He resorted first to a tantric master and was initiated into Hevajra's cycle. Thereafter he continued to move in the circles of tantric yogins, until Śākyamuni himself, surrounded by a vast retinue of monks, urged him in a dream to take monastic vows. He made these vows at the age of twenty-nine in a monastery at Bodhgayā and thereafter devoted himself to scholastic studies, mainly of monastic rule (vinaya), Perfection of Wisdom literature and the tantras. These three classes of later Buddhist scriptures seem to come often to the fore in courses of study during the final Indian Buddhist period, and they certainly provided the main basis for most Tibetan Buddhist practice. Some of Atiśa's teachers were famous yogins who are listed among the conventional set of the Eighty-Four Great Adepts (mahāsiddha), such as Jetāri, Kāṇha, Avadhūtipa, Ḍombhipa and Nāropa. The connection with the tantric scholar Nāropa (956–1040) is perhaps worthy of special note, as this master-yogin was also the revered teacher of Marpa (1012–96), the founder (in retrospect) of the whole Tibetan Kagyüpa order with its several branches.[19] Nāropa seems to have had a considerable reputation both in northern India and Tibet. Thus it is related that before Dromtön met Atiśa and was practicing the art of writing with a teacher who seems to have been nicknamed "Verbal Thorn" (Dré Tserma), he asked him: "Who is really great in India now?" The teacher replied: "When I was in India, Nāropa was the great one. There was also a monk of royal lineage named Dīpaṅkaraśrījñāna, and if he is still around, he should be great too."[20] As soon as Dromtön heard this second name, he felt a great aspiration, and fortunately for him Atiśa had already arrived in Tibet, so there was never any need for him to go to India.

From what is known of his later strict teaching, one might imagine that he would have been scandalized by the teachings of the other great one, whose name was mentioned to him. Yet others could easily revere Nāropa and Atiśa at the same time, perhaps because the difference between their religious practice was not really so great as it might have appeared publicly, when Atiśa was invited to Tibet with the specific task of raising the local standards.

Several efforts were made to persuade him to come, when Ödé was ruling in Gugé and Purang, assisted by his two royal religious brethren, Jangchup-ö and Zhiwa-ö. All the later stories tell how he finally agreed to come because of the self-sacrifice of their aging grandfather, the Royal Lama Yeshé-ö, who was languishing in enemy captivity and having rejected the offer of ransom, urged that the price for this, the weight of his own body in gold, should be used to invite Indian scholars instead. This story, which may have happened in some other case in real life, is probably legendary so far as Yeshé-ö is concerned. According to Rinchen Zangpo's biography, he died of a severe illness in his own palace at Toling, where the Great Translator himself performed the proper funeral rites according to the *Durgatipariśodhana* tradition.[21]

Atiśa had agreed when he left Vikramaśila to return within three years, but returning from Toling, where he bestowed many tantric initiations, he found the route blocked on account of some local fighting beyond Kyirong, and thus was persuaded by Dromtön, who had met him on his journey, to visit Central Tibet. Here he traveled quite extensively, staying in such famous places as Samyé, Tangpoché, Yerpa and Nyetang, where he finally died. Having not fulfilled his promise to return to Vikramaśila, he used to send back there the large sums that he received on his Tibetan travels. After his death Dromtön withdrew to Radreng together with a group of faithful disciples and founded there in 1056 the monastery that was to remain the center of his religious order until it was absorbed by the Gelukpas.[22] Although Dromtön appears to have disapproved of noncelibate tantric Buddhism, Atiśa's attitude, like that of so many of his contemporaries, whether Indian or Tibetan, would seem to have been ambivalent. Having practiced his religion earlier in life under the guidance of famous tantric yogins, he could scarcely be expected to change his views later in order to please a few leading people in Tibet, who wanted a far more thorough "reformation" than he was prepared to countenance. Being well trained in monastic rule (*vinaya*), he could certainly urge these teachings, when such advice was required of him. Probably it is within such a context as this that one should understand a short work of his, which he produced at the request of his royal host in Toling, who wanted a concise treatise in answer to the disagreements that existed on points of doctrine between various scholars in Tibet. Atiśa thus composed the famous *Bodhipathapradīpa* as a "Light on the Path toward Enlightenment."

Although not specifically mentioned, a main disagreement must have been continually present between those who urged the slow progress of a bodhisattva toward enlightenment and those who preferred the far more rapid means, which are promised in so many tantras. The usual way of explaining the existence of such very different ways was to place human beings in three categories, low, medium and high, where only the highest would follow the tantric path. These three grades thus correspond with the three types of religious vow, which may be taken; that of *śrāvaka* (Hinayānist), a bodhisattva (usually understood in this context as a monk of Mahāyānist persuasion) and that of a tantric yogin. Atiśa must have been well aware of such distinctions; yet he begins his little treatise, written for the benefit of Jangchup-ö, by equating the three grades of human beings with the way of a nonreligious man, the way of one who acts religiously for his own benefit (viz., a Hinayānist) and the way of one who acts religiously for the benefit of others as well (viz., a Mahāyānist). He is thus free to continue his treatise commending the life of a Mahāyānist monk as the highest possible. He therefore commends explicitly the same gradual path toward enlightenment as was represented by the teaching of Kamalaśīla toward the end of the eighth century.[23] Thus he can write in the name of his ideal practitioner:

> I must keep to the practice of celibacy,
> Avoiding sin and desire.
> Delighting in the vow of morality,
> I must follow the teachings of the Buddhas.
> I must not want to gain enlightenment
> Quickly and just for myself.
> For the sake of a single living being
> I will delay to the very last limit.
> I will purify the realms
> Inconceivably numberless,
> Known in all ten directions of space
> By the name I have taken.

He then goes on to stress the importance of Wisdom and Means practiced together, where Wisdom means the Perfection of Wisdom in its normal Mahāyāna sense, and Means refers to all the other perfections, generosity and the rest. This is followed by a brief lesson in the doctrine of voidness, namely the voidness of self and the voidness of all the elements of existence. This is in fact the wisdom that one has to realize with the help of scripture (*lung*) and perception (*rikpa*), and thus progressing through the various stages of contemplation one is not far from a Buddha's enlightenment. At this point the treatise suddenly appears to offer another alternative:

> If one wishes to complete easily the components of enlightenment
> By means of the rites of tranquilizing, prospering etc.,
> Which are achieved by the power of mantras,
> And also by the eight great achievements,

The achievement of the auspicious jar (consecration), etc.,
And if one wishes to practice secret mantras,
As given in the *kriyā, caryā* and other tantras,
Then one must give due honor and gifts
For the sake of the Master's Consecration,
And make one's holy lama content
With your austerities and all else besides.
By thus contenting your lama
And so receiving the complete Master's Consecration,
You are cleansed of all sins and become worthy of achieving perfection.
But since it is strictly forbidden in the Great Tantra of Ādibuddha,
Those who practice celibacy should not receive the Secret Consecration
      or that of (the Knowledge of) Wisdom.
If they receive these consecrations,
They break their vow of self-denial,
Since they have practiced that which is forbidden
For those committed to the state of celibate self-denial.
In that a fatal sin is occasioned
By such as have broken their vows,
They assuredly fall into evil rebirths
And no achievement is possible.
In the study and explanation of all tantras
And the performance of *homa* rites, and worship, etc.,
And in receiving the Master's Consecration,
All that is acceptable and no harm is done.[24]

This famous little work of Atiśa's seems to be conceived as a kind of accommodation to the wishes of his host in that it commends in such explicit detail the moral virtues of monastic life in accordance with Mahāyāna teachings about one's primary concern for all other living creatures. Moreover, at the outset, as we noted, such practice is said to be only suitable for the best of the three grades of human beings. Following upon such a discourse, the concluding verses about tantric practices (quoted above in full) suggest a conflict of priorities. Who would not want to complete easily the components of enlightenment using means recommended in the tantras? But is the Master's Consecration sufficient for this purpose? Here we are informed that it removes sins and makes one worthy of achieving perfection, clearly implying that the higher consecrations are necessary for its final realization. This is also the explicit teaching of those tantras that prescribe the series of four consecrations. Yet those who have taken monastic vows cannot receive the Secret Consecration and the Knowledge of Wisdom Consecration. They are therefore given no choice but to follow the gradual path of a Bodhisattva through many rebirths. Also if we take his wording literally Atiśa does not even promise them final success by this means.

Progressing through the various stages of contemplation "one is not far from a Buddha's enlightenment." The whole treatise raises so many questions that one may wonder if Jangchup-ö, who requested it, was satisfied with the results. An easy answer to these apparent difficulties is provided by the theory of the various grades of human beings. Those who are born with keen senses[25] are suitable clients for the higher consecrations. Since they are in a position of advantage over their duller brethren, this can only be because of merits achieved in previous lives. It thus follows that those who cannot aspire beyond the conventional monastic state in their present life should hope to render themselves fit for a higher calling in their next one. Thus the essential fallacy in Atiśa's little treatise is revealed. It was presumably required of him that he should commend the monastic state as highly as possible, for a well-ordered religious life was clearly the chief requirement, if there were to be any noticeable religious reform, and it was for this purpose that he had been invited. However, having commended the monastic life, he could scarcely omit all reference to the higher tantric practices, and thus the inevitable conflict of priorities, to which we have drawn attention, becomes apparent.[26]

A solution could be found to the problem by practicing the higher consecrations as an imaginative process. It is recorded that Rinchen Zangpo meditated upon them precisely in this way and was rebuked by Atiśa, who was twenty-four years his junior, for treating each tantra separately. This is an oft-told story, but may be worth repeating briefly. They were spending the night in a three-story temple. On the ground floor there was a circle of divinities of the *Guhyasamāja Tantra*, on the next floor Hevajra's circle, and on the top floor the circle of Cakrasaṃvara. At twilight the Translator practiced meditation on the ground floor, at midnight on the next floor, and at dawn on the top floor. The following morning when they were having a meal, Atiśa asked: "O Great Translator, how was it that you practiced meditation yesterday at twilight on the ground floor, at midnight on the next floor and at dawn on the top floor?" The Translator replied: "In that way I can produce separately and reabsorb the different sets of divinities." Atiśa's face darkened as he said: "There was indeed need for me to come." The Translator then asked: "How do you understand it?" and Atiśa replied: "I don't understand it like that. Even if one practices all these religious ways with one's thoughts quite subdued, yet fundamentally they all have the same single flavor. It is quite sufficient to experience in one single spot all production and reabsorption."[27]

According to this story, which surely belongs to the cycle of stories about Atiśa, although it is included in Rinchen Zangpo's biography, the Great Translator was duly grateful for this advice and practiced meditation successfully for the first time in his life. The point of the story is obvious enough; any of the higher tantras properly practiced is as effective as any other. One might argue that by practicing several sets, one appreciates more easily the relative nature of all of them, and having worked on so many different tantras Rinchen Zangpo must have acquired great wisdom in that respect. However, the story is of interest not because of its intended application so much as an incidental account of how Rinchen Zangpo himself used the tantras on which he spent his working life as a translator. He became a monk and remained one, lacking altogether Atiśa's earlier training in the company of tantric yogins. Yet he is said to have achieved enlightenment by means of his meditative practices. He is even acclaimed at the end of his biography as an incarnation of the Buddha Śakyamuni himself. One therefore leaves this discussion with the impression that the way of the celibate monk might achieve just as quickly the goal of enlightenment as the much-vaunted way of the higher tantric initiations involving the actual practice of sexual yoga. Atiśa might have been more explicit on this matter in his little treatise, unless he held to the view of tantric yogins that their way is the superior one.

NOTES

1. David Snellgrove, *Indo-Tibetan Buddhism: Indian Buddhists and Their Tibetan Successors* (London: Random House, 1987), 2:386–396.

2. Srong nge appears to be an elision of Drang srong lde, while his brother's name 'Khor re represents 'Khor lo lde. They are thus clearly royal names. See Samten G. Karmay, "The Ordinance of lHa Bla-ma Ye-shes-'od," in *Tibetan Studies in Honour of Hugh Richardson: Proceedings of the International Seminar on Tibetan Studies, Oxford, 1979*, ed. Michael Aris and Aung San Suu Kyi (Warminster: Aris & Phillips, 1980), 150–160.

3. At its greatest extent Spu hrang with its capital at Ya rtse (either Taklakot itself or at an ancient site, identified by Professor Tucci as the village of Semja near Jumla in present-day western Nepal) became a Hindu Buddhist kingdom with rulers who were caste-Hindus, named as Mallas, and speaking an earlier form of the language (Khāskura), which was later to be known as Nepāli. See Giuseppe Tucci, *Preliminary Report on Two Scientific Expeditions to Nepal* (Rome: Instituto italiano per il Medio ed Estremo Oriente, 1956), 43–71, and Prayag Raj Sharma, *Preliminary Study of the Art and Architecture of the Karnali Basin, West Nepal* (Paris: Centre National de la Recherche Scientifique, 1972). Gu ge remained an independent kingdom until the seventeenth century, when it was first taken over by King Seng ge rnam rgyal of Ladakh and then fell into the hands of the fifth Dalai Lama and his Mongol supporters. For a brief account of this unhappy ending see David Snellgrove and Tadeusz Skorupski, *The Cultural Heritage of Ladakh* (Warminster: Aris & Phillips, 1977–1980), 1:86, and in far more detail Luciano Petech, *The Kingdom of Ladakh, c. 950–1842 A.D.* (Rome: Istituto italiano per il Medio ed Estremo Oriente, 1977), 58 ff.

4. See Snellgrove, *Indo-Tibetan Buddhism*, 2:508–526.

5. The important Bon po monastery of Sman ri in Gtsang Province was founded in 1405 and G.yung drung gling not until the mid-nineteenth century. Some small communities later developed in the upper Kāli Gandaki Valley (now in northwestern Nepal) and there is one community in Bhutan, but Bon's main strength has been in Khams and A mdo far to the east.

6. All of which have been referred to in Snellgrove, *Indo-Tibetan Buddhism*, 1:3.

7. See Karmay, "The Ordinance of lHa Bla-ma Ye-shes-'od," 155 and 157. The ten sins are: killing, stealing, adultery, lying, coarse language, angry speech, malevolence, foolish talk, covetousness, and harboring wrong views.

8. See Samten G. Karmay, to whom we are much indebted for bringing this particular text to light, "An Open Letter to Pho-brang Zhi-ba-'od," *The Tibet Journal* 5, no. 3 (1980): 3–28.

9. See Snellgrove, *Indo-Tibetan Buddhism*, 2:451–463.

10. See Snellgrove, *Indo-Tibetan Buddhism*, 1:147–160.

11. Gzhon nu dpal (1391–1476), *Deb ther sngon po* [*Blue Annals*] (New Delhi: International Academy of Indian Culture, 1974), 63 ff. (Tibetan pagination: vol. kha, 4a ff.); George N. Roerich's translation, *The Blue Annals* (Delhi: Motilal Banarsidass, 1976), 69–71. I pay tribute to the amazing amount of work that Roerich has done with the assistance of the Tibetan scholar Dge 'dun chos 'phel in producing his translation, which includes identification of dates (some of which may have to be amended in accordance with the finds of later research) as well as the Sanskrit titles of all quoted works.

12. I accept the name Atiśa as a popular abbreviation of Sanskrit *atiśaya*, meaning "outstanding." The problem of its interpretation and hence its correct spelling has been discussed by Helmut Eimer in his *Berichte über das Leben des Atiśa (Dīpaṃkaraśrījñāna): Eine Untersuchung der Quellen* [*Reports on the Life of Atiśa*] (Wiesbaden: Harrassowtiz, 1977), 17–22.

13. There is a translation of his biography in Snellgrove and Skorupski, *Cultural Heritage of Ladakh*, vol. 2.

14. This remarkable ability attributed to some yogins is known as *rkang mgyogs* in Tibetan; Alexandra David-Neel claims to have met such adepts on her travels, see her *With Mystics and Magicians in Tibet* (London: Penguin, 1936), 183ff.

15. Professor Tucci has suggested as a possible identification a village below the Shipki Pass near the present Indian and Tibetan border on the route between Simla and Toling; see his *Indo-Tibetica* 2: *Rin c'en bzaṅ po e la rinascita del buddhismo nel Tibet intorno al mille* [*Rinchen Zangpo and the Renaissance of Buddhism in Tibet Around the Millenium*] (Rome: Reale accademia d'Italia, 1933), 56.

16. See Snellgrove, *Indo-Tibetan Buddhism*, 1:198–213.

17. Lists may be found in Tucci, *Rinchen Zangpo and the Renaissance of Buddhism*, 39–49. This is the so-called Laghusaṃvara Tantra; see Shinīchi Tsuda, *The Saṁvarodaya-tantra: Selected Chapters* (Tokyo: Hokuseido Press, 1974), 27–45 for useful observations on its identity.

18. This is mainly thanks to the labors of Helmut Eimer, firstly in his *Reports on the Life of Atiśa*, followed by a synoptic study of the biographies with the title of *Rnam thar rgyas pa: Materialien zu einer Biographie des Atiśa (Dīpaṃkaraśrījñāna)* [*Materials for a Biography of Atiśa*], 2 vols. (Wiesbaden: Harrassowitz, 1979). Roerich, *Blue Annals*, 241ff. has a good account of easier access to those who do not read German. Alaka Chattopadhyaya's *Atīśa and Tibet: Life and Works of Dīpaṃkara Śrījñāna in Relation to the History and Religion of Tibet* (Calcutta: Indian Studies: Past & Present,

1967) may provide much useful information for the general reader, but the scope of this book extends unhappily beyond the competence of its well-intentioned compiler, who has not always sought the right advice.

19. For the dates given here for Nāropa see Snellgrove and Skorupski, *Cultural Heritage of Ladakh*, 2:90ff. It differs by sixty years from that put forward by Herbert V. Guenther in his excellent study, *The Life and Teaching of Nāropa: Translated from the Original Tibetan with a Philosophical Commentary Based on the Oral Transmission* (Oxford: Clarendon Press, 1963), to which the reader is referred unhesitatingly.

20. Roerich, *Blue Annals*, 252; Gzhon nu dpal, *Blue Annals*, 225 (Tibetan pagination: vol. ca, 6a).

21. See Snellgrove and Skorupski, *Cultural Heritage of Ladakh*, 2:92.

22. Rwa sgreng, which is some fifty miles northeast of Lhasa, has remained an important monastery within the Dge lugs pa fold. Its high incarnate lama enjoyed the privilege, shared with only two other monasteries, of acting as regent during the minority of the Dalai Lama. See David Snellgrove and Hugh Richardson, *A Cultural History of Tibet* (Boulder: Prajñā Press, 1980), 228, and for its extraordinary topical interest Hugh E. Richardson's article, "The Rva-sgreng Conspiracy of 1947," in *Tibetan Studies in Honour of Hugh Richardson: Proceedings of the International Seminar on Tibetan Studies, Oxford, 1979*, ed. Michael Aris and Aung San Suu Kyi (Warminster: Aris & Phillips, 1980), xvi–xx.

23. See Snellgrove, *Indo-Tibetan Buddhism*, 2:426–436.

24. See Helmut Eimer, *Bodhipathapradīpa: Ein Lehrgedicht des Atiśa (Dīpaṃkaraśrījñāna), in der tibetischen Überlieferung* [*Bodhipathapradīpa: A Doctrinal Poem of Atiśa*] (Wiesbaden: Harrassowtiz, 1978), 156–159, where the edited Tibetan text and his German translation are available. For the passage quoted just above see likewise, 118–121. The Ādibuddha Tantra is the Kālacakra Tantra. The "eight great achievements" surely refer to eight component parts of the Master's Consecration according to this tantra, viz., consecrations with water, crown, stole, vajra and bell, self-lordship, name, sanction and jar (see Snellgrove, *Indo-Tibetan Buddhism*, 1:262–266). I note that a curious list of intended correspondence is given in the Commentary (*Bodhimargadīpapañjika*) as quoted by Eimer (137). For the rites of tranquilizing, prospering, etc., see Snellgrove, *Indo-Tibetan Buddhism*, 1:235–240. Alaka Chattopadhyaya has also translated this text with the help of Lama Chimpa: Chattopadhyaya, *Atiśa and Tibet*, 525–535. The result is not very satisfactory, as they appear to be unfamiliar with much of the terminology relating to consecrations.

25. See Snellgrove, *Indo-Tibetan Buddhism*, 1:117–128.

26. This matter has also been discussed recently by David Seyfort Ruegg, "Deux problèmes d'exégèse et de pratique tantriques" [Two Problems of Tantric Exegesis and Practice], in *Tantric and Taoist Studies in Honor of Professor R. A. Stein*, Mélanges chinois et bouddhiques 20, ed. Michel Strickmann (Bruxelles: Institut belge des hautes études chinoises, 1981), 212–226.

27. Taken direct from my own translation in Snellgrove and Skorupski, *Cultural Heritage of Ladakh*, 2:98.

Chapter 10

THE BÖN RELIGION OF TIBET

Per Kvaerne

Norwegian Tibetologist Per Kvaerne introduces here one of the two organized religious traditions of Tibet, Bön. While he briefly mentions the early history of *bön* and *bönpo* during the imperial period, he distinguishes these (mostly royal mortuary) practices from the very different organized Bön tradition that developed in the tenth and eleventh centuries—at the same time as Buddhism was revived in Tibet—and are practiced to the present day. As Kvaerne points out, to the casual observer, the practices and art of Bön and Buddhism might be difficult to distinguish. But the two traditions define each other as different religions. Key differences lie in their concepts of sacred history and sources of religious authority. It is precisely the Bön tradition's claim that it predated Buddhism in Tibet by several centuries (having flourished in Zhang-zhung, which was taken over by Tibet's rulers) that has led some to associate the religious practices of the ritual specialists called *bönpo* from the Tibetan imperial period with the later organized religion of Bön. As for religious authority, Tönpa Shenrap (as opposed to the Buddha, Śākyamuni) is the source of the Bön religion. The similarities include the establishment, starting in the late eleventh century, of Bön monasteries organized along the same lines as those of the Buddhists, a Bön canon (Kangyur) dating around the fifteenth century, and the practice of discovering hidden "treasure" texts (a tradition shared with the Nyingma order). Kvaerne explains that there is no historical evidence for the claim that the Bön currently practiced is the indigenous religion of Tibet. Despite the different views of the Bönpo about Tibetan history discussed here, there is no philological evidence that their historic texts date to (or before) the imperial period.

Tibet is universally regarded as the homeland of one of the major Buddhist civilizations of Asia. Introduced into Tibet in the seventh and eighth centuries, Buddhism soon became the dominant religion. Although Chinese influences were not altogether absent during the initial period of Buddhist activity in Tibet, it was above all to the Indian subcontinent (including Kashmir and the Kathmandu Valley) that the Tibetans turned for their sacred scriptures and traditions of philosophy, art and learning, and monastic life was organized on the whole according to Indian models.[1]

With its many centers of learning and places of pilgrimage connected with the life of the Buddha Śākyamuni, India became, in the minds of most Tibetans, a holy land of religion. This remained true even after the Muslim conquest of northern India in the twelfth and thirteenth centuries caused Buddhism in India to disappear and gradually brought the flow of Tibetan pilgrims to a virtual standstill.

Not all Tibetans, however, regarded India as the source of their religious traditions. Since the tenth or eleventh century and until the present day there have been two organized religious traditions in Tibet: Buddhism and a faith that is referred to by its Tibetan name, Bön.[2]

Western scholars have adopted the Tibetan term *bön* together with the corresponding adjective *bönpo* to refer to ancient pre-Buddhist as well as later non-Buddhist religious beliefs and practices in Tibet. Hence, in the context of Western scholarship, "Bön" has no less than three significations:

1. The pre-Buddhist religion of Tibet which was gradually suppressed by Buddhism in the eighth and ninth centuries. This religion, only imperfectly reconstructed on the basis of ancient documents, appears to have focused on the person of the king, who was regarded as sacred and possessing supernatural powers. Elaborate rituals were carried out by professional priests known as *bönpo*. It is possible that their religious doctrines and practices were called *bön* (although scholars disagree on this point); certainly they were so designated in the later, predominantly Buddhist historiographical literature. In any case, their religious system was essentially different from Buddhism. Thus, the rituals performed by the ancient Bönpo priests were above all concerned with ensuring that the soul of a dead person was conducted safely to a postmortem land of bliss by an appropriate animal—usually a yak, a horse or a sheep—which was sacrificed in the course of the funerary rites. Offerings of food, drink and precious objects, and, in the case of kings, even of servants and ministers, likewise accompanied the dead. The purpose of these rites was twofold: on the one hand, to ensure the happiness of the deceased in the land of the dead, and on the other, to obtain their beneficial influence for the welfare and fertility of the living.

2. Bön may also refer to a religion that appeared in Tibet in the tenth and eleventh centuries, at the same time that Buddhism, introduced once again from India after a period of decline in Tibet, became dominant. This religion, which has continued as an unbroken tradition until the present day, has numerous and obvious points of similarity with Buddhism with regard to doctrine and practice, so much so that its status as a distinct religion has been doubted. Some scholars (among them the present author in earlier publications) have suggested that it could most adequately be described as an unorthodox form of Buddhism.[3] The fact that the adherents of this religion, the Bönpos—of whom there are many thousands in Tibet and in exile today—maintain that their religion is anterior to Buddhism in Tibet, and, in fact, identical with the pre-Buddhist Bön religion, has tended to be either contradicted or ignored by Western scholars. Tibetan Buddhists, however, also regard Bön as a distinct religion, and it will be argued below that this claim is justified if one emphasizes aspects such as concepts of religious authority, legitimation and history rather than rituals, metaphysical doctrine and monastic discipline.[4]

3. Bön is sometimes used to designate a vast and amorphous body of popular beliefs, including divination, the cult of local deities and conceptions of the soul. Tibetan usage does not, however, traditionally refer to such beliefs as "Bön," and since they do not form an essential part of Buddhism or of Bön (in the sense of the word outlined under point 2 above), a more appropriate term is that coined by R. A. Stein, viz. "the nameless religion."[5]

Even if one leaves this third sense of "Bön" aside, the usual view of Bön in the West has been less than accurate. This is particularly true of the continuous, living religion called "Bön" (point 2 outlined above) which has often been characterized as "shamanism" or "animism," and as such, regarded as a continuation of what supposedly were the religious practices prevalent in Tibet before the coming of Buddhism.[6] It is worth noting that the argument in support of this view is a circular one, the presence of such elements in the pre-Buddhist religion of Tibet being inferred from their existence in present-day popular religious practices. Further, the later, so-called "developed" Bön religion was often described in distinctly unfavorable terms as a perversion of Buddhism, a kind of marginal counter-current in which elements of Buddhist doctrine and practice had either been shamelessly copied, or else inverted and distorted in a manner which was compared with the mediaeval satanistic cults of Europe (no matter whether such cults ever actually existed or not).[7] This view of Bön was, however, not founded on first-hand research, but on certain polemical writings by Tibetan Buddhist critics of Bön, who tended to employ standard terms of polemical invective. It is only since the mid-1960s that a more adequate understanding of Bön has emerged, first and foremost thanks to the efforts of David L. Snellgrove.[8]

The religious art and iconography of Bön in the second sense of the word outlined above are the topics of the book [from which this essay was drawn].

This is the religion that emerged in the tenth and eleventh centuries (at least in its present form) and which still flourishes today. Of the pre-Buddhist (or, if one prefers, the pre-seventh-century) art of Tibet almost nothing is known, and iconographical expressions of folk beliefs are for the most part integrated in either the Bönpo or the Buddhist traditions.

An adherent of the Bön religion is called Bönpo. A Bönpo is a "believer in Bön," and for him Bön signifies "Truth," "Reality" or the eternal, unchanging Doctrine in which Truth and Reality are expressed. Thus, Bön has the same range of connotations for its adherents as the Tibetan word chö (Tibetan chos, translating the Sanskrit term dharma) has for Buddhists.

Although limited to Tibet, Bön regards itself as a universal religion in the sense that its doctrines are true and valid for all humanity. The Bönpos also believe that in former times Bön was propagated in many parts of the world (as conceived in their traditional cosmology). For this reason, it is called "Eternal Bön," yungdrung bön. The importance of the term yungdrung, "eternal, unchanging," which for Tibetan Buddhists, but not for Bönpos, translates the Sanskrit term svāstika, explains the frequent appearance in Bönpo iconography of the swastika, which is its symbol. In Bönpo usage, the term yungdrung corresponds in many respects to the Buddhist term dorjé (Sanskrit vajra). The Bönpo swastika, however, turns to the left, i.e., counter-clockwise, while the Buddhist version turns to the right. This is but one of innumerable examples of a characteristic (although superficial) difference between Bön and Buddhism; in Bön, the sacred movement is always counter-clockwise. This is not, however, an expression of protest, much less of a spirit of perversion; it is, so the Bönpos believe, simply the normal ritual direction which contributes, ultimately, to moral purification and spiritual enlightenment. Several basic terms in the Bön religion contain the word yungdrung; thus, beings who have advanced on the path of enlightenment are known as yungdrung sempa, corresponding to the Buddhist term vajrasattva, but in practice having the same range of meaning as the term bodhisattva. In this volume [from which this essay was drawn] yungdrung sempa will be rendered "Spiritual Hero," stressing the second element of the term sempa (Tibetan sems, "mind"; dpa', "hero").

To the casual observer, Tibetans who follow the tradition of Bön and those who adhere to the Buddhist faith can hardly be distinguished. They all share a common Tibetan heritage. In particular, there is little distinction with regard to popular religious practices. Traditionally, all Tibetans assiduously follow the same methods of accumulating religious merit, with the ultimate end in view of obtaining rebirth in a future life as a human being once again or as an inhabitant of one of the many paradisiacal worlds of Tibetan (Buddhist as well as Bönpo) cosmology. Such practices include turning prayer wheels, hand-held or set in motion by the wind or a stream; circumambulating sacred places such as monasteries or holy mountains; hoisting prayer flags; and chanting sacred formulas or engraving them on stones or cliffs. It is only when these practices are scrutinized more closely that differences appear; the ritual movement is, as already mentioned, always counter-clockwise and the sacred mantra is not the Buddhist "Oṃ maṇi padme hūṃ," but "Oṃ matri muye sale du." Likewise, the cult of the innumerable deities of Tibetan religion, whether Buddhist or Bönpo, may at first appear to be indistinguishable; but again, the deities are, in fact, different (although belonging to the same range of divine categories) with regard to their names, mythological origins, characteristic colors and objects held in their hands or adorning their bodies.

Even a cursory glance at the doctrines of Bön, as expressed in their literature or explained by contemporary masters, reveals that they are in many respects identical with those found in Tibetan Buddhism. It is this fact that until recently led Western scholars to accuse the Bönpos of plagiarism. The view of the world as suffering, belief in the law of moral causality (the "law of karma") and the corresponding concept of rebirth in the six states of existence, and the ideal of enlightenment and Buddhahood, are basic doctrinal elements not only of Buddhism, but also of Bön. Bönpos follow the same path of virtue and have recourse to the same meditational practices as Buddhist Tibetans.

In view of the many manifest similarities between Bön and Buddhism, one may well ask in what the distinction between the two religions consists. The answer, at least to this author, would seem to depend on which perspective is adopted when describing Bön. Rituals and other religious practices, as well as meditational and metaphysical traditions are, undeniably, to a large extent similar, even identical. Concepts of sacred history and sources of religious authority are, however, radically different and justify the claim of the Bönpos to constitute an entirely distinct religious community.

According to its own historical perspective, Bön was introduced into Tibet many centuries before Buddhism and enjoyed royal patronage until it was finally supplanted by the "false religion" (i.e., Buddhism) from India and its priests and sages expelled from Tibet by king Tri Songdetsen in the eighth century. It did not, however, disappear from Tibet altogether; the tradition of Bön was preserved in certain family lineages, and after a few generations it flourished once more, although it never again enjoyed royal patronage.[9]

It is claimed that before reaching Tibet, Bön prospered in a land known as Zhangzhung and that this country remained the center of Bön until it was conquered by the expanding Tibetan empire in the seventh century. Zhangzhung was subsequently converted to Buddhism and assimilated into Tibetan culture, losing not only its independence but also its language and its Bönpo religious heritage in the process. There is no doubt as to the historical reality of Zhangzhung, although its exact extent and ethnic and cultural identity are far from clear. It seems, however, to have been situated in what today is, roughly speaking, western Tibet, with Mount Kailash as its center.[10]

A crucial question—for present-day Bönpos and Western scholars alike—is the authenticity of a specific Zhangzhung language. Just as the greater part of the canonical, sacred texts of the Tibetan Buddhists has been translated from Sanskrit, the scriptures of Bön have, so the Bönpos claim, been translated into Tibetan from the language of Zhangzhung. Numerous texts have titles that are given, first, in a non-Tibetan form, stated to be "in the language of Zhangzhung," followed by a Tibetan translation of the title. As no texts have so far come to light that can be conclusively shown to be of Zhangzhung origin, it has not been possible to identify this language with any degree of precision. The issue of the Zhangzhung language has been hotly debated, especially since the publication of a bilingual Tibetan-Zhangzhung vocabulary by the Danish scholar Erik Haarh in 1968. R. A. Stein, on the other hand, has argued against the existence of an authentic Zhangzhung language.[11] While much more research is needed, it is at the very least clear that the sacred texts of Bön have preserved a large and authentic vocabulary from a Tibeto-Burman linguistic stratum closely linked to languages in the Himalayas and along the Sino-Tibetan border, such as the dialects of Kinnaur (Himachal Pradesh), Tsangla (eastern Bhutan) and the dialects of Gyarong [Gyelrong] (Sichuan). These languages are only distantly related to Tibetan.

Many Zhangzhung words are used in Bönpo texts, quite independently of textual titles, and thus contribute towards giving Bönpo texts a different character from Buddhist Tibetan texts. Such words are (to quote only a few random examples) *shetün*, "heart" (*she thun*, Tibetan *snying*); *nyiri*, "sun" (*nyi ri*, Tibetan *nyi ma*); *werro*, "king" (*wer ro*, Tibetan *rgyal po*); *rang*, "horse" (*hrang*, Tibetan *rta*), etc. Some Zhangzhung words occur in the names of deities presented in this book [from which this essay was drawn], such as *tsamé*, "woman" (*tsa med*, Tibetan *skyes dman*, cf. Kinnauri *tsamé*); *sé*, "god" (*sad*, Tibetan *lha*, cf. Kinnauri *sat*); *ting*, "water" (*ting*, Tibetan *chu*, cf. Kinnauri *ti*).

The ultimate homeland of Bön is, however—so the Bönpos claim—to be found even farther to the west, beyond the borders of Zhangzhung. The Bönpos believe that "Eternal Bön" was first proclaimed in a land called Takzik (Rtag gzigs or Stag gzig). Although the name suggests the land of the Tajiks in Central Asia, it has so far not been possible to make a more exact identification of this holy land of Bön. Takzik is, however, not merely a geographical country like any other; in Bön tradition, it assumes the character of a "hidden," semi-paradisiacal land which latter-day humans can only reach in visions or by supernatural means after being spiritually purified. Takzik, also known as Ölmo Lungring ('Ol mo lung ring), may thus be regarded as a counterpart to the Buddhist holy land of Shambhala.[12]

For the Bönpos, Takzik is the holy land of religion, being the land in which Tönpa Shenrap (Ston pa Gshen rab, "the Teacher Shenrap") was born in the royal family and in due course became enthroned as king. Tönpa Shenrap is believed to be a fully enlightened being, the true Buddha (the word "Buddha" simply means "the Enlightened One") of our world age. The Bönpos possess a voluminous hagiographical literature in which his exploits are extolled.[13] Without entering into details or discussing the many problems connected with the historical and literary genesis of this extraordinary figure, one may at least note that his biography is not, contrary to what has sometimes been claimed by Western scholars, closely related to that of Śākyamuni. Thus, during the greater part of his career, Tönpa Shenrap was the ruler of Takzik or Ölmo Lungring and hence a layman, and it was as such that he incessantly journeyed from his capital in all directions to propagate Bön. It is worth noting that this propagation also included the performance of innumerable rituals. These rituals, which are performed by Bönpos today, thus find their justification and legitimation in the exemplary exploits of Tönpa Shenrap. Contrary to Buddhism, where rituals generally have no direct canonical basis, in Bön, as pointed out by Philip Denwood, "we have whole developed rituals and their liturgies specified in the minutest detail in the basic canon."[14] The propagation of Bön by Tönpa Shenrap also included the construction of temples and stūpas, but not the foundation of monasteries, which are not mentioned at all in his biography. Traveling far and wide and surrounded by his entourage he engaged in the conversion of notorious sinners. His numerous wives, sons, daughters and disciples also played significant roles in this soteriological activity, in a way for which there is no Buddhist parallel. It was only late in life that he was ordained, after which he retired to a forest hermitage, and it was only at this point in his career that he finally succeeded in converting his mighty opponent, the Prince of Demons.[15]

Certain parts of the biography of Tönpa Shenrap are clearly related to figures such as Padmasambhava, the eighth-century Indian yogin and magician who, according to the Buddhists, was invited to Tibet by the king and, subjugating the local gods and demons, founded Samyé (*Bsam yas*), the first Buddhist monastery (c. 779). He may also be compared to Gesar, the hero of the great Tibetan epic who, like Tönpa Shenrap, conducts triumphant campaigns in all cardinal directions against the forces of evil. The historical and literary relationship between these various figures remains to be clarified, but it is at least certain that the entire cycle of biographical material relating to Tönpa Shenrap—whatever its relationship to historical fact—cannot be dismissed as simple plagiarization of Buddhist texts.

By the late eleventh century, the Bönpos had begun to establish monasteries organized along the same lines as those of the Buddhists, and several of these monasteries eventually developed into large institutions with hundreds of monks and novices. The most prestigious Bönpo monastery, founded in 1405, is Menri in the Central Tibetan province of Tsang, north of the Brahmaputra (Tsangpo) River, but there are numerous other monasteries, especially in eastern and northeastern Tibet (Kham and Amdo). Monks are bound by strict rules of discipline, including celibacy. Fully ordained monks are called *drangsong*, a term that in Tibetan usually translates Sanskrit *ṛṣi*, the semi-divine "seers" of the Vedas.[16] Over the centuries the monastic life of Bön has increasingly come under the influence of the tradition of academic learning and scholastic debate that characterizes the dominant Buddhist Gelukpa school, but the tradition of tantric yogins and hermits, living in organized communities or in solitude, has never been abandoned.

The Bönpos have a vast literature which Western scholars are only just beginning to explore. Formerly it was taken for granted in the West that this literature was nothing but an uninspired and shameless plagiarism of Buddhist texts. The last twenty-five years have, however, seen a radical change in the view of the Bön religion. This reassessment was initiated by David L. Snellgrove, who in 1967 made the just observation regarding Bönpo literature that "by far the greater part would seem to have been absorbed through learning and then retold, and this is not just plagiarism."[17]

Subsequently, other scholars have been able to show conclusively that in the case of several Bönpo texts which have obvious, even word-by-word Buddhist parallels, it is not, as was formerly taken for granted, the Bönpo text which reproduces a Buddhist original, but in fact the other way round: the Bönpo text has been copied by Buddhist authors.[18] This does not mean that Bön was never at some stage powerfully influenced by Buddhism; but once the two religions, Bön and Buddhism, were established as rival traditions in Tibet, their relationship, it is now realized, was a complicated one of mutual influence.

The nature of the sacred texts of Bön can only be understood in the context of the Bönpo view of history. Bön tradition holds that the early kings of Tibet were adherents of Bön, and that consequently not only the royal dynasty but the entire realm prospered. This happy state of affairs came to a temporary halt during the reign of the eighth king, Drigum Tsenpo. This king persecuted Bön with the result that a large number of Bön texts were hidden away so that they might be preserved for future generations. For Bönpos, this was the beginning of the textual tradition consisting of "treasures," *terma*, i.e., concealed texts that have been rediscovered at an appropriate time by gifted individuals called "treasure-revealers," *tertön*.[19]

Although Bön was reinstated by Drigum Tsenpo's successor and flourished during the reigns of subsequent kings as it had done before, it was once more persecuted by king Tri Songdetsen in the eighth century. This king is portrayed in mainstream Tibetan tradition as a devout Buddhist, thanks to whose patronage the first Tibetan monks were ordained. Bönpo sources maintain, however, that his motives for supporting Buddhism were, on the one hand, the selfish belief that he could thereby prolong his life, and, on the other hand, the argument put forward by certain evil individuals at his court that the Bönpo priests, already equal to the king in power, would certainly take over the whole government after his death.[20]

Whatever the truth—and leaving aside the question of whether "later historians have made two persecutions out of what was in fact only one"[21]—both Buddhist and Bönpos agree that during the reign of Tri Songdetsen, the Bönpo priests were either banished from Tibet or compelled to conform to Buddhism.

Once again Bön texts were concealed, to be rediscovered when the time was ripe for propagating Bön anew.

The greater part of this vast body of literature, which the Bönpos regard as forming their canon of sacred scriptures, belongs to the class of "treasures," believed to have been hidden away during the successive persecutions of Bön and subsequently revealed by "treasure-discoverers." Bönpos also claim that many of their sacred scriptures were transformed by the Buddhists into Buddhist texts, thus reversing the accusation of plagiarism.

According to Bönpo historical texts, the final rediscovery of their sacred scriptures began early in the tenth century. The first discoveries are said to have been made by chance. Wandering beggars stealing a box from the monastery of Samyé in the belief that it contained gold and later exchanging the contents—which to their disappointment turned out to be only Bönpo books—for food, has an authentic ring; the same is true of an account of Buddhists looking for Buddhist texts, who, finding only Bönpo texts, simply gave them away.[22] Gradually, however, the textual discoveries came to be surrounded by supernatural signs and circumstances. Discoveries of texts were frequently preceded by initiatory preparations, often lasting several years and culminating in visions in which supernatural beings revealed the place where the "treasure" was hidden. Often the "treasure" is not a concrete book at all, but an inspired text arising spontaneously in the mind of the "treasure-discoverer"; such a text is a "mental treasure," *gongter.*[23]

Those texts which were considered by the Bönpos to be derived, ultimately, from Tönpa Shenrap himself, were collected to form a canon. This vast collection of texts (the only edition available today consists of approximately 190 volumes) constitutes the Bönpo Kangyur, forming an obvious parallel to the Tibetan Buddhist canon, likewise called "Kangyur." While no precise date for the formation of the Bönpo Kangyur can be ascertained at present, it should be noted that it does not seem to contain texts which have come to light later than 1386. A reasonable surmise would be that the Bönpo Kangyur was assembled by 1450. The Bönpo Kangyur, which in turn only constitutes a fraction of the total literary output of the Bönpos, covers the full range of Tibetan religious culture; as far as Western scholarship is concerned, it still remains practically unexplored.[24]

A common division of the Bönpo Kangyur is the fourfold one into Sūtras (Mdo), Prajñāpāramitā ('Bum), Tantras (Rgyud) and texts dealing with the higher forms of meditation (Mdzod, "Treasure-house"). For the sake of convenience the Indian (Buddhist) terms are used here and elsewhere, but it must be kept in mind that although the Bönpos employ the same Tibetan terms as the Buddhists, they do not accept their Indian origin, since they trace their religious terminology to Zhangzhung.

Like the Buddhists, the Bönpos also have a vast collection of commentarial, philosophical and ritual texts known as the Tengyur (Bstan 'gyur). The contents are divided into three basic categories: "External," including commentaries on canonical texts dealing with monastic discipline, morality, metaphysics and the biographies of Tönpa Shenrap; "Internal," comprising the commentaries on the Tantras including rituals focusing on the tantric deities and the cult of Ḍākinis, goddesses whose task it is to protect the Doctrine, and worldly rituals of magic and divination; and finally "Secret," a section that deals with meditational practices.[25] For the present study of the iconography of Bön, textual material has been extracted from the Sutra and Tantra sections of the Kangyur, and from the "External" and "Internal" sections of the Tengyur.

A significant genre within Bönpo literature is that of historiographical texts. The importance of this genre lies in the particular perspective on Tibetan history that it presents, a perspective which is radically different from Tibetan Buddhist texts. Thus, in Buddhist texts, the introduction of Buddhism in the seventh and eighth centuries under the patronage of successive Tibetan kings is regarded as a great blessing, pre-ordained by the Buddha Śākyamuni and carried out by saints and scholars from the holy land of India. Thanks to Buddhism, so the Buddhists maintain, Tibetans acquired a higher ethical code, the art of writing, the subtleties of philosophy and the possibility of reaching spiritual enlightenment—in other words, they became a civilized nation.

The picture is altogether different when we turn to Bönpo historical literature. The introduction of Buddhism into Tibet is described as a catastrophe. Writing in 1842, a Bönpo scholar, an abbot of Menri monastery, Nyima Tendzin, described the introduction of Buddhism as ultimately due to "the perverse prayer of a demon" and put into effect when the moment was ripe by "he who acted like a monk but retained the Five Poisons," i.e., the Buddhist saint Śāntarakṣita. The suppression of Bön is referred to as "the setting of the sun of the Doctrine," followed by the dissolution of the Tibetan state and the spread of moral and social anarchy.[26] On the other hand, conciliatory efforts have not been lacking; thus one source suggests that Tönpa Shenrap and the Buddha Śākyamuni were in reality cousins, and their doctrines, consequently, essentially identical.[27]

It is difficult to assess the number of Bönpos in Tibet. Certainly they are a significant minority. Particularly in eastern Tibet, as for example in the Sharkhok area north of Sungpan in Sichuan, whole districts are populated by Bönpos. Another important center is the region of Gyarong [Gyelrong] where several petty kingdoms, fully independent of the Tibetan government in Lhasa as well as of the Chinese Emperor, provided generous patronage for local Bönpo monasteries until the greater part of the region was conquered in a series of devastating campaigns conducted by the imperial Chinese army in the eighteenth century.[28] Scattered communities of Bönpos are also to be found in central and western Tibet; of the ancient Zhangzhung kingdom, however, no trace remains, although Mount Kailash is an important place of pilgrimage for Bönpos as well as Buddhists. Another much-frequented place of pilgrimage, exclusively—as opposed to Mount Kailash—visited by Bönpos, is Mount Bönri, "Mountain of Bön," in the southeastern district of Kongpo.[29] In the north of Nepal there are

Bönpo villages, especially in the district of Dölpo. At a point in history which remains to be determined, Bön apparently exerted a strong influence on the Nakhi [Ch. Naxi] people in Yunnan Province in southwestern China;[30] with this exception, the Bönpos do not seem to have engaged in missionary enterprises. In India, Bönpos belonging to the Tibetan exile community have established (since 1968) a large and well-organized monastery in which traditional scholarship, rituals and sacred dances of Bön have been preserved and are carried out with great vigor.[31]

NOTES

1. For a survey of the early history of Buddhism in Tibet, see David Snellgrove and Hugh Richardson, *A Cultural History of Tibet* (New York: Frederick A. Praeger, 1968), 66–143; and David Snellgrove, *Indo-Tibetan Buddhism: Indian Buddhists and Their Tibetan Successors* (London: Random House, 1987), 381–526.

2. For an overview of Bön, see Per Kværne, "Bon," in *The Encyclopedia of Religion*, ed. Mircea Eliade, vol. 2 (New York: Macmillan, 1987), 277–281. There is no consensus as to the etymology of the word *bön*; the discussion is summed up in David Snellgrove, *The Nine Ways of Bon: Excerpts from the* Gzhi brjid *Edited and Translated* (London: Oxford University Press, 1967), 2.

3. Bön has been described as an unorthodox form of Buddhism by Snellgrove, *The Nine Ways of Bon*; Per Kværne, "Aspects of the Origin of the Buddhist Tradition in Tibet," *Numen* 19, no. 1 (1972): 22–40, and again by Snellgrove, *Indo-Tibetan Buddhism*.

4. I have emphasized this perspective in Kværne, "Bon," and Per Kværne, "The Bön of Tibet: The Historical Enigma of a Monastic Tradition," in *The Renaissance of Tibetan Civilization*, ed. C. von Fürer-Haimendorf (Oracle, Ariz.: Synergectic Press, 1990), 114–119.

5. R. A. Stein, *Tibetan Civilization* (Stanford: Stanford University Press, 1972), 191ff.

6. This understanding of Bön has been consistently maintained by Helmut Hoffmann; see Hoffmann, *The Religions of Tibet* (London: George Allen and Unwin, 1961).

7. Hoffmann, *The Religions of Tibet*, 98. Fifteen years later, he still maintained this view in spite of a radical improvement in the availability of relevant sources. See Helmut Hoffmann, *Tibet: A Handbook* (Bloomington: Indiana University Press, 1975).

8. Especially Snellgrove, *The Nine Ways of Bon*, 1–21 ("Introduction"). For a detailed study of a whole range of Buddhist polemical writings directed against Bön, see Daniel Martin, "The Emergence of Bon and the Tibetan Polemical Tradition," Ph.D. thesis, Department of Uralic and Altaic Studies, Indiana University, 1991.

9. The relevant section of the historical work *Legs bshad mdzod*, written in 1929 but quoting a large number of older sources, has been translated by Samten Karmay,

The Treasury of Good Sayings: A Tibetan History of Bon (London: Oxford University Press, 1972).

10. On the question of Zhangzhung, see Karmay, *The Treasury of Good Sayings*, xxx, and Giuseppe Tucci, *Preliminary* Serie Orientale Roma X, *Report on Two Scientific Expeditions in Nepal*, part 1 (Rome: Instituto italiano per il Medio ed Estremo Oriente, 1956), 71–75.

11. See Erik Haarh, *The Zhang-zhung Language: A Grammar and Dictionary of the Unexplored Language of the Tibetan Bonpos*, Acta Jutlandica XL:1, Humanistisk serie 47 (Aarhus: Universitetsforlaget i Aarhus, 1968); and R. A. Stein, "La langue zhang-zhung du Bon organisé [The Zhang zhung Language of Organized Bon]," *Bulletin de l'ecole Fraçaise d'Extrême Orient* 58 (1971): 232–254.

12. On Takzik and Ölmo Lungring, see Karmay, *The Treasury of Good Sayings*, xxviii; and Graham Coleman, *A Handbook of Tibetan Culture* (London: Rider, 1993), 13–16. On Shambhala, see Edwin Bernbaum, *The Way to Shambhala: A Search for the Mythical Kingdom Beyond the Himalayas* (New York: Anchor Press/Doubleday, 1980).

13. For an overview of this literature, see Per Kværne, "The Canon of the Tibetan Bonpos," *Indo-Iranian Journal* 16, no. 1 (1974): 18–56 and continued in *Indo-Iranian Journal* 16, no. 2 (1974): 96–144. See also Per Kværne, "Peintures tibétianes de la vie de Ston pa gçen rab" [Tibetan Paintings of the Life of Ston pa gshen rab], *Arts Asiatiques* XLI (1986): 36–81.

14. Philip Denwood, "Notes on Some Bonpo Rituals," in *Buddhist Studies: Ancient and Modern*, ed. Philip Denwood and Alexander Piatigorsky (London: Curzon Press; Totowa, N.J.: Barnes & Noble, 1983), 13.

15. Kværne, "Tibetan Paintings of the Life of Ston pa gshen rab," 73–74.

16. Snellgrove, *The Nine Ways of Bon*, 10.

17. Snellgrove, *The Nine Ways of Bon*, 12.

18. Anne-Marie Blondeau, "Le Lha 'dre bka' thang," In *Études Tibétaines dediées à la mémoire de Marcelle Lalou* (Paris: Maisonneuve, 1971), 29–126, especially 45–47, and Samten Karmay, *The Great Perfection* (Leiden: Brill, 1988), 216–223.

19. Karmay, *The Treasury of Good Sayings*.

20. See the Bönpo historical work known as *Grags pa gling grags*, hitherto unpublished and known to exist in the form of two manuscripts only. I am preparing an edition and translation of this text for publication.

21. Karmay, *The Treasury of Good Sayings*, xxxiii.

22. Karmay, *The Treasury of Good Sayings*, 152.

23. For an overview of the traditions of Bönpo "treasures," see Kværne, "The Canon of the Tibetan Bonpos," 27–37.

24. See Kværne, "The Canon of the Tibetan Bonpos."

25. The Bönpo Tengyur is analyzed in Kværne, "The Canon of the Tibetan Bonpos," 114–144. Note that in the context of Bön, the spelling of Tengyur is *brten 'gyur*, "that which is firm (*brten*)," hence implying the firmness of the doctrine.

26. Per Kværne, "A Chronological Table of the Bon po: The bstan rcis of Ñi ma bstan 'jin," *Acta Orientalia* 33 (1971): 227.

27. Per Kværne, "Śākyamuni in the Bon Religion," *Temenos* 25 (1989): 38.

28. On the Bönpo communities in Gyarong, see Patrick Mansier, "La guerre du Jinchuan (Rgyal rong): son contexte politico-religieux [The Jinchuan (Rgyal rong) War: Its Politico-Religious Context]," in *Tibet: Civilisation et société*, ed. Fernand Meyer (Paris: Éditions de la Fondation Singer-Polignac: Éditions de la Maison des Sciences de l'Homme, 1990), 125–142; Samten Karmay, "The Decree of the Khro chen King," *Acta Orientalia* 51 (1990): 141–159; and Roger Greatrex, "A Brief Introduction to the First Jinchuan War (1747–1749)," in *Tibetan Studies: Proceedings of the 6th Seminar of the IATS Fagernes 1992*, ed. Per Kværne (Oslo: The Institute for Comparative Research in Human Culture, 1994), 247–263.

29. Samten Karmay, "A Pilgrimage to Kongpo Bon-ri," In *Tibetan Studies: Proceedings of the 5th Seminar of the International Association for Tibetan Studies, Narita 1989*, ed. International Association for Tibetan Studies, Shōren Ihara, and Zuihō Yamaguchi, Monograph series of Naritasan Institute for Buddhist Studies, 2 (Narita-shi, Chiba-Ken, Japan: Naritasan Shinshoji, 1992), 527–539.

30. Anthony Jackson, *Na-khi religion: An Analytical Appraisal of the Na-khi Ritual Texts, Religion and Society*, vol. 8 (The Hague; New York: Mouton), 1979. The Nakhi have a complex pantheon which at least to some extent is influenced by Bön and in some cases includes deities also found in Bön; cf. Rock 1952.

31. Kværne, "The Bön of Tibet"; and Coleman, *A Handbook of Tibetan Culture*, 208–210.

Chapter 11

THE EVOLUTION OF MONASTIC POWER

R. A. Stein

R. A. Stein can probably be considered France's first great historian of Tibet. He read both Tibetan and Chinese and wrote one of the first survey textbooks of Tibetan history and culture (*La civilisation tibetaine*, 1962; English translation, 1972). The present selection, extracted from *Tibetan Civilization*, offers a useful overview of the development of Tibetan monasticism from the eleventh century. It begins with the revival of Buddhism, first reintroduced from Amdo and then from Ngari (relying on Indian teachers), in Central Tibet. Stein was one of the leading scholars of Tibet to pay attention to the role of eastern Tibet (often referred to simply as Kham in this selection, a term that for centuries included the regions now known as both Kham and Amdo) in the revival of Tibetan Buddhism in Central Tibet. A key feature of this period was the diminished importance of royal or aristocratic lines in favor of monastic centers of power, albeit some led by families of noble lineage. This became a tradition and a hallmark of Tibetan society by the twelfth century, as did a pattern of reliance on outside military and financial support whenever Tibet returned to effective centralized rule for any length of time. This selection sketches the general picture of Tibetan religio-political history from the tenth to the seventeenth centuries, which will be explored in more detail in other chapters that follow.

When the curtain lifts once more and a few gleams of light fall on the scene, Tibetan civilization is definitely taking on the aspect it has retained till modern times. History is no longer concerned with kings but with monasteries and reli-

gious orders. The princes or heads of noble houses are now no more than benefactors and partisans of one ecclesiastical establishment or another. It is the
eleventh century.

In China, after the fall of the Tang (907) and the intervening period of the
Five Dynasties (907–960), the Song dynasty (960–1276) was established. But in
the north-west of the country a new state had taken shape: Xixia or, in both Tibetan and its own Tibeto-Burman language, Minyak. It soon stormed the Chinese towns occupied by the Uighurs (Shazhou, Ganzhou, and so on, in 1038), but
in the west it collided with a recently formed Tibetan kingdom in the Xining
region (Chinese Qingtang; Tibetan Tsongkha), that was headed by one Gyelsé
(Chinese Juesiluo [Gusiluo in the Iwaski article above], 997–1065), whom the
Tibetan chieftains of the region had traveled westwards to find, probably in
Maryül, among the descendants of the royal line. This state, which lasted till
about 1100, was Buddhist. Monks, some of them from Khotan—occupied by the
Muslims since 1006—played a major political part. They had dealings with China
and the Uighurs, both those of Ganzhou, who later settled further south in the
Nan Shan range where they still live under the name of Uighurs, and those of
Turfan who were Buddhists and Manichaeans.

So it was to these parts that Buddhist monks made their way, fugitives from
the persecution and decadence in Central Tibet. Three monks set out via Ladakh
and the Qarluq Turks to the west, passing through Hor (Uighurs) in the north, to
end up in Amdo, on the Yellow River. Ge[wa] Rapsel of the Musu or Musi clan,
an ex-Bönpo from Tsongkha, was converted to Buddhism (832–915 [more recent
scholarship suggests his dates were actually 953–1035]).[1] His ordination as a monk
required the presence of five existing monks. Three Tibetans were found further
south, at Longtang in Kham, and two Chinese were added to make up the quo-
rum. Others came to join the nucleus thus constituted, which soon approached
King Tri of Yarlung with the intention of renewing links with Central Tibet. The
ruins of Samyé were restored and other monasteries were founded.[2]

A new upsurge of Buddhism meanwhile took place in the west through the
efforts of the kings of Ngari. King Khorré had abdicated in favor of his younger
brother Sungé, and taken the robe under the name (Lha Lama) Yeshé-ö. He
decided to send young men to study in India, for the monastic tradition had
been lost, and irregular practices had caused the spread of doubt. In the tenth
and eleventh centuries, married Tantrists had taken the instructions of certain
Tantras literally. These "robber-monks" (*artso bande, aramo bandhe*) kid-
napped and killed men and women, ate them, drank alcohol and indulged in
sexual intercourse. In the face of such developments, the need to be assured of
a sound tradition was felt. The kings as patrons of the established religion were
concerned for the upholding of public morals, just as in Tri Songdetsen's day.
The Tibetan monks they sent to India and the Indian teachers they invited to
Tibet, however, were all firm adherents of the Tantrism then flourishing in
India, not only among isolated yogins, but in the great monastic colleges such

as Nālandā and Vikramaśīla. They were simply careful to offer a symbolic interpretation, especially to the uninitiated and to lay people, of ritual acts which
taken literally would offend common morality. Their reform consisted mainly of
a rigorous distinction between the types of behavior expected at different levels of
mental training and holiness: ordinary men had to regulate their conduct according to ordinary morality. Not for nothing was the most violent diatribe against
Tantric abuses delivered by Lha Lama Jangchup-ö, prince of Purang.[3] Reform
aimed at the re-establishment of monastic discipline.

Two figures dominate this period in western Tibet. Rinchen Zangpo (958–
1055), who was sent to India and Kashmir, showed tremendous industry as a
translator and founded several temples in Gugé—Toling in particular—as well
as, in all probability, Tabo and Nako in Spiti. Atiśa (982–1054), invited to Tibet,
was the founder of the great Kadampa order, from which later came the Gelukpa
order, the official or Yellow Church of the Dalai Lamas and Panchen Lamas.

Atiśa, also known as Dīpaṃkara Śrījñāna, is described as the son of a king of
Zahor, a country noted for Tantrism. He studied all the schools of Buddhism,
including Hīnayāna, but above all the Tantras. These works were taught by the
famous *siddhas* or yogins such as Dombhi, Nāropa and Avadhūtipa, all of them
teachers revered in Tibet. Offered a large quantity of gold to come to Tibet, by
Jangchup-ö, nephew or grand-nephew of Yeshé-ö, the king of Gugé, he arrived
in 1042 and died in Tibet in 1054. He found Buddhism in the process of renewal
through the work of monks from Kham who now became his disciples. The
composition of this group of disciples is significant. The three leading members, Langdarma, Ngoktön and Dromtön, were natives of Ü who had brought
back the tradition of the Vinaya or monastic discipline from Kham, while the
four others were all yogins (*amé* or *neljorpa*).

It was in Kham, at Longtang in the land of Den, that a wandering monk
from Nepal, Smṛiti, had founded a school for the study of the *Abhidharmakośa*,
before moving on to Liangzhou. He taught Dromtön. The latter, at the age of
seventeen, returned to Ü and founded the famous Radreng monastery (north of
Lhasa) in 1057. He became Atiśa's principal disciple. Smṛiti had taught Sanskrit
to Setsün who, in turn, was the teacher of Atiśa's three chief disciples, and who
founded an important faculty of theology at Ölka on the model of the school at
Longtang.

But, in the same part of Kham, the spiritual lineage of Padmasambhava had
also been kept alive through the agency of the translator Vairocana, exiled to
Jinchuan [Gyelrong], where the daughter of a king of that region became his
disciple. This lineage is that of the Dzokchenpa order, which belongs to the
"ancient" (Nyingmapa) unreformed school, and teaches a form of Tantrism in
which some material from Chinese Dhyāna (Chan, Zen) is preserved. A former
Bönpo, Yazi Böntön, and his teacher, Aro, were also there at that time. This
Aro, likewise established at Longtang in Den, had received the teachings of
seven lineages of India, together with seven lineages of China. A point of inter-

est is that, alone among Tibetan writings of this period, it was his chief work, *Entering Into the Yoga of the Mahāyāna*, that Atiśa is recorded as having liked and praised. So we are hardly surprised to find that Dromtön was followed on the abbot's throne at Radreng, from 1065 to 1078, by a great yogin (*amé*), Jang-chup Jungné, who was born at Tsongkha in 1015.[4]

Tantric teachings, with some variations, took root everywhere. On the basis of particular techniques and teachers, different orders and great monasteries were founded in this period. Drokmi, "the man of the grazing lands" (992–1074), acquired from great yogins in India the teaching known as Lamdré ("the path and fruit of action") that made use of sexual practices for mystical realization. His disciple Könchok Gyelpo in 1073 founded the great monastery of Sakya whose future hierarchs were to become so important.

Marpa (1012–1096) also went to India where he learned, among other things, the art of transferring the conscious principle into another body or a paradise (*powa, drongjuk*). But above all he brought back and handed on to his disciple Milarepa the mystical songs (*dohā*) of the Tantric poets of Bengal, and the doctrines called Mahāmudrā, the "Great Seal." Out of the disciples of the poet hermit Milarepa (1040–1123) was formed the Kagyüpa order, whose two main branches were to have extensive influence. Khyungpo the Yogin, born in a Bönpo clan and brought up initially on Bönpo and Dzokchenpa doctrines, founded the branch at Shang in Tsang, dying in 1139. To the east, in Dakpo, Gampopa (1079–1153)—also called Dakpo Lharjé ("physician, or medium, of Dakpo")—founded the Dakpo branch, maintaining doctrinal links with the Kadampa. A little later the school produced major subdivisions whose hierarchs and monasteries played an important political role: the Karmapa, Drigungpa, Tselpa, Pakmodrupa and Drukpa. All these names are derived from the names of monasteries, the suffix -pa denoting membership of a group, or place of birth.

The incredible religious and philosophic ferment of the eleventh century does not stop at that. We have already mentioned the Dzokchenpa tradition, which had been kept up since the ninth century in Kham. Now people tried to link up with that period and with Padmasambhava by discovering "hidden treasures" (*terma*). These were writings which a modern historian would class as apocryphal like prophecies, but which were said to have been concealed in the time of Padmasambhava. Some, it should be added, may have been adaptations of genuine documents if we are to believe their description as rolls of yellow paper, which agrees with the appearance of the Dunhuang manuscripts. From its beginning at this period the fashion grew over subsequent centuries, with Nyangrel Nyima Özer, ruler of Nyang (1136–1203), Guru Chöwang (1212–1273) and many others, including Mingyur Dorjé of Kham in the seventeenth century. We should also recall that at the same period the Kālacakra and the sexagenary cycle were introduced (1027). Two other doctrines and practices which were to play a great part in Tibet (*zhijé* and *chö*) were spread at that time by an Indian yogin, Dampa Sanggyé (who died in 1117), and more especially by a remarkable Tibetan woman, "the Mother" (*Machik*) Lap Drönma (1055–1145 or 1153).

In the following century, this intellectual activity was translated into social or political reality. We know nothing at all about the noble families and local principalities, and only a little about the conditions that allowed the flourishing of rich and powerful monasteries. We shall hear of one feature later on: the succession of abbots from paternal uncle to nephew within a noble family, one brother getting married, the other becoming a monk. In any case, by the twelfth century monasteries are everywhere, some of them being particularly powerful. A century later and they are battling for temporal power; and these internal feuds, in combination with the rivalries of noble houses and the absence of central authority, prepare Tibet for the fate that will henceforth be hers. On re-entering Asian history in the thirteenth century, her participation is no longer active as in the past but passive. Submission to foreign powers is all that will now be possible.

Let us take a look at the forces confronting one another when the Mongols first appeared on the scene. The great Khön family, which had supplied prominent members of the religious community since Tri Songdetsen's time, had made its home at Sakya. Like other great noble clans, it claimed divine descent. It was allied with the Ché family whose divine ancestry accordingly had much in common with theirs. The family connection was carried on in the relations between monasteries. The Khön founded Sakya in 1073; the Ché had founded the monastery of Zhalu, not far away, in 1040. Some centuries later their rulers established marriage ties with the lords of Gyantsé.

Another important noble family with the indispensable distinction of divine origin, the Pakmodru, was connected with the great Lang clan and, through it, with the Gar family that was already powerful in Kham and later to reign at Dergé. The Pakmodru family originally came from Kham where its forbears occupied a district in the valley of the Drichu (the Upper Yangtze), but it took the name of the region where the branch's founder settled. This "precious protector of beings," the "great man of Kham," born in 1110, was a pupil of Gampopa (Dakpo Lharjé) and of one of the Sakyapas. In 1158 he founded the monastery of Til or Tel at the place called Pakmodru, in the Ön district (the south-eastern corner of Central Tibet), and in 1170 he died. He won the territory of the "king of Tsarong" at a game of chess. His religious order derived from both the Kadampas and the Kagyüpas. The monastery was a bone of contention between the abbots of Drigung and those of Taklung. The office of abbot was handed down from uncle to nephew. But the family did not attain political power till later, in the fourteenth century.

Drigung monastery, on a tributary on the Kyichu far to the north-east of Lhasa, was first set up by Minyak Gomring, a disciple of Pakmodrupa (abbot in 1167); however, its real foundation was the work of Drigung Rinpoché (1143–1217), a monk from Den, in Kham, in 1179. The order was attached to the Kagyüpas. The administration, modeled on that of Sakya, comprised an abbot assisted by a civil and military governor who, despite his functions, bore the title of "great meditator (or hermit)" (*gom chen*).

Another monk of the Kagyüpa order, Zhang Rinpoché (1123–1193), founded the monastery of Tsel (1175) and the temple of Tsel Gungtang (1187) on the Kyichu [River] a little east of Lhasa. This monastery became the seat of the Tsel family who were soon to take part in the struggles for power.

One last important counter on the political board remains to be introduced. This is the Karmapa order. Its founder Düsum Khyenpa (1110–1193) was another native of Kham, from the district of Dao (Daofu), and a follower of Milarepa's disciples—Gampopa, Rechung, etc. He first founded, in 1147, the "Karma seat" or "southern camp of Karma," east of the river Ngomchu in Kham, between Riwoché and Dergé. Subsequently in 1155 he established the Karma monastery of Tsur Lhalung (already began in 1154 by Dakpo Gomtsül in Tölung), then in 1185 that of Karma Lhadeng, and lastly, in 1189, that of Tsurpu, the modern seat of the Karmapas and also in the Tölung valley north-west of Lhasa. The order, which stems from the Kagyüpa, owes its name to a Black Hat of *ḍākinīs'* hair in which are brought together all the works (*trinlé* = *karma*) of all the Buddhas. With the abbots of Drigung, the Karmapa "Black Hat" succession claims to have started the system of successive reincarnations of the same person, which was later adopted for the Dalai and Panchen Lamas. Its representatives reign to this day and formerly recognized a related line of incarnate hierarchs, the "Red Hats," starting with Drakpa Senggé (1283–1349).

While these monastic authorities were being set up at the religious, economic, political and military level, the "kings" or heads of principalities left scarcely a trace. In the west, our sources only provide incomplete lists of the kings of Gugé and Ladakh. They had turned towards Nepal and the outlying parts of India (Kulu, Purang and Kashmir). In the east, Gyelsé's sons were competing for mastery in Tsongkha, facing the powerful Xixia kingdom, and part of their domain seems to have formed the nucleus of a principality which was to play its part later on—Ling. With its neighbor, Beri, this little kingdom had been in existence since the end of the twelfth century if isolated references are to be believed. For the rest, there is silence and obscurity.

But now the Mongols appear on the scene. Chinggis Khan, king of the Mongols (Tibetan "Sok"), got as far as Central Tibet by 1206 according to Tibetan sources [actual Mongol incursions in Central Tibet did not occur until 1240, long after Chinggis had died].[5] Greeted by the regent Joga, a descendant of the Yarlung royal family, and by Künga Dorjé, head of the Tselpas, he received Tibet's submission from them. But we are also told that, before leaving, he sent presents to Sakya and invited its abbot, Künga Nyingpo, to come and preach the religion in Mongolia, thus offering himself as a "donor" or patron. By surrendering to alien suzerainty, Tibet was able to preserve her autonomy. In order to wield power in the interior, it was necessary to have a foreign patron. Sakya had been preferred to the Tselpas, though other candidates were waiting in the wings. And the political game grew more complex by virtue of the division of the Mongol empire between several brothers, on the death of Chinggis Khan in 1227 [in fact, this was not the case until 1251, when the Tibetan religions traditions' monasteries and their territories were divided up between the Mongol *khan* Möngke and other princes].

According to a Mongol work the first Karmapa, Düsum Khyenpa, tried to convert Qubilai Khan. Perhaps this is merely a pious anticipation, but it does show how, from the outset, the Karmapas were going to be the Sakyapas' rivals at the court of the Emperors of China—first Mongolian (Yuan) and later Chinese (Ming). In 1221–1222 a Karma lama, Tsangpa Dungkhurwa, was invited to Minyak, i.e., to a Buddhist, Tibetanized Xixia. He was still there when Chinggis Khan conquered that kingdom and died there (in 1227), and received an edict of approval from the queen. Karma Pakshi (1206–1283) was sent for by Qubilai, while still a prince, and met him in Amdo in 1255. Urged to stay with him, he refused, in expectation of conflicts between the Mongol princes. This attitude was to earn him persecution by Qubilai Khan and exile to South China, but prior to that he continued his journey as far as Mongolia (1256). There he took part in theological contests between Buddhists and Daoists at the court of the Emperor Möngke whom he had converted from Nestorian Christianity to Buddhism. However, Möngke died in 1260 and Qubilai took power against his young brother Arik Böke. Karmapa had lost his patron.[6]

The Sakyapas were more fortunate. The "great scholar" Sakya Panchen (1182–1251) had the reputation of having worsted the "heretics" in theological debates in India. So that he might do the same in Mongolia, he was sent for in 1244 by Güyük and Köden, the son and grandson of Chinggis Khan, who had made their headquarters in Koko Nor. In 1244, accompanied by his young nephews Pakpa (1235–80) and Chakna, he met Köden. The invitation was "supported," it seems, by a raid under the general, Dorta, whose army advanced as far as northern Ü, burning Radreng monastery and killing monks, but apparently sparing Drigung monastery. Sakya Panchen gave Köden religious initiation, and is credited with devising a Mongol alphabet. Köden in 1249 gave him an order conferring the rulership of Ü and Tsang on the Sakyapas [see David Jackson's chapter in this collection for the dubious origins of a similar document]. After the deaths of Köden and Sakya Panchen there was a fresh Mongol invasion of Tibet (1252–1253). But Qubilai became patron of the Sakyapas and granted them rulership over all [Central] Tibet's "thirteen provinces": this was in 1253, or in 1260 when he was proclaimed Emperor. The recipient of this authority was Pakpa, under the title of "Teacher of the Emperor" (di shi). He originated a Mongol script, derived from Tibetan writing, which continued in use for nearly a century.

If the Sakyapas had thus officially received the regency of all Tibet, other monasteries did not stand idly by. Profiting by the splitting up of Mongol power, each tried to have its own patron. The Tselpa, Gara, had performed rites for Arik Böke, son of Möngke, about 1260, but was later arrested by Qubilai Khan at Shangdu, the Mongol capital, where he died. Even so, Qubilai became patron of the Tselpas. Meanwhile Qubilai's elder brother, Hülegü, had founded the Ilkhan dynasty (1258–1335) in Iran. Despite some partiality towards the Christians, he was a Buddhist. He was chosen by the Drigungpas as their patron, which he became as early as 1267. Their aim was to turn the tables on the Sakyapas. They received offerings from Hülegü, gained control of Ü and founded the fief of Neudong which was to be very important later on; and in 1285 they descended in force on Jayül, in southern Tibet, and brought an army of Iran Mongols against Sakya. However, the Sakyapas won, helped by an army belonging to Qubilai's son Temürbukha and an army from Tsang, and burned the temple of Drigung in 1290; though Drigung was soon restored at the Sakyapas' own request, and received gifts from the Emperor. This was the first expression of the opposition between Ü and Tsang which was often to be manifested over the centuries.[7]

The Mongol Emperors of China exerted a fairly loose suzerainty over Tibet. They had instituted population censuses (1268, 1287) and tried to set up an administrative organization. But the real power was still contested among great monasteries backed up by important noble families. Sakyapa influence lasted only three-quarters of a century. The Pakmodrupa family had at first been linked with the Drigungpas and their patron Hülegü. But in the fourteenth century, under the "Great *Situ*" Jangchup Gyeltsen and his grandson, the family came to power in southern Tibet, where it was now allied with, now opposed to the Sakyapas and Drigungpas. In the meantime, the Karmapas continued to be welcomed at the Chinese court and took firm root in Kham and south-east Tibet. Here they were to occupy a leading position for centuries, alongside the Sakyapas.

One of the countries in Kham which had close relations with the Karmapas was the "kingdom" of Ling, which in those days included modern Dergé. When the Ming dynasty in China took over the Mongols' policy of bestowing honorary ranks and titles on various heads of religious orders, around 1400, Ling and Gönjo received the title of "kings" and golden seals, on a par with the Pakmodrupas, the Drigungpas and the Taktsangpas of Tsang. The Karmapas went to China in great numbers. They occupied themselves in bringing their moral authority, but often too the force of their military camps, to bear in pacifying the countless feuds and quarrels between indigenous tribes and minor states, followers of Buddhism and Bön.

Meanwhile a great yogin-type saint, Tangtong Gyelpo (1385–1464), celebrated for the building of iron suspension bridges, had opened the route to the

Kongpo aborigines (the Lo), and from them he obtained supplies of iron and rights of passage for Tibetan pilgrims wishing to visit the holy places of Tsari. He had also founded Dergé monastery.

In Central Tibet, Pakmodrupa power was on the wane and a new antagonism between Ü and Tsang was taking shape. The political leaders of the Pakmodrupas reigned in their capital of Nedong, in Yarlung, south of the Tsangpo; their abbots at Tsetang, a little further north. Their ministers, the princes of Rinpung, then took power at Samdruptsé (modern Zhigatsé in Tsang). They made war upon Ü (1481), while another war took place between the Karmapas (on the Tsang side) and Gelukpas (Ü).

For, in the meantime, an event of major importance had taken place—the foundation by Tsongkhapa (1357–1419) of the Gelukpa order. Not that the "reformation" for which he is commonly praised really included any basic innovation in doctrine or ritual. No more than Atiśa, whose teachings he followed, did he neglect the Tantras with all the rituals and meditations that go with them, which he had studied with the Karmapas and Sakyapas. But, like Atiśa and his Kadampa order, he insisted once more on the need for monastic discipline and the gradual path (morality, etc.), for the generality of men and even as a preliminary to total liberation. After a retreat at Radreng, the Kadampa monastery where in 1403 he composed his great work in two volumes (*Lamrim* and *Ngakrim*), he took the decision to mark the renewal of the discipline by founding a new order. At first, this was called "new Kadampa," but later Gelukpa ("those who follow virtuous works") or Gandenpa, from the Ganden monastery, founded in 1409. His reputation as a great theologian and debater earned Tsongkhapa an invitation to China from the Emperor (1408). Being too busy, he sent his disciple, Jamchen Chöjé Shakya Yeshé, who received the title "king of religion" and soon afterwards (1419) founded the great monastery of Sera. Another disciple, Jamyang Chöjé Trashi Penden, had founded—in 1416—the third great monastery in the neighborhood of Lhasa, Drepung, on the pattern of a Tantric monastery in India. These monasteries were regular university cities, and they all contained a variety of faculties, some of which specialized in the Tantras.

Despite the importance of this maintenance of Tantric tradition at the religious and philosophical level, it was its reforming side, its insistence on discipline, that set the movement's tone and political direction. Its affinity with the early Kadampas drew it towards the Pakmodrupas. The fact that their chief monasteries were situated in Ü reinforced this closeness through the territorial opposition between the forces of Ü and Tsang. Gelukpa monasteries were founded at Chamdo (1436–1444) in Kham, and at Trashilhünpo (1447) in Tsang, but the order was unable to gain the upper hand in either of these regions of Karmapa predominance. The princes of Tsang built a fortified monastery at Zhigatsé, close by Trashilhünpo, and even succeeded in keeping control of Lhasa for twenty years (1498–1518) through the instrumentality of the Karmapas. The "Red

Hat" Karmapas allied themselves with the governors of Tsang, who had succeeded the Rinpung princes (sixteenth century).

There were many wars. The monks of Drepung attacked the "people of the camps" (*garpa*), i.e., the Karmapa military camps, in 1546. The reason was that in 1537 the fifth Red Hat had formed an alliance with Drigung and the governor of Tsang, designed to suppress the Gelukpas and their best patrons, the princes of Ganden. The uncertain fate of these temporary alliances and local struggles was to be decided by a fresh Mongol irruption onto the political and military scene.

The influence of the Karmapa and Sakyapa hierarchs at the court of Chinggis Khan and his successors did not amount to an actual conversion of the Mongols to Lamaism. The eighth "Black Hat" Karmapa had fleeting contacts with Dayan Khan (1470–1543) who was then reigning over the Mongols. However, their real conversion was the work of Gelukpas at the time of Altan Khan, Dayan's grandson and king of the Tümed Mongols. The head of the Gelukpas in those days was the abbot of Drepung, later known as the Third Dalai Lama, Sönam Gyatso (1543–1588). The royal patrons of his order, the house of Pakmodru, were then split into two hostile branches. In spite of the support he received from several feudatories of this royal house, even in Tsang, the ruling family of Tsang was still a serious threat, along with the Karmapas, to Ü and the Gelukpas, particularly after they occupied the important position of Samdruptsé. So it was understandable that Sönam Gyatso should approach foreign patrons, as other hierarchs had done in the thirteenth century. Some Tibetan monks had been taken prisoner during expeditions led by Sechen Hung Taiji of the Ordos Mongols in 1566, and by Altan Khan in 1573. To revive the policies of his illustrious ancestor Qubilai Khan, Altan Khan now issued an invitation to Sönam Gyatso, and met him in 1578. With gifts heaped upon him, Sönam Gyatso secured an edict abolishing the Mongols' blood-sacrifices, as well as receiving his famous title of Dalai Lama (*dalai*, meaning "ocean" in Mongol, is a translation of the "gyatso" which occurs in the names of all the Dalai Lamas). The reason he is reckoned the third of the line is that his two previous incarnations were given the same title retrospectively. These were Gedün Drup (1391–1474), a personal disciple of Tsongkhapa and the founder of Trashilhünpo in 1447; and Gedün Gyatso (1475–1542), the first of his incarnations to be recognized as such, who had been abbot of Trashilhünpo in 1520, Drepung in 1517 and Sera in 1526.

The Third Dalai Lama traveled a great deal throughout Kham, Amdo, the Koko Nor region and Inner Mongolia, winning the patronage of the Tümed, Chahar and Khalkha Mongols for the Gelukpas. This the Mongols doubtless saw as a political advantage, for the Third Dalai Lama had scarcely died before his reincarnation was discovered in the person of a great grandson of Altan Khan. He was recognized by a delegation from his Drepung monastery and the princes of Ü, which had gone to Guisui (Köke Qoto [Hohhot], Inner Mongolia) to meet him in 1601.

The Fourth Dalai Lama, Yönten Gyatso, was duly installed on the throne of Drepung; but he was still threatened by the rulers of Tsang—who were aiming at hegemony and whose dependency the fief of Lhasa then was—and by the Karmapas. The latter had not omitted to find a patron of their own among the Mongol princes—Ligdan Khan of the Chahars. But at the same time they weakened their authority through an armed quarrel between the Amdo "Black Hat" and the "Red Hat" who was in alliance with the governor of Tsang. At this juncture the Karmapas had first to sustain an attack by Arslan Khan of the Khalkhas (battle near Dam in 1635), who subsequently turned against the Gelukpas, and then once more against the Karmapas. Arslan was executed by his father, and the Karmapas' remaining ally, Ligdan Khan, died of smallpox on the Koko Nor plain.

Mongol troops had opposed the armies of Tsang several times since 1621 in defense of the young Fifth Dalai Lama, Ngawang Lozang Gyatso (1617–1682). But the final blow to Tsang power and the triumph of the Gelukpas were due to the intervention of Gushri Khan. Having established himself at Koko Nor in 1637, he first crushed the principality of Beri, in Kham, whose religion was Bönpo, and then came to the aid of Dergé, which was by now enlarging itself at the expense of Ling. He went on to subdue the whole of Kham as far as Yunnan (Lijiang), where the Karmapas, till then (1641), had been powerful. A year later, the Tsang sovereign was defeated and killed. The Dalai Lama received authority from Gushri Khan to reign over all [Central] Tibet, but at the same time he had a "governor" (*desi*), nominated by the Mongol, imposed on him.

NOTES

1. Editors' note: Tshe tan Zhabs drung, "Mdo smad grub pa'i gnas chen dan tig shel gyi ri bo le lag dang bcas pa'i dkar chag don ldan ngag gi rgyud mangs [A Zither of Meaningful Words: A Catalogue to the Holy Place for Siddhas in Mdo smad, Mount Dan tig shel and Surrounding Areas]" in 'Jigs med chos 'phags, ed., *Tshe tan Zhabs drung rje btsun 'Jigs med rigs pa'i blo gros mchog gi gsung 'bum*, vol. 3 (Beijing: Minzu chubanshe, 2007), 314. This information was kindly provided by Nicole Willock.

2. Ye shes dpal 'byor, Sum pa mkhan po, *Dpag bsam ljon bzang* [*The Auspicious Wish-Fulfilling Tree*], ed. S. C. Das (Calcutta: xylograph in 316 folios, 1908 [1748]), 177–178 and *Re'u mig* [*Chronological Tables*]; *Une chronique ancienne de Bsam-yas, Sba-bžed* [*An Ancient Chronicle of Samyé, Bazhé*]. Edition of the Tibetan text with French summary by R. A. Stein (Paris: Institut des hautes études chinoises, 1961), 87–88.

3. Ye shes dpal 'byor, *The Auspicious Wish-Fulfilling Tree*, 393.

4. George N. Roerich, *The Blue Annals* (translation of 'Gos Gzhon nu dpal, *Deb ther sngon po*, 1476–1478), 2 vols. (Calcutta: Royal Asiatic Society of Bengal, 1948–1953), 2:1000; H. Hadano, "Kamu no Bukkyō to sono Kādamu-ha narabini Eizō no Bukkyō ni ataeta eikyō ni tuite [The Influence of the Buddhism of Khams on the Bka' dams pa Sect]," *Bunka* 20, no. 4 (July 1956): 703; Dkon mchog lhun grub and Sangs rgyas phun

tshogs, *Dam pa'i chos kyi 'byung tshul* [*A History of Religion*] (Sde dge edition: xylograph. First part [ff. 1–128] written in sixteenth century by Dkon mchog lhun grub, second part [ff. 129–228] completed by Sangs rgyas phun tshogs, 1692), f. 129*b*.

5. Editors' note: These later Tibetan sources have been shown to be mistaken about how early the Mongols arrived in Tibet. See T. V. Wylie, "The First Mongol Conquest of Tibet Reinterpreted," *Harvard Journal of Asian Studies* 37, no. 1 (1977): 103–133.

6. Ye shes dpal 'byor, *The Auspicious Wish-Fulfilling Tree*, f. 275*b*; P. Ratchkevsky, "Die mongolischen Grosskhane und die Buddhistische Kirche [The Mongol Khans and the Buddhist Church]," *Asiatica: Festschrift Friedrich Weller zum 65*, ed. Johannes Schubert and Ulrich Schneider (Leipzig: O. Harrassowitz, 1954); Gtsug lag 'phreng ba, Dpa' bo (1504–64), *Mkhas pa'i dga' ston* [*Feast for Scholars*] (Lho brag: xylograph, 1565), *MA*, ff. 17–18.

7. Gtsung lag 'phreng ba, *Feast for Scholars*, MA, f. 21*a*; Padma dkar po, *Chos 'byung bstan pa'i padma rgyas pa'i nyin byed* [*History of Religion*] (Spungs thang edition: xylograph, [1580]), ff. 160–172; Nges don bstan rgyas, *Karma pa sku 'phreng rim byon gyi rnam thar mdor bsdus* [*Biographies of the Karmapas*] (Sman dgon Thub chen bde chen gling: Xylograph in 236 ff., 1891), ff. 39*b*–88*a*; Hugh Richardson, "The Karma pa Sect," *Journal of the Royal Asiatic Society* (1958): 139–164, (1959): 1–18; Gtsung lag 'phreng ba, *Feast for Scholars*, MA, ff. 17*b*–37*a*.

PART IV

Lamas and Patrons (Thirteenth to Fourteenth Centuries)

TIBET AND THE MONGOLS

Chapter 12

THE PRECEPTOR-DONOR RELATION IN
THIRTEENTH-CENTURY TIBETAN SOCIETY
AND POLITY

Its Inner Asian Precursors and Indian Models

David Seyfort Ruegg

This essay examines one of the most important ideas in the political history of Tibetan Buddhism: the synergistic relationship between leading lamas and temporal rulers, defined here as between religious officiants/preceptors (donees) and their royal donors (in this case, mostly Mongol rulers, starting in the thirteenth century). Ruegg's essay is challenging due to his focus on specific Tibetan terminology and the possible Indic origins of these terms. Yet attention to these details is necessary because the Indo-Tibetan concepts described here are absolutely essential to understanding Tibetan political history and its conceptual foundations. The terms and ideas are so different from those in religious and political ideologies in other cultures, whether Western or East Asian, that the original Tibetan must be clearly understood for the English-language translations to make sense. For instance, the binary of religious and secular so often referred to in the West does not work very well for Tibet. The opposition of "supramundane" and "mundane" is better, and in this binary, the mundane can still be marked or influenced by the religious (for instance, in Tibetan culture, all the worldly protectors as well as harmful spirits are considered mundane, though they would certainly not fit within a definition of the secular). Rather than a secular figure, the donor is in most cases a lay ruler, specifically understood as a religious person, just not an ordained one. Ruegg also discusses a hallmark of Tibetan political ideology: the close relation between the spiritual and temporal described by the expression *chö si zungdrel* or "the union of spiritual and temporal orders." In Tibetan thought, these often are located at more or less the same level, and are sometimes even joined in one and the same person, who is both a lama and a political leader. The latter example, a bodhi-sattva-king, combines in himself both spiritual authority and temporal power. Ruegg dismisses once and for all the theocractic model as applicable to Tibet; instead the hierocratic model, in which religious hierarchs rule, is the appropriate term for governance by figures such as the Dalai Lama.

I

This paper is concerned with a set of Tibetan concepts and their corresponding terminology which pertain to the relationship between the religious or spiritual order on the one side, and the secular or temporal order on the other side, in so far as they are found either coordinated or joined together, especially in thirteenth-century Tibetan society and polity. Within Tibetan and Indian Buddhist thought, the two general categories most relevant to this set of concepts are probably the "supramundane" or "transmundane" (*'jig rten las 'das pa* = *lokottara*) as opposed to the "mundane" (*'jig rten pa* = *laukika*). To refer to this pair of concepts or orders, the expressions "sacred" and "profane" have often been used in the west, but this antithesis—characteristic as it is of a rather different way of thinking—lends itself poorly to the understanding and analysis of our Tibetan (and Indian) source materials, where these two orders sometimes overlap, and where the boundaries between them have in any case been differently drawn.[1] The two western concepts best suited to describe the pair of socio-religious and politico-religious categories under discussion are perhaps spiritual authority and temporal power. The boundary between this pair of ideas is, however, often shifting and somewhat fluid, and their relationship may thus appear as an oscillating and so to say "kaleidoscopic" one.[2]

II

The historically and culturally very significant link existing between a lama as reverend donee (*chöné*, Tib. *mchod gnas*) and his princely or royal donor (*yöndak*, Tib. *yon bdag*) may be taken both as the point of departure and as the focus for a study of the spiritual and temporal orders in Buddhist thought, in Tibet and elsewhere in Inner Asia. At the outset, it needs to be emphasized that, in itself, this relation is not an official or institutional one, but rather, an essentially religious and personal one. For while the *yöndak* (Skt. **dakṣiṇā-pati*) is a royal or princely "master of offerings," the *chöné*—literally "recipient (worthy) of honor(s)/ritual fees," and more generally "honorable, reverend donee"[3] (Skt. *dakṣiṇīya/dakṣiṇeya*, Pali *dakkhiṇeyya*)[4]—functions as an officiant/spiritual counselor/preceptor and as a guru (*lama*, Tib. *bla ma*) to the donor. The latter is usually a lay householder (*khyimdak* = Skt. *gṛhapati*). And the word *yöndak* is in effect an honorific form for *jindak* (Tib. *sbyin bdag* = Skt. *dānapati*), a term that designates the householder who, in the Buddhist structure of society, offers alms (*sbyin pa* = *dāna*, i.e., *āmiṣadāna*) to a monk (*bhikṣu* = *dge slong*).

As for the two words *yönchö* and *chöyön*—"(relationship of) *chöné* and *yöndak*"—they designate both the two components in the relation between the spiritual and temporal orders, and this relationship itself. Grammatically, the terms are copulative compounds, each made up of the terms *yöndak* and *chöné*, and despite the difference in sequence of their two component elements, they have the same reference.

In several modern publications dealing with this theme, *yönchö/chöyön* have been translated by the phrase "patron-priest (relationship)." This rendering is, however, somewhat misleading because it obscures the real nature of the terms of this relation between a monk as religious donee and a prince or king as lay donor. For in Buddhist society, the monk in his capacity as preceptor-donee worthy of honor (*dakṣiṇīya*) is hardly a priest in any usual meaning of this word, being literally a person worthy of ritual gifts (*dakṣiṇā*). As for the householder donor (*sbyin bdag* = *dānapati*), if he might reasonably be compared— in particular in the case of a munificent royal donor or *yöndak*—with a Maecenas or princely patron, in the context of Buddhist ideas on the link between a donor (royal or otherwise) and a religious (*pravrajita* = *rab tu byung ba*) or monk, the notion of "patron" is at the very least problematical, in so far as it may, altogether inappropriately, imply the subordination of the religious to the temporal (as for instance in Caesaropapism or Erastianism). That is, the translation of *yöndak* by "patron" entirely obscures the very fundamental matter of the place in Buddhist society of the householder *dānapati* in relation to the *bhikṣu*.[5] For this reason, the alternative rendering of *yönchö* by "donorchaplain (relationship)," also to be found in some recent publications, is no doubt preferable, provided of course that this choice of words does not lead to prejudging as a foregone conclusion the still open question as to whether the *chöné* was historically the Tibetan successor of the Indian *purohita*, i.e., the court chaplain who functioned as a royal officer at the court of an Indian king.[6]

Probably the closest English equivalent for the copulative compound *yönchö* is "(relationship of) donor and officiant/spiritual preceptor-donee." Similarly, *chöyön* may be rendered by "(relationship of) officiant/spiritual preceptor-donee and donor."

III

Historically, the best-known example of the socio-religious and politico-religious relation between a spiritual preceptor and a ruler has perhaps been the one established, from about 1253/1254, between the Tibetan Lama Pakpa Lodrö Gyeltsen Pelzangpo (1235–1280)—hierarch of Sakya, *chögyel* (Skt. *dharmarāja*) and *drogön* (Skt. *jagannātha* or, so to say, "ethnarch")—and Qubilai Khaghan (r. 1260–1294)—the emperor of the Sino-Mongol Yuan dynasty.

Some immediate historical precursors of this relation may already be found in the links established by earlier Tibetan lamas and hierarchs with other Mongol—and in particular Chinggisid—rulers as well as with rulers of the Tangut king-dom of Xixia (Tib. Minyak) in the region of the upper Yellow River. Thus, in the capacity of a spiritual counselor and preceptor of a king of Minyak, Tibetan sources mention Tsangpa Dungkhurwa (a disciple of Zhangyu Drakpa Tsön-drü Drakpa, 1123–1193), Tsang Sowa Könchok Senggé (a disciple of Karmapa I Düsum Khyenpa, 1110–1193) and Tisri Repa (also a disciple of Zhangyu Drakpa Tsöndrü Drakpa).[7] In addition, the Sakya hierarch Drakpa Gyeltsen (1147–1216) was linked with the Tangut king known to Tibetan sources as Dorjé, and Sakya Paṇḍita Künga Gyeltsen (1182–1251) with the Tangut king known as Bumdé. After the conquest of the Tangut kingdom by the Mongols in 1227, Rangjung Dorjé (Karmapa III, 1284–1339) is stated to have revived the Buddhist teaching in Minyak. Much earlier, Patsap Gomnak (1077–1158, a disciple of Patsap Nyima Drak born in 1055) and the Kāśmīri master Jayānanda (an associ-ate of Patsap Nyima Drak) may have occupied the function of spiritual counsel-ors in Minyak. And there are even indications that the *lachen* Gewasel (Gongwa Rapsel) may have filled such a function in the country of Minyak Ga as early as the ninth/tenth century.[8]

It may be noted that the function filled by these masters has usually been re-ferred to in our sources not as that of *chöné* but as that of *lama* or *lachö*.[9] These three terms, and in particular the first and third, are very frequently employed as equivalents to designate the officiant and spiritual preceptor of a ruler.

The above-mentioned Tsangpa Dungkhurwa has, in addition, been linked with the Mongols by Tibetan sources, which place this *lama* in the time of Chinggis Khan (died 1227). The relation between him and Chinggis is in fact stated by the historian Tsuklak Trengwa to have constituted the first contact between a Mongol ruler and a Tibetan monk, and also the first time a Ti-betan was recognized as a *bandhya/bandé* "reverend (monk)" by a Mongol ruler.[10] Among other earlier Tibetan masters who acted as officiants and pre-ceptors of Mongol rulers prior to Pakpa, Tibetan sources mention the master Tsel Gungtangpa, who functioned as the *lama/lachö* of the consort of the Great Khaghan Ögödei (r. 1229–1241), and Karma Pakśi (Karmapa II, 1206–1283) who was the *lama* of the Great Khaghan Möngke (r. 1251–1259). In the middle 1240s, Pakpa's uncle Sakya Paṇḍita (1182–1251) maintained a relationship with the Chinggisid prince Köden/Ködön (Tib. Godan) who was stationed in the Jangngö (Liangzhou) region. In general, among the Tibetan religious orders (*chöluk*), the Drikhungpa (or Drigungpa) have been linked in this function with Möngke, the Tselpas with Qubilai, the Taklungpas with Ariq Böke (r. 1260–1264, died in 1265), and the Pakmodrupas with Prince Hülegü (the founder of the Ilkhān dynasty in Iran who died in 1265). As for the Sakyapas, they were of course linked first with Prince Köden and then with Qubilai and his imperial successors.[11]

Interestingly, the relation between Sakya Paṇḍita and Köden has been regarded by certain sources as having in some fashion continued the earlier one that existed between Tibetan masters (including Sakya Paṇḍita himself) and the kings of Minyak, whose realm had been subjugated by Chinggis in 1227. Indeed, it is even stated that Köden was a rebirth (*kyewa*) of King Gyelgö, the founder of the Minyak royal dynasty (i.e., Jingzong, r. 1032–1048). And, very curiously, when speaking to Qubilai, Pakpa is reported to have referred to a *lachö* relation having previously existed between himself and the king of Minyak among other rulers. In this view of things, the Mongol empire was seemingly a kind of successor state—as it were by *renovatio*—of Minyak.[12]

An early Tibetan example of the preceptor-donor relation going back to the second half of the eighth century was that existing between Tri Songdetsen and Śāntaghoṣa—i.e., presumably, the Indian master Śāntarakṣita—who is referred to as being the Tibetan ruler's *gewé shenyen* ([*geshé*], Skt. *kalyāṇamitra*). Thus, particularly in earlier times, the term *gewé shenyen* may well have been used to designate what came later to be called the *lachö/chöné*. The latter terms are in fact not included in the Mahāvyutpatti dating to the early ninth century, which also does not register the term *yöndak* (although it does list *jindak* = *dānapati*). But both *chöné* and *yöndak* are words found in other texts dating back to the Old Kingdom. As for the terms *yönchö/chöyön*, they also are not listed in the *Mahāvyutpatti*.[13]

IV

Among the sources available for the present study, it is in Tselpa Künga Dorjé's *Depter Marpo* (otherwise known as the *Hulan Depter*; dated 1346, but with later additions) that the expression *yönchö* is clearly and unambiguously attested for the first time as a copulative compound designating the relation between a donor and preceptor, the reference in the relevant passage being to Qubilai as *yöndak* and Pakpa as *chöné*.[14] Already in the previous century (at the latest) the expression *yönchö* was in use, but in what are (for us) rather less clear contexts (where the expression may not be a copulative compound).[15]

As for the copulative compound *chöyön* of identical reference with *yönchö*, among the sources accessible it has been found in somewhat later texts such as Paṇchen Sönam Drakpa's (1478–1554) *Depter Marpö Dep Sarma* (the *Gyelrap Trülgyi Demik*, dated 1538).[16]

To express what is known as the *yönchö* relation, the Tibetan language possesses an extensive vocabulary, but one that is sometimes ambivalent and oscillating depending on the particular concrete circumstances of the individual participants in this relationship. The general idea of the close relation between the spiritual and temporal orders is especially clearly expressed by the expression *chösi zungdrel* "(dyarchic) conjunction/coordination (literally 'syzygy') of Dharma and Regnum." Other frequently used equivalent terms are *lukzung/luknyi* "two/twin orders" and *tsülnyi* "two/twin systems." In addition, but more rarely, there are attested the terms *tsuklak nyi* "two/twin sciences" and *trim (chenpo) nyi* "two/twin (great) rules." Further terms and concepts relating to the respective features of the two orders are *lama'i jawa* "activity (or duty) of the Lama" and *chökyi jawa* "activity of the Dharma" or *chötrim* "Dharma-rule" in contrast to *jiktengyi/pa'i jawa* "activity of the world (*loka*)," *trimkyi jawa* "activity of rule" and *rgyeltrim* "governance-rule." The copulative compound *lapön* "lama and (civil) officer" may be cited as another expression closely related in meaning to *yönchö*.[17] The renderings "twin" and "coordination" are appropriate in cases where both the spiritual and temporal orders are being thought of as located at more or less the same level (as in the case of the two coordinate branches of the Tibetan government below the Dalai Lamas), whereas these translations will not be suitable when the spiritual order is on the contrary regarded as superordinate to the temporal (as has indeed been the case in very many instances).[18]

Equivalents (at least partial) of *chöné* are *jinné* "recipient of alms" (in relation to a *jindak* = *dānapati* "donor"), *yöné*[19] (= *dakṣiṇīya*) "recipient [worthy] of offerings, ritual gifts/fees (*yön* = *dakṣiṇā*; cf. Pali *dakkhiṇā*)," and *lachö* "honorable (*dakṣiṇīya*) lama, reverend donee." To the extent that these personages are all eminent lamas—i.e., gurus—functioning as officiants and preceptors, the high honorific expression *ula* is applicable to them.

V

In order fully to understand the real nature and the conceptual background of the relation in question between the spiritual and temporal, and of both its terms individually, it is necessary to take into account the old Buddhist concept of alms-giving (*dāna* = *jinpa*, i.e. *āmiṣadāna* = *zangzinggi jinpa*) by a householder (i.e., lay) donor to a monk, who on his part dispenses the gift of Dharma (*dharmadāna* = *chökyi jinpa*). There has thus existed a kind of mutuality and socio-religious solidarity between monk and donor.

But it has to be observed that, in terms of this theory, the monk does not simply teach the Dharma in return for the alms he receives from a donor as a sort of advance payment for his teaching. On the contrary, it is the monk's very nature to be one who realizes and eventually teaches the Dharma. And in Buddhist thought what the donor is deemed actually to receive for his alms is in fact not the Dharma but something rather different, namely religious good (*puṇya* = *sönam* "merit"), the wholesome roots of which he has as it were planted by means of his *dāna* in the good "field" (*kṣetra* = *zhing*) represented by the monk.[20]

With respect to the officiant/spiritual preceptor as donee (*chöné* = *yönné*), it is necessary to attempt to determine the extent to which it might be historically and ideologically legitimate to regard him as the successor, or the substitute, of the Indian *purohita* "chaplain" (Tib. *mdun na 'don*)—the title of a category of official listed in the *Mahāvyutpatti* (3680) which is not, however, normally counted as equivalent to the *chöné* = *lachö*—who came to function as an official at the court of Indian kings.[21]

The same question arises in relation to the offices of master of the realm (Tib. *gu shri* < Ch. *guo shi*) and of imperial master (Tib. *ti shri* < Ch. *di shi*) in the Sino-Mongolian bureaucracy of the Yuan dynasty. A *chöné* could indeed be appointed a *guo shi* or *di shi*, as Pakpa for example in fact was. But this does not imply that, per se, the function of *chöné* can be automatically equated with the official and institutionalized positions of *guo shi* and *di shi*. For, as already observed above, the relation between *chöné* and *yöndak* is essentially a socioreligious and personal one whereas that between *guo shi/di shi* and emperor was evidently an official one of bureaucratic character in the Yuan administration.[22]

Our enquiry thus comes to engage the vexed problem of what Robert Lingat has called the "functionarization" of the Buddhist clergy—i.e., its officialization, institutional bureaucratization and quasi secularization.[23]

VI

Also requiring attention is a process opposed to this "functionarization" of the clergy, namely the process that counteracted the officialization and politicization latent in the *yönchö* relation (and in other parallel relationships between monks and monarchs)—and to which the *chöné* was thus exposed in his capacity of officiant to a royal donor—by favoring what might be termed a "neutralization of the political." This neutralization was achieved, with greater or lesser success, according to the historical and personal situation in which the individual actors actually found themselves at a given time.[24]

The tension—latent or manifest—in the *yönchö* relation between politicization accompanied by secularization and strict Buddhist observance found expression in the thirteenth century in an epigram which the young scholar Chomden Rikrel is reported to have directed against Pakpa's ambiguous situation and in the latter's reply. In his epigram Rikrel blames Pakpa's position in the following words:

"The Teaching of the Buddha is obscured by a cloud of obedience to [imperial] commands [?], the well-being and happiness of beings falls into the hands of the ruler, and the religious of this Iron Age adopts the behavior of an official: it is known that he who [like Pakpa] is ignorant of these three things is no Noble (*pakpa* = *ārya*)."

To this biting criticism Pakpa is stated to have replied:

> "The Jina has declared that his Teaching is subject to increase and decline, the well-being and happiness of beings depend on their karmic action, and one gives teachings to the one destined to be one's disciple: it is known that he who is ignorant of these three things is no scholar."[25]

Thus, against Rikrel's traditionalist, and "Vinayist," conception of the matter, Pakpa has pointedly, and very tellingly, invoked the idea of a guru's being bound to teach those disciples who are karmically linked with him.[26]

Now, in a comparable—but clearly not altogether identical—situation in the following century, a parallel difficulty was met by the traditionalist and "Vinayist" attitude adopted by Butön Rinchendrup (1290–1364), who managed to escape an invitation—no doubt rather a summons—from the Mongol court in Dadu (Taidu, Beijing) and to remain in Tibet to devote himself to the activities and duties normally deemed suitable for a learned monk.[27] Although he thus avoided having to obey the emperor's summons—and risking becoming involved in what could have been a politico-religious relationship of the *yönchö* type with the emperor Toghon Temür (rg. 1333–1368 [1370]), Butön was nonetheless prepared to maintain a more traditionally Buddhist socio-religious link with the *kuzhang* ruler of the Zhalu myriarchy based on the ancient precedent of the relation existing between the Buddha and the lay donor Anāthapiṇḍada.[28] It would doubtless have been much less problematic for Butön—and for Tibetan lamas in general—to establish and maintain the link between the spiritual and temporal orders with a fellow Tibetan Buddhist than to entertain one with a Mongol emperor descended from the great conqueror Chinggis Khan.

VII

With regard to spiritual authority and temporal power in Tibet, these two orders have not only been represented separately by two different persons—the *chöné* = *lachö* and the *yöndak*—but they have also sometimes been conjoined, and exercised together, by one and the same person. This person was the bodhisattva-king in a hierocratic—or, more precisely, "bodhisattvacratic" and "bodhisattva-centric"—polity.

Thus, within the frame of Tibet taken by itself, Pakpa—regarded as he was as the manifestation (*trülpa* = *nirmāṇa*) of the bodhisattva Avalokiteśvara-Lokeśvara—functioned both as a great lama and as the ruler of Central Tibet, thus combining in himself as hierarch the two functions or orders. Moreover, within Tibet, he was also associated dyarchically with the Sakya *pönchens* or great (civil) officers, who took on certain executive functions of rulership. And for a time he was associated with his layman younger brother Chakna Dorjé (1239–1267)—regarded as the *nirmāṇic* manifestation of the bodhisattva Vajrapāṇi—who filled a temporal function as Prince of Bailan.[29] On the other hand, in the larger frame of the Mongol empire, Pakpa was dyarchically linked in a *yönchö* relationship with Qubilai, himself regarded as a *nirmāṇic* manifestation of the bodhisattva Mañjughoṣa.[30]

It is these shifting and multilayered links between a bodhisattva-king or hierocrat and various levels of temporal power that justify describing the relation between the spiritual and temporal order as oscillating and kaleidoscopic.

This structural ambivalence in the function of sovereignty appears to be reflected on the linguistic level in the lexeme *lapön*, which may be used to designate either a dyarchically linked pair of persons, one of whom is a lama and the other is a chief or civil official, or a single person who is both a lama and a chief thus combining the two functions.[31]

It is to be noted that the idea of the bodhisattva-king or hierocrat is by no means reducible to that of theocracy, the Āryabodhisattva—who has entered the transworldly Path of Awakening (*lokottaramārga* = *'jig rten las 'das pa'i lam*, starting with the *darśanamārga* = *mthong lam*)—having of course nothing whatever to do in Buddhist thought with a *theos* of any kind. Indeed, in Tibetan as well as in Indian Buddhism, the idea of a "god" (Tib. *lha*, Skt. *deva*) is connected very much less with a Bodhisattva (and *a fortiori* a Buddha) than with a king. As for the concept of the Bodhisattva-King taking on the function of a ruling monarch as the *nirmāṇic* manifestation (*trülpa*) of a Bodhisattva—such as the Dalai Lamas or Pakpa himself as manifestations of Avalokiteśvara-Lokeśvara, the Mahākāruṇika or "Great Compassionate"—, it is at least in principle distinct from that of the king-as-bodhisattva—in other words the ruler identified with a bodhisattva. This latter idea also is found in Tibet—for example in the cases of the kings Songtsen Gampo, Tri Songdetsen and Relpachen regarded as manifestations respectively of Avalokiteśvara, Mañjuśri and Vajrapāṇi—as well as in Sri Lanka and Southeast Asia.[32]

VIII

An attempt has next to be made to identify in Indian and Tibetan Buddhist thought what may be either historical precedents—or, in the case of the Legend of King Aśoka, a quasi historical precedent—or theoretical models which could have helped underpin the idea of a "constitutional" relation between a spiritual preceptor, or guru, on the one side and the king of/by the Dharma (*dharmarāja* = *chögyel*) or Universal Monarch (*cakravarti-rāja* = *khorlö gyurpé gyelpo*) on the other. Particular attention has also to be given to the situation already mentioned in which the spiritual and temporal orders have been combined together in a single person, the bodhisattva-king or hierocrat.

The search for theoretical models and ancient Indian historical precedents which might have served Tibetan thinkers is, however, no straightforward matter, for our Tibetan sources are not as explicit on the subject as we would wish. Moreover, in view of the many demands doubtless made on their time and energy and of their numberless practical day-to-day concerns and responsibilities, it is likely that neither Pakpa in his relation with Qubilai Khaghan nor his uncle Sakya Paṇḍita in his relation with Prince Köden was ever in a position to compose a full theoretical treatise on the "constitutional" relation between the two orders represented by the officiant/spiritual preceptor and the donor-ruler. It has to be remembered besides that Pakpa died in 1280 at the quite young age of 45.

To be noted in the first place is the fact that the Indian emperor Aśoka does not figure among the precedents and models for the *dharmaraja*-donor of a spiritual preceptor, which have been identified in our sources. In this way, the significance in Tibet of Aśoka was rather less than it was in the Theravādin world of South Asia, where this ruler has been regarded as an exemplar for the *dharmaraja*-donor.[33]

One precedent for the relation between a religious and his donor attested in our Tibetan sources has been that of the link between the Buddha and Anāthapiṇḍada, the munificent householder (*grhapati*) and merchant (*śresthin*) of Śrāvasti. As already pointed out above, this particular relationship has been cited by Dratsepa Rinchen Namgyel as the model for the one obtaining between his master Butön and the *kuzhang* prince of Zhalu in the fourteenth century.

A second precedent is that of Nāgārjuna as the spiritual counselor of a king. This rôle is found in two texts ascribed to this master, the *Suhṛlleka* (where the Śātavāhana ruler De chö is named) and the *Ratnāvalī* (where no king's name is specified). Nāgārjuna is also credited with having composed treatises on morals and statecraft (*nītiśāstra*) such as the *Prajñāśataka*, the *Janaposaṇabindu* and the *Prajñādaṇḍa*. And the *Mañjuśrīmūlakalpa* (liii.867–9) describes him as an ascetic concerned with affairs of the realm (*rājyavṛttin*). A passage from the *Ratnāvalī* (ii.26–28) has been cited in Tsepel's *Religious History of Mongolia* in respect to the relation between Pakpa and Qubilai.[34]

These two precedents are subsumable under the model of the spiritual counselor and his *dānapati*, the latter being a wealthy and munificent merchant in the case of the Buddha and a king in the case of Nāgārjuna.

A further, closely related, model for the relation between the spiritual and temporal orders is the particularly significant one of the Vajrayānist guru and his ruler-disciple. Indeed, according to Tibetan historical traditions, Pakpa owed his rulership and temporal power over Tibet in the frame of the Mongol "universal empire" to the ritual *dakṣiṇā* (*wangyön*) or gift which he received as Qubilai's guru for consecrations (*wang[kur]* = *abhiṣeka*) he conferred on this Mongol emperor.[35]

The matter of the link between the spiritual and temporal orders is, however, complicated by the fact that they were not invariably represented by two different persons in a dyarchic relationship (either in the coordination of two parties or in the superordination of one party to the other). As already observed, spiritual authority was on occasion invested together with temporal rule in a single person, as in the case of Pakpa who—as the *nirmāṇic* manifestation (*trülpa*) of the bodhisattva Avalokiteśvara-Lokeśvara—was considered, within the frame of Tibet, as both a lama hierarch and the ruler of Tibet (in much the same way as the Dalai Lamas have been afterwards).

In summary, beside the (quasi) historical precedents of the Buddha's relation with Anāthapiṇḍada and of Nāgārjuna's relation with contemporary kings, it appears possible to distinguish at least three main theoretical models for the "constitutional" relationship between spiritual authority and temporal power in Tibet at the time in question:

1. the dyarchic model of the *dānapati* (*yöndak*)—a *dharmarāja* (*chögyel*) sometimes viewed also as a *cakravartin* king (*khorlö gyurpé gyelpo*)—and his officiant and spiritual preceptor (*chöné*)—often considered a bodhisattva—the two orders being thus represented by two separate persons;

2. the model of the Vajrayānist guru and his neophyte disciple, namely the ruler recipient of a Consecration from a guru to whom he presents a ritual gift or *dakṣiṇā* (*wang-yön*) (structurally, this model presents itself as a special case of the first, non-Vajrayānist, model);

3. the hierocratic and nirmāṇic one of the bodhisattva-king combining in himself both spiritual authority and temporal power—even when, additionally, this hierarch in turn stands in a *yönchö* relation to a "universal emperor" (e.g., Qubilai in the larger frame of the Mongol empire), or in a dyarchical relationship with a civil officer (e.g., the Sakya *pönchens* in the frame of the smaller unit of Central Tibet), or even associated with a relative (such as in the case of Pakpa's relation to his younger brother Chakna Dorjé, Prince of Bailan). In the case of the bodhisattva-king as hierocrat, the use of the terms *yönchö* and *chöyön* as copulative compounds referring to two separate persons is not appropriate, as it would evidently also not be when Pakpa was associated either with the Sakya *pönchen* or with his brother. But its employment will be relevant when this hierarch is linked with a *yöndak* in the way Pakpa was with Qubilai.

Another lama who filled the role of officiant and preceptor to a Mongol prince at approximately the same time as Pakpa was Ga Anyen Dampa Künga Drak (died in 1303). Considered a manifestation of Gurgyi Gönpo—i.e., Mahākāla, a *yidam* form of Avalokiteśvara—he may be supposed to have functioned as a Vajrayānist guru. Also, like Pakpa, he is reported to have received the title of *guoshi* from the Yuan emperor.[36]

The fact that both Pakpa and Anyen Dampa have been regarded as nirmāṇic manifestations (trülpa) in some way connected with Avalokiteśvara is
likely to be significant in view of this Bodhisattva's well-known identity as
Lokeśvara = Jikten Wangchuk. (Compare the more or less synonymous epithet,
and proper name, jikten gönpo = lokanātha applied to Avalokiteśvara, and also
the title drogön = jagannātha, literally "ethnarch," which was given Pakpa and
other hierarchs.[37])

Although the theoretical models that have been identified above are conceptually distinct, in practice they do not exclude each other. And each of them has
been found applicable, in some particular respect, to Pakpa's functions and
roles as described in our various sources.[38]

IX

When examining here the relationship of the spiritual and temporal orders, and
the yönchö link, our task has above all been to study cultural and religious phenomena, as well as socio-religious and politico-religious ideas, rather than the
political and military history of Inner Asia in the thirteenth and fourteenth
centuries. The latter task has already been carried out by several historians of
the empire of Chinggis Khan and his successors, of the Sino-Mongol Yuan dynasty and of the relations between Tibetans, Mongols and Chinese at that time.
Reference may be made in particular to the recent book by Luciano Petech
entitled Central Tibet and the Mongols.[39]

In the recently published sixth volume of the Cambridge History of China it
has been observed that "the contributions of the Tibetan Buddhist monk Pakpa
have not been accorded a full-scale study . . . [M]ore research is needed on
Pakpa's influence."[40] That Pakpa did exercise considerable influence in Inner
Asia, and even at the Sino-Mongol court, indeed appears likely. As already
noted, however, the Tibetan documentation available does not include any
detailed contemporary treatise on his "constitutional" position as the chöné of
Qubilai, any more than it does on his uncle Sakya Paṇḍita's politico-religious
thinking in the relation into which he entered with Prince Köden.[41] And it appears probable that neither Sakya Paṇḍita nor Pakpa found the opportunity to
theorize in a special treatise this relation as it was developing between them
and Mongol rulers in the middle of the thirteenth century.

One thing however appears abundantly clear. As envisaged in the thirteenth
century, and also in succeeding centuries, in Tibet and elsewhere in Inner Asia,
the yönchö relation linking an officiant and spiritual preceptor with a donor-
ruler was in fact considered possible and meaningful exclusively between a lama
or guru on the one side and a monarch who was a chögyel—i.e., a King of/by the
Dharma (dhannarāja)—on the other side. The officiant and preceptor (chöné/
lachö) might, like Pakpa, be a powerful abbot-prince considered to be the nir-

māṇic manifestation of the bodhisattva Avalokiteśvara-Lokeśvara; or, like Butön, he might be a monk who was highly regarded above all by reason of his eminence as a learned lama. As for the donor-ruler (*yöndak/jindak*), he might be a great emperor and "universal monarch" like Qubilai (who was, moreover, sometimes himself considered to be a manifestation of a bodhisattva); or he might be a king like the Minyak rulers who appointed Tibetan masters as their *lamas* (without either of them being stated in our sources to be the *nirmāṇic* manifestation of great bodhisattvas); or again he might be a princely myriarch like Butön's *kuzhang* donor (considered an emanation of the *lokapāla* and *mahārāja* Vaiśravaṇa). But at all events, in the relationship between the spiritual and temporal orders, the temporal power had to be held by a ruler considered to be a true *dharmarāja*, a king of/by the Dharma.

Furthermore, as already noted, the link between donee and donor was accordingly—and virtually by definition—a religious and personal one rather than an official and bureaucratically institutionalized one. It thus differed significantly from the institutionalized relationships into which the Sino-Mongol *guoshi* and *di shi*—and even the Indian *purohita* as a royal officer—entered.

X

In summary, the *yönchö/chöyön* relation as well as the spiritual and temporal functions of the *chöné* and *yöndak* constituting it can be seen to be rooted—if sometimes only at more than one remove—in certain Buddhist socio-religious concepts, and in what might be called an emerging politico-religious ideology influenced by Buddhist concepts.

Of special importance was in the first place the above-mentioned Indian Buddhist concept of alms-giving (*jinpa* = *dāna*) in the relation between an alms-giver (*jindak* = *dānapati*) and a religious (*rapjung* = *pravrajita*) and almsman (*gelong* = *bhikṣu*) worthy of being honored (*dakṣiṇīya* = *chöné*, [*sugyurpa*]). The donor was of course usually a layman who supplied the monk with material gifts (*āmiṣadāna* = *zangzinggi jinpa*), i.e., alms. For his part the monk is characterized by his gift of the Dharma (*dharmadāna* = *chökyi jinpa*).

As for the gift, or ritual fee (*wangyön*), received by the guru from the neophyte at the time of a Vajrayānist consecration (*wang*[*kur*] = *abhiṣeka*), it was evidently not considered to have the effect of placing the guru in a position of subordination to his disciple.

Technically, the term *chöné* and its equivalent *yönné* (*dakṣiṇīya*) may denote a recipient worthy of receiving such ritual gifts (*yön*: *dakṣiṇā*). The ritual gifts, known as *wangyön*, of rulership over Tibetan provinces that Pakpa is stated to have received for the consecrations he conferred on Qubilai are famous examples. More generally, however, the terms *chöné* and *yönné* denote a religious to be honored, a "reverend donee" in the Buddhist structure of society.[42]

If he is a king or a person of high rank, the donor (*jindak* = *dānapati*) is commonly (though not invariably) referred to as *yöndak* "master of ritual offerings"—corresponding literally to Skt. **dakṣiṇā-pati*, a term that does not, however, appear to be actually attested in Sanskrit sources.

Now, it is doubtless true that the participants in the Inner Asian *yönchö* relation—the *yöndak* and the *chöné*—differ in certain important respects from the participants—the *dānapati* and the *bhikṣu*—in the ancient Indian structure of society just outlined which is founded on the relation between a lay giver of material gifts (*āmiṣadāna*) and a religious, who is the provider of Dharma-teaching (*dhamiadāna*). Still, as noted above, in a Buddhist society and polity the concept of the *yöndak* is hardly rendered adequately by "patron" (at least in most uses of this word) when the relationship into which the preceptor-donee enters with the ruler-donor is based on the dyarchical model of the spiritual preceptor in relation to his *dānapati*, or on the somewhat more specific model of the Vajrayānist guru and his disciple. This question does not of course arise at all in the case of the bodhisattva-king, who combines in himself both the spiritual and temporal orders, and in whom the rulership aspect of sovereignty is subordinate to his religious function.

XI

For any full and well-founded understanding of what, in Tibetan civilization and history, is at stake in the relationship between the spiritual and temporal orders, there is required not only a "rectification of names and terms" but in addition a historical-philological analysis of socio-religious and politico-religious concepts and of the corresponding terminology as used in the sources.

This kind of investigation inescapably raises a number of difficulties of a conceptual and historical nature, as well as many a vexed problem of methodology. Not only are generalizing and comparative—and hence "etic"—analyses to be proposed, but, in addition, a sustained effort needs to be made to take into account categories and terms proper to the Buddhist civilization from which our materials come. Being systemic and structural—and hence "emic"—in nature, these latter categories and terminologies may indeed be expected to be at least as appropriate (if not more so) as the former for the purpose of shedding light on the cultural and intellectual structures inherent in the materials being examined. Indeed, generalizing and comparative, i.e., "etic," interpretations need to be solidly anchored in analyses founded on indigenous, i.e., "emic," categories. Such analysis has moreover to be not only descriptive but also historical, according due importance to the diachronic axis alongside the synchronic one.[43]

In Tibetan and Indian Buddhist thought, two "emic" categories that come close to situating and defining the concepts of spiritual and temporal invoked here are in certain contexts "supramundane" or "transmundane" (*jikterlé depa = lokottara*) and "mundane" (*jikterpa = laukika*).[44]

With regard to the links connecting Tibetan and Indian civilization, beside Indian borrowings (in the proper and strict sense of the word "Indian") Tibetan civilization embraces what can be termed Indic (as distinct from Indian) components. These are elements that (in our present stage of knowledge at least) are not actually attested in India, but which the Tibetans have themselves developed by creatively adopting, adapting and further elaborating ideas—and also terms—that are ultimately of Indian origin. In other words, these Indic elements are *typologically* and *structurally* Indian without having actually been borrowed ready-made from India.[45]

Thus, whilst Tib. *chöné/yönné* are known to translate Skt. *dakṣiṇīya/dakṣiṇeya* (cf. Pali *dakkhiṇeyya*), the idea expressed by these Tibetan terms is, in its full religio-political development, something more than what is actually known under this Sanskrit designation from our Indian sources. No established Sanskrit term is, moreover, known to correspond precisely to the copulative compounds *yönchö/chöyön*.[46]

When investigating such concepts and terms it will, then, be necessary methodologically to steer clear both of the Scylla of radical relativism that deems it right to enclose each civilization hermetically within the boundaries of its categories and concepts—something that represents a distortion of the genuinely systemic, and "emic," approach—and of the Charybdis of ethnocentrism (European or Asian) which, Procrustes-like, would superimpose its own standards and categories on another culture while judging the latter by imposed interpretative grids and templates—something that is a travesty of any truly comparative, and "etic," analysis.[47]

GLOSSARY OF TIBETAN TECHNICAL TERMS

CHÖSI ZUNGDREL "(dyarchic) coordination" (literally "syzygy") of
(chos srid zung 'brel) Dharma and Regnum (said of the spiritual and temporal orders).

CHÖNÉ (determinative compound) "(spiritual) officiant/counselor/
(mchod gnas) preceptor-donee" (literally "recipient [worthy] of honor/ honoraria; reverend donee"; *chöpa pülyülgyi zhingngam chöja*);[48] translates Skt. *dakṣiṇīya/dakṣineya* (cf. Pali *dakkhiṇeyya*) "worthy of honor/an honorarium/ritual fee" and, more generally, "honorable, reverend donee" (cf. *yönné*, and also *chöné*)

CHÖYÖN (1) (copulative compound) "(spiritual) officiant/counselor/
(mchod yon) preceptor-donee (*chöné*) and donor (*yöndak*)" (cf. *yönchö*) [no Indian source for this term is known, but compare

the Sanskrit copulative compound *ṛtvig-yājyau* "officiant and beneficiary of the sacrifice";[49]

(2) (determinative compound) "(ritual) water (offering)" (cf. *yönchö/yonchap*);[50]

(3) = *aghnyā* "not to be killed (cow, as something holy)." [51]

JINDAK
(sbyin bdag)

(determinative compound) "almsgiver, donor" (literally "master of *dāna*").[52]

JINNÉ
(sbyin gnas)

(determinative compound) "(religious) donee" (in relation to a *jindak*) (literally "recipient [worthy] of *dāna*").[53]

LACHÖ
(bla mchod)

(1) (appositional compound) "honorable/reverend lama-donee";[54]

(2) (determinative compound) = *lama chöpa* (= *gurupūjā*).[55]

LAPÖN
(bla dpon)

(1) (copulative compound) "lama and chief/(civil) officer (*pönpo*)";

(2) (appositional compound) "lama who is (also) a *pönpo*";

(3) (honorific for) *pönpo*.[56]

LUKNYI
(lugs gnyis)

"two orders" (said of the spiritual and temporal orders).

LUKZUNG
(lugs zung)

"(dyarchic) coordination of the two orders" (spiritual and temporal).

TRIM (CHENPO) NYI
(khrims chen po gnyis)

"two (great) rules" (said of the spiritual and temporal orders).

TSUKLANYI
(gtsug lag gnyis)

"two sciences" (said of the spiritual and temporal orders) (*tsuklak* = *śāstra* [also *ārṣa/ārṣabha*]).

TSÜLNYI
(tshul gnyis)

"two systems" (said of the spiritual and temporal orders).

ULA
(dbu bla)

(high honorific) "lama" (in his capacity of officiant/counselor/preceptor of a person of high status).

WANGYÖN
(dbang yon)

(determinative compound) "gift/ritual honorarium/fee (*dakṣiṇā*) offered to the guru by a neophyte disciple on receiving a Vajrayānist consecration" (*wang*[*kur*] = *abhiṣeka*).

YÖN
(yon)

(honorific for *lacha* and *jinpa*) "gift, offering, ritual honorarium/fee" (Skt. *dakṣiṇā*; also translates Skt. *argh*[*y*]*a* "water offering," etc.).

YÖNCHÖ
(yon mchod)

(copulative compound) "donor (*yöndak*) and (spiritual) officiant/counselor/preceptor-donee" (cf. *chöyön*).[57]

YÖNDAK
(yon bdag)

(honorific for *jindak* = *dānapati*) "donor" (literally "master of offerings, ritual honorarium/fee," Skt.*dakṣiṇā-pati* [term not attested in the dictionaries]).[58]

YÖNNÉ
(yon gnas)

"recipient [worthy] of *dakṣiṇā*; honorable, reverend donee";[59] translates Skt. *dakṣiṇīya* and equivalent to *chöné* (cf. also *jinné*).

NOTES

1. On the history of this pair of concepts over the past century, see recently P. Borgeaud, "Le couple sacré/profane [The Couple: Sacred/Profane]," *Revue de l'histoire des religions* 211, no. 4 (1994): 387–418.

2. This article is based on the present writer's *Ordre spirituel et ordre temporel dans la pensée bouddhique de l'Inde et du Tibet* [*Spiritual Order and Temporal Order in the Buddhist Thought of India and Tibet*] (Paris: Collège de France, 1995), of which it provides an English summary, together with some additions within the limits of the space available here. In the following, the abbreviation Ruegg, *Spiritual Order and Temporal Order in the Buddhist Thought of India and Tibet* refers to this book; when followed by section and a Roman numeral, the reference is to the sections in part I of the same book. Some aspects of the present topic were treated earlier in D. Seyfort Ruegg, "*Mchod yon, yon mchod* and *mchod gnas/yon gnas*: On the Historiography and Semantics of a Tibetan Religio-social and Religio-political Concept," in *Tibetan History and Language*, ed. E. Steinkellner (Vienna: G. Uray Festschrift, 1991), 441–453, hereafter abbreviated Ruegg, "Historiography and Semantics of a Tibetan Religio-social and Religio-political Concept." In his new *Empereur et prêtre* (Paris, 1995 [also available in English: *Emperor and Priest: The Imperial Office in Byzantium* (Cambridge: Cambridge University Press, 2003)]), G. Dagron reexamines the Western, and in particular the Byzantine and Orthodox, materials, and subjects the notion of Caesaropapism to a critique.

Dictionary references are to the following works: Blo ldan shes rab, Brag g.yab, *Bod brda'i tshig mdzod* [*Dictionary of Tibetan Symbols*] (Dharmasala: Library of Tibetan Works and Archives, 1989); Chos kyi grags pa, Dge bshes, *Brda dag ming tshig gsal ba* [*New Tibetan Dictionary*] (Beijing: Mi rigs dpe skrun hhang, 1981); Zhang Yisun, ed., *Bod rgya tshig mdzod chen mo (Zang-Han da cidian)* [*Great Tibetan-Chinese Dictionary*] (Beijing: Minzu chubanshe, 1985).

3. The lexeme *mchod gnas* is explained in Zhang Yisun, *Great Tibetan-Chinese Dictionary* as *mchod pa 'bul yul gyi zhing ngam mchod bya* "field that is the object of paying honor, or to be honored."

4. Skt. *dakṣiṇīya/ dakṣiṇeya* (cf. Pali *dakkhiṇeyya*)—represented in Tibetan either by *mchod gnas* or *yon gnas (su gyur pa)* (see below)—is known as an epithet of the Buddha, the Pratyekabuddha, and the Saṃgha, or religious community. On the meaning of the expression, cf. F. Edgerton, *Buddhist Hybrid Sanskrit Dictionary* (Delhi: Motilal Banarsidass, 1998).

5. On the unsuitability of the renderings "priest" and "patron," see also Ruegg, "Historiography and Semantics of a Tibetan Religio-social and Religio-political Concept," 441–453.

6. See Ruegg, *Spiritual Order and Temporal Order in the Buddhist Thought of India and Tibet*, section XI, where it is shown that the functions of the Tibetan *mchod gnas* and the Indian *purohita* have been rather different, the latter being a somewhat more official and institutionalized one. To Skt. *purohita* corresponds Tib. *mdun na*

'don (registered in the Mahāvyutpatti; see Yumiko Ishihama and Yoichi Fukuda, eds., *A New Critical Edition of the Mahāvyutpatti: Sanskrit-Tibetan-Mongolian Dictionary of Buddhist Terminology*, Studia Tibetica, No. 16, Materials for Tibetan-Mongolian Dictionaries, Vol. 1 [Tokyo: Toyo Bunko, 1989], 3680), which is not normally regarded as a synonym of *mchod gnas/yon gnas*.

7. For further details on Gtsang pa Dung khur ba and Gtsang so ba (or Gtsang po pā?) Dkon mchog seng ge, see Ruegg, *Spiritual Order and Temporal Order in the Buddhist Thought of India and Tibet*, section V. In his *Central Tibet and the Mongols: The Yüan-Sa skya Period of Tibetan History*, Serie Orientale Roma, vol. 65 (Rome: Instituto italiano per il Medio ed Estremo Oriente, 1990), 6, L. Petech considers these two names to refer to a single person. On the 'Ba' rom pa Ti shrī ras pa Sangs rgyas ras chen (1164/5–1236) and on Rtsa mi, see recently E. Sperling, "Rtsa mi Lo tsa ba Sangs rgyas grags pa and the Tangut Background to Early Mongol-Tibetan Relations," in *Tibetan Studies: Proceedings of the 6th Seminar of the International Association for Tibetan Studies, Fagernes 1992*, vol. 2, ed. Per Kvaerne (Oslo: The Institute for Comparative Research in Human Culture, 1994), 801–824, especially 804.

8. For further details see Ruegg, *Spiritual Order and Temporal Order in the Buddhist Thought of India and Tibet*, section V.

9. In Zhang Yisun, *Great Tibetan-Chinese Dictionary*, the relevant sense of the lexeme *bla mchod* is explained as *mchod yul gyi bla ma*.

10. Gtsug lag 'phreng ba, Dpa' bo (1504–1564), *Dam pa'i chos kyi 'khor los bsgyur ba rnams kyi byung ba'i gsal byed pa mkhas pa'i dga' ston* [*Feast for Scholars: The Development of the Promoters of Buddhism*], 4 vols. (1565; reprint, New Delhi: International Academy of Indian Culture, 1959–1962), 1414–15. See Ruegg, *Spiritual Order and Temporal Order in the Buddhist Thought of India and Tibet*, section IV.

11. Ruegg, *Spiritual Order and Temporal Order in the Buddhist Thought of India and Tibet*, section IV.

12. Ruegg, *Spiritual Order and Temporal Order in the Buddhist Thought of India and Tibet*, section IV and VI.

13. Ruegg, *Spiritual Order and Temporal Order in the Buddhist Thought of India and Tibet*, section III. The word *mchod yon* in the meaning of *argha* is however listed in Ishihama and Fukuda, *A New Critical Edition of the Mahāvyutpatti*, 4338.

14. Kun dga' rdo rje, Tshal pa [1309–1364], *Hu lan deb ther* [*The Red Book*], annotated and ed. by Dung dkar Blo bzang 'phrin las (1363; reprint, Beijing: Mi rigs dpe skrun khang, 1981), 48. See Ruegg, *Spiritual Order and Temporal Order in the Buddhist Thought of India and Tibet*, section VII.

15. Ruegg, *Spiritual Order and Temporal Order in the Buddhist Thought of India and Tibet*, section VII (with note 64).

16. Ruegg, *Spiritual Order and Temporal Order in the Buddhist Thought of India and Tibet*, sections II, VII.

17. Ruegg, *Spiritual Order and Temporal Order in the Buddhist Thought of India and Tibet*, sections I, VIII; cf. section XVII. In Zhang Yisun, *Great Tibetan-Chinese Dictionary*, the lexeme *bla dpon* is defined as (1) *bla ma dang dpon po gnyis ka yin pa zhig*; (2) *bla ma dang dpon po gnyis kyi bsdus ming*; and (3) *dpon po'i zhe sa* (honorific for *dpon po* "chief, [civil] officer"). For the expression *bla dpon sbrag pa* "to combine [the functions of] Lama and officer," see Ruegg, *Spiritual Order and Temporal Order in the Buddhist Thought of India and Tibet*, n. 15 and section VIII.

18. Ruegg, *Spiritual Order and Temporal Order in the Buddhist Thought of India and Tibet*, sections I (especially 24ff.), XVI.

19. In Zhang Yisun, *Great Tibetan-Chinese Dictionary*, the lexeme *yon gnas* is explained as *mchod yul gyi gnas* . . . "(worthy) recipient who is the object of honoring" (cf. the explanation of *mchod gnas* quoted above, note 3); and under *yon gnas rnam bzhi* the same dictionary explains *yon nam mchod pa 'bul ba'i gnas*. Chos kyi grags pa, *New Tibetan Dictionary*, gives *mchod pa'i gnas*, and Blo ldan shes rab, *Dictionary of Tibetan Symbols*, gives *mchod yul gyi gnas bla ma lta bu*.

20. Ruegg, *Spiritual Order and Temporal Order in the Buddhist Thought of India and Tibet*, sections XIII and XVIII, 81.

21. Ruegg, *Spiritual Order and Temporal Order in the Buddhist Thought of India and Tibet*, section XI (and above, 213).

22. Ruegg, *Spiritual Order and Temporal Order in the Buddhist Thought of India and Tibet*, sections X–XI, ed.

23. Robert Lingat, *Royautés Bouddhiques: Asoka et la Fonction Royale à Ceylan* [*Buddhist Kingdoms: Asoka and the Function of Royalty in Sri Lanka*], ed. Gérard Fussman and Eric Meyer (Paris: Éditions de l'École des hautes études en sciences sociales, 1989), 227, 239. See Ruegg, *Spiritual Order and Temporal Order in the Buddhist Thought of India and Tibet*, section XVIII.

24. Ruegg, *Spiritual Order and Temporal Order in the Buddhist Thought of India and Tibet*, section XVIII.

25. The text is to be found, e.g., in Blo bzang tshe 'phel 'Jigs med rigs pa'i rdo rje, Gu shri, *Hor chos 'byung* [*History of Buddhism in Mongolia*], in George Huth, ed. and trans., *Geschichte Des Buddhismus in Der Mongolei: Aus Dem Tibetischen Des 'Jigs Med Nam Mk'a* [*sic*] (Strassburg: K. J. Trübner, 1892), 98–99: *sangs rgyas bstan pa bka' phyag sprin gyis bsgribs//sems can bde skyid mi dpon lag tu shor//snyigs dus dge sbyong dpon po'i brtul zhugs 'dzin//'di gsum ma rtogs 'phags pa min par go/ —bstan la 'phel 'grib yod pa rgyal bas gsungs//sems can bde skyid rang rang las la rag//gang la gang 'dul de la de ston byed//'di gsum ma rtogs mkhas pa min par go//*. See Ruegg, *Spiritual Order and Temporal Order in the Buddhist Thought of India and Tibet*, 83–84.

26. Ruegg, *Spiritual Order and Temporal Order in the Buddhist Thought of India and Tibet*, section XVIII.

27. Ruegg, *Spiritual Order and Temporal Order in the Buddhist Thought of India and Tibet*, section XVIII. See Rin chen rnam rgyal, Sgra tshad pa (1318–1388), *Bu ston*

rnam thar [*Biography of Butön*], f. 23a (cf. f. 35a). Cf. Ruegg, *Life of Bu ston Rin po che* (Rome: Instituto italiano per il Medio ed Estremo Oriente, 1966), 121 (and 156).

28. Ruegg, *Spiritual Order and Temporal Order in the Buddhist Thought of India and Tibet*, sections XIII, XV. For the relation between Bu ston and the myriarch (*khri dpon*) of Zhalu—the *sku zhang* Grags pa rgyal mtshan, who was regarded as the emanation of the *lokapāla* and *mahārāja* Vaiśravana—see Rin chen rnam rgyal, *Biography of Butön*, f. 15a–b (cf. Ruegg, *Life of Bu ston Rin po che*, 93).

29. Presumably, however, neither the Sa skya dpon chen nor Phyag na rdo rje as Prince of Bailan could be properly described as a *yon bdag* of 'Phags pa, so that here we have cases of the relationship of the spiritual and temporal orders without the copulative compound *yon mchod* being strictly speaking applicable.

On the title *pa'i len dbang*, see L. Petech, "Princely Houses of the Yuan Period Connected with Tibet," in *Indo-Tibetan Studies: Papers in Honor and Appreciation of Professor David L. Snellgrove's Contribution to Indo-Tibetan Studies*, ed. T. Skorupski (Tring: Institute of Buddhist Studies, 1990), 257–269, 258. The spelling *sa len dbang*, found in Ngag dbang kun dga' bsod nams, *Sa skya'i gdung rabs* [*Genealogy of the Sakya (Family)*] (Beijing: Mi rigs dpe skrun khang, 1986), 233, appears to be an error for *pa['i] len dbang* "Prince of Bailan," the letters *pa* and *sa* being rather easily confused in Tibetan cursive script.

30. Ruegg, *Spiritual Order and Temporal Order in the Buddhist Thought of India and Tibet*, sections I, IX, XVI. It is to be observed that the three Bodhisattvas in question—Avalokiteśvara, Vajrapāṇi and Mañjughoṣa—are sometimes known as the *rigs gsum mgon po*, i.e., the heads of a triad of spiritual families (*kula*).

31. Ruegg, *Spiritual Order and Temporal Order in the Buddhist Thought of India and Tibet*, section VIII. On this and the expression *bla dpon sbrag pa*, see above, n. 17.

32. Ruegg, *Spiritual Order and Temporal Order in the Buddhist Thought of India and Tibet*, sections I, IX. In the case of a king-bodhisattva, an individual king would be the focus and central figure, who is then identified with a bodhisattva; whereas in the case of a bodhisattva-king it is evidently the bodhisattva who is the central figure, who then manifests himself, *nirmāṇically*, as a king. But the frontier between the two concepts is not always absolute.

33. Ruegg, *Spiritual Order and Temporal Order in the Buddhist Thought of India and Tibet*, sections XIV, XVI.

34. Blo bzang tshe 'phel, *History of Buddhism in Mongolia*, 86–87. See Ruegg, *Spiritual Order and Temporal Order in the Buddhist Thought of India and Tibet*, sections XV–XVI.

35. Ruegg, *Spiritual Order and Temporal Order in the Buddhist Thought of India and Tibet*, section XVI.

36. Ruegg, *Spiritual Order and Temporal Order in the Buddhist Thought of India and Tibet*, sections I (18), VII (39–40), X, XII (54). On Sga A gnyan Dam pa, see Ruegg, *Spiritual Order and Temporal Order in the Buddhist Thought of India and Tibet*, 82.

37. Ruegg, *Spiritual Order and Temporal Order in the Buddhist Thought of India and Tibet*, sections I, IX.

38. Ruegg, *Spiritual Order and Temporal Order in the Buddhist Thought of India and Tibet*, section XVI.

39. Luciano Petech, *Central Tibet and the Mongols: The Yüan-Sa skya Period of Tibetan History*, Serie Orientale Roma, vol. 65 (Rome: Instituto italiano per il Medio ed Estremo Oriente, 1990).

40. Herbert Franke and Denis Crispin Twitchett, *Alien Regimes and Border States, 907–1368*, Cambridge History of China, vol. 6 (New York: Cambridge University Press, 1994), 706–707.

41. In the Tibetan historical literature accessible to me, I have been able to find little that is directly comparable to, e.g., the Mongolian *Chaghan teüke*. In this text are to be found several of the Mongolian equivalents of the terms and concepts discussed in this paper. See K. Sagaster, *Die weisse Geschichte* [*The White History*] (Wiesbaden: Harrassowitz, 1976)

42. There can therefore be no question of the *mchod gnas* either being a "sacrificial priest" ("Opferpriester") or standing to his *yon bdag* in a more or less feudal tribute relationship; see Ruegg, *Spiritual Order and Temporal Order in the Buddhist Thought of India and Tibet*, section II, n. 27. On whether feudalism can serve as a relevant heuristic or analytical concept in the present context, see Ruegg, "Historiography and Semantics of a Tibetan Religio-social and Religio-political Concept," 441–442, 453 n. 37.

43. On this see Ruegg, *Spiritual Order and Temporal Order in the Buddhist Thought of India and Tibet*, part II, 140ff.

44. See Ruegg, *Spiritual Order and Temporal Order in the Buddhist Thought of India and Tibet*, 22f., 90f., 138f. (with bibliography).

45. On this see Ruegg, *Spiritual Order and Temporal Order in the Buddhist Thought of India and Tibet*, part II, 141ff.

46. Compare however the Sanskrit copulative compound *rtvig-yājyau* "officiant and beneficiary of the sacrifice"; see Ruegg, *Spiritual Order and Temporal Order in the Buddhist Thought of India and Tibet*, 56.

47. See Ruegg, *Spiritual Order and Temporal Order in the Buddhist Thought of India and Tibet*, part II. On ethnocentric (Eurocentric, etc.) interpretations in modern international law of the *yon mchod* relation between a lama and a ruler, as well as in some modern ideas about so-called Tibetan feudalism, see Ruegg, "Historiography and Semantics of a Tibetan Religio-social and Religio-political Concept," 441–442, 443–444, 451–452 and n. 37.

48. Zhang Yisun, *Great Tibetan–Chinese Dictionary*.

49. Ruegg, *Spiritual Order and Temporal Order in the Buddhist Thought of India and Tibet*, 56.

50. Ishihama and Fukuda, *A New Critical Edition of the Mahāvyutpatti*, 338 and Śrīdharasena, *Abhidhānaviśvalocanam, or, Abhidhānamuktāvalī of Śrīdharasena*, trans. A. Wayman and L. Jamspal, Monograph series of Naritasan Institute for Buddhist Studies, vol. 3 (Narita, Narita-shi, Chiba-ken, Japan: Naritasan Shinshoji, 1992), 1480 have *argha*; Amarasiṃha, Kīrticandra, Grags pa rgyal mtshan, and S. C. Vidyabhusana,

Amarakoṣa and Its Tibetan Translation, 'Chi med mdzod: A Metrical Dictionary of the Sanskrit Language by Amarasiṃha with Its Tibetan Translation Made by Mahāpaṇḍita Kīrticandra and Yar-luṅs Lo-tsā-ba Grags-pa-rgyal-mtshan, Bibliotheca Indica, work no. 204 (Calcutta: Asiatic Society, 1911), ii, Brahmavarga 32 has *arghya*; Blo ldan shes rab, *Dictionary of Tibetan Symbols* gives *argha*; Chos kyi grags pa, *New Tibetan Dictionary*, indicates both *yon chab* and *zhal bsil*; but Zhang Yisun, *Great Tibetan-Chinese Dictionary*, interprets the expression as a copulative compound: *mchod pa dang yon chab* "offering (*pūjā*) and ritual water offering (*argh[y]a*)," and gives the additional meaning of *sku yon* "offering; emolument, fee."

51. Ishihama and Fukuda, *A New Critical Edition of the Mahāvyutpatti*, 2866: dānapati.

52. Amarasiṃha et al., *A Metrical Dictionary of the Sanskrit Language by Amarasiṃha*, ii, Vaiśyavarga 67 [misreading of *aghnyā* as *arghya* by the Tibetan translator?].

53. Ishihama and Fukuda, *A New Critical Edition of the Mahāvyutpatti*, 6798: dakṣiṇīya.

54. Blo ldan shes rab, *Dictionary of Tibetan Symbols* gives *argha* and Chos kyi grags pa, *New Tibetan Dictionary: mchod pa'i gnas la'ang*; Zhang Yisun, *Great Tibetan-Chinese Dictionary: mchod yul gyi bla ma* (cf. *mchod gnas*).

55. According to Zhang Yisun, *Great Tibetan-Chinese Dictionary*.

56. According to Zhang Yisun, *Great Tibetan-Chinese Dictionary*; see above, n. 17.

57. There also exist uses of the lexeme *yon mchod* where reference does not appear to be made to two different (sets of) persons, in other words where the compound is not a copulative one (but an appositional one?; cf. the uses of the word *bla dpon* listed above, and the Skt. word *rājarṣi* "king-sage," i.e., a royal Ṛṣi). See Ruegg, *Spiritual Order and Temporal Order in the Buddhist Thought of India and Tibet*, 39 n. 64.

58. Śrīdharasena et al., *Abhidhānaviśvalocanam*, 898 has *sattrin* "performer of a *sattra* ceremony."

59. Zhang Yisun, *Great Tibetan-Chinese Dictionary: mchod yul gyi gnas te/dkon mchog gsum lta bu*; cf. s.v. *yon gnas rnam bzhi: yon nam mchod pa 'bul ba'i gnas bźi ste/bla ma dang/'jam pa'i dbyangs/dbyangs can ma/srung ma bcas so/*.

Chapter 13

THE MONGOL CENSUS IN TIBET

Luciano Petech

The Italian scholar Luciano Petech was perhaps the single most important twentieth-century historian of Tibet, having written on just about every period of the country's history. Working against the grain of much mid-century scholarship, Petech utilized both Tibetan and Chinese sources, thus paving the way for later scholars such as Elliot Sperling, who now routinely use Chinese sources to study historical relations among Tibetans, Chinese, Manchus, and Mongols. This article is a detailed study of one specific method of the Mongol administration of Tibet, the census, which was necessary for purposes of tax collection. This census was, as far as we know, the first ever conducted in Tibet; it records just under a quarter million Tibetans living in the farming household units counted by the Mongols in Central Tibet, not including the nomadic population. One interesting revelation of this account is that the three regions (*chölkha*) of Tibet, now typically described as Ü-Tsang, Kham, and Amdo, were in the Mongol period of Sakya rule restricted to what is now the Tibetan Autonomous Region: Ü, Tsang, and Ngari Korsum. Thus, later claims of Sakya rule over the three *chölkha* of Tibet (often implying control of the entire Tibetan Plateau) do not reflect the reality as documented in these kind of practical administrative records from the period of Mongol domination.

It is a known fact that the whole of the financial and military administration of the Mongol rulers of China was based on a systematic survey of the population of their dominions. A first census was taken in 1235 and a second in 1258, both being limited to North China as the South was still independent under the national Song dynasty. These early surveys were followed between 1261 and 1275 by annual calculations, apparently not based upon actual field work; the only one registered in the *Yuan History* as a real census is that of 1270. After the conquest of the South in 1276–79 the Mongol government waited till 1290 before it carried out a general census of the whole of China; it was repeated (probably re-calculated) in the following year, and completed in 1292 by a survey of the agricultural population only. The 1290 census was practically the last. A set of figures given in 1330 refers only to the number of tax-paying families registered with the Ministry of Finance, and it was probably not based on an actual survey.[1]

Census, tribute, militia, and mail service were the four supporting pillars of Mongol rule in all the outer dependencies of the empire; this fundamental principle was valid in Tibet as well. The various sections of the Tibetan-speaking area came under Mongol sway at different times. North-Eastern Tibet (Amdo; called Tufan in the official usage of the Yuan terminology) passed under Mongol influence during the fifties of the thirtieth century and these regions received a separate administration.[2] The date of the formal setting-up of Mongol rule in Central Tibet (Ü-Tsang; Chin. Wusi zang) is 1267–68, when the mail routes with their stages (*jam*) were organized and a census was taken. Both measures were carried out by imperial officials sent out from China, with the collaboration of the administrative staff of the Sakya abbot, whom the emperor Qubilai had chosen as his collaborator and instrument for the new organization of Tibet.[3]

The main source on the 1268 census is *Gya Bö Yiktsang* [*Chinese and Tibetan Documents*], written in 1434 by the monk Śribhūtibhadra.[4] It supplies a fairly detailed account of the Sakya–Mongol partnership, partly drawn from local information but for an even larger portion based indirectly on a Chinese source, as twice stated in the text. This is the *Da Yuan Tongzhi* [*Comprehensive Institutions of the Great Yuan*], an account of Mongol administration in China compiled in 1323; it is no longer extant, except for a section which was recovered and published half a century ago. This blend of authoritative local and Chinese information is the feature that makes *Chinese and Tibetan Documents* so particularly interesting.

The section dealing with the Mongol dominance in Tibet was translated long ago by S. C. Das;[5] the contents were re-arranged in a partly different order and, as usual with him, it is sometimes difficult to recognize the Tibetan and Mongol names in their anglicized garb.

Several later texts drew their treatment of this subject from *Chinese and Tibetan Documents*. They are: the Sakyapa chronicle called *Dzamling Jangchok kyi Tuppé Gyeltsap Chenpo Pelden Sakyapé Dungrap* [*Lineage of the Glorious Sakya*], the *History of Tibet* by the fifth Dalai Lama, the *Autobiography of the*

Fifth Dalai Lama, and Longdöl Lama's account of the benefactors of the Buddhist religion.[6] These secondary sources were utilized by Professor G. Tucci in *Tibetan Painted Scrolls,* and this remains to this day the only Western study of the census in Tibet,[7] since the special article promised by Madame Macdonald has never appeared, as far as I am aware.

The statistical skeleton upon which the census was built is described as follows. The basic unit is the *hordü,* literally "Mongol smoke," meaning a homestead with its fire-place, built on Mongol principles. The elements necessary to form a *hordü* are: "a house (*khangsa*) with at least six pillars supporting the roof; a strip of land sufficient for sowing twelve bushels (*khel*) of Mongol seed (*hor sön*); husband, wife, and children with male and female attendants, six in all; three plowing bullocks, two goats, and four sheep." Clearly this basic unit refers to a middle-peasant family tilling government soil or its own land. It covers the agricultural element of the population and leaves out the other component of Tibetan population, the nomads.[8]

The *hordü* serves as the foundation layer for the pyramid of the larger units. Fifty *hordü* form one *tago* (horse-head). Two *tago* form a *gyakor,* a group of one hundred families. What follows is the usual decimal structure of the Mongol army and people. Ten *gyakor* form a *tongkor* (chiliarchy). Ten *tongkor* form a *trikor* (myriarchy). The *trikor* in Mongol times and even later was the equivalent of a district; it was supposed to contain 4,000 temple serfs and 6,000 serfs of the noble families, but the figures were purely theoretical. On a higher level, ten *trikor* formed a *lu,* which is the Chinese term *lu,* circuit; and ten *lu* normally formed a *zhing,* the Chinese *sheng,* province. Tibet actually contained only three *chölkha* (Mongol *cölge* corresponding to the Chinese *lu*): Ü, Tsang, and Ngari Korsum; thus it was too small to form a regular *sheng.* However, out of respect for the religious character of the country, the emperor Qubilai decreed that Tibet was to be considered as one *sheng.*[9]

The census of 1268 was carried out by two imperial officials called Akön and Mingling: their names seem to be unknown to the Chinese texts. They personally carried out the survey of Tsang, from Ngari to the Zhalu district. In Ü, from Zhalu to Drigung, the work was entrusted to a Tibetan, Sutu Akyi, who incidentally was an ancestor of the fifth Dalai Lama on the maternal side.[10]

The figures of the census are given in some detail, but we cannot deal with them here.[11] Suffice it to say that the total sums were 15,690 *hordü* for Ngari and Tsang and 20,763 for Ü, giving a grand total of 36,453 *hordü* for Central and Western Tibet to which 750 *hordü* in Yardrok (probably Northern Tibet) must be added. *Chinese and Tibetan Documents* remarks that these figures were taken from the paper-roll registers compiled by Shakya Zangpo, who was *pönchen,* i.e., temporal administrator of Sakya, from 1244 to 1275. Working out these results, they go to show that the population of Central and Western Tibet amounted to c. 223,000 souls; as said above, the nomads are not included. The figure seems very low, but we have to remember that China proper under Mongol domination contained only c. fifty million people, and thus the proportion is acceptable.

The results of the 1268 census were copied, not without some mistakes, in later texts.[12] But the original list is always the same; the comparatively few variants found in the later texts cannot be taken to refer to a second census, as it has been supposed.[13]

Having completed the basic census (*rtsa ba'i dud chen rtsis pa*), the two officials proceeded to assign to each myriarchy the upkeep of the postal stages, of which there were twenty-seven. This meant reserving a certain number of *hordü* for the duty of supplying horses, yaks, drivers, caretakers, etc.; in exchange for this service the families concerned were exempted from any other form of taxation. Practically each stage came to form the center of a postal district.[14] The mail service was efficient, at least in the beginning, but the burden on the Tibetan authorities and peasants was such that most of the mail servants preferred to abscond and turn to a life of vagrancy. In 1281 the imperial official Sanggyé, who led an expedition to Tibet after the death of Pakpa, had to make use of the Mongol garrisons to get the mail stages in working order again.[15]

It is usually believed that there was a second census in 1287, but the sources hardly justify this assertion. *Chinese and Tibetan Documents* informs us that "in the earth-dragon year 1268 the imperial envoys Akön and Mingling carried out the basic census of people and land (*rtsa ba'i dud grangs rtsis pa*). Twenty years later, in the fire-hog year 1287, Hoshu and Unukhan, these two, sent by the *trimra chenpo* (perhaps the grand secretariat, *zhongshu sheng*), working in collaboration with the *pönchen* Zhönnu Wangchuk, carried out a revision (*chesel*) of the country."[16] Then follows the list of the *hordü* in each *trikor* according to the registers of Shakya Zangpo as related above; actually the text mentions the revision of 1287 merely in order to emphasize the correctness and trustworthiness of the figures in the basic census.

The *Autobiography of the Fifth Dalai Lama* follows a somewhat different version of the same text. Hoshu and Unukhan are telescoped together into one person: Doshu Anugen, which seems preferable. This looks more like a title than a name; but I am unable to identify the original. The *Autobiography* gives him as companions Ergön and Sutu Akyi, i.e., the same two officials of 1268, and the three together are said to have carried out a counting of the population dividing it by the number of the *hordü* (*mi brtsis dud grangs su bcad*).[17] Possibly the fifth Dalai Lama misunderstood (at least in part) the manuscript of *Chinese and Tibetan Documents* he was following.

We can reach a better understanding of the revision of 1287 by placing it in the frame of the general policy of the Mongol government of the time. During those years Sanggyé, who had become the all-powerful favorite and minister of the emperor, ordered widespread revisions (*lisuan*) in various provinces. For instance, in the tenth month of 1288 he sent twelve officials of the Central Control

Boards (*shengyuan taiguan*) to carry out a financial revision in the six provinces of Jianghuai, Jiangxi, Fujian, Sichuan, Gansu and Anxi.[18] It stands to reason that the proceedings of 1287 in Tibet were but another instance of this policy. We may suppose that these local inspections were meant as preparations for the grand census of 1290; but this is only hypothetical.

A secondary result of the revision was that the *xuanwei shi* Zhönnu Wangchuk (*xuanwei shi* [pacification commissioner] was the chief imperial official in Tibet; practically identical with the *pönchen*) was ordered to provide for the needs of the famished families of the postal and military services in the territory under his jurisdiction; as a reward, Sanggyé sanctioned a grant of 2,500 silver taels (tenth month of 1288).[19]

Much later there was another inspection. Our sole source for this is *Chinese and Tibetan Documents*; the passage is translated here word for word: "Although in the middle royal generation [after Chinggis Khan] the revision of ecclesiastical and secular dependants and the land survey and census were carried out in some fashion, when the Mongol emperor Togön Temur ascended the throne in 1333 he sent the man called Tozhu Anugen and Gechakté Pingchang."[20]

The name Tozhu Anugen is clearly identical with Hoshu Unukhan, to whom the revision of 1287 is attributed; and this tends to support our suspicion that it is a title and not a personal name. As to Gechakté Pingchang, this raises at once the problem of his identification with *pingchang* Kimčaqtai (Jinchatai in Chinese), whose career can be recovered in main outlines from scattered mentions in the basic annals (*benji*) of the history of the Yuan dynasty. On January 10th, 1323, he was appointed head of the Office of Buddhism and Tibet (*xuanzheng yuanshi*).[21] During the short civil war of 1328 which resulted in the restoration of the Qaishan branch of the imperial family, he stayed at the summer capital Shangdu, then in the hands of the faction which opposed the restoration. He hatched a conspiracy against its leader Daula Shah; the plot was discovered and its members were put to death. Kimčaqtai alone escaped, because at the time he was away on military duty. After the end of the war, on November 19th, 1328, he was appointed vice-chancellor (*bingzhang zhengli*) of the Grand Secretariat (*zhongshu sheng*).[22] In February 1329 he received (concurrently?) the presidency of the Supreme Military Council (*qumi yuan*).[23] But already in March 1330 he was subjected to an enquiry by the censorate.[24] Some months later he was dismissed and his property was confiscated; but almost immediately the emperor pardoned him and appointed him provincial *pingchang* of Sichuan. On August 12th, 1331, he was again denounced by a censor for having falsely accused another official and thus caused his ruin, the event going back to 1323–1324; he was also charged with doubtful attitude during the civil war and with inefficiency in handling the revolt raging on the Yunnan–Sichuan border. As a result, he was dismissed and banished with his family to Guangdong; however, his property was not confiscated.[25] After this he vanishes from the basic annals. However, the tables (*piao*) of the officials of the central government list again, for the year 1333 only, a Kimčaqtai as *bingzhang zhengli*, although there is no mention anywhere of a second rehabilitation.[26] In 1336 Gapchakté Pingchang, belonging to the family of the king of the Yugur (i.e., of the *idiqut* of Ui-ghuristan), accompanied the Third Karmapa hierarch Rangjung Dorjé to Tsurpu, from where the latter was to proceed to China.[27] From the Chinese angle, the identity of the Kimčaqtai of 1323–1331 with the one of 1333 may not be wholly beyond doubt. But in any case Gechakté and Gapchakté are one and the same person; in 1334 or 1335 the emperor had sent him to Tibet, apparently on an inspection tour.

After the mention of Gechakté there is a break in the logical sequence of the text of *Chinese and Tibetan Documents*, and what follows deals with a different subject: "During the second term of office of the Ü-Tsang *pönchen* Zhönwang, in the matter of the counting of the population and the census together, with the *hordü*, the following [rules] were observed";[28] then follow the definitions of *hordü*, *tago* and the higher units, as told above. The first term of office of Zhönnu Wangchuk was about 1288 (see above); the second was after the victori-ous campaign against the Drigung sect and monastery in 1290. But we know that the revision took place in 1287; and thus "second term" must be an error for "first term," unless we accept the improbable supposition that the revision of 1287 was registered only after 1290. In any case, there is no relation with the preceding sentences and there may be a gap in the text. It is a pity that no textual compari-son is possible, as this passage was not copied in later sources, as far as I know.

Turning again to the inspection of c. 1335, we must introduce at this point the mention in the *History* of the fifth Dalai Lama of a revision (*phye gsal*) car-ried out by Situ Darma Gyeltsen, apparently a Tibetan monk sent by the em-peror; the context shows that this took place at some date after 1329.[29] No further information on this man is forthcoming, nor is it possible to see any connection with Kimčaqtai. We might suppose that the journey to Tibet of both personages was connected with the tabulation of the tax-paying families of the empire com-piled in 1330, as said above; but this is mere speculation.

Anyhow, it is clear that, while Qubilai maintained a firm grip on Tibet through his census and the subsequent revision, his weak successors tried only once, in 1334 or 1335, to regain a real control over the Tibetan administration, which was slipping fast out of their hands. Only ten years later Jangchup Gyel-tsen of Pakmodru was wresting first Ü and then Tsang from the hands of the Sakyapa; and the last Yuan emperor Toghan Temür had to recognize officially the new situation, which implied the *de facto* independence of Tibet.

Summing up the results of our enquiry, we may conclude that there was only one Mongol census in Tibet consisting of an actual survey of the land and of the population, and this was carried out in 1268. Its results were revised and checked in 1287 and again in about 1335, both times in possible connection with similar efforts in China proper; but they were never replaced by a fresh survey.

NOTES

1. *Yuan shi* [*History of Yuan*] (Baina edition) (Shanghai: Shangwu yinshuguan, 1937), 58.1b. Cf. Herbert Franke, *Geld und Wirtschaft in China unter der Mongolen-Herrschaft* [*Money and Economy in China Under Mongol Rule*] (Leipzig: Harrassowitz, 1949), 128–129.

2. *History of Yuan*, 87.9b–12a, 14a. See also Han Rulin, "Yuanchao zhongyang zhengfu shi zenyang guanli Xizang difang di" [How the Central Government of the Yuan Dynasty Managed Tibet], *Lishi yanjiu* 7 (1959): 51–56.

3. See my paper "Tibetan Relations with Sung China and with the Mongols," in *China Among Equals: The Middle Kingdom and Its Neighbors, 10th–14th Centuries*, ed. Morris Rossabi (Berkeley: University of California Press, 1983), 173–203.

4. Full title: *Rgya Bod kyi yig tshang mkhas pa dga' byed chen mo.* On its author and date see Ariane Macdonald, "Préambule à la lecture d'un *rGya-Bod yig-chan*" [Preamble to the Reading of a *Rgya Bod yig tshang*], *Journal Asiatique* 251 (1963): 83–159. The text is known through a single manuscript (*dbu med*) in the Densapa library, Gangtok; I utilized a microfilm, for which I am indebted to the kindness of Professor K. Enoki, Tokyo. The University of Washington, Seattle, owns a beautiful *dbu can* manuscript, said to have been obtained in the thirties of this century from the late Dr. Joseph Rock. As it agrees word for word with the Densapa manuscript (ms.), I suppose it is a copy of the latter, made at Gangtok for Dr. Rock. The work is here cited as Stag tshang pa, *Chinese and Tibetan Documents* (ms.), and the pagination refers to the Densapa ms.

5. Sarat Chandra Das, "Tibet Under the Tartar Emperors of China in the 13th Century," *Journal of the Asiatic Society of Bengal* (1905):94–102.

6. On these texts see Giuseppe Tucci, *Tibetan Painted Scrolls* (Rome: Libreria dello Stato, 1949), 145–147, 149–150, 154, 165–166.

7. Tucci, *Tibetan Painted Scrolls*, 13–14.

8. Macdonald, "Preamble to the Reading of a *Rgya Bod yig tshang*," 57.

9. Stag tshang pa, *Chinese and Tibetan Documents* (ms.), 130a–b. A more correct text is found in Ngag dbang kun dga' bsod nams, A mes zhabs, *'Dzam gling byang phyogs kyi thub pa'i rgyal tshab chen po dpal ldan sa skya pa'i gdung rabs rin po che ji ltar byon pa'i tshul gyi rnam par thar pa ngo mtshar rin po che'i bang mdzod dgos 'dod kun 'byung* [*Lineage of the Glorious Sakya*] (New Delhi: Tashi Dorji, 1975), 65–66a.

10. Stag tshang pa, *Chinese and Tibetan Documents* (ms.), 143b, 145b; Ngag dbang blo bzang rgya mtsho, *Za hor gyi bande blo bzang rgya mtsho'i 'di nang 'khrul pa'i rol rtsed rtogs brjod kyi tshul du bkod pa du ku la'i gos bzang* [*Autobiography of the Fifth Dalai Lama*], Zhöl Edition, 20b–21a. Cf. Macdonald, "Preamble to the Reading of a *Rgya Bod yig tshang*," 57.

11. Stag tshang pa, *Chinese and Tibetan Documents* (ms.), 144a–145b.

12. Ngag dbang blo bzang rgya mtsho, *Gangs can yul gyi sa la spyod pa'i mtho ris kyi rgyal blon gtso bor brjod pa'i deb ther rdzogs ldan gzhun nu'i dga' ston dpyid kyi*

rgyal mo'i glu dbyangs [*History of Tibet*], in the xylograph edition *Fifth Dalai Lama's Collected Works*, vol. dza (Lhasa), 20b–21a; Ngag dbang blo bzang, Klong rdol Bla ma, *Bstan pa'i sbyin bdag byung tshul gyi ming gi grangs* [*Benefactors of the Teachings*], in *Klong rdol ngag dbang blo bzang gi gsung 'bum* [*Collected Works*], vol. 'a (Lhasa: Kun bde gling, n. d.), 5a–b (translated in Tucci, *Tibetan Painted Scrolls*, 251–252).

13. Macdonald, "Preamble to the Reading of a *Rgya Bod yig tshang*," 56–57.

14. The details of the organization are given in Stag tshang pa, *Chinese and Tibetan Documents* (ms.), 133a, 146a–b.

15. Stag tshang pa, *Chinese and Tibetan Documents* (ms.), 141a.

16. Stag tshang pa, *Chinese and Tibetan Documents* (ms.), 143b.

17. Ngag dbang blo bzang rgya mtsho, *Autobiography of the Fifth Dalai Lama*, 21a.

18. *History of Yuan*, 15.11a, 205.20a.

19. *History of Yuan*, 15.11a.

20. *Bod dbus gtsang du/thog mar hor jing gir rgyal pos/rgya nag rgyal sa lon nas/ rgyal kham byin po mnan/bu rnams la sa bkos byas pa'i dus dang/gzhan yang rgyal po na rims kyi bar ma/lha sde mi sde phye gsal dang: sa rtsi: dud 'grang lugs ci rigs su byung 'dug na'ang/'dir hor rgyal po tho gon the mur rg/ryalsar phebs nas/tho zhu a nu gan bya ba dang/ges chag tha'i phing chang mngags nas.* Stag tshang pa, *Chinese and Tibetan Documents* (ms.), 130a.

21. *History of Yuan*, 28.9a.

22. *History of Yuan*, 32.17a. On the civil war see John W. Dardess, *Conquerors and Confucians: Aspects of Political Change in Late Yuan China* (New York: Columbia University Press, 1973), 31–52.

23. *History of Yuan*, 33.1b.

24. *History of Yuan*, 34.5a.

25. *History of Yuan*, 35.19a–b. For Kimčaqtai's tenure as *pingchang* see *History of Yuan*, 112.26b–28a.

26. *History of Yuan*, 113.1a.

27. Si tu Pan chen Chos kyi 'byung gnas, *History of the Karma Bka-'brgyud-pa Sect: Being the Text of "Sgrub brgyud Karma Kaṃ tshang brgyud pa rin po che'i rnam par thar pa Rab 'byams nor bu zla ba chu sel gyi phreṅ ba"* (New Delhi: D. Gyaltsan and Kesang Legshay, 1972), 111b–112a.

28. *Dbus gtsang dpon chen gzhon dbang skyar ma'i dus/mi rtsis/dud grangs/hor dus* (sic) *bcas pa na 'di btang snang ngo*; Stag tshang pa, *Chinese and Tibetan Documents* (ms.), 130a.

29. Ngag dbang blo bzang rgya mtsho, *History of Tibet*, 76b (translated in Tucci, *Tibetan Painted Scrolls*, 636).

Chapter 14

SAKYA PAṆḌITA'S LETTER TO THE TIBETANS

A LATE AND DUBIOUS ADDITION TO HIS COLLECTED WORKS

David P. Jackson

In this essay, David Jackson argues that one of the most important documents in Tibetan history is a later forgery. The letter discussed here was supposedly written around 1247 by Sakya Paṇḍita (Sapaṇ) to instruct the Central Tibetans to submit to Mongol rule under Sakya regency. It is generally (mis)understood to mark Tibet's entry into the Mongol empire. The details of the belated appearance in Tibetan historical literature may seem ponderous, but Jackson's work on this text suggests that Tibetan historical texts (like all others) need to be treated with some caution when used to make claims regarding earlier periods. Such caution was not observed toward this text by some of the most important historians of Tibet, like Giuseppe Tucci. Tucci concluded on the basis of this letter that Sapaṇ "had negotiated the country's surrender." There are further problems with the letter's authenticity beyond those Jackson discusses, including the fact that it refers to the Mongol census—before a census was taken in Tibet. While Jackson does not speculate about the reasons this text appeared (for the first time) almost four centuries after it was purported to have been written, we might conclude that it was part of an effort to bolster the position of the Sakya. For instance, just as the text of this letter was first made available, Sakya monks were serving as lamas to Mongols again, at the court of Ligdan Khan, the heir to Chinggis Khan's lineage. Whatever the real reason for the late advent of this text, it provides a good example of the need for close attention to a text's production in assessing its place in history.

In the Degé printed edition of Sakya Paṇḍita's collected works there exists a short letter that purports to have been written by Sakya Paṇḍita (Sapaṇ)

(1182–1251) in about 1247, after he reached the Mongol camp in Liangzhou and had an interview with the Mongol prince Köden. It bears the title *Bulop Namla Dringwa* and, if authentic, is one of the earliest sources on Tibetan-Mongolian political and religious relations. Till now it has been accepted as authentic and used as a basic source by scholars. It was translated in full and studied by G. Tucci in his monumental *Tibetan Painted Scrolls*,[1] and was summarized by T. W. D. Shakabpa in his *Tibet: A Political History*.[2] It has also been described or mentioned by several others.[3] There are, however, some important reasons to doubt its authenticity, one being that it is absent from some of the early lists of Sapaṇ's collected works and only enters Tibetan historiography from about the first half of the 16th century.

The earliest evidence for the existence of this letter is its mention in the record of teachings received (*senyik*) of Ngorchen Könchok Lhündrup (1497–1557). In that work, which is entitled *Chökyi Jé Penden Lama Namlé Dampé Chö Töpé Chö Töpé Tsül Selwar Shépé Yigé Tupten Gyépé Nyinché*, the letter is cited by the title *Bulop Namla Dringpa*. It is the sixty-third work in that list.[4] The letter is also listed in the *senyik* of the Gongkar Lama Trinlé Namgyel (fl. c. 1700), a work entitled *Topyik Bumpa Zangpo*. There the letter is cited by the different title *Chöjé Sakya Paṇḍita's Böbang Chila Dampa*, and the text is said to have been four folios long in the manuscript upon which this *senyik* list was based. In the latter list it was the fifty-second work, the last work in volume *dza*.[5]

As for the actual text of the letter, the first place it is known to have turned up is in the *Sakya Dungrap Chenmo* of Amezhap Ngawang Künga Sönam (1597–1659), a work that he completed in 1629.[6] It is found added to the long biography of Sapaṇ, which Amezhap took almost verbatim from the commentary by Lowo Khenchen Sönam Lhündrup (1456–1532) on Sapaṇ's *Khepanam Jukpé Go*.[7] The inclusion of this letter, however, was one of the few instances where Amezhap departed from Lowo Khenchen's account and added some new material from elsewhere, two other important additions being the letter of summons from Köden to Sakya Paṇḍita and the list of Sapaṇ's writings.[8]

The second place the letter turned up in was the edition of Sapaṇ's collected works by Zhuchen Tsültrim Rinchen (1700–1769), Sapaṇ's works forming the fourth main part of the 1736 Degé edition of the *Sakya Kabum*.[9] The letter therefore is listed in the index compiled by Zhuchen (ascribed to the Ngor Khenpo Trashi Lhündrup, 1672–1739),[10] as well as in the almost identical list of Sapaṇ's works recorded in Zhuchen's record of teachings received (*senyik*).[11] In both index and *senyik*, the title is marked with the numerals 9 and 24, thus apparently showing that he found the same work listed in the *senyik*s of Könchok Lhündrup (1497–1557) and Sanggyé Püntsok (1649–1705), who were respectively the 9th (i.e., 10th) and 24th (i.e., 25th) abbots of Ngor. As mentioned above, the work indeed is listed in the record of teachings received of Könchok Lhündrup. However, Zhuchen noted in both the index and *senyik* that the letter is not actually listed in Sanggyé Püntsok's *senyik*, the *Senyik Bang gi gyelpo*.[12] Instead, according to Zhuchen, one finds there the title *Böyül la Ngakpa* [*Eulogy to Tibet*]. This is the title of a work which appears in the Degé edition before the letter (being no. 69 in the Tōyō Bunko reprint edition) and which, according to its colophon, was written when Sapaṇ was in his nineteenth year (1200).[13] Zhuchen decided that this title (which appeared twice in the *senyik* he was using?) must refer to the letter, since "there was no other [similar work?] besides this." He also notes that the letter itself had the title *Böbang Chila Dampa* in the manuscript available to him.[14] One hopes that the actual *senyik* of Sanggyé Püntsok will become available so that one can verify the presence or absence of the letter or of any similarly entitled work in its list. But until it does, it is open to doubt whether it lists this work, since Zhuchen qualifies his citation from the *senyik* of Sanggyé Püntsok in the above way.

The third and last known appearance of Sapaṇ's letter is its quotation in the recent *Hor Chöjung* by Lozang Tadrin (1867–1937), as mentioned by D. Schuh.[15]

Besides its mention in the *senyiks* of Könchok Lhündrup and Gongkar Trinlé Namgyel, and the *Sakya Kabum* index and *senyik* of Zhuchen Tsültrim Rinchen, this letter is not cited in any other list of Sapaṇ's works available to me. It is absent from that in the *senyik* of Ngorchen Künga Zangpo (1382–1456)[16] and also from that of the fifth Dalai Lama Ngawang Lozang Gyatso (1617–1682).[17] It is likewise missing from the lists of Sapaṇ's works found within the biography of Sapaṇ in the *Khejuk Namshé* composed in 1527 by Lowo Khenchen Sönam Lhündrup,[18] in the long biography of Sapaṇ by Rinpungpa Ngawang Jikmé Drakpa (composed in 1579),[19] and in the *Sakya Dungrap Chenmo* of Amezhap Ngawang Künga Sönam.[20] As mentioned above, however, Amezhap did present the letter itself *in extenso* in that genealogical history.

The absence of the letter from those lists is sufficient to show that it was probably a later addition to Sapaṇ's oeuvre. It surfaced as early as the early-16th century, the time when Könchok Lhündrup received the *lung* for Sapaṇ's works. It is curious that Rinpungpa did not list it, for he had access to many works, and he also was quite free in including a number of probably apocryphal letters and treatises among the works he listed. The letter was also not included by Lowo Khenchen in the biography of Sapaṇ placed at the beginning of his commentary on the *Khejuk* which he completed in 1527. In this biography Lowo Khenchen did quote several of Sapaṇ's other letters, as well as some four letters ascribed to Sapaṇ's student Biji Rinchen Drak which he says were recovered from Kham in the time of Gyeltsap Künga Wangchuk (1424–1478; abbot of Ngor 1465–1478).[21]

All of this may not decisively disprove the letter's authenticity, but it does cast doubt on it. There are, moreover, some other dubious features of the letter. Stylistically it is quite unlike anything else I have read in Sapaṇ's works. In general, the letter is colloquial in tone and not at all elegant. I do not recall, for instance, seeing the "*é*" interrogative particle ever used by Sapaṇ elsewhere.[22] The letter, if authentic, was admittedly written in very unusual circumstances and its contents are somewhat unique among Sapaṇ's writings. When I first read the letter some years ago, even without doubting its authenticity I noted its strange style and wondered whether Sapaṇ had not received some official "help" in writing it, such as from a bilingual scribe at the court. It was ostensibly meant to be an official statement and, if authentic, it presumably was the product of close consultations with the Mongols. Another possibility that occurred to me was that it had survived in some Mongolian or Chinese collection of edicts and correspondence, and later had been translated back into Tibetan, thus giving it a strange flavor. Indeed, the work it reminded me of most was the putative letter of summons sent by the Mongol prince Köden to Sapaṇ, a letter which likewise first surfaced as a complete work within the same section of Amezhap's *Sakya Dungrap Chenmo*.

One should not overlook the strong probability that these two letters are closely connected. The letter of summons attributed to Köden has already been investigated by D. Schuh, who has shown it to be not only corruptly transmitted but also, on formal grounds, probably a forgery.[23] Therefore there is all the more reason to doubt the authenticity of the related letter ascribed to Sapaṇ. In this connection one should also take note of the fact that Köden's letter was known to Paṇchen Sönam Drakpa (1478–1554), who quoted part of its beginning in his *New Red Annals* (composed in 1538).[24] As seen above, this is also about the period in which the letter ascribed to Sapaṇ is first known to have been cited in a *senyik*.

In any case, it is not yet possible to determine the authenticity of these materials in a decisive way. Moreover, if the letter is a forgery, one should be able to attribute a motive for it. I must leave that, as well as the detailed examination of its contents and style, to scholars who are specialized in the study of Tibetan political history and Tibeto-Mongolian relations. I do think, however, that all scholars who use this letter should henceforth do so with caution, since it is probably a later accretion to Sapaṇ's collected works, and its ultimate origins are still by no means clear.[25]

NOTES

1. G. Tucci, *Tibetan Painted Scrolls* (Roma: Libreria dello Stato, 1949), 10–12.

2. T. W. D. Shakabpa, *Tibet A Political History* (New Haven: Yale University Press, 1967; reprinted New York: Potala Publications, 1984), 63f.

3. See for instance D. Schuh, "Wie ist die Einladung des fünften Karmapa an den chinesischen Kaiserhof als Fortführung der Tibetpolitik der Mongolen-Khane zu verstehen? [How Is the Invitation of the Fifth Karmapa to the Chinese Imperial Court to Be Understood as a Continuation of the Tibetan Policy of the Mongol Khans?]," *Altaica Collecta* (Wiesbaden: Otto Harrassowitz, 1976), 211f., and *Erlasse und Sendschreiben mongolischer Herrscher für Tibetische Geistliche* [*Missives and Decrees of Mongolian Rulers for the Tibetan Clergy*], Monumenta Tibetica Historica,

Abt. 3, Bd. 1 (St. Augustin: VGH-Wissenschaftsverlag, 1977), xvii, 18, 51f., and 76 n. 125; and J. Szerb, "Glosses on the Oeuvre of Bla ma 'Phags pa: II. Some Notes on the Events of the Years 1251–1254," *Acta Orientalia Hungarica* 34: 264, n. 6.

4. Dkon mchog lhun grub, *Chos kyi rje dpal ldan bla ma dam pa rnams las dam pa'i chos thos pa'i tshul gsal bar bshad pa'i yi ge thub bstan rgyas pa'i nyin byed* [*Religious History*]. (*dbu med* manuscript, 159 ff., First section completed ca. 1550; completed by Sangs rgyas phun tshogs, 1692), 120b. For the full list see Appendix N of *The Entrance Gate for the Wise (Section III): Sa skya Paṇḍita on Indian and Tibetan Traditions of Pramana and Philosophical Debate*. Wiener Studien zur Tibetologie und Buddhismuskunde, vol. 17, 2 parts (Wien: Arbeitskreis für Tibetische und Buddhistische studien Universität Wien, 1987).

5. 'Phrin las rnam rgyal, Gong dkar, *Thob yig bum pa bzang po* [*Teachings Received*] (*dbu med* manuscript, 244 ff.), fascicle *da*, 4b. For the complete list of Sa pan's works from this source, see Appendix M of the study cited in the previous note.

6. Ngag dbang kun dga' bsod nams, A mes zhabs, *'Dzam gling byang phyogs kyi thub pa'i rgyal tshab chen po dpal ldan sa skya pa'i gdung rabs rin po che ji ltar byon pa'i tshul gyi rnam par thar pa ngo mtshar rin po che'i bang mdzod dgos 'dod kun 'byung* [*Lineage of the Noble Sakya*] (New Delhi: Tashi Dorjé, 1975). The letter occurs near the end of Sapan's biography, which extends from 93.6–170.6. See 156.4–162.1 (78b.4–81b.1).

7. Bsod nams lhun grub, Glo bo mkhan chen, *Mkhas pa rnams 'jug pa'i sgo'i rnam par bshad pa rig gnas gsal byed* [*Commentary on (Sakya Paṇḍita's) Explanation of the Introduction for Scholars*] (New Delhi: N. Topgye, 1979). The biography of Sapan is found on 94.4–154.5 (= 47b.4–77b.5).

8. Ngag dbang kun dga' bsod nams, *Lineage of the Noble Sakya*, 60a.4–61a.6 and 67b.1–6.

9. Kun dga' rgyal mtshan, Sa skya Paṇḍita, *Bu slob rnams la spring ba* [*A Message for Disciples*], Collected Works, Dergé Edition, vol. na, 214b–217a. See also the *Sa skya pa'i bka' 'bum* [*Collected Works of the Sakyapa*] (Tokyo: Tōyō Bunko, 1968), vol. 5, 401.3.2–402.4.3.

10. Tshul khrims rin chen, Zhu chen, *Dpal sa skya'i rje btsun gong ma lnga'i gsung rab rin po che'i par gyi sgo 'phar 'byed pa'i dkar chag 'phrul gyi lde mig* [*The Precious Teachings of the Five Sakya Forefathers*], In *Sa skya pa'i bka' 'bum* (Tokyo: Tōyō Bunko, 1969), vol. 7, 329.4.2 (ba 449b.2).

11. Tshul khrims rin chen, Zhu chen, *Dpal ldan bla ma dam pa rnams las dam pa'i chos thos pa'i yi ge don gnyer gdengs can rol pa'i chu gter* [*Record of Teachings Received*], vol. 2 (Dehra Dun: D. Gyaltsan, 1970), 429.1 (= 215a.1).

12. Tshul khrims rin chen, *Record of Teachings Received*, 429.1 (= 215a.1) and Tshul khrims rin chen, *The Precious Teachings of the Five Sakya Forefathers*, 329.4.2 (449b.2): "*gsan yig dbang gi rgyal por bod yul la bsngags pa zhes byung ba 'di min pa gzhan mi 'dug pas yig skyon yin nam snyam/ bod 'bangs spyi la gdams pa zhes dpe dngos la 'dug/.*"

13. Sakya Paṇḍita, *Bod yul la bsngags pa* [*Eulogy to Tibet*], In *Sa skya pa' bka' 'bum*, vol. 5 (Tokyo: Tōyō Bunko, 1968), 395.3.2–396.1.2 (= *na* 202a.2–203a.2). The colophon reads: "*bdag nyid chen po grags pa rgyal mtshan gyi zhabs kyi rdul la reg pas blo gros*

tsang ba'i khon jo sras kun dga' rgyal mtshan gyis lo bcu dgu lon pa'i tshe/ dpal sa skya'i dben gnas yon tan rin po che'i 'byung gnas su nye bar sbyar ba'o//."

14. See above, n. 9.

15. Blo bzang rta mgrin, *'Dzam gling byang phyogs chen po hor gyi rgyal khams kyi rtogs pa brjod pa'i bstan bcos chen po dpyod ldan mgu byed ngo mtshar gser gyi deb ther* [*Great Treatise on the History of Mongolia*] (New Delhi: Lokesh Chandra, 1964), 92a.5–6, as cited by Schuh, *Missives and Decrees of Mongolian Rulers for the Tibetan Clergy*, 192, YIG, and 185, GSER.

16. Ngor chen Kun dga' bzang po, *Thob yig rgya mtsho* [*Teachings Received*], in *Sa skya pa'i bka' 'bum*, vol. 9 (Tokyo: Tōyō Bunko, 1969), 62.1.1–62.3.4 (*ka* 124b.1–125b.4).

17. Ngag dbang blo bzang rgya mtsho, Dalai Lama V, *Zhab pa dang rgya che ba'i dam pa'i chos kyi thob yig gang ga'i chu rgyun* [*Record of Teachings Received*], vol. 2 (Delhi: Nechung and Lakhar, 1971), 126.2–134.1 (*kha* 63b.2–67b.1).

18. Bsod nams lhun grub, *Commentary on (Sakya Paṇḍita's) Explanation of the Introduction for Scholars*, 40.1–43.3 (=20b.1–22a.3).

19. Ngag dbang 'jigs med grags pa, Rin spungs pa, *'Jam pa'i dbyangs dngos smra ba'i mgon po sa skya paN di ta kun dga' rgyal mtshan dpal bzang po'i rnam par thar pa bskal pa bzang po'i legs lam, lam 'bras slob bshad* [*The Biography of Sakya Paṇḍita*] (Derge ed.), vol. 1 (*ka*), 109b–112b.

20. Ngag dbang kun dga' bsod nams, *Lineage of the Noble Sakya*, 60a.4–61a.6.

21. Bsod nams lhun grub, *Commentary on (Sakya Paṇḍita's) Explanation of the Introduction for Scholars*, 30a.3–32a.4; 32a.4–33b.4; 33b.4–34a.4; and 39a.3–42a.6. These are the minor works listed in the index to the *Collected Works of the Sakyapa*, vol. 5, nos. 97, 99, and 32.

22. Kun dga' rgyal mtshan, Sa skya Paṇḍita, *A Message for Disciples*, 401.3.5 (*na* 114b.5): "*de ngas mi shes pa e yin*," and "*khyed kyis lha chos* [line 6] *kyis bskyangs na shakya mu ne'i bstan pa yang phyi'i rgya mtsho'i mtha' tshun chad khyab par mi 'gro ba e yin gsungs so//.*" And on 401.4.2 (115a.2): "*nga bzang por e gtong gnam shes gsungs/.*" All three of the above sentences are from supposed direct quotes of Köden's words. Cf. Köden's letter of invitation, Schuh, *Missives and Decrees of Mongolian Rulers for the Tibetan Clergy*, 32f., line 13: "*khyod kyi chos go ba'i dam bca' dang e 'gal/*" and lines 16–17: "*(sems can) mang po la gnod pa byas na (khyod) mi skrag pa e yin/.*"

23. Schuh, *Missives and Decrees of Mongolian Rulers for the Tibetan Clergy*, 41.

24. Bsod nams grags pa, Pan chen, *Rgyal rabs 'phrul gyi lde mig gam deb ther dmar po'am deb gsar ma* [*New Red Annals: Key to Royal Genealogy*]. Text and partial translation published in G. Tucci, *Deb t'er dmar po gsar ma*, Serie Orientale Roma, vol. 24 (Rome: Instituto italiano per il Medio ed Estremo Oriente, 1971). The origin of this passage of the *Deb ther dmar po gsar ma* was noticed by Schuh, *Missives and Decrees of Mongolian Rulers for the Tibetan Clergy*, 40.

25. *Acknowledgement*: I would like to thank Mr. Y. Fukuda for help in obtaining some of the sources used in this article, and Prof. D. Seyfort Ruegg for several useful comments.

PART V

Centers of Power and Religious Learning
(Fourteenth to Eighteenth Centuries)

Chapter 15

THE RISE OF THE PAKMODRU DYNASTY

Luciano Petech

This selection from Petech's groundbreaking book on the Yuan-Sakya period covers the early consolidation of Pakmodru rule over Central Tibet in the waning years of the Yuan dynasty. Petech describes the rise of the lay leader of the Pakmodru sect, Jangchup Gyeltsen, the single most important political figure of the mid-fourteenth century. Jangchup Gyeltsen began his period as the *de facto* ruler of Tibet still dependent on the formal authority of the Ü-Tsang *xuanwei si* (Pacification Office), a position established by the Yuan dynasty and staffed by the Sakya family. At first, Jangchup Gyeltsen needed to support the weakened authority of the Sakya Pacification Office and the great official (*pönchen*) while effectively ruling in their place. Meanwhile, the Sakya family, which had split into various competing lineages with estates (*labrang*), were struggling among themselves for the right to rule. Jangchup Gyeltsen took advantage of these disputes to bolster his own power. In return for his support, he secured from Sakya's great official a formal submission to the Pakmodru, a written pledge of loyalty, the surrender of some estates, and the seal of office. Near the end of the 1350s came the real end to the Mongol Yuan dynasty's ability to interfere in Tibetan affairs: Jangchup Gyelsten ignored imperial orders, asserted his right to rule Central Tibet, and despite his aggressive stance, was given a seal of authority and the title *taisitu*. Thus the end of Mongol influence on Tibet can be dated to 1358, a decade before the Yuan dynasty was driven from China. The Pakmodrupa regime was the expression of a conscious return to the purely Tibetan tradition and as such took a Tibetan name for the new ruler of Central Tibet (*lhatsün*).

The events of 1349–1354 had laid the foundations for Pakmodrupa rule over both Ü and Tsang. From the point of view of Realpolitik, however, it was neither secure nor final. Looking at it under the constitutional angle, it had no legal existence, as the imperial authority remained unquestioned, the Ü-Tsang *xuanwei si* [Pacification Office] was still functioning, at least on paper, and above all the new strong man continued to pay lip service to the authority of the Sakya lamas.[1] The new structure was still inchoate and only its main outlines were taking shape. Jangchup Gyeltsen's basic conception was the undermining of the power of the various *tripön* [myriarchs] and the establishment of a net of local stewardships (*gzhis kha*) based on forts (*rdzong*; but this term is never used in *Situ's Testament*), held by his old trusted servants.[2] In the long run these stewardships became hereditary, thus giving origin to a new aristocracy existing alongside with those *trikor* that made their submission in time. The new Pakmodrupa policy, however, cannot be dealt with here, as it lies beyond the scope of the present work.

Our main (and almost exclusive) source continues to be *Situ's Testament* by Jangchup Gyeltsen, which grows more and more detailed and discursive as it draws nearer to the time of writing (ca. 1361). It also assumes some special features, such as an increasing preoccupation with matters of etiquette and of precedence during the official conferences. It is also pointedly silent about the relations with the imperial court of abbots and scholars not belonging to the Sakya school. To give an example, the name of the Karmapa Rölpé Dorjé (1340–1383), who in 1358/9 traveled to the Court on the invitation of the emperor, never appears in the text.

In 1356[3] a serious incident took place, viz. the sudden imprisonment of the *pönchen* [great officer, the temporal administrator (of Sakya)] Gyelwa Zangpo by Chökyi Gyeltsen (1332–1359) and his half-brother, the nominal chief abbot Lodrö Gyeltsen (1332–1364), the sons of the *di shi* [imperial preceptor] Künga Gyeltsen. Our text informs us of the fact in a single sentence.[4]

This coup was actually the work of an influential combination between the Lhakhang Labrang [of Sakya monastery], to which the two brothers belonged (and therefore often called the Lhakhangpa) and the lords of Latö Jang. The head of the latter family was Namkha Tenpé Gyeltsen or Namkha Tenpa, usually called Jangpa or (by anticipation) Jangpa *pönchen*. He was the youngest son of Dorjé Gönpo and thus a grandson of the *pönchen* Yöntsün. Already as a young man he received the rank of Situ with the tiger-head button of the third rank and was appointed judge (*janghochi*) of Ü-Tsang. Later he received the title of *guogong* and the gold seal with the rock-crystal button. He appears for the first time in 1352, probably upon his appointment as judge, and at once showed himself hostile to Pakmodru and closely associated with prince Aratnaśiri.[5] The connecting link between the two families was represented by Lama Künchangpa, a cousin of Dorjé Gönpo and a maternal uncle of Lama Lodrö Gyeltsen.

The sources afford not the slightest clue to the reasons and aims of Gyelwa Zangpo's imprisonment. We can only suppose that, since the *pönchen* had completely veered over to the side of Jangchup Gyeltsen and had become his supporter, his capture was an attempt to stem Pakmodrupa rise by laying hold of his main prop within the Sakya administration.

Jangchup Gyeltsen handled the new situation cautiously. Of course he was obliged to procure the liberation of the *pönchen*, if only in order to uphold his own prestige. His first concern was to get hold of the official seal of the *pönchen*, which was in the keeping of the latter's son Drakpa Gyeltsen, at that time residing at Dzongkha. He was summoned to Rinpung, where he arrived safely. Then Jangchup Gyeltsen started leisurely to collect his troops. His slow and prudent action, clearly aimed at avoiding an armed clash, was, however, disturbed by the rash activities of the nephews of the prisoner, who at the head of their *buta* started raiding the border tracts of the Sakya domain. The Lhakhangpa and Jangpa tried to buy them off by offering the cession of some estates, but to no avail. Later Jangchup Gyeltsen himself intervened, placing these mischief makers under a bland arrest.[6]

The imperial officers found themselves in an awkward situation. Zhünnu Gyeltsen, the most prominent member of the *xuanwei si*,[7] who apparently did not know how he and his office should cope with this emergency, proceeded to Rinpung together with the commanders of the military mail stations of the North. Being thus assured at least of the benevolent neutrality of the imperial officials, Jangchup Gyeltsen convened a conference of the foremost political leaders, including Lama Künchangpa, the Lhakhangpa brothers, and Jangpa. The crafty Künchangpa offered to appoint as *pönchen* Pakpa Pelzang, the chief of Gyantsé, subject of course to the approval of the emperor; but the offer was summarily rejected.[8]

The conference assembled at Zhudrok, with the participation of the officials of the *xuanwei si*[9] and of the respected Lama Sönam Lodrö Gyeltsen (1332–1362) of the Düchö branch [of the Sakya]. There was much wrangling about petty ceremonial questions, such as who should bow and take off his bonnet to whom. When business began in earnest, the assembled leaders of Ü left no doubt about their unanimous request of an unconditional liberation of the *pönchen*. Künchangpa, having failed in all his attempts to obtain at least a delay, returned to Sakya to report, and the conference adjourned.[10]

Then another round of negotiations was started by Lama Sharpa (no personal name is given), who banked on the record of his family, of which two members had been Imperial Preceptors; he was seconded by Lama Nyammepa, the old teacher of the Pakmodrupa leader. The lengthy discourses supposed to have been delivered on this occasion are interesting in so far as they show how the history of the Sakya-Yuan period was viewed by its actors and their epigones.

But once more the discussions led to no results. Jangchup Gyeltsen took the stand that the Lhakhangpa brothers were rebels in the eyes of Mongol law and as such were to be punished under the terms of the imperial *jasa* brought to Sakya by Qipčaqtai and by Darma Gyeltsen.[11]

Sharpa brought this uncompromising answer to Sakya, where it was discussed in the council, both Lhakhangpa brothers being present, but in the absence of Jangpa, who was becoming suspicious of the intentions of his relatives and feared they would use him as scapegoat. The council decided to send out once more Lama Künchangpa to arrange a compromise. The Lama negotiated skillfully and for a long time with the Pakmodrupa. To lessen the tension, he even proposed that Gyelwa Zangpo's son Drakpa Gyeltsen should take the place of his father as a hostage at Sakya. The suggestion was flatly refused, but the idea was picked up by the Pakmodru officials in the opposite sense; and Jangchup Gyeltsen had to use his authority to save Künchangpa from being arrested and held as pawn. In the end Künchangpa was sent back to Sakya as the bearer of a formal letter (*chahu*, Chin. *zhafu*), countersigned by him, which amounted to an ultimatum requesting the immediate release of the *pönchen*, the request being backed by a forward move of the troops under the command of *chenpo* Rinchen Zangpo.[12]

The game was up, as Sakya clearly had not the means to oppose armed resistance; so the Lhakhang Labrang had to bow to the inevitable. Gyelwa Zangpo was brought to the Pakmodru camp by Lama Künchangpa. He was received there with great solemnity and with ostentatious rejoicings, of course intended to emphasize the triumph of Pakmodru. The matter had ended with the humiliation of the Sakyapa, whose last attempt at opposition had failed completely. Jangchup Gyeltsen had obtained this success without shedding blood, thanks to his consummate diplomacy backed by an adequate display of military force. The whole proceedings were capped by a memorial sent to the emperor to inform him of the events.[13] It seems, however, that the Lhakhang brothers obtained immunity for their deed, although this is not mentioned expressly in *Situ's Testament*, but only alluded to obliquely in another context. Lodrö Gyeltsen may have kept his empty title of chief abbot, although he was not considered as such by the Pakmodrupa. Chökyi Gyeltsen, who perhaps had committed himself deeper than his half-brother, left in the same year 1356 for Beijing, where he was appointed teacher of the heir-apparent prince Ayuśiridara with the title of *Da Yuan guoshi*; he died in China in 1359.[14]

As to Gyelwa Zangpo, by now a broken reed, he tendered a solemn act of submission to Pakmodru, including a written pledge of loyalty and the surrender of some of his estates. Even his seal of office was handed over to the custody of Jangchup Gyeltsen. Still he kept (at least so it appears) the empty title of *pönchen*, shorn of any vestige of power.[15] He retired to Tongmön in Shang, where he received initiation from Karmapa Rölpé Dorjé.[16] His nephew Könchok Rinchen was considered by some as the acting *pönchen*; but since the imperial decree granting him the tiger-head seal as *fushi du yuanshuai* [vice commander-in-chief] had never been officially promulgated in Tibet, his character of *pönchen* was disavowed;[17] and indeed, he is not included in the official list of the *pönchen*.

Pakmodru military control was secured by the permanent occupation of Chumik, although it was formally an estate belonging to the Zhitok Labrang [of Sakya]; it was heavily garrisoned and placed in the charge of Dorjé Gyeltsen as steward (*gnyer*).[18]

During the New Year's festival of 1357 an imperial envoy called Yilao (possibly a title and not a name) arrived in Tibet. He was the bearer of an imperial decree granting to Jangchup Gyeltsen the rank and seal of Taisitu (*da situ*). Although this title was not quite rare, in this case it implied the recognition by the emperor of his outstanding position in Central Tibet, and the Tibetans seem to have considered this act as the legalization of the new regime. Along with Yilao but independently from him, another envoy called Lugyel *ta shri gön* (Chin. *dashi guan*) brought an edict inviting Lama Sönam Lodrö Gyeltsen to court.[19] These imperial messengers, however high-ranking, were no longer empowered to supervise and interfere with Tibetan administration like Qipčaqtai and Darma Gyeltsen one generation earlier; they were limited to the ceremonial task of inviting to court high lamas. The Yuan government, fully occupied with the mounting revolt in Central China, tacitly gave up trying to reassert its direct authority in Tibet.

A partial exception was represented by an edict addressed to Jangchup Gyeltsen. The Drigungpa had appealed to the emperor and had obtained from him an order to the Pakmodrupa enjoining the restitution of Ön and Ölkha. They followed up this theoretical success by claiming also possession of Gyama, where the local *tripön* had resigned his office. Jangchup Gyeltsen ignored the imperial command and refused every one of these requests. The consequence was serious fighting, chiefly around Gyama. There was also some untoward meddling by the Pakmodru abbot. In the end Jangchup Gyeltsen got his own way and no territorial change took place.[20]

In another field he complied more or less gracefully with the imperial decree which had charged him with providing the means and making the arrangements for the journey of Sönam Lodrö Gyeltsen to Dadu [Beijing]. This gave rise to frictions and small bickerings with the future *dishi*, who had a personal dislike for the Pakmodrupa; consequently, the actual departure was long delayed.

Things at Sakya had remained unsettled; the party struggle there continued and reached its climax with the murder of Lama Künchangpa. The circumstances are obscure and the reasons for the deed are not apparent; we are only told that Jangchup Gyeltsen asked the Jangpa *pönchen* not to interfere and requested a written engagement in this sense, perhaps in order to prevent a private vengeance.[21] When the Pakmodrupa ruler betook himself to Chumik in order to investigate, this affair receded in the background as an even more serious piece of news reached him there: the *pönchen* Gyelwa Zangpo, who in the meantime had delegated his judicial work to Wangtsön, had suddenly died at Lhatsé, where he had been invited by the Lhasa authorities for a conference. The cause of his death was rumored to be either assassination by Wangtsön and his son, or excessive drinking of strong liquor;[22] the first alternative seems to have been generally believed. The event took place at the end of 1357 or in January 1358.

After performing the funeral rites for the deceased, Jangchup Gyeltsen summoned to Chumik the councilors of Sakya, presided over by Lama Dampa Sönam Gyeltsen. The first days after their arrival were occupied by the New Year's festival of 1358, held in the presence of the imperial envoy; on that occasion the latter presented solemnly to the Pakmodrupa the seal of Taisitu. Then the conference adjourned to Sakya itself, where several pending questions were dealt with.[23]

The seal of the *pönchen* had remained in the hands of his son Drakpa Gyeltsen, whom *Situ's Testament* up to this point calls by the title *lopön*. He had been adopted as son by Jangchup Gyeltsen after his reconciliation with Gyelwa Zangpo. At an unknown moment the latter procured for him the office of *nangso*, soon enhanced to *nangchenpa*, by which title he was later known. He inherited the Shang estate.[24] Now he handed over the seal of his father to the conference, which was sitting at the administrative headquarters in the Lhakhang Chenmo. Even the great official seal (*dam kha*) of the Sakya see was abandoned by Lama Dampa to the keeping of Jangchup Gyeltsen, as a sign that the temporalities of Sakya were henceforward to be supervised by him. To give a practical backing to this formal act, the Lhakhang Chenmo itself was opened to Jangchup Gyeltsen, who garrisoned it with about 200 men, of which 130 were retainers (*bza' pa*) of Pakmodru. Khetsün's son Künga Rinchen (1331–1399), who resided at Chumik under Pakmodrupa protection, received from the emperor the title of *guanding guoshi* with the great crystal seal and took up the office of abbot of Zhitok; he was guaranteed the necessary means for the upkeep of his dignity.[25]

Jangchup Gyeltsen, who was in indifferent health, returned to Yarlung. There he settled finally the old question of the Three Valleys (Ön, Ölkha, Dora), which had become acute after the imperial decree on this subject. Eventually the valleys were left in his possession in exchange for an almost complete autonomy for Drigung.[26]

In the meantime the opposition elements within Sakya had gathered at Lhatsé under the leadership of the local chief. Pending the arrival of reinforcements for the Jangpa, they attacked the new monastery of Namring and marched through Latö as far as Zangzang. Jangchup Gyeltsen sent a strong force under *chenpo* Rinchen Zangpo. Before their arrival, the Lhatsé levies under the command of Wangtsön had reached Sakya and laid siege to the Lhakhang Chenmo.

But the Pakmodru troops were timely re-directed toward Sakya and apparently took the besiegers in the back. Their victory was complete and final. It was followed by stern reprisals: Wangtsön was taken and thrown into jail, many of his men fell fighting and the prisoners (464 men in all) were blinded.[27] This ruthless act, the only one of this kind in Jangchup Gyeltsen's long career,[28] stamped out the last embers of opposition in Tsang.

Lhatsé was taken and entrusted in judicial custody to the Lama Dampa and to Butön; this was one of the very few instances in which that great scholar played a half-political role.

At the end of 1358 the *yuanshi* [imperial envoy] Dharmakirti,[29] whom the emperor had sent to bring the formal rescript of invitation to Lama Sönam Lodrö Gyeltsen and to escort him to the capital, had reached Dam. After the New Year's festival of 1359 the usual ceremonies for the state reception of the envoy and of the edict were staged.[30] In the meantime the Imperial Preceptor Künga Gyeltsen had died at the end of 1358.[31] As a consequence, the invitation to Sönam Lodrö Gyeltsen was changed into a nomination as *dishi*, the decree being brought to Tibet by Dharmakirti and by the *yuanshi* Ebu. On the same occasion the *di shi*'s brother Drakpa Gyeltsen received the title of Bailan *wang* and an imperial decree confirmed his possession of Taktsang Dzongkha.[32] Perhaps because of his new status, the traveling preparations for Sönam Lodrö Gyeltsen took a very long time. The caravan gathering in the train of the lama consisted of about 800 men. As they were slowly approaching Pakmodru, Jangchup Gyeltsen stopped them en route, remarking dryly that "if they are soldiers, they are too few; and if they are envoys, they are too many." Things turned well eventually, and the lama visited Samyé and Densatel, Jangchup Gyeltsen offering a lavish hospitality. Then further unpleasantness arose, and the lama returned in high dudgeon to Sakya, where he had trouble with the Jangpa *pönchen*, who permitted the Jé estate to be raided by his men.[33]

Gradually the last questions left open by the tragic events of the preceding years were settled. Wangtsön was spared his life and was placed under custody in Ön. Lama Lodrö Gyeltsen and *pönchen* Jangpa, who had quarreled during the last stages of Gyelwa Zangpo's imprisonment, were compelled to make peace, under a sealed document drawn up in the presence of witnesses. A new commander was appointed to the Lhakhang Chenmo. In 1360 Jangchup Gyeltsen hardened his grip on Sakya by granting, with the concurrence of the Lamas, the title and office of *nyené chenpo* (chief attendant) of the Zhitok to a man he could trust: *chenpo* Pakpa Pelzang of Gyantsé.[34] Then the new Imperial Preceptor and his companions finally departed, being accompanied by Sanghaśrī *du yuanshuai*, whom the emperor had sent to escort them to Dadu.[35]

The most important event of 1360 (at least in Pakmodrupa eyes) was the death of the Pakmodru hierarch Tsezhipa Drakpa Gyeltsen. Jangchup Gyeltsen appointed as his successor his own half-brother Chunyi Sarma Drakpa Sherap

(1310–1370). He caused a great *kumbum* [stūpa] to be erected at Densatel in honor of the deceased, a complicated affair because of the difficulties in the geomantical determination of the site.[36]

The funeral rites had been long and expensive; they also afforded a pretext to the imperial preceptor, who seemed most unwilling to go to the disturbed imperial capital, for turning back on his way, in order to be present at them. Eventually he had to be invited kindly but firmly to proceed at last on his voyage.[37] He arrived at the capital early in 1362, only to die there in the tenth month of the same year; he was the last imperial preceptor at the Mongol court.[38]

On this occasion Jangchup Gyeltsen clarified his position in front of the permanent imperial representatives in Tibet. The officials of the *xuanwei si* were informed that "you continue to say that, since *lopön* Situwa (i.e., Jangchup Gyeltsen) has the greater power, there is no scope for your activity. If things are so, you should give back to the *yuanshi* (the imperial envoy) your tiger-head [button] and your seal; I myself by virtue of my black hand-sign (*thel rtse nag pos*) having arranged for the postal personnel as far as Sok, shall take care that there should be no hindrance whatever. If things are not so, as to the official duties that are in your resort concerning the service to the *yuanshi*, you must perform them with no harm ensuing to ecclesiastical and lay subjects. This was intimated exactly and widely to all."[39] This somewhat contemptuous emphasis on the irrelevance of the normal routine duties of the Yuan officialdom in Tibet, as compared with the effective power of Pakmodru, shows that by 1360 actual authority of the Mongol government in Central Tibet had waned. Henceforward the outward trappings of the *xuanwei si* were maintained, but that body became an empty shell without real contents, although the titles of its members were used by Tibetan noblemen for many years to come.

The Pakmodrupa regime was the expression of a conscious return to the purely Tibetan tradition. An outward sign of this policy was the forcible expulsion of all the "quasi-Mongols" (*hor 'dra'*, i.e., Tibetans who had accepted Mongol dress, customs and language) residing in Sakya and elsewhere.[40] We cannot, however, expatiate here on Jangchup Gyeltsen's reforms.

Just before the departure of the imperial preceptor another prominent person appeared at Densatel and Neudong. As usual, our text gives no name, but employs only the double title of *lopön chenpo* and of *wang*. He was received with adequate honors, both because he was the bearer of an imperial *jasa* and because he was a "scion of the illustrious Sakya family."[41] This helps us in identifying him with Drakpa Gyeltsen (1336–1376),[42] the second son of the Bailan prince Künga Lekpé Jhungné Gyeltsen and younger brother of the new imperial preceptor; we know from other sources that he wore those very titles of *lopön chenpo* and *wang*, because of his origin and because he was famous as a great master of yoga. Since 1354 he had lived with his brother in the new castle of Taktsang Dzongkha, which the emperor in 1360 granted to him in sole ownership. The same imperial edict of 1360 appointed him as the fourth (and last) prince of Bailan and gave him the customary title of *dongzhi* of the right and left, the golden seal, the *tuoshu* of delegation and the mandate that placed him in authority "in the regions where the sun sets." Drakpa Gyeltsen was most emphatically resolved never to go abroad, because conditions in China had become too disturbed, alluding probably to the conflict between the Mongol factions which in 1359 had led to the sack and wholesale destruction of the summer capital Shangdu. As to his role after 1360, we are told very vaguely that he displayed great activity in the field of both ecclesiastical and civil law (*khrims gnyis*). But his political influence was practically nil, in spite of his high connections (he had married the sister of the Jangpa *pönchen* Namkha Tenpa). He lived at Sakya and at Taktsang Dzongkha, in which latter place he died.[43]

We may also add that his third son Namsé Gyeltsen (1360–1408), although he never left Tibet, became at once a special protegé of the last Yuan emperor. When the boy was preparing to take his first monastic vows, Toghan Temür declared him to be equal to his eldest son (*bu'o che* or *sras che ba*) and granted him titles and ranks much higher than those usually pertaining to the Bailan princedom, including the establishment (*wangfu*) reserved to the princes of the blood. But he never met his adoptive father and died at Mönkhang Tsedong Dzong forty years after the end of the Yuan dynasty.[44] Indeed the Bailan princes never played that role of props of the Mongol domination which may have been expected of them.

The office of *pönchen* had become vacant either after the liberation or upon the death of Gyelwa Zangpo. His succession presents a knotty problem, as *Situ's Testament* pointedly avoids giving us clear information. In most of our other texts the third term of office of Gyelwa Zangpo is ignored, and after Wangtsön the list includes the following names: Namkha Tenpé Gyeltsen, Drakpa Gyeltsen, Pelbum, Lochen.[45] The sequence in *Chinese and Tibetan Documents* is different: after Sönampel we find Gyelwa Zangpo for a second time as substitute (*tshab*) for Namkha Tenpé, then Drakpa Gyeltsen, Lochen, Pelbum.[46] It seems at present impossible to unravel the tangle and I shall merely present the scanty bits of information available on these persons, Lochen excepted.

The career of Namkha Tenpé Gyeltsen down to 1356 has been sketched out above. He is said to have been appointed *pönchen* of Ü-Tsang at the age of thirty, and then in the wood-bird year 1345 he received the rank of *Da Yuan guoshi* [dynastic preceptor of the great Yuan] and the crystal seal.[47] It is possible that wood-bird may be a mistake for fire-bird 1357, but the fact remains that Butön, who in 1351 imparted him religious tuition and gave him the religious name Rinchen Pelzangpo, calls him a *pönchen*.[48] He was a disciple of Dolpopa Sherap Gyeltsen (1292–1361), on whose advice he completed and endowed the monastery of Jang Namring, and invited the famous scholar Bodong Choklé Namgyel (1306–1386) to become its abbot.[49] Jangchup Gyeltsen had a poor opinion of him, and some verses of his *sungchem* attribute to him the responsibility for the downfall of Sakya power.[50] In 1364, still bearing the title of *pönchen*, he took part in the funeral ceremonies for Butön,[51] and in 1373 he tendered allegiance to the new Ming dynasty, as we shall see later.

Gyelwa Zangpo's son Drakpa Gyeltsen is a pale figure, mentioned only in connection with the checkered career of his father. He was at first a secretary (*nang so*), then he was promoted chief secretary (*nang chen*). His action during his father's imprisonment was not particularly effective. After the end of that affair, Jangchup Gyeltsen adopted him as his son, a purely formal gesture. In 1358 he inherited the estate of Shang Tongmön, where he died at an unknown date.[52] Drakpa Gyeltsen is always styled *lopön*, implying that he was a monk, at least in his early years. In *Situ's Testament* we find no trace of his appointment as *pönchen*. Only Takshangpa's *Chinese and Tibetan Documents* informs us that the *lopön* Drakpa Gyeltsen received the courtesy title (*ming*) of *pönchen*.

Pelbum (his family name is unknown) was an official in the imperial government. In 1346/7 he was posted in Tibet as a *zhaotao*. Then he went to Beijing, from where he returned to Tibet in 1354 as a *darughači*. In 1357 he was a *nyené chenpo*.[53] In 1359 he asked Karmapa Rölpé Dorjé to bring to Tibet the bones of the imperial preceptor who had died the year before. On this occasion he is termed Sakya *pönchen*.[54] This was apparently an appointment on a caretaker basis, and in 1360 the matter came up for a final decision. The new *dishi* and the imperial *yuanshi* on the eve of their final departure had a meeting near Lhasa with Jangchup Gyeltsen and other officials. They intimated that, upon their own responsibility, they intended to confirm Pelbum as *pönchen* by handing out to him the official seal. They deemed the proposal quite safe, since Pelbum had delivered his son as hostage and taken a pledge to act according to the Pakmodrupa's instructions. Jangchup Gyeltsen's reply is interesting from various points of view:

"Since you lama and your nephew, the councilors of Sakya and the whole *xuanwei si* have signed a letter of agreement (*kha 'cham gyi bca' rtse*), you cannot act against its terms. Pelbum cannot be a *pönchen* because he is not issued from the class (*gyü*) of the disciples (*nye-né*) of Sakya; originally he was the tea-brewer (*soljawa*) of Wangtsön; he is a partisan of the Drigungpa and is the man of the *gompa*; in his innermost heart he belongs to them. In the same manner as a minister of the Tö Hor (Chaghatai) cannot become a minister (*chyingsang*, Chin. *zhengxiang*) of the King of the East (the Yuan), so a disciple (*nye-né*) of the Sakyapa cannot be subservient to the Drigungpa. Pelbum shall not become a *pönchen*. This being the state of fact, choose between me and Pelbum." And they answered: "We choose you." Thus it was decided not to effect the transfer of the seal (*dam rtags*) of *pönchen*, and all those present, starting with the *yuanshi*, were witness to this.[55]

This scene shows how complete had become the control of the Pakmodrupa over the machinery and officialdom of the old order; Jangchup Gyeltsen could dispose at will of the highest office of Central Tibet. The political role of Sakya had indeed played out.

Pelbum having been excluded, who was to become *pönchen*? Our main source gives no further information and turns to other matters. As it is highly unlikely that Drakpa Gyeltsen was ever a *pönchen*, I suggest that perhaps the office remained vacant for some months (or years) and then was given to Namkha Tenpé Gyeltsen, who certainly held it in 1364. By that time it had lost all remnants of authority and prestige and soon became obsolete, although the official list gives some additional names. Jangchup Gyeltsen's scornful verses quoted above are a sad but truthful epitaph to the decay and end of the top-level office in the Sakya government.

Jangchup Gyeltsen had been ill for some time. He had recovered, but age and a strenuous life were apparently starting to tell upon his robust frame. Thus it cannot be wondered if he thought his life-work to be done and began thinking of means to ensure its perpetuation through a smooth passage to worthy successors. We are not told how this decision matured in him; we know only how it was carried out, and this most important act is the last to be registered in his autobiography.

At some time in 1361 he sent Sherap Trashi as his special envoy to the imperial court. His first (but not his main) task was to counter the hostile influence and pernicious slanders of Dharmakirti and of the attendants of the *dishi*, who accused Jangchup Gyeltsen of being a rebel and an enemy of the Sakypa and to have ravaged the Lhakhang Chenmo, turning it into a horse stable. Sherap Trashi proved to be an able negotiator. He interviewed the prime minister and then was received in audience by the emperor, dispelled his suspicions and obtained a favorable decree; the sovereign issued a *jasa* appointing Shakya Rinchen, the second of Jangchup Gyeltsen's three nephews, as the new *tripön* of Pakmodru and confirming all the estates, old and new, belonging to the myriarchy. As a personal reward, Sherap Trashi was granted the estate of Drakkar. Upon his return home, the *jasa* was formally proclaimed at Tel, and Jangchup Gyeltsen prepared to retire from the office of *tripön* after a tenure of almost forty years (1322–1361/2).[56] Almost immediately, however, he reversed his decision. He had found out that Shakya Rinchen had an uncontrollable temper and that his succession would cause opposition and confusion; apparently he had misjudged his nephew's fitness for such a heavy responsibility. Passing over the imperial decree, he decided to keep the office of *tripön* for himself, as long as his health permitted it.[57] Jangchup Gyeltsen retained power in his hands until his death on the 27th day of the tenth month of the wood-dragon year, corresponding to 20th November, 1364.[58] He was succeeded as *tripön* and as ruler of Central Tibet (*lhatsün*) by his eldest nephew Shakya Gyeltsen (1341–1373), hitherto abbot of Tsetang.

The autobiography of Jangchup Gyeltsen closes with a kind of comparative list of the most prominent persons, families, and monasteries, together with short hints to his successor on how to deal with them. It is worthwhile to quote the words by which this cool and shrewd politician judged the shortcomings and the causes of the decay of the Sakyapa and of the Drigungpa, the two main factors of Tibetan history in the Yuan period. "Formerly the prestige of the Drigungpa had expanded in the times of *gompa* Shākya Rinchen; but later the decay of their influence was a consequence of their manifold signs of greed and lawlessness. With the Sakyapa too, the disciples (*nye-né*) were more powerful than the lamas, the state servants (*pönkya*) were more powerful than the high officials (*pön*) and the women were the most powerful of all. Since the prestige of the Sakyapa is now in such a ruinous state, you should take heed of its causes; and if you wish this community of ours to remain intact and happy, all of you must avoid evil actions."[59]

In 1354 the risings in Central China had started, and fourteen years later the dynasty collapsed and the last emperor fled to Mongolia. It is difficult to guess how these events were viewed in Tibet. Although the lamas must have realized that the golden days of lavish Mongol patronage had passed forever, we find nowhere a word of regret. The Tibetan texts merely state the bald fact that the last Yuan emperor had fled and that the new Ming dynasty had seized the throne. At the utmost, there was some fear (soon dispelled) that the war in China could lead to an invasion of Tibet by Ming armies.[60]

Still, we have adequate information on the switching of Sakyapa and Pakmodrupa allegiance (if this term is at all justified) to the new rulers of China. When the Yuan rule vanished, there was in Tibet an "acting *dishi*" called Namkha Pelzangpo. On 16th January, 1373, his envoys arrived at Nanjing bearing tribute, whereupon he was granted the title of Zhisheng Fobao Guoshi. He died at some time before 1381.[61] We do not know who had appointed him nor to which clan or sect he belonged; he was certainly not a member of the Khön family, because the genealogical tree of Sakya contains no member bearing the name Namkha during those years.[62]

The Sakya secular administration recognized the new regime in China when on 23rd February, 1373, Namkha Tenpé Gyeltsen, a former *guogong* of the Yuan, came personally to the court at Nanjing to beg for a fresh title.[63] Thus we meet for a last time with the Jangpa *pönchen*. Whether he had remained in office during all those years, or was out of office but still a prominent person in the government, is a question which must remain open; the Tibetan sources know nothing of his relations with the Ming.

The Khön family followed suit. On 27 October, 1373, the Lama Dampa Sönam Gyeltsen and his nephew Künga Gyeltsen (1344–1420) sent envoys to apply for a new jade seal; but they met with a refusal, because such a seal had already been conferred upon Namkha Pelzangpo. It appears that Künga Gyeltsen had tried to go personally to Nanjing, but stopped in Kham on account of local disturbances.[64] On 23rd August, 1374, envoys from him were received once more at court; this time he was granted the jade seal together with the title of *yuanshi*.[65]

The Pakmodrupa, i.e., Jangchup Gyeltsen's successor Shākya Gyeltsen, had been confirmed by the Yuan emperor (1365) in the titles of Taisitu, *chang guogong* and *guanding guoshi* with power over the three *chölkha*.[66] In 1372 his political importance was recognized and brought to the notice of the emperor by a Ming general engaged in the pacification of Amdo. The sovereign took the initiative of sending him an envoy, confirming his title of *guanding guoshi* and granting him the jade seal.[67] The Pakmodru ruler reciprocated by sending to court his own father Sönam Zangpo carrying suitable presents of religious objects.[68]

Some nobles, who used to receive their titles from the Mongols, carried out the switch-over during the four or five years following the downfall of the Yuan.[69]

Henceforward the international relations of the rulers of Central Tibet were almost exclusively with the Ming, till in the late sixteenth century the Mongols reappeared on the scene in different circumstances but with similar final results.

NOTES

1. It appears that Byang chub rgyal mtshan considered the *chos rje* Bla ma dam pa Bsod nams rgyal mtshan of the Rin chen sgang *bla brang* as the foremost Bla ma of Sa skya.

2. For a list of the *rdzong* established by Byang chub rgyal mtshan see Giuseppe Tucci, trans., *Deb t'er dmar po gsar ma: Tibetan Chronicles by Bsod nams grags pa* (Rome: Instituto Italiano per il Medio ed Estremo Oriente, 1971), 210.

3. The date is given in Stag tshang pa Srībhūtibhadra, *Rgya Bod yig tshang mkhas pa'i dga 'byed chen mo* [Chinese and Tibetan Documents] (Thimphu: Kunsang Top-gyel and Mani Dorji, 1979), 2:172b, as 5th day of the 2nd month of the water-monkey year, a palpable mistake for fire-monkey. It seems to correspond to 7th March, 1356.

4. Byang chub rgyal mtshan, Ta'i Si tu, *Si tu bka' chems* [Situ's Testament], in *Lha rig rlangs kyi rnam thar* (New Delhi: T. Tsepal Taikhang, 1974), 533. Cf. Rgyal mtshan dpal bzang, 'Ba ra ba, *Rje btsun 'Bar ra ba Rgyal mtshan dpal bzang po'i rnam thar mgur 'bum dang bcas pa* [Biography of Gyeltsen Pelzangpo], in *A Tibetan Encyclopedia of Buddhist Scholasticism: The Collected Writings of 'Ba' ra ba Rgyal mtshan dpal bzang*, vol. 14 (Dehradun: Ngawang Gyaltsen and Ngawang Lungtok, 1970), 104b.

5. Dpal bzang chos kyi bzang po, *G.yas ru byang pa rgyal rabs* [Royal Genealogy of Yeru Jangpa], in *Rare Tibetan Historical and Literary Texts from the Library of Tsepon W. D. Shakabpa*, compiled by T. Tsepal Taikhang (New Delhi: Taikhang. 1974), 6a; Byang chub rgyal mtshan, *Situ's Testament*, 496–497.

6. Byang chub rgyal mtshan, *Situ's Testament*, 533–536.

7. As no Mongol *du yuanshuai* [commander-in-chief] was resident in Tibet at that time, Gzhon nu rgyal mtshan, in his character as *san du yuanshuai* and as bearer of

the tiger-head button of the third rank and keeper of the six-cornered seal of the *xuan-wei si*, was for practical purpose the highest official in the permanent imperial organization in Tibet; Byang chub rgyal mtshan, *Situ's Testament*, 553. No holder of the regular *xuanwei shi* [pacification commissioner] title appears in Byang chub rgyal mtshan, *Situ's Testament*, which mentions only the *dben we si pa* or the *mi dpon* of the *dben we si*, always in the plural. Probably the office of *shi* was vacant or had even fallen in abeyance.

8. Byang chub rgyal mtshan, *Situ's Testament*, 537–540.

9. We are informed in this connection that some Mongol troops were still quartered in Tibet; Byang chub rgyal mtshan, *Situ's Testament*, 555.

10. Byang chub rgyal mtshan, *Situ's Testament*, 540–545, 552–557.

11. Byang chub rgyal mtshan, *Situ's Testament*, 561–570.

12. Byang chub rgyal mtshan, *Situ's Testament*, 571–586; Tucci, *Tibetan Chronicles by Bsod nams grags pa*, 209. The date of the letter is given in Stag tshang pa, *Chinese and Tibetan Documents*, 2:172b, as 5th day of the 5th month, corresponding perhaps to 4th June, 1356.

13. Byang chub rgyal mtshan, *Situ's Testament*, 598.

14. Ngag dbang kun dga' bsod nams grags pa rgyal mtshan, *'Dzam gling byang phyogs kyi thub pa'i rgyal tshab chen po dpal ldan Sa skya pa'i gdung rabs rin po che ji ltar byong pa'i tshul gyi rnam par thar pa ngo tshar rin po che'i bang mdzod dgos 'dod kun byung* [A History of the Khön Lineage of Prince-Abbots of Sakya], woodblock print in the Library of the Istituto Italiano per il Medio ed Estremo Oriente, Rome, 154a.

15. Byang chub rgyal mtshan, *Situ's Testament*, 605–609; cf. Stag tshang pa, *Chinese and Tibetan Documents*, 2:172b.

16. Chos kyi 'byung gnas, Si tu Pan chen, *History of the Karma Bka 'brgyud pa Sect: Being the Text of Sgrub brgyud Karma Kaṃ tshang brgyud pa rin po che'i rnam par thar pa Rab 'byams nor bu zla ba chu sel gyi phreṅ ba* [History of the Karma Kagyüpa Sect] (New Delhi: D. Gyaltsan and Kesang Legshay, 1972), 175a; Gtsug lag 'phreng ba, Dpa' bo, *Dam pa'i chos kyi 'khor los bsgyur ba rnams kyi byung ba'i gsal byed pa mkhas pa'i dga' ston* [Feast for Scholars: The Development of the Promoters of Buddhism] (New Delhi: International Academy of Indian Culture, 1959–1962), 488.

17. Byang chub rgyal mtshan, *Situ's Testament*, 619.

18. Byang chub rgyal mtshan, *Situ's Testament*, 611–614, 617; Rgyal mtshan dpal bzang, *Biography of Gyeltsen Pelzangpo*, 104b.

19. Byang chub rgyal mtshan, *Situ's Testament*, 644–647. The rather vague Chinese title means office (*guan*) of a high commissioner (*dashi*). Perhaps the same official brought to Karma Rol pa'i rdo rje the imperial letter inviting him to the capital.

20. Byang chub rgyal mtshan, *Situ's Testament*, 647–654, 659–661.

21. Byang chub rgyal mtshan, *Situ's Testament*, 665–667.

22. Stag tshang pa, *Chinese and Tibetan Documents*, 2:78a; Byang chub rgyal mtshan, *Situ's Testament*, 668–669. Dbang brtson had led a rather effaced life after his

dismissal. We know only that in 1352 he had obtained instruction from Bu ston; David Seyfort Ruegg, *Life of Bu ston Rin po che* (Rome: Instituto Italiano per il Medio ed Estremo Oriente, 1966), 139.

23. Byang chub rgyal mtshan, *Situ's Testament*, 670–672.

24. Byang chub rgyal mtshan, *Situ's Testament*, 680; Stag tshang pa, *Chinese and Tibetan Documents*, 2:76a and 78a.

25. Byang chub rgyal mtshan, *Situ's Testament*, 682–684; Ngag dbang kun dga' bsod nams grags pa rgyal mtshan, *A History of the Khön Lineage of Prince-Abbots of Sakya*, 116a–b.

26. Byang chub rgyal mtshan, *Situ's Testament*, 686–688.

27. Byang chub rgyal mtshan, *Situ's Testament*, 688–690.

28. The man immediately responsible for the atrocious deed was *chen po* Rin chen bzang po; Ngag dbang blo bzang rgya mtsho, *Gangs can yul gyi sa la spyod pa'i mtho ris kyi rgyal blon gtso bor brjod pa'i deb ther rdzogs ldan gzhun nu'i dga' ston dpyid kyi rgyal mo'i glu dbyangs* [*History of Tibet*], in the xylograph edition Fifth Dalai Lama's *Collected Works*, vol. dza (Lhasa), 98b (= Giuseppe Tucci, *Tibetan Painted Scrolls* [Rome: Libreria dello Stato, 1949], 645).

29. Dharmakirti was one of the ten *inaq*, "friends," who took part in the Śakti cult practiced by the emperor Toghan Temür; he was killed in 1364. See Helmut Schulte-Uffelage, trans., *Das Keng-shen wai-shih: eine Quelle zur späten Mongolenzeit* [*The Gengshen waishi: A Source for the Late Mongol Period*] (Berlin: Akademie-Verlag, 1963), 68–69, 98.

30. Byang chub rgyal mtshan, *Situ's Testament*, 691–696.

31. Karma Rol pa'i rdo rje heard of the event in Amdo on 24th January 1359; Chos kyi 'byung gnas, *History of the Karma Kagyüpa Sect*, 178a.

32. Stag tshang pa, *Chinese and Tibetan Documents*, 2:28b.

33. Byang chub rgyal mtshan, *Situ's Testament*, 702–712.

34. 'Jigs med grags pa, *Rgyal rtse chos rgyal gyi rnam par thar pa dad pa'i lo thog dngos grub gyi char 'bebs* [*Lives of the Kings of Gyantsé*], wood-block print in the library of the Istituto Italiano per il Medio ed Estremo Oriente, 12a–b (= Tucci, *Tibetan Painted Scrolls*, 663). The appointment as *nye gnas chen po* (colloquially *nang chen*) was confirmed by the emperor in 1364.

35. Byang chub rgyal mtshan, *Situ's Testament*, 718–721. On 5th March, 1359, the Karma pa met prince Sangaśiri (probably the same person) at Bya kha in Amdo; Chos kyi 'byung gnas, *History of the Karma Kagyüpa Sect*, 178a.

36. Byang chub rgyal mtshan, *Situ's Testament*, 722–728, 740–754.

37. Byang chub rgyal mtshan, *Situ's Testament*, 722–734.

38. Stag tshang pa, *Chinese and Tibetan Documents*, 2:28a–29a. Nearing the capital, he encountered the Karma pa, who was returning home; Chos kyi 'byung gnas, *History of the Karma Kagyüpa Sect*, 181b; Kun dga' rdo rje, Tshal pa, *Deb ther dmar po rnams kyi dang po Hu lan deb ther* [*The Red Book*], ed. Dung dkar Blo bzang 'phrin las (Beijing: Mi rigs dpe skrun khang, 1981), 120. After his death the emperor invited to court Bla ma dam pa Bsod nams rgyal mtshan, perhaps with the intention of appointing

him Imperial Preceptor; but the Bla ma turned down the invitation; Ngag dbang kun dga' bsod nams grags pa rgyal mtshan, *A History of the Khön Lineage of Prince-Abbots of Sakya*, 120a.

39. Byang chub rgyal mtshan, *Situ's Testament*, 734–735.

40. Byang chub rgyal mtshan, *Situ's Testament*, 720; Rgyal mtshan dpal bzang, *Biography of Gyeltsen Pelzangpo*, 105a.

41. Byang chub rgyal mtshan, *Situ's Testament*, 736, 738.

42. Cf. Luciano Petech, "Princely Houses of the Yuan Period Connected with Tibet," in *Indo-Tibetan Studies: Papers in Honour and Appreciation of Professor David L. Snellgrove's Contribution to Indo-Tibetan Studies*, ed. T. Skorupski (Tring: Institute of Buddhist Studies, 1990), 261.

43. Stag tshang pa, *Chinese and Tibetan Documents*, 2:29a; Ngag dbang kun dga' bsod nams grags pa rgyal mtshan, *A History of the Khön Lineage of Prince-Abbots of Sakya*, 175a–b.

44. For more details see Petech, "Princely Houses of the Yuan Period Connected with Tibet," 261–262.

45. Kun dga' rdo rje, *The Red Book* (1961); George N. Roerich, trans., *The Blue Annals* (translation of 'Gos lo tsa ba Gzhon nu dpal, *Deb ther sngon po*, 1476–1478), 2 vols. (Calcutta: Royal Asiatic Society of Bengal, 1948–1953); Tucci, *Tibetan Chronicles by Bsod nams grags pa*. The name Drakpa Gyeltsen is omitted in Tucci, *Tibetan Chronicles by Bsod nams grags pa*.

46. Stag tshang pa, *Chinese and Tibetan Documents*, 2:42b.

47. Dpal bzang chos kyi bzang po, *Royal Genealogy of Yeru jang*, 6a–b. Cf. Ngag dbang blo bzang rgya mtsho, *History of Tibet* (Lhasa), 66a (= Tucci, *Tibetan Painted Scrolls*, 632).

48. Ruegg, *Life of Bu ston Rin po che*, 134.

49. Roerich, *The Blue Annals*, 778; Dpal bzang chos kyi bzang po, *Royal Genealogy of Yeru Jang*, 6b; Dkon mchog lhun grub, Ngor chen, and Sangs rgyas phun tshogs, Ngor chen, *A History of Buddhism: Being the Text of Dam pa'i chos kyi byung tshul legs par bshad pa bstan pa rgya mtshor 'jug pa'i gru chen zhes bya ba rtsom 'phro kha skong bcas* (New Delhi: Ngawang Topgey, 1973), 148b.

50. Quoted in Tucci, *Tibetan Chronicles by Bsod nams grags pa*, 209.

51. Ruegg, *Life of Bu ston Rin po che*, 168. I do not think he can be identified with the *lha btsun* Rin chen dpal on whose request the Bla ma dam pa compiled the *Rgyal rabs gsal ba'i me long* [*The Clear Mirror of Royal Genealogies*], as maintained by Per K. Sørensen in *A Fourteenth-Century Tibetan Historical Work: Rgyal rabs gsal ba'i me long: Author, Date, and Sources: A Case Study* (København: Akademisk Forlag, 1986), 63. The title *lha btsun* was normally reserved to the monks descending from the old Tibetan kings, and not from other royal families. The Byang pa claimed descent from the Mi nyag rulers, not from the ancient Tibetan dynasty.

52. Byang chub rgyal mtshan, *Situ's Testament*, 534–535, 578–580, 669, 677–678, 793: Stag tshang pa, *Chinese and Tibetan Documents*), 2:76a and 79b–80a.

53. Byang chub rgyal mtshan, *Situ's Testament*, 383, 394, 532, 658.

54. Chos kyi 'byung gnas, *History of the Karma Kagyüpa Sect*, 178b; Gtsung lag 'phreng ba, *Feast for Scholars*, 490. Cf. Kun dga' rdo rje, *The Red Book* (1981), 116, where he is called simply *dpon*.

55. Byang chub rgyal mtshan, *Situ's Testament*, 758–759.

56. Byang chub rgyal mtshan, *Situ's Testament*, 769–771; Ngag dbang blo bzang rgya mtsho, *History of Tibet* (Lhasa), 97b–98a (= Tucci, *Tibetan Painted Scrolls*, 545).

57. This information is supplied by Byang chub rgyal mtshan's last will and testament (*Mya ngan 'das chung zhal chems*), written down during his last illness; Byang chub rgyal mtshan, Ta'i Si tu, *Si tu bka' chems* [*Situ's Testament*], in *Rlangs kyi po ti bse ru rgyas pa* (Lhasa: Bod ljongs mi dmangs dpe skrun khang, 1986), 426.

58. Tucci, *Tibetan Chronicles by Bsod nams grags pa*, 210; 'Jigs med grags pa, *Lives of the Kings of Gyantsé*, 14b (= Tucci, *Tibetan Painted Scrolls*, 664). According to Stag tshang pa, *Chinese and Tibetan Documents*, 2:173a, he died in his 63rd year fire-dragon, a palpable mistake for wood-dragon. The date of 1373, found in Roerich, *The Blue Annals*, 218, and too often followed by Western scholars, is due to a misunderstanding by the translator. The Tibetan text (Gzhon nu dpal, 'Gos lo tsa ba, *Deb ther sngon po* [*Blue Annals*] [New Delhi: International Academy of Indian Culture, 1974], 7a) actually refers to the death of Gushri ba, i.e., of Byang chub rgyal mtshan's successor Gushri Shākya rgyal mtshan. But the risk of a misunderstanding is so high that Tucci (*Tibetan Chronicles by Bsod nams grags pa*, 210) felt bound to caution the reader against it.

59. Byang chub rgyal mtshan, *Situ's Testament*, 835–836.

60. Rgyal mtshan dpal bzang, *Biography of Gyeltsen Pelzangpo*, 154a.

61. *Da Ming shi lu* [*Veritable Records of the Ming Dynasty*] (Taipei: Zhongyang Yanjiuyuan Lishi Yuyan Yanjiusuo, 1962–66), Hongwu, 77.4b and 79.1a.

62. The best candidate for identification would be Nam mkha' bstan pa'i rgyal mtshan (1333–1379), abbot of Stag lung thang, on whom see Roerich, *The Blue Annals*, 635–636. The dates too agree perfectly.

63. *Veritable Records of the Ming Dynasty*, Hongwu, 79.1a.

64. *Veritable Records of the Ming Dynasty*, Hongwu, 85.7a–b, and Ngag dbang kun dga' bsod nams grags pa rgyal mtshan, *A History of the Khön Lineage of Prince-Abbots of Sakya*, 179b.

65. *Veritable Records of the Ming Dynasty*, Hongwu, 91.4a.

66. Ngag dbang blo bzang rgya mtsho, *History of Tibet* (Lhasa), 81b (= Tucci, *Tibetan Painted Scrolls*, 638).

67. *Veritable Records of the Ming Dynasty*, Hongwu, 73.4b.

68. *Veritable Records of the Ming Dynasty*, Hongwu, 78.7a. Cf. Zhang Tingyu, et al., *Mingshi* [*History of the Ming*] (Beijing: Zhonghua shuju, 1974), 331.9b (= Tucci, *Tibetan Painted Scrolls*, 692).

69. In 1367 the ruler of Rgyal rtse received from the emperor Toghan Temür the title of *yongluo taifu da situ*, and it seems that his successor got confirmation and enhancement of it in the following years; 'Jigs med grags pa, *Lives of the Kings of Gyantsé*, 17a and 22a (= Tucci, *Tibetan Painted Scrolls*, 664).

Chapter 16

MONASTIC PATRONAGE

IN FIFTEENTH-CENTURY TIBET

Turrell V. Wylie

Turrell Wylie was the first American to teach Tibetan history, at the first program for Tibetan studies, started at the University of Washington in the 1950s. This article is concerned with the rivalry between the two main parts of Central Tibet, Ü and Tsang. The Pakmodru leaders were based in the east, in the Yarlung Valley of the former Tibetan kings, and had strong centers of power in Lhasa and Gyantsé, while their ministers, the Rinpung, eventually broke with them and took control of western Central Tibet, taking Zhigatsé, Gyantsé, and for a time even Lhasa. Wylie noticed a pattern of patronage by the Pakmodru rulers that contrasted sharply with that of their rivals in the west. For instance, in the decade from 1409 to 1419, the main Gelukpa religious festival and four main Gelukpa monasteries were sponsored by local leaders appointed by the fifth leader of the Pakmodru religiopolitical polity, which had ruled Tibet since the fall of the Mongol-Sakya alliance. Although it may seem strange that the leader, Gongma Drakpa Gyeltsen, a monk of the Kagyü Pakmodrupa sect, would sponsor a new religious movement, Wylie explains that "a sectarian liaison developed naturally between the older Pakmodrupa sect and the new Gelukpa order because of their shared affinity with the Kadampa tradition." Each of the Gelukpa institutions was established at a place not far from the local political center of the lay patron, usually in a major Tibetan settlement. Wylie does not exactly give a reason for this, but the vitality of the new tradition may have breathed some life into the Pakmodru polity, which had been weakening. He contrasts the establishment of these institutions with the founding of Yangpachen, a new monastery of the Red Hat Karmapa sect, in 1490, far from the political centers of its sponsors. Wylie's explanation is that this new seat was used as a staging area for military aggression against Lhasa. The fact that Lhasa fell to the Rinpung-Karmapa alliance shortly thereafter lends credence to his theory.

The purpose of this preliminary paper is to review specific cases of patronage extended to the newly founded Yellow-hat Gelukpa sect in the first half of the fifteenth century in order to establish a pattern for such patronage. Then, the founding of the Red-hat Karmapa monastery of Yangpachen in the year 1490 will be reviewed in order to show the geo-political differences from the established pattern.[1]

In chronological order, the cases of Gelukpa patronage to be dealt with are the inauguration of the *Mönlam Chenmo* prayer observance and the founding of the monasteries of Ganden, Drepung, Pelkhor Chödé, Sera, and Trashilhünpo. With the exception of the founding of Trashilhünpo, the Gelukpa patronage cases cited here all occurred during the reign of the fifth Lhatsün of Pakmodru, Gongma Drakpa Gyeltsen (1385–1432).[2] Although this hierarchic ruler of Tibet was himself a monk of the Kagyü Pakmodrupa sect, he was nevertheless a staunch patron of the founder of the Yellow-hat Gelukpa sect, Tsongkhapa (1357–1419), and his disciples.[3]

In the year 1409 Tsongkhapa inaugurated the annual prayer observance *Mönlam Chenmo* in the Lhasa region. The patron for this monastic event was Namkha Zangpo, the *Dzongpön* of Neudzong, an administrative fortress situated on the left bank of the Kyi river near Lhasa.[4] As *Dzongpön*, Namkha Zangpo was an official appointed by Gongma Drakpa Gyeltsen, whose own political headquarters were located at Nedongtsé in the Yarlung valley.[5]

In the same year, Tsongkhapa founded Riwo Ganden Nampar Gyelpé Ling, the first monastery of the Gelukpa sect.[6] This institution was built some 35 miles upstream from the Lhasa area on the left bank of the Kyi River. The chief patron for the founding of Ganden was Drakkarwa Rinchenpel, who had been appointed *Dzongpön* of Ölkha Taktsé, an administrative center not too far from the founding site of Ganden.[7]

In the year 1416, Jamyang Chöjé Trashi Penden, a personal disciple of Tsongkhapa, founded the monastery of Chödra Chenpo Penden Drepung. The patron for this monastic institution was again the *Dzongpön*, Namkha Zangpa.[8] It was built on the right bank of the Kyi river not far from Neudzong, local headquarters of its founding patron.

In the year 1418, Khedrup Chöjé Geden Lekpel Zangpo, a personal disciple of Tsongkhapa, founded the monastery of Pelkhor Chödé at Gyelkhartsé [henceforth called Gyantsé].[9] The founding patron was the local ruler of Gyantsé, Rapten Künzang Pakpa, who had served as *Zimpön* (Chamberlain) to the Pakmodru Gongma, Drakpa Gyeltsen.[10]

In the next year (1419), Jamchen Chöjé Shākya Yeshé, a personal disciple of Tsongkhapa, founded the monastery of Sera Tekchenling just north of Lhasa.[11] Curiously, all but one of the sources used in this paper fail to identify a source of patronage for the founding of Sera monastery. Only the biography of Tsong-khapa mentioned it in this passage: ". . . assistance, for the most part, was sent from Neudzong."[12] Although not identified in this passage, the lay patron would have been, once again, the *dzongpön* of Neudzong, Namkha Zangpo, who is mentioned by name in another context shortly afterwards.[13]

This indirect reference to patronage, together with the silence of the other sources used, would seem to suggest that there was perhaps another source of patronage. Relevant to this suggestion is the fact that this disciple, Jamchen Chöjé, had recently returned from the court of the Ming Emperor Chengzu, where he had been sent by Tsongkhapa as the latter's representative in response to repeated invitations from that Ming emperor.[14] The Ming emperor lavishly rewarded Jamchen Chöjé who, in turn, presented great offerings to Tsongkhapa when he came back from China.[15] The *Vaiḍūrya Serpo* states that Jamchen Chöjé brought sixteen white sandalwood images of the Buddha's venerable disciples from China and used them as the principal icons in the temple of Sera.[16] Thus, it would seem the Ming imperial treasury contributed its share of patronage to the building of Sera monastery.

In 1432, thirteen years after the death of Tsongkhapa, his patron, the Pakmodru *gongma*, Drakpa Gyeltsen, died at Nedongtsé. His death was followed by bitter rivalry within the Lang ruling family for the throne. This rivalry was temporarily abated when the political seat was given to Drakpa Jungné, a nephew of the former *gongma* and a relative of the Rinpung administrator.[17] Before long, dissension arose between the Lang and the Rinpung families. In 1435, Döndrup Dorjé, a son of the Rinpung administrator, seized control of the *dzong* of Samdruptsé [henceforth called Zhigatsé].[18] Yeshé Peljor's *Chronological Tables* laconically state that in the "wood-hare year, Pakdrupa lost the Tsang region to Rinpungpa."[19] This seizure of Zhigatsé *dzong* did not, however, mark an immediate dichotomy in the Tibetan polity. The Rinpung officials continued to support the Pakmodru *gongma* to whom they were related by blood.

In the year 1447 the Yellow-hat monastery of Trashilhünpo was founded close to the *dzong* of Zhigatsé. This institution is attributed to Gendün Druppa (1391–1474), a personal disciple of Tsongkhapa, and the hierarch regarded in Tibetan tradition as the first Dalai Lama.[20] Although the sources used for this paper agree that the founding date for Trashilhünpo was the "fire-hare" year (1447), they do not agree on the identity of the founding patron.

The Fifth Dalai Lama explicity states that the patron was Hor Peljor Zangpo of the Chonggyé family,[21] who had been appointed *dzongpön* of Zhigatsé by the former Gongma, Drakpa Gyeltsen, himself.[22] There is a story that the Chöjé of Ngor, leader of a subdivision of the Sakyapa sect, asked Norbu Zangpo of Rinpung to put a stop to the building of Trashilhünpo, a monastery for the Gelukpa sect; but, the Rinpung administrator refused to do so.[23] This story is directly refuted by the Fifth Dalai Lama on the grounds that the *dzongpön* of Zhigatsé, Hor Peljor Zangpo of Chonggyé, was the patron of Gendün Druppa and the founding of Trashilhünpo.[24]

The Fifth Dalai Lama notwithstanding, this paper accepts as fact that Dön-drup Dorjé of Rinpung seized Zhigatsé in 1435, and that when Trashilhünpo was founded thirteen years later, the *dzongpön* of Zhigatsé was no longer Hor Peljor Zangpo of Chonggyé.[25]

Moreover, other primary sources identify the founding patron as Dargyepa Pön Sönam Pelzang.[26] Unfortunately, the sources consulted so far offer no additional information on this patron. Until such time that Dargyepa Pön Sönam Pelzang can be identified further, it can only be assumed in this paper that he was an official associated in some way with the Rinpung ruler of Zhigatsé who supported the Pakmodru Gongma, at least *pro forma*, at the time Trashilhünpo was founded.

The six cases of monastic patronage given to the Yellow-hat Gelukpa sect in the first half of the fifteenth century reviewed in this study provide data for establishing a triadic pattern for such patronage.

First: the lay patron involved in each case, with the exception perhaps of Trashilhünpo, was a local official appointed by the fifth *lhatsün* of Pakmodru, Gongma Drakpa Gyeltsen, who was known for his patronage of Tsongkhapa and his disciples.

Second: those who received Pakmodru patronage were either the founder of the new Gelukpa sect or one of his disciples; none of whom had had a previous monastic seat of his own.

Third: each of the Gelukpa institutions was established at a place close to, or not far from, the local political center of the lay patron.

This triadic pattern of patronage can now be used for comparison with the founding of Yangpachen, a new monastery of the Red-hat Karmapa sect, in the year 1490.

Döndrup Dorjé, who had seized the office of *dzongpön* at Zhigatsé in 1435, was in time succeeded by a nephew, Dönyö Dorjé, who became a nemesis of the Pakmodru government at Nedongtsé. This new Rinpung ruler of Zhigatsé entered into a patronage alliance with the fourth Red-hat Karmapa hierarch, Chödrak Yeshé (1453–1524).[27] The monastic center of the Red-hat Karmapa sect was at Nenang, a monastery founded in 1333 by the first Red-hat Karmapa, Drakpa Senggé. Nenang was not far from Tsurpü, the chief monastery of the Black-hat Karmapa sect.[28]

In the year 1481, military forces of the Rinpung ruler of Zhigatsé attacked the Lhasa region, but they were defeated.[29] According to the *Chronological Tables*, the Tsang army was led by the Red-hat Karmapa himself.[30]

In 1485 the Rinpung ruler sent a military expedition against the local ruler of Gyantsé in the upper reaches of the Nyang valley, but it was defeated. Another campaign three years later was victorious and Dönyö Dorjé took control of the fortress of Gyantsé, which dominated the southern route from Zhigatsé to the province of Ü.[31]

Two years later in 1490, the fourth Red-hat Karmapa, Chödrak Yeshé, and his patron, Dönyö Dorjé, decided to build the monastery of Yangpachen.[32] This monastery, which became the chief center of the Red-hat sect, was built in the Tölung valley, on the Lhasa side of a mountain pass. Across that pass is the Üyuk valley, whose river flows southwardly, entering the Tsangpo [= Brahmaputra river] east of Zhigatsé.[33]

When the building of this Red-hat monastic center is compared with the triadic pattern of patronage for the Yellow-hat institutions discussed in this paper, it is obvious that the pattern for the founding of Yangpachen is completely different.

First: the lay patron, Dönyö Dorjé, the Rinpung ruler of Zhigatsé, was not a local official loyal to the head of the Pakmodru government at Nedongtsé. On the contrary, he had succeeded his uncle who had usurped the office of *dzongpön* at Zhigatsé. Moreover, by the time Yangpachen was founded, Dönyö Dorjé had already proven his military hostility towards Pakmodru authority in Ü province.

Second: the Red-hat Karmapa Chödrak Yeshé was not the founder, nor a follower, of a newly formed sectarian group. He was the fourth hierarch of a long established sect, whose center had been at Nenang monastery since its founding in 1333.

Third: the new monastic center of the Red-hat Karmapa was not built close to, nor even within a reasonable distance from, the political center of the Rinpung patron at Zhigatsé. In fact, the distance from Zhigatsé to Yangpachen was more than twice that from Yangpachen to Lhasa.

Now, the fact that none of the three points for the founding of the Red-hat monastery agrees with any of the triadic pattern of Yellow-hat patronage already given should not be dismissed simply as coincidental. On the contrary, it is the contention of this paper that the difference between the two patterns suggests that the founding of the Red-hat Karmapa monastery was intended to satisfy needs other than purely religious ones.

This suggestion gains support from the story that Dönyö Dorjé was also a patron of the seventh Black-hat Karmapa hierarch, Chödrak Gyatso (1454–1506). Immediately following reference to the founding of Yangpachen, the Fifth Dalai Lama states that in accordance with the wishes of Jedrung Chödrak Gyatso, Dönyö Dorjé built a monastery near Lhasa; but, due to karmic forces, it did not long survive.[34] Although undated by the Fifth Dalai Lama, the building of this monastery is placed by Sumpa Khenpo after the unsuccessful 1481 campaign against the Lhasa region and the victorious one of 1498.[35] Shakabpa also mentions the founding of the Red-hat monastery of Yangpachen and the Lhasa monastery built for the Black-hat Karmapa in the same sentence, adding that the latter was destroyed by Yellow-hat monks from Sera and Drepung monasteries.[36]

After the founding of Yangpachen and in keeping with their obvious political aspirations for the Lhasa region, the Rinpung ruler of Zhigatsé and the Red-hat Karmapa hierarch increased their hostility towards the Gelukpa sect. The Yellow-hat monastery of Trashilhünpo, located virtually in the shadow of the

Zhigatsé fortress, was particularly vulnerable. Trashilhünpo had been the seat of the First Dalai Lama, Gendün Druppa, from its founding in 1447 until his death in 1474.[37] Gendün Gyatso (1475–1542) was recognized as his rebirth and was brought to Trashilhünpo in 1486.[38] In 1494, four years after the founding of Yangpachen, the Second Dalai Lama moved from Trashilhünpo near Zhigatsé to Drepung monastery near Lhasa.[39] In view of the hostile ambience prevailing at Zhigatsé, this unexplained move may well have been for the personal safety of the Yellow-hat Dalai Lama.

In 1498, combined forces of the Rinpung ruler and the Red-hat Karmapa successfully attacked the Lhasa region. The Neudzong administrator was forced to flee to the Yellow-hat monastery of Kyormolung near Drepung and his territorial domains came under Rinpung control.[40]

The Rinpung/Red-hat Karmapa forces occupied the Lhasa region from 1498 until 1517 and throughout that occupation monks of the Yellow-hat monasteries of Sera and Drepung were excluded from the *Mönlam Chenmo* prayer observances.[41] The Second Dalai Lama left Drepung, again presumably for reasons of personal safety, and traveled extensively in districts southeast of Lhasa. In the year 1509 he founded the monastery of Chökhor Gyel on the border between Ölkha and Dakpo.[42]

By 1517 the power of the Rinpung/Karmapa occupation forces in the Lhasa region declined and the 2nd Dalai Lama once again returned to Drepung monastery.[43] The next year, after two decades of exclusion, monks of Sera and Drepung again participated in the *Mönlam Chenmo*.[44] In the same year (1518), the Second Dalai Lama began construction of Ganden Podrang, the residence at Drepung which served as the seat of the successive Dalai Lamas until the Potala palace was erected in the seventeenth century.[45]

In review, the fact that the founding of Yangpachen monastery for the Red-hat Karmapa sect did not follow the triadic pattern of the Yellow-hat institutions suggests, as noted earlier, that this new monastic center may have been built for other than purely religious reasons. It is the proposal of this paper that this Red-hat monastery was founded, when and where it was, as part of the overall Rinpung/Karmapa campaign to control the Lhasa region.

Such a proposition immediately begs the question: if Lhasa were the goal, why was a new monastery needed when the old Red-hat monastic center of Nenang was not far from the Lhasa region itself? Due to religious orientation, the primary sources consulted do not offer information on such mundane matters as military logistics and tactical maneuvers: consequently, this preliminary paper can only suggest probable causes.

First: during the Rinpung/Karmapa campaign against the Lhasa region in 1481, the monastic center of the Red-hat sect had been at Nenang in the Tsurpü valley. The Red-hat Karmapa himself is said to have led the Tsang army in the campaign; yet, it ended in defeat. After that, and precisely because of its location near the Lhasa region, the Nenang monastery would have been vulnerable, both as a monastic center and a military base of operations. Overt hostile activity at Nenang could well have led to the same fate as that of the Black-hat Karmapa monastery near Lhasa mentioned earlier, which was destroyed by Yellow-hat monks from Drepung and Sera.

Second: Nenang, the old Red-hat monastic center, was not directly on the main northern route from Zhigatsé to Lhasa. It was located up the Tsurpü valley, which branched off from the Tölung valley, west of Lhasa. A route did run from the Tsurpü valley by way of the Nyemo valley to Gyantsé;[46] but, treacherous terrain in places made this route too difficult for heavy travel to Zhigatsé.[47]

Third: lacking specific information, it is impossible to guess what role the fortress at Gyantsé played in the Rinpung/Karmapa military campaign against Lhasa. On the other hand, that fortress did dominate the southern route from Zhigatsé to the province of Ü in general, and the Lhasa region in particular. Can it be mere coincidence that the monastery of Yangpachen was built on the northern route shortly after the Gyantsé fortress on the southern route came under Rinpung control?

Finally, the shortest natural route from Zhigatsé to Lhasa traversed up the Üyuk valley, across a mountain pass, then down the Tölung valley to the Kyi river near Lhasa.[48] This northern route from Zhigatsé was dominated by Yangpachen monastery, which was built in the upper reaches of the Tölung valley. Strategically located, this new Red-hat monastery was close enough to Lhasa to be within military striking distance; yet, far enough away to provide a base for logistical operations secure from immediate intervention by Lhasa forces.

In conclusion, the reasons given in this preliminary paper for the founding of Yangpachen in 1490 are hypothetical and certainly not intended to be exclusive. They are presented as an explanation why the monastery was built where and when it was, and why the 1498 Rinpung/Red-hat Karmapa campaign against Lhasa was successful when the 1481 campaign was not.

Ironically, the long history of Yangpachen, built originally for the Red-hat sect during its struggles with the Yellow-hat sect for supremacy, came to a bitter end in the eighteenth century when the ninth Red-hat Karmapa, accused of treason during war with Nepal, was forbidden to reincarnate by the government of the Dalai Lama. The monastery of Yangpachen was then taken from the Red-hat Karmapa sect and given to the Yellow-hat Gelukpa sect.[49]

NOTES

1. I was able to spend the academic year 1973–1974 doing Tibetan research in Rome thanks to a Fellowship from the American Council of Learned Societies. This preliminary paper on monastic patronage is based in part on that research.

2. On the life of this Phag mo gru ruler of Tibet, see Giuseppe Tucci, trans., *Deb t'er dmar po gsar ma: Tibetan Chronicles by Bsod nams grags pa* (Rome: Instituto italiano

per il Medio ed Estremo Oriente, 1971), 214–219; Giuseppe Tucci, *Tibetan Painted Scrolls*, 3 vols. (Rome: Libreria dello Stato, 1949), I:26–27; II:639; Tsepon W. D. Shakabpa, *Bod kyi srid don rgyal rabs: An Advanced Political History of Tibet*, 2 vols. [text in Tibetan only] (Kalimpong: T. Tsepal, Taikhang, 1976), I:337–344.

3. A sectarian liaison developed naturally between the older Phag mo gru pa sect and the new Dge lugs pa order because of their shared affinity with the Bka' gdams pa tradition. See *inter alia* Tucci, *Tibetan Painted Scrolls*, I:85–86; R. A. Stein, *Tibetan Civilization* (Stanford: Stanford University Press, 1972), 80–81. On the life of Tsong kha pa, see Rudolf Kaschewsky, "*Das Leben des Lamaistischen Heiligen Tsong kha pa Blo bzang grags pa (1357–1419)*" [*The Life of the Lamaist Saint Tsong kha pa Blo bzang grags pa (1357–1419)*], *Asiatische Forschungen*, Band 32, 2 vols. (Wiesbaden: O. Harrassowitz, 1971).

4. Ye shes dpal 'byor, Sum pa mkhan po, *Dpag bsam ljon bzang (Re'u mig)* [*The Auspicious Wish-Fulfilling Tree (Chronological Tables)*], *Śatapitaka*, vol. 8 (New Delhi: International Academy of Indian Culture, 1959), 43; Tucci, *Tibetan Chronicles by Bsod nams grags pa*, 240–241. Also in the same year (1409) Tsong kha pa, with Gong ma Grags pa rgyal mtshan and Nam mkha' bzang po, the *rdzong dpon* of Sne'u rdzong, as patrons, refurbished some of the icons (*rten*) in the Gtsug lag khang of Lhasa (Shakabpa, *An Advanced Political History of Tibet*, I:340). The location of the Sne'u rdzong fortress needs to be made clear. The vague description in the '*Dzam gling rgyas bshad* places the Sne'u rdzong ruins on the left bank of the Kyi river north of Snye thang, but south of the Skyor mo lung monastery, which was in the lower Stod lung valley, downstream from Lhasa. See Turrell V. Wylie, *The Geography of Tibet According to the 'Dzam gling rgyas bshad* (Roma: Instituto italiano per il Medio ed Estremo Oriente, 1962), 76–77. Professor Tucci recorded that, entering the valley of Netang [= Snye thang], the ruins of the castle of Sne'u rdzong were on the left. This would seem to place the fortress across the river from Snye thang. See Giuseppe Tucci, *A Lhasa e oltre* [*To Lhasa and Beyond*] (Roma: La Libreria dello Stato, 1952), 99, 152 n. 35. My Tibetan colleague, Geshe Nawang Nornang, a native of Lhasa, says the Sne'u rdzong ruins are on the left bank of the Kyi river across from the Norbulingka, summer palace of the Dalai Lamas in Lhasa, and that the ruins can be seen from the Snye thang valley. Thus, impressions to the contrary, the fortress of Sne'u rdzong was located in the Lhasa region itself, rather than downstream, across from Snye thang.

5. Some modern scholars give the name of the Phag mo gru headquarters as Sne'u gdong rtse, even when the original sources spell it Sne gdong rtse. See *inter alia* Tucci, *Tibetan Chronicles by Bsod nams grags pa*, folios 75, 96a; Wylie, *The Geography of Tibet*, 32; Alfonsa Ferrari, *Mkhyen brtse's Guide to the Holy Places of Central Tibet* (Roma: Istituto italiano per il Medio ed Estremo, 1958), 10; Ngag dbang blo bzang rgya mtsho, Fifth Dalai Lama, *Bod kyi deb ther dpyid kyi rgyal mo'i glu dbyangs Bod kyi deb ther dpyid kyi rgyal mo'i glu dbyangs* [*History of Tibet*] (Varanasi: Kalsang Lhundup. 1967), 185, where the spelling is Sna gdong rtse. The mixture of spellings may stem from the name of the Sne'u rdzong fortress. In my opinion, the correct orthography for the Phag mo gru headquarters in the Yar klungs valley is Sne gdong

rtse, and the 'u of Sne'u rdzong is the diminutive suffix, indicative of the dependent relationship of this fief near Lhasa to Sne gdong rtse near Rtse thang in Yar klungs. On this point, the locations of Sne gdong rtse and Sne'u rdzong are confused in Tucci, *Tibetan Painted Scrolls*, II, 692 n. 248, which states: "as Neu gdong rtse, the capital of Phag mo gru . . . must not be identified with Gzhis kha 'ne'u rdzong, near Rtse thang, on the Southern bank of the Brahmaputra . . . Sne'u gdong rtse is near Snye thang to the east of the 'Kyid chu . . . to the South of Stod lung. . . ." The actual locations of Sne gdong rtse and Sne'u rdzong are just the reverse; i.e., the former is near Rtse thang, the latter near Snye thang/Lhasa (see footnote 4 of this paper).

6. Ye shes dpal 'byor, *The Auspicious Wish-Fulfilling Tree* (*Chronological Tables*), 43; Shakabpa, *An Advanced Political History of Tibet*, I:431–432; Ferrari, *Guide to the Holy Places of Central Tibet*, 107–108; Wylie, *The Geography of Tibet*, 150.

7. Ngag dbang blo bzang rgya mtsho, *History of Tibet*, 228–229; Tucci, *Tibetan Painted Scrolls*, II:646.

8. Ye shes dpal 'byor, *The Auspicious Wish-Fulfilling Tree* (*Chronological Tables*), 44; Tucci, *Tibetan Chronicles by Bsod nams grags pa*, 240–241; Sangs rgyas rgya mtsho, *Vaiḍūrya ser po* [*The Yellow Beryl*], Śatapitaka, vol. 12, part 1 (New Delhi: International Academy of Indian Culture, 1960), 91; Ferrari, *Guide to the Holy Places of Central Tibet*, 96–97; Wylie, *The Geography of Tibet*, 151.

9. The name of this monastic institution is given as: Dpal 'khor chos sde (Shakabpa, *An Advanced Political History of Tibet*, I:343; Ferrari, *Guide to the Holy Places of Central Tibet*, 59; Wylie, *The Geography of Tibet*, 70), Dpal 'khor bde chen (Ngag dbang blo bzang rgya mtsho, *History of Tibet*, 235), and Dpal 'khor sde chen (Tucci, *Tibetan Chronicles by Bsod nams grags pa*, 190). For a comprehensive treatment, see Giuseppe Tucci, *Indo-Tibetica 4, 1–2: Gyantse ed i suoi monasteri* [*Gyantsé and Its Monasteries*] (Rome: Reale Accademia d'Italia, 1941).

10. Tucci, *Tibetan Chronicles by Bsod nams grags pa*, 190; Ngag dbang blo bzang rgya mtsho, *History of Tibet*, 235; Tucci, *Tibetan Painted Scrolls*, II:646.

11. Ye shes dpal 'byor, *The Auspicious Wish-Fulfilling Tree* (*Chronological Tables*), 44; Sangs rgyas rgya mtsho, *The Yellow Beryl*, 118.

12. Kaschewsky, *The Life of the Lamaist Saint Tsong kha pa*, II, Tafel 573, IX, 16r.

13. Kaschewsky, *The Life of the Lamaist Saint Tsong kha pa*, II, Tafel 574, IX, 16v.

14. Kaschewsky, *The Life of the Lamaist Saint Tsong kha pa*, I, 148–52, 220.

15. The gifts received from the Ming Emperor included such things as Buddhist scriptures and images, monastic robes, fine silks, gold, and silver utensils. See *Ming Shi* [*History of the Ming*] (Beijing: Zhonghua shu ju, 1974), *zhuan* 331, 8677–79.

16. ". . . tsan dan dkar po'i gnas brtan bcu drug . . ." (Sangs rgyas rgya mtsho, *The Yellow Beryl*, 118). In the Indian Buddhist tradition there were sixteen venerable disciples, each of whom was a *sthavira* (Tibetan: *gnas brtan*), also an *arhat* (Chinese: *luohan*). In the Chinese tradition, two more were added, making eighteen *arhats* (*luohan*). Thus, a Qing dynasty text, dealing with Sera monastery, states there were sandalwood images of the eighteen *luohan*. Song Yun, *Weizang tongzhi* [*Comprehensive Gazetteer of Ü-tsang*] (China: Jianxi cun she, 1896), *zhuan* 6, 6b. The discrepancy between the num-

ber of images, sixteen in *Yellow Beryl* and eighteen in *Comprehensive Gazetteer,* is accounted for in the biography of Tsong kha pa, which says there were images of the sixteen *sthaviras,* together with Chinese *upasakas,* made of white sandalwood (. . . *gnas brtan bcu drug/dge bsnyen hwa shang dang bcas pa tsan dan dkar po las grub pa* . . .), Kaschewsky, *The Life of the Lamaist Saint Tsong kha pa,* Tafel 574, IX, 16v.

17. Tucci, *Tibetan Chronicles by Bsod nams grags pa,* 218–219; Shakabpa, *An Advanced Political History of Tibet,* I:344; Tucci, *Tibetan Painted Scrolls,* II:639.

18. Ngag dbang blo bzang rgya mtsho, *History of Tibet,* 213; Tucci, *Tibetan Painted Scrolls,* II:542, 654.

19. Ye shes dpal 'byor, *The Auspicious Wish-Fulfilling Tree (Chronological Tables),* 47: "*shing yos/ . . . /phag gru bas tsang phyogs rin spung* [sic!] *ba la shor/.*"

20. Ye shes dpal 'byor, *The Auspicious Wish-Fulfilling Tree (Chronological Tables),* 48; Sangs rgyas rgya mtsho, *The Yellow Beryl,* 196–197; Shakabpa, *An Advanced Political History of Tibet,* I:366; Ferrari, *Guide to the Holy Places of Central Tibet,* 144–145; Wylie, *The Geography of Tibet,* 137.

21. Ngag dbang blo bzang rgya mtsho, *History of Tibet,* 212; Tucci, *Tibetan Painted Scrolls,* II:642. This 'Phyong rgyas *Rdzong dpon* of Zhigatsé is linked with Dge 'dun grub pa also in Tucci, *Tibetan Chronicles by Bsod nams grags pa,* 236.

22. Ngag dbang blo bzang rgya mtsho, *History of Tibet,* 196; Tucci, *Tibetan Painted Scrolls,* II:639.

23. Tucci, *Tibetan Chronicles by Bsod nams grags pa,* 239–240.

24. Ngag dbang blo bzang rgya mtsho, *History of Tibet,* 212; Tucci, *Tibetan Painted Scrolls,* II:642.

25. The sources give varying accounts of the seizure of Zhigatsé *rdzong* by Rin spungs. One story says Nor bu bzang po became *rdzong dpon* of Zhigatsé in 1435 (Tucci's translation of *Dam pa'i chos kyi 'byung tshul,* Tucci, *Tibetan Painted Scrolls,* II:651; Shakabpa, *An Advanced Political History of Tibet,* I:352). Shakabpa, on the very same page, also states that Nor bu bzang po's son, Don grub rdo rje, seized the office of *rdzong dpon* of Zhigatsé (. . . *rdzong dpon gyi las ka bzungs/*): Shakabpa, *An Advanced Political History of Tibet,* I:352. If Nor bu bzang po were the *rdzong dpon* of Zhigatsé in 1435, there would have been no need for his son, Don grub rdo rje, to seize (*bzungs*) that office. On the other hand, Ye shes dpal 'byor Sum pa mkhan po wrote ". . . beginning from the year wood hare (1435) of the seventh cycle, one of the sons of Nor bzang of Rin spungs, called Kun bzang took the feud of Rin spungs and the other Don grub rdo rje took bSam 'grub rtse . . ." (Tucci's translation, Tucci, *Tibetan Painted Scrolls,* II:654). Elsewhere, Tucci asserts that Don grub rdo rje wrested the fort of Zhigatsé from the 'Phyong rgyas *rdzong dpon* (Tucci, *Tibetan Painted Scrolls,* I:30). Consequently, if Don grub rdo rje seized the *rdzong* of Zhigatsé in 1435, taking that office away from Hor Dpal 'byor bzang po of 'Phyong rgyas, logically the latter would not have been the *rdzong dpon* of Zhigatsé over a decade later.

26. *Tsong kha pa,* Tafel 583, IX, 31r. Variant spellings of this name are: Dar rgyas nang pa Bsod nams dpal ba (*Tsong kha pa,* Tafel 584, IX, 31v); Dar rgyas pa Dpon

Bsod bzang pa (Sangs rgyas rgya mtsho, *The Yellow Beryl*, 197); Dar rgyas Dpon Dpal bzang (Shakabpa, *An Advanced Political History of Tibet*, I:366).

27. For a condensed biography of this Red-hat hierarch, see Si tu Paṇ chen Chos kyi 'byung gnas and Tshe dbang kun khyab, 'Be-lo. *History of the Karma Bka 'brgyud pa [sic] Sect: Being the Text of 'Sgrub brgyud Karma Kaṃ tshang brgyud pa rin po che'i rnam par thar pa Rab 'byams nor bu zla ba chu shel gyi phreng ba* (text in Tibetan only) (1775; reprint, New Delhi: D. Gyaltsan and Kesang Legshay, 1972), vol. 1, 594–624. See also Gzhon nu dpal, 'Gos Lo tsā ba, trans. George N. Roerich, *The Blue Annals* (Delhi: Motilal Banarsidass, 1976), 551–552; Hugh E. Richardson, "The Karma pa Sect: A Historical Note," *Journal of the Royal Asiatic Society* (1958):151–152.

28. On the Gnas nang monastery, see Chos kyi 'byung gnas and Tshe dbang kun khyab, *History of the Karma Kagyüpa Sect*, 253: Roerich, *The Blue Annals*, 530; Ferrari, *Guide to the Holy Places of Central Tibet*, 74, 169. On Tsurpü, see Ferrari, *Guide to the Holy Places of Central Tibet*, 168; Wylie, *The Geography of Tibet*, 150.

29. Ngag dbang blo bzang rgya mtsho, *History of Tibet*, 214; Tucci, *Tibetan Painted Scrolls*, II:642, 654.

30. Ye shes dpal 'byor, *The Auspicious Wish-Fulfilling Tree (Chronological Tables)*, 51–52: *lcags glang/ … /zhwa dmar pas Tsang dmag dbus su drangs/*. In reference to the 1481 Lhasa Campaign, Tucci's translation of Ye shes dpal 'byor, Sum pa mkhan po, *The Auspicious Wish-Fulfilling Tree* reads: ". . . Don yod rdo rje . . . of Rin spungs, was solicited by Zhwa dmar, Kar ma Chos grags rgya mtsho . . . " (Tucci, *Tibetan Painted Scrolls*, II:654). The name of the fourth Red-hat Kar ma pa was Chos grags ye shes; the name given in Tucci, *Tibetan Painted Scrolls*, Chos grags rgya mtsho, was that of the 7th Black-hat Kar ma pa hierarch. Since *The Auspicious Wish-Fulfilling Tree (Chronological Tables)* is not available to me at this time, I do not know if this mixed identification of the Kar ma pa hierarch derives from the original text or from the translator's interpolation.

31. Tucci, *Tibetan Chronicles by Bsod nams grags pa*, 226; Shakabpa, *An Advanced Political History of Tibet*, I, 349.

32. Chos kyi 'byung gnas and Tshe dbang kun khyab, *History of the Karma Kagyüpa Sect*, 609–610; Ngag dbang blo bzang rgya mtsho, *History of Tibet*, 214–215; Tucci, *Tibetan Painted Scrolls*, II:642; Shakabpa, *An Advanced Political History of Tibet*, I:353. Curiously, Shakabpa, *An Advanced Political History of Tibet*, dates the founding of Yangs pa can in the earth-pig year, 1479, without further explanation. Ye shes dpal 'byor, Sum pa mkhan po dates it in 1490; but attributes its founding to Mus rab 'byams pa thugs rje dpal (*Chronological Tables*, 52). I have not found this name in any of the sources consulted other than the *Chronological Tables*.

33. Ferrari, *Guide to the Holy Places of Central Tibet*, 69, 160–161. The sketch map at the end of Ferrari, *Guide to the Holy Places of Central Tibet*, gives a misleading topographical picture of this area. The Snye mo river valley does not intervene between Yangs pa can monastery and the upper reaches of the 'U yug valley as depicted there. (See footnote 48 of this paper for additional data.)

34. Ngag dbang blo bzang rgya mtsho, *History of Tibet*, 215; Tucci, *Tibetan Painted Scrolls*, II:642.

35. See Tucci's translation of the *Dpag bsam ljon bzang* [*The Auspicious Wish-Fulfilling Tree*], Tucci, *Tibetan Painted Scrolls*, II:654.

36. Shakabpa, *An Advanced Political History of Tibet*, I:363. Shakabpa, *An Advanced Political History of Tibet*, again mentions the Black-hat monastery in a brief biographical sketch of the Second Dalai Lama, dating its founding in the earth-pig year, 1479 (I:366). This is the same year he gave for the founding of Yangs pa can (see footnote 32).

37. For a brief biographical sketch of Dge 'dun grub pa, see Kaschewsky, *The Life of the Lamaist Saint Tsong kha pa*, 222; Sangs rgyas rgya mtsho, *The Yellow Beryl*, 194–8; Shakabpa, *An Advanced Political History of Tibet*, I, 365–6.

38. Sangs rgyas rgya mtsho, *The Yellow Beryl*, 98.

39. Sangs rgyas rgya mtsho, *The Yellow Beryl*, 98. Shakabpa, *An Advanced Political History of Tibet*, dates this move to 'Bras spungs in the next year, 1495 (*An Advanced Political History of Tibet*, I:367).

40. Ye shes dpal 'byor, *The Auspicious Wish-Fulfilling Tree (Chronological Tables)*, 53; Tucci, *Tibetan Chronicles by Bsod nams grags pa*, 228; Tucci, *Tibetan Painted Scrolls*, II:654; Shakabpa, *An Advanced Political History of Tibet*, I:354, 367. On Skyor mo lung monastery, see Ferrari, *Guide to the Holy Places of Central Tibet*, 73, 167; Wylie, *The Geography of Tibet*, 77, 149.

41. Sangs rgyas rgya mtsho, *The Yellow Beryl*, 100; Shakabpa, *An Advanced Political History of Tibet*, I:367.

42. Ye shes dpal 'byor, *The Auspicious Wish-Fulfilling Tree (Chronological Tables)*, 54; Sangs rgyas rgya mtsho, *The Yellow Beryl*, 99; Shakabpa, *An Advanced Political History of Tibet*, I:367.

43. Ye shes dpal 'byor, *The Auspicious Wish-Fulfilling Tree (Chronological Tables)*, 55; Sangs rgyas rgya mtsho, *The Yellow Beryl*, 100.

44. Ye shes dpal 'byor, *The Auspicious Wish-Fulfilling Tree (Chronological Tables)*, 55; Sangs rgyas rgya mtsho, *The Yellow Beryl*, 100; Shakabpa, *An Advanced Political History of Tibet*, I:368.

45. Sangs rgyas rgya mtsho, *The Yellow Beryl*, 100; Ferrari, *Guide to the Holy Places of Central Tibet*, 98; Wylie, *The Geography of Tibet*, 152.

46. Hugh E. Richardson gives a brief description of his journey from Lhasa to Gyantsé by way of the Mtshur pu and Snye mo valleys in 1946 (Ferrari, *Guide to the Holy Places of Central Tibet*, 161).

47. According to Geshe Nawang Nornang, the canyon walls along the Gtsang po river between the 'U yug and Snye mo valleys are reportedly so steep in places that people can negotiate the narrow track, but animals cannot.

48. This is the route along which a highway was built in modern times. Geshe Nawang Nornang made the journey from Lhasa to Zhigatsé on this highway by motor vehicle in 1958.

49. Richardson, "The Karma pa Sect," 161–164; Wylie, *The Geography of Tibet*, 78, 150.

Chapter 17

CENTRAL TIBETAN CONFLICT IN THE
SIXTEENTH CENTURY

Guiseppe Tucci

This selection is drawn from Guiseppe Tucci's massive *Tibetan Painted Scrolls* (1948), probably the first Western effort at constructing a survey of the age of monastic hegemony (thirteenth to eighteenth centuries) in Central Tibetan history based on an extensive reading of a broad range of sources. His overarching narrative of Central Tibetan political history has essentially gone unchallenged since the publication of *Tibetan Painted Scrolls*; all subsequent scholarship has worked within this framework without upsetting it. Besides creating a coherent list of regimes—the monastic hegemons—that dominated Central Tibet in this period, what is probably most important about Tucci's account is that it presents a picture of Central Tibet as divided, even if dominated by one ruling family (in Tsang during the late sixteenth and early seventeenth centuries). Rather than a strong centralized state, we see a Central Tibet composed of many different states, something like the Holy Roman Empire in the same period. Central Tibet was plagued by guerrilla warfare and civil war, and many different alliances and strongholds vied for domination or simply tried to survive. The aggression of the Tsang governors and their Rinpung allies was turned against the old ruling family (the Pakmogru) and the newest religious order (the Gelukpa). Given the weakness of the Pakmogru and the lack of strong leadership, the Gelukpa order served as a focal point for resistance to Tsangpa rule. The successful military campaigns of the Tsang governors drove the leader of the Gelukpa, Sönam Gyatso, east from Trashilhünpo to Lhasa to Amdo, Mongolia, and the frontiers of China. He was soon honored with the title "Dalai Lama" and gained strong support for his cause among the Mongols. Whether or not it was his original intention, Sönam Gyatso's long missionary trip (lasting from 1578 until his death in 1588) through Amdo, Kham, and Inner Mongolia laid the foundations for a powerful Gelukpa influence on all these regions for centuries. Among the principal tools of this missionizing was the establishment of Gelukpa monasteries, as well as the incarnation lineages (Mong. *Khutugtu*) that sprang up wherever the monasteries were founded. Tucci's occasional use of terms such as "Lamaism," "the Lamaistic pantheon's supreme deities," "demonology," and "exorcisms" to describe Tibetan Buddhism and related practices are signs of his times, before the end of colonialism in Europe and its attendant demeaning of non-Christian religions.

In the year 1565 Karma Tseten, waging war with his son Pema Karpo as his associate, conquered Samdruptsé, a feud of Neudong[tsé], once assigned to Chonggyé, and later to the princes of Rinpung, who held it by force. Samdruptsé, corresponding to present-day Zhigatsé, was a very important place, lying in a fertile valley and commanding the highroads which met there between Northern Tsang and Ü and the regions north and south of the Tsangpo (Brahmaputra); thus not only did it have a great strategic value, but it was enriched by a prosperous market.

The possession of Samdruptsé meant not only that the Pakmodru had been finally excluded from Tsang, but also that Ü was more than ever exposed to invasion by the lords of Tsang. In 1575 they actually attacked Tsangrong, camped in Gel and then having occupied Gel, Jang and Mön, marched on Kyishö [near Lhasa], where they were stopped, the fifth Dalai Lama says, by the magic formulas of the *kuzhang* of Künzangtsé of Tsetang.[1] In that same year 1575 we find [the soon-to-be Third Dalai Lama] Sönam Gyatso as a peacemaker between the Zhamar and Yarlung.

As we have seen, no event is recorded which does not show, against the background of military events echoed in the biography and in pious narratives, the watchful and suspicious action of the two sects, now pitted one against the other in the fight for supremacy: the Yellow and the Reds.

If the Yellow Sect's prestige grew in Tibet from year to year, their fortune, as we have seen, awakened new suspicion on the Reds' part; they watched the course of events and were fatally led to strengthen their ties with the greatest military and political force then existing in the Land of Snows, the successors of the chiefs of Rinpung now settled in Samdruptsé.

On the other hand the Gelukpa, playing for safety, relied on the Mongols, thus encouraging their desire for expansion; at the same time, they flattered their vanity by naming them paladins of the faith and patrons of a culture much superior to their own, for which they felt a recent convert's boundless devotion. The Gelukpa at the same time claimed to be the apostles of the Buddha's word and believed they were renewing with Mongolia the daring of those Indian missionaries who, several centuries earlier, had brought the Buddha's word into Tibet's desert highlands.

Indeed Mongols and Tibetans have celebrated Sönam Gyatso as an apostle; historians speak of him as a brave propagator of the faith, who introduced a spirit of love and charity into hardened Mongol hearts and by his preaching inspired those restless tribes with mildness.

There is no doubt that his work was a result of evangelizing zeal; the golden times of Tibetan Buddhism were still a living example in men's memories and a monk educated on those glories would naturally be proud to vie with them, but the third Dalai Lama's mission was also inspired by considerations of a more worldly character. We must remember the conditions of Tibet at the time, torn by strife between sects and parties, broken up into a large number of principalities mutually jealous and always ready to take up arms.

Hence Sönam Gyatso's journey to Mongolia could not be simply an apostolic tour, but must be explained mainly by the Tibetan situation and the interests of the Gelukpa who had resolved to obtain help from the new converts, as soon as the threat against them should be about to break out violently.

When the Mongol prince Altan Khan and Sönam Gyatso met, they believed they were living over again Qubilai's and Pakpa's experiences. Both the Mongol chief and the abbot of Drepung were flattered by this return of the past: the former believed himself predestined to his ancestor's glory, while the latter anticipated he would obtain, in that troubled period, the support of a new power appearing on Tibet's frontiers. In whatever direction internal events and their relation with the Reds and with Tsang might develop, it was meanwhile to the Yellows' advantage to secure in Mongolia faithful devotees, who should descend upon Tibetan monasteries no longer as invaders but as pilgrims, not to prey but to offer gifts. Thus Sönam Gyatso's apostolic task was not an exclusively religious mission: it determined Tibet's future political and historical destinies, and we must therefore briefly follow its events, which we already know in their main lines; the subject is amply treated both by the Mongol historian Saghang Sechen and by Jikmé Rikpé Dorjé. The former was a great-grandson of one of the most eminent cooperators in the spread of the Gelukpa among the Mongols, namely Sechen Khung-Taiji.

The third Dalai Lama's biographer relates the same events sometimes alluding to details the other historians ignore; hence, by comparing the different versions, it will be possible to appraise more accurately Sönam Gyatso's religious and political action. Owing to him and to his counselors, the Yellow Sect finally gained the Mongols' support for its cause. We do not mean to say that the Mongols had not already come in contact with Lamaism, which on the contrary had reached several tribes and made converts among them; but conversions were sparse and wavering, divided between the Red Sect, which had a larger number of followers, and the Yellow Sect, which had appeared later and had not been so fortunate in its spread. A case, then, of limited infiltrations, incapable of influencing the Mongol way of life and of overcoming Shamanism, which reigned supreme: at the best, Buddhist islands, which would not prosper, abandoned to themselves in alien and often hostile surroundings, until they should be protected and fostered by the power of the strongest.

The first contact between Tibet and the Ordos had not been peaceful: already in 1573 Altan Khan had led an expedition against North-Eastern Tibet; this conflict however had led to spiritual contacts, for Altan Khan had brought back to his country some lamas, who had planted the first seeds of faith in the Mongol chief's heart. Even earlier, in 1566, Khutugtai Sechen Khung-Taiji of the Ordos had led another expedition, or rather a raid, against Tibet; according to Saghang Sechen its spiritual fruit was that some lamas were taken by him to his camp.[2] These are the meager facts chroniclers tell us: we can only guess what exchanges may then have come about between Tibet and the Ordos, what network of interests may have been established, what prospects of future gains, not merely spiritual but political, were opened up before both Mongols and Tibetans. It is certain anyhow that Khutugtai Sechen Khung-Taiji was influenced by Lamaism to the extent of convincing Altan Khan himself that its doctrines deserved to be received with greater favor. We know only the bare facts, but it is beyond doubt that at a moment when a new situation was being established in Mongolia strong political reasons must have backed the religious conversion. In 1573 the first mission to Drepung took place; beside the monks already mentioned, Dzogé Aseng Lama had arrived in 1571 (*chak luk*) in Altan Khan's headquarters and had spoken to him of the Yellow Sect's newly incarnated chief.[3] Acting on this monk's advice, Altan Khan now sent a mission with gifts and letters containing a formal invitation. Sönam Gyatso, after seriously taking counsel, answered by sending to the Mongol chief's court the master of monastic rules Tsöndrü Zangpo.

In 1577 new envoys arrived from Altan Gyelpo [Tibetan for "king"][4] and announced that the King, who was then in Tsokha (Kokonor) was again insisting that Sönam Gyatso should come to him and preach the Buddha's word; thus repeatedly invited, Sönam Gyatso set out.[5]

His meeting with the King took place on the fifteenth day of the fifth month of the year earth tiger (1578). On this occasion Altan Gyelpo was prodigal in his gifts to the lama: a mandala made of 500 ounces (*sang*) of silver; a golden bowl full of precious stones; white, yellow, red, green and blue silk, twenty bolts of each kind; a hundred horses, ten of which were white, their saddles ornamented with precious stones.

On this occasion the famous proclamation was made of the ethical laws laid down for the Mongols, modifying their cruel customs, forbidding the worship of "*öngön*" or images of the deceased and bloody sacrifices, particularly of horses and camels buried with the corpses of chiefs. Then, in the same spot where the king and the lama had met, a temple was built, which took the name of Tek-chen Chökor Ling: the Chöjé of Tongkor, Yönten Gyatso, was regularly ordained on this occasion.[6]

Next an exchange of titles took place: Sönam Gyatso received from the King the title of Dalai Lama vajradhara, and the King from the Lama that of Chökyi Gyelpo Lhetsangpa.[7]

The Dalai Lama had been covered with gifts, but Altan Khan did not forget the temples of Tibet and the great dignitaries faithful to the new school: he sent Aseng Lama at the head of a mission charged with the distribution of gifts to the Jowokhang in Lhasa, to the monasteries of Sera, Drepung and Ganden, and finally to the princes who had become the Yellow Sect's greatest patrons, namely to those of Tsetang, Gongkar, Gyari, Gamen, while invitations and honors were multiplied.[8]

Then Aseng Lama returned from Tibet, bringing letters from lamas and dignitaries, insisting that Sönam Gyatso should come home. The Dalai Lama did not consent, he wished to carry out his mission to the end. Altan Gyelpo went back to the Sokpo [Mongol] country and Sönam Gyatso went on as far as Litang with the object of founding a monastery there, and named as his representative in the Mongols' country the Tongkor Chöjé, Yönten Gyatso. In the eighth month of that same year embassies came from the Emperor Wanli,[9] bringing him a diploma duly sealed: he conferred upon Sönam Gyatso the title of protector of all lands, and invited him to his court.

This is the Tibetan version of the event; the Chinese version is less detailed: as a preceding attempt to get in touch with the Dalai Lama's predecessor had miserably failed, the court became careful and waited, according to the dynastic histories, until Sönam Gyatso, induced by Altan Khan, should himself seek the Emperor's favor and send him the prescribed gifts. But the prime minister was cautious and hesitated to accept them before the Emperor's consent had reached him. The memory was still fresh of Liu Yun's adventurous expedition: he had left Tibet to do homage to the other "living Buddha" Gendün Gyatso, and in consequence of the Tibetans' suspicions his mission came to grief: many officials of his retinue were killed, the survivors fled. Permission was now given to receive gifts, but nothing is said of titles conferred upon Sönam Gyatso, although it is recognized that the effective power of the Dalai Lama's office began with him and that the authority of other Tibetan chiefs, lay or ecclesiastical, declined and vanished before the Dalai Lama's prestige.[10]

Truly this is the very beginning, almost the premise, of the Yellow Sect's future power. Once having established the principle of incarnation, on which the theological domination exalting the chief of the new sect was founded, Sönam Gyatso remained nevertheless the abbot of Drepung; his prestige as a lama was far superior to his political authority, still scanty and questioned. Rivalry between sects had not been pacified nor the turbulent nobility's restlessness silenced. The function of Dalai Lama practically began only with [the Fifth Dalai Lama

Ngawang] Lozang Gyatso when, in a certain sense, Gushri Khan renewed in his favor the endowment conferred by Qubilai on the Sakya. Tibetan tradition is therefore mistaken when it carries the institution of the Dalai Lamas back to Gendün Drup's times, even before the title itself had been officially conferred, as we have seen, on Sönam Gyatso.

Let us go back to the latter and to his journeys. We see him now continuing to travel to Litang, Garchen in Dokham country, honored on the way by Epel Noyön, and then install the Chöjé Tsöndrü Zangpo as *lopön* of the Püntsok Namgyel Ling monastery. Passing through Janaktang he consecrated the temple of Litang, which had been built by the King of Jamsa Tamché,[11] on whom he conferred the name of Tupten Jamsem Chok Tamchelé Nampar Gyelwa.[12] The same King, in the year 1580, sent two envoys, Kapakshi[13] and Jaka, to invite him to his country. Then he went to Markham where he converted some Bönpo; next to Chamdo Jamling, Denchö Khorling and to the temple of Longtang Drönmé where he was in 1582.[14]

In the meantime, according to the last desire of the King, who had died a short time before, Mongol messengers came to the Dalai Lama to take him to Tsokha; Sönam Gyatso set out again for the North. Passing through Kumbum where he founded a school for the explanation of sacred texts, Jakhyung Drak, Riwo Dentik,[15] Dzomo khar where Jamchen Chöjé had dwelt, in 1584 he arrived in Gelgönpa; he then crossed Pakshingkün [in Gansu],[16] where he concluded a peace between warring Chinese and Hor, and Bakré, and got to Tsokha. There he was met by a delegation of about a thousand horsemen, headed by Dayan Noyan. Having traveled on the territory ruled by the Pön of the Ordos Sechen Khung-Taiji,[17] in the year 1585 he led Dayan Noyan to a deeper understanding of the Law.

The lord of Gurkar "the white tents" of the 40 great clans of the Sokpo [Mongols], invited him into his domains together with Jokhor Noyön;[18] on this occasion, beside preaching the Law he conferred baptism upon these neophytes. In 1586 he received messengers from Altan Khan's son During (Dügüräng) anxious to meet him; he took up his journey again towards the Machu [Yellow River] and arriving in Kökö-hoto (Kharngön, now Hohhot), inhabited by Tibetans and *drokpa* [nomads] together, he consecrated the images that Altan Gyelpo had built, putting the sacred formulas (*dhāraṇī, zung*) into them. The biography then tells how Namotai Khung-Taiji of Chakar (Chahar Mongols) came to meet him,[19] how he then continued towards the right wing (*yeru*) of the Tümed (Tumé Mongols) where he consecrated many temples. Having accomplished the funeral ceremonies in honor of Dügüräng who had died that year, he was loaded with gifts by Dorjé Gyelpo of the Halha[20] (Khalkha Mongols) and received envoys from Jokhor Noyön of the Urat (Oirat Mongols) and the chief of the Kharcheng (Qarachin Mongols) for whom he consecrated a temple.

In 1588 messengers from the Emperor of China finally arrived inviting him to his court and conferring upon him titles and the patent of Guanding Tai *gushri* [Chin. *guoshi*]. He was ready to accept the invitation, when in that same year death struck him down far from his country.

Thus the task Sönam Gyatso had undertaken with such enthusiasm abruptly came to an end. He had established personal relations with many chiefs, consecrated statues and temples, spread the Buddha's word. In the course of a few years the princes of the most important Mongol tribes had officially embraced Buddhism. At the moment of taking leave of Altan Khan, he had named a representative in the person of the Khutugtu of Tongkor, considered as an incarnation of Mañjuśrī; the King of Tümed's example had been followed by the Chahar chiefs and then by the Halha, with whom he installed the "Maidari" Khutugtu. Thus the Yellow Sect had spread among the Mongols with a speed which shows how easily permeable they were to new ideas and how slight was the opposition of Shamanism, which partly crumbled and partly became associated with the demonology and the exorcisms of Lamaism. But however great Sönam Gyatso's success may have been, it cannot be said that his task was completed. The foundations had been laid, but they had to be made fast, lest the fruits of his apostolic labors should be lost.

At that moment recourse was made to the theory of incarnation, so that the supreme ruler of the Gelukpa might carry out his task. No sooner had he died than he was said to have been born again in 1589 as the great grandson of Altan Khan.[21] We are certainly not in a condition to reconstruct the intrigues, which led to this birth of the Yellow Sect's supreme authority in the heart of the Mongol tribes, but the persons guaranteeing the incarnation to be authentic, the presence of the Tibetan court which had accompanied the deceased Sönam Gyatso to that same country during his journey, the official recognition by the envoys of the Tri Rinpoché of Ganden and by other dignitaries of Tibet proper, are facts from which we may assume that the Gelukpa sect had come up with well-laid plan.

The task begun by the third Dalai Lama had not yet yielded its fruits. The abbot of Drepung's rebirth in a princely family of Mongolia served above all to weld still more firmly together the relations between the Yellow Sect and its patrons and to lead towards new developments: the alliance between the young but already triumphant school and the power of Mongol arms. It was certainly not an unimportant event that the head of Tibetan Lamaism should now for the first time see the light in a Mongol tribe; thus the barriers existing between the Country of Snows and the new converts' homeland were broken down at one blow; neophytes became the equals of their masters in the identity of religion; differences of race, language and tradition were annulled and the numerous disasters which the Mongol hordes had repeatedly inflicted on Tibet with their sudden raids were forgotten. The Yellow Church received into its *oikoumene* even those frontier tribes which Tibet, up to that time, had feared or despised, and the tribes took pride in the official recognition of their religious maturity, on which the Dalai Lama's incarnation placed an unchallengeable seal. The new Dalai Lama's kinship guaranteed to the Gelukpa a powerful support in case of need: the Mongols had by now enthusiastically accepted the Buddhist preachings, reaching them through a double channel: the Reds and the Yellows. The prestige conferred upon Altan Khan's descendants by the birth in their midst of the supreme pontiff of a powerful and constantly ascending sect guaranteed the support of their arms, in case that Church were attacked, to which they were now bound by a link more direct than simple devotion.

The newly incarnated Dalai Lama's education was entirely Tibetan, as his guardians were Tibetans; but that the Mongols were flattered by the fact that one of the greatest Lamaist prelates should be of their race, is shown by the honor they did him; first of all, in 1591, by the King of the Tümed.[22]

In the eighth month of that same year the *kuzhang rinpoché* of Künzangtsé, many Tibetan *bhandé* [monks] and Sokpo [Mongols] headed by Mañju Chöjé,[23] kings, queens and Khung-Taiji arrived, each of them to invite him to his own country; finally messengers came from the king of Chahar, and later, when the child had reached Chörten Karpo,[24] Könchok Taiji. In his first years, his principal tutor was the Rinpoché Künzang Tsepa, who in his turn was a fast friend of the Chakdzö Gushri Penden Gyatso,[25] namely the Chakdzö of the third Dalai Lama, to whom the King of China, in 1579, when Sönam Gyatso had received his various titles, had given a Gushri's diploma.[26]

To bear out the miraculous rebirth, according to the prescribed rites, a conclave of the Yellow Sect, on the advice of Tri Rinpoché of Ganden, i.e., Penjor Gyatso of Gyelkhangtsé[27] sent this same Chakdzö as the most qualified person to verify if the child were really an incarnation of the deceased Lama, with whom he had lived in a continued familiarity, as no one else had. The Chakdzö then left Ü, with many delegates of the main Gelukpa monasteries and of the nobility, now supporters of the new sect. Among others there were envoys of the prince of Neudong[tsé], Gongma Miwangchuk Mipam Wanggyur Gyelpo Ngawang Sönam Drakpa Gyeltsen of the clan of Gongri Karpo, lord of all Tibet (*Gangchen namkyi gön chik*) and of the *zhapdrung* of Shün, the *sakyong* of Gyari, the *sakyong* of Ganden, etc. and many other *depön*, who all arrived in Kharngön (Kökö-hota) to meet the incarnated Lama and officially ratify his identity.[28] This took place in the year *chak lang*, 1601. It is obvious that, once the recognition had taken place, the child must be taken to Tibet; not only to receive there an education suited to his dignity, but also because he was the abbot of Drepung and as such it was incumbent upon him to take possession of his monastery. There he would lose all traces of his Mongol origin in the impersonal discipline of monastic life; but the Church would always be ready to use his kinship, if political circumstances required it. The Mongol alliance was now concluded and Tibet's future was marked.

The young Lama, following the road which runs outside the Great Wall of China, arrived in Tsokha (Kokonor) where he stayed for three months as a guest of the King Kholoché; next, although our sources do not give his itinerary, he was in Radreng and Taklung.[29] As he got nearer and nearer to his see, acts of homage became more frequent: the *sakyong* of Ganden Yülgyel Norbu came to meet him, with his son, then the Pönnyer Kudün Rinpoché Chözang Trinlepa of Ganden palace,[30] the Zhelngané Gendün Gyeltsen. When he arrived in Ganden Namgyel Ling and Rasa Trülnanggi Tsuklak Khang, the *sakyong* Trashi Rapten invited him in the feud of Ganden Khangsar, while the prince of Neudong Ngawang Sönam Drakpa and Gyelzangpa did him great honor.[31]

Having taken possession of the Ganden throne in the temple called Chok Tamchelé Nampar Gyelwé Ling, with a great concourse of monks from Sera, Drepung, Ganden, Kyormolung, he then went to Lhasa where he was solemnly initiated before Jowo's image by Ganden Tri Rinpoché Zurpa Zhelngané Sanggyé Rinchen, who acted as abbot (*khenpo*), by the Tri Rinpoché of Ganden as master (*loppön*) and as officiating priest (*letokpa*) the Zhelngané Gendün Gyeltsen.[32] He then took the name of Yönten Gyatso.

The fifth Dalai Lama and the biographers from whom he draws his narrative relate only the young Lama's triumphs and solemn receptions; but it is not certain that every one applauded this incarnation of the Gelukpas' supreme chief among the Mongols, which had suddenly called a foreigner to occupy the abbatial throne of the sect's greatest monastery. It is, perhaps, not improbable that the Tri Rinpoché of Ganden, when he used his great age as an excuse to avoid traveling to Mongolia with the object of confirming the new Dalai Lama's incarnation, did not entirely approve of what had been prepared. Probably it was for this reason that he sent the Chakdzö Gushri in his stead. But as soon as the Dalai Lama came to Tibet, even if such doubts were felt, nothing transpired.

It is natural that the Red Caps and the rulers of Tsang should be surprised and uneasy when they saw how the Yellow Sect was spreading among the Mongols, how the most powerful Mongol chiefs went over to them and what favor the new school enjoyed among them. The situation had completely changed; while the Mongol supporters of the Reds were steadily decreasing and the sect's former penetration among them had given no fruit, we see in the course of a few years, since Altan Khan's invitation, Tümed, Chahar and Ordos under the Gelukpa's influence. Their religious dependence implied the possibility of political developments whose consequences could not but preoccupy Tsang. Up to what point could the Yellows turn their converts' devotion to their own advantage, to get rid of their rivals once for all? It was no longer a case of friction between internal forces, which might have balanced each other; new possibilities were coming to the fore. Might not the Mongols invade Tibet on their new patrons' invitation, and become their temporal arm? This being the case, Tsang went warily, for by this time it could only count on Tibetan forces and on noble families and convents hostile to the Gelukpa. The object was to gain time. No wonder then that the supreme representatives of the Red Sect did not abstain from congratulating the new Dalai Lama. The fifth Dalai Lama relates that the

Garchenné Zhamar Garwang Chökyi Wangchuk[33] wrote him a letter of congratulations (*lekjé zhushok*)[34] which, as we shall see, gave occasion to the conflict which violently broke out a little later between the two sects. The letter was written according to the subtlest rules of rhetoric, in which the Zhamar was past master, but it contained certain passages covertly urging the Dalai Lama to study deeply; these aroused the Yellow Sect's resentment. The Dalai Lama, they said, will take complete vows at the age of twenty, and he will certainly study under the masters chosen to instruct him, but as an incarnation of his predecessor, his knowledge is complete and needs no offers of guidance. Thus the letter, whether it had been written with a disparaging intention or not, hurt the Gelukpa's feelings; although well versed in logic and religion, they had no one capable of rivaling the Zhamar in rhetoric, hence, after long debates, Tsekhapa Depa Gyelchenpa and the Zhukhen Rapjampa Gelek Lhündrup were called upon to compose an answer.[35]

Meanwhile Yönten Gyatso, according to the example of his predecessors and accepting invitations from princes and monasteries, began to travel throughout the whole of Tibet.[36] The object of these journeys was propaganda: to establish direct relations and surround the head of the Yellow Sect with sympathies and support, which might be counted upon when the crisis, which was felt by all to be impending, should break out. That the above-mentioned families had invited him does not mean they all definitely sided with the Gelukpa; in Tibet the heads of monasteries, reincarnated personages and famous lamas enjoy such prestige, and their miraculous powers excite such awe, that any clan able to do so is anxious to receive them as guests and to load them with gifts, no matter to which sect they belong. No wonder, then, that the young Dalai Lama should also tour in Tsang, which was ruled as a feud by its chiefs, now completely independent from Ü, which had become increasingly powerful and menacing. The invitation naturally came both from the ecclesiastical authorities of Trashilhünpo and from the lay authorities living under the new monastery's influence. The latter sent as its official envoy Dradül of Shartsé. Yönten Gyatso naturally had many good reasons not to ignore this invitation: Trashilhünpo was the Yellow Sect's outpost in Tsang, the symbol and the bulwark of the much-opposed school, in a country where the old convents were gaining new vigor, supported by the prudent generosity of the new kings ruling from Samdruptsé; Trashilhünpo's fortunes would naturally have a great interest for the chiefs of the Gelukpa; this journey furnished them with a pretext and an occasion to watch closely the *desi* of Tsang's ventures, to get an idea of his intentions, to see if it was possible to reach an agreement or whether open war was unavoidable.[37]

Let us omit the religious events, ceremonies and sermons recorded on this occasion: the fifth Dalai Lama dwells on them at length and Jikmé Rikpé Dorjé accurately summarizes them. But it is worth recalling that during this visit Yönten Gyatso is said to have converted to his doctrine the wife of the *desi* of Tsang Püntsok Namgyel; she belonged to the Yargyap family.[38]

From these times on, Trashilhünpo's position in the general plan of the Yellow Sect appears clearly: the Panchen Rinpoché, as its abbots were called later on, held aloof from any effective political activity, which he left to the monasteries of Ü, particularly to the one in Drepung, which up to the foundation of the Potala by the fifth Dalai Lama, remained the Gelukpa's active capital. The Panchen claimed for himself supreme spiritual authority, he became the Dalai Lama's guide and master, but he left the management of political affairs to the latter and to his monasteries in Ü. This policy, which later became traditional for the abbots of Trashilhünpo, is certainly due, in part, to the fact that it was in a territory far removed from the school's center, in the country most hostile to the Yellows, a short distance from Samdruptsé, the capital of Tsang.[39]

When Yönten Gyatso got back to Drepung, he met there the Tri Rinpoché Könchok Chöpel,[40] who was to have such a share in future events, as the fifth Dalai Lama's assistant, while from Kokonor new visitors arrived, like Lhatsün Chewa, the son of Kholoché, and Sechen Taiji.

Meanwhile friction with the Karmapa became more acute; as it is always the case when suspicion and ill-will stand between opposite parties and groups, on both sides every pretext was taken to excite men's spirits. Since 1605 the Pakmodrupa, together with the Zhokarnak and others, had raided the camp of the *depa* of Kyishö. The latter then had recourse to arms making the situation more tense, and furnishing new motives for spite between the adverse parties, who took this occasion to vent their accumulated ill-will. We have already seen how, when Yönten Gyatso had come to Tibet from Mongolia, the Zhamar had written him a gratulatory letter in verse which, rightly or wrongly, had been taken in bad part by Zhukhen Rapjampa Gelek Lhündrup; the Zhamar and his secretary Jamyang retaliated, when they got to Lhasa, by writing on silken scrolls hung in front of the Jowo's statue some obscure hints, in an enigmatic form, which were interpreted, when the news was brought to Drepung, as an insult to the Yellow Sect.[41]

Everyone understood that any chance of an agreement had vanished, for the rivals were far too embittered; an open conflict might break out at any moment, any pretext would have sufficed. So the quarrel was renewed concerning certain land in Neu, which Dönyö Dorjé, many years before, had annexed at the instigation of the Zhamar Chödrak Gyatso, founding upon it the *gönpa* [monastery] of Sanakmar. Hence the Gelukpa had suffered great anxiety: they considered the Tsang garrison, in the very heart of their country, a serious menace against their stronghold. Strife was again breaking out on account of that monastery: the prince of Ganden Yülgyel Norbu tried to get back the land and to take possession of the convent; peace was broken: the fifth Dalai Lama lays the initiative at the door of the *desi* of Yar Tsang, but it is natural that, ruling over those lands, the latter should take up arms when confronted by an attempt to wrest them from him. Indeed elsewhere Lopzang Gyatso openly says that in the year 1612[42] an armed coalition was formed by Neudongtsé against the ruler of Tsang, Püntsok Namgyel; Lhagyari, Ja, Yargyap and Chonggyé took part in it. But sources belonging to a different faction, like that of the Sakyapa, protected and favored by the chief of Tsang, say that in 1607 they had recourse to arms in order to beat back an army of Sokpo [Mongols] who had been invited to invade Tibet by Kyishö, and that, although he conquered in 1612–13 a large part of Tibet, from Jang and Nyangtö to Latö and Ü, he could not lay down his arms because his rivals continually broke the peace; this was to be secured only in 1622–23.[43]

The Pakmodrupa had the worst; they lost their old capital Neudong[tsé] and were obliged to give up their feud of Sacha Dzong. But the appearance of the Mongols on the frontier put an end to the military operations which the old nobility was carrying on with the idea of supporting its own interests, while it was actually playing into the hands of the great religious sects.

Meanwhile, as these events were developing in rapid succession, Yönten Gyatso had gone back to Sera[44] and then in 1611 to Drepung, where he performed, together with other lamas particularly versed in the rites of exorcism, great magical ceremonies to ward off incumbent perils.

In Tibet the frontiers between the real and the imaginary are so vague, that an admixture ensues: the invisible forces of prayer and magic ritual are considered more powerful and efficient than material weapons. In moments of extreme danger, men invoke the protection of the Lamaistic pantheon's supreme deities, particularly the terrific deities which obey the manifestations of Jikché represented in a warlike aspect as a defender of Tibet's menaced faith. Hence we must not wonder that the Yellow Sect, in such a moment of extreme peril, when the ruler of Tsang seemed extremely powerful, had recourse to magic in order to obtain the help of the secret forces regulating the world's destinies. And the incumbent danger was truly serious. In 1611 the chief of Tsang, Püntsok Namgyel, attacked and defeated the prince of Yargyap[45] and came to Lhasa, threatening many monasteries, which were barely saved by Könchok Chöpel's intervention.[46] He came to Lhasa not as a conqueror but rather as a visitor to his own domains; the city had passed under Tsang rule a long time before and did not definitely come into the Yellows' hands until the fifth Dalai Lama's times. It must not be forgotten that the Red Caps excluded the Gelukpa from the celebration of the new year *Mönlam*; this sentence must have been confirmed by some measure on the part of temporal authority, which can have been no other than the kings of Tsang, zealous patrons of the Karmapa. Should we stand in need of further proofs, they are to be found in another passage by the same fifth Dalai Lama who says that (perhaps with the intention of improving relations between the Karmapa and the Gelukpa) Tsang, in 1612[47] gave Lhasa to the Ganden Podrang. He had the power to do so, because Lhasa was his territory, ruled by one of his *nyerpa*; one of them was Rapjampa Chömpel.

Having thus come to Lhasa, the *desi* of Tsang wished to be initiated into the 108 rules of Tsepakmé. By thus propitiating the heads of the Yellow Sect, he wished to consign to oblivion the ill-will that war was arousing, and to obtain the good graces of the Gelukpa, who were already preparing to bind an alarming alliance with the Mongols. The ruler of Tsang's request caused a great sensation among the Geluks' followers, who had gathered in Lhasa on this occasion; Yönten Gyatso's court was wavering, but finally decided to refuse, because the Rapjam Sönam Drakpa stated that the *desi's* request could not be granted, since he was an enemy of the Gelukpa doctrines. Though the biography does not say it so plainly, the consequence was that Yönten Gyatso had to seek a safer abode; we accordingly find him in Samyé, seeking refuge in the reliable protection of his tutelary deities, the Tensung and Pekar.[48] Confronted by an armed foe, the lamas had no allies except the almighty divinities on whom, since Padmasambhava's times, the defense of the Law had been conferred, according to legend.

Meanwhile Könchok Chöpel lost no time in gathering round the Gelukpa other monasteries having a noble history in Tibet's religious tradition. Due to this policy, in 1614, the *depa* of Ganden invited and got in touch with the *zhapdrung* of Taklung, Ngawang Namgyel.[49] Taklung was one of Tibet's most ancient convents, it had a glorious history and unlike other Tibetan holy places had remained untouched by the invasions which at various times had laid the country waste. What is more, it was a Kagyüpa convent, which had kept faith with old traditions, but without going to extremes and still preserving many contacts with the Kadampa; this made an understanding with the Gelukpa easier, and their relations had become very close ever since the times of Sönam Gyatso.[50]

While these events were taking place, some great religious dignitaries from Mongolia, on the Chinese frontier (*Gya Sok*), Dotö and Domé, arrived in Lhasa.[51] Among them was Gyelwa Gyatso, *zhapdrung* of Tongkor, Pakpa Chökyi Gyelpo, Pakpa Lhünchok, the incarnated of Baso and others.

Their visit was a matter of politeness and homage; they brought gifts and asked for religious initiations, but the bare lists of visitors preserved by chronicles hide more important events; we can easily imagine, even if information is so scanty, how many relations were thus established, how many messages were exchanged through visitors and how many agreements were entered upon, while the ruler of Tsang and his troops penetrated the Ü region, an impending menace for the Yellow Sect and an obstacle to the fulfillment of its ambitions.

Meanwhile Yönten Gyatso had grown in years, but kept aloof from these rapidly occurring events: studious and addicted to a life of devotion he seems to have left all negotiations and intrigues in the hands of the court dignitaries, who acted on his behalf and perhaps apart from him.

In 1614 he received the supreme ordination and finished his religious education under the Panchen Rinpoché, the Tri Rinpoché Sanggyé Rinchen, the Tri Rinpoché Gendün Gyeltsen, the Zhelngané Chönyer Drakpa, the Zimkhang Gong Trülku and many other famous scholars and masters.[52] A little later the Tongkhor Trülku Jamyang Gyatso arrived with many pilgrims.[53] But internal strife showed no sign of subsiding; in those years Dechen Drakkar and other places were incorporated by the *desi* of Tsang, who was then at the height of his power. The menace of its rivals was closing round the Yellow Sect; a large part of the Ü nobility, fearing for its own fortunes, hesitated.[54]

In 1616 according to the biographer, an embassy arrived, headed by Sönam Lodrö, whom the emperor of China[55] is said to have sent to Yönten Gyatso to confer upon him the title of *Khyapdak Dorjé Sanggyé* with its diploma. The envoys, who naturally brought precious gifts, were received in the assembly hall of Drepung.[56] We find these things in the Tibetan chronicles, but the *History of the Ming* (*Mingshi*) has no record of the embassy.

Tibet's internal situation was growing worse: the *desi* of Tsang was carrying out his hegemonic plans with tireless energy; the Yellow Sect saw many of its patrons conquered and trampled on by the armed forces of Tsang. In 1616 the whole territory of Kyishö had been brought into subjection and Neudong had submitted, so that a large part of Ü and most of Tsang were under the *desi's* unchallenged sway.

The Yellows were in a difficult position: it was due to their insistence that a Mongol army commanded by two of Kholoché's sons entered Tibet and induced the *desi* of Tsang to behave less aggressively; it does not seem that any fighting occurred.

During these happenings, while many misgivings and fears were abroad, Yönten Gyatso died, still young in the twelfth month of 1616, during a very dangerous crisis for the Yellow Sect's career.

The events we have related all center around the vicissitudes of a few eminent families or of the greater convents, but we must not let them delude us into a belief that the small states whose names do not appear in these pages lived peacefully. Even if they did not side with one or the other warring sect or faction, these lesser states were moved to take up arms by long-standing enmities. We can learn many things of this kind from the biography of Künga Rinchen, the Sakyapa lama, who is remembered in history as the reconstructor of the Sakyapa temples and monasteries damaged by warfare or crumbling with age. Reading the story of his life we can see that Tsang, in the middle of the fifteenth century was torn by continual guerrilla warfare.

The Sakyapa, remembering their former greatness, had claims to support; among their obstinate rivals we see the *depa* of Lhakhang Chenmo and the *depa* of Lhasa Dzong. The former was the governor of the Great Monastery which had been turned into a fortress, in the plain to the south of the Drum-chu, which crosses the city of Sakya. Was this governor an official of the Pakmo-dru, as in the times of Jangchup Gyeltsen and of his immediate successors? We have no reason to deny it, but no way of ascertaining it. Neither can we reach any certainty regarding Lhasa Dzong, unless we are to identify this place with Lhatsé on the Tsangpo, not far from Sakya, to the west of Zhigatsé. But whoever these enemies of Sakya may have been, we see them so much more powerful, that they could force the Sakyapa abbot Künga Rinchen to flee from his see and repair to Ü, accepting the abbatial see of another monastery in Nalendra (north of Lhasa); we also find the ancient sympathies for the Sakya stubbornly surviving the vicissitudes of those times, and the princes of Jang and Gyantsé levying troops and rushing to defend the head of the sect, vanquish his enemies, overthrow Lhasa Dzong, restore his former possessions to Künga Rinchen and then Panam, Norbü Khyungtsé, and Drongtsé join in the fight. We then see that friendship waning on the death of the princes of Jang and Gyantsé, the latter passing for a short time to other alliances, and while the might of Gyantsé was crumbling, become the patron of the Sakyapa lamas Zhingshak [Tseten] Dorjé, lord of Samdruptsé, the ancestor of the future Tsang dynasty. In these pages we also find interesting information concerning other wars in which a large part of the Nyang region was implicated, for the succession to the throne of Panam;[57] several princes tried to seize it by armed force, while the abbot of Ngor Könchok Lhündrup protected it. We also find in these records proof of the progressive disappearance of the smaller states absorbed by the larger ones. In the restricted horizon within which these historians and hagiographers moved, every petty incident disturbing their lives acquired a particular relief, and they were inclined to consider it a great event, but in reality these wars were simple encounters between a few armed bands, and the occasion of these warlike exploits was very often quite insignificant: quarrels over grazing rights or limits between different estates, usurpations of pasture grounds (*drok*). In the biographies such small episodes troubling the life of feuds and petty states, reflect the illusion that some aftermath of their ancient greatness was still left to them, and thus arouse a certain interest. Anyhow, whatever way one looks, in Ü and Tsang, peace was nowhere to be found. Nor were internal struggles lacking, like those which had shaken the Pakmodrupa and substantially contributed to their rapid decay. Even in lesser states, like Jang, north of the Brahmaputra, at the end of the sixteenth century internal strife broke out, through the enmity of two factions: Dar and Dong, related by marriage to the Pön of Jang's family; they ended with the defeat of the Dar who, having been vanquished in battle, had the city and their estates sacked by the Dong; the latter, according to the pious biographer who is my source for these events, were protected by the magic arts and defensive ceremonies of the Sakyapa lama, Sönam Wangpo.[58] Not even Gyantsé, now reduced to a small principality in the shadow of its great monastery, was spared internal quarrels, like that recorded by Tāranātha in his autobiography,[59] which furnished the powerful lords of Samdruptsé a pretext to set things right by a military expedition; as they had already done with Norbü Khyungtsé, a citadel ruled by descendants of the celebrated *chögyel* of Gyantsé, whose possession had strategic value.[60]

Thus on one side we see Ü more and more attached to the Yellow Church, the old local nobility, weakened and without a chief, gathered round the sect, and the latter spreading among the Mongols and finding there new patrons and defenders. On the other hand Tsang was cutting loose from the Pakmodrupa, becoming independent, associating with the Reds and taking up its position against the Yellows, lending a religious color to conflicting interests and political rivalries. At the same time the aristocracy did not disarm or give in, indeed it clung almost stubbornly to its old enmities so that, when the moment came to unite for the defense of its very existence against invasion, it was found to be weakened, exhausted and failing.

NOTES

1. Ngag dbang blo bzang rgya mtsho, the Fifth Dalai Lama (1617–1682), *Rje btsun thams cad mkhyen pa bsod nams rgya mtsho'i rnam thar dngos grub rgya mtsho'i shing rta* [Life of the Third Dalai Lama, Sönam Gyatso (1544–1588)], in *The Collected Works (Gsung-'bum) of the Vth Dalai Lama, Ngag dbang blo bzang rgya mtsho*, vol. 8 (Nya) (Gangtok: Sikkim Research Institute of Tibetology, 1992), 89a.

2. Saghang Sechen [Ssanang Ssetsen], *Geschichte der Ost-Mongolen und ihres Fürstenhauses, verfasst von Ssanang Ssetsen Chungtaidschi der Ordus* [History of the Eastern Mongols], ed. and trans. Isaak Jakob Schmidt (St. Petersburg, 1829), 212.

3. Ngag dbang blo bzang rgya mtsho, *Life of the Third Dalai Lama*, 88a.

4. Whose head was A to sa dar kan (see Georg Huth, ed. and trans., *Geschichte des Buddhismus in der Mongolei: Aus dem Tibetischen des Jigs-med nam-mk'a* [sic: 'Jigs med rig pa'i rdo rje] *herausgegeben* [History of Buddhism in Mongolia] [Strassburg: K. J. Trübner, 1892, 1896], 2:214; Saghang Sechen, *History of the Eastern Mongols*, 225). The mission also comprised representatives of Sechen Khung-Taiji (Huth, *History of Buddhism in Mongolia*, 2:214; Saghang Sechen, *History of the Eastern Mongols*, 225). Saghang Sechen, intent on increasing the family's merits, says that the invitation to Altan Khan was made precisely on his great-grandfather's advice.

5. Ngag dbang blo bzang rgya mtsho, Fifth Dalai Lama, *Life of the Third Dalai Lama*, 90. The biography has preserved a schematic but interesting itinerary, whose chief points it will be well to summarize; Tshal zur khang, Dga' ldan rnam par rgyal ba'i gling, 'Phan yul, Rwa sgrengs. In this place to the northeast of Lhasa, he sent back many of the lamas and dignitaries who had accompanied him, namely the Dga' ldan khri rin po che, the *slob dpons* of Se ra and 'Bras spungs, the *rin po che* of Bod mkhar, the Paṇ chen Rig pa seng ge of Gtsang, Sangs rgyas ye shes of Dben sa, Bkra shis rin chen, Nam mkha' byams pa, a master of Yar lungs, the *sde pa* of Gong dkar and Bkra shis rab brtan, who was *sa skyong* of Brag dkar. Next, after a stop in Rwa sgrengs, the journey continued towards Smab thang, where some more of those who accompanied him went back, like Lha btsun Bsod nams dpal bzang po, the Rin po che of Kun bzang rtse, invested with the office of Ma chen. Then, passing through camps of *'brog pa*, Bsod nams rgya mtsho reached the 'Bri chu (i.e., the upper branch of the Yangzi Jiang) at Ngam tsho stod, i.e., Nga ring tsho, Rma chu, the branch of the Huang He born out of that lake. On the bank of the Dmar nag river, the Dpon Dger

rgyas met him to do him honor; then he arrived in Ag chen thang, where many Mongols offered him rich gifts (Ngag dbang blo bzang rgya mtsho, the Fifth Dalai Lama, *Life of the Third Dalai Lama*, 93a) and then to Rma chen spom ra, viz., to the main course of the Rma chu, where Sangs rgyas skyab, *dpon* of that place, welcomed him with great celebrations. After this Altan Khan's first envoys came to meet him with about 800 horsemen: to this group belonged: Yong sha bui [*sic*] Bar ku tai ji, Kha than pā thur, Ma zin pakshi the Mthu med (Saghang Sechen, *History of the Eastern Mongols*, 227: chatan Bagbatur, Mahācin baksi) followed by a great crowd which had gathered there. Bsod nams rgya mtsho went on to A rig dkar po thang, where they offered him 1,000 horses and 1,000 heads of sheep, up to Hang nge, where he consecrated the temple of Phun tshogs rnam rgyal gling, recently built (Ngag dbang blo bzang rgya mtsho, the Fifth Dalai Lama, *Life of the Third Dalai Lama*, 94a). Then great Mongol dignitaries arrived to meet him: about 3,000 persons, headed by Sechen Khung-Taiji and Dayan Noyan, both of royal lineage. He continued his journey through the territory of As dpal no yon, then, as he got nearer and nearer to the place where Altan rgyal po was waiting for him, meetings and rich homages succeeded one another more frequently. Finally the Chos rje Brtson grus bzang po came to receive him with all honors, whom he had previously sent to Altan's court, and the Lo tsā ba Gu shri pak shi who acted as interpreter.

6. Viz., the so-called Tongkor Khutugtu.

7. On the occasion of the temple's consecration there was a fresh exchange of gifts: a diadem (*dbu rgyan*) of gold, a vase, the tiara with the symbols of the five supreme Buddhas, implements for the liturgy of baptism, like the vase for blessed water, etc., a seal made out of a *srang* of gold having engraved upon it the figure of a five-clawed dragon and the inscription, in Mongol characters *Rdo rje 'chang ta la'i bla ma tham ka*, "seal of the Ta la'i bla ma Vajradhara" . . . its container of silver, a cape ornamented with pearls, yellow silk mantles, ornamented with five-taloned dragons' claws, internally lined with leather (*'bol rgan: bol gong, bol gar*, see Sarat Chandra Das, *A Tibetan-English Dictionary* [Delhi: Motilal Banarsidass, 1973], s.v. and Berthold Laufer, "Loan Words in Tibetan," *T'oung Pao*, second series, 17, no. 4/5 [1916]: 49, 166), a waistcoat of yellow silk *tābun*, lined internally with leather, pillows and such things.

8. Ngag dbang blo bzang rgya mtsho, the Fifth Dalai Lama, *Life of the Third Dalai Lama*, 97a.

9. In the text: Wan yi.

10. This is how Zhang Tingyu, et al., *Mingshi* [*History of the Ming*] (Shanghai: Commercial Press, 1930–37), chap. 231, 4a, relates these events. "Then (first Zhengde year, 1506) the Emperor was deceived by recent rumors, according to which in Dbus and Gtsang there was a monk who was able to know the three times: the men of that country called him a living Buddha. The Emperor was glad and wished to know him and he examined the ancient events when, in the times of Yongle and Xuande, Chen Cheng and Hou Xian entered the barbarians' country (Tibet). (The Emperor) ordered the eunuch Liu Yun to go and meet him. The Minister Liangchu (on whom see Zhang Tingyu, *History of the Ming*, chap. 190) and others said, "The teachings pre-

vailing in Tibet (Xifan) are bad and do not correspond to those of the Classics. The Court of our ancestors sent envoys (in those countries) and this took place because, as in those times the world began to be well-ordered, it intended, through those (envoys), to educate fools and check barbarians. (Our ancestors) did not believe in the doctrines of those (peoples) and did not respect them.

"Later, there was peace and many emperors succeeded one another for many generations; only, as (the barbarians) sent envoys to the court, they offered gifts (in exchange), but they never lightly sent their envoys to travel in those lands. Now, if this eunuch is suddenly sent as an official envoy to honor those monks, the court and people, seeing this, will be astonished and (the eunuch) Yun will ask up to several tens of thousands of measures of salt and will begin to ask that hundreds of horses and boats be given him. He will naturally smuggle salt, harassing the stations, and he will wrong officers and private persons. Now in (Sichuan) brigandage seems to have subsided; epidemics do not yet arise, the officers have no reserves, but he will certainly wish to extort money wrongfully from military men and from the people. The latter will bravely give themselves up to adventures. Once more brigands will appear. Moreover, when from Tianchuan (now Tianchuan Xian, in Sichuan) and from Liufan one crosses the frontier, it is necessary to travel for several tens of thousands of *li*, for the space of several years. But on the high roads there are absolutely no mail stations. Where then will they rest? If in the middle of the roads they meet with brigands, how can they defend themselves? This is tantamount to insulting China's prestige, and receiving insults from barbarous foreigners. Such a thing is not possible. We cannot write the letters the emperor has ordered us to write . . .

"The emperor paid no attention (to these representation[s]. When Liu Yun arrived) . . . the living Buddha (Dge 'dun rgya mtsho) fearing that China should wish to harm him, went into hiding and did not show himself. The officials became angry and wanted to take him by force. By night the barbarians attacked them. Two officers fled and about a hundred men died. The wounded were half as many. Yun, riding a fast horse, rapidly fled, thus avoiding death. When he got to Chengdu, he forbade them to speak (of what had happened) and reported to the emperor in an untruthful letter. When the letter arrived, the Emperor Wuzong [d. 1521] had died. Shizong called Yun back and handed him to the judges for punishment.

"In the Jiajing period (1522–1567) the Fawang sent several times offerings of tributes, which came uninterruptedly to Shizong's court. At that time there was (in Tibet) the monk Suonan Jianzuo (Bsod nams rgya mtsho) who knew the past and the future. They called him the living Buddha. The Shunyi wang Anda (Altan Qaghan) held him in great consideration and had much faith in him. In the seventh year of the Wanli period (1579) with the pretext of going to meet the living Buddha, (marching) westward he invaded Wala (Kalmuks, see Zhang Tingyu, *History of the Ming*, chap. 328) but he was defeated. This monk turned him from his inclination to slay and advised him to return to the East. Anda also induced this monk to establish relations with China; from Ganzhou (today Zhangye in Gansu), he sent a letter to Zhang Zhuzheng (the Chief Minister of the Emperor Wanli; Zhang Tingyu, *History of the*

Ming, chap. 213, 14–22) giving himself the name of Shijia Muni Biqui (Śākyamuni Bhikṣu) and, trying to establish with China the relations of a tributary, he sent cere-monial gifts. Zhuzheng dared not accept them and informed the emperor. The latter ordered the gifts to be accepted and allowed that tribute. From that time China knew that there was a living Buddha. This monk possessed extraordinary capacities, by which he was able to subdue men. All the barbarians followed his teaching. Then the Dabao fawang and the Shanhua wang and the other princes revered him and called themselves his disciples. From this time the Western countries acknowledged them-selves obedient to this monk. The barbarian princes had then a nominal authority and were no longer able to issue orders. . . ."

11. King Sa tham is a descendant of one of Ge sar's rivals (see Alexandra David-Neel, *La vie surhumaine de Gésar de Ling* [*The Superhuman Life of Gesar of Ling*] [Paris: Adyar, 1935], 264). The scene upon which these events are said to have taken place is, according to Mme. David-Neel, the Lijiang region, north of Yunnan, Zhong-dian and Adunze. According to Blo bzang rgya mtsho, the country of 'Jam should be placed a little more to the north, towards Batang/Litang (on the relations between Sa tham of 'Jam and the third Dalai Lama see Saghang Sechen, *History of the Eastern Mongols*, 241). The Bum nag thang is in the environs of the Bum la, west of the Yangzi Jiang.

12. Ngag dbang blo bzang rgya mtsho, the Fifth Dalai Lama, *Life of the Third Dalai Lama*, 100a.

13. But in the text: bha si.

14. Ngag dbang blo bzang rgya mtsho, the Fifth Dalai Lama, *Life of the Third Dalai Lama*, 102b.

15. Ngag dbang blo bzang rgya mtsho, the Fifth Dalai Lama, *Life of the Third Dalai Lama*, 102b.

16. 'Phags pa shing kun has nothing to do with the one of Nepal.

17. The latter is the great-grandfather of the Mongol historian Saghang Sechen; he died in 1581, a year after this visit of Bsod nams rgya mtsho. Antoine Mostaert, *Or-dosica*, Bulletin of the Catholic University of Peking, no. 9 (Peking: Catholic Univer-sity of Peking, 1934), 56. On this visit see Saghang Sechen, *History of the Eastern Mongols*, 249. Dayan Noyan was a Tümed chief.

18. The same as 'Ombu C'uhur-Noyon, in Huth, *History of Buddhism in Mongolia*, 1:143, 2:228.

19. Saghang Sechen, *History of the Eastern Mongols*, 255, Amutai Chungtaidschi.

20. Saghang Sechen, *History of the Eastern Mongols*, 225, Nomun Jeke wadschra Chagan.

21. Cfr. Huth, *History of Buddhism in Mongolia*, 1:59, 233; Saghang Sechen, *History of the Eastern Mongols*, 257; Henry Serruys, "Pei-lou Fong-sou: Les coutumes des es-claves septentrionaux de Siao Ta-Heng" [The Customs of the Northern Slaves], *Mon-umenta Serica* 10 (1945): 139.

22. Blo bzang rgya mtsho's spelling is always uncertain: now Thu med, now Mthu med.

23. Ngag dbang blo bzang rgya mtsho, the Fifth Dalai Lama, *'Jig rten dbang phyug thams cad mkhyen pa yon tan rgya mtsho dpal bzang po'i rnam par thar pa nor bu'i 'phreng ba* [*Life of the Fourth Dalai Lama Yönten Gyatso (1589–1616)*], in *The Collected Works (Gsung-'bum) of the Vth Dalai Lama, Ngag dbang blo bzang rgya mtsho*, vol. 8 (Nya) (Gangtok: Sikkim Research Institute of Tibetology, 1992), 14a.

24. Ngag dbang blo bzang rgya mtsho, the Fifth Dalai Lama, *Life of the Fourth Dalai Lama*, 14b.

25. Ngag dbang blo bzang rgya mtsho, the Fifth Dalai Lama, *Life of the Fourth Dalai Lama*, 16a.

26. Ngag dbang blo bzang rgya mtsho, the Fifth Dalai Lama, *Life of the Third Dalai Lama*, 99. [Editor's note: Gushri represents Chinese *guoshi*, meaning "dynastic preceptor," though by this time it had become merely another high religious title, rather than indicating a direct relationship of teacher and student between a lama and an emperor.]

27. Ngag dbang blo bzang rgya mtsho, the Fifth Dalai Lama, *Life of the Fourth Dalai Lama*, 16a.

28. Ngag dbang blo bzang rgya mtsho, the Fifth Dalai Lama, *Life of the Fourth Dalai Lama*, 16b.

29. Ngag dbang blo bzang rgya mtsho, the Fifth Dalai Lama, *Life of the Fourth Dalai Lama*, 21a.

30. Ngag dbang blo bzang rgya mtsho, the Fifth Dalai Lama, *Life of the Fourth Dalai Lama*, 22b.

31. Ngag dbang blo bzang rgya mtsho, the Fifth Dalai Lama, *Life of the Fourth Dalai Lama*, 23–24.

32. Ngag dbang blo bzang rgya mtsho, the Fifth Dalai Lama, *Life of the Fourth Dalai Lama*, 27a.

33. He was the religious patron of princes of Sam 'grub rtse; he was invited, together with his son, by the three sons of Zhing bshag Tshe brtan rdo rje, the founder of the princes of Gtsang's dynasty.

34. Ngag dbang blo bzang rgya mtsho, the Fifth Dalai Lama, *Life of the Fourth Dalai Lama*, 29b.

35. Ngag dbang blo bzang rgya mtsho, the Fifth Dalai Lama, *Life of the Fourth Dalai Lama*, 31.

36. In 1604 came the invitation of the chief of Gong ri dkar po (who was called Lha gzigs mi'i dbang po, like the king of Sne'u gdong) Bka' brgyud rnam par rgyal ba (Fifth Dalai Lama, *Life of the Fourth Dalai Lama*, 31b); followed by that of Dgye re lha btsun (Fifth Dalai Lama, *Life of the Fourth Dalai Lama*, 33a) and that of Skyid shod, extended to him by the Sa skyong g.yul rgyal nor bu, uncle and nephew (Fifth Dalai Lama, *Life of the Fourth Dalai Lama*, 33b).

Yon tan rgya mtsho accepted and then continued his tour towards Mal gro, Rin chen gling chos sde, 'Ol kha; the lay and religious communities of Rdzing phyi, that of Lcang ra, Grum mda', Bang rim, then came to do him homage. Having returned to Skyid shod (Fifth Dalai Lama, *Life of the Fourth Dalai Lama*, 34) and then again to

'Bras spungs, we find him in 1606 in Yar lungs, in 'Phyong rgyas, in Stag rtse, invited there by the prince Bsod nams grags pa, and next in Ri bo sde chen, 'Phyong gyas, Phag sde, Dpal ri sgrub sde, Bkra shis bde chen, Chos lam ring pa and other monasteries which had no prejudices as to system.

He went on to Mkhar thog, Sne'u gdong and other convents, large and small, like Rtse tshogs, Dkon gnyer, Ras chung phug, Ri bo chos gling, Bkra shis chos sde (Fifth Dalai Lama, *Life of the Fourth Dalai Lama*, 35). He then conferred baptism to Rtse zhabs drung rin po che Lha gzigs Mi pham Dbang sgyur rgyal po, and was then invited by Thogs mkhan chen pa Rin chen rgya mtsho, visited Rtse thang, went to the *sde pa* of Rgya ri rdzong and thence continued through Rong chad dkar, E ri sgo chos rdzong, Yar rgyab, where Thu mi sam bhota's descendants ruled; received there with great honor by Srid gsum rnam rgyal, he next passed to Rgyal chen gling, Dol lhun grub (Fifth Dalai Lama, *Life of the Fourth Dalai Lama*, 36b), Lhun po rtse in Gtsang; finally he returned to 'Bras spungs.

37. The Dalai Lama's itinerary went through U yug lung, Shangs Ri bo dge 'phel, Rtse gdong, Sa skya, where he was invited by 'Jam dbyangs kun dga' bsod nams lhun grub bkra shis grags pa rgyal mtshan dpal bzang po, up to Bkra shis lhun po, where he was received with great honors by the Paṇ chen Blo bzang chos kyi rgyal mtshan.

38. Ngag dbang blo bzang rgya mtsho, the Fifth Dalai Lama, *Life of the Fourth Dalai Lama*, 38b.

39. On his way back Yon tan rgya mtsho passed through Lhun po rtse, accepted invitations from the *sde pa* of Rin chen rtse, the prince or Rgyal mkhar rtse, the *zhabs drung* of Gnas rnying Ngag dbang gi dbang po; the Lord of Rgyal Khang chen po and Gong ri dkar po (Fifth Dalai Lama, *Life of the Fourth Dalai Lama*, 40–41).

40. The fifth Dalai Lama wrote a brief biography of Dkon mchog chos phel, his lama and guardian until he came of age. He belonged to the Yar rgyab clan (Fifth Dalai Lama, *'Jam dpal dbyangs chos kyi rje dkon mchog chos 'phel gyi rtogs brjod mkhas pa'i rnga rgyan* [Biography of Könchok Chöpel (1573–1646)], in *The Collected Works (Gsung-'bum) of the Vth Dalai Lama, Ngag dbang blo bzang rgya mtsho*, vol. 8 [Nya] [Gangtok: Sikkim Research Institute of Tibetology, 1992], 3) and was born from Bkra shis rnam rgyal and Lha mo in the year *chu bya*, 1575; he died at seventy-two in the year *shing spre'u*, 1644. At the age of eight he took the first vows in the Sa skya pa monastery Bkra shis chos gling, with the Rin po che Bsod nams rgyal mchog, and he was then baptized by the name of Yon tan rnam rgyal. Having completed his religious education with Grum mda' pa Chos rje Blo bzang chos 'phel, at the age of twelve he took monastic vows and was called Dkon mchog chos phel. Among the monasteries where he studied are mentioned: Rtse thang-Skyid shod, Dpal gsang phu, Sne'u thog, the latter in the territory of Skyid shod. He had as his masters, among others, the Chos rje rin po che Dpal 'byor rgya mtsho, who in the year *me spre'u*, 1596, when he was twenty-four, imparted perfect initiation to him, the Chos rje of Stag lung brag, whom he met when he went for the second time to Rtse thang, Ngag dbang chos kyi rgyal mtshan, Khri chen of Ri bo dga' ldan, the *ācārya* of Ra ba stod Rab byams pa Blo gros

rgyal mtshan, Don grub rin chen of Skyor mo lung, Byams pa chos mchog of Dwags po, Dge 'dun rnam rgyal of Rdzing phyi, etc.

Having become famous for his great learning, he was invited by the *gong ma* of Sne'u gdong rtse and by the prince of 'Phyong rgyas. His meeting with Yon tan rgya mtsho took place in 'Bras spungs, when this Dalai Lama was coming back from his tour in the Gtsang region.

He had a preeminent part in concluding peace between Mongols and Tibetans when the latter invaded Tibet in 1621. See Sangs rgyas rgya mtsho, *Dpal mnyam med ri bo Dga' ldan pa'i bstan pa zhwa ser cod pan 'chang ba'i ring lugs chos thams cad kyi rtsa ba gsal bar byed pa bai dur ser po'i me long* [*A History of the Gelukpa Tradition, the Yellow Beryl*] (Zhol Edition), 74.

41. See the translation of Ye shes dpal 'byor Sum pa mkhan po's *Dpag bsam ljon bzang* in Giuseppe Tucci, *Tibetan Painted Scrolls* (Rome: Libreria dello Stato, 1949), 2:654.

42. Ngag dbang blo bzang rgya mtsho, the Fifth Dalai Lama, *Rgyal kun 'dus pa'i ngo bo khyab bdag he ru ka ngur smrig gar gyis rnam par rol pa gdan gsum tshang ba'i sde dpon rje btsun bla ma dbang phyug rab brtan bstan pa'i rgyal mtshan dpal bzang po'i rtogs pa brjod pa bdud rtsis za ma tog* [*Biography of Wangchuk Rapten Tenpé (1558–1636)*], in *The Collected Works (Gsung-'bum) of the Vth Dalai Lama*, Ngag dbang blo bzang rgya mtsho, vol. 9 (Ta) (Gangtok: Sikkim Research Institute of Tibetology, 1992), 34.

43. Ngag dbang kun dga' bsod nams, *Khams gsum gyi 'dren pa dam pa grub mchog gi ded dpon 'jam pa'i dbyangs bsod nams dbang po'i rnam par thar pa bcud kyi thigs phreng rab tu 'phel ba'i dgos 'dod 'byung ba'i chu gter* [*Life of Sönam Wangpo*], in *The Biographies of Sa skya Lo tshā ba 'jam dpa'i rdo rje (1485–1533), Sṅags 'chan grags pa blo gros (1563–1617), and 'Jam dbyangs bsod nams dbagn po (1559–1621)* (Dehradun, U.P.: Sakya Centre, 1984), 28.

44. Ngag dbang kun dga' bsod nams, *Life of Sönam Wangpo*, 42a.

45. Ngag dbang kun dga' bsod nams, *Life of Sönam Wangpo*, 55a.

46. Ngag dbang blo bzang rgya mtsho, the Fifth Dalai Lama, *Biography of Kön-chok Chömpel*, 11a.

47. Ngag dbang blo bzang rgya mtsho, the Fifth Dalai Lama, *Zur thams cad mkhyen pa chos dbyings rang grol gyi rnam thar theg mchog bstan pa'i shing rta* [*Life of Chöying Rangdröl (1604–1669)*], in *The Collected Works (Gsung-'bum) of the Vth Dalai Lama*, Ngag dbang blo bzang rgya mtsho, vol. 9 (Ta) (Gangtok: Sikkim Research Institute of Tibetology, 1992), 46b.

48. Ngag dbang blo bzang rgya mtsho, the Fifth Dalai Lama, *Life of Chöying Rangdröl*, 43a.

49. Ngag dbang blo bzang rgya mtsho, the Fifth Dalai Lama, *Biography of Kön-chok Chömpel*, 12b.

50. Ngag dbang blo bzang rgya mtsho, the Fifth Dalai Lama, *Za hor gyi ban de ngag dbang blo bzang rgya mtsho'i 'di snang 'khrul pa'i rol rtsed rtogs brjod kyi tshul*

du bkod pa du ku'u la'i gos bzang las glegs bam dang po [Autobiography of the Fifth Dalai Lama], in *The Collected Works (Gsung 'bum) of the Vth Dalai Lama, Ngag dbang blo bzang rgya mtsho*, vol. 5 (Nga) (Gangtok: Sikkim Research Institute of Tibetology, 1992), 70a.

51. Ngag dbang blo bzang rgya mtsho, the Fifth Dalai Lama, *Life of the Fourth Dalai Lama*, 45b.

52. Ngag dbang blo bzang rgya mtsho, the Fifth Dalai Lama, *Life of the Fourth Dalai Lama*, 46b.

53. Ngag dbang blo bzang rgya mtsho, the Fifth Dalai Lama, *Life of the Fourth Dalai Lama*, 48b.

54. Ngag dbang blo bzang rgya mtsho, the Fifth Dalai Lama, *Life of the Fourth Dalai Lama*, 48b.

55. Ngag dbang blo bzang rgya mtsho, the Fifth Dalai Lama, *Life of the Fourth Dalai Lama*, 49a: 'U shu wang. Huth, *History of Buddhism in Mongolia*, 2:321: Zhun shu wang. On this transcription see Laufer, "Loan Words in Tibetan," 432.

56. Ngag dbang blo bzang rgya mtsho, the Fifth Dalai Lama, *Life of the Fourth Dalai Lama*, 49a.

57. These events are also mentioned by Padma dkar po in his autobiography: Padma dkar po (1527–1592), *Sems dpa' chen po padma dkar po'i rnam thar thugs rje chen po'i zlos gar [Biography of Pema Karpo]*, in *Collected Works (gsung 'bum) of Kun mkhyen Padma dkar po*, vol. 3 (Darjeeling: Kargyud Sungrab Nyamso Khang, 1973–1974), 45, 96.

58. On the wars of Byang see Ngag dbang kun dga' bsod nams, *Life of Sönam Wangpo*, 28ff.

59. Tāranātha, *Rgyal khams pa tā ra nā thas bdag nyid kyi rnam thar nges par brjod pa'i deb gter shin tu zhib mo ma bcos lhug pa'i rtogs brjod [Autobiography of Tāranātha]*, in *Rje btsun Tā ra nā tha'i gsung 'bum*, vol. 1 (Ka) (Phun tshogs gling edition), 46.

60. Tāranātha, *Autobiography of Tāranātha*, 27.

Chapter 18

THE HE CLAN OF HEZHOU

A TIBETAN FAMILY IN SERVICE TO THE YUAN
AND MING DYNASTIES

Elliot Sperling

As did Luciano Petech in a previous generation, Elliot Sperling demonstrates the importance of Chinese sources for students of Tibetan history, especially those wishing to understand the rich and diverse Sino-Tibetan borderlands. Given the almost complete absence of Tibetan-language sources for the history of most of Amdo between the Tibetan imperial period and the sixteenth century, Sperling instead examines local sources from the Ming dynasty (1368–1644), such as the *Gazetteer of Hezhou* (*Hezhou zhi*) and centralized compilations of dynastic history: *History of the Ming* (*Mingshi*) and *Veritable Records of the Ming* (*Ming shilu*). He documents the career of the Tibetan leader He Suonan (Sönam) as an official of the Ming dynasty, including two visits to the Ming court and one to Central Tibet as an envoy of the court. This illustrates the key role that figures from this region have played as mediators between China-based polities and Central Tibet. This selection is an abridged version of the original article, omitting a detailed study of the descendants of He Suonan down to 1531 and their campaigns (as far away as Xining and Ganzhou in the Gansu corridor to Xinjiang) on behalf of the Ming dynasty, on the basis of which Sperling concludes: "the information that we derive from these varied references indicates a clear assimilation into the new environment engendered by Ming rule. Most of the time there is little to show that they are Hezhou Tibetans, except for the mention of their descent from He Suonan. Their names are Chinese and their service to the Ming, as mentioned in our sources, is generally directed against Tibetans." Hezhou is now the town of Linxia in Gansu province, south of Lanzhou, and outside the Tibetan culture region.

The establishment of Mongol authority over both Tibet and China in the thirteenth century sharply altered the subsequent history of both countries, and came to exert a deep influence over the future course of Sino-Tibetan relations. The general importance of the era of Mongol domination of Tibet is well accepted, in part due to the work of Professor Petech, who has done much to elucidate the contours of this period and to increase an awareness of the changes in Tibet that grew out of it.

In an article on the Sino-Tibetan borderlands during the Yuan,[1] Professor Petech made a brief reference to Suonanpu, the Yuan pacification commissioner (Ch. *xuanwei shi*) based at Hezhou in Gansu, and to his submission to the Ming shortly after the new dynasty's forces had invested the region. This individual was a fairly important figure in the Hezhou area, and his submission to the Ming was significant in the solidification of the dynasty's hold on that sector of the Sino-Tibetan border. It may therefore be of interest to provide here not only a brief discussion of him and his place in early-Ming Hezhou, but remarks about some of his descendants who also served the Ming.[2]

"Suonanpu" is generally referred to in Chinese sources as either He Suonan or He Suonanpu, transcriptions that have proved to be somewhat problematic. Although the characters that are today read as "Suonan" are easily recognizable as an unambiguous transcription of the Tibetan name Sönam (Bsod nams), other elements of the name have proved a bit more puzzling. The character "pu" may well represent half of a further Tibetan name; in fact a relatively late Chinese source, the nineteenth-century *Ming tongjian* transcribes his Tibetan name as Sonomu Gunbu, an equally unambiguous rendering of Sönam Gönpo.[3] The surname He, however, has seemed more problematic. It was suggested by Satō Hisashi that the name might have been the result of He Suonan being of mixed Chinese-Tibetan descent.[4] In a conversation on this point in 1985, however, Professor Deng Ruiling of the Chinese Academy of Social Sciences kindly directed me to the *Hezhou zhi*, a gazetteer of the Hezhou region wherein is contained biographical information on He Suonan that clearly indicates, as Prof. Deng pointed out, that the character "He" in his name was a Chinese surname bestowed on him by Ming Taizu (r. 1368–1399), the founder of the new dynasty, in recognition of his submission to the Ming.[5]

Further information in the *Hezhou zhi* and in other Ming sources provides us with only a very broad and general outline of the activities of He Suonan and his family, but it is one that is worth delineating for what it tells us of the extension of Ming power into Hezhou. He Suonan, as noted, was the Yuan pacification commissioner at Hezhou, appointed as such within the structure of the dynasty's "Chief Military Commandery of the Pacification Commission for Tibet and Other Regions" (Ch. *Tufan dengqu xuanweisi duyuan shuaifu*) based at Hezhou and created sometime in 1268/1269.[6] However, our sources are not precise about the date of He Suonan's appointment as pacification commissioner nor about very much else;[7] we don't know his date of birth nor that of his death. Nevertheless, in order to elucidate what information we do have on He Suonan we ought to turn first to the biographical remarks on him in the *Hezhou zhi*.[8] This short biography gives us a basic outline of what is known about He Suonan, and presents it in a manner brief enough to be quoted in full, even though most of the information on He Suonan that we find there (with the exception of the comment on the origins of the surname "He") can be found scattered in the *Ming shilu* and in other sources as well; and in spite of the fact that there is obvious confusion on the part of the *Hezhou zhi* between He Suonan's two visits to Ming Taizu's court:

He Suonan, in his youth, was fond of practicing archery and horsemanship. During the late Yuan he served in the Pacification Commission for Tibet and Other Regions (Ch. *Tufan dengqu xuanweisi*). In the third year of the Hongwu period [1370/1371] Dengyu, the Duke of Wei, arrived on the frontier leading a great army. Suonan lead [*sic*] a great group to tender allegiance (to the Ming). Taizu commended his sincerity; he appointed him vice commander (Ch. *zhihui tongzhi*) of the Hezhou guard (Ch. *wei*) and bestowed upon him the family name He. His younger brother Jiang [*sic* = Wang][9] Jianu was appointed assistant commander (Ch. *zhihui qianshi*) and his second son (Ch. *cizi*) He Min assistant commander of the Imperial Bodyguard (Ch. *Jini wei*). Letter patents with round and square seal script dragons (Ch. *zhuanlong jintong gaoming*)[10] were bestowed.

In the fifth year [1372/1373] the secretariat (Ch. *zhongshu*) was ordered to honor the commander (Ch. *zhihui*) of the Western Regions, He Suonan. The imperial orders said:

"The noble gentleman (Ch. *juanzi*) remains faithful by preserving righteousness with humaneness. Therefore humaneness flourishes and righteousness prospers. This is the way of principle. Now the commander of He[-zhou] in the Western [Regions] (Ch. *Xihe*), He Suonan, has been very firm in his faith since tendering allegiance. During an earlier year he was ordered to go to Ü (Ch. *Wusi*) to proclaim Our command. He traveled far, covering a myriad of *li*, and not shrinking from difficulties. Arriving in Ü, his utterances about Our command accorded with the imperial orders. This year he came to the capital with his wife. Now the ceremonial treatment accorded him has been augmented to make it sufficient for the sustenance of his family members."

As a parting present he was given thirty *tan* of rice and an equal amount of wheat. Although his judge (Ch. *zhenfu*), Liu Wen, was of a minor rank, [the emperor] also took his family into consideration and he also got a parting present of ten *tan* of rice and also an equal amount of wheat.

The *Hezhou zhi*, like other sources, leaves little doubt about He Suonan being one of the critical figures in both the establishment of Ming control over the Amdo-Shaanxi frontier area and the course of Ming Taizu's first contacts with Central Tibet. Basic sources for the Ming give the clear impression that he was the first important Tibetan figure to have accepted the new dynasty.

He Suonan visited the Ming court twice, the first visit coming shortly after his acceptance of Ming rule. This submission, we are told, was the result of the dispatch of Xu Yunde, a bureau vice director (Ch. *Yuanwai lang*) in the Ministry of Rites, as Taizu's emissary to Tibetan regions. As stated in a *shilu* entry for June 5, 1369, Xu Yunde carried a proclamation from the emperor announcing the establishment of the new dynasty.[11] He Suonan's submission was formally carried out via the surrender of the seals and credentials granted him by the Yuan to the left regional commander (Ch. *zuo fujiang*) Dengyu, and is noted in a *shilu* entry for July 21, 1370.[12] Thereupon he set out for the Ming capital at Nanjing and arrived at Taizu's court on January 13, 1371, not departing until March 4, of that year.[13] One might be inclined to regard this visit to the court as the one referred to in the imperial orders honoring He Suonan, quoted in the passage from the *Hezhou zhi* given above, for although the date mentioned there is erroneous, it is nevertheless close. However, He Suonan came to the Ming court a second time as well, as described in a *shilu* entry for August 26, 1379, which quotes from the very same imperial orders.[14] Thus, the *Hezhou zhi* has essentially gone astray in its chronology and assigned the date 1372/1373 to an event (i.e., the presentation of the orders while He Suonan was at court) that took place several years later.

After the entries on his first visit to the Ming court the *Ming shilu*, with the exception of one entry for February 27, 1374 (noting the bestowal of silver on him),[15] makes no mention of He Suonan until his second visit in 1379. His trip to Central Tibet, as a representative of Taizu, must therefore have taken place some time between 1371 and 1374 or 1374 and 1379. Although there are *shilu* references to Hezhou mentioning other figures, or sometimes speaking simply of communications from Hezhou from unnamed persons, He Suonan does not appear in them. As we will see below, this was a period in which He Suonan's power in Hezhou was being lessened by Ming administrative measures. Still, one assumes the dearth of references to He Suonan is due, at least in part, to his presence in Central Tibet at some time during one of the two possible periods mentioned above. This mission must have been a fairly important one; it probably constituted one of the Ming court's most important contacts with Tibet up to that time. However we know nothing about it aside from its mention in the imperial orders quoted above. There seems to be no mention of it in Tibetan sources either, leaving us only the possibility of speculation.[16]

There were, of course, other dynamic factors at work in the Hezhou region aside from the appearance of Ming forces and the assertion of Ming dominion in the area. These include the ongoing diminution of the borders of the land area inhabited by Tibetan-speaking populations: a sporadic, but clear, stage following the apogee of Tibetan expansion, the Tibetan imperial era of the seventh to ninth centuries. The Tibetan Empire had projected Tibetan language and Tibetan culture, as well as Tibetan political and military power, over a very wide area. But its collapse left Tibetan enclaves on the frontiers of the former empire with ever-loosening links to Central Tibet. The extreme and sparsely-inhabited distances between the outlying areas of Tibetan habitation in the northeast and the Tibetan cultural center undoubtedly aided this estrangement. By the Yuan period Hezhou and other areas had been out of the political orbit of Central Tibet for several centuries. Along with other frontier areas Hezhou was made subordinate to administrative structures in Shaanxi by the Yuan, and ultimately, as we know, ceased to be home to a Tibetan-speaking population.[17]

He Suonan's role, seen from a distance of several centuries, was to assist in the consolidation of Ming power in Hezhou and, in so doing, to further the Sinicization of the area. As we will observe, He Suonan's submission directly led to Ming military and bureaucratic domination of Hezhou and much later to the decline of the area's Tibetan character. Hezhou's political links to Central Tibet were certainly cut, as we have noted, with the collapse of the Tibetan Empire, a factor which, taken with Hezhou's geographical position, dictated growing links to China. During the Song and Jin periods Hezhou was integrated into the composition of Chinese border provinces.[18] The fact that its political leaders looked to China could not but affect the area's character, even though it is clear that Hezhou did remain a recognizable Tibetan enclave up through the early Ming. The Yuan, as we have mentioned, did not make Hezhou directly a part of the neighboring province of Shaanxi, although the administrative unit to which it belonged, the Chief Military Commandery of the Pacification Commission for Tibet and Other Regions, was controlled through the administrative apparatus of the province.[19]

It is during the Ming period that the nature of Hezhou appears to have clearly changed. This is manifested by the contents of that section of the *Hezhou zhi* dealing with major personages (Ch. *renwu*) of the region.[20] With the exception of He Suonan and his family the entire section apparently mentions only Chinese, as we would normally expect. However, among these Chinese figures we find only a very small number who were originally from the region prior to the Ming.[21] Only in the subsection on the Ming do we begin to come upon a good number of Chinese who clearly seem to be native to Hezhou. Of course in other sections of the *Hezhou zhi* we do find a number of pre-Ming Chinese figures from outside the region mentioned with regard to administration, military activity, etc., during periods such as the Song, when Hezhou was administered as an important defensive frontier. This is surely indicative of the influence and domination that China was able to exert over the region in the centuries following the end of the Tibetan Empire; but the growth of a well-established indigenous Chinese population does not seem to be noticeable until the Ming.

This Ming-era transition is also somewhat in evidence in the administrative history of the region which we may derive from what is set out very concisely in the *Mingshi*;[22] and from relevant information in the *Ming shilu*. In 1371 the Hezhou guard was established and made subordinate to the regional guard (Ch. *duwei*) at Xi'an, the administrative seat of Shaanxi. The *shilu* doesn't mention the specific date of this, but it must have been connected with He Suonan's visit to Taizu's court. He arrived on January 13, 1371, and is mentioned in a *shilu* entry for the following day with his Yuan title of pacification commissioner.[23] However, an entry for January 23, 1371, describes his appointment as vice commander of the Hezhou guard, thus allowing us to assume that the guard unit in question was created on or just prior to that day.[24] The creation of a guard unit simply allowed for the garrisoning of Hezhou by Ming forces. Only after another two years was the area reorganized and brought more solidly into the Ming administrative structure via the creation of the Hezhou prefecture (Ch. *fu*).[25] This prefecture was subordinate to the Shaanxi Branch Secretariat (Ch. *Xing zhongshu sheng*). On August 23, 1374, the Xi'an branch regional guard (Ch. *Xing duwei*) was established at Hezhou. There are several interesting aspects to this event, described in greater detail, as we would expect, in the *Ming shilu* than in the *Mingshi*.[26] The first is the elevation of an otherwise unknown Chinese official, Weizheng, from the position of commander (Ch. *zhihui shi*) of the Hezhou guard to that of regional military commissioner (Ch. *tu zhihui shi*). Clearly, Weizheng had already superseded He Suonan in authority in the Hezhou guard unit. Now he was the highest ranking Ming military official in Hezhou. Although we may suspect that these events happened during the time of He Suonan's mission to Tibet on behalf of the Ming court (his absence from Hezhou during this period may be indicated by the absence of his name in *shilu* entries dealing with the area), we must still reach the conclusion that He Suonan's authority in Hezhou was clearly being reduced at this time. We may note too that while He Suonan is no longer mentioned in the *Ming shilu*, except with reference to his court visit in 1379, some of his descendants do turn up, as we will see, in the *Hezhou zhi* and other sources.

The second aspect to this change in Hezhou's status was the expansion in the scope of the regional bureaucracy's functions. The Xi'an branch regional guard was given administrative jurisdiction and control not only over the Hezhou guard, but over the Eastern Tibet (Ch. Duogan < Tib. Do-kham) and Central Tibet (Ch. Wusi-Tsang < Tib. Ü-Tsang) guards as well. The fact that these units were established at Hezhou, and not in Tibet proper, seems to be somewhat indicative of their role in Tibetan affairs. Essentially garrison structures, these units could at best only have served in defensive or liaison functions vis-a-vis Tibetan border areas. Although they certainly exerted some influence over Tibetans living close to the frontier, evidence does not reveal any real administrative or military role in Tibetan affairs for either of these guard units. Weizheng, when newly appointed as regional military commander, is said to have had overall command of the Hezhou, Eastern Tibet and Central Tibet guard units;[27] but he can hardly be considered to have held power anywhere beyond the confines of the frontier along the Hezhou region. Obscure as he is in Chinese sources, to date he appears to have been quite unknown to Tibetan historians.

On August 25, 1379, a tribal military command (Ch. *junmin zhihui shisi*) was established at Hezhou,[28] reflecting the fact that the region still had to deal with local (and probably also nomadic) Tibetans. Almost a century later, on January 4, 1474, Hezhou was reorganized as a subprefecture (Ch. *zhou*) under Lintao prefecture, and the tribal military command became a common guard unit.[29] One may assume that the population was by that time well Sinicized; hence the decision to eliminate the tribal military command, a structure associated with non-Chinese frontier areas. We should note that the growth in the Chinese presence in Hezhou ought to be seen against the background of the economic opportunities presented by the border trade with Tibet: a trade which had been drawing Chinese merchants to the frontier, much as it had also been drawing Tibetan traders following a period in which Tibet's contacts and dealings with Eastern Turkestan and India had declined with the eclipse of Buddhism in both areas.[30]

The question of the commercial possibilities of the region brings us back again to Weizheng, who superseded He Suonan's authority in Hezhou, and leads us to some remarks on the decline of Tibetan authority in the area during the period following He Suonan's submission to the Ming. These economic possibilities were perhaps vaguely evident to Weizheng; however, we have little information on him aside from the few lines describing him in the *Da ming yitongzhi*, which are later quoted in the *Hezhou zhi*:[31]

> Weizheng, in the third year of the Hongwu period [1370–1371], was appointed commander of the Hezhou guard. He often said that among the people great labor is expended in transport; moreover, tea and cloth are exchanged for grain. Tea and cloth could be given to the lower-level officers (Ch. *junshi*) and they could be ordered to carry on their own mutual trade in order to reduce the labor of the people in the West. The Emperor decreed compliance with this.
>
> When Cheng first arrived the towns under the guard were empty. Thereupon day and night he soothed its people. Hezhou consequently was a region of joy. The court bestowed an Imperial Letter on him as a reward, enabling the restoration of his original surname, Ning (Ch. *pifu Ning xing*).

We learn from this passage that Weizheng was made commander of the Hezhou guard in the very same year (and no doubt at the same time) that He Suonan was made vice commander. Thus, in spite of the greater attention given to He Suonan in our sources, we may conclude that the Ming authorities were quick to move in a Chinese official from outside the region to hold rank over him, thereby cutting away the overall authority which the first *shilu* entries implied that He Suonan had in Hezhou. In this connection too we have the expected impression that Weizheng's primary concern was with the sedentary structures needed for dynastic administration; hence the reference in the passage above to the emptiness of the towns, with no mention of the non-sedentary population. Similarly, his sole recorded idea on the economic aspects of regional life centers on procuring grain. We see in this some very common Chinese views applied to an area that was still largely Tibetan. This dichotomy is of course reflected in Weizheng's appointment over He Suonan. Hezhou, though, must have remained noticeably Tibetan in character until at least well into the fifteenth century, when the tribal military commission was abolished.

As we well know, the major area of trade that sprang up in Hezhou went well beyond the procurement of grain, as described in the passage on Weizheng quoted above. It involved the transport of tea to Hezhou (and to other points along the Tibetan border) where it was traded to Tibetans for horses. It might well be that the potential of this trade was not evident to Weizheng, hence its omission from his proposal. This is difficult to understand, however, for the availability of horses in Hezhou must have been obvious; He Suonan presented them as tribute when he came to Taizu's court, following the mission of Xu Yunde and his own submission to Dengyu.[32] We may even speculate that he had been encouraged to present horses. Perhaps Weizheng's remarks on the horse trade have simply not been preserved. However that may be, a definite interest in securing horses from Hezhou through border trade developed, or became clear, rather quickly. A *shilu* entry for June 8, 1375, tells of the dispatch and subsequent success of the eunuch attendant (Ch. *neishi*) Zhaozheng who was sent to Hezhou with tea and fabrics on what was clearly a preliminary mission to trade for horses.[33] It is from this period that we can probably date the establishment of a tea-horse trading office (Ch. *chama si*) at Hezhou.[34]

This helped to further establish the importance of Hezhou to the Ming and to increase China's interest and influence in the area. The trade undoubtedly helped to draw ever greater numbers of merchants into the area as well. Further elaboration on this subject goes beyond a discussion of He Suonan and his family, however. The point here is simply to underline the significance of He Suonan's submission with regard to the region that he brought into the Ming domains. Once under Ming rule, geography and economic conditions, along with the administrative steps taken by the Ming court, quickly worked to accelerate the assimilation of Hezhou into the Chinese world well beyond the state of affairs existing at the time of He Suonan's submission. . . .[35]

We may briefly conclude by noting several points. He Suonan's submission to the Ming brought a largely Tibetan area into the new dynasty's territory. In one sense, this submission was later manifested by the assimilation of some of

He Suonan's descendants into the Ming bureaucratic and military structure where they helped defend the frontier for the dynasty. Shortly after He Suonan's submission, steps were taken to assure the paramountcy of Ming authority in the area. We assume that He Suonan acquiesced in this undercutting of his own power. Nevertheless, Hezhou remained markedly Tibetan in population for most of the first half of the Ming period. Ultimately, of course, the Tibetan character of the area declined drastically as Hezhou became home to greater numbers of Chinese, eventually becoming a largely Muslim region, which it remains today. The Islamicization of Hezhou is similarly a topic well worth exploring, particularly with regard to the role of regional trade in drawing a Muslim population. That, however, goes beyond the subject of this paper, in which an attempt has been made to elucidate information on the He clan that may be useful in understanding the decline of the Tibetan presence in Hezhou.

NOTES

1. Petech, "Yuan Organization of the Tibetan Border Areas," in *Tibetan Studies: Proceedings of the 4th Seminar of the International Association for Tibetan Studies, Munich 1985*, International Association for Tibetan Studies, ed. Helga Uebach and Jampa Losang Panglung (München: Kommission für Zentralasiatische Studien, Bayerische Akademie der Wissenschaften, 1988), 369–380.

2. Hezhou is today the predominantly Muslim town of Linxia in Gansu, and is no longer part of the Tibetan-speaking world. Under both the Yuan and early Ming Hezhou was an important frontier region for both Tibetans and non-Tibetans. During Tibet's imperial era, from the seventh to ninth centuries, it was incorporated into the Tibetan Empire and has subsequently been known in Tibetan sources by its transcribed form, "Gachu." The basic Chinese source for Hezhou is the *Hezhou zhi* [*Gazetteer of Hezhou*], of which several redactions exist. I have only been able to work with the 1707 version (in six *zhuan*) by Wang Chuanzhen. I am grateful to Dr. Nicola Di Cosmo for obtaining a microfilm of this work for me from the Tōyō Bunko in Tokyo.

3. Xia Xie, *Ming tong jian* [*Comprehensive Mirror of the Ming*] (Beijing: Zhonghua shuju, 1959), 248; cited in Louis Hambis, *Documents sur l'histoire des Mongols à l'époque des Ming* [*Documents on the History of the Mongols in the Ming Period*] (Paris: Presses universitaires de France, 1969), 119.

4. Satō Hisashi, "Gen matsu Min sho no Chibetto josei [The Tibetan Situation from Late Yuan to Early Ming]," in *Mindai Man-mō shi kenkyū*, ed. Tamura Jituzō (Kyoto: Kyōto Daigaku Bungakubu, 1963), 522.

5. Wang, *Gazetteer of Hezhou*, 3:64a. For the sake of consistency within personal names I shall use the Chinese name He Suonan, rather than the Chinese-Tibetan He Bsod nams, throughout this article. The *Gazetteer of Hezhou* generally refers to him as He Suonan, although it notes the variant Suonanpu, which is the common form used in references to him in the *Ming shilu* [*Veritable Records of the Ming (Dynasty)*];

see Wang, *Gazetteer of Hezhou*, 3:33a. The *Mingshi* [*History of the Ming*] uses both He Suonan and He Suonanpu, and in one place even writes Si Suonanpu. Although these discrepancies have been edited out in the most recent version of this source, they are mentioned in notes appended to the *zhuan* in which they occur; see Zhang Tingyu, et al., *Mingshi* [*History of the Ming*] (Beijing: Zhonghua shuju, 1974), 126:3767 and 330:8568. I would like to believe that the surname He, which is a well-attested Chinese surname, was granted because its pronunciation is identical with that of the "He" in Hezhou. It might even be that He Suonan was known in Tibetan partly via a geographical prefix denoting his home area (a custom still common among Tibetans), perhaps as "Ga Bsod nams," thus allowing for the imperially-bestowed surname to easily reflect an existing appellation. This is speculation, of course, as none of the available sources says anything about any reasoning behind the choice of the surname "He."

6. On He Suonan's appointment, see Gu Zuzheng et al., *Ming shilu Zangzu shiliao* [*Tibetan Historical Sources in Veritable Records of the Ming Dynasty*] (Lhasa: Xizang remin chubanshe, 1982), 8. Petech, "Yuan Organization of the Tibetan Border Areas," 370, cites Song Lian, *Yuan shi* [*History of the Yuan*] (1370; reprint, Beijing: Zhonghua shuju, 1976), 60:1429 in adducing the date 1268/1269 for the establishment of the *Tufan xuanweisi Duyuan shuiafu* (i.e., = *Tufan dengqu xuanweisi duyuan shuaifu*; he translates it as "Tufan Government Commissionership"). The passage referred to simply notes that Hezhou was made part of the commission's jurisdiction, but inasmuch as Song, *History of the Yuan*, 63:1565 describes Hezhou as the commission's seat we may tentatively accept 1268/1269 as the date for its establishment.

7. Wang, *Gazetteer of Hezhou*, 1:2b notes only that he was appointed towards the end of the Zhizheng reign period (1341–1368).

8. Wang, *Gazetteer of Hezhou*, 3:64a–64b.

9. All of the other sources on He Suonan's brother that are referred to below give his name as Wang, rather than Jiang. Obviously, in this passage from the *Gazetteer of Hezhou* the omission of one stroke from the former character has changed it into the latter one.

10. I am not familiar with this term. My translation of it is only tentative and may well be incorrect.

11. Gu et al., *Tibetan Historical Sources in the Veritable Records of the Ming Dynasty*, 3, which gives the text of the proclamation.

12. Gu et al., *Tibetan Historical Sources in the Veritable Records of the Ming Dynasty*, 8. On Tengyu, see Zhang, *History of the Ming*, 126:3748–3751; and Edward L. Dreyer and Hok-Lam Chan, "Tengyu," in *Dictionary of Ming Biography*, ed. L. Carrington Goodrich and Chaoying Fang (New York: Columbia University Press, 1976), 1277–1280. It should also be noted that Tengyu had entered Hezhou less than a month before, and at that time had dispatched his own messengers with a proclamation to local Tibetan leaders calling, one assumes, for their submission.

13. Gu et al., *Tibetan Historical Sources in the Veritable Records of the Ming Dynasty*, 9–10 and 11.

14. Gu et al., *Tibetan Historical Sources in the Veritable Records of the Ming Dynasty*, 52. The emperor's orders are also quoted in Zhang, *History of the Ming*, 330:8541. There are differences in the text of the orders as quoted in the *Veritable Records*, the *History of the Ming*, and the *Gazetteer of Hezhou*; while they do not affect the import of the orders, they do produce the following variants:

Zhang, *History of the Ming*: "He Suonanpu has been very firm in his faith since tendering allegiance. Earlier he was sent as an envoy to Dbus tsang (Ch. Wusi-Zang). He travelled far, covering a myriad of *li*, and then returned. All his utterances [there] commended Our ideas. Now he has come to the court with his family. It is fitting that the ceremonial treatment accorded him be augmented."

Gu et al., Tibetan Historical Sources in the Veritable Records of the Ming Dynasty: "The noble gentleman honors the retainment of faithfulness and practices righteousness. Now He Suonanpu has been very firm in his faith since tendering allegiance. Earlier he was sent as an envoy to Dbus tsang to proclaim Our command. He travelled far, covering a myriad of *li*, not shrinking from diligent toil and then returned. All his utterances [there] commended Our ideas. Now he and Liu Wen have come to court, each with their families. It is fitting that the ceremonial treatment accorded them be augmented."

The modern editors of *Tibetan Historical Sources in the Veritable Records of the Ming Dynasty* continue the text of the orders by including the reference to the presentations made to He Suonan and Liu Wen on this occasion within it. The modern editors of the *History of the Ming* have not done so, nor have I.

15. Gu et al., *Tibetan Historical Sources in the Veritable Records of the Ming Dynasty*, 26.

16. We may note that someone carried a missive composed early in 1375 from Ming Taizu to the fourth Kar ma pa, Rol pa'i rdo rje, a missive that has survived to the present day (I deal with it in a forthcoming volume from the Library of Tibetan Works and Archives in memory of Rai Bahadur Athing T.D. Densapa). He Suonan was surely an ideal envoy, for Hezhou's position was clearly considered to have been something of a gateway for Tibet (and for information from Tibet) for the Ming; hence the development (as we will mention below) of Hezhou as the base for Ming guard units assigned to Tibet. A *shilu* entry for May 23, 1372 (Gu et al., *Tibetan Historical Sources in the Veritable Records of the Ming Dynasty*, 37–18) reports a communication from Hezhou on dealing appropriately with 'Jam dbyangs shākya rgyal mtshan, Byang chub rgyal mtshan's successor within the Phag mo gru pa establishment, so as to advantageously influence conditions along the Sino-Tibetan border. If He Suonan was not the bearer of Taizu's missive to Mtshur phu in 1375, might he have gone earlier to Tibet and then have sent back the communication on the Phag mo gru pa?

17. With regard to these last remarks, we may note the earlier cases of the Hexi and Liangzhou regions (in the same general vicinity as Hezhou), where independent Tibetan political power far removed from Central Tibet had succumbed to annexation into a neighboring state, that of the Tanguts (concerning which, see Iwasaki

Tsumoto, "A Study of Ho-Hsi Tibetans During the Northern Song Dynasty," *Memoirs of the Research Department of the Toyo Bunko* 44 [1986]: 57–132); this led to the disappearance of these regions from the map of the Tibetan world. In our own day we may also note the effect of several centuries within which what had formerly been ethnically Tibetan regions divorced from political authority in Central Tibet have continued to shrink, particularly as Muslim populations have expanded into them (e.g., along the frontiers of Ladakh and Amdo which are, interestingly enough, at directly opposite ends of the Tibetan plateau).

18. See Li Xian et al., *Daming yitong zhi* [*Complete Gazetteer of the Great Ming*] (1461; reprint, Taipei: Wenhai chubanshe, 1965), 37:14a; and *Gazetteer of Hezhou*, 1:2b. Tan Qixiang, *Zhongguo lishi ditu ji* [*The Historical Atlas of China*] (Beijing: Ditu chubanshe, 1982), vol. VI, maps 20–21 and 57–58, shows Hezhou's location within the Qinfeng Circuit during the Song and the Lintao Route during the Chin.

19. As described in Song, *History of the Yuan*, 60:1432–1433, the Chief Military Commandery of the Pacification Commission for Tibet and Other Regions held jurisdiction over the following areas along the Tibetan side of the Sino-Tibetan frontier:

The Hezhou circuit and the three districts (Ch. *xian*) attached to it, Dingqiang, Ninghe, and Anxiang;

Yazhou, and the five districts attached to it, Mingshan, Lushan, Baizhang, Rongjing, and Yendao;

Lizhou and the one district attached to it, Hanyuan;

Taozhou and the one district attached to it, Kedang;

Guidezhou;

Maozhou and the two districts attached to it, Wenshan and Wenchuan;

The Mdo smad (Ch. Duosi ma) circuit;

Minzhou;

Tiezhou.

All of the places named can be easily located in Tan, *The Historical Atlas of China*, vol. VII, maps 36–37. The arrangement, whereby the Chief Military Commandery of the Pacification Commission for Tibet and Other Regions remained subordinate to authorities in Shaanxi but not part of the province, is not as unusual as one might think; it calls to mind the administrative arrangements made by the Qing rulers several centuries later for Amdo and eastern Kham.

20. Wang, *Gazetteer of Hezhou*, 3:63a–70b.

21. For the period prior to the Ming this section of the *Gazetteer of Hezhou* has references to only three personages: one each for the Nanbei period and the Song and Yuan dynasties (Wang, *Gazetteer of Hezhou*, 3:63a–63b). Of the three people mentioned, the Yuan figure receives only a few words and his native place is not made clear; it probably was Hezhou. Of the other two, the Nanbei figure is from the area, but he was active there in the first part of the sixth century, well before the area fell to the Tibetan Empire. The Song figure is said to be from Xizhou, an area then just to the east of Hezhou; see Tan, *The Historical Atlas of China*, VI, maps 20–21.

22. Zhang, *History of the Ming*, 42:1009.

23. Gu et al., *Tibetan Historical Sources in the Veritable Records of the Ming Dynasty*, 9–10.

24. See Gu et al., *Tibetan Historical Sources in the Veritable Records of the Ming Dynasty*, 9–10.

25. See Gu et al., *Tibetan Historical Sources in the Veritable Records of the Ming Dynasty*, 19. This *shilu* entry, for January 31, 1373, states that the elevation of Hezhou's status was at the request of the local authorities, and included the establishment of subprefectures (Ch. *zhou*) and districts in the region.

26. See Gu et al., *Tibetan Historical Sources in the Veritable Records of the Ming Dynasty*, 29–30.

27. Gu et al., *Tibetan Historical Sources in the Veritable Records of the Ming Dynasty*, 29.

28. Gu et al., *Tibetan Historical Sources in the Veritable Records of the Ming Dynasty*, 52.

29. Cf. Gu et al., *Tibetan Historical Sources in the Veritable Records of the Ming Dynasty*, 709–710.

30. In another article I have set out some general, preliminary observations concerning this idea with regard to developments elsewhere along the Sino-Tibetan frontier: "The Sichuan-Tibet Frontier in the Fifteenth Century," *Ming Studies* 26 (1988): 37–55.

31. Li, *Complete Gazetteer of the Great Ming*, 37:15b, quoted (with some minor changes and without the final sentence) in Wang, *Gazetteer of Hezhou*, 3:57b–58a. The former work was completed in 1461.

32. Gu et al., *Tibetan Historical Sources in the Veritable Records of the Ming Dynasty*, 9–10.

33. Gu et al., *Tibetan Historical Sources in the Veritable Records of the Ming Dynasty*, 35. Little is known about Zhaozheng aside from the face that he was a eunuch in Ming Taizu's service; see Zhang, *History of the Ming*, 304:7765.

34. Note that the *Da ming yitong zhi* [*Complete Gazetteer of the Great Ming*] dates the establishment of the Hezhou tea-horse trading office to the seventh year of the Hongwu period (1374/1375), a year prior to the date of the *shilu* entry on Zhaozheng's journey to Hezhou; see Li, *Complete Gazetteer of the Great Ming*, 37:14b. Most likely the dispatch of Zhaozheng took place in 1374/1375, and thus the establishment of the tea-horse trading office is dated to that year. The *Da ming yitong zhi* also locates the office in the southeastern part of the Hezhou guard's jurisdiction.

35. Editors' note: The final section of the original article, which detailed the descendants of He Suonanpu down to his great-grandson and his death in the early sixteenth century, was omitted due to space constraints, but can be found in the original publication: Elliot Sperling, "The Ho Clan of Hezhou: A Tibetan Family in Service to the Yuan and Ming Dynasties," in *Indo-sino-tibetica: Studi in Onore di Luciano Petech* (Roma: Bardi, 1990), 359–377.

Chapter 19

BÖN IN CENTRAL AND EAST TIBET

Samten Karmay

Samten Karmay was raised in a Bönpo community in Amdo, trained in the Nyingma and Geluk traditions, received a Ph.D. in London, and teaches in Paris. The two volumes to which these essays serve as introductions are concerned with general surveys of monasteries, temples, hermitages of the Bön religion that have survived or recently been rebuilt in Tibetan regions in the People's Republic of China, and the greater Himalayan region.[1] We see here the immense importance of eastern Tibet, especially at the intersection of southern Amdo and Gyelrong, as a critical reservoir and stronghold for Bönpo culture. The main Central Tibetan Bön monasteries of Menri and Yung-drung Ling in Tsang were established by men who were originally from the east, and nearly two thirds of Menri's abbots were from the eastern Tibetan region of Gyelrong.

While Karmay's assertion that "Bönpo religious establishments never had any political ambition" is true enough for Central Tibet, research on the Gyelrong wars of the eighteenth century has shown that the Bön monasteries there were linked both to the kings of Gyelrong (by family relations) and to the kings' military forces that resisted Qing rule. Moreover, the seventeenth-century King of Beri (in Kham) certainly supported the Bönpos (and likely received support in return) and eventually tried to control or eliminate the Buddhist presence in his expanding kingdom. Karmay traces the history of the main Bön monasteries from the early eleventh century to the present, in both Central and eastern Tibet. The small but important Menri monastery, established in 1405 in Tsang, was known for its strict practice of monastic rules, which set a standard for most other Bön monasteries. We learn something of the relative strength of Bön in contemporary times from the fact that the main Central Tibetan monasteries either have not been rebuilt at all or are shadows of their former selves since the Cultural Revolution, while the monasteries in eastern Tibet have flourished.

The monastic system in the Bön tradition has a long history. It goes back at least to the eleventh century. However, Bön tradition itself traces it back to a period beyond the eleventh century, but this claim remains to be proved.

Although the monasticism of the Bön tradition owns its inspiration to Buddhism, the Bönpo already had established it when the Buddhists began to re-establish their monasteries in the eleventh century. This begins with the six Buddhist monks who returned to Central Tibet from Amdo where they were ordained by Lachen Gewa [Rap]sel (891–975)[2] according to the *Depter Ngönpo* [*Blue Annals*] by Gö Lotsawa Zhönnupel (1392–1481).

In the case of the Bön tradition it started with the disciples of Shenchen Luga. Bönpo chronology ascribes this master to 996–1035. He is also thought to be contemporary with Lotsawa Rinchen Zangpo (958–1055). The disciples of Shenchen Luga established various religious centers, such as temples, hermitages and monasteries.

One of the disciples of this master, Druchen Namkha Yungdrung, is credited with founding a temple in 1072 near the estate of his own family called Dru, a few kilometers to the east of Zhigatsé and north of the Tsangpo river, Central Tibet. It soon developed into a monastery called Yeru Wensakha. The monastery was mainly maintained by the family by providing its abbots. While one brother ensured the line of the family, another would devote himself to religious life and often became the abbot of the monastery. In such an establishment, the monastery is usually considered as belonging to the family as the term *göndak*, the "owner of the monastery" indicates. The ownership always remained the same even when the abbot was not a member of the family.

Wensakha came to be considered as the primary source of the monastic tradition among the Bönpo until the fourteenth century. It was an important center of learning and produced a number of noted writers. Their works became classics for monastic learning in later centuries. The monastery, however, was destroyed by a flood in 1386. With the disappearance of this monastery, a period of monastic culture of the Bön tradition came to an end.

A new era began with the foundation of two monasteries also in Central Tibet. These will be briefly described here as they had a tremendous influence over other Bön monastic establishments.

One of the monks of Wensakha Monastery just referred to was Sherap Gyeltsen. He was the head of one of the colleges of the monastery, but he was absent from the monastery when it was washed away by a flood. He was on a visit to his mother in Gyelrong, eastern Tibet.

On the way back to Central Tibet, news of the flood reached him when he was in Dartsedo. Discouraged, he withdrew himself into a retreat, but there he received good signs that encouraged him to resume his journey on foot back to Central Tibet. He is said to have found various objects in the ruins such as books and musical instruments that belonged to the destroyed monastery. With these objects, taken as an auspicious sign, he founded a monastery on the southern slope of Mount Menri in 1405. The monastery was called Trashi Menri.[3] It is located in a rather secluded place, up the same valley where Wensakha Monastery was located.

With the help of his disciple Rinchen Gyeltsen, a whole system in accordance with the Dru tradition of Wensakha Monastery was re-established with a strong emphasis on the need for abstention from alcoholic drink and the observance of celibacy as the principal guideline of the monastic discipline. These rules are laid out in the *chayik*, the monastic code, and it was read out to the assembly in a solemn ceremony by the disciplinarian once a year. The discipline of the new monastery thus became the model for most Bönpo monasteries in later centuries. It was hard to stick to the rules set out in the *chayik* of Menri Monastery, but it became an established tradition and most monasteries that were founded later were expected to follow its tradition.

However, there were other monasteries which practiced different ritual traditions such as the Shenluk, the "Tradition of Shen" or Zhuluk, the "Tradition of Zhu," but all were expected to follow the same monastic discipline.

The Bönpo were often characterized as being lovers of women and wine (*chang nag la dga' ba*) by the Buddhists, especially the Geluk monastics. In fact, in certain places the members of a monastery or temple were of what one calls *serkhyim*, that is a kind of "semi-monk" who observes only a few out of the many monastic vows. They usually spent a certain amount of time in the year in the monastery and the rest of the time at home in the village helping do household work. The *serkhyim* were not necessarily married men or *ngakpa*.

The founder of Menri Monastery bears the title Nyammé, the "Incomparable One," but in the colophons of books he wrote he describes himself as Shengyi Drangsong, the "monk who follows the Shen," i.e., Sherap Miwo. Amongst his writings there is a detailed commentary of the *Dülwa Lamtü*. It is entitled *Dülhrel Trülgyi Drönmré*. The *Dülwa Küntü* is a classic text devoted to the monastic discipline composed in verse by Metön Sherap Özer (1058–1132).[4] It is these two works that serve as the textual basis of Bönpo monasticism.

Menri Monastery remained small and modest in its development as its founder had wished. Before he died, he appointed his disciple Rinchen Gyeltsen as the abbot of the monastery. Thus Rinchen Gyeltsen bears the title Gyeltsap, the "Apostle." However, the successors of Rinchen Gyeltsen were elected by secret lot from among the qualified monks. There were thirty-two abbots spanning over five hundred and sixty years till around 1966. Its uneasy access did not help it become a great center, but it was highly esteemed for its strict practice of monastic rules. Per Kværne was the first Western scholar to devote an article to the administration of this monastery.[5] The monastery was plundered and finally totally destroyed during the Cultural Revolution, 1966–1976. As of 2002, it still has not been rebuilt.

Yungdrung Ling Monastery was the second in importance to Menri Monastery in Central Tibet.[6] It was founded by Nangtön Dawa Gyeltsen (b. 1796) of Amdo origin in 1834. Although the monastery was a relatively recent establishment in comparison with Menri, it became more prosperous and influential particularly in north-eastern Tibet. The monastery is located on a small plateau at the foot of Mount Ölha Gyelzang to the north of the Tsangpo River facing the Takdruka ferry. It is on the axis of routes leading to Lhasa, Zhigatsé, Gyantsé and Jangtang, the northern plateau. This explains in part the monastery's rapid development. For this strategic reason, the monastery was used as the base of a large People's Liberation Army garrison in the area during the Cultural Revolution; it therefore remained intact till the very last days of the revolution. At the beginning of [the] 1980s, permission was given with funding to rebuild it, but it remains largely symbolic and the temples that have been rebuilt were totally empty when I visited them in 1997.

PERSECUTION AND DESTRUCTION

The history of Bön monasteries is a history of either sectarian persecution or wanton destruction by a foreign invader. The Bönpo religious establishments never had any political ambition and consequently there is no record of their holding any position that had a political significance. This might explain in part why the Bön religion and its monastic tradition somehow survived through the centuries in Tibet in spite of the Bön religion being a non-Buddhist creed among the 80 percent Buddhist population in Central Tibet.

From the eleventh to the fourteenth centuries, no record of general persecution is found apart from a few disputes between two individuals or two religious communities. On the contrary, there are a number of examples of showing good will towards one another. Even after the fourteenth century, a certain number of Bönpo monks of Menri Monastery went to study philosophy at Sakyapa monasteries till Yungdrung Ling Monastery managed to establish its own *tsennyi* studies in the eighteenth century.

In the seventeenth century, Tibet was seething with religio-political conflicts. The rise to political power of the Fifth Dalai Lama (1617–1682) in 1642 calmed down the turmoil in the country. His reign was marked by a remarkable period of peace and tolerance. In 1664, the Fifth Dalai Lama issued a decree appointing Desi Sanggyé Gyatso (1658–1705) as the Regent of Tibet and in the decree the Fifth Dalai Lama recognized Bön as one of Tibet's official religions.[7] This tradition was belatedly revived by the Fourteenth Dalai Lama in India only at the beginning of 1980s. There was therefore no notable persecution during the reign of the Fifth Dalai Lama. On the contrary, the fact that he was deeply interested in the Bön religion is proved by the abundant references to Bön in his autobiography, the *Dukulé Gözang*.

The Regent gives a list of monasteries that were founded by the Fifth Dalai Lama. Amongst these is Sok Tsenden Gön which he mentions rather obliquely saying that it was originally Karma Kagyüpa, but no mention is made regarding whether it had any connection with Bön.[8] However, according to the *Nakchu Sakhülgyi Göndé Khakgi Logyü*, in 1640, during the military campaign of Gushri Khan in Kham, a number of Bönpo and Kagyüpa monasteries suffered destruction.[9] Later in 1668, the Fifth Dalai Lama ordered a Gelukpa monastery to be built for the people of the Sok district, east of Nakchukha, as compensation for the large Bönpo monastery called Sok Yungdrung Ling, four small Kagyüpa monasteries and one small convent called Tsenden Gön that had been destroyed by the Gushri Khan's troops. The new Gelukpa monastery was called Sok Ganden Pelgyé Ling, but it was normally known as Sok Tsenden Gön. However, it was not built on the ruins of Sok Yungdrung Ling as the Bönpo often imply.

However, the Regent seems to have forgotten the very tolerant religious policy that his master maintained throughout his reign. In 1686 under his order, all the Bön religious establishments in the Sertsa district in Khyungpo, Kham, converted to Gelukpa. Four Gelukpa monasteries were then founded for the Sertsa people in four different places: Ganden Trashi Ling in Drodzong; Ganden Tardö Ling in Gangel; Ganden Kapsum Ling in Rimar and Ganden Peljor Ling in Pumar. A lama from Rongpo Ganden Rapten Gön founded by the Fifth Dalai Lama in 1668 was appointed to be in charge of the new monasteries.[10] Rongpo Ganden Rapten Gön is usually known as Rongpo Rapten Gön. Rongpo is a place in the Sok district. The Regent does not mention the names of the Bön religious establishments that he had converted and I have seen no other records mentioning them. It is not clear why the Regent had implemented such a drastic policy of religious conversion by force in this particular place. There were so many other places in the same region where the Bön religion was followed, but no similar action seems to have been taken.

He states: "in Khyungpo Sertsa people believe strongly in Bön (*khyung po gser [ser] tsha khul du bon lugs la dad 'dun che ba* ...) and if the Yungdrung Bön religion is practiced properly ... (citation of a sūtra) one cannot stop them, but during the day the practitioners stay in monasteries. There they fight over the offerings that were made by the faithful just like vultures over corpses. During the night they go to villages and sleep with women. So what they do is very serious sin ... (citation of texts). Thinking for the benefit of myself and them—since they are Bönpo just in name, in reality they behave like laymen—I had them converted to Gelukpa."[11]

It is hard to believe that such was the real reason for which the Regent caused the people of Sertsa to change their faith. It seems that he was not against the religion itself as such, but rather against the Sertsa people who probably resisted the policies of his Gelukpa dominated government in the area. Whatever it may be, this had set a precedent of forced conversion of monasteries belonging not only to the Bön tradition but also to other Buddhist orders. Each time there was a forced conversion the name of the new Gelukpa monastery began with the word *Ganden* or *Genden* following the example of the names of the new monasteries founded by the Fifth Dalai Lama.

Apart from the method of forced conversion, other strategies were used to gain a foothold among a people whose religious tradition was not Gelukpa. This consisted of recognizing a child as a reincarnation in a non-Gelukpa family. That was what happened to the Dru family, which was very prestigious and a strong bastion of Bön as mentioned earlier. The family seat was located to the north of the Tsangpo [River] and a few kilometers to the east of Zhigatsé. It was the Fifth Dalai Lama, who in order to institute the reincarnation series of Panchen Lama, chose a child of the Dru family as the reincarnation of his spiritual master Panchen Lozang Chögyen (1567–1662). The child became the Panchen Lozang Yeshé (1663–1737), but the Fifth Dalai Lama made sure that the family continued to adhere to its own religion. However, another Panchen Lama, Tenpé Wangchuk (1854–1882) was born again in the family. This time, it was the end of the family's own religion. Its seat became known as Trungzhi, the "Base of births" and was made as an estate of Trashilhünpo Monastery.

Another underhanded method was used for enriching their own establishments. In the nineteenth century, it was the intervention by Trashilhünpo Monastery in a dispute between two branches of the Shen family located in the Darding village, a few kilometers to the west of Zhigatsé. The intervention resulted in properties of one of the two families being confiscated and given to a Gelukpa monastery nearby.[12] These are just a few examples of religio-political persecution of a sort under the domination of the Gelukpa government. The Bönpo themselves unfortunately have rarely committed these events to writing.

However, the tendency for non-Gelukpa religious orders to come under persecution was further intensified due to two developments: foreign interference in the internal affairs of Tibet and the gaining of the upper hand by an ultra-fundamentalist section among the Gelukpa monasteries and in government clerical circles.

FOREIGN INTERFERENCE

At the beginning of the seventeenth century, the Zunghar tribes of the Ili district in western Mongolia began to expand their empire. When they became a threat to the Manchu rule over China, the emperor Kangxi had to appeal to the Fifth Dalai Lama (1617–1682) to exert his influence over them since they were of recent conversion to the Gelukpa school. Tibetan authorities in Lhasa maintained good relations with them. However, after the death of the Fifth Dalai Lama, the Manchus began to have political interests in Tibet. Desi Sanggyé

Gyatso was therefore in collusion with the Zunghars in a design to outdo the policies of the Emperor Kangxi concerning Tibet. In 1717, they accordingly began to make incursions into Tibet intended partly to forestall any aggression from the Manchus and on the pretext of defending Gelukpa interests. As their hordes made their way into Tibet, they attacked Bönpo monasteries that they found in their way, looting, burning and murdering monks. As a people of recent conversion, they seem to have had the conviction that they should ransack other religious establishments in Tibet that were non-Gelukpa, such as those of the Nyingmapa and Bönpo. The Nyingmapa suffered particularly at their hands in Central Tibet as they executed several eminent Nyingmapa masters, like Lochen Dharmasri (1654–1717) amongst others, for no valid reasons. Many a Bönpo establishment, such as Shen Darding, had experienced the plunder of the Zunghars. From the accounts of Püntsok Tsering, it is clear that they pillaged and destroyed at least six Bönpo monasteries.[13] The Zunghars were finally expelled by the Tibetans with the help of the Manchu army.

SECTARIAN PERSECUTION

The Gelukpa government in Tibet had a powerful supporter. Since 1720 till 1911 the Manchu influence over Tibet was firmly established and the Gelukpa saw this foreign power as their cherished patron, which it was. At the same time, a certain segment among the Gelukpa began to claim that they were the upholders of the Gelukpa teachings as being the most authentic ones as taught by the Buddha. This of course implied that other Buddhist schools in Tibet and not to mention the Bönpo held false views. The movement came often to be closely associated with the Shukden cult. The deity's antipathy to non-Gelukpa teachings is all the more the object of praise in the ritual texts devoted to this deity.

Amongst other places I should mention here are two areas where this particular movement was very active and where conflicts between the Bönpo and the Gelukpa establishments were particularly fierce. The Sok district contained two important Gelukpa monasteries, Sok Tsenden Gön and Rongpo Rapten Gön as referred to earlier. It was in this area that Pabongkhawa Dechen Nyingpo (1878–1941) of Sera Monastery was active early in the twentieth century. It was he who revived the cult of Shukden in spite of opposition to it by the Thirteenth Dalai Lama. In a forthcoming article I have dealt in some detail with his activities in this area and the revolt of the so-called "Thirty-nine Tribes of Hor" of formally obedient Bönpo against the Tibetan government.

The other place where the relations between the two faiths were similarly strained was Dromo (Chumbi Valley) in southern Tibet. Around 1897 the most active Gelukpa master in this area was Ngawang Kelzang, also of Sera Monastery. He was commonly known as Dromo Geshé Rinpoché and was a disciple and friend of Pabongkhawa Dechen Nyingpo. The cult of Shukden which he set up in this place was based in Dungkar Monastery. The Bönpo monastery in Dromo known as Pümogang had a perpetual struggle with Dungkar for its existence.[14] The conflict between the two monasteries had inspired the composition of a four-line verse of praise to the deity in the propitiatory text by Pabongkhawa Dechen Nyingpo as follows:

> "In the barbarous land where the bad tradition of Shenrap is upheld,
> You made flourish the good path that is complete and faultless.
> With your rapid action of four kinds and many other omens,
> I praise you who are the guide of living beings!"[15]

In 1967 Yongdzin Trijang Lozang Yeshé, the late tutor of the Fourteenth Dalai Lama, wrote a commentary on the propitiatory eulogy to the deity just quoted entitled *Gyelchen Tödrel* (folio 138b). In this work he explains that the phrase "barbarous land" refers to Dromo and thanks to the "four actions of the deity" the Gelukpa tradition was firmly established there. The region was mainly inhabited by a Bönpo population until the Gelukpa penetrated there only in the nineteenth century. Dungkar Monastery was tacitly supported by the Tibetan government in its hostility, but Pümogang seemed to have miraculously survived till the days of the Cultural Revolution.

However, there is yet another region, Gyelrong, where relations between the two faiths were in constant struggle. The exact date of the Buddhist penetration there is not known. Vairocana, a Tibetan Buddhist monk of the eighth century, is said to have resided there, but this is more of a myth than history. In the fifteenth century, Tsakho Ngawang Drakpa, a disciple of Tsongkhapa (1357–1519) and a native of the Tsakho district, [in the] north of Gyelrong, returned to his native country after studying in Central Tibet. He is said to have made a vow to erect 108 monasteries in his native land in the presence of his master. He certainly founded some Gelukpa monasteries in Tsakho and he is said to have used magic against the Bönpo to overcome the latter's opposition to his efforts in conversion.[16] However, the Bönpo people in Gyelrong had to face much more serious hostility in the eighteenth century. Not only had they to fight on a religious front but also a political one. They resisted for nearly thirty years against the Manchu invasion, which was supported and encouraged by the influential Gelukpa lama Changkya Rölpé Dorjé (1717–1786) who had then a high position at the Manchu imperial court of Qianlong. In 1760 the Manchu army finally won the war capturing Sönam Wangdü, the king of Rapten. He was led to Beijing together with more than one thousand people as war prisoners. The king was finally executed. Five horses were attached to his head, hands and feet and then allowed to pull in different directions, a privilege kept for kings in Manchu punishment customs. Yungdrung Lhateng, the royal monastery, was partially destroyed and converted to Gelukpa and was given the name Ganden Tenpel Ling. Gelukpa monks were summoned from Drepung Monastery to administer it. Qianlong issued an edict forbidding the practice of the Bön religion in the area. What is peculiar about this piece of history is that the monastery was totally destroyed during the Cultural Revolution. However, around 1980 the Sichuan government decided to reinstate it for a reason not known to me and even provided funds so that the local Bönpo people could begin to rebuild it as one of their own monasteries.[17]

INTRODUCTION TO GYELRONG IN EASTERN TIBET[18]

Gyelrong is situated to the southeast [*sic*: northeast] of Kham[19] and still remains to this day a very difficult place to get to. The region is now divided into two halves. The northern part is under the administrative unit of the Ngawa (Ch. Aba) "Autonomous Prefecture." Its administrative center is in Barkam. The southern part, which begins just after the Chuchen dzong, comes under the Kandzé (Ch. Ganzi) "Autonomous Prefecture." Its seat of administration is Dartsedo (Ch. Kangding). Both units came under the administration of Chengdu, Sichuan province, although both are completely cut off from the Sichaun basin by the watershed of the massive mountain ranges. Gyelrong therefore no longer exists in its traditional entity. However, in the pre-communist era, it was a Tibetan region with its own history and culture.

The name of this region in Tibetan is spelled as Gyelrong, which is derived from its full name, Gyelmo Tsawa Rong.[20] It is related to the name of the river Gyelmo Ngülchu which is the main river in the region.[21] The toponym Gyelrong in Tibetan usually covers the whole region that had originally included eighteen principalities of varying sizes.[22] The equivalent name of the region in Chinese is often given as Jinchuan, but in fact Jinchuan designates only two principalities in Gyelrong: Tsenla and Chuchen. The Chinese use the name Jiarong for the whole region of Gyelrong. The name Jiarong is obviously a transcription of the Tibetan name Gyelrong.

In Tibetan geographical vocabulary the region is described as *rong*, "gorge." It is one of the four great *rong* (*rongchen zhi*). They are: Kongpo rong, Atak rong,[23] Tsawa rong and Gyelmo rong. The first refers to Kongpo where Mount Bönri is situated;[24] the exact location of the second *rong* remains unknown; the third is the region of Mount Tsawa Karpo in south-east Tibet and the fourth refers to Gyelrong. Indeed, the main valley of the region is long and very narrow. It is cut deep by the huge river called Gyelmo Ngülchu which flows through it.[25] The river starts in the north of the valley from the confluence of Dochu [river] which runs from the area of Dzamtang and Somangchu [river] that flows through the valley of Tsakho. Downstream after about 200 kilometers from the confluence the river is called Dadu in Chinese and here the valley also gradually widens out at a place called Chakzam, "Iron Bridge." From this point the landscape and its inhabitants become explicitly Chinese. The iron suspension bridge over the river is believed to have been originally constructed by the Tibetan engineer Tangtong Gyelpo (b. 1385). It marks the traditional Tibeto-Chinese border in the area.

GYELRONG, AS A SACRED LAND

Gyelrong is also considered as a *beyul*, "hidden land." As is known, there are a number of places in Tibet that are often described as "hidden lands." The term refers to an inaccessible place. The notion of the "hidden land" is also connected with the "sacred geography." From the thirteenth century onwards, there were sporadic Mongol hordes that used to rampage around the country attacking anything they found on their way. Because of this threat, a body of prophetic literature came into existence. It is filled with warnings of the "Hor," a term which refers to Mongol hordes. They would turn up without warning and cause havoc. Gyelrong is described as one of the places where the local people valiantly resisted the Mongol hordes, later the Manchus and still later the Chinese Red Army. In consequence the place was considered a veritable hidden land. It was also a hidden land in the sense that it was the place where the Bön masters claim to have excavated "hidden texts" (*terma*), especially from places around Mount Murdo. Gyelrong was therefore a sacred land for the Tibetans extolled in prophetical texts.[26]

For the Bönpo, it was primarily a "place where textual treasures were concealed" (*terné*) and so a number of "textual rediscoverers" (*tertön*) made visits to Gyelrong. The notion of *terné* in turn has roots in the legendary accounts of the Bönpo sage Drenpa Namkha and his Buddhist disciple Vairocana. They are believed to have dwelt at one time on Mount Murdo. Vairocana was one of the first seven Tibetan Buddhist monks of the eighth century A.D., but he was regarded by the Bönpo and Nyingmapa as one who practiced both Bön and Buddhism. He is, however, said to have been banished to Gyelrong from Central Tibet on an account of having had a liaison with one of the queens of Emperor Tri Songdetsen (r. 742–c. 797).[27] These legendary accounts are important for an understanding of the workings of religious developments in later centuries, particularly in the eighteenth century in Gyelrong. There are caves in the vicinity of Mount Murdo reputed to have been dwelling places of Vairocana.

However, no Bönpo record on Gyelrong has so far been found that goes back beyond the fourteenth century. The founder of the Menri Monastery,[28] Nyammé Sherap Gyeltsen (1356–1415) was a native of Gyelrong. He was first a monk in the Wensaka Monastery in Tsang, Central Tibet. The monastery was founded in 1072.[29] This suggests that monks from Gyelrong studied in this monastery in the fourteenth century. When the latter was destroyed by a flood he founded the Menri Monastery in 1405. Many of the monks who succeeded him as abbots of the Menri Monastery were also from Gyelrong.[30] Both the main Bönpo monasteries Menri and Ralak Yungdrungling[31] in Central Tibet had residential houses for the monk-students coming from Gyelrong (*Gyelrong Khangtsen*) as for monks from other regions.

The natives of Gyelrong are referred to as Gyelrongwa in Tibetan.[32] The Gyelrongwa always considered themselves as Tibetan and they still do to this day. They do not claim any separate ethnic identity from the rest of Tibetans in spite of their native spoken language which is some way from being a Tibetan dialect, but all the same belongs to the Tibeto-Burmese group.[33] Classical Tibetan was the basis of their education and it was their principal means of written communication till around 1950. Even in the present Chinese administrative set up they are rightly treated as Tibetan.[34] And yet it has been denied that the Gyelrongwa are Tibetan on the ground that in their language there is a term for Gyelrong itself.[35]

The Gyelrongwa were reputed to be good craftsmen. Their masonry work was especially appreciated among the Tibetans. This is evidenced by the solidly built houses with stone walls. Another aspect of their architecture is seen in the formidable tall stone towers which are either square, hexagonal or octagonal. They were mainly built for defensive purposes, but also had cultural significance. But above all, it was in their craftsmanship that the Gyelrongwa displayed artistry of a particularly high order, as will be seen below, in the handling of the wood-engravings and paintings.

THE PENETRATION OF THE GELUKPA
IN GYELRONG

Around 1410 a disciple of Tsongkhapa Lozang Drakpa (1357–1419) named Tsakho Ngawang Drakpa, after completing his studies at the feet of the master in Central Tibet, returned to his native land, Tsakho, a district in northern Gyelrong. There is scant information about him. The fact that his name is preceded by the word Tsakho made me presume that he was born in Tsakho. However, he is said to have been born in a place called Sumdo in the principality of Tsenla.[36] This is an interesting indication if it is correct. We will come back to the vicissitude of this principality below. He was no ordinary disciple of Tsongkhapa. In fact, the master praises him in several colophons of works which the master composed at his behest.[37] Tradition has it that he had taken a vow in the presence of his master to found a hundred and eight monasteries in his native land. He certainly managed to convert a few people and founded some small monasteries in Tsakho and even one in the area of Tsenla in the fifteenth century. It was not an easy job for him, for he faced strong resistance from the local people who followed the Bön religion. Subsequently, his establishments remained insignificant throughout the following three centuries. There are tales which tell that he performed magic rites against the Bönpo religious practitioners in order to overcome their opposition to his proselytizing activities.[38] In any case, it is certain that a Gelukpa foothold was established in Gyelrong already in the fifteenth century.

In order to overcome difficulties in converting people the Gelukpa always tried first to convert the chieftain of a locality. The chieftains of Choktsé, Somang and Dzonggak principalities in the Tsakho area were converted to Gelukpa only in later centuries. Their most effective method in converting the local people was to recognize a young boy of a chieftain family. Once the boy becomes a reincarnation as such the prestige of the family increases and the family gets converted usually without any apparent opposition.

In the area of the Choktsé principality, there was a Bön monastery called Barkam Yungdrung Ling. This is said to have been the place of the Bön master Mushen Nyima Gyeltsen (b. 1360).[39] He was a member of the Shen family whose seat was situated in Darding, Tsang, Central Tibet.[40] The monastery therefore followed the religious tradition of the Shen family. The village Barkam has now become a Chinese town serving as the administrative seat of the "Autonomous Prefecture" of Aba (Ngawa). In spite of the intense proselytism of the Gelukpa in the area in the eighteenth century it managed to maintain its own tradition till late in the nineteenth century. A young boy of the Choktsé chieftain family was recognized as the reincarnation of Jangtsé Lozang Lhündrup (1781–1847), the seventy-fourth throne-holder of Tsongkhapa['s seat] in Ganden Monastery in Central Tibet. Lozang Lhündrup himself was a man from Choktsé. The boy was called Khyenrap Tenpé Gyentsen and later he became an abbot of the monastery Tenpelling, formerly Yungdrung Lhateng in Chuchen to which we shall refer below. In 1874, supported by his own family, which was now Gelukpa, and the Manchu court, he turned the Barkam Yungdrungling Monastery into a Gelukpa one and named it Ganden Dargyeling. The forcible conversion of this monastery caused a local war between those people of Tsakho who followed the Gelukpa and the people of Sharkhok (Ch. Songpan) who followed the Bön religion. The latter tried to save the monastery, but they were ultimately defeated. They could give protection only to the lama of the monastery whom they led to Sharkhok where he settled down in the village Trimé.[41]

The Gelukpa had great difficulties in penetrating into southern Gyelrong where the principalities of Trokyap, Chuchen and Geshetsa were situated. They were staunch up-holders of the Bön religion. However, the position of Tsenla principality also in the south was somewhat dubious. At one time, the family of the chieftain followed the Bön religion, at another Buddhism. One of the monasteries founded by Tsakho Ngawang Drakpa is said to be in Sumdo, a place in

Tsenla. The fact that from about the beginning of the fifteenth century Tsenla was already strongly subjected to proselytism by the Gelukpa is also told in a work ascribed to Rongtön Sheja Künrik (1367–1449), a Sakyapa writer born also in Tsenla and originally a Bön follower. The work purports to be contesting the activities of Buddhist proselytism aimed at the court of the king of Tsenla.[42]

In 1731 the king of Tsenla was reluctant to cooperate with the Bön master Sanggyé Lingpa (1705–1735) when the latter was trying to trace a footpath around the sacred Mount Murdo.[43] All this suggests that the royal house of Tsenla was no longer entirely a follower of the Bön religion in the eighteenth century. However, the family was related by blood to the Rapten royal house in Chuchen. Tsenla was the target of the first Manchu military campaign in 1746 and in 1771 it joined Chuchen in putting up resistance against the second Manchu campaign.

The strength of Gelukpa's expansion in Gyelrong, which was slow but solid, is shown by the fact that a number of its monk-students went to study in Central Tibet. All the large Gelukpa monasteries such as Drepung, Sera and Ganden had residential houses for the monk recruits from Gyelrong. At various periods, four of them succeeded in occupying the throne of Tsongkhapa in Ganden Monastery, the highest position a monk could hold in the Gelukpa school. The work on the history of Buddhism in Amdo gives a long list of other monks from Gyelrong who occupied various important positions in the Gelukpa establishments in Central Tibet.[44]

THE BÖN RELIGION IN THE EIGHTEENTH CENTURY IN GYELRONG

In 1731 Sanggyé Lingpa (1705–1735), a Bön "text treasure revealer," traveled from Khyungpo to Gyelrong. His main intention was to turn Mount Murdo into a sacred site and eventually to reveal "hidden texts."[45] It was on this occasion that Kündröl Drakpa (b. 1700) joined him and at the same time became a disciple of the master and was initiated into what is known as Bön Sarma, the New Bön Tradition. This was the beginning of Kündröl's interest in Gyelrong. A little later he flourished there by becoming a prelate at the courts of the Geshetsa, Trokyap and Chuchen royal houses. His main interest was to revive the Bön religion which was under continual threat from the slow but inexorable expansion of the Gelukpa clergy in the northern and eastern areas of Gyelrong. Through this intent, he discovered, thanks to Sanggyé Lingpa, his spiritual mentor, the religious ideology which took the form of the New Bön Tradition. With this new approach to Bön he was able to arouse enthusiasm for the religion among the people, especially the most powerful local kings at the time. He was therefore successful in persuading the kings of Trokyap and Chuchen to undertake major woodblock engraving projects for the printing of the first part of the Bön Canon as well as the engraving of a number of printing woodblocks of the life-stories of Shenrap Miwo.

THE MANCHU CAMPAIGNS AGAINST GYELRONG

In the eyes of the Manchus the inhabitants of such outlying places as Gyelrong beyond the territories of the Manchu imperial rule were barbarians and were not worthy of attention. However, after the conquest of the whole of China proper by the Manchus, it soon became a battleground of religio-political struggle from 1746 onwards, on the one hand between the Bön religion and the Gelukpa school of Tibetan Buddhism and on the other between the Manchus and the principalities of Tsenla and Chuchen in Gyelrong. In 1776 the Manchus finally triumphed in their imperial ambition through military victory over the principalities of Tsenla, called in Chinese Xiao Jinchuan ("Small Jinchuan"), and Chuchen, Da Jinchuan ("Big Jinchuan").

In Chinese historiography, the Mongol imperial rule over China is called the Yuan Dynasty and that of the Manchu rulers the Qing Dynasty making them sound as if the two were just simply Chinese dynasties. This Chinese ethnocentric presentation of history is often faithfully followed by Sinologists. The fact is that neither the Mongols nor the Manchus were Chinese. It was only when the Mongol and Manchu emperors ruled China that Tibet had formed a political association with them just as China herself was part of the Mongol and Manchu empires. In the same vein, the Manchu campaigns in Gyelrong are said to have been launched in order to settle local disputes between "local barbarian chieftains" giving the impression that the region was already under the Manchu rule. The resistance put up by the people of Tsenla and Chuchen in Gyelrong is therefore described as "rebellion." The claim that it was already from the time of the Tang Dynasty (618–907) that the local chieftains received Chinese titles is arguable to say the least.[46] It would be uncritical of us to accept such claims without noting to what extent the control was exercised over these people by the various rulers in China.

From 1720 the imperial court of the Manchus in Beijing had been able to exert its political influence in Tibet and came to embrace, at least in appearance, the new school of Tibetan Buddhism, namely the Gelukpa, which was in power. The Manchu government ostensibly presented itself as the defender of the new school for reasons of political expediency. Even if the Manchu political influence in Central Tibet by 1746 was considerably strong, the Manchus had yet to penetrate into such far flung regions of Tibet as Gyelrong.

In Central Tibet, the Gelukpa had previous political experience, for in 1642 it was with the support of a Mongol force that it was able to vanquish its opponent, Karma Tenkyong Wangpo, the king of Tibet, based in Tsang although the king was the legitimate ruler of the country. The new school, however, came to be overtaken by a movement of fundamentalists within itself which advocated a radical approach to questions of Buddhist theory and practice in Tibet. It was diametrically opposed to the Bön religion, being a non-Buddhist religion, despite the fact that it was recognized as one of Tibet's official religions by the Fifth Dalai Lama (1712–1782) in his edict of 1664. It was therefore no co-incidence that the Manchu empire wanted to bring Gyelrong under its control in its policy of imperial expansion as an extension of its influence in Central Tibet. Moreover, Gyelrong was one of the last regions of Tibet where an appreciable section of the population was still following the Bön religion.

At the Manchu court, there was a very influential Buddhist master in the person of Changkya Khutugtu Rolpé Dorjé (1717–1786) who was a most zealous devotee of the new school. He was certainly keen to lend his power to the expansion of the new school in the places where it had begun to establish itself, but had no great success. The Manchus themselves at the beginning were perhaps not conscious of the religious problems in Gyelrong. Their main interest was the imperial policy of expansion towards the south. As the imperial army became entrenched, the Manchus gradually became aware of the strong resistance put up by the local militia whose faith was opposed to the Gelukpa movement within Gyelrong itself. The Bön leaders in Gyelrong were aware that the Manchus were staunch supporters of the Gelukpa clergy and its theocratic government in Central Tibet. They viewed with skepticism the fact that the Gelukpa clergy in Central Tibet considered the Manchu emperors as the manifestation of Bodhisattava Mañjuśri.

As the war dragged on, the Manchus suspected that the followers of the Bön practitioners in Gyelrong were capable of performing Bön rites against them and the emperor Qianlong was alarmed by the thoughts that it might have had a bad effect on the morale of his fighting men in Gyelrong. On the other hand, the emperor appreciated the Buddhist rites performed by Changkya at the court for the same purpose. Changkya was shrewd enough to foresee that the Gelukpa movement in Gyelrong would benefit if the imperial government embarked on its expansion towards the south and controlled regions like Gyelrong. He therefore lost no opportunity to exert his influence at the court in encouraging the imperial army to destroy the Bön establishments once it was victorious. In 1776 the imperial army, after six years of fighting was at last able to vanquish the enemy, but it was only through the use of Western methods of armament. In the same year the imperial army destroyed Yungdrung Lhateng, the Bön monastery of the Rapten royal house. It was immediately rebuilt in the image of the Gelukpa monastery with a new name. It was invested with full authority over all other Gelukpa establishments in Gyelrong.

The view according to which the emperor Qianlong was anxious not to encourage too strongly the Gelukpa in their proselytism in Gyelrong, lest the influence of Central Tibetan authority in the region might increase does not correspond to the historical reality.[47] This seems to derive from wanting to credit more political genius to the emperor than is likely to have been the case. The fact is that Changkya was not content with just having the Rapten royal monastery rebuilt in accordance with the tradition of the Gelukpa school. He further made sure that the Bön religion in Gyelrong was buried in the ashes of the ground on which the new monastery of the Gelukpa stood. In this, he was very successful, convincing the emperor of the necessity of proscribing the Bön religion in the region, for the emperor went to the extent of issuing an edict plainly authorizing imperial support for the politico-religious domination by new Gelukpa clergy in Gyelrong.[48]

Gelukpa sources state that the emperor issued another edict that particularly forbade the practice of the Bön religion in Gyelrong.[49] However, if that had been the case, the imperial proscription had little effect, because the Bön religion continued to be practiced in large parts of the region in the later eighteenth, nineteenth and twentieth centuries. Although in the eighteenth century Gyelrong was marred by wars, persecution and destruction, there were short periods of intense cultural developments such as gave rise to the practice of wood-engraving, calligraphy, painting, printing, architecture, stone work and writing.

NOTES

1. Editors' note: This article combines two introductions, from Samten G. Karmay and Yasuhiko Nagano, eds., compiled by Dondrup Lhagyal, et al., *A Survey of Bönpo Monasteries and Temples in Tibet and the Himalaya*, Senri Ethnological Reports 38 (Osaka: National Museum of Ethnology, 2003) and Samten G. Karmay, *Feast of the Morning Light: The Eighteenth Century Wood-engravings of Shenrab's Life-stories and the Bön Canon from Rgyal rong*, Senri Ethnological Reports, 57 (Osaka: National Museum of Ethnology, 2005). The source of each part will be obvious from its regional focus.

2. Editors' note: Another scholar suggests his dates were actually 953–1035. Tshe tan Zhabs drung, "Mdo smad grub pa'i gnas chen dan tig shel gyi ri bo le lag dang bcas pa'i dkar chag don ldan ngag gi rgyud mangs [A Zither of Meaningful Words: A Catalogue to the Holy Place for Siddhas in Mdo smad, Mount Dan tig shel and Surrounding Areas]," in 'Jigs med chos 'phags, ed., *Tshe tan Zhabs drung rje btsun 'Jigs med rigs pa'i blo gros mchog gi gsung 'bum*, vol. 3 (Beijing: Minzu chubanshe, 2007), 314. This information was kindly provided by Nicole Willock.

3. Karmay and Nagano, *A Survey of Bönpo Monasteries*, see monastery number 1.

4. Per Kværne, "The Canon of the Tibetan Bönpos," *Indo-Iranian Journal* 16, no. 1 (1974): 18–56 and *Indo-Iranian Journal* 16, no. 2 (1974): 96–144: T. 7.

5. Per Kværne, "Remarques sur l'administration d'un monastère bon-po," *Journal Asiatique* 258 (1970): 187–192.

6. Karmay and Nagano, *A Survey of Bönpo Monasteries*, see monastery number 2.

7. Hugh E. Richardson, "The Fifth Dalai Lama's Decree Appointing Sangs rgyas rgya mtsho as Regent," in *High Peaks, Pure Earth: Collected Writings on Tibetan History and Culture*, ed. Michael Aris (London: Serindia Publications, 1998), 441.

8. Sangs rgyas rgya mtsho, *Dga' ldan chos 'byung Vaiḍūrya ser po [Yellow Beryl]* (Zi ling: Krung go Bod kyi shes rig dpe skrun khang, 1989), 405.

9. *Nag chu sa khul gyi dgon sde khag gi lo rgyus [History of the Monasteries of Nakchu Prefecture]* ([Bod ljongs]: Nag chu sa gnas srid gros lo rgyus rig gnas dpyad gzhi'i rgyu cha rtsom sgrig khang, 1993), 351.

10. Sangs rgyas rgya mtsho, *Yellow Beryl*, 459.

11. Sangs rgyas rgya mtsho, *Yellow Beryl*, 459.

12. Dondrup Lhagyal, "Bonpo Family Lineages in Central Tibet," in *New Horizons in Bon Studies*, ed. Samten Gyaltsen Karmay and Yasuhiko Nagano (Osaka: National Museum of Ethnology, 2000), 444.

13. Karmay and Nagano, *A Survey of Bönpo Monasteries*, see monasteries numbered 15, 19, 22, 54, 27, 34.

14. Karmay and Nagano, *A Survey of Bönpo Monasteries*, see monastery number 8.

15. *gshen rabs[rab] lugs ngan 'dzin pa 'i mtha' 'khob tu/ las bzhi'i rtags mtshan rno myur du ma yis/ tshang la ma nor lam bzang rgyas mdzad pa'i/ skye rgu'i 'dren par gyur pa khyod la bstod/.*

16. Dkon mchog bstan pa rab rgyas, Brag dgon zhabs drung, *Yul mdo smad kyi ljongs su thub bstan rin po che ji ltar dar ba'i tshul gsal bar brjod pa deb ther rgya mtsho [The Ocean Annals of Amdo]* (Lanzhou: Kan su'u mi rigs dpe skrun khang, 1982), 774.

17. Karmay and Nagano, *A Survey of Bönpo Monasteries*, see monastery number 187.

18. This marks the start of the introductory material drawn from Karmay, *Feast of the Morning Light*.

19. [Editors' note: The reference to Gyelrong being southeast of Khams must be a mistake. This region can best be described as being southeast of Amdo, or northeast of Khams.] Whether Rgyal rong is a part of Khams or Amdo, it is sometimes disputed. According to Dkon mchog bstan pa rab rgyas, *The Ocean Annals of Amdo*, it is in Mdo khams, hence Khams (771), but according to Bsam gtan, Dmu dge, *Bod kyi lo rgyus kun dga' me long [History of Tibet]*, Rnga ba bod rigs rang skyong khul gyi rig gnas lo rgyus dpyad yig gdam bsgrigs, Spyi'i deb lnga pa, Bod yig deb gnyis pa (N.p.: Srid gros si kron zhing chen rnga ba bod rigs cha'ang rigs rang skyong u yon lhan khang gi rig gnas lo rgyus dpyad yig gi zhib 'jug u yon lhan khang, 1987), 270, it is in Mdo smad.

20. For the sake of simplification, I have used the transcription Rgyal rong throughout. The name is sometimes written as Rgya rong, which is derived from the phrase *shar phyogs rgyal mo rgya yi rong,* but considered as incorrect. The phrase occurs in texts such as Kun grol grags pa, Smon rgyal, "Par gyi dkar chag srid pa'i sgron me [Catalogue of Blockprints: Lamp of the World]," in *Khams chen ti ka 'grel* (Khro skyabs [Sichuan] edition, Vol. A, f.531a). There is confusion about this name between Tsha ba rong and Rgyal mo tsha ba rong in Buddhist sources; cf. Samten Karmay, *The Great Perfection* (Leiden: Brill, 1988), 26 n. 31. G. van Driem translates the name Rgyal mo rong as "Queen ravine" and further indicates that "the 'Queen' is the native Bön

goddess associated with mount Dmu rdo in the Rgyal mo rong area" (*Languages of the Himalayas*, vol. 1 [Leiden: Brill, 2001], 44.

21. The name of this river is often mistakenly spelled as Rgya mo rngul chu.

22. For references to the list of the eighteen principalities, see Samten Karmay, *Feast of the Morning Light: The Eighteenth Century Wood-engravings of Shenrab's Life-stories and the Bon Canon from Gyalrong*, Senri ethnological reports 57 (Osaka: National Museum of Ethnology, 2005), chapter 5 n. 15.

23. This is normally known as A stag rong in the north (Byang A stag rong). It is therefore situated in the north, but its precise location remains unknown. In the Gesar epic literature, one of the thirty "knights" (*dpa'thul*) is called A stag Lha mo. She is considered to be based in the north. Cf. Samten Karmay, *The Little Luminous Boy: The Oral Tradition from the Land of Zhangzhung Depicted on Two Tibetan Paintings* (Bangkok: Orchid Press, 1998), 500.

24. Cf. Charles Ramble, "The Creation of the Bon Mountain of Kongpo," in *Mandala and Landscape*, ed. A. W. MacDonald (New Delhi: D. K. Printworld,1997), 133–232; Samten Karmay, *The Arrow and the Spindle: Studies in History, Myths, Rituals and Beliefs in Tibet* (Kathmandu: Mandala Book Point, 1998), No. 14.

25. The river 'Bri chu (Salween) in Khams is also called by the same name.

26. Cf. Blo ldan snying po, *Ma 'ongs ba byang gsal ba'i me long [Collected Prophecies and Visionary Revelations of Bonpo Masters of the Past, A Collection of Texts from yang steng Hermitage in Dolpo (northwestern Nepal) by Blo ldan snying po, Tre ston Nam mkha' rgyal mtshan and Yang ston Khri khar wer shi]* (Dolanji [H. P., India]: n.p., 1979), 29.

27. Cf. Karmay, *The Great Perfection*, 17–37.

28. Karmay, *Feast of the Morning Light*, Survey No. 1.

29. Nyi ma bstan 'dzin, *Bstan rtsis ngo mtshar nor bu'i phreng ba [Chronological Table]*. No publication data. See Per Kværne, "A Chronological Table of the Bon po: The bstan rcis of Ñi ma bstan 'jin," *Acta Orientalia* 33 (1971): 205–282.

30. According to Kun bzang blo gros, *Zhang bod kyi bstan 'byung lo rgyus lha rgyud rin chen phreng ba ma bcos gser gyi yang zhun [Bön Religious History of the Zhang Zhung and Tibet]* (Beijing: Mi rigs dpe skrun khang, 2003), 461–465, nineteen out of thirty-three abbots of Sman ri were from Rgyal rong.

31. Karmay, *Feast of the Morning Light*, Survey No. 2.

32. The population of Rgyal rong is about 80,000 (Yasuhiko Nagano, *A Historical Study of the Rgyarong Verb System* [Tokyo: Seishido, 1984], 4).

33. Cf. Nagano, *A Historical Study of the Rgyarong Verb System*, 1.

34. Cf. Nagano, *A Historical Study of the Rgyarong Verb System*, 4.

35. Patrick Mansier, "La guerre du Jinchuan (Rgyal rong): son contexte politico-religieux" [The Jinchuan (Rgyal rong) War: Its Politico-Religious Context]," in *Tibet: Civilisation et société*, ed. Fernand Meyer (Paris: Éditions de la Fondation Singer-Polignac: Éditions de la Maison des Sciences de l'Homme, 1990), 128.

36. Dkon mchog bstan pa rab rgyas, *The Ocean Annals of Amdo*, 774; Shes rab rgya mtsho, "Rje tsha kho mkhan chen ngag dbang grags pa'i rnam thar mdor bsdus ches

phra zegs ma tsam" [Biography of Ngakwang Drakpa]," in *Rnga ba bod rigs rang skyong khul gyi rig gnas lo rgyus dpyad yig gdam bsgrigs*, Deb gsum pa (N.p.: Srid gros si kron zhing chen rnga ba bod rigs cha'ang rigs rang skyong u yon lhan khang gi rig gnas lo rgyus dpyad yig gi zhib 'jug u yon lhan khang, 1987), 67.

37. Shes rab rgya mtsho, "Biography of Ngakwang Drakpa," 68, 69, 71.

38. Dkon mchog bstan pa rab rgyas, *The Ocean Annals of Amdo*, 774.

39. Nyi ma bstan 'dzin (b. 1813), *Sangs rgyas kyi bstan rtsis ngo mtshar nor bu'i phreng ba* (*A Chronological Table of the Bon po*).

40. Cf. Samten Karmay, *The Treasury of Good Sayings: A Tibetan History of Bon* (London: Oxford University Press, 1972), 3–6; Dondrup Lhagyal, "Bonpo Family Lineages in Central Tibet," 437–445.

41. Cf. Sher grags, "'Bar khams zhes pa'i ming gi byung tshul [Origins of the Name Barkam]," in *Rnga ba bod rigs rang skyong khul gyi rig gnas lo rgyus dpyad yig gdam bsgrigs*, Deb gsum pa (N.p.: Srid gros si kron zhing chen rnga ba bod rigs cha'ang rigs rang skyong u yon lhan khang gi rig gnas lo rgyus dpyad yig gi zhib 'jug u yon lhan khang, 1987), 149. On the people of Shar khog one may see Samten Karmay and Philippe Sagant, *Les neuf forces de l'homme: récits des confins du Tibet* [*The Nine Forces of Man: Stories from the Borders of Tibet*] (Nanterre: Société d'ethnologie, 1998).

42. Shes bya kun rigs, *Bon chos kyi bstan pa shan dbye* [*A Discussion of the Doctrinal and Practical Differences Between Bon and Chos*] (Dolanji Village, H.P.: Tashi Dorji: distributor, Tibetan Bonpo Monastic Centre, 1976), 512.

43. Cf. Karmay, *The Arrow and the Spindle*, No. 25, 457. Also see Karmay, *Feast of the Morning Light*, chapter 1.

44. Dkon mchog bstan pa rab rgyas, *The Ocean Annals of Amdo*, 778–779.

45. Karmay, *The Arrow and the Spindle*, No. 25.

46. Mansier, "The Jinchuan (Rgyal rong) War: Its Politico-Religious Context," 126–128.

47. Mansier, "The Jinchuan (Rgyal rong) War: Its Politico-Religious Context," 126–127; Joanna Waley-Cohen, "Religion, War and Empire-Building in Eighteenth Century China," *International History Review* 20, no. 2 (Qing Colonialism Issue) (June 1998): 349.

48. Per Kværne and Elliot Sperling, "Preliminary Study of an Inscription from Rgyal rong," *Acta Orientalia* 54 (1993): 119.

49. Blo bzang chos kyi nyi ma, Thu'u bkwan III, "Bon gyi grub mtha' byung tshul [Origins of the Bon Tenet System]," in *Grub mtha' thams cad kyi khungs dang 'dod tshul ston pa legs bshad shel gyi me long* (Lanzhou: Kan su'u Mi rigs Dpe skrun khang, 1985), 389.

PART VI

Modern Tibet (Seventeenth to Twentieth Centuries)

CENTRAL TIBETAN LEADERSHIP

Chapter 20

THE DALAI LAMAS AND THE ORIGINS OF
REINCARNATE LAMAS

Leonard W. J. van der Kuijp

Who is the Dalai Lama? A man? A monk? A god? Leonard van der Kuijp surveys the prehistory of the Dalai Lama as a divinity, as the bodhisattva Avalokiteśvara. How and when did the Dalai Lamas come to be associated with the most important Buddhist celestial being in Tibet? Van der Kuijp provides answers to these questions in this study of the history of an idea. If the Dalai Lamas are the most famous embodiments of Avalokiteśvara in Tibet, they are by no means the first leaders to have been identified with the bodhisattva. Van der Kuijp places the origins of the tradition as early as the eleventh century, when the institution builder Dromtön was invested with the authority and status of Avalokiteśvara by his Indian guest, the Buddhist scholar Atiśa. In Atiśa's telling, Dromtön was not only Avalokiteśvara but also a reincarnation of former Buddhist monks, laypeople, commoners, and kings. Furthermore, these reincarnations were all incarnations of that very same being, Avalokiteśvara. Van der Kuijp takes us on a tour of literary history, showing that the narrative attributed to Atiśa became a major source for both incarnation and reincarnation ideology for centuries to come.

Two interconnected images appear in the mind's eye when Tibet and Tibetan Buddhism are brought up—the Dalai Lama and the system of reincarnation of lamas and teachers, both lay and monastic. This essay discusses both from a historical perspective by traversing the grounds of Tibetan history as well as Tibetan biographical, autobiographical, and historical literature. What follows is based on what is considered historical fact, and serves to provide a guide to the pertinent features of the lives of the Dalai Lamas from the First Dalai Lama, Gendün Drup (1391–1474) to the current Fourteenth Dalai Lama, Tendzin Gyatso (b. 1935). The origin of the institution of the Dalai Lama is closely connected to the "invention of tradition."[1] The remarks that will be made about the origin of the institution of the Dalai Lama are admittedly speculative, in particular the idea that the men heading this institution are reincarnations of the bodhisattva Avalokiteśvara who was himself the embodiment of the enlightened compassion ensuing upon buddhahood. Ever greater numbers of treasures have been emerging from the extraordinarily rich literary storehouse of Tibetan culture in recent years. Many previously unknown wood-block printed texts and very old, handwritten manuscripts have started to reappear. Only further investigation of these texts will prove whether the following remarks have any validity and are more than probable hypotheses. Such investigation may lead to unanticipated insights into their narrative structures and ideological projects. This means that reading through them, we should always be aware of the historical, political, and religious contexts in which they were written.

ALTAN KHAN'S LEGACY

The title "Dalai Lama" derives from a longer expression that first appears in 1578. Altan Khan (1507–1582), ruler of the Tümed Mongols (Tib. *Sokpo*), gave Sönam Gyatso (1543–1588) the title *Dalai Lama Vajradhara* during a series of meetings that began on 19 June 1578 in Cabciyal, in present-day Qinghai Province, China. The Mongol word *dalai* indicates something vast, expansive, or universal, and therefore commonly denotes "ocean," even though such a large body of water probably fell beyond the experience of the average Mongol. Mongol *dalai* corresponds to Tibetan *gyatso*, the usual equivalent of Sanskrit *sāgara*, all "ocean."

It has become increasingly clear that much Tibetan literature has suffered at the hands of its editors. Sometimes the changes made in a piece of writing are due to careless oversights, other times they are intentional and reflect the editor's own agenda. Provided that the text has not been tampered with—and there is no real guarantee that it has not—the earliest Tibetan historical account of the meeting between Altan Khan and Sönam Gyatso is that found in Mipam Chökyi Gyatso's 1596 biography of Maitri Döndrup Gyeltsen (1527–1587) of Bökhar. The meeting was also recorded in the biography of Sönam Gyatso, which the Fifth Dalai Lama, Ngawang Lozang Gyatso (1617–1682), almost completed in 1646. This biography and its later companion volume, his 1652 biography of his immediate predecessor, the Fourth Dalai Lama, Yönten Gyatso (1589–1616), soon became quite influential because the author was, after all, the Fifth Dalai Lama. He had these texts printed quickly, thereby ensuring a wider circulation than if only handwritten copies had been available. His large autobiography records that he edited the first work and wrote the second while en route to Beijing, to the Qing court of the young Emperor Shunzhi (1638–1661).

This trip took him through largely Mongol populations, which was no coincidence because the Fourth Dalai Lama himself had not been an ethnic Tibetan but rather Tümed Mongol. Yönten Gyatso was in fact Altan Khan's great-grandson. Both texts are as much biographies as they form part of a political and sociological complex in which the Fifth Dalai Lama seeks to establish the theological inevitability and legitimacy of his office, himself, and his institution as the rightful ruler of Tibet, in addition to emphasizing his metaphysical ties to the ruling house of Altan Khan. This was a project he had started with his 1643 chronicle of Tibetan political history. These works display his keen awareness of the power of the "right" language and he was indeed a great master in shaping public opinion. The fact that he is often called "the Great Fifth" testifies to his political savvy and organizational skills and those of his immediate entourage. With him also began the so-called "bodhisattvacratic" governance of Tibet.

Turning to the Mongols, we find that Altan Khan's anonymous biography in verse, which cannot have been earlier than 1607, records the meeting between Altan Khan and the Third Dalai Lama. This work should hold particular authority for no other reason than that the author explicitly states that he bases this narrative on an earlier work by Sarmai (alias Uran Tanggharigh Dayun Kiya), a member of the party the Khan had dispatched in 1574 to invite Sönam Gyatso to Mongolia. The Fifth Dalai Lama writes that the Khan had given Sönam Gyatso the title *Dalai Lama Vajradhara*, although the full Mongol title[2] found in this work is longer.

Shortly after his birth, Sönam Gyatso was recognized as the reincarnation of Gendün Gyatso (1475–1542). The latter was the second Zimkhang Okma "Lower Residence" reincarnate lama of Drepung monastery and consequently later also came to be known as the Second Dalai Lama. During his lifetime, Drepung became the largest and probably most influential Geluk institution, which traced its origins back to Tsongkhapa Lozang Drakpa (1357–1419) and his immediate disciples. Gendün Gyatso's residence there was the Ganden Podrang, which had originally served as the residence where the Phakmodru rulers stayed when they visited the monastery. The Ganden Podrang had been called the Dokhang Ngönpo or "Blue Stone House" until the Phakmodru ruler, Ngawang Trashi (r. 1499–1564), donated it to Gendün Gyatso. Gendün Gyatso himself had already been recognized as the reincarnation of Gendün Drup, one of Tsongkhapa's last students and founder of Trashilhünpo in 1447.[3] Gendün Drup in turn was posthumously recognized both as the first "Lower Residence" reincarnate lama and as the First Dalai Lama.

Hierarchs of other traditions in Tibetan Buddhism gave Sönam Gyatso respect commensurate with his ranking as one of many reincarnate lamas populating the Tibetan religious landscape. Contemporaneous sources such as the biographies of hierarchs from the Karma sect of the Kagyü, those of the Fifth

Karmapa Zhamar Könchok Yenlak (1525–1583) and the tenth Karmapa Zhanak Wangchuk Dorjé (1556–1603), simply make reference to him as the "(supreme) incarnation of Drepung," or the *chöjé* "religious lord of Drepung." Maitri Döndrup's biographer often follows the same practice, at one point calling Sönam Gyatso the reincarnation of both Avalokiteśvara and Domtön Gyelwé Jungné (1005–1064), a motif we will return to below.

REENACTMENT OF AN OLDER RELATIONSHIP

Both the earliest Tibetan and the earliest available Mongol accounts of the meeting between Altan Khan and Sönam Gyatso display many similarities. Absent from both, however, is an acknowledgement that the two were consciously reenacting a much earlier relationship that had existed between the Mongol emperor Qubilai Khan (r. 1260–1294), who inaugurated the Yuan dynasty in 1276, and Pakpa Lodrö Gyeltsen (1235–1280), Tibetan hierarch of the Sakya School. Later narratives do explicitly record that each recognized the other as the reincarnation of these earlier men. The Fifth Dalai Lama writes in his biography of Sönam Gyatso that when the latter taught the six-syllable prayer of Avalokiteśvara to Altan Khan and his entourage, the Khan said:

> In the past, when the monastery of Pakpa Shingkun[4] was constructed, I was Sechen Gyelpo [= Qubilai Khan] and you were Lama Pakpa. You consecrated the monastery. . . .

This suggests that Altan Khan had been Qubilai in a previous life while Sönam Gyatso had been Pakpa. It is likely no coincidence that Pakpa and his personal possessions appear in the Fifth Dalai Lama's autobiography with unusual frequency. The Fifth Dalai Lama cites several sources he used in his study of Sönam Gyatso, including a complete biography Kharnak Lotsawa Jampel Dorjé had written. While this work has not come down to us, a large fragment of Kharnak Lotsawa's manuscript on the development of the Geluk School has. Here Kharnak Lotsawa treats Sönam Gyatso and his journey to Qinghai in a surprisingly perfunctory manner. After the Khan had invited Sönam Gyatso to visit him, Kharnak Lotsawa writes:

> Sönam Gyatso set out northwards in the Year of the Tiger [1578]. At that time, the Tibetanized Mongol chief Karmapel paid him obeisance with respect and worship, including gifts. Then in the year of the earth hare [1579], at the age of thirty-six Sönam Gyatso met with Athen Gyelpo (i.e., Altan Khan) in Tsokha. He sated all the Mongols by teaching Buddhism to establish them in virtue. Then he went to Pelden Chökhorling Monastery [which he founded with Altan Khan] and then went down to Chamdo in Kham. . . .

Whatever the merits of identifying Altan Khan with Qubilai, tradition has never problematized Pakpa's incorporation into the reincarnations of the Dalai Lamas. As addressed later, this is a result of the specific role tradition has assigned Avalokiteśvara. For political and religious reasons, the Sakya School, particularly members of the ruling family at Sakya Monastery who were distant relations of Pakpa, were understandably disinclined to recognize Sönam Gyatso as a reincarnation of their ancestor. Moreover, the School held the opinion that Pakpa was an emanation—not reincarnation—of Mañjuśrī, the symbol of enlightened wisdom. The School held this position in recognition of Pakpa's learning. In fact, from quite early on, the School also held that Sachen Künga Nyingpo (1092–1158), Pakpa's great-grandfather and the School's first patriarch, was a reincarnation of Avalokiteśvara. Yet in none of the writings from this School do we find Pakpa referred to as a reincarnation of Sachen.

We should keep in mind that when Altan Khan initially granted Sönam Gyatso the title "Dalai Lama," it was a relatively minor and by no means unique event despite that from the seventeenth century onward it came to play a significant role in Tibetan political and religious history starting with the Fifth Dalai Lama. There is evidence that at least one other hierarch, Gyelwa Künga Trashi (1536–1605), of the Kagyü School and sixteenth abbot of Taklung, also enjoyed the patronage of the Khan, though perhaps not on the same scale as that with Sönam Gyatso. Gyelwa Künga Trashi's biography reports that he traveled twice to regions where the Tümed Mongols lived. The first trip was from 1578 to 1581, the second from 1589 to 1593. During that first trip the Khan gave Gyelwa Künga Trashi the title *Dezhin Shekpa*, a *tamka* seal forged from eighty-five *sang* pieces, a *jasa* edict, and thousands of pieces of silver. Gyelwa Künga Trashi and the Khan met once more in the fall of 1578, on which occasion the Khan made him an offering of a large container made from fifteen hundred pieces of silver. The Khan no doubt made this offering in consideration of the various Buddhist teachings Gyelwa Künga Trashi had conferred.

A DOUBLE-EDGED SWORD DECISION

The reasons for the Geluk School's incredible success in their missionary work among the Mongols remain to be investigated. Probably one reason was that Sönam Gyatso was an incarnate lama while Gyelwa Künga Trashi was not. Part of the explanation would surely include the doings of Pelden Gyatso, Sönam Gyatso's financial secretary, who was entrusted with the task of finding his late master's reincarnation. He rejected Könchok Rinchen (1590–1655)[5] as the primary and only Tibetan candidate for Sönam Gyatso's subsequent reincarnation. After some deliberation, he chose instead Yönten Gyatso, an ineffectual and rather tragic figure whose main claim to fame was being the Khan's great-grandson. Pelden Gyatso and his decision are open to some skepticism and we may question his motives. The decision turned out to be a double-edged sword: on the one hand, it was a master stroke ensuring the allegiance of a large segment—but by no means all—of the Mongol tribal federations to the institution of the Dalai Lama and to its associated *labrang*, or "corporation." The *labrang* was the repository of the economic resources of the institution of which incarnate lamas formed a transient part. His decision also ensured that the patronage with these Mongols continued as did the economic success of the *labrang*. The downside was that his decision brought the intertribal conflicts between the different Mongol groups to Tibet, a development which had disastrous consequences for the future of the country as a sovereign entity. Matters came to a head in 1720 when the Qing Emperor Kangxi (1654–1722) stationed his military in Tibet to protect it from the Zunghar Mongols' political and military ambitions.

Yönten Gyatso's successor, the Fifth Dalai Lama, was a towering figure. With him began the Ganden Podrang governance of Tibet. Many of the best aspects of the institution of the Dalai Lama were due to his skills and those of his right-hand men, the *desi* "rulers," the most ambitious and influential among them being Sönam Chöphel (d. 1657) and Sanggyé Gyatso (1653–1705). Compared with Yönten Gyatso, the Sixth and Twelfth Dalai Lamas fell short in their learning, political acumen, and sheer pleasure in wielding power. The Sixth Dalai Lama, Tsangyang Gyatso (1683-?1706), was very much disinclined to play the expected role of his office and rather more inclined to live up to the "Tsangyang" of his name, meaning "pure sonority." Despite having been novitiated, he wore his hair long, and lived the life of a poet and artist. Several collections of poems have been attributed to him. In 1705, he was deposed. Although he likely died around 1706, there is a long narrative—probably apocryphal—of his later years and the life he led as a wandering *yogi*.

The Seventh Dalai Lama, Kelzang Gyatso (1708–1757), was not formally installed until 1720. During his reign, a formal governing cabinet with him as head was established and lasted until 1959, although the landed nobility ultimately thwarted his rule. For similar reasons the Eighth to Twelfth Dalai Lamas played rather negligible roles in the rule of Tibet. The Ninth through Twelfth were also at the mercy of a succession of regents, their political ambitions and interests, and those of their families. None of these Dalai Lamas lived beyond twenty-one and it is likely their untimely deaths resulted from foul play.

The Thirteenth Dalai Lama, Tupten Gyatso (1876–1933), represents a radical break with this sequence, not least because of his contact with the world beyond Tibet. Having been in exile once in Mongolia and once in British India, he sought to introduce unprecedented political and social innovations. He even unilaterally declared Tibet an independent state. Ultimately, however, his policies proved ineffective against the resistance the conservative clergy brought to bear against them. He was the most important successor of the Fifth Dalai Lama and so it is little wonder that the *stūpa* containing his remains at the Potala is second only to that of the Great Fifth in terms of size, ornamentation, and splendor.

The present Fourteenth Dalai Lama has been a potent force and rallying point for the Tibetans ever since China claimed sovereignty over Tibet in the 1950s. Going into exile in India in 1959 and headquartered in Dharamsala, a small Indian town nestled in the Himalayan foothills, he has become increasingly present on the international scene and is a much-sought public speaker on both religious and non-religious subjects. In 1989 the Nobel committee awarded him their Peace Prize partly in recognition of his insistence that the "Tibet question" be resolved through peaceful means.

SIGNIFICANCE OF ATIŚA

How did the institution of the Dalai Lama and the idea that he was a reincarnation of Avalokiteśvara begin and gain potency? What meanings are attached to Avalokiteśvara for Tibetan self-understanding? To answer these questions in brief we must go back in Tibetan history to at least the eleventh century, when the Bengali Buddhist monk Atiśa (ca. 982–1054) and his party finally reached the Tibetan Plateau in the early summer of 1042. Their arduous journey had taken them through the sweltering plains of northern India to what is now the Terai of southern Nepal. The Terai abruptly transforms upwards into the Himalaya foothills which steadily rise for those on foot or horseback. Almost without warning the foothills give way to the lush and fertile Kathmandu Valley, into which Atiśa led his group. There the small, determined group stayed for about a year, after which they set out for the Tibetan highlands.

Atiśa made the trek at the invitation of and with the financial support of Jangchup-ö (984–1078), ruler of Gugé, a remote region of far western cultural Tibet.[6] Yet he and his followers felt no sense of urgency to travel on to Gugé. Crossing into the Tibetan frontier at Nagarkot (Tib. *Belpo dzong*), they stayed about a year at the residence of the Sanskritist and translator Naktso Lotsawa Tsültrim Gyelwa (1011–c. 1068), in Mangyül, Gungtang. Atiśa spent most of the rest of his life in Tibet, but through his activities and those of the body of disciples he attracted, he was able to found the Kadam School of Tibetan Buddhism. This term derives from Atiśa's disciplines taking the *Gyelwé ka* "word of the Buddha" and Atiśa's *dam ngak* "oral instructions" as functionally equivalent. Hence *ka* + *dam*, and we find the term *kadampa* "of or having to do with the Kadam" already attested in the early second half of the eleventh century.

The Kadam School likely originated from a sense of community, both intellectual and spiritual-meditative, that grew out of the absolute authority members invested in their master's teachings. This is not to say that it was a unified or monolithic entity. All the earliest sources on the tradition describe with refreshing candor the tensions, conflicts, and outright pettiness among its founding members, even while Atiśa was still alive. These sources depict in brutal and eloquent detail the jealousies and competitions for the master's favors that filled the days of many of his disciples. Yet it was Atiśa's charisma and authority that held these men together. His teachings, encapsulated in written texts, formed the ultimate basis and authority from which the ideology of the Dalai Lama evolved conceptually until it crystallized into the institution of the Dalai Lama with its concrete, bodily manifestations starting from Sönam Gyatso.

This process was a local development, one that likely had its origins in a branch of the Dom (alt. Drom) ['Drom] clan, among whom Domtön Gyelwé Jungné was a member. Clan membership and self-identification with a clan, although remaining strong throughout the Tibetan cultural area as manifest in the majority of Tibetan biographical and autobiographical literature which takes pains to trace both patrilineal and matrilineal clans and sub-clan affiliations of its subjects, gradually erodes in importance as they were slowly supplanted by Indic Buddhist social and religious concepts.

Naktso Lotsawa journeyed to northern India at his king's behest to invite Atiśa back to Tibet. He wrote a sketch of his journey, which although it has not come down to us, a significant portion is found in the *Biography and Itinerary of the Lord Atiśa: A Source of Religion Written by Domtön Gyelwé Jungné*. Many crucial portions of this work have been written in the first-person singular and detail Naktso's travels into the subcontinent to invite Atiśa to come to Tibet, which both support the hypothesis that much of the text was in fact an autobiography. Yet we find that it has in fact come to be attributed to Domtön, who appears in different guises as Naktso's helper. It is clear that Domtön and his guises are simply manifestations of Avalokiteśvara. In other words, Avalokiteśvara functions as a kind of "bodhisattva ex machina" taking on this role from the beginning and in every way directing the narrative. He appears, for example, in the guise of a white man when Naktso and his party arrive in Nagarkot. Resting there with his party in a rented bamboo hut to shelter from the blistering heat, Naktso, "suffering from the heat and crazed by fatigue," has a vision of this white man who tells him:

> Don't sleep! Don't sleep! Get up quickly!
> Don't go to sleep! Get up now and get on the road!
> If you were to fall asleep, you will lose your precious life.
> I am the tutelary deity of all of Tibet.

The owner of the hut was in fact about to burn the hut down to kill the party for the gold he knew Naktso was carrying.

Later in the text we encounter the idea that Tibet is Avalokiteśvara's special domain. In this context "Tibet" covers the area as measured from Nagarkot northwards. It is important to keep in mind that Atiśa and his disciples taught religious practices centered on Avalokiteśvara widely throughout Tibet. This reflects their mission, which was in part to spread their version of Buddhism among the many non-Buddhists populating the Tibetan cultural area at that time. Of special significance may have been the Kashmiri nun Lakṣmī's introduction and propagation of a special variety of Avalokiteśvara-related practice. Whereas monks in the confines of their monasteries of Tantric hermits in the wilds of the Tibetan plateaus performed many such practices, Lakṣmī made it a point to move beyond the monastery and isolated hermitage to include the laity, both male and female, in a quasi-Tantric short-term fasting practice that she structured around the bodhisattva. We cannot underestimate the impact of this kind of grassroots Buddhism.

AVALOKITEŚVARA AND HIS REINCARNATIONS

As stated earlier, Tibetans conceive of the institution of the Dalai Lama as a set in the open-ended series of Avalokiteśvara's reincarnations. In Indian Buddhist lore, Avalokiteśvara's home is Mount Potala located in southern India, although he then came to be relocated to central Tibet. Early exponents of the Kadam School were quick to universalize him as the patron-bodhisattva of the entire Tibetan cultural area. Textual sources suggest that one community in which this concept took hold was the area of western Tibet governed by descendants of the imperial families whose political and ideological aspirations were, if not major players in the origin, assuredly its beneficiaries. Other communities in which this concept played an overarching role were those with some connection to Domtön. As we find in an important but at first localized corpus of Kadam literature, Atiśa recognized Domtön as Avalokiteśvara, thus legitimating the proposition that he therefore physically embodied the spirit of intelligent compassion and had done so during a number of previous incarnations.

In the final and only redaction that we have, the title of this corpus in twenty chapters is *Accounts of Rebirths of Dom Gyelwé Jungné* [*Drom rgyal ba'i 'byung gnas kyi skyes rabs*]. Certainly, the phrase "Accounts of Rebirths" suggests the same kind of authority as that of the *jātaka* tales of the previous lives of the historical Buddha. The nineteenth, and by far longest chapter, explains at considerable length the ideologies that had developed around Tibetan imperial history and imperial families. It goes on to argue that a spiritual link existed between Domtön and Songtsen Gampo, the first king of Tibet under a centralized government, a link based on the supposition of them both being reincarnations of Avalokiteśvara. The dating of the text is problematic, especially in view of the fact that it is first extensively cited in the fifteenth century. Strikingly, the earliest available biographical sketches of Domtön do not suggest a connection with Avalokiteśvara, nor describe him as a reincarnation. This includes the longest sketch compiled around the mid-thirteenth century and found in a handwritten manuscript, the *Golden Rosary of the Kadampa*.

In terms of ideology, this nineteenth chapter is intimately connected with the *Kachem Kakhölma* [*Bka' chems ka khol ma*] "Kakhölma Testament," a work the king himself allegedly authored. Although in view of linguistic and other grounds, this is surely a pious fiction. A tradition current by at least the end of the 12th century held that Atiśa had retrieved an ancient manuscript of this work in Lhasa towards the end of the 1040s. One of the central arguments of the *Kakhölma Testament* is the ontological equivalence of Songtsen Gampo with Avalokiteśvara. There is no reliable evidence that this equation had any precedent.

Tibetan literature of the eleventh century begins to elaborate on the motif of the "Three Protectors of Tibet," in which we find equivalences drawn between three bodhisattvas and three Tibetan rulers who according to tradition played important roles in the development of Tibetan Buddhism. They are 1) Avalokiteśvara and Songtsen Gampo; 2) Mañjuśrī and Tri Songdetsen; and 3) Vajrapāṇi and Relpachen. This motif appears in Kadam, Sakya, and Kagyü literature, where it designates important masters belonging to these schools. It occurs in at least two different forms in early Kadam literature. We also find these same three bodhisattvas being equated with three of Atiśa's disciples.[7] Another schema equates them with Atiśa's three "brother" disciples,[8] although we do not know how far back this tradition goes or its motivation.

Interestingly, we also find three "Bodhisattva Protectors" in the tradition surrounding the masters of the main corpus of Kālacakra teachings, albeit here in reverse chronological order: Avalokiteśvara and Puṇḍarīka; Mañjuśrī and Yaśas; and Vajrapāṇi and Sucandra. These three men were the rulers of the mythical kingdom of Śambhāla. The Kālacakra texts in which we find this set of three dyads of equivalence entered Tibet shortly before the middle of the eleventh century. We can but wonder about the impact it had on local sensibilities. Equating bodhisattvas with rulers was not new, neither in the subcontinent nor in early Tibet. A text in the Tibetan Buddhist canon attributed to Vairocana and written around 800 speaks of Tri Songdetsen as a bodhisattva. The Tibetan canon also contains a supposed translation of a letter attributed to Buddhaguhya in which the author suggests that Songtsen Gampo is the reincarnation of Avalokiteśvara.

HONORING AND PRESERVING THE *DOM* PATRIMONY

The *Kakhölma Testament* does not mention Domtön, for which reason I am inclined to believe that this work emerged from an environment in which Domtön, his associates, and the traditions growing out of their teachings initially had no stake. If that is the case, then we must reconcile at least two initially separate lines of argument: the first in the *Kakhölma Testament* in which Songtsen Gampo is equated with Avalokiteśvara, the second in *Accounts of Rebirths* in which we find a similar scenario but with Domtön at the center.

The *Kakhölma Testament* has come down to us in three different recensions of which the longest is clearly connected to the ruling house of west Tibet. I would therefore argue that the use made of the *Kakhölmà Testament* in the nineteenth chapter of the *Accounts of Rebirths* was to create an environment conducive to establishing Songtsen Gampo as one of Domtön's previous births. Unfortunately, there is no way to date this compendium with any certainty.

The corpus of early Kadam texts focusing on Domtön was not widely known for several centuries. Four men played essential roles in the preservation and ultimate dissemination of a major portion of the corpus: Namkha Rinchen (1214–1286), Zhönnu Lodrö (1271–?), Nyima Gyeltsen (1225–1305), and Gendün Drup, posthumously recognized as the First Dalai Lama. All four were members of the same Dom clan to which Domtön belonged. This can hardly be coincidence and it is therefore likely that these men were making efforts to preserve and honor their clan patrimony, although none of these men likely imagined their activities would have such a profound impact on later events. The Fifth Dalai Lama and his last regent Sanggyé Gyatso were well aware of the ways in which this early Kadam literature could be used as religious propaganda. Thus it is no surprise that the Fifth Dalai Lama had printing blocks of a major portion of this corpus carved.

CONCEPT OF THE *TÜLKU*

These systems of reincarnation, equivalence, and correspondence are predicated upon the metaphysics and phenomenology of reincarnation and the attendant complex concept of the *tülku* (alt. *trülku*). To put it succinctly, the *tülku* is the "earthly" manifestation of buddhahood. Through its limitless compassion and gnosis, this buddhahood generates the *tülku*, which provides a basis for the various qualities associated with the sainthood of the *bodhisattva*.[9] The idea of one Tibetan being the reincarnation of another earlier one is an important concept, though one whose origins are difficult to establish. Tibetan tradition asserts that the *tülku* phenomenon began with Karma Pakshi (1206–1283), the second hierarch of the Karma branch of the Kagyü School. Karma Pakshi recognized himself as the reincarnation of Düsum Khyenpa (1110–1193) and later of Avalokiteśvara, a recognition that his disciples came to embrace. There were many other Tibetan masters whose students considered them reincarnations of this Bodhisattva. We have already seen that Sachen Künga Nyingpo of the Sakya School was held to be one, while other examples include Yapsang Chökyi Mönlam (1169–1233), whom the *Totingma* or "Totingma Testament"—a work similar to the *Kakhölma Testament*—prophesies as a reincarnation of Songtsen Gampo, and then Dölpopa Sherap Gyeltsen (1291–1362).

Later traditions holding that the Karma reincarnations were unprecedented in history are, however, incorrect. There is ample evidence that a number of other individuals had been considered *tülkus* during the thirteenth century. Although the metaphysics of the *tülku* easily allow for the possibility of an individual being the rebirth of a previous human master whose spiritual attainments—real, assumed, or self-proclaimed—served as convincing evidence of his enlightenment, it is only sporadically attested in Indian Buddhism. One example might be in Advayavajra's eleventh-century commentary on Saraha's songs, where we encounter the phrase *jetsüngyi trülpé ku* or "reincarnation of the holy lord."[10] In the Indo-Tibetan environment, we find clear allusions to this phenomenon in the autobiography of Tropu Lotsawa Jampépel (1172–1236), where he refers to *tülku* Mitrayogin and *tülku* Vikhyātadeva, both Indian Buddhist masters. The earliest attestation of a Tibetan being recognized, or representing himself, as a reincarnation of another Tibetan master took place in the Kadam School in the second half of the twelfth century. We find the Tantric master Chökyi Gyelpo (1069–1144) of Könpu considering himself to be a rebirth of Naktso. We further find the Kadam master Gyer Zhönnu Jungné recognized as the reincarnation of both a bodhisattva as well as Ja Yülpa Chenpo, also known as Zhönnu Ö (1075–1138). Zhönnu Ö figures among the most important Kadam masters of his day, one whose influence spread throughout Central Tibet and into the southern borderlands. It is in fact recorded that some two thousand monks attended his cremation.

In the thirteenth century, we also find the first attempts at creating a lineage of female reincarnations. Drowa Zangmo was consort to Götsangpa Gönpo Dorjé (1182–1258), himself regarded as the reincarnation of the Tibetan saint Milarepa. Drowa Zangmo died around 1259, after which a certain Künden Rema (1260–ca. 1339) was soon recognized as her next incarnation. This lineage was short-lived, in fact ending with Künden Rema.

In summary, it appears that the concept of Avalokiteśvara as Tibet's patron-bodhisattva first emerged in the eleventh century, although his identification and association with Songtsen Gampo, first ruler of a unified Tibet, may go back earlier. A small group from the Kadam School, in spiritual allegiance with their master Domtön, elaborated on this theme in a series of texts which proposed relations of equivalence between Domtön and the bodhisattva. They equated the site of Domtön's monastery of Reting [Radreng] with Mount Potala, the residence of Avalokiteśvara in south India. Finally, it appears that the bodhisattva moved once again from Radreng to Lhasa with the Fifth Dalai Lama's construction of the Potala Palace.[11]

NOTES

1. See Eric Hobsbawm and Terence Ranger, eds., *The Invention of Tradition* (New York: Cambridge University Press, 1992).

2. *Ghayiqamsigh vcira dara sayin coghtu buyantu dalai,* Tib. *vajradhara dspal* [sic] *bzang po bsod nams rgya mtsho,* in which "coghtu buyantu dalai," Tib. *dpal bzang po bsod nams rgya mtsho,* inverts the order of Sönam Gyatso's full religious name which

he received at age four from Bsod nams grags pa (1478–1554) in 1547. "Ghayiqamsigh vcira dara" means "wondrous Vajradhara," where *vajradhara*, "Thunderbolt-bearer" connotes not only his expertise in tantric theory and practice, but more importantly his buddhahood.

3. Later, this monastery was to become the seat of the Panchen Lamas from the late sixteenth century onward.

4. That is, Dpal gyi sde chen in Shingkun (Lintao in Gansu province).

5. Son of Chos rgyal phun tshogs bkra shis (1547–1602), the twenty-second abbot of Drigung monastery.

6. Editor's [Martin Brauen] note: "Cultural Tibet" includes all areas that share some form of Tibetan culture and language, including the modern Tibetan Autonomous Region, Amdo, Kham, Ladakh, Bhutan, Sikkim, and other areas. The area this term covers is far greater than what has ever been unified in "Political Tibet."

7. That is, Avalokiteśvara with Dromtön; Mañjuśrī with Rngog legs pa'i shes rab; and Vajrapāṇi with Khu ston brston' grus g.yung drung (1011–1075).

8. Here Avalokiteśvara with Gzhon nu rgyal mtshan (1031–1106); Mañjuśrī with Po to ba Rin chen gsal (1027–1105); and Vajrapāṇi with Tshul khrims 'bar (1033–1103).

9. *Sprul sku*, Skt. *nirmāṇakāya*, "emanation body," the form in which the Buddha appears to ordinary beings or "form of magical apparition." The third of three *kāya*, besides the "truth body" or Skt. *dharmakāya*, Tib. *chos sku* and the *longs sku*, Skt. *sambhogakāya* "enjoyment body."

10. Editors' note: This text from Buddhist India has been preserved in Tibetan translation.

11. Suggested further reading: Karénina Kollmar-Paulenz, *Erdeni tunumal neretü sudur: die Biographie des Altan qagan der Tümed-Mongolen: ein Beitrag zur Geschichte der religionspolitischen Beziehungen zwischen der Mongolei und Tibet im ausgehenden 16. Jahrhundert* [*Erdeni tunumal neretü sudur: The Biography of Altan qagan-Tümed Mongol: A Contribution to the History of the Religious Political Relations Between Mongolia and Tibet at the Turn of the Sixteenth Century*] (Asiatische Forschungen, Bd. 142. Wiesbaden: Harrassowitz, 2001); Thub bstan rgya mtsho, Glenn H. Mullin, and Christine Cox, *Path of the Bodhisattva Warrior: The Life and Teachings of the Thirteenth Dalai Lama* (Ithaca, N.Y.: Snow Lion, 1988); Per K. Sørenson, *Divinity Secularized: An Inquiry Into the Nature and Form of the Songs Ascribed to the Sixth Dalai Lama* (Wien: Arbeitskreis für Tibetische und Buddhistische Studien, Universität Wien, 1990); Shen Weirong, *Leben und historische Bedeutung des ersten Dalai Lama Dge' 'dun grub pa pdal bzang po (1391–1474), ein Beitrag zur Geschichte der Dge lugs pa Schule und der institution der Dalai Lamas* [*The Life and Historical Significance of the First Dalai Lama Dge' 'dun grub pa pdal bzang po (1391–1474), a Contribution to the History of the Dge lugs pa School and the Institution of the Dalai Lamas*] (Sankt Augustin: Institut Monumenta Serica, 2002); Bstan 'dzin rgya mtsho (Dalai Lama XIV), *Freedom in Exile: The Autobiography of the Dalai Lama* (San Francisco: HarperPerennial, 1991); Ya Hanzhang, *The Biographies of the Dalai Lamas*, trans. Wang Wenjiong (Beijing: Foreign Languages Press, 1991).

Chapter 21

THE FIFTH DALAI LAMA

Kurtis R. Schaeffer

Kurtis Schaeffer describes the career of a man who is in all likelihood the single most important figure in the shaping of the modern image of Tibet as a place under the protection of the Dalai Lamas. The Fifth Dalai Lama was the first Dalai Lama to hold real political power in Central Tibet (the thirteen myriarchies of Ü-Tsang), thanks to the support of the Mongol ruler, Gushri Khan, whom the Dalai Lama in turn recognized as the king of all of Tibet. The sources examined here, covering nearly fifty years and thousands of pages, were key to generating the understanding of the Dalai Lama as simultaneously the bodhisattva Avalokiteśvara and the ruler of Central Tibet. The "Great Fifth" and his regent, Sanggyé Gyatso, embarked on a massive literary, architectural, and institutional campaign to create a cultural hegemony for Gelukpa influence over the entire Tibetan Plateau, reforming religious and secular practices and especially the Lhasa landscape in the process. Aside from their literary output and the building of the Potala Palace, they made Lhasa a lively center of international exchange, with resident Armenians, Mongols, Newārs, and Indians, not to mention Tibetans from all over the plateau who brought elements of this cultural renaissance back to their own home regions, helping shape the current vision of Tibetan nationalism.

The Fifth Dalai Lama, known to Tibetan history simply as the "Great Fifth," is renowned as the leader under whom Tibet was unified in 1642 in the wake of bitter civil war. The era of the Fifth Dalai Lama—roughly the period from his enthronement as leader of Tibet in 1642 to the dawn of the eighteenth century, when his government began to lose control—was the formative moment in the creation of a Tibetan national identity, an identity centered in large part upon the Dalai Lama, the Potala Palace of the Dalai Lamas, and the holy temples of Lhasa. During this era the Dalai Lama was transformed from an ordinary incarnation among the many associated with particular Buddhist schools into the protector of the country. In 1646 one writer could say that, due to the good works of the Fifth Dalai Lama, the whole of Tibet was now centered under a white parasol of benevolent protection. And in 1698 another writer could say that the Dalai Lama's government serves Tibet just as a bodhisattva—that saintly hero of Mahāyāna Buddhism—serves all of humanity.[1] In what follows we will survey the career of this important Tibetan leader by focusing on his youth and education, his assumption of power over Tibet, the role of Lhasa as a cultural center under his rule, the competition for authority in Lhasa, the Dalai Lama's literary corpus, the intriguing circumstances of his death, and finally his status as the bodhisattva Avalokiteśvara and as a buddha.

YOUTH, EDUCATION, AND EARLY TEACHING

The Fifth Dalai Lama was born into a noble family in the Yarlung Valley, near the tombs of the Tibetan kings. According to the biography by Möndrowa Jamyang Wanggyel Dorjé,[2] the Dalai Lama's birth was portended by his mother's dreams. The account of the first years of his life, 1617 to 1619, is largely taken up with a description of his birth. The years 1620 to 1621 find the Dalai Lama engaged in "youthful play." Most importantly, it is during this period that this young resident of Chonggyé was recognized as the reincarnation of the Fourth Dalai Lama. In 1622 the Dalai Lama was taken to the central Tibetan institution that was to be his home base for years to come, Drepung Monastery. His first years there were taken up with learning to read. At the beginning of 1623, the Dalai Lama undertook one of the first of the numerous public rituals he was to perform during his life, granting a large feast for [the] New Year. In the fourth month of that year, the Dalai Lama celebrated the Sagadawa Festival (Skt. Vaiśākha Pūrnamā Pūjā). In that same month he embarked on a tour of central Tibet, travelling from Rigo to Chekar Dzong, on to Tsetang, and finally back to Drepung. Such annual tours of central Tibet were to form a constant obligation for the young Dalai Lama.

In 1622 the Dalai Lama began his studies at Drepung Monastery under Lingmé Zhapdrung Könchok Chöpel (1573–1646). The latter was a central figure in the young life of the Dalai Lama, and he would continue serving as tutor until 1646. In 1625, the Dalai Lama first met another figure who was to be prominent in his education, the First Panchen Lama, Lozang Chökyi Gyeltsen (1570–1662). He received many teachings from the Panchen Lama, and, more importantly, he took novice vows under both the Panchen Lama and Lingmé

Zhapdrung. It was under the Panchen Lama that he began studying Mahāyāna literature, and the next few years found him deeply enmeshed in the study of classical Buddhist literature. The years 1630 to 1632 were especially productive years, as during this time the teenaged Dalai Lama undertook studies in *Prajñā-pāramitā*, *Madhyamaka*, *Vinaya*, and *Abhidharma*, all under the tutelage of Lingmé Shapdrung. In 1630 the Dalai Lama began his own career as a teacher by discoursing on the *Book of the Kadam* to a large crowd.

THE FIFTH DALAI LAMA ASSUMES POWER OVER TIBET

In 1637 the Fifth Dalai Lama met with the Mongol leader who would become his greatest ally, Gushri Khan, who had come on pilgrimage to visit the great monasteries of central Tibet. At their first meeting, Gushri Khan offered 4,000 measures of silver and sat to hear teachings from the young incarnation. This meeting made a great impression on the Mongol leader, for that night he dreamt that he beheld a gigantic Dalai Lama, wearing a golden scholar's hat, floating above the Ganden Kangsar. By the end of the year, encouraging signs appeared to both the Dalai Lama's retinue and to Gushri Khan, portending, from the perspective of Möndrowa's hindsight, the impending victory over the Geluk's enemies that would be brought about by the collaboration of [the] Mongol leader and the Geluk incarnation. On one occasion, while Gushri Khan was travelling by night, a great white light came from the north, illuminating all the bushes and the pebbles along the path. When he asked about the significance of this omen, he was told that "this is very auspicious. The stainless teaching of Lord Tsongkhapa will spread in all regions and grow. This is a sign that you, the king, will perform all actions toward that end." Gushri Khan accepted this prophecy and went once more to Lhasa, where he received teachings and oral transmissions from the Dalai Lama. Now filled with faith in the teaching of Tsongkhapa, Gushri Khan dedicated himself to the protection of the Geluk School. In Möndrowa's estimation, "even though some had blocked the golden bridge between central Tibet and India, and had blocked the hundred rivers of offering to the monks of Ü and Tsang, this king repaired them." Together, Gushri Khan and the Dalai Lama, now referred to as *yönchö* ("patron-spiritual teacher" or "donor-donee"), went to the Rasa Trülnang Temple, "the Vajrāsana of Tibet," where the Dalai Lama blessed Gushri Khan and gave him the title "Upholder of the Teaching, King of the Dharma" or Tendzin Chökyi Gyelpo, the title by which Möndrowa refers to Gushri Khan henceforth. Möndrowa describes the Dalai Lama's blessing with vivid imagery:

The elephant trunk of the words and their connected blessing of our world-protecting master was raised high. Then with a golden vase completely filled with ten-million [types of] the nectar of merit, [the Dalai Lama] empowered the king in order to benefit and soothe all the people and cover [them] with one all-encompassing white umbrella.

So blessed, Gushri Khan put his ten fingers together at his heart and said that he must return to Mongolia. Toward the end of the year 1638 Gushri Khan returned to Tibet with three hundred people to whom the Dalai Lama gave teachings. At this time the Dalai Lama also began to bestow full monastic vows upon others, exercising his new status as a full monk. Earlier, in the third month of the same year, he had taken full monastic vows from the Panchen Lama in the presence of ten monks of Sera and Drepung and in the presence of the Jowo (Śākyamuni). At this time he was given the name Ngawang Lozang Gyatso. In 1642 Gushri Khan—now styled by Möndrowa as "this King who grasped the three worlds [of gods, humans, and serpents]"—asked the Dalai Lama to come to Tsang, now firmly in the hands of the Mongol leader and his army. It was in Zhigatsé that the Mongol king offered the thirteen myriarchies of Tibet to the Dalai Lama, as if he were offering a maṇḍala. The relationship of these two as donor and donee was now firmly established, "just as it was earlier between Chögyel Pakpa and Sechen Gyelpo [Qubilai Khan]." Because of this momentous event, "the whole of the Snow-land was covered by a single white umbrella of prosperity and happiness." Gushri Khan had "achieved dominion over all the earth with a golden wheel that is victorious over all regions. [He] bound the crown that is the seal of the kingdom to [his] head, opened the hundred doors of [such] auspicious acts and took hold [of Tibet]." In Möndrowa's account, the new arrangement between Gushri Khan and the Dalai Lama was met with widespread praise. Abbots from every Geluk, Kagyü, and Druk religious establishment came to meet the Dalai Lama, despite the fact that, as Möndrowa boasts, "in the presence of this our Omniscient Lama, other scholars were like fireflies in the presence of the sun, making it difficult to be impressed with their qualities." The Dalai Lama gave a teaching on the Book of the Kadam to a large assembly at Trashilhünpo: "not just thinking of the faithless, but also of all the lay and clerical people of Tsang, [he] planted the seeds of good karma, and wished to accomplish the desires of the people of Tsang."

In 1645 the Dalai Lama set his sights on the establishment of a permanent location from which to rule. In this endeavor he was influenced by prophecies "explained by those with the untarnished clear eyes of Dharma," which stated that

when great fortresses were established on Menpori, Chuwori, and Hepori in this glorious Snowland, the harvest of the Victor—in which the life root of the precious teaching naturally dwells—grew ever greater like the waxing moon, and perfect happiness gathered in the human realm, knowing no exhaustion, like rain during summer time . . .

Gushri Khan and the Dalai Lama agreed "to carry the burden of the precious teaching" by building a fortress in Lhasa. Thus the Dalai Lama granted that a new palace be constructed on Mount Marpori, a palace that would be known as the Potala. Here Möndrowa makes a clear equation between Avalokiteśvara and the Dalai Lama, averring that "our protector of the Snowland, this very Avalokiteśvara, came from Drepung to the Potala in order to subdue the land."

In the spring of 1645 the Dalai Lama performed purification rituals along the outline of the future building's foundation, after which the foundation was laid for the construction of the new palace. Usually at that time of year great winds would blow through the valley. But now not even a little wind came up, and the sky was completely clear. A tent of rainbows wrapped the hill without interruption and a rain of flowers fell. Such wonders "were an object of perception for all, high and low." In addition, Gushri Khan beheld a divine mansion in the sky, with many immortal sons and daughters making offerings. The king and the lama remained on the hill for some time, taking tea on the hill that was to be Avalokiteśvara's residence in Tibet. With the new palace well underway, the Dalai Lama's position of power in Lhasa was firm.

LHASA AS CULTURAL CENTER

Throughout the 1640s the influence of the Dalai Lama's new government grew, in great part due to the work of the Dalai Lama's senior advisors, the regents of the government, who were technically in charge of administrative affairs. It was Sönam Rapten (1595–1658, assumed office in 1643), who was most instrumental in guiding the Dalai Lama's rise to power, though traditional biographies tend to downplay his influence so as to portray the Dalai Lama as de facto leader of Tibet. By 1651 the Dalai Lama had achieved considerable renown throughout Asia, so much so that Emperor Shunzhi (1638–1661) invited the Tibetan leader to pay a visit to Beijing. He began his journey in 1652 and arrived in Beijing the next year.

China was certainly not the only country with which the Dalai Lama's government had relations, nor the only culture with which it interacted during the latter half of the seventeenth century. It is well known that during this period Lhasa was host to a multitude of foreign travelers. Armenians maintained a fixed trading outpost, Mongols travelled to Lhasa on diplomatic missions, and Newār artisans were continuously employed as painters, sculptors, and builders. Indians were also present in Lhasa during this period. According to the Dalai Lama's autobiography, nearly forty Indian guests resided at his court at some time or other during the thirty-seven years between 1654 and 1681,[3] though it appears that the 1670s were the greatest period of Indian activity at the court. The majority of Indians mentioned were intellectuals heralded as experts either in the medical arts or the language arts. This South Asian presence at the Dalai Lama's court coincides in part with the emergence of new intellectual trends in certain regions of India itself at that time.

Some of the Indian scholars visiting Lhasa under the patronage of the Dalai Lama spent considerable periods of time there. Gokula, a Brahman scholar from Varanasi, spent the entire decade from 1654 to 1664 either residing in Lhasa or travelling between India and Lhasa. Varanasi appears to have been the most common point of origin for the trip to Tibet, as fully ten of the forty Indian scholars are said to have come from that city. However, this does not necessarily mean that all ten were natives of that city. For example, although Gokula is said to be a scholar of Varanasi, a letter addressed to him from the Dalai Lama relates that he was born in the Indian region of what is now Kerala.

A visit to the Dalai Lama could be economically rewarding for those Indian scholars who made the trip, for the Dalai Lama bequeathed a variety of items to his visitors, most usually gold, but also cotton, tea, clothing, silk, Chinese red satin, and provisions for the road. Indeed, many of the dated entries in the Fifth Dalai Lama's autobiography report no more than that the Dalai Lama met a certain Indian and gave him certain goods. In 1677, for instance, he gave to two mendicants from Mathurā, named Hemagiri and Nīlakantha, three measures of gold each, while to a Brahman of Varanasi named Sītādāsa he gave two measures of gold. He also provided a travel document allowing the three travelers to move as they wished between India and Tibet. Such travel documents, what we might call passports, were routinely issued to Indian visitors by the Dalai Lama.

In addition to these records of material gifts, a few passages from the autobiography hint at conversations about culture. For example, an entry from 1677 records the Dalai Lama questioning two Brahmans from Varanasi on their skills and religious background. The two Brahmans, Jīvanti and Ganera, respond that they are learned in the science of mathematics and are followers of Viṣṇu. Whenever the Dalai Lama offers descriptive remarks about his Indian guests, they are nothing but laudatory, praising both India and its scholars. In a letter to the grammarian Gokula dated 1663 the Fifth Dalai Lama addresses him as a "son of the world's grandfather, Brahman, supreme in effort among those who speak of the Vedas." In a letter written in 1670 he praises Varanasi as "the great city where gather many scholars of vast intellect, skilled in all linguistic and philosophical topics," and he bids the scholars farewell as they prepare to return south through the Himalayas, having illuminated the darkness of Tibet with the moonlight of Pāṇini's grammar. Though we cannot make too much of these passages, they do at least suggest that in the seventeenth century, the court of the Dalai Lama held Varanasi in high regard because of its visiting scholars.

COMPETING FOR AUTHORITY IN LHASA

Though the Fifth Dalai Lama and his government were largely in control of the political and cultural affairs of central Tibet, this does not mean that they were without competition, even from within the Geluk School. A short work composed by the Fifth Dalai Lama, entitled *Guidelines for Seating Arrangements at the Mönlam Chenmo Festival of Lhasa* (1675), exemplifies such struggles for power in its prescription of cultural practices surrounding the ritual calendar of Lhasa.[4] The ostensible purpose of the work was to establish a hierarchical seating arrangement for monks participating in the Mönlam Chenmo Festival, an annual event founded by Tsongkhapa in 1409. The more pressing concern, however, was to establish the monks of the Dalai Lama's own Drepung Monastery at the top of that hierarchy, while placing the monks of Sera Monastery, the other large Geluk institution near Lhasa, in a secondary position. To this end the Dalai Lama's *Guidelines* focuses on one crucial point—he argues that individuals and sectarian groups should not foment discord in the Buddhist monastic community, the *sangha*, for to do so vitiates the authority of the *sangha* as a unified moral body in the eyes of the lay public, thereby bringing negative karma upon those who perpetuate such discord.

The Dalai Lama then addresses the matter of hierarchy within the *sangha*, building his argument almost exclusively on canonical citations strung one after the other. It is a given, he argues, that when so many monks gather for a single event, there will be present both those who are models of virtue and some who know little virtue. The latter are often inappropriately motivated by the desire to gain a name for themselves or their particular faction, and thus are led to disrupt the proceedings. Not only do such people bring a bad reputation to the *sangha* as a whole, but they bring unthinkable suffering upon themselves. As the Dalai Lama describes the troubles that have plagued the Mönlam Chenmo Festival in past years, it becomes plainly obvious that his criticisms are directed not at the full set of participants but are targeted specifically on the monks of Sera Monastery. Because certain monks of Sera have sought gains for themselves, without thinking of the *sangha* as whole, the festival has been delayed, extra rules have become necessary, and the aisles needed for the proper performance of ritual have been blocked. More seriously, fighting has broken out over seating arrangements, usually provoked by the inmates of Sera. A Mongolian monk of the Jé College at Sera even hit a discipline officer from Drepung, and then received praise from his abbot.

By contrast, says the work, the monks and officials of Drepung have promoted a communal perspective and have "sought friendship with the troublemakers, whatever their impure previous actions." It is in this spirit of harmony that the Dalai Lama has decided to impose strict seating arrangements for the festival, all of which, as one might expect, favor the monks of Drepung. Earlier he has argued that, according to the *vinaya*, the eldest among the *sangha* are to be accorded the highest respect at all times. It now becomes clear that the monks of Drepung are in his estimation the "elders" of the *sangha*. Thus, under the guise of reforming the *sangha* and maintaining order at this massive festival, the Dalai Lama shifts both moral and administrative authority to his own monastery. He accomplishes this by arguing that his institution has continually fulfilled the intentions of Buddhist scripture, whereas the monks of Sera have failed to do so. It is his monastery which has lived up to classical ideals of the Buddhist saṅgha, and now it is his monastery that is in charge of the largest public ritual in central Tibet.

WRITINGS OF THE FIFTH DALAI LAMA

The Fifth Dalai Lama was also a most prolific author. He composed over twenty-five volumes of writing, a corpus that covers nearly every aspect of Buddhist thought and practice. He is particularly well known for being one of the most prodigious authors of autobiographical literature in the history of the Himalayan plateau. The Dalai Lama's autobiographical corpus consists of three principal works amounting to some 2,500 folios. The first of these works is a four-volume record of texts and teachings he had received. Suggestively entitled *River Ganga's Flow*, we might be tempted think of the work as a massive survey of Tibetan literary history rather than a single person's reading list. The second work, entitled *Fine Silken Dress*, is a three-volume account of the Dalai Lama's life from 1617 to 1681, covering all save his last year.[5] This work, a veritable mine of political, social and cultural detail, is the single most important portrait of courtly life at the Potala from the 1640s to the middle of 1681. The final work is an account of the many visions of gods, kings, queens, and demons that the Dalai Lama experienced between the ages of six and fifty-six. Together these three works fit well into the traditional three-fold rubric for life writing, which distinguishes external, internal, and arcane aspects of the subject's life.

The Fifth Dalai Lama is also renowned as a writer of history, though this reputation stems entirely from a single, early work. One year after he took the throne as leader of central Tibet, he composed a history of Tibetan political institutions entitled *Song of the Spring Queen: The Annals of Tibet*. This influential history begins with a short life of the Buddha and a brief discussion of the Kālacakra Tantra, then moves quickly to the history of imperial Tibetan rulers. The central chapters detail the political institutions of Ü and Tsang in Central Tibet from the twelfth to the beginning of the seventeenth century, including sections on the Sakya, Phakmodru, and Rinpung hegemonies. The concluding chapter lauds the Fifth Dalai Lama's Mongolian patron, Gushri Khan, who had requested the work's compilation. In this work the Fifth Dalai Lama is occasionally critical of other historians, and he states in the conclusion that his work is meant to correct "the foolish and baseless words of proud and haughty 'learned men.'" Throughout the book are interspersed examples of ornate poetry, giving the work a tone of both formal eloquence and rhetorical authority. In both style and content, *Song of the Spring Queen* is one of the most important historical works on central Tibet that we possess.

One cannot discuss the writings of the Fifth Dalai Lama without also mentioning those of the fifth regent, Sanggyé Gyatso. The latter would be a prolific writer during his twenty-four years as ruler (1679–1703), and much of his work complements that of the Dalai Lama. Sanggyé Gyatso was perhaps the most influential writer on secular arts and sciences that Tibet has ever produced. From his early 1681 work on governance to his 1703 history of medicine, he touched on subjects as varied as language arts, building techniques, the politics of ritual, funeral rites, astrological and calendrical theories, methods of healing, and rules for court servants. Sanggyé Gyatso spent much of the 1690s molding a public vision of the Fifth Dalai Lama. His literary activities between 1693 and 1701 were almost entirely concerned with the Fifth Dalai Lama's life, death and legacy, marshalling the vast resources of canonical literature in what is surely one of the great biographical projects of Tibetan literature. In all, the regent devoted more than 7,000 pages to extolling the Fifth Dalai Lama from a variety of perspectives—a staggering amount of writing by any account, and likely the largest biographical project ever attempted in Tibet. Sanggyé Gyatso's writing efforts during these few years were not random occasions, but were almost certainly connected with major events such as the 1695 installation of the Fifth Dalai Lama's remains in the great *stūpa*, the completion of the Potala's Red Palace in which the *stūpa* was housed, and the 1697 enthronement of the Sixth Dalai Lama.

Rather than to slavishly follow the standard canons of tradition, both the Fifth Dalai Lama and Sanggyé Gyatso argued with them, remade them, and—using the advantage of their position as rulers of Tibet for over six decades combined—implemented a new vision of Tibetan culture by means of wide-ranging reforms. Over the course of their careers they sought to systematize Tibetan cultural life and practice in a number of specific areas through writing, systematizing bodily practices in the form of medical treatises, spatial practices in ritual manuals, time in the form of astrological writings and the institution of an officially sanctioned New Year, administrative practice in the form of rules for court servants, and religious discourse in the form of polemical, historical, and philosophical writings. Although their vision remains to be borne out in detail, it is probably no exaggeration to say that the corpus of writing left by the Dalai Lama and his regent represents the boldest attempt ever to create a broad cultural hegemony in Tibet.

THE DEATH OF THE FIFTH DALAI LAMA

In 1679, after thirty-three years of leadership, the Dalai Lama abdicated his rule over Tibet to Sanggyé Gyatso. He died three years later, on 7 April 1682, though few were to know of his death until more than a decade later.[6] In April of 1695 the desiccated body of the Fifth Dalai Lama was removed from the wooden casket in which it had been placed the day after his death thirteen years earlier. Wrapped in silk and cotton, packed with cinnamon, saffron, camphor, and salts, the body had mummified over the years, and it was now time to install it in the sixty-foot-tall golden reliquary housed in the recently completed Red Palace of the Potala. Known as the Single Ornament of the World, this *stūpa* was intended to form an essential part of ritual and political life not only within the massive Potala but also in the nearby city of Lhasa and its environs and more widely throughout Tibet. At least, this is what Sanggyé Gyatso hoped as he prepared to unveil the reliquary to the public and reveal the long-hidden fact of the Dalai Lama's death.

The lengthy mummification presented some practical problems. From 1682 to 1695 the corpse of the Great Fifth had been preserved in a sandalwood casket, wrapped in cotton and packed in two types of salt. Because of the effects of this preservation, Sanggyé Gyatso admitted, the all-important relics gathered after cremation would not be forthcoming and thus will not be available for the people's benefit as had been the case with the previous Dalai Lamas. But this is no cause for dismay; one merely needed a substitute—in this case, embalming salt. This salt was efficacious because it had been in contact with the body of Dalai Lama, a fact which alone should be reason enough to accept the efficacy of its blessing power. In order to convince people of this, Sanggyé Gyatso composed a reasoned defense of the Dalai Lama's salt relics in November of 1697, issuing it as a proclamation that very month. The timing of the proclamation was not coincidental. It fell between two events of crucial import for the continuing success of the Dalai Lama's government—the announcement of the Fifth Dalai Lama's death and the enthronement of the young Sixth Dalai Lama. The Fifth Dalai Lama had now been dead for fifteen years, and his tomb had been complete for three, yet knowledge of these events did not extend beyond the few privileged insiders at the Potala court.

The regent had begun to reveal the secret in June of 1697. In that month he laid the groundwork for revealing the existence of a new Dalai Lama by providing select people with an account of the transference of consciousness from the Fifth Dalai Lama to the Sixth, an event that would have occurred fifteen years earlier. In November of 1697 he had the proclamation and the account read to large assemblies at the major monasteries around Lhasa—Drepung, Sera, and Ganden—as well as at the Trashilhünpo Monastery in Tsang. According to Sanggyé Gyatso's biography of the Sixth Dalai Lama, during the proclamations the skies were clear and there were many wondrous signs, such as a rain of flowers at Trashilhünpo. In Lhasa, two laymen read the account of the transference of consciousness to citizens gathered in a public park. As the people heard the news of the Dalai Lama's death some years earlier, an old woman remarked that "from that year to now the regent has accepted the responsibility of Dharma and worldly affairs. Not even knowing the dusk, we now see the dawn!"

The "dawn" in this case was of course the coming of the new Dalai Lama, and the timing of these proclamations was no doubt planned carefully to prepare the lay citizens of Lhasa and the thousands of resident[s] of its monasteries for the upcoming enthronement of the Sixth Dalai Lama, an event of great pomp that was to occur on 8 December of the same year. Most people reportedly met the news with a mixture of sorrow and joy, and they wept a great deal. As the proclamation and the account were read at Sera Monastery, each monk present was given a portion of the embalming salt, and each commoner was given a small molded figurine of the Dalai Lama made of materials mixed with the salt, a memento of the previous Dalai Lama in expectation of the next.

THE DALAI LAMA AS AVALOKITEŚVARA AND AS BUDDHA

At the beginning of his autobiography, the Fifth Dalai Lama goes to great lengths to de-emphasize his status as author, authority, and unique subject. In his auto-biographical writing he presents as a very human figure simply recounting the mundane details of everyday life. Yet the Fifth Dalai Lama.is also considered by tradition to be the reincarnation of a previous Buddhist master, the Fourth Dalai Lama, as well as the incarnation of that ever-benevolent celestial being, the bodhisattva Avalokiteśvara. The contrast between his self-effacing presentation and his sublime public status can be seen by comparing the tone of his autobio-graphical production with the praise Möndrowa accords him. Even more strik-ing is the contrast between the Dalai Lama's self-presentation and the writings dedicated to him by his regent and most zealous biographer, Desi Sanggyé Gyatso. Let me thus conclude with a few remarks about this latter set of writ-ings, which we might consider an elaboration on Möndrowa's early effort.

Not content with the Dalai Lama's self-presentation in his autobiographical writings, Sanggyé Gyatso contributed a further 5,000 folios of biographical work, much of which is concerned with extolling the Dalai Lama as Avalokiteśvara. His most concentrated effort in this regard is no doubt the introduction to his 1,000-folio supplement to the Dalai Lama's *Fine Silken Dress*, where he assem-bles fifty-eight biographical narratives of the various incarnations of Avalokite-śvara. Expectedly, the last of these narratives deals with the Fifth Dalai Lama himself, who, Sanggyé Gyatso argues, is at once the incarnation of Avalokite-śvara and the rebirth of those numerous masters of the past, who also happen to have been incarnations of Avalokiteśvara. The tone of this hagiographic project contrasts starkly with the self-deprecation of its subject. For example, Sanggyé Gyatso writes that it is by definition impossible to capture in words the fullness of the Dalai Lama's activities as Avalokiteśvara, for "what person," he asks, "can speak of the profound, vast, and ineffable interior life of this holy omniscient one and not exceed the bounds of propriety?" The Dalai Lama, by contrast, suggests in his introductory remarks to *Fine Silken Dress* that it is all but impos-sible not to exaggerate. Nevertheless, the tension between the two writers may be more a matter of rhetorical technique than anything else. The Dalai Lama's modesty fits the norms of the autobiographical genre while also being expressive of the bodhisattva Avalokiteśvara's character as a model of empathetic compassion. The regent's laudatory style was shaped by this same vision, and it was only because his persistent and lengthy efforts to promote the cult of this same bodhisattva in the person of the Dalai Lama that the Dalai Lama's government and its rule from the Potala Palace continued to be perceived as the center of Avalokiteśvara's benevolent reign in Tibet.

Sanggyé Gyatso was not the first to associate the Dalai Lama with Avalokiteśvara. In 1646 Möndrowa was already placing this identity at the center of his hagiographic efforts. Indeed, the first chapter of this work consists in the main of a defense of this notion that the Dalai Lama was Avalokiteśvara. Möndrowa even goes so far as to equate the Fifth Dalai Lama with the Buddha himself. In an apologetic tone, Möndrowa assures the reader that his subject's enlightened activities are beyond description. The Dalai Lama "is no different from the Victor of the Three Times and his Sons," he writes. "Because he is indivisible from them, the total accumulation of facets of his life story are inconceivable and inexpressible. His manner is not a matter for *arhats*, *śrāvakas*, *bodhisattvas*, or *vajradharas*, so even if one were to make an effort eon upon eon, one could not tell even a fraction of his life story, because how could it be a matter for normal, foolish people?" Though the middle chapters of *Life of the Dalai Lama* are devoted largely to chronological narrative, in the conclusion Möndrowa returns to praise the Dalai Lama:

> His worship-worthy body, blazing with the brilliance created by turning the wheel of Dharma day in and day out, is not sullied by even a speck of evil. He performs unceasing good works that open a hundred doors to welfare and happiness. His fame for having completely learned the five great knowledge systems—language, logic, plastic arts, medicine, and inner knowledge, as well as divination, poetics, synonymy, and prosody, together comprising the ten knowledge systems, encompasses the three lands with a white umbrella of garlands. All *Dharma*—the essence and extent of what can be known—have entered his mind. He has seen the end of the ocean of our philosophical systems and others. He has become a lord of those who speak of scripture and reasoning. The melodies of his Dharma explanations fill the ears of all intelligent people with nectar. His voice of debate confounds backward speakers with a thunderous downpour of diamonds. The sensitivity in his elegant compositions creates a charming delight that makes the hearts of scholars grow joyful. Countless acts such as this delight like nectar the minds of all fortunate beings.

A measure of Möndrowa and Sanggyé Gyatso's success at promoting the enlightened qualities of the Fifth Dalai Lama can be gleaned from an anecdote from Lhasa related by Sir Charles Bell in the early part of the twentieth century.

In describing folk memories of the Fifth Dalai Lama's death, more than two centuries after the event, Bell notes that "you will hear from some of the simpler folk that it is only since this calamity that the branches [of the weeping willows around Lhasa] drooped, whence they call it the 'tree of sorrow.' Even those who use the ordinary name, 'Chinese Willow,' aver that since those days all the trees and flowers have drooped a little."[7] Likely I make too much of this anecdote, yet I very much doubt whether the willows around Lhasa would still be drooping more than two centuries later without the help of Sanggyé Gyatso in memorializing his master, the Fifth Dalai Lama.

NOTES

1. A number of sources and studies have informed this essay. Two accounts of the Fifth Dalai Lama's political career have become standard reference works: Giuseppe Tucci, *Tibetan Painted Scrolls* (Rome: Libreria dello Stato, 1949), 57–66, and Zahirud-din Ahmad, *Sino-Tibetan Relations in the Seventeenth Century* (Roma: Instituto italiano per il Medio ed Estremo Oriente, 1970), 108–145. A number of additional studies dedicated to the Fifth Dalai Lama have appeared in the last several decades. Luciano Petech, "The Dalai Lamas and Regents of Tibet," in *Selected Papers on Asian History* (Roma: Instituto italiano per il Medio ed Estremo Oriente, 1988) provides dates for all the Dalai Lamas and their regents, while in *China and Tibet in the Early XVIIIth Century: History of the Establishment of Chinese Protectorate in Tibet* (Leiden: Brill, 1950), Petech surveys the history of the closing years of the era of the Fifth Dalai Lama. Samten Gyaltsen Karmay introduced the corpus of visionary autobiography in *Secret Visions of the Fifth Dalai Lama: The Gold Manuscript in the Fournier Collection* (London: Serindia Publications, 1988). Samten Karmay ("The Rituals and Their Origins in the Visionary Accounts of the 5th Dalai Lama," in *Religion and Secular Culture in Tibet: Tibetan Studies: Proceedings of the Ninth Seminar of the International Association for Tibetan Studies, Leiden 2000*, Brill's Tibetan Studies Library, vol. 2, International Association for Tibetan Studies, ed. Henk Blezer and A. Zadok [Leiden: Brill, 2002], 21–40) follows up on his earlier work. Vladimir Uspensky ("The Illustrated Manuscripts of the 5th Dalai Lama's 'The Secret Visionary Autobiography' Preserved in the St. Petersburg Branch of the Institute of Oriental Studies," *Manuscripta Orientalia* 2, no. 1 [1996]: 54–65) describes a related collection of visionary autobiography. Ariane Macdonald ("Un portrait du cinquième Dalaï Lama [A Portrait of the 5th Dalai Lama]," in *Essais sur l'art du Tibet*, ed. Ariane MacDonald and Yoshiro Imaeda [Paris: Librairie d'Amérique et d'Orient, 1977], 119–156) details a statue of the Dalai Lama. Yumiko Ishihama ("A Study of the Seals and Titles Conferred by the Dalai Lamas," in *Tibetan Studies: Proceedings of the 5th Seminar of the International Association for Tibetan Studies, Narita 1989*, vol. 2 [Narita: Naritasan Shinshoji, 1992], 501–514) compiles evidence of the investitures granted by the Dalai Lama. Ishihama ("On the Dissemination of the Belief in the Dalai Lama as a Manifestation

of the Bodhisattva Avalokiteśvara," *Acta Asiatica* 64 [1993]: 38–56) offers an insightful reading of the Fifth Dalai Lama's autobiography and related works as they pertain to the cult of Avalokiteśvara. Hugh Richardson (*Ceremonies of the Lhasa Year*, ed. Michael Aris [London: Serindia, 1993]) offers firsthand accounts of the annual rituals performed in and around Lhasa, many of which have their origins in the era of the Fifth Dalai Lama. Gray Tuttle ("A Tibetan Buddhist Mission to the East: The Fifth Dalai Lama's Journey to Beijing, 1652–1653," in *Power, Politics, and the Reinvention of Tradition: Tibet in the Seventeenth and Eighteenth Centuries. Proceedings of the 10th Seminar of the International Association for Tibetan Studies, Oxford University 2003*, ed. Bryan J. Cuevas and Kurtis R. Schaeffer [Leiden: Brill, 2006], 65–87) details the Dalai Lama's important diplomatic trip to China. In the same volume, Kurtis R. Schaeffer ("Ritual, Festival, and Authority Under the 5th Dalai Lama," 187–202) discusses Sanggyé Gyatso's adaptation of Lhasa ritual life around the figure of the Fifth Dalai Lama. The Fifth Dalai Lama's history of Tibet has been translated into English in its entirety by Ahmad (1995). Ahmad (*Life of the Fifth Dalai Lama*, vol. 4, Teil 1 [New Delhi: Aditya Prakashan, 1999]) translates the first half of the first volume of Sanggyé Gyatso's three-volume continuation of the Dalai Lama's autobiography. All of the essays contained in Françoise Pommaret (*Lhasa in the Seventeenth Century: The Capital of the Dalai Lamas* [Leiden: Brill, 2003]) pertain to a greater or lesser degree to the Fifth Dalai Lama. Nathalie Bazin (*Rituels Tibétains: visions secrètes du Vᵉ Dalaï Lama [Tibetan Rituals: Secret Visions of the 5th Dalai Lama]* [Paris: Réunion des Musées Nationaux, 2002]) offers a glimpse of many ritual implements described in the visionary autobiographies of the Dalai Lama. Fernand Meyer ("The Potala Palace of the Dalai Lamas in Lhasa," *Orientations* 18, no. 7 [1987]: 14–33) introduces artistic features of the Potala. Hugh Richardson ("The Fifth Dalai Lama's Decree Appointing Sangs rgyas rgya mtsho as Regent," in *High Peaks, Pure Earth: Collected Writings on Tibetan History and Culture*, ed. Michael Aris [London: Serindia Publications, 1998], 440–461) translates an important source for the history of the Dalai Lama's regents. Christoph Cüppers ("A Letter Written by the Fifth Dalai Lama to the King of Bhaktapur," *Journal of the Nepal Research Center* 12 [2001]: 39–42) introduces the form and content of the Dalai Lama's many diplomatic letters. Kristina Lange (*Die Werke des Regenten Sangs rgyas rgya mc'o [1653–1705]: eine philologisch-historische Studie zum tibetischsprachigen Schrifttum [The Works of Regent Sang rgyas rgya mtsho (1653–1705): A Philological and Historical Study of Tibetan Literature]* [Berlin: Akademie-Verlag, 1976]) provides a preliminary bibliography of Sanggyé Gyatso's writings. Michael Aris (*Hidden Treasures and Secret Lives: A Study of Pemalingpa [1450–1521] and the Sixth Dalai Lama [1683–1706]* [London: Kegan Paul, 1989]) describes the transfer of consciousness from the Fifth to the Sixth Dalai Lama.

2. 'Jam dbyangs dbang rgyal rdo rje, Smon 'gro ba [Möndrowa], *Rgyal dbang thams cad mkhyen pa ngag dbang blo bzang rgyo mtsho'i mtshan thos pa'i yid la bdud rtsir byed pa'i rnam thar mtho na ba don ldan mchog tu dga' ba'i sgra dbyang sar ga gsum pa* [*Life of the Dalai Lama*], 128 folios (Cultural Palace of Nationalities, Beijing, catalog number 002555). The present narrative of the Fifth Dalai Lama's life up to the year 1646

is taken from Möndrowa's important work. I gratefully acknowledge the assistance of Leonard W. J. van der Kuijp, who provided me with a photocopy of Möndrowa's *Life of the Dalai Lama*. I would also like to thank Christoph Cüppers of the Lumbini International Research Institute (LIRI), who generously made available to me an extremely useful digital text of Möndrowa's *Life of the Dalai Lama*.

3. Ngag dbang blo bzang rgya mtsho, *Za hor gyi ban de ngag dbang blo bzang rgya mtsho'i 'di nang 'khrul ba'i rol rtsed rtogs brjod kyi tshul du bkod pa du ku'u la'i gos bzang* [*Autobiography of the Fifth Dalai Lama*] (Lhasa: Bod ljongs mi dmangs dpe skrun khang, 1989).

4. Ngag dbang blo bzang rgya mtsho, "Lha ldan smon lam chen mo'i gral 'dzin bca' yig," in *Bod kyi snga rabs khrims srol yig cha bdams bsgrigs* (Lhasa: Bod ljongs tshogs tshan rig khang gi bod yig dpe rnying dpe skrun khang, 1989, 324–345).

5. Ngag dbang blo bzang rgya mtsho, *Autobiography of the Fifth Dalai Lama*.

6. The following is largely taken from Sangs rgyas rgya mtsho, *Mchod sdong 'dzam gling rgyan gcig rten gtsug lag khang dang bcas pa'i dkar chag thar gling rgya mtshor bgrod ba'i gru rdzings byin rlabs kyi bang mdzod* [*Account of the Building and Installation of the Fifth Dalai Lama's Stupa*] (Beijing: Bod ljongs mi rigs dpe skrung khang, 1990); Sangs rgyas rgya mtsho, *Thams cad mkhyen pa drug ba blo bzang rin chen tshangs dbyangs rgya mtsho'i thun mong phyi'i rnam par thar pa du ku la'i 'phro 'thud rab gsal gser gyi snye ma* [*Biography of the Sixth Dalai Lama*], ed. Bod ljongs mi dmangs dpe skrun khang (Lhasa: Tshe ring phun tshogs, 1989); and Sangs rgyas rgya mtsho, *Pur tshwa me 'dzin ma'i dkar chag dad pa'i sa bon gyis bskyed pa'i byin rlabs ro bda'* [*Accounts of the Fifth Dalai Lama's Remains*], unpublished blockprint.

7. Charles A. Bell, *The Religion of Tibet* (1928; reprint, New Delhi: Motilal Banarsidass, 1992), 135–136.

Chapter 22

EXPERIENCE, EMPIRICISM, AND THE FORTUNES

OF AUTHORITY

TIBETAN MEDICINE AND BUDDHISM ON THE EVE

OF MODERNITY

Janet Gyatso

Where can one draw the line between the authority of tradition to focus our observations of the physical world and observation's potential to challenge accepted beliefs? If Buddhist tantric theory states that there are channels of energy running up and down the center of the human torso and these are not found upon inspection, how can one adjudicate between the Buddha's word and empirical observation? In Tibet these questions were never more poignant than in the medical arts, for the visceral reality of the human body consistently confronted the claims of the medical tradition. Janet Gyatso places the fulcrum point at which empirical knowledge began to offer an abiding challenge to traditional knowledge of the body in the late seventeenth century, when the Fifth Dalai Lama's rule ushered in a renaissance age for art, science, and government. In Lhasa the court physicians at the Potala advanced pharmacology by rigorously collecting, comparing, and cataloging plants. They imported new treatments from Nepal and India. And they began, according to Gyatso, to perform autopsies upon human cadavers for the first time in Tibetan history. In detailing select vignettes from the lives of several key physicians at the Lhasa court and isolating the central challenge that empiricism as a discipline brings to traditional authority, Gyatso signals the emergence of a promising subfield in Tibetan historical studies—the history of science.

Sometime around 1670, Darmo Menrampa, one of an inner group of physicians close to the Fifth Dalai Lama, set up a laboratory in a park in Lhasa. He and his students proceeded to dissect four human corpses—two male, two female, two old, two young—in order to count their bones. He wrote briefly of the event in an anatomical treatise, after surveying received tradition on how to count the bones in the body, which were classically said to add up to 360. This number, Darmo notes, is explained in the texts as entailing that one count the sections of the skull as four. But, he says, "My students and I based ourselves instead on there being nine sections of the skull, and thus [we count] 365."[1]

We have to admire Darmo's deftness. The number of bones that the physician and his acolytes "determined with precision, and through naked illustration" confirms the canonical number of 360. He also hints at the possibility of variation, if, for example, one were to recognize a different number of sections in the skull. But then Darmo goes on to call into question the notion of a definitive count altogether, suggesting a horizon of undecidability. Such undecidability would ensue if, instead of counting—as he and his students did—only the bones near in size to "the span between fingertip and elbow and the width of a finger," one were also to reckon "the numerous small bones that are merely the size of a roasted bean."

The idea that properties of the physical world cannot be represented definitively by canonical doctrine might remind us of issues germane to the birth of Western empiricism. Darmo's experiment may also be striking for its simultaneity with the public anatomy lessons of the Amsterdam Guild of Surgeons, especially memorable from a famous painting by Rembrandt. But Tibet had no part in the European Enlightenment. It saw no radical revolution in science, no salient notion of innovation, no widespread and publicly touted recourse to repeated dissection and further experimentation.[2] Still, Darmo's corpse dismemberment in the Tibetan capital encapsulates a climactic moment in the history of medicine in Tibet. Part and parcel of a series of momentous social changes— which culminated in the consolidation of a centralized Tibetan state under the rule of the Dalai Lamas—was that medicine came into its own as a system of knowledge distinct from mainstream Buddhism. The process by which this unfolded involved kinds of arguments and practices that we often associate with the birth of modernity. Participants in a growing network of physicians flourishing under the patronage of the Dalai Lama's court, medical theorists and historians like Darmo were caught up in debates about what constituted the authoritative sources for medical knowledge, and how to construe the history of that knowledge. A notable part of these debates was a distinctively medical empiricism, with far-reaching implications for the prestige of medicine and its practitioners as well as for the larger issue of how medicine relates to Buddhism.

Considering these developments in light of the question of modernity promises to enhance both our sense of that notion and our understanding of Tibetan history. To recognize features—and I am arguing that *some* features can be so identified, but not *all* or exactly the same ones—of what is defined as modernity in a variety of historical contexts suggests that modernity might be a generalizable process. That process, although by no means universal, can be recognized in other times and places besides its emergence in full force as "the modern West." Such a realization stands apart from anything we might say about actual influence or interaction, although as our historiographical practice develops, we may become better at discerning connections between European modernity or science and the medicine being practiced under the Ganden Podrang government and the surrounding cosmopolitan culture of seventeenth-century Central Tibet. In any event, what follows is not meant to claim that seventeenth-century Tibetan society achieved full modernity. It is only to say that *some* aspects of that society bear comparison with such moments around the world.

What this paper will do, then, is to examine attitudes and values associated with modernity—among them, a questioning of religious authority, a valuing of empirical evidence, a probative attitude to texts and practices, and a recognition of cultural difference—in the particular ways they developed in specifically Tibetan conditions. To recognize the variety of circumstances that can give rise to such attitudes is both to discover the broad descriptive power of the category of "modernity" and to appreciate the rich range of its instances. Furthermore, to take a category like modernity and use it heuristically to study a time and place where no such indigenous category is named does not necessarily force our interests upon an incommensurate object. Rather, if the category is both apropos and general enough—"gender" would be another example; so would "culture" or "religion"—it can help us to recognize connections and identify patterns that we might not have otherwise seen.[3]

This essay will focus on a few inflections of what I am identifying as empiricism in the shifting camps of Tibetan medical science from around the end of the fifteenth century through the momentous events of the seventeenth century and their legacy in the following years. I explore two salient clusters of ideas that contributed to such empiricism, both of which fell under the larger Tibetan rubric of "experience."[4] One had to do with the special kind of knowledge that, unlike book learning, is acquired only in practice, guided by a teacher and involving daily immersion in the illnesses of individual patients. The other concerned the particular type of knowledge that comes from direct perception, that is, from contact between the sense organs of the researcher and something in the material world. These two senses of experience overlapped, but the second is more specific and pointed. Importantly, it has a special authority of its own; in the polemical rhetoric of the medical writers under discussion, it could trump what was predicted by ideology or doctrinal system.

Germane to this entire investigation will be a troubling of the boundaries of "science" vs. "religion" in Tibet, that is, between medicine and mainstream Buddhist modes of writing and thinking, during the period under discussion. Buddhism and medicine grew up together in Tibet in a shared universe of institutions, conceptions, and modes of discourse. Buddhist texts certainly also were concerned with versions of both kinds of experience just mentioned. Still, there is a telling distinctiveness in the way that medicine came to construe the significance of direct perception and hands-on practice.

BACKGROUND: INSTITUTIONS AND LITERATURE

The emergence in Tibet of professional medicine was a gradual process that began with the kings of the Yarlung dynasty.[5] From everything we can tell from Tibetan historiography, the early Tibetan kings sponsored the visits of a stream of physicians from India, Nepal, Kashmir, China, Persia, and other areas of western Asia. The process started in earnest at the court of Songtsen Gampo (seventh century). An astonishing number of titles of medical works are recorded from this period that either were translated from other languages or were new works composed in Tibetan. By the time of Tri Desongtsen (late eighth century), there are reports of the title of "court physician" (*lamen*) in the royal court, a position that remained through the twentieth century, along with the granting of land and inherited rights to medical clan lineages, including the releasing of such clans from military duty.[6]

After the fall of the dynasty (ninth century), patronage for medical learning was provided by the emerging Buddhist monastic centers. The premier translator of Indic Buddhist works in the "new" period, Rinchen Zangpo (eleventh century), also translated the medical work *Aṣṭāṅgahṛdaya*, whose presentation of Ayurvedic tradition was especially influential for medicine in Tibet.[7] It was probably during the next century that Yutok Yönten Gönpo (1126–1202) and his students codified the work known as the *Four Treatises* (*Gyüzhi*), although the text attributes its authorship to the Buddha.[8] The *Four Treatises* became the principal "root" medical text in Tibet. Already major Buddhist teachers and writers, such as Gampopa (1079–1153) and Jetsün Drakpa Gyeltsen (1147–1216), had been serving as physicians and composing medical works. Special schools for medical learning, sometimes conjoined with curricula in astrological calculation, began to be established at the major monasteries: at Sakya Mendrong during the twelfth century; at Zhalu, which specialized in the *Astanga* system, and Tsurpu, which saw much eclectic medical scholarship, in the fourteenth century; and at É'i Chödra at Bodong in the early fifteenth century. By the time the Chang line of physicians was consolidating at Chang Ngamring, the old Tibetan capital, in the fifteenth century, there were oral medical examinations and regimes of memorization. There was also much medical learning at Latok Zurkhar, which became the home of the other major line of Tibetan medicine, the Zur. The Drigung Kagyü developed its own medical tradition, branching off from the Zur.

By the early seventeenth century several key medical centers were thriving in the Lhasa area, at Drepung, Shika Samdruptsé, and Tsé Lhawangchok, where more formal methods of examination were established. These centers were the springboard for the further nurturing of medical learning under the reign of the Fifth Dalai Lama and the establishment by his regent, Desi Sang-gyé Gyatso, of the Chakpori Medical College on a hill in the middle of Lhasa. Chakpori served as the nucleus of the medical academy in Tibet until the Cultural Revolution. Other medical schools continued to appear at monastic centers, now in eastern Tibet, including at Dergé, Pelpung, Katok, Kumbum, and Labrang Trashikhyil. Some of these institutions developed curricula that were at odds with medical orthodoxy at Chakpori, creating the conditions for debate and dissent.

In fact, medical practice in Tibet was far from limited to these monastic learning centers. Healing traditions also abounded in tantric circles, and oracle mediums were involved with healing as well. But even for the medicine fostered by the monastic schools, we know little of the sociology of practice, regarding, for example, what percentage of practicing physicians were actually trained in those schools, what the lay–monastic breakdown was, to what extent physicians actually used medical writings, and so on, let alone all the questions one might raise about the economics and daily practice of medicine. We can only venture, for example, that the degree of professionalization for Tibetan medicine probably never approached that achieved in Chinese medicine through the centralized bureaucratization of qualifying examinations for physicians and, by the Song dynasty, regulations that physicians keep standardized case records.[9] On another note, we can also observe that there seems to have been an unusually widespread familiarity among Tibetans with dissected bodies, due to the long-standing practice of dismembering human corpses to feed vultures; such charnel grounds were used to gather stray body parts for the making of certain ritual instruments, and they also served as sites for Buddhist meditations on death.

Lacking at this point detailed sociological knowledge for the period under discussion, I will restrict my attention to insights we can glean from the scholastic medical literature. This already provides a huge and rich body of data, with many indications of tensions, debates, and changing mentalities and practices, as well as a heterogeneous array of medical traditions, from the Ayurvedic physiology of the three humors, to Chinese-influenced pulse diagnostics, to methods of surgery indebted to western Asian medicine. By the fourteenth century, writing a commentary on the *Four Treatises* had become a major way for medical scholars to demonstrate their learning and debate points of controversy. Other common literary genres included instructions that supplemented the root text, manuals for the preparation of medicines, manuals for medicinal plant recognition, and manuals of therapeutic techniques.[10] Another key genre that provides clear evidence of an effort to identify medicine as a separate tradition is the historical overview of medical personalities, literature, and institutions. Two very influential examples of this special medical history were written at the height of the consolidation of medical tradition, in the sixteenth and seventeenth centuries.[11]

"WRITING FROM EXPERIENCE"

One other distinctive medical genre that may be traced to the sixteenth century is the *nyamyik*, a "writing from experience." This genre serves well as a flash-point for the emerging empiricist dimensions of the medical mentality, and not only because of its name. In fact, the label only infrequently actually appears in a text's title.[12] Beyond the occasional specification that a given text was written on the basis of the author's experience,[13] being a *nyamyik* appears to be a matter mostly of reader reception. Frequently the term is only retrospectively applied, as is the case for the famous but oddly titled *Jewa ringsel* (*Relic of Ten Million*), a work describing medical practices written in the fifteenth century.[14] It may well be that the term was only used after the sixteenth century, with the explic-itly labeled collection of one hundred *nyamyik* by Gongmenpa.[15] The entire conception of a prestigious genre written by an elite expert class may be the product of the very period we are looking at.

One of the main purposes of the *nyamyik* seems to be to convey the special kind of knowledge that comes from hands-on practice, that is, the first sense of experience sketched above. In general, the content of the *nyamyik* seems to be construed as superior to the results of mere book learning.[16] Desi even ventures in his own *nyamyik* that the *Four Treatises* are of little use for actually treating patients, other than to provide information on recognizing medicinal plants, the basic structures of medical knowledge, and the location of the channels in the body. Even previous *nyamyiks* didn't support actual treatment sufficiently, he claims, prescribing "one medicine for one hundred diseases" and failing to describe the course of an illness fully from beginning to end.[17] That is what Desi implies his own *nyamyik* will provide. Thoroughness based on hands-on experience becomes the signal virtue of the *nyamyik*. In the eighteenth century Dergé Lamen maintains, "I wrote this *nyamyik* from my own experience and what I have become familiar with. This would be equivalent to a vast textbook of what has been heard of the kind actions [of former teachers]."[18] The point is developed further in the nineteenth century, with the influential *nyamyik* of Kongtrül, who chastises physicians who have never had "oral teachings from an experienced teacher and experience based on a long period of familiarization." Kongtrül stresses that merely checking the pulse and urine (the basic diagnos-tic tools of the *Four Treatises*) is not sufficient to diagnose disease. He insists instead upon asking the patient a set of detailed, particular questions and listen-ing carefully to the responses.[19]

The upshot of the increasing demand for more reliance on experience-based training was that the *Four Treatises* fell out of clinical use, even though the medical colleges still compelled students to memorize it.[20] At least by the nine-teenth century, authors of *nyamyiks* could speak directly of the *Four Treatises'* limitations. Kongtrul describes the many sources to which he had to resort for information that was lacking in the root text, and Mipam can distinguish the way he read pulses based on his own experience from an array of authoritative precedents in Tibet and China alike.[21] Innovation, if not actual deviation from the authoritative was always a risky business in Tibetan literary culture. What could be gained from bringing forth one's own experience to surpass the root text can be seen in the rhetoric of prestige surrounding the fact that so-and-so wrote a *nyamyik*.[22] Equally, the information that a *nyamyik* conveyed became valuable property. In the sixteenth-century collection of one hundred, each *nyamyik* was dedicated to one of the author's students, whose name and often clan or toponyms were specified. Here the *nyamyik* would be a kind of patrimony, a possession to be guarded against competitors.

THE WEIGHT OF EXPERIENCE

To the extent that the *nyamyiks* described what was learned idiosyncratically in the clinic and recorded information not known in the *Four Treatises*, the genre reflected an important direction in which medical practice was moving by the sixteenth century. The possibility of newness and innovation had definitely become an open question in learned medical circles.

There can be no question that in tandem with this move was a recurring insistence on the value of textual study and the learning of system.[23] Certainly such a value is evident in the perduring popularity of writing commentaries to the *Four Treatises*, which reminds us once again of the shared universe of values between medicine and Buddhist scholasticism. We often find three principal sources of valid knowledge—scriptural authority, logic, and experience—valued in the medical commentaries of the period.[24] The pair "empirical examination and critical analysis" is also invoked.[25] But the medical writers very frequently emphasized experience in particular, and denigrated the barrenness and even dangerousness of a physician who had only book learning.[26]

A critique of book learning alone and a valuing of experience are also encountered in Buddhist rhetoric, especially with regard to meditative practice and spiritual advancement. But differences can be detected. Tibetan Buddhist writers display a decided ambivalence about experience as a valid source of knowledge, unless it has been thoroughly informed by "right view" on key points of doctrine. The issues involved might be compared to debates about empiricism and the relation between mind, matter, and divine design in early modern Europe.[27] In Tibet, neither Buddhist nor medical writers considered experience ever to be entirely free of ideational content. Hence their presumption that it is necessary to educate experience in the right way; left uneducated, experience is subject to emotional prejudice and error. But although medical writers worried about physicians who practiced only on the basis of their experience, they showed far less suspicion of experience as a category as such than we do in Buddhist epistemology and meditation theory.[28] Experience appears to have been unambiguously a good thing in medical learning, even if it could not suffice on its own.

I would suggest there was a fundamental disparity in basic orientation that overdetermined this difference. The goal of medical practice, the orienting horizon of what constituted success, was the patient's recovery. The ascertainability of this telos—its empirical demonstrability—is of an entirely different order than that of the Buddhist summum bonum of "enlightenment." The success of the latter was determined by a far more socially complex set of criteria than the pretty indisputable fact of whether or not a patient died.[29]

I suspect that the very different ways these goals were ascertained affected the mentalities of their respective traditions in far-reaching ways. But we can also note more generally a greater respect for the realities of the physical world in medicine than in Buddhism, particularly in the substantial medical commentaries that were being written by the sixteenth century, and whose debates will be considered below. There is sometimes an openness to the physical world revealing itself in ways that no discursive knowledge can fully anticipate. One detects a confidence that there is something out there that has its own integrity—the number of bones in the body, say—that stands fully apart from what any text might say, and that one can consult and find new information from. This becomes particularly clear in the second, more specific notion of experience at play in medical tradition by this point, namely, the authority of direct observation. In the following section I consider arguments that sometimes turned on "what can be seen in actuality" or what is known "through direct perception" as a way to prove someone else's theory wrong.[30] While we might find some analogue in classical Buddhist epistemology regarding the role of direct perception in moments of meditative breakthrough, that is a very different matter, since what is perceived then is not everyday reality. And on those few occasions when Buddhist polemicists did invoke some obvious fact in the everyday world, it was more a rhetorical ploy than a precise argument. For Buddhist theory, what appears to direct perception in the conventional world will on close analysis prove to be but an illusion.[31] Again, the contrast is instructive. On no account will we find the medical tradition arguing that the physical death of a patient is an illusion.

With their ultimate goals so disparate (and despite the frequent characterization of the Buddha himself as healer par excellence), medicine in Tibet has struggled with classical Buddhist doctrine throughout its history. Some of these struggles issue simply from a discrepancy of system: is illness to be understood as bad karma, or more physicalistically, as an imbalance in the humors of the body? Although these very different kinds of etiology coexist in the *Four Treatises*, they do so sometimes in an uneasy mix. What's more, in actual medical practice, a truly weighty implication emerged in those moments that the physical world could be perceived as having a reality of its own, as when Darmo resorted to the body itself to determine the number of its bones. We begin to recognize in some quarters of the emerging medical academy both the suspicion, and then an unease with that suspicion, that the "word of the Buddha" itself could be subject to correction.

WHEN SYSTEMS COLLIDE: THE CHANNELS OF THE BODY

Empirical evidence in its most overtly physicalistic sense posed on several occasions an estimable challenge to Buddhist revelation. How this challenge was mounted, and then fielded, is illustrated well by a debate around the anatomy of the channels.

The *Four Treatises* describes four kinds of channels that transmit substances and energies through the body: 1) initial "growth channels," which give rise to the fetus's body; 2) "channels of being," matrices of channels at the brain, heart, navel, and genitals responsible for perception, memory, and reproduction; 3) "connecting channels," which consist of two main sets of "soul channels," one white and one black, that control the nervous and the cardiovascular systems; and 4) "life channels" through which a life force moves around the body. There was debate in the commentaries about what these categories actually refer to and exactly where in the body the channels are. But the discussion took a new turn entirely when, in the fifteenth century, a medical writer casually remarked that the life channels follow along the path of *lalana* and *rasana*.[32]

This writer was referring to the tantric conception of the "central channel," a straight tube that runs between the crown of the head and the genitals, and two others, *lalana* and *rasana*, that run along its sides; the three are well known in Indic and Tibetan Buddhist tantras as the basis for yogic cultivation. But starting in the fifteenth century there developed in Tibet a sustained effort to locate this tantric system within the medical system of channels in the *Four Treatises*.

A generation or so later, Sönam Yeshé Gyeltsen identified the tantric channels not only with the life channels, which in any case had always been viewed as derivative of the tantric system, but also with the more properly medical growth channels, and especially with the connecting channels.[33] He called the medical white soul channel, often understood to be the spinal column, the "outer" *lalana* and labeled the black soul channel, which is something like the vena cava, the "outer" *rasana*. This seems to be the first time a medical writer equated the medical nervous and cardiovascular systems with these two tantric channels. But we already see a device to make the equation palatable—a distinction between an "outer" version and an "inner" one. This device mirrors a larger tendency to distinguish the average human body—in this case, the medical body—from the body of the meditator or indeed that of a buddha. And it serves to avoid a very large problem: the central channel, *lalana*, and *rasana* are simply not visible in the average body in the way they are described in the tantras. Clearly, people had been looking inside corpses to find these channels, and the discrepancy had already been noted several centuries before.[34] What is new now is the increasing attention to the problem on the part of the medical community. And yet it has not really been solved: in Sönam Yeshé Gyeltsen's solution, the real, or correct—the inner—*lalana* and *rasana* are still invisible.

Different writers tried different schemes. The brilliant Kyempa was most interested in locating the most important tantric channel, the central one, which, controversially, he identified with the spinal column itself.[35] This would seem promising, since like the central channel, the spinal column is a single straight channel running from the top of the torso to the bottom. It took the master commentator Zurkharwa Lodrö Gyelpo (b. 1509) to disqualify this attractive solution—largely because it fails to respect the signal characteristics of the central channel as described in the tantras.[36] The deft answer he proposes instead is emblematic of where medicine was headed by the latter part of the sixteenth century.

Like other participants in this fray, Zurkharwa let the embryonic growth channels be the tantric channels.[37] In a way, this is a safe solution; those initial channels disappear once the child's body is fully formed. So, although he does not say this, there is no chance to disprove their existence later by investigation. But apparently, finding the tantric channels in the first weeks of life did not satisfy the quest to locate them in the adult body. So Zurkharwa also had recourse to the earlier suggestion that lined up the two side tantric channels with the white soul channel (the spinal column) and the black soul channel (the vena cava) in the adult body. However, a close reading of his language reveals that he doesn't actually equate them. At one point, he says that *rasana* "gives rise" to the black soul channel,[38] but this seems to only have the general sense that, as he says elsewhere, all of the wind channels in the body are the central channel, all of the blood channels in the body are *rasana*, and all of the liquid channels are *lalana*.[39] As for the central channel itself, he indicates his agreement with a variety of tantric passages that describe it, but he does so in the context of the growth channels. The upshot is that he actually locates the central channel only in the general channel (*soktsa*) that grows in the embryo's body.[40] So he rejects the views of those who argue that the central channel "always exists," i.e., in the adult body.[41] He certainly never physically pinpoints any of the tantric channels the way he does the medical channels, whose location with respect to the spine, for example, he can specify by digit.

Here and elsewhere Zurkharwa is quite conscious of a larger question of incommensurability.[42] But when he raises the possibility that it could be inappropriate to introduce ideas into medicine from what is clearly another system—that of the tantras—he doesn't jump at the chance to disqualify the medical effort to find the tantric channels in the physical body. He almost sounds like a modern historian when he argues instead that in fact it *is* appropriate to bring tantric ideas into medical description, for the medical system has always had multiple sources, which included the Vedas and disparate Buddhist sources like the Vinaya, the *Suvarnaprabhasottama*, and the *Kālacakra*. But the signature of his complex polemics is all too evident when he maintains that while the *Four Treatises* system "roughly accords" with the tantric one, it is important to separate the terminology, for the *Four Treatises* is not talking about the same thing as the tantras are, which is the fruits of meditation. Whatever is tantric about the anatomy of the *Four Treatises* is "hidden."[43] Note that in the process Zurkharwa has sustained his allegiance to tantric truths.

Indeed, Zurkharwa rejects as "invalid" the argument of previous writers that the tantric channels are merely matters of meditation, existing in the imagination but not present in the average body, since if they were, they would be visible in corpses.[44] Others came up with the theory that the tantric channels do exist concretely in the body but evaporate at death, just as the mind does. Zurkharwa's reason for rejecting all of these views is telling: if the tantric channels were only a matter of the imagination, the fruits of tantric yoga would not be obtained. The next major *Four Treatises* commentator, Desi Sanggyé Gyatso (1653–1705), makes a similar argument for the physicality of the tantric channels: yogis can attain immortality by holding the winds in the central channel.[45]

In arguing for the concrete efficacy of exercises involving the tantric channels, Zurkharwa and Desi would probably say (if they were reading this essay) that they were having recourse to another kind of empirical truth: the evident efficacy (from their perspective) of tantric practice. It is significant that they are committed to this efficacy being physically based. That already says a lot about the ambitions of the period to establish tantric ideology in some sort of physical reality, and I will return to this below. Note for now that while the influential Desi repeats most of Zurkharwa's solution verbatim,[46] the subtlety of the ambiguation is such that the question continues to dog the medical commentators, and major nineteenth- and twentieth-century writers are still at pains to demonstrate that what Zurkharwa and Desi established was the validity of the tantric system.[47] But that perduring ambiguity also meant that the door had been opened for dissent. Lingmen Trashi (b. 1726), close student of the polymath Situ Chökyi Jungné at the outlying medical center at Pelpung, might have been far enough from the dominion of Desi's Chakpori to offer a more rigorously empirical account. He is willing to concede that the soul channel is sometimes called an outer central channel; this distinction lines up with his general approach: to treat the human body differently from that of a buddha.[48] But regarding that human body, Lingmen has little patience for anything that is not directly observable. He can declare categorically that the tantric channels are out of court in an anatomy of the medical, i.e., "material," body. The tantric system is meant solely as a map for meditation.[49]

THE SEVENTEENTH CENTURY, MEDICINE, AND THE WORD OF THE BUDDHA

The move to separate tantric anatomy from the medical eventuated in writers such as Lingmen setting aside tantric anatomy as invalid for medical knowledge. In another debate that similarly pits scripture against empirical evidence,[50] Lingmen explicitly invokes what he has seen directly in medical examinations and autopsies in order to disprove anatomical statements in the *Four Treatises*.[51] Still, the fact that influential writers like Desi and Zurkharwa were motivated to find someplace for a separate functioning of tantric anatomy indicates that the latter was hard to displace entirely.

There can be no question that the medical writers were grappling with a knotty set of issues about authority. Although we can find examples of commentators overtly correcting the *Four Treatises*' statements, these tend to be cautious and minor. More commonly, the *Four Treatises* was upheld, in displays of loyalty that are more important for what they say socially than for what they actually meant to the practice and theory of medicine, which was evolving. A twentieth-century commentator's warning probably reflects a long-standing sentiment: "If [the channels are] explained other than this, that is, if one makes a claim that goes against . . . the tantras that explain the natural condition of the body's channels, that would establish a position that invalidates scripture. [Therefore] it is best to abandon personal arrogance and follow the experts [as represented in scripture]."[52]

Both the display of compliance to system and the urge to distance medicine from it make eminent sense for the tumultuous period leading to the centralization of the Tibetan state in the seventeenth century. The patrons of medical writers like Zurkharwa and Sönam Yeshé Gyeltsen—warring factions such as the Rinpung clan lords and the Karmapa lamas, jockeying for power during the sixteenth century—made for much political insecurity. The final hegemony of the Fifth Dalai Lama's government in the Potala in the seventeenth century coincided with the aspirations of the Qing dynasty in Tibet, which meant serious vulnerability for renegade monasteries and intellectuals.[53] We are only beginning to appreciate the extent of the impact of cultural contact between Tibetans and the Chinese empire during this period.[54] But one undoubted effect of the consolidation of a centralized government in Tibet was a consolidation of the fortunes of the medical academy.

The combination of increased bureaucratization of the Tibetan state and the highly rationalized apparatus of the Chinese empire created a climate that conferred status on public accountability and empirical testing.[55] A principal agent in creating that status was the Great Fifth himself, who actively sought out medical experts from abroad, for his own well-being but also clearly with a view toward broadening the profession's repertoire of diagnostic, therapeutic, surgical, and pharmacological tools. Again, the signal is that the *Four Treatises* do not contain everything one needs to know to practice medicine successfully. The Dalai Lama's search for supplements, both foreign and local, to medical knowledge in Tibet was wide-ranging. He brought an Indian physician to his court in 1675 for that physician's expertise in cataract operation, a technique that he induced Darmo to master, and which the latter performed successfully on the Dalai Lama himself.[56] The Dalai Lama also invited a Chinese expert in eye treatments, along with other physicians from South Asia, for whom he sent emissaries to India. He put his own court physicians in contact with these foreign experts, encouraging them to study the new techniques; new medical works were also translated into Tibetan. His catholic vision extended to the past as well. Old works of Tibetan medicine were sought in archives, recognized as important, edited, and carved for block printing; biographies were codified of the founders of medical tradition in Tibet; several scholars attempted to codify a definitive edition of the *Four Treatises*.[57]

We also read repeatedly of the granting of lands and income to monastic medical schools. State support of medical learning reached its climax when the regent Desi Sanggyé Gyatso finally established a new medical school at Chakpori in 1696, thus fulfilling the wishes of the Dalai Lama conveyed to the Desi decades earlier, after the medical school at Drepung had declined. Perhaps for the first time in medical academia, the new school would admit both monk and lay students.[58] The granting of "tax monks" for assuring student enrollment, the degree of trans-Tibetan enrollment, and the standardization of medical examinations, degrees, and sites for plant collection in Central Tibet all reached new specificity. The Desi's other great accomplishment for medicine was overseeing the production of a spectacular set of medical paintings illustrating anatomy, pharmacology, therapeutics, and other vignettes of medical theory, practice, and learning.[59] In striking ratification of our thesis about empiricism during this period, the Desi records how his artists executed the anatomical drawings by looking at real corpses.[60] It is also reported that he employed artists to draw plants based on local knowledge of particular specimens. The Desi was aware that drawing from life produced new knowledge that surpassed the *Four Treatises*.[61] The set's precise images constituted "unprecedented paintings which provide direct instruction that can introduce [medical learning] as if pointing to it with the finger."[62]

Yet the revelatory visions at the base of the Desi's agenda—seeing Chakpori mountain as the heaven of the Medicine Buddha, glorifying the tomb of the Great Fifth and its place in Lhasa[63]—show that we must also remain alert to other dimensions of this moment. In their actions with regard to state, religion, and medicine alike, agents like the Great Fifth and the Desi were creating what is now loosely called the Tibetan "theocracy," a state whose very essence was founded upon the entire edifice of the Tibetan Buddhist universe of imagination—tantric and otherwise.[64]

It is not too much to say that the stridently authoritative political climate infected intellectual life in the monastery as well as in the practical sciences.

Ironically, the political climate fostered conservatism at the very time of the sweeping moves toward rationalization. This conservatism was not the same as censorship, however; prominent medical scholars of the period protecting the root text or looking for the tantric channels in the empirical body were simply part and parcel of the same worldview that was being built into the whole political and cultural basis of Tibet. Tantric meditation is efficacious in the real world; the words of the Buddha are true.

The upshot, then, was a dual movement. The same medical colleges that were being given fiscal autonomy and experimental license were also ordered to conduct prayer ceremonies every day for the health of government officials. Nowhere do we see this twofold urge better than in a long-running debate in Tibet about which Zurkharwa quips, "Whenever three or more people gather, it gets discussed."[65] The debate is none other than the very grave question of whether or not the *Four Treatises* is the "word of the Buddha." If it is, it is a sacred revelation on par with the other canonical teachings of the Buddha, translated into Tibetan from the holy language of Sanskrit. If not, it would have been composed by Tibetans in Tibetan.[66] This is a familiar issue in Tibet: demonstrating a text to be an authentic translation from an Indic original had long been the dividing line between a true Buddhist teaching and a debased apocrypha by an impudent upstart. If the root text was originally Tibetan, rather than Indic, its authority could be in jeopardy.

Evidence for Tibetan composition of the *Four Treatises* had already been noticed as early as the thirteenth century,[67] but it was Zurkharwa who worked it out most explicitly. He drew on arguments devised for another, parallel debate, also at issue by the thirteenth century, regarding the authorship of the so-called treasure scriptures and the nature of the word of the Buddha.[68] Yet again, the contrast is stark: where the advocates of the Buddhist treasure scriptures always concealed their Tibetan composition and constructed elaborate ways to keep authorship attributed to the Buddha, Zurkharwa is driven in one of his essays to finally blurt it out: "If [the *Four Treatises*] were not made to appear as if it were Buddha word, Tibetans—wise, dumb, and middling alike—would have a hard time believing it."[69]

Zurkharwa makes the *Four Treatises* instead a *śastra*, a genre that in Buddhism denotes highly regarded writings, but not the work of the Buddha himself.[70] In one essay he builds three positions—on the outside the *Four Treatises* is Buddha word, on the inside it is a *śastra* written by an Indian scholar, and secretly (this always connotes the deepest truth) it is a *śastra* written by a Tibetan. Then he shows the first two to be untenable anyway. The *Four Treatises* mentions tea, not typically mentioned in Indian *śastras*; it describes diagnostic methods using pulse and urine, not known in Indian medicine: these and other facts show the text must be a Tibetan composition. This kind of evidence, noted even prior to Zurkharwa, is emblematic of the empiricist mentality and historical sense that the medical writers could muster.[71] And once again Lingmen,

writing in eastern Tibet in the eighteenth century, illustrates this mentality
even more clearly: Indian medical texts like the *Aṣṭāṅgahṛdaya* consider goat
meat to be good, he declares, while the *Four Treatises* considers it to be one of
the worst kinds of meat; this shows the Tibetan character of the *Four Treatises*,
a work that accords with the cold climate of Tibet.[72]

What illustrates the tension surrounding such empiricism is the striking fact
that the Desi himself accedes to so many of the same arguments about the Tibetan character of the *Four Treatises*, but still makes it Buddha word. The Medicine Buddha, he avers, granted the text to the Tibetan compiler Yutok, who then
fixed it in a few spots for the Tibetan context.[73] We cannot read this position
without thinking about the Desi's political investment in the power of the word
of the Buddha. But the risks in making the medical root text anything but the
word of the Buddha are already evident a century earlier in Zurkharwa's obvious caution: how he saves his most radical statement for a separate essay;[74] how
in his more widely known commentary he is oblique, avoiding overt discussion
of Tibetanness and focusing rather on the status of kinds of *śastra*;[75] and how in
a third work he bemoans the delicacy of the question, insisting that in the end
it is undecidable and what is really important is to realize that the *Four Treatises*
is highly valuable and should be respected *as if* it were Buddha word.[76]

THE ALTERNATE SPACE OF MEDICINE

The high stakes of empiricist leanings for the learned centers of medicine in
Tibet have as their background the larger debate about the value of an individual's direct experience vis-à-vis a doctrinal system. We have seen how that
larger issue had specific valences for medicine. Personal clinical experience was
sometimes construed as more valid than system and as capable of producing
innovation. But personal experience also fleshes out and even owes its existence
to system—as when foreign physicians, invited by the Dalai Lama, teach new
techniques that Tibetan physicians then practice. It has been instructive to
compare the salience of experience in medicine with its status in scholastic
Buddhist discussions; this has suggested, for one thing, that medicine had more
tolerance for the innovation that direct experience fosters.

Much of that difference is doubtless attributable to the higher investment
that the Tibetan state had in Buddhism—its ethics, its institutions, its imagery,
its ritual regalia, the status of its scholastic doctrine—than the more circum-
scribed world of academic medical theory and practice. But once we take stock
of how fundamental the entire universe of Buddhism had become to the society
that the Tibetan government represented, we confront the limitations of the
heuristic distinction between Buddhism and medicine. There was much mutual
indebtedness, and both participated in the larger mix that constituted the texture
of Tibetan life, especially in the very cosmopolitan Tibetan capital during the

centuries we are considering. Medicine had some very special things, symbolic and otherwise, to offer. But we would probably still do well to consider that mix under the general banner of Buddhism in this more expansive sense, even if medicine sometimes represented a dissent from Buddhist scriptural authority.

In essence medicine provided a special spin to experience, even if it shared an interest in it with mainstream Buddhist scholasticism. For both kinds of experience identified in this paper, the medical versions were distinctively all about the physical. The thick world of practice that informed *nyamyik* writing, for example, had for the physician everything to do with the idiosyncrasy of the material world—the texture of daily routine; the cultivation of habits of clinical technique; the development of "dexterity," an often-cited virtue; familiarity with plants; and most of all, the variability and indeed unpredictability of the course of illness itself. Even more so, the force of the second, more specific sense we have identified for experience—direct contact with the empirical—was actually about the authority of the physical world. Here especially, the evidence that polemicists like Zurkharwa and Lingmen could cite to decide a dispute was there to be seen by the eye: unpredictable again, it had a reality of its own, of a different order beyond the grasp of system.

The case par excellence of the recalcitrant physical fact that exceeds system is the death of the patient. I speculated above that its possibility on the horizon defined the field of medicine in fundamental ways. I would add now that this special allegiance to materiality conjoined, in the particular historical circumstances of seventeenth-century Tibet, with a recognition on the part of the Dalai Lama's government that medicine provided a special service in a Buddhist society. The externality of the physical world became, as it were, the rare case of a reality standing outside system, and it therefore could serve as a checkpoint, an independent confirmation of what often seemed otherwise to be an all-encompassing Buddhist universe. I suspect that these were the stakes in the channel debate: medicine offered a vehicle by which to confirm the truth of the systems of tantric yoga, in turn a very key ingredient of the reincarnation system that founded the office of the Dalai Lama. Even if empirical evidence was not actually forthcoming to prove the physical existence of the tantric channels, the medical thinkers almost made it so. But however the debate came to be decided (differently by each of the commentators), the important point is that the (in)visibility of the channels—along with the larger question of what could be seen, or proven, through dissection—had been put on the table, forever to be reckoned with.

The Lhasa government created a special institutional space for medical learning, a place apart, to a degree not seen before. But medicine had already created a place apart for itself by virtue of its distinctive kinds of arguments and practices. Still, in the volatile case of the authorship of the *Four Treatises*, the limits and risks of such a separation meant that an argument against the Buddha's authorship could only be advanced with extreme caution and some amount of dissimulation. But it would be wrong to conceive of these medical thinkers as thoroughgoing empiricists who only had to stay out of the punishing way of the "Church." Buddhist ideology and tantric truths were as basic to the medical writers' worldviews as was their interest in saving patients from death. We can even note cases where the dynamic went in the other direction, whereby something like tantric thinking could also serve to legitimize the medical. As one example, tantric theorizations of subtle matter sometimes helped medical theory to talk about imperceptible functions in the body.[77]

If, then, we find an uneasy tension remaining between the claims of perceptibility and the claims of soteriological transformation, the tension may turn out to be mainly in our own eyes. In the particular circumstances of seventeenth-century Buddhist Tibet, medicine helped provide the government with the grounds for an episteme in which the ideals and images of religion could coexist with the everyday practices of governance and power, together to display a coherent universe.

NOTES

I am grateful to Charles Hallisey for conversations that were critical in the conceptualization of this essay, and to Yang Ga of the Tibetan Medical College in Lhasa and Harvard University and Thupten Phuntsok of the Central University for Nationalities in Beijing for much information and insight on some of the historical issues discussed herein.

1. This and the following quote from Blo bzang chos grags, Dar mo Sman rams pa (b. 1638), "Rus pa'i dum bu sum brgya drug cu'i skor bshad pa" [Explanation of 360 Bones], in *Bod lugs gso rig sman rtsis ched rtsom phyogs bsdus* (Lhasa: Sman rtsis khang, 1996), 22–24, excerpted from his unpublished *Gser mchan rnam bkra glegs bam gan mdzod.*

2. The degree of the revolution in European science in the early modern period is itself subject to question: see Steven Shapin, *The Scientific Revolution* (Chicago: University of Chicago Press, 1996).

3. I took a similar approach to the issues of individualized selfhood, the writing of autobiography in Tibet, and modernity in Janet Gyatso, *Apparitions of the Self: The Secret Autobiographies of a Tibetan Visionary* (Princeton: Princeton University Press, 1998).

4. The common Tibetan terms are *myong ba* and *nyams*, or some combination thereof. See Janet Gyatso, "Healing Burns with Fire: The Facilitations of Experience in Tibetan Buddhism," *Journal of the American Academy of Religion* 67, no. 1 (1999): 113–147.

5. The following is based largely on Blo gros rgyal po, Zur mkhar ba (b. 1509), *Sman pa rnams kyis mi shes su mi rung ba'i shes bya spyi'i khog dbubs* [Pitched Tent] (Chengdu: Si khron Mi rigs dpe skrun khang, 2001), 287–321; and modern surveys

such as Dkon mchog rin chen (b. twentieth century), *Bod kyi gso rig chos 'byung bai durya'i 'phreng ba* [*History of Tibetan Medicine*] (Lanzhou: Kansu'u Mi rigs dpe skrun khang, 1992) and Khro ru Tshe rnam (1928–2004), "Bod lugs gso rig slob grwa rim byung gi lo rgyus gsal ba'i gtam dngul dkar me long" [History of Tibetan Medical Education], in *Bod sman slob gso dang zhib 'jug* 1 (1996): 1–11. See also Christopher I. Beckwith, "The Introduction of Greek Medicine Into Tibet in the Seventh and Eighth Centuries," *Journal of the American Oriental Society* 99, no. 2 (1979): 297–313; and Fernand Meyer, *Gso ba Rig pa: Le système médical tibétain* [*The Tibetan Medical System*] (Paris: Centre National de la Recherche Scientifique, 1981).

6. Blo gros rgyal po, Zur mkhar ba, *Pitched Tent*, 291–299.

7. See Claus Vogel, ed., *Vagbhata's Astangahrdayasamhita, the First Five Chapters of Its Tibetan Version* (Wiesbaden: F. Steiner, 1965); Vagbhata, *Vagbhata's Astangahr-dayasamhita*, ed. Rahul Peter Das and Ronald Eric Emmerick (Groningen: Forsten, 1998); and R. E. Emmerick, "Sources of the *Four Tantras*," *Zeitschrift der Deutschen Morgenländischen Gesellschaft* 3, no. 2 (1977): 1135–1142.

8. Yon tan mgon po, G.yu thog (1126–1202), *Bdud rtsi snying po yan lag brgyad pa gsang ba man ngag gi rgyud* [*Four Treatises*] (Lhasa: Bod ljongs mi dmangs dpe skrun khang, 1992).

9. See Christopher Cullen, "*Yi'an*: The Origins of a Genre of Chinese Medical Literature," in *Innovation in Chinese Medicine*, ed. Elizabeth Hsu (Cambridge: Cambridge University Press, 2001), 297–323.

10. The Tibetan labels are *lhan thabs, sman sbyor, 'khrungs dpe,* and *lag len.*

11. Blo gros rgyal po, Zur mkhar ba, *Pitched Tent*, and Sangs rgyas rgya mtsho, Sde srid (1653–1705), *Dpal ldan gso ba rig pa'i khog 'bugs legs bshad bai dur ya'i me long drang srong dgyes pa'i dga' ston* [*Beryl Mirror*] (Lanzhou: Kan su'u Mi rigs dpe skrun khang, 1982).

12. Sometimes a work self-identifies as a *nyams yig*, e.g., Blo gros mtha' yas, Kong sprul (1813–99), *'Tsho byed las dang po la nye bar mkhor ba'i zin tig gces par btus pa bdud rtsi'i thigs pa* [*Advice to Novice Physicians*], in *Gso rig skor gyi rgyun mkho gal che ba bdam sgrig*, ed. Yon tan rgya mtsho et al. (Beijing: Mi rigs dpe skrun khang, 1988), 2.

13. E.g., Chos grags rgya mtsho, Sde dge bla sman (eighteenth century), *Nad sman sprod pa'i nyams yig* [*Writing from Experience on Giving Medicine to the Sick*], in *Gso rig skor gyi rgyun mkho gal che ba bdam sgrigs*, ed. Yon tan rgya mtsho et al. (Beijing: Mi rigs dpe skrun khang, 1988), 417–418.

14. *Bye ba ring srel.* See Sangs rgyas rgya mtsho, Sde srid, *Techniques of Lamaist Medical Practice, Being the Text of Man ngag yon tan Rgyud kyi lhan thabs zug rngu'i tsha gdung sel ba 'i katpu ra dus min 'chi zhags gcod pa'i ral gri* (Leh: S. W. Tashigangpa, 1970), 566 and 568–569.

15. Dkon mchog phan dar, Gong sman (1511–77), *Nyams yig rgya rtsa: The Smallest Collection of Gong sman Dkon mchog phan dar's Medical Instructions to the Students* [*One Hundred Writings from Experience*] (Leh: Lharje Tashi Yangphel Tashigang, 1969). See also the sources listed by Sangs rgyas rgya mtsho, Sde srid, *Techniques of Lamaist Medical Practice*, 566–569.

16. Such a sentiment is not necessarily at odds with the prestige accorded to medical scholarship in other contexts, regarding which see Kurtis Schaeffer, "Textual Scholarship, Medical Tradition, and Mahayana Buddhist Ideals in Tibet," *Journal of Indian Philosophy* 31 (2003): 621–641.

17. Sangs rgyas rgya mtsho, Sde srid, *Techniques of Lamaist Medical Practice*, 566–567.

18. Chos grags rgya mtsho, Sde dge bla sman, *Writing from Experience on Giving Medicine to the Sick*, 401.

19. Blo gros mtha yas, Kong sprul, *Advice to Novice Physicians*, 1–3.

20. Zur mkhar ba already notes that the *Four Treatises' Bshad brgyud* is rarely read: Blo gros rgyal po, Zur mkhar ba, *Rgyud bzhi'i 'grel pa mes po'i zhal lung* [*Oral Instructions of the Progenitors, Commentary on the Four Treatises*], 2 vols (Beijing: Krung go'i Bod kyi shes rig dpe skrun khang, 1989), 1:95. See also Sangs rgyas rgya mtsho, Sde srid, *Techniques of Lamaist Medical Practice*, 566. Certainly by the twentieth century, physicians almost always used recent *nyams yigs* as their actual handbooks, usually Blo gros mtha yas, Kong sprul, *Advice to Novice Physicians*, or one of the ones by Mkhyen rab nor bu (1883–1962).

21. Blo gros mtha yas, Kong sprul, *Advice to Novice Physicians*, 32–33; Mi pham rgya mtsho, 'Jam mgon 'Ju (1846–1912), *Bdud rtsi snying po'i rgyud kyi 'grel pa drang srong zhal lung las dum bu bzhi pa phyi ma rgyud kyi rtsa mdo chu mdo'i tika* [*Commentary on the Final Treatise*]. In *Gso rig skor gyi rgyun mkho gal che ba bdam sgrigs*, ed. Yon tan rgya mtsho et al. (Beijing: Mi rigs dpe skrun khang, 1988), 260–262.

22. See Dkon mchog rin chen, *History of Tibetan Medicine*, 187 and 188.

23. Schaeffer, "Textual Scholarship." See also Sangs rgyas rgya mtsho, Sde srid, *Techniques of Lamaist Medical Practice*, 569, emphasizing his own recourse to authoritative works (*lung*) and reasoning (*rigs*), even after arguing that experience is most essential.

24. I.e., *lung* (Skt. *agama*), *rigs* (Skt. *yukti*), and *myong ba*. See, e.g., Blo gros rgyal po, Zur mkhar ba, *Commentary on the Four Treatises*, 3; Sangs rgyas rgya mtsho, Sde srid, *Techniques of Lamaist Medical Practice*, 569.5.

25. (*Rtag*) *dpyad* (Skt. *vicara*) is sometimes a synonym for *myong ba*: Byams pa 'phrin las (b. 1928) [quoting Sde srid], "Sde srid sangs rgyas rgya mtsho'i 'khrungs rabs dang mdzad rjes dad brgya'i padma rnam par bzhad pa'i phreng ba" [Desi Sanggyé Gyatso's Rebirths and Acts], in *Byams pa 'phrin las kyi gsung rtsom phyogs bsgrigs* (Beijing: Krung go'i Bod kyi shes rig dpe skrun khang, 1997), 415.

26. E.g., Sangs rgyas rgya mtsho, Sde srid, *Techniques of Lamaist Medical Practice*, 566, railing against "nyams len byed mi mi 'dug" (those who are not people who practice), even while also insisting on the need for learning. Cf. Smin gling Ngag dbang sangs rgyas dpal bzang's criticism of Darmo and others who are "attached to the words of the *Great Treatise* (= *Four Treatises*) but fail to do practice; leaving behind clinical examination, they murder patients." Quoted by Byams pa 'phrin las, *Gangs ljongs gso rig bstan pa'i nyin byed rim byon gyi rnam thar phyogs bsgrigs* [*Biographies of Tibetan Medical Teachers*] (Beijing: Mi rigs dpe skrun khang, 2000), 318.

27. Jonathan I. Israel, *Radical Enlightenment: Philosophy and the Making of Modernity 1650–1750* (Oxford: Oxford University Press, 2001), 252–256, 477–485, 535–540.

28. Gyatso, "Healing Burns with Fire."

29. For an early example of death as a key issue in medical ethics, see Ye shes gzungs, Sum ston pa (twelfth century), "'Grel ba 'bum chung gsal sgron nor bu'i 'phreng mdzes" [Commentary on the Smaller Prajnaparamita Sutra: Beautiful Rosary of Bejeweled Shining Lights], in *G.yu thog cha lag bco brgyad*, vol. 1 (Lanzhou: Kan su'u Mi rigs dpe skrun khang, 1999), especially 297 seq.

30. Tib. *dngos su mthong zhing* or *mngon sum du.*

31. Cf., for example, Candrakirti's arcane analysis of the status of things that are directly perceived: Mervyn Sprung, trans., *Lucid Exposition of the Middle Way* (London: Routledge and Kegan Paul, 1997), 60–63.

32. Rnam rgyal dpal bzang, Byang pa (1395–1475), *Bshad Rgyud kyi 'grel chen bdud rtsi'i chu rgyun* [*Continuous Stream of Amrita, a Commentary on the Explanatory Treatise*] (Chengdu: Si khron Mi rigs dpe skrun khang, 2001), 90.

33. Bsod nams ye she rgyal mtshan (fifteenth to sixteenth centuries), *Dpal ldan bshad pa'i rgyud kyi 'grel pa bklag pa don tham chad grub pa* [*Commentary on the Explanatory Treatise*] (photocopy of ms. held in Lhasa), 63a–82a. His position is likely based on an innovation of his father, the famed scholar Byang pa Bkra shis dpal bzang, whose commentary on this part of the *Rgyud bzhi* [*Four Treatises*] is not available at present. In a previous version of this essay I mistakenly identified the author of *Commentary on the Explanatory Treatise* as Byang pa Bkra shis dpal bzang: Janet Gyatso, "The Authority of Empiricism and the Empiricism of Authority: Tibetan Medicine and Religion on the Eve of Modernity," *Comparative Studies of South Asia, Africa, and the Middle East* 24, no. 2 (2004): 83–96.

34. Rgyal mtshan dpal, Yang dgon pa (1213–58), *Rdo rje lus kyi sbas bshad*, in *The Collected Works* (*Gsung 'bum*) *of Yang dgon pa Rgyal mtshan dpal* (Thimphu: Kunsang Topgey, 1976), vol. 2, 434–435.

35. Tshe dbang, Skyem pa (fifteenth century), *Rgyud bzhi'i rnam bshad* [*Explanation of the Four Treatises*] (Xining: Mtsho sngon mi rigs dpe skrun khang, 2000), 129.

36. Blo gros rgyal po, Zur mkhar ba, *Commentary on the Four Treatises*, 133, 152, and 159.

37. Blo gros rgyal po, Zur mkhar ba, *Commentary on the Four Treatises*, 152 seq.

38. Tib. *bskyed cing.* Blo gros rgyal po, Zur mkhar ba, *Commentary on the Four Treatises*, 162. He also says that *lalana* and *rasana* are the basis (*gzhi*) of the white and black soul channels (133); or exist "in connection" (*dang 'brel ba*) with them (165).

39. Blo gros rgyal po, Zur mkhar ba, *Commentary on the Four Treatises*, 155.

40. Blo gros rgyal po, Zur mkhar ba, *Commentary on the Four Treatises*, 133.10–12. This *srog rtsa* is different from the black and white *srog rtsa* specified under the heading of the "connecting channels" in the mature body. See also Blo gros rgyal po, Zur mkhar ba, *Commentary on the Four Treatises*, 166.20–22 seq. Zur mkhar ba and others also consider the *Four Treatises'* fourth kind of channel, the life channel, as a place to juxtapose the tantric system of channels, but these discussions largely quote tantric

sources and avoid specific medical anatomy: Blo gros rgyal po, Zur mkhar ba, *Commentary on the Four Treatises*, 166–174. I examine the interesting details of this debate more fully in my forthcoming book, entitled *The Way of Humans in a Buddhist World: Contributions to an Intellectual History of Tibetan Medicine.*

41. Blo gros rgyal po, Zur mkhar ba, *Commentary on the Four Treatises*, 133.

42. Blo gros rgyal po, Zur mkhar ba, *Commentary on the Four Treatises*, 154.

43. Blo gros rgyal po, Zur mkhar ba, *Commentary on the Four Treatises*, 133 and 154.

44. *Mi 'thad pa.* Cf. Sangs rgyas rgya mtsho, Sde srid, *Gso ba rig pa'i bstan bcos sman bla'i dgongs rgyan Rgyud bzhi'i gsal byed bai dur sngon po'i ma lli ka* [*Blue Beryl*], 2 vols (Leh: D. L. Tashigang, 1981), vol. 2, 152). He calls this view "stupid."

45. Sde srid, *Blue Beryl*, vol. 2, 173–174.

46. Compare Sangs rgyas rgya mtsho, Sde srid, *Blue Beryl*, vol. 2, 151 seq., and Blo gros rgyal po, Zur mkhar ba, *Commentary on the Four Treatises*, 153 seq.

47. See, e.g., Blo gros mtha yas, Kong sprul, *Rnal 'byor bla na med pa'i rgyud sde rgya mtsho'i snying po bsdus pa zab mo nang di don nyung ngu'i tshig gis rnam par 'grol ba sa bon snang byed* [*Commentary on the Profound Inner Meaning*], in *Zam mo nang gi don zhes bya ba'i gzhung gi rtsa 'grel* (Xining: Mtsho sngon Bod lugs gso rig slob grwa chen mo, 1999), 57–333. This is reportedly also the position of a *Four Treatises* commentary by 'Ju Mi pham. For a recent example by the twentieth-century scholar Tsültrim Gyeltsen, see Frances Garrett and Vincanne Adams, "The Three Channels in Tibetan Medicine," *Traditional South Asian Medicine* 8 (2008): 86–114.

48. Gling sman bkra shis (b. 1726), *Gso ba rig pa'i gzhung Rgyud bzhi'i dka' 'grel* [*Commentary on Difficult Points in the Four Treatises*] (Chengdu: Si khron Mi rigs dpe skrun khang, 44–45).

49. Gling sman bkra shis, *Commentary on Difficult Points in the Four Treatises*, 46; "material" = *gdos bcas.*

50. See Gyatso, "The Authority of Empiricism," 89–90.

51. Gling sman bkra shis, *Commentary on Difficult Points in the Four Treatises*, 478: "*bdag gis ni pho mo mang po'i ro bshas pa mthong/rang gis kyang gri snying blangs pas pho mo thams cad snying rtse cung zad g.yon phyogs brang ngos la bsten pa mthong.*"

52. Translation adapted from Garrett and Adams, "The Three Channels in Tibetan Medicine," 19.

53. For an overview of the period, see Tsepon W. D. Shakabpa, *Tibet: A Political History* (New Haven: Yale University Press, 1967); and Luciano Petech, *China and Tibet in the Early XVIIIth Century: History of the Establishment of Chinese Protectorate in Tibet* (Leiden: Brill, 1972).

54. An admirable beginning is Françoise Pommaret, ed., *Lhasa in the Seventeenth Century: The Capital of the Dalai Lamas* (Leiden: Brill, 2003).

55. The archival sources for this period are substantial, but our information depends for the moment largely on the secondary work of contemporary Tibetan scholars who are systematically combing the lengthy biographies and autobiographies of the key figures in the period; examples include Dkon mchog rin chen, *History of*

Tibetan Medicine, and some of the essays in Byams pa 'phrin las, *Byams pa 'phrin las kyi gsung rtsom phyogs bsgrigs [Collected Writings]* (Beijing: Krung go'i Bod kyi shes rig dpe skrun khang, 1997).

56. The physician is styled "(R)manaho." Dkon mchog rin chen, *History of Tibetan Medicine*, 99; Byams pa 'phrin las, *Biographies of Tibetan Medical Teachers*, 315, quoting the Fifth's autobiography, *Duku'ula'i gos bzang*.

57. Dkon mchog rin chen, *History of Tibetan Medicine*, 100–104; Byams pa 'phrin las, "Desi Sanggyé Gyatso's Rebirths and Acts," 414–417.

58. Byams pa 'phrin las, "Desi Sanggyé Gyatso's Rebirths and Acts," 417, states that Chakpori was founded in 1695, quoting *Duku'ula'i gos bzang*, vol. *cha*, f. 335, but the block-print edition of that text does not provide the date that he seems to have interpolated into his quotation. Most scholars identify the date of the founding of Chakpori as 1696, e.g., Thub bstan tshe ring, Lcags ri dge rgan, "History of Chakpori," 150.

59. Yuri Parfionovitch, Gyurme Dorje, and Fernand Meyer, eds., *Tibetan Medical Paintings: Illustrations to the Blue Beryl Treatise of Sangye Gyamtso (1653–1705)*, 2 vols. (London: Serindia Publications, 1992). For a history of the set, see Byams pa 'phrin las, "Bod kyi gso rig Rgyud bzhi'i nang don mtshon pa'i sman thang bris cha'i skor la rags tsam dpyad pa" [Analysis of the Medical Paintings that Illustrate the Meaning of the *Four Treatises*], in *Byams pa 'phrin las kyi gsung rtsom phyogs bsgrigs* (Beijing: Krung go'i Bod kyi shes rig dpe skrun khang, 1997), 370–381.

60. Byams pa 'phrin las, "Desi Sanggyé Gyatso's Rebirths and Acts," 425–426, quoting Sangs rgyas rgya mtsho, Sde srid, *Blue Beryl*.

61. For example, he notes that when you look at an actual body you see that, in contrast to what the *Four Treatises* claims, the heart tip faces left in both male and female: Byams pa 'phrin las, "Desi Sanggyé Gyatso's Rebirths and Acts," 425–426.

62. "*Dmar khrid mdzub tshugs su ngo sprod sngon med kyi bris cha.*" Byams pa 'phrin las, "Desi Sanggyé Gyatso's Rebirths and Acts," 424, quoting Sangs rgyas rgya mtsho, Sde srid's *Mchod sdong 'dzam gling rgyan gcig rten gtsug lag khang dang bcas pa'i dkar chag thar gling rgya mtshor bgrod ba'i gru rdzings byin rlabs kyi bang mdzod* [Account of the Building and Installation of the Fifth Dalai Lama's Stupa] (Beijing: Bod ljongs mi rigs dpe skrung khang, 1990), f. 281.

63. Byams pa 'phrin las, "Desi Sanggyé Gyatso's Rebirths and Acts," 419, quoting Sangs rgyas rgya mtsho, Sde srid's *Baidurya Ser po [Yellow Beryl]*. Sde srid's *Account of the Building and Installation of the Fifth Dalai Lama's Stupa* is also a key source here: it has been studied by Schaeffer in "Controlling Time and Space in Lhasa," paper delivered to the annual meeting of the American Academy of Religion, Toronto, November 2002.

64. For striking images of the rituals of the Tibetan state by the mid-twentieth century, see *Ceremonies of the Lhasa Year*, ed. Michael Aris (London: Serindia, 1993).

65. Blo gros rgyal po, Zur mkhar ba, "Rgyud bzhi bka' dang bstan bcos rnam par dbye ba mun sel sgron me" [Distinguishing the Four Treatises as Buddha Word or Composition], in *Bod kyi sman rtsis ched rtsom phyogs bsdus*, ed. Bod Rang skyong

ljongs Sman rtsis khang (Lhasa: Bod ljongs Mi dmangs dpe skrun khang, 1986), 64. I treat this debate in detail in my forthcoming work *The Way of Humans*.

66. See also Samten Karmay, "The Four Tibetan Medical Treatises and Their Critics." Reprinted in *The Arrow and the Spindle: Studies in History, Myths, Rituals and Beliefs in Tibet* (Kathmandu: Mandala Book Point, 1998), 228–237.

67. Karmay, "The Four Tibetan Medical Treatises and their Critics," 230 n. 15. Others who argued for Yutok's authorship included Bo dong Phyogs las rnam rgyal (1376–1451) and Stag tshang Shes rab rin chen (b. 1405).

68. See Janet Gyatso, "The Logic of Legitimation in the Tibetan Treasure Tradition," *History of Religions* 33, no. 1 (1993): 97–134.

69. Blo gros rgyal po, Zur mkhar ba, "Distinguishing the Four Treatises as Buddha Word or Composition," 70.

70. Cf. Zur mkhar ba's detailed discussion in Blo gros rgyal po, Zur mkhar ba, *Commentary on the Four Treatises*, 4 seq.

71. See list in Karmay, "The Four Tibetan Medical Treatises and Their Critics," 234–237.

72. See Gling sman bkra shis, *Commentary on Difficult Points in the Four Treatises*, 4–8.

73. Sangs rgyas rgya mtsho, Sde srid, *Beryl Mirror*, 274–276.

74. Blo gros rgyal po, Zur mkhar ba, "Distinguishing the Four Treatises as Buddha Word or Composition."

75. Blo gros rgyal po, Zur mkhar ba, *Commentary on the Four Treatises*, 21–22. Here he vacillates between calling the *Four Treatises* śastra and another category of scriptures composed by figures other than the Buddha but in some sense inspired by the Buddha (*rjes su gnang ba'i bka*), which therefore still count as canonical. I am saving the details of this intricate argument for my forthcoming book.

76. Blo gros rgyal po, Zur mkhar ba, *Pitched Tent*, 311–313.

77. An example would be the invocation of the invisibility of the tantric central channel as a model for the imperceptibility of certain fine channels connected to the liver: 'Bri gung Dkon mchog 'gro phan dbang po (b. 1631), "Gso ba rig pa'i gzhung lugs chen po dpal ldan rgyud bzhi'i dka' gnad dogs sel gyi zin bris mdo" [Notes on a Discourse Clearing Away Doubts About the Four Treatises], in *'Bri gung gso rig gces bsdus*, ed. 'Bri gung Chos grags et al. (Beijing: Mi rigs dpe skrun khang, 1999), 134–138.

T<small>IBET AND THE</small> M<small>ANCHUS</small>

Chapter 23

THE ADMINISTRATION OF TIBET DURING THE
FIRST HALF-CENTURY OF CHINESE PROTECTORATE

Luciano Petech

In another essay from the vast corpus of mid-twentieth century Italian scholarship on Tibetan history, Luciano Petech describes the political institutions of Tibet, focusing in particular on the role the Manchu Qing dynasty played in restoring stability after the period of invasions and civil wars experienced in the eighteenth century. When Petech refers to Tibet in this selection, he is only concerned with Central Tibet, especially the thirteen myriarchies, which were governed by the Fifth Dalai Lama and his regents under the authority of the Khoshud Mongols, starting with Gushri Khan. Beginning with the rule of Tibet by the last Khoshud Mongol, Lajang [Lhazang] Khan, Petech examines the structures of power and leadership positions set up, mostly by the Manchu Qing in the process of trying to stabilize Central Tibet in the eighteenth century. The pattern is clear: while the Qing empire built most of the governing structures, fashioned more or less out of preexisting institutions or under powerful leading figures, Tibetans generally ruled themselves according to their own dictates. The Qing representatives in Tibet were mainly concerned with Tibet's foreign relations, and the military forces stationed there were more protection from outsiders than an occupying force to control the Tibetans.

In dealing with the administrative organization of Tibet, we must of course distinguish between the Tibetan government and the Chinese supervising bodies.

I. THE TIBETAN GOVERNMENT

To give an account of the Tibetan government between 1705 and 1751, we meet with a difficulty concerning the theoretical foundations of the state: it is difficult to give a satisfactory solution, according to our Western ideas, to the question of the headship of the Tibetan state. The only way of throwing light upon this problem lies through a detailed enquiry into the true character of the highest offices of the state.

As for the lower sections of the administrative machinery, on which the information available is rather scanty, they remained throughout this period much the same as they had gradually come into existence during the preceding century.

We shall now proceed to examine one by one the main features of the Tibetan government.

A. THE DALAI LAMA

The temporal rights of the Dalai Lama go back to the donation made in 1642 by the Khoshud ruler Gushri Khan to the Fifth Dalai Lama.[1] Its terms are not very clear, at least not from our Western point of view. So much is sure, the donation recognized to the Dalai Lama the undisputed supremacy over the Tibetan church. It placed also all the resources of the state at his disposal for the purpose of furthering the welfare of the Lamaist religion, through the grant of sovereign rights over the thirteen provinces (*trikor* [also called myriarchies]) of Tibet.

At that time the Dalai Lama was not equipped with the proper machinery for undertaking the actual administration, nor possessed an adequate military strength of his own to give it a solid backing. Perhaps also it was not expected of a holy personage of such a high standing that he should directly concern himself with administrative work.[2] It was on these considerations that the office of *desi* was created, to carry on the government of the country; the only temporal right reserved to the Dalai Lama was to decide the appeals brought before him against the judicial decisions of the *desi*.[3] But only a few years afterwards the Fifth Dalai Lama asserted his capacity and willingness to carry out a personal government, by appointing the *desi* at his will for rather short terms (a nominal right of confirmation remaining with the Khoshud Khan), by closely controlling him, and quite often by taking direct action without reference to the *desi*. When the Dalai Lama in his old age left the reins of the government in the trusted hands of Sanggyé Gyatso (1679), the above-sketched process underwent an involution, and the Dalai Lama seemed once more to drop out of active politics. The personality of the Sixth Dalai Lama was certainly not made for stopping this development; that gay toper was more than content to leave the worries of government to the experienced *desi*. But a new principle had been established once and for all, viz. that the Dalai Lama, besides his undisputed theoretical right of sovereignty, was able and willing to act as the head of the state, if circumstances were favorable.

The catastrophe of 1706 sharply changed the situation, and the factual conditions of the Dalai Lama in the following forty-five years influenced also his political status. From 1706 to 1720 there was a complete eclipse. First the see was practically vacant for several years, because the puppet of Lajang Khan, unrecognized by the greater part of the church, enjoyed no authority whatsoever, not even in the spiritual sphere. Then for three years the Zunghars maintained the fiction of governing in the name of an absent Dalai Lama. All this completely ruined his temporal prospects. When the Chinese installed the Seventh Dalai Lama in Lhasa (1720), they completely ignored his theoretical rights; neither was he in a position to stand up for their enforcement. The Tibetan government then set up did recognize the religious supremacy of the Dalai Lama; but politically it was and remained a creation of the Chinese. This is what makes the great difference between the period before 1706 and that after 1720. Before 1706 the government was practically (not so theoretically) appointed by the Dalai Lama and controlled by him; the long minority of the Sixth Dalai Lama under the tutelage of the *desi* is an exception in appearance only. After 1720 the government was appointed by the Chinese, and, because of the distance and bad organization, was little or not at all controlled by them. Nevertheless it was to be expected that with the slackness of Chinese supervision and the coming of age of the Dalai Lama, the latter would have slowly increased his influence; there were several signs pointing that way. But the outcome of the civil war of 1727/8, which was partly also an attempt at restoration of the power of the Dalai Lama, seemed to ruin forever all his prospects of a temporal rule. Suspected of complicity in the murder of Khangchenné, he was exiled to Gartar, and all temporal authority became vested in Polhané. Even after the Dalai Lama's return, he had absolutely no political power and was strictly limited to his religious functions.[4] We are justified in saying that the donation of Gushri Khan, unrecognized by the Chinese, lapsed in 1717/20, and that the Dalai Lama returned to the conditions in which he was in the 16th century: a much respected spiritual chief without a valid title to temporal rule. The events of 1750 and his firm and able handling of the situation offered him a chance of reaching at last that worldly power after which he and his predecessors had striven for some centuries. The Chinese emperor thought it advisable to tacitly recognize the right of the Dalai Lama to the sovereignty in Tibet. This right was not sanctioned in a formal act, but was taken as granted and considered as having been always exercised, even if through deputies. In any case, the year 1751 saw not so much the revival of Gushri Khan's old donation, as the establishment of a quite new title of sovereignty for the Dalai Lama. And indeed he had become not so much the successor to the power of the Fifth Dalai Lama, who had controlled the government without actually undertaking it, but the heir, with some limitations, to the sovereignty of Polhané; that is, he conducted the government with the assistance of his council, but was in some degree controlled by the Chinese. In 1642 there had been no actual differentiation between religious and political power. In 1706 this distinction was sharply drawn, and the two powers rested in separate hands. In 1751 the powers were reunited in the same person.[5]

The powers of the Dalai Lama after 1751 are set forth with sufficient clearness in *The Veritable Records of the Shizong [Yongzheng] Emperor* and in the *Weizang tuzhi [Topographical Description of Central Tibet]*.[6] They were considerable, because every important decision of the ministers must be referred to the Dalai Lama for his sanction; the appointments of the district governors, provincial commanders and officers of the army were made by him on the proposal of the council and with the approval of the *ambans*. On the other hand, he could act only through the medium of the council of *kalön*. But this system of government was organized in such a way that it allowed ample scope for the energy and enterprise of the Dalai Lama, particularly if Chinese supervision was inefficient. What an energetic pontiff could do under this system, without substantially modifying it, is shown by the life work of the Thirteenth Dalai Lama.

B. THE KHOSHUD KHAN

Gushri Khan conquered Tibet with his own forces and handed it as a gift to the Fifth Dalai Lama. His position henceforward was that of a "defender of the faith," i.e., he had the responsibility of the military defense of Tibet and of the protection of the Dalai Lama. The army and everything connected with it were in the exclusive charge of the Khan. Though Gushri Khan and his successors were not in permanent residence in Lhasa, we see them intervening personally every time a danger from outside is threatening the Tibetan government. Apart from this, they did not interfere with the administration. Even the appointment of the *desi*, at first a right belonging to them, soon slipped out of their hands. Their relations with the Dalai Lama in this period were somewhat indefinite. They were not his subordinates; they could not dictate their policy to him. Theirs was rather the position of a powerful ally, not that of a protecting power in the modern sense.

When Lajang Khan carried out his coup in 1705/6, he took over all the powers formerly belonging to the *desi*. In his double capacity as political and military chief, he was to all purposes the absolute ruler of Tibet; the Dalai Lama was a puppet in his hands and the Chinese emperor only a benevolent and distant ally. Thus he wielded such power as not even Gushri Khan had ever enjoyed. It looked like the establishment of an absolute and hereditary Mongol monarchy in Tibet. But the Zunghar storm shattered at one blow the Khoshud power. The reason for this is that the basis had become too slender for supporting such a far-reaching policy. We must remember that in 1658 the sons of Gushri Khan had divided the heritage, the younger sons keeping the Kokonor territories along with the greater part of the clansmen, and the first-born inheriting his father's rights in Tibet and the headship of the remaining clansmen.[7] When the storm broke out, the Khoshuds under Lajang Khan were too few to pose effective resistance to the invader, and their power was easily crushed beyond possibility of redress.

C. THE REGENT

Under this title I gather two distinct though related offices: the *desi* of 1642–1706 and the "king" of 1728–1750. Enough has already been said of the character of both. The *desi* was originally only an official (though the highest in the state) appointed by and depending from the Khoshud Khan at first, and later from the Dalai Lama. During the Fifth Dalai Lama's old age and the Sixth's minority, Sanggyé Gyatso gathered all power in his hands and made his office the actual head of the state, practically uncontrolled and acting quite on his own authority even in matters of foreign policy.[8] But this disproportionate increase of the *desi*'s authority depended merely on the overpowering personality of its holder and on the non-entity of the Dalai Lama; it can be doubted whether it would have survived the death of Sanggyé Gyatso. Such as it was, Lajang Khan cut short the importance of the office. The son and successor of Sanggyé Gyatso was a mere tool in his hands, and after some months the office was abolished altogether.

The office of *sakyong* filled by Taktsepa under Zunghar occupation was closely connected with that of *desi*, but had not by far the same importance. It enjoyed little authority, and the country was ruled, or rather ruthlessly kept in submission, directly by the Zunghar commander.

In 1721 the Chinese refused to reestablish the post of *desi*, which reminded them of Sanggyé Gyatso's unfriendly policy towards them during the nineties of the seventeenth century. It is true that the president of the council of ministers was given the title of *desi* by the people, but his office bore quite a different character, as he was only a primus inter pares.

The new regent appointed, or rather recognized, by the Chinese in 1728 bore after 1740 the title of *wang*, or "prince," for the Chinese, but "king" for the European missionaries. And a king in truth he was. Polhané and after him Gyurmé Namgyel exercised their power in their own name and authority, without reference to the Dalai Lama. The Chinese supervision was merely nominal; it was non-existent in internal affairs and limited itself to the control of external relations. The rule of the regent was absolute. The council of ministers had sunk to a mere executive organ, and the provincial administration was controlled by the nominees of the regent. The right to *ulak*, or compulsory transport service for government officials, had become a monopoly of the regent. The aristocracy was repressed and kept strictly under control. As the office was hereditary, none of the conditions for the continuance of a royal dynasty were lacking; the

Chinese would perhaps have placed it under stricter control, but certainly would not have abolished it. But Gyurmé Namgyel's folly destroyed the work of Polhané. The office and the title were done away with, never to return again.

The "regents" (gyeltsap) that we meet again in Tibetan history,[9] represented no permanent office, but, like the regents in European monarchies, managed the government of the Dalai Lama during the latter's minority; they were mostly high dignitaries of the church. When the Dalai Lama came of age at eighteen, the office of regent naturally ceased. This is the reason why more than one regent was tempted to do away with the Dalai Lama before he reached his eighteenth year, in order to perpetuate his own authority. But these officials were only a sort of temporary caretaker of the Dalai Lama's sovereignty, and enjoyed no independent authority.

D. THE COUNCIL OF KALÖN

The executive duties under the head of the state, whoever he might be, were performed by a council of four ministers called kalön. This council is known to have existed between 1642 and 1705/6, but we hear very little about its activity. Under Lajang Khan it enjoyed little standing or power, and as a matter of fact [is] seldom if ever mentioned in Tibetan or Chinese sources. But we know from the Breve Relazione of Fr. Domenico da Fano that during the period 1707–1711 the council existed and was composed of four Mongol jaisang, to the exclusion of Tibetans. Their main functions seem to have been judicial.[10]

The council was renewed by the Chinese in 1721, but was given a very different character. Its status was no longer that of an administrative body, but it ranked as the head of the state; it was a sort of collective praesidium (as in the Soviet constitution) or directory (as in the French constitution of 1795), with no authority superior to it, except for loose Chinese supervision. Its composition had also changed. The members were no longer Khoshud chiefs or Tibetan professional officials accustomed to routine work under the superior direction of the head of the state; they were great Tibetan nobles, hereditary chiefs of districts, each of whom cared above all for his own territory and considered the council only as the fighting ground for his personal ambitions, not as a living organism. This change in character was much for the worse. Free from efficient supervision and unaccustomed to teamwork, the members soon ceased to function collegiately, and each of them acted for himself, not departmentally but territorially. If this council had lasted, it would have dissolved Tibet into a loose federation of feudal states. But the result of the struggle in its midst was its utter collapse and the civil war of 1727/8.

The council as reconstituted in 1728 had again a different character. Composed at first of two members, then of three, then once again of four, it was the executive organ of the regent. Its members were at first trained professional officials, who came from the finance department or from other public offices. Its authority was at first limited to Ü, Tsang being placed under the direct administration of the ruler. When the council was expanded, the representatives of the old territorial aristocracy found again their entrance in it; probably about the same time its authority was tacitly extended to Tsang. These ministers can scarcely be said to have formed a council. Each *kalön* was in charge of a department of the administration (the texts do not give particulars on this score) and was responsible directly to the "king" and not to the council as a whole. In the last part of Polhané's reign the ministers even ceased to hold regular meetings in the council house, each *kalön* transacting his official business at his home and reporting directly to the "king." It was a state of affairs which reminds us vaguely of the U.S.A. cabinet.

The council of 1721 had been too powerful. After it was smashed, the Chinese court went to the opposite extreme, and the council of 1728 was again, as under Lajang Khan, a shadowy body unable to check or restrain the power of the "king." It was only in 1751 that the just balance of powers was found. The personnel of Polhané's and Gyurmé Namgyel's council was taken over by the Chinese, as they had taken over Lajang Khan's officials in 1721; in their dependencies the Chinese always stood for continuity of the tradition. But the nature of the council changed again. By law, the number of members was fixed at four. The Chinese insisted on its resuming the character of a collective body. It was to meet in the council house and all decisions were to be taken by common agreement and under common responsibility; no departmental specialization was allowed. The character of the council as a committee of professional administrators was on the whole maintained, although it was not always possible, especially under minorities of the Dalai Lama, to avoid its being influenced by the most powerful noblemen. On the whole the council, or *kashak* as it is usually called, may remind us of a Western European council of ministers, and the more so since in the course of time a measure of departmental specialization was gradually established. It served its purpose remarkably well and maintained its character for 200 years down to 1959.

The council had a staff of its own; the highest officials were the two *kashak drönnyer*. We may suppose that their functions consisted (as in the following century) in transmitting the orders of the council and supervising their execution.[11] There was also an unknown number of secretaries or writers of the council (*kashak drungyik*; later shortened into *kadrung*).

It does not appear that the later-day distinction between lay officials (*shödrung* or *drungkhor*) and ecclesiastic officials (*tsedrung*) was formally in existence; as the Dalai Lama had no political functions during the whole of this period, his establishment and its staff had little or nothing to do with the government. And indeed the *drungkhor* alone are mentioned in our texts.[12]

Little is known about the several departments of the central government during these years. We only have some scattered information about the judiciary, the finance department, the army, the *ulak* and postal service, and the provincial government.

E. JUDICIARY

On the organization of Tibetan justice the Tibetan texts are nearly silent. According to the *Weizang tuzhi* [*Topographical Description of Central Tibet*], at the head of the judiciary there was the *nangso chak*.[13] But I never met with such a title in the Tibetan texts of this period.

Fr. Domenico da Fano, writing in 1713, gives a sketch of the judiciary under Lajang Khan's rule. Criminal justice belonged to the council of ministers. Cases in which no capital offense was involved, were heard by a lesser council formed of eight *jaisang*. Civil suits in Lhasa were dealt with by the governor of the town and a law officer with the title of vice-governor. The task of the governor was to examine the cases, to preside over the proceedings and to supervise the execution of the sentence. But death sentences were given by the king alone, or in his absence by the council of ministers.[14]

Fr. Orazio della Penna too gives us a short and less clear sketch of judicial organization in 1730.[15] In Lhasa normal jurisdiction was exercised by the three city magistrates (*mipön*),[16] who heard cases daily in their residence. From their decisions litigants could appeal to the officials whom Della Penna calls "revisors of the cases"; I suppose these are the magistrates called in the *Biography of the Lord of Men* with the literary title of *trimkyi zhelchekhen*, judges of the law.[17] Their normal style was *sherpang*; they were two in number, both of them lay officials.[18] From these revisors the appeal went through the council of ministers to the ruler, and in very special cases to the Dalai Lama. Fr. Orazio seems to make no distinction between civil and criminal cases.

Fr. Cassiano da Macerata does not speak of the judiciary; he merely mentions in passing the three *mipön* of Lhasa, whom he calls *kutubal* (Hind. *kotvāl*); their retinue included twelve *korciapa* (*korchakpa*) or policemen.[19]

Although it is nearly impossible to check the accounts of the Capuchin Fathers with other sources, still, as the authors were eyewitness, we can assume them to be fairly accurate, with due allowance made for possible misapprehensions and inaccuracies.

In the times of the Khoshud Khans, judicial power in the provincial towns seems to have been in the hands of a provincial magistrate (*trimkyi khalopa*). But no trace of this office is found after the Zunghar invasion, and in the times of Polhané judicial power lay with the civil governor (*dzongpön*). The appeal from these tribunals, if allowed, went to the council of ministers at Lhasa.

The law applied in Tibetan courts was the old code traditionally attributed to king Songtsen Gampo and revised first by Jangchup Gyeltsen of Pakmodru and a second time by the Fifth Dalai Lama and the *desi* Sanggyé Gyatso.[20] The edition of this code used in the eighteenth century comprised forty-one sections in three volumes.[21]

On the practical working of Tibetan justice we are informed by the Italian missionaries and the Chinese documents. In Lhasa the seat of the tribunal was in the *labrang*, i.e., the buildings alongside the Trülnang temple. Litigation was discouraged by the parties being compelled to deposit a certain sum with the court; small disputes were therefore usually settled out of court. Criminal law was very severe, even barbarously so. Capital punishment was inflicted for a large number of crimes. Its forms were beheading, drowning, or the *kyang-shing*, a square vertical frame crossed by two beams in the shape of an X, to which the culprit was tied and shot at with arrows. Highway robbery with murder was usually punished with the *kyangshing*; for less grave cases there was exile to a fortress in the southern districts, where the criminals invariably died of hunger and thirst in the jails of the governor. Simple robbery was punished by cutting off the right hand, or (in lighter cases) by the bastinado. Adultery was punished by a fine or a whipping; common brawls by a fine. For many other crimes there was imprisonment, of the particularly cruel Tibetan kind; no food and no clothing were provided for the prisoner, who was dependent on the support of his relatives. Private vengeance was strictly forbidden. The fines realized were kept by the *mipön*, who at the end of each year handed over the total amount to the council of ministers.

Procedure was swift and the case was judged at once, normally on the day after its filing. The employment of advocates was permitted, but the time allowed to them for their speeches was severely limited. In civil suits the proofs admitted were written documents or oral witness. In criminal cases ordeal was freely used, mostly by compelling the accused to extract a white stone out of a cauldron of boiling oil, or by licking or grasping a red-hot iron.[22]

F. THE FINANCE DEPARTMENT

The finance department (*tsikhang*) was given special care. We have already spoken of Polhané's reforms there. Otherwise, for this period we have only stray references in the Tibetan texts, but no direct evidence.[23] What we can glean from our texts is this. The department seems to have been under the particular control of one of the ministers. The managing directors were the three *tsipön* (finance director), who often went on tours to control the finances of the provincial governors.

The most important part of the finance department was the central treasury, situated then as well as now in the *labrang* palace; at its head there was one (perhaps more) official called *chakdzöpa* (treasurer).[24] After the reorganization by Polhané, it was a well-arranged establishment, and the accounts were carefully kept on ledgers (*depter*).[25]

The private treasury of the Dalai Lama (treldé chakdzö) is not much in evidence during this period; we have only a few stray references and its importance seems to date from the reforms of 1792.[26]

Of course the autonomous temporal dominion of the Panchen had a separate financial organization, with its own finance directors and treasury.

Tibetan finance was then wholly based on natural produce. In this period and for a long time afterwards there were no Tibetan coins. For centuries the only minted metal in circulation had been the rupees coined by the three kingdoms of Nepal (till 1768). The Chinese introduced their silver taels, which soon became very popular.[27] But although important for trade purposes, money had little or no importance in the finance administration.

The income was mainly derived from direct taxation. We may safely surmise that, notwithstanding the lapse of years and the many abuses which crept in and which Polhané strove to eliminate, the assessment was still based on the general census taken by order of the Fifth Dalai Lama in 1663. Its results were carefully recorded, and to these records probably refer the mention of 300 ledgers at the time of Polhané's reorganization. These ledgers contained also the cadastre or land survey, and all rentals due and changes of property were duly registered in them.[28] It seems that in the capital all the ground belonged to the government, and purchases of plots of building land were more in the character of a perpetual lease.[29] Monasteries and their property were exempt from taxation. For the remaining population, the taxpaying unit was the tep or household (lit. threshold). Each tep must pay a fixed contribution yearly (lakyong, lakbap), consisting basically of a certain number of khel (about two pounds) of barley.[30] Taxation was always in kind, several other items being accepted instead of barley: cattle, sheep carcasses, cloth, butter, iron, rarely cash. Owing to the exemptions granted to the enormous estates of the monasteries, the taxpaying population was comparatively small and composed of the poorest elements of the people. No wonder that taxation was quite oppressive and that the taxpayers often complained of their unbearable conditions.

The taxes were collected and stored by the provincial governors. Each of them had under him two chakdzöpa (treasurers) in charge of finance, customs and public works.[31] Once a year the governors transmitted their accounts and the net balance of their revenue to Lhasa.

Another source of income was derived from the custom duties of the various barriers and toll gates at the frontier. We know these duties to have been heavy and practically left to the will of the custom officers; the letters of the Italian missionaries are full of complaints about the irritating oppressiveness of the customs people, and this in spite of the letters of exemption which the missionaries nearly always obtained from the government. The market duties too yielded a considerable income. Since 1738 a small yearly contribution of 5,000 taels was also regularly paid by the Chinese treasury out of the custom revenue of Dajianlu [Dartsedo].

The main items of expense, besides the costs of general administration, were firstly the subsidies regularly paid to some of the great monasteries, the occasional gifts to sanctuaries or to great lamas, and the sums spent on certain periodical feasts, particularly the great *Mönlam* festival held yearly at Lhasa during the first fortnight of the first month.[32] Secondly there was (chiefly for the period of Polhané's rule) the military expenditure, both for the Tibetan standing army and for the contribution towards the supplies of the Chinese garrison.

G. THE ARMY

The Tibetan standing army was created by Polhané. Before his time, the Tibetan government had depended on the regional and feudal levies, which were summoned every time an emergency occurred. As a general rule, every five families had to give a soldier for the militia (*yülmak*) and had to supply him with arms, accoutrements, food and pay. An exception was Ngari; in this important strategic region every single family had to give a soldier. The militiamen were gathered together by the provincial governors and assigned to the various corps (infantry and cavalry) according to the financial means of their families. The officers were drawn from the more well-to-do families. The general expenses of the militia were paid by the province to which they belonged. As soon as the war for which they were summoned was over, the militiamen returned to their homes. The lowest officer rank was that of the *dingpön*; higher ranks were the *gyapön* (commander of one hundred) and *rupön*. Military affairs at the district headquarters were entrusted to a *gyapön* or a *rupön*, according to the importance of the district. This military commander was equal in rank with the district governor (*dzongpön*), and this fact gave origin to the system of dual governorship, which was prevalent in Tibet before 1951. At the top of the military organization there were the *dapön* or provincial generals. There were three *dapön* in Tsang and only one in Ü; a second Ü *dapön* was added in 1751. Their charge was in this period the apanage of a few noble families: Changlochenpa, Pulungwa, Rampawa in Tsang; Bumtangpa in Ü. Their authority, however, did not extend to Ngari, which had a special organization; supreme civil and military authority there was vested in the two *garpön*, on whom see later. The armament of the militia was primitive; it consisted of swords, lances and bows and arrows, with some blunderbusses. The artillery consisted mainly of swivels, though there were some large cannon mounted on carts with large wheels; but their use in open warfare was quite exceptional.[33]

The Tibetan militia described above was not very reliable, took time to assemble, was undisciplined and ill-armed and, being composed of husbandmen, could not be kept under arms for any long period. Polhané saw the inconvenience of this state of affairs, and after the civil war he began organizing and training a small but efficient professional army of 10,000 horse and 15,000 foot, on which he bestowed much care. Well officered by the most trusted comrades of Polhané, men who had proved their mettle in the battles of the civil war, this army soon became a quite respectable force. No part of it seems to have been quartered in or near Lhasa, a town which had already the Chinese garrison to lodge. It was distributed in various provincial garrisons and in great detachments in the northern districts, on the watch against the Zunghars. Its absence from the capital prevented it from taking part in the upheaval of 1750 and saved it from disbandment. But of course the new ecclesiastic government did not bestow on the army the same fostering care as the regent had done, and its efficiency declined; this was sadly experienced during the Gurkha war of 1791/2. At the side of the standing army, the militia organization was of course still maintained.

H. POSTAL SERVICE AND ULAK

For the conveyance of traveling officials and of government dispatches, the system prevailing in Tibet from olden times was that of the *ulak*, a word of Turkish origin denoting socage, or compulsory labor due by the population to the government. In this case it meant (and still means today) the supplying of porters, drivers and horses or yaks, sometimes for quite long periods. As the traveling season coincides with the agricultural season, it meant a heavy burden on the shoulders of the people, who had to give away men and beasts sometimes even for three or four months, just when they were most needed in the fields. Besides being oppressive and irritating, the system was not made for efficiency or speed. In 1729 Polhané reformed this service too, on the model of the Chinese mail stages system, which he had seen at work after 1721. The service was entrusted to officers sent from Lhasa and was carried out by means of good horses belonging to the central government. It stretched from Lhasa to Ngari on the one hand and to Dokham on the other.[34] This system was expensive, but so efficient that the Chinese entrusted to it the carriage of their own mail. We have seen how this gave origin to a grave inconvenience, viz. that the Tibetan government could stop at will communications between Lhasa and Peking. The Chinese therefore after 1751 resumed their own postal service; Polhané's mail disappeared and the Tibetan government again employed the *ulak*, or else used the Chinese mail, when the ambans chose to authorize it.

   Ulak was also due for public works and for several other purposes. It should have been a service due to the Dalai Lama alone, but Polhané appropriated it more and more for his private use, making money out of it. When Fr. Cassiano journeyed to Lhasa in winter 1740/41, he found that *ulak* service was granted by Polhané to traveling merchants, evidently against payment.[35] Of course it was of common occurrence that Polhané allowed his favorites to enjoy the same privilege. One of the first things the Chinese did in 1751 was therefore to remove these abuses. Henceforward and down to the end *ulak* was only due to officials or other men holding a document to this effect issued case for case by the Dalai Lama's government, the use of which was strictly controlled.[36]

I. PROVINCIAL GOVERNMENT

The government of the districts had been traditionally the task and privilege of the local aristocracy. Even when the political power of the nobles declined, the Lhasa government continued to appoint the local aristocrats to these posts; basing themselves on their private estates, they could be trusted to administer a district more easily and with less expense than a governor sent out from Lhasa. The title of these district governors was *depa*, and the office not seldom passed from father to son.[37] Of course when the central government grew weak, these governors became half independent and acted quite at their own will. Of greater units, in this period there were only three, the governments of Ü (always under direct control of the central government), Tsang and Ngari. There were apparently no single officials appointed to control the district governors of the east and north of the country. The district governor was thus the basis of the government machinery outside Lhasa. The Chinese recognized their importance and tried to bring them together to rule the whole country. But this attempt to entrust the biggest provincial rulers with the central government failed lamentably. In the civil war we see Tsang, Ngari and the districts of the other regions acting as independent units, forming alliances and raising armies on their own account. This sliding back of Tibet towards the century-old anarchy, which had been ended in 1642, was energetically halted by Polhané. Tsang he maintained under his personal rule (except for the new temporal rights of the Panchen), and Ü was governed as before directly from Lhasa. As to the southeastern, eastern and northern districts, the details of his action against the local governors escape us. The process was very gradual and moderate, and provoked no concerted resistance. Step by step he placed his own men in charge of the districts. As these favorites often preferred to remain in Lhasa, actual government of the districts was carried out by their protégées or even slaves; this made provincial government still more strictly dependent from Lhasa. At the end of his twenty years' rule, the great provincial lords had disappeared from the scene. Tibet was divided in fifty-three districts; of these, fifty-two were governed by officials appointed by and dependent from the government of Lhasa. The fifty-third district was represented by the autonomous principality of Sakya.[38]

The modern organization of the districts in its broad outlines goes back to the reforming work of Polhané, of which the main characteristics were the following. At the head of a district, of which there were thirty in Ü alone, there was a civil governor (*dzongpön* or *dzongdö*) and a military commander with equal status. The former was exclusively charged with the administrative affairs and with the maintenance of law and order. This system then underwent a slow evolution, and before 1950 the two governors (both called *dzongpön*), appointed usually for a period of three years, were on a foot of complete equality and the distinction between civil and military had become obsolete. In some outlying districts (e.g., Naktsang, Saga), where the population consisted chiefly of nomads, the local governor had the title of *gopa*, which probably indicated a more rough-and-ready and flexible administration.

Of the great historical provinces of Ü, Tsang, Kham and Ngari, the two first were not administrative units, but merely geographic and ethnic expressions; the district governors were directly subordinate to the central government. Kham was largely independent under its numerous local chiefs; there was, however, in the northern part of that region a representative of the central government, styled the Do *garpön*.[39] His functions were indefinite, but possibly more on the lines of a resident in vassal states. Ngari occupied a particular position. This great province was a late addition to Tibet (1684) and was still considered as a territory enjoying a special status. Since the times of Lajang Khan, it had been the fief of Khangchenné and of his brother. About 1730 Polhané took it away from the Gazhi family, entrusting it to his elder son Yeshé Tseten. After the death of Polhané, the murder of Yeshé Tseten and the end of Gyurmé Namgyel, the Chinese did away with this last remnant of feudal independence, and refused to recognize more than the bare title of duke of Ngari for the son of Yeshé Tseten, without political rights. Still, the administration of Ngari continued to present deep differences from that of the rest of Tibet. In the four districts which compose the province, there was no dual government; there was only one *dzongpön*, in charge of both civil and military affairs. Over the four *dzongpön*, there were at the head of the province two governors called *garpön*.[40] Ngari was thus the only greater province which preserved its individuality.

As we have seen, the militia was under the control of the district governors. The standing army was instead under the central government. There was a moment in which its commanders seemed to be about to become a political power; that was in 1751, when the five *dapön* in Ü and Tsang received a greater sphere of influence and seem to have exercised a sort of supervision over the local government. But these political powers did not last for long, as it was but natural in a country governed by an ecclesiastic government.

Provincial finance was in the hands of the district governors, who remitted the surplus to Lhasa. The regular control and audit by government accountants appears to be a later institution.

Summing up the changes of the Tibetan government from 1642 to 1751, we may conclude that the *desi* can be counted as the actual head of the state from 1642 to 1705, except in the years from 1655 to 1679, when he sank to a mere puppet whose strings were pulled by the Dalai Lama. From 1706 to 1717 Lajang Khan was the absolute ruler of Tibet. Then for three years Central Tibet was under military occupation by the Zunghars. From 1721 to 1727 the supreme power was wielded by the council of ministers under the chairmanship of Khangchenné.

From 1728 to 1750 we have the hereditary monarchy of Polhané and Gyurmé Namgyel. It is only from 1751 that we may date the actual sovereignty of the Dalai Lama. This statement may appear to contradict some of the accepted opinions. But I think that in replying in this manner to the question put at the beginning of this chapter, I am expounding the only conclusion we can reach after a careful perusal of contemporary sources.

II. CHINESE SUPERVISION

A. THE AMBAN

With the solitary exception of Heshou, sent out by Kangxi in 1709, there was no permanent representative of the emperor residing in Lhasa till after the conquest of that city by the Chinese in 1720. Even afterwards, the representative was withdrawn in 1723, and during the following four years we find only officials sent to Lhasa on a special mission, but none in permanent residence. The office of the two *ambans*,[41] as it existed till 1912, was established only in 1728. There was a senior and a junior *amban*, but the distinction has been always a purely formal one, both enjoying in point of fact the same authority. After the death of A'erxun in 1734, one post remained vacant during the following years, and there was only one *amban* in Lhasa. It was only in 1748 that the emperor reinforced the old rule, which was then scrupulously observed as long as the office lasted. The first *ambans* (Senggé and Mala) held office for five years, but after them it became the practice, and soon the rule, that an *amban* should remain in Tibet for a maximum of three years; and sometimes he was recalled home even before the end of his term.

During the rule of Polhané and his son, the duties of the *ambans* consisted mainly in holding the command of the small Chinese garrison, ensuring communications with Peking and reporting to the emperor on the doings of the "King." We hear sometimes of their intervention in matters of external relations; but otherwise they never interfered with the Tibetan government.[42] In 1751 the powers of the *ambans* were greatly increased. Besides commanding the garrison and having exclusive charge of the postal service, their advice had to be taken by the council of *kalön* on every important affair; this gave them a broad right of supervision on the actions of the government. Still, direct intervention of the *ambans* in administrative work was at first of rare occurrence.[43] As a regular practice, it came later, as the result of the reforms carried out in 1792 after the Gurkha war.[44]

The staff of the *ambans* in the period under consideration was not large. It comprised one or two military officers of rank not above lieutenant-colonel, and several *ǰarghuchi* and *bichēchi*. The latter were the writers of the *ambans*, and it was to them that the clerical work of the residence was entrusted;[45] they also formed the personal suite of all officials sent to Trashilhünpo to pay homage to the Panchen. As to the *jarghuchi*, the meaning of this name as given by the dictionaries is "judge." But they hardly can have functioned as such in Lhasa, because there was no independent Chinese judiciary in Tibet during this period. From the Tibetan sources we gather firstly that they were superior in rank to the *bichēchi* and secondly that they were quite often sent out on mission to Trashilhünpo and elsewhere, when the *amban* himself preferred to remain in Lhasa. Sagaster[46] has shown that the Chinese equivalent is *yuanwailang*, second-class secretary of the *Lifanyuan*.[47] Their functions were probably those of a secretary to the residence. It was only in 1751 that the offices of the ambans were organized in a proper manner, with the employ of a sufficient number of Manchu banner officers.

B. THE GARRISON OF LHASA

A Chinese garrison in Lhasa was first established in 1721, and its commander then carried out the same functions as the ambans after 1728. It was withdrawn in 1723, and permanently reestablished in 1728 after the civil war. In 1748 or 1749 its strength was reduced to a mere skeleton of a few officers and men, but after 1751 it remained till the twentieth century a considerable body, numbering (at least on paper) 1,500 men. It was composed of Manchu banner men and Chinese soldiers from the western provinces in varying proportions. At first it was quartered in Lhasa itself, but it was shifted in 1733 to the Drazhi barracks north of the town, which remained henceforward their permanent quarters. The garrison was under the direct orders of the *amban*s, but we may suppose that the actual command of the force was held by the senior military aide-de-camp to the *amban*s. The troops were paid by the Chinese exchequer, and the money arrived regularly from China in heavily escorted convoys.[48] The supplies were partly purchased on the spot (with funds contributed by the Tibetan government) and partly imported from China.[49]

In the period under consideration the garrison was always concentrated in Lhasa. The only exception was the field force of 1,500 drawn from the garrison and stationed every summer from 1730 to 1733 in the fortified military zone of the Tengri nor. It was commanded by officers appointed directly by the emperor, but a right of inspection was reserved to the *amban*s. Apart from this, there were no other detachments. It was only after 1792 that a small force was permanently stationed at Zhigatsé, to guard the Panchen.

C. THE CHINESE MAIL SERVICE

Immediately after their expedition of 1720 the Chinese organized a postal relay system on their usual model[50] on the Dajianlu—Litang—Batang—Lhari—Lhasa route. It was based on a series of relay stations, providing food, lodging and fresh mounts for the official couriers. The stages were guarded by Chinese soldiers distributed along the route and based on the two garrisons of Chamdo and Lhari. The system ceased to function at the time of the civil war, and in 1728 the Chinese preferred to entrust their communications to Polhané's newly established mail service; hence the breakdown of 1750. The postal service was reestablished on the old lines in 1751, and functioned remarkably well for a century and a half, even after the old stage system had fallen into decay in China proper with the advent of Western systems of communication.

D. TIBETAN AFFAIRS AT PEKING

In Peking Tibetan affairs were at first managed through the Grand Secretariat (*neige*). When the Grand Council (*junjichu*) was established in 1729–1732, at first with the character of a Bureau of Military Affairs, it took over also the responsibility for Tibetan affairs. The *ambans* in Lhasa normally corresponded directly with the Grand Council. But in times of crisis they were directed to forward their dispatches through the provincial governor of Sichuan. The reason for this seemingly peculiar arrangement was that any military action in Tibet, if such became necessary, would have to be organized by the Sichuan authorities. It was better therefore that they should possess a direct knowledge of the relevant documents and memorials (of which a copy always remained with them), than if they had to be informed of Tibetan events by dispatches sent out from Peking.

Questions concerning Tibetan tribute missions and the trade relations between Tibet and Kokonor-Gansu-Mongolia were treated by the Mongolian Superintendency (*Lifanyuan*), which seems at times to have had some say also in the appointment of lower officials to Lhasa.

NOTES

1. See Giuseppe Tucci, *Tibetan Painted Scrolls*, 2 vols. (Rome: Libreria dello Stato, 1949), 1:57–66.

2. This dislike was still felt even in the present century; Charles Alfred Bell, *The Religion of Tibet* (Oxford: Clarendon Press, 1931), 191.

3. *Rappresentanza dei Padri Cappuccini*, etc., in Luciano Petech, *I Missionari Italiani nel Tibet e nel Nepal* [*Italian Missionaries in Tibet and Nepal*], 7 vols. (Rome, 1952–1956), 3:144.

4. On this fact both the Chinese and the Italian missionaries agree. A Chinese document of *yichou*/XII = January 14th, 1748, states clearly that "the Dalai Lama presides over Buddhism in the western countries, while Pho lha nas governs the Tibetan people"; *Gaozong shilu* [*Veritable History of the Gaozong (Reign) of the Qing*] in

Manzhou diguo guowu yuan, ed., *Da Qing lichao shilu* (vols. 58–67). Taipei reprint: Huawen shuju, 4664 *juan* (Tokyo: Okura Shuppan Kabushiki Kaisha, 1937–1938), 280:4a–5a. Father Costantino da Loro, in a letter dated Lhasa, September 22th, 1741, writes: "The Grand Lama at present has not the slightest power; he must only attend to the welfare of the living, transferring on them his merits"; in Petech, *Italian Missionaries in Tibet and Nepal*, 2:35.

5. This development and changing conditions of the powers in Tibet did not pass unperceived by the keen intelligence and great experience of the members of the Congregation of Propaganda Fide in Rome, who from the letters dispatched by the Lhasa missionaries drew nearly the same conclusions as I have. In the minute (in Italian) of a memorial sent by Cardinal Belluga to the king of Spain in order to obtain from him funds for the Tibetan mission, the situation in Tibet is summarized as follows: "Before 1720 Tibet belonged to the Grand Lama, both in the spiritual and in the temporal. He appointed a man with the title of king (the Khoshud Khan) to defend the realm, giving him powers over everything connected with military affairs, with the faculty of appointing the officers of the army. He appointed also another man to act as his vice-regent (the *sde srid*) to govern the whole kingdom in his name, in respect of both civil and political affairs, with his council of state composed of four persons. . . . In 1721 the emperor placed on the throne a Tibetan, giving him complete powers in things temporal, which earlier belonged to the Grand Lama, and left to the latter the spiritual only, with the revenues sufficient for his support." Petech, *Italian Missionaries in Tibet and Nepal*, 3:176.

6. Editors' note: A translation of the relevant passage from *The Veritable Records of the Shizong [Yongzheng] Emperor [Shizong shilu]* in Manzhou diguo guowu yuan, ed., *Da Qing lichao shilu*, Taipei reprint: Huawen shuju, 4664 *juan* (Tokyo: Okura Shuppan Kabushiki Kaisha, 1937–1938) is given in the appendix of Luciano Petech, *China and Tibet in the Early Eighteenth Century* (Leiden: Brill, 1972), 256–261, under the heading: Doc. XI. Ma Jie and Sheng Shengzu, *Weizang tuzhi* (1792) = *Topographical Description of Central Tibet*, translated by W. W. Rockhill in his "Tibet: A Geographical, Ethnographical and Historical Sketch, Derived from Chinese Sources," *Journal of the Royal Asiatic Society* (1891):1–133, 188–291.

7. Luciano Petech, "Notes on Tibetan History of the Eighteenth Century," *T'oung Pao* 52, no. 4–5 (1966): 266–267.

8. Cfr. his intervention in the struggle between Galdan and Kangxi; Zahiruddin Ahmad, *Sino-Tibetan Relations in the Seventeenth Century* (Roma: Instituto italiano per il Medio ed Estremo Oriente, 1970), 286–323.

9. On the series of the Tibetan regents see Luciano Petech, "The Dalai Lamas and Regents of Tibet," in *Selected Papers on Asian History* (Roma: Instituto italiano per il Medio ed Estremo Oriente, 1988), 236–257.

10. "When the king is absent, there are four princes with the title of Ciesani, who govern the country; they are at present Tartars"; Petech, *Italian Missionaries in Tibet and Nepal*, 3:16.

11. We know from Fr. Cassiano that there were also some *mgron gnyer* at the court of the ruler, with the functions of comptrollers of the household (*maestri di casa*); Petech, *Italian Missionaries in Tibet and Nepal*, 4:113. Fr. Gioacchino da S. Anatolia describes these court *mgron gnyer* as chamberlains (*camerieri*); Petech, *Italian Missionaries in Tibet and Nepal*, 3:239. In these functions they were attached also to great personages other than the Dalai Lama. Fr. Gioacchino da S. Anatolia (letter of November 20th, 1724) mentions a *mgron gnyer* of the father of the Dalai Lama; Petech, *Italian Missionaries in Tibet and Nepal*, 1:126.

12. E.g. Rol pa'i rdo rje, Lcang skya II, *Rgyal ba'i dbang po thams cad mkhyen gzigs rdo rje 'chang blo bzang bskal bzang rgya mtsho'i zhal nas kyi rnam par thar pa mdo tsam brjod pa dpag bsam rin po che'i snye ma* [*Life of the Seventh Dalai Lama*] (Unpublished block print), 384b.

13. William Woodville Rockhill, "Tibet: A Geographical, Ethnographical and Historical Sketch, Derived from Chinese Sources," *Journal of the Royal Asiatic Society* 23 (1891): 200. Rockhill wrongly reconstructed the title as *nang mdzod phyag*. We may recall that at the court of the princes of Gtsang in the fifteenth century there was a *nang so chen mo*, with the functions of a chief justice; Giuseppe Tucci, *Indo-Tibetica* 4,1 *Gyantse ed i suoi monasteri* [*Gyantsé and Its Monasteries*] (Rome: Reale Accademia d'Italia, 1941), IV/II:276; and Tucci, *Tibetan Painted Scrolls*, 1:35.

14. Petech, *Italian Missionaries in Tibet and Nepal*, 3:16–17.

15. In Petech, *Italian Missionaries in Tibet and Nepal*, 3:65–66.

16. This title means "chief of men." The Lhasa *mi dpon* are well attested in Rol pa'i rdo rje, *Life of the Seventh Dalai Lama*, 498a etc. In the nineteenth and twentieth century there were only two *mi dpon*, both lay officials; Ram Rahul, *The Government and Politics of Tibet* (Delhi: Vikas Publications, 1969), 35.

17. Tshe ring dbang rgyal, Mdo mkhar zhabs drung, *Dpal mi'i dbang po'i rtogs brjod pa 'jig rten kun tu dga' ba'i gtam* [*A Biography of the Lord of Men*] (unpublished block print).

18. Rahul, *The Government and Politics of Tibet*, 37. The Chinese texts know them by the imperfect transcription *xie er bo mu*.

19. Petech, *Italian Missionaries in Tibet and Nepal*, 4:135.

20. Tucci, *Tibetan Painted Scrolls*, 37.

21. *Weizang tuzhi*, in Rockhill, "Tibet: A Geographical, Ethnographical and Historical Sketch," 216.

22. Della Penna, in Petech, *Italian Missionaries in Tibet and Nepal*, 3:65–70. Fr. Domenico da Fano, in Petech, *Italian Missionaries in Tibet and Nepal*, 3:15–17. Desideri, in Petech, *Italian Missionaries in Tibet and Nepal*, 6:26, 76–78; Clements R. Markham, George Bogle, and Thomas Manning, *Narratives of the Mission of George Bogle to Tibet and of the Journey of Thomas Manning to Lhasa* (London: Trübner and Co., 1876), 101–102; *Weizang tuzhi* in Rockhill, "Tibet: A Geographical, Ethnographical and Historical Sketch," 129, 216–218; Sarat Chandra Das, "Tibetan Jails and Criminal Punishments," *Journal of the Asiatic Society of Bengal* (1894):5–8.

23. The Chinese manual of administration *Lifanyuan zeli* (edition of 1816) partly translated by Rockhill in "Tibet: A Geographical, Ethnographical and Historical Sketch," refers to a later period, after the reforms of 1792. So does ch. 9 of the *Weizang tuzhi* (on administration), in Rockhill, "Tibet: A Geographical, Ethnographical and Historical Sketch."

24. The Bla brang *phyag mdzod* is mentioned also in Rol pa'i rdo rje, *Life of the Seventh Dalai Lama*, 538b. Later the treasurer was popularly known by the abbreviation *bla phyag*.

25. The treasury and finance offices in the Bla brang are described by Desideri, in Petech, *Italian Missionaries in Tibet and Nepal*, 6:26. This description holds also good for modern conditions; Bell, *The Religion of Tibet*, 196.

26. E.g., Rol pa'i rdo rje, *Life of the Seventh Dalai Lama*, 385a.

27. Desideri, in Petech, *Italian Missionaries in Tibet and Nepal*, 6:69. Bogle's Memorandum on the trade of Tibet (of December 12th, 1774), in Markham, "Narratives of the Mission of George Bogle to Tibet," 128–129; better and more detailed is Bogle's Memorandum on the money and merchandise of Tibet (of April 19th, 1779), in D. B. Diskalkar, "Bogle's Embassy to Tibet," *The Indian Historical Quarterly* 9 (1933): 431–432.

28. In 1724 the purchase by the Capuchins of a piece of land in Lhasa, for the purpose of building a small convent and a church, was registered in the books (*libri camerali*) of *la varanga* (sic., for *lavaranga, bla brang*). Fr. Gioacchino da S. Anatolia's Ragguaglio, in Petech, *Italian Missionaries in Tibet and Nepal*, 3:215.

29. In a report of the Procurator General of the Capuchins to the Congregation of Propaganda Fide about the financial situation of the mission, dated November 9th, 1730, it is stated that "in Lhasa it is not permissible to sell immovable property, which according to the law of the realm remains as property of the *varanga* (*bla brang*), which is like the Reverend Apostolic Chamber in the Church State." Archives of Propaganda Fide, Rome, *Scr. Congressi*, vol. 20, f. 286b.

30. Tucci, *Tibetan Painted Scrolls*, 69–70.

31. Joseph Marie Amiot et al., *Mémoires concernant l'histoire, les sciences, les arts, les mœurs, les usages, &c. des Chinois* [*Memoirs on the History, Sciences, Arts, Customs, Habits and So Forth of the Chinese*] (Paris: Nyon, 1776), 150.

32. Fr. Cassiano da Macerata gives a detailed account of the enormous expenses of the *Smon lam* ceremonies; Petech, *Italian Missionaries in Tibet and Nepal*, 4:123–127.

33. There is no special account of the Tibetan army, and the above sketch is based mainly on the scattered evidence found in various texts. Some incomplete accounts, extracted from the *Da Qing yitong zhi*, depicting conditions about 1740, are found in Amiot, *Mémoires . . . des Chinois*, 142–143, 147, and in Andrea Becker, *Eine chinesische Beschreibung von Tibet aus dem 18. Jahrhundert* [*A Chinese Description of Tibet from the Eighteenth Century*] (Ph.D. diss., Ludwig-Maximilians-Universität [München], 1976), 22, 24. Cf. also the short account of the Tibetan militia in the time of Lajang Khan given by Desideri, in Petech, *Italian Missionaries in Tibet and Nepal*, 6:79–80.

34. Tshe ring dbang rgyal, *A Biography of the Lord of Men*, 326a.

35. Petech, *Italian Missionaries in Tibet and Nepal*, 4:72.

36. Several European travelers have given accounts of *ulak* traveling arrangements. A graphic description can be read, e.g., in chapters 23–25 of Wilhelm Filchner, *Om mani padme hum: meine China- und Tibet expedition, 1925/28 [Om mani padme hum: My China and Tibet Expedition, 1925/28]* (Leipzig: F. A. Brockhaus, 1929).

37. On the provincial *sde pa* see Desideri in Petech, *Italian Missionaries in Tibet and Nepal*, 6:76.

38. Letter of Fr. Costantino da Loro, dated Lhasa, October 11th, 1741, in Petech, *Italian Missionaries in Tibet and Nepal*, 2:41, where the number actually given is twenty-three; this must be, however, a mistake. On the administration of Sa skya see Charles William Cassinelli and Robert Brainerd Ekvall, *A Tibetan Principality* (Ithaca: Cornell University Press, 1969).

39. E.g., Rol pa'i rdo rje, *Life of the Seventh Dalai Lama*, 306a.

40. For conditions in Mnga' ris in the thirties of the present century see Giuseppe Tucci and E. Ghersi, *Cronaca della Missione scientifica Tucci nel Tibet Occidentale (1933) [Chronicle of the Tucci Scientific Mission in Western Tibet (1933)]* (Roma: Reale Accademia d'Italia, 1934), 251; Giuseppe Tucci, *Santi e briganti nel Tibet ignoto (Diario della spedizione nel Tibet occidentale 1935) [Sadhus and Brigands of Unknown Tibet (Diary of the Expedition to Western Tibet 1935)]* (Milano: Ulrico Hoepli, 1937), 177–178.

41. For the meaning and origin of the name, see Luciano Petech, *China and Tibet in the Early XVIIIth Century: History of the Establishment of Chinese Protectorate in Tibet* (Leiden: Brill, 1972), 87. The Chinese official title was *zhu Zang da chen*.

42. Fr. Costantino da Loro, in his already quoted letter of October 15th, 1741 writes that the *amban* "does not interfere on any account with the government of Tibet, but attends only to the command of the Chinese soldiers"; Petech, *Italian Missionaries in Tibet and Nepal*, 2:74. The above quoted letter of Fr. Costantino da Loro, dated Lhasa, September 22nd, 1741, says that the whole kingdom "is subject to the great emperor of China; but he does not interfere on any account with its government, as he has granted its despotic rule to the present king Mivang Cugiab (Mi dbang sku zhabs)," Petech, *Italian Missionaries in Tibet and Nepal*, 2:35.

43. George Bogle writes that the *ambans* "seldom interfere in the management of the country"; Letter of December 5th, 1774, published by Diskalkar, "Bogle's Embassy to Tibet," 424.

44. On the reforms of 1792 see William Woodville Rockhill, *The Dalai Lamas of Lhasa and Their Relations with the Manchu Emperors of China, 1644–1908* (Leiden: Oriental Printing-Office, E. J. Brill, 1910), 53.

45. William Frederick Mayers and G. M. H. Playfair, *The Chinese Government: A Manual of Chinese Titles, Categorically Arranged and Explained, with an Appendix* (Shanghai: Kelly and Walsh, 1897), n. 181.

46. Shes rab dar rgyas and Klaus Sagaster, *Subud erike: "Ein Rosenkranz aus Perlen": die Biographie des 1. Pekinger Lcang skya Khutukhtu Ngag dbang blo bzang chos ldan, verfasst von Ngag dbang chos ldan alias Shes rab dar rgyas [Subud Erike: "A Pearl Rosary": The Biography of the 1st Peking Lcang skya Khutukhtu Ngag dbang blo bzang*

chos ldan, written by Ngag dbang chos ldan alias Shes rab dar rgyas], Asiatische Forschungen, 20 (Wiesbaden: Harrassowitz, 1967), 106 n.

47. Mayers and Playfair, *The Chinese Government: A Manual of Chinese Titles*, n.
164.

48. In 1744 two Chinese Christian officers arrived at Lhasa with one of these convoys. Letter of Fr. Orazio della Penna dated Lhasa, September 1st, 1744; in Petech,
Italian Missionaries in Tibet and Nepal, 158–159.

49. *Shengzu shilu* [*Veritable Records of Shengzu*], in *Manzhou diguo guowu yuan*,
ed. *Da Qing lichao shilu*, Taipei reprint: Huawen shuju, 4664 *juan* (Tokyo: Okura
Shuppan Kabushiki Kaisha, 1937–1938), 299, 5b.

50. On the Chinese postal service under the Manchu dynasty see J. K. Fairbank
and S. Y. Têng, "On the Ch'ing Tributary System," *Harvard Journal of Asiatic Studies*
6 (1941): 135–246. On the transmission of Qing documents, see J. K. Fairbank and S. Y.
Têng, "On the Transmission of the Ch'ing Documents," *Harvard Journal of Asiatic
Studies* 4 (1939): 12–46.

Chapter 24

LOBJANG DANJIN'S REBELLION OF 1723

Katō Naoto

Katō Naoto treats an event of high drama: the betrayal of the Khoshud Mongols of Kokonor, to whom the Qing emperor had promised the restoration of their former dominion over Central Tibet, first held, however lightly, by Gushri Khan and then later by Lajang Khan. The emperor offered this in return for the Khoshuds' vital assistance in driving out the Zunghar Mongols from Lhasa. When the Qing empire withdrew its troops and left Tibet in the hands of Tibetans instead, the leader of the Qinghai Khoshud Mongols, Lobjang Danjin, challenged the Qing empire in Qinghai. Naoto makes use of contemporary Manchu sources, a special strength of Japanese scholarship on Tibetan history. One of the more revealing elements of these documents is that they make clear that Tibet was considered a separate country outside the borders of the Qing empire, even according to a 1722 high-level Qing secret memorial. Moreover, the Qing were quite eager for the Seventh Dalai Lama to take control of Tibet, which would have restored the tradition of religious rule the Fifth Dalai Lama had established earlier. The Tanguts referred to in these documents are the Amdo Tibetans, who were thought of as a distinct people from the Central Tibetans. The Khoshud and Tangut uprising against the Qing was to have epoch-changing consequences for Amdo; most of its territory, and large portions of Kham as well, that had been under the sway of the Khoshud Mongols came under the influence of the Qing court by 1724.

INTRODUCTION

The rebellion instigated by Lobjang Danjin in 1723 (Yongzheng 1) in Qinghai (Köke naghur/Kokonor) was, as already noted by Luciano Petech who described it as "the most important turning point in the history of Qinghai,"[1] an event that exerted no small influence on the history of Mongolia and Tibet and even on the Qing dynasty's rule of foreign peoples. On the basis of Qing historical sources such as the first part of the *Qinding pingding zhunge'er fanglüe* (*Authorized Military Record of the Subjugation of the Zunghar*; abbreviated below: *Subjugation of the Zunghar*) and the *Huangchao fanbu yaolüe* (*Summary Exposition of Frontier Parts of the Present Dynasty*), Tibetan historical sources and missionary records, Petech published a study of Tibet's relations with China and Mongolia[2] in which he touched on this rebellion.[3] Then, availing himself of the *Da Qing Shizong jingtian changyun jianzhong biaozheng wenwu yingming kuanren xinyi daxiao zhicheng Xian huangdi shilu* (abbreviated below: *Shizong shilu* [*Veritable Records of Shizong*]; records of other reigns follow this example) and other Chinese historical materials, Satō Hisashi clarified many points that had remained unclear in Petech's study and, carefully comparing the place names and so forth appearing in the *Neifuyutu* (Palace Treasury Map) of the Gengwulong era with other accounts, made a comprehensive study of this rebellion.[4]

The results of the above two detailed studies made a considerable contribution towards elucidating the relations obtaining between the Qing on the one hand and Qinghai and Tibet on the other during the first half of the eighteenth century, a subject that had hitherto constituted a blank in the study of this period. The reason that we have nevertheless undertaken to write the present paper is that there has since appeared some new historical material.

In 1971 a collection of material entitled *Nian Gengyao zouzhe* (*Confidential Memorials of Nian Gengyao*) was published by the National Palace Museum (Guoli Gugong Bowuyuan) in Taipei. It contains the confidential memorials presented to the throne by Nian Gengyao, who in his capacity as governorgeneral (*zongdu*) of Sichuan and Shaanxi and general-in-chief for the pacification of distant lands (*fuyuan dajiangzhun*) was the supreme commander on the Chinese side responsible for the suppression of Lobjang Danjin's rebellion and subsequent countermeasures, as well as Yongzheng's instructions in reply to these memorials, correspondence between Nian Gengyao and his subordinates, and other documents. In particular, the 333 documents that have been photographically reproduced in their original form in volumes 1 and 2 date from the period between the first month of Yongzheng 1 and fourth month of Yongzheng 3, which corresponds to the time when Nian Gengyao was dealing with matters relating to Qinghai and Tibet, culminating in Lobjang Danjin's rebellion, and they may be described as historical sources of the first order for acquainting oneself with details of this rebellion. Since we have elsewhere already given a review of the content of this collection of material,[5] we do not wish to repeat ourselves here. It may, however, be noted that although Satō utilized the Chinese-language documents contained in this collection,[6] to date use has not yet been made of the Manchu documents, which account for the greater part of the collection.

In addition to the above material, the confidential memorials of Chinese government officials other than Nian Gengyao who were involved with Qinghai at the time are also preserved at the Palace Museum in Taipei and are to be found, together with those of Nian Gengyao, in a photographically reproduced collection of material published by the Palace Museum under the title of *Gongzhong dang Yongzheng chao zouzhe* (*Confidential Memorials of Yongzheng's Reign Among the Documents of the Palace Museum*).[7]

Our aim in the present paper is to reexamine Lobjang Danjin's rebellion on the basis of the many new facts that have come to light in these sources which have now become available. (The spelling of Mongolian and Tibetan names generally follows that given in Fuheng's 1750 *Qinding Xiyu tongwen zhi* [*Authorized Polyglot Dictionary of the Western Regions*].)

I

With the accession to the throne of Yongzheng following the death of Kangxi there arose the question of whether to withdraw the Chinese troops stationed in Tibet. In 1717 (Kangxi 57) Cewang Arabtan (Tsewang Rapten), the leader of the Zunghars (Jünghar), had sent his elder cousin Cering Dondub (Tsering Döndrup) to kill Lajang Qaghan of the Khoshuds (Qoshuud), who was the *de facto* "king" of Tibet.[8] At the request of Khoshuds residing in Qinghai, the Chinese had dispatched troops[9] and, after having routed Cering Dondub's forces,[10] they had kept stationed in Lhasa for more than two years as many as 3,000 troops, including 500 Chahar troops and 1,200 Green Bannermen from Sichuan, on the grounds that "although Tibet has already been subjugated, it is of great urgency and importance to keep troops stationed there."[11] On the second of the first month, Yongzheng 1, Yansin (Yanxin), acting general-in-chief for the pacification of distant lands, and Nian Gengyao, governor-general of Sichuan and Shaanxi, submitted the following memorial to the emperor:

> As a result of our investigations, we have found that in the past [Chinese] soldiers have never set foot in Tibet. Some years ago, on account of Cewang Arabtan's having sent troops and raised a disturbance [there], the previous Emperor (Kangxi) dispatched officers and men for the enhancement of Imperial authority, and they entered [Tibet] from two routes for the purpose of subduing the rebels, whereupon the latter met with a crushing defeat and fled to far distant regions. When I, Yansin, led my troops into Tibet some years ago, the previous Emperor gave me instructions to the

effect that "when you have advanced with your forces into Tibet and pacified it, in the event that the Dalai Lama and the people of Qinghai do not
ask your forces to remain, it would be splendid if you could withdraw all
your forces." Later, after we had pacified the land of Tibet, the living Buddhas (*qubilghan*) and Tanguts all requested that the forces remain for a
short time to watch over them, and so we kept our troops stationed there.
Considering the matter now, it appears inconceivable that the rebels
will again enter Tibet. There have been difficulties involved in stationing
troops for more than two years in order to guard [Tibet] and in transporting rice to a locality situated several thousand *li* [from Inner China], and
it also requires considerable levies on grain crops. At present, even though
we do attempt to purchase [grain] here and distribute it among the troops,
the prices of grain and so forth are gradually rising because Tibet is a
small country. In addition, our troops are suffering from having been
outside the borders [of China] for a long period of time, and the Tangut
soldiers and people also desire the affair to be brought to a conclusion.
Not only that, but if we keep the troops in such a remote region for any
length of time, it is impossible to anticipate what they will end up doing.
However, the Dalai Lama is still young in years and has been instated
only recently, nor is there anyone in Tibet to administer all the affairs of
state. If [state affairs] are not dealt with in such a manner as to appease the
minds [of the Tanguts], this will run contrary to the previous emperor's
desire for "extreme benevolence in pacifying distant lands." In our humble opinion it would be advisable to have the Dalai Lama, numerous
local abbots (*qambu/ khenpo*) and the leaders of the Tibetan people elect
someone who is trusted and serious-minded and has the trust of the
Tanguts to attend to all the affairs of state in the capacity of majordomo
(*depa*) of Tibet. Since this majordomo will not be someone who has been
appointed [by the Chinese], if it should later turn out that he is incompetent, it will not prove difficult to immediately replace him. In the fourth
to fifth months of the first year of the Yongzheng era and by the time the
new grass has sprouted we intend withdrawing the troops at present stationed in Tibet, the Mongolian troops via the Murui-usu route and the
Manchu and Green Banner troops via the Barkham route. In addition, we
shall station one thousand Green Bannermen from Sichuan in Chamdo
for a short period, under the supervision of an able vice-commander
(*fujiang*) whom we shall choose, in order to protect the land of Tibet. We
shall also inform the Dalai Lama of Your Majesty's thoughts of compassion towards the Tanguts and have the Tanguts set up courier stations
along the route from Lhasa to Chamdo in preparation for sending reports
relating to military secrets. We shall have the Dalai Lama understand
that, in the event of the rebels reentering Tibet, they should promptly report the matter to Chamdo, whereupon we will be able to immediately

lead troops to their relief. In this manner we will be able to always keep
the Dalai Lama under our protection and also win the hearts of the Tanguts. It will also lead to a considerable saving in grain levies. Once Cewang
Arabtan has sent an envoy to receive punishment and has truly submitted
[to our country], then we shall withdraw all government forces stationed
in Chamdo. But [these matters] are military secrets, and it is extremely
important that they be interconnected. After we have received Your instructions as to whether or not they ought to be dealt with in this manner,
we intend writing another confidential memorial and reporting to Your
Majesty. It was for this reason that we have respectfully submitted this as
a secret memorial. We await Your Majesty's orders.[12]

The Dalai Lama in question, namely the seventh Dalai Lama Kelzang Gyatso,
had been installed following the Chinese subjugation of Cering Dondub. The
course of events leading to his instatement has been dealt with in detail by Petech,[13] and we rely heavily on his account. This Dalai Lama had the support
and assistance of Dashi Baghatur, the paramount chief of Qinghai (and tenth
and youngest son of Gushri Qaghan, progenitor of the Qinghai Khoshuds), his
son Lobjang Danjin, and *dayiching qoshuuchi* Chaghan Danjin, a man of considerable influence among the tribes.[14] After the defeat of Cering Dondub, the
Chinese saw no problems in installing this Kelzang Gyatso as Dalai Lama, but
they did have reservations about placing the control of Tibet in the hands of the
Khoshuds, and so they established an administrative body composed of six
members, two each from the Khalkhas, the Tibetans and the Khoshuds.[15] The
two members from the Khoshuds were Lobjang Danjin and Abuu (son of Qor-
oli, the eldest son of Bayan Abughai Ayushi, in turn the fourth son of Gushri
Qaghan),[16] the latter an imperial brother-in-law (*erfo*) and residing in Alashan.
But at the time in question, namely, Yongzheng 1, it was Abuu and the Khalkha
Cewang Norbu (Tsewang Norbu—adopted son of Todo Erdeni, who belonged
to the Khalkha left wing, Jodba)[17] who remained in Tibet and were in actual
control of military affairs there. Cewang Norbu, in particular, had been given
the post of acting general for the pacification of the west (*shulidingxi jiangzhun
yinwu*) by the Qing[18] and, according to Nian Gengyao, he was "a grand minister
in command of troops and stationed [in Tibet] in order to deal with all matters
concerning Tibet, and his function is to supervise the troops."[19]

As will be considered in greater detail below, it was a cause of considerable
malcontent to the Qinghai Khoshuds that the withdrawal of the Chinese forces
should be effected in such a manner that their control over Tibet be left unrecognized and instead control of Tibet be entrusted to the Tibetans themselves.
In reply to the memorial quoted above, Yongzheng made the comment that
"although your memorial is sound, I remain undecided,"[20] and he summoned
Nian Gengyao to Peking. As a result it was decided to withdraw the troops as
proposed in the memorial,[21] and the control of Tibet, including military affairs,

was placed almost completely in the hands of the Tibetans themselves.[22] The Mongolian troops among the Chinese forces stationed in Lhasa withdrew as planned via the Murui-usu route, namely, from the Murui-usu River through Tsaidam, and they passed through the border region between Tibet and Qing-hai in about the middle of the seventh month of that year.[23] According to the report submitted by commander-in-chief (*dutong*) Sirentu (Xiluntu), who was stationed at Chaghan Tologhai on the southeastern shores of Kokonor, the sol-diers were short of arrows, gun powder and bullets, many of their tents, pots and other daily necessities were beyond repair, and their horses and livestock were emaciated and of insufficient numbers,[24] and it is to be surmised that the troops were not in a very good condition after their sojourn of more than two years in Tibet. On the grounds that not only were Abuu's troops few in number and their weapons unserviceable but Abuu himself was a descendant of Gushri Qaghan and his troops could not be deployed in Qinghai, Nian Gengyao had him leave Xining on the ninth of the tenth month for his home in Alashan.[25] The Chahar troops that had been brought in by Cewang Norbu,[26] on the other hand, were in a better state than those of Abuu and numbered 400; to these were added their children and servants, making a total of about 500, and of these 400 were kept at Xining under the charge of commander-in-chief Uge (Wuge), while the remaining 73 soldiers were placed under the com-mand of Cewang Norbu and sent home via Hengcheng and Ordos on the 15th of the 10th month.[27]

Details of the conditions in Tibet following the withdrawal of the Chinese forces may be found in Petech's study.[28] According to a confidential memorial submitted by Nian Gengyao, a lama by the name of Tsültrim Zangpo Rap-jampa,[29] who arrived in Xi'an from Tibet on the ninth of the fifth month, Yong-zheng 1, brought the following information:

> At present there is no trouble whatsoever in Tibet. But the seal conferred [by the Qing dynasty] on the [present] Dalai Lama is smaller than that of the previous Dalai Lama. Because the Tanguts are all stupid and ig-norant, they give credence to the rumor that, because the seal is small, the present Dalai Lama may be smaller than the previous Dalai Lama, and they do not appear to act promptly if one sends documents stamped with that seal. They are now saying that they will be obliged to bring out the seal conferred on the Dalai Lama during the Yüan dynasty and use that.[30]

In response this report Nian Gengyao asked that a seal a little larger than that of the Northern Yüan be made. Tsültrim Zangpo further stated that

> the present Dalai Lama is a fine person with a lucid mind. The Tanguts all want the present Dalai Lama to administer the affairs of state. But the

Dalai Lama says that, because he has taken the tonsure, he can on no account attend to state affairs.[31]

Nian Gengyao also did not desire the advent of a majordomo, and he maintained that it would be best for Tibet if the seventh Dalai Lama himself assumed control of government:

> Rather than vice-minister (*shilang*) Orai (Olai) going [to Tibet] to nominate a majordomo, it would be far better if the Dalai Lama devoted himself to the affairs of state. If Your Majesty (Yongzheng) were to send the Dalai Lama a message persuading him of this matter and putting him in a mind to undertake the task, and if he were to administer the affairs of state in the manner of the fifth Dalai Lama, the Tanguts would obey him and it would greatly benefit political affairs. . . .[32]

It is thus evident that, following the withdrawal of the Chinese forces, there was clearly some bewilderment within Tibet, and the Chinese were at this point also undecided in regard to their future policy towards Tibet.

II

In the tenth month of Kangxi 61 (1722) the princes (*taiji*) of Qinghai held a conference at which they ostensibly pledged to halt brigandage, not to shelter fugitives, and to consolidate mutual relations.[33] But after the conference they secretly reached the following agreement:

> From the time of our grandfathers up until the present we have together acted in accordance with the orders of Amughulang Khaghan (Kangxi) of the Qing dynasty. But when we consider the matter in recent times, it has brought us no benefit whatsoever. Because Lajang Khaghan's own conduct was wrong, he was killed by Cewang Arabtan and Tibet was occupied. Our soldiers advanced together with the Chinese, routed Cering Dondub, and requested the instatement of the Dalai Lama. There was earlier an instruction from Amughulang Khaghan to the effect that "once you have taken Tibet, appoint a *khaghan* from amongst yourselves." But since then, despite our attempts to appoint a *khaghan* from amongst ourselves, we have had no communication on this matter even though three or four years have elapsed. There is probably no longer any hope of our being able to appoint a *khaghan*. From the time of our grandfathers up until the present we have been on friendly terms with the Zunghars. But because Lajang Khaghan acted wrongly, they became our enemies. But of what concern to us [is the Lajang Khaghan incident]? Now, during the

twelfth month, let each *taiji* promptly send someone to Cewang Arabtan and have him speak there as follows: "[The Zunghars and Khoshuds] have been friendly with one another since the time of their grandfathers, and this friendly relationship exists still today. Henceforth let us act of one heart and one mind. If we continue to follow Amughulang Khaghan, there will again be no advantage to us." Let us quickly send people to advise [Cewang Arabtan] of these matters. [The Khoshud *taiji*] deliberated and pledged themselves in this manner.[34]

This information had been obtained by Cewang Norbu while in Tibet from elder clan cousins living in Qinghai, and on the second of the fourth month, Yongzheng 1, it was passed on to Gao Qizhuo, governor-general of Yunnan and Guizhou, who then reported it to the emperor on the fifth day of the same month. This does not appear to have been the first such anti-Chinese assembly, for the same report went on to state:

> Noyan and others of Kokonor are now seeking to join forces with Cewang Arabtan, but it seems to us (Cewang Norbu's elder clan cousins) that Noyan and others of Kokonor have in the past held repeated meetings and made pledges, yet their words have still not been implemented and have all been suspended. Although repeated consultations have been held in the past, they have all been discontinued. . . .[35]

After obtaining this information, Gao Qizhuo strengthened the defenses along the principal roads leading into Tibet and contacted those concerned.

Lobjang Danjin sent a person by the name of Durai Jayisang to Cewang Arabtan,[36] and it was not only Lobjang Danjin who sent a messenger to Cewang Arabtan; Chaghan Danjin also dispatched a person by the name of Bayartu Qoshu-uchi to Zunghar on the tenth of the second month, Yongzheng 1,[37] and he reached Cewang Arabtan's place of residence on the twenty-sixth day of the fourth month.[38]

As was noted earlier, not only Nian Gengyao but also Yongzheng had no intentions whatsoever of placing the control of Tibet in the hands of the Qinghai Khoshuds. This was partly because of Tibetan opposition to any such measure,[39] but also because the Chinese feared any expansion of the Qinghai Khoshuds and the possibility of their uniting with the Zunghars. But the Qinghai side had faith in the promise (quoted above) made by Kangxi, namely, "Once you have taken Tibet, appoint a *khaghan* from amongst yourselves," and they expected it to be fulfilled. These expectations were only natural for the Khoshuds, who had ruled Tibet since the time of their progenitor, Gushri Khaghan, and it was the breach of this promise that was to become a major factor in Lobjang Danjin's subsequent anti-Chinese actions, a fact of which the Chinese were also fully aware.[40]

It was in such circumstances that on the 12th of the 1st month, Yongzheng 1, Yongzheng gave instructions that consultations be held concerning rewards for the Khoshud *taiji* of Qinghai who had participated in the subjugation of Cering Dondub in Tibet and that a report be submitted to the throne.[41] The results of the deliberations of the princes and grand ministers to whom this task was assigned are given below.[42] In the case of *beise* Danjung (Tensung), who had died prior to the bestowment of these rewards, he was posthumously conferred the title of commandery prince, with the emperor sending an envoy to perform a memorial service in his honor, and granted 200 taels of silver in recognition of his services[43] during the advance into Tibet.[44]

REWARDS GRANTED TO QINGHAI *TAIJI* IN YONGZHENG 1

Imperial Prince (*qinwang*) Lobjang Danjin
   → 200 taels of silver and 5 pieces of satin
Commandery Prince (*junwang*) *dayiching qoshuuchi* Chaghan Danjin
   → title of imperial prince
Beile (*beiluo*) Erdeni Erke Toghtonai
   → title of commandery prince
Beise (*beizi*) Baljur Arabtan
   → title of *beile*
Beise *mergen dayiching* Lachab
   → title of *beile*
Bulwark Duke (*fuguogong*) Galdan Dashi
   → title of defender duke (*zhenguo gong*)
Bulwark Duke Dondub Dashi
   → title of defender duke
Chuyiragh Nomchi
   → title of *beile*
Beile Arabtan Ombu
   → 100 taels of silver
Duke (*gong*) Norbu Püngchugh
   → 50 taels of silver
Beise Danjung
   → posthumous title of commandery prince and 200 taels of silver
   (*Veritable Records of Shizong*, fasc. 4, 32b–33b)

The two figures to wield influence at this time in Qinghai were Lobjang Danjin and Chaghan Danjin.[45] Following the death of his father Dashi Bātur,[46] Lobjang had become paramount chieftain, and being the only person in Qinghai to have been conferred the title of "imperial prince" by the Qing dynasty,[47] he was, as it were, the head of the Qinghai Khoshuds. Chaghan, on the other hand, had considerable influence among the tribes and also had strong connections with Tibet, and one of the reasons for his being conferred the title of imperial prince in the above list of awards was doubtless that the Chinese wished to prevent power being concentrated in the hands of Lobjang. But there then arose a question concerning the territory that had formerly been under the jurisdiction of the late Danjung, who had been posthumously conferred the title of commandery prince.

According to a secret memorial dated the ninth of the fifth month, Yongzheng 1, and submitted by Yue Zhongqi, provincial military commander (*tidu*) of Sichuan, he had left Chengdu on the twenty-fourth of the fourth month of that year under orders from Nian Gengyao[48] and had reached Songpan to the north of Chengdu and near the border between Shaanxi province and Qinghai on the fourth of the fifth month.[49] There he had received the following report from squad leader (*bazong*) Tang Yimei, whom he had sent to gather intelligence from across the border:

> Danjung's wife has already been taken away by Chaghan Danjin, and because Danjung's concubine had not been on friendly terms with his wife, she is still in the region of Dzongkhar where they had originally been grazing their livestock. In this tribal domain there are those who have followed after Chaghan Danjin and those who remain in Dzongkhar.[50]

Danjung and Chaghan Danjin were both descended from Ilduchi, the fifth son of Gushri Khaghan, and Danjung was the son of Chaghan's younger brother Gender. Chaghan's inheritance of the territory formerly under the jurisdiction of Danjung, his nephew, was "recognized" by Yongzheng in the sixth month of Yongzheng 1,[51] but it had in fact already been "occupied" by Chaghan.[52] In addition, as is suggested by the above report, there existed deep-rooted animosities inside Danjung's former territory, and the situation required prompt action.[53]

As regards the size of the territory in question, it is described in Yue Zhongqi's report to Nian Gengyao in the eighth month of Yongzheng 1 in the following terms:

> According to the register drawn up by Chaghan Danjin, Danjung's domain was of no more than 900 households. But according to a register secretly sent [to the Chinese] by a former *jayisang* of Danjung, it comprised 2,560 households. Furthermore, this figure does not include Tanguts. I (Yue Zhongqi) have always known that Danjung's was a powerful domain in Kokonor, and the *jayisang's* register is certain to be true.[54]

This "arbitrary"[55] action on the part of Chaghan did not make a good impression on Nian Gengyao, Yue Zhongqi and other Chinese government officials involved with Qinghai,[56] and it also appears to have been regarded as impermissible by the *taiji* of Qinghai. For example, *mergen dayiching* Lachab, the son of

Chaghan's elder brother Mergen Noyan, denounced Caghan's exclusive possession of the territory in question, took some of Danjung's former retainers into his own fold, and reported the matter to Lobjang Danjin.[57]

For Lobjang, Chaghan's action represented an expansion of the latter's sphere of influence[58] and was a serious matter that could lead to the decline of his own influence among the tribes and, in the words of Lobjang himself, had to be "dealt with squarely"[59] by him in his capacity as paramount chieftain of Qinghai. Yet, in spite of these circumstances, Yongzheng continued to support Chaghan.[60] This was the result of Yongzheng's consultations with imperial prince Yi, Longkodo (Longgeduo), Rashi (Lashi) and other brains in his administration.[61] The reasons for this stand were that, as has already been noted, they feared power being concentrated in the hands of Lobjang Danjin and also that, if Chaghan's dominium was not recognized, there was a strong possibility that he would resort to drastic measures.[62]

As a result of these Chinese policies towards the Khoshuds, ranging from the decision on rewards to the question of Danjung's former territory, animosities among the *taiji* in Qinghai began to surface. As was pointed out earlier, the Qinghai Khoshuds, especially their leader Lobjang Danjin and those associated with him, had been greatly disappointed at the breach on the part of the Chinese of their "promise," and because of their contacts with the Zunghars they were apprehensive about information being leaked from within the tribes to the Chinese side.[63] Then, towards the end of the fifth month of Yongzheng 1, Lobjang took action to rid the tribes of those forces hindering their unification.

III

First of all, Lobjang Danjin attacked Erdeni Erke Toghtonai (Erteni Erkhe Toktoné),[64] Sonom Dashi (Sönam Trashi),[65] and Galdan Dashi (Ganden Trashi).[66] In the aforementioned rewards Erdeni Erke Toghtonai had been conferred the title of "commandery prince," and this appears to have rankled Lobjang Danjin, for there is a record stating that he attempted to divest him of this title.[67]

According to one of Nian Gengyao's confidential memorials, dated the sixth of the sixth month, Yongzheng 1, Nian Gengyao had received the following report from left vice-minister (*zuoshilang*) Cangsheo (Changshou) of the ministry of war, who had been involved in the negotiations with Qinghai taking place at Xining:

> Lobjang Danjin's troops have appeared and will attack Erdeni Erke. We should dispatch troops and you yourself ought to go to Xining.[68]

In response to this Nian Gengyao decided to write a letter in Mongolian and send it to Erdeni Erke:

... I understand that some of your brothers are sending troops to attack you. Be well prepared. At present I am having the troops of our country gather provisions and fodder along the border. Even if their troops should come, be sure to defend yourselves. Have no fear. Our large forces will immediately go to your assistance.[69]

But Yongzheng made the following comment on this:

It stands to reason, and in the event of any trouble it will be advisable to act accordingly, for otherwise it will impair China's reputation and make the hearts of those in the outer provinces [of Mongolia, Tibet and Qing-hai] turn cold [towards us].[70]

The reason for this comment by Yongzheng was that Nian Gengyao had no intentions of dispatching troops to the relief of Erdeni Erke, for he was advocating a policy of nonintervention in the internal strife among the Qinghai Khoshuds.

The people of Qinghai are all descendants of Gushri Khaghan, and if they should now forget their great indebtedness to our country and kill their own flesh and blood, it is of no concern whatsoever to us, and if Lobjang Danjin is really able to eradicate Erdeni Erke, let them reduce by themselves their own strength as they please. . . .[71]

This standpoint of his was also influenced by the following practical considerations:

Even though one may maintain that we must always protect those who have looked towards us, it is at present just the time when grass has sprouted on the steppes of Mongolia and the horses are well-fed, and if we were to raise troops now and set off to attack them, we would only waste the strength of our own forces when they fled far off into the distance on their well-fed horses.[72]

Yongzheng's comments on this view were:

If Erdeni Erke should seek to enter [Inner China], let him enter and protect him. Otherwise it will later lead to error in the path of pacifying distant lands and showing kindness to foreigners. Erdeni Erke [and others] are on our side and most deserving of our pity. If we now let them [into Inner China], they will be of assistance at a later date.[73] ([. . .] added by a later hand)

He further gave orders that they be protected, and this policy was subsequently to become the basic stance of the Qing dynasty, proving to be extremely effective. In the form of a "decree from the Yongzheng Emperor"[74] and with some degree of intimidation Nian Gengyao then conveyed to Lobjang Danjin that he wished to have the reasons for the latter's actions explained.

But before that could be done Erdeni Erke was defeated by Lobjang Danjin[75] and made good his escape to Ganzhou via Suyoukou.[76] Sonom Dashi was taken prisoner because his elder brother Dondub Dashi informed Lobjang Danjin that "Sonom Dashi is an ally of China,"[77] and he was held in custody by Dondub Dashi. But with the assistance of his retainers he later escaped on the fifteenth of the tenth month and, with more than 300 followers, went to Jiayuguan,[78] from where he dispatched a messenger by the name of Metechi Jayisang to seek protection from the Chinese garrison at Bulunggir.[79] As in the case of Erdeni Erke, the Chinese granted him generous protection.[80] Galdan Dashi, on the other hand, was attacked by Arabtan Ombu (Rapten Wönpo) and others and fled to seek protection in Ganzhou, where he was made to reside together with Erdeni Erke.[81]

To date there have come to light no new historical sources describing the details of Lobjang Danjin's movements from the time after his attack on Erdeni Erke until the end of the eighth month, but the course of events was probably as outlined by Satō Hisashi,[82] with Yongzheng sending Cangsheo and others to Lobjang in an attempt to bring this incident to a peaceful conclusion.[83] But in actual fact movements running directly counter to this were under way throughout Kham (Xikang). A letter of censure in Tibetan, dated "eighth of seventh month, *guimao* (Yongzheng 1)," was sent to the eight leaders of Kham who had neglected to visit Nian Gengyao by a functionary named Dzung Ren, who exercised jurisdiction over the "Manchurian Emperor's territories of Barkham and so forth." This letter contains the following passage:

> . . . If you do not come [to pay your respects], it will mean that you have turned against the Great Lord (Yongzheng). I will see to it that you are punished in accordance with the law. On no account will I forgive you [your offense]. . . .[84]

The bewildered leaders contacted Lobjang Danjin, who had general control over them, in Qinghai. Although not directly from Lobjang himself, a charge was later made by his mother against the Chinese for this action, which was denounced as an unwarranted action against "our people" and the possibility of an insurrection by the Tibetans was also hinted at.[85] The fact that such an incident occurred within Qinghai at this time when the Chinese forces were withdrawing from Tibet would suggest that the Chinese were exerting a form of pressure on Qinghai.

According to the report submitted by the messenger Cangsheo, Lobjang Danjin told him that he had resorted to the course of action that he had taken because Erdeni Erke Toghtonai and Chaghan Danjin had attempted to occupy

Tibet and had made a false charge to the Chinese accusing him of allying with the Zunghars and seeking to instigate a rebellion, and it was now only a question of time before he would attack Chaghan.[86] Chaghan, on the other hand, asserted that Lobjang had assembled the *taiji* of Qinghai at Bar Tologhai and intended taking possession of Tibet and Qinghai, while the Mongolians stated that Lobjang was having people call him *Dalai qong tayiji* and had forbidden the *taiji* to use the titles conferred on them by the Chinese, demanding that they instead use their former titles.[87]

IV

As was noted earlier, Chaghan Danjin's "inheritance" of Danjung's former territory was "recognized" by Yongzheng shortly after Lobjang Danjin's attack on Erdeni Erke Toghtonai, and in order to dispose of the formalities of the matter Yongzheng sent Danai, imperial guardsman first class of the Qian-Qing Gate (*Qian-Qingmen toudeng shiwei*), to Chaghan.[88] That the Chinese should have taken such an action, which would incite Lobjang at a tense time just when he was moving to rid the tribes of any pro-Chinese elements, was based on their understanding that Chaghan's forces would be quite capable of resisting Lobjang's attacks,[89] and it was also, as already mentioned, probably because there was a need to prevent power in Qinghai being concentrated in the hands of Lobjang. But Chaghan's appropriation of Danjung's former territory provided Lobjang with a perfect excuse for attacking him.

Danai arrived back in Xi'an on the twenty-third of the eighth month, Yongzheng 1,[90] after having seen to the formalities of Chaghan's inheritance of Danjung's former territory, and on the same day Cangsheo received the following report from Yue Chaolong, acting vice-commander of Hezhou:

> Prince Chaghan Danjin has sent someone to say, "We were unable to check Lobjang Danjin's first assault. If we are unable to check his second attack, we wish to cross the border into China."[91]

This first attack on Chaghan Danjin by Lobjang Danjin took place on the seventeenth of the eighth month.[92] Chaghan proved to be no match for Lobjang and was routed, fleeing through Laoyaguan into Hezhou.[93] Nian Gengyao's reaction to this was as follows, but it was already too late to do anything.

> The disposition of the Mongolians is such that they are afraid of those who are powerful, and this is not at all surprising. But Chaghan Danjin's domain is known for its strength, and it ought not to be easily defeated. The reason for this outcome was perhaps that the messenger sent by Lobjang Danjin had returned from Cewang Arabtan, but he did not allow

him to meet anyone and instead fabricated a false report, misled people, and intimidated them. . . .[94]

Lobjang Danjin then attacked a garrison of the Chinese army near Xining, but was put to rout. Once the *taiji* of Qinghai realized that the Zunghar reinforcements on whom they had been counting would not be coming, they gradually dissociated themselves from Lobjang and were won over by the Chinese, who then went on to suppress this rebellion within a short span of time, while Lobjang fled to the Zunghar Cewang Arabtan.[95]

Although it is true that Lobjang Danjin had hoped to unify Qinghai and bring Tibet under his control, it was partly out of considerations of defense against the Zunghars that the Chinese should have dealt with a confrontation within Qinghai—namely, the conflict between the Lobjang faction and Erdeni Erke Toghtonai (who was pro-Qing), Chaghan Danjin (who stood intertribally opposed to Lobjang) and others—as an act of hostility against the Qing dynasty, and therefore a rebellion, and should have taken immediate measures to suppress it.[96] The reasons for Lobjang's having acted as he did may be inferred from the following letter sent by Nian Gengyao to Lobjang when the latter attacked Chaghan Danjin.

When you earlier attacked Erdeni Erke Toghtonai and people said that you had turned traitor, I took no heed since you have received great favors from successive emperors, and so how could you turn traitor? When viceminister Cangsheo went with an imperial decree to mediate between you, you did not obey the decree, nor did you recognize your wrong and submit a memorial to the emperor, and not only that, but you also said that you wished to acquire the title of *khaghan* and that you wished to be given Tibet and placed in charge of all the land of Tibet and Qinghai and to act as *dalai bātur*, and you would not be satisfied unless we took Erdeni Erke Toghtonai's title and gave it to you. Furthermore, your statement "After having decided the matter with Chaghan Danjin, I will myself go to Jingcheng (Peking) or else send someone to submit a memorial on the reasons [for my action] to the emperor" was a serious violation of the law. The land of Tibet was originally a place, which your grandfather Gushri Khaghan established by spreading the way of the law. In the decree issued by the Emperor Shengzu Ren (Kangxi) it is quite clear that "when the business [of expelling the Zunghar Cering Dondub from Tibet] has been concluded, everything will be restored to its original state." Not once have we said that [our Chinese army] will occupy and take possession of Tibet. In fact when Cewang Arabtan sent troops to kill your [Khoshud] Lajang and occupy Tibet, because you were totally incapable of revenging yourselves and reestablishing Tibet, His Majesty (Kangxi) dispatched a large army, spent tens of millions of taels, and defeated the rebels, took Tibet and installed the Dalai Lama. The laws established by your grandfather were once again disseminated. In spite of the fact that at the moment the matter has not yet been brought to a conclusion, can you say that you now want to retrieve Tibet immediately? The [Khalkha] duke Cewang Norbu is a grand minister in command of troops and stationed [in Tibet] in order to deal with all matters concerning Tibet, and his function is to supervise the troops. What has [this] got to do with your wrath? You do not make zealous efforts like your ancestors and are still dissatisfied even though we allow you to inherit [the title of] imperial prince and make you paramount chieftain of Qinghai saying that you want to assume the title of *khaghan*. Erdeni Erke Toghtonai is a commandery prince appointed by the emperor, and it was quite outrageous and the height of presumption for you to arbitrarily attack him, even though he is quite innocent, and to say that you want us to deprive him of his title and give it to you. . . . Under no circumstances will we grant you the title of *dalai qong tayiji*. If at that time you again wish to be appointed paramount chieftain of Qinghai and imperial prince, it will be too late.

It was, in other words, not possible for Nian Gengyao to nullify Kangxi's decree, and the only grounds he had for questioning the justifiableness of Lobjang Danjin's conduct aiming at the unification of Qinghai and the control of Tibet was that "at the moment the matter has not yet been brought to a conclusion." But Nian Gengyao's basic attitude towards Qinghai was:

> Lobjang Danjin should himself come forward in supplication, for since all [of Qinghai] has already become liege to His Majesty, it all belongs to His Majesty regardless of whether [the Chinese] should take your territory or not. . . .[97]

Yongzheng was also in agreement with this view.[98] This was diametrically opposed to Lobjang's understanding (of which the Chinese were of course fully cognizant), which regarded the Khoshud control of not only Qinghai but also Tibet as quite proper ever since the time of Gushri Khaghan.

CONCLUSION

The reason for Lobjang Danjin's rebellion has been described by Petech in the following terms:

> One of the causes of the revolt was Lobjang Danjin's frustrated ambition to be placed in some form at the head of the Tibetan government. His

rash and badly prepared rebellion meant the final break with his former associate Caghan Danjin, who remained loyal.[99]

In addition to this, Satō Hisashi has noted that the rewards given to Lobjang Danjin for his military services in Tibet were scanty[100] and that he aspired to becoming the ruler of Qinghai and Tibet.[101]

These reasons are all convincing, but they fail to provide any positive explanation as to why Lobjang Danjin should have on the one hand been so desirous of controlling Tibet and on the other hand taken action to oust Chaghan Danjin and other forces opposed to him among the Khoshuds at this particular point in time.

In the present paper I have reexamined these issues on the basis of original historical sources from the Chinese side such as the *Nian Gengyao zouzhe*, only recently made available, and within the context of major political changes accompanying the death of Kangxi and Yongzheng's accession to the throne. An underlying factor in the reasons for Lobjang Danjin's rebellion was, namely, the fact that, on the occasion of the subjugation of Cering Dondub in Tibet, Kangxi had promised to entrust the control of Tibet to the Qinghai Khoshuds and that their leader Lobjang and other *taiji* of Qinghai were expecting this promise to be fulfilled. But even after the pacification of Tibet this promise was not acted upon, and in Qinghai the *taiji* held repeated meetings where he suggested that they dissociate themselves from the Chinese and join forces with the Zunghar Cewang Arabtan. It was at such a time that Kangxi died and Yongzheng ascended the throne, and although the *taiji* of Qinghai were rewarded for their earlier services rendered during the advance into Tibet, Khoshud control over Tibet was not recognized and the rewards consisted mainly of conferral of relatively high titles on the pro-Chinese faction within the tribes. In addition, with this change in emperors Yinti (fourteenth son of Kangxi), who had been in charge of military affairs in this region, including the subjugation of Cering Dondub, was summoned to Peking[102] and an almost total withdrawal from Tibet was decided upon. At the same time a tense situation developed within Qinghai when Chaghan Danjin, whose influence among the tribes rivaled that of Lobjang, appropriated *beile* prince Danjung's former territory. Because Lobjang now made actual moves to unify the tribes, Yongzheng, fearful of an alliance with the Zunghars, not only endorsed Chaghan's action but also recognized his inheritance of Danjung's former territory. Lobjang and his followers, objecting to these developments, made a raid on Chaghan and eventually attacked a Chinese garrison. The main causes behind Lobjang Danjin's rebellion were, in other words, a major change in the situation brought about by Yongzheng's accession to the throne and the active political intervention in Qinghai on the part of the Chinese as evidenced in their bestowment of rewards and treatment of Chaghan.[103]

NOTES

1. Luciano Petech, "Notes on Tibetan History of the 18th Century," *T'oung Pao* 52, no. 4–5 (1966): 276–292.

2. Luciano Petech, *China and Tibet in the Early XVIIIth Century: History of the Establishment of Chinese Protectorate in Tibet*, T'oung Pao, Monographie I (Leiden: Brill, 1972).

3. Petech, *History of the Establishment of Chinese Protectorate in Tibet*, 95–98; Petech, "Notes on Tibetan History of the 18th Century," 288–289.

4. Satō Hisashi, "Robuzan Danjin no hanran ni tsuite" [On Lobjang Danjin's Rebellion], *Shirin* 55, no. 6 (Kyoto: Shigaku Kenkyūkai, 1972).

5. Katō Naoto, "Kokuritsu Kokyū Hakubutsuin hen *Nen Kōgyō sōshō*" [Confidential Memorials of Nian Gengyao, National Palace Museum], *Tōyō Gakuhō* 60, no. 3–4 (1979).

6. Satō, "On Lobjang Danjin's Rebellion," 32, and "Postscript."

7. On this collection of material there have appeared reviews by Kanda Nobuo, "Kyūcyūtō yōseicyō sōshyō" [Secret Memorials of the Yongzheng Period], *Tōyō Gakuhō* 60, no. 1–2 (1978) and Saeki Tomi, "Kyūcyūtō yōseicyō sōshyō" [Secret Memorials of the Yongzheng Period], *Tōyōshi Kenkyū* 37, no. 3 (1978).

8. *Veritable Records of Shengzu*, fasc. 278, *xinsi*, 4th month, Kangxi 57; Petech, "Notes on Tibetan History of the 18th Century," 227; Petech, *History of the Establishment of Chinese Protectorate in Tibet*, 30–37.

9. *Veritable Records of Shengzu*, fasc. 289, *gengxu*, 10th month, Kangxi 59.

10. *Veritable Records of Shengzu.*, fasc. 289, *xinyou*, 10th month, Kangxi 59. After their entry into Tibet, Cering Dondub's troops had been considerably reduced in numbers through illness and other causes (*Veritable Records of Shengzu*, fasc. 277, *yihai*, 1st month, Kangxi 57), and it has been suggested that Cering himself died in Tibet (Eva S. Kraft, *Zum Dsungarenkrieg im 18. Jahrhunder: Berichte des Generals Funingga, aus einer mandschurischen Handschrift übers und an Hand der chinesischen Akten erläutert* [*On the Zunghar War in the 18th Century: Explanations of General Funingga's Reports in Manchu Handwriting. . . .*] [Leipzig: O. Harrassowitz, 1953], 83). There is much concerning Tibet during its occupation by Cering Dondub that has hitherto remained unclear, but recently Morikawa Tetsuo has been studying the subject primarily on the basis of new historical material (Tetsuo Morikawa, "On the Documents of the Kangxi Period of Köke Qota-yin Tümed Qosigu [The Tümed Banner of Köke Khota]," in *Proceedings of the Fifth East Asian Altaistic Conference, December 26, 1979–January 2, 1980, Taipei, China*, ed. East Asian Altaistic Conference and Chieh-hsien Ch'en [Taipei: National Taiwan University, 1980], 131–139).

11. *Veritable Records of Shengzu*, fasc. 291, *jiwei*, 2nd month, Kangxi 60.

12. Manchu confidential memorial from Yansin and Nian Gengyao dated 2nd of 1st month, Yongzheng 1 (Taipei National Palace Museum, ed. *Nian Gengyao zouzhe* [*Nian Gengyao's Memorials*], vol. 1 [Taipei: Taipei National Palace Museum, 1977], 63–67).

13. Petech, "Notes on Tibetan History of the 18th Century," 266–281.

14. Petech, "Notes on Tibetan History of the 18th Century," 281–287.

15. Petech, "Notes on Tibetan History of the 18th Century," 287–289.

16. Fuheng, *Qinding Xiyu tongwen zhi* [*Authorized Polyglot Dictionary of the Western Regions*] 1750, fasc. 17; Petech, "Notes on Tibetan History of the 18th Century," 288.

17. Petech, "Notes on Tibetan History of the 18th Century," 287.

18. *Veritable Records of Shengzu*, fasc. 294, *jiawu*, 9th month, Kangxi 60.

19. Manchu letter from Nian Gengyao to Lobjang Danjin dated 11th of 9th month, Yongzheng 1 (Taipei National Palace Museum, ed., *Nian Gengyao's Memorials*, vol. 2, 723–728).

20. Manchu comments by the emperor on the confidential memorial given in n. 12 (Taipei National Palace Museum, ed., *Nian Gengyao's Memorials*, vol. 1, 67).

21. *Veritable Records of Shizong*, fasc. 5, and *Subjugation of the Zunghar*, fasc. 11, *jiachen*, 3rd month, Yongzheng 1.

22. See n. 21; Petech, *History of the Establishment of Chinese Protectorate in Tibet*, 85; and Petech, "Notes on Tibetan History of the 18th Century," 338.

23. Manchu confidential memorial from Nian Gengyao dated 16th of 10th month, Yongzheng 1 (Taipei National Palace Museum, ed., *Nian Gengyao's Memorials*, vol. 1, 138–141).

24. Manchu confidential memorial from Nian Gengyao dated 2nd of 7th month, Yongzheng 1 (Taipei National Palace Museum, ed., *Nian Gengyao's Memorials*, vol. 1, 95–97). In accordance with a written directive from Nian Gengyao dated 11th of 5th month, Yongzheng 1 (Taipei National Palace Museum, *Nian Gengyao's Memorials*, vol. 2, 711–712), Sirentu moved from Tsaidam to Chaghan Tologhai, which was where meetings of the Qinghai *taiji* were usually convened. Nian Gengyao cautioned Sirentu against causing any friction there and ordered him to report not only the progress of the withdrawal of the Chinese army but also any other information he might obtain. As support, he also sent 500 musketeers (100 horse and 400 foot) from Xining to Chaghan Tologhai.

25. Manchu confidential memorial from Nian Gengyao dated 16th of 10th month, Yongzheng 1 (Taipei National Palace Museum, ed., *Nian Gengyao's Memorials*, vol. 1, 132–137); see also abstract of this memorial in *Veritable Records of Shizong*, fasc. 12, and *Subjugation of Zunghar*, fasc. 12, *renxu*, 10th month, Yongzheng 1. Petech writes that this Abuu later participated in the subjugation of Lobjang Danjin (Petech, "Notes on Tibetan History of the 18th Century," 289), but this is probably a misunderstanding.

26. See the confidential memorial given in n. 25. Petech states that the troops commanded and stationed in Tibet by Cering Norbu on the occasion of the subjugation of Cering Dondub were "Qinghai Mongolian troops" (Petech, "Notes on Tibetan History of the 18th Century," 287), but they were probably "Chahar troops" as stated in this memorial.

27. See n. 25.

28. Cf. Petech, *History of the Establishment of Chinese Protectorate in Tibet*, Chapter 7 ("Tibet and the New Policy of Yongzheng"), 91–112.

29. Manchu confidential memorial from Nian Gengyao dated 11th of 5th month, Yongzheng 1 (Taipei National Palace Museum, *Nian Gengyao's Memorials*, vol. 1, 80–84), Tsültrim Zangpo, who had been appointed the new lama official to Dajianlu, left Xi'an for his new post on the 20th of the same month.

30. Manchu confidential memorial from Nian Gengyao dated 24th of 5th month, Yongzheng 1 (Taipei National Palace Museum, *Nian Gengyao's Memorials*, vol. 1, 86–88). The seal in question is probably that bestowed upon the new Dalai Lama by Kangxi at the time of the advance into Tibet (cf. *Veritable Records of Shengzu*, fasc. 285, imperial edict dated *yiwei*, 9th month, Kangxi 58, and deliberations and report thereon [*Veritable Records of Shengzu*, fasc. 286, *xinyou*, 12th month, Kangxi 58]).

31. See n. 30.

32. See n. 30.

33. Chinese confidential memorial from Gao Qizhuo dated 5th of 4th month, Yong-zheng 1 (Taipei National Palace Museum, ed., *Gongzhong dang Yongzheng chao zou-zhe* [*Secret Memorials of the Yongzheng Period*], vol. 1 [Taipei: Taipei National Palace Museum, 1977], 164–168).

34. See n. 33.

35. See n. 33.

36. Undated Manchu confidential memorials from Nian Gengyao (judging from their content, probably sent during 2nd month, Yongzheng 2; Taipei National Palace Museum, ed., *Nian Gengyao's Memorials*, vol. 2, 673–676, 684–686).

37. Manchu confidential memorial from Nian Gengyao dated 25th of 1st month, Yongzheng 2 (Taipei National Palace Museum, ed., *Nian Gengyao's Memorials*, vol. 1, 334–339). In addition, Arabtan Ombu sent Erdeni Tayiji together with Lobjang's messenger (Manchu confidential memorial given in n. 36, Taipei National Palace Museum, ed., *Nian Gengyao's Memorials*, vol. 2, 673–676).

38. Manchu confidential memorial given in n. 37 (Taipei National Palace Museum, ed., *Nian Gengyao's Memorials*, vol. 1, 334–339).

39. Undated Chinese confidential memorial from Nian Gengyao (Taipei National Palace Museum, ed., *Nian Gengyao's Memorials*, vol. 1, 51–52).

40. See n. 19.

41. *Veritable Records of Shizong*, fasc. 3, and *Subjugation of the Zunghar*, fasc. 11, *renchen*, 1st month, Yongzheng 1.

42. *Veritable Records of Shizong*, fasc. 4, *yihai*, 2nd month, Yongzheng 1.

43. See, for example, *Veritable Records of Shengzu*, fasc. 281, entry for *jiazi*, 10th month, Kangxi 57.

44. *Veritable Records of Shizong*, fasc. 4, *yihai*, 2nd month, Yongzheng 1.

45. Chinese confidential memorial from Nian Gengyao dated 20th of 6th month, Yongzheng 1 (Taipei National Palace Museum, ed., *Nian Gengyao's Memorials*, vol. 1, 14–15).

46. He died in the second half of 1714 (cf. *Veritable Records of Shengzu*, fasc. 260, *yichou*, 9th month, Kangxi 53).

47. *Veritable Records of Shengzu*, fasc. 270, *yimao*, 12th month, Kangxi 55.

48. Two Chinese confidential memorials from Yue Zhongqi dated 24th of 4th month, Yongzheng 1 (Taipei National Palace Museum, ed., *Secret Memorials of the Yongzheng Period*, vol. 1, 205–206, 206–207).

49. Chinese confidential memorial from Yue Zhongqi dated 9th of 5th month, Yongzheng 1 (Taipei National Palace Museum, ed., *Secret Memorials of the Yongzheng Period*, vol. 1, 236–238).

50. See n. 49.

51. *Veritable Records of Shizong*, fasc. 8, *mouchen*, 6th month, Yongzheng 1.

52. A letter from vice-minister Cangsheo (Changshou to Nian Gengyao, which arrived on 13th of 5th month, Yongzheng 1, has "Chaghan Danjin has occupied Danjung's tribal domain" (Chinese confidential memorial from Nian Gengyao dated 14th of 5th month, Yongzheng 1 [Taipei National Palace Museum, ed., *Nian Gengyao's Memorials*, vol. 1, 8–9]), and Nian Gengyao also criticized this action.

53. See nn. 49 and 57.

54. Undated Chinese confidential memorial from Nian Gengyao (judging from its content, probably sent around 15th of 8th month, Yongzheng 1; Taipei National Palace Museum, ed., *Nian Gengyao's Memorials*, vol. 1, 58). In addition, Danjung's former territory is described as having been "extremely extensive, exceeding even the area comprising of Ningxia, Liang[zhou], the Helanshan [Mts.] to the north of Gan[zhou] and Su[zhou], and the Kundulun [River]" (undated Chinese confidential memorial from Nian Gengyao [Taipei National Palace Museum, ed., *Nian Gengyao's Memorials*, vol. 1, 40–42]).

55. See n. 52.

56. See nn. 49, 52, and 57.

57. Undated Manchu confidential memorial from Nian Gengyao (judging from its content, probably sent during 11th month, Yongzheng 1; Taipei National Palace Museum, ed., *Nian Gengyao's Memorials*, vol. 2, 676–680). According to the account given by Yue Zhongqi when he reached Nian Gengyao on the 17th of the 6th month, Yongzheng 1, the situation in Danjung's former territory was as follows:

The key figures handling administrative affairs in Danjung's domain were taken away under duress by Chaghan Danjin, but now they have all fled and returned. In addition, some have gone to stay with the *beile* prince Lajab. The women in the service of Danjung's two wives have also all fled. Chaghan Danjin is at present preparing to depart in one or two days with five to six hundred troops, and he is speaking falsely, saying, "Because Lobjang Danjin took all of Danjung's domain, I will go myself to put a halt to it." But the truth of the matter is that he is pursuing [the inhabitants of] Danjung's domain in an attempt to kill them. . . . (Chinese confidential memorial from Nian Gengyao dated 20th of 6th month,

Yongzheng 1 [Taipei National Palace Museum, ed., *Nian Gengyao's Memorials*, vol. 1, 14–15]).

Allowing Chaghan Danjin to inherit Danjung's former territory in such circumstances represented a gamble, as Nian Gengyao himself was aware (Taipei National Palace Museum, ed., *Nian Gengyao's Memorials*).

58. See n. 54.

59. Manchu confidential memorial from Nian Gengyao dated 7th of 10th month, Yongzheng 1 (Taipei National Palace Museum, ed., *Nian Gengyao's Memorials*, vol. 1, 123–124); see also n. 19.

60. See Chinese confidential memorial from Nian Gengyao dated 17th of 5th month, Yongzheng 1 (Taipei National Palace Museum, ed., *Nian Gengyao's Memorials*, vol. 1, 6–8) and the comments added by Yongzheng to the confidential memorial given in n. 52.

61. See n. 60.

62. According to Cangsheo's views as expressed in the confidential memorial given in n. 52, "If Danjung's domain is not given to Chaghan Danjin to supervise, . . . then an emergency may arise at any time in Xihai, and he will seek to side with foreign norms (*viz.* the Zunghars) . . . ," and this view was to a certain degree held in common by the Chinese (cf. Chinese comments added by Yongzheng to the confidential memorial given in n. 60).

63. This is also evident from the fact that when Lobjang later attacked some tribal members, it was because they had leaked internal information to the Chinese (cf. nn. 64, 65, and 66).

64. The son of Gümbü (Mgon po), son of Gushri Qaghan's third son, Dalantai (*Waifan Menggu Huibu wanggong biaozhuan* [*Biographies of the Princes and Dukes of the Outer Provinces, Mongolia and the Muslim Region*], fasc. 81). According to Satō, "on the occasion of Galdan's uprising, [Gümbü] acted as guide to envoys in the Chinese operations against Cewang Arabtan and supplied provisions, fodder, camels and horses. He also took no part in the private league of the Qinghai *taiji* and remained loyal to the Qing dynasty" (Satō Hisashi, "Kinsei Seikai shoburaku no kigen [The Origins of the Tribal Domains of Early Modern Qinghai] [1]," *Tōyōshi Kenkyū* 32, no. 1 [1973/74]: 96). One reason for Lobjang Danjin's attack on Gümbü's son Erdeni Erke was that he had leaked internal information to the Chinese (undated Manchu edict of Yongzheng [judging from its content, probably issued in middle or towards end of 6th month, Yongzheng 1; Taipei National Palace Museum, ed., *Nian Gengyao's Memorials*, vol. 2, 800–801]).

65. He issued from the line of Gushri Qaghan's eighth son, Sangara, and his pasturage bordered on that of Lobjang Danjin (see Satō, "The Origins of the Tribal Domains of Early Modern Qinghai [2]"). According to Nian Gengyao, he regularly provided the Chinese with information (undated Chinese confidential memorial [annex?] from Nian Gengyao [judging from its content, probably sent during 6th month, Yongzheng 1; Taipei National Palace Museum, ed., *Nian Gengyao's Memori-*

als, vol. 1, 35]). It may also be noted that his name is the same as that of Erdeni Erke's second son.

66. He belonged to the lineage of Gushri Qaghan's eldest son, Dayan, and lived on the southern banks of the Datong River (Zhang Mu, *Menggu youmu ji* [*Record of the Mongol Nomads*], fasc. 12). He was also attacked on the grounds that he had leaked information to the Chinese (see imperial edict given in n. 64).

67. Manchu letter to Lobjang given in n. 19.

68. Manchu confidential memorial from Nian Gengyao dated 6th of 6th month, Yongzheng 1 (Taipei National Palace Museum, ed., *Nian Gengyao's Memorials*, vol. 1, 89–94).

69. See n. 68.

70. See Manchu comments added by Yongzheng to the confidential memorial given in n. 68 (Taipei National Palace Museum, ed., *Nian Gengyao's Memorials*, vol. 1, 91).

71. See n. 68.

72. See n. 68.

73. See Manchu comments added by Yongzheng to the confidential memorial given in n. 68 (Taipei National Palace Museum, ed., *Nian Gengyao's Memorials*, vol. 1, 89–90).

74. See n. 68. In his Manchu comments appended to this confidential memorial, Yongzheng wrote as follows in regard to this seemingly presumptuous action on the part of Nian Gengyao:

Your sending [of a decree to Lobjang Danjin] represents my will and its wording accords with the draft that I sent to you. I was most delighted to see it. This will be the end of the matter. But anyone other than you would not have dared to act in this manner, and anyone other than I would not be delighted in this manner. It is this that may be described as selfless service in the true sense and as the intimacy of ruler and subject like that of water and fish. . . .

But this was followed with a warning not to go too far:

It is Arabtan Ombu and Lobjang Danjin who are the most abominable. Do not on any account confuse the relative importance of matters. . . .

75. *Veritable Records of Shizong*, fasc. 8, and *Subjugation of the Zunghar*, fasc. 11, *renxu*, 6th month, Yongzheng 1.

76. *Veritable Records of Shizong*, fasc. 8, and *Subjugation of the Zunghar*, fasc.11, *jiazi*, 6th month, Yongzheng 1.

77. Manchu confidential memorial from Nian Gengyao dated 16th of 12th month, Yongzheng 1 (Taipei National Palace Museum, ed., *Nian Gengyao's Memorials*, vol. 1, 264–268).

78. See n. 77.

79. Manchu confidential memorial from Nian Gengyao dated 7th of 11th month, Yongzheng 1 (Taipei National Palace Museum, ed., *Nian Gengyao's Memorials*, vol. 1, 175–176).

80. See nn. 77 and 79.

81. See n. 76, the imperial edict given in n. 64, and Manchu confidential memorial from Nian Gengyao dated 19th of 1st month, Yongzheng I (Taipei National Palace Museum, ed., *Nian Gengyao's Memorials*, vol. 1, 309–311). The original sources do not tell us whether or not it was Arabtan Ombu who attacked Galdan Dashi, but we have followed the account given in the *Veritable Records of Shizong* (see n. 76). Arabtan Ombu was at this time on an expedition to appropriate the wife Changmar of Lajang Qaghan's second son Surza (who had been taken prisoner at the time of the Zunghar invasion of Tibet and sent to Ili) and her pasturage (Manchu confidential memorial from Nian Gengyao dated 11th of 11th month, Yongzheng 1 [Taipei National Palace Museum, ed., *Nian Gengyao's Memorials*, vol. 1, 178–184]), and they may have come into conflict at this time. This Changmar also appears to have been leaking information in Qinghai to the Chinese (Manchu confidential memorial from Nian Gengyao dated 8th of 5th month, Yongzheng 1 [Taipei National Palace Museum, ed., *Nian Gengyao's Memorials* , vol. 1, 77–80]), and her pasturage was situated in the basin of the Boru Chüngkeg River (see confidential memorial given in n. 65).

82. Satō, "On Lobjang Danjin's Rebellion."

83. *Veritable Records of Shizong*, fasc. 9, and *Subjugation of the Zunghar*, fasc. 11, *jimao*, 7th month, Yongzheng 1.

84. Manchu letter from Cangsheo to Nian Gengyao dated 24th of 9th month, Yongzheng 1 (Taipei National Palace Museum, ed., *Nian Gengyao's Memorials*, vol. 2, 728–733).

85. See n. 84.

86. *Veritable Records of Shizong*, fasc. 10, and *Subjugation of the Zunghar*, fasc. 12, *gengwu*, 8th month, Yongzheng 1.

87. See n. 86. The title *dalai qong tayiji* is identical to that conferred by the fifth Dalai Lama on Dalai Baghatur Dorji, the sixth son of Gushri Qaghan, who became the representative of the *taiji* of Qinghai following the latter's death (Petech, "Notes on Tibetan History of the 18th Century," 267).

88. The Manchu letter from Nian Gengyao to Danai dated 20th of 6th month, Yongzheng 1 (Taipei National Palace Museum, ed., *Nian Gengyao's Memorials*, vol. 2, 718–720) represents the written directive in question, and in it Nian Gengyao advises Danai to carefully observe how Chaghan Danjin changes following his "inheritance" and warns him against conveying Yongzheng's words of commendation immediately upon meeting with Chaghan.

89. Chinese confidential memorial from Nian Gengyao dated 22nd of 8th month, Yongzheng 1 (Taipei National Palace Museum, ed., *Nian Gengyao's Memorials*, vol. 1, 21). Yongzheng's dispatch of Danai took into full consideration Lobjang Danjin's attack on Chaghan Danjin (undated Manchu imperial edict [judging from its content,

probably issued towards end of 8th month or early in 9th month, Yongzheng 1; Taipei National Palace Museum, ed., *Nian Gengyao's Memorials*, vol. 2, 788–789]).

90. Manchu confidential memorial from Nian Gengyao dated 22nd of 8th month, Yongzheng 1 (Taipei National Palace Museum, ed., *Nian Gengyao's Memorials*, vol. 1, 103–104).

91. Undated Manchu imperial edict (according to *Veritable Records of Shizong*, fasc. 11, issued on *Jichou* [12th], 9th month, Yongzheng 1; Taipei National Palace Museum, ed., *Nian Gengyao's Memorials*, vol. 2, 785–787). This edict reached Nian Gengyao on the 13th of the 9th month (Manchu confidential memorial from Nian Gengyao dated 18th of 9th month, Yongzheng 1 [Taipei National Palace Museum, ed., *Nian Gengyao's Memorials*, vol. 1, 105–118]).

92. Chinese confidential memorial from Nian Gengyao dated 3rd of 9th month, Yongzheng 1 (Taipei National Palace Museum, ed., *Nian Gengyao's Memorials*, vol. 1, 22). According to a comment added by Yongzheng (Manchu comment [Taipei National Palace Museum, ed., *Nian Gengyao's Memorials*, vol. 1, 288] on Manchu confidential memorial from Nian Gengyao dated 28th of 12th month, Yongzheng 1 [Taipei National Palace Museum, ed., *Nian Gengyao's Memorials*, vol. 1, 287–291]), when Lobjang Danjin crossed the Yellow River and attempted to capture Chaghan Danjin, the reincarnated lama Chaghan Nomun Qaghan is said to have spread his robes on the ground and remonstrated with Lobjang (although the truth of this incident remains to be confirmed). The annex to the Chinese confidential memorial from Nian Gengyao dated 19th of 1st month, Yongzheng 2 (Palace Museum Archives [Gugong Bowuyuan Wenxianguan] in Beiping, ed., *Wenxian congbian* [*Collection of Documents*], vol. 5 [Beijing: Guoli Beiping gugong bowuyuan wenxianguan, 1930]) probably represents the reply to Yongzheng's query.

93. Manchu confidential memorial from Cangsheo deated 27th of 8th month, Yongzheng 1 (Taipei National Palace Museum, *Secret Memorials of the Yongzheng Period*, vol. 28, 614–628). In dealing with this situation, Yongzheng sent Cangsheo a letter instructing him to give Chaghan Danjin all necessary goods and assistance, and at the same time he dispatched Hūwashan (Huashan), vice-minister (*shaoqing*) of the court of the imperial stud (*tai pusi*) to give him protection (two undated Manchu imperial edicts [judging from their content, issued around 13th or 14th of 9th month, Yongzheng 1]). These two edicts were issued at about the same time; one of them (Taipei National Palace Museum, ed., *Nian Gengyao's Memorials*, vol. 2, 787–788) was directed at Nian Gengyao and Fan Shijie, acting governor (*xunfu*) of Xi'an, and gave instructions concerning material and financial aid for Chaghan, while the other (Taipei National Palace Museum, ed., *Nian Gengyao's Memorials*, vol. 2, 769–770) contained military directions for Nian Gengyao. The latter reached Nian Gengyao in the first watch (*xu*) of the 15th of the same month, and after having considered it together with an edict (see n. 91) that he had received two days earlier, he submitted a memorial (see n. 91) listing nine countermeasures. Yongzheng then suggested that Nian Gengyao help Chaghan regain his strength and use him to subjugate Lobjang,

while Nian Gengyao proposed that he himself use Erdeni Erke Toghtonai's troops, and although this proposal was not adopted (Manchu edict in reply to the confidential memorial given in n. 91 [Taipei National Palace Museum, ed., *Nian Gengyao's Memorials*, vol. 2, 793–794]), it indicates that even at this stage the Chinese still had a high estimation of the influence exerted by Chaghan and Erdeni Erke in Qinghai. Subsequently the greater part of Chaghan's forces did not gather around him in Hezhou, and because Lobjang was furthermore giving it out that he would capture Chaghan, Nian Gengyao charged Hūwashan with the task of moving 90 members of Chaghan's kin and followers from Hezhou (which they left on the 3rd of the 11th month) to Lanzhou (which they reached on the 8th; Manchu confidential memorial from Nian Gengyao dated 11th of 11th month, Yongzheng 1 [Taipei National Palace Museum, ed., *Nian Gengyao's Memorials*, vol. 1, 188–189]).

94. Undated Chinese confidential memorial from Nian Gengyao (judging from its content, probably sent towards end of 9th month, Yongzheng 1; Taipei National Palace Museum, ed., *Nian Gengyao's Memorials*, vol. 1, 56).

95. In regard to these events, see Katō Naoto, "Robusan Danjin no hanran to Shinchō—hanran no keika o chūshin to shite" [Lobjang Danjin's Rebellion and the Qing Dynasty: With a Focus on the Course of the Rebellion], *Tōyōshi Kenkyū* 45, no. 3 (Kyoto: Seikei Shoin, 1986) and Satō, "On Lobjang Danjin's Rebellion," 8–19.

96. See for example the imperial edict given in n. 91. In addition, Ishihama Yumiko, using the Chinese confidential memorials contained in *Nian Gengyao's Memorials*, vol. 1, has made a detailed and suggestive study of this question: "Gushri Han ōke no Ghibetto ōken sōshitsu katei ni Gansuru ichi kōsatsu—Ropusan-Danjin (Blo bzang bstan 'dzin) no 'hanran' saikō" [A Study of the Process Whereby the Royal House of Gushri Qaghan Lost Its Sovereignty Over Tibet: A Reconsideration of Blo bzang bstan 'dzin's "Rebellion"], *Tōyō Gakuhō* 69, nos. 3–4 (1988).

97. See n. 19.

98. Manchu letter from Nian Gengyao to Lobjang Danjin's mother dated 28th of 9th month, Yongzheng 1 (Taipei National Palace Museum, ed., *Nian Gengyao's Memorials*, vol. 2, 733–736).

99. Chinese comment added by Yongzheng to a "copy" of the letter given in n. 98 that had been sent to him (Taipei National Palace Museum, ed., *Nian Gengyao's Memorials*, vol. 2, 736).

100. Petech, "Notes on Tibetan History of the 18th Century," 289.

101. Satō, "On Lobjang Danjin's Rebellion," 20.

102. Satō, "On Lobjang Danjin's Rebellion," 21.

103. *Veritable Records of Shizong*, fasc. 4, *gengshen*, 2nd month, Yongzheng 1.

Chapter 25

ARISTOCRACY AND GOVERNMENT IN TIBET

1728–1959

Luciano Petech

Another essay from the indefatigable Luciano Petech, this is one of the best summaries of the history of Central Tibet in the nineteenth century. The period was marked by the premature death of all but the thirteenth of the Dalai Lamas and the rule of a regent-lama in his stead. The external conflicts that Central Tibet had with the Dogra rulers of Ladakh and the Gurkha rulers of Nepal did not involve the Qing at all, and the failure to deal with the British in India indicates how little engaged the Qing was with Tibet by this time. Few have challenged Petech's assessment that, in Central Tibet at least, the nineteenth century was a "period of stagnation," but this may well prove to be an exaggeration, the result of too little research having been done on this period. One unnoticed difference during this time was the prominent place of Amdo lamas who essentially ruled Tibet (during the series of young Dalai Lamas who never actually ruled Central Tibet). The longest reigning Amdo regent was the Tsomönling Trülku, who dominated Tibet from 1819 to 1844. In 1860 the power to appoint the regent was taken over by an assembly of leading men in Lhasa (called the *tsongdu*, which was created for this purpose but later became important in ruling Tibet). Petech's study of the aristocracy and the small circle of families that practically ruled Central Tibet under the Dalai Lamas is essential for understanding modern Tibetan history.

THE HISTORICAL FRAME

The internal history of Tibet under Manchu suzerainty (1720–1912) and during the brief period of *de facto* independence (1912–1951) has not yet been adequately treated as a whole. Worst off is the central period, about 1751–1904, for which we have practically only the book of Shakabpa, *Tibet, A Political History*.[1] It is unscholarly in its handling of the Tibetan texts, and Chinese sources are not utilized at all; nevertheless it supplies a large amount of new information, including some texts not yet accessible to Western scholars, and can render good service as a first introduction to Tibetan history of the period under consideration. There are adequate studies for the periods 1720–1751[2] and 1904–1959,[3] and the Chinese angle has been set forth by Li Tie-Tseng.[4] As it is not my aim to give here a complete account of Tibetan modern history, I shall limit myself to pointing out some landmarks.

The Manchu suzerain power, finally established in Tibet in 1720, tried in succession several ways of controlling the country and its peculiar aristocratic-theocratic society; the most prolonged experiment consisted in a sort of resurrection of the old monarchy under the house of Polha (1728–1750). It collapsed in 1750 with the murder of the "king" by the imperial representatives, and the ensuing changes were final; henceforward wavering ceased and Tibet received on that occasion her final political set-up, which was to last with few modifications till 1912. Its main feature was the restoration of the temporal power of the Dalai Lama, in abeyance since 1682; he was to act through a council of four ministers (*kalön*). The Tibetan government was supervised by two imperial residents (Manchu *amban*; Chinese *zhu Zang banshi dachen*), who down to the end were always Manchu and never Chinese.

The Nepalese wars of 1788 and 1791–1792[5] ended with the intervention of an imperial army, which dictated peace at the gates of Kathmandu. They also gave occasion for some administrative reforms, the most important being the enhancement of the *ambans'* powers of intervention, and the new procedure for selecting the re-incarnations of the Dalai Lama, the Panchen and other high churchmen; this was to take place through the presentation by the ecclesiastical authorities of three candidates, the final choice to be made by drawing lots from a golden bowl in the presence of the *ambans*. Formally, there were no further changes until 1912. Of course the practical working of the institutions and the actual measure of imperial influence and control depended on the local political situation, and even more on the efficiency of the Manchu supervising agencies; the latter declined sharply after the Opium War (1839–1842).

The nineteenth century was a period of stagnation, with little apparent change. There were three major events, which broke the somnolent peace prevailing in the country.

The first was the outbreak in 1844 of very strong and vocal protest of the clergy against the long rule of the regent, the Tsomönling *trülku* Ngawang Jampel Tsültrim, in office since 1819. At that time Manchu supervision was still fairly efficient; the government sent to Tibet a special commissioner (Qishan), who had the regent tried by a judicial committee of the highest dignitaries of the church and sentenced him to deposition and exile. The ensuing troubles were quelled with adroitness not devoid of firmness.[6] Imperial authority was still unchallenged and everybody bowed to it. But it was to be for the last time.

In 1862 there was a sharp conflict between the regent, the Radreng *trülku* Ngawang Yeshé Tsültrim Gyeltsen (in office 1845–1855 and since 1856), and the monks of Drepung. This time the inefficient and corrupt *amban* Manqing let events grow over his head. The regent fled to China, where he died almost at once, and power passed in the hands of the former *kalön* and duke Shedra Wangchuk Gyelpo; the Peking government could only recognize the fait accompli.[7] The reappearance of a lay regent might have portended a new trend in Tibetan history; but Shedra's death, after only two years as regent, allowed power to return to the high clergy as a matter of course.

Lastly in 1871 there was the reaction of a part of the clergy against Pelden Döndrup, an ambitious monk of Ganden, who was aiming at gathering all power in his hands. He tried to forestall the mounting opposition by a coup d'état, which cost their life to some ministers and other officials; but in the end Pelden Döndrup failed, fled to Ganden, had to quit this haven of refuge, and on the point of being overtaken by the soldiers of the government, committed suicide.[8] The Chinese *ambans* had successfully intervened in the last stages of the coup, and their action, coupled with the general revival of Manchu power in the seventies of the nineteenth century, brought about a temporary increase of imperial authority in Tibet[9] at least as far as external relations are concerned.

On a different plane was the Thirteenth Dalai Lama's assertion of power in 1895, when he compelled the regent to resign. This resulted in the permanent direct rule of a Dalai Lama, for the first time in that century: all his predecessors since 1804 had died either before or immediately after reaching the full age of eighteen. His assumption of ruling powers went off without serious friction, at least outwardly; and yet it led to consequences much more far-reaching than the dramatic convulsions of 1844, 1862 and 1871. These had concerned only a small circle of the higher clergy, as well as some of the foremost noble families, and had no lasting effects either upon or within the prevailing system. On the other hand the action of the young Dalai Lama in 1895 created, or rather revived, a center of power, which increasingly overshadowed Manchu suzerainty and eventually inherited its position in Tibet. On the immediate plane, coupled with the disastrous result of the Sino-Japanese war of 1894–1895, it led to a strong decrease of the influence of the *ambans*.

As for external wars, the first years of the nineteenth century saw almost complete peace till the Dogra invasion of 1841. It failed disastrously; but also the Tibetan counterstroke and the attempt of the Lhasa government to oust Gulab Singh from Ladakh met with an equally dismal failure. The treaty then concluded recognized the annexation of the purely Tibetan kingdom of Ladakh to the Indian state of Jammu and Kashmir. No Chinese troops had taken part in the war, and the *amban* Mengbao played a passive role, merely reporting to the emperor the facts as if the victories in the first campaign were due to his orders and leadership.[10]

The war with Nepal (1854–1856) is a subject that has been grossly neglected till very recently and is still insufficiently known,[11] as the Chinese documents are scarce, the Tibetan texts give almost no information, and most of the Nepalese documents still await publication. It ended with Tibet paying an indemnity, promising a small annual tribute and allowing a Nepalese representative in Lhasa, with jurisdiction over the Nepalese subjects residing in Tibet. In this case too the paramount power took no action and could only secure a platonic assurance of "respect to the emperor" in the final draft of the peace treaty.

By then the Lhasa government had come to realize that Chinese military power in the Himalaya was a thing of the past and that there was no possibility of a renewal of the campaign of 1792. This led them to take a mild interest in military matters; but its only practical result was seen in 1863–1864, when the Sichuan provincial authorities signally failed to stamp out the "rebellion" (i.e., the national resistance) of the chief of Nyarong. It was a Central Tibetan expeditionary force who succeeded in bringing the war to an end; the Nyarong chief Gönpo Namgyel perished in the flames of his castle besieged by the Lhasa troops. The emperor recognized the fact by granting to the Dalai Lama the government of that region, a situation which lasted until 1908 in spite of an abortive attempt to reintroduce direct Chinese rule in 1896–1897.

Small local affairs, such as the periodical trouble with the semi-independent principality of Powo, were of no great consequence.[12]

The border frictions with British India, which started in earnest in 1887 and climaxed in the entry of Colonel Younghusband and his force in Lhasa in 1904, ushered in a hectic period. It saw in turn the flight of the Dalai Lama to Mongolia, his short-lived return at the end of 1909, the attempt of the dying Manchu regime to gain cheap laurels by energetic action in Tibet, the flight of the Dalai Lama to India and his final return to Lhasa upon the collapse of the Chinese empire, to maintain himself as absolute ruler of Tibet down to his death in 1933. These events are well known and we need not expatiate upon them here.

THE TIBETAN GOVERNMENT

The political institutions of Tibet during the last two centuries have been described several times.[13] For our purpose a short sketch may suffice, supplemented by the glossary of administrative terms at the end.

The government of Tibet was basically divided into a secular and an ecclesiastical branch. The latter lies outside the scope of my study. Suffice it to know that there were 175 ecclesiastic officials (*tsedrung*) and that the highest among them was the chief abbot (*chikhyap khenpo*; the Chinese called him simply *khenpo*); the office was created at the time of the Gurkha wars of 1788–1792. He was the head of the ecclesiastic establishment[14] and acted as a link between the Dalai Lama, to whom he had always direct access, and the *yiktsang*. The latter, composed of four lama officials (*khendrung* or *dedrung*, popularly called *drung-yik chenmo*), was a sort of ecclesiastic counterpart to the council of ministers. Its chairman was the senior member (*khendrung chewa*, sometimes shortened into *khenché*), who usually held the half-Chinese title of *da lama*. Their main task was the control of the numerous and wealthy monasteries. Only the three great convents of Drepung, Sera and Ganden in the neighborhood of Lhasa were directly subordinate to the Dalai Lama.

The cadre of the lay officials (*shödrung*, usually called *drungkhor*) consisted of 175 members, all of them belonging to the aristocracy; they alone filled the government posts reserved to the secular element. Their rank was determined according to the Chinese system, introduced in 1792. However, only five of the nine Chinese ranks were in normal use, viz. those from the third to the seventh inclusive. The Dalai Lama and the Panchen were outside and above official rank. Only the ministers and the holders of Chinese titles (*gong, taiji, jasak*) were entitled to the third rank. Most of the higher officials belonged to the fourth, and the title *rimzhi* (fourth rank) was a sort of general style for most of the upper bureaucracy. Sometimes the emperor granted to an official a personal rank higher than the one normally belonging to his post; e.g., a *kalön* could be promoted to the second rank.

The highest office in the state was after 1907 that of the grand ministers (*lönchen*), whom the Dalai Lama, then at Xi'an, appointed to help the regent in conducting the government. At first they were three, but vacancies were not filled again after the death of the original incumbents. After 1926 there was only one, now styled minister of state (*silön*). In 1939 the post practically fell into abeyance. It was revived in 1950, when two ministers of state were appointed; but in 1952 it was abolished altogether. The grand (or state) ministers are some-times said to have enjoyed the second rank; but it seems that this was never of-ficially settled. Their task was to act as connecting link between the Dalai Lama and the council of ministers. They did not, however, take part in the de-liberations of that body, but merely forwarded its proposals to the ruler together with their own opinion. Their actual influence on affairs was always much less than the name would indicate.

Before 1907, and in practice even after that date, the lay branch of the Ti-betan government was topped by the council of ministers, called *kalön shak lhen gyé*, usually shortened into *kashak*; this was actually the name of their of-fice rooms near the Trülnang, the cathedral of Lhasa. As the highest adminis-trative agency in Tibet, during most of this period it enjoyed the right of direct access to the Dalai Lama; this privilege was withdrawn in 1907. The *kashak* was one of the two really significant offices open to the nobility, and often contributed decisively to the shaping of Tibetan policy. The history of the *kashak* is therefore of great relevance for the study of the practical functioning of Tibetan institutions. After the reforms introduced by the Chinese in 1792–1793 it was placed under the control of the *ambans*, but otherwise left paramount in current administration.

The *kashak* was formed by four officials of the third rank, whose full title was *ké gunglön*, usually shortened into *kalön*; the literary style was *dünnadön*, sometimes also *sawang*. At the beginning of the nineteenth century they came to be called in common parlance *shappé* (lotus feet).[15] As shown by the *Shingji* roll, the *kalön* in charge, as well as the *lönchen* and *silön*, were not included in the official list of the 175 *shödrung*; evidently they were considered as outside and above the professional government service.[16] The *kalön* were on an equal footing and there was no chairman of the council; seniority conferred merely a gradation of prestige and of ceremonial precedence. However, during the last years the *kalön lama* took seniority regardless of the date of appointment.[17] They acted as a committee, without departmental specialization. Quite often one of them was sent out on a special task (as *chikhyap*) consisting in a mission (*dönchö*) to outlying districts, or accompanying the *amban* in his tours of inspection. After 1750 three of them were laymen and one an ecclesiastic, with the title of *kalön lama*; but during the period 1804–1878 no seat was reserved for the clergy and all the four ministers were laymen.[18] In 1878 a supernumerary ecclesiastical member was added, increasing thus to five the number of the ministers; but in 1894 the scheme of 1751 was restored, and henceforward the *kashak* consisted of three laymen and one *lama*. This number was never exceeded, except that sometimes joint or deputy members of the council were appointed, but with a lower standing. Only during the last six or seven years of its existence a beginning with departmental specialization was made.

The *kashak* had a considerable staff at its disposal. It consisted of five secretaries (*kashak drungyik*, usually shortened into *kadrung*), who were responsible for its clerical work. Of these, the two Grand Secretaries (*kadrung chewa*) were of the sixth rank, and the three Lesser Secretaries (*kadrung chungwa*) were of the seventh rank. Other members of the staff were the three *kashak drönnyer*, shortened into *kadrön* (sixth rank); they presented to the council the petitions and reports of the lower officials and generally maintained the liaison with the bureaucracy. There was also a subordinate secretarial section called *kashö*, concerned mainly with ecclesiastical affairs and manned by several *drungyik* of the seventh rank.

The revenue and expenses of the state were controlled by the account department (*tsikhang*), headed by three lay officials of the fourth rank called *tsipön*; at some date in the late twenties of the present century a fourth *tsipön* was added. They were assisted by three or four accountants (*tsipa*; sixth rank). Although in theory subordinate to the *kashak*, theirs was the other significant office open to laymen alone, because the *tsipön*, together with the *khendrung*, were the spokesmen or leaders of discussion in the National Assembly (*tsokdu*), at which the *kalön* were not allowed to be present, and they reported the opinion of the Assembly to the *kashak*. Another source of influence was their control of the school of finance (*tsilap*), which entailed a considerable say in the new appointments to government service.[19]

There were three treasuries. The main one was the *labrang chakdzö*, in the premises adjoining the Trülnang. It was controlled by three treasurers (*labrang chakdzöpa*, usually shortened into *lachak*; fourth rank), one lay and two ecclesiastic. Then there was the private treasury of the Dalai Lama (*treldé chakdzö*), housed in the Potala palace (*tsé*); it was headed by three treasurers (*tsetrel chakdzöpa*, usually shortened into *tsechak*; fourth rank), one lay and two ecclesiastic; however, the lay *tsechak* was regarded during his term of office as a *tsedrung* and sat with the monks at the ceremonies, audiences with the Dalai Lama, etc.[20] Lastly there was the reserve treasury (*namsé gendzö*) in the Potala, seldom mentioned in the texts; it was under the direct responsibility of the *kashak* and was drawn upon only in a national emergency.

The financial administration of the army was in the charge of two paymasters (*pokpön*; fourth rank), one lay and one ecclesiastic.

There was no well-graded judiciary. Outside the capital the district governors acted also as judges in civil and criminal cases. Special judicial officers were found in Lhasa only (all of them of the fifth rank). They were: the city magistrates of Lhasa (*mipön*; two laymen); the magistrates of the walled dependency of the Potala (*zhöl depa* or *zhölnyer*; two laymen, one monk), in charge of the state dungeons there and having jurisdiction for some twenty-six miles up the Kyichu valley and nineteen down it;[21] and the *sherpang* (two laymen), who acted as law advisers to the *kashak* when the latter, sitting as court of appeal, decided serious cases brought before it from Lhasa and Central Tibet. Indirectly their jurisdiction extended to most of the country. They were also responsible for the care of the Trülnang cathedral.

Military organization, based upon the local militia (*yülmak*) and in later times upon a small standing army, normally lacked a central command. When it was necessary to send out a considerable body of troops on an expedition, one of the *kalön* took its command. Only in 1913 the Dalai Lama created the permanent post of commander-in-chief, with the title of *chikhyap dapön* (abridged in *chida*), changed almost at once into *makgi chikhyap* (abridged in *makchi*). After 1934 there were permanently two *makchi*, one monk and one lay. Otherwise the highest officers of the army were the provincial generals (*dapön*; fourth rank), at first three in Tsang[22] and one in Ü. In 1751 one was added in Ü and after the middle of the nineteenth century another was appointed in Tsang, but permanently detached to Dingri. After 1913 other *dapön* were created, such as the commander of the Dalai Lama's bodyguard and one or two to command large units in Eastern Tibet. Other officers were the twelve wing commanders (*rupön*;

fifth rank), the twenty-four commanders of hundred (*gyapön*; sixth rank) and the 120 captains (*dingpön*; seventh rank); but numbers and ranks of these officers are found in the Chinese texts only, and they were outside the cadre of the 175 *shödrung*.

The structure of the central government sketched above was in existence already in the twenties of the eighteenth century. Almost all the relevant titles of office can be met with in the Tibetan texts of the time and in the letters and reports of the Italian missionaries.[23] There was no substantial modification during the whole of the following two hundred years. And this is another instance of the innate conservatism of Tibetan traditional society.

For the purposes of provincial administration, most of the regions under the direct control of the Lhasa government were divided into districts (*khül*; but they are now called *dzong*, which is properly the castle serving as headquarters), the great majority of which were situated in the two provinces of Ü and Tsang. At the time of the Thirteenth Dalai Lama there were fifty-two *dzong*, to which the small independent principality of the Sakya abbots should be added. Each *dzong* was in charge of one or two governors (*dzongdö*, more usually *dzongpön*; the Chinese and Nepalese continued to use the earlier title *depa*), appointed for a term of three years; in the case of two governors (*dzongdrel*), either both laymen, or more commonly one lay and one monk. The governors of the outlying *dzong* of Naktsang, Nakchu and Saga bore the title of *göpa*; those of Rongshar and Nyanang the title of *shöpa*. The heads of twenty-three important districts (eight single *dzongpön*, eleven double *dzongpön*, two *göpa*, two *shöpa*) were of the fifth rank; twenty-seven governors (eighteen single, eight double, one *göpa*) were of the sixth rank; two *dzongpön* (single) were of the seventh.[24] They were responsible for the collection of revenue, for law and order and for the hearing of civil and criminal cases arising in their districts.[25] Often a *dzongpön*, especially when young and belonging to a family of the higher nobility, was an absentee; he stayed on in Lhasa and his duties were performed by a steward (*nyerpa*).

Besides, there was a certain number of government estates (*zhika*), their stewards (*zhidö*) ranking on the average below the *dzongpön*; three were of the sixth rank, the rest of the seventh. Districts and estates together were usually called *dzongzhi*, a collective name for the administrative units outside Lhasa.

Some outlying regions were under a special administration. In Ngari Korsum, or Western Tibet, two commissioners called *Tö garpön* (fifth rank, but locally fourth) supervised the four *dzong* and the numerous nomad clans of the region. In Amdo (Northeastern Tibet) there was till about the middle of the nineteenth century a commissioner called *Do garpön*, whose functions concerned above all trade and the control of local monasteries. Kham (Eastern Tibet) was subject to a sort of general supervision by the *dzongpön* of Markham (fifth rank, but locally fourth). When the administration of Nyarong was entrusted to the Dalai Lama in 1865, his representative (*chikhyap*) supervised in some form the various chieftains of Kham down to 1911.[26] In 1918 the Dalai

Lama created the post of governor-general of Eastern Tibet (*Domé chikhyap*, usually abridged into *dochi*), held concurrently by one of the *kalön*. A parallel post of governor-general of the South (*Lhokha chikhyap*, abridged as *lhochi*) was established in 1927 with authority over the several *dzong* and estates of Dakpo and Kongpo; but its importance and prestige were not high. Another special officer (*Dromo chikhyap*, in short *drochi*) was in charge of the Chumbi valley.[27]

There were at first no fixed rules for appointment and advancement in officialdom. Between 1751 and 1788 membership of the *kashak* was practically by direct inheritance from father to son. This custom was abolished by the Chinese, and in later times a young nobleman had to follow a sort of administrative career, starting with his first official appointment (*zhap sarwa*) usually on New Year's day and following either the financial branch up to *tsipön* or the treasury service up to *lachak* or the military career up to *dapön*. These three offices were the usual stepping stones from which the judgment and trust of the Dalai Lama (or of the regent) raised him to a seat in the *kashak*. A kind of intermediate stage was represented by the joint ministers (*kalön lepar*) and by the deputy ministers (*katsap*). The office of *kalön* could be held only once. There is not a single instance of a *kalön* being reinstated after dismissal or retirement. When the Thirteenth Dalai Lama wanted to redress the injustice done on the three ministers he had abruptly dismissed in 1903 for giving him advice which the events proved sound, he did not appoint them to the *kashak* again, but created for them the new post of grand minister.

According to Chinese regulations, a vacancy in the council and among the *dapön* was to be filled upon the presentation by the *amban* (acting upon the advice of the Dalai Lama or of the regent) of two names in order of preference; the final choice was reserved to the emperor.[28] But mostly it was a mere formality, as Peking constantly appointed the man presented as first choice, thus ratifying the proposal of the Tibetan government.

ARISTOCRACY AND THEOCRACY

After 1751 Tibet was under the temporal rule of the Dalai Lama. In this theocratic state the nobility held a sort of subordinate partnership, the forms of which have now to be studied.

It is usually said that Tibet was a feudal country down to 1951,[29] with the qualification that the nobility was flanked and up to a certain point dominated by the Yellow Church and its great monasteries. On the whole this picture is correct, but remains somewhat vague; the composition of the aristocracy and the measure of their participation in the central government have yet to be worked out.

The Tibetan nobility, like every other aristocracy, underwent radical changes during the ages. The great noble families of the time of the monarchy (c. 600–841), such as Takdra, Chokro, Chim, etc., vanished after the end of that period and the victory of Buddhism, to be replaced by new ones; in recent times very few houses (Lhagyari, Dokhar, Tönpa) could claim an ancestry going back to monarchical times. In the same way the nobility of Sakyapa times was largely superseded by new families in the course of the Pakmodru period (fourteenth century). The topmost layer of Tibetan aristocracy, as it existed in the time of the Thirteenth Dalai Lama, came into being in the first half of the eighteenth century and was the most lasting result of Polhané's rule. We could even say that the high peerage of today (the *depön*) is formed by the descendants of Polhané's council of ministers; but this would be an over-simplification. This, however, was the last change of great import. The vested interests then created were consolidated under the dyarchy of the Dalai Lamas and of the Manchu emperors and were crystallized down to the end of traditional Tibet after 1951.

The first enlargement of this hard core came in 1792 as a result of the Gurkha war. A second was due to the Thirteenth Dalai Lama, who included in the upper nobility some of his favorites (Tsarong is a typical instance); at the same time a few of the oldest families faded into the background (e.g., the Tönpa). All this enlarged the circle of the ruling families, but did not substantially alter its composition. Regeneration within the nobility was a comparatively slow affair; its most active factor was the institution of the *makpa*, on which see below. This system resulted in changing the lineage proper of most of the noble families.

Political influence within the central government was restricted to the nobility of Ü and Tsang. The latter region prevailed in the eighteenth century, because of the privileged position given to it by Polhané. Predominance passed soon to Ü (chiefly after 1792); but Tsang always preserved a substantial share of power. This regional rivalry lost its meaning after the flight of the sixth Panchen to China in 1923 as most of the great families of Tsang gradually shifted their residence to Lhasa and its district.

The clearest evidence of the political influence of a family was membership in the *kashak*. That body was always a stronghold of the aristocracy, and even more so during the long span of time (1804–1878) when no seat was reserved for an ecclesiastical member. The interplay of clerical supremacy, Manchu suzerainty and aristocratic power during the nineteenth century influenced to some extent the inner balance of the *kashak*, giving preponderance in turn to the upper nobility, to the old lower nobility and to new families; however, it is difficult to get a clear picture on this point. As for the great feudal lords of the southeast (e.g., Lhagyari and Powo), their influence remained restricted to the local plane and they never participated in the central government.

The administrative machinery functioned as a partnership between clergy and nobility; no commoner was normally admitted to middle or high office. If such a thing happened, his ennoblement was a necessary preliminary step (Tsarong is again the typical instance).[30] The economic position of the aristocracy was firm and secure, except for possible confiscations for crimes or misdemeanors. Therefore, the noble class was not exposed to any appreciable pressure from below. On the other hand, the apportionment of offices between clergy and aristocracy was rigidly determined by law and custom, and no direct clash between the two components of Tibetan polity was possible. Thus the social and political status of the nobility as a whole could oscillate only between very narrow limits. Substantially, the power and wealth of the aristocracy in 1950 was not much different from what it had been in 1750.[31]

This pattern shows some striking similarities with the only possible parallel within European polity of about the same period: the nobility of the Papal State in its last stages. There too we notice the same stable social frame, the same partnership with the clergy (but only on the administrative, not on the policy-making level) and, on the whole, the same stagnation and lack of real renovation.

As to the economic and social aspects of the aristocracy, the basic fact is that the power of the nobility rested on their landed estates and serfs, and thus on agriculture; there were no nobles among the cattle-raisers and the nomads, although some families had herds of cattle in addition to land. But, as said above, I deliberately exclude this subject from my account and refer the reader to Pedro Carrasco's *Land and Polity in Tibet* and to the recent studies by M. C. Goldstein.[32] The family based on the estate shows some peculiarities which makes it something very different from a European noble family. Polyandry is not perhaps the main factor, mainly because the fathership of a son is attributed by convention to the chief or first husband. Much more relevant is the institution of *makpa*, the son-in-law who enters the family of his wife to all effects and takes its name. This is not simply a means for ensuring the continuation of a family in the case of absence of male heirs. Not seldom the lineage by *makpa* is parallel to the survival of the direct male descendance; sometimes *makpa* lineage overshadows the direct one, i.e., becomes the main branch of the family. Typical examples are found chiefly in the house of Shedra.

There are some instances of the continuance of a family being suddenly cut off because of a sentence of death upon its head or on the whole of its male members. An instance of total extirpation and of absolute severance, without any appreciable connection between old and new family, seems to be that of the Ngapö family, wholesale executed by order of the Chinese representatives in 1728; however, the documents on the case are not sufficiently clear. A less radical instance is that of the foundation of a new Tsarong family after its head and heir had been killed in 1912. In this case government gave to the transfer of the estate the formal shape (of course a forced one) of a succession by *makpa*, although male members of the original house were still alive. In any case, the basic element of continuity seems to be the landed estate, not descent by blood.

On the other side the original estate (*pazhi*) has not such a paramount importance as to supply the family with its only and unchangeable name; fairly often the name of the estate is flanked by the name of the family mansions in Lhasa. Official documents, such as the *Shingji* roll, prefer the estate name and their example will be followed here.[33]

TABLE 25.1

Family	Seats 1728–1844	Seats 1844–1959
Dokhar	3	3
Gazhi	4	1
Palha	3	2
Shedra	3	2
Zurkhang	2	2
Samdrup Podrang	2	2
Tön	3	–
Sarjung	–	3
Trimön	1	1
Ngapö	–	2
Tsarong	–	2
Yutok	–	2
Hor Khangsar	1	1
Lhalu	–	2
Drongtsé	1	–
Lhading	1	–
Twenty-one families	–	1 each

Coming now to the actual composition of the ruling class, the distribution of political influence as reflected in membership of the *kashak* is shown by table 25.1. It lists the seats held by various families during the first and the second halves of the period under consideration (1728–1844 and 1844–1959). The date of 1844 is that of the deposition of the Tsomönling regent; it has no particular meaning in this context, but simply affords a convenient division into two equal portions for a period of about 230 years.

We can legitimately draw some conclusions. First, the circle to which real power was limited was much smaller in the first period (eleven families) than in the later period (thirty-four families). Secondly, the noble houses that held a seat twice or more times, i.e., those who at one time or the other were politically very important, are only fourteen, out of the more than two hundred listed in *The Aristocracy of Central Tibet*.[34] And this shows that social differences within the aristocracy were much more marked than it appeared on the surface.

TITLES AND SUBDIVISIONS OF THE ARISTOCRACY

The Tibetans distinguish three classes within their aristocracy:

1. *yapzhi*, i.e., the families of former Dalai Lamas; they are now six, including that of the present Dalai Lama;

2. *depön*, the highest peerage, including five families;
3. the rest of the aristocracy (*kudrak*; in their capacity as landholders called *gerpa*), about two hundred families, most of whom never played a political role.

Of course the first two classes monopolized most of the power received by the aristocracy, the *depön* (except the Lhagyari house) more so than the *yapzhi*; the latter were handicapped by the unwritten rule that during the lifetime of a Dalai Lama his relatives were debarred from the *kashak*. The Thirteenth Dalai Lama was the first to circumvent it by creating for his nephew the new post of minister of state (*silön*).

The Tibetan aristocracy could receive Chinese titles from the emperor. In 1751 the Qianlong emperor had laid down that henceforward no Tibetan could hold the title of prince (*wang*), nor that of duke of the first degree (*chenguo gong*). Thus the highest title available was that of duke of the second degree (*fuguo gong*), followed by that of *taiji* (in four degrees). The additional distinction of *jasak* could be granted to a first-class *taiji*. Heredity was by decreasing degrees; thus the son of a *gong* became a first-class *taiji*, the son of the latter a second-class *taiji* and so on. The rule did not apply to those houses to whom the emperor granted the privilege of "heredity forever."

At the end of the empire the houses officially holding rank in "heredity forever" were the following: the Polha or Changchen house (*gong*); Hor Khangsar (*jasak* first-class *taiji*); Samdrup Podrang (first-class *taiji*); Gazhi (first-class *taiji*). The *gong* title belonging to the three *yapzhi* houses of Langdün, Pünkhang and Lhalu seems to have been inherited by courtesy only, without imperial sanction.

In 1912 the emperor ceased to be the *fons honorum*. Only once, in 1919, the Thirteenth Dalai Lama tried to exercise this privilege, as the *de facto* successor to the vanished imperial authority, by confirming the *gong* title to Changchen, Pünkhang and Lhalu. Then the matter remained in abeyance and the *gong* title seems to have become a matter of custom, reserved to the houses who had enjoyed it under Manchu rule.

Occasionally the emperor granted the *gong* title for life only, as a very special distinction; the father of the fourth Panchen and Shedra Wangchuk Gyelpo are instances in case. Much more common was the grant of the personal title of *taiji*, an usage which was continued by the Dalai Lama after 1912.

Lastly, I point out once more, at some risk of repeating myself, that my enquiry regards a strictly limited field, i.e., that portion of the Tibetan aristocracy which was in contact with, and participated in, the actual functioning of central power. The exclusion of notables and landowners of purely regional importance practically reduces the field of research to the nobility of Ü and Tsang, with the addition of the premier families of Kongpo and Dakpo. Within this field a narrower selection has been effected by including only those families which had access to power at its highest level, that of the *kashak*. But if I had adhered strictly to these principles, I would have left out some houses of such prestige and influence as to render their exclusion wholly unjustifiable. Therefore, the last section includes some families who, although they never held a seat in the *kashak*, have at one time or another occupied an outstanding place, because of their social position and their traditional connection with the military career.

NOTES

1. Tsepon W. D. Shakabpa, *Tibet: A Political History* (New York: Potala Publications, 1984).

2. Luciano Petech, *China and Tibet in the Early XVIIIth Century: History of the Establishment of Chinese Protectorate in Tibet* (Leiden: Brill, 1972).

3. Alastair Lamb, *The McMahon Line: A Study in the Relations Between India, China and Tibet, 1904–1914* (London: Routledge & Kegan Paul, 1966). Hugh Richardson, *Tibet and Its History* (London: Oxford University Press, 1962).

4. Li Tieh-Tseng, *Tibet, Today and Yesterday* (New York: Bookman Associates, 1960).

5. By far the best account of this conflict is that by Leo E. Rose, *Nepal: Strategy for Survival* (Berkeley: University of California Press, 1971), 50–67, based mainly on Chinese texts and unpublished Nepalese documents. The other recent study by Bhairava Dat Sanwal, *Nepal and the East India Company* (New York: Asia Publishing House, 1965), 74–84, brings nothing new, except for some sidelights from British-Indian documents.

6. See Luciano Petech, "The Dalai Lamas and Regents of Tibet," *T'oung Pao* 47 (1959): 388–389. The relevant Chinese documents are summarized by Suzuki Chūsei, "A Study of a Coup d'état at Lhasa in 1844," in *Oriental Studies Presented to Sei Wada in Celebration of His Seventieth Birthday* (Tokyo, 1960), 553–564 (in Japanese). The Tibetan point of view, ignoring the role of Qishan, is expressed by Shakabpa, *Tibet, A Political History*, 180. The deposed regent was at first sent to Manchuria, then was allowed to settle on the Gansu-border, where he died in 1854; William Frederick Mayers and G. M. H. Playfair, *The Chinese Government: A Manual of Chinese Titles, Categorically Arranged and Explained, with an Appendix* (Shanghai: Kelly and Walsh, 1897), 116.

7. Luciano Petech, *Aristocracy and Government in Tibet: 1728–1959* (Rome: Instituto italiano per il Medio ed Estremo Oriente, 1973), 174–177.

8. The sources for this event are particularly meager. The account of Shakabpa, *Tibet, A Political History*, 189–190, is the best. The Chinese documents (mainly Mu Zong, *Da Qing Lichao Shilu* [*Veritable Records of the Court of the Great Qing*], 313.14.b–16a) give few details, but supply the names of the six officials killed by the order of Dpal ldan don grub. On the manner of his death (suicide pact with a *jasak bla ma*) see also Charles Alfred Bell, *The Religion of Tibet* (Oxford: Clarendon Press, 1931), 158.

9. Rose, *Nepal: Strategy for Survival*, 123.

10. A serious study of this conflict is a desideratum. For the moment, two one-sided accounts can be utilized. Shakabpa, *Tibet, A Political History*, 177–180, gives the Tibetan angle; and Margaret Welpley Fisher, Leo E. Rose, and Robert A. Huttenback, *Himalayan Battleground: Sino-Indian Rivalry in Ladakh* (New York: Praeger, 1963), 49–59, reflects mostly the Chinese point of view, giving in the Appendix a translation of the relevant passages of Meng Bao, *Xizang Zou Shu* [*Memorial and Decrees of Meng Bao, Amban in Tibet 1839–1844*] (c. 1851).

11. Recent accounts are those by Sanwal, *Nepal and the East India Company*, 284–286, and Ramakant, *Indo-Nepalese Relations, 1816 to 1877* (Delhi: S. Chand, 1968), 257–261; they bring no fresh information. The first serious study of the subject is due to Rose, *Nepal: Strategy for Survival*, 108–118.

12. Sometimes these frictions, usually due to the Lhasa government attempting to annex the country or to the ruler (the Ka nam *sde pa*) refusing to pay tribute, degenerated into full-fledged war. Such was the case in 1835–1838 (see under Bshad sgra and Zur khang, Petech, *Aristocracy and Government in Tibet: 1728–1959*, 163–164, 146), in 1910 when Spo bo utterly wearied out a Chinese expeditionary force (see Shakabpa, *Tibet, A Political History*, 238–239; Lamb, *Relations Between India, China and Tibet, 1904–1914*, 276–277), and in 1927–1931, when the principality was finally extinguished and its territory annexed (see under Mtsho sgo, Petech, *Aristocracy and Government in Tibet: 1728–1959*, 140).

13. The last and perhaps the most complete account is that in Ram Rahul, *The Government and Politics of Tibet* (Delhi: Vikas Publications, 1969), 22–50. A dry list of offices classified according to rank is found in Bshad sgra, Bka' blon and Nor nang, Bka' drung, *Yig bskur rnam gzhag* [*Terminology for Correspondence*], ed. G. Tharchin (Kalimpong, 1956), 164–166; another, of course in Chinese transcription, is given by Mayers and Playfair, *The Chinese Government: A Manual of Chinese Titles*, 111–112. An account of the Tibetan government, rather muddled and incomplete, but important because of its early date is that by Sarat Chandra Das, *A Journey to Lhasa and Central Tibet* (London: John Murray, 1904), 230–256. Another, quite good but not detailed, is that by David Macdonald, *The Land of the Lama* (London: Seeley Service and Co., 1929), 55–62 and 116–120. Also Richardson, *Tibet and Its History*, 18–27, is helpful.

14. In the thirties and forties of the present century it was the practice for the *spyi khyab mkhan po* to be treated as an additional member of the *bka' shag*, or at least called in frequently to their discussions. He therefore became a link between the *bka' shag* and the regent (Hugh Richardson, in personal communication).

15. Some instances are found already in De mo, Qutuqtu, *Rgyal ba'i dbang po thams cad mkhyen gzigs chen po rje btsun blo bzang bstan pa'i dbang phyug 'jam dpal rgya mtsho dpal bzang po'i zhal snga nas kyi rnam par thar pa mdo tsam brjod pa 'dzam gling tha gru yangs pa'i rgyan* [*Life of the Eighth Dalai Lama*] (Vol. Ka of the gsung 'bum of the Eighth Dalai Lama), e.g., 193a, 196a, 197b, 199a, 204b. The title *zhabs pad* grows more common in De mo, Qutuqtu, *Rgyal ba'i dbang po thams cad*

mkhyen pa blo bzang pa'i byung gnas ngag dbang lung rtogs rgya mtsho dpal bzang po'i zhal snga nas kyi rnam par thar pa mdor mtshon pa dad pa'i yid 'phrog [*Life of the Ninth Dalai Lama*] (unpublished blockprint), at least in its first pages. Blo bzang sbyin pa, *Rab 'byams rgyal ba'i spyi gzugs skyabs mgon paṇ chen thams cad mkhyen pa rje btsun blo bzang dpal ldan bstan pa'i nyi ma phyogs las rnam rgyal dpal bzang po'i zhal snga nas kyi sku gsung thugs kyi rnam par thar pa 'dzam gling mdzes rgyan* [*Life of the Fourth Panchen Lama*] (Vol. Ka of the Fourth Paṇchen Lama's *gsung 'bum*), does not use it.

16. Tibetan text published in Petech, *Aristocracy and Government in Tibet: 1728–1959*, 240–249.

17. Hugh Richardson, in personal communication.

18. See Petech, *Aristocracy and Government in Tibet: 1728–1959*, 220.

19. Hugh Richardson, in personal communication.

20. Hugh Richardson, in personal communication.

21. Charles Alfred Bell, *Portrait of the Dalai Lama* (London: Collins, 1946), 266.

22. There is some evidence going to show that in the first quarter of the eighteenth century there were two *mda' dpon* in Gtsang (*Gtsang ljongs kyi kha lo pa zung*; Tshe ring dbang rgyal, Mdo mkhar, *Dpal mi'i dbang po'i rtogs brjod pa 'jig rten kun tu dga' ba'i gtam* [*Life of Pho lha nas*] (unpublished blockprint), 57b, 127a, 190a, and one in Kong po, the latter post being hereditary in the O rong family.

23. The documents issued to the missionaries by the Tibetan governments between 1714 and 1741 (Luciano Petech, *I missionari italiani nel Tibet e nel Nepal* [*Italian Missionaries in Tibet and Nepal*], 7 vols. [Rome, 1952–1956], 3:183–214) are particularly interesting in this connection. They show that control over taxation, building activity, etc., in and near Lhasa was already in the hands of the *lha gnyer, zhol gnyer* and *mi dpon*, while the *bla brang phyag mdzod* acted as public register of land. On the other side some offices mentioned there vanished soon after; such were the *lcang srung ba* (forestry officer; probably replaced by the *shing gnyer*) and the *darogha*, a Mongol term which at least in some instances seems to be equivalent to the Tibetan *'go pa* (see the six *darogha* of Nag chu in Sangs rgyas rgya mtsho, *Thams cad mkhyen pa drug ba blo bzang rin chen tshangs dbyangs rgya mtsho'i thun mong phyi'i rnam par thar pa du ku la'i 'phro 'thud rab gsal gser gyi snye ma* [*Biography of the Sixth Dalai Lama*] (unpublished blockprint, 438b).

24. This list is based on Bshad sgra et al., *Terminology for Correspondence*, 164–166, with slight modifications from the *Shingji* roll; Petech, *Aristocracy and Government in Tibet: 1728–1959*, 240–249.

25. For the relations between central and local government see the discerning remarks of Melvyn C. Goldstein, "Taxation and the Structure of a Tibetan Village," *Central Asiatic Journal* 15, no. 1 (1971): 170–182.

26. Except for an abortive attempt to reintroduce direct Chinese rule in 1896–1897, which ended with the retrocession of Nyag rong to the Dalai Lama; see Li, *Tibet, Today and Yesterday*, 64. The Tibetan officials were expelled from Nyag rong by Zhao

Erfeng in the summer of 1911; Lamb, *Relations Between India, China and Tibet, 1904–1914*, 274.

27. For some other offices of secondary or nominal importance we may refer to the glossary of the original book in which this appeared.

28. There are many instances of this procedure in Meng Bao, *Memorial and Decrees of Meng Bao*, and Wu Feng Pei, ed., *Qing Ji Chou Zang Zou Du* [*Qing Dynasty Memorials and Documents Concerning Tibet*].

29. But see the discerning remarks of Pedro Carrasco Pizana, *Land and Polity in Tibet* (Seattle: University of Washington Press, 1959), 207–208.

30. As M. C. Goldstein rightly remarks, "although it was possible for the ruler to ennoble commoners . . . , such events were extremely rare"; Melvyn C. Goldstein, "Serfdom and Mobility: An Examination of the Institution of 'Human Lease' in Traditional Tibetan Society," *Journal of Asian Studies* 30, no. 3 (1971): 523.

31. However, some of its new members, such as Tsha rong and Spo mda' tshang, grew very rich; and increasing contact with India after about 1934 tended to increase also the successful trading ventures of several noble families (Hugh Richardson, in personal communication).

32. Pedro Carrasco Pizana, *Land and Polity in Tibet* (Seattle: University of Washington Press, 1959); Goldstein, "Taxation and the Structure of a Tibetan Village," 1–27; Goldstein, "The Institution of 'Human Lease' in Traditional Tibetan Society," 521–534.

33. Tibetan text published in Petech, *Aristocracy and Government in Tibet: 1728–1959*, 240–249.

34. Prince Peter of Greece, *The Aristocracy of Central Tibet: A Provisional List of the Names of the Noble Houses of U-Tsang* (Kalimpong: Tharchin, 1954).

ECONOMY AND TRADE

Chapter 26

GOLD, WOOL, AND MUSK

TRADE IN LHASA IN THE SEVENTEENTH CENTURY

Luce Boulnois

Lucette Boulnois was one of the most important scholars of Tibetan economic history. Her 1983 *Poudre d'or et monnaies d'argent au Tibet (principalement au 18ème siècle)* [*Gold Dust and Silver Coins of Tibet (Mainly in the 18th Century)*] is one of the
earliest, still among the most important, and unfortunately one of the least cited monographs on the subject. She examined Western-, Nepalese-, and Chinese-language
sources to paint a picture of the importance of precious metals to Tibet's economy as
well as its engagement with the rest of Asia. This article describes the previous (seventeenth) century and demonstrates, against the usual image of Tibet, that trade and
commerce were supported by the Tibetan government, included the active participation of monks, and were quite international in scope, with nearly one hundred commercial firms in Lhasa. The rulers of the Kathmandu Valley were to play a key role in
the Tibetan economy, in the process invading Tibet five times over two centuries. She
also shows that the rise of the Gelukpa establishment was linked to and benefited
from the stability that came with Mongol and later Manchu involvement in Central
Tibet. Finally, she places the Tibetan economy in the context of international trade,
with which it was intimately linked.

Lhasa, city of golden temples and prostrating pilgrims, "Lassa or Barantola,
Residence of the Great Lama" as the maps of the time show, was not only a holy
city and a political capital; it was also a great center for commercial trade which
focused on it dreams that were material as well as secular.

Tibet already had the reputation of being a country of commerce and merchants, where the government favored trade, where every traveler or pilgrim brought something to sell, where everyone had the right to buy and sell without either shop or license (everyone except, in principle, the monks, but this rule could be circumvented).

Trade—the country was, in any case, unable to do without it; the lack of certain commodities required it. Internal trade between farmers and nomadic stockbreeders, external trade with neighboring countries, was a necessity. Tibet had, still has, unbalanced economic resources: it lacked commodities of prime necessity, foodstuffs, products of the textile and metallurgical industries; it had, on the other hand, in abundance and beyond its own needs, products desired abroad. Some of them fed a major and far-reaching commercial trade, an important source of enrichment; the commodities of primary necessity were the object of trade of survival and proximity.

These different types of trade existed for centuries. Contrary to our current notion of a country closed, forbidden, isolated, and therefore mysterious, Tibet, in the seventeenth century and especially in the second half of the century, offers the image of a country open to foreign merchants and missionaries. At least this is what can be deduced from the contemporary Indian, Nepalese, Chinese, Armenian and Western accounts that have come down to us, testifying to the vitality of trade and the diversity of travelers who reached Lhasa at that time.

WITH GREAT RISK AND DIFFICULTY: GOD SAVE THE TRAVELER!

Communications were difficult, however, in the first place because of geographical obstacles: the cold, snow and altitude of this fortress-plateau surrounded by the highest mountains in the world—the Himalayas, Kunlun, Hengduan, where even the passes lie at more than 5,000 meters—a plateau blocked in its interior by other mountain ranges; salt marshes to the north-west, considerable distances to travel, vast regions almost uninhabited or infested by bandits, deserts without pasture. Added to this, for those who came from overseas, were the risks of storms, pirates, dead calm, deadly reefs and other perils of the sea, before reaching the terra firma of India. From all these voyages, on both land and sea, one did not always return; besides murder, drowning and other violent deaths, exhaustion and disease overcame many travelers, merchants or missionaries, pilgrims or sailors. Further on, we will see the risks to profits and of material losses, plundered caravans, goods lost or seized, travel costs and delays en route.

THE POLITICAL CONDITIONS OF TRADE

The free flow of commercial movements depended however on the political situation, a factor more powerful than snow and bandits. During the seventeenth

century, the political situation was often troubled in Tibet; a long period of politico-religious conflict mirrors the struggle for ascendancy between different
groups, religious orders, monasteries, princely families: Gelukpa against Karma
Kagyüpa, the "kingdom" of Ü (Lhasa) against the "kingdom" of Tsang (Zhigatsé).
And especially, the turbulence that shook the Mongol world affected the political
and religious situation of Tibet (or rather, before 1642, of the different Tibets),
through the game of alliances and wars involving eastern and western Mongols,
Manchus in rampant expansion—Ming China until 1644, then Manchu China
(Qing). One can imagine that in periods of open war, commercial trade was
sometimes interrupted, diverted or limited; but to recover immediately, or link
up in another way. On the other hand, external trade was also conditioned by the
evolution of Mogul India and the establishment in India of Western maritime
and mercantile powers: after the decline of the Portuguese, the seventeenth century saw the rapid expansion of the Dutch and the British.

The trade of survival—which included various types of barter, such as grain
for salt, salt for tea, tea for butter—was widely prevalent inside the country.
Moreover, a system of trading grain for salt seems to have existed for centuries on
the borders of the Tibetan plateau and the Himalayan valleys of India, Nepal,
Bhutan, all along the Himalayas. This system, which could still be observed in
the 1960s, is based on the lack of salt within the land-locked Himalayan populations. On the other hand, the high Tibetan plateau is rich in deposits—especially
lake deposits—of food salt. As for the Tibetans, they lack grain, fruits and vegeta-
bles. This system of barter supported a precarious regional economy and brought
about a circulation of goods almost independent, locally, of the great political
disturbances of the kingdoms, even though part of the grain likely contributed
to feeding Lhasa. The great import-export trade between nations is a completely
different story.

The importance of trade with Tibet for all the surrounding countries is reflected in the military episodes, international treaties and rivalries between
kingdoms, to take over the trade routes to Lhasa, to obtain certain privileges
and monopolies, one country supplanting another. An apparently dull form of
war, but war all the same, and sometimes open war, large-scale trade is the field
of action for the great predators.

In Asia, the sixteenth century had been the century of the Portuguese, of the
transfer through their hands, by way of Indian and Indonesian ports, of a good
part of the wealth in spices, gold, indigo, cotton fabrics and silks; of a slide towards the Indian ports of the commercial overland flow across Asia, somewhat
devitalizing the routes that were called (later) the "Silk Route." But from the
beginning of the seventeenth century Portuguese power began to decline. Other
predators were arriving: the Netherlands and England. The "East Indies Companies," trading companies with shareholders and monopolies, supported by
their governments, are successively created: in 1601 the British East India Company, in 1602 the Dutch V. O. C. (Vereenigde Oost-Indische Compagnie); the
French Compagnie des Indes only in 1664. Little by little, with difficulty but

effectively, the Dutch and British forced the Portuguese from all their strong-holds in India and Indonesia (Goa essentially remained theirs) and set them-selves up triumphantly in the mercantile channels; they all had their "factories" in the great cities and ports, particularly in Surat, on the west coast of India, in Gujarat, then a Mogul province. Surat, which was until the end of the seventeenth century the principal port in India, "the source and life of all the trade of the East Indies" according to one traveler of the time; Surat, where Gujarati, Mogul, Persian, Arab, Armenian, Jewish, central Asian Turkic, British and Dutch and, later and briefly, French, merchants all flocked. The products of all the West, the Middle East, Indonesia, China and all of India were traded there. The products ending up in Tibet or coming from there passed through Surat.

Trade with the West was a source of enrichment for the Mogul Empire. And the Moguls lent a hand to the process. This set of circumstances constituted new breath: it is not by chance that this same period saw trans-Himalayan trade with Tibet expand, a currency appear in Tibet, and Lhasa filled with foreign merchants.

THE APPEARANCE OF CURRENCY IN TIBET

Towards the end of the sixteenth century, central Tibet, which until then had not used metal coins and would have known, it is said, only barter in kind, began to make use of silver coinage. This currency was not made in Tibet by the Tibet-ans but, curiously enough, came to them from the south, from Nepal: in a way, they bought their currency, not being able, for religious reasons, it is said, to make it themselves.

In Nepal, the Newar kings of the Malla dynasty who reigned over the Kath-mandu Valley had themselves begun making silver currency only after 1565; until then they had contented themselves with copper coins. This monetary evolution, realized after agreement with the Mogul emperor, marks at the same time an economic boom and an intensification of trade in these regions.

Subsequently, King Mahendra Malla who had struck the first silver coinage, or one of his successors, concluded with the government of Lhasa an agreement according to which Tibet would henceforth be supplied with silver coinage by the king of Kathmandu, according to the following device: with silver ingots provided by the Tibetans, the Kathmandu mint would make half-rupee coins; these coins (very similar to the half-rupees made for Nepal) would then be re-turned to Tibet, the Nepalese taking, in the process, a profit obtained in part in replacing a small proportion of the silver in the coins by the same weight of copper. This strange contract ended in 1792, following the serious problems in the eighteenth century, but functioned perfectly well, it seems, during the sec-ond half of the seventeenth century.

These coins were used in central Tibet: Lhasa, Zhigatsé, Gyantsé, the richest districts, the most populated, the ones closest to southern influences. They were never used outside Tibet. Considering the value of silver at this time, the fact that there was no smaller denomination than this half-rupee coin (however, people broke these coins into pieces to obtain smaller denominations), it can be assumed that this silver currency was not suitable for small day-to-day expenditures by the population, which, undoubtedly—not having copper coins at their disposal either—still practiced barter in kind for small-value trade.

It seems that this contract had been imposed on the Tibetans; a number of factors enabled the Nepalese to put pressure on them: the desire the Tibetans might have had to profit from the increased development of trade with Mogul India, mutual need, Tibet's military weakness at the time in question. We will see further on how this device was, if not imposed, at least re-imposed and confirmed about 1643.

TRANS-HIMALAYAN TRADE:
THE NEPALESE ROUTE

Over the course of the seventeenth century, Tibet-Nepal trade was going to burgeon more than ever, benefiting from two politico-economic circumstances: first, from 1642—when the Fifth Dalai Lama was established in Lhasa as political and religious sovereign of a large, more or less unified Tibetan state extending from Kham to the borders of Ladakh—the development of Lhasa as administrative, religious and commercial capital, giving rise to the influx of aristocratic families, the concentration of craftsmen and artists for the construction of religious and civil buildings, the appearance, all in all, of a richer clientele; second, a period of prosperity for the Mogul empire and active trade with countries overseas. This commercial boom, which drew the flow of goods in towards the big Mogul cities, was to make the fortune of, among others, the Malla kingdoms of the Kathmandu Valley in the role of forwarding agents where they succeeded in imposing themselves between Tibet and its southern trading partners: India and the West.

This trade to the south had as centers, in Tibet, mainly Lhasa and Zhigatsé. Via the double Nepalese route Kuti–Kathmandu and Kyirong–Kathmandu, crossing the Himalayan range fairly easily, goods coming from central Tibet were sent in large part to Patna, in Mogul India. The Nepalese route was the most convenient, the least difficult, the most sure. Infinitely more difficult was the route between Lhasa and Kashmir via the western Tibetan plateau; moreover, Ladakh, worried about Mogul policies, closed its borders from about 1643 to 1664, which contributed even more to the diverting of the flow of trade to the Nepalese route; as for the journey via Bhutan, it would have been shorter and fairly practical if it had not been closed politically. Therefore, large-scale trade, for these reasons, already preferred the Nepalese route.

Between Tibet and Nepal, religious, political and economic relations are ancient. From the seventh century A.D. at least, when the major routes to central Tibet by way of Kuti and Kyirong were frequented by merchants, pilgrims and Buddhist missionaries. Commercial relations flourished with the setting up of Newar shopkeepers and craftsmen in Lhasa and Zhigatsé. Ambiguous relations, dictated by geography, embellished by religion and threatened by conflicts of vested interests, imposed by force, periodically exploding into wars and invasions, but always resumed.

Since 1967, a year-round (at least theoretically) road suitable for motor vehicles, built by Chinese engineers, allows travel from Kathmandu to Lhasa in twenty-nine hours by bus, spread over three or four days. Before that, the route unfolded to the rhythm of pack animals and human feet. For example, Ippolito Desideri left Lhasa on 28 April 1721 and arrived in Kuti, then a border town, on 30 May: that is to say, a month on the road. Not wanting to face the Nepalese hot season, he stayed in Kuti for six and a half months; setting off again on 14 December, he passed Nesti (the old frontier) two or three days later and arrived in the Kathmandu Valley on 27 December: thirteen days plus thirty-two days, that is to say, forty-five days, if one did not stop, between Lhasa and Kathmandu. Two other missionaries, Johannes Grueber and Albert d'Orville, who made the same trip in 1662, state: four days from Lhasa to the foot of the first range, plus one month up to Kuti, plus five days from Kuti to Nesti, plus five days from Nesti to Kathmandu; total: forty-four days without stopping. These times represented a moderate pace, with horses in Tibet, on foot in Nepal. Heavily loaded trade caravans, those that used yaks for pack animals, could be slower. One could, moreover, be forced to stop here or there for a few days. It was necessary as well to take the seasons into account: one did not travel willingly in either the height of the monsoon in Nepal, or the depths of winter over the Himalayan passes. Further south, for the crossing of the plains, through forests infested with malaria, one would definitely avoid the summer. But in spite of all these obstacles, this route via Nepal remained the favorite of merchants and travelers.

At that time, to go from Kathmandu to the big trade centers of India, merchants had to cross a zone of moderately high mountains, then a low range, then the Terai—plains dangerous because of malaria; one then entered, via Gorrochepur (Gorakhpur) among others, Mogul territory; one ended up in Patna, whose wealth and commercial importance are described by many travelers; from there goods left again for Bengal, or Agra, Multan, Lahore, Kabul, or the ports of India's western coast, and particularly Surat. Kabul was the emporium for the land routes to Balkh, "Great Tartary" and, in short, all of central Asia, as well as Kandahar and Isfahan.

The crossing of Nepal was made in great part using human porterage: the image still familiar today of the porter with his big basket—though the porter is sometimes a woman. In the southern plain one entered the Indian domain of the bullock cart. Bullock cart all the way to Surat; boats on the Ganges between Patna and Bengal, mules, horses, camels and carts to Kabul. But between the southern Nepalese Terai and Patna, it was necessary as well—like Desideri in his unhappy experience in 1722—to face forests haunted by tigers, the rapaciousness of extortionate local Mogul authorities, the peril of highwaymen, before reaching the safety of the big merchant city.

One of the reasons for the dominance of the Nepalese route is that the Newar kings of the Malla dynasty that ruled the whole of the Kathmandu Valley, mainly the kings of Kathmandu—despite the attempts of the neighboring Gurkha kingdom to take their place—succeeded in imposing themselves as exclusive middlemen between Lhasa and northern India on the two main routes, Kyirong–Kathmandu and Kuti–Kathmandu. For this, they resorted to the army and invasion—first, about 1630, and a second time about 1645–1650—and achieved their ends; that is to say, a treaty which conclusively established their privileges and monopolies. By the terms of this treaty, Newar merchants were authorized to set up thirty-two firms in Lhasa; a representative of the king of Kathmandu would be accredited in Lhasa to ensure the protection of their interests; Newar merchants engaged in trade with Tibet would be exempted from all taxes and customs duties; if they died in Tibet, their possessions would go back to Nepal and not to the Tibetan government; all trade from Tibet to India, even that conducted by non-Newar merchants, would be routed through the Kathmandu Valley and by no other route (such as Sikkim or Bhutan). The governments of the Dalai Lama and the Malla kings would jointly control the fortified towns of Kyirong and Kuti, which meant command of the two Lhasa–Kathmandu routes. Furthermore, Tibet would pay Nepal a symbolic amount in gold and silver, and finally, a major clause: Nepal would act as Tibet's mint; Nepal would supply Tibet with silver coins and for that would use silver ingots provided by Tibet or would purchase silver with gold provided by Tibet. This monetary clause is perhaps only the reaffirmation at this point of a situation already in existence. What is certain is that from 1645, the Malla kings and the Newar merchants occupy a position of monopoly and have a stranglehold on Tibet–Nepal–India trade which they will hold on to for more than a century, and beyond the fall of the Malla kings. This situation seems to have been accepted by the Tibetans, who probably also found advantage in it.

But what, then, were these products so precious that, despite great difficulty and danger, made merchants come from the snowbound heart of Asia or from beyond the oceans?

PRODUCTS EXPORTED BY TIBET

In the seventeenth century Tibet was world famous for the following products: musk, gold, medicinal plants, yak tails, "shawl" wool, and a few other articles. All these rare and precious products are fully described in the accounts of merchants and missionaries, among the geographers and historians, in dictionaries and trade handbooks of the time, especially for the second half of the century.

Of these precious materials, surely the most famous, in the West, is musk. We know that this substance, used in medicine and making perfume in Europe and Asia (in Europe, today, medical usage has disappeared and its use in perfume-making is extremely reduced), is produced by a small quadruped resembling a fawn, the musk deer, whose scientific name is *Moschus moschiferus*. It haunts the wooded mountains of eastern Asia: the Himalayas, Tibet, Tonkin, Altai, Korea, Manchuria, Siberia. It has always been hunted for the profit to be derived from its musk pouch, a small outgrowth that only the males have, situated under the stomach, associated with the animal's sexual activity. This small pouch, which weighs from twenty to thirty grams, is lined inside with glands that secrete a thick, oily, brown-red colored substance, giving off a very powerful odor: pure musk. The value of musk varies according to its region of origin, that from Siberia and Korea being less than that of the Himalayas. In the seventeenth century, the most sought after on the international market are the musks of Tibet and Tonkin, especially because of their greater purity, guaranteed by government controls; musk was often adulterated in various ways by dishonest vendors. The animal has been hunted for so many centuries that it is now protected as a species at risk of extinction; but at the time we are focused on, it seems that it was abundant.

European perfume-makers and doctors of the time used at least as much musk as their colleagues in Persia, China or the Indies; this is attested to by therapy treatises from that period. The uses of musk varied according to the medical systems in various countries, but they included use as a heart tonic, antispasmodic, and treatment for snake venom, to help in childbirth and to soothe small children, and for a great number of the most varied ailments. The French merchant Jean-Baptiste Tavernier, who lived in India between 1638 and 1668, purchased in one particular year, at one time, 7,673 pouches, plus 452 ounces in bulk—that is to say, a total of more than 92 kilograms—from Tibetan merchants in the city of Patna, which seems to have been at the time, along with Kabul, one of the big markets for Asian musk. For this purchase he paid the equivalent of 14,357 French *livres*, or francs, of his time; but he writes that rather than being paid in gold or silver coin, the vendors much preferred to exchange the musk for coral and amber.

According to Tavernier, in order to maintain Tibet's trade reputation, the "king" instituted an inspection of merchandise: musk pouches had to be presented open for inspection in Lhasa, so that the contents could be verified, because people often adulterated this substance, mixing in blood from the animal or its mashed flesh, or adding lead to increase the weight; after the inspection, the Tibetan government inspector sealed the pouches and they left for Nepal,

India, the rest of the world, and also, of course, to Xining, of which we will speak further on.

From Patna, the musk could continue its way to Delhi, Agra, Surat; from there, putting out to sea bound for a port on the Persian Gulf or the Red Sea, or directly to Europe by going around Africa; from the Red Sea, to the ports of Arabia and Alexandria. And from Kabul, via the overland routes, the musk was routed towards central Asia, to Kandahar, Isfahan, Tauris and the Mediterranean shores of the Middle East.

Tibet's longest standing reputation in the economic sphere, apart from musk, was as a producer of gold. This reputation goes back, unbroken, to earliest antiquity, without doubt as far back as the time of Herodotus who, in the fifth century B.C., handed down to us a tradition of "ant's gold" which still amuses and intrigues many researchers. Today, what is considered to be the most probable hypothesis for this is that specks of gold were to be found in the ground—in which an infinite number of marmots made their burrows—in then uninhabited regions located in present-day Ladakh. In throwing out the earth as they burrowed, these marmots brought to light particles of gold, which neighboring populations came to gather up. It was paid in tribute to the king of Persia.

Tibet's gold-bearing reputation, in general, continued from century to century. It is, moreover, well-founded; but the importance of the production, and even more that of reserves, have undoubtedly been continually exaggerated. It is, nevertheless, a fact that for two thousand years and more, Tibet continually produced gold dust from successive sites. If, in the seventeenth century, stories of nuggets as big as a sheep's liver and mountains peppered with gold, were already nothing more than legend, gold-washing and the working of shallow mines supplied the state treasury in the form of taxes, the growth of monastic wealth in the form of offerings, the growth of private wealth, the decoration and architecture of palaces and temples, and external trade. This was where Nepal obtained the gold that the Newar goldsmiths and statue makers used. It was not minted into coins, but left as Tibetan gold dust, held in small leather sacks containing a half-*tola* (about 5.8 grams) called "*sarshu*," which were easily transported: gold was accepted everywhere.

From time to time (even today!) one sees the reappearance of some fantastic rumor attributing fabulous gold mines to Tibet: in the same way the two Jesuit missionaries who crossed Tibet and Nepal in 1662, Grueber and d'Orville, related (in *China Illustrata*, by Athanasius Kircher) that in the region of the town of Changur, capital of a kingdom occupying north-east Tibet, situated fifteen days' travel from Lhasa, between Lhasa and Kokonor, were "fourteen gold mines, the quantity of which supplied all of India." According to a personal communication from Ren Xinjian (Institute of History, Sichuan Academy of Social Sciences), the town of Changur is Dengke in the county of Dergé. Dengke is situated on the left (eastern) bank of the Yangzi River, in the province of Sichuan, about 98° E and 32° 30' N. There certainly was gold in this area, but not so much as to supply all of India!

What could seriously attract foreign merchants, then, was not so much the quantities of gold that Tibet could supply, but the price at which it could supply it. Now, it seems that Tibetan gold was very cheap, on the spot, compared to what a non-producing country could buy from the Spanish, the Portuguese, in Africa and in India. The price ratio between gold and silver at the end of the century was of the order of 1 to 14, or 1 to 15 in the West (1 gram of gold being worth 14 to 15 grams of silver), 1 to 10 in China, and in Tibet it could go down to 1 to 10, 1 to 9 and even lower. There was, therefore, a good, attractive market there. Furthermore, unlike many countries, Tibet did not hinder the export of gold produced on its territory. The passage of gold through Nepal was the monopoly by the Malla kings. However, we know that Tibet also exported gold to Ladakh, and to Xining for the Chinese market, and that Armenian merchants purchased it in Lhasa and Xining to take back to India.

At the beginning of the eighteenth century, the "gold-bearing" rumor of Tibet reached the ears of Peter the Great, who dreamed of seizing "the Dalai Lama's gold." He did not have time to carry out his plan. There is, however, an edict from him from which it emerges that he had conceived a plan to send to Lhasa, on the pretense of engaging in trade, informants expert in mining. It was perhaps these "Muscovites," supposed merchants, that Ippolito Desideri reported in Lhasa during his stay in the city from 1716 to 1721. But it is not known for how long they were there.

Another category of export from Tibet in the seventeenth century, was (and still is) medicinal plants and other materia medica. At that time, it was not a question, like today, of fritillary, *Cordyceps sinensis* or snow lotus, but rhubarb, worm-seed (*Artemisia, maritima*), mamiron, zedoary, peonies and medicinal mallows. Everyone knows medicinal rhubarb, which was consumed in large quantities in Europe; the most highly rated varieties were those from Tibet and Tartary; much of it passed through Patna and Kabul, marketed in the form of dried sections of roots and rhizomes; it was prescribed in Europe as a purgative, tonic agent, digestive and astringent; in Nepal, for snake bite and stomach trouble. From Tibet came, as well, worm-seed, an artemisia, a known anti-helminth remedy, also used, according to Tavernier, by the Persians, the British and the Dutch, in place of anise, in their sweets. An export from the southern Himalayan regions of Tibet, more especially around Dzongkha and Kirong, was zedoary, a word that seems to cover several non-poisonous aconites such as *Aconitum heterophyllum*, prescribed for snake bite, various digestive problems, the "fevers," and as a tonic and antidote. *Mamiron*, which was used as a treatment for eye diseases, was also derived from a Tibetan plant. Medicinal animal products also made up part of Tibetan exports (they are still used in Chinese medicine): besides musk, already mentioned, leopard bone, bear bile, bezoars (internal concretions) from cows, newly grown stag horn, boiled and dried scorpion, all products that were plentiful in Kham at that time.

The trading of furs was much more important than today: there was little heating and for months travelers were exposed to severe temperatures. Tibet was abundant in martens; the snow leopard was not yet scarce; the fox and the wolf were abundant. In spite of the brake that Buddhism represents, Tibetans and Mongols of this period hunted a lot—with less skill than the Russians, claims Tavernier.

Among the oldest of Tibet's export products, yak tails must also be mentioned, marketed across India under the name of *"chowry"* (Skr. *chamara*): superb white and black plumes, the strands of which can reach two meters in length. These tails served as fly swatters, but were also symbols of power, decorating standards or staffs of command in the Turkish, Indian and Chinese worlds. Later, there will be industrial uses for yak tails. There should be no mistake: this was not a gimmick, it was an item of export found on trading lists, from antiquity, all through the centuries.

So far we have listed the rare, precious or curious products that most attracted the attention of foreigners; more common, but perhaps equally profitable (we lack the figures) were the basic products of the Tibetan economy: those of its flocks and herds. Sheep, goats, yaks, hybrids of yak and cow, horses, mules, asses, camels (the latter in the north), a few pigs here and there, totaled millions of head. Further along we will touch on the products of the "shawl" goat, exported particularly to the West, and horses, exported to China. It seems that at that time Tibet exported a heavy yak-hair serge, raw sheep's wool and woolen cloth. The accounts at our disposal do not mention a massive export of raw sheep's wool as will be seen later, in the nineteenth and twentieth centuries (today's sheep breeds provide, in particular, carpet and blanket wool). On the other hand, they report products that seem to have disappeared from the country: a gray felt known as "silver and iron," fine woolen cloth and "a very beautiful woolen cloth that resembles silk," made in Tsetang in central Tibet. There seems to have been at that time a high-quality textile craft industry. Tibetan carpets are already mentioned as well.

That Tibet could have been a producer of silk is something that seems curious to us today; and yet, two witnesses present in Lhasa in 1720—an Italian missionary and a Chinese officer—each separately testify that Tibet was selling silkworm cocoons and Tibetan silk (the Chinese princess who was given in marriage to a king of Tibet in the seventh century, is she not supposed to have introduced sericulture to Tibet?). Desideri also mentions a wild silk, a "tree silk" produced on the borders of Bhutan and sold throughout the whole of Tibet. There is nothing surprising in that: Assam, which is not far from there, also produced a well-known wild silk.

One does not often see the production of borax mentioned. Borax or sodium borate, abundant in Tibetan lakes, was used in the past for metal soldering, and was an important object of trade in the nineteenth century. On the other hand, one finds articles mentioned for the seventeenth century that seem to have disappeared from Tibetan soil: iron from the region of Kuti, paper from Dakpo, lapis lazuli from Lhorong Dzong, turquoise from Chaya (Tibet was a modest producer and a big user and importer of turquoise); rock crystal from the Yarlung region seems to have lost its importance, although tourists see small pieces of it offered for sale. Also mentioned as products at the end of the seventeenth century are an incense paste made of various vegetable substances, used for religious fumigation, and bowls of veined wood, very much sought after.

TRANS-HIMALAYAN IMPORTS

But what did Tibet import from the south, in exchange for all the precious products—gold, musk—that went out?

Tibetans obtained food products from among their neighbors: grain from border trade; more grain from the Kathmandu Valley—at that time called the Nepal Valley—as well as sugar, chilies and various vegetable produce. They also imported food products from China, particularly tea. Having no factories for the production of metal goods, they also imported small agricultural implements, weapons (swords and knives, bullets, gun hammers), padlocks and locks; also mentioned are, at least for the very end of the seventeenth century, glass bottles, small mirrors, silk and cotton fabric, pieces of copper and copper objects, dying products like "manjit" or madder, which dyes red, odoriferous products for making incense, Kashmiri saffron. No less essential than the foodstuffs, the coins used in Tibet were, as we have seen, imported from Nepal.

Imports reported with the most insistence by Western merchants (no doubt because they concerned them more) are those of precious materials: Tibet was a buyer of amber, coral, turquoise, conches, pearls and precious and semi-precious stones, as well as articles made of gold and silver.

We know the importance of coral, turquoise and amber in the Tibetan civilization: necklaces, earrings and reliquaries are inlaid with coral and turquoise, and decorated with large amber beads; wealthy and highly placed people, lay and religious, have rosaries of coral, amber, pearls, rock crystal and lapis lazuli. Amber, coral and turquoise are almost part of everyone's wardrobe, and statues in temples are profusely adorned with them.

All or nearly all the coral imported by the Tibetans came from the shores of the Mediterranean. In the seventeenth century, red coral, or pink, used in jewelry, was gathered mainly in nine Mediterranean fishing zones situated on the coasts of Sardinia, Corsica, Sicily, Catalonia and Majorca and on the Barbary Coast of Algeria and Tunisia. The coral was marketed most often in the form of grains or beads, polished in the workshops of Marseilles or Italy. They were made into necklaces, bracelets and rosaries. The largest pieces, which went to sculptors, became cameos, large brooches and statuettes. For the Eastern market, unpolished pieces were also shipped so that foreign artists could work them in their own way. It was customary in the West to set aside fine intact branches, which were rare, and give them as they were to kings and churches. This custom crossed the seas, since Desideri, in 1720, notes that the Tibetans, to whom blood sacrifices were repugnant, offered to their lamas and to their "idols," on the altars, such things as lamps, Chinese silks, gold and silver, perfumes to burn, or "branches of coral and other curiosities."

The crates of coral passed through Alexandria, the ports of the Red Sea and Persian Gulf, Surat; from the coasts of the Mediterranean, they traveled to Persia—Isfahan, whence Armenian merchants took them to Kabul, Balkh, Agra, Patna, Leh, Lhasa, Xining. Why such infatuation, so lasting, so universal, for coral? The beauty, the color, the virtues attributed to it of protection against evil forces, demons, bad luck. It is, no doubt, about the first century A.D. that coral, via the routes and the flow of trade that developed then, found a place among the precious materials particularly prized in Buddhism.

Amber, as well, was (and still is) very much in demand in Tibet. It was extracted in Burma and China; but even more sought after was European amber, produced since antiquity in one sole coastal region of eastern Prussia, on the shores of the Baltic. Armenian merchants went to Danzig (Gdansk) for their supply to take back to Asia; they even took an order for the "king of Tibet." According to Tavernier, four Armenians, after a trip to Tibet, went to Danzig "to have a quantity of yellow amber figures made, which represented all sorts of animals and monsters, that they were going to take to the King of Bhutan . . ." (Bhutan is one of the names by which Westerners referred to, at that time, not the Bhutan of today, but central Tibet). To their great regret, they were unable to find a large enough piece to fill one of the orders of the "king of Tibet": "a figurine in the form of a monster, which has six horns, four ears, four arms with six fingers on each hand." Tavernier is Christian, and Huguenot: his description of the "monster" reflects this; he deplores this lure of gain because "it is a vile business to supply instruments of idolatry to this poor people." For him, these Armenians too easily come to terms with religion.

Amber sold then in Patna from 250 to 300 rupees for a good piece of nine French ounces (about 275 grams), while the same weight in small unpolished, unworked pieces went for only 35 to 40 rupees.

Tibet also imported conches—Buddhist symbol and musical instrument in the temples—gathered on the shores of India; as well, pearls from the Persian Gulf, turquoise from Persia, precious stones from India.

TIBET–LADAKH TRADE

The western Tibetan plateau is the habitat of a goat which, in this terribly cold climate, produces a downy under-coat that can be removed by carding, spun and made into an extraordinarily warm wool, fine and light. It has been known for centuries in the world by the name of "cashmere," because it is mainly through the Kashmiri weavers and their famous shawls that it is widely known, originally, in Europe.

This wool was exported raw to Ladakh, whose capital, Leh, was a crossroads for caravans between Tibet, Kashmir and Yarkand; worried about Mogul designs, the king of Ladakh closed its borders in 1643, but in 1664 he fell subject to the Mogul empire. Then, after a politico-religious war with central Tibet, he was definitively forced, in 1684, by his Indian overlord and his Tibetan conqueror, to submit to a system that regulated the exploitation of "shawl" wool in favor of Kashmir: first, the province of Ngari, the western part of the Tibetan plateau, a big producer of this wool, became, definitively, a province under the authority of central Tibet, and its revenue would go to Lhasa; all the "shawl" wool would be sold to a single intermediary—the government of Ladakh. Ladakh could keep for itself only the production from the Rutok district, which its royal agents would come to get; all the rest would be resold exclusively, by perpetual monopoly, to Kashmir, through the intermediation of four authorized merchants. It is, in fact, for a long time, Kashmir which derived profit from this wonderful wool; it supplied the industry that made the famous shawls, put weavers, dyers and embroiderers to work, constituted a major component of the Kashmiri economy and filled Europe, Russia and northern India with these marvelous products. Here again, Tibet was selling its products raw, and others were growing rich; the same is true for the Ladakhis. Lack of labor force or know-how? Lack of interest? Or constraint?

The treaty of 1684 between Ladakh and Lhasa concerned not only wool but also a product which had become essential—tea. It came from China—then the sole producer—from Sichuan, on the other horizon of Tibet, by way of a route that passed through Lhasa. Any obstacle to the arrival of the caravans hit the Ladakhis at the heart of their way of life. The 1684 treaty stated that tea would continue to be supplied to Ladakh by Tibetan caravans, at the rate of 200 loads per year. If this meant yak-loads, from 90 to 100 kilograms, this represented 18 to 20 metric tons of tea.

Another clause established the regular dispatching every two years of a caravan departing Leh and carrying to Lhasa the "tribute" from the kingdom of Ladakh; and on return to Leh, the caravan brought tea. This tribute caravan, called the lapchak caravan, existed for almost three centuries.

It is understood that the crossing of Tibet from the west was not the route preferred by merchants. The trip from Leh to Lhasa, via Gartok, past Mount Kailash and over the Mayum pass, meant, first of all, three months in wild, almost uninhabited, very cold regions, up to Lhatsé; then three or four more weeks to Lhasa. Desideri reckons 168 days of travel for a trip which in fact, because of a necessary halt, lasted from 17 August 1715 to 18 March 1716. For the first three

months of the journey, it was necessary to carry all of one's own food—tea, butter, barley flour, dried meat for the men, grain, flour or peas for the horses—
because there was nothing to eat. In addition, there was, like everywhere in Tibet
and especially in all regions that were little inhabited, great risk of bandits. This
is why it was not customary to travel alone: one organized a strong, well armed
caravan, or joined a large caravan, merchant or official, and placed oneself under its protection.

From Lhasa, crossroads of routes to the Himalayas, south and west, there
radiated two more major "routes," whatever concrete sense one gives to this
word, two classic routes to Mongolia and especially China: the Xining route
and the Sichuan route.

THE XINING ROUTE

Xining, the Chinese city at the gates of the empire, was the emporium for trade
between Tibet, China and the Mongol kingdoms; the ties between the latter
and the Dalai Lama were, we know, close in the seventeenth century—political
and religious ties. It was also through Xining that one passed to go from Lhasa
to Beijing and Jehol (Chengde), the two residences of the Qing emperors, after
1644. A route of merchants, ambassadors, taken by princes and Dalai Lamas,
the Xining–Lhasa route seems to have played, then, a role as important as that
of Lhasa–Kathmandu.

Today the trip is made in five days by car. Until 1955, it was a journey of three
to four and a half months, on horseback for the men, on the backs of camels and
yaks for the goods (camels only between Xining and Nakchu). It was, by the old
route, a little more than 2,100 kilometers and it was necessary to cross a desolate
windy plateau and the Tangla pass at 5,200 meters. But there again, what was
feared most, were the bandits, up to Nakchu. For the rest, the journey was less
hard than in Ngari.

What did one buy, what did one sell in Xining? The Tibetan products already mentioned: gold, musk, furs, woolen cloth, wool, stag horns, medicinal
plants, leathers and skins; products coming from overseas via Nepal and Lhasa,
like coral and amber, conches, gems. Chinese products: tea, silks, porcelains,
which China exported everywhere in the world; agricultural implements, domestic tools and utensils, food products, cloth, paper; and a lot of silver in ingots, which Tibet bought to supply its mint, silver that was going, in part, to take
the road to Kathmandu to return to Tibet in the form of half-rupee coins, and
that, for the other part, was going to be worked for lay and religious jewelry and
ornamentation.

Xining was also an important market for livestock (cattle, horses, sheep, yaks,
camels and so on), the horses being bred by the Mongols—among others, by

those of the "Banners" of Kokonor. The military requirement for horses was always the determinant factor in Chinese relations with its nomad neighbors, breeders of horses. Already, for centuries, a system of trading horses for tea, closely controlled by the Chinese state, ensured, through its inspection offices in Xining and other locations, these indispensable acquisitions. Although this trade took place on the borders, it nevertheless concerned Lhasa because it was there that a good part of the tea ended up. After a troubled period around the end of the Ming dynasty, in the 1630s and 1640s, trade resumed under the Qing dynasty. The exchange ratio, under the latter dynasty, ranged from 36 to 72 kilograms of tea for one horse, depending on the quality of the latter. The tea came mainly from Sichuan. From the second half of the seventeenth century, it undoubtedly also followed the "Sichuan route" to reach Lhasa, via Dajianlu (Dartsedo/Kangding) and Kham.

THE SICHUAN ROUTE

In fact, it was probably only after the middle of the seventeenth century, after a part of Kham passed into the control of the Lhasa government, that this Sichuan "route" acquired the commercial importance for which. it was known in the nineteenth and twentieth centuries, when it was the tea route, and Dajianlu, now Kangding, was for the Chinese the door to Tibet and the big tea port for the Tibetans. Similarly, its military importance also dates only from the beginning of the eighteenth century.

This route presents the disadvantage of very difficult terrain (the modern route, built in 1955–56, crosses fourteen mountain ranges). The Lhasa–Dajianlu section went through Medrogongkar, Tramdo, Atsa, Lhari, Shopado, Lhorong Dzong, Chamdo, Batang and Litang, and represented 2,753 kilometers; it was then 498 kilometers from Dajianlu to Chengdu. Lhasa–Dajianlu was made in a minimum of eighty-four day-stages. Thus, the tea took about three months to arrive in Lhasa from China; part of it continued the journey to Leh, about four more months. Between the Chinese border and that of Ladakh, in the course of more than seven months of travel, the tea doubled in price many times.

At these speeds, it can be seen how, for a merchant who invested in a caravan of goods for distant buyers, a round trip, and consequently the return of profit, could mean a lapse of time of two or three years. Apart from the time on the road, it was also necessary for the agent or merchant to take time to sell his merchandise and buy other goods; it was necessary, as well, to allow for forced halts for necessary rest, for climatic reasons, waiting for new pack animals whose delivery could take a long time, waiting for local government permits and waiting for the goodwill of customs officers.

Most certainly, journeys by sea were not quick either: Father Alexander of Rhodes, embarking at Lisbon on 4 April 1619, rounds the Cape of Good Hope on 20 July and arrives in Goa on 9 October; in the other direction, Ippolito Desideri, embarking at Pondicherry on 21 January 1727, will drop anchor at Port-Louis in Brittany only on 11 August. Such were the conditions of trade: those who went, went for a long time—a job for men who were young, hardy, little attached to their comfort, curious to see the world and without fear. There was no lack of them.

FOREIGN MERCHANTS IN LHASA

The second half of the seventeenth century is certainly the period in which Lhasa found within its walls the greatest variety of foreign merchants. While the Tibetans themselves ventured very little outside the boundaries of their country (one sees them in the countries bordering on Tibet but scarcely further than Patna or Leh or Xining, never in Surat, Isfahan or Bukhara, let alone on the shores of the Mediterranean), they had no objection to merchants from other countries setting themselves up in Tibet.

The longest established were the Newar of the Kathmandu valley. Buddhists like the Tibetans, often married to Tibetans, they formed several colonies of merchants, silversmiths and goldsmiths in Lhasa and in a few other Tibetan centers, from at least the thirteenth century. At the end of the sixteenth, they already benefited from a right of extraterritoriality, which was subsequently renewed several times.

Besides their activities as silversmiths and goldsmiths, casters of statues, sculptors of wood, whose works are still found in many Tibetan temples and monasteries, they set up commercial firms, whose descendants left Tibet only after 1950. We saw above that a treaty between the government of Kathmandu and that of the Dalai Lama, about 1645, reorganized the system in firmly ensuring for the Newar merchants a privileged situation in Lhasa, and in Nepal itself, the near monopoly of the transit trade between Tibet and India, as well as the very profitable monopoly of minting the silver coins used in Tibet.

It was also in the seventeenth century, under the government of the Fifth Dalai Lama, that Muslims settled in Tibet and received as a gift from the Tibetan government, in the vicinity of Lhasa, a park, called the "garden of the Khaché" ("Kashmiris' garden"), with the right to build a mosque and establish a cemetery there. Most of these Muslims were Kashmiri merchants; spread among Lhasa, Tsaparang, Zhigatsé and Gyantsé, they traded in all products; their role in trade between Tibet, Nepal, Kashmir, Ladakh and the rest of India, became more important; they had in their hands the "shawl" wool trade. In Lhasa they set up, at the end of the seventeenth or at the beginning of the following century, fifty-six commercial firms. It was Muslim caravaneers who were given the responsibility of running the lapchak caravan to Lhasa.

Originally, many of these Kashmiri Muslims had first been established in Ladakh at the end of the sixteenth century; from there their commercial interests (especially involved in "shawl" wool) were extended to Tibet. The closing of the kingdom of Ladakh between 1643 and 1664 pushed other Muslims to Nepal, and from Nepal to Tibet; still others, also of Kashmiri origin, had first emigrated to the plains of India and from there embarked upon business right up to Tibet.

For convenience and security, these merchant communities, Newar as well as Kashmiri, were organized with a head merchant, or several head merchants, representing them, protecting their rights, sorting out their disputes; in addition, the Newar had an official, representative of their king; the Kashmiris seem to have gained fewer privileges than the Newar.

Another category of Muslims who will make a place for themselves in Lhasa and Zhigatsé, perhaps not before the end of the seventeenth century, is that of the Chinese Muslims originally from Gansu. These merchants dealt in Chinese silks and pearls, perhaps freshwater pearls from Siberian lakes and rivers.

The Tibetan authorities seem to have willingly tolerated these foreigners, non-Buddhist but not proselytizing, and devoted to business. Contrariwise, phases of favor and disfavor alternated with regard to Christian missionaries, who appear from 1624, do not engage in business, but do try to convert.

Also reported in Lhasa, right at the beginning of the eighteenth century, are merchants from Bhutan, "Tartar" merchants, that is to say Mongols, and, subject to the observation made above, "Muscovite" merchants; finally, a category of merchants on which we are best informed: the Armenians.

The Armenians—they are everywhere in the seventeenth century: in Persia, India, Tibet, one finds them at all the major crossroads of trade and commerce. Many originally come from New Julfa (Iulfa, Zulfa), a suburb of Isfahan where, in 1605, the king of Persia, Shah Abbas, had forced the transfer of 1,200 Armenian families from Julfa on the Araxe in Armenia. These families established a merchant colony that sent its agents everywhere, from Europe to Tibet by way of Persia and India, and later, spread here and there through families and communities.

Originally, they were of course Christians. In Persia and in Mogul India, though theoretically having the right to remain so, they were subject to so much pressure, harassment and taxation, that some, to avoid this, became Muslims.

They were solidly established in the port of Surat; they had been, for a long time, in Agra, Patna, Madras, Hooghly—in Calcutta before Calcutta, as it were. They took sides, later, with the British, and played a big role in the setting up of the East India Company in Calcutta in fact and in the granting by the Moguls to the British of firmans and trade privileges. The Armenian network stretched from Delhi to Kabul, from Kandahar to Balkh, to Bukhara, to Tabriz, to Trebizonde; in fact, they sent agents, as we have seen, just as easily to Danzig as to Lhasa and Xining. They were forwarding agents in all merchandise; through them passed Kashmiri shawls, gold, musk, spices, a thousand and one types of

Indian fabrics, cottons and silks, rhubarb, coral, amber, pearls, yak tails and saffron, padlocks, knives and bullets, paper, glass bottles, tea and cardamom. They were skillful, organized, experienced, they always spoke several languages; they made a vocation of commerce; peaceably, they succeeded.

Nevertheless, the period of their activity in Tibet was brief; the traces we have of them go from the 1680s to the year of the Zunghar invasion, 1717. After the capture of Lhasa and the years of trouble and violence that followed, one no longer saw them again in Tibet; nor, moreover, the mysterious "Muscovites" either. The Newar, the Kashmiris and the Chinese Muslims stayed.

RICH COUNTRY, POOR COUNTRY?

These imports of precious materials (silks, gems, amber, coral, pearls) are difficult to associate in our minds with a relatively small population, made up essentially of peasants and livestock breeders living a life that is materially crude, even rudimentary, as simple as that of its many monks. Who, then, made up the Tibetan clientele capable of buying this luxury merchandise? The religious and lay aristocracy that was concentrated, at that time, in Lhasa and Zhigatsé? Those responsible for the construction and ornamentation of temples and palaces, starting with the Potala? Did the feudal landlords become wealthy, did a class of well-to-do merchants come into existence? What proportion of the imported precious materials stayed in Tibet, and what proportion, arriving in Lhasa, continued the journey to Xining or to Kathmandu to reach other foreign buyers?

One at least partial answer to these questions is, of course, the concentration of these precious materials in the temples and monasteries, to which rumor soon attributed fabulous treasures, treasures constantly growing, never put back into circulation in the economy but consecrated, fixed, to the veneration of the deities (those of the Potala and Trashilhünpo, the most famous, will be plundered in the eighteenth century by enemy armies, but the rumor will long outlive them). Was there not, however, some exaggeration, on the part of observers, as to the real importance of this category of imports in Tibet's balance of trade?

On the other hand, if we compare the bulk of exports—which include precious materials, gold and musk in particular, plus an unknown quantity of wool products and all the other products mentioned above—with the bulk of imports—where it is necessary to count big essential purchases like tea, currency, the silver ingots for making it, and all the other merchandise enumerated above (though having very little data at our disposal)—one is tempted to think that what left Tibet was sold cheap compared to the world market price (then resold at a much higher price in other countries)—in any case, this is certain for gold—while in the opposite direction, Tibet bought at high prices. In the process, there was profit to be made, which consequently attracted foreign merchants. More-over, we have seen that Tibet exported, almost exclusively, unfinished products (unrefined gold, unprocessed musk, unwashed "shawl" wool, medicinal herbs in bulk) and imported many manufactured products that included the cost of the work, the most striking example being its own currency.

Chapter 27

THE CIRCULATION OF ESTATES IN TIBET

Reincarnation, Land, and Politics

Melvyn C. Goldstein

Melvyn Goldstein outlines in this essay the importance of agricultural estates and the agricultural workers, largely bound to the land, who made these corporate estates productive. Aside from the luxury goods and nomad products described in the previous and following essays, such estates were the main form of wealth generation, and therefore became a contested commodity in their own right. The description of this circulation of estates is based on studies of Central Tibet, but how widespread such a system was in other parts of Tibet has yet to be thoroughly studied. The "National Assembly" discussed here is the same institution also called simply "the Assembly" (*tsongdu*) by Petech in a previous essay, though it was not so much national in the sense that we mean this in modern nation-states because the body was representative only of the Lhasa elite and the abbots of the three great Gelukpa monastic seats (Sera, Ganden, and Drepung). The monastic representatives might have included monks from Amdo and Kham, but they did not represent those regions per se since the areas were not part of the Dalai Lama's polity. As with the empowering and composition of the Kashak, the Manchu Qing dynasty played a key role in repurposing the existing Tibetan institution of reincarnate lama lineages as the ruling power, in the form of the lama regents (*gyeltsap*, as opposed the earlier position of *desi*, which is often translated the same way) who dominated Central Tibet in the late eighteenth and nineteenth centuries.

One of the most salient features of traditional political life in Tibet was the intense and pervasive competition for power and prestige that took place within the ranks of the politically relevant, particularly within the aristocratic lay-official segment of the government. Plots, disputes, and confiscations were key elements in the dynamics of the system. Although this competition appears, synchronically, to be part of a stable circular process, when the Tibetan political system is viewed diachronically, the apparent stability is seen to be part of a larger, ongoing process of change. Thus, while it is possible to analyze the "structure" of this competition from a synchronic point of view, a diachronic perspective is necessary to understand the forces which have generated it, as well as the overall nature of the system.

Critical to the diachronic perspective is the idea of reincarnation succession. Although the idea of reincarnation is widespread, Tibet was unusual in using it as a mechanism for political succession. The rulers of Tibet, the Dalai Lamas, were succeeded by children who were considered their incarnations. This paper shows how features inherent in reincarnation as a mode of political succession, together with economic-ecological factors regarding land, generated an inevitable "circulation of estates," which, in turn, produced the political competition and conflict that were characteristic of the traditional Tibetan political system at any synchronic point in time. Moreover, reincarnation generated a process of change which, had the Chinese not come in 1950, would have ultimately transformed the system. In this paper, the nature of this process as well as its synchronic manifestations will be discussed.

Although the Fifth Dalai Lama (and the Gelukpa sect) first came into power in Tibet in 1642, their position underwent a variety of vicissitudes in the early part of the eighteenth century. During this period Tibet fell under the control of the Manchu emperors of China. For the Dalai Lamas, the civil war of 1728 in particular led to the diminution of their temporal authority and the emergence of aristocratic rule. Richardson writes of the fate of the Seventh Dalai Lama:

> It was therefore decided to remove the Dalai Lama from Lhasa and in 1728 he was invited to Peking. He set out on the journey but was taken no further than Litang where he stayed for seven years, after which he was allowed to return to Lhasa on the strict condition that he refrain from political activity.[1]

At this same time, the Tibetan Council of Ministers was reconstituted under the leadership of Polhané, the aristocrat who had been victorious in the civil war. He completely overshadowed the Council and in 1740 was awarded the title of "prince" or "king" by the Manchu emperor. After his death in 1747, he was succeeded by his son. This son, however, ruled arrogantly and ruthlessly and was assassinated in 1750 by the Emperor's representatives in Lhasa.

Following this, the emperor abolished the office of "king" and restored the Council of Ministers to its earlier position of importance. Furthermore, the emperor in 1751 restored to the Seventh Dalai Lama much of the temporal authority that had earlier been exercised by the Fifth Dalai Lama. From this point on there were no more "kingly" interludes and the line of Dalai Lamas ruled (at least in name) until 1959. The year 1751, therefore, will be used as a base line for the process discussed in this paper.

The Dalai Lama is an emanation (incarnation) of the bodhisattva Avalokiteśvara. A bodhisattva is an "enlightened being" who postpones his final entry into nirvāṇa to work to liberate all sentient creatures from the misery of samsaric existence. Avalokiteśvara, the bodhisattva of compassion, thus continually returns to human form through the line of the Dalai Lamas and the Dalai Lama is not, like the Pope, the representation of the deity, but rather a manifestation of it.

When reincarnation is used as a principle of succession, legitimization of the individual selected as the incarnation is of critical importance to the successful operation of the system. In other words, the selection mechanism must eliminate doubts as to whether the person chosen is the "real" incarnation. In Tibet, this was achieved through an elaborate selection procedure that was interlaced with supernatural supports. The speeches and comments of the late Dalai Lama were examined for possible clues as to where he would be reborn. Other unusual occurrences, such as strange cloud formations or a shift of the position of the corpse of the late Dalai Lama toward a particular direction, were analyzed by high lamas, oracles, the regent, and high ranking government officials. The regent and other high dignitaries also visited a holy lake in which visions concerning the Dalai Lama's rebirth were traditionally seen. All these preliminary examinations of cryptic, supernatural signs ended with the dispatch by the regent of one or more search parties composed of government officials and high lamas to areas where it was deemed probable that the late Dalai Lama would return to Tibet. In these areas, the search parties investigated stories of wondrous or strange births and ultimately administered a series of tests to the prospective candidates. Neither the children under consideration nor their parents were told by the search party that they were searching for the incarnation of the late Dalai Lama.[2] Typical tests consisted of showing the candidates several pairs of articles such as rosaries or walking sticks, one of which had been the personal possession of the late Dalai Lama. Selection of the objects belonging to the late Dalai Lama was taken as confirmation of being the incarnation since it indicated residual knowledge of the past, and the ability to recall events of one's past life was a characteristic of bodhisattvas.

On the basis of the reports sent by the search parties, and after consultation with important religious leaders and government officials, the regent informed the National Assembly[3] of the situation. Guided by him, the Assembly accepted one candidate as Dalai Lama. The selection process, therefore, not only incorporated supernatural supports but also included in the decision-making process all the politically relevant segments (aristocracy, monk officials, monastic elements). So long as the chosen candidate was alert and seemingly intelligent, it was of little consequence who he was, and on some occasions the selection was made by lottery.[4]

Although the Tibetan system dealt efficaciously with the potential problem of legitimacy, continuity of rule could not be attained. With succession by reincarnation there must, of necessity, be interim periods when the newly found incarnation (here the Dalai Lama) is a minor. All such succession systems must consequently have some mechanism to handle these interim periods. In Tibet, the age of majority for the ruler was eighteen years of age. This represented a significant span of time and the Tibetan solution was a regent who ruled in the Dalai Lama's name.

Beginning in 1757, when the seventh Dalai Lama died, the Manchu Emperors of China selected regents from among the great "incarnate" religious figures of the Gelukpa sect (the so-called "Yellow Hat" sect of the Dalai Lama). The regency became the prerogative of a small number of incarnate Gelukpa religious lamas. But the problem of continuity in reincarnation succession also existed for the regents, since they, too, were incarnations. Like the Dalai Lamas, when one of these incarnations died a child was selected as his reincarnation and thus a continuity across time was achieved for the named incarnation. I shall call such a lineage of reincarnations an incarnation line. Six different incarnation lines (each, as we shall see, a corporate unit) were represented among the eleven lama regents who ruled after 1757 (see table 27.1).

As a result of both natural misfortune and more sinister machinations, regents came to rule Tibet most of the time. When viewed diachronically, the Dalai Lamas were little more than legitimizing figureheads. From 1757 to 1895 the apex position in the Tibetan government was actually held by regents. Even when a Dalai Lama such as the Eighth managed to reach majority, a regent was retained to administer secular affairs. The following table illustrates this graphically.

By examining the above figures (which were abstracted from Petech),[5] one can see that from 1751–1950 there was a shift in ruler on the average of every 13 years, with regents ruling 77 percent of the time. If we exclude the reign of the Thirteenth Dalai Lama (1895–1933) from this, regents ruled approximately 94 percent of the time.

With this in mind, let us now examine selected aspects of the socio-economic system. Significant wealth in Tibet meant land and serfs to work the land. The aristocracy, in the form of corporate families, all held hereditary estates (with serfs), which were the foundation of their income. Religious institutions, however, were also corporately organized and held estates with serfs. Of particular interest to us is the religious corporation called *labrang*. The literal translation of *labrang* is "lama's house," and this delimits the general meaning. The *labrang* was a named, property owning corporation, control over which was transmitted through a line of incarnate lamas. Although these were usually a part of larger monasteries, they were autonomous units with full control over

TABLE 27.1

REIGNS OF DALAI LAMAS AND REGENTS

Dalai Lama	Ruled	Regent	Ruled
7th Kelzang Gyatso (1708–57)	1751–57	Demo I	1757–77
8th Jampel Gyatso (1758–1804)	1781–1804*	Tsemönling I	1777–86
9th Lungtok Gyatso (1806–15)		Kundeling I	1789–1810
10th Tsültrim Gyatso (1816–37)		Demo II	1811–19
		Tsemönling II	1819–44
11th Khedrup Gyatso (1838–56)		Radreng I	1845–62
		Shedra** (*aristocrat*)	1862–64
12th Trinlé Gyatso (1856–75)	1873–75	Dedruk	1864–72
		Kundeling II	1875–86
13th Tupten Gyatso (1876–1933)	1895–1933	Demo III	1886–95
		Radreng II	1934–41
		Takdrak	1941–50

*The eighth Dalai Lama was very otherwordly and the regent was kept even though he reached majority age. The regent actually ruled during his reign.
**Shedra was a Council Minister who, in the confusion of the coup of 1862, was charged with restoring order by the Manchu *amban* and confirmed by the emperor. This was an exceptional situation, and on his death in 1864, a high lama was again selected.

their resources. Originally one of these might have consisted of no more than a lama with a few monk servants who were supported by the gifts of patrons, and in fact, most *labrang* are not huge and wealthy. However, it often happened that a particular incarnation, because of his learning or spirituality, acquired a reputation and a large following who gave him numerous gifts. Gradually the wealth of his *labrang* grew and with it the number of associated monks. Those *labrang* that became very wealthy built their own residences and even their own monasteries and hermitages, all of which were under the direct control of the lama and not the monastery they were initially affiliated with. They were the possessions of the line of lamas. On the lama's death, the corporation was controlled by stewards until the newly found incarnation reached majority age. What is important, then, is that many of these *labrang* became holders of huge estates. This was particularly the case with the regents, whose *labrang*s became fantastically wealthy during the reign of their lama. For example, when Takdrak became regent in 1940 he was an old, relatively unknown lama with a small, inconsequential *labrang*. However, when he turned over the reins of government to the Dalai Lama in 1950, his *labrang* ranked among the largest. In other words, the rulers for most of Tibet's history were intimately involved in the estate-serfdom system. Moreover, because the regents were reincarnations, their infant successors could not immediately become regent (for the infant Dalai Lama). Thus, no single incarnation line (*labrang*) could continuously control the regency and there were actually six regent incarnation lines which, over the past 200 years, held the regency and came to possess tremendous land and serf holdings (see table). Each time the regent changed, the new one always represented a corporate interest different than his predecessor, and inevitably increased the holdings of his unit.

The corporations of the regents were not the only ones to acquire numerous estates and serfs. So too did the families of the Dalai Lamas. The (natal) family of the Dalai Lama was "ennobled" and became a part of the highest stratum of the Tibetan aristocracy. Each such family received estates sufficient to match, on an economic scale, their newly found social status. A recent Chinese Communist publication claims that the family of the Fourteenth Dalai Lama possessed (i.e., received) twenty-seven estates,[6] a figure which is not too unreasonable. Certainly they acquired huge land and serf holdings.

Every change of ruler, whether Dalai Lama or regent, entailed a new demand on land (estates). Given the fact that the ruler changed on the average of every thirteen years, we see that reincarnation succession produced a recurrent demand on the basic economic resource in Tibetan society: land. However, while the demand was ever expanding, the supply was fixed. New estates were not created through the conversion of previously virgin land to agricultural purposes. The reasons for this seem to have been techno-environmental in nature. Tibetan traditional agricultural technology simply was not capable of converting marginal pasture areas into profitable farm land. Even under the modern technology of the Chinese Communists, one usually reads of increasing yields and only rarely of opening new lands. Nevertheless, what concerns us here is that the only source available for the satisfaction of this recurrent demand consisted of the estates already in existence. On a recurrent basis, then, some holders of estates inevitably had to lose their holdings in order for the demands of the rulers to be satisfied. This was what actually occurred. There was an inevitable "circulation of estates."

The inevitable "circulation of estates" produced a pattern of pervasive and intense competition among elements of the politically relevant segments of Tibetan society. Space limitations preclude an intensive analysis of this competition, but I should like to discuss briefly certain aspects of it, particularly with respect to the aristocracy.

The formal governmental structure consisted of a network of hierarchically arranged permanent offices staffed by a bureaucracy. This bureaucracy was divided into two segments: one comprising only lay aristocrats and the other only Gelukpa monks. I shall hereafter refer to the former as lay officials and the latter as monk officials.

Lay officials were recruited exclusively from an aristocracy that was essentially a closed status group, membership in which was ascribed through birth. It comprised approximately 200[7] named corporate families which, at the rate of six people per family, would have totaled 1,200 people out of a population of 1–3 million. Each of these corporate families held one or more agricultural estates. The most important type of estate closely resembled the manorial estate of feudal Europe. This estate was divided into *demesne* and tenement land, the former being the land held by the lord and the latter the land held by the serfs. Such estates were the basic source of aristocratic power and wealth.

The aristocracy controlled a large segment of Tibet's arable land, and although the total land it held was quantitatively less than that held by either the monasteries or the government, their economic importance was still considerable. While the aristocracy formed a status group in the Weberian sense, complete with a distinctive "style of life" and a variety of differential status symbols and rights, internally it was differentiated with respect to prestige evaluation and wealth. Since this internal stratification played an important role in the political system, let me briefly indicate the four substrata.

The highest and most prestigious element of the aristocratic substrata was called *yapzhi*. This substratum comprised all the corporate families that were descendants of the ennobled natal family of one of the Dalai Lamas. In 1950 there were only six such *yapzhi* families.[8]

The next substratum consisted of four families and was called *depön*. These families were descended from ancient aristocratic lineages, some claiming descent from families extant during the age of the great Tibetan empire (seventh to ninth centuries A.D.). Like the *yapzhi* families, each of the *depön* families possessed extensive estate holdings.

Beneath these two was the somewhat larger, but still very prestigious, substratum called *midrak* which consisted of approximately fifteen families. Each of these families at one time had distinguished itself in government service, and from that derived its special status. This distinguished service generally meant the attainment of one of the highest governmental offices such as that of Council Minister.

The remaining 175 or so aristocratic families were lumped together in the status called "common" or *kyüma*. Because of its residual character and its large size there was considerable variation among the families within it with regard to the number and size of estates they held and their overall wealth. A few actually equaled in wealth some of the *midrak* families, but most did not, having only one or two small estates. In fact, many were extremely poor. What is therefore most characteristic of the dichotomy between the three numerically small but high strata and the large lower one was that in addition to the difference in prestige, the lower families were also decidedly inferior in terms of economic and political resources. Consequently, while it was theoretically possible for the officials from the "common" families to attain any, even the highest, governmental positions, generally the top twenty-five families of the superior substrata dominated and almost monopolized the most important and powerful government offices and therefore the effective decision making apparatus of the lay segment of the bureaucracy.

This differentiation in estates and prestige was directly related to the circulation of estates. It has been indicated that in every generation some estate holders had to lose estates in order to satisfy the inevitable demand for estates produced by reincarnation succession. But since estates were the most prized economic possession, they were not voluntarily given up by families, and the basic means of redistribution was confiscation. In every generation, then, some estate holders lost estates through confiscation, while a few others received new estates.

However, all estate holders were not equally threatened. Aristocratic holders were in much more precarious straits than their religious counterparts. The rulers of Tibet were lamas and a basic orientation of the government was to provide an environment in which religion—the monastic system—could flourish. Since the monks were in large part subsidized through their estates, confiscation of monastic estates hit directly at the vitality of organized religion and was rarely done. This is not to say that religious estates were never confiscated. There were rare instances of confiscation of the estates of monasteries and *labrang* whose leaders had committed serious political offenses. For example, in 1895, after an abortive plot to kill the Dalai Lama, the ex-regent (Demo Rinpoché) and his brother were imprisoned for life and all of the estates he acquired in this incarnation were confiscated. However, to leave the monks an economic base, the estates acquired by the previous Demo incarnations were left in the hands of his monastic followers. Similarly, in 1948 a plot of the Radreng ex-regent against the present regent was uncovered. The ex-regent (Radreng) was imprisoned (and then murdered in prison) and many estates belonging to his *labrang* and allied monasteries were confiscated. But, in general, although monastic-*labrang* estates were sometimes confiscated, they normally were confiscated only as a result of very serious crimes and the confiscation was usually not permanent. After some lapse of time, many, if not most, of the confiscated estates were returned to the "innocent" monks of the monasteries in question.

The aristocracy had no such leverage, and it was from this group that the major portion of estates was confiscated. However, even within the aristocracy not all families were equally threatened. Small families possessing only one estate were not in real danger since confiscation of their lone estate meant, in effect, denoblement, and this action was taken only for serious crimes when the aim was clearly the destruction of the family rather than the mere acquisition of an estate. The main source of estates, then, was the multiple estate holders, and for the most part, the thirty or so high status families were the primary targets.

But since estates were hereditary, and since the owners held formal land tenure documents issued by the government, the ruler could not simply take back an estate. Some excuse was needed. Usually this excuse involved some question concerning validity of the title or some offense against the government on the part of the owner. Confiscated estates reverted to the government and remained as such until the ruler redistributed them.

For example, the historical section of the title document of the Tsechokling monastery's Puzhi estate in Trengo (Central Tibet) states that the estate was confiscated by the government (the regent) as a consequence of a dispute that arose between the collateral relatives of an aristocratic family all of whose immediate members had died. The dispute afforded the regent the opportunity to intervene and decide that none of the disputants had "valid rights" to the estate and that the estate should revert to the government. He then redistributed it to the *labrang* of one of his teachers. Another example involved an estate which had been willed to a bride's family by a relative and subsequently brought by her into a marriage-merger. After about a year the couple was divorced and the bride claimed the estate should revert to her and her newly born daughter. The husband's family protested and said the estate should remain with it and an infant son. The ensuing dispute was referred to the government for adjudication. The regent was hostile toward the bride's family and ended the controversy by confiscating the estate. Later he gave it to his own religious corporation (*labrang*).

The above two examples reveal an important difference between the reasons for the confiscation of religious and aristocratic estates. Whereas religious estates were only confiscated for very serious crimes against the state, aristocratic estates were confiscated for relatively minor reasons. Thus, not only did aristocrats permanently lose ties to their confiscated estates but they were victimized for reasons which would never be sustained for the religious sector.

The dangers inherent in this type of situation led various segments of the aristocracy to employ very different strategies in the political area. The segment comprising officials from the powerful, high status families were interested in competing for positions with high authority. Each of the larger families attempted to manipulate its resources so as to maintain a continuity of people in high positions across generations. They carefully tried to prepare a younger member of their corporate family unit so that he would have the necessary experience to obtain high positions when the elder official from the family was ready to retire. This strategy often entailed procuring positions which, in terms of income, cost the family money in the short run. But the fact that the young official was adequately prepared for higher position was well worth the investment. The motivation behind this warrants some comment.

One obvious motivating factor was the differential prestige accruing to government position. Relative prestige and rank were important determinants of interpersonal behavior. Lhasa was not only the political center of the polity, it was also the hub of Tibetan "high society." The elegant life style of the capital emphasized rank and prestige through various institutionalized asymmetrical deference patterns. Clothes, seating arrangements, titles, honorifics in speech, and so forth, all mirrored differences in governmental rank. Entrance into high governmental position meant that the individual and his family received deferential behavior from lower officials and their families not only in official contexts, but also socially. Wealth without high governmental status did not confer social esteem among the status conscious Lhasa society.

But high governmental status meant more than social esteem. It meant power and authority and this was certainly the fundamental motivating factor. Power and authority, however, had an added dimension in Tibetan politics. This is what Tibetans sometimes verbalized as "defense" or "protection."

The circulation of estates insured that the stakes of the political game would always be high. The threat of loss of estate was a real one, and for many officials the acquisition of a high governmental post was perceived as protection against their being easily victimized. The higher the position of a government official, the more resources he had available to retaliate for attacks against himself. In any case, both the status and the protection motives led the larger families to adopt a strategy aimed at obtaining high positions in the government, in many instances regardless of their salary or income potential.

A second category consisted of a handful of officials, lay and monk, who were primarily oriented toward directly influencing the highest level of decision making by becoming favorites of the ruler. This was the high risk strategy. Fabulous wealth and power awaited the successful, while demotion and poverty were the lot of the losers.

For the overwhelming majority of the aristocratic government officials, however, the primary motivation was not prestige, nor power, nor protection. Rather, it was the acquisition of wealth. These officials were oriented toward obtaining lucrative government posts, and since most of the lucrative jobs were located in the provinces, these officials spent a large part of their time outside of the capital. Although a few tried to use wealth obtained in the provinces to procure high positions, most tried to avoid becoming deeply entangled in the intense political machinations of the capital.

The results of this differentiation in terms of political strategies is clearly seen when we examine those who in fact held the high posts in the government in this century. For example, from 1900–1950 there were 41 council ministers. Twelve of these were monk officials, and 29 were lay officials. Of the lay officials, 72 percent were from *midrak* or higher families, and of the remaining 28 percent, 14 percent were from very wealthy families. Thus, a total of 86 percent of the lay council ministers were either from *midrak* or higher status or from very wealthy families. Of the 12 monk officials, 33 percent were from aristocratic families, and 33 percent from a type of wealthy corporate monastic family (*shaktsang*) which was perpetuated by adoption of close relatives. Thus, even in the monk official segment, wealthy corporate units dominated. This pattern of domination of the important government positions by the large families could be shown to pervade all the important positions in the government.

The circulation of estates was paralleled by what might be called a circulation of victims. Upon entering office every new ruler, particularly the regents, sought to build a network of loyal supporters among the government officials. The most obvious source of supporters were those disgruntled officials who had been victimized by the last administration. There was, therefore, a circulation of the larger families from in-group to out-group status and vice versa. Across generations the victimized eventually regained their status and prestige, although usually not their estates. The manner in which this circulation operated and the way aristocratic officials entered into alliances and client relations is too complex to be discussed here. Nonetheless, it is clear that the circulation of estates generated an intense pattern of competition for high office among the larger aristocratic families who were seeking in that way to secure their positions. Someone was going to be victimized with each shift of ruler, and the focus of political life for the larger families was to defend themselves against victimization. The mass of smaller families, on the other hand, were interested not so much in prestigious and authoritative positions, but rather in posts where they would derive economic benefits in the form of a good income. However, although the strategies these different segments adopted were markedly different, ultimately all were integrated into the competition system. The smaller families had of necessity to approach higher officials to obtain lucrative posts and often came to be associated as clients of large families. Kinship ties with larger families were also relevant here. Even though a smaller family might not be actively involved in the political arena, the dominance of particularistic values in the day-to-day operation of the Tibetan government insured that no one could ever be completely neutral or safe from the inherent and ever-lurking threat of partial or complete ruination. Consequently, even the smaller families were to an extent drawn into this web of political competition.

Now that the effects of the circulation process on the nature of political competition have been discussed, the diachronic consequences of this process must be examined. Given the existence of this circulation of estates and given the fact that the aristocracy was the main source for the confiscation of estates, one would expect that over the two hundred year period the process existed (1751–1950) the economic base of the aristocracy would have deteriorated and the aristocratic segment would have become increasingly impoverished. Unfortunately, there is no quantitative comparative data either on the number of aristocratic families extant in 1751 or the percent of arable land they held at that time. Nonetheless, if we examine the state of the aristocracy in 1950, its condition is consistent with this assumption of a process of gradual deterioration.

In the twentieth century the aristocracy held land less than either the government or the religious (monastic and *labrang*) segments of society. Carrasco[9] states that in 1917 the monasteries held 42 percent of the land, the government 37 percent, and the aristocracy only 21 percent. Moreover, of the two hundred or so aristocratic families, a large percent were in a state of relative impoverishment. They were not poor compared to poor peasants, but wealthy "taxpayer" peasants[10] were often much better off economically. In any case many families did not have wealth adequate to sustain the aristocratic style of life. These poor aristocrats usually could not afford either basic aristocratic status symbols such as owning a house and maintaining horses in Lhasa, or ritual necessities such as the various dresses and ornaments required for special government functions. Mrs. Taring (a Tibetan aristocrat) comments in passing in her autobiography[11] that "some estates could not meet the family needs and therefore trade was greatly exercised among the nobility." In some instances the plight (and debts) of these impoverished aristocrats became so bad that they gave up government service and ceded their estates to a monastery (the main moneylenders) in return for a guaranteed income for the rest of their lives.

But the deterioration of the aristocracy has not gone unimpeded and several important factors have acted to restrain the rate of decline. First, it should be reiterated that several of the important recipients of the flow of estates were the families of the Dalai Lamas. Since these became the highest level of the aristocracy, the total amount of land alienated from the aristocratic segment was lessened. This, however, as the large number of poor aristocrats indicates, did not increase the viability of individual families and merely exacerbated the gulf between the wealthy aristocratic families and the rest. On the whole, then, while the cumulative result of the circulation of estates was the ever increasing domination of land by the monastic and government segments, the rate of this alienation, due to the institutionalized mobility of the Dalai Lama's family, was less rapid than might otherwise be thought.

Another important brake on this process was the increasing involvement of the aristocracy in trade and commerce. Aristocrats, particularly in this century, engaged widely in intra- and international trade which, of course, again served to impede the decline of the aristocracy as an economically important segment.

While these factors slowed the inevitable deterioration of the aristocracy, they did not reverse it. It seems likely that had this process continued without outside interference, eventually the system would have been transformed. The seeds of its own destruction were clearly built into it. It is interesting to note with respect to this that the only known attempt at revolution (i.e., changing the system rather than the incumbents) in Tibet was masterminded in 1933 by an aristocrat, and throughout the twentieth century it has been elements of the aristocracy who have favored and tried to implement major changes.

CONCLUSIONS

This paper has shown how the characteristic form and processes of the political system in Tibet derived from the interaction of a cultural rule—political succession by reincarnation—and the techno-environmental matrix in which it existed—the absence of new sources of economically viable agricultural land. It also has shown how these inevitably produced a "circulation of estates" and how this in turn generated the intense and pervasive competition patterns that so characterized the traditional Tibetan polity. Furthermore, it has shown how, from a diachronic perspective, the system was inherently unstable and the deterioration of the aristocratic segment could only have ended in a radical change in the political system itself.

Finally, it is suggested that the Tibetan example illustrates the importance of considering cultural as well as ecological/materialistic variables in explaining synchronic structure diachronically. Whatever the initial causes of the institutionalization of reincarnation succession in Tibet, once begun, it itself became a critical force in shaping the structure of the political system. Thus, it would seem that the type of intense competition characteristic of Tibetan politics will emerge whenever a cultural rule institutionalizes recurrent demand for a resource which is at once paramount in importance and fixed in quantity.

NOTES

1. Hugh Richardson, *A Short History of Tibet* (New York: E. P. Dutton, 1962), 52.

2. The parents of the candidates suspect only that their son is being considered for one of the numerous lesser incarnation lines. The fourteenth Dalai Lama gives an excellent account of this selection procedure in his autobiography: Bstan 'dzin rgya mtsho, Dalai Lama, *My Land and My People* (New York: McGraw-Hill, 1962), 20–25.

3. The National Assembly was really the platform for the great Gelukpa monasteries.

4. This is, of course, the author's "outsider" point of view. Tibetans consider the selection of the correct child to be a matter of great consequence. It should also be noted with respect to the use of lotteries, that H. E. Richardson (personal communication) contends that even when the Manchu emperor ordered the use of the lottery method the candidate chosen was invariably the one the Tibetans had already decided upon. In any case, my point is simply that for the system to work it made little difference who was selected so long as he was selected in the "proper" manner.

5. Luciano Petech, *China and Tibet in the Early 18th Century* (Leiden: Brill, 1950).

6. "Lhasa's New Look," *Peking Review* 41 (1971): 12.

7. Prince Peter, *The Aristocracy of Central Tibet* (Kalimpong: Tharchin, 1954) lists 205 families, including about 50 Trashilhünpo aristocratic families.

8. Merger-marriages with other families accounts for the discrepancy.

9. Pedro Carrasco, *Land and Polity in Tibet* (Seattle: University of Washington Press, 1959), 86.

10. See M. Goldstein, "Taxation and the Structure of a Tibetan Village," *Central Asiatic Journal* 15, no. 1 (1971): 1–27, and "Serfdom and Mobility: An Examination or the Institution of 'Human Lease' in Traditional Tibetan Society," *Journal of Asian Studies* 30, no. 3 (1971): 521–534, for a discussion of these serfs.

11. R. D. Taring, *Daughter of Tibet* (London: John Murray, 1970), 6.

Chapter 28

THE GEO-HISTORY OF LONG-DISTANCE TRADE IN TIBET 1850–1950

Wim van Spengen

This article represents in an abridged form the original research eventually published in the most detailed economic history of Tibet, Wim van Spengen's *Tibetan Border Worlds: A Geo-historical Analysis of Trade and Traders* (2000). Due in part to the limitations of Tibetan-language source materials, relatively little has been written about the economy of Tibet. This article takes advantage of the burgeoning Western (English, German, French) travel literature from the mid-nineteenth century onward to analyze Tibetan trade. The method of analysis draws on the work of Fernand Braudel, which introduces the idea of regional economic-worlds (*économies-mondes*) and defines each of these in terms of an internally cohesive set of relations, a "movement-space" (*espace-mouvement*). Van Spengen applies these concepts to the Tibetan plateau and delineates a distinct network of trade relations in connection to the regional economic-worlds of China and British India. By viewing the Tibetan economic space in relation to these neighboring economic-worlds, he is able to trace variations in products, markets, and routes, thereby placing Tibet in the context of world economic history as well.

It is the purpose of this study to identify the main structural characteristics of long-distance trade within the particular geo-historical setting of Tibet during the period 1850 to 1950. It is this historically transitional period, which forms the background to our discussion of long-distance trade within the Tibetan culture world at large.[1] The choice for the period concerned is justified because it covers the final days of disintegration of Central Tibet as an ecclesiastical state based on a long-distance trade in luxury goods. But it is also the time of the rise of Tibet as a politically defined national state under the Thirteenth Dalai Lama. In addition, the period under review shows the decline of foreign merchant communities and the corresponding rise of Tibetan trade initiatives in outlying regions as a response to wider processes of geo-political change. The "frontier" character of Tibet gave way to contending imperialist spheres of interest, ultimately leading to a Chinese-dictated Indo-Tibetan boundary in the Himalayan region. In fact, this "frontier" character forms the structural geo-historical background against which the following discussion of a changing Tibetan trading region has been set. Even so, change has not been uniform for a variety of geographical and historical reasons. It is the stated purpose of this study not to overlook those differences.

The thus defined broad geo-historical setting will be conceptualized with the help of Braudel's major analytic category of *économie-monde* as developed in his *Civilisation Matérielle*.[2] An *économie-monde*, according to Braudel, is an economically autonomous part of the world, essentially capable of being self-sufficient. It is a major *espace-mouvement* in terms of its trade flows and perhaps its civilization. In an Asian setting and application, Braudel, somewhat surprisingly, distinguishes only one *économie-monde*, which marches under the rather illogical name of *Extrême-Orient*, because it comprises the sub-regional economies, or rather the *économies-mondes*, of both India and China, the Malayan world acting as a pivot of exchange.[3] Tibet in this view is thought to have been linked to the long-standing Chinese "wing," as were Korea, Indo-China, Yunnan and Mongolia.[4] The Indian "wing," although a great national market, is thought of as less integrated than the Chinese one, and in Braudel's view appears more clearly on the international scene with the rise of British India.

The idea of fluctuating prosperity of an *économie-monde* in response to a long-term secular trend, although in itself insufficiently understood, is an attractive complementary feature of Braudel's theorizing, as it allows for the historical dynamics of regional organization to be incorporated in our analysis. The prosperity, for example, of the Tibeto-Himalayan economy in the seventeenth century, was undoubtedly linked to the flourishing of the adjacent Indian and Chinese *économies-mondes*. When by the beginning of the nineteenth century an overall decline had set in, especially in China, Tibet too, gradually lost its economic vigor, only to be drawn slowly into the orbit of a rising and gradually better integrated British-Indian *économie-monde*. Within this particular geo-historical setting, Tibet developed into an economic-geographic transitional zone, linked up in Braudelian terms with the fortunes of its neighboring *économies-mondes*.[5]

THE TRADITIONAL BARTER COMPLEX

Geographically speaking, Tibet consists of a mountain-fringed mosaic of greater and lesser plateau, gently sloping towards the great river trenches in the southeast of the country. Its highest stretch of mountainous tableland is the desolate Changtang, located in the north-central part of Tibet. On this high tableland roam a few hardy nomads, but the major nomad countries are to be found in the broad band of grassland which runs along the rim of the Changtang from Amdo in the northeast via Central Tibet to the Indian border in the southwest. Areas of settled agriculture and sedentary farming generally follow the lower lying river valleys in the south and the southeast of the country. But in many of the higher areas elsewhere in Tibet, as well as those in the Himalaya, pastoralism both in its full-blown and mixed forms are part and parcel of the local economies.

Nomadism and related activities in Tibet are still insufficiently documented, although we do have a number of written reports and monographs of varying quality at our disposal.[6] From these, as well as from a number of erratic references across a disparate set of complementary sources, we have to distil the meaning and importance of Tibetan nomad life and its role in the traditional barter complex.

"The chief economic wealth of Tibet lies in its nomad cattle-breeding districts. Deprive Tibet of its cattle-breeding regions and the country would starve."[7] This shrewd observation by a Russian Tibetanist, who crossed the Changtang in 1925, highlights the importance of Tibet's nomad countries. And indeed it was the wool production based on extensive yak and goat keeping that made a viable enterprise out of the high-altitude Tibetan economy at large. The one problem which Tibet's herders shared with many other nomads in the world was that they needed foodgrains to supplement their meat and milk based diet. The sedentary farmers of the drier Tibetan West however, were not always capable of producing enough food to supplement the nomad's diet with the necessary grain. Fortunately, the Tibetan nomad economies themselves were seldom lacking in productive capacity and were generally able to produce a surplus of animal products, in particular wool. These could be exchanged for larger consignments of foodgrains, if necessary even from beyond Tibet's borders. In addition there was the salt for which there was ample demand in the cis-Himalayan region and eastern Tibet. The general picture of exchange is completed by large imports of tea from China which found their way all over Tibet. Thus, the traditional Tibetan barter complex rested, with considerable regional variations, in the exchange of wool and salt for foodgrains and tea, the latter of which may be regarded as a daily necessity within a Tibetan context.

As pointed out before, nomad countries in Tibet are mainly to be found along the southern and eastern rim of the Changtang. These pastoral *pays* are not of equal prosperity, due to a variety of reasons. Combe, who edited the observations of "a Tibetan on Tibet" (viz. Paul Sherap, or Dorje Zodba), gives a brief overview of the nomad countries Dorje was personally acquainted with, and though impressionistic, the few pages convey the image of a number of widely disparate nomad societies.[8] First of all, there are differences in resource base, the eastern and northeastern nomad countries generally enjoying higher precipitation, and consequently having better grazing grounds than their counterparts in western Tibet.[9] But whether a nomad country made a more prosperous impression or not also depended on its external relations. The differences in wealth noted by Dorje Zodba in the 1910s and 20s must have been at least partly related to their location *vis-à-vis* potential buyers of nomad products, or to their capacity to control crucial transport routes. Contrary perhaps to popular wisdom, an economy founded on pastoralism is not infrequently an economy of relatively high involvement in the market.[10] According to Khazanov, there are two different forms of nomad interaction with the outside world. Firstly, there is direct trade and barter with both agricultural and urban societies. Secondly, there takes place mediation or participation in the trade between different sedentary societies, in the form of transport and middleman services.[11]

The first form is mainly an example of "vertical trade," that is the local exchange of animal products of the plateau-dwelling nomads for the grain of the valley-resident farmers. It is this trade to which a Tibetan nomad still referred when the American anthropologists Goldstein and Beall conducted research in the Pala nomad country of western Tibet in 1987:

> "You see," he said, "we live off the products of our animals. Every year our sheep provide wool, skins, meat, milk and butter which we use for food and clothes as well as for bartering with villagers to obtain barley, tea and so forth."[12]

The inclusion of tea in an otherwise home-produced set of trading articles as referred to in the above citation, shows once more the important position of tea in the barter complex under discussion.

The second form of nomad trade is less dependent on the productive capacity of nomadism per se, but more on the power of transportation offered by its yaks, *dzos* (a crossbreed), goats and sheep. The control over pack-animals in combination with a favorable location astride distinct ecozones, as well as a thorough knowledge of routes in difficult terrain, made the nomads and semi-nomads of Tibet's border areas often into middlemen-transporters in a trans-regional and cross-cultural trade. If the right combination of animal control, favorable location, ecosystematic complementarity and sufficient demand existed, long-distance caravan trading and the supplying of caravan traders were sometimes more profitable for the nomads than was the direct exchange of pastoral for agricultural products. In addition, a specialized animal trade developed in some border areas, which provided a sort of mixture between the two forms mentioned above. Examples of the latter were the large-scale trade in Amdo-bred cavalry horses for the Chinese army at the Gansu horse fairs,[13] as well as the annual sale of tens of thousands of sheep to Nepal at the time of a major Hindu festival.[14]

The nomad way of life is one of inherent mobility. The necessary shifts of nomad camps to assure continuous and good grazing feature prominently in daily and seasonal routines. But as pasture-grounds, in particular around the fixed winter encampments, had the character of non-alienable land owned by specific clans or tribes,[15] movements tended to be restricted in space. Moreover, groups of herders that were living nearer to the settled agricultural areas stood in varying degrees of dependency to monasteries and feudal chiefs, the liens involved being ever so many restrictions to the free movement of nomad subjects.[16] Even the independent Golok nomads of the upper Huanghe or Machu basin in eastern Tibet were subject to the supreme moral authority of the lamas and depended for the barter of their animal products on the regional monasteries in the neighboring valley-areas.[17] In a wider sense then, their movements too, were necessarily structured, not to say restricted. Beyond this world of local exchanges lay the regional networks of nomad and related middlemen trade. Especially in the drier parts of western Tibet, insufficient grain could be grown to feed the nomad populations outside the valleys. Consequently, a whole system of Trans-Himalayan grain imports had developed over the centuries which were paid for by salt and wool.

THE SALT FOR GRAIN BARTER

The salt trade had its productive origin in the lakelands of Central Tibet and the Tsaidam basin. Latter-day research has discovered forty-six kinds of salt minerals in the saline lakes, among which fourteen are borates.[18] The borates, in the form of raw borax or tincal, commanded a good sale in Europe, in particular during the first half of the nineteenth century. The demand by the European porcelain industry was met almost exclusively by the Tibetan trade, but the discovery of borax in the Italian province of Tuscany, as well as its chemical production later on in the century, brought to an end this lucrative trade.[19] As some of the nomads must have been involved in the first stages of this long-distance trade, it may have brought a certain wealth to their communities, which however declined at the eclipse of their monopoly. The borax-digging at Puga in Ladakh, for example, was already past its heyday in 1847.[20] The export of borax from Tibet to China however, continued unabated.[21]

What was left was the export of non-borate salts for daily use in the Himalayan border lands, insofar as they could compete with imported sea salt from the south. Salt from the Tsaidam basin in Northeastern Tibet was brought to the eastern Tibetan province of Kham, where it formed one of the staple trades.

The salt was brought down by the nomads from Amdo and exchanged for the barley of the densely-settled agricultural valleys along the Yangzi (Drichu) and Yalung (Dzachu).[22] Southeastern Tibet obtained its supplies of salt from the brine wells on the banks of the Mekong at Yenching or Tswakhalo,[23] but its sphere of influence being small, it had to compete with salt coming down from the Tsaidam basin and the Nakchuka area, which harbored at Nakchu a kind of transit market for the products of many Central Tibetan nomad countries. Salt, then, was an important trade product for the nomads, as they alone possessed the transport capacity and the spatial mobility making possible the exploitation of salt at its places of production.[24]

The general picture that arises is one of a number of salt-producing regions where nomads fetched the salt and brought it down to seasonal markets, monasteries and villages. From there it was transported onwards to a series of frontier fairs along the Sino-Tibetan and Himalayan borders. In exchange for the salt, several grains found their way into Tibet, in particular its western parts where the climate showed less clemency than in its eastern reaches. The main food imports in western Tibet consisted of barley and to a far lesser extent wheat. Rice, for the higher classes, was imported from Tsayül and Pemakö, both low-lying regions in southeastern Tibetan territory. But as these were far away from the main centers of population, additional rice of a superior quality was brought in from Assam, Bhutan and Nepal.[25] Trade in the Sino-Tibetan borderlands was of a different character. The trade between Tibet and China was largely monopolized by merchants from the eastern Tibetan province of Kham. These were either private traders doing business on their own account or on behalf of monasteries.[26]

THE TEA AND WOOL TRADE OF TIBET

For more than a thousand years already Tibet is the land of great tea drinkers.[27] Tea for the Tibetan market was almost exclusively grown in the Chinese province of Sichuan, where the prefecture of Yachao was the collecting center of a number of tea-growing districts.[28] The trade at Yachao was controlled by Chinese tea firms,[29] which prepared the tea for export to Tibet by packing quantities into coarse rectangular bricks.[30] From Yachao the tea was carried to the Sino-Tibetan frontier town of Daqianlu by way of human porterage, as the terrain to be crossed was too mountainous to allow for the use of pack-animals. The porterage was performed by "a very nationality of porters," the so-called Giama Rongbas (from Gyelmo rong?), who inhabit the cultural fringe land between the two towns.[31] From Yachao, the tea carriers saw their loads over a distance of some two hundred kilometers to Daqianlu [Dartsedo], where the tea generally changed hands from Chinese to Tibetan traders. With old-established firms, business was put through without a written contract, but the use of paper, being introduced from China, gained in importance in the early decades of the twentieth century.[32]

Daqianlu, familiarly known as the Shanghai of Tibet,[33] yet harboring a mere five thousand inhabitants,[34] was a veritable node of trade routes.[35] Although Chinese-ruled since the beginning of the eighteenth century, the town had been able to retain its Tibetan atmosphere, as it really lay well within the Tibetan culture region which was thought to extend right up to the Dong river a few kilometers to the east of the town. Daqianlu was the major break-of-bulk point for a variety of goods leaving and entering the eastern Tibetan province of Kham, human porterage as a mode of transport at this point being replaced by pack-animals and vice versa.[36]

Tea too, was subject to this operation. Thus the Tibetan purchaser removed the less durable Yachao wicker-work and repacked the tea in relatively small brick-like loads, a number of which were tightly sewn together in a yak-skin cover, especially the better quality teas destined for the Lhasa market.[37] In addition, Chinese and Tibetan duties had to be paid at Daqianlu for fixed quantities and qualities of tea entering and leaving the town.[38] After that the tea was ready for its onward journey into the highlands of Tibet.[39]

The tea trade of Tibet was in the main an inward-looking affair. Tea steadily came to pervade even the remotest districts, though sometimes by enforced sales to the local populations.[40] In contrast, the wool trade was largely an outwardly directed phenomenon, based on an externally generated demand and involving relations far beyond the grasp of the ordinary nomad farmer. In particular after 1890, wool increasingly found its way to Europe and America, where the coarse Tibetan sheep wool was used in the carpet-making industry. But before this international "boom" trade gained full shape in the early decades of the twentieth century, the fame of the Tibetan wool rested in another supra-regional circuit, that of the shawl-wool or *pashm* of western Tibet.

Pashm is the fine wool of a particular type of goat, whose main habitat is to be found in the region between Lake Pangong on the Ladakh border and Lake Manasarovar near the sacred peak of Kailash.[41] Together with musk, a natural perfume, it was one of the two products for which Tibet was known to the outside world since the Middle Ages. By the fifteenth century, this fine Tibetan wool commanded a regular sale in Kashmir, where it was manufactured into woolen products of high quality, in particular shawls. With the coming of the British in India, the Kashmir-oriented framework of trans-Himalayan trade came under pressure from the South. In 1812, the intrepid traveler William Moorcroft reached Gartok in disguise, and after a few days succeeded in procuring eight loads of the passionately desired shawl-wool in a neighboring village. To break the Ladakhi monopoly on Tibetan wool, the import of *pashm* along the newly established Sutlej route through the British-protected state of Bashahr was silently encouraged. After 1815, Rampur, the capital of Bashahr, began to develop into a real transit-trading center of shawl-wool, while Kinnaur, towards the Tibetan border, emerged as a smuggler's nest of *pashm* wool.[42]

The wool trade of northeastern Tibet, which tapped the nomad countries that were to be found in the Tsaidam basin, the Kokonor Lake region, and the Upper Huanghe or Machu reaches, only seems to have become important and of sufficient scale to be noticed by outsiders by the 1890s.[43] During the eighteenth and the greater part of the nineteenth century, most of the wool from this area was traded with the non-Chinese residents of the Xining region, wool never having been popular with the Chinese. But with the growing Chinese hold over Xinjiang after the defeat of Yakub Beg in 1877, and the reluctant opening up of China to western interests in the second half of the nineteenth century, a reorientation of the northeastern wool trade of Tibet took place in an eastward direction.[44] As the Gansu borderlands were predominantly inhabited by Chinese Muslims (or Hui), the growing number of Sino-Tibetan contacts in this area meant first and foremost a Tibetan-Hui encounter, in time creating a multi-faceted Tibetan-Hui economic and cultural interface.[45] Through these Hui intermediaries, the Tibetan wool eventually reached Tianjin on the northeast China coast, from where it was shipped to Europe and America.[46] By 1895, the wool had already assumed some importance in the economy of northeastern Tibet,[47] and by the 1920s, World War I and its post-war economic boom had provided a tremendous stimulus to all participants in the wool trade. The heyday of Chinese wool exports occurred in the mid-1920s[48] but afterwards the trade declined, firstly as a result of the disturbed nature of the Ningxia and Gansu states in the late 1920s, and secondly by growing Japanese influence in Manchuria in the 1930s, which discouraged foreign capital. The Japanese invasion of China in 1937 gave the coup de grace to the Tibet-Tianjin wool trade, eliminating the eastern half of the trade route up to Baotou on the Middle Huanghe.[49]

With the increased demand for wool in the second half of the nineteenth century, two developments in the wool trade of northeastern Tibet took place. Firstly, the growing importance of a few wool collecting market towns and monasteries along Amdo's Gansu frontier, and secondly, the growing number of Hui (Chinese Muslims) venturing into the Tibetan nomad lands to buy the wool on the spot for the lowest price. The first development became visible in the rise of Tankar [Tongkhor], a Tibetan frontier town to the west of Xining, as a wool collecting center.[50] The great monastic towns of Kumbum and Labrang too, through the development of their neighboring trade villages, provided the necessary infrastructure for the growing trade of wool.[51] In addition, Jyekundo, near the southern border of Amdo, emerged as a great wool collecting center.[52] But as the distance from Jyekundo to Tankar (and Xining) was considerable, and the intervening stretch of country subject to Golok robbery,[53] the wool from Jyekundo also found its way out of Tibet via the Sichuan frontier markets of Songpan and Daqianlu. From there it was transported to the wool mills of

Shanghai,[54] that is to say until about 1918, after which renewed hostilities in the Sino-Tibetan borderland disrupted this very lucrative trade.[55] Tankar, however, remained by far the biggest wool exporting market of northeastern Tibet, because of the transport advantages it enjoyed.[56]

The Tibet-Tianjin wool trade rested, at least partly so, in the possibility of cheap river transport down the Huanghe to Baotou, a burgeoning break-of-bulk point on the northern loop of the Middle Huanghe near the Ordos desert. Here the wool was repacked and subsequently transported by camel to Tianjin, and after 1923 by rail to Peking.[57] The river transport between Lanzhou and Baotou was a monopoly of the Hui, but it is the Tibetan side of their trade which deserves closer scrutiny in the context of this study.

There is an extremely interesting chapter in Ekvall's *Cultural Relations on the Kansu-Tibetan Border*,[58] describing the economic and cultural interaction between the Chinese Muslims of West Gansu and the nomadic Tibetans of Amdo. The Hui venturing into Tibetan territory were mostly Muslims from Xining, Hezhou, and especially Taozhou.[59] In fact, the Hui came to occupy the supreme role of economic middlemen and cultural brokers between the widely disparate Tibetan and Chinese societies involved. In this respect they resemble the Sharba of Songpan,[60] and also their Bhotia confrères of Kumaon along the Indo-Tibetan border. Their success as middlemen can be partly explained by their location on the Sino-Tibetan border, and partly by their knowledge of Tibetan, which gave them a tremendous advantage in borderland commerce.[61] Having access to both Chinese manufactures and Tibetan nomad products, they could work an exchange, which greatly enriched themselves, and at the same time guaranteed a further strengthening of Hui-Tibetan trade contacts.

The wool brought back from these trading ventures into Tibetan territory, was either sold to Chinese representatives of foreign export firms resident in Tankar or the big monasteries of Kumbum and Labrang,[62] or brought down to Lanzhou, or even Baotou by the Hui themselves, in the hope of maximizing their profit margin. This could well be done, as the river transport on the Huanghe was largely a Muslim monopoly and fruitful schemes of collaboration existed between the buyers and transporters of wool.[63]

The collapse of the Tibet-Tianjin wool trade at the end of the 1930s, due to geo-political strife and outright war, had only limited repercussions on the Tibetan nomads. Their wool exports could be partly re-channeled via Songpan and Daqianlu, and even when the latter route had become impracticable because of civil war in Sichuan, as well as renewed Sino-Tibetan frontier fighting, part of the wool produced in the northern nomad countries found its way to foreign markets via Lhasa and Kalimpong.[64] Until 1930, some of the wool also reached Russia by way of a relatively undisturbed Xinjiang.[65]

The reorientation of the Tibetan wool trade to the South emphasized a locational shift of long-distance trade through the Central Himalayas which had already become noticeable from the end of the nineteenth century onwards. By the turn of the twentieth century, Kalimpong had definitively replaced Kathmandu as the entrepot of Trans-Himalayan trade, even to the extent that Newar merchants from Kathmandu shifted their locus of activity to Kalimpong.[66]

By 1944 wool comprised over 90 percent of Tibet's annual exports, some destined for the American east coast.[67] The international wool trade had come to dominate the Tibetan economy to the extent that the Tibetans were greatly at a loss when World War II cut the export to foreign markets. In the decade before the war, the southward-bound wool trade via Kalimpong had become an arena of competition for the Marwari from India and a class of newly arisen traders from central and eastern Tibet. One of the most powerful among the latter was Yarpel Pangda Tsang from Kham, who had become the Tibetan government's major trade agent.[68] The fortunes of Pangda Tsang rested in particular in the wool trade, though Marwari competition had by no means been broken. Already in January 1932, the thirteenth Dalai Lama had written a letter to the American journalist Suydam Cutting, strange to say, one of the few contacts of Tibet with America, in which he pointed out the importance of passing by Marwari middlemen trade at Kalimpong:

> From now onward if Pangda Tsang could deliver the wool at a fixed price to the buying agents of the big American wool merchants at Kalimpong (trade town of northern Bengal) without having to pass through the hands of the Malwaris (woolen merchants of Kalimpong) and thereby doing away with the middlemen's profit, it would be of great advantage to the government.[69]

Cutting succeeded in establishing a few trade contacts and for a couple of years some of the wool from Tibet found its way directly to the American market. But the war cut off the export and the Tibetans were temporarily without this source of revenue. Thus it should come as no surprise, that when the Americans Ilia Tolstoy and Brooke Dolan visited Tibet in the autumn of 1942, they were approached by Pangda Tsang, asking them when the United States would again buy Tibetan wool.[70]

Almost imperceptibly we have moved in our analysis from the traditional barter trade in salt and grain to the growing importance of a long-distance commerce in tea and wool, the latter in particular being subject to the vagaries of the world market and the geo-political predicament of its transport lines. Growing trade in the wake of the Younghusband expedition tended to emphasize the British-Indian connection, a process being reinforced by the internal chaos in China in the 1920s and 30s, when the overland trade bound for Tibet, except that for tea, was diverted via Calcutta and other Indian centers.[71] The locational shift of the Tibetan wool trade is but one example of this process of spatial reorientation. This largely externally induced process also brought changes in the long-distance trade of luxury goods, a one-time important pillar of Tibetan prosperity. It is to this trade and to the versatility of its fairs and markets that we turn now.

THE LONG-DISTANCE TRADE IN LUXURY GOODS

Behind the above, almost self-evident caption of this section lie hidden two conceptual problems: what is long-distance trade and what do we understand by luxury goods? These questions are important, because in a Tibetan context, trade beyond the local exchange of daily necessities has, in variable degrees, always formed an important pillar of the Tibetan economy. It seems likely that many areas in Tibet would not have been economically so viable as they were without extensive involvement in long-distance trade.

But when may this trade be called long-distance, and who was actually involved in it? Within the context of this study, long-distance trade has been defined as that form of commercial activity which involves the crossing of international boundaries, or the penetration into a non-familiar culture or society, or both.

This section focuses in particular on the flexibility of traders along the large-scale and genuine long-distance extremity of the continuum mentioned above. The trade on this end was usually in non-essential, luxury products, generally low weight for value, easily transportable, and high in price. To this category belonged traditionally much sought-after commodities like amber and musk, but also coral and turquoise, supplemented by silk from China and indigenous cotton from Nepal. With the rising importance of the British-Indian *économie-monde*, these were partly replaced by cheap Indian-made textiles, as well as a whole array of modern European goods for the use and entertainment of the richer classes in Tibet. The almost chronic disturbances in a fading imperial China and the birth pangs of the new republic, reduced Tibetan contact with the Chinese *économie-monde* considerably, but of course the proximity of eastern Tibet to China could and can never be nullified or neglected in terms of potential economic integration. However, the historically specific trade situation that arose from these circumstances with regard to Tibet in the first half of the twentieth century, was one of an increased orientation towards the south, i.e., India, where the *Pax Britannica* guaranteed a safety of roads and the unrestricted movement of goods, except for salt. In particular after the Younghusband expedition of 1904, trade steadily increased and became of a more intentionally organized and large-scale nature.

PILGRIMAGE, FAIRS, AND TRADE

Within a Tibetan regional setting, the mobility of the nomad was generally matched by the mobility of the pilgrim. Pilgrimage as a devotional and penitential exercise had always been an important aspect of the Tibetan culture world and restless was the search for merit to fulfill one's destiny. Many were the places where natural energy and magical powers were thought to enrich the pilgrim's *karma*, and mountains, monasteries and caves were the object of many a protracted journey.[72] Near these power-places sprang up a brisk trade, carried on by a host of mendicant monks and itinerant traders. Punctuated by the religious calendar of a particular place or establishment, the fair or *mela* attached could well develop into an important seasonal market place characterized by the harmonious blend of commercial enterprise and spiritual devotion. Periodicity of the more secular oriented markets was naturally influenced by population density and aggregate demand. It was also subject to the seasonal going of trails, winter being the preferred time of trade and travel. Some of the more important markets specialized in a limited number of goods and products like tea, wool, and horses. Favorably located break-of-bulk points between major ecozones sometimes developed into small trading towns, which acted as entrepots and control centers of caravan traffic. Sometimes too, a hierarchy of seasonal *melas* at different altitudes existed in certain transitional areas.

In discussing the traditional trade of Tibet, the prominent place of pilgrimage deserves further elaboration. What makes pilgrimage relevant in the context of this study is its close relation to economic activity, in particular trade. Though it is impossible to tell whether pilgrimage created trade or vice versa, it seems undeniable that the large flows of pilgrims generated by Lhasa and a few other centers contributed to the growth of a network of international exchange, spanning the length and breadth of Central Asia.[73] But regional centers of pilgrimage too, drew numerous worshippers.

Lhasa as the supreme focus of pilgrimage in the Tibetan Buddhist world, harboring its highest incarnation, the Dalaï Lama, attracted pilgrims from all over Tibet and even beyond. Particularly at the times of a major festival, such as the great Mönlam Prayer following the Losar or New Year celebrations, the population of Lhasa, which was ordinarily perhaps fifteen to twenty thousand, swelled to four or five times this number.[74] Trashilhünpo too, the seat of the Panchen Lama near Zhigatsé, drew tens of thousands of pilgrims, single audiences at major celebrations bringing together six thousand pilgrims and lookers-on before the great Living Buddha.[75] Numbers of pilgrims to other famous places of pilgrimage, such as the sacred mountains of Kailash, Kawakarpo, and Takpa Siri also ran into the thousands, especially during the years of "High Pilgrimage," which occurred in twelve-year cycles.[76] All these must have generated considerable flows of pilgrims, creating a culturally defined *espace-mouvement*, which however was also characterized by concomitant forms of commercial activity, ranging from the peddler's hawking to the prince's caravan trade.

The high mobility of people in the context of pilgrimage, the scale at which it took place, as well as the vast distances covered by the pilgrims, all contributed to the likelihood of trade. Pilgrims were sometimes away for over two years[77] and had to barter their way to Lhasa and other places. The pilgrimage of farmers and herders was often combined with petty trade[78] their cattle being used as walking merchandise. In addition, they might have saved some of their agricultural surpluses while still at home, which were now carried in the form of bundles of tea, parcels of gold dust, and silver talents.[79] Devotees generally managed to combine religion with a little business and the shops of Lhasa and the fairs of Kailash definitely felt their presence.[80]

At times of great religious festivals, supra-regional fairs under the protection of the monasteries saw the gathering of numerous trading pilgrims. The demand generated by the seasonal clustering of large numbers of pilgrims also brought together traders from all over Central Asia and adjoining countries. In addition, fakirs, mendicants, and charlatans tried their luck, performing their tricks and selling their magical medicines.[81]

Of course, not all of these fairs were of the same importance. In fact, there was a whole hierarchy of greater and lesser sacred places with their corresponding fairs, structurally perhaps not unlike the geographer's Central Place system. Sacred places of different levels had corresponding pilgrim fields, creating a kind of nested hierarchy ultimately encompassing the entire population of Tibet and its culturally related border worlds.[82] In practice, such a set-up meant that some fairs were held less often than others, were of longer duration, and offered a greater variety of goods, in addition to a high or even temporarily increased degree of sacredness of the locality involved. The twelve-year "High Pilgrimage" and corresponding Khumb mela near Kailash is a good example of the latter.[83] Let us briefly cast a glance now at two very specific Tibetan items of luxury trade, that were often to be seen at places of pilgrimage: medicinal herbs and precious stones.

Temporary and chronic illness has always been part and parcel of the *condition humaine*, and pilgrims too, did not escape that predicament. Weakened perhaps by insufficient food on their long journey across high passes, quite a few of them were afflicted by strange ailments that needed to be cured. As the mountainous areas of the Himalayas and eastern Tibet yield many an officinal herb of proven effect, herb collectors and medicine sellers plied their trade successfully at the crowded fairs. Monasteries too, were sometimes centers of herbal medicine preparation.[84] At the fairs, herbs also changed hands from collectors to wholesalers, who transported greater quantities to the lowland markets of India and China.[85] This trade had already a long history and may be traced back to the seventeenth century.[86] Especially the rhubarb trade developed into a long distance commerce of stable profit and great range. We shall briefly return to this trade in a following section.

The step from herbal medicines to precious stones such as traded at the fairs of Tibet, is less than one might think at first sight. In a world full of symbolism as traditional Tibet undoubtedly was, gem-stones had their own meaning attuned to the need of the hour. One of them was the healing power stones were thought to possess, and consequently their appreciation as medicine ranked next to their valuation as ornaments. Turquoise, for example, the widely appreciated gem-stone of Tibet, was in high demand in both qualities.[87] In addition, coral, pearls, amber, rubies and jade found their way into Tibet, the low weight for value quality making them a preferred item for the itinerant traders plying the fairs. Precious stones came from Afghanistan, India, Burma, and Turkestan,[88] but less so from the Himalayas.[89] If they could afford it, Tibetans spent fortunes on ornamentation.[90] Consequently, precious stones commanded a glorious sale, and not only in pilgrim centers.

Tibetan pilgrimage came to extend beyond its immediate cultural domain from the beginning of the nineteenth century onwards. An exception to this general statement was the Kathmandu valley in Nepal, which had already been visited for centuries by Tibetans, especially in wintertime.[91] Since the era of the seventeenth-century Malla kings, when free circulation across the Himalaya was still the rule, Tibetans increasingly had come to create their own niche in valley society, a position best visible near the stupas of Bodnath and Swayambunath.[92] The German scholar Kurt Boeck, in his well-illustrated book on his journey to India and Nepal in 1898, gives an interesting impression of what he calls the Tibetan village of Bodnath.[93] According to him, Tibetans visited the Kathmandu valley in wintertime to exchange salt, yak tails, and woolen blankets for grain, and in addition were dealing in gold dust, turquoise, agate, rubies, and other precious stones, together with medicinal herbs.[94] They still did so recently at the time of the Tibetan New Year.[95]

Apart from these pilgrimages and trading ventures into the Kathmandu valley, journeys to places well outside the Tibetan cultural sphere of influence, in particular India, did become fashionable in the course of the nineteenth century.[96] The holiest place to visit for the Tibetans was Bodh Gaya, where Buddha attained enlightenment under a *pipal* tree. As the Indian plains are scorching hot in summertime, these journeys of pilgrimage too, took place during the winter season, over time accelerated in pace and volume by the beginnings of railway transport in the Ganga Plain, and the increasing orientation of Central Tibet towards a rising British-Indian *économie-monde*. These journeys of pilgrimage, especially in its extended form throughout the northern plains and the Indian Himalayas, were instigated by the rich who gained merit by paying poor people to go on pilgrimage for them. From the beginning of the twentieth century onwards, they came to regard Kalimpong in the Sikkim Himalaya as their main point of departure. However, it also became the refuge of stranded pilgrims, who, venturing into the plains, had lost all their money and now tried to make ends meet by selling off their personal belongings.[97] The more successful traders and pilgrims on their way to Bodh Gaya, often passed through Calcutta, satisfying both their natural curiosity for things beyond the Tibetan ken and their passion for trade.[98]

To avoid a one-sided picture, it should be mentioned here that similar developments took place in eastern Tibet, though on a smaller scale. With the rise of Daqianlu on the Sino-Tibetan border, quite a few Tibetans, ventured into China, especially to the great pilgrim mountain of Emei Shan in southern Sichuan[99] and even beyond.[100] Urga in Mongolia too, as the seat of a primary Living Buddha, became the object of pilgrimage and trade for Tibetans from Amdo, as well as for monastic trade missions from all over Tibet.[101] The two-year stay of the Dalai Lama in Urga (1904–1906) may temporarily have emphasized its renown as a center of pilgrimage.

Thus, pilgrimage to sacred places, whether by private pilgrims or monastic missions, had a definite economic effect becoming visible in the commercial activities accompanying major religious festivals. In fact, these fairs as they were commonly called, may be defined as annual gatherings of buyers and sellers at a particular place and time for the purpose of trade, often following a religious function, and accompanied by forms of amusement and entertainment. However, when the scale of the trade increased, fairs often assumed a more secular character, in which the exchange of goods came to dominate the religious celebrations.

FROM THE SACRED TO THE PROFANE

In the period under investigation, the "long" century between 1850 and 1950, fairs gradually shed their aura of being predominantly religious festivals. The larger the fair, the greater the attraction for full time traders, who in the course of the nineteenth century came to consider monetary profit to be the leading motive for their attendance. For them the fairs were not places of karmic restoration, but arenas for economic competition. In order to maximize profits they sought to realize optimal locational conditions by turning footloose, visiting theaters of commercial exchange, even when these were not, strictly speaking, the product of a religious festival. Specialized itinerant traders became a regular feature of fairs that were more a response to the changing geo-historical conditions of long-distance trade than the slavish following of the pilgrim crowds near incarnated buddhas or sacred mountains. In particular the Himalayan border regions became the scene of a whole series of frontier fairs that reflected the growing orientation of southern Tibet on a rising British-Indian *économie-monde*.

The distinguishing feature of fairs as commercial gatherings was their theoretical openness to all trade and traders, irrespective of their provenance. As such they could flourish in times of limited political interference and in areas outside effective governmental control, "frontier" conditions that were satisfied in the "long" nineteenth century of Tibet and its borderlands. But if we look at the geographical distribution of fairs, it is also clear that they were commonly held in fringe zones of different ecozones and culturally disparate *économies-mondes*. Though Tibet cannot properly be called an *économie-monde*, both the ecozonal and the cultural fringe argument hold in regard to the location of its fairs. The European parallel, in particular with regard to the great medieval fairs of France and Germany, is interesting, but cannot be given any space here.[102]

The above theorizing fits well in with Braudel's characterization of India and China in terms of the development of their fairs.[103] India, according to Braudel, is the land of fairs *par excellence*.[104] Perhaps this may be explained by the decentralized nature of its political organization over much of its history, in contrast to China, where fairs only seem to have flourished in times of disintegration of the Chinese central polity. From the moment onwards that fresh political unity was achieved, and the Chinese bureaucracy restored to its former efficiency, fairs in the interior of China declined, but remained intact in a few frontier zones.[105] This distinction between India and China may well explain the relative preponderance of fairs along the Himalayan border of Tibet, and their paucity along the Sino-Tibetan one. Consequently, the presence of itinerant traders and peddlers, on which the fair as a commercial phenomenon rested, was far more pronounced in Tibet's southern reaches than in its eastern ones, at least for the period under discussion.

Fairs along the Sino-Tibetan border were far less common than in the Himalayan region. This does not mean that commercial exchange was unimportant. In fact, the volume of Tibet's China trade had always been greater than its trade with India, and on top of that, more institutionalized. Since the beginning of the eighteenth century already, Daqianlu and Xining had grown as the major break-of-bulk points between China and Tibet. Trade was in the hands of Chinese merchants, though with the crumbling of Chinese power in the second half of the nineteenth century, Tibetan traders were able to make successful inroads into this monopoly.[106] Fairs comparable to those in the Himalayan border world were only to be found near places of supra-regional exchange like Kumbum, mentioned earlier in this chapter, Jyekundo,[107] or Ragya,[108] the latter being but a relatively tiny affair. Although annual tribal fairs did exist on the Sino-Tibetan border,[109] large ones seem to have been the exception rather than the rule. In fact, these borderlands had developed into a smuggler's paradise for tea, musk, opium, and modern weapons, a sort of Sino-Tibetan "Wild West," in which Songpan, and in particular the neighboring hamlet of Matang, occupied a prominent place.[110]

The slow extinction of fairs in the Himalayan region and their virtual disappearance along the Sino-Tibetan border in the period under review, had everything to do with the rise of a more professionalized trade circuit, focusing on urban markets and a few through-going transport routes, like the one across the Jelep La to Kalimpong, or the main Tibet-China road via Daqianlu. Fairs dwindled insofar as they were meant to provide a wholesale market for specialized traders. The latter increasingly shifted their activity to the towns, where the grander scale of the business precipitated new forms of a capitalist-oriented trade in the hands of a few trading families or firms. Wholesale trade came of age, and developed quite independently from the traditional trade circuits center-ing on the fairs and local markets. The bigger itinerant traders established them-selves as resident merchants, who through their commercial agents tried to de-velop direct lines of exchange with a few merchants or institutions on the other side of the border.

To make the picture of Tibet as a trading region complete, we still have to focus on the transformation of traditional, long-distance trade in luxury goods by foreign traders to a more open, yet increasingly government-controlled trade. And as the government of Tibet had close links with the bigger monasteries, it should come as no surprise that these are relevant to our discussion.

THE ECCLESIASTICAL STATE AND TRADE

It is quite likely, though not proven beyond any doubt, that the rise of the Ge-lukpa order in Central Tibet, and its consolidation into a kind of ecclesiastical state in the seventeenth century was at least partly related to the wealth generated by long-distance trade.[111] In fact, the whole issue deserves a separate investiga-tion, which goes beyond the limits set for this study. According to Snellgrove and Richardson,[112] the great monasteries of central and eastern Tibet, already from the fourteenth century onwards, grew rich on their China trade, which, disguised as "tribute missions" to the emperor's court, served no other purpose than the trade in luxury goods.[113] These "government"-controlled trade mis-sions were really large caravans equipped by the leading monasteries of Tibet, who in doing so succeeded in amassing more wealth than was probably good for them. In addition, the heyday of the seventeenth century Gelukpa administra-tion, saw the flocking of hundreds of foreign traders to Lhasa, of whom Kashmiri, Newari, and Chinese were the most important.[114] Lhasa, as the center of the Ti-betan Buddhist world, also received a kind of tribute missions, for example the lapchak from Ladakh,[115] which connected Central Tibet to the Afghan and Kashmir-Yarkand trade circuits. As outlined elsewhere, trade was partly of a tran-sit nature, which explains perhaps the 197 Kashmiri trading houses in Lhasa in the eighteenth century.[116] The location of Central Tibet between major civiliza-tions and ecozones, made it into an ideal transit-corridor at a time when railways and cheap transport by sea had not yet arisen. Moreover, the highlands of Tibet were a distinct ecozone in themselves, from which many a special product could be procured. Trade was of a luxury nature, goods of low weight for value like musk, rhubarb, gold and precious stones, dominating the scene.

Musk, a natural perfume derived from the indigenous musk-deer, from .times immemorial had served to put Tibet on the mental map of Asian and even European long-distance traders. Medieval Arab sources mentioned it in connection with Tibet.[117] Marco Polo too, knew of it,[118] and William Finch, an early seventeenth century merchant, drew attention to it in his 1611 report.[119] The French traveler Tavernier tells us of musk from Tibet being sold at Patna as early as 1692,[120] and Bogle refers to it as one of the principal commodities, together with gold dust, with which the Tibetans paid for their imports from Bengal.[121] Musk over the centuries, remained a very lucrative business, even attracting agents from European firms to the Tibetan borderlands. In the second half of the nineteenth century, markets for musk developed in Xining, Daqianlu, Lijiang and Darjeeling, part of the commodity offered being in transit from Lhasa.[122]

Rhubarb, valued as a drug, also played an important role in long-distance trade, especially towards China, where the Chinese held a virtual monopoly over its export to Europe in the eighteenth century.[123] But in Tavernier's time, a century earlier, rhubarb was also brought to Gorakhpur and Patna in northern India.[124] In the nineteenth century, Muslim traders from Xining exported quantities of rhubarb to Kiakhta on the Russo-Mongolian border,[125] Xining being the chief depot for the rhubarb trade in northeastern Tibet.[126] Daqianlu was another major center of the rhubarb export in the Sino-Tibetan borderlands.[127]

Gold too, was an important item in keeping the balance of Tibetan trade upright. Over the centuries, the gold of Tibet had acquired a mythical reputation, but a Tibetan El Dorado did not exist, and quantities mined were relatively small.[128] Gold digging and washing took place at several localities in northwest and eastern Tibet,[129] the gold being transported to Lhasa and Zhigatsé[130] and a few of the larger monasteries along the major trade route with China, like Litang,[131] and Batang.[132] Actually, very little of the Tibetan gold found its way to India,[133] rather, Indian silver rupees were coming in, so as to pay for the wool exported to Ladakh and Kashmir. However, gold did flow out of Tibet into China, Tibet's major trading partner until the early twentieth century. According to Shuttleworth,[134] 30,625 pounds sterling in Tibetan gold entered Daqianlu alone for the year 1913.[135]

The precise extent to which monasteries were involved in trade will probably always remain a relative mystery. Where Tibetans chose to write down their life experiences, these had not, with few exceptions, to do with economic affairs. Moreover records which may have existed at one time, were largely destroyed after the Chinese takeover. Which leaves us with the writings of outsiders, mainly travelers and a few scientist-explorers. It is to one of the former that we owe the following immortal observation, which, as a mirror of the time in which it was written, i.e., the late 1930s, succinctly summarizes the relation of the sacred to the profane: "the monks of Tibet, though cloistered from the vulgar world, have a nice sense of business."[136]

This situation was the outcome of a long historical process, in which the conditions and demands of everyday life, as well as the continual growth in power of the monasteries, had necessarily led to a considerable softening of the originally strict monastic observance.[137] This in turn created the ideological basis for a further involvement in trade, even to such an extent that it became institutionalized within the monastic organization.[138] Incarnations turned secular insofar as they could make big money,[139] but perhaps there is some stereotyping involved in painting the monasteries and the Living Buddhas as the greatest traders of Tibet.[140] After all, there were big and small monasteries, rich and poor *gönpas*,[141] and among the monks "all the graduated shades of poverty and wealth that you see in mundane cities."[142] Nevertheless, it is true that monasteries were important economic centers,[143] some of which had deteriorated into dens of exploitation for local villagers and visiting pilgrims.[144] It is quite likely, however, that reform measures under the stern rule of the thirteenth Dalai Lama (1895–1933), counteracted the worst excesses.[145] Anyway, monasteries had grown rich by their legitimate functions, and sometimes by their illegitimate actions. Their pivotal position in Tibetan society made them into "immense reservoirs, into which flowed, by a thousand channels, all the wealth of these vast regions."[146] Their strong financial position made them engage in money-lending,[147] as well as trade,[148] and there was a tendency for the bigger monasteries to monopolize certain products and trade flows, which led to occasional clashes with private traders and among themselves.[149]

From the 1880s onward, there was a definite tendency among the higher classes to grow more and more luxurious in their style of living.[150] This was inevitably brought about by the foreign trade of Tibet and the arrival of goods of foreign origin. The latter were increasingly brought to Tibet by the Tibetans themselves. Actually, the rise of a British-Indian *économie-monde* in the course of the nineteenth century tempted Tibetan traders to try their luck beyond the immediate Tibetan pale and a class of widely traveled Tibetans came into existence.[151]

During the period of Bell's direct diplomatic involvement with Tibet (1910–1921), a growing number of Tibetans went abroad.[152] This was definitely facilitated by the outcome of the Younghusband expedition of 1904. Political obstacles for commerce across the Himalaya were removed, and a few British-controlled trade marts established inside Tibetan territory.[153] In the course of the process, the Indo-Tibetan trade via Darjeeling shifted to the newly arisen town of Kalimpong, which was more suitably located for the caravans coming down from the Jelep La and the Natu La.[154] The most important items of trade were in the hands of a few families, whose agents resided in Kalimpong and elsewhere. Although there were some wealthy private traders in Lhasa, most of the trading families served in one way or another the interests of the Tibetan government and the monasteries on which its power rested.[155]

A good example is the Pangda Tsang family "consortium," which had branches in Calcutta, Shanghai, and Peking.[156] Its origin dated back to the privileges received from the thirteenth Dalai Lama after the Chinese occupation of

Lhasa in 1912. In a few years, Pangda Tsang created a trading imperium that extended across the length and breadth of Tibet. In due time, he had his elder son, Yarpel, sent to Peking with the intention of setting up a commercial agency, while two others went to eastern Tibet, in order to tap the Southwest China trade.[157] In India the network included Kalimpong and Calcutta.[158] In fact, the Pangda Tsangs belonged to those traders who controlled large sections of the Tibet-China trade as earlier referred to. Other trading families from Kham were Sadu Tsang, "the all-embracing merchant,"[159] Gyanak Tsang, and Andru Tsang, the later resistance-leader against the Chinese in the 1950s.[160] With the rising tide of disturbances along the Sino-Tibetan border in the 1930s, most of these corporate trading families settled in Kalimpong.[161] Yarpel Pangda Tsang, after the death of his father, quickly developed into the most important trader of Tibet, effectively being for years the government's commercial agent in the British-controlled trade mart at Yatung,[162] and later in Kalimpong.[163] Basically, the fortunes of Pangda Tsang rested on the wool trade as described earlier in this study. It was Yarpel Pangda Tsang who asked Brooke Dolan and Ilia Tolstoy on their visit to Tibet in 1942 when the United States would buy wool again.[164]

The 1930s and 40s saw a proliferation of the Lhasa-Calcutta trade via Kalimpong.[165] Apart from the big shots in the Tibet trade mentioned above, many a smaller trader succeeded in earning a decent livelihood. And if the regular trade failed, there were always the many sidelines by which he could try to make ends meet. Gambling and smuggling were among the most common strategies to overcome temporary misfortune.[166] The sale of imitation stones or adulterated musk provided yet another.[167] And then there was of course the opium, and Tibet was not a newcomer for that matter.[168] The Tibetans did a brisk trade during World War II, especially when the Burma road to China had been cut, and a transit trade developed to Lijiang in northern Yunnan by way of Kalimpong, Gyantsé, Lhasa and Chamdo.[169] After the war, trade and commerce continued to flourish, and as such may be regarded as the most dynamic aspect of the Tibetan economy in the years just prior to the Chinese take-over.[170]

THE GEO-HISTORY OF TIBETAN TRADE: AN INTERPRETATION

Let us briefly recapitulate. Traditional trade in Tibet and its borderworlds rested on the local and regional exchange of salt, wool, grain and tea. In addition to this barter complex, there was a long-distance trade in luxury goods like musk, medicinal herbs, and precious stones, which initially focused on monastic fairs and supra-regional places of pilgrimage. On top of that, and perhaps increasingly so with monastic and government control over its mining operations, gold too, by virtue of its low weight for value, served as a long-distance bridging trade commodity, in particular in its quality as payment for the numerous tea imports from China into Tibet.

With the growing impact of the British-Indian *économie-monde* in the nineteenth century, the long-distance trade in wool acquired new dimensions. Locationally speaking, it shifted from Ladakh to the Indo-Tibetan borderlands further eastwards and institutionally it was being organized on an ever grander scale. Over time it became monopolized by rising border groups of Bhotia traders. The resulting trade networks centered in particular on the Bhotia villages of Garhwal and Kumaon. The partly self-imposed geo-political isolation of Nepal, to the detriment of its one-time supreme trade route via Kathmandu, equally expressed itself in the rise of a number of Bhotia communities as long-distance traders along Nepal's northern border. The trade of these Bhotia communities flourished in particular during the second half of the nineteenth century, but suffered from the opening of British-controlled trade marts in Tibet after the Younghusband expedition and the opening of the Chumbi valley route to Central Tibet via the Sikkimese Jelep La.

In addition to this locational funneling via a few routes, trade became increasingly controlled, not to say monopolized, by a few bigger merchants, who had settled in the newly arisen towns of Darjeeling, and especially Kalimpong. These merchants were not only members of age-old trading communities like the Kashmiri and Newari, but also concerned a class of newly arisen Tibetan traders hailing from Kham, who had managed, with the support of privileges received from the Tibetan government, to monopolize the wool trade across the Central Himalayas. They had left their eastern Tibetan trading fields, not because the Chinese *économie-monde* had suddenly ceased to exist, but because political disturbances and geo-political strife made for very unsettled conditions all along the Sino-Tibetan border in the 1930s.

Thus, the trade relations of Tibet underwent a definite spatial reorientation. The Chinese wing of Braudel's *super économie-monde* lost out to a rising Indian wing during the period 1850–1950. The pull of the Indian *économie-monde* made itself more clearly felt when the rise of a British colonial empire in India made possible an enhanced internal coherence of movements by a bout of road and railway building during the second half of the nineteenth century. China lagged behind in this respect, but after the revolution of 1911, transport networks in the latter country too, slowly improved. The increased mobility of goods and people which showed as a result, allowed for an intensification of old and new forms of economic activity, especially in the form of market places near zones of cultural and ecological transition, as well as at specific break-of-bulk points. Tibet in this view was a kind of transitional zone, which, though culturally speaking an *espace-mouvement*, cannot be considered the same in economic terms. On the contrary, its internal movements and external relations were mainly conditioned by the fragmentary nature of its polity and its location *vis-à-vis* neighboring *économies-mondes*. Its reorientation towards the South was therefore only a derived, and partial one, if only because the regional population clusters in the eastern and southeastern provinces of Amdo and Kham could and can never escape their locational proximity to China.

NOTES

1. The present study is essentially a shortened and revised version of chapter 4 of my Ph.D. thesis, "Tibetan Border Worlds: A Geo-historical Analysis of Trade and Traders," University of Amsterdam, 1992.

2. F. Braudel, *Civilisation matérielle, économie et capitalisme, XVe–XVIIe siècle* [*Material Culture, Economy and Capitalism: 15th–17th Centuries*], 3 vols. (Paris: Armand Colin, 1979), 3:12.

3. Braudel, *Material Culture, Economy and Capitalism: 15th–17th Centuries*, 3:451.

4. Braudel, *Material Culture, Economy and Capitalism: 15th–17th Centuries*, 3:14.

5. This view has been further worked out in W. van Spengen, "Géographie politique, géographie historique braudelienne et régionalité culturelle du Tibet" [Political Geography, Braudelian Historical Geography, and Cultural Regionality of Tibet], *Géographie et Cultures* 7 (Fall 1993): 55–74.

6. A. Tafel, *Meine Tibetreise: Eine Studienfahrt durch das nordwestliche China und durch die innere Mongolei in das östliche Tibet* [*My Tibet Travels: A Study Tour Through Northwestern China and Inner Mongolian in Eastern Tibet*], 2 vols (Stuttgart, Berlin, Leipzig: Union Deutsche Verlagsgesellschaft, 1914); G. A. Combe, *A Tibetan on Tibet* (1926; reprint, Kathmandu: Ratna Pustak Bhandar, 1975), 100–117; George N. Roerich, *Trails to Inmost Asia: Five Years of Exploration with the Roerich Central Asian Expedition* (1931; reprint, Moscow: Izdatel'stvo, Nauka, 1967), 35–149; R. B. Ekvall, *Cultural Relations on the Kansu-Tibetan Border* (Chicago: University of Chicago Press, 1939), 48–82; R. B. Ekvall, *Fields on the Hoof: Nexus of Tibetan Nomadic Pastoralism* (New York: Holt, Rinehart and Winston, 1968); F. Kingdon-Ward, "Tibet as a Grazing Land," *The Geographical Journal* 110, nos. 1–3 (1948): 60–75; M. Hermanns, *Die Nomaden von Tibet. Die sozial-wirtschaftlichen Grundlagen der Hirtenkulturen in A mdo und von Innerasien: Ursprung und Entwicklung der Viehzucht* [*The Nomads of Tibet. The Socioeconomic Underpinnings of the Shepherding Culture of Amdo and Inner Asia: The Origin and Development of Animal Husbandry*] (Wien: Verlag Herold, 1949); N. Norbu, *A Journey Into the Culture of Tibetan Nomads: Bod 'brog gi shes rigs* (Arcidosso: Shang-Shung Edizioni, 1983); G. E. Clarke, *China's Reforms of Tibet, and Their Effects on Pastoralism* (Brighton, Institute of Development Studies, Discussion Paper, No. 237, 1987); and M. C. Goldstein and C. M. Beall, *Nomads of Western Tibet. The Survival of a Way of Life* (London: Serindia Publications, 1989).

7. Roerich, *Trails to Inmost Asia*, 39.

8. Combe, *A Tibetan on Tibet*, 103–115, end map.

9. Kingdon-Ward, "Tibet as a Grazing Land," *Tibet and Its Birds*, ed. C. Vaurie (London: H. F. and G. Witherby Ltd., 1972), 11, 19.

10. A. Khazanov, *Nomads and the Outside World* (Cambridge: Cambridge University Press, 1984), 202.

11. Khazanov, *Nomads and the Outside World*, 202.

12. Goldstein and Beall, *Nomads of Western Tibet*, 49.

13. Ekvall, *Cultural Relations on the Kansu-Tibetan Border*, 56; cf. H. Serruys, *Sino-Mongol Relations During the Ming, Vol. 3—Trade Relations: The Horsefairs (1400–1600)* (Bruxelles: Institut Belge des Hautes Etudes Chinoises, 1975), 86.

14. H. Harrer, *Sieben Jahre in Tibet* [*Seven Years in Tibet*] (Wien: Ullstein, 1952), 56; M. Brauen, ed., *Peter Aufschneiter: sein Leben in Tibet* [*Peter Aufschneiter: His Life in Tibet*] (Innsbruck: Steiger Verlag, 1983), 38, 44.

15. R. B. Ekvall, "Some Differences in Tibetan Land Tenure and Utilization," *Sinologica* 4, no. 1 (1954): 46–47.

16. M. C. Goldstein, "On the Political Organization of Nomadic Pastoralists in Western Tibet: A Rejoinder to Cox," *Himalaya Research Bulletin* 8, no. 3 (1988): 15–17.

17. A. Guibaut, *Ngolo-Setas, deuxième expedition, Guibaut-Liotard au Tibet, 1940* [*Ngolo-Seta: The Second Guibat-Liotard Expedition in Tibet, 1940*] (Paris: J. Susse, 1947), 219; B. Chakrabarty, "The Unknown Country of Golok-Setas," *Tibetan Review* 17, no. 5 (1982): 18–20.

18. G. Shi Yang and L. Bing Ziao, "Borate Minerals on the Qinghai-Xizang Plateau," *Geological and Ecological Studies of Qinghai-Xizang Plateau* (Beijing: Science Press; New York: Gordon and Breach, 1981), 1724–1725.

19. C. W. Brown, "'The Goat Is Mine, the Load Is Yours': Morphogenesis of 'Bhotiya-Shauka,' U.P., India" (Ph.D. diss., University of Lund), *Lund Studies in Social Anthropology* No. 1, 1984, 117–119.

20. T. Thomson, *Western Himalaya and Tibet: A Narrative of a Journey Through the Mountains of Northern India, During the Years 1847–8* (1852; reprint, Kathmandu: Ratna Pustak Bhandar, 1979), 66.

21. A. Hosie, *Report on a Journey to the Eastern Frontier of Thibet* (London: His Majesty's Stationery Office, 1905), 27.

22. E. Teichman, *Travels of a Consular Officer in Eastern Tibet: Together with a History of the Relations Between China, Tibet and India* (Cambridge: Cambridge University Press, 1922), 175.

23. C. H. Desgodins, *Le Thibet d'après la correspondance des missionaires* [*Tibet, from the Correspondence of Missionaries*] (Paris: Librairies Catholique de l'Oeuvre de Saint-Paul, 1885), 343–344.

24. The best outline on the salt trade in western Tibet has been given by the Austrian engineer Peter Aufschneiter, who lived and traveled extensively in the area during and shortly after World War II. See M. Brauen, *Peter Aufschneiter*; cf. Van Spengen, "Political Geography, Braudelian Historical Geography, and Cultural Regionality of Tibet," 75.

25. C. R. Markham, *Narratives of the Mission of George Bogle to Tibet and of the Journey of Thomas Manning to Lhasa* (1876; reprint, New Delhi: Manjusri Publishing House, 1971), 119; W. W. Rockhill, "Tibet: A Geographical, Ethnographical and

Historical Sketch, Derived from Chinese Sources," *Journal of the Royal Asiatic Society* 23, no. 1 (1891): 11–33, no. 2, 237, note 2; S. G. Burrard, *Records of the Survey of India*, vol. 8, part 1 (Dehra Dun: Office of the Trigonometrical Survey, 1915), 18; C. Wessels, *Early Jesuit Travellers in Central Asia, 1603–1721* (The Hague: Martinus Nijhoff, 1924), 249; C. Bell, *The People of Tibet* (1928; reprint, London: Oxford University Press, 1968), 118; B. N. Aziz, *Tibetan Frontier Families: Reflections of Three Generations from Dingri* (New Delhi: Vikas Publishing House, 1978), 96–97.

26. Hosie, *Report on a Journey to the Eastern Frontier of Thibet*, 29; O. Coales, "Economic Notes on Eastern Tibet," *The Geographical Journal* 54, no. 4 (October 1919): 244.

27. Cf. Van Spengen, "Political Geography, Braudelian Historical Geography, and Cultural Regionality of Tibet," 79.

28. E. C. Baber, *Travels and Researches in Western China*, Royal Geographical Society Supplementary Papers, vol. 1, part 1 (London, John Murray, 1882), 193; A. Hosie, *Three Years in Western China. A Narrative of Three Journeys in Ssuch'uan, Kuei-chow, Yün-nan* (New York: Dodd, Mead and Co., 1890), 93.

29. T. T. Cooper, *Travels of a Pioneer of Commerce in Pigtail and Petticoats: Or, an Overland Journey from China Towards India* (London: John Murray, 1871), 171; Rockhill, *The Land of the Lamas*, 277; F. M. Bailey, *China—Tibet—Assam. A Journey, 1911* (London: Jonathan Cape, 1945), 33.

30. Baber, *Travels and Researches in Western China*,194; F. W. Bailey, "Journey Through a Portion of South-Eastern Tibet and the Mishmi Hills," *The Geographical Journal* 34, no. 4 (April 1912): 334.

31. Burrard, *Records of the Survey of India*, part 2, 233; Cooper, *An Overland Journey from China Towards India*, 187.

32. Combe, *A Tibetan on Tibet*, 142–143.

33. H. Stevenson, "Notes on the Human Geography of the Chinese-Tibetan Borderland," *The Geographical Review* 22, no. 4 (October 1932): 616.

34. D. C. Graham, "A Trip to Tatsienlu," *Journal of the West China Border Research Society* 2 (1924–25): 34.

35. J. H. Edgar, "Notes on Trade Routes Converging at Tachienlu," *Journal of the West China Border Research Society* 4 (1930–31): 5–8.

36. Baber, *Travels and Researches in Western China*,196; A. von Rosthorn, *On Tea Cultivation in Western Ssuch'uan and the Tea Trade with Tibet via Tachienlu* (London: Luzac, 1895); Burrard, *Records of the Survey of India*, vol. 2, 233; W. Limpricht, *Botanische Reisen in den Hochgebirgen Chinas und Osttibet* [*Botanical Journey in the Highlands of China and Eastern Tibet*] (Dahlem bei Berlin: Verlag des Repertorium, 1922), 143; A. Migot, *Tibetan Marches*, translated from the French (London: The Travel Book Club, n.d., ca. 1957), 89.

37. Rockhill, *The Land of the Lamas*, 278; Burrard, *Records of the Survey of India*, part 2, 233; Combe, *A Tibetan on Tibet*, 143.

38. Baber, *Travels and Researches in Western China*, 195; Rockhill, *The Land of the Lamas*, 277, 280.

39. See M. H. Duncan, *The Yangtze and the Yak. Adventurous Trails in and out of Tibet*, (Alexandria, Va./Ann Arbor, Mich.: Edwards Brothers, 1952), 67, figure 18; for a more detailed discussion on the distributive trade in Tibet, see Van Spengen, "Political Geography, Braudelian Historical Geography, and Cultural Regionality of Tibet," 80.

40. Burrard, *Records of the Survey of India*, part 2, 388.

41. E. C. Ryall, "Explorations in Western Tibet, by the Trans-Himalayan Parties of the Indian Trigonometrical Survey," *Proceedings of the Royal Geographical Society* 1 (1879): 446.

42. A. Gerard, *Account of Koonawur in the Himalaya* (1841; reprint, New Delhi: Indus Publishing Company, 1993), 116.

43. Rockhill, *The Land of the Lamas*, 111.

44. J. Fletcher, "A Brief History of the Chinese Northwestern Frontier," in *China's Inner Asian Frontier: Photographs of the Wulsin Expedition to Northwest China in 1923*, ed. M. E. Alonso (Cambridge, Mass.: The Peabody Museum of Archaeology and Ethnology, Harvard University, 1979), 38.

45. J. N. Lipman, "The Border World of Gansu, 1895–1935" (Ph.D. diss., Stanford University, 1981), 117–119.

46. J. Scott, "A Short Journey Through Northwestern Kansu and the Tibetan Border Country," *Journal of the Royal Central Asian Society* 21, part 1 (January 1934): 18–37.

47. Cf. Rockhill, *The Land of the Lamas*, 90.

48. Lipman, "The Border World of Gansu, 1895–1935," 116.

49. Cf. S. Cammann, *Trade Through the Himalayas: The Early Attempts to Open Tibet* (Princeton: Princeton University Press, 1951), 43ff.

50. S. C. Rijnhart, *With the Tibetans in Tent and Temple: Narrative of Four Years' Residence on the Tibetan Border, and of a Journey Into the Far Interior* (Edinburgh and London: Oliphant, Anderson and Ferrier, 1901),134, 230; Tafel, *My Tibet Travels*, vol. 1, 181; Coales, "Economic Notes on Eastern Tibet," *The Geographical Journal* 53, no. 4 (April 1919): 242; Fletcher, "A Brief History of the Chinese Northwestern Frontier," 30.

51. For Kumbum, see Rockhill, *The Land of the Lamas*, 90; W. Carey, *Travel and Adventure in Tibet: Including the Diary of Miss Annie R. Taylor's Remarkable Journey from Tau-chau to Tachienlu Through the Heart of the Forbidden Land* (London: Hodder and Stoughton, 1902), 155; Li An-che, "Our Pilgrimage to a Sacred Kountain," *Asian Horizon* 2 (summer 1948), photo and caption following page 40; for Labrang, see K. Futterer, "Land und Leute in Nordost-Tibet" [Land and People in Northeast Tibet], *Zeitschrift der Gesellschaft für Erdkunde, Berlin* 35, no. 5 (1900): 326; Tafel, *My Tibet Travels*, vol. 2, 313; E. Fürholzer, *Arro! Arro! So sah ich Tibet* [Aro! Aro! The Tibet I Saw] (Berlin: Wilhelm Limpert-Verlag, 1942), 199, photo; Fletcher, "A Brief History of the Chinese Northwestern Frontier," 28; see also G. T. Tsybikov, *Un pèlerin bouddhiste au Tibet* [A Buddhist Pilgrim in Tibet] (Paris: Éditions Peuples du Monde, 1993), 33–49.

52. Teichman, *Travels of a Consular Officer in Eastern Tibet*, 92.

53. Tafel, *My Tibet Travels*, vol. 2, 152.

54. Teichman, *Travels of a Consular Officer in Eastern Tibet*, 97.

55. Combe, A Tibetan on Tibet, 141.

56. Coales, "Economic Notes on Eastern Tibet," 242.

57. G. Köhler, "Die Bedeutung des Huang Ho innerhalb des nordwest-chine-sischen Verkehrsnetzes" [The Importance of Huang He Within the Northwestern Chinese Traffic System], Petermanns Geographische Mitteilungen 96 (1952): 85–89.

58. Ekvall, Cultural Relations on the Kansu-Tibetan Border, 48–62.

59. Tafel, My Tibet Travels, vol. 2, 248; J. F. Rock, The Amnye Machen Range and Adjacent Regions. A Monographic Study, Serie Orientale Roma, 12 (Roma: Istituto italiano per il Medio ed Estremo Oriente, 1956), 65.

60. Tafel, My Tibet Travels, vol. 2, 309.

61. Ekvall, Cultural Relations on the Kansu-Tibetan Border, 51, 61.

62. Tafel, My Tibet Travels, vol. 1, 181, 347n; vol. 2, 313.

63. Lipman, The Border World of Gansu, 1895–1935, 120.

64. A. W. Radhu, Caravane tibétaine [Tibetan Caravans], adapté en français par Roger du Pasquier d'après les mémoires inédits de l'auteur (Paris: Fayard, 1981), 167–168. [Editors' note: Available in English as: Abdul Wahid Radhu, Islam in Tibet: Tibetan Caravans, trans. Jane Casewit, ed. Gray Henry (Louisville: Fons Vitae, 1997).]

65. W. Bosshard, "Politics and Trade in Central Asia," Journal of the Central Asian Society 16, part 4 (1929): 447–448.

66. R. Uprety, Nepal-Tibet Relations, 1850–1930 (Kathmandu: Puga Nara, 1980), 166–167.

67. Brown, "The Goat Is Mine, the Load Is Yours,"115.

68. H. Stoddard, Le Mendiant de l'Amdo [The Beggar from Amdo], recherches sur la Haute Asie, vol. 9 (Paris: Société d'ethnographie; Nanterre: Service de publication du Laboratoire d'ethnologie et de sociologie comparative, Université de Paris X, 1985), 77–78.

69. C. S. Cutting, The Fire Ox and Other Years (New York: Charles Scribner's Sons, 1940), 177–178.

70. I. Tolstoy, "Across Tibet from India to China," The National Geographic Magazine 90, no. 2 (August 1946): 178.

71. Macdonald, The Land of the Lama, 125.

72. A. M. Blondeau, "Les pèlerinages tibétains" [Tibetan Pilgrimages], in Sources Orientales, vol. 3—Les pèlerinages (Paris: Editions du Seuil, 1960), 203–245; K. Dowman, The Power-places of Central Tibet: The Pilgrim's Guide (London: Routledge and Kegan Paul, 1988); V. Chan, Tibet Handbook (Chico, Calif.: Moon Publications, 1994). See also G. T. Tsybikov, Un pèlerin bouddhiste au Tibet [A Buddhist Pilgrim in Tibet], translated from the Russian (orig. ed. 1919) and critical ed. by Bernard Kreise, preface by A. M. Blondeau (Paris: Éditions Peuples du Monde, 1993).

73. Blondeau, "Tibetan Pilgrimages," 212.

74. C. Bell, "A Year in Lhasa," The Geographical Journal 63, no. 2 (February 1924): 95; cf. the eighteenth-century Capuchin missionary figure of 80,000 inhabitants as quoted by D. Snellgrove and H. Richardson, A Cultural History of Tibet (Boulder: Prajna Press, 1980), 224.

75. S. Hedin, *Trans-Himalaya. Discoveries and Adventures in Tibet* (London: Macmillan and Co., 1910–1913), vol. 1, 304; see also plates 111 and 112.

76. C. A. Sherring, *Western Tibet and the Indian Borderland* (1906; reprint, Delhi: Cosmo Publications, 1974), 283; Duncan, *The Yangtze and the Yak*, 132; Blondeau, "Tibetan Pilgrimages," 210; for further details see Van Spengen, "Political Geography, Braudelian Historical Geography, and Cultural Regionality of Tibet," 91–92.

77. Cf. Tafel, *My Tibet Travels*, vol. 2, 253.

78. Pedro Carrasco, *Land and Polity in Tibet* (Seattle: University of Washington Press, 1959), 213.

79. Markham, Bogle, and Manning, *Narratives of the Mission of George Bogle to Tibet and of the Journey of Thomas Manning to Lhasa*, 83.

80. Sherring, *Western Tibet and the Indian Borderland*, 159, 283–284.

81. See for example the eyewitness report on the Kumbum *mela* by Rijnhart, *With the Tibetans in Tent and Temple*, 115.

82. Cf. S. M. Bhardwaj, *Hindu Places of Pilgrimage. A Study in Cultural Geography* (Berkeley: University of California Press, 1973), 6–7, for an example from the Indian Himalayas.

83. Sherring, *Western Tibet and the Indian Borderland*, 28; Hedin, *Trans-Himalaya: Discoveries and Adventures in Tibet*, vol. 1, 191.

84. Cf. Harrer, "My Life in Forbidden Lhasa," 162.

85. A. Heim, *Minya Gongkar: Forschungsreise ins Hochgebirge von Chinesisch Tibet* [*Minya Gongkar: Expedition Into the High Mountains of China's Tibet*] (Bern-Berlin: Verlag Hans Huber, 1933), 65, and figure 45 facing page 56.

86. Finch 1611, as quoted by A. Stein, "Routes from the Punjab to Turkestan and China Recorded by William Finch (1611)," *The Geographical Journal* 51, no. 1 (January 1918): 173; Tavernier 1692, as quoted by S. Lévi, *Le Népal. Etude historique d'un royaume hindou* [*Nepal: Historic Study of a Hindu Kingdom*] (Paris: Ernest Leroux, Annales du Musée Guimet, tome 17, vol. 1, 1985), 94; F. B. Hamilton, *An Account of the Kingdom of Nepal and the Territories Annexed to This Dominion by the House of Gorkha* (1819; reprint, New Delhi: Manjusri Publishing House, 1971), 86.

87. M. N. Walker-Watson, "Turquoise—the Gemstone of Tibet," *Tibetan Review* 18, no. 6–7 (1983): 17; cf. W. Filchner, *Kumbum Dschamba Ling: Das Kloster der hunderttausend Bilder Maitreyas* [*Kumbum Jamba Ling: The Monastery of One Hundred Thousand Maitreya Images*] (Leipzig: F. A. Brocjhaus, 1933), 413.

88. Ryall, "Explorations in Western Tibet," 450; E. Kawaguchi, *Three Years in Tibet* (1909; reprint, Kathmandu: Ratna Pustak Bhandar, 1979), 453–454; A. B. Calhoun, "Burma—an Important Source of Precious and Semi-precious Stones," *Engineering and Mining Journal* 127, no. 18 (May 4, 1929): 708 ff.; H. H. P. Deasy, *In Tibet and Chinese Turkestan* (London: T. Fisher Unwin, 1901), 156; for amber, see C. Jest, "Valeurs d'échange en Himalaya et au Tibet: l'ambre et le musc" [Exchange Values in the Himalayas and Tibet: Amber and Musk], in *De la voûte céleste au terroir, du jardin au foyer* (Paris: Editions de l'Ecole des Hautes Etudes en Sciences Sociales, 1987), 228–230.

89. A. M. Heron, "The Gem-stones of the Himalaya," *The Himalayan Journal* 2 (April 1930): 21.

90. W. Gill, *The River of Golden Sand: The Narrative of a Journey Through China and Eastern Tibet to Burma*, 2 vols. (London: John Murray, 1880), 2:107.

91. Hamilton, *An Account of the Kingdom of Nepal*, 212–213; H. A. Oidfield, *Sketches from Nepal* (1880; reprint, New Delhi: Manjusri Publishing House, 1974), vol. 1, 11; Snellgrove and Richardson, *A Cultural History of Tibet*, 202.

92. D. Wright, *History of Nepal* (1877; reprint, Kathmandu: Nepal Antiquated Book Publishers, 1972), 27; Lévi, *Nepal: Historic Study of a Hindu Kingdom*, vol. 2, 319, 332, 336.

93. K. Boeck, *Durch Indien ins verschlossene Land Nepal: Ethnographische und photographische Studien Blätter* [*Through India to Isolated Nepal: Ethnographic Studies and Photographic Plates*] (Leipzig: Verlag von Ferdinand Hirt und Sohn, 1903), 293–301; see also the frontispiece of the same book.

94. Boeck, *Through India to Isolated Nepal*, 294.

95. A. W. Macdonald, personal communication, Paris.

96. Blondeau, "Tibetan Pilgrimages," 218–219.

97. Blondeau, "Tibetan Pilgrimages," 219.

98. Richardus, *The Dutch Orientalist Johan van Manen: His Life and Work* (Leiden: Kern Institute, 1989), 41.

99. Cooper, *An Overland Journey from China Towards India*, 176; Baber, *Travels and Researches in Western China*, 42; Hosie, *Report on a Journey to the Eastern Frontier of Thibet*, 9; Hackmann, *Walks on the Borders of China, Tibet and Burma*, 9.

100. See for example M. Cable, F. Houghton, R. Kilgour, A. McLeish, R. W. Stuart, and O. Wyon, *The Challenge of Central Asia* (London: World Dominion Press, 1929), 95: "Yunnanfu Where There is a Tibetan Colony of Resident Traders."

101. G. Tsybikoff, "Journey to Lhasa," *The Geographical Journal* 23 (1904): 96; F. Ossendowski, *Beasts, Men and Gods* (London: Edward Arnold, 1922), 235.

102. But see A. Allix, "The Geography of Fairs," *Geographical Review* 12 (1922): 532–569; H. Pirenne, *Histoire économique et sociale du moyen âge* [*Economic and Social History of the Middle Ages*] (1933; reprint, Paris: Presses Universitaires de France, 1969), 83–89; F. Braudel, *La Méditerranée et le monde méditerranéen à l'époque de Philippe II* [*The Mediterranean and the Mediterranean World in the Age of Philip II*], 2 vols., seconde édition revue et augmentée (Paris: Librairie Armand Colin, 1966), 1 :347–350; Braudel, *Material Culture, Economy and Capitalism: 15th–17th Centuries*, vol. 2, 63–75.

103. Braudel, *Material Culture, Economy and Capitalism: 15th–17th Centuries*, vol. 2, 104–109.

104. Braudel, *Material Culture, Economy and Capitalism: 15th–17th Centuries*, vol. 2, 106–107.

105. Hypothesis put forward by E. Balazs as quoted by Braudel, *Material Culture, Economy and Capitalism: 15th–17th Centuries*, vol. 2, 109.

106. Desgodins, *Tibet, from the Correspondence of Missionaries*, 337; H. Bower, *Diary of a Journey Across Tibet* (1894; reprint, Kathmandu: Ratna Pustak Bhandar, 1976), 282.

107. See the lively description of the annual fair at Bkra shis dgonpa by F. Grenard, *Tibet: The Country and Its Inhabitants* (London: Huchinson and Co., 1904), 128–130.

108. Rock, "The Unexplored Amnye Machen Range," 162, see also photo on 157.

109. Duncan, *The Yangtze and the Yak*, 100.

110. Bird, *The Yangtze Valley and Beyond*, 333, 424; Tafel, *My Tibet Travels*, vol. 2, 248.

111. Cf. M. Gaborieau, *Récit d'un voyageur musulman au Tibet* [*Story of a Muslim Traveler to Tibet*] (Paris: Librairie Klincksieck, 1973), 17–18.

112. Snellgrove and Richardson, *A Cultural History of Tibet*, 156.

113. Cf. J. K. Fairbank and S. Y. Têng, "On the Qing Tributary System," *Harvard Journal of Asiatic Studies* 6 (1941): 135–246.

114. Gaborieau, *Story of a Muslim Traveler to Tibet*, 14–36; T. T. Lewis, "The Tuladhars of Kathmandu. A Study of Buddhist Tradition in a Newar Merchant Community" (Ph.D. diss., Columbia University, 1984). Markham, Bogle, and Manning, *Narratives of the Mission of George Bogle to Tibet and of the Journey of Thomas Manning to Lhasa*, 258–291.

115. L. Petech, *The Kingdom of Ladakh, c. 950–1842 A.D.* (Roma: Istituto italiano per il Medio ed Estremo Oriente, 1977), 161–162; Radhu, *Tibetan Caravan*; J. Bray, "The Lapchak Mission from Ladakh to Lhasa in British Indian Foreign Policy," *The Tibet Journal* 15, no. 4 (Winter 1990): 75–96.

116. L. Boulnois, *Poudre d'or et monnaies d'argent au Tibet (principalement au XVIIIe siècle)* [*Powdered Gold and Silver Coins in Tibet (Prinicaplly in the Eighteenth Century)*] (Paris: Editions du Centre National de la Recherche Scientifique, 1983), 129, after Chinese sources.

117. S. Hedin, *Southern Tibet: Discoveries in Former Times Compared with My Own Researches in 1906–08* (Band I–IX) (Stockholm: Lithographic Institute of the General Staff of the Swedish Army, 1917–1922), vol. 1, 50–52.

118. Marco Polo, *The Travels of Marco Polo*, after the complete Yule-Cordier edition of 1903/20, reprinted (New York, Dover Publications, 1992), 45.

119. Stein, *La civilisation tibétaine* (Paris: l'Asiathèque, 1987) (édition definitive, réédition revue et augmentée de l'édition de 1962; Paris: Dunod), 173.

120. As quoted by Lévi, *Nepal: Historic Study of a Hindu Kingdom*, vol. 1, 93.

121. Markham, Bogle, and Manning, *Narratives of the Mission of George Bogle to Tibet and of the Journey of Thomas Manning to Lhasa*, 6, 115, 183.

122. Rockhill, *Diary of a Journey Through Mongolia and Tibet in 1891 and 1892*, 71; F. Weiss, "Die Provinz Yunnan, ihre Handels- und Verkehrsverhältnisse" [Yunnan Province, Its Trade and Transportation Conditions], *Mitteilungen des Seminars für Orientalischen Sprachen* 14 (1912): 41; Burrard, *Records of the Survey of India*, vol. 1, 22, vol. 2, 330; J. W. Gregory and C. J. Gregory, *To the Alps of Chinese Tibet* (London: Seeley Service and Co., 1923), 205; Sagant, "Ampleur et profondeur historique des

migrations népalaises" [The Extent and Historical Depth of Nepalese Migrations], *L'Ethnographie* 120, no. 77–78 (1978): 112; see also Jest, "Exchange Values in the Himalayas and Tibet," 230–237.

123. S. Cammann, *The Land of the Camel: Tents and Temples of Inner Mongolia* (New York: The Ronald Press Company, 1951), 32n.

124. Lévi, *Nepal: Historic Study of a Hindu Kingdom*, vol. 1, 94; cf. V. Jacquemont, *Correspondance de V. Jacquemont avec sa famille et plusieurs de ses amis pendant son voyage dans l'Inde (1828–1832)* [*Correspondence of V. Jacquemont with His Family and Several of His Friends During His Voyage in India (1828–1832)*] (Bruxelles: Wouters, Raspoet et Cie, Imprimeurs-Libraires, 1843), nouvelle édition, vol. 1, 173.

125. N. M. Przehevalsky, *Mongolia, the Tangut Country and the Solitudes of Northern Tibet*, 2 vols. (London: S. Low, Marston, Searle and Rivington, 1876), 2:70n.

126. Prejevalsky, *Mongolia, the Tangut Country and the Solitudes of Northern Tibet*, vol. 2, 83; G. Kreitner, *Im fernen Osten. Reisen des Grafen Bela Szechenyi in Indien, Japan, China, Tibet und Birma in den Jahren 1877–1880* [*In the Far East. Travels of Count Bela Szechenyi in India, Japan, China, Tibet and Burma in the Years 1877–1880*] (Wien: Alfred Holder, 1881), 727–728.

127. Rockhill, *The Land of the Lamas*, 283–284.

128. Boulnois, *Powdered Gold and Silver Coins in Tibet*, 71–85.

129. Peter Lindegger, *Griechische und römische Quellen zum peripheren Tibet* [*Greek and Roman Sources on Tibet's Peripheries*], Opuscula Tibetana, Fasc. 14 (Rikon/Zürich: Tibet-Institute, 1982), 183, map, 44–45n; Boulnois, *Powdered Gold and Silver Coins in Tibet*, end map.

130. Burrard, *Records of the Survey of India*, vol. 1, 22.

131. Gill, *The Narrative of a Journey Through China and Eastern Tibet*, 93; Rockhill, *Diary of a Journey through Mongolia and Tibet in 1891 and 1892*, 357.

132. Cooper, *An Overland Journey from China Towards India*, 417.

133. Ryall, "Explorations in Western Tibet," 449; Shuttleworth, "A Wool Mart of the Indo-Tibetan Borderland," 557.

134. Shuttleworth, "A Wool Mart of the Indo-Tibetan Borderland," 557.

135. Cf. Hosie, *Report on a Journey to the Eastern Frontier of Thibet*, 80.

136. J. Hanbury-Tracy, *Black River of Tibet* (London: Frederick Muller Ltd., 1938), 58.

137. G. Tucci, *The Religions of Tibet* (London: Routledge and Kegan Paul, 1980), 110–111.

138. Cf. Tsarong, "Economy and Ideology on a Tibetan Monastic Estate in Ladakh: Processes of Production, Reproduction and Transformation" (Ph.D. diss., University of Wisconsin, Madison, 1987).

139. Prejevalsky, *Mongolia, the Tangut Country and the Solitudes of Northern Tibet*, vol. 2, 46–47; Tsybikoff, "Journey to Lhasa," 746; Rock, "The Unexplored Amnye Machen Range," 161.

140. Carrasco, *Land and Polity in Tibet*, 213.

141. Cutting, *The Fire Ox and Other Years*, 195.

142. E. R. Huc and J. Gabet, *Travels in Tartary, Thibet and China, 1844–1846*, foreword by Paul Pelliot (London: George Routledge and Sons, 1928), translated from the original French edition, Paris, 1850 (reprint, New York: Dover Publications 1987), vol. 2, 59; cf. A. David-Néel as quoted by R. Middleton, *Alexandra David-Neel: Portrait of an Adventurer* (Boston and Shaftesbury: Shambala, 1989), 121; G. N. Patterson, *Requiem for Tibet* (London: Aurum Press, 1990), 52.

143. Tucci, *The Religions of Tibet*, 130.

144. Huc, *Travels in Tartary, Thibet and China, 1844–1846*, vol. 1, 89, 92; W. Gill, "Travels in Western China and on the Eastern Border of Tibet," *The Journal of the Royal Geographical Society* 48 (1878): 93; A. D. Carey, "A Journey Round Chinese Turkistan and Along the Northern Frontier of Tibet," *Proceedings of the Royal Geographical Society* 9, no. 12 (1887): 731–752; Hosie, *Report on a Journey to the Eastern Frontier of Thibet*, 45; Filchner, *Kumbum Monastery*, 12.

145. C. Bell, *Portrait of the Dalai Lama* (London: Collins, 1946), 49.

146. Huc and Gabet, *Travels in Tartary, Thibet and China, 1844–1846*, vol. 2, 180.

147. Rockhill, *Diary of a Journey Through Mongolia and Tibet in 1891 and 1892*, 357; Futterer, "Geographical Sketch of Northeast Tibet," 326; Hosie, *Report on a Journey to the Eastern Frontier of Thibet*, 45; Carrasco, *Land and Polity in Tibet*, 213.

148. Desgodins, *Tibet, from the Correspondence of Missionaries*, 334–335; Bower, *Diary of a Journey Across Tibet*, 282; Kawaguchi, *Three Years in Tibet*, 458; Bell, *The People of Tibet*, 125; Filchner, *Kumbum Dschamba Ling*, 218.

149. Stein, *La civilisation tibétaine*, 92; cf. Macauley, *Report of a Mission to Sikkim and the Tibetan Frontier*, 16, 44.

150. Kawaguchi, *Three Years in Tibet*, 456.

151. Cf. Van Spengen, "Political Geography, Braudelian Historical Geography, and Cultural Regionality of Tibet," 102 for an elaboration on the subject.

152. Bell, *The People of Tibet*, 109.

153. A. Lamb, *British India and Tibet, 1766–1910* (London and New York: Routledge and Kegan Paul, 1986), 256ff.

154. Bell, *The People of Tibet*, 113; G. Tucci, *To Lhasa and Beyond. Diary of an Expedition to Tibet in the Year MCMXLVIII* (Roma: Libreria della Stato, 1956), 10.

155. Carrasco, *Land and Polity in Tibet*, 213; cf. Brauen, *Peter Aufschneiter*, 158.

156. Bell, *The People of Tibet*, 130.

157. Cf. Gregory and Gregory, *To the Alps of Chinese Tibet*, 112.

158. Radhu, *Tibetan Caravan*, 168; Stoddard, *The Beggar from Amdo*, 77.

159. A. Winnington, *Tibet: Record of a Journey* (London: Lawrence and Wishart, 1957), 185–189.

160. G. T. Andrugtsang, *Four Rivers, Six Ranges: Reminiscences of the Resistance Movement in Tibet* (Dharamsala: Information and Publicity Office of H.H. the Dalai Lama, 1973), 9–10.

161. Radhu, *Tibetan Caravan*, 168.

162. Patterson, *Requiem for Tibet*, 38.

163. Peter, *A Study of Polyandry*, 474.

164. Tolstoy, "Across Tibet from India to China," 172, 178.

165. Tucci, *To Lhasa and Beyond*, 12.

166. Bell, *The People of Tibet*, 117; Tucci, *To Lhasa and Beyond*, 33.

167. J. Hanbury-Tracy, *Black River of Tibet*, 181; A. David-Néel, "Les marchands tibétains" [Tibetan Merchants], *France-Asie* 9, no. 83 (1953): 284–293, part 1; *France-Asie* 9, no. 84 (1953): 398–409, part 2.

168. J. W. Edgar, *Report on a Visit to Sikhim and the Thibetan Frontier* (1874; reprint, New Delhi: Manjusri Publishing House, 1969), 45–47; Hosie, *Report on a Journey to the Eastern Frontier of Thibet*, 28; W. Stötzner, *Ins unerforschte Tibet: Tagebuch der deutschen Expedition Stötzner 1914* [*Into Unexplored Tibet: Diary of the German Stötzner Expedition 1914*] (Leipzig: Verlag von K F. Koehler, 1924),107; Harrer, *Seven Years in Tibet*, 141; S. Goswami, "The Opium Evil in Nineteenth Century Assam," *The Indian Economic and Social History Review* 19, nos. 3–4 (1982): 365–376; J. Norbu, *Warriors of Tibet: The Story of Aten and the Khampas' Fight for Freedom of Their Country* (London: Wisdom Publications, 1986), 71.

169. Peter Goullart, *Forgotten Kingdom* (London: John Murray, 1955), 102–105.

170. T. W. Wiley, "Macro Exchanges: Tibetan Economics and the Roles of Politics and Religion," *The Tibet Journal* 11, no. 1 (1986): 10, cf. T. W. Shakya, "1948 Tibetan Trade Mission to United Kingdom," *The Tibet Journal* 15, no. 4 (Winter 1990): 98.

INSTITUTIONAL GROWTH BEYOND CENTRAL TIBET

Chapter 29

THE KINGDOM OF DERGÉ

Lauran R. Hartley

Lauran Hartley addresses the important question of whether the famous eastern Ti-betan polity of Dergé was a state in any sense that reflects modern political usage of the term. She isolates many elements that fit that definition within the history of the polity, and in so doing urges historians to reconsider the geopolitical make-up of east-ern Tibet. The example of Dergé reflects the situation of much of the Tibetan-Chinese frontier in the modern period, with small polities caught between larger, more centralized regimes. The details of local administration make clear that Tibetans ruled themselves at the regional and local levels. Furthermore, Hartley illustrates very well how the secular representatives of power were not, despite their importance to the neighboring Qing and Central Tibetan governments, the sole local or regional powers. Instead, religious institutions in the form of monasteries, sometime with vast estates and real political power, actually dominated eastern Tibetan areas. With the exception of Labrang monastery, discussed in chapter 30, no religious institution exer-cising power in early modern Tibet has been given a book-length study. This is partly because information about the economic and social role of these monasteries is often found only in Chinese sources from the twentieth century, such as the *Socio-Histori-cal Investigation* that Hartley examines in this essay.

THE KINGDOM OF DERGÉ

BACKGROUND

While the political designations of Dergé have varied from "principality," "king-dom," and "district"[1] to "quasi-autonomous state,"[2] "independent state,"[3] and even "a self-contained kingdom . . . which was almost autonomous,"[4] all sources attest to this territory's long history and cultural significance. In this paper, I will focus on the period from 1862, when Dergé was attacked by a neighboring principality, to 1910, when the Chinese commander Zhao Erfeng established direct imperial rule. I refer to Dergé as a "kingdom" given that the local ruler was traditionally referred to as a *gyelpo* (king) and *sakyong* (protector of the land). The appellation "Dergé" is said to be an abbreviation for *dezhi gechu* (the four accomplishments and the ten virtues), a title bestowed by Pakpa upon a celebrated lama of a local ruling family in the thirteenth century.[5] Although the House of Dergé (*Dergé tsang*) officially accepted the teachings of the Sakya religious tradition at that time, the influence of the royal family and the sect reached its peak only after they acquired adjacent territories with the assistance of Gushri Khan in the mid-seventeenth century, at which point the kingdom's territory extended over 78,000 sq. km.[6] With the estab-lishment of its central monastery, Lhündrupteng, the capital of Dergé Gönchen began to thrive. Long famous for its fine saddles, copperware, and silver work, by the mid-eighteenth century the kingdom became equally renowned for its print-ery and the publishing of many important texts.[7] The dialect of Dergé was re-garded as the standard for Kham dialect (*Kham ké*), and even a special Dergé style of calligraphy developed. Traversed by the northern and more arduous of two trans-Kham routes, Dergé was more likely to be visited by monk-scholars, pilgrims, and traders than by political or military envoys, who preferred the south-ern route with more settlements and supplies, and where resistance to outsiders was less common.[8] Nevertheless, the kingdom had strong cultural and religious ties to Lhasa and the Sakya principality in Central Tibet, and the House of Dergé traced its ancestry back to Gar Tongtsen, the renowned minister of the Tibetan Empire during the seventh century.[9]

Dergé was reportedly the most densely populated and the "richest agricul-tural manufacturing district of eastern Tibet."[10] According to most sources, the population at the turn of this century was roughly 45,000.[11] Nomadic families comprised less than 30 percent.[12] Rockhill (1891) estimated the population to be about 32,000 (8,000 families), with an additional monastic population of 10,000. This suggests that nearly one-fourth of the people were religious clerics,[13] a fig-ure that accords with two more recent Chinese reports.[14]

RELATIONS WITH LHASA AND PEKING

In terms of Dergé's relationship with earlier regimes in China, contact from the fourteenth through seventeenth centuries was characterized by imperial patronage of religious teachers in Dergé. This changed—at least from the perspective of the Manchu court—in 1727 when imperial policy dictated the partitioning of Kham, so that areas west of the Yangtze-Mekong[15] divide fell under Tibet and the jurisdiction of the Lhasa *amban*,[16] while east of the divide was governed indirectly through local rulers. The latter territories were considered tributaries under the Sichuan governor-general, but practical imperial presence was limited to the commissariat officers and escorts at Litang, Batang, and Chamdo, along the southern road.[17] Imperial efforts at a twofold political division of Kham were further complicated by an overlay of monastic alliances, through which important monasteries in Central Tibet appointed abbots and collected taxes in their affiliate monasteries of eastern Kham, as did the Sakya in Dartsedo, Hor, and Dergé.[18]

Nevertheless, contact between the imperial court and Dergé Gönchen increased—along with Manchu imperial patronage—and Dergé flourished as a cultural center. In 1728, the forty-fourth king of Dergé, Tenpa Tsering (1678–1739), received the title "pacification commissioner of Dergé" from the Yongzheng Emperor. In 1733, this was changed to "goodwill commissioner."[19] At the same time, financial support from the Manchu court assisted in the construction of the Dergé printery in 1729, and the subsequent printing of the entire Kangyur and Tengyur, as well as the complete works of five Sakya teachers.[20] When the Qianlong Emperor had 10,000 sets of the Kangyur and Tengyur distributed among Mongol and Tibetan princes and lamas in 1793, the provincial government of Sichuan was ordered to allocate 180,000 taels of silver, weighing 800 pounds, to Dergé for the printing of additional copies.[21]

Despite these imperial influences, direct Chinese administration was not established in Dergé until 1908, when Zhao Erfeng captured the capital, Dergé Gönchen. During most of the Qing dynasty, Manchu imperial authority was limited to patronage and titles granted by the court to local rulers.[22] Lhasa's influence was also limited, though Dergé was technically under the jurisdiction of the Ganden Podrang government from 1865 to 1908.[23] Yet, even during this period, Rockhill pointedly observed that the presence of Chinese settlers was limited and that control by either Lhasa or Peking was virtually nonexistent. Jyekundo, just north of Dergé, was "the only town in that region where Chinese merchants are allowed to reside."[24] Limited Chinese influence is also attested in other travel accounts,[25] including a survey conducted as late as 1940 that found that in only two of 103 Dergé households were both parents Chinese.[26] Rockhill summarized the situation in 1890 accordingly:

> The position of the Chinese throughout this part of the country is still extremely precarious, especially in Dérgé. Tungshin [Ch. *tongshi*, agent or envoy][27] from Xining and Chengdu visit this region yearly to collect the "horse tax" of eight tael cents (about ten cents of our money) for each family, the only one payable by this people to the Chinese government. Once in five years the chiefs under the governor-general of Sichuan send

a "little tribute" mission to Chengdu and every ten years a "great tribute" mission to Peking. Unlike the Mongol chieftains, who are obliged to go in person when paying tribute, those of eastern Tibet hardly ever visit the capital, sending their stewards or some small officer in their stead.[28]

There were only six Manchu imperial military posts in the Kham region, three of which were not established until the 1880s, and none was in Dergé. These officers were reported to "have absolutely no authority over the native chiefs, their duties being confined to protecting and administering the Chinese trade, reporting to Daqianlu [Dartsedo] on the condition of the country, forwarding government couriers, officials, troops, funds, etc."[29] Officers were occasionally appealed to by native chiefs to arbitrate disputes, but their decisions were not binding. Finally, Rockhill noted that throughout much of Kham, "Chinese silver bullion was not received; only Indian rupees were current."[30] At the same time, he remarked, "The *gandan tangka*[31] of Lhasa is not current in eastern Tibet except at a heavy discount."[32]

In his study of political administration in Sichuan, Adshead (1984) concludes that for the Qing dynasty, Kham was a "mosaic of mountain principalities, neither China nor Tibet, which controlled the roads between Chengtu and Lhasa, the lifeline of the Chinese presence in the Gelukpa theocracy."[33] Rockhill also concluded that Dergé was one state in eastern Tibet that was "independent of both China and Lhasa."[34] However, when rulers of Dergé increasingly found their kingdom under attack by neighboring states or challenged internally by opposing factions, one strategy the king used to secure his rule was to appeal to either Peking or Lhasa for support. Ultimately, this tactic would in itself compromise Dergé's sovereignty.

THE NYARONG CAMPAIGN

In 1862, the state of Nyarong, bordering Dergé to the southeast with similar claims to *de facto* independence, invaded Dergé territory under the leadership of Nyarong chief Gönpo Namgyel. Within a year, troops from Nyarong had seized the capital of Dergé. I would contend that such acts of aggression from neighboring states led to a significant shift in the balance of power for the formerly self-governing states in northern Kham in relation to both Peking and Lhasa. The situation in Dergé after the Nyarong campaign illustrates how local rulers in Kham were more frequently compelled to seek an alliance with either the Lhasa Ganden Podrang government or the Sichuan provincial administration in order to maintain their increasingly compromised autonomy. Furthermore, both Lhasa and Peking readily took advantage of the ensuing internal struggles to assert greater control in the area.

With reference to several primary sources, Tashi Tsering (1985) notes that the Nyarong army had reached the peak of its campaign in 1862 and had conquered all of Dergé by early 1863. He adds that the tribes of Dergé offered little resistance, especially those along the eastern border, which were on favorable political terms with Nyarong. Once the resistance centered in the western Drichu (Yangtze) area was defeated, the queen of Dergé, Chöying Zangmo, and her son, Chimé Takpé Dorjé, were taken hostage and the capital, Dergé Gönchen, seized.[35] Suspecting the whole of Dergé would rise in revolt, the Nyarong chief also took many high incarnate lamas and important Dergé officials hostage in Nyarong. Among these were Pelpung Wöngen Rinpoché, a few lamas from Dzokchen and Katok monasteries, and some of the *dünkor* and *hordra* officials; it is said that the lamas and the *dünkor* officials were thrown into the Nyarong river.[36] Several ministers of Dergé fled to Lhasa,[37] along with refugees from three of the Hor states bordering Dergé, which also sought military assistance against Nyarong.[38]

At this opportunity to extend its influence in Kham, the General Assembly in Lhasa passed a resolution to intervene and Kalön Pünlung Püntsok Tsewang Dorjé was chosen to lead an expedition to Nyarong. He left with troops on February 9, 1863, recruiting a substantial number of men en route from the ecclesiastical states of Riwoché, Drayap, and Chamdo.[39] According to Petech, the Nyarong chief was hard pressed in Dergé by "both Chinese and their local allies . . . (but) held out successfully for quite a time and *enrolled in his forces many lamas of the monasteries subject to Dergé*."[40] By September 1864, Pünlung and his Lhasa forces occupied Dergé and forced Gönpo's troops back to Nyarong.[41] However, the Lhasa troops reportedly looted and inflicted much violence upon the local Dergé population.[42] Significantly, Petech adds, "An unpleasant aftermath of the victory *was a widespread purge of Nyingmapa elements*, suspected of collusion with Gönpo Namgyel."[43]

In June 1865, Lhasa made further advances upon Nyarong, whereupon the abducted queen, her son, and Pelpung Wöngen Rinpoché escaped to Dergé.[44] Within two months, the Nyarong fortress was surrounded and set on fire. Gönpo Namgyel and his two sons died in the blaze, and his followers were arrested.[45] Lhasa then insisted on an indemnity of 200,000 taels from Peking before withdrawing. Adshead suggests that Lhasa was fully aware that the responsibility for payment would belong to Chengdu and that the provincial governor would be unable to pay this amount. Lhasa promptly placed Nyarong under its permanent administration.[46] The high commissioner (*chikhyap*) appointed by Lhasa to Nyarong also exercised jurisdiction over Hor and Dergé.[47] Carrasco cites two sources that note that Dergé paid a tribute in silver, and provided labor, transport, and a bodyguard to the Tibetan commissioner in Nyarong. Evidence of the king's closer ties with Lhasa can also be found in Gele (Tib. Gelek):

Throughout this incident, Chimé Takpé Dorjé[48] completely leaned towards the Tibetan authorities. It is said that after he was released from the Xinlong [Nyarong] prison, he took more than 1,000 loads of gold, silver, and property to Tibet and offered expensive gifts to Tibetan government officials in thanks for the Tibetan troops having saved his life and to gain the [continued] attention and protection of the Tibetan government. Also, he was allowed to bring officials of all levels and their entourages to visit various places in Tibet to make religious offerings.[49]

Perhaps to further strengthen his new alliance with Lhasa, in 1870 King Chimé Takpé Dorjé married Tseten Drölkar, daughter of Tibetan general Dokhar *sé* Tsewang Norbu, who helped lead the expeditionary force from Lhasa.[50] Barber (1882) provides details of their wedding, the preliminaries of which "included a contract by which the Depas [chieftains or headmen] 'tied their heads' (*gotak*) to Lhasa, without, however promising to aid openly in the annexation of their territory."[51] Reportedly, most people of Dergé were "disinclined" to acknowledge this "submission." According to Baber's informant, the decision to turn to Lhasa for assistance in the Nyarong war followed "a vain appeal for assistance to the Chinese government."[52] From the accounts above, we can see how the independence of Dergé as it approached the twentieth century was increasingly compromised *vis-à-vis* outside forces.

SECULAR AUTHORITY IN DERGÉ

In the wake of the Nyarong campaign, two factions arose during what are referred to in the *Dergé Chöjung* (*Religious History of Dergé*) as "various periods of chaotic and uncontrolled thinking among members of the Dergé royal family, the chaplains (*üla*), and the district chiefs."[53] According to Gele, this conflict began during the trip that King Chimé Dorjé made with his thirty chiefs (*da touren*) to thank Lhasa for its support during the Nyarong affair.[54] These chieftains are the same reluctant *depa* to whom Baber referred above. The following section examines the role of local chieftains and other players in the administration of Dergé, which in its totality possessed the characteristics of an "internally differentiated" state apparatus that "exercised its power over a territorially demarcated area" and itself constituted "a site of power struggle"—all qualities that have been used to define a "state."[55]

LAND ADMINISTRATION AND THE OFFICIALDOM

The system by which land in Dergé was granted to hereditary officials in exchange for administrative responsibilities constituted a decentralized bureaucracy, the highest levels of which employed more than two hundred aristocrats. There were four types of land management systems in the kingdom:[56] land held directly by the king for his own subsistence, land allocated to the top two ranks of officials under the king, land granted for monastic estates, and land leased directly to *trelpa* (taxpayers). *Trelpa* paid three types of dues for the land they essentially leased: 1) dues in grain; 2) dues in kind (butter, hay, etc.) per household and in gunpowder, fuel, fodder, and money for printing books, which was assessed on a village basis; and 3) labor, which entailed land cultivation, construction, transportation, and military service.[57] Some of the wealthier *trelpa* employed *khölpa* (servants) to work their land. However, the majority of *khölpa* worked for officials who were reportedly granted the servants with their land by the king.

The territory of Dergé was divided into twenty-five districts (*dzongkha* or *dechok*)[58] headed by local chieftains (*depa*) whose official tenure ranged from seven years to life.[59] Most chieftains held a hereditary and life-term position, and some were "practically semi-independent."[60] The highest secular political body in the king's court was the council of ministers (*nyerchen*), which was comprised of the chief or head official from each of the designated districts: Yilhung in the east, Garjé in the south, Drongpa in the west, and Sershül in the north.[61] Along with the *chakdzö* (treasurer), *drungyik* (secretary), and *sölpön* (major domo), they constituted the first rank of officials and spent most of their time in the capital itself.[62]

According to the *Dergé Chöjung*, the second stratum of officials consisted of thirty-three *dzonggo* (district headmen) (see table 29.1). I am quite certain that these district officials are the same thirty major headmen (*da touren*) mentioned in Du Yongbin and in Gele, where he writes of thirty chiefs who accompanied the king to Lhasa after the Nyarong campaign.[63] In other sources, they are referred to alternately as the "thirty ministers,"[64] "thirty hereditary clan leaders,"[65] or *depa* (chief or headman).[66] I am unable to account for why the number of *dzonggo* (thirty-three) exceeds the number of districts (twenty-five). Perhaps some districts were further divided into subdistricts. According to the Dergé *semo* and her son, Dergé was comprised of thirty districts (*dzong*) each headed by a "duke" (*lönpo*). However, in a few additional districts that had no traditional *lönpo*, the king would select a *dzongpön* from among the *hordra* or *dünkor* (see below) to administer the district.[67] This might account for the discrepancy between the thirty-three *dzonggo* listed in the *Dergé Chöjung* and the thirty "chiefs," "*da touren*," "ministers," or "hereditary clan leaders" mentioned in other sources. I can find no other satisfactory explanation for the discrepancy. According to Rockhill, each district official had a *makpön* (military officer)[68] and the privilege of hosting high officials traveling across the land, which provided a considerable source of income.[69] But the position of district officials in nomadic communities was more limited:

> All the pastoral tribes called in Tibetan drupa or drukpa ['brog pa] are ruled by chiefs called depa [sde pa], who have no other officials under them. They have, as far as my observation goes, very little authority; in case of war they lead their men, and in time of peace they see that the pasture lands of their tribes are not encroached upon; they levy the

TABLE 29.1
LOCAL CHIEFS OR HEADMEN

Dergé Chöjung[i]	Teichman (if cited)[ii]	Dergé Chöjung	Teichman (if cited)
Kutsé		Maror	Marong
Khardo	Kargung?	Meshö	Mesho
West Khardo		Tsamdo	Tsando
Khordo		Dzamtok	
Chakra		Dzingpa	Dzenko
Joda		Dzapa	Tzako
Nyakshik	Nyashi	Dzokchen	Dzogchen
Terlhung	Dehlung	Wara	
Denchödé		Zurgyü	
Denma		Yerap	
Pelyül	Beyu	Rakchap	Racha
Pewar		Rapten	
West Pewar		Rida	
Polu	Spo lu	Sa ngen	
Wöntö		Samar	
West Wöntö		Horpo	Horbo
Barong		Barong	

[i] Karma rgyal mtshan, ed. *Mdo smad chos rgyal Sde dge'i rgyal rabs las 'phros pa'i chos kyi 'byung tshul mdo tsam brjod pa gzur gnas blo ldan dgyes pa'i tambu ra* [*A Brief Religious History from the* History of the Dergé Kings: *Lute to Please the Impartial Mind*]. Hong Kong: Ya gling dpe skrun khang, 1994, 77. Note that the districts of the four chief ministers (*gnyer chen*) are not included here.

[ii] Teichman, *Travels of a Consular Officer in Eastern Tibet*, 208. Teichman also includes a district called "Desho," which would appear to be Sde shod, but which was not included among the districts listed in the *Sde dge chos 'byung*.

various taxes for China, for Lhasa or Dergé, as the case may be, and sometimes arbitrate quarrels among their clansmen, but generally the people settle such matters between themselves.[70]

The *Dergé Chöjung* lists an additional forty-one aristocratic retinue appointees (see table 29.2). The *dünkor* also included *chi pöngo* (outer officials) from Gamongna Sokmotsang, Nyakshik Setsa, and Gojo Samdrup. They were specifically noted to be exempt from the military service tax. Presumably, the remaining *dünkor* officials were responsible for providing soldiers to protect Der-

TABLE 29.2

THE ARISTOCRATIC RETINUE

(*DÜNKOR KHAK*)

Dilgo	Puma	Chaktsa
Atup	Jetol	Chepa
Drenkhor	Nera	Jokhong
Chudo	Juchen	Namsé
Yalok	Juchung	Yago
Böntok	Zhimo	Ngentré
Lhoru	Sokmo	Ngenchung
Jagö	Drumo	Ripuk
Sakar	Utsa	Khardo
Malok	Drebö	Khardo Matang
Chakta	Atri	Drayap
Hocho	Nezhi	Namchung
Jara	Okma	Raru
Lukra	Gakhar	

See Karma rgyal mtshan, ed. *A Brief Religious History from the* History of the Derge Kings, 78–79.

gé's borders when necessary. This list seems to consist of important family names, which were primarily derived from or used as the toponymic identifying where the family's estate was located.

Finally, there were eighty local representatives (*hordra*)[71] who held this title in exchange for functioning as a local representative or deputy. These are apparently the same "village headmen" discussed by Carrasco,[72] who notes that they were selected from the third rank of officials and their position was often hereditary.[73] As representatives of the king, the village heads were responsible for administering *ulak*, the corvée tax consisting of supplies provided by the local people for transporting officials, outsiders, and their loads. They could also grant land to *trelpa* on the king's behalf.[74] One traveler reported that the village headmen were nearly all hereditary and responsible for presiding over the assemblies of the people, communicating orders from superior authorities and deciding the share of each villager in the labor services.[75] Based on the statement in Gele (1984) of there being more than one hundred "*da xiao touren*" (big and petty chiefs) in Dergé, I would conclude that the *hordra* are identical to the minor officials (*xiao touren*) mentioned in his account and those of others.[76] The village heads were assisted by *göpa* (leaders?) who were selected from among the common people to aid in collecting taxes, managing the labor services and requisitions, and other affairs; but the *göpa* had no official rank. According to Carrasco, third-rank officials also included bureaucrats who resided in the capital and served as assistants to the *nyerpa*.

Carrasco has contrasted the independent character of a landed nobility in Dergé with the bureaucratic aristocracy of the Lhasa government, where "instead of local chiefs performing duties in the central government, we have officials of the central government paid in land."[77] He notes that the growth and development of the bureaucratized nobility and monk-officials reduced the chance for local leaders to become excessively powerful. Officials in Central Tibet were less likely to set themselves up as territorial rulers in their estates, because the larger and more centralized Ganden Podrang administration often required the presence of its nobility in Lhasa. Carrasco views the Central Tibetan administration as having developed from an organizational structure based on territorial chiefs to a bureaucratic one where "personal estates even if hereditary become, rather than small principalities, salary lands easily resumable by the state if the need arises."[78]

In contrast, in the small states of eastern Tibet, such as Dergé, hereditary *depa* or *lönpo* maintained a high degree of local power. Though the land of Dergé was allegedly considered the property of the king and granted to these first two ranks of officials in exchange for administrative services,[79] the king's four chief ministers (*nyerchen*) and many of the local chieftains wielded a significant degree of authority. Eric Teichman, the British consul stationed at Dartsedo (Daqianlu) in the early twentieth century, observed that the chieftains of the three "largest and most important" districts—Garjé, Sershül, and "Adu"—were "exceptionally powerful."[80] A more recent Chinese source reports that the seven most important districts were Yilhung, Wönpotong, Kharsumdo, Meshö, Kutsé, Polu, and "Chita."[81] The *Dergé Chöjung* notes that only the chieftains of Khardo, Wöntö, Pewar, and Yerap were *dzongpön* within the Dergé system.[82] Presumably the other chiefs had their own indigenous and local authority. Chen (1949) notes that, because of the king's presence in Dergé, the administrative system there was more centralized than in other areas of Kham.[83] Nevertheless, the division of land among hereditary local chiefs enabled alternative foci of power that could counter the authority of the king. This would place the king *primus inter pares*, if local districts became exceptionally powerful or allied with one another.

INTERNAL DISSENT AFTER
THE NYARONG CAMPAIGN

Further evidence for the authority wielded by local chiefs can be found in oral histories recorded by Gele in his 1984 study, *Ganzi Zangzu zizhi zhou shi hua* (*Oral History of the Ganzi Tibetan Autonomous Prefecture*). Again, it was Gele who claimed that the succession struggle that would engulf Dergé for nearly forty years began during the trip that King Chimé Dorjé made with his thirty chiefs to thank Lhasa for its support during the Nyarong affair.[84] During this excursion, a member of the king's entourage killed a staff member of the Manchu imperial bureau in Zhigatsé. The Manchu imperial *amban*[85] in Lhasa ordered that the assassin be handed over, but the thirty chiefs refused. Reportedly fearing the *amban's* wrath, the king himself gave up the assassin. When the party returned to Dergé, the chiefs contested the king's authority. In order to mediate the conflict, the king called all the chiefs to his administrative compound in Dergé Gönchen for a council. However, not only did the thirty chiefs refuse to attend the meeting, they also severely beat the king's father-in-law.[86] Allegedly, Chimé Dorjé angrily announced, "I only want the common people, I don't want the thirty chiefs." According to Gele's sources, the chiefs at that time evidently wielded considerable power *vis-à-vis* the king:

> It is said that the thirty chiefs then organized many people to gather in front of the palace of the *tusi*,[87] dancing a *guozhuang*[88] that used satirical lyrics to ridicule the *tusi*:
> "The beautiful sky is a guesthouse in paradise;
> the moon and stars are its happy travelers;
> and one by one, clouds are the farewell gift.
> The beautiful site of Gongya[89] is a guesthouse in paradise;
> the thirty chiefs are its happy travelers,
> and thirty embroidered belts are the farewell gift."
> After this song, they threw thirty belts at the palace front and abruptly left. Henceforth, the *tusi's* relationship with the chiefs was completely broken. When the thirty chiefs returned to their own villages, they each governed on their own and officially declared that they would not obey Chimé Dorjé's rule.
> As Chimé Dorjé was not able to exercise his power as *tusi*, he became angry and sent a mission to the governor-general's office in Sichuan in order to petition the following: "The emperor himself has granted [the title of] *xuanwei shi* to [the] Dergé [king]. The thirty chiefs' present betrayal of the *tusi* was an illegal action, a rebellion. Governor-general, please send troops to suppress them."[90]

The governor-general of Sichuan, Lu Chuanlin, had already been seeking to incorporate the lands of the various *tusi* of northern Kham into a single territory.[91] The policy he sought—*gaitu guiliu*—was customary administrative practice for the Ming and Qing imperial courts in the area along China's southwestern border. It entailed replacing the local hereditary ruler, king, or chief (Ch. *tusi*) with a nonhereditary appointee from the central government, thus bringing the area under direct control. Having already sent General Zhangji to

Nyarong, Lu Chuanlin then ordered his advance upon Dergé to subjugate it militarily:

> The Qing troops entered Dergé and were stationed in Zechenlong [Tib. *Zhechen lung*]. The Qing military commander ordered the thirty chiefs to Zechenlong for a meeting. When the thirty chiefs arrived in Zechenlong, the commander Zhangji ordered that they be arrested. The chiefs resisted and opposed him. The Qing troops opened fire and killed one of the chiefs, named "Zhuomo." The remaining chiefs hurried back to their administrative villages, organized the people, declared a rebellion, and led the local people to surround the Qing military encampment. They cut off their water supply, forcing the Qing to agree to negotiate. At the negotiation table, the chiefs proposed the detainment of Chimé Dorjé and his wife. The Qing troops had to do as they were told and arrested Chimé Dorjé, his wife, and the two sons, who were all taken to Chengdu and interrogated [circa 1895]. Shortly after, Chimé Dorjé and his wife died in the Chengdu prison [circa 1898]. The two surviving sons were named Baba and Ajia (some sources say Jiangbai Renqing [Tib. Jampel Rinchen] and Duoji Cengge [Tib. Dorje Senggé]). They were released and welcomed back to Dergé. Dorje Senggé inherited the position of *tusi*, becoming the forty-eighth *tusi*. . . . Jampel Rinchen became a monk.[92]

Gele notes that there are both official and local oral accounts of this affair, though other accounts discussing the royal family's deposition[93] do not include the story of the chiefs' satirical demonstration in front of the king's palace. Additional evidence for the relative autonomy of several local chiefs can be found in Babar (1882), who cites an account by T. T. Cooper, who in 1868 noted that the people of Dergé were "very warlike, and appear to be divided into several clans, constantly engaged in deadly feuds with each other, but uniting in one common cause against attacks from without."[94] Another source notes that as late as 1942, when King Tsewang Düdül died and the Situ Rinpoché of Pelpung monastery was selected to administer Dergé, a powerful chief named "Xiake Daodeng" (Tib. Shargé ??) opposed this appointment and had Situ Rinpoché ousted after just one month.[95] Having examined the administration of land in Dergé, one sees how such concentrations of local authority might arise—or rather, how strongholds were accommodated in a decentralized administration where the king's power was not consummate.

RELIGIOUS AUTHORITY IN DERGÉ

Considering that only tangential reference was made to the involvement of any monks in the Nyarong campaign in the accounts above, it may be surprising to read the following observation by Rockhill some twenty years later:

From Jyekundo to Tachienlu [Dajianlu, Tib. Dartsedo], a distance of about 600 miles, I passed forty lamaseries, in the smallest of which there were 100 monks, and in five of them from 2000 to 4000. Although the greater part of Kham is not under their direct rule, *they are everywhere the de facto masters of the country.* In their hands is nearly all the wealth of the land, acquired by trading, donations, money-lending, and bequests. Their landed property is enormous, their serfs (*miser*)[96] and bondsmen (*tseyo*) swarm.[97] (Italics added.)

Given that Jyekundo lies just north of Dergé and Dartsedo lies 588 miles east of Dergé Gönchen, Rockhill's observation must have applied to a significant part of Dergé's territory. What lay behind his assessment? By what means did the monasteries of Dergé wield authority and how did their position *vis-à-vis* the king differ from that of the lay chiefs?

LAND ADMINISTRATION AND THE MONASTERIES

Monasteries held estates in much the same way as did the noble officials, but in a more "corporate"[98] sense, rather than as individuals or families. Monastic estates in Dergé were worked by peasants, called *lhadren*, who either leased land and had their own equipment or worked the land as servants.[99] According to Carrasco (1959), the *lhadren* generally lived under better conditions than the *trelpa* subject to district and local chiefs. He adds that they were often protected by their monastic lords from the oppression of the chiefs.[100] Sometimes a monastery was exempt from land taxes, in which case its subjects were more affluent, but the living standard of most *lhadren* remained at or below subsistence level.

A useful source for information regarding the political and economic privileges enjoyed by monasteries in Dergé is *Sichuan sheng Ganzi zhou Zangzu shehui lishi diaocha* [*A Socio-Historical Investigation of the Tibetans in Ganzi Prefecture, Sichuan Province*]. This work is the result of a 1958–59 survey and largely concurs with what is cited in Carrasco (1959). According to *A Socio-Historical Investigation*, monasteries held 24 percent of Dergé's total land area[101] and were granted labor for maintaining their estates. This source mentions that Pelpung monastery—one of the largest in Dergé—held 2,000 *mu*[102] of land and had a few hundred taxpaying households. An earlier source claims that the same monastery held more than 6,000 *mu* of land with 400 households of *khölpa*.[103] Ten percent of these holdings were tilled by *khölpa* who gave a percentage of their yield solely to the Dergé king, 25 percent were tilled by *khölpa* who split their yields evenly with the monastery, and 45 percent were tilled by *khölpa* who offered 40 percent of a predetermined yield to the monastery. The remaining 20 percent of the monastery's land was reportedly "managed and tilled without any pay by *khölpa*."[104] Lhündrupteng, the main monastery of the capital, was reported to have collected 134,000 *jin*[105] of barley each year. Monasteries in nomadic areas, such as Dzokchen monastery, had the right to control pastures nearby.

MONASTIC BUREAUCRACIES AND THE COMMUNITY

A monastery often served as a sort of community center with a variety of functions. Information provided in A *Socio-Historical Investigation* supports Rockhill's observations of the monastery's financial activity, which included special offices for business and usury. While monastic estates had no courts or jails, they did have military equipment, as attested above. This furthered the monastery's ability to serve a fortresslike role in protecting the local population. As Samuel (1982) notes, "Monasteries in East Tibet into the twentieth century served as places where local peasants and nomads could store their produce safely and where they themselves could take refuge against bandits. The monasteries also mediated in disputes between nomadic groups."[106] Lamas were generally more numerous in agricultural areas than in nomadic areas.[107] Yet Dzokchen monastery, one of the largest in Kham, was located in a nomadic area. In his discussion of this *gönpa*, Rockhill notes that nomads (*drokpa*) are "so exposed to forays of the Golok[108] who are distant only two days ride to the east, that many prefer to live near villages or large lamaseries, where they can find refuge in case of need, even if the grazing is not so good."[109]

According to Carrasco, monastic hierarchs could participate in governmental affairs. While they could not appropriate their office in the same way as did hereditary lay officials, it was not uncommon for more influential lamas to be related to Dergé officials or aristocratic families in neighboring territories. A monastic hierarch could not obtain personal revenue from the land in the same way as an individual landowner, but several held considerable financial and political power, which was bolstered militarily:

> Nor do the lamas confine themselves to the use of peaceful means in furtherance of their policy; there is as much of the soldier about them as there was in the Templars, with whom they offer many points of resemblance. The larger lamaseries are rather fortified camps than the abodes of peace-loving Buddhist monks; every lama is well-armed, well-mounted, and always ready for the fray, whether it be to resist the local chiefs or the Chinese, or to attack a rival lamasery. Their declaration of war is unique of its kind. In times of peace lamas wear no trousers, only a long kilt called *shamta,* so when about to start on a military expedition, when they will be for days in the saddle, a nether garment becomes indispensable, and the order goes forth to convert their shawls (*zan*) into breeches. I was

assured that frequently when the weaker party learns that its enemy has thus made clear a determination to fight, it sues for peace without waiting for the attack.[110]

Accordingly, the possibility that religious clerics were involved in the Nyarong campaign is less surprising than one might suppose. Further evidence of their worldly capabilities can be seen in the organization of the monasteries themselves, which were highly bureaucratized and included personnel responsible for military affairs.

The following summary of the monastic organization is based largely on information found in *A Socio-Historical Investigation* and Carrasco (1959).[111] Most of the larger monasteries (*gönpa*) were comprised of several *dratsang* (Ch. *zhongyuan*), within which were various *khangtsen* (Ch. *xiaoyuan*). Each *khangtsen* elected a *gezang* (Ch. *gesang*), who then collectively elected a *khenpo* (abbot; Ch. *kanbu*) from among the high lamas of the monastery or would invite an abbot from another monastery. The abbot was also called a *gönpön* (monastery official) and generally held the position for a three- or four-year term. He supervised the monastic bureaucracy, which included the following monk-officials:

- The *nyerpa* (Ch. *xiangzi, guanjia*) was the main administrator in charge of economic affairs.
- The *gekö* (Ch. *gegu*) was responsible for enforcing the monastery's code of law, in particular ensuring that monks adhered to monastic rules.
- There were two to four *geyok* (Ch. *geyao, geyue*) in the larger monasteries. They helped the *gekö* enforce the law and were responsible for military-related work. They were chosen from among the *gesang* and had a term of one year.
- The *wuma* (Ch. *zhangjing lama*) was responsible for leading the recitation of scriptures and explaining them.
- The *lhawa* (Ch. *fashen lama*) was responsible for invocations, prognostications, and divinations.
- The *tsongpön*, also called a *nyerpa*, managed the business-related activity. This post was held by a wealthy merchant in the area who was either publicly elected or appointed.

The *Dergé Chöjung* provides an extensive list of monasteries in Dergé, representing all 5 traditions: 61 Nyingmapa; 44 Sakyapa; 26 Kagyüpas; 18 Gelukpa; and 10 Bönpo.[112] Li (1947) provides figures regarding the monastic population at selected monasteries. However, Li's figures differ significantly from those found in other accounts, such as Peltrül Rinpoché's record of Nyingma monasteries, and I can find no satisfactory explanation for these discrepancies. For example, the monastery of Dzokchen is said to traditionally have had more than 850 monks,[113] yet Li reports only 257 monks.[114] In another example, Li cites the population of Yakzé monastery as 62, while Peltrül Rinpoche has recorded a total of 225.[115] Some monks may not have been in residence and fighting against Chinese incursions must have taken a large toll in fatalities, but this figure still seems severely underestimated.

Li cites a total resident monastic population in Dergé of only 2,576, of whom 88 were nuns.[116] Be that as it may, most nuns apparently resided in Sakhok, Yilhung, and Pelpung, the only places reported to have nunneries.[117] Whereas the largest numbers of monks were between the ages of 20 and 29, nuns were concentrated between the ages of 55 and 64.[118] This reflects the social structure in Kham, where women were often in charge of estates and more likely to take vows only at a later age. According to A Socio-Historical Investigation, there were a total of 5,700 lamas in Dergé, comprising 24 percent of the population and 52 percent of the male population, of whom only 2,500 lived in monasteries.[119] However, as discussed above, this would mean a total population of 22,000 people, far less than earlier estimations for the larger territory of Dergé. According to A Socio-Historical Investigation and several other sources, the Sakya monasteries were "most powerful" among the monasteries of Dergé. However, A Socio-Historical Investigation also points to a special relationship that the king had with the wu da jia miao (five major monasteries).[120] The significance of this relationship, in a kingdom where authority was relatively decentralized, though important, cannot be dealt with here.

NOTES

1. William W. Rockhill, "Tibet: A Geographical, Ethnographical and Historical Sketch," Journal of the Royal Asiatic Society 23 (1891): 227.

2. Michael Aris, Lamas, Princes and Brigands: Joseph Rock's Photographs of the Tibetan Borderlands of China (New York: China House Gallery, China Institute of America, 1992), 17.

3. Pedro P. Carrasco, Land and Polity in Tibet (Seattle: University of Washington Press, 1959), 223.

4. Robert Ford, Captured in Tibet (1957; reprint, Hong Kong: Oxford University Press, 1990), 49.

5. Li Anche, "Dege: A Study of Tibetan Population," Southwest Journal of Anthropology 3 (1947): 279. This lama, Sgam ston Bsod nams rin chen, subsequently established a monastery for 1,000 monks in the southern part of what came to be the Sde dge kingdom. According to Xie Qihuang, Zangzu chuantong wenhua cidian [Dictionary of Traditional Tibetan Culture] (Lanzhou: Gansu renmin chubanshe, 1993), 797, he had served as the gsol dpon (housekeeping official, who attends to important domestic affairs, travel arrangements, etc.) of the great 'Phags pa. See Leonard W. J. van der Kuijp, "Two Courts of the 'Phags pa Era," Zhongguo zangxue/China Tibetology (Special supplement) (1992): 288–292, for a discussion of this position and what it may

have entailed in different courts and at different times. Based on his findings, I would translate *gsol dpon* here as "major domo." Once Bsod nams rin chen received the appellation "Sde dge," the name was adopted by his family, who ruled what would become the territory of Sde dge.

6. Carrasco, *Land and Polity in Tibet*, 144. [Editors' note: By way of comparison, West Virginia is smaller and Maine larger.]

7. Josef Kolmaš, "Dezhung Rinpoche's Summary and Continuation of the *Sde dge'i rgyal rabs*," *Acta Orientalia Academiae Scientiarum Hungaricae*, Tomus XLII (1) (1988): 121; and R. A. Stein, *Tibetan Civilization* (Stanford: Stanford University Press, 1972), 82–83, 287.

8. S. A. M. Adshead, *Province and Politics in Late Imperial China: Viceregal Government in Szechwan, 1891–1911*, Scandinavian Institute of Asian Studies Monograph Series, no. 50 (London and Malmo: Curzon Press, 1984), 55.

9. Kolmaš, "Dezhung Rinpoche's Summary and Continuation of the *Sde dge'i rgyal rabs*," 121. C.f. van der Kuijp, "Two Courts of the 'Phags pa' Era," who identifies inconsistencies among various accounts of this geneaology.

10. Rockhill, "Tibet: A Geographical, Ethnographical and Historical Sketch."

11. Li estimates the population at that time to have been 48,500 (Li, "Dege: A Study of Tibetan Population," 280). Carrasco cites a figure of 45,500 from official British documents of 1910 (Carrasco, *Land and Polity in Tibet*, 144). Traditionally, Sde dge was said to comprise *"khri skor bdun"* (seven units of 10,000) (Skal bzang chos sgrol [*alias* Sde dge *sras mo*], interviewed by the author, Chengdu, PRC, September 1, 1997). However, we should keep in mind that the population unit *"khri skor"* was a rough estimate based on varying family sizes used for census purposes in Tibetan areas during the Yuan dynasty. Given the otherwise general concurrence, it seems likely that this "calculation" should be considered more figuratively.

12. Li, "Dege: A Study of Tibetan Population," 283. This estimate is based only on the territory of Sde dge located east of the 'Bri chu River. See n. 14 below.

13. Rockhill observed there were "very few nuns in Eastern Tibet" (Rockhill, "Tibet: A Geographical, Ethnographical and Historical Sketch," 212). This is supported by Li, who recorded a total of only eighty-eight nuns in eastern Sde dge (Li, "Dege: A Study of Tibetan Population," 285).

14. In *Sichuan sheng Ganzi zhou Zangzu shehui lishi diaocha* the population in 1958 was recorded as 22,000, of which 5,700 were monks; see Sichuan sheng bianjizu, *Sichuan sheng Ganzi zhou Zangzu shehui lishi diaocha* [*A Socio-Historical Investigation of the Tibetans in Ganzi Prefecture, Sichuan Province*] (Chengdu: Sichuan sheng shehui kexueyuan chubanshe, 1985), 106. Li reports that the total population of Sde dge in the 1940s was only 11,172, of whom 2,576 were monks (Li, "Dege: A Study of Tibetan Population," 283). In real terms, these figures are much lower than Rockhill's, because they include only the territory of Sde dge lying east of the 'Bri chu (Yangzi River; Ch. Jinsha jiang "Golden Sand River"). By the Kah tog Agreement of 1932, land west of the river was placed under Lhasa's jurisdiction and eastern Sde dge was incorporated into Xikang. In addition, extensive fighting embroiled most of Kham in the

early twentieth century, significantly reducing Sde dge's population with death and emigration. For one account of what transpired in Sde dge, especially in the monasteries, during the Chinese Communist takeover, see Chögyam Trungpa and Esmé Cramer, *Born in Tibet* (London: Allen & Unwin, 1966), 116–117.

15. These rivers are locally referred to as the 'Bri chu and the Rdza chu, respectively.

16. See Josef Kolmaš, "The Ambans and Assistant Ambans of Tibet (A Chronological Study)," *Achív orientální*, supplementa VII (Prague: The Oriental Institute, 1994), for a chronological summary of the *ambans* or representatives of the Manchu imperial court sent to Tibet from the seventeenth to the early twentieth century.

17. Adshead, *Province and Politics in Late Imperial China*, 29. From that time on the extreme north of Kham administratively fell under the Xining *amban*, and the extreme south under the Yun-Gui governor-general.

18. Adshead, *Province and Politics in Late Imperial China*, 56.

19. Li, "Dege: A Study of Tibetan Population," 281. The first of these two titles was probably *anfushi*, a title of rank 5b awarded to chieftains of southwestern aboriginal tribes; see Charles O. Hucker, *A Dictionary of Official Titles in Imperial China* (Stanford: Stanford University Press, 1985), 104. The subsequent title was likely *xuanweishi*, a commissioner of rank 3b and one of the most prestigious titles granted during the Yuan, Ming, and Qing dynasties to local hereditary chiefs along China's southwestern border; see Hucker, *A Dictionary of Official Titles in Imperial China*, 251. Cf. Luciano Petech, "Yuan Organization of the Tibetan Border Areas," in *Tibetan Studies: Proceedings of the 4th Seminar of the International Association for Tibetan Studies, Schloss Hohenkammer, Munich 1985*, ed. International Association for Tibetan Studies, Helga Uebach, and Jampa Losang Panglung (München: Kommission für Zentralasiatische Studien, Bayerische Akademie der Wissenschaften, 1988), for a discussion of this position in Kham during the Yuan dynasty.

20. See Kolmaš, "Prague Collection of Tibetan Prints from Derge," *Bulletin of Tibetology* 7, no. 2 (1971): 13–19.

21. Li, "Dege: A Study of Tibetan Population," 281–282.

22. Rockhill, "Tibet: A Geographical, Ethnographical and Historical Sketch," 349; and Gele, *Ganzi Zangzu zizhi zhou shi hua* [*Oral History of the Ganzi Tibetan Autonomous Prefecture*] (Chengdu: Sichuan minzu chubanshe, 1984), 260.

23. This occurred in the aftermath of the Nyarong campaign, which will be discussed below.

24. Rockhill, "Tibet: A Geographical, Ethnographical and Historical Sketch," 205–206. Cf. P. K. Kozlov, ed., *Mongoliia i Kam*, vol. 1, 2nd ed. (Moskva: Gosudarstvennoe Izdatel'stvo Geograficheskoi Literaturi, 1947), 279, who reported that ten Chinese, primarily traders from Sichuan, were living in Sde dge dgon chen at the turn of this century.

25. See, for example, the account of one Russian explorer who describes how his Chinese guide feared for his life upon arriving in Sde dge and neighboring areas in 1899: A. H. Kaznakov, "Moi Puti po Mongolii i Kamu," in *Mongoliia i Kam: Trudy*

ekspeditsii Imperatorskago Russkago geograficheskago obshchestva, sovershennoi v 1899–1901, vol. 2, 1st ed., ed. P. K. Koslov (St. Petersburg: Gerold, 1907), 67.

26. Li, "Dege: A Study of Tibetan Population," 292–293. In a sample survey taken near Sde dge dgon chen in 1940, Li identified three types of households on the basis of ethnicity: Tibetan families: 7 households with male head; 55 households with female head; 22 matrimonial households. Sino-Tibetan families: 17 households—38 males, 45 females; Chinese families: 2 households—6 males, 7 females.

27. Robert Henry Matthews, *Matthews' Chinese-English Dictionary*, rev. American ed. (Cambridge: Harvard University Press, 1969), 969.

28. Rockhill, "Tibet: A Geographical, Ethnographical and Historical Sketch," 222.

29. Rockhill, "Tibet: A Geographical, Ethnographical and Historical Sketch," 221–222.

30. Rockhill, "Tibet: A Geographical, Ethnographical and Historical Sketch," 208.

31. This refers to traditional Tibetan coins, which were recognized by other countries as having exchange value with the Indian rupee. In *Tibet: A Handbook* (Bloomington: Research Institute for Inner Asian Studies, 2nd print., 1986), 185, Helmut Hoffman notes that from 1750 to 1790 a Nepalese coin called a *tamka* was used in Tibet. In 1792, the Dga' ldan Pho brang administration discontinued use of the *tamka* and established its own system of currency with coins bearing a Tibetan inscription—apparently, the first *dga' ldan tamka*. By 1890, paper notes called *srang* were introduced. These appeared in denominations equivalent to five, ten, twenty-five, and one hundred *tamka*s.

32. Rockhill, "Tibet: A Geographical, Ethnographical and Historical Sketch," 208 n. 1. Cf. the remarks of Edward Colburne Baber, *Travels and Researches in Western China*, Royal Geographical Society Supplementary Papers, vol. 1, part 1 (London: John Murray, 1882), 104.

33. Adshead, *Province and Politics in Late Imperial China*, 20.

34. Rockhill, "Tibet: A Geographical, Ethnographical and Historical Sketch," 218.

35. See Tashi Tsering, "Nyag Rong Mgon po rnam rgyal: A 19th Century Khams pa Warrior," in *Sounding in Tibetan Civilization: Proceedings of the 1982 Seminar of the International Association for Tibetan Studies*, ed. Barbara Nimri Aziz and Matthew Kapstein (Delhi: Manohar Publications: 1985), 199; and Luciano Petech, *Aristocracy and Government in Tibet: 1728–1959* (Rome: Instituto italiano per il Medio ed Estremo Oriente, 1973), 178. Petech says that the queen was "widowed" and that the prince was her son. Thus, we would have to understand that the "prince" was already king at this time. This is supported by Gele, who cites the *Xikang jian sheng ji (Records of the Establishment of Xikang Province)*, noting that 'Chi med rtag pa'i rdo rje "lost power for one year when Zhandui [Nyag rong] tribes seized power" (Gele, *Oral History of the Ganzi Tibetan Autonomous Prefecture*, 285). C.f. the recollection of the queen's own granddaughter, who currently lives in Chengdu. She insists that she has never heard of any such abduction, though she is aware such claims appear in contemporary historical accounts (Skal bzang chos sgrol [*alias* Sde dge sras mo], interview).

36. Karma rgyal mtshan, ed., *Mdo smad chos rgyal Sde dge'i rgyal rabs las 'phreng pa'i chos kyi 'byung tshul mdo tsam brjod pa gzur gnas blo ldan dgyes pa'i tambu ra* [A Brief Religious History from History of the Dergé Kings: *Lute to Please the Impartial Mind*] (Ganze: Hong Kong Asian Press, 1994), 56–57.

37. Tashi Tsering, "Nag Rong Mgon po rnam rgyal," 198–199.

38. Petech, *Aristocracy and Government in Tibet: 1728–1959*, 120–121. Interestingly, the kingdom of Gling tshang did not face such advances by Mgon po rnam rgyal, for the reported reason that the aggressor's daughter was married to the Gling tshang king (Jigme Lingtsang [*alias* Gling tshang sras], interviewed by the author, Chengdu, PRC, 1 September 1, 1997).

39. Tashi Tsering, "Nag Rong Mgon po Rnam rgyal," 209.

40. Petech, *Aristocracy and Government in Tibet: 1728–1959*, 120; italics added.

41. According to Jigme Lingtsang, it was a member of the powerful Bya rgod tshang family in Sde dge (*Blon po* Pad ma rnam rgyal?) who feigned loyalty to Mgon po rnam rgyal but then contacted Lhasa for assistance. Jigme Lingtsang [*alias* Gling tshang sras], interview.

42. *Da Qing lichao shilu* [*Veritable History of the Qing*], Mu tsung (134.25a–26b, 147.30a–31a). Cited in Petech, *Aristocracy and Government in Tibet: 1728–1959*, 120.

43. Petech , *Aristocracy and Government in Tibet: 1728–1959*, 121; italics added.

44. According to Smith, the queen, her son, and Dpal spungs Dbon sprul were released after Kong sprul Rinpoche, also a victim of the purges, healed an important Dge lugs pa lama. This helped ease the adamantine manner in which some Dge lugs pa clergy had been urging the Lhasa troops to raze Dpal spungs monastery; see Gene E. Smith, "Preface," in Kong sprul Blo gros mtha' yas, *Kongtrul's Encyclopaedia of Indo-Tibetan Culture*, ed. Lokesh Chandra (New Delhi: International Academy of Indian Culture, 1970), 33.

45. Petech, *Aristocracy and Government in Tibet: 1728–1959*, 121; and Tashi Tsering, "Nag Rong Mgon po Rnam rgyal," 211.

46. Adshead, *Province and Politics in Late Imperial China*, 57; and E. Teichman, *Travels of a Consular Officer in Eastern Tibet* (Cambridge, England: Cambridge University Press, 1922), 5.

47. Adshead, *Province and Politics in Late Imperial China*, 57; and Petech,.*Aristocracy and Government in Tibet: 1728–1959*, 256.

48. Ch. Jiagema.

49. Gele, *Oral History of the Ganzi Tibetan Autonomous Prefecture*, 259.

50. Petech, *Aristocracy and Government in Tibet: 1728–1959*, 76–77; Adshead, *Province and Politics in Late Imperial China*, 86; and Karma rgyal mtshan, ed., *A Brief Religious History*, 57.

51. Baber, *Travels and Researches in Western China*, 99.

52. Baber, *Travels and Researches in Western China*,98.

53. Karma rgyal mtshan, ed., *A Brief Religious History*, 57.

54. Gele, *Oral History of the Ganzi Tibetan Autonomous Prefecture*, 259.

55. These characteristics are drawn from John Schwarzmantel, *The State in Contemporary Society: An Introduction* (New York: Harvester Wheatsheaf, 1994), 8–11. This is, of course, only one perspective on what constitutes a modern "state." What Sde dge lacked was "centrality," emphasized by both Schwarzmantel and Geoffrey Samuel, "Tibet as a Stateless Society and Some Islamic Parallels," *Journal of Asian Studies* 41, no. 2 (1982): 215–229. Perhaps one better versed in political theory than I could use the evidence that cases such as the administration of Sde dge provide to challenge the notion that "centrality" need be a defining feature of a "state."

56. Hanseng Chen, *Frontier Land Systems in Southernmost China: A Comparative Study of Agrarian Problems and Social Organization Among the Pai Yi People of Yunnan and the Kamba People of Sikang* (New York: International Secretariat, Institute of Pacific Relations, 1949), provides valuable information regarding land administration from a 1940 survey of Kham. For his discussion of Sde dge, Carrasco, *Land and Polity in Tibet*, relied on Chen's survey and on the observations of Rockhill. The summary here directly draws upon these three works and Du Yongbin. The latter identifies only three systems, grouping monastic estates with the land allotted to nobles (Yongbin Du, "Dege tusi de tedian" [The Dergé Tusi's Characteristic Features], *Xizang yanjiu* 3 [1991]: 67).

57. Carrasco, *Land and Polity in Tibet*, 145.

58. Carrasco, *Land and Polity in Tibet*, 145; and Teichman, *Travels of a Consular Officer in Eastern Tibet*, 208.

59. Carrasco, *Land and Polity in Tibet*, 144.

60. Teichman, *Travels of a Consular Officer in Eastern Tibet*, 208.

61. Karma rgyal mtshan, ed., *A Brief Religious History*; 77. The role of four "chief ministers" (*gnyer chen*) was also mentioned by Dhong thog Rinpoche (interviewed by the author, Bloomington, Indiana, January 1997) and in an autobiographical piece on Dil mgo Mkhyen brtse Rin po che; see Orgyan Topgyal Rinpoche, *Khyentse Özer: International Journal of the Rigpa Fellowship* 1 (August 1990): 13. However, the term *blon chen* is also used for this position in some works, such as the *Sde dge'i rgyal rabs*. Cf. Petech, *Aristocracy and Government in Tibet: 1728–1959*, 8, who notes that *blon chen* was used to designate the chief ministers in Lhasa. Note that Sga rje and Ser shul are two of Sde dge's largest districts.

62. Chen, *Frontier Land Systems in Southernmost China*, 82. According to the Sde dge *sras mo* (princess), the king traditionally appointed two *phyag mdzod* to his court and they were considered senior to the *snyer chen*. She also clarified that what is referred to by Chen as *gsol dpon* was more commonly called a *gzim dpon* (chamberlain), the most favored among the king's servants and the only one allowed access to the ruler's sleeping quarters (Skal bzang chos sgrol, interview).

63. Du, "The Dergé Tusi's Characteristic Features," 68; Gele, *Oral History of the Ganzi Tibetan Autonomous Prefecture*.

64. Orgyan Topgyal Rinpoche, *Khyentse Özer*.

65. Cited in Carrasco, *Land and Polity in Tibet*, 145. According to Carrasco, this second rank of officials were called tingkoo (Tib. *lding dpon?* or *lding sku* [*tshab*]?),

from whom he claims the most talented were selected as *gnyer ba*. This contradicts information provided in the *Sde dge chos 'byung*, which specifies four districts from which the *gnyer chen* were selected. The Sde dge *sras mo* confirmed that *gnyer pa* are one and the same as *gnyer chen* and that these were selected by district (Skal bzang chos sgrol, interview).

66. Evidently, a clear treatment of these terms could constitute an entire article in itself. Baber (*Travels and Researches in Western China*, 97)—one of the earliest sources cited here—refers to the king of Sde dge as the "Chief Deba" and the local chiefs as simply "Debas." Tashi Tsering also uses *sde pa* when referring to the leaders of 'Ba' and Li thang (Tashi Tsering, "Nag Rong Mgon po Rnam rgyal," 199). Rockhill mentions a *sde pa* of Sde dge being locally addressed as *dpon pa* (Rockhill, "Tibet: A Geographical, Ethnographical and Historical Sketch," 185). C.f. Petech, *Aristocracy and Government in Tibet: 1728–1959*, 12, who notes that district governors in the Lhasa government were originally referred to as *sde pa* but later called *rdzong dpon*.

67. Skal bzang chos sgrol and Jigme Lingtshang, interview.

68. Rockhill, "Tibet: A Geographical, Ethnographical and Historical Sketch," 219.

69. Rockhill, "Tibet: A Geographical, Ethnographical and Historical Sketch," 191–192.

70. Rockhill, "Tibet: A Geographical, Ethnographical and Historical Sketch," 189.

71. Karma rgyal mtshan, ed., *A Brief Religious History*, 79–80. The Sde dge sras mo described the *hor 'dra* as deputy "police" who served under the *blon po* (district officials). They were responsible for administering taxes and in some instances were promoted to the position of *rdzong dpon* (Skal bzang chos sgrol, interview).

72. Carrasco, *Land and Polity in Tibet*, 71. The duties for the village headmen as described by Carrasco are notably similar to the duties of Tibetan *hor 'dra* as defined in Zhang Yisun [Krang Dbyi sun] et al., *Bod rgya tshig mdzod chen mo* (*Zang-Han da cidian*) [*Great Tibetan-Chinese Dictionary*] (Beijing: Minzu chubanshe, 1985), 3071.

73. Chen, *Frontier Land Systems in Southernmost China*, 82; Rockhill, "Tibet: A Geographical, Ethnographical and Historical Sketch," 219, and Carrasco, *Land and Polity in Tibet*, 72.

74. Carrasco, *Land and Polity in Tibet*, 72; and Rockhill, "Tibet: A Geographical, Ethnographical and Historical Sketch," 219.

75. Launay, cited in Carrasco, *Land and Polity in Tibet*, 71.

76. For example, Du, "The Dergé Tusi's Characteristic Features," 68.

77. Carrasco, *Land and Polity in Tibet*, 222.

78. Carrasco, *Land and Polity in Tibet*, 226.

79. Carrasco, *Land and Polity in Tibet*, 28, 144.

80. Teichman, *Travels of a Consular Officer in Eastern Tibet*, 208. I was not able to positively identify "Adu," which Teichman says is located in the north. However, Jigme Lingtsang mentioned parenthetically in our interview that A du (sp?) was a "Hor pa state."

81. Du, "The Dergé Tusi's Characteristic Features," 68. I am unable to ascertain the Tibetan name for "Chita," but it may refer to "Chu rdo," as listed among the *mdun skar*.

82. Karma rgyal mtshan, ed., *A Brief Religious History*, 77.

83. Chen, *Frontier Land Systems in Southernmost China*, 83–84.

84. Gele, *Oral History of the Ganzi Tibetan Autonomous Prefecture*, 259.

85. See n. 27.

86. Recall that this probably refers to the Tibetan general Mdo mkhar sras Tshe dbang nor bu, who helped lead the expeditionary force from Lhasa into Sde dge to defeat the Nyag rong chief. See n. 59.

87. *Tusi* is the Chinese term for local leaders allegedly appointed to administer lands in the southwestern frontier. Here it refers to the king. In actuality, most *tusi* were already powerful local leaders to whom the Manchu imperial court granted a title with varying degrees of impact—usually very little—on the actual administration of the area. See van der Kuijp, "Two Early Sources for the History of the House of Sde dge," 10, for a discussion of the earliest Tibetan attestations of this title and its implications.

88. This most likely refers to a *sgor bro* dance in Tibetan.

89. This is the Chinese name for the capital, Sde dge dgon chen.

90. Gele, *Oral History of the Ganzi Tibetan Autonomous Prefecture*, 260. According to the Sde dge *sras mo*, her father (Rdo rje seng ge) was summoned to Chengdu, but never imprisoned (Skal bzang chos sgrol, interview).

91. Gele, *Oral History of the Ganzi Tibetan Autonomous Prefecture*.

92. Gele, *Oral History of the Ganzi Tibetan Autonomous Prefecture*, 260.

93. These accounts include Adshead, *Province and Politics in Late Imperial China*, 86; Teichman, *Travels of a Consular Officer in Eastern Tibet*, 6–7, 26; and Petech, *Aristocracy and Government in Tibet: 1728–1959*, 194–195. Petech also cites the *Veritable History of the Qing*, 410.10a–11a, 412.1a–2a, which I have not personally consulted.

94. Baber, *Travels and Researches in Western China*, 101.

95. Sichuansheng bianjizu, *A Socio-Historical Investigation of the Tibetans in Ganzi Prefecture, Sichuan Province*, 110.

96. The translation of the term *mi ser* as "serf" continues to be a controversial topic. Rockhill's account is one of the earliest to use the term "serf."

97. Rockhill, "Tibet: A Geographical, Ethnographical and Historical Sketch," 215–216. Italics added.

98. Carrasco, *Land and Polity in Tibet*, 219.

99. Carrasco, *Land and Polity in Tibet*, 147.

100. Carrasco, *Land and Polity in Tibet*, 149.

101. Sichuansheng bianjizu, *A Socio-Historical Investigation of the Tibetans in Ganzi Prefecture, Sichuan Province*, 106.

102. 1 *mu* = .16 acres of land.

103. Kuang Haolin, *Zhongguo jindai shaoshuminzu jingji shigao* [*The Historical Account of Modern Minorities' Economy in China*] (Beijing: Minzu chubanshe, 1992), 130.

104. Kuang, *The Historical Account of Modern Minorities' Economy in China*, 135–136.

105. 1 *jin* = .5 kilogram.

106. Samuel, "Tibet as a Stateless Society and Some Islamic Parallels," 221 n. 10.

107. Li, "Dege: A Study of Tibetan Population," 289.

108. *Mgo log* is the name of a nomadic tribe that had an exceptional reputation as fighters. For an interesting article on its leadership in the early twentieth century, see Lodey Lhawang, "The Conferring of Tibetan Government Ranks on the Chieftains of Golok," *Lungta* 8 (1992?).

109. Rockhill, "Tibet: A Geographical, Ethnographical and Historical Sketch," 232–233.

110. Rockhill, "Tibet: A Geographical, Ethnographical and Historical Sketch," 216–217.

111. See Sichuansheng bianjizu, *A Socio-Historical Investigation of the Tibetans in Ganzi Prefecture, Sichuan Province*, 106–112; and Carrasco, *Land and Polity in Tibet*, 147–151.

112. Karma rgyal mtshan, ed., *A Brief Religious History*, 80–83. C.f. Li, "Dege: A Study of Tibetan Population," 283–285, who recorded thirty-four monasteries in the area of Sde dge lying east of the 'Bri chu (Yangzi River) and classified them on the basis of their nomadic or agricultural location. A useful source for tracing these names is Peter Kessler, *Laufende Arbeiten zu einem ethnohistorischen Atlas Tibets (EAF) 40,1. Die historischen Königreiche Ling und Derge* [*Ongoing Work Toward an Ethno-historical Atlas of Tibet (EAF) 40,1, the Historic Kingdoms Ling and Derge*], XI, 143 S.: Ill., Kt. + 2 Beil., 2 Kt.-Beil (Rikon/Zürich: Tibet-Inst, 1983).

113. 'Jam dpal blo gros, Dpal sprul, *Bod na bzhugs pa'i rnying ma'i dgon deb* [*Record of Nyingma Monasteries in Tibet*] (Dalhousie: Paltul Jampal Lodoe, 1965), 79.

114. Li, "Dege: A Study of Tibetan Population," 285.

115. 'Jam dpal blo gros, *Record of Nyingma Monasteries in Tibet*, 86.

116. Li, "Dege: A Study of Tibetan Population," 283.

117. Li, "Dege: A Study of Tibetan Population," 285.

118. Li, "Dege: A Study of Tibetan Population," 288.

119. Sichuansheng bianjizu, *A Socio-Historical Investigation of the Tibetans in Ganzi Prefecture, Sichuan Province,*106.

120. Sichuansheng bianjizu, *A Socio-Historical Investigation of the Tibetans in Ganzi Prefecture, Sichuan Province.*

Chapter 30

LABRANG

A TIBETAN BUDDHIST MONASTERY AT THE CROSSROADS OF
FOUR CIVILIZATIONS

Paul Nietupski

If there is no easily recognizable state apparatus in the northeast that we might readily compare with the Central Tibetan government, what was the political structure of Amdo? This essay by Paul Nietupski, a portion of his first book-length treatment of Labrang monastery, offers the beginnings of an answer. The book focuses on the surviving photographs taken by the Griebenows, a Protestant missionary family active around Labrang in the early twentieth century. The photographs are an important source for this history in their own right, and bear detailed investigation. Here Nietupski offers an overview of Labrang as a political center. Just as the last essay's study of the Dergé kingdom represented a typical pattern for the Kham region, this essay on Labrang represents a typical pattern for Amdo: there were few principalities or kingdoms, but many monasteries that held real political power. Labrang, for instance, controlled an area about the size of Switzerland, through a complicated network of estates, subordinate rulers and monasteries, and representative political envoys. The multiethnic nature of the frontier in Amdo was especially important to Labrang's development. First, the Mongols who ruled Amdo until 1724 were key to the monastery's foundation and later continued their support. In fact, the main sponsor, the Khoshud Mongol Prince Erdeni Jinong, known in Chinese as the "Henan Qinwang," was the same man called Chaghan Danjin in Katō Naoto's article above. His decision to forego participation in the 1723–24 uprising against the Qing meant that Labrang experienced growth at a time when most of the other major monasteries in Amdo had been destroyed and were trying to rebuild. Later, in the twentieth century, cooperation with the Chinese was necessary as well, especially in the face of Muslim aggression.

Labrang monastery is located in the Amdo region of Tibet, more specifically in what Tibetans refer to as Khagya Tsodruk. Amdo occupies the northeast corner of the Tibetan Plateau, north of the steep valleys and high passes of Kham, and east of the high Northern Plains of Tibet. Most of Amdo, including the Labrang region, averages over 10,000 feet above sea level, and has the severe climate and unique vegetation, animal life, and ecosystem peculiar to high-altitude environments. The monastery itself is located at about 8,400 feet (2,820 meters) above sea level. The Labrang region of Amdo borders on China, Muslim territories and Mongolia. It is also near the Hexi corridor section of the ancient "Silk Road," the main conduit for economic, military, and cultural exchanges between Asia and Europe.

The Griebenows and all foreign visitors marveled at the variety and numbers of animal and plant species in Amdo and Labrang. It was a wild, rugged land, in this respect analogous to the early North American "Wild West," or Alaska. Untapped and seemingly unlimited resources in remote places with severe climates populated by tough, intensely territorial mountain people with a strange religious culture all gave an exotic image to the Labrang region of Amdo in the eyes of foreign visitors.

Labrang monastery's natural setting is indeed striking. It is located in a high valley that descends from the 18,000-foot-high glacier-capped peaks that surround the Tibetan Plateau. The upper passes are narrow, but they widen into high plateaus with grassy plains suitable for livestock in the summer months. Valleys below the tree line separate into forests that teemed with wildlife in the first half of the twentieth century. Labrang monastery itself stands in a relatively narrow, winding valley amidst fields of barley and tall grasses once surrounded by evergreen forests. In the early twentieth century neighboring regions were accessible only by narrow trails along steep gorges; there were no roads to Labrang until 1940. The Labrang valley continues to twist down in elevation to the northeast, finally ending in the Yellow river lowlands in nearby China. Nearly all sources describe the descent along this valley as a place where the culture obviously changes from Tibetan to Chinese. This cultural geography confirms the comment that most Tibetans live on the Tibetan Plateau and the Chinese prefer the lower elevations, each choosing the environment more conducive to the maintenance of their cultures and lifestyles.[1]

The Amdo region boasts many rivers, including the Drichu (Yangtze) and the Machu (Yellow) rivers. The Yellow river valley passes through the center of the Labrang region, from the Ragya monastery down to the confluence of the Yellow and Sangchu (Xiahe) rivers, not far from Labrang monastery and modern-day Lanzhou. This region contained the greatest number of monasteries in Amdo, including Labrang.

The monastery itself, by far the largest and most influential political and religious institution in Amdo in the first half of this century, is located on the
Sangchu river, a tributary of the Yellow river, on the Xiahe or Kalawat plateau,
just south of the Hui market town of Linxia. It is about 103 kilometers from
Linxia, and about 285 kilometers west-southwest from Lanzhou, the capital city
of Gansu province. There were trails to the other border towns, Choné (Choni)
and Songpan to the south, to the Tibetan highlands to the west and southwest,
to Kumbum, other monasteries and Xining city to the northwest, to local towns
east of Labrang, and to Lanzhou.

Few accurate population statistics exist for Labrang in the early twentieth
century, much less for earlier times. Apa Alo, the local leader during the Griebenow mission, describing Amdo in the early twentieth century, gives some at
least approximate data:

> Amdo consists of about two million square kilometers of territory,[2] is sur-
> rounded by mountains, notably the Amnyé Machen mountains. According
> to estimates made in the 1930s there were about 600 ethnic groups in
> Amdo. The political structure can be roughly described as a regionally vari-
> able mixture of large estates or small kingdoms with inherited titles and
> powers, towns built up around major monasteries, and open, unsettled ter-
> ritories claimed by groups of nomads. There were altogether about one and
> a half million people in Amdo. Buddhism was the primary religion.[3]

Labrang Monastery was an important Tibetan cultural center and an important trading center located at a strategic intersection of major ethnic groups.

LABRANG'S CULTURAL HERITAGE

The Tibetan Buddhists describe the Sangchu valley in poetic terms. The valley
is visualized as more than just a valley; the eight Buddhist auspicious signs[4] and
the seven attributes of royalty[5] are implicit in the mountain peaks, and in the
twisting, forested valleys, rivers, and high plains. Certainly this sense of inspiration from the environment is not misplaced, nor is the image of a jewel of Buddhist dharma in a remote high-altitude mountain valley, since Labrang monastery
was a major center of Tibetan religious culture, with a rich and distinctive heritage. The enchanting image is reinforced by the predictions which the Tibetans
find in classical Indian Buddhist literature about Buddhism coming to Labrang.[6]
These visions and predictions have been living for centuries in Amdo's religious
history and cultural imagination.

Long before Labrang monastery was founded, Amdo's culture was diverse:
Chinese Buddhism from the Tang dynasty courts had considerable influence
in the region, the pre-Tibetan Bön religion was established throughout Amdo,

and in the ninth and tenth centuries new influences from central Tibet took root in Amdo. As Amdo developed political and trade links with the Chinese and the Mongols and when Labrang was founded in the early eighteenth century, it became a major conduit for Tibetan Buddhist culture to Mongolia. All of these diverse influences contributed to make Labrang monastery evolve into a dynamic cultural, religious, economic, and political environment.

The historical beginnings of Labrang are interesting because they evolve out of one of the most important periods of Tibetan civilization. The Fifth Dalai Lama, Ngawang Lozang Gyatso (1617–1682), is linked to Labrang through his 1653 meeting with the first Jamyang Zhepa (1648–1721), then a precocious five-year-old who was to become the founder of Labrang monastery. This meeting took place while the Dalai Lama was in Amdo en route to a diplomatic meeting with the Chinese.[7] Years later, the Fifth Dalai Lama was to confer full ordination on Jamyang Zhepa in Lhasa, when the novice was twenty-seven years old.[8]

After receiving full ordination Jamyang Zhepa devoted some twenty-five years to the rigorous study of Buddhist scriptures, including the full range of Buddhist philosophies, psychologies, and mystical subjects. He mastered the ritual arts, ritual dance, and mandala science. He studied unflaggingly under the tutelage of numerous scholars and adepts in the major monastic establishments in central Tibet, concentrating on the Kadampa and Gelukpa teachings. It is said that he became very austere, thin and frail.[9]

Meanwhile, the capable Fifth Dalai Lama kept the Tibetan political world in a rather delicate balance. An astute political negotiator, the Fifth Dalai Lama visited China in 1651–53, keeping Tibet's imperial eastern neighbor at bay through prudent diplomacy, and at the same time making use of Mongolian assistance to consolidate the central Tibetan realm and absorb western Tibet and Ladakh. The Fifth Dalai Lama's death in 1682 upset the balance in central Tibet. His ministers decided to try to maintain equilibrium in the kingdom by concealing their leader's passing. This deception lasted until 1697, during which time Jamyang Zhepa played a part in the central Tibetan government's attempts to maintain stability. Jamyang Zhepa participated in the ordination ceremony of the Sixth Dalai Lama at Trashilhünpo Monastery in Zhigatsé in 1697, but with young Tsangyang Gyatso's rejection of his monastic vows and his position as Sixth Dalai Lama, the subsequent occupation of Lhasa by the Zunghar Mongols in 1705, and the Sixth Dalai Lama's flight in 1706, central Tibet was in turmoil. Jamyang Zhepa left an unstable political environment in Lhasa when he accepted the Mongolian invitation to found a monastery in remote Amdo.[10]

His 1695 meeting with the local Khoshud Mongol Prince Erdeni Jinong, known in Chinese as the "Henan Qinwang" (Prince of the Henan district)[11] and in Tibetan as the "Sokpo Gyelpo," and several local Tibetan families marks the original conception of Labrang. Though he had initially declined the request, in 1709 Jamyang Zhepa finally went to Amdo to establish a monastery.[12] Thus it came to pass that the Amdo-born Khenpo Lozang Gyeltsen, or the first

Jamyang Zhepa, went back to his original home in Amdo from Drepung monastery's Gomang college,[13] and brought Labrang monastery from its humble beginnings in a tent to its development as a major community institution.

Part of the complex twentieth-century governance of Labrang originated and evolved from the thirteenth-century Mongols Chinggis and Qubilai Khan, who initiated the connection of Mongol khans to Tibetan lamas. This connection was continued by the seventeenth-century Mongol ruler Gushri Khan, who invaded Tibet to assist the Fifth Dalai Lama. Gushri Khan's grandson was the locally influential Prince Erdeni Jinong, the "Henan Qinwang," the highest-ranking nobleman of the Khoshud Mongols in Amdo.

The Mongol Henan Qinwang was the preeminent ruler in Amdo south of the Machu river.[14] (In Chinese *he* means "river" and *nan* means "south.") His descendant in power in the 1920s and 1930s was the "Mongolian Prince," Künga Peljor, one of the twenty-nine Mongol princes in Amdo.[15] As the highest ranking Mongolian prince, his influence extended even over parts of Gansu, Qinghai and Sichuan, including the region around Lake Kokonor (*Kokenuur*). Künga Peljor died in 1940 and his wife Lukho and daughter Trashi Tsering ruled[16] until Trashi Tsering married Amgön, or Kelsang Döndrup, Apa Alo's son and the nephew of Jamyang Zhepa.

By the early eighteenth century, the Mongol tribes had largely adopted Tibetan language, lifestyles, and religion. Of all the peoples present in the region the Mongols enjoyed the strongest sense of solidarity and peaceful coexistence with the Tibetans. This was doubtless the result of the Mongol sponsorship of the monastery and the Mongols' faith in Tibetan Buddhism. The local Mongols, with a royal palace located at Labrang, were responsible for financing much of the original construction of Labrang monastery in the early eighteenth century and maintained significant but gradually declining political influence through the period of the Griebenow Mission. The approximately 15,000 Mongol subjects[17] in the modern period lived primarily in the Labrang territories and recognized the religious and secular authority of Labrang monastery as endorsed by the Mongol prince.

The monastery's formal name is Genden Shedrup Dargyé Trashi Yesu Khyilwé Ling, but it is most commonly known as Labrang Trashikhyil or simply Labrang. A *labrang* is actually a Tibetan teacher's personal property. It may include religious books and materials as well as buildings, land, wealth, and even tax revenues. Labrang was the *labrang* of the lineage of the Jamyang Zhepas.[18] After the death of the first Jamyang Zhepa, the second through fourth Jamyang Zhepas inherited, or more accurately, continued the lineage of Jamyang Zhepas in their office (i.e., their *labrang*) at Labrang. The Tibetans believed that these boys were enlightened or powerful beings, the living emanations of the first Jamyang Zhepa.

The actual date of the founding of Labrang monastery was planned to coincide with the 300th anniversary of Tsongkhapa's founding of Ganden monastery in central Tibet.[19] Its beginnings were modest—a large tent located on the site where the main assembly hall would be built, with a congregation of five monks. The hall was built in 1711 using that of Drepung Monastery in central Tibet as a model.[20] The monastery grew over the years to include well over one hundred buildings, accommodating its population of between 3,000 and 5,000 monks, depending on the time of year. By the twentieth century there were

> six *Sūtra* Halls, forty-eight Buddha temples, thirty-one palaces for the Jam-yang Zhepas and the senior Lamas, thirty mansions for the incarnate Lamas, eight government buildings, six big kitchens, one printing house, two main meeting halls, over five hundred prayer-wheel rooms, and more than five hundred common monks' cells.[21]

Over the years the monastery grew slowly not only in its physical size, but also in terms of its political mechanisms and its role in Amdo. The second Jam-yang Zhepa (1728–1791) was installed as leader of Labrang only after overcoming disputes over his legitimate claim to the title. He prevailed, was ordained by the famous scholar Changkya Rölpé Dorjé, and made significant contributions to the monastery. The second Jamyang Zhepa enlarged Labrang's existing structures and sponsored the construction of new buildings, among them the Kālacakra Temple (1763) and the Medical College (1784). He was also the first Jamyang Zhepa to hold the position of abbot of nearby Kumbum Monastery for one term, a practice that was followed by the later Jamyang Zhepas.

Like his predecessors, the third Jamyang Zhepa (1792–1856) was a native of the region. His identity was established early in his life, after which he began his monastic studies and training. He was ordained in Lhasa by the Panchen Lama in 1812. The third Jamyang Zhepa was known for his ascetic practices. He followed the *vinaya* rules strictly and exemplified the Buddhist teachings on humility and moral conduct. He always found time to help even novice monks in their studies and would assist them in the most menial tasks. He became famous for his ability to maintain a stable state of meditation, even while traveling on horseback. Though he did not undertake much new construction to the monastic complex at Labrang, he oversaw the completion of the Medical College begun by his predecessor.

The fourth Jamyang Zhepa (1856–1916), a native of Kham, was different from the other Jamyang Zhepas in that he traveled extensively to solicit funds for new structures at Labrang. He was educated at Labrang and in Lhasa. In 1881 he built a major religious structure at Labrang, the Hevajra Temple, and in 1898 made a historically important diplomatic visit to the Buddhist community at Wutai shan in China.

The fifth Jamyang Zhepa, second son of Gönpo Döndrup of the locally significant Alo family, was born in 1916 and died on April 14, 1947. His full name was Lozang Jamyang Yeshé Tenpé Gyeltsen Pelzangpo (also known as Pelshül Ngawang Tsöndru; in Chinese, Huang Zhengguang).[22] He was unique as a child and was identified as the reincarnation of the fourth Jamyang Zhepa in 1919 by the interregnal regent of Labrang, the ninth Panchen Lama.[23] His family arrived at Labrang on August 6, 1919, and he was enthroned at age five.[24]

The fifth Jamyang Zhepa's older brother, Apa Alo, was the most important military figure in the area. He led the Tibetan militia and forged an independent claim to authority with the aid of Chinese military and political figures. His authority derived from his gradual rise to political power and was legitimated by his younger brother's status as incarnate lama of Labrang monastery, who, at least according to the Tibetan tradition, was the final authority in religious and secular matters at Labrang monastery and in all of its territories.

The fifth Jamyang Zhepa's 1919 entry into Labrang was a grand affair; the rinpoché (the "reverend") and his entourage stopped en route at many regional monasteries and encampments, and were greeted in Labrang by about one thousand troops of the predominantly Hui Ninghai Army bearing gifts from the Qinghai authorities (Ninghai was the name given to the local Chinese Republican forces in the Ningxia-Qinghai area). Ngawang Tendar, the fifth Jamyang Zhepa's uncle, accepted financial authority for Labrang from the Manager Li Zongzhe (Tibetan: Tsöndru Gyatso), and Jamyang Zhepa's father, Gönpo Döndrup, assumed political responsibility. The party was met with drums, bells, conches, shawms and long horns. The streets were full of people, all of the monastic officials were present, and "there were tears in the eyes of many."[25] The Alo family—Gönpo Döndrup, his spouse, Apa Alo, and the rest of his children— were very well received by the Mongol prince.[26] Further, Pei Zhenjun, the army general of Lanzhou, and Zhu Geliang,[27] representing the Chinese Republican authorities in Lanzhou, came to honor the arrival of Jamyang Zhepa. Local rulers sent representatives as well.

It is not surprising, therefore, that the Alo family was given special status as the protector and vessel of the incarnate precious one, the rinpoché, or in the local dialect, "alak." When the family arrived at Labrang, its already dynamic history took yet another major turn with the gaining of religious and political prestige in Labrang. It was this family of authorities that allowed permanent residence to a foreign Christian mission and family, the Griebenows. Marion Griebenow was about twenty-two and Blanche about twenty-three when they started their mission at Labrang. Jamyang Zhepa entered the monastic system as successor to his inherited throne in 1919, and was about six years old when the Griebenows arrived.

The current sixth Jamyang Zhepa is Jetsün Lopzang Jikmé Tupten Chökyi Nyima Pelzangpo, identified after the Chinese took control of Amdo in 1950. The monastery and community were largely destroyed by officially sponsored vandalism in the 1950s and mid-1960s, and further damaged by fire in the 1980s. But these are later chapters in Labrang's history.

Labrang's governance has at various times been under the military and political control of the Mongol princes, the Hui militarists and regional Tibetan leaders. Until the Chinese Communist era, however, daily administration at

Labrang was primarily in the hands of the Labrang Tibetans, regardless of the battles with the Qinghai troops and the claims of the Chinese. Its location and turbulent political history have created Mongol, Muslim Hui and Chinese enclaves in the area, creating a mosaic of cultures on their shared borders. This account, a necessarily brief unraveling of the tightly wound patterns of cultures, religions, and politics in Labrang and Amdo, aims to provide an overview of the complex cultural identifications, changes, peaceful cooperation, and bloody conflicts that took place at Labrang between 1700 and 1950.[28]

NOTES

· 1. See Susan Naquin and Chun-fang Yu, eds., *Pilgrims and Sacred Sites in China* (Berkeley: University of California Press, 1992), 11: "Chinese were by preference lowlanders."

2. Editors' note: About the size of Kansas, though this covers only part of what is now considered Amdo.

3. See Huang Zhengqing and Lun Shi, *Huang Zhenqing Yu Wushi Jiamuyang* [*Huang Zhengqing and the Fifth Jamyang*] (Lanzhou: Gansu renmin chubanshe, 1989), 1–3; Hwang krin ching [Huang Zhengqing], *Hwang krin ching blo bzang tshe dbang dang kun mkhyen lnga ba chen po sku mched zung gi rnam thar ba rjes su dran pa zag med ye shes kyi me long (A blo spun mched kyi rnam thar)* [*Biography of Apa Alo*], Klu tshangs rdo phrug, trans. (Beijing: Mi rigs dpe skrun khang, 1994); Li Anche, *Labrang: A Study in the Field by Li An Che*, ed. Chie Nakane (Tokyo: Institute of Oriental Culture, The University of Tokyo, 1982). Also published as: Li An-che, *History of Tibetan Religion: A Study in the Field* (Beijing: New World Press, 1994).

4. The eight auspicious symbols: *Bkra shis rtags brgyad*: conch, umbrella, victory banner, fish, vase wheel, knot of infinity, and lotus.

5. Dkon mchog bstan pa rab rgyas, Brag dgon zhabs drung, *Yul mdo smad kyi ljongs su thub bstan rin po che ji ltar dar ba'i tshul gsal bar brjod pa: Deb ther rgya mtsho* [*The Ocean Annals of Amdo*], Śatapiṭaka Series, 226, ed. Lokesh Chandra (New Delhi: Sharada Rani, 1977), 2a.3–4. *Rgyal srid rin chen sna bdun*, the seven jewels of a king: *cakra*, the wheel [of law]; *hastin*, elephant; *aśva*, horse; *maṇi*, jewels; *mantrin*, minister; *senāpati*, general; *strī*, queen.

6. "In the northern part of a northern country the study and practice of the *Prajñāpāramitā* will flourish." Dkon mchog bstan pa rab rgyas, *The Ocean Annals of Amdo*, 2a.3–4. According to the *Lha mo dri ma med pa'i 'od lung bstan pa*, "the dharma will flourish in the land of the red-faced ones 2500 years after the enlightenment." Dkon mchog bstan pa rab rgyas, *The Ocean Annals of Amdo*, 2a.3–4.

7. Dkon mchog bstan pa rab rgyas, *The Ocean Annals of Amdo*, 3a.1.

8. Dkon mchog bstan pa rab rgyas, *The Ocean Annals of Amdo*, 2b.2–3a.1.

9. Yon tan rgya mtsho [Yönten Gyatso], *Chos sde chen po bla brang bkra shis 'khyil: mkhas grub 'bum sde'i rol mtsho mdo sngags bstan pa'i 'byung gnas dga' ldan bshad*

sgrub bkra shis 'khyil gyi skor bzhad gzhung dal 'bab mdzod yangs las nye bar sgrub pa sngon med legs bshad ngo mtshar bkra shis chos dung bzhad pa'i sgra dbyangs [*Religious History of Labrang Tashikhyil Monastery*] (Paris: Privately published, 1987), 15.

10. The Dalai Lamas, the Jamyang Zhepas, and the large number of other "lineages of reborn Tibetan Buddhist lamas" are the institutionalization of the Buddhist belief that a spiritually advanced person can choose his or her birth in a succeeding lifetime. Hence, the Dalai Lama in the early twentieth century was the thirteenth and the Jamyang Zhepa the fifth incarnations in those particular lines. The procedure for identifying reborn Buddhist lamas has been discussed elsewhere in detail. See John Avedon, *In Exile from the Land of Snows* (New York: Knopf, 1984); Franz Michael, *Rule by Incarnation: Tibetan Buddhism and Its Role in Society and State* (Boulder, Colo.: Westview, 1982); and others.

11. Mongolian sources identify this person as Boshugtu Jinong, but Erdeni may be the title added to Jinong, "Viceroy." Thanks to Christopher Atwood for information about the Mongols here and throughout, lexical suggestions, and clarification of key events in Chinese history.

12. Eleventh cycle, earth female-buffalo year, Dkon mchog bstan pa rab rgyas, *The Ocean Annals of Amdo*, 1a.4–2a.1; Yon tan rgya mtsho, *Religious History of Labrang Monastery*, 29.

13. Huang Zhengqing and Lun Shi, *Huang Zhengqing and the Fifth Jamyang*, 5.14–6.1.

14. Here we have yet another claim of sovereignty in this region, in addition to the Chinese, Muslim, and Tibetan claims.

15. The "twenty-nine" refers to the twenty-nine separate "banners" or principalities among the Mongols of Qinghai. Künga Peljor (Gungga Baljur), the prince of the Khoshud South Leading Banner (the official name of his principality) was the highest ranking, but he did not directly rule over the other twenty-eight princes.

16. Hwang krin ching, *Biography of Apa Alo*, 142.

17. Li, *Labrang*, 27.

18. Compare the *menhuan* structure among Muslims in China. The ethnic minority identity and small-kingdom or semi-independent state situation functioned in similar ways in different cultures.

19. See Yon tan rgya mtsho, *Religious History of Labrang Monastery*, 30.

20. See Yon tan rgya mtsho, *Religious History of Labrang Monastery*, 16.

21. Huang Zhengqing and Lun Shi, *Huang Zhengqing and the Fifth Jamyang*, 6.11; for detailed descriptions of the major structures in pre-Communist Labrang, see the Dkon mchog bstan pa rab rgyas, *The Ocean Annals of Amdo*; Bstan 'dzin dpal 'bar (Tenzin Palbar), *Nga'i pha yul gyi ya nga ba'i lo rgyus* [*The Tragedy of My Homeland*] (Dharamsala: Narthang Publications, 1994); Heather Stoddard, *Le Mendiant de l'Amdo* [*The Beggar from Amdo*] (Paris: Société d'Ethnographie, 1986); Yon tan rgya mtsho, *Religious History of Labrang Monastery*; Skal bzang dkon mchog rgya mtsho, Rgya zhabs drung tshang, *Thub bstan yongs su rdzogs pa'i mnga' bdag kun gzigs ye shes kyi nyi ma chen po 'jam dbyangs bzhad pa'i rdo rje 'phreng lnga'i rnam par thar ba*

mdor bsdus su skod pa [*Biography of the Fifth Jamyang Zhepa*] (Nanjing: n.p., 1948); Li, *Labrang*; Cao Ruigai, ed., *Labuleng Si* [*Labrang Monastery*] (Beijing: Wenwu chubanshe, 1989); and others.

22. Huang Zhengqing and Lun Shi, *Huang Zhengqing and the Fifth Jamyang*, 2.

23. Hwang krin ching, *Biography of Apa Alo*, 239. Regents were appointed to handle monastery affairs during the period after the death of an incarnate lama and before the discovery of his successor.

24. After the death of the fifth Jamyang Zhepa on April 14, 1947, the ninth Panchen Lama took over as regent once again, until the sixth Jamyang Zhepa was enthroned.

25. Huang Zhengqing and Lun Shi, *Huang Zhengqing and the Fifth Jamyang*, 33.

26. Huang Zhengqing and Lun Shi, *Huang Zhengqing and the Fifth Jamyang*, 53.

27. Hwang krin ching, *Biography of Apa Alo*, 32–33.

28. "Study of Gansu's ethnic conflicts and compromises may enhance our understanding of peripheral China and peripheral Islam—a double-edged comprehension of perception and behavior on frontiers." Jonathan N. Lipman, "Ethnicity and Politics in Republican China: The Ma Family Warlords of Gansu," *Modern China* 10, no. 3 (1984): 289. I likewise suggest that study of Labrang will enhance our comprehension of the monastery itself and offer a quadrupled comprehension of perception of behavior on the frontiers.

TIBET IN A GLOBAL CONTEXT

Chapter 31

UNITING RELIGION AND POLITICS IN
A BID FOR AUTONOMY

LAMAS IN EXILE IN CHINA AND AMERICA

Gray Tuttle

Until recently, little was known about the lives and times of Tibetans active in China. The wrenching turmoil of the late twentieth century has made it difficult even to conceive that Tibetan religious leaders might have actively missionized Chinese-speaking populations in China in the early part of the century and, even if one wanted to pursue such questions, sources of information were scarce. The situation has changed in last two decades, thanks in large part to a new generation of scholars that seeks to understand the place of Tibetan intellectuals and institutional leaders within their East Asian context during the early modern period. Gray Tuttle asks: Who went to China to promote Tibetan Buddhism in the early decades of the twentieth century? How did they move between two languages, two cultures, two political environments, two cultural worlds? Tuttle follows several leaders as they establish political connections in China. He argues that politics especially must not be divorced from religion when considering the place of Tibetan Buddhism in China during the Republican period. The Panchen Lama—the second highest incarnation series in Tibetan Buddhism after the Dalai Lama—was provided a special office in Nanjing upon his praise of the Nationalist government. And if the Nationalists utilized the reputation of Tibetan religious leaders toward their own ends in Tibetan cultural regions, Tibetan Buddhist masters also sought to employ the political and military strength of the new government to further their goals in the new geopolitical landscape of modern China.

An examination of the activities of Tibetan lamas in China in the early decades of this century reveals the repetition of centuries-old traditions as well as innovations associated with modernity. Most interesting for those who are familiar only with the current interest in Tibetan Buddhism in America is the fact that many of the strategies for propagating Buddhism to a non-Tibetan audience and seeking support for an autonomous Tibetan polity have earlier antecedents. The spread of Tibetan Buddhism in China, and later in the West, has been intimately linked to the political status of exiled Tibetan lamas. For this reason, this chapter discusses the connection between certain prominent Tibetan lamas' search for political patronage and the Tibetan Buddhist mission. The host of other Tibetan Buddhists with little interest or involvement in politics who helped to disseminate their religion in China and in America must unfortunately be neglected here. However, I should add that, both in China and America, ethnic Tibetan and Mongol lamas who focused more exclusively on teaching religion were important forerunners, preparing the ground, so to speak, for the later political activities of the lamas who are the subject of this chapter.

Viewing the activities of Tibetans in China in the early twentieth century allows us to discern patterns that provide significant parallels to the current place of Tibetan Buddhism in contemporary America. The assertion that these lamas were merely the pawns of Chinese politicians is a commonplace, while few Americans have a historically informed perspective on the current Dalai Lama's relations with the American government. I contend that all of these lamas, past and present, have exercised an agency that elevates their roles above that of pawns in someone else's game. At the same time, I recognize the very real context of events (or, in Buddhist terms, the nexus of causes and conditions) that serves to limit these actors' choices. Among the issues I will discuss are the enduring role of nationalism in prompting Tibetan "missions" abroad, the initial religious nature of such missions, their gradual politicization, and finally a combination of religious and political activities that has been a characteristic feature of Tibetan Buddhism for centuries.[1]

In the study of the cross-cultural transfer of Buddhism and globalization, the Tibetan Buddhist example holds a special place. Even before the Mongol successors of Chinggis Khan became patrons of Tibetan Buddhism from the Middle East to China, this religion had been linked with prominent political leaders. The origins of some Tibetan Buddhists' orientation toward patrons from outside Tibetan regions date back to the time of the Western Xia state (1038–1227). Lamas from a branch of the Kagyü school became spiritual preceptors to the ethnically Tangut rulers of the Western Xia state and were still serving in this role when Chinggis Khan eliminated the state and the dynastic family to whom the Tibetan Buddhists had been ministering. Within a few short decades, branches of the Kagyü school and the Sakya school had all come under the sway and received the patronage of various descendents of Chinggis Khan.[2] This relationship—the Chinggisid patronage of various Tibetan Buddhist religious schools and the claim on their associated properties—led to a vast dispersal of Tibetan Buddhism over much of East Asia, and even parts of the Middle East.

This first wave of Tibetan Buddhism's "global" dispersal was less the result of a mission undertaken by Tibetans than a requirement of their relationship with the rulers of the Mongol empire. Qubilai Khan (1260–1294) must be given the greatest credit for ensuring the enduring relationship between the Chinese empire and Tibetan Buddhism. Through the relationship between Lama Pakpa Lodrö Gyeltsen (1235–1280) and Qubilai Khan, a close bond between China and Tibet and between the religious and political functions of Tibetan lamas in the service of the state was established. Certain elements of this "contract" remained prominent in Sino-Tibetan relations into the twentieth century, though there was rarely direct continuity; these instances represent an enduring, rather than an unbroken, tradition. In his *Tibetan Nationalism: The Role of Patronage in the Accomplishment of a National Identity*, Christiaan Klieger described this Tibetan tradition as follows: "Tibetan culture provides a mechanism whereby forces and personnel from the 'outside' can be utilized . . . to economically and ideologically support the perceived continuation of Tibetan cultural patterns."[3] I explore how certain lamas engaged with "outside" resources, spreading their religion while simultaneously pursuing political goals.

On the one hand, disciples of Tibetan Buddhism in China and America shared an interest in potent ritual activity and the prestige associated with being the patron (and student) of prominent religious figures. On the other hand, teachers shared the desire to propagate their religion and receive patronage. Elsewhere I have explored why Tibetan Buddhism was so popular in the early twentieth century among Chinese Buddhists, and also the link between Angarika Dharmapala and Master Taixu (Tai Hsü). A key figure in supporting Tibetan Buddhism in China, Taixu embraced the Tibetan tradition of uniting religious and secular concerns. He was briefly educated in a Buddhist school inspired by Dharmapala.[4] In this essay, I will focus on a scarcely explored connection between Tibetan Buddhist mission activity and the political goals of exiled lamas. As these varied interests make obvious, a union of religious and secular matters was involved in forging the modern relations between Tibetans and their Chinese and American disciples.

The Tibetan understanding of the proper relation between religion and politics can be traced back to the end of the Tibetan empire in the eighth century, but was set in place most firmly in the time of Pakpa and Qubilai. Far from a conception of the separation of church and state, the Tibetan idea of the inextricable connection between religion and politics (*chos srid zung 'grel*) implies that these are not two opposing fields of activity which are meant to be kept separate. Rather, the linking of these two arenas is seen as perfectly appropriate in Tibet. As the current Dalai Lama stated in his autobiography, "religion and politics do mix."[5]

Tibetan society, since at least the time of the fifth Dalai Lama in the seventeenth century, had been accustomed to the notion of a joint religious and secular rule.[6] When the global wave of nationalism closed in on Tibet from British India and Han China, the thirteenth Dalai Lama tried to centralize these two aspects of leadership under his personal control more effectively than had any Tibetan leader in the past. With his success in this endeavor, other lamas found their positions—which shared similar features of joint religious and political rule, but on a local level—challenged. Unable to resist the Dalai Lama's military and political power, some Tibetan Buddhist hierarchs fled to China. Although modern Chinese may have shared some of the Western beliefs in the separation of the "church" and state, Tibetan Buddhists certainly did not.

Globalization was largely a product of the spread of nationalism. The appearance of first a British, then a Chinese army bent on redefining the relations of power in the very heartland of Tibet forced the Tibetans to take a more active role in the world of nations. The thirteenth Dalai Lama, Tupten Gyatso (1876–1933), was able to elevate his role to what is commonly perceived today to be an ideal model for Tibetan leadership: a truly unified secular and religious head of state. His innovation was actually taking into his hands all the secular power that had so often been associated *in principle* with religious leadership. By tightening his control over Tibet and modernizing, as much as possible, the Tibetan administration, the Dalai Lama hoped to assert Tibet's independence. Nevertheless, his efforts to create a compact national territory caused tensions in the larger Tibetan cultural world, parts of which did not necessarily recognize the supreme authority of a central Tibetan government. Just as Tibet had broken with China when the Chinese attempted to administer Tibet directly, so the leaders of heretofore self-governing Tibetan regions resisted the authority of the centralizing policies of the Tibetan government in Lhasa. Some of these leaders turned to their enemy's enemy, China, in order to counter these efforts at nation building.

At least partially, the Chinese aggression toward Tibet throughout the twentieth century has involved a similar contestation of power. Whereas the thirteenth Dalai Lama felt that he should exercise dominion over all culturally Tibetan regions, the Chinese believe that they have rightful dominion over all of the former Qing frontier dependencies, which included Tibet. The real source of the Tibetans' current claim to independence is that the central Tibetans succeeded in driving out the Chinese forces at the end of the Qing dynasty. On the other hand, the monastic polities that resisted the centralization of Tibet under the rule of the thirteenth Dalai Lama were not successful in resisting central Tibetan aggression. Therefore, they—like the current (fourteenth) Dalai Lama— were forced to seek support outside of Tibet proper. The impetus of nationalism that drove the Tibetans to consolidate a Tibetan nation in the first half of this century is not entirely different from the forces of nationalism that impelled the Chinese to exert control over Tibet in the second half of the century. In both cases, smaller polities, which wished to be separate and independent (but were not recognized as such by the international community), were forcibly incorporated into a larger community on the basis of nationalistic motivations.

Within a decade of his return from exile, the thirteenth Dalai Lama's efforts to centralize and militarily maintain a Tibetan nation-state resulted in the alienation of one of the most important figures in the Tibetan Buddhist world, the Panchen Lama. The Chinese were happy to receive the lama when he arrived in Chinese territory and provided for his basic needs for many years.[7] Similarly, India and the United States would later support the fourteenth Dalai Lama against the "communist menace" of the PRC.[8] Although the circumstances of these two lamas' going into exile are not identical, the parallels are striking. Neither was forcibly ejected from his home territory. Rather, in each case the stronger power tried to coerce the weaker but legitimate authority to adjust to a reduction of autonomy. When both lamas felt that their lack of cooperation would soon lead to their imprisonment, they fled into exile. Another example of a lama driven into exile did not share this common fate. The Norlha Khutugtu (1865–1936), the spiritual and political leader of territory in Kham, was actually imprisoned by the Tibetan government and only went into exile after he escaped his captors.[9] He arrived in Beijing late in 1924,[10] just as the Panchen Lama himself was making his way to the Chinese capital overland.

TEACHING RELIGION TO FOREIGNERS

Rather than playing prominent roles in the politics of a fragmented China, during their early years in China, the Panchen Lama and the Norlha Khutugtu were involved almost exclusively in spreading Tibetan Buddhist teachings. The Panchen Lama was careful to maintain a low political profile at first. Part of the tension between the Dalai Lama and the Panchen Lama had been over the latter's relations with the Qing state and the British in India. During his early years in China, while the Panchen Lama was still hoping to quickly return to Tibet, he did not want to add to the accusations that could be leveled against him. The fourteenth Dalai Lama was to face a similar dilemma in both 1951 and 1957. At these times, his acceptance of proffered American aid would only have confirmed the Chinese condemnation of imperialist intrigue in Tibet, while he still held out hope for a working relationship with the Chinese. The Dalai Lama was also careful not to meet directly with these foreign agents.[11] Likewise, in his early years in China, the Panchen Lama only sent representatives to deal with political officials, while he propagated religion.

The Panchen Lama's first teachings were directed at Mongolian, Tibetan, and Chinese adherents of Tibetan Buddhism at the sites of the old imperially supported Tibetan Buddhist temples in and around the capital, Beijing. However, he quickly moved into contexts that were purely Chinese, both ethnically and in terms of the form of Buddhism practiced. In these communities, the Panchen Lama largely focused on teaching about Buddhist figures that were shared with his Chinese Buddhist brethren. At the same time, he infused his teachings with elements unique to Tibetan Buddhism, especially emphasizing the esoteric aspects of the Buddhist figures. Once he had won a substantial following and the government's recognition of his religious status, the Panchen Lama sought to create a bureaucratic administration to support his interests.

Meanwhile, the Norlha Khutugtu pursued Chinese government assistance in claiming his domains but failed to secure it. At best, he was given permission to try, but without resources this was an impossible task. As there was no way to return to the combined political and religious position that had formerly been his, the Norlha Khutugtu was also limited temporarily to religious activities among the Chinese. Unlike the Panchen Lama, however, he seems to have focused on presiding over rituals whose precedents were of long standing in imperial China. As the Qing elite were no longer a viable audience, he adapted these traditions by making them available to the Chinese Buddhist laity. Although a prominent local politician aided him, his actual support appears to have come from a very broad base of the Chinese Buddhist community in Sichuan province. In these early years in China, then, these two prominent Tibetan Buddhist hierarchs focused their attention primarily on spreading Tibetan Buddhism among the Chinese, without ever losing sight of their longer-term goals.

When the Dalai Lama first came to America, he was allowed entry only as a religious leader and not as the leader of the Tibetan government-in-exile. Even in this capacity, his entry into the United States was blocked until 1979. As early as 1977 a student of Tibetan Buddhism in the Carter administration had secured official permission for the Dalai Lama to come to America, but it was two years before all obstacles were cleared.[12] Like the two lamas in China, the Dalai Lama initially spent his time abroad in religious contexts, offering Buddhist teachings to relatively small crowds from 1979 to 1985. In 1981, he brought esoteric Tibetan Buddhism to America in the form of an elaborate ceremony and practice known as the Kālacakra Tantra. The first group to attend this ritual numbered only twelve hundred, but this number nearly doubled each time the event reoccurred over the next decade.[13] As will become clear, the Dalai Lama was not the first to share this esoteric ritual with a foreign culture in modern times; in this, too, he followed a precedent. Thus, the Dalai Lama—like the lamas in exile in China—was only able to participate directly in American politics after he had built up a religious base of support abroad.

The Panchen Lama's first activities in China were perfectly consonant with his being a prominent religious leader. Seeing the death and destruction caused by the ravages of warlord battles, he offered prayers for those killed. Shortly thereafter he sent an open telegram to all the warlords, requesting that they cease fighting one another so that peace and prosperity might return to China.[14] He favored no side but made only vague statements about his support of the central government based in Beijing. Moreover, when the government invited the Paṇchen Lama to the National Reconstruction Meeting in 1925—which brought together the rulers of northern China with the "father" of Republican China, Sun Yat-sen—he studiously avoided becoming too involved in Chinese politics. He sent a representative to the conference while he stopped at the sacred Buddhist pilgrimage site of Mount Wutai and gave Buddhist teachings there until the conference ended.[15]

This instance of first contact with the central Chinese government set the pattern that the Paṇchen Lama was to follow for several years: sending representatives to deal with political matters while he frequented temples and expounded on Buddhist topics, thus eschewing direct involvement in politics. Aside from considering how the Tibetan government would respond to his having dealings with that of China, the Paṇchen Lama also might have been aware of the Chinese condemnation of monks who involved themselves in political affairs. Unlike Tibetan society, Chinese culture had little tolerance for religious figures who were active in politics.[16] For instance, Taixu was pejoratively labeled a "political monk."

At least at first, the expectations governing the behavior of the fourteenth Dalai Lama in America largely mirrored this Chinese attitude. The Dalai Lama was limited to traveling abroad only as a religious figure with restrictions placed on what he could say and do.[17] For example, in 1987 he was reprimanded by the U.S. State Department for addressing the U.S. Congressional Human Rights Caucus. Somehow this activity was deemed "inconsistent with his status as a respected religious leader" and a violation of the terms of his visa.[18] This has certainly changed in recent years, as it did for the Paṇchen Lama in his later years in China. Yet, despite the fact that the fourteenth Dalai Lama has obviously embraced a very political role in America, emphasizing this fact—as this essay consistently does—will no doubt be perceived by some as insulting to Tibetan Buddhism in general and the current Dalai Lama in particular. Yet he himself has said that, "I find no contradiction at all between politics and religion."[19] In any case, the pattern followed by the Dalai Lama for many years was very similar to that of the Paṇchen Lama upon his arrival in China: he acted as a religious figure, visiting local political leaders wherever he went but taking no direct role in politics.

When the Paṇchen Lama first arrived in Beijing, he taught at Yonghe Gong, which had served as the main imperial Tibetan Buddhist temple under the Qing dynasty. Though some ethnic Chinese were pursuing the study of Tibetan Buddhism at Yonghe Gong at that time, the audience would have been primarily ethnic Mongolian Tibetan Buddhists, as this group comprised the principal monastic population of the temple. This instance demonstrates the subtle yet significant role Mongols continued to play in "globalizing" Tibetan Buddhism. Just as the earliest Chinese scholar of Tibetan Buddhism (Yu Daoquan) studied at the ethnically Mongol Tibetan Buddhist monastery of Yonghe Gong, so the first American scholars of Tibetan Buddhism (Robert Thurman and Jeffrey Hopkins) studied in an ethnically Mongol Tibetan Buddhist monastery in New Jersey. This monastery, by far the earliest one in America, catered to and was supported by an immigrant Kalmyk Mongolian community.[20]

The Panchen Lama's first contact with a purely ethnic Chinese audience seems to have taken place in the first few months of 1925. His two-and-a-half-month-long southern tour into the heartland of Chinese culture in Jiangnan, south of the Yangtze River, marked the first instance of a Tibetan Buddhist reaching large ethnically Chinese audiences. This visit to Jiangsu and Zhejiang was especially significant because the region was the heart of active Chinese Buddhist education and training. Holmes Welch has described how these two provinces represented the best and the brightest of Chinese Buddhism. In fact, according to his figures, the number of Buddhist monks and laity in these two provinces outnumbered those in most of the other provinces combined.[21]

In April of 1925, the Panchen Lama transmitted the long-life (Amitayus) Buddha's mantra according to the esoteric tradition. The long-life Buddha cycle of teachings was especially significant coming from him, as he was understood to be an emanation of Amitābha, who is closely associated with Amitayus. This transmission linked the recipients to the Panchen Lama through a powerful set of religious beliefs; he was the master and they the disciples. The Panchen Lama clearly built a religious following oriented toward Tibetan Buddhist practice, though initially he did this through Buddhist teachings and deities shared by Tibetan and Chinese Buddhism.

The Panchen Lama also traveled to a second of the four Buddhist sacred mountains in China, the island Mount Putuo. The island was home to a very concentrated Chinese Buddhist monastic population that was well known for the intensity of its study and practice.[22] He blessed with the touch of his hand the fourteen hundred monks who had gathered to see him; to each he also gave two silver dollars. This was a significant financial contribution at the time, especially for a refugee who had fled home due to lack of funds.[23] On the next day, he lectured to two thousand monks on the Buddhist theories of birth, old age, sickness, and death, as well as on the three trainings in ethics, meditation, and wisdom. He also transmitted the esoteric mantras of Tārā and Avalokiteśvara. This gathering was a historic occasion, marking as it does the first time in the history of Sino-Tibetan relations that a Tibetan Buddhist taught so many Chinese monks.

In late July 1925, the provisional chief executive of China and temporarily the dominant warlord of north China, Duan Qirui, invited the Panchen Lama to the capital to receive the government's official recognition. Duan's recognition of the Panchen Lama was based on earlier models dating back as far as the Yuan dynasty. The tradition since the Mongol rule of China had been that rulers of China—whether Mongol, Han, or Manchu—would award respected

Tibetan Buddhist hierarchs elaborate religious titles and accompanying symbols of respect.[24] The most recent example, which Duan followed fairly closely, was the Qing court's treatment of the thirteenth Dalai Lama: "the Qing court, by imperial decree, conferred on him an additional title, inscribed in a gold leaf album, of 'The Loyally Submissive Viceregent, Great, Good, Self-Existent Buddha of Heaven.'"[25] On August 1, Duan bestowed the title "Propagator of Honesty, Savior of the World" on the Panchen Lama and gave him a certificate printed on plates of gold and a golden seal as symbols of his new honor.[26] Thus, Duan demonstrated no new ability to "utilize" the Panchen Lama's presence in China in the service of the struggling Chinese nation-state. Though aware of the need to preserve the integrity of the former Qing dynasty's borders, he was unable to conceive of any modern methods of employing Tibet's second most famous hierarch to this end. In fact, the only innovation that came about as a result of the Panchen Lama's interaction with this conservative leader of China was undertaken at the Panchen Lama's request. After receiving these honors, the Panchen Lama requested that he be permitted to set up his own offices within China.

The Norlha Khutugtu, on the other hand, had little success either gaining assistance from the government or teaching the Chinese in his early years in the north. His lack of a common language seems to have hindered his ability to communicate, especially in north China. He was from the eastern Tibetan region of Kham, which had its own dialects. In addition, the Norlha Khutugtu was trained in the Nyingma school of Tibetan Buddhism, whereas most of the Tibetans living in China proper at that time were adherents of the Geluk school. These differences may well have made it difficult for the Norlha Khutugtu to find disciples or venues in which to teach.

The Norlha Khutugtu's one successful contact with a Chinese politician while living in Beijing is described in two separate biographical accounts printed in a single volume. One account tells how he reached the president of China, Duan Qirui, through the practice of a great "dharma" which was "in response to a need" (*ganying dafa*).[27] Duan was said to be very surprised by this, and the event apparently increased his respect for the Norlha Khutugtu. The biography also implied that Duan studied the Buddha Dharma with the lama, though it does not state this directly and no other source confirms it.

In addition, Duan apparently "gave the Norlha Khutugtu permission to return to Kham to try to retake his lost territory."[28] The language of the biography suggests that the Norlha Khutugtu was seeking support for his former rule, rather than that the Chinese were seeking to utilize his good services to retake the area. The northern Chinese had their own problems at the time, and Tibet was far away and far from a priority. Another version of the Norlha Khutugtu's biography adds that Duan gave him one thousand Chinese *yuan* in cash.[29] Be that as it may, by the autumn of 1925, Duan was already losing the support of the warlords who had placed him in control of the Beijing government.[30] When Duan resigned his office in April 1926, the Norlha Khutugtu was left without even this weak patronage.

This problem was solved when a warlord leader of Sichuan province, named Liu Xiang, heard about the Norlha Khutugtu.[31] His career as a teacher to Chinese Buddhists blossomed in the next three years, during which time he built up a huge following in Chongqing. We are told that after the Norlha Khutugtu transmitted the esoteric teachings, his disciples numbered over ten thousand. In the words of his biographer, "the Guru went from none to an abundance [of students]." The one English-language biography I have found of the Norlha Khutugtu simply states that he "was invited to Sichuan by Gen. Liu Xiang to preach Buddhism [in] 1926 and won many converts to the faith."[32] It is doubtful whether the Norlha Khutugtu would have considered his disciples "converts," as most were probably already Buddhists, but Tibetan Buddhism and Chinese Buddhism probably appeared different enough to the Western observer to merit this term.

The Norlha Khutugtu's ritual activities were marked by a combination of tradition and modernity that is remarkably similar to Tibetan Buddhist practices in the West today. For example, in the spring of 1927, he held a "Dharma assembly for peace" (*heping fa hui*) that lasted forty-nine days. The event was held on the second floor of a Chinese company's office in Chongqing. Common laypeople were permitted to attend the esoteric ceremony.[33] Both of these conditions were new in the realm of Sino-Tibetan relations. Under the auspices of the Qing dynasty, such rituals were performed at court-supported temples dedicated to the practice of Tibetan Buddhism. Only the Buddhist elite and the imperial family would have taken part in such ceremonies, though they too had been for the benefit of both the dynasty (and by extension, the country) and the people.

In other respects this situation also anticipated the modern, and soon to be global, diffusion of Tibetan Buddhism. Instead of being initiated by the state, these ceremonies were privately sponsored by common people with business connections. At the same time, they were public events, open to anyone, rather being restricted to an imperial elite. Westerners accept as normal the events of 1991, when the Dalai Lama taught in New York's Madison Square Garden and a sand maṇḍala was displayed at the IBM office building, but the Norlha Khutugtu was the pioneer in this move into nonreligious space. Even the Panchen Lama continued to teach in temples or imperial palaces until the 1930s.

The next spring, in 1928, the Norlha Khutugtu held a one-hundred-day "great Dharma assembly for prayers" (*qidao da fa hui*). At this assembly, a vajra-maṇḍala was constructed. Though such maṇḍalas had previously been constructed in imperially sponsored temples or within the imperial palace, this new public construction of a maṇḍala again anticipated exiled Tibetan Buddhist activities on the global stage. In introducing this phenomenon's appearance in America, Jensine Andresen noted that the first public display of a sand maṇḍala took place in China, and this particular occurrence predates the one she noted by four years. As in the United States, where some fifty maṇḍalas were constructed between 1988 and 1997, this became somewhat of a regular practice in China.[34] Moreover, this activity did not merely draw an anonymous fringe of Chinese Buddhists; many officials sent either telegrams or representatives to attend such ceremonies.

If the Norlha Khutugtu's main goal in coming to China had been to regain power in his native region of Kham, he had made little direct progress in his first five years of exile. He gained permission to make the attempt and secured limited financial support, but far from the contested region and from a warlord on his way out of power. Nevertheless, his time was not entirely wasted, as he built up a large following among the Chinese in Sichuan. In the end, the Norlha Khutugtu's efforts at cultivating Chinese Buddhists as his disciples had the positive result of bringing him to the attention of the central government. As was the case for the Panchen Lama, only after all of China united under the Nationalist government was the Norlha Khutugtu's influence actually brought to bear on political questions.

Sometime after the Panchen Lama had received his title and honors from the government, he requested the right to set up offices to handle his affairs. The first such office was apparently located in a temple in Beijing with government approval. However, at that time, the government neither funded nor otherwise oversaw the offices. Far from being part of a government ploy to enlist the services of this prominent Tibetan Buddhist in Chinese schemes, the offices were the result of Tibetan initiative. On the basis of linguistic evidence, the Panchen Lama appears to have adapted an old Qing institution to his own purposes.[35] I suspect that their principal reason for existence was to handle the business affairs that accompanied the massive donations made by the Panchen Lama's Buddhist followers. For most of 1926, the Panchen Lama was teaching in Chinese Buddhist temples around the capital. In mid-September he gave an initiation into the tantric practice of the Amitābha Buddha to lay and monastic Buddhists. One feature of tantric initiation is the often substantial donations made to the teacher of such liberating techniques. It seems likely that these initiates' donations provided both the reason and the funding for creating offices that would handle the Panchen Lama's affairs.

From late 1926 until early 1929, the Panchen Lama lived among the Mongol adherents of Tibetan Buddhism in Inner Mongolia. During this period, he started to perform initiations into the Kālacakra Tantra. The ceremonies that conferred these initiations attracted enormous crowds (eighty thousand Mongols were said to have attended each of the first three initiations into this tantra) and brought the Panchen Lama much prestige and many rich donations. As Andresen noted in researching the Kālacakra tantra in America, "economically, western patronage of Kālacakra provides an important source of financial support for exiled Tibetans."[36] The growth of the number and the institutional development of the Panchen Lama's offices were no doubt given great impetus by similar donations.

THE POLITICIZATION OF THE TIBETAN BUDDHIST MISSIONS ABROAD

The real politicization of the Tibetan Buddhist leaders in China did not occur until 1929, after the success of Chiang Kai-shek's Northern Expedition had suppressed the warlords of north China and opened the way for a truly centralized government. The new Nationalist government was much more willing to involve these Tibetan Buddhist lamas in the politics of China. The Panchen Lama had sent his envoys to offer his congratulations to the new regime in Nanjing in the spring of 1928. By January 11 of the following year, the "Office of the Panchen's resident in [the capital] Nanjing to handle official affairs (*Banchan zhu* [*Nan*]*jing bangong chu*)" was officially established. For the first time in the history of modern China, the government had created a special office for a Tibetan Buddhist hierarch. To mark the establishment of this office, the government issued a proclamation of its opening, a chart of the organization of the office, and detailed rules and regulations to guide how affairs were to be managed there.[37] In the meantime, the Panchen Lama established additional offices, one in Taiyuan (located on the main road between Inner Mongolia and Nanjing) and one in Kham.[38] In this way, the previously religious nature of the Panchen Lama's role in exile was transformed into an official one, with a political administration.

After having established these offices, the Panchen Lama remained in Inner Mongolia for two more years. During this period, he communicated with Chiang Kai-shek, the leader of China. Judging from the content of the letters exchanged between the two men, it seems that the Panchen Lama was trying to see what sort of political support he could gain from Chiang Kai-shek. Specifically, in April 1930, he requested military supplies—five thousand rifles, a quarter of a million rounds of ammunition, five thousand uniforms, and funds to pay soldiers—to be used against a bogus Nepalese "invasion" of Tibet.[39] The Nationalists, who probably understood this request as the attempt to create a private army that it was, shrewdly linked the supplying of these items to the Panchen Lama's agreement to provisions that would have eliminated Tibetan autonomy entirely, at least in principle. So he refused these conditions and received no military aid. Despite the official cooperation and ongoing communication between these two men, neither the Nationalist government nor the Panchen Lama was to have their wishes fulfilled at that time. The similarity between this situation and the negotiations that arose between the Tibetan government and the CIA in 1951 is remarkable and will be discussed later.

In 1929, just months after having established the Panchen Lama's office in the capital, the central government summoned the Norlha Khutugtu from

Sichuan province to the capital in Nanjing. Once there, he was made a member of the Mongolian and Tibetan Affairs Commission. An office similar to the Panchen Lama's, called the "Office of the Khutugtu's resident in [the capital] Nanjing to handle affairs" (*Hutuketu zhu [Nan]jing banshi chu*),[40] was then established, while three branch offices were eventually set up in Chongqing, Chengdu, and Kangding [Daqianlu/Dartsedo]. The concentration of these three offices in the single province of Sichuan demonstrates the more limited scope of the Norlha Khutugtu's influence compared to that of the Panchen Lama.[41] Because his influence was most important for securing the loyalty of the Tibetans in Kham, he was also made a member of the commission to establish the province of Xikang.

The Norlha Khutugtu's presence in the capital was also important for the foreign community. The Nationalist government could counter Tibetan claims that the contested Tibetan region of Kham belonged to Tibet if they had a spokesman from that region within their own government. In the 1933 supplement to *Who's Who in China*, the compilers gullibly reported that the Norlha Khutugtu was the "former secular and religious ruler of Xikang [Kham]."[42] This was an obvious error in fact, as the Norlha Khutugtu had only ruled a small portion of Kham. Nevertheless, the ignorance of westerners living in China and the prestige conferred on this individual by the Chinese government were a powerful combination. Not only was the Norlha Khutugtu given positions within institutions that dealt with Inner Asia, he was also made a member of the legislature (*lifa weiyuan*). Though this governmental body was actually powerless in the Nationalist party-state, few foreigners were fully aware of this at the time. Thus, after an initial period of avoidance of or exclusion from the political realm, both the Panchen Lama and the Norlha Khutugtu had been welcomed into the Chinese government bureaucracy. However, although their influence was brought to bear on the ethnic and territorial problems China faced at that time, these men were pursuing their own interests as well.

While the Panchen Lama and the Norlha Khutugtu were being officially recognized in these various capacities by Chiang Kai-shek, the Dalai Lama was also in communication with China's new leader. In 1928 the Nationalist government claimed that it would remain true to Sun Yat-sen's policy of "equality for all nationalities of the country." Encouraged by this stance, the Dalai Lama sent his resident representative to Nanjing. This exchange, which was heralded as "the beginning of contact between Tibet and the KMT [Nationalist] government," followed the initiative of the Panchen Lama by almost half a year, giving the impression that the central Tibetans were trying to keep up with the Panchen Lama's efforts.[43]

Given the presence of the Panchen Lama's office in the capital since early 1929, the central Tibetan government must have begun to worry about the possibility that he could undermine its de facto independence by cooperating too closely with the Chinese. Later that year, the abbot of the Yonghe Gong monastery in Beijing, who had been appointed to the post by the Dalai Lama, went to Nanjing and conveyed to Chiang Kai-shek that the Tibetan government was friendly to China and welcomed the Panchen Lama's return. The abbot, Könchok Jungné, continued on to Tibet, carrying Chiang's message to the Dalai Lama. When he returned to China in 1931, he was made the Dalai Lama's chief resident representative in Nanjing. Adapting a former Qing religiopolitical institution to the modern context of overtly political offices, the Dalai Lama transferred an abbot at what had béen the primary imperial Tibetan Buddhist temple in the old capital in Beijing to serve as his representative to the Chinese government at the new capital. Thus, in 1931 an "Office of Tibet" was set up in Nanjing.[44] Originally, the Chinese had wanted the office to be called merely the "Dalai Lama's Representative Office" (Tib. *Tā la'i don gcod khang*), which would have put it on par with the Panchen Lama's office. However, his representatives insisted that the office represented Tibet and not merely the Dalai Lama.[45]

The creation of this office in China was a significant precedent for the later globalization of such offices. At present, the Dalai Lama's government-in-exile has Offices of Tibet in New York, Geneva, London, New Delhi, Paris, Zürich, Budapest, Moscow, Tokyo, Taipei, Washington, D.C., and Kathmandu, as well as in South Africa and Australia.[46] The first of these overseas offices were CIA-sponsored centers for the coordination of a National Security Agency (NSA) Special Group program built "around the Dalai Lama to heighten a sense of nation among his refugee constituency and to keep his cause before the international community." This 1.7-million-dollar program was funded by the NSA. An annual budget of US$150,000 was given to the fourteenth Dalai Lama's older brother, Gyalo Döndrup, to run the first two offices set up in New York and Geneva.[47] Ken Knaus, the former CIA officer in charge of Tibetan operations, reported that in 1963 the U.S. State Department was willing to allow a New York office as an "unofficial embassy" for Tibet and informed India of this permission.[48] Unlike the Panchen Lama and the Norlha Khutugtu's offices, these new Offices of Tibet are similar to the Dalai Lama's office in China, having served political purposes from the start.

Knaus credited an American adviser to the Tibetans with the idea of creating these offices, though he acknowledged that Gyalo Döndrup "readily recognized that they would provide the Dalai Lama with unofficial representation."[49] Given that Gyalo Döndrup had been intimately familiar with the offices in China, I suspect that he played a significant role in the creation of these CIA-funded offices.[50] In any case, the Dalai Lama's offices in China, and initially in the United States and elsewhere, were very different from those of the Panchen Lama and the Norlha Khutugtu in China in that they did not provide for a religious mission. They were purely political offices, functioning principally as unofficial embassies. Since 1974, when the United States eliminated such aid to the Tibetans as part of its renewed relations with China,[51] the various Offices of Tibet have come to coordinate both the religious and political roles of the Dalai

Lama. In this respect they now resemble those of his fellow Tibetans in China earlier in the century.

UNITING RELIGION AND POLITICS

Although I have been able to periodize the Tibetan Buddhist mission to China into neatly divided "religious" and "political" sections, the men examined here would certainly not have compartmentalized their lives in the same way. I suspect that they would have felt neither that they were using religion to achieve political ends nor that their involvement in politics was merely some "expedient means" to be employed in the spread of religion. Rather, they likely felt that the political and religious concerns were linked in a most natural way. They were Buddhist leaders and had been ousted from their rightful place in the cultural context in which they were raised. Given these circumstances, they did whatever was necessary and appropriate within the confines of the situation and their worldview to restore themselves to power. In the meantime, spreading Tibetan Buddhism allowed them both to practice the religion so central to their world and to build up the political power that accompanies being a celebrity in the modern world.

From 1931 to 1935, the Norlha Khutugtu's popularity grew immensely. His biography states that he had disciples from all provinces of China.[52] He traveled and taught in Beijing, Tianjin, Chongqing, Shanghai, Hangzhou, Guangzhou, Nanchang, Wuhan, and Changsha, while being based in the capital, Nanjing.[53] He taught an impressive array of Tibetan tantric cycles over the six years when he was based in the capital. These included cycles of teachings dedicated to Amitābha Buddha, the Medicine Buddha, the bodhisattvas Avalokiteśvara and Green Tārā, Padmasambhava, and a host of tantric deities previously unknown to the Chinese. His disciples set up the the Norlha Students' Society to provide funds to support his living and travel expenses, as well as for the publication of his teachings.[54] We are told that he initiated twenty thousand disciples into the esoteric teachings of Tibetan Buddhism. Although no gender ratio can be determined, the Norlha Khutugtu's biography, unlike those of other figures in China at that time, does mention that he had women disciples.[55] His experience anticipated that of dozens of teachers who have come to America: without the status of the Panchen or Dalai Lamas, such men have relied on a devoted following of students. Devotees' supporting their lama was certainly nothing new to the Tibetan Buddhist tradition; however, the formation of particular societies dedicated to this purpose appears to be a modern phenomenon that has reached new heights in America.[56]

Prior to 1929, the Norlha Khutugtu had had a decidedly local influence tied closely to his home region, as it was nominally controlled from the very provincial capital in which he lived. After 1929, the Norlha Khutugtu became a national figure for the Chinese. He represented the interests of the nation and not just the local concerns of an exiled Tibetan Buddhist leader. By embracing this role, he both gave the Chinese Nationalists his religious and political support and earned for himself their trust. The differences between the current Dalai Lama's relationship to foreign governments and the Norlha Khutugtu's relationship with the Chinese government are most pronounced in this respect. Although the Dalai Lama has become an international figure, he has never been offered or accepted a position or title from any other government body.

For the Norlha Khutugtu, the culmination of this trust was the Nationalist government's conferral of the title pacification commissioner of Xikang. This abrupt assignment to an officially political role was occasioned by the Communist Long March through the Norlha Khutugtu's native Tibetan region of Kham. In August 1935, the Norlha Khutugtu went to Kangding and assembled the important religious and political figures of the region to explain the position of the Nationalist government and the threat of the Communists.[57] Nevertheless, he failed to prevent the Communist advance, or even to return to his homeland before his death in 1936. In the end, although the Norlha Khutugtu was able to use the influence gained over all his years of missionizing in China to secure the support of the Chinese government in returning to his homeland, he failed to retake his former domains.

Meanwhile, the differences between the Paṇchen Lama and Chiang Kai-shek had been resolved by February 1931, when the Nationalists invited the Paṇchen Lama to the National Conference to be held later that year. He accepted and on May 4 was welcomed to Nanjing by a huge crowd of people—official representatives from all government ministries, councils, and commissions, as well as "several tens of thousands of citizens and students."[58] The next day the Paṇchen Lama met with Chiang Kai-shek and throughout the period was housed in his headquarters. From that time, the Paṇchen Lama took a stand in support of Chinese policy toward Tibet while the Chinese government solidly backed the Paṇchen Lama. No doubt this open and public acknowledgment of the position that China had consistently maintained toward Tibet was the deciding factor in the close relations the Chinese government then adopted toward the Paṇchen Lama. A similar situation governed the United States' support for the Dalai Lama. In 1951, when the fourteenth Dalai Lama was in India trying to decide whether to return to an occupied Tibet, the State Department conditioned support for Tibetan autonomy upon the Dalai Lama's disavowal of the Seventeen Point Agreement made with the Chinese, as well as a promise to resist the Communist regime. At that time, the Dalai Lama refused to agree to such externally imposed conditions and was refused overt aid by the Americans.

By late 1932, the Nationalist government rewarded the Paṇchen Lama for his support of China's titular sovereignty over Tibet. They publicly granted him a title that suggested a more political orientation while preserving the religious elements of its precedents: Protector of the Nation, Propagator of Transformation, Great Master of Infinite Wisdom. With such government recognition, he enjoyed an enormous surge in popularity. The Chinese government also committed itself to supplying an annual subsidy of 120,000 *yuan* to the Paṇchen Lama.[59] Likewise, when the Dalai Lama repudiated the Seventeen Point Agreement in 1959, the U.S. government agreed to support him and his government-in-exile with a yearly subsidy of US$175,000.[60]

As with the Norlha Khutugtu, the conferral of official recognition brought with it a whole new level of missionizing activity. The most important were Kālacakra rituals. Although the Paṇchen Lama had given the Kālacakra initiation to enormous crowds in Tibetan Buddhist Inner Mongolia, the practice of this ritual among the Chinese was unprecedented. The first ceremony, held in the Forbidden City in Beijing, accommodated as many as one hundred thousand people by some estimates. The second, held in 1934 in Hangzhou, was said to have been attended by some seventy thousand.[61] Admittedly, these numbers represent a tiny proportion of the Chinese population at that time (roughly 500 million), nevertheless, it represents over 150 times the proportion of Americans who have attended the Dalai Lama's Kālacakra ceremonies in the United States. Few Americans or Tibetans are aware that the performance of the Kālacakra for foreign audiences was first popularized in China.

The growth of the Paṇchen Lama's religious popularity was accompanied by an increasing political importance. At the end of 1932, he was granted a purely political office for the first time. He was to serve as the Western Borderland Publicity Commissioner, whose job it was "to publicize the desires of the central government to the borderland . . . [and] to propagate, *with the help of religious belief,* the Three People's Principles, teachings of the late Director-General Sun Yat-sen."[62] In this way, the Tibetan Buddhists had brought the Chinese around to their perspective: religion and politics had to go hand in hand when trying to settle relations between China and Tibet. Following a different tradition, in the United States propaganda was handled by a public relations firm hired by the CIA to help the Tibetans make their anti-Communist case in 1959.[63]

In return for his help, throughout 1933 the Chinese government assisted the Paṇchen Lama in negotiating with the Tibetan government permission for the Paṇchen Lama's return to Tibet. His last major public appearance in China, just days after the second Kālacakra ceremony, was to be his best attended event. According to Chinese sources, he lectured in Shanghai to a crowd of three hundred thousand on the topic "Mongolia and Tibet are China's important frontiers." By July 1934 he had set off for the western borderlands to carry out his duties and, it was hoped, return to Tibet. Like the Norlha Khutugtu, the Paṇchen Lama had finally secured the support of the Chinese government in his attempt to return to his former domains. Also like the Norlha Khutugtu, he was ultimately to die (in 1937, in the borderlands between China and Tibet) unsuccessful in his effort to return to his former position of authority.

CONCLUSION

Despite their cooperation with Chinese politicians, these Tibetan Buddhists were pursuing their own goals. In order to return to their previous positions, they sought the financial and military backing that only the Chinese government could have provided. In fact, as religious figures cooperating with the Chinese government, they established an important pattern for the future of Sino-Tibetan relations. As is still the case today, Chinese politicians were forced to work with the religious leaders of Tibet to try to maintain control over the populace in the region.

At the same time, these men invented and adapted strategies for dealing with the new challenges of a modernized world. They taught religion and gathered disciples when there was no way to enter into the political life, but accepted and often initiated political contacts and institutions when this was possible. Finally, they succeeded in combining religion and politics in an almost seamless fashion, linking their religious activities with their political causes.

For those who are privy to the world of Tibetan Buddhism in America today, this may well sound a familiar note. With regard to nationalism, the current Dalai Lama—whether or not he coordinated his plans with the American government—has fulfilled the 1963 goal of the NSA's Special Group: he continues to serve as the key rallying point for the Tibetan nationalist movement. And, like the lamas in China, he taught religion to foreigners as long as he felt that that was his only option. In his *The Making of Modern Tibet*, Grunfeld cynically (though probably accurately) described this early period as one in which "[Tibetan] Buddhist monasteries, study groups, rural communes, and even an accredited college . . . have converted hundreds, if not thousands, to their religious beliefs—thereby creating a large, receptive audience for their political beliefs."[64] He also prophetically noted, as he completed the writing for the first edition in 1985, that the Dalai Lama's "spiritual role . . . far outweighs his political functions—for the time being."[65]

This balance of religion and politics did change after 1985. As Grunfeld reported in his second edition, the Dalai Lama has always officially come to the United States only as a religious leader of the Tibetan people. However, since the "Tibet lobby" has enlisted a powerful law firm to serve as its United States agents for the Tibetan government-in-exile, the Dalai Lama has had decidedly more of an international political force.[66] At present, he, like the lamas before him in China, has also succeeded in uniting religion and politics abroad, as anyone who has attended one of his large public events will readily acknowledge. Whatever the different causes that resulted in these diverse missions to China and now to the world, the strategies have remained true to tradition while at the same time evolving in new—but surprisingly parallel—directions.

NOTES

1. In this analysis I am indebted to the work of the prominent late Tibetologist, Dung dkar Blo bzang 'phrin las, *The Merging of Religious and Secular Rule in Tibet*, trans. Chen Guansheng (Beijing: Foreign Languages, 1991), and David Ruegg, *Ordre spirituel et ordre temporel dans la pensée Bouddhique de l'Inde et du Tibet [Spiritual Order and Temporal Order in the Buddhist Thought of India and Tibet]*, Publications de l'Institut de Civilisation Indienne (Paris: Collège de France, 1995).

2. Ruegg, *Spiritual Order and Temporal Order in the Buddhist Thought of India and Tibet*, 34–37.

3. P. Christiaan Klieger, *Tibetan Nationalism: The Role of Patronage in the Accomplishment of a National Identity* (Berkeley, Calif.: Folklore Institute, 1992), 20.

4. Gray Tuttle, *Tibetan Buddhists in the Making of Modern China* (New York: Columbia University Press, 2005).

5. Bstan 'dzin rgya ratsho, Dalai Lama XIV, *Freedom in Exile: The Autobiography of the Dalai Lama* (New York: HarperCollins, 1990), 202.

6. Franz Michael, *Rule by Incarnation: Tibetan Buddhism and Its Role in Society and State* (Boulder, Colo.: Westview, 1982), 40–50.

7. Ya Hanzhang, *Biographies of the Tibetan Spiritual Leaders Paṇnchen Erdenis*, trans. Chen Guansheng, Li Peizhu (Beijing: Foreign Languages, 1994), 258–260.

8. Ken Knaus, *Orphans of the Cold War: America and the Tibetan Struggle for Survival* (New York: Public Affairs, 1999), 275.

9. Han Dazai, *Kang-Zang Fojiao yu Xikang Nona Hutuketu yinghua shilüe [Brief Account of Kham-Tibetan Buddhism and the Manifestation of the Norlha Khutugtu of Kham]* (Shanghai: Yujia jingshe, 1937), fols. 4r, 8v. I want to thank Professor Lawrence Epstein and Peng Wenbin of the University of Washington for alerting me to the presence of this text.

10. Two conflicting dates are given in Han (*Brief Account of Kham-Tibetan Buddhism and the Manifestation of the Norlha Khutugtu*) for his arrival in Beijing: Mar. 15, 1924 (fol. 4v) and Oct. 15, 1925 (fol. 8v). Other sources, including Holmes Welch, *The Buddhist Revival in China*, Harvard East Asian Series, 33 (Cambridge, Mass.: Harvard University Press, 1968), 175, indicate that he was present in Beijing in 1924, so I have accepted this date.

11. Knaus, *Orphans of the Cold War*, 88–103, 140. Instead, a chain of intermediaries informed him (at least partially) of the negotiations of his older brothers. However, it should be noted that they were not officially the Dalai Lama's representatives and at times followed their own agenda.

12. Roger Hicks and Ngakpa Chogyam, *Great Ocean: An Authorized Biography of the Buddhist Monk Tenzin Gyatso His Holiness the Fourteenth Dalai Lama* (1984; reprint, New York: Penguin, 1990), 164.

13. Rick Fields, *How the Swans Came to the Lake: A Narrative History of Buddhism in America* (Boulder, Colo.: Shambala, 1981), 378; Jensine Andresen, "Kālacakra: Textual and Ritual Perspectives" (Ph.D. diss., Harvard University, 1997), 15–16.

14. Ya, *Panchen Erdenis*, 261.

15. Fabienne Jaguo, "A Pilgrim's Progress: The Peregrinations of the 6th Panchen Lama," *Lungta* 1, no. 10 (1996): 6, 14.

16. Welch, *The Buddhist Revival in China*, 157.

17. Hicks and Ngakpa Chogyam, *Great Ocean*, 164.

18. Tsering Shakya, *The Dragon in the Land of Snows: A History of Modern Tibet Since 1947* (London: Pimlico, 1999), 416.

19. Bstan 'dzin rgya mtsho, *Freedom in Exile*, 203.

20. Fields, *How the Swans Came to the Lake*, 291–293.

21. Welch, *The Buddhist Revival in China*, 251.

22. Welch, *The Buddhist Revival in China*, 239.

23. These were probably Mexican silver dollars.

24. For photographs of Qing examples of a golden certificate, see entry 74, and of a golden seal, entry 71, in *A Collection of the Historical Archives of Tibet* (Beijing: Wenwu chubanshe, 1995).

25. Ya Hanzhang, *The Biographies of the Dalai Lamas*, trans. Wang Wenjiong (Beijing: Foreign Languages, 1991), 263.

26. Ya, *Panchen Erdenis*, 264; Danzhu Angfen, *Liwei Dalai lama yu Banchan erdeni nianpu* [*Chronicle of the Genealogy of the Dalai Lama and Panchen Erdeni*] (Beijing: Zhongyang minzu daxue chubanshe, 1998), 637–638.

27. Han, *Brief Account of Kham-Tibetan Buddhism and the Manifestation of the Norlha Khutugtu*, fol. 4v. What exactly occurred is left to the reader's imagination.

28. Han, *Brief Account of Kham-Tibetan Buddhism and the Manifestation of the Norlha Khutugtu*, fol. 4v.

29. Han, *Brief Account of Kham-Tibetan Buddhism and the Manifestation of the Norlha Khutugtu*, fol. 8v.

30. Joseph K. H. Cheng, Richard C. Howard, and Howard L. Boorman, eds., *Biographical Dictionary of Republican China*, 3 vols. (New York: Columbia University Press, 1970), 3:335.

31. Han, *Brief Account of Kham-Tibetan Buddhism and the Manifestation of the Norlha Khutugtu*, fols. 4v, 8v–9r.

32. Jerome Cavanaugh and Chinese Materials Center, *Who's Who in China, 1918–1950, with an index*, 1933 supplement ed. (1933; reprint, Hong Kong: Chinese Materials Center, 1982), 82.

33. Han, *Brief Account of Kham-Tibetan Buddhism and the Manifestation of the Norlha Qutugtu*, fol. 4v.

34. Andresen, "Kālacakra," 238.

35. For details, see Tuttle, *Tibetan Buddhists in the Making of Modern China*, 198.

36. Andresen, "Kālacakra," 17.

37. Danzhu Angfen, *Chronicle of the Genealogy of the Dalai Lama and Panchen Erdeni*, 639.

38. In May 1929 and April 1930, respectively; see Danzhu Angfen, *Chronicle of the Genealogy of the Dalai Lama and Panchen Erdeni*, 640.

39. Li Pengnian and Fang Qingqiu, eds., *Jiushi Banchan neidi huodong ji fanzang shuoxian dang'an xuanbian* [*Selections from the Archives Concerning the Ninth Panchen's Activities in China and the Restrictions on His Return to Tibet*] (Beijing: Zhongguo Zangxue chubanshe, 1992), 15–17.

40. In Tibetan, this institution was simply called Norlha's Representative Office (Nor lha don gcod khang); see Thub bstan sangs rgyas, *Rgya nag tu Bod kyi sku tshab don gcod skabs dang gnyis tshugs stangs skor gyi lo rgyus thabs bral zur lam* [*Experiences of a Former Tibetan Representative in China, 1930–1939*] (Dharamsala: Library of Tibetan Works and Archives, 1982), 44.

41. Han, *Brief Account of Kham-Tibetan Buddhism and the Manifestation of the Norlha Khutugtu*, fols. 5r, 9r; Sichuan sheng difang zhi bianji weiyuanhui, Sheng zhi renwu zhi bianji and Ren Yimin, eds., *Sichuan jinxiandai renwu zhuan* [*Biographies of Sichuan's Contemporary Figures*], vol. 1 (Chengdu: Sichuan sheng shehui kexueyuan chubanshe, 1985), 291.

42. Cavanaugh and Chinese Materials Center, *Who's Who in China*, 81.

43. Ya, *Dalai Lamas*, 341; Thub bstan sangs rgyas, *Experiences of a Former Tibetan Representative in China*, 25–26.

44. Ya, *Dalai Lamas*, 342, 345–346; Melvyn Goldstein, *A History of Modern Tibet, 1913–1951: The Demise of the Lamaist State* (1989; reprint, Delhi: Bishen Singh Mahendra Pal Singh, 1993), 214, 219; Thub bstan sangs rgyas, *Experiences of a Former Tibetan Representative in China*, 55, provided an English translation of this office's name in Tibetan transcription, the "Bureau of Tibet" (Tib. Be 'u ru 'u/Ob/Kri bi kri).

45. For a full history of the office, see: Thub bstan sangs rgyas, *Experiences of a Former Tibetan Representative in China*.

46. The official Web site of the Tibetan Government-in-exile: www.tibet.com.

47. Knaus, *Orphans of the Cold War*, 275, 282.

48. Knaus, *Orphans of the Cold War*, 283, 310.

49. Knaus, *Orphans of the Cold War*, 282.

50. Gyalo Döndrup frequented the Tibet Office while studying in Nanjing from 1947 to 1949. However, his relations with this office and the conservative officials it represented were tense. Knaus, *Orphans of the Cold War*, 48–49; Mary Craig, *Kundun: A Biography of the Family of the Dalai Lama* (Washington, D.C.: Counterpoint, 1997), 134.

51. Knaus, *Orphans of the Cold War*, 310.

52. Han, *Brief Account of Kham-Tibetan Buddhism and the Manifestation of the Norlha Khutugtu*, fol. 5v.

53. Han, *Brief Account of Kham-Tibetan Buddhism and the Manifestation of the Norlha Khutugtu*, fol. 9r.

54. Welch, *The Buddhist Revival in China*, 175.

55. Han, *Brief Account of Kham-Tibetan Buddhism and the Manifestation of the Norlha Khutugtu*, fols. 3r, 6v. He also tried to improve the status of women in Kham.

56. Alexander Berzin, *Relating to a Spiritual Teacher* (Ithaca, N.Y.: Snow Lion, 2000), 16.

57. Han, *Brief Account of Kham-Tibetan Buddhism and the Manifestation of the Norlha Khutugtu*, fol. 9r.

58. Ya, *Panchen Erdenis*, 271–272; Danzhu Angfen, *Chronicle of the Genealogy of the Dalai Lama and Panchen Erdeni*, 641.

59. Danzhu Angfen, *Chronicle of the Genealogy of the Dalai Lama and Panchen Erdeni*, 642; Jaguo, "A Pilgrim's Progress," 16.

60. Knaus, *Orphans of the Cold War*, 275, 310.

61. Ya, *Panchen Erdenis*, 274, 284.

62. Ya, *Panchen Erdenis*, italics added.

63. Knaus, *Orphans of the Cold War*, 204.

64. Thomas A. Grunfeld, *The Making of Modern Tibet*, rev. ed. (1985; reprint, New York: M. E. Sharpe, 1996), 209.

65. Grunfeld, *The Making of Modern Tibet*, 210.

66. Grunfeld, *The Making of Modern Tibet*, 230–240; see also Shakya, *The Dragon in the Land of Snows*, 412–416.

Chapter 32

PROGRESSIVES AND EXILES

Heather Stoddard

This selection is drawn from Heather Stoddard's important 1985 book, the first detailed scholarly history of modern Tibet. Stoddard compels us to pay special attention to Tibet's connections to both China and India in the late nineteenth and early twentieth centuries, while also highlighting the role of Khampas in Central Tibetan politics and economy. Her pioneering research in this single concise selection anticipates later work on a number of important figures who connected Tibet and China in the crucial decades of the early twentieth century, including Geshé Sherap Gyatso, Püntsok Wanggyel, Rapga Pandastang, Babu Tharchin, and of course the focus of her own work: Gendün Chöpel. Later scholarship by Melvyn Goldstein, Imgard Mengele, Donald Lopez, Carole McGranahan, Du Yongbin, Peng Wenbin, Gray Tuttle, Isrun Engelhardt, and others has elucidated or extended her foundational research on these eminent personalities, though there are still many other figures she discusses who deserve further exploration. This is an abridged version of the original French version, which omits a long section that gives the story of the founding and dismantling of the Tibet Progressive Party.

With the benefit of hindsight and the help of unpublished documents from the India Office in London, as well as the oral accounts of Tibetan witnesses and various Chinese sources—which unfortunately remain very scarce—I will attempt to retrace here the careers of several Tibetans who appeared on the political scene from 1925 to 1933. Mentioned here and there in various sources, these

Tibetans did not, from the outset, represent a political party or even an organized group, and it is only by examining their individual life stories that a better understanding of their aspirations for Tibet's sociopolitical change may be gained. At first sight, several among them clearly identified themselves with China. Their pro-British sympathies were nonexistent, so to speak. With the exception of Künpel-la and Changlochen and several other young aristocrats from Lhasa, the Tibetans in question were all from the border regions of the Tibetan Plateau, mainly from Kham and Amdo in eastern Tibet. They were concerned not so much with the future of the religious state as with the political survival of their provinces, which were threatened by the negotiations taking place among the Chinese, British, and Tibetan governments. The continuous aggression from the Chinese during the first half of the twentieth century, their personal knowledge of both China and India, and their growing political awareness led them to concern themselves with the long-term future of Tibet as a whole.

Each striving in their own way for what they referred to as the "real" Tibet, they formed a heterogeneous group, united by a common goal and a common ideal: the renewal of a government they considered "tyrannical"[1] and the reunification of Tibet. Most of them ended up as exiles whose paths crossed in Kalimpong in the mid-1940s.

The first whom I will discuss is Künpel-la, who became renowned as the Thirteenth Dalai Lama's great favorite during the last years of his reign and is mentioned in most accounts of that period. This young monk was born into a family of humble peasants and was trained in the difficult art of carving xylographic blocks for the printing of religious texts in the Norbulingka. In 1925, when Tsarong was demoted, Künpel-la became the lama's most influential attendant. Shortly after, the Dalai Lama established a new governmental department, the Drapzhi Lekung, to deal with the manufacture of ammunition, coins, and bills, as well as electricity production.[2] These hitherto three distinct sectors were from then on grouped and managed jointly by Tsarong and Künpel-la. The quality of paper currency was improved, light weapons and bullets were manufactured, and additional arms were imported from India. Lhasa was provided with electricity with the help of Ringang, an engineer trained in England.

Künpel-la created a new regiment of around one thousand men recruited from among the youngest sons of well-off peasant and noble families, which he established in a large garrison known as the Drongdrak Makkar, to the west of the Drapzhi hydropower plant.[3] The new regiment was meant to reinforce troops stationed on the eastern front in Kham.

The three Pangdatsang brothers, more of whom will be said later, closely collaborated with Künpel-la in this undertaking. Two of the brothers, Topgyel and Rapga, who were responsible for defending the eastern border in Kham, relied on him for military reinforcement.[4] Although the loyalty of officers from Central Tibet was questionable at times, the two Khampa brothers had Künpel-la's absolute trust. Yarpel, the eldest brother established in Lhasa, was a trader and transport entrepreneur for the government. He took an active interest in the manufacture of currency and also imported from India the quota of arms and ammunition authorized by the British. . . .

Künpel-la took a "keen interest in modern civilization," and in order "to please his master," had the first two automobiles shipped to Tibet, one of which was exclusively reserved for the Dalai Lama's use. The other, a black A-4 Austin, was used by Künpel-la. . . .[5]

It was also Künpel-la who was responsible for the first film projection in Lhasa. Two clever Muslim traders from Ladakh,[6] who knew of his partiality for the "new world" and who were well aware of his power that "surpassed that of all ministers together," requested his permission to buy a film projector (such endeavors required the Dalai Lama's special authorization). Künpel-la himself organized the first showing, which was attended, for the most part, by members of the high nobility:

> They were so eager to see this promised marvel that they pushed and shoved each other in the room where the projector had been installed, almost causing it damage. Infuriated, the host, despite the fact that he himself was a commoner, seized an electric torch and began beating the most undisciplined among them regardless of their rank and even expelled several of them. The showing could finally begin.[7]

One day in December 1933, the Dalai Lama fell ill; he took to his bed and died on the evening of the following day. According to the account Charles Bell obtained from the clerk who witnessed the Dalai Lama's last days, during the night Künpel-la sent for the Nechung *chöjé*, or state oracle, who administered a medicinal powder to the ailing leader. Jampa-la, the doctor, said that the oracle had given the wrong medicine, and shortly afterward the oracle administered another remedy, this time in accordance with the doctor's prescription. The next day, the Dalai Lama remained bedridden all day without uttering a word and passed away in the evening. . . . Since 1912, the Thirteenth Dalai Lama had firmly held the reins of power and had taken responsibility for all the decisions regarding his country. As a result, his sudden death left the government in a state of confusion.

At first, the Assembly discussed the nomination of Künpel-la as prime minister together with Langdün,[8] the late Dalai Lama's nephew, who was considered incompetent. The procedure of appointing two prime ministers was in conformity with the governmental system, in which each post was occupied by two officials, one lay and the other religious. It seems that Künpel-la suggested this to the Dalai Lama just before his death, along with a proposal to suppress the Council of Ministers [the Kashak], which the lama did not find to his taste. The Kashak was rapidly informed of its potential suppression and, fearing that Künpel-la might use his regiment to remain in power, kept close watch on his person and property. Had Künpel-la been designated as prime minister together with Langdün, there would have been no need to appoint a regent for the interregnum period. Such a decision would have restricted monastic power since the regency was a means by which the church had controlled the government since the end of the eighteenth century.

Künpel-la was accused of the Dalai Lama's death, arrested, and clapped in irons in the Potala prison on January 10, 1934.[9] W. Donaldson, the British representative in Lhasa at the time, reported a month later, on February 21: "There seems to be a danger that Künpel-la and the Progressive Party may be overthrown by the monks though he has the support of lay officials. There is an unconfirmed report of his arrest."[10]

At the same time, Künpel-la's brother and father, his friend Tashi Döndrup, as well as the Dalai Lama's physician and the state oracle were either arrested or interrogated.[11]

Künpel-la sympathizers Changlochen, Kapshöpa, and Yutok sent a petition to the Assembly, which in the interim had become the highest governmental organ. In order to appease his numerous supporters both lay and religious, Künpel-la was released and questioned before the Assembly where, according to reports gathered by the British, he behaved with courage and honesty. When accused of having concealed his master's death for several days, he answered that he had acted according the late Dalai Lama's wishes. The clerk who witnessed the Dalai Lama's last moments testified in favor of Künpel-la and proclaimed his innocence, declaring that Künpel-la had always carried out his master's orders.[12]

However, although he was acquitted, a rumor that he had frequently opposed the Dalai Lama began to circulate. The claim in the Thirteenth Dalai Lama's official biography that he himself determined the moment of his death in fact refers to the prophecy in his Testament announcing his forthcoming death, which would compel the people to repent their sins.

The Dalai Lama had been very upset by the misunderstanding between himself and the Panchen Lama and had hoped that they would one day be reconciled and that his spiritual brother would return to Tibet. Fearing Chinese intervention, Künpel-la disagreed with his master on this question, and because he had expressed his discontent before the Assembly when the issue was raised, he prevented any decision in favor of the Panchen Lama's return. The weakened and exhausted Dalai Lama had contained his anger before his protégé: "the anger entered into him and did not issue from his mouth." Thus the people did indeed hold the *Chensel* responsible for the Precious Protector's departure for the (Celestial) "Field."[13]

In the end, Künpel-la was stripped of his fortune and sent, with a hundred *dotsé* in his *ambak*, to the Monastery of Black Waters (Chapnak) in Kongpo, a week's journey to the east of Lhasa. Tashi Döndrup and Jampa-la, the physician, were also sent into exile. The oracle was imprisoned in Lhasa.

Charles Bell's account subtly implies that the lama's death may have been due to the machinations of his entourage.[14] Upon his ascension to power, the Dalai Lama had already suffered two attempts on his life. The fates with which the other Dalai Lamas met throughout the nineteenth century leave little room for doubt as to the causes of their disappearance.[15] Throughout his life, the Thirteenth Dalai Lama had irritated the Manchus and the Chinese Republicans. In this case, however, Künpel-la appears to be innocent. He depended entirely on his master for his status and influence, and his subsequent career confirms his devotion to his country.

The oracle and the physician seem more dubious. The Nechung Oracle's predecessor had revealed the ex-regent Demo's plot at the end of the nineteenth century, but so far there is no specific information concerning the oracle's role on the night of the Thirteenth Dalai Lama's death.[16] The physician's case, however, is a different matter. He was sent into exile at the same time as Künpel-la,[17] but his movements and whereabouts remained obscure until 1943, when the British identified him as the owner of a photography studio, known as the "Home Studio," at Ten Mile in Kalimpong.[18] He is then reported to have studied English at St. Andrews School and is identified as Jampa Ösel (Chang Fangkun), a Chinese secret agent. Later in 1946, he was arrested and imprisoned in Calcutta. He was charged with being a propagandist in the pay of the Chinese and of gathering information in northern India, Bhutan, Nepal, and Tibet. He was deported to China on December 31, 1946.[19] Again, the contemporary sources' lack of information regarding this personage is probably not mere coincidence. In any case, there is a ten-year lapse between the Thirteenth Dalai Lama's death and Jampa Ösel's reappearance in Kalimpong. Perhaps the Chinese approached him following his exile. The question remains unanswered. A close study of Tibetan and Chinese sources might one day shed some light on the physician's role that night.[20]

Several months after Künpel-la was banished, Lungshar's "Republican" plot was exposed. Found guilty of high treason and condemned to losing his eyesight, this exuberant character ended his life as an invalid, cared for by his wife, who eventually obtained his release. The members of his party, known as the "Happy Union," who were later exiled, included Sönam Gyelpo, better known as Changlochen. This former "duke" was born into the noble Changlochen family and was a descendant of the Polhané family.[21] He became a well-known writer in Lhasa and wrote "most of the texts that defined the party's political orientations and goals."[22] The available sources provide very little information on this personage. He was stripped of his title and rank for having participated in the military conspiracy of 1925. In 1932 he was sent as *dapön* to Kham, where he probably met another military commander recently appointed by the Dalai Lama, the *rüpon* Topgyel Pangdatsang. In 1933, Changlochen returned to Lhasa, where he was appointed governor (*garpön*) of western Tibet, which, for a Lhasa noble, was another form of exile. He sent a servant in his place, and according to one source, in the same year he obtained the position of assistant at the weapons factory of Drapzhi, which was then run by Künpel-la.[23] By then, the three names of Pangdatsang, Künpel-la, and Changlochen had become closely linked.

Changlochen was banished following Lungshar's downfall and joined Künpel-la at the Monastery of Black Waters,[24] where, according to Charles Bell, the latter's fortune had taken a surprising turn.[25] Owing to his singular charm and qualities, he became so popular with the monks who were responsible for guarding him that he was elected head of the monastery. Thus together with Changlochen, he was able to leave Kongpo on the pretext that the Black Waters environment was unsuitable for their health.[26] In the autumn of 1936, they crossed the border at Tawang into Bhutan in order to make their way down to Calcutta.[27] On December 19, the two refugees reached Kalimpong, where they met with a number of officials . . . [and] the two men established themselves in Kalimpong, where Künpel-la was hired as a foreman in a wool depot.[28] He probably obtained the job thanks to the intervention of Yarpel Pangdatsang, who was one of the largest Tibetan wool exporters at the time. Charles Bell gives the following account:

> After Künpel-la's arrival in Kalimpong, Chinese officials tried to persuade him to come to China, saying that he would be paid a salary there. They desired to use him against Tibet, as a discontented element, as the Chinese government in the case of the Panchen Lama and the officers who accompanied the latter. But Künpel-la stood firm against the temptation.[29]

Rapga and Topgyel, the two Pangdatsang brothers stationed at Markham, reacted strongly to the Dalai Lama's death and Künpel-la's arrest. They confiscated the army's weapons and ammunition and rose against the Tibetan government. In Lhasa, the family residence was surrounded and the eldest brother, Yarpel, who was suspected of conspiring with his rebel brothers, was threatened with arrest.

The different sources describing these events give conflicting stories. Some say it was a small rebellion,[30] whereas others claim it was an attempt on the part of the Khampas to establish an autonomous or even an independent state between Central Tibet and China. Although the rebellion is somewhat eclipsed by the fragmentary presentation of events provided by the available sources, it formed part of a coherent whole, the origins of which may be traced back to the beginning of the twentieth century:

> On the tenth day of the fifth Tibetan month in the year of the water-mouse (1912), the Dalai Lama left Kalimpong for Tibet via the Dzalep-la pass. At Yatung, he remained a week at the residence of the British trade agent, David Macdonald. From there, he wrote to the monasteries and

chieftains in eastern Tibet encouraging them in their opposition to the
Chinese and promising them early liberation.

Two hundred monks from Sera, Ganden and Drepung volunteered to
escort the Dalai Lama back to Lhasa. They were led by Ragashar. At the
same time, two well-known Khampas, Nyima Gyelpo Pangdatsang of
Markham and Chopatshang of Gonjo, voluntarily brought an armed escort
of Khampas to join the Dalai Lama. They were to protect him day and
night until Lhasa was reached.[31]

Nyima Gyelpo invested the reward he received for his loyalty to the Dalai
Lama in trade. He first established trade links with India and gradually developed a network throughout the whole of Tibet. The eldest of his sons, Yarpel,
was sent to open a branch office in Beijing, and the two younger brothers, Topgyel and Rapga, returned to eastern Tibet to manage the business there and to
establish trade links with southwestern China. In India, the network extended
from Kalimpong to Calcutta.

Other important trading families from Kham, such as the Sadutsang,
Gyanaktsang, and Andrutsang,[32] established themselves at that time and a powerful Tibetan bourgeoisie began to emerge. They were open to trade opportunities in Asia and even in the West, and began familiarizing themselves with the
"new" world and adopting some of its customs, like that of sending their children abroad, to China or India, in order to receive a modern education.

After Nyima Gyelpo was killed in a family vendetta in Lhasa, Yarpel returned from Beijing to take his father's place as head of the family and settled
down in Lhasa. He rapidly became the most important tradesman of Tibet.
He was appointed trade agent by the government and worked many years in
Yatung.

Owing to the Dalai Lama's support, he became one of the few laypersons of
common origin to be given the grade of "fourth-rank officer" (*rimzhi*), which
allowed him to make his entry into Lhasa's high society. In British files, he is
referred to by the title of *kushap*, which is normally only attributed to sons of
noble families.[33] Yarpel was also one of the few, in such a conservative society,
to wear his hair short.[34]

The Pangdatsang fortune was built on the export of wool.[35] In 1932 the Dalai
Lama made the following request to the British:

> It would be very advantageous for the Tibetan government if Pangdatsang
> could from now on deliver the wool at a fixed price to the representatives
> of the great American wool trader at Kalimpong without having to go
> through the Malwaris, and thus avoid all intermediaries.[36]

S. Cutting took charge of the matter and put the Tibetan porters and American
buyers into contact.

Topgyel, the youngest of the three brothers, was a renowned warrior who, in the late 1940s, became the military leader of a large portion of Kham. A *rüpon* in Markham since 1930,[37] Topgyel, "unlike most Tibetan officials, was interested in the Khampas, the fiercest and most populous of all Tibetan peoples, as individuals, and not as mere tools to serve his purpose. They loved him for it, as much as they respected him for his fighting record."[38] . . .

Rapga, the second eldest brother, was the intellectual of the family. He was "intelligent, sharp, and well-read." In his youth, he amused himself by "shooting at eggs which servants held up for him." He had been a "mad rider" in his youth, and "gambled recklessly on horses during his stay in India." He pursued political and military studies in India and China and knew both countries well.[39]

According to W. D. Shakabpa's version, by rebelling, Rapga and Topgyel intended to establish Kham as an independent state and had distributed political pamphlets to this end. They captured the town of Markham and drove out Colonel Nornang, the Tibetan government's representative. However, their political aspirations did not spark the reaction they had hoped for, and two or three months later government troops from Chamdo, led by Tetong Gyurmé Gyatso, launched a counterattack. Defeated, the Khampas fled to the other side of the Drichu [river] to Batang, which was under Chinese control, taking with them many rifles and three machine guns that the British had given to the Tibetan government. All attempts at negotiation failed, and the Chinese, neither wishing to help Topgyel nor agreeing to send him back, allowed him to remain in Batang with the intention of using the Khampas for their own political purposes.

In Lhasa, Yarpel's house was surrounded, so a group of monks from Pangda residing in one of the great monasteries around Lhasa acted as emissaries and presented a statement to the Kashak denying any contact between Yarpel and his brothers. The government accepted this claim following Yarpel's offer to compensate for the military expenses incurred in putting down his brothers' rebellion. According to this officially accepted version, Yarpel had no idea of his brothers' intentions and activities.[40]

However, *Who's Who in Tibet* informs us that Yarpel was one of Künpel-la's close partisans and provides a different interpretation of the Markham uprising and Topgyel's role:

Appointed *rupön* in the Tibetan army in 1930 and sent to Kham. In 1934 he rebelled against the Tibetan government and took three machine guns, one hundred rifles and one hundred men to Batang where he surrendered to the Chinese government. He did this on account of a rumor that the Tibetan government had imprisoned his elder brother Pangda-tsang II (Yarpel) and had seized his house and property. He has managed to avoid fighting against the Tibetan troops in eastern Tibet and is said to be in communication with the Commissioner in Kham in order to arrange for his surrender on the condition that no action is taken against him by the Tibetan government.[41]

This last version differs entirely from that given by W. D. Shakabpa. Indeed, according to the British, Topgyel rebelled against the Tibetan government because the latter had imprisoned his brother. Thus Yarpel was not arrested following the rebellion of his two brothers in Kham. We may deduce then that Yarpel, along with several other close supporters of Künpel-la, had fallen into disgrace. Yarpel was subsequently freed because, as a major tradesman in international exchange, he was needed by the government. According to this version, the Pangdatsang brothers sought to avoid any conflict with the Tibetan army and to negotiate their return. There is no mention of Kham becoming an independent state.

Rapga Pangdatsang gives his own version of the events. We have two sources, one in English recorded by the British reporter G. Patterson, and the other in Tibetan, published in the *Melong* on December 24, 1936. G. Patterson, who met Topgyel and Rapga in the late 1940s in Kham, gives the following account:

> In the jockeying for power in Tibet following the death of the thirteenth Dalai Lama, Rapga and Topgyay (Topgyel) rebelled against the Tibetan Government and, with their armed Khampas, marched on Chamdo to try and seize power. They were defeated through counter intrigue by the lamas and, fighting a retreating battle, crossed over the River Yangtze into Chinese-occupied Tibet. Here the Chinese were alarmed at so large a force of armed Tibetans appearing, even in retreat, and the governor of the province, General Liu, ordered his troops to engage them immediately. After a protracted struggle through the mountains and valleys of Kham, sometimes fighting Chinese Nationalists, and sometimes the retreating forces of the Chinese Communists on the "Long March" from Jiangxi to Yenan in North China, they were ultimately defeated and the remnants of the army scattered. Rapga and Topgyay fled, the former making his way to Kalimpong in North India, near the western Tibetan border, while Topgyay disguised himself and disappeared down country in China.[42]

Rapga passed through Batang and Litang, where General Liu invited him to Ya'an. Considered a "guest of honor," Rapga was supposed to have been escorted by ten men. Distrusting the warlord's intentions, Rapga found a way to escape. . . .

After a year in India, Rapga published an explanation concerning his political activities in the *Melong* dated December 24, 1936, with a photograph showing him in Guomindang military attire. The article, in which Tharchin speaks for Rapga in the third person, reveals Rapga's point of view, but the author's awkward and cryptic language, combined with his use of metaphor and disregard for grammatical form, make it difficult to translate:

> Having attended both military and political schools in India and China, Rapga returned to India a second time and made the following

statement: the majority of monasteries in Kham were behind him. Following the Thirteenth Dalai Lama's death, tension prevailed in Markham as a result of intrigues among the ministers in Lhasa whose actions went against the lama's will. Rapga, having learned of the death of Tibet's Great Protector, was determined to keep on serving his master who had entrusted him with the responsibility over border matters in this volatile period that was "as fragile as an eggshell." Just as he was about to open negotiations with officials from the Tibetan government, several officials in Kham, thinking only of themselves and forgetting the country, let unfounded stories spread, to the detriment of the people and Tibet. In the end Rapga no longer knew to which country he belonged and thus left for India, taking to heart the well-being of his people and above all keeping in mind the late Dalai Lama's prophecy that the country was in danger of losing its territory in face of the military might of its two great neighbors, India and China, regardless of the fact that their religion and that of Tibet derive from the same source, and that the Chinese government has committed itself in this respect.[43] When Rapga passed through Sichuan, the Chinese general Liu Zaigyen[44] made grand promises to him, including that of appointing him military leader of Kham. Convinced that he would derive no benefit from such a situation, since this territory was exploited by the two neighbors,[45] Rapga escaped by means of subterfuge and traveled to Nanjing. After one year in India, he rejoiced in watching the Lotus, source of joy for Tibet, blossom anew.[46] He met at this time the Chinese representative, Wang Musong,[47] who insisted that he return to China, where he now resides and where he is well cared for.

He had believed in the possibility of a fate determined by his karma: a special task in harmony with the Thirteenth Dalai Lama's will. As a result he studied in China and in India. However, if this karma was not meant for him, he will be happy to spend the rest of his life taking care of himself, spending his meager savings, in this era when human life is worthless and when at any time a friend may be used to reward yesterday's foe.

Rapga's two accounts, that of 1936 and that of 1949, complete each other. He admits that in 1936 he found himself in an ambivalent and frightening situation, from both a moral and a political point of view. Having devoted his life to the future of Tibet, he sought to justify his rapprochement with China in the eyes of his people. His discourse remains coherent, as opposed to other available accounts of his life as well as the British reports accusing him of duplicity.[48] His devotion to the Dalai Lama is beyond doubt. He felt betrayed after his master's death by the representatives of the interim government.

After his sojourn in China, he again returned to Kalimpong. On July 28, 1938, the following brief notice entitled "Kuchar Künpel-la" appeared in the *Melong* (p. 13): "Recently the *kuchar* (Künpel-la), Chang kung (the duke

Changlochen) and Rapga, son of Pangdatsang, were invited by the magistrate sahib for tea. . . . They are eagerly studying English."

The reactions within the Tibetan government in the first years of the inter-regnum period—which resulted in the exile, whether voluntary or forced, of the most progressive figures of Tibet—reveal a struggle for power not only among various factions, personalities, and the traditional elite groups (the nobility and the church) but also between conservatives and those who sought an alternative solution for Tibet that was more adapted to the twentieth-century world. The Thirteenth Dalai Lama, who came from a modest peasant background, at-tempted through his reforms to improve the lot of his people, by abolishing for instance the heavy transport tax (*ula*). He restricted the privileges of the nobility and elevated a number of men of modest origin to the highest functions.[49] His military policy, aimed at strengthening his country against its powerful neigh-bors, was challenged by the majority of Tibetans, who continued to consider Tibet as the seat of wisdom and center of the spiritual world.

A number of other young Tibetans from Kham and Amdo also studied in China, especially at the Central Academy of Political Studies in Nanjing.[50] Three among them, Wangdu Norbu, Meru Samshak, and the *tsedrung* Lopön-la, be-longed to the entourage of the Panchen Lama, who was then established in the Guomindang capital. Wangdu Norbu, the Panchen Lama's nephew, appears, also in Guomindang military uniform, next to Rapga in the photograph pub-lished in the *Melong* dated December 24, 1936. The caption reads as follows:

> Wangdu Norbu, nephew of the Panchen Rinpoche, brought up and edu-cated in China. He has graduated from the Guomindang Military Acad-emy and was trained in the following fields: military arts, strategy, cartog-raphy, telegraphy, and Morse code. He has also received religious and political training in his own culture and has faithfully served the Panchen Lama for many years. He is serving in Nanjing as a chargé of protocol at the Bureau of Western Affairs, where he ensures the maintenance of good relations between Tibetan and Chinese officials.

The Nanjing Academy also admitted three members from a Batang family: the famous Baba (in other words, "originally from Batang") Püntsok Wangyel,[51] one of the first Tibetan Communists; his elder brother, Kelzang Tsering;[52] and their uncle Jiang Xinxi.[53] Ngawang Kelzang (a close companion of Püntsok Wangyel)[54] and the Fourteenth Dalai Lama's brother, Gyalo Döndrup, also studied there.[55]

In comparison with the "derisory" military training dispensed by the British in Lhasa, the education the young Tibetans received in China was more thor-ough, and consisted of practical training combined with studies in philosophy and political science. However, the Tibetans found that their studies were, in practice, of little use to them. The case of Jiang Xinxi perfectly illustrates their situation: after having brilliantly completed his studies and finished first in his class, he received the title of "liaison officer stationed in Tibet."[56] He was subsequently admitted to the Department of National Defense (Guofangbu), where a number of his Han Chinese peers occupied high posts. However, he exercised no real power, whether he found himself in Chinese-controlled Tibetan territory or in Nanjing. Thus, while he praised Sun Yat-sen's *Sanmin Zhuyi (Three Principles of the People)*, Jiang Xinxi complained about the gap between theory and practice, since, despite the theoretical equality among the "Five Races," the Guomindang never placed a person of non-Chinese origin in a position of power.

Later, when the formidable Muslim warlord Ma Bufang, who then controlled Qinghai province, was informed of Jiang Xinxi's discontent, he offered him a post in Xining, but the latter refused. Perhaps, like Rapga with Liu Wenhui, he found it difficult to trust such a pitiless warrior. Perhaps he was searching for an alternate solution adapted to Tibet's situation.

Fed with the dominant political theories of that time—those of Sun Yat-sen and Marx—the Tibetans trained in China found themselves on a razor edge. The Khampas and Amdowas had always felt disdained and misunderstood by the Tibetan government, who considered them at best as provincial or tribal, and at worst as bandits. They felt that they had been betrayed, that they had been "sold" to the Chinese following the creation of the two provinces of Qinghai and Xikang. Yet China was their immediate neighbor with whom they had maintained commercial and religious ties since at least the thirteenth century. These relations had changed, however: the new republican and later revolutionary China, which preached a doctrine of equality and democracy, held the promise of a warm welcome and a modern education, and until the early forties, granted self-rule to their territories, at least in theory. Following the havoc wreaked by the warlords Ma Bufang and Liu Wenhui, and confronted with the selfish attitude of the Lhasa officials who were concerned solely with their own interests, it is not difficult to understand why the ideology of the Republican or Communist parties appealed so strongly to the politicized youth of eastern Tibet.

The *Sanmin Zhuyi* written by Sun Yat-sen—father of the Chinese Revolution—underwent its final formulation in 1924, a year after the reorganization of the Guomindang [(Chinese) Nationalist Party] following the Soviet line. Its first principle, nationalism, aimed at the Manchus as early as 1905, turned into a reaction against foreign imperialism.[57] This attitude prevailed during the period of the Guomindang's collaboration with the newly founded Communist Party and the Soviet Union, which supported both parties in view of a national revolution. The recovery of sovereign rights and the overthrow of foreign power and privileges constituted the new order:

> Our race is threatened and will certainly disappear one day. The causes for its disappearance may be found in the triple foreign oppression: ethnic, political, and economic. . . . Foreigners always say that the Chinese are like "scattered sand" (and indeed) with regard to the principle of nation-

alism we are scattered sand, we don't really have national unity. . . . If only we realized that each (of us) is an oppressed citizen.[58]

How did the Tibetans of Nanjing see themselves? They were not Chinese; they had their own culture, which differed largely from Chinese culture, a difference made obvious in the exercise of power even after the political changes. Furthermore, they were worlds apart from their aristocratic fellow countrymen who had received an English education and had merely learned "to be proud of their English accents, to dance the latest tango, and really nothing else besides."[59] Indeed, the Tibetan nobles identified with the English they had seen in India who, like them, had been born to rule. Unlike the inhabitants of the eastern border regions, they had not been exposed to continuous Chinese harassment and, for the most part, they felt neither threatened nor concerned by the events taking place beyond their borders. Since the death of the Thirteenth Dalai Lama, the doors of the armory had remained locked,[60] and the idea of war was not taken seriously in the Holy City. The Tibetanized English used by the Tibetan military commanders to order their troops was the subject of mirth for the British residing in Tibet at that time, as was the Tibetan military orchestra's innocent and clumsy rendering of "God Save Our Gracious King," which they never fail to recall with amusement in their accounts.

This situation, which subtly reflected the naïveté of some and the thirst for power of others, lasted until 1950, when the Chinese reached the gates of Central Tibet.

As we have seen, the young Tibetans educated in China followed an altogether different path. Most came from modest or common backgrounds, generally from merchant families, and were admitted to the Guomindang schools when the Guomindang still represented a revolutionary force. Chiang Kai-shek himself was trained by the Soviets in Moscow and headed the Military Academy of Whampoa near Canton in the twenties. It was in this academy that not only the best generals of the Guomindang but also those of the Chinese Communist Party were trained.

At the time the authoritarian character of the Guomindang was not yet influenced by Communism or Fascism. It represented a new form of politics inspired in part by the USSR but without the latter's doctrinal aspect and in part by the fallen Empire but without the sacramental aspect of Confucian orthodoxy. The Chinese were looking for their own answers.[61]

Carried away by his idealism, Sun Yat-sen made the following declaration during the first Guomindang conference in 1922: the "right to self-determination of China's different nations is recognized. Thus, a free and united China will be founded on the voluntary association of these nations."[62] Mao Zedong followed his example in 1930 in a similar statement, according to which "national minorities" had the right to separate from the central government and to create their own state.[63]

Both the Guomindang and the Communist Party eventually hardened their nationalist policy—which was devised along the Soviet model—and the rights of "nations" or "minorities" were increasingly restricted until they were left with no choice but to become part of the new China. For the Communists, this hardening came as a result of the direct and, in some cases, painful contact with the non-Han populations during their Long March.

Nevertheless, the Internationalist ideal survived and continued to inspire a number of Tibetans, including Püntsok Wanggyel. That Rapga Pangdatsang embraced the Republican ideal is certain. He translated the *Sanmin Zhuyi* into Tibetan and drew his inspiration from the works of Marx. According to an article published in the *Melong*, he was driven by his love for his country. A tragic love, since his country denied him the heroic role he dreamed of playing and compelled him to seek refuge in China, which had provided him with much of his training.

In January 1975, Rapga Pangdatsang said:

The *Sanmin Zhuyi* was intended for all peoples under foreign domination, for all those deprived of human rights. It was especially destined for Asian peoples. For these very reasons I translated it. At the time, many new ideas spread throughout Tibet, but only among the elite and the educated and they did not serve anyone else. The masses were too ignorant to be receptive to such ideas and, moreover, had no rights.[64]

Geshé Sherap Gyatso, a master at Gomang College in Drepung, left Tibet in 1937 at the age of 53. His proposals for reform, which he wanted to include in the new xylographic Lhasa edition of the 108 volumes of the Buddhist canon or Kangyur, did not go down well. Contrary to custom, his editor's name is not mentioned in the Thirteenth Dalai Lama's official biography.[65] According to Rahul Sankrityayan, an Indian specialist on Buddhism who visited the *geshé* several times in Lhasa in 1934, this Gelukpa master was the "first Tibetan to rejoice at the success of Mao Zedong and the Communist Party in China" and to hope for reforms that would initiate a new era in Tibet.[66]

Both Tibetan and Chinese sources fail to mention the events that led to his exile. Snellgrove and Richardson briefly remark:

It may be healthy to mention some literary rebels and innovators, if only to indicate that a few exist. Doyül Sherap, a favourite of the thirteenth Dalai Lama, was later banished, and he went to China where he recently became president of the Chinese Buddhist Association. He is said to have translated into Chinese Tsongkhapa's *Lamrim* (Survey of the Doctrine).[67]

The other rebel they mention is his disciple Gedün Chöpel, who had left Tibet earlier in November 1934. Other written sources regarding Geshé Sherap include a paragraph in Shakabpa's political history, an article by Tharchin published in the *Melong*, a few references in the London India Office files, a number of official documents and publications of the People's Republic of China, and an obituary in the *Sheja*, the official bulletin of the Tibetan government in exile.

W. D. Shakabpa does not mention the reasons for the Gelukpa master's departure and simply states that "despite the fact that he was highly respected as a learned master and as editor of the Kanjur under the orders of the thirteenth Dalai Lama, his work did not prove entirely satisfactory."[68] He therefore left for China.

Tharchin's account, published in the *Melong*, is based on information published at an earlier date in the same newspaper:

Geshé Sherap left Lhasa for Calcutta via Kalimpong at the beginning of 1937, accompanied by Lu Wuyuan, a Chinese military official. After a grand farewell party in Calcutta attended by members of both the Tibetan and Chinese communities, as well as Francis Younghusband and Gedün Chöpel, the two travelers boarded a boat to China. In Nanjing, the Guomindang offered him an official, high-ranking post, and he remained in the country, where he taught Buddhism for many years. When the Communists took power and Chiang Kai-shek fled to Taiwan, Geshé Sherap found himself in a difficult situation. After reflecting on how best to serve the Buddhist doctrine, he proceeded to Kumbum Monastery in northern Amdo near Xining, in order to devote himself to the Dharma. But the Communists, "like a deluge," reached even that remote region, and the *geshé* struggled to remain afloat on the boat of Dharma without being submerged by the "red waves." He tried his best to achieve two aims: to prevent the "atheist" Communists from entering the Great Land of Dharma, i.e., Tibet, and to build a barrier around the country so as to preserve its independence. He also attempted to harmonize relations between Tibet and China, between the Fourteenth Dalai Lama and the new Chinese leaders, in accordance with the traditional priest-patron relation and in continuity with the great era of the Manchu Emperor Qianlong.[69]

In this account, Tharchin makes no mention of exile, or the reasons for which this great master left his country at the age of fifty-three (which is considered elderly by Tibetans), after an outstanding and uninterrupted career as monk and teacher of the Dharma, to join the Chinese Republicans. Nor does he mention that in April 1944 Geshé Sherap arrived at Nakchuka, north of Lhasa, at the *de facto* border between the territory governed by the Depa Zhung [the Lhasa government] and Qinghai province. Geshé Sherap was escorted by fifty

Chinese soldiers. According to British sources, it is likely that he took with him several copies of the printed, bilingual edition of his own translation of Sun Yat-sen's *Sanmin Zhuyi* published by the Guomindang Bureau, several copies of which were found circulating in Lhasa in the months that followed.[70] The Tibetan government authorized the *geshé* to return to Lhasa on the condition that his escort remained behind. But he turned back to Xining via the Changtang.

According to W. D. Shakabpa, the government refused the *geshé* permission to return to Lhasa (with or without his Chinese escort), fearing the trouble his influence over the monks of the Three Seats might create.[71]

In May 1945, Geshé Sherap was appointed an alternate member of the Guomindang's Sixth Supervision Committee.[72] He then returned to his country, and according to Tharchin, went to Kumbum.

There are two opinions with regard to Geshé Sherap's relationship with the Communists: that of R. Sankrityayan, himself a Communist, who claims that Geshé Sherap rejoiced at Mao's rise to power, and that of Tharchin, who depicts the *geshé* in the "boat" of Dharma and refers to him as striving to prevent his own and Tibet's destruction by the "red waves."

According to the *Sheja*'s obituary, which attempts to rehabilitate the *geshé*, whom the Tibetans in exile for a long time considered to be in the pay of the Communists, he fled from the Liberation Army's troops to Nakchuka but was eventually captured, and the Chinese Communists used his name to spread their ideas in radio broadcasts.[73]

W. D. Shakabpa also expresses the widely shared feeling that Geshé Sherap was used as a political tool by the Chinese.[74] However, his subsequent career in the People's Republic of China contradicts this simplistic interpretation and suggests that the truth probably lies somewhere between R. Sankrityayan and Tharchin's perspectives. If Geshé Sherap translated the *Sanmin Zhuyi*, he was undoubtedly one of the Tibetan progressives of his time. After all, the theories of the "father" of the Chinese Revolution applied just as well to Tibet as they did to China, and could be easily adapted to the Buddha's doctrine.[75]

In the early 1940s, relations between the young Tibetans from eastern Tibet and China underwent a radical change. This change was prompted by the publication of Chiang Kai-shek's *China's Destiny* in 1944. In this work he exposed his new political philosophy, based on a racist distortion of China's history. The Chinese, Manchus, Mongols, Tibetans, and Hui (Chinese Muslims) are reduced to the status of tribes and considered members of the same race. The five thousand years of Chinese history bear witness to their common destiny, and their fusion into one race was achieved by their assimilation into Han civilization. The work displays an evolutionist interpretation of Chinese history, based on the conventional prejudiced attitude of the Han Chinese with regard to their barbarian neighbors. All ideas of democracy, equality, and freedom of choice are completely abandoned. Thus the Tibetans discovered in 1942 that the process of their assimilation by China had been taking place over the last thirteen hundred years, in other words, since the foundation of the Tibetan state in the seventh century, which marked the first military and diplomatic contacts between the two countries. There is no longer any mention of an independent or autonomous Tibet but only of unconditional assimilation.[76]

This ideological turnaround was accompanied by a large-scale offensive of which eastern Tibet became the center stage at the beginning of 1943.

On March 16, Yarpel Pangdatsang received a report in Lhasa that signaled the massing of twenty thousand troops in Sichuan near the Tibetan border. The Republican government denied all responsibility for the presence of these troops, while the Khampas lived in fear of a major Chinese attack and of losing another large piece of their territory. A month later, on April 14, General Ma Bufang and three thousand Muslim troops from Qinghai began advancing toward Sichuan and the general dispatched another ten thousand troops to [Central Tibet's] northern frontier with Amdo.[77]

The Tibetan government had responded in March by suspending the transport of all merchandise throughout its territory until a tripartite agreement was reached. The British government, which had allied itself to China during World War II, announced that "it would be out of place to provide Chongqing with a reason to complain," and increased pressure on the Tibetans to compromise. On April 15, when the Tibetan government was informed that Ma Bufang's troops had entered Qinghai, it authorized the transport of nonmilitary goods and medicine.[78]

The conflict stemmed from Chiang Kai-shek's order to build an alternate supply route through Dzayül in southern Tibet after the Japanese had severed the Burma roadway linking India to China in 1942. The Tibetan government, which had not been consulted on the matter beforehand, refused entry to Chinese engineers and the transport of materials and equipment on its territory. The government's categorical refusal infuriated Chiang Kai-shek, who responded with threats, although the military governors of Sichuan and Yunnan—with the exception of Ma Bufang and his cavalry—probably did not relish the idea of a war with Tibet, given the situation in China and the low morale of Chinese troops at the time.

Despite its strong stance, the Tibetan government was especially anxious to avoid the intervention of Ma Bufang, whose troops in Tibet were reputed to be invincible. The Nechung Oracle was consulted and recommended the performance of a special ritual to ward off all danger from the Muslim soldiers. All the government officials participated in the grand *torgyak* procession. In the *torma* (the central offering of the ritual), an effigy with the appearance of a Muslim soldier (possibly Ma Bufang) was burned.[79] As one British official commented, not without humor, after the ceremony "all was quiet on the northern front." At the end of the month, a deadly epidemic spread among Ma Bufang's soldiers. In spite of this "divine intervention,"[80] the Tibetan government finally consented to the transport of goods along the normal routes and the crisis died down.

However, the concentration of troops in southwest China became more and more oppressive, and there was a rush of British reports signaling the dramatic increase of Chinese troops in Kham. By August 1943, there were three thousand troops in Jyekundo, as opposed to two hundred four years previously. By October, their numbers had reached six thousand. At Dergé, a new garrison of two hundred soldiers was established. Five hundred troops were sent to Kandzé and Gyarong. The Chinese used the friendly relations between Tibet and Japan as a pretext for their presence, claiming that the Japanese were building airfields on Tibetan territory.[81] The British located around twenty radio units throughout the Chinese-controlled part of Kham, as well as ten airports, six of which were functioning and four of which were still under construction.

The building of a road network had begun with the construction of a road from Xining in the north through Amdo to the town of Jyekundo, which represented a major crossroads between Amdo and Kham. The new road reached a point located five days' march from Jyekundo, and once it was completed, the journey would take only seven days by truck. The construction of another road through eastern Kham, from Dartsedo to Jyekundo, was under way, and Chiang Kai-shek intended to extend it farther into Tibet.[82]

Toward the end of 1943, a report sent via Kalimpong stated that Chongqing had sent a fifteen-day ultimatum to the Tibetan government with the following clauses: 1) the bureau of external relations must be closed, and only China had the authority to conduct Tibet's foreign relations; 2) Tibet must cooperate with China in the construction of a road between the two countries; 3) Tibet must ensure that China had access to proper landing areas; and 4) the Chinese must have total freedom of movement throughout Tibet.[83]

Given China's military and diplomatic threats, its new ideological orientation, and the road projects under way in the eastern part of their provinces, the anxiety of the eastern Tibetans is perfectly understandable. One after the other, they left China for Kalimpong.

In Lhasa, however, the Guomindang's attempts following the Thirteenth Dalai Lama's death to establish an official representative in the Tibetan capital met with failure. Once the conflict had subsided, Chiang Kai-shek's threats were perceived as a political maneuver rather than a real declaration of war and no longer impressed the government in Lhasa, which discreetly but determinedly continued to pursue its conservative policy of independence and neutrality.

For the Chinese, the most effective, long-term way to control the country was through penetration using modern communication means and motorized transport, namely the radio and aircraft.

It is relevant to mention here other figures from the peripheral Himalayan regions, such as Abdul Wahid, a young Muslim from Ladakh, whom Richardson received in Lhasa in 1944:

He was educated at Tindale Biscoe's school in Srinagar and at Aligarh University. With his interest in Indian politics and in politics generally, he is a misfit in Lhasa. He claims to be making efforts to unite the Lhasa Ladakhis or at least form a party of younger men for the purpose of strengthening the Ladakhis position here. . . . Abdul Wahid also claims to be keenly interested in Tibetan independence.[84]

Son of an important Ladakhi family and in charge of Ladakh's annual tribute for the Dalai Lama, Abdul Wahid headed the mission for one year. Drawn by the religion and people of the Tibetan Plateau, he returned to Lhasa from 1942 to 1943, after having completed his studies at the Muslim University of Aligarh. In Lhasa he became a close friend of Tetong, a young noble and friend of the progressives, with whom he had long political discussions. In 1944, he went to Kalimpong, where he was introduced to Rapga Pangdatsang and his entourage. It so happened that the latter's wife had been formerly married to Abdul Wahid's uncle, one of the traders who had, with Künpel-la's help, brought the first film projector to Tibet in the early 1930s.[85]

A few months beforehand, on November 23, 1943, the political attaché in Sikkim reported the recent arrival in Kalimpong of Kelzang Trashi, "a young anti-Chinese Tibetan, who studied at the Political Institute in Chongqing," and of two young men from Batang with the following comment:

They studied in Nanjing and possess very anti-Chinese views. On being offered a job by the Chinese government, they refused. They have submitted a plan of revolt to Surkang, present Tibetan foreign minister, and seem to have high hopes of obtaining help and advice from the British government. They are at present working with a Tibetan trader. Trading they say may help them to keep clear of suspicion from any of the Chinese Secret Service men employed in Lhasa and Kalimpong.[86]

Unfortunately, the available India Office files make no further mention of their request for help. We only know that their attempts to convince both the Tibetans in Lhasa and the British in Kalimpong failed.

The description of the two Babas, confirmed by other sources, allows us to identify one of them as Püntsok Wanggyel and the other as either his brother Kelzang Tsering or his friend Ngawang Kelzang.[87]

Kelzang Tsering had already been involved in the political game taking place in Kham in the early 1930s:

Gesang ceren [Kelzang Tsering], the Commissioner for the Guomindang Affairs of Xikang, with the support of the masses easily disarmed the garrison force of Liu Wenhui at Batang, and in March 1932, declared the establishment of an autonomous regime.[88]

As commissioner for Xikang, it was Kelzang Tsering's duty to disarm Liu Wenhui, who acted independently and uncontrollably. However, by declaring Kham, located between Central Tibet and China, an autonomous state independent from Chinese authority, Kelzang Tsering was exceeding his prerogatives. Later the Guomindang government put an end (by what means?) to his regime, and he disappeared from the political scene.

H. Richardson gives his version of the incident (specifying that Püntsok Wanggyel and his brother were born of a mixed, Chinese-Tibetan union):

> In 1932 Kelzang Tsering, claiming to act for Chiang Kai-shek, enlisted some support from local tribes and evicted Liu Wenhui's governor from the town. The latter had driven the Tibetans back to the Yangtse. The attack by Liu's forces, after the conclusion of an armistice by a National Government representative, was in Tibetan eyes, considered an act of treachery. It probably caused some embarrassment to the National Government by exposing its lack of control over provincial governors. Kelzang Tsering soon came into conflict with a powerful freebooter lama of the neighborhood who secured support from the Tibetan forces, and eventually occupied Batang but later had to evacuate it (with the return of Liu Wenhui).[89]

In a very interesting but unfortunately single article on the first Tibetan Communists, T. N. Takla—one of the few Tibetan Sinologists and a member of the progressive group in Kalimpong in the 1940s—retraces the career of Püntsok Wanggyel. The latter was born in c. 1920 and was the son of a cobbler named Gora Ashé. At the age of seven, he was sent to the American mission and then to the Chinese school at Batang. He went to China to complete his studies, and during World War II he was admitted to the Guomindang's Central University of Political Studies, the lay counterpart of the military institute of Whampoa. By then Communist infiltration among Chinese intellectuals and the Guomindang was quite deep. It was during this period that Püntsok Wanggyel was approached by a member of the Communist Party, which he eventually joined. His friend Ngawang Kelzang, another Baba trained in China, became a member of the party around the same time. Püntsok Wanggyel was accused of "indiscipline" because of his clandestine activities and expelled from the university in 1942.[90]

According to T. N. Takla, the two friends returned to Tibet and then went to Kalimpong, where they worked for six months at the Melong, the newspaper published by Tharchin. The article does not mention the interview they had in Lhasa with the minister Surkang—the Tibetan government, even in exile, has never admitted that during this period it was approached by several eastern Tibetans in view of restructuring the government—but it does mention that the two Babas submitted a project to the British government in which they demanded radical political, social, and economic reforms for Tibet and requested help. Besides a few interviews with a local British officer, their project received no response. Although T. N. Takla does not mention the meeting with Surkang, it seems obvious that such a project would have first been presented to the Tibetan government.

It was not only the publication of Chiang Kai-shek's work and the ambiguity of the Tibetan students' position in China that led Püntsok Wanggyel to formulate his reform project, but also his own personal experience of the war on the Sino-Tibetan border from 1942 to 1943, in which he took part on the Tibetan side against the Republican troops. Defeated and very impressed by the potential power of China, he withdrew to the Tsakur region, where he founded (or proposed to found) a revolutionary government of eastern Tibet. He then traveled to Lhasa and Kalimpong, accompanied by Ngawang Kelzang, to present his project. The discussions having failed, he returned to China, where he rejoined Mao Zedong's side in Yenan and further confirmed his commitment to the Communist cause. In 1944, he settled with his brother and his uncle in Lhasa, where he obtained work as a music teacher at the Guomindang school. At the same time, he founded a secret organization known as the "association of young Tibetans under oath."[91]

According to Abdul Wahid, who met Püntsok Wanggyel in Kalimpong and who became a close friend of his despite their diverging political opinions and the fact that the Khampa attempted to rally the Muslims to communism, Püntsok Wanggyel was an "authentic Tibetan Nationalist" who upheld pan-Tibetan theories and believed in the creation of a federation that would comprise all the Tibetan regions and ethnic groups, including Ladakh.[92]

> Like Rapga Pangdatsang with the Guomindang, this young and brilliant Tibetan sought to use the Chinese Communists in order to achieve his ideal of a new socialist Tibet. He and his group of partisans in Lhasa fought for a "real Tibet," and his thesis—the project mentioned above, which he presented to the Tibetan government—consists of two parts: one in which he discusses the Tibetan feudal society and the role of the Tibetan nobility, and the other in which he presents a program of preliminary measures and reforms aimed at changing Tibetan society. Because of his thesis, which he wrote in Chinese, he was watched by the Tibetan government and his entourage was advised to cut all ties with him.[93]

NOTES

1. India Office Library/Political & Secret/12/4211, 36/file39 (1) Ext. 5750, cf. p. 101.

2. Rnam rgyal dbang 'dud, *Bod dmag gi lo rgyus* [*History of the Tibetan Army*] (Dharamsala: Bod gzhung shes rig par khang, 1976), 21; Tsepon Wangchen Deleg Shakabpa, *Tibet: A Political History*, (New Haven: Yale University Press, 1967), 267.

3. Rinchen Dolma Taring, *Daughter of Tibet* (London: John Murray, 1970), 109; Dbang phyug bde ldan, Zhwa sgab pa, *Bod kyi srid don rgyal rabs: An Advanced Political History of Tibet*, Vol. 2 (Kalimpong: T. Tsepal, Taikhang, 1976), 299.

4. In the Tibetan version, Zhwa sgab pa, *An Advanced Political History of Tibet*, 330, remarks that Rapga Pangdatsang "had a deep and sincere relationship with the Thirteenth Dalai Lama and Künpel-la."

5. Abdul Wahid Radhu, *Caravane tibétaine* [*Tibetan Caravan*], adapted into French by Roger du Pasquier from the unedited English-language memoirs of the author (Paris: Fayard, 1981), 145. [Editors' note: Available in English as Abdul Wahid Radhu, *Islam in Tibet: Tibetan Caravans*, trans. Jane Casewit, ed. Gray Henry (Louisville: Fons Vitae, 1997)].

6. On Abdul Wahid's uncles, see below, and his book: Radhu, *Tibetan Caravans*.

7. Radhu, *Tibetan Caravans*, 145.

8. Zhwa sgab pa, *An Advanced Political History of Tibet*, 2:315.

9. Zhwa sgab pa, *An Advanced Political History of Tibet*, 2:316.

10. India Office Library/Political & Secret/12/4178.

11. Zhwa sgab pa, *An Advanced Political History of Tibet*, 2:316.

12. Sir Charles Bell, *Portrait of the Dalai Lama* (London: Collins, 1946), 386.

13. Bell, *Portrait of the Dalai Lama*, 386.

14. Bell, *Portrait of the Dalai Lama*, 384–385. Palasé, a friend of Charles Bell, suggests that the spirit of Nyarong Lama, who committed suicide following his implication in the attempt to assassinate the Dalai Lama, incited the state oracle to administer a deadly remedy to the pontiff in December 1933. Bell (*Portrait of the Dalai Lama*, 50) mentions the "holy pill" and in his *Tibet, Past and Present* (Oxford: The Clarendon Press, 1924, 124) he wrote: "it is possible that when the regent or the *amban* wished to poison the young Dalai Lama they bribed the Court Physician to give him a poisoned pill."

15. See R.-E. Huc, *Souvenirs d'un voyage dans la Tartarie et le Tibet pendant les années 1844, 1845, 1846* [*Memories of a Voyage in Tartary and Tibet in the Years 1844, 1845, 1846*] (Paris: Librairie générale française, 1962), 350–351; Ekai Kawaguchi, *Three Years in Tibet* (Madras: The Theosophist Office, 1909), 318; Clements R. Markham, *George Bogle, and Thomas Manning, Narratives of the Mission of George Bogle to Tibet and the Journey of Thomas Manning to Lhasa* (New Delhi: Mañjuśrī, 1971), xcv–xcviii; Shakabpa, *Tibet: A Political History*, gives a detailed account of the deaths of the Dalai Lamas—174 (Ninth Dalai Lama); 176 (Eleventh Dalai Lama); 190 (Twelfth Dalai Lama)—without suggesting that they were assassinated.

16. Zhwa sgab pa, *An Advanced Political History of Tibet*, 2:73.

17. Zhwa sgab pa, *An Advanced Political History of Tibet*, 2:316.

18. India Office Library/Political & Secret/12/4210, 23 November 1943 (cf. p. 348). An unusual occupation for a Tibetan at the time.

19. India Office Library/Political & Secret/12/4211, 36/file39 (1), D448 NEF/46, 3 August 1946.Zhwa sgab pa, *An Advanced Political History of Tibet*, 2:316, refers to the physician as Byams pa ye shes.

20. Bell, *Portrait of the Dalai Lama*, 392.

21. Luciano Petech, *Aristocracy and Government in Tibet: 1728–1959* (Rome: Instituto italiano per il Medio ed Estremo Oriente, 1973), 215.

22. Radhu, *Tibetan Caravans*, 156.

23. Petech, *Aristocracy and Government in Tibet*, 215.

24. India Office Library/Political & Secret/12/4185A Col. 36/20. *Who's Who in Tibet* 1938, 10.

25. Bell, *Portrait of the Dalai Lama*, 392.

26. See India Office Library/Political & Secret/12/4178, p. 357, for a less romanticized version.

27. India Office Library/Political & Secret/12/4185A Col. 36/20. *Who's Who in Tibet* 1938, 10.

28. *Melong*, January 2, 1937, 6.

29. Bell, *Portrait of the Dalai Lama*, 393.

30. Robert Ford, *Captured in Tibet* (London: Harrap, 1957), 49.

31. Shakabpa, *Tibet: A Political History*, 242–243.

32. Radhu, *Tibetan Caravans*, 168. Adruk Gönpo Tashi, a member of the Andrutshang family, became one of the great heroes of the Tibetan guerrillas. Blo bzang Bstan dzin, Ri kha, "Mdo smad kyi mkhas pa [{Gedun Chompel}, the Scholar from Amdo]," in *Rgyun mkho'i chos srid she bya gnas bsdus* (Varanasi: Legs bshad gter mdzod khang, 1972), 207–214, provides a short biography.

33. India Office Library/Political & Secret/12/4202, p. 348, January 1, 1946; see also Radhu, *Tibetan Caravans*, 168.

34. Radhu, *Tibetan Caravans*, 168.

35. See Eric Teichman, *Travels of a Consular Officer in Eastern Tibet* (Cambridge, England: Cambridge University Press), 96–97, on the potential importance of Tibetan wool.

36. Suydam Cutting, *The Fire Ox and Other Years* (London: Collins, 1947), 177.

37. *Melong*, December 24, 1936, 12.

38. George Patterson, *Tibetan Journey* (London: Faber and Faber, 1954), 24.

39. Ford, *Captured in Tibet*, 79; George Patterson, *God's Fool* (Garden City, N.Y.: Doubleday, 1954), 23, for descriptions of Rapga Pangdatsang, whom both Englishmen met in Kham in the late 1940s.

40. Patterson, *God's Fool*, 208; see also Michel Peissel, *Les Cavaliers du Kham* [*The Cavaliers of Kham*] (Paris: Lafont, 1972), 25.

41. India Office Library/Political & Secret/12/4185A Col. 36/20. *Who's Who in Tibet* 1938, 53.

42. Patterson, *God's Fool*, 208.

43. The author refers here to the traditional priest-patron relationship.

44. Liu Wenhui; see below.

45. In other words, the governments of Tibet and Sichuan.

46. The Fourteenth Dalai Lama, who had just been recognized. The lotus is the symbol of Avalokiteśvara, of whom the Dalai Lamas are considered an incarnation.

47. Probably Huang Musong, the head of the condolence mission in Lhasa following the Thirteenth Dalai Lama's death. See Richardson, A *Short History of Tibet*,
141–143.

48. India Office Library/Political & Secret/12/4211, 36/file39 (1) Ext.6642 D.O. 3(7)–
L/46/80, 9 (a), from Richardson to Mr. Hopkinson: "refutation by one's government is
always the fate of the unmasked spy or conspirer."

49. Bell, *Portrait of the Dalai Lama*, 140–141; Radhu, *Tibetan Caravans*, 153–155;
Tada Tokan, *The Thirteenth Dalai Lama* (Tokyo: Toyo Bunko, 1965), 65.

50. Nanjing Zhongyang zhengzhi xuexiao. Several Tibetan students were also
admitted to the Boading junguan daxuexiao and to the Huangpu junguan xuexiao
(Whampoa).

51. T. N. Takla, "Notes on Some Early Tibetan Communists," *Tibetan Review* 2
(1969): 7–9, 17. His Chinese name is Min Zhicheng.

52. Tieh-Tseng Li, *Tibet, Today and Yesterday* (New York: Bookman Associates,
1960), 161, 278 n. 137), 279 n. 145. Richardson, *A Short History of Tibet*, 135.

53. Kimura Hisao, *Chibetto Senkô Junen* [*Ten Years Disguised in Tibet*] (Tokyo:
Mainichi Shinbun, 1958), 196. His Chinese name means "River (the four rivers of
Kham) New West"; I don't know his Tibetan name.

54. Takla, "Notes on Some Early Tibetan Communists," 9.

55. Radhu, *Tibetan Caravans*, 189, 252–254.

56. *Zhu Zang lianluo canmou.*

57. Wm. Theodore de Bary, ed., *Sources of Chinese Tradition*, vol. 2 (New York:
Columbia University Press, 1960), 106.

58. Sun Yat-sen, *San Min Chu I: Les Trois Principes du Peuple* [*The Three Principles
of the People*], French translation by J. Marcuse (1913; reprint, Taipei: Comité de compilation de l'histoire du Kuomintang, 1971), 76, 115, 119.

59. Radhu, *Tibetan Caravans*, 78–79, evokes his education in India, which was dispensed for the purpose of training "good subjects" for the British Empire.

60. India Office Library/Political & Secret/12/4210, Coll.36/39, cf. p. 348, December 5, 1943, concerning the armory at the base of Chakpori: "To have the doors un-
locked, one must give warning five days in advance and nobody takes care of the
weapons. The door is sealed with the seals of the Dalai Lama, the regent, the Kashak
and the military commander. Representatives of each must be present when the
doors are opened."

61. C. P. Fitzgerald, *The British of Communist China* (London: Pellican, 1964), 59.

62. Chiang Kai-shek, *China's Destiny and Chinese Economic Theory*, trans. Philip
Jaffee (London: D. Dobson, 1947), 40 n. 17.

63. J. Teufel Dreyer, *China's Forty Millions: Minority Nationalities and National
Integration in the People's Republic of China* (Cambridge, Mass.: Harvard University
Press, 1976), 63–64.

64. Interview in Kalimpong, January 1975.

65. Thub bstan byams pa tshul khrims bstan 'dzin, Phur bu lcog yongs 'dzin sprul
sku, *Ngo mtshar rin po che'i 'phreng ba* [*The Biography of the Thirteenth Dalai Lama*],

vol. Kha. ('Bras spungs lha sa: Dga' ldan pho brang, 1940), f. 241a: the Lhasa Kangyur was edited between 1921 and 1933, over a period of twelve and a half months; f. 202b: a few years previously, Geshé Sherap is mentioned as coeditor of the *Complete Works* of Büton Rinchendrup, published between 1916 and 1918.

66. Rahul Sankrityayan, "Introduction au *Pramanavarttika*: 'Sanskrit Palm-leaf Manuscripts in Tibet,'" *Journal of the Bihar and Orissa Research Society* 21 (1935): 21–26.

67. D. Snellgrove and H. Richardson, *A Cultural History of Tibet* (Boulder, Colo.: Prajna Press, 1968), 245.

68. Shakabpa, *Tibet: A Political History*, 290.

69. *Melong*, January 1, 1951.

70. India Office Library/Political & Secret/12/4201, April 30, 1944: "A famous *geshe*, Sherab Gyatsho has recently arrived at Nagchuka. He is reputed to be very pro-Chinese and keen on spreading Chinese propaganda. The Tibetan government has asked him to return (to China) via Jyekundo." May 14, 1944: "Fifty soldiers accompanied *geshe* Sherab." December 1, 1944: "Copies of the book *San Ming Truh Yi* printed in both Tibetan and Chinese have been seen in Lhasa. The Tibetan version was written by *geshe* Sherab. . . . The books were published by the Guomindang bureau and were perhaps brought to Nagchuka by the *geshe* himself."

71. Zhwa sgab pa, *An Advanced Political History of Tibet*, II:380–381.

72. See Shirob Jaltso entries in *Who's Who in Communist China* (Hong Kong: Union Research Institute, 1970), vol. II.

73. June 1981, 25–26; see also Radhu, *Tibetan Caravans*, 172; Holmes Welch, *The Buddhist Revival in China* (Cambridge, Mass.: Harvard University Press, 1968), 177, 336–337; Holmes Welch, *Buddhism Under Mao* (Cambridge, Mass.: Harvard University Press, 1972), 10, 19, 54, 65–66, 113, 144, 174, 176, 211, 286–287, 325–328, 355; Li Naimin, ed., *Tibet 1950–1967* (Hong Kong: Union Research Institute, 1968), Shirob Jaltso entries, 1, 46, 178, 179, 186, 188; Xianggang fojiao lianhehui, Xianggang fojiao sengqie lianhehui, Yulian yanjiusuo, eds., *Zhongguo dalu Fojiao ziliao huibian, 1949 nian zhi 1967 nian* [*Sourcebook on Buddhism in Mainland China 1949–1967*] (Hong Kong: Union Research Institute, 1968), Xirao Jiacuo entries, 100, 119 sqq. His complete works are published in three volumes in Tibetan *poti* format: Shes rab rgya mtsho, 'Bras klu 'bum rdo sbis lha rams pa shes rab rgya mtsho'i gsung 'bum [*Collected Works of Dobi Geshé Sherap Gyatso of Drepung Lumbum*].

74. Zhwa sgab pa, *An Advanced Political History of Tibet*, 1:11, 2:381.

75. Editors' note: Stoddard refers here to an earlier citation of Tsung-lien Shen and Shen-chi Liu, *Tibet and the Tibetans* (Stanford: Stanford University Press, 1953), 64–65: members of the clergy "could be most conservative as well as ultraradical; they are conservative when conservatism pays. Once the new social forces are unleashed, they are likely to break ranks with the aristocrats, with whom there has always been keen tension. Already there is a rumor of Buddho-Marxism in the making."

76. Chiang, *China's Destiny and Chinese Economic Theory*, 38. [Editors' note: The references here to 1942 and 1944 reflect earlier versions of the Chinese-language

edition of *China's Destiny* (*Zhongguo zhi ming yun*), some of the variations of which are discussed in the 1947 English translation.]

77. India Office Library/Political & Secret/12/4210, Coll.36/39, 197: March 16, 1943; April 14, 1943.

78. India Office Library/Political & Secret/12/4210, Coll.36/39, 197: March 16, 1943; April 14, 1943. See also Shakabpa, *Tibet: A Political History*, 286.

79. India Office Library/Political & Secret/12/4210, Coll.36/39, 102: June 6, 1943.

80. India Office Library/Political & Secret/12/4210, Coll.36/39, 102: June 30, 1943.

81 .India Office Library/Political & Secret/12/4210, Coll.36/39, 102: October 3, 1943. The following year the figures given (May 29, 1944) were: for Jyekundo: 3,500–4,000; Dergé: 250; Kandzé: 400–500; Dartsedo: 2,500–3,000, etc., thus a total of roughly 10,000 Chinese troops in Kham.

82. India Office Library/Political & Secret/12/4210, Coll.36/39, 102: October 23, 1943.

83. India Office Library/Political & Secret/12/4210, Coll.36/39, 102: October 23, 1943.

84. India Office Library/Political & Secret/12/4201, August 20, 1944.

85. Radhu, *Tibetan Caravans*, 145.

86. India Office Library/Political & Secret/12/4201, November 23, 1943.

87. According to other oral sources, Püntsok Wanggyel's brother was called Kelzang Wangdu. Kelzang is used as a component in the names of several politicized Khampas of that time. This leads to some confusion even among Tibetans, who easily confuse or change names, including those of their kin. Moreover, the British often made reports according to hearsay from more or less reliable sources. Unless I am mistaken, there was Ngawang Kelzang who was the political companion of Püntsok Wanggyel; Kelzang Tsering, a militant and member of the Guomindang, who was active in Kham in the early 1930s; Kelzang Wangdu, who presented an essay to Richardson concerning the relations between Kham and its two neighbors, Central Tibet and China; and finally, Kelzang Trashi, mentioned by the British on November 23, 1943, as a former Chongqing student.

88. Li, *Tibet, Today and Yesterday*, 161.

89. Richardson, *A Short History of Tibet*, 135.

90. Takla, "Notes on Some Early Tibetan Communists," 8–9.

91. Kimura, *Ten Years Disguised in Tibet*, 178, and oral communication.

92. Radhu, *Tibetan Caravans*, 172.

93. Radhu, *Tibetan Caravans*, 241–243, 249–259, 267.

Chapter 33

THE GENESIS OF THE SINO-TIBETAN AGREEMENT

OF 1951

Tsering Shakya

Tsering Shakya examines one of the key turning points in Tibetan history. In 1951 Tibet was forcibly subsumed under the People's Republic of China, an event marked both symbolically and practically by the Seventeen-Point Agreement. Shakya correctly points out the importance of international affairs to this agreement, the only one of its kind in the process of the consolidation of the modern Chinese state. Given that the Chinese launched their invasion of areas of Kham under Lhasa rule the same day that the United States sent troops into North Korea, it seems that the Chinese communists were thinking strategically about when the international community might be least likely to take the side of the Tibetans. Shakya makes clear how little effective international support there was for Tibet. What is most remarkable about the early proposal and final agreement is the degree of real autonomy granted to the Tibetans and the recognition of the importance of religion, both in the person of the Dalai Lama as the ruler and with respect to the monasteries, which sought to protect their socioeconomic position. China's willingness to negotiate such matters for over a year demonstrates how much they needed such an agreement to solidify their weak claim on Tibet.

In 1991, the Chinese Government launched a year-long celebration to mark the fortieth anniversary of the signing of what is officially known as "the Agreement of the Central People's Government and the Local Government of Tibet on Measures for the Peaceful Liberation of Tibet." The Agreement is more commonly known as the "Seventeen-Point Agreement," signed between Tibet and China in Beijing on 23rd May 1951, and the celebrations forty years later included an exhibition in Beijing of the original documents, with receptions held at Chinese embassies abroad to publicize the event.[1] The Chinese media took the opportunity to publish detailed coverage of their achievements in Tibet over the past forty years.

What was interesting about this celebration was that the Chinese government resurrected the agreement after ignoring it for nearly thirty years. From 1959 until the time of the celebration, the Chinese had made little or no reference to the agreement. In the past the Chinese government's stated view was that the Dalai Lama's flight into exile and the abortive revolt of 1959, made the agreement invalid. In their words he had "torn up the agreement."[2] Moreover, the agreement had been superseded by the establishment of an Autonomous Region of Tibet and subsequent constitutional changes in China.

The Dalai Lama and the Tibetan exile organizations had argued that the agreement had been signed under duress and was therefore invalid. On arrival in India in 1959, the Tibetan leader had publicly repudiated the agreement. On 20th June 1959, in a statement to the press, he announced that:

> The agreement which followed the invasion of Tibet was [also] thrust upon its people and government by the threat of arms. It was never accepted by them of their own free will. The consent of the Government was secured under duress and at the point of the bayonet. My representatives were compelled to sign the Agreement under threat of further military operations against Tibet by the invading armies of China leading to utter ravage and ruin of the country. Even the Tibetan seal which was affixed to the Agreement was not the seal of my representatives in Peking, and [has been] kept in their possession ever since.[3]

Although the question of the legal validity of the agreement and its status in contemporary politics is a perplexing one, for China the agreement is of great historical significance in that it represents the legal and historical basis for Chinese rule in Tibet. The nationwide celebration aimed, internally and internationally, to demonstrate the legality of Chinese rule in Tibet, and it was not an accident that the celebration occurred at a critical period in Sino-Tibetan history. The agreement is also of great importance to Tibetans in Tibet, particularly those in the government who argued that Tibet must be regarded as a special case because it had signed the Seventeen-Point Agreement, unlike other regions or minority groups. This point was made by Ngapö Ngawang Jikmé at the Second Plenary Session of the Fifth Tibet Autonomous Region's Congress, when he delivered a lengthy speech detailing for the first time his account of the signing of the Seventeen-Point Agreement.[4]

Despite the historical importance of the agreement and its significance in contemporary Sino-Tibetan politics, the topic has received scant attention from scholars, and we know very little about what occurred during the process of negotiation. Discussion of the subject has been marred by polemic from those who either support the Chinese or the Tibetans' claim; but there are also a number of objective factors preventing scholarly research on the subject. Most published sources are questionable or they are deliberately distorted to support one or the other side; the question of source materials will be examined in detail below. In addition, it may be argued that the events of 1951 are too recent and that until the archives in Beijing and Lhasa are made available for scholarly inspection it will not be possible to reach any definite conclusion on the subject.

The topic is politically sensitive to the Chinese and the Tibetans. On the one hand, if it is proved as claimed by the Dalai Lama, that the agreement was signed under duress and enforced by the Chinese under threat of military action, it would mean that the Chinese presence in Tibet is illegal; if on the other hand, it is shown that the Tibetans voluntarily accepted the agreement, it would mean that the Chinese entry into Tibet was legitimate. Given the stakes that are involved it is understandable that the subject is a sensitive one and that much of the official writing on the topic has obscured rather than shed light on what happened.

The topic is dealt with at some length in Melvyn Goldstein's *A History of Modern Tibet, 1913–1951: The Demise of the Lamaist State* (University of California Press, 1989). However, at the time of its publication the recent account given by Ngapö was not available to Professor Goldstein. Ngapö's account sheds important light on what occurred during the meeting. His account can be regarded as presenting a near accurate description of the time, and it can be assumed that the Chinese concur with his account, which was distributed and published in the *Tibet Daily*.[5] However, the majority of the articles published on the topic as a part of the fortieth anniversary tended to adhere to the official line and do little to add to our knowledge of the diplomacy surrounding the signing of the agreement.

It is interesting to note that not only Ngapö, the head of the Tibetan delegation, but also most of the other senior Tibetan delegates have written their own accounts of the negotiations. Lhautara Tupten Tendar, a monk official who was the second most senior member of the Tibetan team, wrote an account which was published in Tibet for internal distribution for the members of the Political Consultative Committee.[6] There also exists a biography of Lhautara written by his secretary and published by the Library of Tibetan Works and Archives, Dharamsala.[7] Two other Tibetan members of the delegation, Khemé Sönam Wangdü[8] and Sampo Tendzin Döndrup have also written their accounts.[9] A number of valuable sources in British archives and the published papers on the foreign relations of the United States also throw some light on the subject. The

United States in particular was involved in Tibetan affairs at the time and attempted to influence Tibetan decisions on the subject.[10]

This paper does not seek to provide a legal or theoretical interpretation of the agreement. Drawing on published and unpublished sources I have tried to examine the events and the process leading to the signing of the agreement. The paper merely seeks to add to our factual knowledge of the events surrounding the signing of the agreement. To understand how the agreement came about, we have to go back to the eve of the founding of the People's Republic of China. When the Communists came to power in October 1949, they were quick to make their claim that Tibet was an integral part of China, and during the founding celebrations of the PRC, Zhu De, the commander-in-chief of the People's Liberation Army (PLA), announced that one of the last remaining tasks for the PLA was the liberation of Tibet. Despite their rhetoric, the Chinese found that Tibet was for all intents and purposes independent of China. There were no Chinese present in Lhasa and the Guomindang representative had been expelled from Tibet.

The new Chinese Government urged the Tibetans to send a negotiating team to discuss the Tibet problem. In December 1949 the Tibetan Government appointed a negotiation team headed by Tsipön Shakabpa, one of the few Tibetan officials with a fairly good knowledge of the outside world and experience of negotiations with foreign powers, having a year earlier led a successful trade mission to the U.S., Britain and China.[11] Shakabpa was instructed to meet the Chinese representative either in Singapore or Hong Kong, but not on any account to go to Beijing for discussions. When the Tibetan team arrived in India and sought British permission to conduct negotiations either in Hong Kong or Singapore, the British refused to allow the negotiations to take place in territories under their rule and advised the Tibetans that the discussions should take place in New Delhi. The Chinese refused to accept the venue for the meeting and insisted that the Tibetan group should go to Beijing. However, there took place in Delhi a long and unofficial negotiation between Shakabpa and the Chinese ambassador, which lasted almost a year. Meanwhile the Chinese had also dispatched a number of emissaries overland, including the Dalai Lama's elder brother, Tupten Norbu, who was in Kumbum monastery in Qinghai, and Geda Rinpoché, who was the head lama of Beri monastery in Kardzé. Geda had traveled to Chamdo and met with Ngapö, who refused to allow him to proceed to Lhasa. While waiting for instructions from the Kashak in Lhasa, Geda Rinpoché died in Chamdo. The Chinese believed that he was assassinated by the Tibetans and the death of Geda Rinpoché furthered the Chinese suspicion that foreign powers were trying to thwart Chinese attempts to communicate with Lhasa.

On 16th September the newly appointed Chinese ambassador to India, Yuan Zhongxian, met with the Tibetan delegation in Delhi. At the meeting the Tibetan delegation stressed that the traditional relationship between Tibet and China had been one of priest and patron (*mchod yon*).[12] They also said that there were no foreign imperialist influences in Tibet. The Chinese ambassador told the Tibetans that China could never accept Tibetan independence and gave a copy of the "Common Programme," telling them to study articles 50 to 53.[13]

Yuan also gave them a proposal which listed three points:

(1) Tibet must be regarded as part of China;
(2) China would be responsible for Tibet's defense;
(3) All trade and international relations with foreign countries would be handled by the PRC.[14]

Shakabpa replied that he would inform the Kashak of the proposals. On 19th September Shakabpa sent a telegram to Lhasa with the Chinese three-point proposal, recommending that the Kashak accept the proposals. Shakabpa suggested that the point about Tibet being part of China should be accepted only in name.[15] On the point regarding defense Shakabpa recommended that there was no need to station a Chinese army in Tibet, since neither India nor Nepal were a threat to Tibet's security. However, in the event of danger, Tibet should request Chinese assistance. Thirdly, Tibet should insist on the right to maintain direct trade and cultural relations with Nepal and India. Shakabpa also requested that his mission should be allowed to proceed to Peking for further negotiations.

In retrospect we cannot say whether the Shakabpa mission would have achieved a peaceful and better solution to the status of Tibet if it had been allowed to proceed: his request was turned down. The Kashak was not prepared to negotiate with the Chinese since they believed the Chinese proposals would have far-reaching consequences, a strong reaction which may have been influenced by the increasing American willingness to supply aid to Tibet: the Tibetan Government hoped that the U.S.A. might provide a last chance for Tibet's survival. By September 1951 the Chinese believed that the Tibetans were deliberately delaying giving a response to their three-point proposal. The Kashak, meanwhile, had observed the growing tension over the possible involvement of China in the Korean War, and instructed Shakabpa to wait and watch the international situation. The Tibetans therefore never communicated Shakabpa's compromise proposal to the Chinese.

On 6th October 1950, the Chinese launched a full-scale military invasion of Tibet and the primitive Tibetan defenses in Chamdo collapsed with little resistance. The Chinese made it clear that the failure of the mission to proceed to Peking and the obstacles placed by Britain and India had forced them to adopt a military solution. An editorial in the *People's Daily* on 17th November stated:

The British Government deliberately delayed issuing transit visas for Hong Kong to the Lhasa delegation, making it impossible for them to come to Peking. According to reports from various sources, when the

Lhasa delegation were loitering in India, the British High Commissioner Nye and other foreign imperialist elements used every effort to persuade the delegation not to come to any agreement with the Chinese People's Government. Then on the 12th August, when the Indian Government saw that the operations of Chinese Government's forces to enter Tibet were about to begin, they informed the Chinese Government that the British Government had withdrawn its refusal to issue visas to the Tibetan delegation and that facilities for the departure of the delegation for Peking were available. But more than two months have passed and still "the stairs have been created but no one has come down." It is obvious that the delay of the Lhasa delegation in coming to Peking to carry on peaceful talks is the result of instigation and obstruction from foreign states who must bear the responsibility for obstructing and sabotaging the peaceful talks. It is only necessary for the local Tibetan authorities to strive to correct their former errors and abandon the erroneous position of relying on foreign influences to resist the entry of the People's Liberation Army and the Tibetan question can still be settled peacefully.

It appears that the Tibetans also shared the view that the Chinese attack was prompted by the failure of Britain to provide a visa for the Tibetan negotiating team to travel to China by way of Hong Kong. Shakabpa said in an interview with Reuters in Calcutta that "Chinese forces had entered Tibet. This was because his delegation had been delayed in India due to visa difficulties."[16] What is most significant about Shakabpa's negotiation in Delhi is that it shows the extent of the shift that occurred in the Tibetans' position. It is clear that the position adopted by the Tibetans before the Chinese military action in Chamdo was to preserve the status enjoyed by Tibet since 1913. If the negotiation had taken place in a relatively natural atmosphere and one that was free of Chinese intimidation, it is most likely that the Tibetans would not have given in to Chinese pressure.

The failure of the Tibetans to respond to proposals made by the Chinese through diplomatic channels in Delhi and through various emissaries who came to Lhasa does not in itself explain the reasons for the Chinese use of force. Beijing feared that the Tibetans had been advised by foreign powers not to negotiate and to hold out until the Chinese could be pressurized into making a compromise with the Tibetans. The Chinese would have assumed that there was a possibility that foreign powers might deploy troops in Tibet to bolster the regime and as a means of containing the spread of Communism westward into the Indian sub-continent. The Sino-Tibetan discussion was taking place under the shadow of the Korean war and there was growing concern as to whether the Chinese were going to join the North Korean side or not. The Chinese were concerned about the American intentions and feared that the U.S.A. would use the Korean war as a pretext for the invasion of China: this is crucial to understanding later developments in Tibet. The Chinese would have been aware that while in Delhi Shakabpa and Tibetan officials had held meetings with the American Ambassador Loy Henderson; American interest in the region cannot be ruled out. On 7th October 1950, the day when the Americans crossed the 38th Parallel, the Chinese decided to support the North Koreans and deployed PLA troops in the Korean war. On that same day 40,000 PLA troops from the south-west military region led by Zhang Guohua crossed the Drichu river and attacked Tibetan garrisons in Eastern Tibet. The date of the Chinese attack was very significant in that it was the same date that China announced its military support for the North Koreans. I believe that the decision to invade Tibet was taken in conjunction with their thinking over the Korean situation. The Chinese decision to use force was not only aimed at bringing the Tibetans to the negotiating table but it was also an explicit warning to foreign powers that China was prepared to use military means to find a solution to the Tibet problem and would resist any foreign intervention.

The Chinese caught the Tibetans by surprise. On 19th October 1950 Ngapö Ngawang Jikmé, then the commander of the Tibetan army in Eastern Tibet and governor of Kham, surrendered to the Chinese. The news of the fall of Chamdo and the fear of the imminent arrival of PLA troops in Lhasa alarmed officials in government circles. The regent, Kashak and abbots of the three great monasteries held a meeting to discuss the situation; it was evident that they did not know how they should respond to the invasion. There were factions who advocated all-out war with the PLA, while others felt a negotiated settlement should be reached. One thing was clear: no one was willing to take charge.[17]

Ngapö and his officials feared that the Dalai Lama and the members of Kashak might have escaped to India. Ngapö wrote a report to Lhasa. Because he did not know who was in charge in Lhasa, the report was addressed to "Whoever is in power in Lhasa."[18] The report gave a glowing account of the behavior of the PLA and stressed the futility of resisting the Chinese army. He advised Lhasa that a peaceful agreement should be reached with the Chinese.

On 7th December 1950, two messengers (Gyeltsen Püntsok and Dzamlingpa Püntsok Dorjé) arrived in Lhasa with a message from Ngapö. They brought a letter addressed to the Dalai Lama and the Kashak which contained the eight-point proposal given to Ngapö by the Chinese. This was the most comprehensive proposal made by the Chinese to date and it included the three-point proposal that Yuan Zhongxian, the Chinese ambassador in Delhi, had put to the Kashak two months earlier. The eight points were:

(1) China's policy would be based on the unity and equality of all nationalities.
(2) Tibet was to remain under the rule of the Dalai Lama.
(3) Tibetan religion would be protected by the state.
(4) China was to help Tibet to reform her army and build a common defense against external aggression.

(5) China was to provide Tibet with expert guidance in matters relating to agriculture, animal husbandry, commerce and industry.

(6) Administrative reform in Tibet was to be undertaken only after mutual consultation between China and Tibet.

(7) Those who had collaborated with the Americans, the British and the Kuomintang [Guomindang] would not be persecuted.

(8) Tibet was to be assured that the central government would not support anti-Tibetan elements like the Trashilhünpo and Radreng [Reting] factions.[19]

On 12th December 1950 the National Assembly discussed the eight proposals received from Chamdo. At the same time the Kashak and the abbots of the three monasteries held a secret meeting on the security of the Dalai Lama. It was agreed that it was not safe for the Dalai Lama to remain in Lhasa. Some argued that the Chinese could not be trusted and that the Communists' offer was "trying to lure a fly with honey spread on a sharp knife."[20] In the end, due to growing fear that the Chinese would march into Lhasa, the National Assembly agreed to negotiate with the Chinese. Shortly after the arrival of the messengers from Chamdo, Ngapö had secretly dispatched a separate message which stated that he was no longer free to act independently and was conforming to the wishes of his captors and that the government should take any action necessary, without worrying about Ngapö himself or other officials.[21]

On the night of 16th December 1950, the Dalai Lama, dressed as a commoner, accompanied by two tutors and the members of the Kashak, left Lhasa for Dromo, a small town near the Indo-Tibetan border. Before the Dalai Lama left Lhasa, Lukhangwa Tsewang Rapten and Lozang Trashi were appointed as the joint caretaker prime ministers (*srid tshab*). The Dalai Lama and the Kashak also appointed Sampo Tendzin Döndrup and Khenchung Tupten Lekmön to proceed to Chamdo to assist Ngapö. The delegation reached Chamdo in the end of February, and Sampo handed Ngapö the letter from the Kashak, which authorized him to hold discussions with the Chinese. The letter also stated that he (Ngapö) must insist on Tibetan independence and must not accept the stationing of PLA troops in Tibet.

Ngapö thought the points were unrealistic and that there was no scope for discussion with the Chinese, since it was clear that they were determined to gain control of Tibet. Sampo also gave him a five-point written statement as the starting point for discussions with the Chinese:

(1) There is no imperialist influence in Tibet; the little contact Tibet had with the British was the result of the travels of the thirteenth Dalai Lama to India. As for the relationship with the United States, this was only commercial.

(2) In the event of foreign imperial influence being exerted on Tibet, the Tibetan government would appeal to China for help.

(3) Chinese troops stationed in Kham should be withdrawn.

(4) The territories taken by Manchu China, the Kuomintang [Goumindang] and the new government of China must be returned to Tibet.

(5) The Chinese Government should not be influenced by the followers of the Panchen Lama and Radreng factions.[22]

Ngapö knew that the five points would be unacceptable and that they might infuriate the Chinese. He asked Sampo if he had received any oral instruction from the Kashak. Sampo did not even know whether they were to negotiate with the Chinese at Chamdo or were to proceed directly to Beijing. When Ngapö gave the statement to the Chinese, they repudiated it point by point:

(1) It was clear that the British and American imperialists had interfered in the internal affairs of China. It was evident from the fact that they had prevented the negotiating team from leaving India.

(2) The defense of the Motherland was the prime objective of the PLA and it was imperative that the PLA should defend the frontiers of the Motherland.

(3) The existing political system and the status of the Dalai Lama would not be altered. However, in the event of the Dalai Lama going into exile, he would lose all his power and status.

(4) Tibet would enjoy regional autonomy.

(5) China would not interfere in internal political rivalry and factions.[23]

In January 1951, the Tibetan Government dispatched Surkhang Dzasa and Chöpel Tupten to New Delhi to meet with the Chinese ambassador and discuss a venue for a meeting. They agreed that the meeting would be held in Peking and that for the duration of the meeting, Chinese troops would not proceed any further into Tibet. Unknown to the Dalai Lama and the Kashak in Dromo, Ngapö had met with Wang Chimen, the commander of the Chinese forces and secured his agreement that the negotiations should take place in Lhasa. Ngapö immediately radioed Lhasa for permission for a small delegation of Chinese to proceed to Lhasa for discussions. The two prime ministers, Lhukhang and Lozang Trashi in Lhasa accepted Ngapö's suggestion and authorized a Chinese delegation to come to Lhasa for discussions. At the same time Ngapö received a telegram from the Dalai Lama, via the Chinese embassy in Delhi, instructing him to proceed to Beijing for discussions. Ngapö later wrote that since the Dalai Lama's order superseded instructions from the *kalöns*, on 22nd March his party in Chamdo reluctantly proceeded to Beijing.[24]

When Shakabpa was appointed to negotiate with the Chinese, he was instructed that the venue should be either Hong Kong or Singapore because it was agreed that once the Tibetan delegation was in Beijing, they would be exposed to an unacceptable degree of Chinese pressure. But in Dromo the Kashak felt that once a Chinese delegation had been allowed to come to Lhasa, even if the negotiation failed there was a danger that the delegation may set themselves up in Lhasa as the representatives of the new Chinese Government. Since the main Tibetan objective at the time was to keep any Chinese presence out of Lhasa, it seemed wise to prevent them from gaining a foothold in the city. However, it seems to me that the decision to shift the venue to Beijing was a crucial mistake by the Tibetans.

The Kashak also appointed Lhautara Tupten Tendar and Khemé Sönam Wangdü to proceed to Beijing via India. They were assisted by Takla Püntsok Trashi as the Chinese interpreter and Sendu Lozang Rinchen as the English interpreter. The delegation was provided with a written document with the names of five representatives; Ngapö Ngawang Jikmé was named as the chief Tibetan representative. The delegation was given instructions that it should on no account accept Chinese sovereignty over Tibet. The delegation was to refer all important points back to Dromo for consultation, and for that purpose a direct wireless communication would be established between Beijing and Dromo. It was clear that although Ngapö was appointed as the chief representative, he did not have any authority to make decisions without further consultation with the Kashak and the Dalai Lama. The delegation was also given a ten-point verbal proposal which they were to raise with the Chinese.

On their way to Beijing, the Tibetan delegation went to Delhi where, on 24th March, they met with the Indian Prime Minister, Jawaharlal Nehru. Lhautara presented a letter from the Dalai Lama and asked Nehru's advice on the forthcoming talks. The Tibetans also asked whether India could mediate between Tibet and China.[25] Nehru made no comment on this point. According to Lhautara, Nehru advised them that the Chinese would insist on three points. Firstly, the Tibetans would have to accept the Chinese claim that Tibet was a part of China. According to Nehru, Chinese claims over Tibet were internationally recognized. Secondly, the Tibetans would have to surrender the right to conduct their own external affairs. Thirdly, the Tibetans *must not agree* to the stationing of Chinese troops in Tibet, since this would have serious repercussions on India. Nehru's statement was a great disappointment for the Tibetan delegation. Now the Tibetan delegation was leaving for Beijing in the knowledge that India was not prepared to support Tibetan independence.[26]

Ngapö, the chief representative, Sampo Tendzin Dündup and Khenchung Tupten Lekmön arrived in Beijing on 22nd April. Lhautara and Khemé Sönam Wangdü arrived four days later on 26th April 1950. While the Tibetan delegation was in Beijing, they were informed that the Panchen Rinpoché and his retinue would be arriving in Beijing and the Chinese asked if they would come to the railway station to welcome him. Ngapö, not wanting to give any impression of formal recognition of the Panchen Rinpoché, suggested that only the junior members of the Tibetan delegation, Sampo, Takla and Sendu Rinchen, should go to the railway station. The presence of the Panchen Lama and his retinue were to become a major stumbling block during the course of the negotiations.

Lhautara and Khemé brought further instructions from the Kashak, which stated that at first the delegation must make a claim for Tibetan independence and argue that the past relationship between Tibet and China had been that of "priest and patron." If the discussion reached deadlock, then they could accept Tibet as part of China, on the following conditions namely that:

(1) Tibet must enjoy full internal independence.[27]
(2) No Chinese troops would be stationed in Tibet.
(3) The Tibetan army would be responsible for defense.
(4) The Chinese representative to Lhasa, his personal staff and guards must not exceed one hundred men.
(5) The Chinese representative must be a Buddhist.[28]

The Tibetan delegation discussed the proposals and agreed that these terms would be unacceptable to the Chinese. Ngapö send a telegram to Dromo stating that it was impossible not to accept Chinese troops in Tibet and that there would otherwise be no scope for discussion. The Kashak's reply once again insisted that no Chinese troops should be deployed in Tibet, but they proposed a strange solution: the existing Tibetan army could be incorporated into the Chinese army and would be responsible for defense.[29]

The Tibetan delegation met once again to discuss the Kashak's reply. Ngapö stated that the Kashak had already agreed to make a major concession in accepting Tibet as part of China, and therefore all other issues were only minor. He scornfully remarked, "Who would have heard of a Communist Buddhist?" The remark implied that the Kashak was not well informed. Then Ngapö stated that there was no point in referring all the matters back to Dromo, since the Kashak had agreed on the most important point. Moreover, there would be a considerable delay if every single point were referred back to Dromo, from where the Kashak and the National Assembly would take days to reply. In the event of a long delay the Chinese might resume their military actions.[30]

On 29th April 1951, the Tibetan and Chinese delegations met in an army headquarters in Beijing. The Chinese group was headed by Li Weihan, who was one of the key members of the Communist Party. Li had studied in France in the early 1920s and was one of the cofounders of the French section of the CCP. In 1944 he became director of the Party's United Front Work Department and the Chairman of the Nationalities Affairs Commission of the State Council. Li was assisted by Zhang Guohua, who was the leader of the 18th Corps of the Second Field Army, which led the PLA's invasion of Tibet, and Zhang Jingwu, another PLA officer who was directly involved in the invasion of Tibet, together with Sun Zhiyuan. The significance of Li's appointment, and of the fact that the negotiations were carried out by the United Front section of the

Party, was that the Chinese regarded the Tibetan issue as essentially one of internal affairs. The United Front Work Department was primarily concerned with gaining control and influence over non-Communists and minority groups. The Tibetan delegation was not aware of the significance of this. As far as the Tibetans were concerned they were dealing with the Chinese.

On the first day the formal meeting only lasted for half an hour. They merely agreed to draw up a written statement on their respective positions and then the meeting ended. On the second day, Li Weihan presented a proposal, which was more or less the same as the proclamation issued by the South-West Military Command in Chamdo after its capture by the PLA. Li suggested that the Tibetan delegation should study the proposal and that then they should meet again. The meeting was resumed on 2nd May, when the Chinese delegation explained each point of their proposal. According to Püntsok Trashi Takla the Chinese delivered their position rather like a lecture, with a mixture of Communist interpretation of recent history and their nationalities policy.

When Ngapö opened the discussion, he declared that Tibet had been an independent country and the past relationship with China had been one of priest-patron and that there was no need to deploy Chinese troops in Tibet.[31] Li Weihan responded by saying that the question of the status of Tibet was not under discussion and Chinese sovereignty over Tibet was nonnegotiable. He added that it was a historical fact that Tibet formed an integral part of China, and her claim over Tibet was internationally recognized. He went on to say that the purpose of the meeting was to discuss the proposal that had been submitted and that no other issues should be added to the agenda.[32] It was clear to the Tibetan delegation that the Chinese could not be moved from their position and, moreover, the Tibetans had no maneuvering points to counter tight control by the Chinese over the agenda for the discussion. It became apparent to the Tibetan delegation that what was expected of them was to ratify the proposal presented to them.[33] In subsequent meetings the Chinese and Tibetan delegation discussed each of the articles of the Seventeen-Point Agreement. In fact much of the discussion centered around semantic issues, as the newly coined Communist terminology which was used in the text was difficult to translate into Tibetan.[34] The Tibetan delegation made some minor changes in the wording. This discussion of semantics suggested that there was a general agreement.

But by the 10th of May the meeting threatened to break down. The Chinese were proposing that the Central Peoples' Government (CPG) would set up a Military and Administrative Commission in Tibet. Lhautara asked what the functions of the Commission would be. Li Weihan stated that the Commission would be responsible for the implementation of the agreement and would "decide" all important political and military issues. Lhautara pressed further saying that this would contradict the assurance that the power and status of the Dalai Lama and the existing political system would not be altered (meaning that the final decision would be made by the Tibetan Government). At this point Li

Weihan got irritated and said: "Are you showing your clenched fist to the Communist Party? If you disagree then you can leave, whenever you like. It is up to you to choose whether Tibet would be liberated peacefully or by force. It is only a matter of sending a telegram to the PLA group to recommence their march into Tibet."[35]

The meeting ended abruptly, and for several days the Tibetan delegation was taken on a sightseeing tour. Lhautara writes that he feared the Chinese might have already ordered the PLA to march into Tibet. He asked Ngapö to find out from the Chinese if they had. The Chinese insisted that it was necessary to set up the "Military and Administrative Commission" in Tibet. The Commission would be the representative of the CPG and be responsible for the implementation of the agreement. It would also be responsible for "unifying the command of all armed forces in Tibet in order to safeguard the national defense." Li Weihan also tried to reassure the Tibetans that they should observe the behavior of the PLA for a while. In time they would see that the PLA were making a constructive contribution in Tibet.[36] Moreover, he told the Tibetans that "the PLA movement into Tibet is the established policy of the Central Government, since Tibet is an integral part of Chinese territory and all China must be liberated." It was evident that the key to Chinese policy in Tibet was the establishment of the Military and Administrative Commission. This would form a parallel administrative organ. It was clear that the Chinese were determined not to compromise on this point.

In the end the Tibetans decided not to raise any objections and the meeting was resumed. There were no other points of disagreement. However, they were anxious that the Kashak might not approve of the agreement. Ngapö told the Chinese that if the Dalai Lama and the Kashak approved the agreement, it was all well and good. But should they repudiate the agreement and the Dalai Lama escape abroad, they would need some form of guarantee that the power and the status of the Dalai Lama would be protected. Therefore the Tibetan delegation proposed a new clause to the agreement, which stated that in the event of the Dalai Lama going into exile, he could remain outside Tibet for four or five years and during this period he would maintain his existing status and power. The Dalai Lama could observe the prevailing conditions and progress from outside and if he chose to return to Tibet, his status would be reinstated. The Chinese made no objections, but insisted that this should not be included in the main agreement and that it would form part of a separate clause.[37] This was to become the first article of a seven-part secret agreement. Another important clause stated that after the establishment of the Tibet Military Commission, one or two members of the Kashak would hold positions in the Commission. Other clauses dealt with the phasing out of Tibetan currency, and the right of the Tibetans to maintain a small police force.

On 17th May 1951, the two delegations met to discuss the draft of the agreement. When the meeting opened Li Weihan stated that now the problems concerning the "Central" (*dbus gzhung*) and the "Local" (*sa gnas gzhung*) government had been resolved. However, there remained the internal problem, arising from the conflict between the thirteenth Dalai Lama and the ninth Panchen Rinpoché. It was imperative that this was also solved. Therefore Li Weihan asked Ngapö what instructions he had received from the Kashak regarding the 10th Panchen Rinpoché. Ngapö said he was sent to Peking to discuss relationships between Tibet and China, and he did not have any power to discuss internal affairs of Tibet. If the Chinese Government wanted to discuss the issue, it should be dealt with separately.[38]

Li Weihan went on to say: "This is your internal business, but at the same time in order to solve the Tibetan issue, it is impossible not to discuss the question. This question must be settled! Regarding the method for reconciliation between the Dalai Lama and Banqen [Panchen] Lama, mutual agreement must be reached through negotiation."[39] He also stated that if this issue was not solved then there was no point in signing the agreement. The threat irritated Ngapö who announced that he was happy to return to Chamdo and he would be instructing the other Tibetan delegates to return to Lhasa. At this point the meeting again broke down, and the Tibetan delegations returned to their hotel.[40]

The Chinese decision to raise the question of the Panchen Rinpoché was no doubt prompted by a strong lobbying campaign carried on by his supporters in Beijing. However, it is also a well-known Chinese negotiating tactic of "dislocating" the other side by raising a totally unexpected issue and effectively making use of their weakness.[41] It was apparent from Ngapö's response that the issue was a sore point for the Tibetans. The Chinese had raised the issue to gain maximum concessions, and it was also an implicit warning that if Ngapö and his delegation failed to sign the agreement, they had other means of mobilizing support in Tibet.

It was interesting that Ngapö stubbornly refused to discuss the Panchen Rinpoché issue although he knew that the Dalai Lama and the Kashak had agreed to recognize the 10th Panchen Rinpoché. When he heard that the Panchen Rinpoché had arrived in Peking, Ngapö had immediately telegrammed the Kashak and advised that they recognize the 10th Panchen Rinpoché otherwise there would be difficulties in reaching an agreement with the Chinese. The Kashak replied that they had received representations from the Trashilhünpo authorities, who had appealed to the Dalai Lama to recognize the same 10th Panchen Rinpoché. The Dalai Lama and the Kashak had reached the decision to accept their request.[42]

Back in Beijing the deadlock continued. One morning at 9 o'clock, Sun Zhiyuan accompanied by Baba Püntsok Wanggyel came to the hotel where Ngapö was staying to discuss the issue of the Panchen Rinpoché. Ngapö adamantly refused to be drawn into this discussion. Sun Zhiyuan insisted the issue must be settled. The meeting lasted until 6 o'clock in the evening when Sun Zhiyuan finally suggested that they could agree to the phrase that "the relation-

ship between the Dalai Lama and the Panchen Lama should be based on the
amicable relationship that existed between the thirteenth Dalai Lama and the
ninth Panchen Lama." Ngapö raised no objection. Later this became clauses
five and six of the agreement.[43]

On 23rd May, the Chinese and Tibetan delegations signed the final copy of
the agreement. The preamble stated that Tibet had been part of China for the
past "hundred years or more" and that imperialist forces had caused disunity
between the Tibetan and Han nationalities. It further stated that "The Local
Government of Tibet did not oppose imperialist deception and provocation, but
adopted an unpatriotic attitude towards the great Motherland." The first article
stated that "the Tibetan people shall return to the big family of the Motherland,
the People's Republic of China."

During the course of the meeting the Chinese asked Ngapö if he was empowered with authority to sign the agreement. Ngapö replied that he had been
given full authority to sign. They also asked if the delegation had brought their
seals to place on the document. Ngapö told the Chinese that he did not have
the seal. It was true that other members of the delegation did not have their
seals with them, but Ngapö was in possession of the seal of the governor of
Kham, which he could have affixed to the document. Ngapö later told Pala that
he refused to use the original seal because he wanted to show that he did not
approve of the Agreement.[44] The Chinese proposed that new seals should be
made, which the Tibetan delegation agreed to. Later Tibetan exiles claimed
that the Chinese forged seals and affixed them to the document.

As far as the Chinese were concerned the agreement came into effect immediately after the signing. It is not clear why the Tibetans did not insist upon
keeping the agreement secret until the Kashak and the Dalai Lama had the
chance to ratify the agreement. It may be that it was beyond the power of the
Tibetan delegation to prevent the Chinese from publicizing the agreement.
The extensive international publicity given to the signing of the agreement gave
China a major propaganda and diplomatic victory. The international community accepted the agreement as a *fait accompli*. For the Chinese it was a political
necessity that they should announce to the world the peaceful resolution of the
Tibetan problem.

The Tibetan delegation dispatched a telegram to Dromo, informing the
Kashak and the Dalai Lama that an agreement and a secret clause had been
signed. The Dalai Lama wrote that he first heard of the agreement on the 26th
May in Dromo, on Radio Peking. The Dalai Lama described his initial reaction to the announcement:

We first came to know of it from a broadcast which Ngapö made on Peking Radio. It was a terrible shock when we heard the terms of it. We were
appalled at the mixture of Communist clichés, vainglorious assertions
which were completely false, and bold statements which were only partly

true and the terms were far worse and more oppressive than anything we had imagined.[45]

The Tibetan government was clearly shocked and alarmed by the terms of the agreement. Some officials urged the Dalai Lama to leave Dromo and seek asylum in India. Others felt they should wait until members of the delegation returned to Tibet and gave their explanation. From Dromo the Kashak immediately dispatched a telegram to Ngapö requesting the full text of the agreement and the secret clause. The delegation was instructed to remain in Peking until further notice. Ngapö replied that because of the secret nature of the separate agreement, he was not willing to dispatch it on the wireless. He bluntly stated that the agreement had been signed and that if the Kashak was not satisfied with the agreement then they should send a new team to Beijing.[46] The Tibetan delegation left Beijing in two groups, the Chinese telling Ngapö that he must return via Chamdo because they feared for his safety. In reality the Chinese were suspicious that Ngapö might not return to Tibet and would remain in India. Ngapö and Tupten Lekmön returned by the land route.

The Tibetan government in Dromo clearly found it unacceptable that the agreement compromised Tibet's independent status and, moreover, they were concerned that the Tibetan delegation had agreed to the deployment of Chinese troops in Tibet. Ngapö was not empowered to sign the agreement and his decision to sign the agreement was clearly *ultra vires. This would have been sufficient grounds for repudiating the agreement.*[47] Yet the Kashak did not want to denounce the agreement immediately without hearing what the Tibetan delegation had to say. They were suspicious that the delegation in Beijing might have been coerced into signing the agreement. The Tibetans once again turned to the United States for help.

In this short article I do not wish to deal at length with the American involvement in the affair. It is sufficient to point out that the U.S. clearly wanted the Tibetans to repudiate the agreement. They made representations to the Dalai Lama, and influential members of the Tibetan Government advised that the agreement should be renounced and that the Dalai Lama should seek asylum abroad. Moreover the Americans explicitly warned that the Tibetans could only expect their support if they denounced the agreement. In the end for various reasons the Tibetans did not heed the advice from the Americans.

There was a strong faction which was adamant that the Dalai Lama should return to Lhasa and accept the agreement as the best possible solution. This group was led by the most influential section of Tibetan society: the abbots of the three great monasteries who had recently arrived from Lhasa to urge the Dalai Lama to return. They were supported by the Dalai Lama's senior tutor Ling Rinpoché. The faction which advocated that the Dalai Lama should seek asylum and repudiate the agreement was led by Pala Tupten Öden, Surkhang Wangchuk Gelek and Trijang Lobsang Yeshé. This faction was supported by

Shakabpa and Tupten Norbu, the Dalai Lama's elder brother, who had been responsible for mustering international support.

In Dromo a meeting attended by thirty officials was held to decide whether the Dalai Lama should return to Lhasa or seek asylum in India. Tsipön Namseling Peljor Jikmé opened the meeting by stating that the Seventeen-Point Agreement was a mistake and it must be repudiated. He urged the meeting to petition the Dalai Lama to leave for India. Namseling was followed by Drönyik Chenmo Chöpel Tupten, who was a monk official and exercised considerable influence over the religious community. He was in favor of accepting the agreement and of the Dalai Lama returning to Lhasa. He stated that the agreement was correct and he did not believe that the Tibetan delegates had sold Tibet out. "We have looked for foreign support but it has been fruitless and in the future it is unlikely that the foreign governments will support us. Therefore it is best that the Dalai Lama should return to Lhasa."[48]

Shokhang Dündup Dorjé supported Chöpel Tupten and said that for over a year Shakabpa had been in India seeking international support, and what had been achieved? He urged them to accept the agreement and to return with the Dalai Lama to Lhasa. The majority of the religious and secular officials endorsed the sentiments expressed by Chöpel Tupten and Shokhang. Later Shokhang told his son, "No matter what happens, we have made up our mind to persuade His Holiness the Dalai Lama to return to Lhasa. On no account should he go abroad."[49]

Tsipön Namseling Peljor Jikmé, who openly advocated that the Dalai Lama should leave for India was only a fourth rank official. Although there were a number of high ranking officials who were in favor of denouncing the agreement, none of them spoke at the meeting. This faction concentrated on influencing the Dalai Lama personally. It was thought that the Dalai Lama's family was in favor of him seeking asylum in India. The meeting did not discuss in detail the Seventeen-Point Agreement. Khemé and Lhautara made a detailed report to the Kashak and were told that the final decision would be made in Lhasa. Khemé and Lhautara were not granted an audience with the Dalai Lama, and this was meant to show his disapproval of the agreement.[50]

At the end of September 1951, the National Assembly met to discuss the agreement in Lhasa. The meeting was attended by over three hundred officials. Normally the *zhapé* (members of Kashak) were not allowed to attend the meeting. Ngapö told the two prime ministers that he should be given the opportunity to address the meeting, along with the other members who signed the agreement, because as the head of the delegation he should explain the terms of the agreement and that he wished to clear his name from the allegations and rumor that he had been offered bribes by the Chinese.[51]

When the meeting began, the members of the delegation who had gone to Beijing were seated in a separate area. Ngapö was the first to speak. He opened the meeting by stating that neither he nor any member of the delegation had accepted any bribes from the Chinese. He had only received a photo of Mao and a box of tea as presents during his stay in Beijing. Ngapö spoke for nearly an hour and a half. He explained the instructions he had received from Dromo. He argued that the agreement did not endanger the status and the power of the Dalai Lama, nor would it harm the religious and political system of Tibet. Therefore he urged the Assembly to accept the agreement. If however the Assembly decided to repudiate the agreement, maintaining that he (Ngapö) had acted without full authorization, then he was willing to accept any punishment that the Assembly imposed on him, including the death sentence. After Ngapö had given his speech, the delegation to Beijing left the meeting.[52]

The National Assembly finally recommended the Dalai Lama to accept the agreement. The memorandum from the Assembly to the Dalai Lama stated that the agreement did not threaten the status and power of the Dalai Lama and that the religious and political system of Tibet would not be in danger. Zhang Jingwu, the newly appointed Chinese representative to Tibet, had been urging the Dalai Lama to issue a public acceptance of the agreement since his arrival in Tibet. Now that the National Assembly had accepted the agreement, it was no longer possible to stall a public announcement. The National Assembly had also recommended that the Dalai Lama should make such an announcement.

On 20th October 1951, a year and thirteen days after the Chinese invasion of Chamdo, a letter of acceptance of the agreement was drafted and given to Pün-tsok Trashi Takla to translate into Chinese. When the letter was shown to Zhang Jingwu, he immediately objected to the use of the terms "China and Tibet" (*Rgya-Bod*). He insisted that since they regarded Tibet as a part of China, and that the term "China" naturally included Tibet, the use of the terms "Tibet and China" implied separate nations. Zhang Jingwu wanted the letter to use the terms "central government" (*dbus gzhung*) and "local government" (*sa gnas gzhung*).[53] On 24th October 1950, the letter was dispatched as a telegram to Mao:

> The Tibet Local Government as well as the ecclesiastic and secular people unanimously support this agreement, and under the leadership of Chairman Mao and the Central People's Government, will actively support the People's Liberation Army in Tibet to consolidate national defense, drive out imperialist influences from Tibet and safeguard the unification of the territory and the sovereignty of the Motherland.[54]

A few days later, on 28th October, the Panchen Rinpoché made a similar public statement accepting the agreement. He urged the "people of Zhigatsé to give active support" to carrying out the agreement.[55]

The National Assembly and the Dalai Lama's acceptance of the Seventeen-Point Agreement ended the independence Tibet had enjoyed since 1911. Tibet became a region of China. The most vocal supporters of the agreement came from the monastic community: they felt that the agreement gave a guarantee that Tibet's traditional social system would not be altered and that the Chinese had no interest but to secure their symbolic claim over Tibet. Tibet's traditional elite was governed by narrow self-interest. The preservation of the existing social order (which safeguarded their power and privileges) was seen as synonymous with the legal status of Tibet.

In the end for the Tibetan elite the Seventeen-Point Agreement to some extent met the need to safeguard Tibet's cultural and social independence. The agreement guaranteed that (1) the existing political system would function as before; (2) the power and privileges of the ruling elite would be protected; and (3) religious freedom would be protected. Moreover, the agreement did not even mention the words "socialism" or "communism." It merely stated that "various reforms" would be carried out according to the local conditions and the wishes of the Tibetan people. As a result many Tibetans were willing to accept the agreement.

Finally there were strong factions in Tibet who felt that the agreement was acceptable and that Communist China and Buddhist Tibet could co-exist peacefully. This section was led by the religious community, whose main concern was the protection of the "existing system." The Tibetans' acceptance was not based on a legal interpretation of the agreement, which transformed Tibet's international legal status from one of an independent state to a region of China. In the Tibetans' view their independence was not a question of international legal status, but as Dawa Norbu writes, "Our sense of independence was based on the independence of our way of life and culture, which was more real to the unlettered masses than law or history, canons by which the non-Tibetans decide the fate of Tibet."[56]

However, in the final analysis, it must be recognized that the Chinese would not have secured the agreement had they confined themselves to diplomatic means. As we have seen, the Tibetans were determined initially to maintain their independence. It was only after the Chinese had invaded and the Tibetans' attempts to secure international support had failed that Tibet was forced to seek a dialogue with the Chinese. Once the Chinese had shown their military might the Tibetans had no choice but to reach a diplomatic compromise. This was the first formal agreement between Tibet and Communist China and it established the legal basis for Chinese rule in Tibet.

NOTES

1. Some Western governments refused to attend these functions as a protest against the abuse of human rights in Tibet.

2. "How the Tibetan Reactionaries Sabotaged the 17-Article Agreement," *Peking Review* (May 1959):16–19.

3. A statement issued by the Dalai Lama at a Press Conference held in Mussoorie on 20th June 1959.

4. Nga phod Ngag dbang 'jigs med, *Rang skyong ljongs mi dmangs 'thus tshogs rgyun mthud kyi kru'u rin nga phod ngag dbang 'jigs med kyis rang skyong ljongs kyi skabs lnga pa'i mi dmangs 'thus tshogs du thengs gnyis pa'i thog gnang ba'i gal che'i gsungs bshad* [Ngapö Ngawang Jikmé's Speech at the Second Plenary Session of the Fifth Tibet Autonomous Region's Congress] (Lhasa, 1989).

5. I have been told that the speech was published in the *Tibet Daily*, but I have not seen a published copy. The copy in my possession is a typeset copy marked for internal distribution only.

6. Thub bstan bstan dar, Lha'u rta ra, "Bod zhi bas bcings 'grol 'byung thabs skor gyi gros than tshan bcu bdun la ming rtags bkod pa'i sngon rjes su" [The 17-Point Agreement for the Peaceful Liberation of Tibet], in *Bod kyi rig gnas lo rgyus rgyu cha bdam bsgrigs*, vol. 1, ed. Bod rang skyong ljongs chab gros lo rgyus rig gnas dpyad gzhi'i rgyu cha U yon lhan khang (Lhasa: Bod ljongs mi dmangs dpe skrun khang, 1982), 88–117.

7. Bstan 'dzin rgyal mtshan, *Lha'u rta ra'i lo rgyus* [History of Lhautara] (Dharamsala: Library of Tibetan Works and Archives, 1988).

8. Bsod nams dbang 'dus, Khe smed, *Rgas po'i lo rgyus 'bel gtam* [Tale of an Old Man] (Dharamsala: Library of Tibetan Works and Archives, 1982).

9. Bstan 'dzin don grub, Bsam 'grab po brang, *Mi tshe'i rba rlabs 'khrugs po* [The Agitated Waves of Life] (Rajpur: privately published, 1987).

10. See Robert Ford, "Foreign Relations of the United States," *East Asia* 6 (1951): 1696–1743.

11. For details of Shakabpa's Mission to Britain, see "1948 Tibetan Trade Mission to United Kingdom: An Essay in Honour of Tsipon Shakabpa," *The Tibet Journal* 15, no. 4 (1990): 97–114.

12. Here I have used the term "priest and patron" as used by Tsepon W. D. Shakabpa in his book *Tibet: A Political History* (New Haven: Yale University Press, 1967), 229. Generally the term "priest and patron" gives a misleading rendering of the Tibetan term *mchod yon*. For a discussion on the topic, see D. Seyfort Ruegg, "*Mchod yon, yon mchod* and *mchod gnas/yon gnas*: On the Historiography and Semantics of a Tibetan Religio-social and Religio-political Concept," in *Tibetan History and Language*, ed. E. Steinkellner (Vienna: G. Uray Festschrift, 1991), 440–453.

13. Shakabpa writes that he was given a booklet, and does not seem to be aware that it was actually the "Common Programme" and that articles 50–53 were the basis of the Communist policy towards minority groups.

14. Dbang phyug bde ldan, Zhwa sgab pa, *Bod kyi srid don rgyal rabs: An Advanced Political History of Tibet*, 2 vols. (Kalimpong: T. Tsepal, Taikhang, 1976), 2:420.

15. Zhwa sgab pa, *An Advanced Political History of Tibet*; in Tibetan, "*bod ming tsam gyi rgyal khongs zhal bzhes gnang rgyu.*" The term *ming tsam* (only in name) is used as a rendering of the Western term "suzerainty."

16. Public Record Office, London, FO 371–84469.

17. Soon after the Chinese invasion the Regent Taktra was ousted from power and on 17th November 1951 the Fourteenth Dalai Lama assumed full political power.

18. Nga phod Ngag dbang 'jigs med, *Speech at . . . the Fifth Tibet Autonomous Region's Congress.*

19. The eight-point proposal was recorded in the monthly report (15th December 1950) from the Indian Mission in Lhasa. Public Record Office, London, DO (Dominion Office) 35/3096.

20. Public Record Office, London, DO (Dominion Office) 35/3096.

21. Public Record Office, London, DO (Dominion Office) 35/3096.

22. Lu'o Yus hung, "Bod zhi bas bcings 'grol skor gyi nyin tho gnad bshus," *Bod kyi rig gnas lo rgyus rgyu cha bdam bsgrigs,* vol. 1, ed. Bod rang skyong ljongs chab gros lo rgyus rig gnas dpyad gzhi'i rgyu cha U yon lhan khang (Lhasa: Bod ljongs mi dmangs dpe skrun khang, 1982), 117–170.

23. Takla Püntsok Trashi, "The Seventeen-Point Agreement Between Tibet and China in 1951," unpublished paper, 1991.

24. Nga phod Ngag dbang 'jigs med, *Speech at . . . the Fifth Tibet Autonomous Region's Congress.*

25. Thub bstan bstan dar, "The 17-Point Agreement for the Peaceful Liberation of Tibet," 104. This account of the meeting was confirmed by Takla Püntsok Trashi. Indian records of the meeting slightly differ from the account given by Lhautara. The Indian records make no mention of Tibet's request for the Government of India (GOI) to mediate between China and Tibet.

26. Thub bstan bstan dar, "The 17-Point Agreement for the Peaceful Liberation of Tibet."

27. In Tibetan, "nang khul du rang btsan rang bdag."

28. Nga phod Ngag dbang 'jigs med, *Speech at . . . the Fifth Tibet Autonomous Region's Congress.*

29. Nga phod Ngag dbang 'jigs med, *Speech at . . . the Fifth Tibet Autonomous Region's Congress.*

30. Nga phod Ngag dbang 'jigs med, *Speech at . . . the Fifth Tibet Autonomous Region's Congress.*

31. Thub bstan bstan dar, "The 17-Point Agreement for the Peaceful Liberation of Tibet," 105.

32. Interview with Takla Püntsok Trashi.

33. A writer with long experience of negotiating with the Chinese noted, "It can be argued that limiting the agenda in one's favor is a common tactic of international negotiations and no monopoly of the Chinese. Yet the Chinese seem to attach a special importance to the agenda, and the intensity with which they insist on the inclusion or exclusion of certain subjects surprises many international negotiators. Agreement to put a subject on the agenda seems to imply to the Chinese a certain concession on the matter. The Chinese do not share the view widely held in western countries that agreement on the agenda does not necessarily prejudice the nature of a negotiation." Oguru Kazuo, "How the 'Inscrutables' Negotiate with the 'Inscrutables': Chinese Negotiating Tactics *vis-à-vis* the Japanese," *The China Quarterly* 79 (1979): 528–552. The Tibetans' experience seems to confirm Oguru Kazuo's statement. For the Chinese to

place the question of the status of Tibet on the agenda would be seen as recognizing Tibet's separate identity. As far as the Chinese were concerned, Tibet was an integral part of the PRC and it did not matter what the Tibetans thought about their status.

34. On words such as "the People" and "Liberation," see Huang Mingxin, "The Tibetan Version of the 17-Article Agreement," *China's Tibet* (Autumn 1991):12–15. It is interesting to note that author writes, "In the Tibetan language, there was no word which meant 'China.' When the Tibetans use the word, '*Rgya nag*' this excludes the Tibetans, and explicitly recognizes Tibetan separateness from China."

35. Thub bstan bstan dar, "The 17-Point Agreement for the Peaceful Liberation of Tibet," 106–107. In his account published in Tibet Lhautara does not mention the incident. However, he writes that, as instructed by the Kashak, he objected to the deployment of the PLA in Tibet and therefore the meeting broke down for several days.

Accounts published in India by members of the delegation agree that the meeting broke down because of Lhautara's questioning and Li Weihan's statement. See Bstan 'dzin don grub, *The Agitated Waves of Life*, 109. A biography of Lhautara by his former secretary Tendzin Gyeltsen (Bstan 'dzin rgyal mtshan, *History of Lhautara*, 20–21) also confirms the threat made by Li Weihan. In an interview Püntsok Trashi Takla also concurred this account.

36. Jiang Ping, "Great Victory for the Cause of National Unity and Progress," *China's Tibet* (Spring 1991):8–9.

37. Nga phod Ngag dbang 'jigs med, *Speech at . . . the Fifth Tibet Autonomous Region's Congress*.

38. Nga phod Ngag dbang 'jigs med, *Speech at . . . the Fifth Tibet Autonomous Region's Congress*.

39. Jiang Ping, "Great Victory for the Cause of National Unity and Progress," 8.

40. Nga phod Ngag dbang 'jigs med, *Speech at . . . the Fifth Tibet Autonomous Region's Congress*.

41. Kazuo, "Chinese Negotiating Tactics *vis-à-vis* the Japanese," 535.

42. Nga phod Ngag dbang 'jigs med, *Speech at . . . the Fifth Tibet Autonomous Region's Congress*.

43. Nga phod Ngag dbang 'jigs med, *Speech at . . . the Fifth Tibet Autonomous Region's Congress*.

44. Pala Tupten Woden, Oral History Collection of the Library of Tibetan Works and Archives, Dharamsala.

45. Bstan 'dzin rgya mtsho, The Dalai Lama, *My Land and My People* (1962; reprint, New York: Potala Corp., 1985), 88.

46. Nga phod Ngag dbang 'jigs med, *Speech at . . . the Fifth Tibet Autonomous Region's Congress*.

47. There are two grounds on which an agreement could be rejected: (1) if it can be shown that duress was applied to the individual members of the delegation and (2) if that delegation exceeded their instructions or acted at variance with them. It is difficult to argue that the individual members of the Tibetan delegation were coerced. However, the second argument could be applied to this case. Though Ngapö himself

had written that he was instructed to consult Dromo before signing any agreement, clearly he did not do so.

48. Thub bstan bstan dar, "The 17-Point Agreement for the Peaceful Liberation of Tibet," 110–111.

49. Shokang Soinam [Sönam] Dagyal, "Escorting the Representative of the Central Government to Tibet," *China's Tibet* (Spring 1991):12–14.

50. Interview with Takla Püntsok Trashi.

51. Nga phod Ngag dbang 'jigs med, *Speech at . . . the Fifth Tibet Autonomous Region's Congress.*

52. Nga phod Ngag dbang 'jigs med, *Speech at . . . the Fifth Tibet Autonomous Region's Congress.*

53. Interview with Takla Püntsok Trashi.

54. *Tibet: Myth vs. Reality* (Beijing: Beijing Review Publications, 1988), 134.

55. *Tibet: Myth vs. Reality*, 135–137. Statement by Bainqen Erdini and Officials of the Bainqen Kambu Liji.

56. Dawa Norbu, "Tibetan Response to Chinese Liberation," *Asian Affairs* 62 (1975): 266.

FULL REFERENCES TO ORIGINAL ARTICLES

PART I. THE PREHISTORY OF THE TIBETAN PLATEAU

1. Mark Aldenderfer and Zhang Yinong, "The Prehistory of the Tibetan Plateau to the Seventh Century A.D.: Perspectives and Research from China and the West Since 1950," *Journal of World History* 18, no. 1 (2004): 1–55. Excerpts. Reprinted with kind permission from Springer Science and Business Media.

2. Bryan Cuevas, "Some Reflections on the Periodization of Tibetan History," *Revue d'Etudes Tibétaines* 10 (April 2006): 44–55.

3. Peter Schwieger, "Geschichte als Mythos: Zur Aneignung von Vergangenheit in der Tibetischen Kultur: Ein Kulturwissenschaftlicher Essay" [History as Myth: On the Appropriation of the Past in Tibetan Culture: An Essay in Cultural Studies], *Asiatische Studien* 54, no. 4 (2000): 945–974. Translated for this volume by Alison Moffat.

PART II. IMPERIAL TIBET (SEVENTH TO TENTH CENTURIES)

NARRATIVES OF TIBETAN ORIGINS

4. Matthew Kapstein, "Remarks on the *Mani Bka' 'bum* and the Cult of Avalokiteśvara in Tibet," in *Reason and Revelation*, ed. Steven Goodman and Ronald Davidson (Albany: SUNY Press, 1992), 79–94 (notes on 163–169). Reprinted by permission from the State University of New York Press © 1992. State University of New York. All Rights Reserved.

5. David Seyfort Ruegg, "On the Tibetan Historiography and Doxography of the 'Great Debate of Samyé,'" in *Tibetan Studies: Proceedings of the 5th Seminar of the International Association for Tibetan Studies, Narita 1989*, ed. Ihara Shören and Yamaguchi Zuihö (Narita-shi, Chiba-Ken, Japan: Naritasan Shinshoji, 1992), vol. 1, 237–244.

IMPERIAL POLITICS

6. Fang Kuei Li and W. South Coblin, *A Study of Old Tibetan Inscriptions* (Nang-kang: Academia Sinica, 1987), chapters 1 and 2, 3–24.
7. Christopher I. Beckwith, "The Tibetans in the Ordos and North China: Consider-ations on the Role of the Tibetan Empire in World History," in *Silver on Lapis: Tibetan Literary Culture and History*, ed. Christopher I. Beckwith (Bloomington: The Tibet Society, 1987), 3–12.

PART III. TIBETAN REVIVALS (TENTH TO
TWELFTH CENTURIES)

8. Tsutomu Iwasaki, "The Tibetan Tribes of Hexi and Buddhism During the North-ern Song Period," *Acta Asiatica* 64 (1993): 17–37.
9. David Snellgrove, "Rulers of Western Tibet," in *Indo-Tibetan Buddhism: Indian Buddhists and Their Tibetan Successors* (Boston: Shambhala, 1987), vol. 1.
10. Per Kværne, *The Bon Religion of Tibet* (Boston: Shambhala, 2001), 9–23.
11. R. A. Stein, "The Evolution of Monastic Power," in *Tibetan Civilization* (Stanford: Stanford University Press, 1972), 70–83. Translated by J. E. Stapleton Driver. Copy-right © 1972 by Faber and Faber Ltd. Used by permission of the publisher.

PART IV. LAMAS AND PATRONS: TIBET AND THE MONGOLS
(THIRTEENTH TO FOURTEENTH CENTURIES)

12. David Seyfort Ruegg, "The Preceptor-Donor (Yon Mchod) Relation in Thirteenth-Century Tibetan Society and Polity, Its Inner Asian Precursors and Indian Models," in *Tibetan Studies: Proceedings of the 7th Seminar of the International Association for Tibetan Studies*, ed. Ernest Steinkellner (Graz: Verlag der Österreichischen Akedemie der Wissenschaften, 1997), vol. 2, 857–872.
13. Luciano Petech, "The Mongol Census in Tibet," in *Tibetan Studies in Honour of Hugh Richardson: Proceedings of the International Seminar on Tibetan Studies, Oxford, 1979*, ed. Michael Aris and Aung San Suu Kyi (Warminster, England: Aris & Phillips, 1980), 233–238.
14. David P. Jackson, "Sakya Paṇḍita's Letter to the Tibetans: A Late and Dubious Ad-dition to His Collected Works," *The Journal of the Tibet Society* 6 (1986): 17–24.

PART V. CENTERS OF POWER AND RELIGIOUS LEARNING (FOURTEENTH TO EIGHTEENTH CENTURIES)

15. Luciano Petech, "Rise of Phag mo gru," in *Central Tibet and the Mongols: The Yüän-Sakya Period of Tibetan History* (Rome: Istituto Italiano per il Medio ed Estremo Oriente, 1990), 119–137.
16. Turrell V. Wylie, "Monastic Patronage in 15th-Century Tibet," *Acta Orientalia* 34 (1980): 319–328.
17. Giuseppe Tucci, "Gtsang Against Dbus," in *Tibetan Painted Scrolls* (Roma: Libreria dello Stato, 1949), 46–57.
18. Elliot Sperling, "The Ho Clan of Hezhou: A Tibetan Family in Service to the Yuan and Ming Dynasties," in *Indo-sino-tibetica: Studi in Onore di Luciano Petech* (Roma: Bardi, 1990), 359–377.
19. The Central Tibetan extract is from Samten G. Karmay and Yasuhiko Nagano, eds., compiled by Dodrup Lhagyal et al., *A Survey of Bonpo Monasteries and Temples in Tibet and the Himalaya* (Osaka: National Museum of Ethnology, 2003), 1–9. The Eastern Tibetan extract is from Samten Gyaltsen Karmay, *Feast of the Morning Light: The Eighteenth-Century Wood-engravings of Shenrab's Life-stories and the Bon Canon from Gyalrong* (Osaka: National Museum of Ethnology, 2005), 1–8.

PART VI. MODERN TIBET (SEVENTEENTH TO TWENTIETH CENTURIES)

CENTRAL TIBETAN LEADERSHIP

20. Leonard W. J. van der Kuijp, "The Dalai Lamas and the Origins of Reincarnate Lamas," in *The Dalai Lamas: A Visual History*, ed. Martin Brauen (Chicago: Serindia, 2005), 14–31.
21. Kurtis R. Schaeffer, "The Fifth Dalai Lama Ngawang Lopsang Gyatso," in *The Dalai Lamas: A Visual History*, ed. Martin Brauen (Chicago: Serindia, 2005), 64–91.
22. Janet Gyatso, a revised version of "The Authority of Empiricism and the Empiricism of Authority: Medicine and Buddhism in Tibet on the Eve of Modernity," *Comparative Studies of South Asia, Africa and the Middle East* 24 (2) (2004): 83–96. Copyright 2004, All Rights Reserved. Reprinted by permission of the publisher.

TIBET AND THE MANCHUS

23. Luciano Petech, "The Administration of Tibet During the First Half-Century of Chinese Protectorate" and "Conclusion," in *China and Tibet in the Early Eighteenth Century* (Leiden: Brill, 1972), 217–243.
24. Katō Naoto, "Lobjang Danjin's Rebellion of 1723," *Acta Asiatica: Bulletin of the Institute of Eastern Culture* 64 (1993): 57–80.
25. Luciano Petech, *Aristocracy and Government in Tibet: 1728–1959* (Rome: Istituto Italiano per il Medio ed Estremo Oriente, 1973), 3–21.

TRADE AND COMMERCE

26. Luce Boulnois, "Gold, Wool and Musk: Trade in Lhasa in the Seventeenth Century," in *Lhasa in the Seventeenth Century: The Capital of the Dalai Lamas*, ed. Françoise Pommaret (Leiden: Brill, 1983), 133–156.
27. Melvyn C. Goldstein, "The Circulation of Estates in Tibet: Reincarnation, Land and Politics," *Journal of Asian Studies* 32, no. 3 (1973): 445–455. Copyright © 1973 by the Association of Asian Studies. All Rights Reserved. Reprinted with the permission of Cambridge University Press.
28. Wim van Spengen, "The Geo-History of Long-Distance Trade in Tibet 1850–1950," *Tibet Journal* 20, no. 2 (1995): 18–63. Abridged.

INSTITUTIONAL GROWTH BEYOND CENTRAL TIBET

29. Revised extract from Lauran Hartley, "A Socio-Historical Study of the Kingdom of Sde-dge (Derge, Kham) in the Late Nineteenth Century: Ris-med Views of Alliance and Authority," M. A. thesis, Indiana University, 1997, 7–35. Edited for this volume and reprinted with permission of the author.
30. Paul Nietupski, "Labrang in History," *Labrang: A Tibetan Buddhist Monastery at the Crossroads of Four Civilizations* (Ithaca, N.Y.: Snow Lion, 1999), 15–25.

TIBET IN A GLOBAL CONTEXT

31. Gray Tuttle, "Uniting Religion and Politics in a Bid for Autonomy: Lamas in Exile in China and America," in *Buddhist Missionaries in the Era of Globalization*, ed. Linda Learman (Honolulu: University of Hawai'i Press, 2005), 210–232. Copyright © 2005 University of Hawai'i Press.
32. Heather Stoddard, "Progressistes et exiles" [Progressives and Exiles], in *Le Mendiant de l'Amdo* [*The Beggar from Amdo*] (Nanterre: Société d'ethnographie, 1985), 69–94. Translated for this volume by Veronique Martin.
33. Tsering Shakya, "The Genesis of the Sino-Tibetan Agreement of 1951," in *Tibetan Studies: Proceedings of the 6th Seminar of the International Association for Tibetan Studies, Fagernes, 1992*, ed. Per Kværne (Oslo: Institute for Comparative Research in Human Culture, 1994), 739–754.

BIBLIOGRAPHY

NON-ASIAN LANGUAGES REFERENCES

Adshead, S. A. M. *Province and Politics in Late Imperial China: Viceregal Government in Szechwan, 1891–1911*. Scandinavian Institute of Asian Studies Monograph Series, no. 50. London and Malmo: Curzon Press, 1984.

Ahmad, Zahiruddin, trans. *Life of the Fifth Dalai Lama*, vol. 4, Teil 1. New Delhi: Aditya Prakashan, 1999.

——, trans. *A History of Tibet by the Fifth Dalai Lama of Tibet*. Bloomington: Indiana University, Research Institute for Inner Asian Studies, 1995.

Aldenderfer, Mark. "Domestic *rdo-ring*? A New Class of Standing Stone from the Tibetan Plateau." *Tibet Journal* 28 (2004): 1–23.

——. "Early Human Occupations of the Tibetan Plateau and Andean Altiplano." Paper presented at the American Association for the Advancement of Science, Seattle, Wa., 2004.

——. "Archaeology and Ethnicity in Far Western Tibet: The Evidence from Dindun." In *Discoveries in Western Tibet and the Western Himalayas: Essays on History, Literature, Archaeology and Art: PIATS 2003, Tibetan Studies, Proceedings of the Tenth Seminar of the International Association for Tibetan Studies, Oxford, 2003*, ed. A. Heller and G. Orofino. Leiden: Brill, 2003.

——. "Moving up in the World: Archaeologists Seek to Understand How and When People Came to Occupy the Andean and Tibetan Plateaus." *American Scientist* 91, no. 6 (2003): 542–550.

——. "Piyang: A 10th/11th C A.D. Tibetan Buddhist Temple and Monastic Complex in Far Western Tibet." *Archaeology, Ethnology & Anthropology of Eurasia* 4, no. 8 (2001): 138–146.

——. "Roots of Tibetan Buddhism." *Archaeology* 54, no. 53 (2001): 610–612.

——. "The Pleistocene/Holocene Transition in Peru and Its Effects Upon the Human Use of the Landscape." *Quaternary International* 53, no. 4 (1999): 11–19.

——. *Montane Foragers: Asana and the South-Central Andean Archaic.* Iowa City: University of Iowa Press, 1998.

Aldenderfer, M. and H. Moyes. "Excavations at Dindun: A Pre-Buddhist Village Site in Far Western Tibet." In *Essays of the International Conference on Tibetan Archaeology and Art*, ed. W. Huo and Y. Li. Chengdu, China: Center for Tibetan Studies, Sichuan Union University, 2004, 47–69.

Allix, A. "The Geography of Fairs." *Geographical Review* 12 (1922): 532–569.

Amiot, Joseph Marie, et al. *Mémoires concernant l'histoire, les sciences, les arts, les mœurs, les usages, &c. des Chinois* [Memoirs on the History, Sciences, Arts, Customs, Habits and So Forth of the Chinese]. Paris: Nyon, 1776.

An, Z., et al. "Paleoliths and Microliths from Shenja and Shuanghu, Northern Tibet." *Current Anthropology* 23, no. 5 (1982): 493–499.

Andrugtsang, Gompo Tashi. *Four Rivers, Six Ranges: Reminiscences of the Resistance Movement in Tibet.* Dharamsala: Information and Publicity Office of H.H. the Dalai Lama, 1973.

Archives of Propaganda Fide, Rome, *Scr. Congressi*, vol. 20.

Ardussi, John and Michael Aris. "Foreword." In *Tibetan Histories: A Bibliography of Tibetan-Language Historical Works*, ed. Dan Martin and Yael Bentor. London: Serindia, 1997, 9–12.

Aris, Michael. *Lamas, Princes and Brigands: Joseph Rock's Photographs of the Tibetan Borderlands of China.* New York: China House Gallery, China Institute of America, 1992.

——. *Hidden Treasures and Secret Lives: A Study of Pemalingpa (1450–1521) and the Sixth Dalai Lama (1683–1706).* London: Kegan Paul, 1989.

Aris, Michael, Wa-gindra, and Bstan 'dzin chos rgyal. *Sources for the History of Bhutan.* Wiener Studien zur Tibetologie und Buddhismuskunde, Heft 14. Vienna: Arbeitskreis für Tibetische und Buddhistische Studien, Universität Wien, 1986.

Assmann, Jan. *Religion and Cultural Memory.* Trans. Klaus Hansen. Stanford: Stanford University Press, 2006.

Avalokiteśvaraguṇa-Kāraṇḍavyūhaḥ. In *Mahāyānasūtrasaṃgrahah*, Buddhist Sanskrit Texts No. 17, ed. P. L. Vaidya. Darbhanga, 1961.

Avedon, John. *In Exile from the Land of Snows.* New York: Knopf, 1984.

Aziz, Barbara N. *Tibetan Frontier Families: Reflections of Three Generations from Dingri.* New Delhi: Vikas Publishing House, 1978.

Baber, Edward Colburne. *Travels and Researches in Western China.* Royal Geographical Society Supplementary Papers, vol. 1, part 1. London: John Murray, 1882.

Bacot, Jacques, F. W. Thomas, and Ch. Toussaint. *Documents de Touen-houang relatifs à l'histoire du Tibet* [Dunhuang Documents Concerning the History of Tibet]. Paris: P. Geuthner, 1940.

Bailey, F. M. *No Passport to Tibet.* London: Rupert Hart-Davis, 1957.

———. *China—Tibet—Assam: A Journey*, 1911. London: Jonathan Cape, 1945.

———. "Journey Through a Portion of South-Eastern Tibet and the Mishmi Hills." *The Geographical Journal* 34, no. 4 (1912): 334–347.

Bazin, Nathalie, ed. *Rituels Tibétains: visions secrètes du Ve Dalaï Lama* [*Tibetan Rituals: Secret Visions of the 5th Dalai Lama*]. Paris: Réunion des Musées Nationaux, 2002.

Becker, Andrea. "Eine chinesische Beschreibung von Tibet aus dem 18. Jahrhundert" [A Chinese Description of Tibet from the Eighteenth Century]. Ph.D. diss., Ludwig-Maximilians-Universität (München), 1976.

Beckwith, Christopher I. *The Tibetan Empire in Central Asia*. Princeton: Princeton University Press, 1993.

———. "Tibetan Science at the Court of the Great Khans." *Journal of the Tibetan Society* 7 (1987): 5–11.

———. "The Revolt of 755 in Tibet." In *Contributions on Tibetan Language, History and Culture. Wiener Studien zur Tibetologie und Buddhismuskunde* 10, vol. 1, ed. Ernst Steinkellner and Helmut Tauscher. Wien: Arbeitskreis für Tibetische und Buddhistische Studien, Universität Wien, 1983, 1–16.

———. "The Introduction of Greek Medicine Into Tibet in the Seventh and Eighth Centuries." *Journal of the American Oriental Society* 99, no. 2 (1979): 297–313.

Bell, Charles Alfred. *The Religion of Tibet*. 1928; reprint, New Delhi: Motilal Banarsidass, 1992.

———. *Portrait of the Dalai Lama*. London: Collins, 1946.

———. *The Religion of Tibet*. 1931; reprint, Oxford: Clarendon Press, 1946.

———. *The People of Tibet*. London: Oxford University Press, 1928.

———. "A Year in Lhasa." *The Geographical Journal* 63, no. 2 (1924): 89–101.

Bellezza, J. *Antiquities of Upper Tibet: Pre-Buddhist Archaeological Sites on the High Plateau. Findings of the Upper Tibet Circumnavigation Expedition, 2000*. Delhi: Adroit Publishers, 2002.

———. *Antiquities of Northern Tibet, Pre-Buddhist Archeological Discoveries on the High Plateau, Findings of the Changthang Circuit Expedition, 1999*. Delhi: Adroit Publishers, 2001.

———. "Buddhist Archaeological Sites in Northern Tibet: An Introductory Report on the Types of Monuments and Related Literary and Oral Historical Sources." *Kailash* 19, no. 1–2 (2000): 1–142.

Bernbaum, Edwin. *The Way to Shambhala: A Search for the Mythical Kingdom Beyond the Himalayas*. New York: Anchor Press/Doubleday, 1980.

Bhardwaj, Surinder Mohan. *Hindu Places of Pilgrimage: A Study in Cultural Geography*. Berkeley: University of California Press, 1973.

Bird, Isabella L. *The Yangtze Valley and Beyond: An Account of Journeys in China, Chiefly in the Province of Sze Chuan and Among the Man-tze of the Somo Territory*. London: J. Murray, 1899.

Blondeau, Anne-Marie. "Le 'Découvreur' du *Maṇi bka' 'bum* était-il Bon po?" In *Tibetan and Buddhist Studies*, ed. Louis Ligeti, vol. 1. Budapest: Akadémiai Kiado, 1984, 77–123.

———. "Le *Lha 'dre bka' thang*." In *Études Tibétaines dediées à la mémoire de Marcelle Lalou*. Paris: Maisonneuve, 1971, 29–126.

——. "Les pèlerinages tibétains" [Tibetan Pilgrimages]. In *Sources Orientales*, vol. 3, *Les pèlerinages*. Paris: Editions du Seuil, 1960, 203–245.

Boeck, Kurt. *Durch Indien ins verschlossene Land Nepal. Ethnographische und photographische Studien Blätter* [*Through India to Isolated Nepal: Ethnographic Studies and Photographic Sheets*]. Leipzig: Verlag von Ferdinand Hirt und Sohn, 1903.

Bogle, George. *Memorandum on the Money and Merchandise of Tibet (of April 19th, 1779)*. In D. B. Diskalkar, "Bogle's Embassy to Tibet," *The Indian Historical Quarterly* 9 (1933): 431–432.

Borgeaud, P. "Le couple sacré/profane" [The Couple: Sacred/Profane]. *Revue de l'histoire des religions* 211, no. 4 (1994): 387–418.

Bosshard, W. "Politics and Trade in Central Asia." *Journal of the Central Asian Society* 16, no. 4 (1929): 447–448.

Boulnois, Luce. *Poudre d'or et monnaies d'argent au Tibet (principalement au XVIIIe siècle)* [*Powdered Gold and Silver Coins in Tibet (Principally in the Eighteenth Century)*]. Paris: Editions du Centre national de la recherche scientifique, 1983.

Bower, Hamilton. *Diary of a Journey Across Tibet*. London: Rivington, Percival and Co., 1894.

Boyle, John Andrew, trans. *The Successors of Genghis Khan*. New York: Columbia University Press, 1971, 241.

Brantingham, P. Jeffrey, et al. "Speculation on the Timing and Nature of Late Pleistocene Hunter-gatherer Colonization of the Tibetan Plateau." *Chinese Science Bulletin* 48, no. 14 (2003): 1510–1516.

——. "The Initial Upper Paleolithic in Northeast Asia." *Current Anthropology* 42 (2001): 735–747.

Brantingham, P. J., John W. Olsen, and George B. Schaller. "Lithic Assemblages from the Chang Tang Region, Northern Tibet." *Antiquity* 75 (2001): 319–327.

Braudel, Fernand. *Civilisation matérielle, économie et capitalisme: XVe–XVIIe siècle* [*Material Culture, Economy and Capitalism: 15th–17th Centuries*], vol. 3. Paris: Armand Colin, 1979.

——. *La Méditerranée et le monde méditerranéen à l'époque de Philippe II* [*The Mediterranean and the Mediterranean World in the Age of Philip II*], vol. 2, seconde édition revue et augmentée. Paris: Librairie Armand Colin, 1966.

Brauen, Martin, ed. *Peter Aufschneiter: sein Leben in Tibet* [*Peter Aufschneiter: His Life in Tibet*]. Innsbruck: Steiger Verlag, 1983.

Bray, John. "The Lapchak Mission from Ladakh to Lhasa in British Indian Foreign Policy." *The Tibet Journal* 15, no. 4 (1990): 75–96.

Bronk-Ramsey, C. "OxCal Program v3.8." In *Radiocarbon Accelerator Unit*. Oxford: University of Oxford, 2002.

Broughton, Jeffrey. "Early Chan Schools in Tibet." In *Studies in Ch'an and Hua-yen*, ed. Robert M. Gimello and Peter N. Gregory. Honolulu: University of Hawai'i Press, 1983, 1–68.

Brown, Charles W. "The Goat Is Mine, the Load Is Yours": Morphogenesis of 'Bhotiya-Shauka' U.P., India." Ph.D. diss., University of Lund, Lund Studies in Social Anthropology no. 1. 1984.

Brown, Peter. "The First Modern East Asians?: Another Look at Upper Cave 101, Liujiang, and Minatogawa 1." In *Interdisciplinary Perspectives on the Origins of the*

Japanese, ed. K. Omoto. Kyoto, Japan: International Research Center for Japanese Studies, 1999, 105–130.

Bstan 'dzin rgya mtsho, Dalai Lama XIV. *Freedom in Exile: The Autobiography of the Dalai Lama*. San Francisco: HarperPerennial, 1991.

——. *My Land and My People*. 1962; reprint, New York: Potala Corp., 1985.

——. *My Land and My People*. New York: McGraw-Hill, 1962.

Burrard, Sidney Gerald. *Records of the Survey of India*, vol. 8., part I. Dehra Dun: Office of the Trigonometrical Survey, 1915.

Burridge, Kenelm. *Someone, No One: An Essay on Individuality*. Princeton: Princeton University Press, 1979.

Bu ston Rin chen grub. *History of Buddhism (Chos-ḥbyung)*. Trans. E. Obermiller. Heidelberg: In kommission bei O. Harrassowitz, 1931–32.

Cable, M., et al. *The Challenge of Central Asia*. London: World Dominion Press, 1929.

Calhoun, A. B. "Burma: An Important Source of Precious and Semi-precious Stones." *Engineering and Mining Journal* 127, no. 18 (1929).

Campbell, Archibald. "Note on the Valley of Choombi." *Journal of the Royal Asiatic Society* N. S. 7, 1875.

Cammann, Schuyler V. R. *The Land of the Camel: Tents and Temples of Inner Mongolia*. New York: Ronald Press, 1951.

——. *Trade Through the Himalayas: The Early British Attempts to Open Tibet*. Princeton: Princeton University Press, 1951.

Carey, A. D. "A Journey Round Chinese Turkistan and Along the Northern Frontier of Tibet." *Proceedings of the Royal Geographical Society* 9, no. 12 (1887): 731–752.

Carey, W. *Travel and Adventure in Tibet. Including the Diary of Miss Annie R. Taylor's Remarkable Journey from Taochao to Tachienlu Through the Heart of the Forbidden Land*. London: Hodder and Stoughton, 1902.

Carr, David. *Time, Narrative and History*. Bloomington: Indiana University Press, 1986.

Cassinelli, Charles William and Robert Brainerd Ekvall. *A Tibetan Principality*. Ithaca, N.Y.: Cornell University Press, 1969.

Cavalli-Sforza, L. Luca. "The Chinese Human Genome Diversity Project." *Proceedings of the National Academy of Sciences of the United States of America* 95 (1998): 11501–11503.

Chakrabarty, P. B. "The Unknown Country of Golok-Setas." *Tibetan Review* 17, no. 5 (1982): 18–20.

Chan, Victor. *Tibet Handbook*. Chico, Calif.: Moon Publications, 1994.

Chandola, Khemanand. *Across the Himalayas: A Study of Relations Between Central Himalayas and Western Tibet*. Delhi: Patriot Publishers, 1987.

Chang, D. H. S. "The Vegetation Zonation of the Tibetan Plateau." *Mountain Research and Development* 1, no. 1 (1981): 29–48.

Chang, Kwang Chih. *The Archaeology of Ancient China*. New Haven: Yale University Press, 1986.

Chattopadhyaya, Alaka. *Atīśa and Tibet: Life and Works of Dīpaṃkara Śrījñāna in Relation to the History and Religion of Tibet*. Calcutta: Indian Studies: Past & Present, 1967.

Chayet, Anne. *Art et Archéologie du Tibet* [*Art and Archeology of Tibet*]. Paris: Picard, 1994.

Chen, C. "The Microlithic of China." *Journal of Anthropological Archaeology* 1, no. 3 (1984): 79–115.

Chen, C. and Wang, X. "Upper Paleolithic Microblade Industries in North China and Their Relationships with Northeast Asia and North America." *Arctic Anthropology* 26, no. 2 (1989): 144–145.

Chen, Hanseng. *Frontier Land Systems in Southernmost China: A Comparative Study of Agrarian Problems and Social Organization Among the Pai Yi People of Yunnan and the Kamba People of Sikang.* New York: International Secretariat, Institute of Pacific Relations, 1949.

Chu, J., et al. "Genetic Relationships of Populations in China." *Proceedings of the National Academy of Sciences of the United States of America* 95 (1998): 11763–11768.

Chung, K. "On Zhangzhung." *Bulletin of the Institute of History and Philology Academia Sinica* 4 (1960): 137–154.

Clarke, G. E. *China's Reforms of Tibet, and Their Effects on Pastoralism.* Brighton: Institute of Development Studies, Discussion Paper, no. 237, 1987.

Coales, O. "Economic Notes on Eastern Tibet." *The Geographical Journal* 54, no. 4 (1919): 242–247.

Coleman, Graham. *A Handbook of Tibetan Culture.* London: Rider, 1993.

Combe, G. A. *A Tibetan on Tibet.* London: T. Fisher Unwin, 1926.

Cooper, Thomas Thornville. *Travels of a Pioneer of Commerce in Pigtail and Petticoats: or, an Overland Journey from China Towards India.* London: John Murray, 1871.

Courant, Maurice. *L'Asie centrale aux XVIIe et XVIIIe siècles empire kalmouk ou empire mantchou?* [*Central Asia in the 17th and 18th Centuries: Kalmyk Empire or Manchu Empire?*] Lyon: A. Rey, imprimeur-éditeur; Paris: Librairie A. Picard & fils, 1912.

Crone, Patricia. *Pre-industrial Societies: New Perspectives on the Past.* Oxford: Blackwell, 1989.

Cullen, Christopher. "*Yi'an*: The Origins of a Genre of Chinese Medical Literature." In *Innovation in Chinese Medicine*, ed. Elizabeth Hsu. Cambridge: Cambridge University Press, 2001, 297–323.

Cüppers, Christoph. "A Letter Written by the Fifth Dalai Lama to the King of Bhaktapur." *Journal of the Nepal Research Center* 12 (2001): 39–42.

Cutting, Suydam. *The Fire Ox and Other Years.* New York: Charles Scribner's Sons, 1940.

Dabringhaus, Sabine. *Das Qing-Imperium als Vision und Wirklichkeit: Tibet in Laufbahn und Schriften des Song Yun (1752–1835)* [*The Qing Empire as Vision and Reality: Tibet in the Life and Writings of Song Yun (1752–1835)*]. Stuttgart: Franz Steiner Verlag, 1994.

Dagron, G. *Empereur et pêtre.* Paris, 1995. [Also available in English: *Emperor and Priest: The Imperial Office in Byzantium.* Cambridge: Cambridge University Press, 2003].

Dardess, John W. *Conquerors and Confucians: Aspects of Political Change in Late Yuan China.* New York: Columbia University Press, 1973.

Das, Sarat Chandra. *A Tibetan-English Dictionary.* 1902; reprint, Delhi: Motilal Banarsidass, 1973.

———. "Tibet Under the Tartar Emperors of China in the 13th Century." *Journal of the Asiatic Society of Bengal* (1905): 94–102.

———. *A Journey to Lhasa and Central Tibet.* London: John Murray, 1904.

———. "Tibetan Jails and Criminal Punishments." *Journal of the Asiatic Society of Bengal* (1894):5–8.

Datta, C. L. *Ladakh and Western Himalayan Politics, 1819–1848: The Dogra Conquest of Ladakh, Baltistan, and West Tibet, and Reactions of the Other Powers.* New Delhi: Munshiram Manoharlal Publishers, 1973.

———. "Significance of the Shawl-wool Trade in Western Himalayan Politics." *Bengal Past and Present* 84, no. 1 (1965): 16–28.

David-Néel, Alexandra. "Les marchands tibétains [Tibetan Merchants]: Part I." *France-Asie* 9, no. 83 (1953): 284–293.

———. "Les marchands tibétains [Tibetan Merchants]: Part II." *France-Asie* 9, no. 84 (1953): 398–409.

———. *With Mystics and Magicians in Tibet.* London: Penguin, 1936.

———. *La vie surhumaine de Guésar de Ling* [*The Superhuman Life of Gesar of Ling*]. Paris: Adyar, 1935.

Davidson, Ronald M. *Tibetan Renaissance: Tantric Buddhism in the Rebirth of Tibetan Culture.* New York: Columbia University Press, 2005.

Deasy, Henry Hugh Peter. *In Tibet and Chinese Turkestan.* London: T. Fisher Unwin, 1901.

Demiéville, Paul. "Récents travaux sur Touen-houang" [Recent Work on Dunhuang]. *T'oung Pao* 56, no. 1/3 (1970).

———. "Deux documents de Touen-houang sur le Dhyâna chinois" [Two Dunhuang Documents on Chinese Dhyāna]. In *Essays on the History of Buddhism Presented to Professor Zenryu Tsukamoto.* Kyoto: Nagai Shuppansha, 1961.

———. *Le concile de Lhasa* [*The Council of Lhasa*]. Paris: Institut Hautes Etudes Chinoises, 1952.

Denwood, Philip. "Notes on Some Bonpo Rituals." In *Buddhist Studies: Ancient and Modern,* ed. Philip Denwood and Alexander Piatigorsky. London: Curzon Press; Totowa, N.J.: Barnes & Noble, 1983, 12–19.

Desgodins, C. H. *Le Thibet d'après la correspondance des missionaires* [*Tibet, from the Correspondence of Missionaries*]. Paris: Librairies Catholique de l'Oeuvre de Saint-Paul, 1885.

Diskalkar, D. B. "Bogle's Embassy to Tibet." *The Indian Historical Quarterly* 9 (1933): 431–432.

Dondrup Lhagyal. "Bonpo Family Lineages in Central Tibet." In *New Horizons in Bon Studies,* ed. Samten Gyaltsen Karmay and Yasuhiko Nagano. Osaka: National Museum of Ethnology, 2000, 429–508.

Doolaard, A. Den. *Prinsen, priesters en paria's: Reizen door India en Thailand* [*Princes, Priests and Pariahs: Travel Through India and Thailand*]. Amsterdam: Em. Querido's Uitgeverij, 1962.

Dowman, Keith. *The Power-places of Central Tibet: The Pilgrim's Guide.* London: Routledge and Kegan Paul, 1988.

Dreyer, Edward L. and Hok-lam Chan. "Tengyu." In *Dictionary of Ming Biography,* ed. L. Carrington Goodrich and Chaoying Fang. New York: Columbia University Press, 1976, 1277–1280.

Drompp, Michael. "The Writings of Li Te-yü as Sources for the History of T'ang-Inner Asian Relations." Ph.D. diss., Indiana University, 1989.

Dudjom Rinpoche, Jikdrel Yeshe Dorje. *The Nyingma School of Tibetan Buddhism.* Trans. G. Dorjé and M. Kapstein. vol. 1. London: Wisdom, 1991.

Duncan, M. H. *The Yangzi and the Yak: Adventurous Trails in and out of Tibet.* Alexandria, Va. and Ann Arbor, Mich.: Edwards Brothers, 1952.

Edgar, J. H. "Notes on Trade Routes Converging at Tachienlu." *Journal of the West China Border Research Society* 4 (1930–31): 5–8.

Edgar, J. W. *Report on a Visit to Sikhim and the Thibetan Frontier.* Calcutta: Bengal Secretariat Press, 1874.

Edgerton, F. *Buddhist Hybrid Sanskrit Dictionary.* Delhi: Motilal Banarsidass, 1998.

Eimer, Helmut. *Rnam thar rgyas pa: Materialien zu einer Biographie des Atiśa (Dīpaṃkaraśrījñāna)* [*Materials for a Biography of Atiśa*]. 2 vols. Wiesbaden: Harrassowitz, 1979.

——. *Bodhipathapradīpa: Ein Lehrgedicht des Atiśa (Dīpaṃkaraśrījñāna), in der tibetischen Überlieferung* [*Bodhipathapradīpa: A Doctrinal Poem of Atiśa*]. Wiesbaden: Harrassowitz, 1978.

——. *Berichte über das Leben des Atiśa (Dīpaṃkaraśrījñāna): Eine Untersuchung der Quellen* [*Reports on the Life of Atiśa*]. Wiesbaden: Harrassowitz, 1977.

Ekvall, Robert B. *Fields on the Hoof: Nexus of Tibetan Nomadic Pastoralism.* New York: Holt, Rinehart and Winston, 1968.

——. "Some Differences in Tibetan Land Tenure and Utilization." *Sinologica* 4, no. 1 (1954): 39–48.

——. *Cultural Relations on the Gansu-Tibetan Border.* Chicago: University of Chicago Press, 1939.

Elston, R. and P. J. Brantingham. "Microlithic Technology in Northern Asia: A Risk-Minimizing Strategy of the Late Paleolithic and Early Holocene." In *Thinking Small: Global Perspectives on Microlithization,* ed. Robert Elston and Steven Kuhn. Washington, D.C.: Archaeological Papers of the American Anthropological Association 12, 2002, 103–116.

Emmerick, R. E. "Sources of the *Four Tantras.*" *Zeitschrift der Deutschen Morgenländischen Gesellschaft* 3, no. 2 (1977): 1135–1142.

Etler, D. "The Fossil Evidence for Human Evolution in Asia." *Annual Review of Anthropology* 25 (1996): 275–301.

Fairbank, J. K. and S. Y. Têng. "On the Ch'ing Tributary System." *Harvard Journal of Asiatic Studies* 6 (1941): 135–246.

Farquhar, David. "Emperor as Bodhisattva in the Governance of the Qing Empire." *Harvard Journal of Asian Studies* 38, no. 1 (1978): 5–34.

Ferrari, A. *Mkhyen brtse's Guide to the Holy Places of Central Tibet.* Roma: Istituto italiano per il Medio ed Estremo, 1958.

Filchner, Wilhelm. *Kumbum Dschamba Ling: Das Kloster der hunderttausend bilder Maitreyas* [*Kumbum Jamba Ling: The Monastery of One Hundred Thousand Maitreya Images*]. Leipzig: F. A. Brocjhaus, 1933.

——. *Om mani padme hum: meine China- und Tibet expedition, 1925/28* [*Om mani padme hum: My China and Tibet Expedition, 1925/28*]. Leipzig: F. A. Brockhaus, 1929.

——. *Das Kloster Kumbum in Tibet: Ein Beitrag zu seiner Geschichte* [*The Kumbum Monastery in Tibet: A Contribution to Its History*]. Berlin: Ernst Siegfried Mittler und Sohn, 1906.

Fisher, Margaret Welpley, Leo E. Rose, and Robert A. Huttenback. *Himalayan Battleground: Sino-Indian Rivalry in Ladakh.* New York: Praeger, 1963.

Fletcher, Joseph F. "A Brief History of the Chinese Northwestern Frontier." In *China's Inner Asian Frontier: Photographs of the Wulsin Expedition to Northwest China in 1923*, ed. M. E. Alonso. Cambridge, Mass.: The Peabody Museum of Archaeology and Ethnology, Harvard University 1979.

Ford, Robert. *Captured in Tibet.* 1957; reprint, Hong Kong: Oxford University Press, 1990.

——. "Foreign Relations of the United States." *East Asia* 6 (1951): 1696–1743.

Franke, Herbert. *Geld und Wirtschaft in China unter der Mongolen-Herrschaft* [*Money and Economy in China Under Mongol Rule*]. Leipzig: Harrassowitz, 1949.

Franke, Herbert and Denis Crispin Twitchett. *Alien Regimes and Border States, 907–1368.* Cambridge History of China, vol. 6. New York: Cambridge University Press, 1994.

Francke, August Herrmann, ed. and trans. *Antiquities of Indian Tibet, Part II: The Chronicles of Ladakh and Minor Chronicles.* 1926; reprint, New Delhi, Madras: Superintendent Government Printing, 1992.

——. *Antiquities of Indian Tibet.* Calcutta: S. Chand & Co., Ltd., 1926.

——. *Antiquities of Indian Tibet.* Archaeological Survey of India 38, Part 1: Personal Narrative. Calcutta: Superintendent Government Printing, 1914.

——. *A History of Western Tibet: One of the Unknown Empires.* London: S. W. Partridge & Co., 1907.

von Fürer-Haimendorf, Christoph. *Himalayan Traders: Life in Highland Nepal.* London: J. Murray, 1975.

Fürholzer, E. *Arro! Arro! So sah ich Tibet* [*Aro! Aro! The Tibet I Saw*]. Berlin: Wilhelm Limpert-Verlag, 1942.

Futterer, K. "Geographische Skizze von Nordost-Tibet" [Geographical Sketch of Northeast Tibet]. *Ergänzungsheft zu Petermanns Geogr. Mitteilungen* 143 (1903).

——. "Land und Leute in Nordost-Tibet" [Land and People in Northeast Tibet]. *Zeitschrift der Gesellschaft für Erdkunde, Berlin* 35, no. 5 (1900).

Gaborieau, Marc. "Pouvoirs et autorité des soufis dans l'Himalaya" [The Powers and Authority of the Sufis in the Himalayas]. In *Prêtrise, pouvoirs et autorité en Himalaya* [*The Priesthood: Their Powers and Authority in the Himalayas*], ed. Véronique Bouillier and Gérard Toffin, vol. 12. Paris: EHESS, collection Purusârtha, 1989, 215–238.

——. *Récit d'un voyageur musulman au Tibet* [*Story of a Muslim Traveler to Tibet*]. Paris: Librairie Klincksieck, 1973.

Gai, P. "Microlithic Industries in China." In *Paleoanthropology and Paleolithic Archaeology in the People's Republic of China*, ed. Rukang Wu and John W. Olsen. New York: Academic Press, 1985, 225–242.

Garrett, Frances and Vincanne Adams. "The Three Channels in Tibetan Medicine." *Traditional South Asian Medicine* 8 (2008): 86–114.

Gasse, F., J. Fontes, E. Van Campo, and K. Wei. "Holocene Environmental Changes in Bangong Co. Basin (Western Tibet)." *Paleogeography, Paleaoclimatology, Palaeoecology* 120 (1996): 79–92.

Gerard, A. *Account of Koonawur in the Himalaya.* London: James Madden and Co., 1841.

Gill, William John. *The River of Golden Sand: The Narrative of a Journey Through China and Eastern Tibet to Burma.* 2 vols. London: John Murray, 1880.

——. "Travels in Western China and on the Eastern Border of Tibet." *The Journal of the Royal Geographical Society* 48 (1878).

Goertz, Hans-Jürgen. *Umgang mit Geschichte: Eine Einführung in die Geschichtstheorie [Handling History: An Introduction to Theory of History].* Reinbek bei Hamburg: Rowohlt Taschenbuch Verlag, 1995.

Goodrich, L. Carrington and Chaoying Fang, eds. *Dictionary of Ming Biography.* New York: Columbia University Press, 1976.

Goldstein, Melvyn. *The Snow Lion and the Dragon: China, Tibet, and the Dalai Lama.* Berkeley: University of California Press, 1997.

——. *A History of Modern Tibet, 1913–1951: The Demise of the Lamaist State.* 1989; reprint, Delhi: Bishen Singh Mahendra Pal Singh, 1993.

——. *A History of Modern Tibet, 1913–1951: The Demise of the Lamaist State.* Berkeley: University of California Press, 1989.

——. "On the Nature of the Tibetan Peasantry: A Rejoinder." *Tibet Journal* 13, no. 1 (1988): 61–65.

——. "On the Political Organization of Nomadic Pastoralists in Western Tibet: A Rejoinder to Cox." *Himalaya Research Bulletin* 8, no. 3 (1988): 15–17.

——. "Serfdom and Mobility: An Examination of the Institution of 'Human Lease' in Traditional Tibetan Society." *Journal of Asian Studies* 30, no. 3 (1971): 521–534.

——. "Taxation and the Structure of a Tibetan Village." *Central Asiatic Journal* 15, no. 1 (1971): 1–27, 170–182.

Goldstein, Melvyn C. and C. M. Beall. *Nomads of Western Tibet: The Survival of a Way of Life.* London: Serindia, 1989.

Goldstein, Melvyn and Matthew Kapstein, eds. *Buddhism in Contemporary Tibet: Religious Revival and Cultural Identity.* Berkeley: University of California Press, 1998.

Goodrich, L. Carrington and Chaoying Fang, eds. *Dictionary of Ming Biography.* New York: Columbia University Press, 1976.

Goswami, S. "The Opium Evil in Nineteenth-Century Assam." *The Indian Economic and Social History Review* 19, no. 3–4 (1982): 365–376.

Goullart, Peter. *Forgotten Kingdom.* London: John Murray, 1955.

Graham, D. C. "A Trip to Tatsienlu." *Journal of the West China Border Research Society* 2 (1924–1925), 33–37.

Greatrex, Roger. "A Brief Introduction to the First Jinchuan War (1747–1749)." In *Tibetan Studies: Proceedings of the 6th Seminar of the IATS Fagernes 1992,* ed. Per Kværne. Oslo: The Institute for Comparative Research in Human Culture, 1994, 247–263.

Gregory, J. W. and C. J. Gregory. *To the Alps of Chinese Tibet.* London: Seeley Service and Co., 1923.

Grossberg, Lawrence, et. al, eds. *Cultural Studies.* London: Routledge, 1992.

Guenther, Herbert V. "Review: Mahāmudrā. Lobsang P. Lhalungpa." *Journal of the American Oriental Society* 109, no. 1 (1989): 151.

——. "'Meditation' Trends in Early Tibet." In *Early Chan in China and Tibet*, ed. W. Lai and L. Lancaster. Berkeley: Asian Humanities Press, 1983.

——. *The Life and Teaching of Nāropa: Translated from the Original Tibetan with a Philosophical Commentary Based on the Oral Transmission.* Oxford: Clarendon Press, 1963.

Guibaut, André. *Ngolo-Setas: Deuxième expedition, Guibaut-Liotard au Tibet, 1940* [*Ngolo-Seta: The Second Guibaut-Liotard Expedition in Tibet, 1940*]. Paris: J. Susse, 1947.

Gyatso, Janet. "The Authority of Empiricism and the Empiricism of Authority: Medicine and Buddhism in Tibet on the Eve of Modernity." *Comparative Studies of South Asia, Africa, and the Middle East* 24, no. 2 (2004): 83–96.

——. "Healing Burns with Fire: The Facilitations of Experience in Tibetan Buddhism." *Journal of the American Academy of Religion* 67, no. 1 (1999): 113–147.

——. *Apparitions of the Self: The Secret Autobiographies of a Tibetan Visionary.* Princeton: Princeton University Press, 1998.

——. "The Logic of Legitimation in the Tibetan Treasure Tradition." *History of Religions* 33, no. 1 (1993): 97–134.

Haarh, Erik. *The Yarlung Dynasty.* Denmark: University of Copenhagen, 1969.

——. *The Zhang-zhung Language: A Grammar and Dictionary of the Unexplored Language of the Tibetan Bonpos.* Acta Jutlandica. XL:1. Humanistisk serie 47. Aarhus: Universitetsforlaget i Aarhus, 1968.

——. "The Identity of Tsu-chih-chien, the Tibetan 'King' Who Died in 804 A.D." *Acta Orientalia* 25 (1960): 121–170.

Hackmann, Heinrich. *Vom Omi bis Bhamo: Wanderungen an den Grenzen von China, Tibet und Birma* [*From Omi to Bhamo: Walks on the Borders of China, Tibet, and Burma*]. Berlin: Karl Curtius, 1907.

Hagen, T. *Nepal: The Kingdom of the Himalayas.* London: Robert Hale and Company, 1972.

Hambis, Louis. *Documents sur l'histoire des Mongols à l'époque des Ming* [*Documents on the History of the Mongols in the Ming Period*]. Paris: Presses universitaires de France, 1969.

Hamilton, Francis Buchanan. *An Account of the Kingdom of Nepal and the Territories Annexed to This Dominion by the House of Gorkha.* Edinburgh: Archibald Constable and Co., 1819.

Hanbury-Tracy, John. *Black River of Tibet.* London: Frederick Muller Ltd., 1938.

Hansen, Klaus P. *Kultur und Kulturwissenschaft: Eine Einführung* [*Culture and Cultural Studies: An Introduction*]. Tübingen: Francke Verlag, 1995.

Hanson, Andrew D., et al. "Upper Upper Oligocene Lacustrine Source Rocks and Petroleum System of the Northern Qaidam Basin, NW China." *American Association of Petroleum Geologists Bulletin* 85, no. 4 (2001): 601–619.

Harrer, Heinrich. "My Life in Forbidden Lhasa." *The National Geographic Magazine* 108, no. 1 (1955).

——. *Sieben Jahre in Tibet* [*Seven Years in Tibet*]. Wien: Ullstein, 1952.

Harrison, Paul. "A Brief History of the Tibetan Kangyur." In *Tibetan Literature: Studies in Genre*, ed. José Ignacio Cabezón and Roger R. Jackson. Ithaca, N.Y.: Snow Lion, 1996, 70–94.

Hedin, S. *Southern Tibet: Discoveries in Former Times Compared with My Own Researches in 1906–08* (Band I–IX). Stockholm: Lithographic Institute of the General Staff of the Swedish Army, 1917–1922.

———. *Trans-Himalaya: Discoveries and Adventures in Tibet*. London: Macmillan and Co., 1910–1913.

Heim, A. *Minya Gongkar: Forschungsreise ins Hochgebirge von Chinesisch Tibet* [*Minya Gongkar: Expedition Into the High Mountains of China's Tibet*]. Bern-Berlin: Verlag Hans Huber, 1933.

Heinrich, Klaus. "Funktion der Genealogie im Mythos" ["The Function of Genealogy in Myth"]. In *Parmenides und Jona*, 1982, S. 11–28, 163–167, abgedruckt in: ders., *Vernunft und Mythos: Ausgewählte Texte* [*Reason and Myth: Selected Texts*], Frankfurt: Fischer Taschenbuch Verlag 1983, 11–26.

Hermanns, M. *Die Nomaden von Tibet. Die sozial-wirtschaftlichen Grundlagen der Hirtenkulturen in Amdo und von Innerasien: Ursprung und Entwicklung der Viehzucht*. [*The Nomads of Tibet. The Socioeconomic Underpinnings of the Shepherding Culture of Amdo and Inner Asia: The Origin and Development of Animal Husbandry*]. Wien: Verlag Herold, 1949.

Heron, A. M. "The Gem-stones of the Himalaya." *The Himalayan Journal* 2 (1930): 21.

Hobsbawm, Eric J. *Nations and Nationalism Since 1780: Programme, Myth, Reality*. Cambridge: Cambridge University Press, 1992.

Hobsbawm, Eric and Terence Ranger, eds. *The Invention of Tradition*. New York: Cambridge University Press, 1992.

Hoffmann, Helmut. *Tibet: A Handbook*. Bloomington, Ind.: Research Institute for Inner Asian Studies, 1986.

———. *Tibet: A Handbook*. Bloomington, Ind.: Research Institute for Inner Asian Studies, 1976.

———. *Tibet: A Handbook*. Bloomington: Indiana University, 1975.

———. *The Religions of Tibet*. London: George Allen and Unwin, 1961.

———. *Die Religionen Tibets: Bon und Lamaismus in ihrer geschichtlichen Entwicklung* [*The Religions of Tibet: Bon and Lamaism in Their Historical Development*]. Freiburg: K. Alber, 1956.

Hosie, A. *Report on a Journey to the Eastern Frontier of Thibet*. London: His Majesty's Stationery Office, 1905.

———. *Three Years in Western China: A Narrative of Three Journeys in Ssu-chúan, Kuei-chow, and Yün-nan*. London: G. Philip & Son, 1890.

Huang, W. "The Prehistoric Human Occupation of the Qinghai-Xizang Plateau." *Götinger Geographische Abhandlungen* 95 (1994): 201–219.

Huc, Evariste Régis. *Travels in Tartary, Thibet and China, 1844–1846*. Trans. William Hazlitt. Ed. Paul Pelliot. New York: Harper & Bros., 1928.

Hucker, Charles O. *A Dictionary of Official Titles in Imperial China*. Stanford: Stanford University Press, 1985.

Huth, Georg, ed. and trans. *Geschichte des Buddhismus in der Mongolei: Aus dem Tibetischen des Jigs-med nam-mk'a* [sic: 'Jigs med rig pa'i rdo rje] *herausgegeben* [*History of Buddhism in Mongolia*]. 2 vols. Strassburg: K. J. Trübner, 1892, 1896.

Imaeda, Yoshiro. "Note Préliminaire sur la formule *Oṃ Maṇi Padme Hūṃ* dans les Manuscrits Tibétains de Touen Houang" [A Preliminary Note on the Formula

Oṃ Maṇi Padme Hūṃ in Tibetan Manuscripts of Dunhuang]. In *Contributions aux études sur Touen Houang*. Genève, Paris: Droz, 1979, 71–76.

——. "Documents Tibétains de Touen-Houang concernant le concile du Tibet" [Tibetan Documents from Dunhuang Concerning the Tibetan Council]. *Journal Asiatique* (Paris: Société asiatique) 1975:125–46.

Institute of Archaeology, Chinese Academy of Social Science and Bureau of Cultural Relics, Tibet Autonomous Region. *Qugong in Lhasa: Excavations of an Ancient Site and Tombs*. 1999. (In Chinese with an English abstract.)

Ishihama, Yumiko. "On the Dissemination of the Belief in the Dalai Lama as a Manifestation of the Bodhisattva Avalokiteśvara." *Acta Asiatica* 64 (1993): 38–56.

——. "A Study of the Seals and Titles Conferred by the Dalai Lamas." In *Tibetan Studies: Proceedings of the 5th Seminar of the International Association for Tibetan Studies, Narita 1989*, vol. 2. Narita: Naritasan Shinshoji, 1992, 501–514.

Ishihama, Yumiko and Yoichi Fukuda, eds. *A New Critical Edition of the Mahavyutpatti: Sanskrit-Tibetan-Mongolian Dictionary of Buddhist Terminology*. Studia Tibetica, No. 16, Materials for Tibetan-Mongolian Dictionaries, Vol. 1. Tokyo: Toyo Bunko, 1989.

Israel, Jonathan I. *Radical Enlightenment: Philosophy and the Making of Modernity 1650–1750*. Oxford: Oxford University Press, 2001.

Iwasaki, Tsumoto. "A Study of Ho-xi Tibetans During the Northern Song Dynasty." *Memoirs of the Research Department of the Toyo Bunko* 44 (1986): 57–132.

Jackson, Anthony. *Na-khi Religion: An Analytical Appraisal of the Na-khi Ritual Texts*. Religion and Society, Vol. 8. The Hague; New York: Mouton, 1979.

Jackson, David P. *The Entrance Gate for the Wise (Section III): Sa skya Paṇḍita on Indian and Tibetan Traditions of Pramana and Philosophical Debate*. Wiener Studien zur Tibetologie und Buddhismuskunde. Vol. 17, 2 parts. Wien: Arbeitskreis für Tibetische und Buddhistische studien Universität Wien, 1987.

Jacobsen-Tepfer, E., V. D. Kubarev, and D. Tseveendorj. *Mongolie du Nord-Ouest: Tsagaan Salaa/Baga Oigor. Répertoire des Pétroglyphes d'Asie centrale* [*Mongolia of the Northwest: Tsagaan Salaa/Baga Oigor. Index of Central Asian Petroglyphs*], Fascicule no. 6, 2 vols., ed. Jakov A. Sher and Henri-Paul Francfort. Paris: De Boccard, 2001.

Jacquemont, Victor. *Correspondance de V. Jacquemont avec sa famille et plusieurs de ses amis pendant son voyage dans l'Inde (1828–1832)* [*Correspondence of V. Jacquemont with His Family and Several of His Friends During His Voyage in India (1828–1832)*]. Bruxelles: Wouters, Raspoet et Cie, Imprimeurs-Libraires, 1843.

Jamyang Norbu. *Warriors of Tibet: The Story of Aten, and the Khampas' Fight for the Freedom of Their Country*. London: Wisdom, 1986.

Jäschke, H. A. *A Tibetan-English Dictionary: with Special Reference to the Prevailing Dialects: to Which Is Added an English-Tibetan Vocabulary*. 1881; reprint, Delhi: Motilal Banarsidass, 1980.

Jest, Corneille. "Valeurs d'échange en Himalaya et au Tibet: l'ambre et le musc" [Exchange Values in the Himalayas and Tibet: Amber and Musk]. In *De la voûte céleste au terroir, du jardin au foyer*. Paris: Editions de l'Ecole des Hautes Etudes en Sciences Sociales, 1987, 228–230.

Jian, Ni. "A Simulation of Biomes on the Tibetan Plateau and Their Responses to Global Climatic Change." *Mountain Research and Development* 20 (2000): 80–89.

Kämpfe, Rainer. "Die Innere Mongolei von 1691 bis 1911" [Inner Mongolia from 1691 to 1911]. In *Die Mongolen: Beiträge zu ihrer Geschichte und Kultur* [*The Mongols: Examinations of Their History and Culture*], ed. Michael Weiers. Darmstadt: Wissenschaftliche Buchgesellschaft, 1986.

Kapstein, Matthew T. "The Indian Literary Identity in Tibet." In *Literary Cultures in History*, ed. Sheldon Pollock. Berkeley: University of California Press, 2003.

——. "Remarks on the *Mani bka' 'bum* and the Cult of Avalokiteśvara in Tibet." In *Tibetan Buddhism: Reason and Revelation*, ed. Ronald Davidson and Steven D. Goodman. Albany: SUNY Press, 2000, 79–93.

——. "The Purificatory Gem and Its Cleansing." *History of Religions* 28, no. 3 (Feb. 1989): 217–44.

——. "The Limitless Ocean Cycle." In *Soundings in Tibetan Civilization: Proceedings of the 1982 Seminar of the International Association for Tibetan Studies*, ed. Barbara Nimri Aziz and Matthew T. Kapstein. Delhi: Manohar, 1985, 358–371.

Karmay, Samten G. *Feast of the Morning Light: The Eighteenth-Century Woodengravings of Shenrab's Life-stories and the Bon Canon from Gyalrong*. Senri ethnological reports, 57. Osaka: National Museum of Ethnology, 2005.

——. "The Rituals and Their Origins in the Visionary Accounts of the 5th Dalai Lama." In *Religion and Secular Culture in Tibet: Tibetan Studies: Proceedings of the Ninth Seminar of the International Association for Tibetan Studies, Leiden 2000*, ed. Henk Blezer and A. Zadok. Brill's Tibetan Studies Library, v. 2/2. International Association for Tibetan Studies. Leiden: Brill, 2002, 21–40.

——. "The Four Tibetan Medical Treatises and Their Critics." Reprinted in *The Arrow and the Spindle: Studies in History, Myths, Rituals and Beliefs in Tibet*. Kathmandu: Mandala Book Point, 1998, 228–237.

——. *The Arrow and the Spindle: Studies in History, Myths, Rituals and Beliefs in Tibet*. Kathmandu: Mandala Book Point, 1998.

——. *The Little Luminous Boy: The Oral Tradition from the Land of Zhangzhung Depicted on Two Tibetan Paintings*. Bangkok: Orchid Press, 1998.

——. "A Pilgrimage to Kongpo Bon-ri." In *Tibetan Studies: Proceedings of the 5th Seminar of the International Association for Tibetan Studies, Narita 1989*. Ed. International Association for Tibetan Studies, Shōren Ihara, and Zuihō Yamaguchi. Monograph series of Naritasan Institute for Buddhist Studies, 2. Narita-shi, Chiba-Ken, Japan: Naritasan Shinshoji, 1992, 527–539.

——. "The Decree of the Khro chen King." *Acta Orientalia* 51 (1990): 141–159.

——. *The Great Perfection*. Leiden: Brill, 1988.

——. *Secret Visions of the Fifth Dalai Lama: The Gold Manuscript in the Fournier Collection*. London: Serindia, 1988.

——. "An Open Letter to Pho brang Zhi ba 'od." *The Tibet Journal* 5, no. 3 (1980): 1–28.

——. "The Ordinance of lHa Bla ma Ye shes 'od." In *Tibetan Studies in Honour of Hugh Richardson: Proceedings of the International Seminar on Tibetan Studies,*

Oxford, 1979, ed. Michael Aris and Aung San Suu Kyi. Warminster: Aris & Phillips, 1980, 150–160.

———. *The Treasury of Good Sayings: A Tibetan History of Bon*. London: Oxford University Press, 1972.

Karmay, Samten and Philippe Sagant. *Les neuf forces de l'homme: récits des confins du Tibet* [*The Nine Forces of Man: Stories from the Borders of Tibet*]. Nanterre: Société d'ethnologie, 1998.

Kaschewsky, Rudolf. *Das Leben des Lamaistischen Heiligen Tsong kha pa Blo bzang grags pa (1357–1419)* [*The Life of the Lamaist Saint Tsongkhapa Lozang Drakpa (1357–1419)*]. Asiatische Forschungen, Band 32, 2 vols. Wiesbaden: O. Harrassowitz, 1971.

Kawaguchi, Ekai. *Three Years in Tibet*. Madras: The Theosophist Office, 1909.

Kaznakov, A. H. "Moi Puti po Mongolii i Kamu." In *Mongoliia i Kam: Trudy ekspeditsii Imperatorskago Russkago geograficheskago obshchestva, sovershennoi v 1899–1901*, vol. 2, 1st ed., ed. P. K. Koslov. St. Petersburg: Gerold, 1907.

Kessler, Peter. *Laufende Arbeiten zu einem ethnohistorischen Atlas Tibets (EAF) 40,1. Die historischen Königreiche Ling und Derge* [*Ongoing Work Toward an Ethnohistorical Atlas of Tibet (EAF) 40,1, the Historic Kingdoms Ling and Derge*]. XI, 143 S.: Ill., Kt. + 2 Beil., 2 Kt.-Beil. Rikon/Zürich: Tibet-Inst, 1983.

Khazanov, Anatoly M. *Nomads and the Outside World*. Cambridge: Cambridge University Press, 1984.

Kingdon-Ward, F. "Tibet as a Grazing Land." *The Geographical Journal* 110, no. 1–3 (1948): 60–75.

Köhler, G. "Die Bedeutung des Huang Ho innerhalb des nordwest-chinesischen Verkehrsnetzes" [The Importance of Huang He Within the Northwestern Chinese Traffic System]. *Petermanns Geographische Mitteilungen* 96 (1952): 85–89.

Kollmar-Paulenz, Karénina. *Erdeni tunumal neretü sudur: die Biographie des Altan qagan der Tümed-Mongolen: ein Beitrag zur Geschichte der religionspolitischen Beziehungen zwischen der Mongolei und Tibet im ausgehenden 16. Jahrhundert* [*Erdeni tunumal neretü sudur: The Biography of Altan Qagan, Tümed Mongol: A Contribution to the History of the Religious Political Relations Between Mongolia and Tibet at the Turn of the Sixteenth Century*]. Asiatische Forschungen, Bd. 142. Wiesbaden: Harrassowitz, 2001.

Kolmaš, Josef. "The Ambans and Assistant Ambans of Tibet (A Chronological Study)." *Achív orientální*, supplementa VII. Prague: The Oriental Institute, 1994.

———. "Dezhung Rinpoche's Summary and Continuation of the *Sde-dge'i rgyal-rabs*." *Acta Orientalia Academiae Scientiarum Hungaricae* 42, no. 1 (1988): 119–152.

———. "Prague Collection of Tibetan Prints from Derge." *Bulletin of Tibetology* 7, no. 2 (1971): 13–19.

Kozlov, P. K. *Mongoliia i Kam*, vol. 1, 2nd ed. Moskva: Gosudarstvennoe Izdatel'stvo Geograficheskoi Literaturi, 1947.

Kraft, Eva Susanne. *Zum Dsungarenkrieg im 18. Jahrhunder: Berichte des Generals Funingga, aus einer mandschurischen Handschrift übers und an Hand der chinesischen Akten erlaütert* [*On the Zunghar War in the 18th Century: Explanations of*

General Funingga's Reports in Manchu Handwriting . . .]. Leipzig: O. Harras-sowitz, 1953.

Kreitner, Gustav. *Im fernen Osten. Reisen des Grafen Bela Szechenyi in Indien, Japan, China, Tibet und Birma in den Jahren 1877–1880* [*In the Far East. Travels of Count Bela Szechenyi in India, Japan, China, Tibet, and Burma in the Years 1877–1880*]. Wien: Alfred Holder, 1881.

Kuang, Haolin. "On the Temple Economy of the Tibetan Areas in Modern Times." *Social Sciences in China* 12, no. 3 (1991): 123–155.

Kuhle, M. "Reconstruction of the 2.4 km² Late Pleistocene Ice Sheet on the Tibetan Plateau and its Impact of the Global Climate." *Quaternary International* 45/46 (1998): 71–108.

——. "The Pleistocene Glaciation of Tibet and the Onset of the Ice Ages: An Auto-cycle Hypothesis." *GeoJournal* 17 (1988): 581–595.

Kværne, Per. "The Literature of Bön." In *Tibetan Literature: Studies in Genre*, ed. José Ignacio Cabezón and Roger R. Jackson. Ithaca, N.Y.: Snow Lion, 1996, 138–146.

——. "The Bön of Tibet: The Historical Enigma of a Monastic Tradition." In *The Renaissance of Tibetan Civilization*, ed. C. von Fürer-Haimendorf. Oracle, Ariz.: Synergectic Press, 1990, 114–119.

——. "Śākyamuni in the Bon Religion." *Temenos* 25 (1989): 33–40.

——. "Bon." In *The Encyclopedia of Religion*, ed. Mircea Eliade. Vol. 2. New York: Macmillan, 1987, 277–281.

——. "Peintures tibétianes de la vie de Ston-pa-gçen rab" [Tibetan Paintings of the Life of Ston pa gshen rab]. *Arts Asiatiques* XLI (1986): 36–81.

——. "The Canon of the Tibetan Bonpos." *Indo-Iranian Journal* 16, no. 2 (1974).

——. "Aspects of the Origin of the Buddhist Tradition in Tibet." *Numen* 19, no. 1 (1972): 22–40.

——. "A Chronological Table of the Bon po: The bstan rcis of Ñi ma bstan 'jin." *Acta Orientalia* 33 (1971): 205–282.

——. "Remarques sur l'administration d'un monastère bon-po." *Journal Asiatique* 258 (1970): 187–192.

Kværne, Per and Elliot Sperling. "Preliminary Study of an Inscription from Rgyal rong." *Acta Orientalia* 54 (1993), 113–125.

Lalou, Marcelle. "Les Textes Bouddhiques au temps du Roi Khri srong lde bstan" [Buddhist Scriptures at the Time of King Khri srong lde bstan]. *Journal Asiatique* 341 (1953): 313–353.

Lamb, Alastair. *British India and Tibet, 1766–1910*. London and New York: Routledge and Kegan Paul, 1986.

——. *The McMahon Line: A Study in the Relations Between India, China and Tibet, 1904–1914*. London: Routledge and Kegan Paul, 1966.

——. *Britain and Chinese Central Asia: The Road to Lhasa, 1767 to 1905*. London: Routledge and Kegan Paul, 1960.

Lancaster, R. Lewis and Whalen Lai, eds. *Early Chan in China and Tibet*. Berkeley: Asian Humanities Project, 1983.

Lange, Kristina. *Die Werke des Regenten Sangs rgyas rgya mc'o (1653–1705): eine philologisch-historische Studie zum tibetischsprachigen Schrifttum* [*The Works of Re-*

gent Sang rgyas rgya mtsho (1653–1705): A Philological and Historical Study of Tibetan Literature]. Berlin: Akademie-Verlag, 1976.

Laufer, Berthold. "Loan Words in Tibetan." *T'oung Pao*, second series, 17, no. 4/5 (1916): 403–552.

Lehmkuhl, F. "Extent and Spatial Distribution of Pleistocene Glaciations in Eastern Tibet." *Quaternary International* 45/46 (1998): 123–134.

——. "Late Pleistocene, Late-glacial, and Holocene Glacial Advances on the Tibetan Plateau." *Quaternary International* 38/39 (1997): 77–83.

Lehmkuhl, F. and F. Haselein. "Quaternary Paleoenvironmental Change on the Tibetan Plateau and Adjacent Areas (Western China and Western Mongolia)." *Quaternary International* 65/66 (2000): 121–145.

Leroux, Ernest. *Annales du Musée Guimet*. Tome 17, I. 1905.

Lévi, Sylvain. *Le Népal: étude historique d'un royaume hindou* [*Nepal: Historic Study of a Hindu Kingdom*]. Paris: Le Toit de monde; Errance: Armand Colin, 1985.

Lévi-Strauss, Claude. *Strukturale Anthropologie II* [*Structural Anthropology II*]. Frankfurt: Suhrkamp, 1992.

Lewis, T. T. "The Tuladhars of Kathmandu: A Study of Buddhist Tradition in a Newar Merchant Community." Ph.D. diss., Columbia University, 1984.

"Lhasa's New Look." *Peking Review* 41 (1971).

Li Anche. *Labrang: A Study in the Field by Li An Che*. Ed. Chie Nakane. Tokyo: Institute of Oriental Culture, The University of Tokyo, 1994. Also published as: Li An-che, *History of Tibetan Religion: A Study in the Field*. Beijing: New World Press, 1982.

——. "Dege: A Study of Tibetan Population." *Southwest Journal of Anthropology* 3 (1947): 279–293.

Li, Fang-kuei. "Notes on Stag sgra Klu khong." In *Contributions on Tibetan Language, History and Culture*. Wiener Studien zur Tibetologie und Buddhismuskunde 10, vol. 1, ed. Ernst Steinkellner and Helmut Tauscher. Wien: Arbeitskreis für Tibetische und Buddhistische Studien, Universität Wien, 1983, 175–181.

Li, Tieh-Tseng. *Tibet, Today and Yesterday*. New York: Bookman Associates, 1960.

Limpricht, W. *Botanische Reisen in den Hochgebirgen Chinas und Osttibet* [*Botanical Journey in the Highlands of China and Eastern Tibet*]. Dahlem bei Berlin: Verlag des Repertorium, 1922.

Lindegger, Peter. *Griechische und römische Quellen zum peripheren Tibet* [*Greek and Roman Sources on Tibet's Peripheries*]. Opuscula Tibetana, Fasc. 14. Rikon/Zürich: Tibet-Institute, 1982.

Lingat, Robert. *Royautés Bouddhiques: Aśoka et la Fonction Royale a Ceylan* [*Buddhist Kingdoms: Aśoka and the Function of Royalty in Sri Lanka*]. Ed. Gérard Fussman and Eric Meyer. Paris: Editions de l'Ecole des hautes etudes en sciences sociales, 1989.

Lipman, Jonathan N. "Ethnicity and Politics in Republican China: The Ma Family Warlords of Gansu." *Modern China* 10, no. 3 (1984): 285–316.

Liu, J., G. Yu, and X. Chen. "Palaeoclimate Simulation of 21 ka for the Tibetan Plateau and Eastern Asia." *Climate Dynamics* 19 (2002): 575–583.

Lodey Lhawang. "The Conferring of Tibetan Government Ranks on the Chieftans of Golok." *Lungta* 8 (1992): 13–17.

Macauley, C. *Report of a Mission to Sikkim and the Tibetan Frontier.* Calcutta: Bengal Secretariat Press, 1885.

Macdonald, Ariane A. "Un portrait du cinquième Dalaï Lama" [A Portrait of the Fifth Dalai Lama]. In *Essais sur l'art du Tibet,* ed. Ariane MacDonald and Yoshiro Imaeda. Paris: Librairie d'Amérique et d'Orient, 1977, 119–156.

——. "Une Lecture des Pelliot Tibétan 1286, 1287, 1038, 1047, et 1290: Essai sur la formation et l'emploi des mythes politiques dan la religion royale de Sroñ bcan sgam po" [A Reading of the Pelliot Tibetan (Manuscripts) 1286, 1287, 1038, 1047, and 1290: Essay on the Formation and Use of Political Myths in the Royal Religion of Srong btsan sgam po]. *Études Tibétaines* 203 (1971): 190–391.

——. "Préambule à la lecture d'un *Rgya Bod yig can*" [Preamble to the Reading of a Rgya Bod yig tshang]. *Journal Asiatique* 251 (1963): 53–159.

Macdonald, A. W. "Une note sur les mégaliths Tibétains" [A note on Tibetan megaliths]. *Journal Asiatique* 24 (1963): 63–76.

Macdonald, David. *The Land of the Lama.* London: Seeley Service and Co., 1929.

Mackerras, Colin. *The Uighur Empire According to the Tang Dynastic Histories: A Study in Sino-Uighur Relations, 744–840.* Columbia, S.C.: University of South Carolina Press, 1973.

Madsen, D., et al. "Dating Shuidonggou and the Upper Paleolithic Blade Industry in North China." *Antiquity* 75 (2001): 706–716.

Mansier, Patrick. "La guerre du Jinchuan (Rgyal rong): son contexte politico-religieux" [The Jinchuan (Rgyal rong) War: Its Politico-Religious Context]. In *Tibet: Civilisation et société,* ed. Fernand Meyer. Paris: Éditions de la Fondation Singer-Polignac: Éditions de la Maison des Sciences de l'Homme, 1990, 125–142.

Markham, Clements R., George Bogle, and Thomas Manning. *Narratives of the Mission of George Bogle to Tibet and of the Journey of Thomas Manning to Lhasa.* 1876; reprint, Bibliotheca Himalayica, series 1, vol. 6, New Delhi: Mañjuśrī Publishing House, 1971.

Martin, Daniel. "The Emergence of Bon and the Tibetan Polemical Tradition." Ph.D. thesis, Department of Uralic and Altaic Studies, Indiana University, 1991.

Martinez, Matias and Michael Scheffel. *Einführung in die Erzähltheorie* [An Approach to Narrative Theory]. München: C. H. Beck, 1999.

Matisoff, James A. "Sino-Tibetan Linguistics: Present State and Future Prospects." *Annual Review of Anthropolology* 20 (1991): 469–504.

Matthews, Robert Henry. *Matthews' Chinese-English Dictionary.* Rev. American ed. Cambridge: Harvard University Press, 1969.

Mayers, William Frederick and G. M. H. Playfair. *The Chinese Government: A Manual of Chinese Titles, Categorically Arranged and Explained, with an Appendix.* Shanghai: Kelly and Walsh, 1897.

Mehra, Parshotam. *The Younghusband Expedition: An Interpretation.* London: Asia Publishing House, 1968.

Meisezahl, R. O., ed. *Die grosse Geschichte des tibetischen Buddhisus nach alter Tradition rÑiñ ma'i čhos 'byuñ čhen mo* [The Great History of Tibetan Buddhism's Old Tradition Rnying ma'i chos 'byung chen mo]. Monumenta Tibetica Historica, vol. 3. Sankt Augustin: VGH Wissenschaftsverlag, 1985.

Meyer, Fernand. "The Potala Palace of the Dalai Lamas in Lhasa." *Orientations* 18, no. 7 (1987): 14–33.

——. *Gso ba Rig pa: Le système médical tibétain* [*The Tibetan Medical System*]. Paris: Centre national de la recherche scientifique, 1981.

Michael, Franz. *Rule by Incarnation: Tibetan Buddhism and Its Role in Society and State*. Boulder, Colo.: Westview, 1982.

Middleton, Ruth. *Alexandra David-Néel: Portrait of an Adventurer*. Boston: Shambhala, 1989.

Miehe, G. "On the Connexion of Vegetation Dynamics with Climate Changes in High Asia." *Paleogeography, Paleaoclimatology, Palaeoecology* 120 (1996): 5–24.

Migot, Andre. *Tibetan Marches*. Trans. Peter Fleming. London: The Travel Book Club, 1957.

Miller, Roy A. "Review of: A. Róna-Tas, *Tibeto-Mongolica: The Tibetan Loanwords of Monguor and the Development of the Archaic Tibetan Dialects*." *Language* 44, no. 1 (1968): 147–168.

Moorcroft, W. "A Journey to Lake Mánasaróvara in Un-dés, a Province of Little Tibet." *Asiatick Researches* 12 (1818): 447.

Morikawa, Tetsuo. "On the Documents of the Kangxi Period of Köke Qota-yin Tümed Qosigu (The Tümed Banner of Köke Khota)." In *Proceedings of the Fifth East Asian Altaistic Conference, December 26, 1979–January 2, 1980, Taipei, China,* ed. East Asian Altaistic Conference and Chieh-hsien Ch'en. Taipei: National Taiwan University, 1980, 131–139.

Mostaert, Antoine. *Ordosica*. Bulletin of the Catholic University of Peking, no. 9. Peking: Catholic University of Peking, 1934.

Nagano, Yasuhiko. *A Historical Study of the Rgyarong Verb System*. Tokyo: Seishido, 1984.

Naquin, Susan and Chun-fang Yu, eds. *Pilgrims and Sacred Sites in China*. Berkeley: University of California Press, 1980.

Newland, Guy. "Debate Manuals (Yig cha) in dGe lugs Monastic Colleges." In *Tibetan Literature: Studies in Genre,* ed. José Ignacio Cabezón and Roger R. Jackson. Ithaca, N.Y.: Snow Lion, 1996, 217–228.

Ngag dbang blo bzang rgya mtsho. *A History of Tibet*. Trans. Zahiruddin Ahmad. Bloomington: Indiana University Research Institute for Inner Asian Studies, 1995.

Ni, J. "A Simulation of Biomes on the Tibetan Plateau and Their Responses to Global Climate Change." *Mountain Research and Development* 20 (2000): 80–89.

Nietzsche, Friedrich. *Untimely Meditations*. Cambridge: Cambridge University Press, 1997.

Nora, Pierre. *Les lieux de mémoire* [*Places of Memory*]. Paris: Gallimard, 1984.

Nünning, Ansgar. *Metzler Lexikon Literatur- und Kulturtheorie: Ansätze—Personen— Grundbegriffe* [*Metzler Lexikon of Literary and Cultural Theory: Approaches— People—Basic Concepts*]. Stuttgart, Weimar: Metzler, 1998.

Oldfield, H. A. *Sketches from Nepal*. London: W. H. Allen, 1880.

d'Ollone, H. M. G. *Les derniers barbares: Chine, Tibet, Mongolie (Mission d'Ollone 1906–1909)* [*The Last Barbarians: China, Tibet, Mongolia (The Ollone Mission 1906–1909)*]. Paris: Pierre Lafitte, 1911.

Orgyan Topgyal Rinpoché. *Khyentse Özer: International Journal of the Rigpa Fellowship*. Vol. 1 (August). London: Rigpa Fellowship, 1990.

d'Orléans, Henri. *Du Tonkin aux Indes, janvier 1895–janvier 1896* [*From Tonkin to India, January 1895–January 1896*]. Paris: Calmann Lévy, 1898.

Ossendowski, Ferdinand. *Beasts, Men and Gods.* London: Edward Arnold, 1898.

Osterhammel, Jürgen. *China und die Weltgesellschaft; Vom 18. Jahrhundert bis in unsere Zeit* [China and Global Society; from the 18th Century to Our Time]. München: C. H. Beck, 1989.

Overpeck, Jonathan, et al. "The Southwest Indian Monsoon Over the Past 18,000 Years." *Climate Dynamics* 12 (1996): 213–225.

Panglung, Jampa L. "Die metrischen Berichte über die Grabmäler der tibetischen Könige" [The Metric Reports on the Tombs of the Tibetan Kings]. In *Tibetan Studies.* München: Kommission für Zentralasiatische Studien, Bayerische Akademie der Wissenschaften, 1988, 336–367.

Pant, S. D. *The Social Economy of the Himalayans.* London: George Allen and Unwin, 1935.

Parfionovitch, Yuri, Gyurme Dorje, and Fernand Meyer, eds. *Tibetan Medical Paintings: Illustrations to the Blue Beryl Treatise of Sangye Gyamtso* (1653–1705), 2 vols. London: Serindia, 1992.

Patterson, George N. *Requiem for Tibet.* London: Aurum Press, 1990.

——. *God's Fool.* Garden City, N.Y.: Doubleday, 1954.

Petech, Luciano. "Western Tibet: Historical Introduction." In *Tabo: A Lamp for the Kingdom,* ed. Deborah Klimburgh-Salter. London: Thames and Hudson, 1997, 229–255.

——. "Princely Houses of the Yuan Period Connected with Tibet." In *Indo-Tibetan Studies: Papers in Honour and Appreciation of Professor David L. Snellgrove's Contribution to Indo-Tibetan Studies,* ed. T. Skorupski. Tring: Institute of Buddhist Studies, 1990, 257–269.

——. *Selected Papers on Asian History.* Roma: Instituto italiano per il Medio ed Estremo Oriente, 1988.

——. "The Dalai Lamas and Regents of Tibet." In *Selected Papers on Asian History.* Roma: Instituto italiano per il Medio ed Estremo Oriente, 1988.

——. "Ya tshe, Gu ge, Pu rang: A New Study." In *Selected Papers on Asian History.* Serie Orientale Roma LX. Roma: Instituto italiano per il Medio ed Estremo Oriente, 1988.

——. "Yuan Organization of the Tibetan Border Areas." In *Tibetan Studies: Proceedings of the 4th seminar of the International Association for Tibetan Studies, Schloss Hohenkammer, Munich 1985,* ed. International Association for Tibetan Studies, Helga Uebach, and Jampa Losang Panglung. München: Kommission für Zentralasiatische Studien, Bayerische Akademie der Wissenschaften, 1988, 369–380.

——. "Tibetan Relations with Sung China and with the Mongols." In *China Among Equals: The Middle Kingdom and Its Neighbors, 10th–14th Centuries,* ed. Morris Rossabi. Berkeley: University of California Press, 1983, 173–203.

——. *The Kingdom of Ladakh, c. 950–1842 A.D.* Rome: Istituto italiano per il Medio ed Estremo Oriente, 1977.

——. *Aristocracy and Government in Tibet: 1728–1959.* Rome: Instituto italiano per il Medio ed Estremo Oriente, 1973.

——. *China and Tibet in the Early XVIIIth Century: History of the Establishment of Chinese Protectorate in Tibet.* Leiden: Brill, 1972.

——. "Notes on Tibetan History of the 18th Century." *T'oung Pao* 52, no. 4–5 (1966): 276–292.

——. *I missionari italiani nel Tibet e nel Nepal* [*Italian Missionaries in Tibet and Nepal*]. 7 vols. Rome, 1952–1956.

——. *China and Tibet in the Early XVIIIth Century: History of the Establishment of Chinese Protectorate in Tibet*. Leiden: Brill, 1950.

Peter, Prince of Greece. *A Study of Polyandry*. The Hague: Mouton, 1963.

——. *The Aristocracy of Central Tibet: A Provisional List of the Names of the Noble Houses of U-Tsang*. Kalimpong: Tharchin, 1954.

'Phags pa Blo gros rgyal mtshan and Constance Hoog. *Prince Jiṅ-gim's Textbook of Tibetan Buddhism: The Śes-bya rab-gsal (Jñeya-prakāśa)*. Leiden: E. J. Brill, 1983.

Pirenne, H. *Histoire économique et sociale du moyen âge* [*Economic and Social History of the Middle Ages*]. 1933; reprint, Paris: Presses Universitaires de France, 1969.

Polkinghorne, Donald E. "Narrative Psychologie und Geschichtsbewusstsein: Beziehungen und Perspektiven" [Narrative Psychology and Historical Consciousness: Relations and Perspectives]. In *Erzählung, Identität und historisches Bewusstsein. Die psychologische Konstruktion von Zeit und Geschichte (Erinnerung, Geschichte, Identität 1)*, ed. Jürgen Straub. Frankfurt a.M: Suhrkamp, 1998, 12–45.

Polo, Marco. *The Travels of Marco Polo*, after the complete Yule-Cordier edition of 1903/1920. New York: Dover, 1992.

Pommaret, Françoise, ed. *Lhasa in the Seventeenth Century: The Capital of the Dalai Lamas*. Leiden: Brill, 2003.

Prasad, R. R. *Bhotia Tribals of India: Dynamics of Economic Transformation*. New Delhi: Gian Publishing House, 1989.

Prejevalsky, Nicholaus Michailovitch. *Mongolia, the Tangut Country and the Solitudes of Northern Tibet*. 2 vols. London: S. Low, Marston, Searle and Rivington, 1876.

Qian, Y., et al. "Multiple Origins of Tibetan Y Chromosome." *Human Genetics* 106 (2000): 453–454.

Radhu, Abdul Wahid. *Caravane tibétaine* [*Tibetan Caravan*]. Adapté en français par Roger du Pasquier d'après les mémoires inédits de l'auteur. Paris: Fayard, 1981. [Available in English as: Radhu, Abdul Wahid. *Islam in Tibet: Tibetan Caravans*. Trans. Jane Casewit. Ed. Gray Henry. Louisville: Fons Vitae, 1997.]

Rafiqi, Abdul Qaiyim. *Sufism in Kashmir: From the Fourteenth Century to the Sixteenth Century*. Varanasi: Bharatiya Publishing House, 1972.

Rahul, Ram. *The Government and Politics of Tibet*. Delhi: Vikas, 1969.

Ramakant. *Indo-Nepalese Relations, 1816 to 1877*. Delhi: S. Chand, 1968.

Ramble, Charles. "The Creation of the Bon Mountain of Kongpo." In *Mandala and Landscape*, ed. A. W. MacDonald. New Delhi: D. K. Printworld, 1997, 133–232.

——. "Kog: A Deserted Settlement in Mustang." *Ancient Nepal* 139 (1995).

Ramble, Charles and Christian G. Seeber. "Dead and Living Settlements in the Shöyul of Mustang." *Ancient Nepal* 138 (1995): 107–130.

Ratchkevsky, P. "Die mongolischen Grosskhane und die Buddhistische Kirche" [The Mongol Khans and the Buddhist Church]. In *Asiatica: Festschrift Friedrich Weller zum 65*, ed. Johannes Schubert und Ulrich Schneider. Leipzig: O. Harrassowitz, 1954.

Regamey, Constantin. "Motifs Vich-nouites et Śivaïtes dans le *Kāraṇḍavyūha*" [Vaisnava and Śaivaite Motifs in the *Kāraṇḍavyūha*]. In *Études Tibétaines dediées à la mémoire de Marcelle Lalou*. Paris: Maisonneuve, 1971, 411–433.

Ren, G. "Decline of the Mid-to-late Holocene Forests in China: Climate Change or Human Impact." *Journal of Quaternary Science* 15 (2000): 273–281.

Ren, Guoyu and Hans-Juergen Beug. "Mapping Holocene Pollen Data and Vegetation of China." *Quaternary Science Reviews* 21, no. 12 (2002): 1395–1422.

Renfrew, Colin. "At the Edge of Knowability: Towards a Prehistory of Languages." *Cambridge Archaeological Journal* 10, no. 1 (2000): 7–34.

Richardson, Hugh E. "The Fifth Dalai Lama's Decree Appointing Sangs rgyas rgya mtsho as Regent." In *High Peaks, Pure Earth: Collected Writings on Tibetan History and Culture*, ed. Michael Aris. London: Serindia, 1998, 440–461.

——. *Ceremonies of the Lhasa Year*. Ed. Michael Aris. London: Serindia, 1993.

——. "The Fifth Dalai Lama's Decree Appointing Sangs rgyas rgya mtsho as Regent." *Bulletin of the School of Oriental and African Studies* 43 (1980): 329–344.

——. "The First Tibetan Chos byung." *The Tibet Journal* 5, no. 3 (1980): 62–73.

——. "The Rva sgreng Conspiracy of 1947." In *Tibetan Studies in Honour of Hugh Richardson: Proceedings of the International Seminar on Tibetan Studies, Oxford, 1979*, edited by Michael Aris and Aung San Suu Kyi. Warminster: Aris & Phillips, 1980, xvi–xx.

——. "Ministers of the Tibetan Kingdom." *The Tibet Journal* 2, no. 1 (1977): 10–27.

——. *A Short History of Tibet*. New York: E. P. Dutton, 1962.

——. *Tibet and Its History*. London: Oxford University Press, 1962.

——. "The Karma pa Sect: A Historical Note." *Journal of the Royal Asiatic Society* (1959): 1–18.

——. "The Karma pa Sect: A Historical Note." *Journal of the Royal Asiatic Society* (1958): 139–164.

——. *Ancient Historical Edicts at Lhasa and the Mu tsung/Khri gtsug lde brtsan Treaty of A.D. 821–822*. London: Royal Asiatic Society of Great Britain and Ireland, 1952.

Ricœur, Paul. *Zeit und Erzählung, Bd. I: Zeit und historische Erzählung* [*Time and Narrative, Vol. I: Time and Historical Narrative*]. München: Fink, 1988.

Rijnhart, Susan Carson. *With the Tibetans in Tent and Temple: Narrative of Four Years' Residence on the Tibetan Border, and of a Journey Into the Far Interior*. Edinburgh and London: Oliphant, Anderson and Ferrier, 1901.

Robinson, James Burnell. "The Lives of Indian Buddhist Saints: Biography, Hagiography and Myth." In *Tibetan Literature: Studies in Genre*, ed. José Ignacio Cabezón and Roger R. Jackson. Ithaca, N.Y.: Snow Lion, 57–69.

Rock, Joseph F. *The Amnye Machen Range and Adjacent Regions: A Monographic Study*. Roma: Instituto italiano per il Medio ed Estremo Oriente, Serie Orientale Roma, XII, 1956.

——. *The Na-khi Nāga Cult and Related Ceremonies*. Roma: Instituto italiano per il Medio ed Estremo Oriente, Serie Orientale Roma, IV, pt. 1–2, 1952.

——. "Seeking the Mountains of Mystery: An Expedition on the China-Tibet Frontier to the Unexplored Amnye Machen Range." *The National Geographic Magazine* 57, no. 2 (1930): 181.

Rockhill, William Woodville. *The Dalai Lamas of Lhasa and Their Relations with the Manchu Emperors of China, 1644–1908*. Leiden: Oriental Printing-Office, E. J. Brill, 1910.

——. *Diary of a Journey Through Mongolia and Tibet in 1891 and 1892.* Washington, D.C.: Smithsonian Institution, 1894.

——. "Tibet: A Geographical, Ethnographical and Historical Sketch, Derived from Chinese Sources." *Journal of the Royal Asiatic Society* 23 (1891): 1–133, 185–291.

Roerich, George N. "The Epic of King Kesar of Ling." *Journal of the Royal Asiatic Society of Bengal, Letters* 8 (1942): 277–311.

——. *Trails to Inmost Asia: Five Years of Exploration with the Roerich Central Asian Expedition.* New Haven: Yale University Press, 1931.

——. *The Animal Style Among the Nomad Tribes of Northern Tibet.* Prague: Seminarium Kondakovianum, 1930.

Roerich, George N., trans. *The Blue Annals* (translation of 'Gos lo tsa ba Gzhon nu dpal, *Deb ther sngon po*, 1476–1478), 2 vols. Calcutta: Royal Asiatic Society of Bengal, 1948–1953.

Rose, Leo. *Nepal: Strategy for Survival.* Berkeley: University of California Press, 1971.

von Rosthorn, A. *On Tea Cultivation in Western Sichuan and the Tea Trade with Tibet via Tachienlu.* London: Luzac, 1895.

Rowley, D., R. Pierrehumbert, and B. Currie. "A New Approach to Stable Isotope-based Paleoaltimetry: Implications for Paleoaltimetry and Paleohypsometry of the High Himalaya Since the Late Miocene." *Earth and Planetary Science Letters* 188 (2001): 253–268.

Ruegg, David Seyfort. *Ordre spirituel et ordre temporel dans la pensée bouddhique de l'Inde et du Tibet* [*Spiritual Order and Temporal Order in the Buddhist Thought of India and Tibet*]. Paris: Collège de France, 1995.

——. "Mchod yon, yon mchod and mchod gnas/yon gnas: On the Historiography and Semantics of a Tibetan Religio-social and Religio-political Concept." In *Tibetan History and Language*, ed. E. Steinkellner. Vienna: G. Uray Festschrift, 1991, 441–453.

——. *Buddha-nature, Mind and the Problem of Gradualism in a Comparative Perspective: on the Transmission and Reception of Buddhism in India and Tibet.* London: School of Oriental and African Studies, 1989.

——. "Deux problèmes d'exégèse et de pratique tantriques" [Two Problems of Tantric Exegesis and Practice]. In *Tantric and Taoist Studies in Honor of Professor R. A. Stein*, Mélanges chinois et bouddhiques 20, ed. Michel Strickmann. Bruxelles: Institut belge des hautes études chinoises, 1981, 212–226.

——. *Life of Bu ston Rin po che.* Roma: Instituto italiano per il Medio ed Estremo Oriente, 1966.

Russell, Jeremy. "A Brief History of the Taglung Kagyu." *Chö yang* (Journal of the Council for Religious and Cultural Affairs of H. H. the Dalai Lama) 1, no. 1 (1986): 120–126.

Ryall, E. C. "Explorations in Western Tibet, by the Trans-Himalayan Parties of the Indian Trigonometrical Survey." *Proceedings of the Royal Geographical Society* 1 (1879).

Ryder, C. H. D. "Exploration and Survey with the Tibet Frontier Commission, and from Yangzi to Simla via Gartok." *The Geographical Journal* 26, no. 4 (1905).

Sagant, Phillipe. "Ampleur et profondeur historique des migrations népalaises" [The Extent and Historical Depth of Nepalese Migrations]. *L'Ethnographie* 120, no. 77–78 (1978).

Sagaster, K. *Die weisse Geschichte* [*The White History*]. Wiesbaden: Harrassowitz, 1976.

Saghang Sechen [Ssanang Ssetsen]. *Geschichte der Ost-Mongolen und ihres Fürstenhauses, verfasst von Ssanang Ssetsen Chungtaidschi der Ordus* [*History of the Eastern Mongols*]. Ed. and trans. Isaak Jakob Schmidt. St. Petersburg, 1829.

Sanwal, Bhairava Dat. *Nepal and the East India Company*. New York: Asia Publishing House, 1965.

Schaeffer, Kurtis R. "Ritual, Festival, and Authority Under the Fifth Dalai Lama." In *Power, Politics, and the Reinvention of Tradition: Tibet in the Seventeenth and Eighteenth Centuries. Proceedings of the 10th Seminar of the International Association for Tibetan Studies, Oxford University, 2003*, ed. Bryan J. Cuevas and Kurtis R. Schaeffer. Leiden: Brill, 2006, 187–202.

——. "Textual Scholarship, Medical Tradition, and Mahayana Buddhist Ideals in Tibet." *Journal of Indian Philosophy* 31 (2003): 621–641.

——. "Controlling Time and Space in Lhasa." Paper delivered to the annual meeting of the American Academy of Religion, Toronto, November 2002.

Schäfer, Jörg, et al. "The Limited Influence of Glaciations in Tibet on Global Climate Over the Past 170,000 Years." *Earth and Planetary Science Letters* 194 (2002): 287–297.

Schaller, G. *Wildlife of the Tibetan Steppe*. Chicago: University of Chicago Press, 1998.

Schmidt, B. *Kognitive Autonomie und soziale Orientierung: Konstruktivistische Bemerkungen zum Zusammenhang von Kognition, Kommunikation, Medien und Kultur* [*Cognitive Autonomy and Social Orientation: Constructivist Comments on the Relationship Between Cognition, Communication, Media and Culture*]. Frankfurt: Suhrkamp, 1994.

Schrader, Heiko. *Trading Patterns in the Nepal Himalaya*. Saarbrücken: Verlag Breitenbach, 1988.

——. *Erlasse und Sendschreiben mongolischer Herrscher für tibetische Geistliche: Bin Beitrag zur Kenntnis der Urkunden des tibetischen Mittelalters und ihrer Diplomatik* [*Missives and Decrees of Mongolian Rulers for the Tibetan Clergy: Contribution to the Knowledge of the Deeds of the Middle Ages and Its Tibetan Diplomatics*]. St. Augustin: VGH-Wissenschaftsverlag, 1977.

——. "Wie ist die Einladung des fünften Karma-pa an den chinesischen Kaiserhof als Fortführung der Tibetpolitik der Mongolen-Khane zu verstehen?" [How Is the Invitation of the Fifth Karma-pa to the Chinese Imperial Court to Be Understood as a Continuation of the Tibetan Policy of the Mongol Khans?]. In *Altaica Collecta*, ed. Walther Heissig. Wiesbaden: Otto Harrassowitz, 1976, 209–244.

——. *Untersuchungen zur Geschichte der tibetischen Kalenderrechnung* [*Studies on the History of the Tibetan Calendrical Calculations*]. Wiebaden: F. Steiner, 1973.

Schuhmann, Hans Wolfgang. *Buddhismus: Stifter, Schulen und Système* [*Buddhism: Donors, Schools and Systems*]. Olten: Walter Verlag, 1976.

Schulte-Uffelage, Helmut, trans. *Das Keng-shen wai-shih: eine Quelle zur späten Mongolenzeit* [*The Gengshen waishi: A Source for the Late Mongol Period*]. Berlin: Akademie-Verlag, 1963.

Schwarzmantel, John. *The State in Contemporary Society: An Introduction*. New York: Harvester Wheatsheaf, 1994.

Schwieger, Peter. *Teilung und Reintegration des Königreichs von Ladakh im 18. Jahr-hundert: Der Staatsvertrag zwischen Ladakh und Purik aus dem Jahr 1753 [Partition and Reintegration of the Kingdom of Ladakh in the 18th Century: The 1753 Treaty Between Ladakh and Purik]*. Monumenta Tibetica historica; Abteilung III; Diplomata et epistolae; Bd. 7. Bonn: VGH Wissenschaftsverlag, 1999.

———. "Zur Rezeptionsgeschichte des *Gsol 'debs le'u bdun ma* und des *Gsol 'debs le'u bsam pa khun grub ma* [The Reception History of the *Gsol 'debs le'u bdun ma* and the *Gsol 'debs le'u bsam pa khun grub ma*]." *Zentralasiatische Studien* 21 (1989): 29–47.

Searle, John R. *The Construction of Social Reality*. New York: Free Press, 1995.

Serruys, Henry. *Sino-Mongol Relations During the Ming, Vol. III—Trade Relations: The Horsefairs (1400–1600)*. Bruxelles: Institut Belge des Hautes Etudes Chinoises, 1975.

———. "Early Lamaism in Mongolia." *Oriens Extremus* 10 (1963): 197–200.

———. "Foreigners in the Metropolitan Police During the 15th Century." *Oriens Extremus* 8 (1961): 59–83.

———. "Some Types of Names Adopted by the Mongols During the Yuan and Early Ming Period." *Monumenta Serica* 17 (1958): 353–355.

———. "Pei-lou Fong-sou: Les coutumes des esclaves septentrionaux de Siao Ta-Heng" [The Customs of the Northern Slaves]. *Monumenta Serica* 10 (1945): 117–208.

Tsering Shakya. *The Dragon in the Land of Snows: A History of Modern Tibet Since 1947*. London: Pimlico, 1999.

———. "1948 Tibetan Trade Mission to United Kingdom: An Essay in Honour of Tsipon Shakabpa." *The Tibet Journal* 15, no. 4 (1990): 97–114.

Shapin, Steven. *The Scientific Revolution*. Chicago: University of Chicago Press, 1996.

Sharma, Prayag Raj. *Preliminary Study of the Art and Architecture of the Karnali Basin, West Nepal*. Paris: Centre National de la Recherche Scientifique, 1972.

Shen Weirong. *Leben und historische Bedeutung des ersten Dalai Lama Dge' 'dun grub pa dpal bzang po (1391–1474), ein Beitrag zur Geschichte der Dge lugs pa Schule und der institution der Dalai Lamas [The Life and Historical Significance of the First Dalai Lama Dge' 'dun grub pa dpal bzang po (1391–1474), a Contribution to the History of the Dge lugs pa School and the Institution of the Dalai Lamas]*. Sankt Augustin: Institut Monumenta Serica, 2002.

Sherring, C. A. *Western Tibet and the Indian Borderland*. London: Edward Arnold, 1906.

Shes rab dar rgyas and Klaus Sagaster. *Subud erike: "Ein Rosenkranz aus Perlen": die Biographie des 1. Pekinger Lcang skya Khutukhtu Ngag dbang blo bzang chos ldan, verfasst von Ngag dbang chos ldan alias Shes rab dar rgyas [Subud Erike: "A Pearl Rosary": The Biography of the 1st Peking Lcang skya Khutukhtu Ngag dbang blo bzang chos ldan, written by Ngag dbang chos ldan alias Shes rab dar rgyas]*. Asiatische Forschungen, 20. Wiesbaden: Harrassowitz, 1967.

Shiba, Yoshinobu. "Sung Foreign Trade: Its Scope and Organization." In *China Among Equals: The Middle Kingdom and Its Neighbors, 10th–14th Centuries*, ed. Morris Rossabi. Berkeley: University of California Press, 1983, 89–115.

Shuttleworth, H. L. "A Wool Mart of the Indo-Tibetan Borderland." *The Geographical Review* 13, no. 4 (1923): 552–555.

——. "Border Countries of the Punjab Himalaya." *The Geographical Journal* 60, no. 4 (1922): 264–268.

Simon, Christian. *Historiographie: Eine Einführung* [*Historiography: An Introduction*]. Stuttgart: Ulmer, 1996.

Singh, J. "A Brief Survey of Village Gods and Their Moneylending Operations in Kinnaur District of Himachal Pradesh, Along with Earlier Importance of Trade with Tibet." In *Wissenschafts-geschichte und gegenwärtige Forschungen in Nordwest-Indien*. Dresden: Staatliches Museum für Völkerkunde, 1990, 246.

Skorupski, Tadeusz. *A Catalogue of the Stog Palace Kangyur*. Vol. 4, *Bibliographia Philologica Buddhica, Series Maior*. Tokyo: The International Institute for Buddhist Studies, 1985.

Smith, E. Gene. "Preface." In Kong sprul Blo gros mtha' yas, *Kongtrul's Encyclopaedia of Indo-Tibetan Culture*, ed. Lokesh Chandra. New Delhi: International Academy of Indian Culture, 1970.

——. *University of Washington Tibetan Catalogue*. Seattle: University of Washington, 1969.

Snellgrove, David. *Indo-Tibetan Buddhism: Indian Buddhists and Their Tibetan Successors*. London: Random House, 1987.

——. *The Nine Ways of Bon: Excerpts from the Gzhi brjid Edited and Translated*. London: Oxford University Press, 1967.

Snellgrove, David and Hugh Richardson. *A Cultural History of Tibet*. Boston: Shambhala, 1995.

——. *A Cultural History of Tibet*. Boulder: Prajñā Press, 1980.

——. *A Cultural History of Tibet*. New York: Frederick A. Praeger, 1968.

Snellgrove, David and Tadeusz Skorupski. *The Cultural Heritage of Ladakh*. Warminster: Aris & Phillips, 1977–1980.

Sørensen, Per K. *Tibetan Buddhist Historiography: The Mirror Illuminating the Royal Genealogies*. Wiesbaden: Harrassowitz, 1994.

——. *Divinity Secularized: An Inquiry Into the Nature and Form of the Songs Ascribed to the Sixth Dalai Lama*. Wien: Arbeitskreis für Tibetische und Buddhistische Studien, Universität Wien, 1990.

Sørensen, Per K. and Bsod nams rgyal mtshan. *A Fourteenth-Century Tibetan Historical Work: Rgyal rabs gsal ba'i me long: Author, Date, and Sources: A Case Study*. Fontes Tibetici Havnienses. København: Akademisk Forlag, 1986.

Sperling, Elliot. "Rtsa mi Lo tsa ba Sangs rgyas grags pa and the Tangut Background to Early Mongol-Tibetan Relations." In *Tibetan Studies: Proceedings of the 6th Seminar of the International Association for Tibetan Studies, Fagernes 1992, vol. 2*, ed. Per Kværne. Oslo: The Institute for Comparative Research in Human Culture, 1994, 801–824.

——. "The Sichuan-Tibet Frontier in the Fifteenth Century." *Ming Studies* 26 (1988): 37–55.

Spiegel, Gabrielle M. "Geschichte, Historizität und die soziale Logik von mittelalterlichen Texten [History, Historicity, and the Social Logic of Medieval Texts]." In *Geschichte schreiben in der Postmoderne: Beiträge zur aktuellen Diskussion*, ed. Cristoph Conrad and Martina Kessel. Stuttgart: Philipp Reclam, 1994.

Sprung, Mervyn, trans. *Lucid Exposition of the Middle Way.* London: Routledge and Kegan Paul, 1997.

Śrīdharasena. *Abhidhānaviśvalocanam, or, Abhidhānamuktāvalī of Śrīdharasena.* Trans. A. Wayman and L. Jamspal. Monograph series of Naritasan Institute for Buddhist Studies, vol. 3. Narita, Narita-shi, Chiba-ken, Japan: Naritasan Shinshoji, 1992.

Stein, A. "Routes from the Punjab to Turkestan and China recorded by William Finch (1611)." *The Geographical Journal* 51, no. 1 (1918): 173.

Stein, R. A. *La civilisation tibétaine.* Paris: l'Asiathèque, 1987.

———. *La civilisation tibétaine* (réedition revue et augmentée). Paris: l'Asiathèque, 1981.

———. *Tibetan Civilization.* Stanford: Stanford University Press, 1972.

———. "La langue zhang-zhung du Bon organisé" [The Zhangzhung Language of Organized Bon]. *Bulletin de l'ecole Fraçaise d'Extrême Orient* 58 (1971): 232–254.

———. *Une chronique ancienne de Bsam-yas, Sba-bzĕd* [An Ancient Chronicle of Samyé, Bazhé]. Edition of Tibetan text with French summary. Paris: Institut des hautes etudes chinoises, 1961.

Stevenson, H. "Notes on the Human Geography of the Chinese-Tibetan Borderland." *The Geographical Review* 22, no. 4 (1932): 599–616.

Stoddard, Heather. *Le Mendiant de l'Amdo* [The Beggar from Amdo]. Recherches sur la Haute Asie, vol. 9. Paris: Société d'ethnographie; Nanterre: Service de publication du Laboratoire d'ethnologie et de sociologie comparative, Université de Paris X, 1985.

Stötzner, W. *Ins unerforschte Tibet: Tagebuch der deutschen Expedition Stötzner 1914* [Into Unexplored Tibet: Diary of the German Stötzner Expedition 1914]. Leipzig: Verlag von K F. Koehler, 1924.

Straub, J. "Personale und kollektive Identität: Zur Analyse eines theoretischen Begriffs" [Personal and Collective Identity: On the Analysis of a Theoretical Concept]. in *Identitäten: Erinnerung, Geschichte, Identität* 3, ed. Aleida Assmann and Heidrun Friese. Frankfurt a.M: Suhrkamp, 1998.

Su, B., et al. "Y chromosome Haplotypes Reveal Prehistorical Migrations to the Himalayas." *Human Genetics* 107 (2000): 582–590.

———. "Y-chromosome Data Evidence for a Northward Migration of Modern Humans Into Eastern Asia During the Last Ice Age." *American Journal of Human Genetics* 65 (1999): 1718–1724.

Suzuki, Chūsei. "A Study of a Coup d'État at Lhasa in 1844." In *Oriental Studies Presented to Sei Wada in Celebration of His Seventieth Birthday.* Tokyo: n.p., 1960, 553–564.

Szerb, J. "Glosses on the Oeuvre of Bla ma 'Phags pa: II. Some Notes on the Events of the Years 1251–1254." *Acta Orientalia Hungarica* 1980.

Takeuchi, Tsuguhito. "The Tibetans and Uighurs in Pei-t'ing, An-hsi (Kucha), and Hsi-chou (790–860 A.D.)." *Kinki Daigaku kyōyōbu kenkyū kiyō. Bulletin of Universities and Institutes* 17, no. 3 (1986): 51–68.

Tang, H. and J. Hare. "Lithic Tool Industries and the Earliest Occupation of the Qinghai-Tibetan plateau." *Artefact* 18 (1995): 3–11.

Taring, Rinchen Dolma. *Daughter of Tibet.* London: John Murray, 1970.

Tashi Tsering. "Nag Rong Mgon po rnam rgyal: A 19th Century Khams pa Warrior." In *Soundings in Tibetan Civilization: Proceedings of the 1982 Seminar of the*

International Association for Tibetan Studies, ed. Barbara Nimri Aziz and Matthew Kapstein. Delhi: Manohar, 1985, 196–214.

Thomas, Frederick William. *Tibetan Literary Texts and Documents Concerning Chinese Turkestan, II*. London: Royal Asiatic Society, 1951.

Thomson, T. *Western Himalaya and Tibet: A Narrative of a Journey Through the Mountains of Northern India, During the Years 1847–8*. London: Reeve and Co., 1852.

Thub bstan rgya mtsho, Glenn H. Mullin, and Christine Cox. *Path of the Bodhisattva Warrior: The Life and Teachings of the Thirteenth Dalai Lama*. Ithaca, N.Y.: Snow Lion, 1988.

Tibet: Myth vs. Reality. Beijing: Beijing Review Publications, 1988.

Tolstoy, I. "Across Tibet from India to China." *The National Geographic Magazine* 9, no. 2 (1946): 178.

Torroni, A., et al. "Mitochondrial DNA Analysis in Tibet—Implications for the Origin of the Tibetan Population and its Adaptation to High Altitude." *American Journal of Physical Anthropology* 92 (1994): 189–199.

Traill, G. W. "Statistical Report on the Bhotia Mehals of Kamaon." *Asiatick Researches* 17 (1832): 1–50.

Trungpa, Chögyam and Esmé Cramer. *Born in Tibet*. London: Allen & Unwin, 1966.

——. *Born in Tibet*. Boston: Shambhala, 1995.

Tsarong, Paljor. "Economy and Ideology on a Tibetan Monastic Estate in Ladakh: Processes of Production, Reproduction and Transformation." Ph.D. diss., University of Wisconsin, 1987.

Tsuda, Shinichi. *The Saṃvarodaya-tantra: Selected Chapters*. Tokyo: Hokuseido Press, 1974.

Tsybikov, G. T. *Un pèlerin bouddhiste au Tibet* [*A Buddhist Pilgrim in Tibet*]. Paris: Éditions Peuples du Monde, 1993.

Tsybikoff, G. "Journey to Lhasa." *The Geographical Journal* 23 (1904).

Tucci, Giuseppe. *Sadhus et Brigands du Kailash: Mon Voyage au Tibet Occidental* [*Sadhus and Brigands of Kailash: My Voyage to Western Tibet*]. Paris: Editions R. Chabaud (1st edition in Italian, 1937), 1989.

——. *English Version of Indo-Tibetica*. Lokesh Chandra, ed. New Delhi: Aditya Prakashan, 1988.

——. *The Religions of Tibet*. London: Routledge and Kegan Paul, 1980.

——, trans. *Deb t'er dmar po gsar ma: Tibetan Chronicles by Bsod nams grags pa*. Roma: Instituto italiano per il Medio ed Estremo Oriente, 1971.

——. *Minor Buddhist Texts, Part II*. Roma: Istituto italiano per il Medio ed Estremo Oriente, 1958.

——. *Preliminary Report on Two Scientific Expeditions in Nepal*. Serie Orientale Roma X, pt. 1. Roma: Instituto italiano per il Medio ed Estremo Oriente, 1956.

——. *To Lhasa and Beyond: Diary of an Expedition to Tibet in the Year MCMXLVIII*. Roma: Libreria della Stato, 1956.

—— "The Sacral Character of the Kings of Ancient Tibet." *East and West* 6 (1955/6): 197–205.

——. *A Lhasa e oltre* [*To Lhasa and Beyond*]. Roma: La Libreria dello Stato, 1952.

——. *The Tombs of the Tibetan Kings*. Roma: Instituto italiano per il Medio ed Estremo Oriente, 1950.

——. *Indo-Tibetica 4, 1–2: Gyantse ed i suoi monasteri* [*Gyantsé and Its Monasteries*]. Roma: Reale Accademia d'Italia, 1941.

——. *Santi e briganti nel Tibet ignoto (Diario della spedizione nel Tibet occidentale 1935)* [*Sadhus and Brigands of Unknown Tibet (Diary of the Expedition to Western Tibet 1935)*]. Milano: Ulrico Hoepli, 1937.

——. *Indo-Tibetica 3,2 templi del Tibet occidentale e il loro simbolismo artistico; pt. 2, Tsaparang* [*The Temples of Western Tibet and Their Artistic Symbolism: Part 2, Tsaparang*]. Roma: Reale accademia d'Italia, 1936.

——. *Indo-Tibetica 3,1. I temple del Tibet occidentale e il loro simbolismo artistic; Parte I: Spiti e Kunavar* [*The Temples of Western Tibet and Their Artistic Symbolism: Part 1, Spiti and Kunavar*]. Roma: Reale accademia d'Italia, 1935. [English trans. New Delhi, 1988]

——. *Indo-Tibetica 2: Rin c'en bzañ po e la rinascita del buddhismo nel Tibet intorno al mille* [*Rinchen Zangpo and the Renaissance of Buddhism in Tibet Around the Millenium*]. Roma: Reale accademia d'Italia, 1933.

Tucci, Giuseppe and E. Ghersi. *Cronaca della Missione scientifica Tucci nel Tibet Occidentale (1933)* [*Chronicle of the Tucci Scientific Mission in Western Tibet (1933)*]. Roma: Reale Accademia d'Italia, 1934.

Tulku Thondup Rinpoché. *Hidden Teachings of Tibet: An Explanation of the Terma Tradition of the Nyingma School of Buddhism*. London: Wisdom, 1986.

Turner, Victor. *Vom Ritual zum Theater: Der Ernst des menschlichen Spiels* [*From Ritual to Theater: The Human Seriousness of Play*]. Frankfurt: Campus Verlag, 1989.

——. *Vom Ritual zum Theater: Der Ernst des menschlichen Spiels* [*From Ritual to Theater: The Human Seriousness of Play*]. New York: Performing Arts Journal Publications, 1982.

Tuttle, Gray. "A Tibetan Buddhist Mission to the East: The Fifth Dalai Lama's Journey to Beijing, 1652–1653." In *Power, Politics, and the Reinvention of Tradition: Tibet in the Seventeenth and Eighteenth Centuries. Proceedings of the 10th Seminar of the International Association for Tibetan Studies, Oxford University, 2003*, ed. Bryan J. Cuevas and Kurtis R. Schaeffer. Leiden: Brill, 2006, 65–87.

——. *Tibetan Buddhists in the Making of Modern China*. New York: Columbia University Press, 2005.

Underbill, Anne P. "Current Issues in Chinese Neolithic Archaeology." *Journal of World Prehistory* 11 (1997): 103–160.

Uprety, Prem Raman. *Nepal–Tibet Relations, 1850–1930*. Kathmandu: Puga Nara, 1980.

Uray, Géza. "L'emploi du tibétain dans les chancelleries des états du Kan-sou et de Khotan postérieur a la domination tibétaine" [The Use of Tibetan in the Chancelleries of the States of Gansu and Khotan After Tibetan Domination]. *Journal Asiatique* 269 (1981): 81–90.

——. "Khrom: Administrative Units of the Tibetan Empire in the 7th–9th Centuries." In *Tibetan Studies in Honour of Hugh Richardson*. Warminster: Aris & Phillips, 1980, 310–318.

———. "The Old Tibetan Sources of the History of Central Asia up to 751 A.D.: A Survey." In *Prolegomena to the Sources on the History of Pre-Islamic Central Asia*, ed. J. Harmatta. Budapest: Akadémiai Kiadó, 1979, 275–304.

———. "Notes on a Chronological Problem in the Old Tibetan Chronicle." *Acta Orientalia Academiae Scientiarum Hungaricae* 21 (1968): 292–297.

———. "On the Tibetan Letters *Ba* and *Wa*: Contribution to the Origin and History of the Tibetan Alphabet." *Acta Orientalia (Academiae Scientiarum Hungaricae)* 5, no. 1 (1955): 101–122.

Uspensky, Vladimir L. "The Illustrated Manuscripts of the 5th Dalai Lama's 'The Secret Visionary Autobiography' Preserved in the St. Petersburg Branch of the Institute of Oriental Studies." *Manuscripta Orientalia* 2, no. 1 (1996): 54–65.

Vagbhata. *Vagbhata's Astangahrdayasamhita*. Ed. Rahul Peter Das and Ronald Eric Emmerick. Groningen: Forsten, 1998.

van der Kuijp, Leonard W. J. "Tibetan Historiography." In *Tibetan Literature: Studies in Genre*, ed. José Ignacio Cabezón and Roger R. Jackson. Ithaca, N.Y.: Snow Lion, 1996, 39–56.

———. "Two Courts of the 'Phags pa Era." *Zhongguo zangxue/China Tibetology* (Special supplement) (1992):288–292.

van Driem, George. "Tibeto-Burman Phylogeny and Prehistory: Languages, Material Culture, and Genes." In *Examining the Farming/Language Dispersal Hypothesis*, ed. Peter Bellwood and Colin Renfrew. Oxford: McDonald Institute for Archaeological Research, University of Cambridge, 2002, 233–249.

———. *Languages of the Himalayas: An Ethnolinguistic Handbook of the Greater Himalayan Region*. 2 vols. Leiden: Brill, 2001.

———. "Neolithic Correlates of Ancient Tibeto-Burman Migrations." In *Archaeology and Language II: Archaeological Data and Linguistic Hypotheses*, ed. Roger Blench and Matthew Spriggs. London: Routledge, 1998, 67–102.

van Spengen, Wim. *Tibetan Border Worlds: A Geohistorical Analysis of Trade and Traders*. New York: Kegan Paul International, 2000.

———. "Géographie politique, géographie historique braudelienne et régionalité culturelle du Tibet" [Braudelian Historical Geography and Cultural Regionality of Tibet]. *Géographie et Cultures* 7 (Fall 1993): 55–74.

———. "The Nyishangba of Manang: Geographical Perspectives on the Rise of a Nepalese Trading Community." *Kailash* 13, no. 3–4 (1987): 131–277.

Vater, Heinz. *Einführung in die Textlinguistik: Struktur, Thema und Referenz in Texten* [*Introduction to Textual Linguistics: The Structure, Theme, and Reference Texts*]. München: Fink W. Robel, 1994.

Vaurie, Charles. *Tibet and Its Birds*. London: H. F. and G. Witherby Ltd., 1972.

Vitali, Roberto. *Early Temples of Central Tibet*. London: Serindia, 1990.

Vogel, Claus, ed. *Vagbhata's Astangahrdayasamhita, the First Five Chapters of Its Tibetan Version*. Wiesbaden: F. Steiner, 1965.

Waley-Cohen, Joanna. "Religion, War and Empire-Building in Eighteenth-Century China." *International History Review* 20, no. 2 (Qing Colonialism Issue; June 1998): 336–352.

Walker-Watson, Martin N. "Turquoise: The Gemstone of Tibet." *Tibetan Review* 18, no. 6–7 (1983).

Walsh, E. H. "Elective Government in the Chumbi Valley." *Journal and Proceedings of The Asiatic Society of Bengal* N. S. 2, no. 7 (1906): 303–308.

Wang, D. "A Further Typological Study of Neolithic Culture in Yunnan." *Journal of Tibetan Archaeology* 1 (1994): 91–108.

Wang, Ming-ke. "Searching for Qiang Culture in the First Half of the Twentieth Century." *Inner Asia* 4 (2002): 131–148.

——. *Economy and Society: An Outline of Interpretive Sociology.* Ed. Guenther Roth and Claus Wittich. Trans. Ephraim Fischoff. Berkeley: University of California Press, 1978.

——. *The Religion of India: The Sociology of Hinduism and Buddhism.* Glencoe, Ill: The Free Press, 1962.

Weiss, F. "Die Provinz Yunnan, ihre Handels- und Verkehrsverhältnisse" [Yunnan Province, its Trades and Transportation Conditions]. *Mitteilungen des Seminars für Orientalischen Sprachen* 14 (1912).

Wessels, C. *Early Jesuit Travellers in Central Asia.* The Hague: Martinus Nijhoff, 1924.

Wheatley, Paul. "Langkasuka." *T'oung Pao* 44 (1956): 404–408.

White, Hayden. *Metahistory: The Historical Imagination in Nineteenth-Century Europe.* Baltimore: Johns Hopkins University Press, 1973.

Winnington, A. *Tibet: Record of a Journey.* London: Lawrence and Wishart, 1957.

Wright, D. *History of Nepal.* Cambridge: Cambridge University Press, 1877.

Wylie, Turrell V. "The First Mongol Conquest of Tibet Reinterpreted." *Harvard Journal of Asian Studies* 37, no. 1 (1977): 103–133.

——. "A Standard System of Tibetan Transcription." *Harvard Journal of Asiatic Studies* 22 (1959): 261–267.

Ya, Hanzhang. *The Biographies of the Dalai Lamas.* Trans. Wang Wenjiong. Beijing: Foreign Languages Press, 1991.

Yang, G. Shi and Li Bing Ziao. "Borate Minerals on the Qinghai-Xizang Plateau." In *Geological and Ecological Studies of the Qinghai-Xizang Plateau.* Beijing: Science Press, 1981, 1724–1725.

Yang, Lien-sheng. "Historic Notes on the Chinese World Order." In *The Chinese World Order: Traditional China's Foreign Relations,* ed. John K. Fairbanks. Cambridge: Harvard University Press, 1968, 20–33.

Yeshé De Research Project. *Light of Liberation: A History of Buddhism in India.* Crystal Mirror Series 8, ed. E. Cook. Berkeley: Dharma Publishing, 1992.

Zhang, David and S. Li. "Optical Dating of Tibetan Human Hand and Footprints: An Implication for the Palaeoenvironment of the Last Glaciation of the Tibetan Plateau." *Geophysical Research Letters* 29, no. 5 (2002): 1069.

Zheng, B. and N. Rutter. "On the Problem of Quaternary Glaciations and the Extent and Patterns of Pleistocene Ice Cover in the Qinghai-Xizang (Tibet) Plateau." *Quaternary International* 45/46 (1998): 109–122.

TIBETAN-LANGUAGE REFERENCES

Anonymous. *Dpal ldan Sa skya dgon gyi lo rgyus dang khri pa rim byon gyi rnam thar mdor bsdud* [*Brief History of Sakya Monastery*]. Lhasa: Bod ljongs mi rigs dpe skrun khang, 1987.

Bdud 'joms Rin po che. "Gangs ljongs rgyal bstan yongs rdzogs kyi phyi mo snga 'gyur rdo rje theg pa'i bstan pa rin po che ji ltar byung ba'i tshul dag cing gsal bar 'brjod pa lha dbang g.yul las rgyal ba'i rnga bo che'i sgra dbyangs (Rnying ma'i chos 'byung)" [The Religious History of the Nyingma]. In *Collected Works*, vol. 1. Kalimpong: Dupjung Lama, 1979. Translation: Dudjom Rinpoche, Jikdrel Yeshe Dorje. *The Nyingma School of Tibetan Buddhism: Its Fundamentals and History*. Trans. and ed. Gyurme Dorje in collaboration with Matthew Kapstein. Boston, Mass.: Wisdom, 1991.

Bkra shis dpal bzang, Byang pa (1395–1475). *Dpal ldan bshad pa'i rgyud kyi 'grel pa bklag pa don thams cad grub pa* [Commentary on the Exposition Tantra]. (photocopy of manuscript).

Blo bzang chos grags, Dar mo Sman rams pa (b. 1638). "Rus pa'i dum bu sum brgya drug cu'i skor bshad pa" [Explanation of 360 Bones]. In *Bod lugs gso rig sman rtsis ched rtsom phyogs bsdus*. Lhasa: Sman rtsis khang, 1996, 22–24.

Blo bzang chos kyi nyi ma, Thu'u bkwan III. "Bon gyi grub mtha' byung tshul" [Origins of the Bön Tenet System]. In *Grub mtha' thams cad kyi khungs dang 'dod tshul ston pa legs bshad shel gyi me long*. 1802; reprint, Lanzhou: Kan su'u Mi rigs Dpe skrun khang, 1985, 378–390.

Blo bzang chos kyi rgyal mtshan. *Bcom ldan 'das 'khor lo bde mchog yab yum la mngon bar bstod pa'i rab tu byed pa* [Explanation of the Chakrasamvara Cycle]. Selected writings of Blo bzang chos kyi rgyal mtshan, 1st Panchen Lama, on Kalachakra, no. 7.

Blo bzang 'phrin las, Dung dkar. *Dung dkar tshig mdzod chen mo* [Dungkar's Tibetological Great Dictionary]. Beijing: Krung go'i Bod rig pa'i dpe skrun khang, 2002.

Blo bzang rgya mtsho. *Bod kyi lo rgyus gzhon nu dga' ba'i gtam phreng* [General Tibetan History]. Lanzhou: Kan su'u mi rigs dpe krun khang, 1997.

Blo bzang rta mgrin. *'Dzam gling byang phyogs chen po hor gyi rgyal khams kyi rtogs pa brjod pa'i bstan bcos chen po dpyod ldan mgu byed ngo mtshar gser gyi deb ther* [Great Treatise on the History of Mongolia]. New Delhi: Lokesh Chandra, 1964.

Blo bzang sbyin pa. *Rab 'byams rgyal ba'i spyi gzugs skyabs mgon paṇ chen thams cad mkhyen pa rje btsun blo bzang dpal ldan bstan pa'i nyi ma phyogs las rnam rgyal dpal bzang po'i zhal snga nas kyi sku gsung thugs kyi rnam par thar pa 'dzam gling mdzes rgyan* [Life of the Fourth Panchen Lama]. Vol. *Ka* of the Fourth Panchen Lama's *gsung 'bum*. Unpublished blockprint.

Blo bzang tshe 'phel 'Jigs med rigs pa'i rdo rje, Gu shrī. *Hor chos 'byung* [History of Buddhism in Mongolia]. In Huth, Georg, ed. and trans., *Geschichte Des Buddhismus in Der Mongolei: Aus Dem Tibetischen Des 'Jigs Med Nam Mk'a* [sic]. Strassburg: K. J. Trübner, 1892.

Blo bzang ye shes. *Sha kya'i dge slong Blo bzang ye shes kyi spyod tshul gsal bar byed pa 'od dkar can gyi phreng ba* [Biography of the Second Panchen Lama]. Trashilhünpo Edition. (*Paṇ chen thams cad mkhyen pa chen po rje btsun blo bzang ye shes dpal bzang pa'i bka' 'bum*, vol. *Ka* [400 fols.]).

Blo gros mtha' yas, Kong sprul (1813–99). *Rnal 'byor bla na med pa'i rgyud sde rgya mtsho'i snying po bsdus pa zab mo nang di don nyung ngu'i tshig gis rnam par 'grol ba sa bon snang byed* [Commentary on the Profound Inner Meaning]. In *Zab mo nang gi don zhes bya ba'i gzhung gi rtsa 'grel*. Xining: Mtsho sngon Bod lugs gso rig slob grwa chen mo, 1999, 57–333.

———. *'Tsho byed las dang po la nye bar mkhor ba'i zin tig gces par btus pa bdud rtsi'i thigs pa [Advice to Novice Physicians]*. In *Gso rig skor gyi rgyun mkho gal che ba bdam sgrig*, ed. Yon tan rgya mtsho et al. Beijing: Mi rigs dpe skrun khang, 1988.

———. *Shes bya kun khyab mdzod: The Treasury of Knowledge*, 4 vols. Paro: Ngodrup and Sherab Drimay, 1976.

———. *Zab mo'i gter dang gter ston grub thob ji ltar byon pa'i lo rgyus mdor bsdus bkod pa rin chen baidūrya'i phreng ba [History of Treasure Literature]*. In *Rin chen gter mdzod chen mo: A Reproduction of the Stod-lung Mtshur-phu Redaction of 'Jam-mgon Kong sprul's Great Work on the Unity of the Gter-ma Traditions of Tibet, with Supplemental Texts from the Dpal-spungs Redaction and Other Manuscripts*. Paro: Ngodrup and Sherab Drimay, 1976.

———. *Rin chen gter mdzod chen mo: Treasury of Rediscovered Teachings*. Paro: Ngodrup and Sherab Drimay, 1976.

Blo gros mtha' yas, Kong sprul, ed. *Gdams nag mdzod (sic) [A Treasury of Instructions and Techniques for Spiritual Realization]*. Vol. 1–12. Delhi: N. Lungtok and N. Gyal tsan, 1971.

Blo gros rgyal po, Zur mkhar ba (b. 1509). *Sman pa rnams kyis mi shes su mi rung ba'i shes bya spyi'i khog dbubs [Interior Analysis of General Knowledge Required for Physicians]*. Chengdu: Si khron Mi rigs dpe skrun khang, 2001.

———. *Rgyud bzhi'i 'grel pa mes po'i zhal lung [Oral Instructions of the Progenitors, Commentary on the Four (Medical) Tantras]*. 2 vols. Beijing: Krung go'i Bod kyi shes rig dpe skrun khang, 1989.

———. "Rgyud bzhi bka' dang bstan bcos rnam par dbye ba mun sel sgron me" [Distinguishing the Four Medical Tantras as Scripture or Treatise]. In *Bod kyi sman rtsis ched rtsom phyogs bsdus*, ed. Bod Rang skyong ljongs Sman rtsis khang. Lhasa: Bod ljongs Mi dmangs dpe skrun khang, 1986, 64–71.

Blo ldan shes rab, Brag g.yab. *Bod brda'i tshig mdzod [Dictionary of Tibetan Language]*. Dharmasala: Library of Tibetan Works and Archives, 1989.

Blo ldan snying po, Khyung po sprul sku. *Ma 'ongs ha byang [sic] gsal ba'i me long [Collected Prophecies and Visionary Revelations of Bonpo Masters of the Past, A Collection of Texts from Yaṅ steṅ Hermitage in Dolpo (northwestern Nepal) by Blo ldan sñiṅ po, Tre ston Nam mkha' rgyal mtshan and Yaṅ ston Khri khar wer shi]*. Dolanji (H. P., India): n.p, 1979.

Bsam gtan, Dmu dge. *Bod kyi lo rgyus kun dga' me long [History of Tibet]* (Rnga ba bod rigs rang skyong khul gyi rig gnas lo rgyus dpyad yig bdams bsgrigs, Spyi'i deb lnga pa, Bod yig deb gnyis pa). N.p.: Srid gros si kron zhing chen rnga ba bod rigs cha'ang rigs rang skyong u yon lhan khang gi rig gnas lo rgyus dpyad yig gi zhib 'jug u yon lhan khang, 1987.

Bsam gtan rgyal mtshan, Mkhar rme'u. "Btsan po lha sras dar ma dang de'i rjes su byung ba'i rgyal rabs mdor bsdus" [Concise Genealogy of the Emperors and Princes After (Lang) Dharma]. *Krung go'i Bod kyi shes rig* 1 (1990): 81–103.

Bshad sgra, Bka' blon and Nor nang Bka' drung. *Yig bskur rnam gzhag [Manual of Correspondence]*. Ed. G. Tharchin. Kalimpong: n.p., 1956.

Bsod nams dbang 'dus, Khe smad. *Rgas po'i lo rgyus 'bel gtam* [*Tale of an Old Man*]. Dharamsala: Library of Tibetan Works and Archives, 1982.

Bsod nams grags pa, Paṇ chen (1478–1554). *Rgyal rabs 'phrul gyi lde'u mig gam deb ther dmar po gsar ma* [*New Red Annals: Key to Royal Genealogy*]. In *Tibetan Chronicles of Bsod nams grags pa. Vol. I. Tibetan Text, Emendations to the Text, English Translation and an Appendix Containing Two Minor Chronicles.* Serie Orientale Roma XXIV, ed. and trans. G. Tucci. Rome: Instituto italiano per il Medio ed Estremo Oriente, 1971.

Bsod nams lhun grub, Glo bo mkhan chen (1456–1532). *Mkhas pa rnams 'jug pa'i sgo'i rnam par bshad pa rig gnas gsal byed* [*Commentary on (Sakya Paṇḍita's) Explanation of the Introduction for Scholars*]. New Delhi: N. Topgye, 1979.

——. *Rje btsun bsod nams lhun grub legs pa'i 'byung gnas rgyal mtshan dpal bzang po'i rnam par thar pa* [*Life of Sönam Lhundrup*]. Manuscript in the Library of Tōyō Bunko, Tokyo. [compiled 1514?].

Bsod nams rgyal mtshan. *Rgyal rabs gsal ba'i me long* [*The Clear Mirror of Royal Genealogies*]. Ed. Bronislav I. Kuznetsov. 1368/9; reprint, Leiden: Brill, 1966.

Bsod nams rtse mo (1142–82). *Chos la 'jug pa'i sgo* [*Introduction to Buddhism*] [1167]. In *Sa skya bka' 'bum*, Bibliotheca Tibetica 1, compiled by Bsod nams rgya mtsho, vol. *Nga*, ff. 263b–317a. Tokyo: Tōyō Bunko, 1968–69.

Bstan 'dzin don grub, Bsam 'grub po brang. *Mi tshe'i rba rlabs 'khrugs po* [*Agitated Waves of Life*] Rajpur: Privately published, 1987.

Bstan 'dzin dpal 'bar (Tenzin Palbar). *Nga'i pha yul gyi ya nga ba'i lo rgyus* [*The Tragedy of My Homeland*]. Dharamsala: Narthang Publications, 1994.

Bstan 'dzin rgyal mtshan. *Lha'u rta ra'i lo rgyus* [*History of Lhautara*]. Dharamsala: Library of Tibetan Works and Archives, 1988.

Bstan 'dzin rin chen rgyal mtshan, Dkar ru (b. 1801). *Gangs ti se 'i dkar chag* [*Guide to Mount Tisé*]. In *Gangs Ti se'i dkar c'ag: Bon po Story of the Sacred Mountain Ti se and the Blue Lake Mapaṅ* (Serie Orientale Roma LXI), ed. and (partly) trans. Namkhai Norbu and R. Prats. 1844/47; reprint, Rome: Istituto Italiano per il Medio ed Estremo Oriente, 1989.

Bu ston. *Bu ston chos 'byung* [*Butön's Religious History*]. Beijing: Krung go'i bod kyi shes rig dpe skrun khang, 1988.

Byams pa 'phrin las (b. 1928). *Gangs ljongs gso rig bstan pa'i nyin byed rim byon gyi rnam thar phyogs bsgrigs* [*Biographies of Tibetan Medical Teachers*]. Beijing: Mi rigs dpe skrun khang, 2000.

——. *Byams pa 'phrin las kyi gsung rtsom phyogs bsgrigs* [*Collected Writings*]. Beijing: Krung go'i Bod kyi shes rig dpe skrun khang, 1997.

——. "Bod kyi gso rig rgyud bzhi'i nang don mtshon pa'i sman thang bris cha'i skor la rags tsam dpyad pa" [Analysis of the Medical Paintings That Illustrate the Meaning of the Four Tantras]. In *Byams pa 'phrin las kyi gsung rtsom phyogs bsgrigs*. Beijing: Krung go'i Bod kyi shes rig dpe skrun khang, 1997, 370–381.

——. "Sde srid sangs rgyas rgya mtsho'i 'khrungs rabs dang mdzad rjes dad brgya'i padma rnam par bzhad pa'i phreng ba" [Desi Sanggyé Gyatso's Rebirths and Acts]. In *Byams pa 'phrin las kyi gsung rtsom phyogs bsgrigs*. Beijing: Krung go'i Bod kyi shes rig dpe skrun khang, 1997, 402–442.

Byang chub rgyal mtshan, Ta'i Si tu. *Si tu bka' chems [Situ's Testament]*. In *Rlangs kyi po ti bse ru rgyas pa*. Lhasa: Bod ljongs mi dmangs dpe skrun khang, 1986.

———. *Si tu bka' chems [Situ's Testament]*. In *Lha rig rlangs kyi rnam thar*. 1361; reprint, New Delhi: T. Tsepal Taikhang, 1974.

Chandra, Lokesh, ed. *The Collected Works of Bu ston*, part 17 *(tsa)*. New Delhi: International Academy of Indian Culture, 1969.

Chos dpal dar dpyang (13th century). *Bla ma 'i gsung dri ma med pa bsgrigs pa [Life of Chak Lotsawa]. Biography of Dharma-svāmin (Chag Lo tsa ba Chos rje dpal). A Tibetan Monk Pilgrim. Original Tibetan Text Deciphered and Translated by G. Roerich*. Patna: K. P. Jayaswal Research Institute, 1959.

Chos grags rgya mtsho, Sde dge bla sman (18th century). *Nad sman sprod pa'i nyams yig [Record of Experiences of Giving Medical Treatment for Illnesses]*. In *Gso rig skor gyi rgyun mkho gal che ba bdam sgrigs*, ed. Yon tan rgya mtsho et al. Beijing: Mi rigs dpe skrun khang, 1988, 401–418.

Chos kyi 'byung gnas, Si tu 08 (1699–1774). *Sgrub brgyud karma kaṃ tshang brgyud pa rin po che'i rnam par thar pa rab 'byams nor bu zla ba chu shel gyi phreng ba [History of the Karma Kagyu School]*. In *Ta'i Si tu pa Kun mkhyen Chos kyi 'byung gnas bstan pa'i nyin byed kyi bka' 'bum*. Vols. 11–12. 1775; reprint, Sansal, Dist. Kangra, H.P., India: Palpung Sungrab Nyamso Khang, 1990.

Chos kyi 'byung gnas, Si tu Paṇ chen. *History of the Karma Bka 'brgyud pa Sect: Being the Text of "Sgrub brgyud Karma Kaṃ tshang brgyud pa rin po che'i rnam par thar pa rab 'byams nor bu zla ba chu sel gyi phreṅ ba" [History of the Karma Kagyüpa School]*. 2 vols. 1775; reprint, New Delhi: D. Gyaltsan and Kesang Legshay, 1972.

———. *Ma Ni bka' 'bum chen mo: Version "B" of the Life of the Famed gter-ston Gu-ru Chos-kyi-dbang-phyug Recounted in Terms of His Instructions on the Avalokiteśvara Practice*. Thimphu: Kunsang Topgey, 1976.

Chos kyi grags pa, Dge bshes. *Brda dag ming tshig gsal ba [New Tibetan Dictionary]*. Beijing: Mi rigs dpe skrun Khang, 1981.

Chos kyi nyi ma, Thu'u bkwan. *Grub mtha' shel gyi me long [The Crystal Mirror of Philosophical Systems]*. 1802; reprint, Delhi: Ngawang Gelek Demo, n.d..

De bzhin gshegs pa thams cad kyi bgrod pa gcig pa'i lam chen gsung ngag rin po che'i bla ma brgyud pa rnam thar [Biography of Dezhin Shekpa].

De Jong, J. W. *Mi la ras pa'i rnam thar [Biography of Milarepa]*. S-Gravenhage: Mouton, 1959.

De mo Khutugtu. *Rgyal ba'i dbang po thams cad mkhyen gzigs chen po rje btsun blo bzang bstan pa'i dbang phyug 'jam dpal rgya mtsho dpal bzang po'i zhal snga nas kyi rnam par thar pa mdo tsam brjod pa 'dzam gling tha gru yangs pa'i rgyan [Life of the Eighth Dalai Lama]* Vol. *Ka* of the *gsung 'bum* of the Eighth Dalai Lama. Unpublished wood-block print.

De mo Khutugtu. *Rgyal ba'i dbang po thams cad mkhyen pa blo bzang pa'i byung gnas ngag dbang lung rtogs rgya mtsho dpal bzang po'i zhal snga nas kyi rnam par thar pa mdor mtshon pa dad pa'i yid 'phrog [Life of the Ninth Dalai Lama]*. Unpublished wood-block print.

Dge 'dun rgya mtsho, Second Dalai Lama. *Gsung 'bum [Collected Works]*. Vol. *Ra*.

Dge legs dpal bzang po, Mkhas grub (1385–1438). *Collected Works: Reproduced from a Set of Prints from the 1897 Lha-sa old Zhol (Dga' ldan phun tshogs gling)*. New Delhi: Gurudeva, 1982.

Dkon mchog bstan pa rab rgyas, Brag dgon zhabs drung. *Yul mdo smad kyi ljongs su thub bstan rin po che ji ltar dar ba'i tshul gsal bar brjod pa: Deb ther rgya mtsho* [*The Ocean Annals of Amdo*]. Śatapiṭaka Series, 2226, ed. Lokesh Chandra. New Delhi: Sharada Rani, 1977.

——. *Yul mdo smad kyi ljongs su thub bstan rin po che ji ltar dar ba'i tshul gsal bar brjod pa deb ther rgya mtsho* [*The Ocean Annals of Amdo*]. Lanzhou: Kan su'u mi rigs dpe skrun khang, 1982.

Dkon mchog 'gro phan dbang po, 'Bri gung (b. 1631). "Gso ba rig pa'i gzhung lugs chen po dpal ldan rgyud bzhi'i dka' gnad dogs sel gyi zin bris mdo" [Notes on a Discourse Clearing Away Doubts About the Four Medical Tantras]. In *'Bri gung gso rig gces bsdus*, ed. 'Bri gung Chos grags et al. Beijing: Mi rigs dpe skrun khang, 1999, 134–138.

Dkon mchog lhun grub, Ngor chen (1497–1557). *Chos kyi rje dpal ldan bla ma dam pa rnams las dam pa'i chos thos pa'i tshul gsal bar bshad pa'i yi ge thub bstan rgyas pa'i nyin byed* [*Record of Teachings Received*]. Dbu med manuscript, 159 ff.

Dkon mchog lhun grub, Ngor chen [1497–1557], and Sangs rgyas phun tshogs. *Dam pa'i chos kyi byung tshul legs bshad bstan pa'i rgya mtshor 'jug pa'i gru chen* [*Religious History*]. In *A History of Buddhism: Being the Text of Dam pa'i chos kyi byung tshul legs par bshad pa bstan pa rgya mtshor 'jug pa'i gru chen zhes bya ba rtsom 'phro kha skong bcas*. New Delhi: Ngawang Topgey, 1973 [first section completed ca. 1550; completed by Sangs rgyas phun tshogs, 1692]. See also Sde dge edition: First part (ff. 1–128) written in sixteenth century by Dkon mchog lhun grub, completed ca. 1550; second part (ff. 129–228) completed by Sangs rgyas phun tshogs, 1692.

Dkon mchog phan dar, Gong sman (1511–77). *Nyams yig rgya rtsa: The Smallest Collection of Gong sman Dkon mchog phan dar's Medical Instructions to the Students* [*One Hundred Teachings on Medical Experience*]. Leh: Lharje Tashi Yangphel Tashigang, 1969.

Dkon mchog rin chen (b. 20th century). *Bod kyi gso rig chos 'byung bai durya'i 'phreng ba* [*History of Tibetan Medicine*]. Lanzhou: Kansu'u Mi rigs dpe skrun khang, 1992.

Dpal bzang chos kyi bzang po. *G.yas ru byang pa rgyal rabs* [*Royal Genealogy of Yeru Jang*]. In *Rare Tibetan Historical and Literary Texts from the Library of Tsepon W. D. Shakabpa*. Compiled by T. Tsepal Taikhang. New Delhi: Taikhang, 1974.

Dpal ye shes, Gu ge Khyi thang pa. *Byang chub sems dpa' lo tsā ba Rin chen bzang po'i 'khrungs rabs dka' spyad sgron ma rnam thar shel phreng lu gu rgyud* (*Biography of Rin chen bzang po*). In D. L. Snellgrove and T. Skorupski, *The Cultural Heritage of Ladakh, Vol. 2: Zangskar and the Cave Temples of Ladakh*, 92. Warminster: Aris & Phillips, 1980.

Gling sman Bkra shis (b. 1726). *Gso ba rig pa'i gzhung rgyud bzhi'i dka' 'grel* [*Commentary on Difficult Points in the Four Tantras*]. Chengdu: Si khron Mi rigs dpe skrun khang, 1988.

Grags pa rgyal mtshan, *Bod kyi rgyal rabs* [*Genealogy of Tibet('s Kings)*]. In *Sa skya pa'i Bka' 'bum* (Tokyo: Tōyō Bunko, 1968), vol. 4, 295–296. Trans. in Giuseppe

Tucci, "The Validity of Tibetan Historical Tradition," in *India Antiqua: A Volume of Oriental Studies Presented by His Friends and Pupils to Jean Philippe Vogel, C.I.E., on the Occasion of the Fiftieth Anniversary of His Doctorate* (Leiden: Brill, 1947), 309–322.

Grags pa smon lam blo gros, Nel pa. *Sngon byung gi gtam me thog phreng ba. Nel pa Paṇḍitas Chronik Me tog Phreṅ ba [Nelpa Paṇḍita's Chronicle: A Rosary of Flowers]* (Studia Tibetica, Band I). Ed. and trans. H. Uebach. 1283; reprint, Munich: Kommission fur Zentralasiatische Studien, Bayerische Akademie der Wissenschaften, 1987.

Grags pa smon lam blo gros, Ne'u (Nel pa) paṇ di ta. "Sngon gyi gtam me tog phreng ba" [Ancient Tales: A Rosary of Flowers]. In *Rare Tibetan Historical and Literary Texts from the Library of Tsepon W. D. Shakabpa.* New Delhi: Taikhang, 1974.

Gtsug lag 'phreng ba, Dpa' bo (1504–1564). *Dam pa'i chos kyi 'khor los bsgyur ba rnams kyi byung ba'i gsal byed pa mkhas pa'i dga' ston [Feast for Scholars: The Development of the Promoters of Buddhism]*, 4 vols. Lho brag wood-block print 1565; reprint, New Delhi: International Academy of Indian Culture, 1959–1962.

Gu ru, Chos kyi dbang phyug. *Ma ṇi bka' 'bum chen mo: Version "A" of the Life of the Famed gter-ston Gu-ru Chos-kyi-dbang-phyug Recounted in Terms of His Instructions on the Avalokiteśvara Practice.* Thimphu: Kunsang Topgey, 1976.

Gzhon nu dpal (1391–1476). *Deb ther sngon po [Blue Annals].* 2 vols. Chengdu: Si khron mi rigs dpe skrun khang, 1984.

——. *Deb ther sngon po [Blue Annals].* New Delhi: International Academy of Indian Culture, 1974.

Hwang krin ching [Huang Zhengqing]. *Hwang krin ching blo bzang tshe dbang dang kun mkhyen lnga ba chen po sku mched zung gi rnam thar ba rjes su dran pa zag med ye shes kyi me long (A blo spun mched kyi rnam thar) [Biography of Apa Alo].* Trans. Klu tshangs rdo phrug. Beijing: Mi rigs dpe skrun khang, 1994.

'Jam dbyangs dbang rgyal rdo rje, Smon 'gro ba. *Rgyal dbang thams cad mkhyen pa ngag dbang blo bzang rgya mtsho'i mtshan thos pa'i yid la bdud rtsir byed pa'i rnam thar mtho na ba don ldan mchog tu dga' ba'i sgra dbyang sar ga gsum pa [Life of the (Fifth) Dalai Lama].* Cultural Palace of Nationalities, Beijing (catalog number 002555).

'Jam dpal blo gros, Dpal sprul. *Bod na bzhugs pa'i rnying ma'i dgon deb [Record of Nyingma Monasteries in Tibet].* Dalhousie: Paltul Jampal Lodoe, 1965.

'Jigs med grags pa. *Rgyal rtse chos rgyal gyi rnam par thar pa dad pa'i lo thog dngos grub gyi char 'bebs [Lives of the Kings of Gyantsé].* Wood-block print in the library of the Istituto italiano per il Medio ed Estrem Oriente, 1479–1481.

Karma chags med. *Thugs rje chen po'i dmar khrid phyag rdzogs zung 'jug gi skor [Instruction on the Great Compassionate One].* In *Collected Works,* vol. 2. Bir, H.P.: Kandro, 1974.

Karma rgyal mtshan, ed. *Mdo smad chos rgyal Sde dge'i rgyal rabs las 'phros pa'i chos kyi 'byung tshul mdo tsam brjod pa gzur gnas blo ldan dgyes pa'i tambu ra [A Brief Religious History from the History of the Derge Kings: Lute to Please the Impartial Mind].* Hong Kong: Ya gling dpe skrun khang, 1994.

Khetsun Sangpo. *Biographical Dictionary of Tibet and Tibetan Buddhism.* Dharamsala, H.P.: Library of Tibetan Works and Archives, Headquarters of H. H. the Dalai Lama, 1973.

Khro ru tshe rnam (1928–2004). "Bod lugs gso rig slob grwa rim byung gi lo rgyus gsal ba'i gtam dngul dkar me long" [History of Tibetan Medical Education]. *Bod sman slob gso dang zhib 'jug* 1 (1996): 1–11.

Krang dbyi sun [Zhang Yisun], ed. *Bod rgya tshig mdzod chen mo (Zang-Han da cidian)* [Tshig mdzod chen mo, *Great Tibetan-Chinese Dictionary*]. Beijing: Minzu chubanshe, 1985.

Kun bzang blo gros. *Zhang bod kyi bstan 'byung lo rgyus lha rgyud rin chen phreng ba ma bcos gser gyi yang zhun* [*Bön Religious History of Zhang Zhung and Tibet*]. Beijing: Mi rigs dpe skrun khang, 2003.

Kun dga' bzang po, Ngor chen. *Thob yig rgya mtsho* [*Teachings Received*]. In *Sa skya pa'i bka' 'bum*, vol. 9. Tokyo: Tōyō Bunko, 1969.

Kun dga' rdo rje, Tshal pa (1309–1364). *Deb ther dmar po* (recte: *Hu lan deb ther*) [HD/ HD-1, *The Red Annals*]. 1363; reprint, Gangtok: Namgyal Institute of Tibetology, 1961.

—— (i.e., Si tu Dge ba 'i blo gros) (1309–1364). *Deb ther dmar po rnams kyi dang po hu lan deb ther* [*Red Annals*]. [HD-2, *The Red Book*]. Annotated and ed. by Dung dkar Blo bzang 'phrin las. 1363; reprint, Beijing: Mi rigs dpe skrun khang, 1981.

Kun dga' rgyal mtshan, Sa skya Paṇḍita (1182–1251). "Nga brgyad ma'i 'grel pa" [Commentary on the Eight Is]. In *Collected Works of the Great Masters of the Sa skya sect of Tibetan Buddhism*, vol. 5, ed. Bsod nams rgya mtsho. Tokyo: Tōyō Bunko, 1968.

——. *Biography of Sa skya pa Grags pa rgyal mtshan (Bla ma rje btsun chen po'i rnam thar*; included in *Mkhas pa rnams 'jug pa'i sgo*). In *Sa skya bka' 'bum*, compiled by Bsod nams rgya mtsho, 15 vols., vol. *Tha*, Bibliotheca Tibetica I/1–15. Tokyo: Tōyō Bunko, 1968–69.

——. *Bod yul la bsngags pa* [*Eulogy to Tibet*]. In *Sa skya pa'i bka' 'bum*, compiled by Bsod nams rgya mtsho, 15 vols., vol. 5, Bibliotheca Tibetica I/1–15, vol. 5. Tokyo: Tōyō Bunko, 1968.

——. *Bu slob rnams la spring ba* [*A Message for Disciples*]. In *Collected Works*, Derge Edition, vol. *na*, 214b–217a.

Kun grol grags pa, Smon rgyal. "Par gyi dkar chag srid pa'i sgron me" [Catalogue of Blockprints: Lamp of the World]. In *Khams chen ti ka 'grel*, Khro skyabs (Sichuan) edition, vol. A, ff 520a–541a.

Lde'u Jo sras. [*History of Buddhism*; also *Lde'u chos 'byung*]. Ed. Chos 'dzoms. 1230–1240?; reprint, Lhasa: Bod ljongs mi dmangs dpe skrun khang, 1987.

Lhar bcas 'gro ba'i mchod sdong jo bo dngul sku mched gsum sngon byung gi gtam dang brjod pa'i rin chen vaiḍūrya sngon pa'i dbang [*Guide to Khojarnath*]. 1880; reprint, Dharamsala, 1988.

Lu'o Yus hung. "Bod zhi bas bcings 'grol skor gyi nyin tho gnad bshus." *Bod kyi rig gnas lo rgyus rig gnas dpyad gzhi'i rgyu cha bdams bsgrigs*, vol. 1. Ed. Bod rang skyong ljongs chab gros lo rgyus rig gnas dpyad gzhi'i rgyu cha u yon lhan khang. Lhasa: Bod ljongs mi dmangs dpe skrun khang, 1982, 117–170.

Ma ṇi bka' 'bum: A Collection of Rediscovered Teachings Focussing Upon the Tutelary Deity Avalokiteśvara (Mahākaruṇika) (sic); Reproduced from a Print from the No Longer Extant Spungs thang (Punakha) Blocks by Trayang and Jamyang Samten. 2 vols. New Delhi: Trayang and Jamyang Samten, 1975.

Mi pham rgya mtsho, 'Jam mgon 'Ju. *Bdud rtsi snying po'i rgyud kyi 'grel pa drang srong zhal lung las dum bu bzhi pa phyi ma rgyud kyi rtsa mdo chu mdo'i tika* [*Commentary on the Final (Medical) Tantra*]. In *Gso rig skor gyi rgyun mkho gal che ba bdams sgrigs*, ed. Yon tan rgya mtsho et al. Beijing: Mi rigs dpe skrun khang, 1988.

Mkhas pa Lde'u. *Rgya bod kyi chos 'byung rgyas pa* [*Expansive Religious History of India and Tibet*; also *Lde ston gyi chos 'byung*]. *Gangs can rig mdzod*, 3. Ed. Chab spel Tshe brtan phun tshogs. 1260–61?; reprint, Lhasa: Bod rang skyong ljongs spyi tshogs tshan rig khang, 1987.

Nag chu sa khul gyi dgon sde khag gi lo rgyus [*History of the Monasteries of Nakchu Prefecture*]. [Bod ljongs]: Nag chu sa gnas srid gros lo rgyus rig gnas dpyad gzhi'i rgyu cha rtsom sgrig khang, 1993.

Nga phod Ngag dbang 'jigs med. *Rang skyong ljongs mi dmangs 'thus tshogs rgyun mthud kyi kru'u rin nga phod ngag dbang 'jigs med kyis rang skyong ljongs kyi skabs lnga pa'i mi dmangs 'thus tshogs du thengs gnyis pa'i thog gnang ba'i gal che'i gsungs bshad* [*Ngapö Ngawang Jikmé's Speech at the Second Plenary Session of the Fifth Tibet Autonomous Region's Congress*]. Lhasa, 1989.

Ngag dbang blo bzang, Klong rdol bla ma (1719–94), *Klong rdol ngag dbang blo bzang gi gsung 'bum* [*Collected Works*]. Lhasa: n.p., n.d.

———. *Bstan pa'i sbyin bdag byung tshul gyi ming gi grangs* [*Benefactors of the Teachings*]. In *Klong rdol ngag dbang blo bzang gi gsung 'bum* [*Collected Works*], vol. 'a. Lhasa: Kun bde gling, n.d.

Ngag dbang blo bzang rgya mtsho, Fifth Dalai Lama. "Lha ldan smon lam chen mo'i gral 'dzin bca' yig" [Guidelines for Seating Arrangements at the Mönlam Chenmo Festival of Lhasa]. In *Bod kyi snga rabs khrims srol yig cha bdams bsgrigs*. Lhasa: Bod ljongs tshogs tshan rig khang gi bod yig dpe rnying dpe skrun khang, 1989, 324–345.

———. *Za hor gyi ban de ngag dbang blo bzang rgya mtsho'i 'di nang 'khrul ba'i rol rtsed rtogs brjod kyi tshul du bkod pa du ku'u la'i gos bzang* [*Autobiography of the Fifth Dalai Lama*]. Lhasa: Bod ljongs mi dmangs dpe skrun khang, 1989.

———. *Zhab pa dang rgya che ba'i dam pa'i chos kyi thob yig gang ga'i chu rgyun. Record of Teachings Received: The Gsan yig of the Fifth Dalai Lama Ngag dbang blo bzang rgya mtsho*, 4 vols. Delhi: Nechung and Lakhar, 1971.

———. *Lha ldan gtsug lag khang gi dkar chag: A Guide to the Great Temple of Lhasa by His Holiness Ngag dbang Blo bzang Rgya mtsho, the Great Fifth Dalai Lama*. Delhi: Ngawang Gelek Demo, 1968.

———. *Bod kyi deb ther dpyid kyi rgyal mo'i glu dbyangs* [*History of Tibet by the Fifth Dalai Lama*]. Varanasi: Kalsang Lhundup, 1967.

———. *Gangs can yul gyi sa la spyod pa'i mtho ris kyi rgyal blon gtso bor brjod pa'i deb ther rdzogs ldan gzhun nu'i dga' ston dpyid kyi rgyal mo'i glu dbyangs* [*History of Tibet*]. In the xylograph edition of *Collected Works of the Fifth Dalai Lama*, vol. *dza*. Lhasa: n.p., 1643.

———. *Rgyal kun 'dus pa'i ngo bo khyab bdag he ru ka ngur smrig gar gyis rnam par rol pa gdan gsum tshang ba'i sde dpon rje btsun bla ma dbang phyug rab brtan bstan pa'i rgyal mtshan dpal bzang po'i rtogs pa brjod pa bdud rtsis za ma tog* [*Biography of Wangchuk Rapten Tenpé (1558–1636), composed 1676*]. In *The Collected Works*

(Gsung-'bum) of the Vth Dalai Lama, Ngag-dbang blo-bzang rgya-mtsho. Sikkim Research Institute of Tibetology, Gangtok, 1992. Vol. *Ta,* 55 folios.

———. *'Jig rten dbang phyug thams cad mkhyen pa yon tan rgya mtsho dpal bzang po'i rnam par thar pa nor bu'i 'phreng ba* [*Life of the Fourth Dalai Lama Yönten Gyatso (1589–1616)*]. In *The Collected Works (Gsung-'bum) of the Vth Dalai Lama, Ngag-dbang blo-bzang rgya-mtsho.* Sikkim Research Institute of Tibetology, Gangtok, 1992. Vol. 8 (*Nya*), 52 folios.

———. *'Jam dpal dbyangs chos kyi rje dkon mchog chos 'phel gyi rtogs brjod mkhas pa'i rnga rgyan* [*Biography of Dkon mchog chos 'phel (1573–1646), composed 1644*]. In *The Collected Works (Gsung-'bum) of the Vth Dalai Lama, Ngag-dbang blo-bzang rgya-mtsho.* Sikkim Research Institute of Tibetology, Gangtok, 1992. Vol. 8 (*Nya*), 19 folios.

———. *Rje btsun thams cad mkhyen pa bsod nams rgya mtsho'i rnam thar dngos grub rgya mtsho'i shing rta* [*Life of the Third Dalai Lama, Sönam Gyatso (1544–1588)*]. In *The Collected Works (Gsung-'bum) of the Vth Dalai Lama, Ngag-dbang blo-bzang rgya-mtsho.* Sikkim Research Institute of Tibetology, Gangtok, 1992. Vol. 8 (*Nya*), 109 folios.

———. *Za hor gyi ban de ngag dbang blo bzang rgya mtsho'i 'di snang 'khrul pa'i rol rtsed rtogs brjod kyi tshul du bkod pa du ku'u la'i gos bzang las glegs bam dang po.* [*Autobiography of the Fifth Dalai Lama*]. In *The Collected Works (Gsung-'bum) of the Vth Dalai Lama, Ngag-dbang blo-bzang rgya-mtsho.* Sikkim Research Institute of Tibetology, Gangtok, 1992. 3 vols.: vols. *Ka* (364 fols.), *Kha* (281 fols.), *Ga* (246 fols.).

———. *Zur thams cad mkhyen pa chos dbyings rang grol gyi rnam thar theg mchog bstan pa'i shing rta* [*Life of Chöying Rangdrol*]. In *The Collected Works (Gsung-'bum) of the Vth Dalai Lama, Ngag-dbang blo-bzang rgya-mtsho.* Sikkim Research Institute of Tibetology, Gangtok. 1992. Vol. *Ta,* 121 folios.

Ngag dbang blo gros, Stag sgang Mkhas mchog (19th century). *Gu bkra'i chos 'byung = Bstan pa'i snying po gsang chen snga 'gyur nges don zab mo'i chos kyi byung ba gsal bar byed pa'i legs bshad mkhas pa dga' byed ngo mtshar gtam gyi rol mtsho* [*Guru Trashi's Religious History*]. Beijing: Krung go'i Bod kyi shes rig dpe skrun khang, 1990.

Ngag dbang 'jigs med grags pa, Rin spungs pa. *'Jam pa'i dbyangs dngos smra ba'i mgon po sa skya paṇ ḍi ta kun dga' rgyal mtshan dpal bzang po'i rnam par thar pa bskal pa bzang po'i legs lam* [*The Biography of Sakya Paṇḍita*]. In *Lam 'bras slob bshad,* Sde dge wood-block print, vol. 1 (*ka*).

Ngag dbang kun dga' bsod nams, A myes zhabs (1597–1660). *'Dzam gling byang phyogs kyi thub pa'i rgyal tshab chen po dpal ldan sa skya pa'i gdung rabs rin po che ji ltar byon pa'i tshul gyi rnam par thar pa ngo mtshar rin po che'i bang mdzod dgos 'dod kun 'byung* [*A History of the Khön Lineage of Prince-abbots of Sakya, 1629*]. New Delhi: Tashi Dorjé, 1975. Also: Wood-block print in the Library of the Istituto italiano per il Medio ed Estrem Oriente, Rome. Also: *Sa skya'i gdung rabs.* Beijing: Mi rigs dpe skrun khang, 1986.

———. *Khams gsum gyi 'dren pa dam pa grub mchog gi ded dpon 'jam pa'i dbyangs bsod nams dbang po'i rnam par thar pa bcud kyi thigs phreng rab tu 'phel ba'i dgos 'dod 'byung ba'i chu gter.* In *The Biographies of Sa-skya Lo-tshā-ba 'jam-dpa'i-rdo-rje*

(1485–1533), Sṅags-'chaṅ grags-pa-blo-gros (1563–1617), and 'Jam-dbyaṅs-bsod-nams-dbaṅ-po (1559–1621). Dehradun, U.P.: Sakya Centre, 1984.

Ngag dbang, Phyong rgyas. *Sngon med pa'i bstan bcos chen po bai dur dkar po las 'phros pa'i snyan gron nyis brgya brgyad pa.* In *The Vaidurya g.ya' sel of Sde srid Sangs rgyas rgya mtsho, together with the Snyan gron nyis brgya brgyad pa: Two Works Clarifying and Elucidating Controversial Points in the Author's Monumental Astronomical and Astrological Treatise, the Vaidurya dkar po.* 64 fols. New Delhi: T. Tsepal Taikhang, 1971.

Nges don bstan rgyas. *Karma pa sku 'phreng rim byon gyi rnam thar mdor bsdus [Biographies of the Karmapas].* Sman dgon Thub chen bde chen gling: Xylograph in 236 ff., 1891.

Nor brang O rgyan. *Bod sil bu'i byung ba brjod pa shel dkar phreng ba [History of the Fragmented Period of Tibet].* Lhasa: Bod ljongs mi dmangs dpa skrun khang, 1991.

Nyi ma bstan 'dzin (b. 1813). *Sangs rgyas kyi bstan rtsis ngo mtshar nor bu'i phreng ba [A Chronological Table of the Bon po].*

Nyi ma 'od zer, Mnga' bdag Nyang ral (1124/36–1192/1204?). *Chos 'byung me tog snying po sbrang rtsi'i bcud [A Religious History: The Distilled Sweet Essence of Flowers].* Paro: Ugyen Tempai Gyaltsen, 1979.

———. *Chos 'byung me tog snying po'i sbrang rtsi'i bcud [A Religious History: The Distilled Sweet Essence of Flowers],* also *Rnying ma'i chos 'byung chen mo, mnga' bdag nyang gi chos 'byung [Nyang's Religious History], Dam chos chos 'byung.* In *Die grosse Geschichte des tibetischen Buddhismus nach alter Tradition rŃying ma'i chos 'byung chen mo. Faksimile-Edition der Berliner Handschrift (Staatsbibliothek, Preussischer Kulturbesitz, Hs. or. 1640) des Geschichtsbuches Chos 'byuṅ Me tog sñiṅ po'i sbraṅ rci'i bcud, auch mŃa' bdag Ṅaṅ gi Chos 'byuṅ genannt, verfasst von Ṅaṅ Ral pa can (1136–1204 A.D.).* Monumenta Tibetica Historica, Abteilung I: Scriptores, Band 3, ed. R. O. Meisezahl. c. 1175–1190?; reprint, Sankt Augustin, 1985.

———. *Chos rgyal mes dbon rnam gsum gyi rnam thar rin po che'i phreng ba [Biographies of the Three Dharma Lords (of Imperial Tibet: Songtsen Gampo, Tri Songdeutsen, Tri Tsukdetsen)].* Paro: Ugyen Tempai Gyaltsen, 1979.

———. *Thugs rje chen po'i rgyud rang byung ye shes [Avalokiteśvara Tantra, Self-generating Pristine Awareness].* Paro: Ugyen Tempai Gyaltsen, 1979.

Padma dkar po (1527–1592). *Chos 'byung bstan pa'i padma rgyas pa'i nyin byed [History of Buddhism].* Spungs thang edition, xylograph, 1575, revised 1580.

'Phrin las rnam rgyal, Gong dkar. *Thob yig bum pa bzang po [Teachings Received].* Kathmandu: Rgyal yongs sa chen dpe skrun khang, 2008.

Rgyal mtshan dpal, Yang dgon pa. *Rdo rje lus kyi sbas bshad.* In *The Collected Works (Gsung 'bum) of Yang dgon pa Rgyal mtshan dpal,* vol. 2. Thimphu: Kunsang Topgey, 1976, 421–497.

Rgyal mtshan dpal bzang, 'Ba ra ba. *Rje btsun 'bar ra ba rgyal mtshan dpal bzang po'i rnam thar mgur 'bum dang bcas pa [Biography of Gyeltsen Pelzangpo].* In *A Tibetan Encyclopedia of Buddhist Scholasticism: The Collected Writings of 'Ba' ra ba Rgyal mtshan dpal bzang,* vol. 14. Dehradun: Ngawang Gyaltsen and Ngawang Lungtok, 1970, 1–443.

Rig pa'i ral gri. *Thub pa'i bstan pa rgyan gyi me tog.* Nepal National Archives; reel no. L493/2.

Rin chen nor bu. *Bod kyi lo rgyus slob gzi blo gsar jug pa'i bab stegs [Teaching Material of Tibetan History].* Lanzhou: Kan su'u mi rigs dpe skrun khang, 1996.

Rin chen rnam rgyal, Sgra tshad pa (1318–88). *Bu ston rnam thar [Biography of Butön].* In *Bu ston Gsung 'bum,* vol. 27. Zhol, Lhasa: wood-block print, n.d.

Rnam rgyal dpal bzang, Byang pa (1395–1475). *Bshad rgyud kyi 'grel chen bdud rtsi'i chu rgyun [Continuous Stream of Amrita, a Commentary on an Exposition Tantra].* Chengdu: Si khron Mi rigs dpe skrun khang, 2001.

Śākya rin chen sde, Yar lung Jo bo. *Yar lung jo bo'i chos 'byung [Yarlung Jowo's Religious History].* 1376; reprint, Chengdu: Bod ljongs mi dmangs dpe skrun khang, 1987.

Sangs rgyas rdo rje. *Dpal 'brag pa rin po che zhabs drung ngag dbang rnam rgyal kyi rnam thar [Biography of Zhapdrung Ngawang Namgyel].* Thimphu: 'Brug gzhung rdzong kha gong 'phel lhan tshogs (Dzongkha Development Commission), 1999.

Sangs rgyas phun tshogs, Ngor chen (1649–1705). *Rgyal bar rdo rje 'chang kun dga' bzang po'i rnam par thar pa legs bshad chu bo 'dus pa'i rgya mtsho [Biography of Ngor Kun dga' bzang po].* 1688, Sde dge print.

Sangs rgyas rgya mtsho, Sde srid, (1653–1705). *Pur tshwa me 'dzin ma'i dkar chag dad pa'i sa bon gyis bskyed pa'i byin rlabs ro bda' [Account of the Fifth Dalai Lama's Remains].* Lhasa: wood-block print, 1697.

———. *Mchod sdong 'dzam gling rgyan gcig rten gtsug lag khang dang bcas pa'i dkar chag thar gling rgya mtshor bgrod ba'i gru rdzings byin rlabs kyi bang mdzod [Account of the Building and Installation of the Fifth Dalai Lama's Stūpa].* Zhöl Edition, 767 fols. Reprint: Beijing: Bod ljongs mi rigs dpe skrung khang, 1990.

———. *Thams cad mkhyen pa drug ba blo bzang rin chen tshangs dbyangs rgya mtsho'i thun mong phyi'i rnam par thar pa du ku la'i 'phro 'thud rab gsal gser gyi snye ma [Biography of the Sixth Dalai Lama].* Ed. Tshe ring phun tshogs. Lhasa: Bod ljongs mi dmangs dpe skrun khang, 1989.

———. *Thams cad mkhyen pa drug ba blo bzang rin chen tshangs dbyangs rgya mtsho'i thun mong phyi'i rnam par thar pa du ku la'i 'phro 'thud rab gsal gser gyi snye ma [Biography of the Sixth Dalai Lama].* Lhasa: Unpublished wood-block print, n.d.

———. *Drin can rtsa ba'i bla ma ngag dbang blo bzang rgya mtsho'i thun mong spyi'i rnam thar du ku la'i gos bzang glegs bam gsum pa'i 'phros bzhi pa [Continuation of Autobiography of the Fifth Dalai Lama].* Lhasa: Zhöl Edition, 3 Vols.: Nga (360 fols.); Vol. Ca (338 fols.), Cha (383 fols.).

———. *Dpal mnyam med ri bo dga' ldan pa'i bstan pa zhwa ser cod pan 'chang ba'i ring lugs chos thams cad kyi rtsa ba gsal bar byed pa baiḍūrya ser po'i me long [Yellow Beryl, A History of the Gelukpa School, 1698].* Lhasa: Zhöl Edition, 419 fols., 1698; reprint, Beijing: Krung go'i bod kyi shes rig dpe skrun khang, 1989. Also: *Vaiḍūrya ser po Śatapitaka,* vol. 12, part 1. New Delhi: International Academy of Indian Culture, 1960, and *Bai DUr ser po: A History of Dga'-ldan.* New Delhi: Ngawang Gelek Demo, 1980.

———. *Dpal ldan gso ba rig pa'i khog 'bugs legs bshad bai dur ya'i me long drang srong dgyes pa'i dga' ston [Beryl Mirror].* Lanzhou: Kansu'u Mi rigs dpe skrun khang, 1982.

———. *Gso ba rig pa'i bstan bcos sman bla'i dgongs rgyan rgyud bzhi'i gsal byed bai dur sngon po'i ma llika [Blue Beryl].* 2 vols. Leh: D. L. Tashigang, 1981.

———. *Bstan bcos bai dur dkar po las dri lan 'khrul nang g.ya' sel don gyi bzhin ras ston byed* (Tōhoku No. 7035), 1685–88, 473 fols. [*The Vaidurya g.ya' sel of Desi Sangs rgyas rgya mtsho*]. New Delhi: T. Tsepal Taikhang, 1971.

———. *Techniques of Lamaist Medical Practice, Being the Text of Man ngag yon tan Rgyud kyi lhan thabs zug rngu'i tsha gdung sel ba 'i katpu ra dus min 'chi zhags gcod pa'i ral gri.* Leh: S. W. Tashigangpa, 1970.

Sa skya pa'i bka' 'bum [*Collected Works of the Sakyapa*]. Tokyo: Tōyō Bunko, 1968.

Sba zhed rgyas pa. Une chronique ancienne de Bsam yas: Sba bzhed [*An Ancient Chronicle of Samyé: The Account of Ba*]. Textes et Documents, I, ed. R. A. Stein. Paris: Institut des hautes études chinoises, 1961.

Shākya rin chen sde, Yar lung Jo bo. *Yar lung Jo bo'i chos 'byung* [*Yarlung Jowo's Religious History*]. 1376; reprint, Chengdu: Bod ljongs mi dmangs dpe skrun khang, 1987.

Sher grags. "'Bar khams zhes pa'i ming gi byung tshul" [Origins of the Name Barkam]. In *Rnga ba bod rigs rang skyong khul gyi rig gnas lo rgyus dpyad yig gdam bsgrigs*, Deb gsum pa. N.p.: Srid gros si khron zhing chen rnga ba bod rigs cha'ang rigs rang skyong u yon lhan khang gi rig gnas lo rgyus dpyad yig gi zhib 'jug u yon lhan khang, 1987, 148–151.

Shes bya kun rigs, Rong ston. *Bon chos kyi bstan pa shan dbye* [*A Discussion of the Doctrinal Differences Between Bön and Chos*]. Dolanji Village, H.P.: Tashi Dorji: distributor, Tibetan Bonpo Monastic Centre, 1976.

Shes rab 'byung gnas (1187–1241). "Chos rje 'jig rten mgon po'i rnam thar phyogs bcu dus gsum ma" [Biography of Jikten Gönpo]. In *The Collected Writings of 'Bri gung chos rje 'Jig rten mgon po rin chen dpal*, I. New Delhi: n.p., 1969.

Shes rab rgya mtsho. "Rje tsha kho mkhan chen ngag dbang grags pa'i rnam thar mdor bsdus ches phra zegs ma tsam" [Biography of Ngawang Drakpa]. In *Rnga ba bod rigs rang skyong khul gyi rig gnas lo rgyus dpyad yig gdam bsgrigs*, Deb gsum pa. N.p.: Srid gros si kron zhing chen rnga ba bod rigs cha'ang rigs rang skyong u yon lhan khang gi rig gnas lo rgyus dpyad yig gi zhib 'jug u yon lhan khang, 1987, 67–73.

Skal bzang dkon mchog rgya mtsho, Rgya zhabs drung tshang. *Thub bstan yongs su rdzogs pa'i mnga' bdag kun gzigs ye shes kyi nyi ma chen po 'jam dbyangs bzhad pa'i rdo rje 'phreng lnga'i rnam par thar ba mdor bsdus su skod pa* [*Biography of the Fifth Jamyang Zhepa*]. Nanjing: n.p., 1948.

Sne tshogs rang grol, Rgod tshang ras pa. *Gtsang smyon he ru ka phyogs thams cad las rnam par rgyal ba'i rnam thar rdo rje'i theg pa'i gsal byed nyi ma'i snying po* [*Biography of Gtsang smyon Heruka*, 1547]. In *The Life of the Saint of Gtsang*, ed. Lokesh Chandra, preface by E. Gene Smith. New Delhi: Sharada Rani, 1969.

Srībhūtibhadra: Dpal 'byor bzang po, G.yas ru; Stag tshang pa. *Rgya Bod kyi yig tshang mkhas pa'i dga' 'byed* [*Chinese and Tibetan Documents*]. 2 vols. 1434; reprint, Thimphu: Kunsang Topgyel and Mani Dorji, 1979.

———. *Rgya bod yig tshang mkhas pa'i dga' 'byed chen mo* [*Chinese and Tibetan Documents*]. Manuscript held in the Densapa Library, Gantok, Sikkim, India, 1434.

Tāranātha. *Myang yul stod smad bar gsum gyi ngo mtshar gtam gyi legs bshad mkhas pa'i 'jug ngogs* [*Miraculous Tales of the Upper, Middle, and Lower Nyang Regions*]. Lhasa: Bod ljongs mi dmangs dpe skrun khang, 1983.

——. "Khrid brgya'i brgyud pa'i lo rgyus" [History of the Transmisssion of the *One Hundred Instructions*]. In *Gdams nag mdzod* (sic): *A Treasury of Instructions and Techniques for Spiritual Realization*, vol. XII, ed. Kong sprul blo gros mtha' yas. Delhi: N. Lungtok and N. Gyaltsan, 1971, 356–357.

——. *Rgyal khams pa tā ra nā thas bdag nyid kyi rnam thar nges par brjod pa'i deb gter shin tu zhib mo ma bcos lhug pa'i rtogs brjod* [*Autobiography of Tāranātha*]. In *Gsung 'bum*, Phun tshogs gling wood-block print edition. Vol. *Ka*. 331 folios.

Thang yig gsar rnying nas byung ba'i bod chen po'i srid lugs [*The System of Government of Greater (Imperial) Tibet from the Old and New Tang (Dynastic) Records*]. Xining: Mtsho sngon Mi rigs dpe skrun khang, 1983.

Thub bstan bstan dar, Lha'u rta ra. "Bod zhi bas bcings 'grol 'byung thabs skor gyi gros than tshan bcu bdun la ming rtags bkod pa'i sngon rjes su" [The 17-Point Agreement for the Peaceful Liberation of Tibet]. *Bod kyi rig gnas dpyad gzhi'i lo rgyus rgyu cha bdams bsgrigs*, vol. 1. Ed. Bod rang skyong ljongs chab gros lo rgyus rig gnas dpyad gzhi'i rgyu cha u yon lhan khang. Lhasa: Bod ljongs mi dmangs dpe skrun khang, 1982, 88–117.

Thub bstan phun tshogs. *Bod kyi lo rgyus spyi don padma ra'a ga'i lde mig* [*General History of Tibet*]. Beijing: Mi rigs dpe skrun khang, 1996.

——. "Bod sil bu'i skabs kyi dus tshigs 'ga' zhig la dpyad pa" [Analysis of the Periodization of the Time of Tibet's Disunity]. *Krung go'i bod kyi shes rig* 1 (1990): 57–62.

Thub bstan sangs rgyas. *Rgya nag tu bod kyi sku tshab don gcod skabs dang gnyis tshugs stangs skor gyi lo rgyus thabs bral zur lam* [*Experiences of a Former Tibetan Representative in China, 1930–1939*]. Dharamsala: Library of Tibetan Works and Archives, 1982.

"Thugs rje chen po dang phyag rgya chen po zung 'jug tu nyams su len tshul rjes gnang dang bcas pa" [The Way to Practice the Union of Avalokitésvara and Mahamudra, together with the Authorization]. In *Sgrub thabs kun btus* (Sde dge ed.), vol. *Ga*, ff. 1–8.

Tshe brtan phun tsbogs, Chab spel, and Nor brang O rgyan. *Bod kyi lo rgyus rags rim gyu'i phreng ba* [*Turquoise Necklace: A General History of Tibet*], 3 vols. Lhasa: Bod ljongs dpe rnying dpe skrun khang, 1989-1991.

Tshe ring dbang rgyal, Mdo mkhar zhabs drung. *Dpal mi'i dbang po'i rtogs brjod pa 'jig rten kun tu dga' ba'i gtam* [*Life of Polhané*]. Unpublished wood-block print, 1733.

——. *Mi dbang rtogs brjod* [*Biography of the King (Polhané)*]. 1733; reprint, Chengdu: Si khron mi rigs dpe skrun khang, 1981.

Tshe dbang nor bu, Kaḥ thog Rig 'dzin (1698–1755). *Rgyal ba'i bstan pa rin po che byang phyogs su 'byung ba'i rtsa lag bod rje lha btsan po'i gdung rabs tshig nyung don gsal yid kyi me long* [*Genealogy of Tibetan Kings*]. 1745; reprint in *Bod kyi lo rgyus deb ther khag lnga* (*Gangs can rig mdzod*, 9), ed. Chab spel Tshe brtan phun tshogs. Lhasa: Bod ljongs bod yig dpe rnying dpe skrun khang, 1990.

——. *Bod rje lha btsan po'i gdung rabs mnga' ri «ris» smad gung thang du ji ltar byung ba'i tshul deb gter «ther» dwangs shel 'phrul gyi me long* [*Genealogy of the Kings of Ngari Gungtang*]. In *Bod kyi lo rgyus deb ther khag lnga* (*Gangs can rig mdzod*, 9), ed. Chab spel Tshe brtan phun tshogs. Lhasa: Bod ljongs bod yig dpe rnying dpe skrun khang, 1990.

Tshe dbang, Skyem pa (15th century). *Rgyud bzhi'i rnam bshad* [*Explanation of the Four Tantras*]. Xining: Mtsho sngon mi rigs dpe skrun khang, 2000.

Tshul khrims rin chen, Zhu chen. *Dpal ldan bla ma dam pa rnams las dam pa'i chos thos pa'i yi ge don gnyer gdengs can rol pa'i chu gter* [*Record of Teachings Received*], vol. 2. Dehra Dun: D. Gyaltsan, 1970.

——. *Dpal sa skya'i rje btsun gong ma lnga'i gsung rab rin po che'i par gyi sgo 'phar 'byed pa'i dkar chag 'phrul gyi lde mig* [*Catalog of the Writings of the Five Sakya Forefathers*]. In *Sa skya pa'i bka' 'bum*, vol. 7. Tokyo: Tōyō Bunko, 1969.

Yang dgon pa, Rgyal mtshan dpal (1213–58). *Rdo rje lus kyi sbas bshad* [*The Vajra Body Account of Ba*]. In *The Collected Works (Gsung 'bum) of Yang dgon pa Rgyal mtshan dpal*, vol. 2. Thimphu: Kunsang Topgey, 1976, 421–497.

Ye shes gzungs, Sum ston pa (12th century). "'Grel ba 'bum chung gsal sgron nor bu'i 'phreng mdzes" [*Commentary on the Smaller Perfection of Wisdom Scripture: Beautiful Rosary of Bejeweled Shining Lights*]. In *G.yu thog cha lag bco brgyad*, vol. 1. Lanzhou: Kansu'u Mi rigs dpe skrun khang, 1999, 158–312.

Ye shes dpal 'byor, Sum pa mkhan po. *Dpag bsam ljon bzang (Re'u mig)* [*The Auspicious Wish-Fulfilling Tree (Chronological Tables)*]. Śatapitaka, vol. 8. New Delhi: International Academy of Indian Culture, 1959.

Ye shes dpal 'byor, Sum pa mkhan po. *Dpag bsam ljon bzang* [*The Auspicious Wish-Fulfilling Tree*]. 1748; reprint, Ed. S. C. Das. Calcutta: xylograph in 316 folios, 1908.

Yon tan mgon po, G.yu thog (1126–1202). *Bdud rtsi snying po yan lag brgyad pa gsang ba man ngag gi rgyud* [*Secret Instructional Tantra on the Eight Branches (of Medicine)*]. Lhasa: Bod ljongs mi dmangs dpe skrun khang, 1992.

Yon tan rgya mtsho. *Chos sde chen po bla brang bkra shis 'khyil: mkhas grub 'bum sde'i rol mtsho mdo sngags bstan pa'i 'byung gnas dga' ldan bshad sgrub bkra shis 'khyil gyi skor bzhad gzhung dal 'bab mdzod yangs las nye bar sgrub pa sngon med legs bshad ngo mtshar bkra shis chos dung bzhad pa'i sgra dbyangs* [*Religious History of Labrang Tashikhyil Monastery*]. Paris: Privately published, 1987.

Zhwa sgab pa, Dbang phyug bde ldan [Shakabpa, Tsepon W. D.]. *Bod kyi srid don rgyal rabs: An Advanced Political History of Tibet.* 2 vols. Kalimpong: T. Tsepal, Taikhang, privately published, 1976.

——. *Bod kyi srid don rgyal rabs: An Advanced Political History of Tibet.* 2 vols. Dharamsala: Dharamsala Tibetan Cultural Printing Press, 1986.

CHINESE-LANGUAGE REFERENCES

Bureau of Cultural Relics, Tibet Autonomous Region. "Xizang Xiaoenda xinshiqi shidai yizhi shijue jianbao" [Brief Report on the Excavation of Xiaoenda Neolithic Site in Tibet]. *Kaogu yu wenwu* (Xi'an: Shanxi sheng kaogu yanjiusuo) 1 (1990): 28–43.

Bureau of Cultural Relics, Tibet Autonomous Region and Department of History, Sichuan University. *Changdu Karou* [*Karou: A Neolithic Site in Tibet*]. Beijing: Wenwu chubanshe, 1985.

Cao Ruigai, ed. *Labuleng Si* [*Labrang Monastery*]. Beijing: Wenwu chubanshe, 1989.

China Tibetology Institute, Archaeology Department of Sichuan University and Bureau of Cultural Relics, Tibet Autonomous Region. "Xizang zhada xian piyang dongga yizhi gumu qun shijue jianbao" [Brief Report of a Preliminary Excavation of Ancient Tomb Groups in Piyang-Dongga Site of Zhada County in Tibet]. *Kaogu* (Beijing: Kexue chubanshe) 6 (2001): 14–31.

——. "Xizang Zhada xian Gebusailu mudi diaocha" [Survey of the Gebusailu Cemetery in Zhada County, Tibet]. *Kaogu* (Beijing: Kexue chubanshe) 6 (2001): 39–14.

Da Ming shi lu [*Veritable Records of the Ming Dynasty*]. Taipei: n.p., 1954.

Da Qing Lichao Shilu Zongmu [*Veritable Records of the Court of the Great Qing*].

Da Qing Shizong jingtian changyun jianzhong biaozheng wenwu yingming kuanren xinyi daxiao zhicheng Xian huangdi shilu [*Veritable Records of Shizong*].

Duan Qingbo. "Xizang xishiqi yicun" [Microlithic Remains in Tibet]. *Kaogu yu wenwu* (Xi'an: Shanxi sheng kaogu yanjiusuo) 5 (1989): 87–109.

Du Yongbin. "Dege Tusi de tedian" [The Dergé Tusi's Characteristic Features]. *Xizang yanjiu* (Lhasa: Xizang yanjiu bianjibu) 3 (1991): 66–74.

Fuheng. *Qinding pingding Zhun'ge'er fanglüe.* [*Authorized Military Record of the Subjugation of the Zunghar*]. 1772; reprint, Beijing: Quanguo tushuguan wenxian suowei fuzhi zhongxin: Faxing Xinhua shudian Beijing faxing suo, 1990.

——. *Qinding Xiyu tongwen zhi* [*Authorized Polyglot Dictionary of the Western Regions*]. China, 1750. (Also available as *Kintei Seiiki dōbunshi*. Tōkyō: Tōyō Bunko, 1961–1964.)

Gai Pei and Wang Guodao. "Huanghe shangyou Layihai xishiqi yizhi fajue baogao" [Excavation Report on a Microlithic Site at Layihai, Upper Yellow River]. *Acta Anthropologica Sinica* (Beijing: Kexue chubanshe) 2 (1983): 49–59.

Gai Pei and Wei Qi. "Hutouliang Jiushiqishidai wanqi yizhi de faxian" [Discovery of the Late Paleolithic Site at Hutouliang, Hebei]. *Vertebrata Palasiatica* 15, no. 4 (1977): 287–300.

Gaozong shilu [*Veritable History of the Gaozong (Reign) of the Qing*]. In *Da Qing lichao shilu* (vols. 58–67), ed. Manzhou diguo guowu yuan. Taipei reprint: Huawen shuju 4664 *juan*. Tokyo: Okura Shuppan Kabushiki Kaisha, 1937–1938.

Ge Le. *Ganzi Zangzu zizhi zhou shihua* [*History of the Kardzé Tibetan Autonomous Prefecture*]. Chengdu: Sichuan minzu chubanshe, 1984, 260.

Gugong Bowuyuan Wenxianguan in Beiping, ed. *Wenxian congbian* [*Collection of Documents*]. 5 vols. Beijing: Guoli Beiping gugong bowuyuan wenxianguan, 1930.

Gu Zuzheng et al. *Ming shilu Zangzu shiliao* [*Tibetan Historical Sources in Veritable Records of the Ming Dynasty*]. Lhasa: Xizang renmin chubanshe, 1982.

Han Dazai. *Kang-Zang Fojiao yu Xikang Nona Hutuketu yinghua shilüe* [*Brief Account of Kham-Tibetan Buddhism and the Manifestation of the Norlha Khutugtu of Kham*]. Shanghai: Yujia jingshe, 1937.

Han Rulin. "Yuanchao zhongyang zhengfu shi zenyang guanli Xizang difang di" [How the Central Government of the Yuan Dynasty Managed Tibet]. *Lishi yanjiu* (Beijing: Kexue chubanshe) 7 (1959): 51–56.

Han Zang duizhao cihui [*Chinese-Tibetan Bilingual Dictionary*]. Beijing: Minzu chubanshe, 1976.

He Qiang. "Xizang Gongga xian Changguogou xinshiqi yizhi diaocha baogao" [A Report on the Investigation of the Neolithic Sites in Changguogou, Gongkar County, Tibet]. *Xizang Kaogu* (Chengdu: Sichuan daxue chubanshe) 1 (1994): 28.

Huang Bufan. "Shangshu sipian gu zangwen yiwen de chubu yanjiu" [Preliminary Study of the Translation of Classical Tibetan in Four Articles of the *Shangshu*]. *Yuyan yanjiu* 1 (1981): 203–232.

Huang Zhengqing and Shi Lun. *Huang Zhengqing yu wushi Jiamuyang* [*Huang Zhengqing and the Fifth Jamyang*]. Lanzhou: Gansu renmin chubanshe, 1989.

Huo Wei. "Jin shinian Xizang kaogu de faxian yu yanjiu" [Archaeological Findings and Research in the Last Ten Years]. *Wenwu* (Beijing: Wenwu chubanshe) 3 (2000): 85–95.

——. "Zai lun Xizang daibing tongjing de youguan wenti" [A Further Discussion on Questions Related to a Bronze Mirror with Handle from Tibet]. *Kaogu* (Beijing: Kexue chubanshe) 11 (1997): 61–69.

——. "Xizang Qugong cun shishimu chutu de daibing tongjing jiqi xiangguan wenti chu tan" [A Preliminary Discussion of the Bronze Mirror with an Iron Handle Unearthed at the Qugong Cyst Tomb, Tibet]. *Kaogu* (Beijing: Kexue chubanshe) 7 (1994): 650–661.

Huo Wei and Li Y. "Xizang Zhada xian Piyang-dongga yizhi 1997 nian diaocha yu fajue" [Survey and Excavation of the Piang-Dongga Site in Tsamda County, Tibet, in 1997]. *Acta Archaeologica Sinica* (Beijing: Kaogu zazhishe) 3 (2001): 397–426.

——. *Ali diqu wenwu zhi* [*A Survey of the Cultural Relics in Ngari Prefecture*]. Lhasa: Xizang renmin chubanshe, 1993.

Kang Furong. *Qinghai ji* [*Account of Qinghai*]. In *Zhongguo fangzhi congshu* [Series of Chinese Local Gazetteers]. Taipei: Chengwen chubanshe, 1968.

Kuang Haolin. *Zhongguo jindai shaoshuminzu jingji shigao* [*The Historical Account of Modern Minorities' Economy in China*]. Beijing: Minzu chubanshe, 1992.

Li Fang-kuei. "Tufan da xiang Lu Dongzan kao" [On the Tibetan Minister Lu Dongzan]. *Papers on the International Conference on Sinology*. Taipei: n.p., 1981, 369–378.

——. "Ma Zhongying kao" [On Ma Zhongying]. *Guoli Taiwan daxue wenshizhe xuebao* (Taibei: Guoli Taiwan daxue chuban weiyuanhui) 7 (1956): 1–8.

Li Jifu. *Yuanhe jun xian tu zhi* [*Gazetteers of Tang Dynasty*]. Taipei, 1973.

Li Xian et al. *Daming yitong zhi* [*Complete Gazetteer of the Great Ming*]. 1461; reprint, Taipei: Wenhai chubanshe, 1965.

Li Y. "Jilong luo long gou de Yaluzangbu jiang zhongshangyou de shiqi yicun: jianlun Xizang gaoyuan xishiqi yicun de xiangguan wenti" [Deposits of Stone Implements in the Kyirong Area and the Upper and Middle Reaches of the Yarlung Tsangpo River: A Reference to Some Correlative Questions About the Microlithic Implements in Tibet]. *Nanfang minzu kaogu* (Chengdu: Sichuan daxue chubanshe) 4 (1991): 47–63.

——. "Lun Xizang de xishiqi" [On the Microlithic Implements of Tibet]. *Xizang yanjiu* (Lhasa: Xizang yanjiu bianjibu) 1 (1994): 126–132.

Liu Jingzhi and Zhao H. "Xizang Gongga xian Changguogou xinshiqi shidai yizhi" [The Changguogou Neolithic Site in Gongkar, Tibet]. *Kaogu* (Beijing: Kexue chubanshe) 4 (1999): 1–10.

Liu Xu. *Jiu Tang shu* [Old Tang Annals]. 16 vols. Beijing: Zhonghua shuju: Xinhua shudian Shanghai faxingsuo faxing, 1975.

Liu Yunxin. *Datong xianzhi* [*Account of Datong County*]. Part 2. In *Zhongguo fangzhi congshu*. Taibei: Chengwen chubanshe, 1970.

Liu Z. "Xizang gaoyuan mafamu hu dongbei an deng san ge didian de xishiqi" [Microlith from Three Sites on the Northeast Shore of Mapham Lake in Tibet]. *Nanjing daxue xuebao* (Nanjing: Nanjing daxue xuebao bianjibu) 4 (1981): 87–96.

Liu Z. and F. Wang. "Xizang gaoyuan duogeze yu zhabu didian de jiushiqi— Jian lun gaoyuan gu huanjing dui shiqi wenhua fenbu de yingxiang" [Paleoliths from the Duogeze and Zhabu Sites of the Tibetan Plateau—On the Paleo-Environmental Influence on the Distribution of Stone Culture on the Tibetan Plateau]. *Kaogu* (Beijing: Kexue chubanshe) 4 (1986): 289–299.

Ma Jie and Sheng Shengzu. "Weizang tuzhi" [Topographical Description of Central Tibet] 1792; also available in William Woodville Rockhill, "Tibet: A Geographical, Ethnographical and Historical Sketch, Derived from Chinese Sources," *Journal of the Royal Asiatic Society New Series* 23 (1891): 1–133, 185–291.

Meng Bao. *Xizang Zoushu* [*Memorial and Decrees of Meng Bao, Amban in Tibet 1839–1844*]. (c. 1851). [Lhasa]: Xizang shehui kexueyuan Xizang xue Hanwen wenxian bianjishi, 1985.

Ming Shi [*History of the Ming*]. Beijing: Zhonghua shuju, 1974.

Nian Gengyao zouzhe [*Confidential Memorials of Nian Gengyao*]. 2 vols. Taipei: Guoli Gugong Bowuyuan, 1971.

Ouyang Xiu and Song Qi. *Xin Tang shu* [*New Tang Annals*]. 20 vols. Beijing: Zhonghua shuju, 1975.

Qian F. and Wu X. "Zang bei gaoyuan geting shiqi chubu guancha" [A Preliminary Observation on the Stone Artifacts Collected from Geting on the Northern Tibetan Plateau]. *Renleixue xuebao* (Beijing: Kexue chubanshe) 7 (1988): 75–83.

Qing shi lu [*Veritable Record of the Qing*], edition 1. Beijing: Zhonghua shuju, 1985.

Shizong shilu [*Veritable Records of Shizong*]. In *Da Qing lichao shilu*. (vols. 18–57), ed. Manzhou diguo guowu yuan. Taipei reprint: Huawen shuju ed. 4664 *juan*. Tokyo: Okura Shuppan Kabushiki Kaisha, 1937–1938.

Shengzu shilu [*Veritable Records of Shengzu*].

Sichuan sheng bianjizu. *Sichuan sheng Ganzi zhou Zangzu shehui lishi diaocha* [*A Socio-Historical Investigation of the Tibetans in Kardzé Prefecture, Sichuan Province*]. Chengdu: Sichuansheng shehui kexueyuan chubanshe, 1985.

Sichuan sheng Litang xianzhi bianzuan weiyuanhui. *Litang xianzhi* [*Litang County Gazetteer*]. Chengdu: Sichuan renmin chubanshe, 1996.

Sima Guang. *Zi zhi tong jian* [*The Comprehensive Mirror in Aid of Government*]. 10 vols. Beijing: Zhonghua shuju, 1956.

Song Lian. *Yuan shi* [*History of the Yuan*]. 1370; reprint, Beijing: Zhonghua shuju, 1976.

Song shi [*History of the Song*].

Song Yun. *Weizang tongzhi* [*Comprehensive Gazetteer of Ü-tsang*]. China: Jianxi cun she, 1896.

Suolang Wangdu. "Xizang kaogu xin faxian zongshu" [A Brief Summary of New Archaeological Discoveries in Tibet]. In *Nanfang minzu kaogu* [*Southern Ethnology and Archaeology*], 4 vols., ed. Tong E. Chengdu: Sichuan daxue chubanshe, 1991, 9–24.

——. *Naidong xian wenwuzhi*. [*A Survey of Cultural Relics in Nedong County*]. Lhasa: Xizang renmin chubanshe, 1986.

Taipei National Palace Museum, ed. *Nian Gengyao zouzhe* [*Nian Gengyao's Memorials*], vols. 1 and 2. Taipei: Taipei National Palace Museum, 1977.

Tan Qixiang. *Zhongguo lishi ditu ji* [*The Historical Atlas of China*]. Beijing: Ditu chubanshe, 1982.

Tong E. *Zhongguo xinan minzu kaogu lunwen ji* [*Collected Papers on Ethnoarchaeology in Southwest China*]. Beijing: Wenwu chubanshe, 1990.

——. "Xizang gaoyuan shang de shoufu" [Hand Axe from the Tibetan Plateau]. *Kaogu* (Beijing: Kexue chubanshe) 9 (1989): 822–826.

——. "Xizang kaogu zongshu" [A Summary of the Archaeology of Tibet]. *Wenwu* (Beijing: Wenwu chubanshe) 9 (1985): 9–19.

——. "Zhongguo xinan diqu: Renlei keneng de fayuandi" [Southwest China: A Possible Place of Origin for Human Beings]. *Sichuan daxue xuebao* (Chengdu: Sichuan renmin chubanshe) 3 (1983): 3–14.

——. "Shi lun chuan xibei shiguanmu de zuqun wenti" [A Tentative Study of the Ethnicity of Stone Coffin Burials in Northwestern Sichuan]. *Kaogu* (Beijing: Kexue chubanshe) 2 (1978): 34–45.

Waifan Menggu Huibu wanggong biao zhuan [*Biographies of the Princes and Dukes of the Outer Provinces, Mongolia and the Muslim Region*].

Wang Chuanzhen. *Hezhou zhi* [*Gazetteer of Hezhou*]. 1707.

Wang Yao. *Tufan jinshilu* [*Records of Tibetan Epigraphs*]. Beijing: Wenwu chubanshe, 1982.

Wu Fengpei, ed. *Qing Ji Chou Zang Zou Du* [*Qing Dynasty Memorials and Documents Concerning Tibet*].

Xiage Wangdui. "Shi xi Xizang shiqian shiguan zang de leixing yu niandai" [A Tentative Analysis of Types and Dates of Prehistoric Stone Coffin Burials in Tibet]. *Xizang yanjiu* (Lhasa: Xizang yanjiu bianjibu) 4 (1998): 40–44.

Xia Xie. *Ming tong jian* [*Comprehensive Mirror of the Ming*]. Beijing: Zhonghua shuju, 1959.

Xibei minzu xueyuan zangwen jiaoyanzu [Nub byang mi rigs slob grwa chen mo'i bod yig slob dpyod tsu'u], ed. *Zang Han zidian* [*RgyAbod (sic) ming mdzod; Tibetan-Chinese Dictionary*]. Lanzhou: Gansu renmin chubanshe, 1979.

Xie Qihuang. *Zangzu chuantong wenhua cidian* [*Dictionary of Traditional Tibetan Culture*]. Lanzhou: Gansu renmin chubanshe, 1993.

Xu Song. *Song huiyao jigao* [*Draft Compendium of Institutions During the Song*]. Beijing: Guoli Beijing tushuguan, 1936.

Yan Kejun. *Tieqiao jinshi ba* [*Epigraphical Notes by Tieqiao*].

Yuan shi [*History of Yuan*]. Baina edition. Shanghai: Shangwu yinshuguan, 1937.

Yu Daojuan. *Zang Han duizhao Lasa kouyu cidian* [*Bod rgya shan sbyar gyi lha sa'i kha skad tshig mdzod = The Colloquial Lhasa Tibetan-Chinese Dictionary*]. Beijing: Minzu chubanshe, 1983.

Zhang Mu. *Menggu youmu ji* [*Record of the Mongol Nomads*].

Zhang Tingyu et al. *Mingshi* [*History of the Ming*]. Beijing: Zhonghua shuju, 1974.

Zhang Wei. *Longyou jinshi lu* [*Epigraphic Records of Longyou*].

Zhang Yisun [Krang Dbyi sun] et al. *Zang Han da cidian* [*Bod rgya tshig mdzod chen mo = Tibetan-Chinese Dictionary*]. Beijing: Minzu chubanshe: Xinhua shudian faxing, 1985.

Zhao H. "Xizang Qugong chutu de tiebing tongjing wenti yanjiu" [Questions Concerning a Bronze Mirror with an Iron Handle Unearthed in Qugong, Tibet]. *Kaogu* (Beijing: Kexue chubanshe) 7 (1994): 47–52.

———. "Lun Xizang Bangda yizhi, Qugong wenhua yu Xizang de shiqian wenming" [On the Bangga Site, Qugong Culture, and Prehistoric Civilization in Tibet]. Paper presented at the International Academic Conference on Tibetan Archaeology and Art, Beijing, 2002.

Zhongguo shehui kexueyuan, Kaogu yanjiusuo, Xizang Zizhiqu Wenwuju [Institute of Archaeology, Chinese Academy of Social Science and Bureau of Cultural Relics, Tibet Autonomous Region]. "Xizang Guoga xian Changguogou xinshiqi shidai yizhi" [The Changuogou Neolithic Site in Gongkar County, Tibet]. *Kaogu* (Beijing: Kexue chubanshe) 4 (1999): 1–10.

———. *Lasa Qugong* [*Qugong in Lhasa: Excavations of an Ancient Site and Tombs*]. Beijing: Zhongguo dabaike quanshu chubanshe, 1999.

———. "Xizang Lasa shi Qugong cun xinshiqi shidai yizhi diyici fajue jianbao" [Brief Report on the First Excavation of Qugong Neolithic Site in Lhasa, Tibet]. *Kaogu* (Beijing: Kexue chubanshe) 10 (1991): 873–881.

———. "Xizang Lasa shi Qugong cun shishimu fajue jianbao" [Brief Report on the Excavation of the Qugong Burials in Lhasa, Tibet]. *Kaogu* (Beijing: Kexue chubanshe) 10 (1991): 927–931.

JAPANESE-LANGUAGE REFERENCES

Enoki Kazuo. "Ōshō no Kiga Keiryaku ni Tsuite" [Wang Shao's Administration of Xihe]. *Mōko Gakuhō* (Tokyo: Mōko Kenkyūjo) 1 (1940).

Hadano Hakuyu. "Kamu no Bukkyō to sono Kādamu-ha narabini Eizō no Bukkyō ni ataeta eikyō ni tuite" [The Influence of the Buddhism of Khams on the Bka' dams pa sect of Tibetan Buddhism]. *Bunka* 20, no. 4 (July 1956): 697–719.

Ishihama Yumiko. "Gushi Han ōke no Chibetto ōken sōshitsu katei ni Gansuru ichi kōsatsu Ropusan-Danjin (Blo bzang bstan'dzin) no 'hanran' saikō" [A Study of the Process Whereby the Royal House of Gushi Qayan Lost Its Sovereignty Over Tibet: A Reconsideration of Blo bzang bstan 'dzin's "Rebellion"]. *Tōyō Gakuhō* (Tokyo: Tōyō Kyōkai Chōsabu) 69, no. 3–4 (1988).

Iwasaki Tsutomu. "Sōdai Kasei Chibettozoku to Bukkyō" [The Tibetan Tribes of Hexi and Buddhism During the Northern Song Period]. *Tōyōshi kenkyū* (Kyoto: Seikei Shoin) 46, no. 1 (1987).

———. "Seika Kenkoku to Sōkazoku no Dōkō" [The Founding of Xixia and the Movements of the Zongge Tribe]. In *Nakamura Jihei Sensei Kaki Kinen Tōyōshi Ronsō* [Collection of Papers on Oriental History in Honor of the 70th Birthday of Professor Nakamura Jihei]. Tokyo: Tōsui Shobō, 1986.

———. "Sōdai Kasei Chibetto no Kenkyū" [A Study of Hexi Tibetans During the Northern Song Dynasty]. *Memoirs of the Research Department of the Tōyō Bunko* XLIV. Tokyo: Tōyō Bunko, 1986, 57–132.

———. "Sokajō Kakushira Seiken no Seikaku to Kito" [The Character and Designs of the Gusiluo Regime of Zonggecheng]. *Chūō Daigaku Ajiashi Kenkyū* (Tokyo: Chūō Daigaku) 2 (1978).

Kanda Nobuo. "Kyūcyūtō yōseicyō sōshyō" [Secret Memorials of the Yongzheng Period]. *Tōyō Gakuhō* (Tokyo: Tōyō Kyōkai Chōsabu) 60, nos. 1–2 (1978): 179–183.

Katō Naoto. "Robusan Danjin no hanran to Shinchō—hanran no keika o chūshin to shite" [Lobjang Danɉin's rebellion and the Qing Dynasty: With a Focus on the Course of the Rebellion]. *Tōyōshi Kenkyū* (Kyoto: Seikei Shoin) 45, no. 3 (1986).

——. "Kokuritsu Kokyū Hakubutsuin hen *Nen Kōgyō sōshō*" [Confidential Memorials of Nian Gengyao, National Palace Museum]. *Tōyō Gakuhō* (Tokyo: Tōyō Kyōkai Chōsabu) 60, no. 3–4 (1979).

Nagasawa Kazutoshi. "Toban no Kasei shinshutsu to Tō-Zai Kōtsū" [Tibet's Domination in Hexi and the Communication Between the West and the East]. *Shikan* (Tokyo: Waseda Daigaku Shuppanbu) 46 (1956): 71–81.

Saeki Tomi. "Kyūcyūtō yōseicyō sōshyō" [Secret Memorials of the Yongzheng Period]. *Tōyōshi Kenkyū* (Kyoto: Seikei Shoin) 37, no. 3 (1978).

Satō Hisashi. "Daruma-ō no Zaii Nenji ni Tsuite" [On the Chronology of the Reign of Lang Darma]. *Shirin* (Kyoto: Shigaku Kenkyūkai) 46 (1963): 741–767 (quoted from the reprint in *Chūsei Chibetto shi kenkyū, Studies on the Medieval History of Tibet* [Kyoto: Dōhōsha, 1986], 9–42).

——. "Kinsei Seikai shoburaku no kigen" [The Origins of the Tribal Domains of Early Modern Qinghai] [1, 2], *Tōyōshi Kenkyū* (Kyoto: Seikei Shoin) 32, no. 1 (1973/74).

——. "Ṛobuzan Danjin no hanran ni tsuite" [On Lobjang Danɉin's Rebellion]. *Shirin* (Kyoto: Shigaku Kenkyūkai) 55, no. 6 (1972).

——. "Gen matsu Min sho no Chibetto josei [The Tibetan Situation from Late Yuan to Early Ming]." In *Mindai Man-mō shi kenkyū*, ed. Tamura Jituzō. Kyoto: Kyōto Daigaku Bungakubu, 1963.

——. "Daruma-ō no Shison ni Tsuite" [On the Descendants of Lang Darma]. *Tōyō Gakuhō* 46, no. 4 (1963): 476–516 (quoted from the reprint in *Studies on the Mediaeval History of Tibet* [Kyoto: Dōhōsha, 1986], 43–88).

——. "Gen matsu Min sho no Chibetto josei" [Tibetan Women in the Late Yuan and Early Ming]. In *Mindai Man-mō shi kenkyū*, ed. Tamura Jitsuzō. Kyoto: Kyoto Daigaku Bungakubu, 1963, 522.

Suzuki Ryūichi. "Geruse Seitō Toban ōkoku no ōgō" [*Rgyal sras*: The Royal Title of the Kingdom of Tufan in Qingtang]. *Yasuda Gakuen Kenkyū Kiyō* (Tokyo: Yasuda Gankuen) 25 (1985).

Ueyama Daishun. "Donkō to Tonkō no bukkyō" [Ðonkō and Buddhist Teaching in Dunhuang]. *Tōhō Gakuhō* [*Journal of Oriental Studies*] (Kyoto: Tōhō Bunka Gakuin Kyoto Kenkyūjo: Hatsubaisho Ibundō) 35 (1985): 169.

Yamaguchi Zuihō. "Daruma-ō no habutsu wa kyokō" [A Fraud in the Description of the Ancient Guge Kingdom]. *Tōhō* 8 (1992): 67–69.

——. "Daruma-ō Satsugai no Zengo" [The Circumstances of the Murder of Lang Darma]. *Naritasan bukkyō kenkyūju kiyō* (Narita-shi, Chiba-ken, Japan: Naritasan bukkyū kenkyūju) 5 (1980): 1–27.

——. "Daruma-ō Nishi to Toban no Bunretsu" [The Two Sons of Lang Darma and the Fragmentation of Tibet]. *Komazawa Daigaku bukkyōgaku bu ronshū* (Tokyo: Komazawa Daigaku bukkyōgaku bu) 11 (1980): 214–233.

——. "Toban Shihai Jidai 3: Tonkō no Bukkyōkai" [Dunhuang Under Tibetan Rule 3: Buddhist Circles in Dunhuang]. In *Kōza Tonkō 2, Tonkō no Rekishi 2* [Lectures on

Dunhuang 2: History of Dunhuang], ed. Enoki Kazuo. Tokyo: Daitō Shuppansha, 1980, 227–228.

——. "'Toban' no kokugo to 'Yōdō' no ichi; Fukoku-den to dai shō Yōdō no kenkyū" [The Name Tufan and the Location of the Yangtung: A Study of the *Fu kuo chuan* and the Greater and Lesser Yangtung]. *Tōyō Gakuhō* 58 (1977): 55–95.

INDEX

Tibetan proper names and terms are presented phonetically followed by *Wylie transliteration in italics*. Boldface numbers indicate **main readings** for topics concerned. Italicized numbers indicate *tables, maps,* or *figures*.